THE
NATIONAL
GEOGRAPHIC
DESK
REFERENCE

CONTRIBUTING GEOGRAPHERS

Chief Consultant: Roger M. Downs, Ph.D.
Professor and Head, Department of Geography,
Pennsylvania State University

Frederick A. Day, Ph.D.
Professor of Geography, Department of Geography,
Southwest Texas State University

Paul L. Knox, Ph.D.
University Distinguished Professor and Dean,
College of Architecture and Urban Studies,
Virginia Polytechnic Institute and State University

Peter Haynes Meserve, Ph.D.
Associate Professor of Geography and Geology,
Department of Natural Sciences and Mathematics;
Head, Environmental Studies,
Columbia College, Missouri

Barney Warf, Ph.D.
Professor and Chair,
Department of Geography, Florida State University

A Stonesong Press Book

Printed in U.S.A.

Library of Congress Cataloging-in-Publication Data

The National Geographic desk reference : a geographical reference
    with hundreds of photographs, maps, charts, and graphs.
        p.   cm.
        Includes bibliographical references.
        ISBN 0-7922-7082-7. (reg.) — ISBN 0-7922-7083-5 (dlx.)
        1. Geography Handbooks, manual, etc.   I. National
Geographic Society (U.S.)
    G123.N38   1999
    910—dc21   99-23549
                                        CIP

THE
NATIONAL
GEOGRAPHIC
DESK
REFERENCE

NATIONAL
GEOGRAPHIC

WASHINGTON, D.C.

A STONESONG PRESS BOOK

CONTENTS

PART I

Geography Past and Present

In this SeaWiFS satellite composite mosaic, high concentrations of chlorophyll from phytoplankton in the oceans range from green to yellow to red. On land, tan denotes little or no vegetation; dark green indicates dense vegetation.

What Is Geography?

Geography gives us a way to look at the Earth as a whole—both the physical world and its people. Geography is much more than the name of the world's highest mountain or longest river or the capital of Brazil. As a science, it seeks to understand *where* things are and *how* and *why* they got there by studying—with an emphasis on location—the connections and interactions among people, places, and environments. Geography looks at how people and their activities adapt to and change their surroundings. To do this, geography must draw upon and integrate the knowledge of many different disciplines.

Geographers divide this broad field of study into physical geography and human geography.

Physical geography draws on the sciences of geology, climatology, biology, ecology, hydrology (the study of water), pedology (soil science), and other natural sciences. **Human geography** encompasses cultural anthropology, economics, political science, history, demography, and other social sciences. Geography links these disciplines to determine why things happen in a particular location. **Cartography**, the art and science of mapmaking, provides geographers with their most basic tool—a graphic representation of a geographic setting.

As technology continues to shrink our world and people become increasingly interdependent, a knowledge of geography can help us understand and manage these changes—in our

Geographic Perspectives

The book *Geography for Life: National Geography Standards 1994* (developed by the Geography Education Standards Project on behalf of the National Geographic Society, the American Geographical Society, the Association of American Geographers, and the National Council for Geographic Education) describes four perspectives from which a geographically informed person sees and understands the world:

■ The spatial perspective: Geography is concerned with the spatial dimension of human experience (space and place). The essential issue of "whereness"—embodied in specific questions such as Where is it? Why is it there?—helps in contemplating the context of spatial relationships where the human story unfolds.

■ The ecological perspective: Understanding Earth as a complex set of interacting living and nonliving elements is fundamental to realizing that human societies depend on diverse ecosystems for food, water, and all other resources. People who regularly inquire about connections and relationships among life-forms, ecosystems, and human societies possess an ecological perspective.

■ The historical perspective enriches the geographic perspective by asking the questions When? and Why then? and Why is the event significant? These questions can yield a clearer understanding of past and contemporary events.

■ The economic perspective asks how diverse peoples earn a living and how they are connected through trade in goods and services. Previously isolated economies are entering the global economy, and technological changes accelerate transportation and communication. The result is increasing interdependence among all societies in a world where decisions made in distant places regularly impact local economies.

own neighborhoods and cities as well as nationally and internationally. More than ever, human activities—for example, clearing rain forest to make room for farmland—have direct consequences, both local and global, that affect the planet in sometimes obscure ways. Geography gives us a framework for understanding those connections so that we can make informed decisions about them.

Geography also exposes us to worlds different from our own so we can see and appreciate their richness and beauty. This knowledge allows us to view the Earth and its people through focused lenses, opening our minds to different points of view and ways of life. When we understand how humans and the Earth's physical forces and places are intertwined and interdependent—and constantly changing—the world becomes an even more fascinating place.

A small boy gains a new perspective on the world as he views the enormous globe at the Boston Science Museum.

The History of Geography

The word **geography** comes from the Greek words *geo* and *graphia,* meaning to write about or describe the Earth. In ancient Greece, geography often meant tales of travel, adventure, and discovery such as Homer's *Iliad* and *Odyssey,* written in the ninth century B.C Although Homer's epics survive, few similar accounts of travels by earlier peoples—the Phoenicians, Egyptians, Chinese, and Polynesians, for instance—have come down to us.

Beginning with ancient Greeks such as Aristotle, who attempted to explain the size and nature of the Earth scientifically, curiosity about geography has been an important stimulus in the development of modern science. In their attempts to measure and plot places on the Earth and establish their relationships in terms of distance and direction, early mathematicians, astronomers, and mapmakers developed the instruments needed to make more

accurate scientific observations. In addition, the discoveries of European explorers in the 16th and 17th centuries reinforced the value of direct observation, accurate measurements, and collection of specimens—a change in approach that countered long-standing and mystical beliefs about the Earth and its people.

The Early Contributors to Geography

One of the first geographers was **Eratosthenes** (circa 276-194 B.C.), head of the great library at Alexandria in Egypt. He plotted the known world, from the British Isles to Sri Lanka and from the Caspian Sea to Ethiopia, on maps that were among the most detailed and accurate of the time. Eratosthenes developed an early framework for mapping the Earth using meridians and parallels—a system similar to the latitudes and longitudes proposed by the Greek astronomer and mathematician Hipparchus a century later.

Eratosthenes' most amazing accomplishment—a remarkably accurate estimate of the size of the Earth—was not fully appreciated for centuries. He noted that on the summer solstice—longest day of the year—the sun was almost directly overhead in Syene, which lies just north of the Tropic of Cancer at modern-day Aswan in southeastern Egypt. On the same day and time in Alexandria, however, the rays of the sun fell at an angle to the vertical of about a fiftieth of a circle. Assuming that the Earth was a sphere, he then multiplied the estimated distance between Syene and Alexandria by 50 to calculate a circumference of some 28,566 miles (46,000 km), which is about 14 percent too large—the actual circumference is 24,840 miles (40,000 km). Minor errors contributed to this difference: Syene was actually about 37 miles north of the Tropic of Cancer, not directly on it; the calculation assumed the Earth was a perfect sphere, whereas it is slightly flattened at the Poles; and the distances were inaccurately measured, not by instruments but by travel times, which then were converted to units of measure.

For hundreds of years most geographers, skeptical of Eratosthenes' measurement, used the smaller figure of 18,000 miles (28,962 km), calculated by the Greek philosopher **Posidonius** (circa 135-50 B.C.). Because his measurements showed the Earth to be so large, Eratosthenes concluded that the seas formed a huge interconnected ocean. He was right, but his idea went unverified for 18 centuries, until the expedition of Portuguese explorer Ferdinand Magellan completed its circumnavigation of the Earth in 1522.

Though not a geographer, the Greek astronomer **Hipparchus** (circa 190-126 B.C.) contributed significantly to the science of map-making. Believed to have invented the astrolabe, or star measurer, he recorded the positions of about a thousand of the brighter stars, creating the first accurate star map around 134 B.C. He plotted the position of each star by its latitude (the distance north or south of the Equator) and longitude (the distance east or west of a chosen point). Subsequently he developed a similar framework, based on a measurement system using 360 degrees as its base, to plot positions on the Earth's surface.

While the ancient Greeks and others were expanding their geographic knowledge outward from the Mediterranean, a geographer from China was discovering the Mediterranean cultures. In 128 B.C. **Chang Ch'ien** (died 114 B.C.) was dispatched westward by the Han emperor to negotiate with China's rivals. His adventures carried him to Babylonia, and on his return he wrote a description

Why Are There 360° in a Circle?

A degree is a fraction of a circle, and there are 360° in each of the imaginary circles around the surface of the Earth. But where did that number come from? The Babylonians—who devised the base 60, or sexagesimal, number system (our modern system is base 10, or decimal)—are believed to have been the first to divide a circle into 360° (6 times 60). Some historians think that the base 60 system derives from the approximate length in days of a calendar year, but others claim that the Babylonians probably chose 60 because it is divisible by so many other numbers. Hipparchus, who invented the formal system of latitude and longitude, divided each Earth circle into 360°, each degree having 60 minutes and each minute having 60 seconds.

of the land route across inner Asia to Persia and the Mediterranean. His reports helped establish the ancient Silk Road, over which commerce between East and West flowed for centuries.

Like many of his predecessors, the Greco-Roman geographer **Strabo** (circa 64 B.C.-A.D. 23) summarized and criticized the work of earlier geographers, including Eratosthenes. He probably compiled information at the library of Alexandria, then controlled by Rome. The result of Strabo's encyclopedic work was the 17-volume *Geographica*, which survives intact except for the seventh volume (only a summary remains). His *Geographica* presents a detailed picture of his era's knowledge of geography, history, science, mathematics, and politics.

A physical geographer as well, Strabo wrote about volcanoes, the origins of seas, and the effects of riverine siltation on seas and coastlines. Like several predecessors, he separated the world into parallel zones—the uninhabited arctic and tropics and the habitable temperate zone. Perhaps most important, Strabo's writings preserve a record of the lost works of many of his predecessors.

Claudius Ptolemy (circa A.D. 90-168) of Alexandria, an astronomer and head of the great library at Alexandria, also synthesized the work of early geographers, including Hipparchus. Like Hipparchus, Ptolemy believed in a geocentric universe, in which the planets revolve around the Earth. This mistaken concept came to be called the Ptolemaic system.

Ptolemy's eight-volume *Geography* plotted the Earth using three methods of projection. It was also an early gazetteer, or geographic index, giving coordinates for 8,000 places, which he based largely on reports from Roman soldiers and other travelers. His view of geography was basically cartographic—that is, he thought of geography as the location of places and things. His book also served as an early atlas, featuring a world map and 26 regional maps, as well as tables of latitudes and longitudes.

Using Posidonius' erroneous 18,000-mile calculation of the Earth's circumference, Ptolemy overestimated the east-west extent of the Old World by 55 degrees and underestimated the circumference of the Earth by 25 percent. Thus his maps showed distances shorter than actual. Thirteen centuries after his death, Ptolemy's book with its erroneous maps was translated into Latin, later encouraging Christopher Columbus to attempt to reach Asia by voyaging westward from Europe.

The Middle Ages: 500 to 1400

Known as the Middle Ages, the nine centuries bridging the classical and modern epochs saw the focus of scientific geography shift from "Dark Age" Europe to dynamic Islam, which controlled virtually all the Mediterranean littoral except Italy. As early as the seventh century, Arabic scholars were translating works of ancient Greeks; in the ninth century they translated Ptolemy's eight-volume *Geography*. Soon Arab geographers and explorers were compiling their own important geographies.

Islam's conquest of Palestine and the holy city of Jerusalem during the A.D. 600s later impelled western European knights and peasants to launch the dozen or so Crusades beginning in A.D. 1095, which broadened geographic horizons and forever changed the relationship of East and West. Roman Catholic priests began to travel widely, making contact with China and India. European maritime exploration advanced with the daring voyages of the Vikings, whose high-prowed long ships bore settlers eastward up Russian rivers and westward to the shores of North America.

The Moroccan geographer **al-Idrisi** (circa 1100-1165) traveled extensively throughout the Mediterranean and eventually joined the court of the crusader king Roger II in Sicily. There he compiled an important geography later known as *The Book of Roger*. In addition, he created 70 sheets of detailed and fairly accurate regional maps.

Ibn Battuta: A Tireless Traveler

Ibn Battuta's 29 years of travels began in 1325, when at age 21 he undertook the pilgrimage to Mecca, some 3,000 miles (4,827 km) from his birthplace in Tangier, Morocco. Joining several caravans along the way, he made the trip in 10 months. For most of the rest of his life, his wanderlust kept him on the move through Asia, Africa, and Europe. On a trip through Egypt, he visited Cairo and the Nile, but scholars doubt that he actually saw the pyramids—he describes them as cone-shaped. In all, he traveled 75,000 miles (120,675 km), three times the distance covered by Marco Polo, his European contemporary.

Another Arab historian and geographer, Moroccan **Ibn Battuta** (1304-1369), was called the traveler of Islam. He journeyed across Africa and Asia and parts of Europe—from Spain to China and from Timbuktu to the steppes of Russia—in a trek that lasted three decades. On his return, he spent two years writing a narrative of one of history's most remarkable wanderlusts.

Arab historian **Ibn Khaldun** (1332-1406), born in Tunis, Tunisia, wrote two influential books. His *Kitar al-'ibar*, or *Universal History*, records the history of Muslim North Africa and the Berbers, and his *Muqaddimah*, or *Introduction to History*, is one of the earliest works on the philosophy of history that does not take a religious approach. In it, he describes his theories of how societies rise, decline through decay and corruption, and fall. A recurring theme is the relationship of humankind and the physical environment.

European interest in geography revived in the 13th century, partly because of the writings of **Marco Polo** (1254-1324?), a Venetian trader and traveler who recorded his many years of observations and adventures journeying through Central and Southeast Asia. With his father and uncle, Polo spent 24 years in Asia, much of it in service to the Mongol ruler Kublai Khan. After returning to Venice, he was imprisoned by its Genoese conquerors, and there he recorded his many geographic and cultural observations. His *Description of the World* was widely read throughout Europe and provided new insights into China.

The Age of Discovery: 1400 to 1600

Portugal's **Prince Henry** (1394-1460), later known as Henry the Navigator, supported far-reaching endeavors in navigational science that lifted his nation to prominence as a center for cartography, astronomy, and nautical instrumentation. Their development was vital to the success of the explorers of the time, who had to determine their location at sea and to map the places they visited. These systematic scientific explorations, which vastly increased human knowledge of the world, were motivated largely by Europe's commercial and political needs, including gold for the minting of coins and faster trade routes to the spices of India and the silk of China. While maritime horizons broadened, overland contacts shrank as the fall of the Mongol empire curbed the Catholic Church's missionary work in China.

By the late 1400s, Portugal led the way in financing expeditions of discovery. Prince Henry's explorers ventured south from Lisbon and Sagres ever farther down the west coast of Africa. To his base at Sagres the prince attracted scientists and mariners who created better charts and improved compass, astrolabe, quadrant, and ship design. Not until 1487 did Bartholomeu Dias round the Cape of Good Hope and Cape Agulhas and enter the Indian Ocean, blazing the trail that Vasco da Gama followed in 1497 to reach India. Spain also understood the practical value of these expeditions, a factor in its sponsorship of Christopher

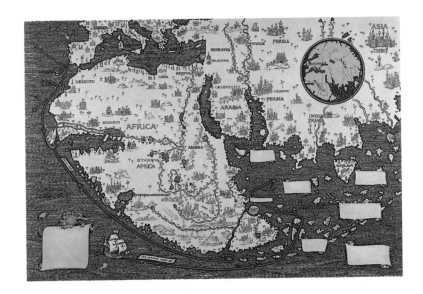

A 15th-century Venetian map shows geographic misconceptions increasing with distance from the Mediterranean. A century of successful European voyages of exploration saw dramatic improvements in map accuracy and a proliferation of globe- and mapmaking.

The Portuguese explored Africa's west coast for 70 years, finally sailing around the Cape of Good Hope—just beyond today's Capetown, South Africa—and discovering a seaway to India.

Columbus, an Italian from Genoa. Amerigo Vespucci, for whom the New World was named, sailed under Portugal's flag in 1501, creating charts of the South American coastline and recording observations of the cultures he saw. These epochal voyages fostered an explosion of geographic knowledge and a matching spurt of maps and globes. Most notable were the voyages by Spain's Juan de la Cosa, whose 1500 *Chart of the World* received the advice of Columbus; by the German mapmaker Martin Waldseemüller (see page 24); and by his countryman Martin Behaim, whose magnificent 1492 globe unfortunately could not reflect Columbus's discoveries.

An early 16th-century German theologian, **Sebastian Münster** (1488-1552), contributed to the science of (Continued on page 15)

Explorers as Geographers

The explorers and trailblazers who sought new lands and peoples were, in a sense, geographers as well. The reports of their journeys and the knowledge they gained helped mapmakers, geologists, biologists, and anthropologists—as well as the general public—better understand the Earth. In this selected listing, the world's best known and a few lesser-known explorers appear in chronological order.

EXPLORER	DATES OF DISCOVERY	WHERE THEY WENT AND WHY
Phoenicians	3000-800 B.C.	World's earliest sailors built trading posts throughout the Mediterranean. First to use the North Star for navigation. Explored as far as Britain and possibly the Azores and Africa's Cape of Good Hope.
Ancient Egyptians	2500-1493 B.C.	Maritime traders in the Mediterranean by 2500 B.C. Searched east coast of Africa for Punt, mythical home of their ancestors, and for ivory, ebony, silver, and gold.
Ancient Polynesians	1500 B.C.-A.D. 1000	About 1500 B.C., traveled from southeast Asia to Australia; settled Fiji by 1300 B.C., most of Oceania between A.D. 300 and 800 (Hawaii, A.D. 500; New Zealand, A.D. 800).
Alexander the Great (Greece)	334-323 B.C.	Conquests carried him eastward to Afghanistan, the Hindu Kush, and India and southward to Egypt. Took with him geographers, engineers, botanists, and historians.
Pytheas of Massalia (Greece)	ca. 325 B.C.	Sailed from the Mediterranean around Spain to Britain, and possibly to Iceland or Norway, in search of tin and amber.
Chang Ch'ien	ca. 138-123 B.C.	This diplomat's explorations of central and western Asia helped establish the ancient Silk Road, the largely overland trade route linking Asia and Europe.
Erik the Red (Norway)	A.D. 986	Explored Greenland, proposing its colonization by settlers from overcrowded Iceland. His son Leif Eriksson continued the search for new lands and is thought to have touched Canada at Baffin Island, Labrador, and Newfoundland.
Marco Polo (Italy)	1271-1295	Accompanying his merchant father and uncle, helped open 7,000-mile overland route from Venice to Shangdu, China; returned after 24 years and wrote influential book describing peoples, sights, and cultures of Asia.
Cheng Ho (China)	1405-1433	Commanded fleets of as many as 317 ships on seven voyages to lands bordering the China Sea and Indian Ocean, including the east coast of Africa, seeking to gain respect for the new Ming Dynasty. China soon closed its doors to foreign contact.
Bartholomeu Dias (Portugal)	1487-1488	First European to round the tip of Africa seeking an eastward route to Asia.
Christopher Columbus (Italy)	1492-1504	Sailing for Spain in search of a westward route to Asia, landed in the Bahamas and the Caribbean islands and later reached Central and South America.
Vasco da Gama (Portugal)	1497-1499	Following Dias's route down the west coast of Africa, sailed around the Cape of Good Hope to Calicut, India, the first recorded voyage from Europe to India.

EXPLORER	DATES OF DISCOVERY	WHERE THEY WENT AND WHY
John Cabot (England)	1497	Italian-born navigator and trader reached coastal Canada believing it was Asia; established England's claims in North America.
Amerigo Vespucci (Spain and Portugal)	1499-1507	Sailed in Spanish and Portuguese explorations to South and Central America; recognized existence of a continent west of Europe and east of Asia and coined the term "New World."
Pedro Álvars Cabral (Portugal)	1500-1501	First European to reach Brazil.
Vasco Núñez de Balboa (Spain)	1502-1513	Founded Darien in northeast South America, the first stable European settlement on the American mainland; crossed the Isthmus of Panama and became the first European to see the Pacific Ocean.
Juan Ponce de Leon (Spain)	1513-1521	Discovered and explored Florida in his search for the Fountain of Youth.
Hernán Cortés (Spain)	1518-1521 1524-1526	Sailing from Cuba with 600 men, entered the interior of Mexico and conquered the Aztec empire. Later explored southeast to Honduras.
Ferdinand Magellan (Spain)	1519-1521	A Portuguese sailing for Spain and seeking a westward route to Asia, Magellan led the first expedition to circumnavigate the world. Threaded the Strait of Magellan, sailed across the Pacific, killed in the Philippines. The circumnavigation was completed by Juan Sebastián del Cano in 1522.
Francisco Pizarro (Spain)	1524-1525 1526-1527 1531-1533	Explored the Pacific coast of South America from Panama to Peru. Later conquered the Incas of Peru.
Pánfilo de Narváez (Spain)	1527-1528	Sent by the King of Spain on an unsuccessful mission to conquer Florida.
Álvar Núñez Cabeza de Vaca (Spain)	1527-1536 1541-1544	One of four survivors of the failed Narváez quest, Cabeza de Vaca was shipwrecked off Texas coast, captured by Indians, and spent eight years wandering southwestern North America; later explored southern Brazil.
Jacques Cartier (France)	1535	Discovered passage past Newfoundland to the St. Lawrence River, later used by the French to settle in America.
Hernando de Soto (Spain)	1539-1542	As governor of Florida, battled Indians from Tampa Bay to western Tennessee and Mississippi; discovered the Mississippi River.
Francisco de Coronado (Spain)	1540-1542	Explored western Mexico and southwestern U.S., reaching Kansas; members of his party were the first Europeans to see the Grand Canyon.
Anthony Jenkinson (Britain)	1557-1571	Attempted to reach China across Russia and central Asia; his observations helped guide later explorers.
Matteo Ricci (Italy)	1578-1610	Jesuit priest traveled by sea to China to convert the Chinese. Produced a map of the world that persuaded Europeans that Cathay was actually China.
Yermak Timofeyevich (Russia)	1579-1585	Crossed the Ural Mountains and captured Siber, a Mongolian Empire outpost; launched Russian expansion across Siberia.

EXPLORER	DATES OF DISCOVERY	WHERE THEY WENT AND WHY
Samuel de Champlain (France)	1603-1615	Established Quebec City as the first French colony in the Americas and explored Lake Champlain, the Ottawa River, and the Great Lakes.
John Smith (England)	1607-1614	Explored and mapped Chesapeake Bay and the New England coast.
Henry Hudson (Holland, England)	1609-1611	Seeking a northern passage to Asia for Dutch interests, sailed up the Hudson River to Albany; on later English voyage discovered Hudson Bay.
Jean-Baptiste Tarvernier (France)	1638-1668	Traveled India as a gem dealer; wrote book about the caste system and other aspects of Indian culture.
Abel Janszoon Tasman (Holland)	1642-1643 1644	Discovered New Zealand, Tasmania, and Fiji and circumnavigated Australia, proving it was an island continent.
Louis Jolliet and Jacques Marquette (France)	1673	Explored interior North America from Michigan down the Mississippi River, paving the way for France's claim to the Mississippi Valley.
Henry Kelsey (England)	1690-1692	Explored Canada from Hudson Bay west to the Saskatchewan River and Great Plains.
Vitus Bering (Russia)	1741	A Dane, explored Alaska's Pacific coast for Russia; first to reach North America from the west.
Daniel Boone (America)	1775	Blazed the Wilderness Road from Tennessee through the Cumberland Gap into Kentucky.
Samuel Wallis (England)	1766-1768	First European to land in Tahiti.
James Cook (England)	1768-1771 1772-1775 1776-1779	Made three Pacific voyages: first to Tahiti, second to New Zealand, and third to Hawaii, where he was the first European to land. Mapped the west coast of Canada and was first to cross the Antarctic Circle (1773).
James Bruce (Scotland)	1768-1773	One of the first Europeans to explore Africa, mostly Ethiopia; located source of Blue Nile.
Alexander Mackenzie (Scotland)	1789-1793	Explored Canada by boat from Great Slave Lake to the Beaufort Sea; later crossed the Rockies and descended the Bella Coola River to the Pacific. First to cross the continent north of Mexico.
Mungo Park (Scotland)	1795-1797 1805-1806	Explored the basin of the Niger River in West Africa.
Alexander von Humboldt (Germany)	1799-1804	Traveled widely in Cuba, Mexico, and South America, writing extensively about their geology, geography, and natural history.
Meriwether Lewis and William Clark (U.S.)	1804-1806	Sent by President Thomas Jefferson to explore the Louisiana Purchase; traveled from St. Louis across the Rocky Mountains to the Pacific and back.

EXPLORER	DATES OF DISCOVERY	WHERE THEY WENT AND WHY
Hugh Clapperton Scotland) Richard Lander (Britain)	1825-1827 1830	Jointly explored lower reaches of Africa's Niger River. In a second journey Lander codiscovered its mouth.
Jedediah Smith (U.S.)	1826-1829	Sought a link between Great Salt Lake and the Pacific; first American to enter California from the east; explored the California coast.
René Caillé (France)	1827-1828	First European to report on Timbuktu in Africa; published a book of his travels across the Sahara.
Richard and John Lander (Britain)	1830	Their discovery of the mouth of the Niger River ended a 30-year British search.
Charles Darwin (Britain)	1831-1836	Darwin's world-roaming voyage as an amateur naturalist on the Beagle yielded the observations that led to his theory of evolution.
Charles Wilkes (U.S.)	1838-1842	Explored Melanesia, including Fiji, and confirmed the existence of Antarctica.
David Livingstone (Britain)	1841-1873	First European to cross Africa, opening trade routes for Europe; sought the source of the Nile but died before reaching it.
John Charles Frémont (U.S.)	1842-1847	Mapped much of the U.S. west of the Mississippi and established U.S. claims in Oregon.
Richard Francis Burton and John Hanning Speke (Britain)	1857-1859	Seeking the headwaters of the White Nile, found Lake Tanganyika; Speke also discovered Lake Victoria.
John Hanning Speke and James Augustus Grant (Britain)	1860-1863	Speke found Ripon Falls, on Lake Victoria, which proved to be the source of the White Nile.
Robert O'Hara Burke and William John Wills (Australia)	1860-1861	First to cross Australia from south to north.
Samuel and Florence Baker (England)	1861-1865	Explored tributaries of the Nile in Ethiopia; discovered Lake Albert.
Nikolay Przhevalsky (Russia)	1870-1885	In four expeditions to central Asia, crossed the Gobi and brought back scientific data and botanical collections.
John Wesley Powell (U.S.)	1869	Explored the Grand Canyon by boat, traveling some 1,000 miles in 98 days.
Luigi D'Albertis (Italy)	1872-1877	Early explorer of New Guinea's interior.

EXPLORER	DATES OF DISCOVERY	WHERE THEY WENT AND WHY
Henry Morton Stanley (Britain)	1874-1877	Journalist explored Lake Victoria, discovered Lake Edward, and traced the length of the Congo River.
Francis Younghusband (Britain)	1886-1904	Crossed China from Peking to India; explored the Karakoram Range and Pamirs; led a small army into Lhasa, capital of Tibet, to establish trade and political relations for Britain.
Sven Hedin (Sweden)	1890-1935	Swedish geographer charted central Asia and the Tibetan Plateau.
Roald Amundsen (Norway)	1903-1906 1911-1912	First to sail through the Northwest Passage (1903–1906) and to reach the South Pole (1911).
Cândido Rondon (Brazil)	1907-1914	Surveyed the Mato Grasso Plateau of Brazil.
Ernest Shackleton (England)	1908-1909 1914-1916	Twice failed to reach the South Pole.
Robert E. Peary (U.S.)	1909	After four attempts, believed to have reached the North Pole.
Robert Falcon Scott (Britain)	1910-1912	Lost the race with Amundsen to the South Pole.
Roy Chapman Andrews (U.S.)	1922-1930	Led five zoological expeditions to the Gobi; discovered important dinosaur fossils.
Joseph Rock (U.S.)	1922-1949	Botanist searched central China for plants and native lore.
Richard E. Byrd (U.S.)	1926 1929	First to fly over the North Pole (1926) and South Pole (1929).
C. William Beebe (U.S.)	1934	Dived in bathysphere off Bermuda to a record depth of 3,028 feet (923 m).
Claudio Villas Boas (Brazil)	1943-1973	With his brothers Orlando and Leonardo, explored the southern Amazon Basin to study Indian cultures.
Jacques Piccard (Switzerland)	1960	Dived to deepest known point in ocean, the Pacific's Mariana Trench, 35,800 feet (10,912 m); his father, balloonist Auguste Piccard, designed bathyscaphe to explore ocean depths.
Yuri Gagarin (Russia)	1961	First man in space.
Alan B. Shepard, Jr. (U.S.)	1961	First American in space.
John Glenn (U.S.)	1962	First American to orbit the Earth.
Ralph Plaisted (U.S.)	1968	First to travel to North Pole via snowmobile; first confirmed (by airplane instruments) arrival at North Pole.
Neil A. Armstrong (U.S.)	1969	First to walk on the moon; flew on Apollo 11 with Buzz Aldrin and Michael Collins.
Ranulph Fiennes (Britain)	1979-1981	First to travel around the world via the Poles.

(Continued from page 9) cartography by making the first separate maps of the continents, published in 1540. His book *Cosmography* (1544) noted the effects of rivers and floods on the Earth's surface and also discussed earthquakes, rock types, metals, and mining. Widely translated, it was a standard text on geography for more than a century.

The Growth of Geography: 1600 to 1900

The spate of world exploration that began in the 1400s and the wealth of knowledge it amassed changed geography as a science. Geography retained its connections to cartography and was often taught in universities in conjunction with astronomy and mathematics, a reflection of its navigational ties. But geographers also expanded their descriptions of human cultures and the natural world, both geological and biological.

Known as Varenius, **Bernhard Varens** (1622-1650) was a German scholar whose influential work *Geographia Generalis,* published the year he died, concerned aspects of physical geography as well as mapmaking and navigation. His approach to geography was mathematical and depended on travelers' direct observations of peoples and places. At the age of 27 he published a book on the history and geography of Japan and followed it with a second volume on Japanese religion. Varens accepted the heliocentric theory of Nicolaus Copernicus—that the Earth and other planets revolve around the sun—as opposed to the Ptolemaic theory of a geocentric universe. Until the mid-1700s, his work and that of **Philip Cluver,** or Cluverius (1580-1622), a German who wrote mainly country descriptions, were important geographic references.

British geographer **Nathanael Carpenter** (1589-1628) explored the theoretical aspects of geography. He followed the distinction first made by Varens between general geography— the study of the Earth as a whole—and special geography, the physical and human geography of regions. His work *Geographie Delineated Forth in Two Books* describes the motions of the Earth, climate zones, and distances between places.

The 1700s saw a flowering of geography books; especially popular were compilations containing detailed descriptions of countries— including forms of government and economies—and their peoples and cultures. One of these, *Geography Anatomiz'd,* or the *Compleat Geographical Grammar,* published by Patrick Gordon in 1699, had been through 20 editions by 1754.

A founder and first secretary of the American Philosophical Society (1743), **Benjamin Franklin** (1706-1790) conducted scientific studies of the Gulf Stream during several of his eight transatlantic voyages. His description, published in 1786, was the first to record the current's course, speed, temperature, and depth.

Naturalist **Georges-Louis Leclerc, Comte de Buffon** (1707-1788) organized the 44-volume *Histoire Naturelle,* or *Natural History,* a massive, detailed compendium about the Earth and living things. His emphasis on the interrelationship between humans and the environment is significant to geography today. Besides noting the many positive changes in human existence that civilization had yielded, he observed that humans can effect negative changes. For example, Buffon suggested that deforestation and drainage of marshes might cause temperature increases. He believed that people needed to clear land for farms and cities, but cautioned that once these were established, the remaining forests were resources that should be managed with care and foresight.

The German philosopher **Immanuel Kant** (1724-1804), who taught physical geography at the University of Königsberg, first defined geography's role as a discipline that could unify many disparate areas of knowledge into an understanding of the world as a whole. According to a biographer, he also "freed geography from its tight bonds with theology."

A six-volume description of the Earth and its people written by **Conrad Malte-Brun**

(1775-1826) bears the unwieldy title *Universal Geography or a Description of All Parts of the World on a New Plan according to the great natural divisions of the globe accompanied with analytical synoptical and element tables.* Half of the first volume covers geographic theory, including physical geography, animals, and civilizations. The remaining five and a half volumes contain extensive country descriptions.

Often called the father of modern geography, German naturalist **Alexander von Humboldt** (1769-1859) was probably the most widely admired man of the 19th century. In 1799, having acquired a background in geology and mining, he set forth with French botanist Aime Bonpland on a five-year trip to explore the American continents. In South America they navigated the Orinoco River and collected thousands of botanical and geologic specimens, and off South America's west coast Humboldt

Alexander von Humboldt was still at work at age 87 in his study in Berlin.

studied ocean currents and temperatures. From observations of Andean volcanoes he conceived a theory of the origin of the Earth's crust. He measured the decline in magnetic intensity from the Poles toward the Equator and the rate that temperature decreased with elevation. As one way to understand the geography of the Earth and its life-forms, he suggested using isothermal lines (marking equal temperature levels) on a world map.

Back in Paris, Humboldt turned his knowledge of the natural world into 19th century best-sellers. In his sixties, after moving to Berlin, he accepted Tsar Nicholas I of Russia's commission to explore mineral resources in Siberia. Finally he began organizing the gathered knowledge of his life into the five-volume work *Cosmos.* This encyclopedia of geography and geology, which treats the Earth as a single organic system, sold tens of thousands of copies. His contributions to plant geography, climatology, oceanography, geology, and volcanology were profound; Charles Darwin claimed that Humboldt was responsible for shaping the course of his life, calling him "the greatest scientific traveler who ever lived." Like Humboldt, **Carl Ritter** (1779-1859), a German contemporary, profoundly influenced the shape of geography as a discipline. His life's work was a 19-volume series titled *Die Erdkunde,* meaning Earth science, which covered Asia, Africa, and in particular the Sinai peninsula and Palestine. Unlike Humboldt, Ritter worked largely with material compiled from the observations of others. Though often obscure as a writer, he was a powerful lecturer; one of his forums was Germany's first academic chair of geography, at the University of Berlin. He envisioned geography as a science that examined the relationship of all forms of nature to human beings, which exist in harmony and unity as evidence of God's plan.

The first American to write about the geography of the New World was **Jedidiah Morse** (1761-1826), a clergyman. He completed his first book, *Geography Made Easy,* in 1784 before obtaining a theology degree at Yale University.

Publication of *The American Geography* followed in 1789, and *American Universal Geography* in 1793. Presidents of both Yale and Harvard recommended his books as texts. Though he largely drew upon published material, Morse became known as the father of American geography. His son, artist Samuel F. B. Morse, developed the telegraph and the Morse code.

Another American nongeographer, **Thomas Jefferson** (1743-1826), pursued a lifelong interest in geography and was instrumental in encouraging its study. While President of the United States, he sent Meriwether Lewis and William Clark on their 1804-1806 western expedition "to enlarge our knowledge of the geography of our continent . . . to give us a general view of . . . its population, natural history, productions, soil, and climate." The only book Jefferson wrote—*Notes on the State of Virginia*, published in 1780-81—was essentially a regional geography.

Geographic Societies

During the 1800s, several societies formed in Europe and North America to promote the study of geography. In France, the largely academic Societé de Géographie de Paris, founded in 1821, furthered the practical interests that geography served, in particular the country's commercial and colonial ventures. The Geographical Society of Mexico appeared in 1833. Great Britain's Royal Geographical Society, established in 1830, was composed of both scholars and laymen. This active organization sponsored many overseas explorations, including expeditions to the Arctic and Australia. Today national and in many cases state or provincial geographic societies exist in most countries of the world.

In the United States, three prominent geographic organizations founded between 1851 and 1904 continue to support research and encourage discussion of geographic topics: the American Geographical Society, the National Geographic Society, and the Association of American Geographers.

The American Geographical Society was formed in New York in 1851 "for the collection and diffusion of geographical and statistical information." Its founders, who included wealthy philanthropists as well as editors and publishers, had two goals: To provide geographic and statistical information about less explored parts of the United States and to supply United States businessmen with similar information about foreign countries with which they traded. The society publishes the quarterly journal *Geographical Review,* pamphlets, a magazine, and books (including brief country geographies for the general public entitled *Around the World*), all written by professional geographers. It sponsors fellowships and lecture programs and performs research under contract to U.S. corporations.

In 1888 Gardiner Greene Hubbard and 32 other prominent Washingtonians established the National Geographic Society in Washington, D.C., "for the increase and diffusion of geographic knowledge." Its membership was to be broadly based, open to all who were interested in geography. After Hubbard died in 1897, Alexander Graham Bell, inventor of the telephone and Hubbard's son-in-law, became the Society's second president. Bell's goal was to make NATIONAL GEOGRAPHIC magazine, which at the time contained mostly technical articles, more appealing to a wider audience. In 1899 he hired a young schoolteacher named Gilbert H. Grosvenor to serve as the first paid full-time editor, and the magazine began its evolution into one of the most widely recognized, highest-circulation publications in the world.

Today the National Geographic Society also produces television specials, publishes books and National Geographic WORLD and NATIONAL GEOGRAPHIC TRAVELER magazines, and sponsors scientific research and exploration and the National Geography Bee. In cooperation with the American Geographical Society, the Association of American Geographers, and the National Council for Geographic Education, it is also active in setting standards and developing educational materials in geography for public schools.

Largely in response to the National Geographic Society's focus on attracting memberships from educated laymen and the public at large, the geographer William Morris Davis founded the Association of American Geographers in Philadelphia in 1904 as a society for "mature geographic scholars." The association "advances professional studies in geography and encourages the application of geographic research in education, government, and business." Today it has 7,200 members in 71 countries, manages funded geography projects, sponsors nearly 50 specialty groups in a variety of geographic fields, and publishes two journals, *The Professional Geographer* and *The Annals of the Association of American Geographers*.

In 1925 the Society of Woman Geographers was formed in New York City as a forum for the exchange of experiences and ideas of women who have conducted research in geographic disciplines and recorded their work in permanent form—written, photographic, or artistic. The society, which maintains headquarters in Washington, D.C., awards fellowships to aid young women studying for advanced degrees in geography or its allied sciences.

Geography After 1900

By the late 1800s, the growing trend toward specializations in the sciences was sparking debate about the proper content of geography as an academic subject. Some scholars wanted to abandon its human side because they felt its inclusion made the subject less scientific. Others proposed that geography should focus on regional studies, where the relationship between physical and human elements remained relevant. Still others suggested relinquishing its geophysical aspects. Eventually, the idea that geography's purpose was to be a unifying science—one that could connect human society with the environment and nature—gained the most support. That concept remains central to geographic thought today.

Reflecting this trend, by the early 1900s universities were establishing separate departments of geography. Study increasingly emphasized geography's human aspects, geared to applications in fields such as urban planning, land use, and resource management. Beginning in the 1950s and '60s, geography also became more statistical in approach, stressing spatial distributions, model-building, and other tools that help geographers track and predict the patterns of events in different places.

Geography Today

The desire to explore and understand the physical world and its peoples gave birth to geography as a field of study. Modern geography continues that tradition, with an increasing emphasis on understanding how humans are changing the physical Earth in ways both good and bad. A key role of geographers is, and will continue to be, to help explain, predict, and manage the global consequences of local and regional conditions and problems. Today geography goes beyond its original Greek definition, "to write about the Earth"; it is a science

that can help us better understand and protect our home planet.

Geographers at Work

Geographers work in a wide variety of jobs in government, business, and education. Most specialize in one of many subfields: The Association of American Geographers' nearly 50 specialty groups include applied geography, biogeography, cartography, cultural geography,

The work of today's geographers spans many disciplines. Members of the Oceanographic Survey use a sextant to map the Flores Sea, in Indonesia (above); a scientist uses Landsat images to study terrain patterns on Cape Cod, Massachusetts (left); teachers participate in a National Geographic Society Geography Education Program summer workshop (left, below).

geomorphology, historical geography, geography education, medical geography, political geography, and urban geography.

The topics they pursue are as diverse as the world itself. Geographers study such phenomena as population growth and movements, the spread of diseases, and the depletion of resources. They work side by side with urban planners, developers, environmentalists, government officials, corporate managers, military leaders, politicians, economists, biologists, and practitioners and researchers in many other fields. Many are teachers, and others specialize in understanding a specific world region, such as Asia, Latin America, or Africa.

Geographic Skills and Tools

All geographers must hone the skills needed to collect and organize information (often in vast amounts), make sense of that information, and use it to generate sound conclusions. Their data come from a variety of sources, including maps, field interviews, reference materials, and other statistical and published data. In recent years, such technological advances as computers and satellite imagery have revolutionized the ways geographers work with and analyze information to see the Earth in ways not possible in the past. Aerial photography and satellite images, for example, have dramatically altered the visual aspects of geographic information and interpretation. Perhaps the contemporary geographer's most powerful tool is the **geographic information system** (GIS).

A GIS uses computers to store, revise, analyze, manipulate, model, and display geographic data. The data can be derived from maps, reports, statistics, satellite images, surveys, land records, and more. A GIS is a database with a difference: All its information is linked to a geographic, or spatial, reference. Products from a GIS include reports, statistical models, spatial analyses, and maps. Many types of specialized GIS's are also available.

One way to view a GIS is to imagine several layers of specialized, or thematic, maps resting on a basic reference map. An urban planner, for example, may have a GIS whose layers contain separate maps of roads, bus routes, locations of shopping centers, and population information. Once all these maps are registered to a basic grid of the area, the GIS digitally combines the layers, enabling the planner to analyze the data in many different ways—for example, to see how well existing bus routes serve area shopping centers or to determine the impact of a proposed housing development on nearby roads and highways.

Though GIS's can help cartographers in producing maps, their most important application is to help geographers identify and analyze spatial patterns and processes. To accomplish this, the systems pull together enormous amounts of information and produce complex models and analyses that would be time-consuming and difficult if not impossible to prepare manually. As decision-making tools, GIS's are used in such diverse areas as environmental management, agriculture, utilities management, urban and land-use planning, marketing and demographic analysis, hazards management, and emergency and transportation planning. GIS's are still evolving, yet they are already revolutionizing the way geographers, as well as researchers and professionals in many other fields, seek answers and solutions.

Computer technology is also being used to create, enhance, and interpret images from low Earth-orbit satellites, giving geographers yet another tool for gathering information that was previously difficult or even impossible to obtain.

Underlying all this technology, however, is the geographer's traditional and most valued tool—maps.

Maps and Globes

Maps are graphic representations of selected aspects of the surface of Earth or another body. No map can cover every possible characteristic of a location—the result would contain so much information that the map would be unreadable. The state of California, for example, can be represented in many different ways: As a road map for travelers, as a relief map showing topography (the relative elevations and positions of such features as lakes, mountains, and canyons), as a geologic map illustrating kinds of rocks and mineral resources, as a demographic map showing location and density of population, or as a satellite map picturing the Earth from space, to name just a few.

A globe is the most accurate way to represent our spherical Earth in its true proportions. From a practical standpoint, however, globes offer limited detail, are expensive, and are difficult to store or carry around. In addition, a person looking at a globe can see only half the world at a time, whereas a map can give the viewer a complete look at the Earth's surface.

When maps portray a curved surface on a flat sheet of paper, accuracy is sacrificed. Map projections—the process of transferring information from a curved surface to a flat one—and the various kinds of maps are discussed later in this section.

Maps of the Past

EARLY MAPMAKERS

People probably created maps before they could write. Some of the oldest surviving maps—scratched on clay tablets and showing features such as canals, gates, walls, and houses—date back more than 4,000 years to early Mesopotamia. Early Egyptian maps illustrate similar features, along with tombs and

This ancient map, incised on a clay tablet and found in Iraq, is thought to be one of the world's oldest (circa 2300 B.C.). It appears to show a river valley; the curved lines on each side may represent hills or mountains. Top is east.

shrines. Most of these maps had practical uses—to indicate boundaries or provide directions—although a few attempted to show the stars and planets.

Another early map, known as the Bedolina, was carved on a cave wall in northern Italy between 2000 and 1500 B.C. Probably representing the plan of a small inhabited area, it contains symbolic carvings of what may be fields, streams, and wells, along with pictures that were probably added much later of humans, animals, and houses.

The ancient Greeks viewed the Earth as a whole and attempted to show graphically its size and shape—then a subject of much debate. Support for the theory that the Earth was spherical dates back to Pythagoras in the sixth century B.C. By the fourth century B.C., most

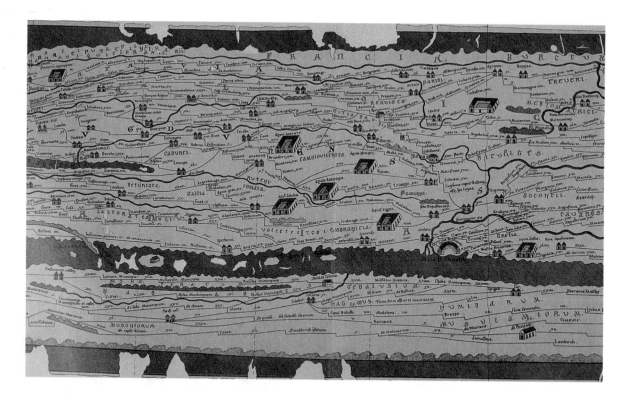

The Romans' approach to mapmaking was largely practical, to chart their extensive road system. This Roman map (above) is based on another from the first century A.D. that shows roads and towns in France, then a Roman province. This web of palm-frond ribs and shells (left), depicting part of the Pacific Ocean, re-creates the type of map used by Micronesian navigators perhaps as early as 1500 B.C. Usually 18 to 24 inches square, such maps showed wave patterns and swells, which the early navigators interpreted to guide their Pacific migrations. Seashells or bits of coral marked the locations of islands.

Greek scholars held this opinion. About 350 B.C. Aristotle advanced a series of arguments to prove the Earth was round: He maintained that during a lunar eclipse, the Earth projects a circular shadow on the moon; and that as a person travels from north to south, new constellations come into view and familiar ones disappear.

The geodetic work of the early Greeks, including Eratosthenes' calculation of Earth's size and use of a system of parallels and meridians, culminated in the monumental work of Claudius Ptolemy in the second century A.D. Ptolemy's eight-volume *Geography* discusses methods of map projection, globe construction, map preparation, and mathematical geography.

His map of the known world, with its tables of latitudes and longitudes, was a considerable achievement for the time, and his contributions to cartography were not surpassed for at least 1,300 years.

Mapmaking in ancient China paralleled that of the Greeks, beginning about the sixth century B.C. Three maps drawn on silk and found in a Han Dynasty tomb date to about 200 B.C. Like their European counterparts, the Chinese used a grid system, although it was not based on a 360° system of latitude and longitude.

MAPMAKING IN THE MIDDLE AGES

Although the science of mapmaking enjoyed little progress in Europe during the Middle Ages, scholars and mapmakers in China and the Islamic world made significant contributions. The first known printed map was created by the Chinese about A.D. 1155, more than three centuries before maps were printed in Europe. Scientific in their approach, Chinese cartographers knew the principles of geometry and used tools familiar to Europeans of the time, including the gnomon, or vertical shaft, sighting tubes, leveling poles, odometer, chains and ropes for ground measurements, and—by the 11th century—magnetic compass bearings.

Beginning in the 800s Islamic mapmakers began to build on Ptolemy's work, which had been translated into Arabic. The world map compiled by the Arab cartographer and geographer al-Idrisi for King Roger II of Sicily in 1154 surpassed any made elsewhere in Europe at the time.

By the late 1200s mariners were sailing by a new kind of navigation map called a **portolan chart**, from the Italian for pilot chart. The earliest portolans outlined the coasts of the Mediterranean and Black Seas. Highly accurate, they carried place names and a rose of wind directions. Eventually portolans included the coastlines of the British Isles, continental Europe, and the west coast of Africa. Their appearance paralleled that of the magnetic compass, causing the portolans to be oriented to the north instead of eastward, as earlier

This surviving piece of a map of the known world of 1513 was drawn on a gazelle hide by Piri Reis, a Turkish mariner. It depicts findings of early discoverers, including South American rivers, a few Caribbean Islands, and exotic animals such as parrots, monkeys, and an elephant.

charts were. With the advent of the compass, the charts' wind rose metamorphosed into the compass rose. Thanks to these advances, mariners could sail directly from one port to another without having to hug the shoreline.

REDISCOVERY IN THE RENAISSANCE

By the 1400s European scholars were rediscovering the works of Ptolemy. The introduction of the printing press in that century made his maps and manuscripts more available to scholars. At the same time, improvements in shipbuilding and navigation were heralding the beginning of the age of exploration. The information gathered by the great sailors and explorers of the day—Dias, Columbus, Cabot, Magellan, and others—significantly improved the accuracy of maps. Their voyages also convinced most educated Westerners that the world was indeed a sphere while China still clung to the concept of a flat Earth and round heaven.

The first map to contain the name "America" was published in 1507 by Martin Waldseemüller, who had read Amerigo Vespucci's reports. The map, which focused largely on portions of South America, was also the first to show that North and South America were not connected to Asia.

The era's leading cartographer was Gerardus Mercator (1512–1594) of Flanders, who gave sailors a valuable navigational tool when he developed the Mercator projection in 1569. He adjusted the spacing of meridians and parallels in such a way that all lines of constant bearing—called rhumb lines (or constant azimuths or loxodromes)—could be drawn as straight lines, even though the Earth is curved. Sailors using such a map could steer by a constant compass setting based on the bearing of the straight line that connected their home and destination ports, correcting for the variation of true from magnetic north. A year after Mercator's death, a son published *Atlas, or Cosmographical meditations upon the creation of the universe, and the universe as created.* "Atlas" in the title, which refers to the mythological figure who was condemned to support the sky on his shoulders, marks the first known use of the term for a collection of maps.

The accuracy and usefulness of maps increased greatly from the 1500s to 1800s thanks to the wealth of information gathered by explorers all over the world. The table on pages 10–14 summarizes their accomplishments.

MAPS SINCE THE 1700S

Mapmaking became more scientific with the invention of better tools and instruments, such as the telescope, the sextant, and an accurate timepiece known as the chronometer. The demand for maps for both civil and military purposes increased in the 1700s and 1800s, and national survey organizations were established in several European nations to create territorial maps. One of the earliest surveys, of France, was authorized by Louis XV in 1746. The Great Trigonometric Survey of India, conducted by the British from 1802 to 1843, established the height of Mount Everest at 29,002 feet (8,840 m), since revised to 29,028 feet (8,848 m).

In the United States, the U.S. Coast and Geodetic Survey was founded in 1807 as the nation's premier mapping agency. The U.S. Army Corps of Topographical Engineers, established in 1838, mapped much of the West through the exploits of John C. Frémont, F. V. Hayden, and others. In 1879 the U.S. Geological Survey (USGS) was formed to coordinate all U.S. land surveys; it publishes and sells maps of all parts of the United States. During World War II, the U.S. military became involved in mapping other parts of the world, and the National Imagery and Mapping Agency (NIMA) continues that mission today. (See Sources of Further Information at the end of Part I for ways to contact these organizations.)

One of the most ambitious cartographic projects has been the creation of the International Map of the World (IMW), which the German geomorphologist Albrecht Penck proposed to the Fifth International Geographical Conference in 1891. Sheets for the map were first printed after World War I, and the cooperative project has continued ever since, occasionally interrupted by wars and other political tensions. Created on a scale of 1:1,000,000, each sheet in the series covers 4° of latitude and 6° of longitude, except those sheets that are poleward of 60° latitude. (See Map Projections, p. 35.) A similar but separate project, the World Aeronautical Chart, originated during World War II to meet the military's need for aeronautical charts. This chart, for which all sheets have been completed, also uses a scale of 1:1,000,000.

Cartographic Changes

In the three years between the first and second revisions to the sixth edition of the National Geographic *Atlas of the World,* society cartographers made nearly 3,500 place-name changes on its maps. Between 1992 and 1995 they changed the spelling *Kazakhstan* to *Kazakstan* (an alteration made by its citizens to show independence from Russia and in 1997 changed back to *Kazakhstan*), added the route of the English Chunnel (the Channel tunnel), revised the shrinking shoreline of the Aral Sea, and added the nations of Eritrea and Palau. They also adjusted the borders between Oman and Yemen and between Saudi Arabia and the United Arab Emirates.

National Geographic Society cartographers make continual changes to world maps, reflecting both physical and political developments.

Today, almost every inch of the Earth's land area has been mapped, some areas in greater detail than others; seafloors too have been extensively charted, though generally in less detail than the land. However, maps must be continuously revised to reflect changes in boundaries, place-names, human structures, and natural phenomena.

Kinds of Maps

Maps are classified in two ways, by scale—either large or small—and by function. A large-scale map shows a relatively small area in substantial detail; an example is a city map that locates urban blocks and buildings. A small-scale map depicts a relatively large area much less minutely, indicating the location of a city, for instance, relative to surrounding rivers, mountains, and political boundaries.

Maps perform two basic functions, labeled **general reference** and **thematic**. A general reference map shows location, either absolute (such as a place at 30° N latitude and 100° W longitude) or relative (the site of one place as it relates to the known position of another place: for example, a map that tells a tourist the direction and distance from the White House to the U.S. Capitol). General reference maps present natural features such as rivers, coastlines, and mountains and man-made features such as highways, railways, and cities and other political subdivisions.

Often produced by government agencies, general reference maps are called base maps. Most base maps depict an area's topography, either as contour lines connecting points of equal elevation or in gradations of color to indicate relief. Color relief maps often include features such as mountain ranges in exaggerated scale because the surface of the Earth is relatively smooth. On a true-to-scale 1:1,000,000 three-dimensional plastic relief map, for example, Mount Everest would be only a third of an inch (8.5 mm) high.

Unlike general reference maps, thematic maps emphasize a specific theme or topic, perhaps illustrating the distribution of average annual rainfall for a region or the locations of various crops. (This information may also be represented on a general reference map. On

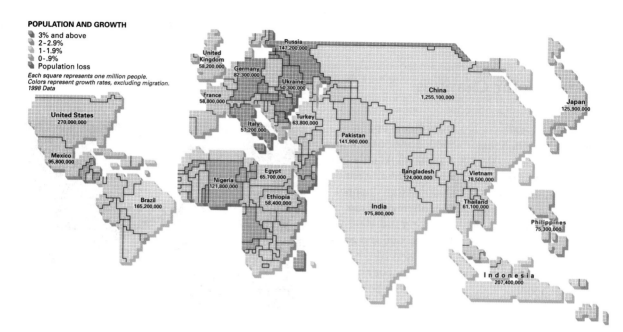

POPULATION AND GROWTH

- 3% and above
- 2 - 2.9%
- 1 - 1.9%
- 0 - .9%
- Population loss

Each square represents one million people.
Colors represent growth rates, excluding migration.
1998 Data

United Kingdom 58,200,000

Russia 147,200,000

Germany 82,300,000

Ukraine 50,300,000

France 58,800,000

China 1,255,100,000

Japan 125,900,000

United States 270,000,000

Turkey 63,800,000

Italy 57,200,000

Mexico 95,800,000

Pakistan 141,900,000

Bangladesh 124,000,000

Vietnam 78,500,000

Nigeria 121,800,000

Egypt 65,700,000

Brazil 165,200,000

Ethiopia 58,400,000

Thailand 61,100,000

India 975,800,000

Philippines 75,300,000

Indonesia 207,400,000

A cartogram designed to depict the rates of world population growth by nation uses color and proportional size to graphically convey the population increase of various nations relative to one another. It shows India and Nigeria as much larger than their physical geographic areas actually are (above). A color key makes clear the theme of a map of the South China Sea—pink highlights the areas where coral reefs are most threatened. The country names and borders on such a map are used as reference points only (right). A large-scale topographic map of the Chugach Mountains of southern Alaska uses both color and contour lines to clearly identify land classes and elevations, respectively.

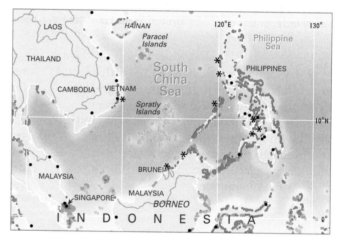

Estimated potential threat to coral reefs
(from coastal development, marine-based pollution, overexploitation of marine resources, and inland pollution and erosion)

■ High ■ Medium ■ Low

• **Metropolitan area greater than 200,000**
✻ **Natural stress occurrence 1986 -1996**
(including hurricanes and typhoons, bleaching, and crown-of-thorns sea star infestations)

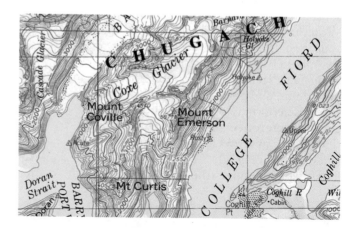

thematic maps, features such as towns and rivers are intended only as reference points.) Thematic maps can provide a graphic complement to words and statistics. A **cartogram** is an abstract thematic map that presents geographic areas on a basis of statistical factors, such as states' population densities proportionate to their land areas. A cartogram comparing the population densities of Connecticut and Nevada, for example, would show Nevada, which is much larger in area than Connecticut, as smaller because Nevada's population is much smaller.

A third type of map is the **chart** (from the Latin word *charta*, meaning document); mariners sail by nautical charts, and airplane pilots fly by aeronautical charts. A **plan** is a large-scale map of a small area, and **plats** and **cadastral** maps record property boundaries.

Extraterrestrial objects have also been mapped. Maps of the moon have been drawn since the 1600s, and their accuracy and number increased greatly in the 1960s in preparation for the first manned lunar landing, in 1969. In 1994 NASA launched the spacecraft Clementine to map the entire surface of the moon. During the mission, the satellite took thousands of high-resolution and infrared images, used laser ranging to map part of the surface, and gathered data on the moon's gravity with radar tracking.

NASA has sent a series of spacecraft to Earth's neighboring planets: Mariners to Venus, Mars, and Mercury; Vikings to land on Mars; Magellan to map Venus; Mars Observer to Mars; Galileo to Jupiter and its moons; Voyagers 1 and 2 to the outer planets and beyond; Mars Pathfinder and the *Sojourner* rover to Mars; Ulysses to the polar regions of the sun; Mars Global Surveyor to Mars; and Cassini to explore Saturn and its moon Titan.

The U.S. Geological Survey and National Imagery and Mapping Agency produce maps from these missions. Today astronomers are mapping the universe in hopes of uncovering clues to its origins.

A surveyor braving sub-zero temperatures uses a transit in the Sverdrup Islands in Canada's Northwest Territiories.

How Maps Are Made

SURVEYING

Cartographers create their varied maps from data derived from surveys, which today include data collected by remote sensing. Surveying is the science of determining the exact size, shape, and location of a given land or undersea area.

Surveys were probably made as long ago as 1400 B.C. by the Sumerians and Egyptians, who left behind boundary stones and clay tablets showing land plots and city plans. The Romans improved the Egyptian surveying instruments and invented their own, such as the water level (to establish the grades of their famous aqueducts) and the plane table (to record angles and help construct the extensive Roman road system).

By the 16th century, surveyors were able to measure an area accurately by applying the principle of **geometric triangulation**, first described by the Dutch astronomer Gemma

The Metric System: Derived from the Earth

In 1790 France established a commission to devise a new form of measurement based on a fraction of the Earth's size—1/10,000,000 of the distance at sea level from the North Pole to the Equator, or one-fourth of the Earth's circumference. Because surveying the entire distance was impossible, the French decided instead to measure a portion of a meridian, which could be used to calculate the Earth's circumference. Such a portion had to begin and end at sea level and lie approximately midway between the Pole and the Equator. The meridian selected was the 2nd East, and the section ran from near Dunkerque, France, to the vicinity of Barcelona, Spain.

In 1792 two astronomers who were also geodesists were sent to survey the line, which took six years. By the end of 1799 the French had completed the calculations that established the meter—defined as 1/40,000,000 of the circumference of the Earth—as the basic unit of the metric system. The definition of a meter has since been revised: A 1983 revision uses the distance that light travels in a vacuum in 1/299,792,458 of a second. Today most countries have adopted the metric system, called the International System of Units, as their official form of measurement. Metric calculation is slowly gaining acceptance in the United States.

Frisius in 1533. In triangulation, the surveyor measures the length of one side of a triangle—a baseline—and two of the triangle's three angles, permitting an easy calculation of the length of the other two sides. The procedure creates two new lines from which other triangles can be formed, a process that continues until the entire area has been surveyed. Surveyors place markers or stations as reference points for these triangles.

In 1620 Edward Gunther introduced to Britain the surveying chain, giving surveyors a standard form of measurement (60 feet; 18 m) that was used until steel measuring tapes replaced it in the early 20th century. Angle-measuring instruments were also developed at this time. Invention of the theodolite, which measures both horizontal and vertical angles, is credited to Leonard Digges of London in 1555, but it was not used widely until Jonathan Sisson added the telescope about 1720. Today remote-sensing technology—including aerial photography, electronic distance measuring, and satellite imaging—has revolutionized the science of surveying.

REMOTE SENSING

Remote sensing is the gathering, storing, and extracting of geographic information from great distances when the gatherer makes no physical contact with the target. The process usually covers large areas.

Aerial photography was the first form of remote sensing, beginning in 1858 with photographs taken from a hot-air balloon near Paris. Photography from balloons continued until the advent of airplanes at the turn of the century. By the 1930s aerial cameras regularly obtained series of overlapping photographs, which experts on the ground later corrected for distortions. The science of making measurements from photographs is known as **photogrammetry**.

Since the 1960s, electronic distance measuring devices have allowed surveyors to obtain extremely precise measurements. Laser measuring systems, on the ground and from satellites, chart distances by recording the time a beam of visible or infrared light takes to reach and then return from a distant reflector.

Today remote sensing is most often

Landsat satellites survey the Earth in strips 115 miles (185 km) wide (above). More than 560 color images from satellite data were combined to make a portrait of the 48 contiguous states (left).

performed by instruments mounted on high altitude aircraft or satellites, which enable scientists and cartographers to capture information invisible to human eyes by recording electromagnetic waves. Emitted by every object on the Earth's surface, these waves range from long, low-frequency radio waves to short, high-frequency gamma rays. Within this spectrum are various wavelength bands, or spectral regions, including microwaves, infrared, visible light, ultraviolet, and x-rays. Each object on

Earth emits a spectral signature, or place in the electromagnetic spectrum, that computers can analyze and identify.

Once remote-sensing data have been gathered, scientists apply image-processing techniques to extract the specific information they need—for example, to create a digital image showing the locations of water. They do this by telling the computer to process only certain spectral bands, a method known as theme extraction. The computer then converts these

Fighting Disease from Space

Images from satellites such as Landsat are giving health officials worldwide a head start in fighting infectious diseases. The satellite data allow scientists to detect changes in the habitats of disease carrying organisms such as insects and rodents, which might trigger epidemics, and to alert local health officials to adopt defensive strategies. In NASA-sponsored tests, Landsat images and remote-sensing technology located areas of heavy mosquito breeding in rice fields in California, malaria-prone areas in Mexico, and in a New York State test, likely landscapes for Lyme disease.

GPS—A New Way to Pinpoint Location

Thanks to the 24 satellites of the U.S. Department of Defense's Global Positioning System (GPS), persons operating a car, boat, or airplane equipped with a GPS receiver will always know exactly where they are, often to within a few meters. Developed for military use in the 1970s, the GPS is also becoming widely available to the public, and the list of civilian applications is burgeoning. Oil companies employ GPS to pinpoint drilling sites in remote areas. Mappers take observations in the field with GPS and superimpose plots into the GIS systems. To help forecast the weather, meteorologists can measure the delays of GPS signals caused by changes in the atmosphere. Geophysicists using GPS and a technique called carrier tracking, monitor slight changes in the Earth's crust that may help predict earthquakes. Other uses, such as systems designed to help blind persons move about safely, are also being developed.

Just as chronometers revolutionized navigation in the 1700s, precise timekeeping is also essential to GPS. Each satellite carries sophisticated atomic clocks, and signals broadcast by the satellites include their exact locations and the time sent.

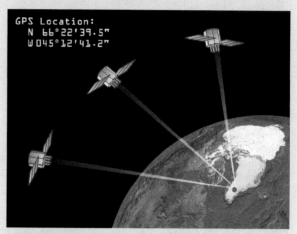

GPS Location:
  N 66°22'39.5"
  W 045°12'41.2"

Time and location data from three satellites are needed to provide information on latitude and longitude to receivers on Earth; a fourth satellite is needed to provide information on altitude. Computers in the receiver, applying the geometric principle of triangulation, can then determine a receiver's location.

digital images into photographic images, which can be used to make maps, predict weather, locate areas of deforestation and mineral deposits, identify crops and their problems, track oil spills, find long-lost archaeological sites, assess flood damage, detect surface changes over time, and identify hundreds of other physical patterns and processes. As the technology develops, government, academia, and business are continuing to find new applications for these images.

The best known satellite images have come from NASA's series of Landsat satellites. The first, originally called the Earth Resources Technology Satellite (ERTS), was launched in 1972. At this writing, Landsat 4 and 5 were operational, though aging; they are managed by Space Imaging, a private firm. Landsat 6

failed at launch. The launch of Landsat 7, which will be operated jointly by NASA and the U.S. Geological Survey, took place in April 1999. The satellites have provided a wealth of information about the Earth to scientists in a range of specialties, as well as to mapmakers.

As the U.S. and Russian governments drop security restrictions on data gathered from reconnaissance satellites, private companies are increasingly using this information for nonmilitary applications, such as seeking potential energy sources, monitoring pollution, and analyzing building sites. Several U.S. companies are building and/or launching their own high-resolution satellites. Some of these can focus on targets as small as homes and yards, raising concerns about the right to privacy.

THE CARTOGRAPHER'S JOB

Who will use the cartographer's map? For what purpose? These are the first questions the mapmaker asks at the outset. The answers will influence decisions about area and features to display, scale and size, type of projection, level of detail, and appropriate symbols.

Maps created by using elements from an existing map or base map as a foundation are called **derived** maps. The cartographer compiles new information from a variety of sources to customize, verify, and update the base map. Road maps are derived maps, often including data from topographic maps, road surveys, and aerial photographs.

After considering a map's purpose, cartographers must determine the level of detail to include so that the map does not become overcrowded with information and therefore hard to read. Such editing must also maintain a uniform level of detail. At times the cartographer must generalize or omit features because of limitations of scale or space. For example, the coves, inlets, and bays of the Cape Cod shoreline would appear on a large-scale map of Massachusetts, but be smoothed out on a small-scale map of the United States. (See Scale, page 33.)

Today's maps are increasingly created with the help of computers. By linking geographic information systems (see GIS discussion on page 20) with graphics software and electronic prepress systems, cartographers can create and revise maps much faster and cheaper than by hand. GIS software permits them to access and manipulate information from databases of stored maps and other geographic data, such as population, land use, and water resources. The resulting layered map files feed into personal computers, which employ illustration software to complete the map by adding symbols, type, and graphics. Then the map can be transferred electronically to an image processor and plotted directly to film or to a printing plate. Maps are usually printed on offset or gravure presses. Print-on-demand

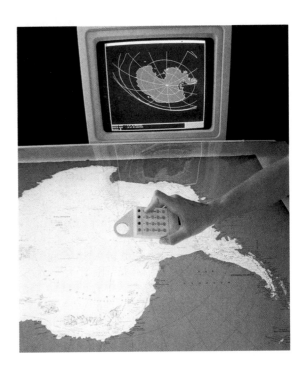

Hand-held digitizers help turn printed maps into computer-readable information, which can then be revised and refined much quicker than traditional methods of mapmaking (top). Scientists studying a rain forest use a GPS receiver to determine their exact location (above).

systems, which produce individual or customized maps directly from a computer, are becoming more widely available.

PARTS OF A MAP

To describe the essential components of a map, cartographers often use the acronym TODAL-SIGS, developed by educator Jeremy Anderson. It stands for title, orientation, date, author, legend, scale, index, grid, and surrounding places. The **title** describes what the map shows and sometimes the time period. **Orientation** denotes the way it is placed on the paper, traditionally but not always with north at the top, and with an arrow or compass rose. The **date** tells when the map was made, an important indicator of reliability. The **author** is the compiling cartographer, agency, or company that developed, researched, and drew the map. **Legend**, **scale**, and **grid** are described in the paragraphs that follow. The **index** is the alphabetical listing of the map's features and place-names, cross-referenced to their grid location on the map, and in atlases to the map page number. The acronym's final S was added by later cartographers, who felt that an additional feature of a good map is its identification of **surrounding places** that border the mapped area, such as states, countries, mountains, or oceans.

LEGEND

The legend, or key, contains the information the user needs to understand a map's symbols. Cartographers depend on symbols and other typographic elements to present information that would be impossible to fit on a map in words. Knowing the meaning of a map's symbols is essential to gleaning all the information it contains. For example, the categories of populations of towns and cities and their relative size may be depicted by different styles and sizes of typefaces, as well as by town-spot symbols of different sizes and shapes. Lines of different widths, types (broken or solid), and colors can represent the kinds of roads shown, from gravel-covered back roads to interstates. Administrative and political boundaries such as

Maps are indispensable tools for visitors to unfamiliar locations. Tourists in London's Trafalgar Square use a city map to get their bearings.

state and county lines can be shown in different colors or line widths.

Point symbols such as triangular flags may indicate the locations of golf courses, and silhouettes of airplanes may locate airports. Contour lines and relief shading are symbolic representations that convey elevations and other topography. Colors can reveal geographic features—green for vegetation, blue for water, brown for deserts. Different mapmakers often choose different symbols, requiring the user to review the key or legend before reading a map.

What's in a Name?

Cartographers must frequently determine the current and official name of a geographic place or feature. The official source for U.S. names is the U.S. Board on Geographic Names (BGN). Created in 1890 to ensure that the federal government uses geographic names consistently, it also fields questions about and resolves problems with geographic names and accepts proposals for new names from the general public. In cooperation with the U.S. Geological Survey (USGS), BGN maintains a database of nearly two million names of physical and cultural geographic features in the United States. This database, which can be accessed through a USGS Web site, gives users the federally recognized name of a feature, the state and county where it is located, latitude and longitude, elevation (where available), population (of incorporated cities and towns), and names that may have designated the feature in the past.

Names of foreign geographic features are maintained on the GEOnet Names Server by the National Imagery and Mapping Agency (NIMA). This database, also available to the public, contains some 3.3 million features and is updated monthly.

SCALE

Most maps are drawn to scale, meaning that a distance measurement on the map is proportionally related to the actual distance on the Earth. Three types of scales are used. The **graphic**, or **bar**, **scale**, commonly seen on road maps, is a line that looks like a ruler and shows the length of a certain distance on the map, for example 40 miles. The **verbal**, or **word**, **scale** is a sentence that states the relationship of map distance to actual distance—for example, "One inch represents 10 miles." The **representative fraction** (**RF**) indicates the ratio to which the map was drawn, such as 1:63,360, meaning that 1 inch on the map equals 63,360 inches (one mile) on land (distance on the map is always expressed as one). Because the scale is a ratio, any unit of measurement can be used; thus 1:63,360 holds equally true for inches, centimeters, or feet.

Maps are normally classified as small scale or large scale, though they also may be medium scale. Large-scale maps may use a 1:63,360 or larger scale and show detailed surface features such as creeks, ponds, hills, and man-made structures, including streets, buildings, and airports. Small-scale maps, which usually depict entire countries or continents, may be 1:1,000,000 and smaller and give only a general view of surface features. Maps with medium scales fall between these two classifications.

GRID

To provide a frame of reference for locating points on a street or regional map, cartographers superimpose a **grid** of lettered rows and numbered columns to form a matrix of squares. An index of places usually accompanies this type of map, citing the grid coordinates of each place-name. For example, the index may show Pheasant Drive at D-6, meaning that the street appears somewhere in the

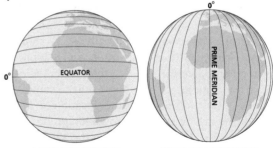

Latitude is the distance north or south of the Equator, and longitude is the distance east or west of the prime meridian.

LINES OF LATITUDE   LINES OF LONGITUDE

The Old Royal Observatory, in Greenwich, England, lies along the prime meridian, or line of 0° longitude.

Longitude: Just a Matter of Time

Longitude is easiest calculated by using clocks—one that shows Greenwich time and one that shows local time. Here's how it works. The Earth takes 24 hours to rotate a full 360°, traveling 15° of longitude each hour. If you know the difference in hours, minutes, and seconds between Greenwich Mean Time (also called Universal Time) and your local time, you can multiply that difference by 15 to determine the degrees longitude of your time zone. Be sure to take into account daylight saving programs.

For early mariners at sea, calculating longitude was not always so easy. They lacked a seagoing clock that could withstand the stresses of swings of temperature and humidity and a ship's motion, and reliably tell the time in their home port or some other location of known longitude. During the 1730s English clockmaker John Harrison perfected a chronometer whose workings employed a mix of metals that achieved this reliability. Now the mariner, knowing the time at a fixed point and a local one (because he had a second clock or could calculate local time by sextant and astronomical tables), could pinpoint local longitude.

In 1884, 24 nations accepted the international time zone system. The 24 time zones are aligned with meridians at 15-degree intervals, each representing one hour. In some locations, the time-zone lines do not exactly follow the meridians, but adjust to accommodate local borders or other political features. The International Date Line, the point at which each new day begins and each old day ends, follows the 180th meridian—halfway around the world from Greenwich—for much of its length.

square formed where D and 6 intersect. On a globe or a flat map, the lines of latitude and longitude produce another type of grid, called a **graticule**, of immense practical value to navigators and surveyors. Latitude and longitude are also used to form the grid used in flat maps of countries, regions, and the world, such as those found in atlases.

LATITUDE AND LONGITUDE

Before mapmakers could create a flat map of the world, they needed lines of reference to pinpoint locations on the globe. These lines originated with the ancient Greek astronomer Hipparchus, who devised a coordinate system using a grid of lines known as **latitude** (parallels) and **longitude** (meridians) and measured in degrees. Latitude is based on a physical aspect of the Earth, the Equator, at 0° latitude. It lies midway between the North Pole (90° north latitude) and South Pole (90° south latitude) and divides the Earth into the Northern and Southern Hemispheres. Longitude, which measures angular distance along the Equator, has no physically fixed point for starting or ending. To establish uniformity in recording longitude, an international agreement in 1884 made Greenwich, England, the location of the **prime meridian**, which extends to 180° east longitude and 180° west longitude. Lines of longitude meet at the North and South Poles.

The distance covered by a degree of longitude varies depending on its distance from the Equator; it can be anywhere from 69.171 miles (111.290 km) at the Equator to zero at either Pole. Because of the oblate shape of the Earth, degrees of latitude also vary in distance covered according to distance from the Equator, but only slightly. At the Equator a degree of latitude is 68.708 miles (110.551 km), and at the Poles it is 69.403 miles (111.669 km).

Map Projections

Even though the only accurate way to portray the Earth's surface is on a globe, travelers over

CONICAL

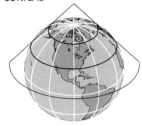 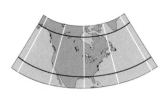

CYLINDRICAL

 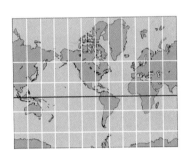

AZIMUTHAL

 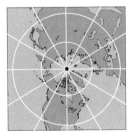

Cartographers through the centuries have used these three basic types of projection.

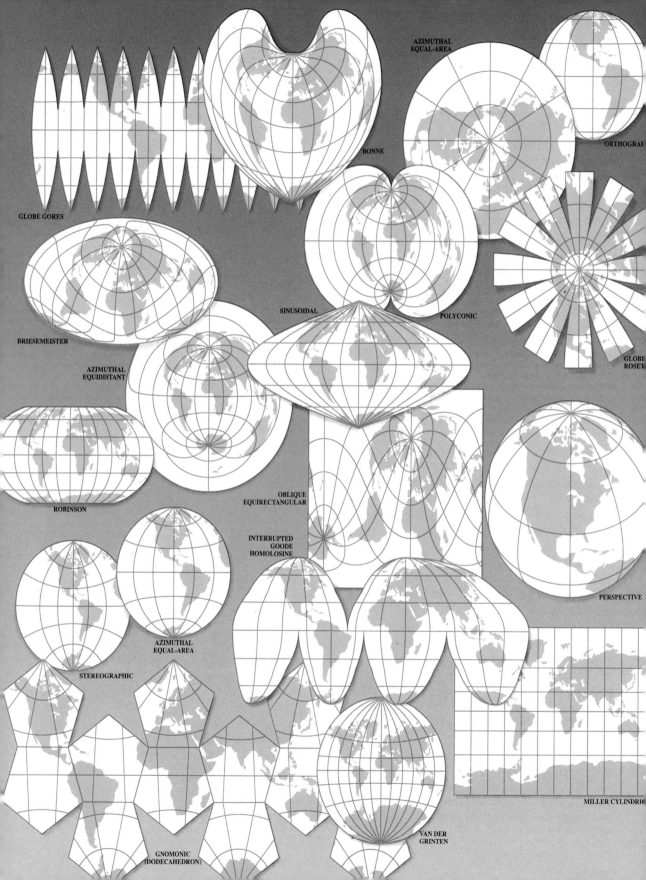

GLOBE GORES

BONNE

AZIMUTHAL
EQUAL-AREA

ORTHOGRAF

BRIESEMEISTER

SINUSOIDAL

POLYCONIC

GLOBE
ROSET

AZIMUTHAL
EQUIDISTANT

ROBINSON

OBLIQUE
EQUIRECTANGULAR

INTERRUPTED
GOODE
HOMOLOSINE

PERSPECTIVE

AZIMUTHAL
EQUAL-AREA

STEREOGRAPHIC

MILLER CYLINDRIC

GNOMONIC
(DODECAHEDRON)

VAN DER
GRINTEN

The Shortest Distance Between Two Points Is . . . a Circle?

Great circle is the term used to describe the largest circle that can be drawn around a sphere such as a globe. Specifically, it is the circle made on the surface of the sphere by any plane that passes through the sphere's center. On any globe, there are an infinite number of great circles. On the Earth, the Equator is the only line of latitude that forms a great circle. Each meridian, or line of longitude, forms half of a great circle.

The phrase "great circle route" describes the shortest distance between two points. When a string is stretched between any two points on a globe, it marks the great circle route. If a ruler connects the same two places on a flat map, the route is different and appears shorter. However, because of the distortion caused by projecting a round object onto a flat surface, the map route only *looks* shorter.

A signpost gives great circle distance (in miles) to various parts of the world from this spot in Canada's Yukon Territory.

the centuries have much preferred to carry flat and foldable charts, posing a continuing challenge to mapmakers. Because there is no perfect way to portray the curved Earth on a flat surface without causing distortion of some kind, the cartographer employs a **projection** to minimize the effects of this distortion.

A projection is a system for transferring information about a round object such as a globe to a flat piece of paper or other surface. Each of the three basic types of projections—cylindrical, conical, and azimuthal—has many possible variations. Created mathematically, map projections can be envisioned physically. A **cylindrical projection** can be pictured by imagining a globe as a translucent

Through the ages, map projections have appeared in a variety of interesting shapes, from hearts and stars to circles and rectangles. All distort the Earth's surface in some way (opposite).

sphere, with a light placed inside that prints an image of the globe's features onto a rolled sheet of paper surrounding it. Although the areas near the middle of the globe will appear accurately, the meridians, which on a globe come together to form a point at the Poles, will be equally spaced from top to bottom. This "stretching" of the meridians at the higher latitudes in a cylindrical map projection—like the Mercator—causes landmasses nearer the Poles to look much larger than they really are.

The idea of using a cone to create a map projection was Ptolemy's. To picture a **conical projection**, imagine the open part of a paper cone resting on a globe, its point above the North Pole and its edge touching a latitude above the Equator. If a light shining inside the globe projects and prints an image of its features onto the cone, the parallels will appear to

VAN DER GRINTEN

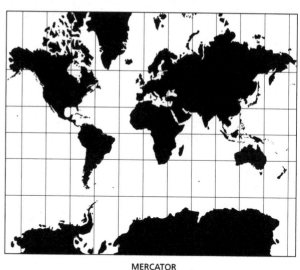

MERCATOR

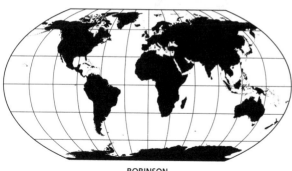

ROBINSON

MOLLWEIDE

WINKEL TRIPEL

The projection usually chosen for general reference, world coverage purposes is the Winkel Tripel, used since 1998 by the National Geographic Society. It replaced the Robinson projection, adopted in 1988, and the VDG, which preceded the Robinson and was used by the Society for most of its political maps since 1922. All projections distort. The useful Mollweide projection compresses and shears shapes at high latitudes, as does the Mercator, which also distorts the relative sizes of landmasses in high latitudes; for example, Brazil and Alaska appear about the same size, but Brazil is nearly six times larger than high-latitude Alaska.

become smaller as they approach the Poles, as they do on a globe, but their spacing will differ. (This problem can be solved mathematically, however, so that the circles are spaced at equal distances.) When the cone is cut, a flat map unfolds, shaped like a fan. The 1507 Waldseemüller map used Ptolemy's conical projection. Such projections are particularly useful for showing areas like the coterminus United States that lie in the middle latitudes.

The **azimuthal**—or **plane,** or **zenithal**—**projection** designates one point of the globe—which can be anywhere—as the center of the map. Imagine an image that would be projected onto a flat piece of cardboard resting on the North Pole. If the point of focus is at the Equator, the projection is equatorial; if the center lies somewhere between the Equator and one of the Poles, the projection is oblique.

On a **gnomic** azimuthal projection, all great circles appear as straight lines. This type of map is used by pilots who fly along **great circle routes** (see sidebar).

More than a hundred world map projections have been invented. All deform the shapes of landmasses, some enlarge or shrink them, and all skew distances or directions. The cylindrical Mercator projection produces a **conformal map** showing the true shapes of small areas, but not correct sizes. **Equal area projections** such as the Mollweide depict all regions in correct relative size, but distort shapes in the higher latitudes. In **interrupted projections**, the oceans (or continents) are cut into pieces to show their relative sizes more clearly. Because all projections have advantages and disadvantages, the intended use of the map determines the one chosen.

SOURCES OF FURTHER INFORMATION

1. A full account of the history of geography may be found in *The Geographical Tradition*, by David N. Livingstone (Blackwell Publishers, 1992). The author tracks the evolution of geography from the times of the early explorers to contemporary applications that focus on social and environmental problems.

2. For a wealth of information on the dozens of different map projections and their histories, see John P. Snyder's book *Flattening the Earth: Two Thousand Years of Map Projections* (University of Chicago Press, 1993). This heavily illustrated volume, intended for a general audience but a little technical at times, traces map development chronologically from the time of Ptolemy to the present day.

3. To learn how maps reflect the beliefs and times of the cultures that developed them, read *Maps and Civilization: Cartography and Culture in Society*, by Norman J. W. Thrower (University of Chicago Press, 1996). The author, a professor of geography at the University of California, Los Angeles, traces the history of the map from prehistoric times to the present day and includes information on the modern-day map-making of governmental and institutional organizations.

4. For a fascinating account of how John Harrison solved the problem of determining longitude at sea, see Dava Sobel's book *Longitude: The True Story of a Lone Genius Who Solved the Greatest Scientific Problem of His Time* (Walker & Company, 1995).

5. Numerous U.S. government agencies provide map information. Among major sources, the Geography and Map Division of the Library of Congress has 4 million maps, 50,000 atlases, and 8,000 reference books—one of the most comprehensive collections in the world (phone 202-707-6277). The National Imagery and Mapping Agency, formerly the Defense Mapping Agency, makes available aeronautical, nautical, topographic, and hydrographic maps and charts (Internet site is http://www.nima.mil). Landsat images are available at NASA's Jet Propulsion Laboratory Internet site, http://www.jpl.nasa.gov. The U.S. Geological Survey offers educational pamphlets, brochures, and maps via their Internet site (http://www.usgs.gov) or by phone 1-800-USA-MAPS (1-800-872-6277).

6. The History of Cartography project at the University of Wisconsin, Madison, is publishing a multivolume series of illustrated books titled *The History of Cartography*. The University of Chicago Press has published three cartographic histories to date, and five more are planned. Each is devoted to a region and time period. The three currently available are *Cartography in Prehistoric, Ancient, and Medieval Europe and the Mediterranean* (1987); *Cartography in the Traditional Islamic and South Asian Societies* (1992); and *Cartography in the Traditional East and Southeast Asian Societies* (1994).

7. Popular books about maps and cartographers include *How to Lie with Maps* (University of Chicago Press, 1991), *Drawing the Line: Tales of Maps and Cartacontroversy* (Henry Holt, 1996), *Cartographies of Danger: Mapping Hazards in America* (University of Chicago Press, 1997), and *Maps with the News* (University of Chicago Press, 1989), all by Mark Monmonier; *The Map Catalog* (3rd. ed., Vintage/Tilden Press, 1992), which lists sources for maps of all kinds; *The Mapmakers*, by John Noble Wilford (Vintage Books, 1982); and *The Power of Maps*, by Denis Wood (The Guilford Press, 1992).

8. The Map Machine section of the National Geographic Society's Internet site (http://www.nationalgeographic.com) provides dozens of online links to libraries, government agencies, and organizations that contain information on cartography and related subjects.

PART II

Physical Geography

California's Yosemite
National Park, located in
the Sierra Nevada, is famous
for its spectacular scenery.
The Merced River passes
through magnificent
Yosemite Valley, lined with
great precipices of granite
that rise 4,000 feet
from the valley floor.

Introduction

Physical geography is the study of Earth's natural environments, the composites of physical and biological processes and patterns ranging in scale from local to global. Physical geography draws on the sciences of astronomy, meteorology, climatology, geology, hydrology, pedology, and ecology.

While physical geography encompasses surface features such as mountain ranges and lagoons, streams and sand dunes, it also includes understanding the composition and processes of the atmosphere and the weather, climates, geology, and other forces of nature that shape landforms and landscapes. Particular combinations of natural processes result in the different environments found on Earth's surface. Many of the processes are global in scale, and the types of environments therefore occur in predictable global patterns.

A physical geographer understands that the grasslands and continental climate of South Dakota's badlands are the result of meteorological and geological processes: Weathering weakened underlying sandstones and shales; fluvial processes eroded stream channels; and meteorologic processes created a dry climate unable to support much vegetative cover.

Having an understanding of the physical processes at work on Earth enables us to anticipate and respond more effectively to natural changes. We can understand the effects of El Niño on global weather and Peru's anchovy fishery, and a volcanic eruption's effects on people, livestock, streams, and vegetation. By applying what we know of physical geography, we can understand the consequences of our actions, whether building a mall, damming a river, or clear-cutting a rain forest.

Planet Earth

Formation and Composition

Earth formed at the same time as the rest of our solar system, approximately 4.6 billion years ago. The foundation of understanding Earth's origins remains the solar nebular theory proposed by French astronomer Pierre-Simon Laplace (1749-1827) in 1796. Laplace held that the sun and the planets each coalesced from a rotating cloud of cooling gases and dust in one arm of the Milky Way galaxy. The sun and the individual planets gained mass as their gravitational pull attracted debris from space, ranging in size from dust to asteroids. Earth and the other planets continued to accrete mass until the **solar wind**—energy and ions flowing from the sun—blew away most of the remaining gases and dust within one million years of the sun's formation.

Over the next billion years, Earth's surface evolved from a thin basalt crust to include granitic continental masses on shifting plates above a still molten interior. Gases from volcanic eruptions provided the beginnings of the first permanent atmosphere. Gradually precipitation accumulated to form Earth's first bodies of water. Then, about 3.8 billion years ago, life in the form of bacteria and algae first appeared within those bodies of water. Once airless, waterless, and lifeless, Earth became the blue planet. Oceans covered nearly three-fourths of its surface, making the entire planet appear blue from space. Earth continues to change; it

is, as Canadian geologist J. Tuzo Wilson noted, "a living mobile thing."

When Earth was first accumulating space debris and therefore mass, gravity attracted hydrogen and helium gases to form an atmosphere, but the solar wind blew away this atmosphere, leaving Earth rocky, like other planets relatively close to the sun—Mercury, Venus, and Mars. Jupiter, Saturn, Neptune, and Uranus, planets farther from the sun and its solar wind and high temperatures, retained these gases. As Earth's magnetic field continued to become stronger, it deflected the solar wind; gravity held gases close to the surface, and a second atmosphere then began to accumulate.

Two hundred million years after Earth formed, volcanoes began to erupt, and **lava**, which is molten rock, released dissolved gases to form the second atmosphere. This **outgassing**, comparable to opening a can of carbonated beverage and having the dissolved carbon dioxide bubble out of solution, created a second atmosphere that Earth's developing magnetic field protected from the solar wind. Outgassing created an atmosphere mostly of carbon dioxide, water vapor, and nitrogen.

In addition to outgassing, condensation and photosynthesis were also important in creating an atmosphere and a **hydrosphere**, or all water on Earth. About 400 million years

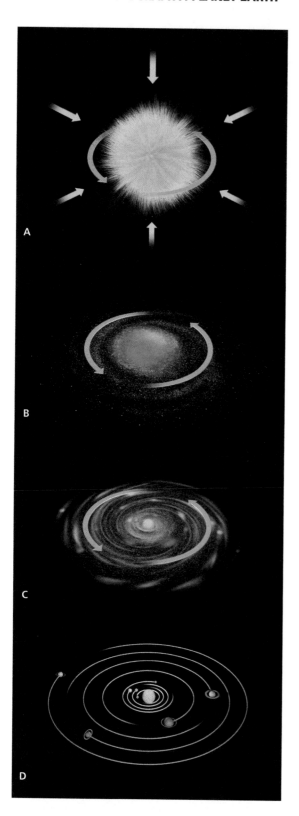

after outgassing started, Earth cooled sufficiently for **condensation** to begin to take place. When water vapor cools, it condenses to become cloud droplets that combine and fall as rain and snow. Rain and snow accumulated to form the first bodies of water on Earth. Condensation removed water vapor and dissolved carbon dioxide from the atmosphere. When carbon dioxide combined with condensed water it formed carbonic acid droplets that made Earth's earliest bodies of water very acidic. The earliest life began in these acidic waters.

Based on the fossil record, life is believed to have begun about 3.8 billion years ago with anaerobic bacteria. Around 3.5 billion years ago, aquatic algae began to remove carbon dioxide from seawater and to release free oxygen through **photosynthesis**, the process by which plants convert carbon dioxide to oxygen and glucose. At first, little oxygen from the algae made it into the atmosphere because of the slow rate of photosynthesis. In addition, iron dissolved in the oceans from sediments combined with free oxygen to form hematite, thus decreasing the amount of oxygen that was available to escape into the atmosphere.

By 570 million years ago the amount of oxygen in the atmosphere had increased from about one percent to ten percent, and when plants appeared on land—about 420 million years ago—greater amounts of oxygen were produced. Eventually land animals evolved, starting with insects and followed by amphibians and reptiles. Although the relative proportion of atmospheric oxygen has varied over the last 100 million years, the present atmospheric level of 21 percent was probably reached about 20 million years ago.

Earth's gravity continues to attract dust and meteoroids, as it has since the beginning. Recent research shows that these particles contribute little mass to Earth, but they do add small amounts of water to our atmosphere. Meteoroids that streak into our atmosphere

The solar nebular hypothesis states that a rotating cloud of gases and dust (A) contracts gravitationally, forming a sun and flat disk of debris (B), which creates planets (C). Solar wind blows off remaining gases and debris (D).

Chicxulub Crater and the K-T Boundary

About 65 million years ago an asteroid more than 6 miles in diameter struck what is now the Yucatán Peninsula of Mexico. The impact created the Chicxulub Crater, more than 180 miles wide, and caused a gigantic dust cloud. The dust eventually settled as a layer of iridium-rich clay now found within sedimentary rock layers beneath the Atlantic and Pacific Oceans and on most northern land masses. The dust cloud may have caused temperatures to drop around the world. This global cooling following the impact is linked to the extinction of dinosaurs and more than half of all plant and animal species. Significant differences in the fossil record separate the Cretaceous (K) period of the Mesozoic era from the Tertiary (T) period of the Cenozoic era, marking the K-T boundary. The K stands for *Kreide*, German for Cretaceous. (See Geologic Time chart, below.) Other events at this time, including huge lava eruptions in what is now India, caused atmospheric changes that may have contributed to the mass extinctions.

and burn up before impact are called meteors or falling stars. Larger meteoroids and asteroids that pass through the atmosphere and slam into Earth create impact craters that are found throughout the world. Meteor Crater, nearly a mile in diameter and 575 feet deep, is located near Winslow, Arizona. Asteroid impacts have been critical in Earth's biological history by contributing to mass extinctions, particularly the extinction of dinosaurs 65 million years ago, at the end of the Mesozoic era.

This asteroid crater shows the typical formation resulting from an impact of an asteroid with Earth's surface.

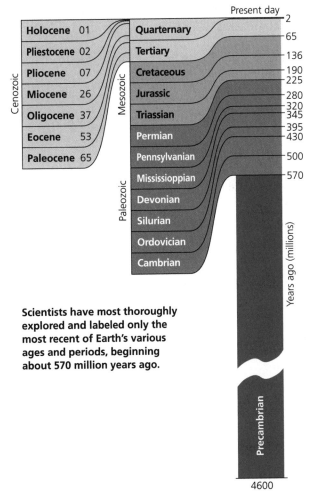

Cenozoic		Mesozoic		Years ago (millions)
				Present day
Holocene	01	Quarternary		2
Pliestocene	02	Tertiary		65
Pliocene	07	Cretaceous		136
				190
				225
Miocene	26	Jurassic		280
Oligocene	37	Triassic		320
				345
Eocene	53	Permian		395
				430
Paleocene	65	Pennsylvanian		500
		Mississioppian		570
		Devonian		
		Silurian		
		Ordovician		
		Cambrian		

Paleozoic

Precambrian

4600

Scientists have most thoroughly explored and labeled only the most recent of Earth's various ages and periods, beginning about 570 million years ago.

Earth Structure

Earth's minerals and rocks, like all matter, are composed of **elements**, basic substances that cannot be broken down chemically. So far 112 elements have been discovered, including oxygen, silicon, aluminum, and iron. Though the relative percentages of elements making up the planet have remained constant since its formation, the internal structure of Earth itself is not homogeneous. During the first billion years, heat from three sources—meteorite impacts, gravity's compression of magma and other inner Earth material, and the radioactive decay of some elements—caused melting within the planet. The high temperatures caused the elements to separate into layers on the basis of their density. Heavy elements such as iron and nickel concentrated nearer Earth's center, and lighter elements such as oxygen and silicon combined with other elements to form most surface rocks and minerals.

Earth now has four major layers: a crust, an underlying mantle, an outer core, and an inner core. While we can easily observe only the crust, we know about the other three layers because some of their minerals and rocks have risen to the surface. Diamonds, for example, have risen from the mantle. Evidence for the structure and composition of inner Earth is primarily obtained by recording and interpreting seismic waves generated by earthquakes.

Earth's crust is the thinnest and least dense of the four layers and floats on the mantle. The oceanic crust forming the ocean floors is from three to seven miles thick and is composed of **mafic rocks**, igneous rocks rich in magnesium and iron. Continental crust, ranging from 6 to 45 miles in thickness, makes up landmasses and is thickest under mountain ranges. **Felsic rocks**, containing more feldspar and silica than mafic rocks, make up the continental crust and are less dense than mafic rocks. The difference in density between the two crusts is significant when studying plate tectonic theory, an explanation of how Earth's major surface features form. (See Plate Tectonics, page 130.)

Below the crust is the denser rock of the mantle, which extends about 1,790 miles toward the core. Croatian physicist Andrija Mohorovičić (1857-1936) discovered the difference between crustal and mantle density by measuring how fast seismic waves travel through the layers; he found that the waves travel faster in the denser rocks of the mantle. The boundary between crust and mantle is called the **Mohorovičić discontinuity**, or **Moho**, in his honor.

Temperature and pressure increase with depth in the mantle and result in some layering within the mantle in terms of composition and rigidity. Of particular significance for plate tectonics is that between depths of 60 and 200 miles, the increasing heat melts a small percentage of the mantle, allowing overlying tectonic plates to move around.

Beneath the mantle are the two layers of Earth's core: a liquid outer core 1,400 miles thick and a solid inner core with a 750-mile radius. The **Gutenberg discontinuity**, named for German geophysicist Beno Gutenberg (1889-1960), marks the contact between the

Abundant Elements of Earth's Crust

ELEMENT	PERCENTAGE OF CRUST BY WEIGHT
Oxygen	46.6
Silicon	27.7
Aluminum	8.1
Iron	5.0
Calcium	3.6
Sodium	2.8
Potassium	2.6
Magnesium	2.1
Total	**98.5**

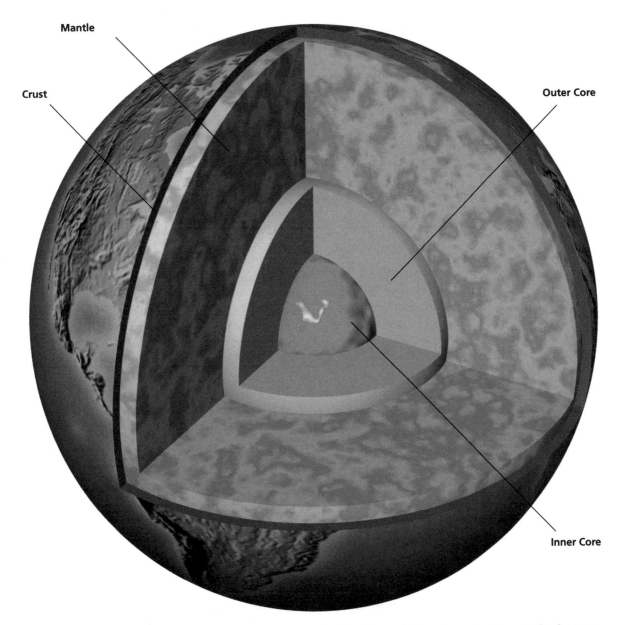

The behavior of seismic waves during earthquakes has revealed that the crust is less dense than the mantle, the outer core is liquid rock, and the inner core is solid.

mantle and outer core, where seismic waves undergo changes in speed. Wave speed varies according to differences in a material's composition and phase, such as whether it is in liquid or solid phase. Iron is the most common element in the outer and inner cores, but based on variations of core densities observed by geophysicists, other elements such as sulfur must also be present.

While Earth rotates on its axis, rotating convection currents in the outer core may generate the magnetic field that surrounds

Earth and may cause the solid inner core to spin slightly faster than the rest of the planet. The extra speed allows the inner core to complete an extra revolution every 140 years, and the interaction between the inner and outer cores may be the cause of the 130 reversals of the north and south magnetic poles over the past 65 million years.

Dimensions and Shape

The dimensions of the sun and planets reflect the total amount of space debris captured by each. Earth is now about 24,900 miles in circumference and 7,900 miles in diameter. It is the largest of the four planets closest to the sun.

Earth is an oblate ellipsoid rather than a perfect sphere, meaning that its circumference at the Equator is greater than at the Poles. Its roundish shape is caused by the planet's gravitational pull, which is equal in all directions and creates a sphere with all surface points an equal distance from the center. Because Earth rotates on its axis, however, the greatest centrifugal or outward force is at the Equator; this variation causes the relative difference between the equatorial diameter and the polar diameter. The diameter of Earth at the Equator is less than one percent greater than the diameter between the Poles, a difference that does not noticeably affect surface processes but does affect mapping and projections. (See Map Projections, page 35.)

Improved technology, such as the global positioning system (GPS), enables increasingly accurate measurement of Earth's shape by **geodesists**, mathematicians who study Earth's measurements. A geoid is the most accurate and specific description of Earth's shape because it incorporates major surface irregularities such as mountains and trenches. Visualizing Earth as a sphere, however, is sufficient for understanding the variations in amounts of solar energy reaching Earth—which affect the formation and patterns of climates and ecosystems—and the equal pull of gravity around the planet.

Motions and Tilt

As the solar system formed, the rotating cloud of gases and dust evolved into planets revolving around the sun. Earth's orbit around the sun is elliptical, and each complete orbit takes one terrestrial year, or about 365.25 days; each day equals one rotation on Earth's axis. The orbit is elliptical and not circular because of the gravitational attraction of other planets. Earth's distance from the sun varies from 91 million miles, the **perihelion** (from *peri*, Latin for "around," and *helios*, Greek for "sun"), in early January to 94 million miles, the **aphelion** (from *apo*, Greek for "away from"), in early July.

As Earth revolves around the sun, it also rotates on its axis. This rotation has immense consequences for Earth's environments and for human societies. First, our day-night, or **diurnal-nocturnal**, system is the direct result of each location on Earth rotating into the sun's radiation at dawn and out of the rays at dusk. Second, rotation produces the **Coriolis effect**, named for 19th-century French mathematician Gaspard Gustave de Coriolis (1792-1843). The effect is seen in the deflection of winds and ocean currents to the right of their original path in the Northern Hemisphere and to the left in the Southern Hemisphere. (See Global Winds

Moving Magnetic Poles

Geographers have long been aware that Earth's north and south magnetic poles shift their locations because of movements within the planet's core. This slow relocation means that cartographers must update the **angle of declination** between magnetic north and geographic north or true north on topographic maps. For some locations in higher latitudes the compass reading for magnetic north can change as much as six minutes per year.

and Ocean Currents, page 80.) Third, the axis of rotation forms our geographic North Pole and South Pole; with the Equator halfway between, the Poles constitute the basis for latitude and longitude in locating ourselves with a coordinate grid system. (See Latitude and Longitude, page 35.) Finally, the differential rotation between Earth's inner and outer cores creates the magnetic field that deflects solar wind, thus protecting Earth's surface from harmful ionizing radiation; this rotation also produces the north magnetic pole

and the south magnetic pole, used for navigational purposes.

Earth tilts on its axis 23.5 degrees away from perpendicular to the plane of its orbit around the sun. The angle of tilt is constant with reference to stars: In the Northern Hemisphere the geographic North Pole points toward Polaris, the North Star. The tilt changes continuously with reference to the sun during Earth's annual revolution, which causes the amount of solar energy received on Earth to vary throughout the year at all locations.

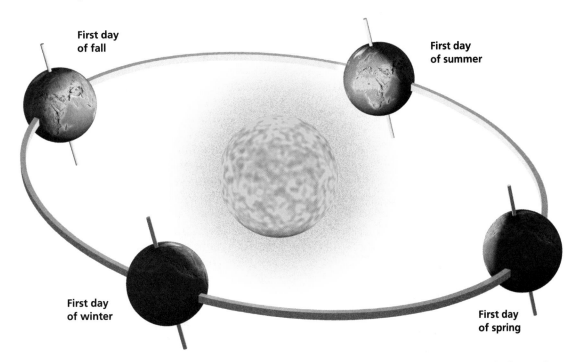

First day of fall

First day of summer

First day of winter

First day of spring

Seasons change when Earth reaches the solstice and equinox positions. Note that the North Pole is tilted away from the sun as winter begins and toward the sun as summer begins.

Seasons

Earth's shape, orbit around the sun, rotation, and tilt combine to cause seasonal variations in the amount of solar energy each latitude receives. The amount of solar radiation is measured in **langleys,** which were first described by American physicist and inventor Samuel P. Langley (1834-1906). Seasonal variations of langleys in turn govern weather, climate, and vegetation. As Earth travels around the sun, the latitude at which sunlight strikes the surface directly (at 90 degrees) changes slowly and constantly. At one point in Earth's path around the sun, the North Pole has its maximum tilt away from the sun. On this day—the **winter solstice** in the Northern Hemisphere, falling on or around December 21—the solar equator is at the Tropic of Capricorn, at latitude 23.5° south. There is no sunlight north of the Arctic Circle at latitude 66.5° north, and no nighttime south of the Antarctic Circle.

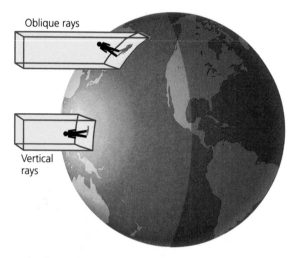

Oblique rays

Vertical rays

Latitude, or distance from the Equator, determines the seasonal variations in temperature. At the Equator the sun's rays are at their most intense. With increased distance from the Equator, the sun's rays become more angled and, therefore, less intense.

The winter solstice marking the traditional start of winter in the Northern Hemisphere is the summer solstice in the Southern Hemisphere. On the solstice all locations north of the Equator receive their fewest langleys of solar energy for the year due, in part, to shortened daylight hours: When the North Pole tilts away from the sun, less of the Northern Hemisphere is sunlit, so days are shorter. In addition, energy is spread over more area and is therefore less intense when sunlight hits Earth at more oblique angles. The coldest weather usually follows the winter solstice by about a month due to **thermal inertia**, the resistance of land and water to temperature change.

Seasons change as Earth orbits the sun and the North and South Poles slowly continue to reorient relative to the sun. Six months after the winter solstice, on or around June 21, Earth is at the **antipode**, the location in its orbit opposite its position at the winter solstice, with the North Pole tilting its maximum toward the sun. On this day, the **summer solstice,** the solar equator is the Tropic of Cancer, latitude 23.5° north. The region south of the Antarctic Circle is dark, and all points north of the Arctic Circle have 24 hours of light, which is why Alaska and other regions north of the Arctic Circle are called lands of the midnight sun. The summer solstice marks the start of summer in the Northern Hemisphere and winter in the Southern Hemisphere.

Between the two solstices, as Earth continues to revolve around the sun, each latitude experiences its own rate of change in the number of daylight hours and the angle of the sun's rays. The changing amount of solar energy reaching different latitudes is reflected in warming and cooling north and south of the Equator, respectively. At two points in Earth's orbit around the sun, on or around March 21 and September 23, Earth's axis is at a 90-degree angle to the sun: The solar equator *is* the Equator, and all locations on the globe receive 12 hours of sunlight. Spring and fall begin on these **equinoxes**, when night (Latin *nox*) is equal (Latin *aequus*) to day at all latitudes.

Seasonal changes in the number of hours and angle of sunlight occur around the world, but there are greater changes in the number of langleys and therefore greater impact on the environments at higher latitudes than those near the Equator. Areas between the Tropics of Cancer and Capricorn have relatively minor annual variation in daylight hours and angle of sunlight, while between the tropics and the polar circles seasonal variations increase. Pole-ward of the Arctic and Antarctic Circles day-light varies in length between zero and 24 hours, and the angle of sunlight varies from zero to 23.5 degrees above the horizon. These

Latitudes and Sunlight Hours During the Summer Solstice

LOCATION	LATITUDE	DAYLIGHT HOURS (APPROXIMATE)
Guantanamo, Cuba	20° N	13 hours
Cairo, Egypt	30° N	14 hours
Beijing, China	40° N	15 hours
Prague, Czech Republic	48° 51′ N	17 hours

systematic seasonal shifts and variations in solar energy are key to understanding global winds and ocean currents, and by extension climates and ecosystems. (See Global Winds and Ocean Currents, page 80.)

Weather

Atmosphere

Gravity holds Earth's **atmosphere**, a thin layer of gases that is the medium for weather and climate, near the surface. The atmosphere insulates the surface from temperature extremes and protects Earth from most space debris and from dangerous radiation such as gamma rays. While nearly all atmospheric gases are within about 20 miles of Earth and weather occurs within 10 miles, some gases penetrate the upper layer of the soil, and a few gas molecules are found 6,000 miles above Earth.

Composition

The atmosphere is divided into the **homosphere**, from Earth's surface to an altitude of about 50 miles, and the **heterosphere**, above the homosphere. There is a fairly uniform mixture of gases stirred by winds in the homosphere, and in the heterosphere atmospheric gases tend to separate based upon their densities.

Local and regional variations in the homosphere's composition are mostly limited to **particulates**, solid or liquid particles, and **aerosols**, microscopic particulates. Over time, fluctuations also occur in a few variable gases that form a small percentage of the atmosphere but have a disproportionately large impact on Earth's weather and climate by affecting temperature and precipitation. Two nonvariable gases, oxygen and nitrogen, make up 99 percent of the volume of dry air, excluding water vapor. Nitrogen comprises 78 percent of the atmosphere, but it rarely reacts with other gases and is insignificant in meteorological processes. Oxygen, at almost 21 percent of the atmosphere, is vital in respiration and is an active agent of the geologic processes of

A view of Earth from space, shot during the Apollo 11 mission to the Moon, shows Australia at the lower left and North America at the upper right.

Sunsets

At midday, a clear sky appears blue because the sun's rays, especially the shorter wavelength blue rays, are scattered when they contact molecules of atmospheric gases. **Rayleigh scattering,** described in 1881 by English physicist John William Strutt, third Baron Rayleigh (1842–1919), also affects solar radiation in the evening and morning. At dawn and dusk the sun's rays pass through more atmosphere as they approach Earth than they do at midday, and the sky appears orange or red because blue rays are too scattered to be seen. Aerosols and dust increase the amount of scattering and make sunsets red and more colorful.

Tambora volcano, on Sumbawa in the Lesser Sunda Islands, erupted in 1815 and lost nearly 3,700 feet from its estimated height of 13,000 feet. The eruption also released tons of sulfurous aerosols that interfered with solar radiation. The following year was called the year without a summer in Europe and the United States because it was cooler than usual.

weathering (see Weathering and Mass Wasting, pages 159), but like nitrogen it is insignificant in meteorological processes.

Far more important to weather and climate are the variable gases water vapor and carbon dioxide, and of the two, water vapor is more variable. Exposed surface water, atmospheric temperature, and altitude are key factors in the amount of vapor in the air. Above tropical deserts and polar regions water vapor may make up less than 0.1 percent of the lower atmosphere's volume, while water vapor may reach 4 percent over equatorial rain forests. As the atmosphere thins and cools with increasing altitude, there is progressively less water vapor present. Atmospheric water vapor is essential for the processes of condensation and precipitation, and it is also the medium by which energy, stored within water vapor molecules as latent heat, is transferred around the planet. (See Earth's Radiation Balance, page 58.)

Carbon dioxide is the other variable gas important to weather and climate and on average makes up only .035 percent of the atmosphere. The amount of carbon dioxide decreases in summer when increased photosynthesis by plants converts it to oxygen and carbon, and it increases in winter when lower temperatures stop plant growth in the mid-latitudes and prevent photosynthesis. Atmospheric levels of carbon dioxide and other gases that warm our atmosphere are extremely important in the greenhouse effect that heats Earth. (See Heat and Temperature, page 63.)

In addition to gases, Earth's atmosphere also contains aerosols and particulates that result from natural and industrial processes. Aerosols are light enough to remain suspended in the atmosphere indefinitely and can significantly affect weather and climate. Large concentrations of aerosols, especially sulfurous aerosols from volcanic eruptions, reduce the amount of solar energy that reaches Earth's surface and can cause short-term global cooling. Many smaller particulates—including volcanic dust, sea salt, meteoric dust, ashes from forest fires, and other by-products from combustion—act as nuclei for condensation of cloud droplets.

Aerosols, particulates, and atmospheric gases become **pollutants** when their concentrations increase to levels that threaten the health of living things or else substantially change existing atmospheric conditions. Aerosol and particulate pollutants include lead and asbestos as well as ash and dust and are generated by internal combustion engines, industrial processes, and waste disposal. Waste incineration and combustion of fossil fuels are primarily responsible for gaseous pollutants such as carbon monoxide, sulfur oxides, nitrogen oxides, and hydrocarbons.

In the heterosphere, gases separate based upon their densities and **ionize**—that is, gain a positive or negative electric charge—by absorbing ultraviolet and x-ray radiation from the sun. Molecular nitrogen dominates the atmosphere from 50 to 120 miles above Earth, at which point oxygen becomes dominant to 660 miles above Earth. Helium and hydrogen form the highest layers of the atmosphere respectively, but their density is so low that exact boundaries for these layers do not exist.

Structure

Earth's atmosphere changes as altitude increases, with significant differences occurring in composition, electrical charge, pressure, and temperature. The atmosphere is divided into layers, from the troposphere, the lowest level, to the exosphere, more than 300 miles above Earth's surface. In the **troposphere**, from the surface to about six miles above Earth, temperature declines with altitude because the primary heat source for the air is the ground. (See Earth's Radiation Balance, page 58.) Most weather is confined to the troposphere because it holds more than 95 percent of water vapor and 80 percent of all atmospheric gases. The decline in temperature with altitude results in instability and vertical mixing of the atmosphere. On average, the temperature in the troposphere drops 3.5°F per 1,000 feet: This is called the **environmental temperature lapse rate**. Occasionally a layer of warmer air will flow over cooler air; the resultant inversion can trap pollutants and particulates as well as cause fogs to form in the lower air.

The top of the troposphere's boundary with the stratosphere is called the **tropopause**. At the tropopause, temperatures begin to increase because the ozone layer warms the air. The altitude of the tropopause increases slightly in summer because surface temperatures warm the air, which then rises. It also varies year-round by latitude because the centrifugal force that increases the Earth's diameter at the Equator also increases the troposphere to an altitude of 11 miles; at that altitude, the lapse rate drops temperatures to –110°F. Above the Poles, the tropopause averages only five miles high and the lapse rate drops temperatures to –60°F.

The **stratosphere**, above the tropopause, extends to about 28 miles above Earth. Temperatures rise with altitude to the **stratopause**, the upper limit that marks the boundary between the stratosphere and mesosphere. Within the stratosphere, the ozone layer warms atmospheric gases by absorbing ultraviolet radiation. Few atmospheric changes can occur in the stratosphere or higher thermal layers because the tropopause, essentially an inversion layer, severely limits mixing between the lower and upper atmospheres.

Within the stratosphere, ultraviolet (UV)

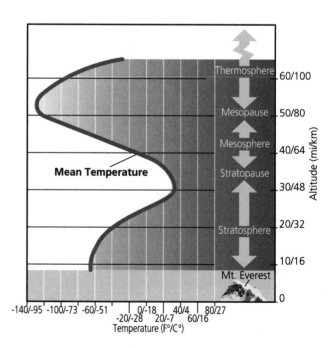

To the naked eye, the atmosphere looks simply like "air," but there are distinct layers with differing composition, electrical charge, pressure, and temperature.

Ozone Hole

By the mid-1980s researchers had confirmed a dramatic thinning in the ozone layer above Antarctica—what is now called an ozone hole. For more than a decade, scientists had identified the mechanisms involved in ozone depletion, tracing it to the escape of chlorofluorocarbons (CFCs) from air conditioners and aerosol sprays into the atmosphere. Since 1975, the ozone hole over Antarctica has increased annually, to nine million square miles in 1993; an ozone hole over the Arctic was detected in 1989. Ozone holes are seasonal; they shrink in winter, then increase over the Poles in spring when sunlight reappears and activates chlorine compounds on ice cloud crystals, changing the compounds from inert to active forms capable of destroying ozone. The reduced ozone layer has been tied to the increasing incidence of skin cancer and cataracts, which can cause blindness. This global threat to human health resulted in nearly a hundred countries signing the revised Montreal Protocol and agreeing in 1990 to phase out CFCs.

radiation from the sun creates and perpetuates an **ozone layer** that protects life on Earth from deadly levels of ultraviolet radiation. Ultraviolet radiation is the energy source for splitting a free oxygen molecule into two ions; each ion then combines with a free oxygen molecule to form ozone. Ozone is then split by UV radiation into free oxygen and an ion that combines with another ion to form a free oxygen molecule. This cycle of creation and destruction of ozone absorbs most UV radiation. While ozone molecules are found throughout the stratosphere, the concentrated ozone layer occurs near the stratopause.

Ultraviolet rays are a high-energy form of radiation that can kill or mutate exposed cells. Life on Earth started 3.5 billion years ago in oceans partially because water was a protection against most UV radiation, and there was no free oxygen to create a protective ozone layer. Ultraviolet rays are divided into ultraviolet A (UVA), ultraviolet B (UVB), and ultraviolet C (UVC), of which UVC has the shortest wavelength and is most dangerous to humans and other life. The ozone layer absorbs almost all UVC rays and much UVB radiation.

Temperatures decline in the **mesosphere** (the layer above the stratosphere, about 28 to 50 miles above Earth) with increased distance from the ozone layer. Few gases are found in the mesosphere and in the **thermosphere**, about 50 miles to 310 miles above Earth, because the distance from Earth is so great that there is little gravity; thus the atmosphere is thin. Temperatures drop to −130°F at the mesopause, 50 miles high, and begin to increase with altitude in the thermosphere, to perhaps 2,200°F.

The ionization of atmospheric gases creates the **ionosphere**, a region within the thermosphere where high-frequency radio signals are reflected back to Earth and where solar winds form luminescent atmospheric displays called auroras. Due to Earth's curvature, radio receivers cannot always receive direct signals from a radio station. Different ionized layers form from the sun's radiation; during the nighttime the lowest level (D), which absorbs radio waves, dissipates while beyond D the F layer remains and reflects the waves, especially in the AM radio band. During the day the presence of the D layer interferes with long-distance AM radio transmission and reception.

Earth's Radiation Balance

Earth's weather and climate systems involve continual vertical and horizontal movement within the atmosphere's troposphere. Solar radiation provides the energy for these movements. Earth maintains a **radiation balance**: Energy coming from the sun must eventually be equaled by energy radiated and reflected from Earth. Understanding how the sun's radiant energy is intercepted by Earth and transformed into different forms of energy is necessary to understand the spatial patterns of weather and climate.

Energy

Energy, the ability to move solids, liquids, and gases, is the key to all change on Earth's surface. Radiant energy from the sun is the basis of atmospheric movement as well as waves and ocean currents. Heat generated in Earth's interior is an example of **sensible heat**—that is, heat felt or sensed as warmth—and it is the basis of plate-tectonic movements.

There are several forms of energy—radiant, kinetic, chemical, and electrical—and each can be converted to another form. Radiant energy from the sun, for example, is converted to

sensible heat in the ozone layer when absorbed by ozone molecules, and sensible heat in the lower atmosphere is converted to the kinetic energy of motion when air that has been warmed expands and rises. Radiant energy from the sun, the kinetic energy of wind, and even the chemical energy stored in fossil fuels—originally derived from radiant solar energy—can all be converted to electrical energy for human use and convenience.

Energy can also be stored as **latent energy** in water, which changes its physical state—a **phase change**—from solid to liquid to gaseous forms within Earth's temperature range. Phase changes enable energy to move from one location to another without any loss. When water evaporates and becomes water vapor, the sensible heat that caused the evaporation is stored in the water vapor molecules and released when the vapor condenses to form water droplets. A comparable storage and release of energy occurs when ice melts and then refreezes. Winds move latent energy when they blow water vapor or cloud droplets to different locations. Global winds and ocean currents circulate this latent energy around Earth by moving water vapor and water.

Solar Energy

Radiant energy from the sun can be converted into other useful forms of energy, including electricity. Location on Earth, however, strongly influences the economic viability of using solar energy because the angle and duration of sunlight plus atmospheric interference determine the amount of energy available for use. Cloud-free areas in lower latitudes, such as southern Arizona, have greater amounts of available solar energy than the fog- and cloud-shrouded Pacific coast of Washington. Active and passive solar-energy systems convert radiant energy to sensible heat that warms air or water in a building. A **passive solar energy system** circulates heat through a structure by convection or conduction, whereas an **active solar-energy system** requires a pump for circulation. Photovoltaic cells convert radiant energy to electricity. Increased use of solar energy depends on its cost relative to that of other energy sources, especially fossil fuels.

(See Atmospheric Pressure and Winds, page 71 and Ocean Currents, page 80.)

Solar Radiation and the Solar Constant

Radiant energy travels in a wavelike path and extends over a limited portion of the **electromagnetic spectrum**, which includes all wavelengths and types of electromagnetic radiation. The spectrum ranges from gamma rays and x-rays to radio waves; each type of energy is distinguished by its wavelength—the distance between wave crests, which can range from billionths of an inch to miles long. Visible light, as seen in a rainbow's colors, ranges in wavelength from 0.4 microns (blue light) to 0.7 microns (red light); green light, reflected by chlorophyll in plants, is a combination of yellow and blue light, with wavelengths of 0.4 microns to 0.6 microns.

The temperature of any surface determines what wavelengths and therefore what types of energy are radiated. At 11,000°F, the surface of the sun radiates mostly in the visible light range, although ultraviolet (.01 to 0.1 microns) and near-infrared energy (0.7 to 3 microns) are also radiated. In contrast, radiation from Earth's surface—which averages 60°F, peaks at the 10-micron wavelength, which is in the thermal-infrared range.

The amount of energy radiated from a surface is also determined by its temperature. At 11,000°F, an area on the sun's surface emits about 160,000 times more energy than an equal area on Earth, and Earth, 93 million miles from the sun, intercepts only a small percentage of this solar energy. The surface temperature of the sun is relatively constant, so the amount of energy emitted by the sun and intercepted by Earth is relatively constant. The **solar constant**, the energy intercepted by Earth, is two langleys per minute; this means that in one hour the amount of energy intercepted on one square foot of land is enough to heat three pints of water by 1°F.

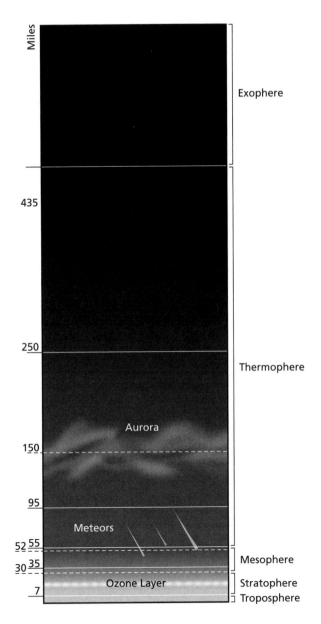

Above our heads is an invisible ocean of gases hundreds of miles thick. The layers of the atmosphere are largely defined by temperature and composition, and vary with latitude and season.

Remote Sensing and Atmospheric Windows

Remote sensing involves observing Earth from satellites, planes, balloons, and the space shuttle. Earth's atmosphere interferes with the passage of radiant energy and can cause images to appear fuzzy or bluish from scatter and be incomplete from missing absorbed energy. Multispectral sensors and the film used in high-altitude photography are designed to detect energy wavelengths only in **atmospheric windows**, those wavelengths not scattered or absorbed by the atmosphere.

Insolation

Of the sun's radiation reaching toward Earth—a stream of radiant energy called **insolation**—only about 52 percent passes through the atmosphere to reach Earth's surface. The atmosphere selectively absorbs, reflects, and scatters the remaining 48 percent. The quantity of solar radiation that reaches Earth also depends on its path through the atmosphere and the angle at which it strikes the surface. The amounts vary with the seasons and with latitude; latitudes farther from the solar equator receive less intense radiation. (See Diagram: Latitudes, Angle of Sunlight, and Intensity, page 52; see also Seasons, page 52.)

Gas molecules in Earth's atmosphere absorb approximately 23 percent of insolation, mostly in the ultraviolet and near-infrared wavelengths. Although absorption converts insolation to sensible heat, it does not contribute much to warming the atmosphere near Earth's surface because it occurs at higher altitudes. Ozone in the stratosphere absorbs much of the ultraviolet radiation, and dust, water vapor, and aerosols absorb some solar radiation in the troposphere, mostly in the near-infrared wavelengths.

Cloud droplets, ice crystals, and dust in the atmosphere reflect about 17 percent of insolation away from Earth. The amount of reflected insolation varies more than absorption or scatter because clouds are the primary cause of atmospheric reflection, and the amount of cloud cover depends on geographical variations of weather and climate. How thick a cloud is determines its **albedo**, or reflectivity. A cloud 16,440 feet thick reflects more than 80 percent of insolation, while less than 40 percent is reflected when a cloud is 165 feet thick.

About 8 percent of insolation is scattered when the radiation strikes the atmosphere's gas molecules, dust, and cloud droplets. Some of the scattered energy may reach the Earth's surface, but most is lost to space. Gas molecules scatter the shorter wavelengths of energy, and dust and water droplets scatter longer wavelengths, mostly in the near-infrared wavelengths. The shortest of the visible light waves, blue light, is scattered more than other wavelengths, resulting in Earth's blue sky.

On average, 52 percent of insolation reaches Earth's surface, where it is either reflected or absorbed and converted to the kinetic energy that creates and moves weather. Different surfaces on Earth have differing **albedos** because of their roughness and color. Surface albedos may be as little as 3 percent or as much as 95 percent. The albedo of water is especially important to understanding Earth's radiation balance because more than 70 percent of Earth's surface is ocean, and the angle of sunlight—which affects albedo—varies so much between latitudes. At the solar equator, water has an albedo approaching 3 percent, and the albedo of water remains low—below 10 percent—within 70° north and south latitudes of the solar equator. Near the North and South Poles, where the angle of insolation can approach zero, the albedo of water approaches

Landsat images register surface radiation, or heat. In Boston, relatively warm urban areas appear light blue, cool areas of vegetation appear red, and water is black.

100 percent. Other factors, such as cloud cover and wave activity, affect the albedo of water, but as a global average the albedo for Earth's oceans is about 8 percent.

The albedo of different types of terrestrial surfaces also varies considerably. Roads that are blacktop, with an average albedo of 5 percent to 10 percent, and lighter-colored concrete, with an albedo of 20 to 30 percent, are major

reasons why urban areas tend to absorb more insolation than rural areas and heat up, forming urban heat islands. (See Urban Heat Islands, page 65.) Snow—especially freshly fallen snow—has an albedo up to 95 percent, which contributes to the lack of absorption and therefore the lack of heat in polar regions. The albedo of chlorophyll in grasses, trees, and crops is usually between 15 and 20 percent;

the albedo of deciduous trees increases in winter when the trees lose their leaves.

Of Earth's total insolation, about 46 percent is absorbed by the planet's surface, providing energy for weather systems; 6 percent is reflected by the surface and, along with 25 percent reflected or scattered by clouds and atmosphere, is lost to space. The remaining energy (23 percent of the total) is absorbed in the atmosphere by gases and dust, but this energy is not concentrated near the surface and does not affect surface weather.

Global Radiation Balance

All solar energy absorbed by Earth's surface and atmosphere is eventually radiated out to space; without this radiation balance energy would accumulate and Earth's temperature would constantly increase. The amounts of incoming and outgoing radiation are not in balance either annually or regionally. Energy from insolation stored in plants by photosynthesis may be released and radiated out to space millions of years later when coal, a fossil fuel formed from swamp vegetation, is burned. Polar regions may annually radiate twice as much energy to space as they receive directly from insolation; this "extra" energy is absorbed between 30° north and south latitudes and is then carried by winds and ocean currents to the polar regions.

While all solar energy absorbed by Earth is eventually lost to space as radiant energy, the atmosphere prevents immediate loss of much of this absorbed energy. Earth radiates energy in thermal infrared wavelengths, of which about 90 percent is absorbed by carbon dioxide and other gases in the atmosphere. This absorbed energy warms Earth's lower atmosphere through the greenhouse effect. (See Greenhouse Effect, page 63.) Ultimately, the energy absorbed by Earth is radiated into space, balancing insolation.

Energy absorbed by Earth's surface is also transported to the atmosphere and north and

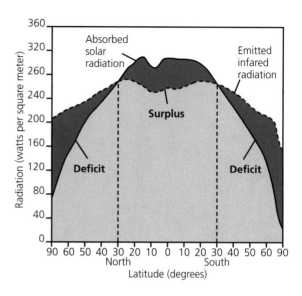

The difference between solar radiation absorbed and infrared radiation emitted is largely determined by latitude.

south to the polar regions by other mechanisms. Much moves as latent energy after solar energy changes water into vapor. When the vapor condenses as water again, often as cloud droplets, the energy is radiated into space or absorbed by the atmosphere, from which it is later lost to space. Surface energy also moves as sensible heat by conduction or convection; conduction warms the lowest atmosphere by its contact with the surface, whereas convection moves air upward and helps keep the troposphere mixed.

The transport of energy by winds and ocean currents from the tropics to upper latitudes is a critical part of the global energy balance and global weather patterns. About 20 percent of the energy absorbed near the Equator is transported poleward as latent or sensible heat energy by global systems of wind and ocean currents. Overall, global winds transport more energy from the tropics to the polar regions than ocean currents do, but the two systems move different kinds of energy: Air masses move water vapor with latent energy; ocean currents slowly move large amounts of sensible heat. (See Global Winds and Ocean Currents, page 80.)

Heat and Temperature

Differential heating of Earth's surface and lower atmosphere creates weather—local winds, global winds, ocean currents, and precipitation. **Heat** is the amount of thermal energy—a form of kinetic energy—that flows among air, water, and rock. **Temperature** is how much thermal energy a substance contains. Differences in temperatures cause heat to flow between substances, and temperature measures the average, not the total, amount of thermal energy a substance contains. As a result denser substances can contain more energy but have lower temperatures than other substances. Water has a much higher heat capacity than dry beach sand and is transparent, allowing energy to be distributed deeper. As a result, with equal inputs of radiant energy, sand and water may contain equal amounts of thermal energy, but the surface temperature of sand will be higher; more heat will flow from the sand to your feet than from the water.

Air temperature is measured on two major scales: Fahrenheit, used mostly in the United States, and Celsius, once called the centigrade scale and now used by scientists and the rest of the world. The scales use the freezing point of water as their base—0 degrees—but the Fahrenheit scale uses saltwater while the Celsius scale uses freshwater. On the Fahrenheit scale, freshwater boils at 212°F and the average temperature of the human body is 98.6°F; on the Celsius scale, freshwater boils at 100°C and average body temperature is 37°C.

Thermometers are used to measure temperature. **Mercury thermometers** have thin, sealed glass tubes containing liquid mercury that expands and rises as it warms and contracts and sinks as it cools. Alcohol is used instead of mercury when especially cold temperatures are to be measured because alcohol freezes at –170°F while mercury freezes at –38°F. Thermostats use bonded bimetallic strips of metals—brass and iron, for example—that expand and contract at different temperatures causing the bonded strip to bend. The temperature is calculated by how much the strip bends.

The U.S. National Weather Service has standardized the collection of temperatures by using shelters to prevent thermometers from absorbing radiant energy that would raise temperatures and to protect them from precipitation that would cool them. This ensures accurate measurements that are also comparable from one site to another. The shelters are ventilated so that the air inside is not warmed by conduction from the shelter itself; they thus have the same air temperature as outside the shelter. All thermometers are set to measure air temperature at four to six feet above the ground to ensure comparability.

Greenhouse Effect

The warming of Earth's lower atmosphere, the troposphere, is often compared to how air inside a greenhouse warms. Although the analogy is not perfect, there are important similarities, and the term greenhouse effect refers to how Earth's atmosphere warms. **Global warming** is caused by atmospheric pollutants that have increased the greenhouse effect. Greenhouse gases, including carbon dioxide, methane, and nitrous oxide, have increased this century due to more industrial activity. For example, the concentration of carbon dioxide in the atmosphere is estimated to be increasing by 1.4 percent annually.

The air in greenhouses warms in part because the glass walls and roof of the building, like Earth's atmosphere, allow only certain wavelengths to pass through. Not much solar radiation is absorbed or reflected by the glass because it's clear; instead, the glass allows the visible and shorter wavelengths of solar

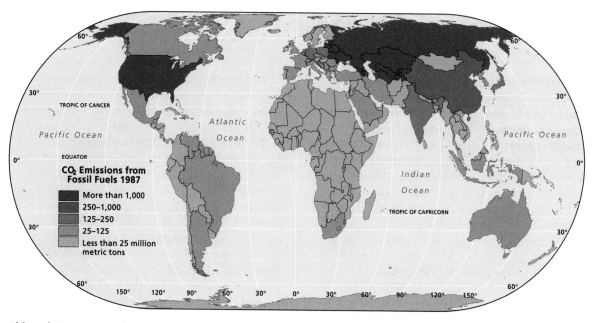

CO₂ Emissions from Fossil Fuels 1987

More than 1,000
250–1,000
125–250
25–125
Less than 25 million metric tons

Although European nations are generally as industrialized as the United States, Europe's emissions of carbon dioxide (CO₂) are lower because of its conservation measures and less dependence on fossil fuels for energy production.

radiation to pass through to be absorbed by the surfaces of the plants and other objects inside. Longer wavelengths, especially thermal infrared energy radiated by the plants and other surfaces, do not pass back through the glass and therefore are absorbed by the air trapped within the greenhouse, warming it. By trapping the air inside, a greenhouse captures sensible heat, and the interior stays warm overnight.

The warming of Earth's lower atmosphere is a more complex process than that of a greenhouse. Thermal energy from Earth's surface is transferred to the troposphere, warming it by radiation, conduction, and convection. Water vapor in the air contains its own latent energy that, when released by condensation, also warms the atmosphere. Most of Earth's radiant energy is absorbed by the atmosphere and then reradiated back to the surface, extending the warming process of the lower atmosphere.

More than 90 percent of Earth's surface radiation is intercepted and absorbed by

greenhouse gases—water vapor, carbon dioxide, ozone, nitrous oxide, and methane—in the atmosphere, and the rest is lost to space. The greenhouse gases are called that because absorbed radiant energy warms them. Each greenhouse gas takes up specific wavelengths; together these gases take in most terrestrial radiation of wavelengths between 2.5 and 8 microns, as well as most wavelengths greater than 15 microns. Water vapor absorbs the widest range of wavelengths and greatest quantity of radiation. Carbon dioxide absorbs the second largest amount of radiation and contributes to global warming because the burning of fossil fuels has increased the atmospheric concentration of the gas. Methane, nitrogen oxide, and other atmospheric gases also absorb surface radiation, although in relatively minor amounts.

Surface radiation, convection, conduction, and the transfer of latent heat in the form of water vapor contribute to the warming of Earth's atmosphere. Of the four mechanisms,

Urban Heat Islands

Large cities tend to be warmer than rural areas; they become **urban heat islands.** Buildings lose heat, and concrete and asphalt have high heat capacities compared to the lower heat capacities of rural fields and soil. Also, there is little surface water present to absorb thermal energy by evaporation. Temperature contrasts between larger urban areas and their rural surroundings are even greater during nighttime and during winter because urban heating increases as rural temperatures drop.

latent heat transfers three times more thermal energy to the atmosphere than conduction and convection combined. The energy is ultimately converted to long-wave radiation that is lost to space.

The Greater Tokyo metropolitan area is the largest urban area in the world. A vast urban heat island, Tokyo also contends with air and water pollution.

Vertical Temperature Change

As Earth's energy is transferred to the atmosphere, most of the warming occurs nearer the surface. The resulting decline in temperature with increased altitude has important implications for atmospheric mixing and surface conditions. Several factors can interfere with this environmental temperature lapse rate, and as a consequence pollutants can accumulate at or near the surface to become a health hazard.

On average, air temperature decreases 3.5°F per 1,000 feet of elevation or altitude—the **environmental temperature lapse rate.** Two major factors cause this lapse rate: Radiation is more intense and more likely to be intercepted and absorbed by greenhouse gases close to Earth's surface, and because air thins with increasing altitude, the amount of water vapor and other greenhouse gases available to absorb radiation decreases proportionately. Tall mountains, even Kilimanjaro and others near the Equator, are cold and often snow covered year-round.

Several atmospheric events, including rapid overnight cooling, can modify the environmental temperature lapse rate and cause temperatures to rise with increased elevation or altitude as a warmer layer of air overlies cooler air. Often these **inversions**, which trap the lower and cooler air, occur within a few hundred feet of the surface. **Radiation inversions** are caused by overnight cooling of the lower atmosphere and most often occur during winter in the higher latitudes, when longer nights

Glaciers cap Kibo Peak, Mount Kilimanjaro, year-round due to the environmental lapse rate—the decrease in temperature that accompanies elevation.

coincide with clear skies: As the surface cools, less energy is radiated, and the air in contact with the ground becomes cooler. An **advectional inversion** occurs when cooler air moves under warmer air already in an area. Terrain is often a factor in the formation of advectional inversions because cooler air is denser and drains into low-lying areas called **frost pockets**.

Upper-air inversions—above several thousand feet—trap lower air over areas as large as the Sahara, affecting far greater areas than do inversions that occur near the surface. Subsidence is associated with cold air masses over midlatitude continents, especially during winter. The subtropical latitudes centered on the Tropics of Cancer and Capricorn have upper-air inversions caused by subsidence of air that rose at the Equator and, after cooling and moving away from the Equator, returned to the surface.

Diurnal and Seasonal Temperature Patterns

Atmospheric temperatures and related changes in humidity, condensation, pressure, and winds vary daily and seasonally, as well as geographically. Diurnal heating patterns reflect the time lag between Earth's absorption of

solar radiation and the subsequent reradiation of long-wave energy to the atmosphere. Air temperatures usually bottom out and begin to increase at Earth's surface about 30 minutes after sunrise, when the surface has absorbed solar energy and then starts to radiate long-wave energy. Temperatures increase as the sun rises and Earth absorbs and radiates increasing amounts of energy. Peak insolation occurs at noon, but the temperature continues to rise for two to three hours, even though the amount of insolation decreases as the sun drops in the sky. Temperatures peak in mid-afternoon because of the time lag between surface absorption and radiation of energy. After the peak, temperatures fall as the rate of surface radiation decreases. The radiation and temperature cycles begin again at sunrise.

Seasonal heating patterns also reflect a time lag between Earth's reception of insolation and its release of that energy as radiation. Not all solar radiation absorbed at the surface is reradiated during the following day or week. Some energy is conducted into the ground; after accumulating, it is released slowly through conduction back to the surface. In the mid- and higher latitudes, where seasonal variations in insolation are greater than those near the Equator, there is usually a one-month time lag between the amount of insolation and the resulting air temperature. January and July are usually the coolest and hottest months respectively even though insolation is lowest in December and greatest in June. (See Climate Controls and Classification, page 114.)

Compared to soil and rock, water is particularly slow to release heat and thus changes temperature more slowly; water therefore increases the lag time for diurnal and seasonal heating. Water has a high heat capacity. Because of circulation by currents and waves and because sunlight penetrates deeper into water than soil, energy is stored at greater depths in the water and is released more slowly into the atmosphere. As a result, the seasonal time lag for coastal high and low temperatures may be closer to two months, compared with one month for inland locations. Most coastal locations have cooler days and warmer nights than inland locations because air over water heats and cools more slowly than air over land. Areas that have little water or water vapor warm rapidly during the day and cool quickly at night; even the Sahara can have freezing temperatures.

Temperature extremes on Earth, especially record high temperatures, usually occur in drier areas. In North America, the highest temperature yet recorded was 134°F in Death Valley, July 10, 1913; the highest temperature yet recorded on Earth—136.4°F—was at El Azizia, Libya, September 13, 1922. Record low temperatures in winter are found at high latitudes where insolation is minimal and at higher elevations where the air is thin; the lack of water vapor and the high albedo of snow and ice in both locations allows rapid cooling.

Spatial Temperature Patterns

Local surface conditions affect the amounts of insolation absorbed, the timing of long-wave radiation, and therefore the temperatures of limited areas. Terrain is an especially important local factor: Slope **aspect**, the direction a slope faces, affects the angle and duration of solar radiation and consequently the amount of moisture in the soil. During early summer in the Rockies and other alpine areas in the Northern Hemisphere, north-facing slopes stay cooler and retain snow longer than south-facing slopes. Surface moisture and temperature can vary dramatically within short distances, as between a streambed and the prairie through which it runs. Lower areas that accumulate water, such as marshes or swamps, may have smaller daily temperature ranges than drier slopes nearby.

Three global temperature maps can show major temperature patterns and reveal the major factors affecting average January temperatures, average July temperatures, and annual average temperature range. January

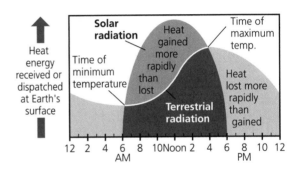

Although solar radiation peaks near midday, temperatures peak later in the day, because the Earth does not warm or cool instantly. During the day heat builds, and after the sun sets, it is gradually lost. This diagram shows the pattern at the equinoxes—when the day and night are each 12 hours long.

and July are usually the coldest and warmest months in the Northern Hemisphere and the warmest and coldest months in the Southern Hemisphere. The annual average temperature range is the difference between the January and July averages. (See Map: Isotherms, page 74.)

Annual temperature *ranges* are used instead of just average annual temperatures because the extreme high and low temperatures throughout the year are most limiting to vegetation and ecosystems. For example, the average annual temperatures for Seattle and Kansas City are nearly identical—about 53°F. In Seattle, however, average January and July temperatures are 41°F and 65°F, an average annual temperature range of 24°F; in Kansas City, the January average is 26°F and the July average 79°F, a range of 53°F. Seattle has far milder temperatures than Kansas City, and its annual temperature range produces far less environmental stress on vegetation and people.

The maps of average January and July temperatures use **isotherms**, lines of equal temperature, that show distinct geographic patterns resulting from five primary temperature controls: latitude, elevation, land-water contrast, global wind patterns, and ocean currents. Latitude, and its correlation to insolation, is clearly shown in the two maps on page 74 by the progressively cooler monthly temperatures farther from the Equator. Ocean temperatures show latitudinal influences more clearly than those of continents because water-surface conditions are much more homogeneous than those on land.

Higher elevations are associated with thinner air, and mountains are typically colder than surrounding low-lying areas. Tall mountain ranges such as the Andes and Himalaya are distinctly colder than their foothills, as are highland areas such as the interior plateaus of Mexico and Ethiopia. In Mexico City, at an elevation of 7,570 feet, average July temperatures may be 10°F cooler than in Veracruz, at sea level on the Gulf of Mexico. Elevational changes are often compared to latitudinal changes because the effects on temperature ranges are so similar. Vegetation reflects this vertical distribution of temperatures on mountains; climbing up the east slope of the Sierra Nevada takes a hiker through a sequence of vegetation types from desert sagebrush to alpine tundra.

Large water bodies, especially oceans, have a strong moderating influence on temperatures because they absorb and release energy slowly. Smaller water bodies, even those the size of the Great Lakes or the Baltic Sea, may freeze in winter and have no moderating influence. The isotherms for oceans show that *cooler* temperatures exist farther poleward over water than over continents in summer while *warmer* temperatures prevail farther poleward than on continents in winter. Thermal inertia affects the atmospheric temperatures over coastal areas; from San Diego to Seattle and Brownsville to Bar Harbor, coastal communities tend to have cooler summers and warmer winters than inland areas at the same latitude.

Maritime influences on coasts and inland areas depend partly on ocean current temperatures and on the global winds prevailing at those locations. Ocean currents tend to be warmer off the east coasts of continents and cooler off the west coasts. (See Map: Ocean Currents, page 87.) As a result, summer temperatures are usually cooler on North America's west coast than on its east coast. In San

Francisco the warmest month (September, due to the time lag) has an average temperature of 65°F because of the cool California Current; in Norfolk, Virginia, at the same latitude on the East Coast, the warmest month (July) has an average of 78°F because of the warm Gulf Stream.

Global winds, which circle the globe, blow the moderating effects of water onshore until either mountains interfere or distance causes the maritime influence to dissipate. January isotherms for North America and Europe show the different influences that the Rockies, which run north-south, and the Alps, which run east-west, have on the maritime effects blown inland by westerly winds. The Rockies severely limit the inland extent of maritime temperatures from the Pacific Ocean, while the east-west trending Alps do not keep the maritime influences of the Atlantic Ocean from moderating temperature patterns more than a thousand miles inland at Budapest and Bratislava.

Temperatures and Humans

Comfort, and in some cases health, is influenced by ambient air temperature, with air circulation and humidity contributing to its impact on people. High temperatures may be debilitating if heat causes the body's core temperature to rise to 102°F or higher, and colder temperatures that lower body temperature below 95°F may cause hypothermia. In summer, the National Weather Service reports the **heat index**, which combines temperature and relative humidity to show the apparent temperature felt by humans, in order to warn individuals of possible health threats.

Cold air temperatures cool people far more rapidly when it's windy or breezy than when it's calm. Ordinarily, a warm layer of air near the skin insulates the human body, but wind displaces this layer with cooler air. As a result, more heat is conducted and convected away from the body. A **windchill index**, sometimes referred to as a windchill equivalent temperature

Verkhoyansk, Russia

Verkhoyansk, Russia, just north of the Arctic Circle in Siberia, has an average annual temperature range of 118°F, one of the largest of any settlement in the world: July averages 60°F and January's average is –58°F. The region around Verkhoyansk is a landlocked part of the world's largest landmass and is almost 4,000 miles from the maritime influences of the Atlantic Ocean. The Sea of Okhotsk, an arm of the Pacific Ocean, is 600 miles east of Verkhoyansk, but the prevailing global winds at this latitude are westerlies that have a negligible maritime influence on temperatures after traveling so far. As inhospitable as the temperatures in Siberia are, the former Soviet government and the tsarist government before that used prison labor to develop the region's abundant coal, gold, and molybdenum resources. Russian author Aleksandr Solzhenitsyn's *The Gulag Archipelago* described the Soviet system of prison camps.

(WET), combines air temperatures and wind speeds to create a measure of how rapidly people lose heat and are chilled at different wind speeds.

Concern over energy conservation has resulted in two measures that relate ambient air temperatures to costs for heating and cooling buildings: The air temperature in many buildings is kept near 70°F, a comfortable temperature for most people at rest. **Heating-degree days** are based on multiplying the number of degrees outside temperatures are below 65°F by the number of hours per day those temperatures last; these values are then totaled for an entire year. Values vary dramatically across the continental United States, from 100 (Miami) to 10,000 (International Falls, Minnesota). Hotter temperatures create a need for air-conditioning, and **cooling-degree days** can be calculated in a comparable fashion for outside temperatures greater than 65°F. Miami's rating on this scale is more than 4,000 whereas cities along the United States–Canada border, such as International Falls, have ratings below 500.

Windchill Index

WIND SPEED (MPH)	THERMOMETER READING (°F)												
	50	40	30	20	10	0	–10	–20	–25	–30	–35	–40	–45
Calm	50	40	30	20	10	0	–10	–20	–31	–36	–42	–47	–52
5	48	37	27	16	6	–5	–15	–26	–52	–58	–64	–71	–77
10	40	28	16	4	–9	–24	–33	–46	–65	–72	–78	–85	–92
15	36	22	9	–5	–18	–32	–45	–58	–74	–81	–88	–95	–103
20	32	18	4	–10	–25	–39	–53	–67	–81	–88	–96	–103	–110
25	30	16	0	–15	–29	–44	–59	–74	–86	–93	–101	–109	–116
30	28	13	–2	–18	–33	–48	–63	–79	–89	–97	–105	–113	–120
35	27	11	–4	–20	–35	–51	–67	–82	–92	–100	–107	–115	–123
40	26	10	–6	–21	–37	–53	–69	–86	–93	–102	–109	–117	–125

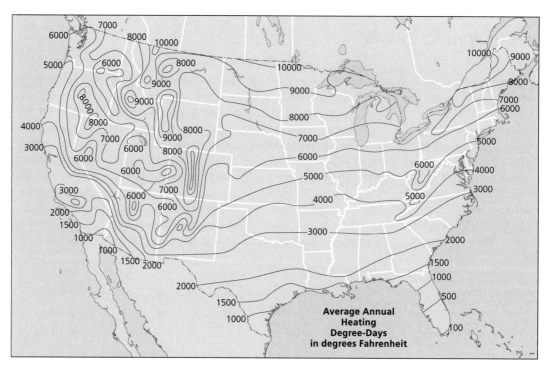

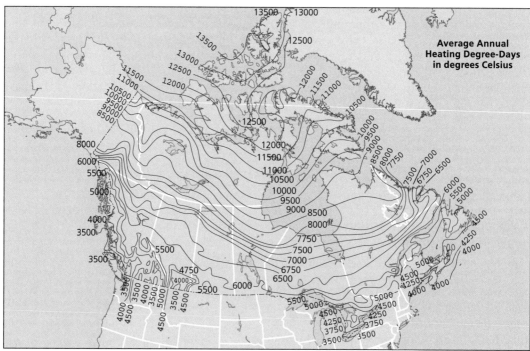

In the United States, heating degree-day totals are calculated according to a base temperature of 65°F (top); in Canada, the base temperature is 18° Celsius. Heating degree-days are considerably higher in Canada due to its northern position.

Atmospheric Pressure and Winds

As solar energy warms Earth, the resulting diurnal and seasonal patterns of surface radiation create related patterns of atmospheric warming and atmospheric pressure. **Wind**, the result of horizontal atmospheric pressure differences, moves clouds, air masses, and particulates locally and around the globe. Understanding the factors affecting atmospheric pressure, wind speed, and direction provides the basis for understanding not only local weather but also global precipitation patterns and climates.

Atmospheric Pressure

Earth's atmosphere, held near the surface by gravity, exerts pressure on all surfaces, much as water does in a pool. The weight of the overlying column of air creates **atmospheric pressure**, and the amount of pressure is comparable to the height of the column of air above a location. While increases in altitude are matched by decreases in atmospheric pressure, horizontal pressure variations can occur at any given altitude because of changes in temperature and other factors.

Barometers, invented by Italian physicist and mathematician Evangelista Torricelli (1608–47) in 1643, are used to measure atmospheric pressure. These measurements are translated into **isobars**, lines connecting points of equal atmospheric pressure, allowing high and low pressure areas to be shown on weather maps. Early barometers used mercury to measure atmospheric pressure: When a glass tube full of mercury is turned upside down, the mercury drops to the level that the pressure of the outside atmosphere supports. Average sea-level atmospheric pressure of 29.92 inches is a physical measurement of the height of the mercury regardless of the diameter of the tube. This principle of atmospheric support of liquid in a tube also allows a pump to raise water from a well. Water has lower specific gravity than mercury, so hand pumps can raise well water slightly more than 32 feet vertically before the weight of the water in the pipe is heavier than that of the atmospheric column.

Atmospheric pressure, the weight of overlying air, decreases with increasing altitude both because there is less overlying air and because gravitational pull decreases with altitude. At Earth's surface, average atmospheric pressure is 14.7 pounds per square inch; this is more familiarly measured as 29.92 inches (of mercury) or 1,013 millibars. In Denver, the Mile High City, atmospheric pressure is 12.2 pounds, or 83 percent, of that at sea level; at 18,500 feet, on the slopes of Mount McKinley in Alaska, pressure is 7.35 pounds, or 50 percent. Lower atmospheric pressure affects respiration because each lungful of air has proportionally fewer oxygen molecules. Mountain climbers who do not take the time to acclimatize to thinner air at higher elevations may experience **hypoxia**, or altitude sickness, because less oxygen gets into their blood.

Horizontal pressure variations cause winds and are mapped using isobars; these maps can then be used to predict the movement of storms and weather systems. (See Weather Map, page 85.) An isobar is a line connecting points of equal atmospheric pressure, so that high-pressure areas (**anticyclones**) and low-pressure areas (**cyclones**) are shown. To adjust for different surface elevations, the barometric reading for each point is calibrated to a sea-level equivalent. Denver, for example, is at an elevation of nearly 5,300 feet, and under average daily conditions it should have an atmospheric pressure of 24.95 inches. New Orleans,

Altimeters

Altimeters are used to determine the altitude of aircraft above sea level by measuring outside atmospheric pressure and comparing that reading to sea-level pressure. The altitude of the aircraft can be calculated because atmospheric pressure decreases regularly with increasing height above the ground. Radar altimeters determine altitude by measuring the time a radio signal takes to beam down to Earth and return. (Radar stands for radio detection and ranging.)

Changes in atmospheric pressure associated with changes in weather, however, can result in incorrect measurements of altitude. When a low-pressure system moves into an area, for example, pressure readings may drop by 2 or 3 percent, and a given reading in an aircraft will incorrectly be translated to a higher altitude. For safety purposes, pilots must adjust their altimeters based on local weather conditions reported by the Federal Aviation Administration.

at sea level, has a barometric level of 29.92 inches, and a comparison of the two cities would show the effect of elevation on the change in pressure, not the effect of the horizontal pressure differences that move weather systems.

Pressure Variations

Horizontal atmospheric pressure variations occur primarily because of differences in temperature. When Earth's atmosphere is warmed by the greenhouse effect the kinetic energy of greenhouse gases increases, causing gas molecules to move more rapidly and spread farther apart. The result is a decrease in the density of the atmosphere that reduces the atmospheric pressure. Record low pressures are found in cyclones; the lowest yet recorded is 25.69 inches in the eye of a typhoon north of the Pacific Ocean island of Guam in 1979. Atmospheric pressure in the eye of a tornado is probably lower, but that has not yet been measured due to the destructive force of the winds.

When air cools, atmospheric pressure increases because the lower kinetic energy causes the gases to compress, increasing air's density. The record high pressure yet measured is 32.01 inches in Siberia during the winter of 1968. Antarctica may have higher atmospheric pressures, but these have not been officially recorded.

Atmospheric pressure varies horizontally at higher altitudes as well as on Earth's surface. Differential rates of heating of different types of surfaces affect not only surface atmospheric pressure, but also the overlying columns of air: When warmed surface air expands, it also rises, thus creating lower surface pressure. In turn, the rising column of air compresses at higher altitudes and has higher pressure at those altitudes than that of surrounding air. High-pressure areas near the surface, where air has cooled or upper air has settled and compressed, tend to have less dense overlying air that is lower pressure than the surrounding air at that higher altitude.

While most horizontal variations in atmospheric pressure can be explained by differences in the rates of heating and cooling on Earth's surface, water vapor concentration in the air and the presence of atmospheric convergence or divergence also contribute to pressure differences. Increased amounts of water vapor, a variable gas, tend to lower atmospheric pressure because water vapor is less dense than either the nitrogen or oxygen that it displaces. **Atmospheric convergence** occurs when winds meet and compress air at their point of convergence. **Atmospheric divergence** occurs when winds blow away from each other and leave lower atmospheric pressure at the location of the divergence. (See Wind, page 74.)

Patterns of Atmospheric Pressure

An idealized global pattern of surface atmospheric pressure shows five pressure bands circling Earth, with two high-pressure areas centered over the North and South Poles. The **intertropical convergence zone (ITCZ)** along the Equator is a low-pressure zone created by intense solar radiation and heating. As heated air rises at the Equator it creates an upper-level high-pressure zone, from which the upper air diverges and moves away from the Equator. By the time the diverging air moves approximately 30 degrees north and south of the Equator, this upper air has cooled and is denser than surrounding air. It then descends, creating high-pressure surface zones near the Tropics of Cancer and Capricorn. At about 60° north and south latitudes—between the high-pressure zones at the tropics and the high-pressure zones over the Poles—lie low-pressure surface zones; these pressure zones are created by the convergence of air moving from the tropical and polar high-pressure zones.

Differences in surface characteristics, especially between water and land, modify this idealized global pressure pattern. For example, in the case of Eurasia, the continental landmasses of Europe and Asia, continent and ocean contrasts in heating and cooling are also reflected in differences in atmospheric pressure. The Eurasian landmass cools more than its surrounding oceans—the Atlantic, Arctic, Pacific, and Indian Oceans—in winter and consequently tends to have higher surface pressure; in summer the landmass warms more rapidly than the oceans and develops lower surface pressure. The winds over Eurasia reflect this seasonal change in pressure. The Siberian high-

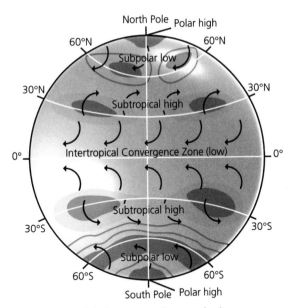

The ITCZ and global patterns of atmospheric pressure are marked above by darker red in the areas of high pressure and lighter red and gray in low-pressure areas; arrows show wind direction.

pressure area is a well-developed winter phenomenon, with an average pressure of 30.56 inches, and an average pressure below 29.53 inches in summer.

Maps of Earth's January and July surface pressures show the interacting effects of latitude and landmasses on global pressure bands. The Equatorial low-pressure zone is relatively well defined, but isobars rarely follow latitudes exactly because of the different pressure systems over the oceans and continents; Eurasia and North America clearly distort the pattern of isobars. Seasonal shifts in average pressure follow the solar equator but are more pronounced over the continents than the oceans, a consequence of water having higher thermal capacity than land. In Africa, for example, isobars shift over greater distances between seasons than they do over the Atlantic Ocean. Isobars show that global pressure bands are less distorted in the Southern Hemisphere, where there is far less land—especially around 60° south latitude—to create competing pressure regions. Finally, global pressure patterns

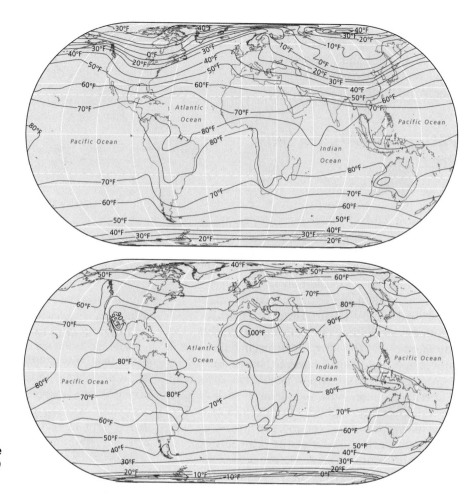

Isotherms show average temperatures around the world in January (above) and July (below).

can be temporarily disturbed by large periodic events such as El Niño. (See Climatic Change, page 121.)

Wind

Wind is the horizontal movement of air in response to differences in atmospheric pressure. If the movement is up or down, it is called an updraft or downdraft. When atmospheric pressure at one location is higher than the pressure at surrounding locations at the same altitude, air flows to equalize this imbalance. Usually the **pressure gradient** between two locations is the result of differen-

tial surface heating, but other factors, such as convergence or divergence, can also affect atmospheric pressure.

Although wind is the force that moves weather systems from place to place, up- and downward movements of air drafts are also part of the pressure system driving global and local winds; they are also the basis of some local weather conditions. Rising air at the ITCZ creates a zone of low surface pressure at the **horse latitudes**, near 30° north and south latitude, where descending air and high surface pressure dominate. The horse latitudes were called that by mariners sailing from Europe to the West Indies with horses aboard their ships. If ships became becalmed, horses were thrown

Wind Speed

Wind speeds are measured in **knots** (one knot is one *nautical mile*, or 6,076 feet) or miles per hour by anemometers, which indicate wind speed by how fast an array of cups that catch the wind can rotate. Francis Beaufort (1774–1857), a British naval officer, devised a system of descriptions in 1805 based on wind effects on the surface. The **Beaufort scale** is still used to describe estimated wind speeds. For example, a moderate breeze—a force four on the Beaufort scale—moves small tree branches, lifts leaves and paper from the ground, and measures from 13 to 18 miles per hour. The current world record for wind speed is 231 miles per hour, measured on Mount Washington, New Hampshire, in 1934. The reading was for one gust, and winds greater than 185 miles per hour have been recorded there for a five-minute interval. Westerly winds are usually strong in this region, and winds flowing over Mount Washington are constricted between the mountain and overlying air layers, causing an increase in wind speed.

overboard to conserve water for the crew. These low- and high-pressure zones are key causes of global winds. (See Global Winds and Ocean Currents, page 80.)

Regional or local updrafts may be the centers of cyclonic storms ranging in size from tornadoes to hurricanes. (See Weather Systems, page 98.) **Thermals**, local updrafts caused by rapid heating of local surfaces, can create dust devils and are used by glider pilots as well as soaring hawks and vultures to climb to higher altitudes.

All winds, whether local, regional, or global, have two defining characteristics—speed and direction, each of which is the result of several interacting factors. Wind speed is the result of the competing influences of pressure gradient and friction. The greater the pressure differential over a given distance, the faster the wind, but pressure gradients cannot be directly correlated to surface wind speeds because different types of terrain slow wind based on their roughness.

Friction, particularly friction created by large objects on the ground, affects wind velocity and wind flow or turbulence. Buildings, trees, and snow fences can decrease the speed of wind, while the flat surfaces of ice, lakes, oceans, or smooth desert often have faster winds than cities or forests. Wind that is 65 miles per hour over a calm ocean may be only 40 mph over rough terrain, while the same pressure gradient may cause winds to reach speeds of 100 mph at 3,000 feet above the influence of surface friction. Windmills are more efficient when located at higher local elevations, and kites fly more easily the higher they soar above the ground because the decrease in friction allows faster winds.

A second effect of friction on wind is to increase air turbulence. Instead of flowing smoothly from high to low pressure, wind blows in gusts or eddies when buildings, hills, and other objects slow, channel, or deflect it. Turbulence can also form at higher altitudes when a **jet stream**—an extremely rapid, high-altitude wind—an updraft, or a mountain causes wind shear that interferes with smooth wind flow. Clouds with a wave pattern can be evidence of high-altitude turbulence, although clear-air turbulence (CAT) also occurs and is an occasional hazard for aircraft.

Wind direction is controlled by pressure gradient, friction, and the Coriolis effect. Pressure gradients are greatest at right angles to the isobars and extend directly from high to low pressure. Winds follow the pressure gradient if they flow for short distances or if they are along the

Beaufort Scale of Wind Force

BEAUFORT NUMBER	GENERAL DESCRIPTION	LAND AND SEA OBSERVATIONS FOR ESTIMATING WIND SPEEDS	WIND SPEED 30 FEET ABOVE GROUND (km/hr)
0	Calm	Smoke rises vertically. Sea like mirror.	Less than 1
1	Light air	Smoke, but not wind vane, shows direction of wind. Slight ripples at sea.	1–5
2	Light breeze	Wind felt on face, leaves rustle, wind vanes move. Small, short wavelets.	6–11
3	Gentle breeze	Leaves and small twigs moving constantly, small flags extended. Large wavelets, scattered whitecaps.	12–19
4	Moderate breeze	Dust and loose paper raised, small branches moved. Small waves, frequent whitecaps.	20–28
5	Fresh breeze	Small leafy trees swayed. Moderate waves.	29–38
6	Strong breeze	Large branches in motion, whistling heard in utility wires. Large waves, some spray.	39–49
7	Near gale	Whole trees in motion. White foam from breaking waves.	50–61
8	Gale	Twigs break off trees. Moderately high waves of great length.	62–74
9	Strong gale	Slight structural damage occurs. Crests of waves begin to roll over. Spray may impede visibility.	75–88
10	Storm	Trees uprooted, considerable structural damage. Sea white with foam, heavy tumbling of sea.	89–102
11	Violent storm	Very rare; widespread damage. Unusually high waves.	103–118
12	Hurricane	Very rare; much foam and spray greatly reduce visibility.	119 and over

Equator, where there is no Coriolis effect. Friction affects wind direction by slowing wind speed and reducing the Coriolis effect.

Winds have their direction diverted by the Coriolis effect: to the right of the pressure gradient in the Northern Hemisphere and to the left in the Southern Hemisphere. Usually the deflection is between 10 degrees and 50 degrees and depends on wind velocity and distance. Increased wind speed and increased travel distance result in greater deflection from the Coriolis effect because both result in winds traveling farther over the Earth. In North America winds curve to their right; a north-to-south pressure gradient does not result in a north wind but a northeast wind. Winds are named for the direction from which they come. A north-to-south pressure gradient in Australia results in a northwest wind because it is deflected to its left.

The Coriolis effect, first described by French mathematician Gaspard-Gustave de Coriolis (1792–1843) in 1835, influences winds, ocean currents, and even missiles. As Earth rotates, the entire surface travels eastward as part of the rotational motion. The rate of eastward motion at the surface depends on the latitude because Earth is a sphere and different latitudes have different circumferences around Earth's axis. At the Equator the surface rotates at more than a thousand miles per hour, but at 40° north latitude—about the latitude of Denver and Philadelphia—the surface rotates at less than 800 miles per hour. Winds, like all motion parallel to the surface, incorporate the eastward movement from their latitude of origin into their trajectories. As a result the path of wind blowing from one latitude to another will be offset because of the difference between the wind's rate of eastward movement and the surface's rate of eastward movement.

For example, a pressure gradient from Houston, at 30° north latitude, to Minneapolis, at 45° north latitude, will initiate a southerly wind incorporating an eastward movement. As the wind moves farther north—where the circumference around a latitude is smaller and the surface rotates more slowly—the eastward movement of the wind is faster than that of the Earth. As a result, the wind ends up east of Minneapolis—to the right of the original direction. By the same process, a wind blowing from Minneapolis to Houston starts with a smaller eastward component than is present in Houston. When the wind arrives in Houston, the city has rotated farther east than the wind and the wind appears to have curved to its right.

Friction affects wind direction indirectly by slowing wind speed and therefore reducing the Coriolis effect. The reduction of friction with increasing altitude contributes to wind-direction variations at different heights; pressure gradients can also vary with altitude and therefore change wind directions. Balloonists change their altitudes in order to change their direction of travel. At altitudes above 3,000 feet, where surface friction is negligible, wind speed is usually fast enough that the Coriolis effect is increased until it actually balances the effect of the pressure gradient. As a result wind direction is parallel, rather than perpendicular to isobars, and is called a **geostrophic wind**.

Local and Regional Winds

Local winds are caused by short-term, often diurnal, temperature changes that create short-term pressure gradients. Land breezes and sea or lake breezes are local winds caused by the diurnal differences in temperature and pressure over land and water. During the day, when land warms more rapidly than water, a sea breeze blows from the cooler, higher pressure air over water toward the warmer, lower pressure air over the land. These breezes may reach several hundred yards to several miles inland before their momentum is stopped, partly because of friction over the surface. In addition, the pressure gradient becomes less sharp farther inland from the beach. At night, a land breeze forms when the pressure gradient reverses—after land has cooled more quickly than a lake or ocean.

As with other local winds, relative temperatures are the key to the pressure gradient and relative air movement. Sea and land breezes usually form during summer, in lower latitudes, and under clear skies—conditions that often generate temperature differences between land and water. Sea breezes are usually stronger than land breezes because temperature and pressure differences are greater during daytime when land has warmed faster than water.

Differential heating in hilly terrain causes another set of local winds: mountain and valley breezes. In daytime, slopes—especially those facing the sun—warm more and therefore have lower atmospheric pressure than surrounding air at the same altitude. As the less dense air warmed by a slope rises, the cooler and denser surrounding air flows toward the slope, creating a valley breeze. At night, slopes—especially upper slopes in thinner air—radiate energy and cool more rapidly than lower slopes; the cooler, denser air descends from the upper slopes as a mountain breeze.

Seasonal differences in heating affect these winds. Valley breezes tend to be stronger in summer than winter because higher summer temperatures create lower atmospheric pressure along slopes than those in winter. Mountain breezes are stronger in winter when lower temperatures cause air to become denser and have higher pressure than during summer.

Regional winds, which affect larger areas for longer periods than local winds do, can also be caused by cold, dense air descending from higher elevations. These winds, often more pronounced in the colder temperatures of winter, are the **katabatic winds** associated with glaciers, high plateaus, and mountains. Katabatic winds in Europe, such as the mistral

of southern France and the bora along the Dalmatian Coast, are channeled by valleys in the Jura Alps and Dinaric Alps and can reach speeds of one hundred miles per hour, powerful enough to topple railroad cars. Other katabatic winds are the tabu of Alaska and the glacial winds in Antarctica.

A second type of regional wind is also related to mountains—the **chinook** of the Rockies, called the föhn in Europe. Chinook winds occur in mountains when air blown up the windward side descends. As a result, chinooks are compressionally warmed and have extremely low relative humidity. Chinooks can

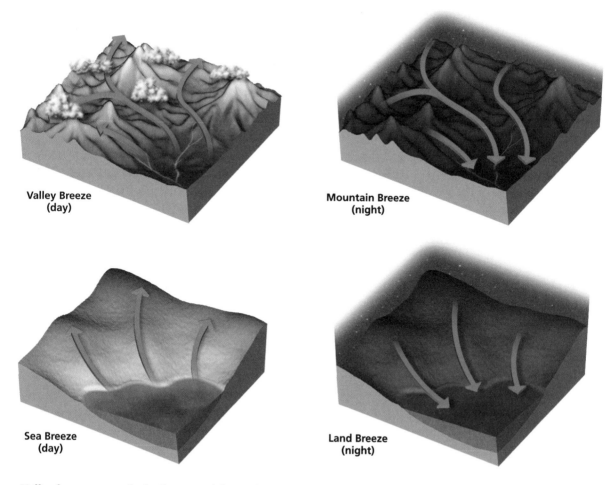

Valley Breeze (day)

Mountain Breeze (night)

Sea Breeze (day)

Land Breeze (night)

Valley breezes occur in daytime as cool dense air warms and rises up warm mountain slopes, while **mountain breezes** occur at night when the air is cooled and descends downslope. **Sea breezes** occur in daytime when cooler sea air rushes inland to replace sun-warmed land air, and **land breezes** occur at night when the cooled land air rushes back out to sea.

gust to one hundred miles per hour, and temperature changes can be extremely rapid: In Alberta, Canada, chinook winds raised air temperature 38°F in four minutes on January 6, 1966. **Santa Anas** are easterly winds blown over the Sierra Nevada from high pressure areas in Utah and Nevada into southern California, where they contribute to the fall fire season by dehydrating vegetation. A comparable wind, the **zonda**, occurs in Argentina after air has blown over the Andes.

Monsoons

Monsoons are regional winds that reverse direction between summer and winter and dominate coastal Asia from Pakistan to Japan. Weaker versions of monsoons also occur in western Africa and northern Australia. Eurasia cools in winter and forms a high pressure area—the Siberian high; in summer the landmass warms and forms a low pressure area. Monsoons in Eurasia are limited to tropical and subtropical locations around its periphery, so other factors are clearly involved. Recent studies show that the position of a monsoon is affected by the shifting of the solar equator and ITCZ, as well as by changes in the polar jet stream. In summer, the low pressure ITCZ shifts northward over southern Asia causing strong onshore sea breezes that extend from the Indian Ocean to the South China Sea. In winter, the ITCZ shifts southward to the Indian Ocean and northern Australia, contributing to land breezes from Eurasia. This shifting of the ITCZ reinforces the effect of the seasonal pressure changes over Eurasia and its surrounding oceans. In addition, in winter the jet stream splits around the east-west trending Himalaya, and one branch travels south bringing wet weather systems from the Mediterranean to the Hindu Kush. By summer this southern branch dissipates and moves north of the Himalaya, allowing warm air masses to blow onshore, bringing moisture with them.

Monsoons are complex winds that several

billion Asians and Africans rely on because they bring moisture and rainfall essential for growing crops. (See Bioregions, page 227.) Even though monsoons are seasonably predictable, the duration and amount of monsoonal winds and rain vary from summer to summer. Occasionally, as in the mid-1980s in the African Sahel, monsoons fail to occur and the resulting summer drought contributes to conditions that cause starvation and hundreds of thousands of deaths.

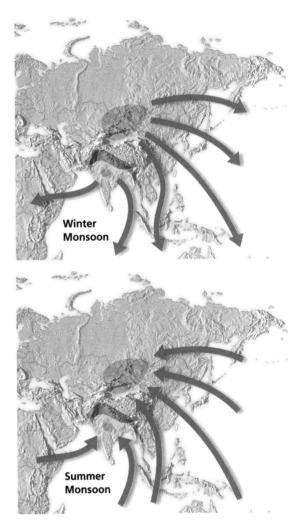

In Asia, land-based winter monsoon winds are relatively dry. Summer monsoon winds originate over warm oceans and bring drenching rains.

Global Winds and Ocean Currents

Global atmospheric pressure zones and the Coriolis effect create a global circulation system of surface and high-altitude winds as well as ocean currents moved by surface winds. Global winds move weather systems, and therefore heat energy and moisture, around the world; heat and moisture are also redistributed by ocean currents. Understanding the spatial and temporal patterns of global circulation is key to understanding seasonal patterns of climates.

Causes of Atmospheric Circulation

Unlike local or regional winds, which are seasonal and limited to one continent or region, global winds blow throughout the year and circle Earth. While global winds are consistent features of Earth's environment, their paths shift in response to changes in regional pressure systems and the movement of the solar equator. These shifts, however, are limited, and global winds provide a consistent basis for generating precipitation patterns and global climates.

Surface high- and low-pressure systems create pressure gradients that drive global winds and also cause upper-air pressure gradients. A cycle of air, called a **Hadley cell**, for English meteorologist George Hadley (1685–1763), illustrates how pressure systems relate to each other and to global winds. In 1735, Hadley described the cells that came to be named for him. Hadley cells link the low-pressure zone at the Equator—the intertropical convergence zone (ITCZ)—with the high-pressure zone at

the horse latitudes to the north and south. Air rises at the Equator because of intense solar heating, leaving lower pressure at the surface and increasing air pressure high above the Equator as more air rises to the higher altitude. This rising air will eventually return to the surface when it loses heat by radiation to space and therefore becomes denser than surrounding air. The air descends at 30° north and south latitudes, creating the surface high-pressure zones found at the horse latitudes.

High-pressure areas centered on the Poles and low-pressure zones around 60° north and south latitudes are also part of the global pressure system. Polar highs are caused by extremely low temperatures. In the Southern Hemisphere, for example, air pressure in the horse latitudes may average 30.42, but the pressure at 60° degrees south latitude may average 29.42. While the linkage between surface and high-altitude pressure systems explained by the Hadley cell is well documented for low latitudes, no similar cells form poleward of the horse latitudes.

In addition to pressure zones, the patterns of global winds reflect the influence of the Coriolis effect. The **westerlies** circle the globe at more than 40 miles per hour; as a rule, they are diverted about 45 degrees to the right or left from the pressure gradient because of the Coriolis effect. As a result global winds do not blow from north to south (or south to north) between pressure systems. Instead, winds tend to blow from a quadrant, or between two cardinal directions: The westerlies blow from the southwest in the Northern Hemisphere and from the northwest in the Southern Hemisphere.

Surface Patterns of Atmospheric Circulation

Earth's global atmospheric circulation system is a pattern of wind and pressure zones centered on the doldrums at the ITCZ. The doldrums, horse latitudes, and polar anticyclones (areas of high atmospheric pressure) are zones that create global pressure gradients. As a result, two consistent wind zones are created in each hemisphere: the **trade winds**, or **easterlies**, and the **westerlies**. Near the North and South Poles, winds are often easterly, but they are more inconsistent than winds in other zones of global circulation.

North and south of the doldrums are the trade winds, which were known to sailors long before Columbus used them on his first voyage to the Americas in 1492. The trades are more consistent than other global winds; they blow from the eastern quadrant almost 80 percent of the time because the pressure gradient between the horse latitudes and doldrums is so consistent. While the pressure gradient for the trades is from high to low pressure, or north to south in the Northern Hemisphere, the Coriolis effect deflects the wind to a northeast wind. In the Southern Hemisphere, with a south-to-north pressure gradient and a leftward Coriolis effect, the trade winds are southeasterly.

The horse latitudes, a high-pressure zone with inconsistent winds, are centered on 30° north and south latitudes. The surface high pressure along these latitudes causes air to flow outward to the Equator and toward higher latitudes.

Just poleward of the horse latitudes, between 35° and 60° north and south of the solar equator, are the westerlies. Winds blowing toward the Poles from the high-pressure zones at the horse latitudes become southwesterlies in the Northern Hemisphere and northwesterlies in the Southern Hemisphere. The westerlies are interrupted in the Northern Hemisphere by continents whose pressure systems and mountains interfere with smooth airflow and cause increased variability in wind direction; most weather systems in these midlatitudes still travel from west to east. In the Southern Hemisphere—especially south of South America, Africa, and Australia, and north of Antarctica—there is less land area to impede winds, which allows the westerlies to be more consistent than in the north.

At higher latitudes than the westerlies are polar easterlies. These winds blow from the high pressure caused by extremely cold temperatures at the Poles to the relatively lower pressure at 60° north and south latitudes where the polar fronts are located. Polar easterlies are curved to the west by the Coriolis effect, which is strongest at the Poles. The Antarctic has higher pressure and more consistent winds than the Arctic because of increased cooling from its larger ice-covered surface area. Winds at both Poles, however,

Global Circulation and Sailing

Sailors named different global winds and pressure systems based on their influence on sailing. The lack of consistent winds at the Equator and along the Tropics of Cancer and Capricorn resulted in sailors being becalmed. If they were immobile for days, they ate or tossed livestock overboard; hence, the name horse latitudes. English poet Samuel Taylor Coleridge (1772–1834) described the experience of windlessness in "The Rime of the Ancient Mariner": *Day after day, day after day/ We struck, nor breath nor motion;/As idle as a painted ship/Upon a painted ocean.* Westerly and easterly winds were named for the directions from which the winds consistently blew; easterlies are also called trade winds, a term derived from *trado*, Latin for "direction."

The Roaring Forties

During the 1700s and 1800s, before steam power replaced sails, sailing from the Atlantic to the Pacific Ocean around Cape Horn at the southern tip of South America was more hazardous and time-consuming. Rounding the Horn involved tacking into the roaring forties, strong westerlies between 40° and 50° south latitude. Delays of a month or more were possible; some captains chose to sail 8,500 miles eastward across the Atlantic to the Pacific to avoid the strong winds.

are less consistent than those in other global wind zones because of changes in the location and the intensity of the polar pressure systems.

Earth's global wind patterns are far more variable than the system described above. Seasonal shifts in the intensity of insolation and temperature cause the surface pressure conditions to change and therefore affect global winds. The distribution of continents and oceans creates pressure systems that displace global wind patterns; major mountain ranges may also interrupt their flow. Passing storms and frontal activity also disturb wind patterns.

One of the most important influences on global wind patterns is the seasonal shift of the intertropical convergence zone (ITCZ), caused by the movement of the solar equator. During summer in the Northern Hemisphere, when the solar equator coincides with the Tropic of Cancer, the entire global wind system shifts slightly north. In winter, when sunlight shines vertically down on the Tropic of Capricorn, the system shifts slightly south. Precipitation patterns also shift north and south in response to the movement of global pressure zones and winds. Southern California's weather, for example, is affected by the doldrums shifting northward in summer, causing hot, dry weather, and by the westerlies shifting south in winter, causing a rainy season with moisture from the Pacific Ocean.

In general, the ITCZ shifts farther north and south between seasons over continents than it does over oceans; water has greater thermal capacity than land, resulting in a slower rate of change in water temperature. Over the Atlantic and central Pacific the ITCZ shifts less than five degrees between seasons, half as much as it shifts over Central America and Africa. Other pressure systems can affect this seasonal shift in the position of the ITCZ: In the monsoon region of South Asia and the Indian Ocean, the ITCZ can shift almost 40 degrees between seasons. The high temperature and low pressure over land in summer bring the ITCZ north to the Himalaya, and the low temperature and high pressure over land in winter force it south of the Seychelles.

In addition to affecting the seasonal shift of the ITCZ over southern Asia, regional pressure systems affect global winds in other locations. **Anticyclones** are consistent high-pressure features over cold waters of the Atlantic, Pacific, and Indian Oceans; these ocean anticyclones form in both the Northern and Southern Hemispheres and center on latitudes 30° north and south. The outward wind flow from these anticyclones modifies wind patterns of the trades, horse latitudes, and westerlies.

Upper-Air Wind Patterns

The upper-air wind component of the global circulation system differs from surface winds in direction and speed because pressure systems and the Coriolis effect vary with altitude. A low-pressure system at the surface causes a high-pressure system at greater altitude because rising air is eventually compressed, making it denser than surrounding air. The result is a high-altitude pressure gradient that may be the reverse of what is occurring on the surface, with high-altitude winds blowing in the opposite direction of surface winds.

Differences in pressure gradient alone would change upper wind directions, but the Coriolis effect also varies with altitude. High-altitude winds have greater velocity than surface winds because there is less friction at higher altitudes, and the Coriolis effect increases with speed. At 3,000 feet above the ground, the influence of surface conditions is negligible, and upper-air wind speeds can exceed a hundred miles per hour.

At higher altitudes, increased wind speeds bring the pressure gradient and Coriolis effect into balance, causing upper-air winds to blow in straight lines parallel to isobars, lines connecting points of equal atmospheric pressure. When isobars parallel latitudes around the globe, patterns that occur at the Equator and in the midlatitudes, **geostrophic winds** occur. Circular isobars mark cyclones and anticyclones that cause high-altitude **gradient winds** to follow circular paths around the pressure centers.

Most upper-air winds in the midlatitudes and in the tropics are geostrophic westerlies; the midlatitude westerlies are especially important in directing weather systems over North America and Eurasia. In the midlatitudes, an overall upper-level pressure gradient exists from higher pressure nearer the tropics to lower pressure nearer the Poles. The Coriolis effect curves the resulting upper-air winds toward the east in both hemispheres. At the tropics, the upper-air pressure gradient from the high-pressure zone over the ITCZ poleward to the low-pressure zones over the horse latitudes also results in geostrophic westerlies.

Midlatitude, upper-air westerlies vary in velocity between seasons because of seasonal changes in temperature and pressure. These westerlies also follow a meandering path of low-pressure areas centered on the Aleutian Islands and Iceland, high-pressure areas cen-

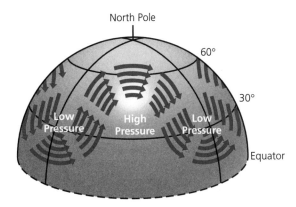

When Rossby waves show strong amplitude—north-south movement—cold polar air is transported toward the Equator and warm air is moved poleward.

tered on the North Pacific and Atlantic Oceans, and other large weather systems. Polar regions are cool in summer but are extremely cold in winter, while tropical temperatures are consistently warm year-round. As a result there is a greater temperature gradient in winter than in summer; winter, therefore, has greater pressure gradients that cause faster winds. Wind speeds in the upper-air westerlies are difficult to specify, but they may average more than 50 miles per hour; **jet streams** in the westerlies are much faster, up to 150 miles an hour. (See Jet Streams, page 84.)

The path of upper-air westerlies meanders between air masses and traces a series of curves called **Rossby waves**, for Swedish-American meteorologist Carl Rossby (1898–1957) who first described them in the late 1930s. Rossby waves roughly parallel the polar fronts, and their paths reflect a balance between the Coriolis effect and the vortices created by cyclones and anticyclones. On average, between two and five Rossby waves exist in the upper-air westerlies at any one time, and there are fewer waves in winter because increased speed caused by greater pressure gradients tends to lengthen the waves.

Much of the influence that the upper-air westerlies have on midlatitude weather is a result of the amplitude of the Rossby waves—

how far north or south each wave extends. When Rossby waves extend farther south, more heat energy is transferred between latitudes. In the United States, cooler air masses can reach into the Sunbelt and cause frost damage to orchards, and warmer air masses may reach Canada. At other times Rossby waves can have minimal amplitude and therefore transfer little heat between latitudes. Shifts in amplitude can occur within days because of the formation and disappearance of air masses, making weather prediction challenging.

On occasion, a Rossby wave can become so large that the wave can be cut off from its source area. It then becomes an air pocket that forms a cyclone or anticyclone depending upon its temperature and source area, and it can persist for several weeks, interrupting the movement of weather systems through the area. Such an air pocket can block the usual eastward movement of weather in the midlatitudes and perpetuate weather conditions. Wet weather systems that were blocked in 1988 caused drought, and in 1993 a blocking system that kept dry weather systems from moving into the Midwest caused floods.

Jet Streams

Jet streams are the fastest of the upper-air winds and are influential in directing the movement of surface weather systems. The speed of a jet stream ordinarily varies between 50 and 150 miles per hour, and **jet streaks**, short sections of jet streams, may top 200 miles

per hour as they circle the globe. These speeds are the result of intense pressure gradients in the upper atmosphere and are found only in zones of great temperature contrast. These contrasts are especially strong at the tropopause above fronts, where tropical and arctic air masses meet. Jet stream speeds are, like those of the upper-air westerlies, faster in winter when temperature contrasts are greater.

While lower-latitude jet streams exist, such as the subtropical jet stream, the **polar-front jet stream** affects more of the world's populated regions. As its name implies, the polar-front jet stream parallels the polar fronts, following the Rossby waves. As it travels eastward, the jet stream literally pulls along the top of surface weather systems, while surface friction slows the systems to one-third the speed of the jet stream. During the summer months, the polar-front jet stream is centered at about 45° north and south latitudes, but in winter the cooling of the polar regions causes it to move about 10 or 15 degrees closer to the Equator.

The polar-front jet streams reinforce the effect of the upper-air westerlies on surface weather; together, they increase the eastward motion of weather systems. Most of the global exchange of heat energy also occurs at the polar fronts, as Rossby waves in the midlatitude westerlies; the polar-front jet stream also guides the exchange of tropical and arctic air masses. As a consequence the midlatitudes experience far greater day-to-day weather variations than other latitudes.

Weather Prediction

Weather proverbs such as "Red sky in the morning, sailor take warning," have given way to computer modeling for predicting the weather. Accurate forecasting requires predicting how rapidly and from what locations surface and high-altitude winds will bring new weather systems. Modeling and mapping of atmospheric conditions has improved with greater understanding of atmospheric processes, improved data, and faster computers.

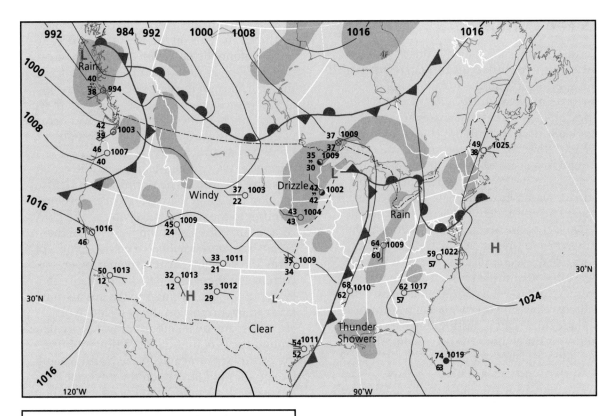

WEATHER SYMBOLS

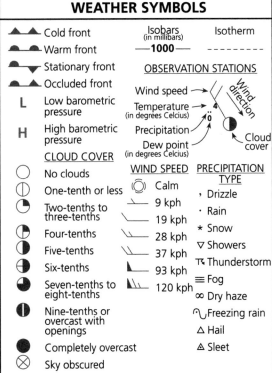

▲▲	Cold front
●●	Warm front
▼	Stationary front
●▲	Occluded front
L	Low barometric pressure
H	High barometric pressure

Isobars (in millibars)
—1000—

Isotherm
– – – – –

OBSERVATION STATIONS

Wind speed →
Temperature → (in degrees Celcius)
Precipitation →
Dew point → (in degrees Celcius)

Wind direction
Cloud cover

CLOUD COVER

○	No clouds
◍	One-tenth or less
◔	Two-tenths to three-tenths
◓	Four-tenths
◑	Five-tenths
◒	Six-tenths
◕	Seven-tenths to eight-tenths
◍	Nine-tenths or overcast with openings
●	Completely overcast
⊗	Sky obscured

WIND SPEED

◎	Calm
⌐	9 kph
⌐	19 kph
⌐	28 kph
⌐	37 kph
◤	93 kph
◤⌐	120 kph

PRECIPITATION TYPE

Symbol	Type
,	Drizzle
·	Rain
＊	Snow
▽	Showers
⊺	Thunderstorm
≡	Fog
∞	Dry haze
⌒	Freezing rain
△	Hail
△	Sleet

A representative weather map uses commonly accepted conventions to depict warm, cold, and occluded fronts, isobars to join areas of similar air pressure, isotherms to connect areas of similar temperature, and a variety of means to show the amount of cloud cover, wind speed, and type of precipitation. Altogether, an amazing amount of weather information is available to knowledgeable weather map readers.

Ocean Currents

Earth's global wind system is the driving mechanism for surface **ocean currents**, which transport heat from the tropics to the polar regions, influence the location of major fisheries, and affect coastal climates around the world. Surface currents are continuous, nearly circular flows, or **gyres**, of surface water that extend to a depth of about 300 feet and are centered in the horse latitudes. (See Earth's Surface Ocean Currents map, opposite.) Deep-water currents ranging in depth from about 2,000 feet to the ocean floor also flow from Antarctica to Greenland and the Bering Strait. These deep-water currents, called **density currents**, are caused by decreases in water temperature to below 30°F and increases in salinity. They support major fishing grounds and are important in distributing oxygen and nutrients throughout the oceans, but they do not affect climates significantly.

Surface currents are relatively slow, averaging one or two miles per hour, and their motion is the result of frictional drag on the water surface by the global wind system. **Waves**, the up-and-down motion of the ocean's surface, are also the result of the frictional drag of wind, but their motion is temporary and caused by storms and local or regional winds. **Tides**, the regular rise and fall of ocean levels, are caused by the gravitational pull of the moon and sun. (See Waves and Coastal Landforms, page 197.) Ocean currents move continuously because the trade winds and westerlies are constant. Current speeds are far slower than wind speeds because water has great inertia, and the kinetic energy of wind transfers directly only to the ocean surface.

Surface ocean currents flow in **gyres** because landmasses divert currents sideways and the Coriolis effect causes the currents to flow at a 45-degree angle to the prevailing wind direction. When the trade winds blow in the North Atlantic, the northeasterly winds result in an easterly ocean current.

While ocean currents average a few miles per hour, currents on the west side of ocean gyres—along the east coasts of landmasses—tend to flow up to several miles per hour faster than currents on the east side of oceans—or along west coasts. The centers of gyres are west of the centers of the oceans themselves because of Earth's eastward rotation. For example, the North Atlantic's gyre is centered near Bermuda. Water accumulates near the center of a gyre because of the Coriolis effect: Earth's rotation causes an increase in ocean level to be offset to the west of the center of the gyre. As a result, currents on the west side of the oceans are constricted between the centers of gyres and coastlines. Thus, the narrower currents on the west—narrower because the center of the gyre is closer to the coast—travel faster than currents on the east side, which are wider; an equal amount of water circulates around the gyre in the same amount of time—the continuity principle. In the North Atlantic Ocean, the Gulf Stream on the west side of the ocean flows more than five miles per hour, while the Canary Current on the east side often moves at less than one mile per hour.

Gyres affect climates primarily because water temperatures affect atmospheric humidity. When the trade winds cause ocean currents to flow parallel to the Equator, the water warms by absorbing insolation. When the Gulf Stream and Brazil Current curve away from the Equator alongside east coasts because of the Coriolis effect, the water warms the coasts and increases the specific humidity in the area. (See Global Climate Patterns, page 116.) When an ocean current, such as the California Current, heads back to the Equator after traveling to polar regions, it has cooled between 5° and 10°F and, though it still moderates temperature extremes, it cannot increase humidity or precipitation significantly.

Ocean currents have a range of other impacts on humans: Fishing and shipping are affected by **upwelling**—cold, deep water rises to replace surface water—and by water temperatures. Most of the commercial fisheries in

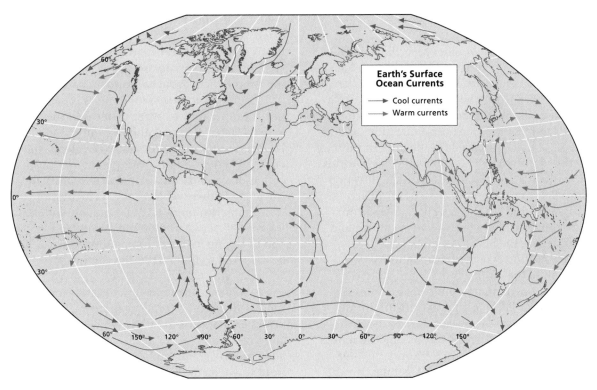

Cool currents convey cold water from the Poles to the tropics; warm currents convey warmer water from the tropics toward the Poles. Ocean currents are profoundly affected by prevailing winds.

the world's oceans are found in waters whose temperatures are below 35°F and where currents cause upwelling. Off the west coast of South America, for example, the cool Peru Current, once called the Humboldt Current, moves north along the coast until it is pulled away from Ecuador as part of the South Pacific gyre, causing nutrient-rich lower waters to upwell and support the food chain for anchovies and other fish. Ocean currents also impact shipping routes: The cooling but still-warm North Atlantic Drift keeps the ports of Norway ice-free during winter, whereas pack ice blocks the coasts of Greenland and Newfoundland.

El Niño and the Southern Oscillation (ENSO)

El Niño, a periodic reversal of the pattern of current flow and water temperatures in the mid-Pacific Ocean, is related to changes in weather around much of the world; La Niña, another periodic event in the mid-Pacific, also affects global weather. The exact causes of El Niño have not yet been confirmed, but there seem to be links between changes in the direction of the trade winds and in Pacific Ocean currents. In normal years, the trade winds and the North and South Equatorial Currents flow to the west, and warm water accumulates near Borneo and Indonesia. In this western region of the Pacific Ocean water levels can reach 18 inches higher than levels at the eastern edge, and the accumulation of warm water can cause atmospheric pressure over the western Pacific to drop.

In October or November preceding an El Niño, the low pressure over the western Pacific changes to higher pressure while the higher pressure in the east falls. This southern oscillation of atmospheric pressure causes the trade winds to fail, if not to reverse direction, and the ITCZ to be displaced five degrees or more farther south than is usual. As the trade winds stop, the equatorial currents reverse direction as the accumulation of warm water near Indonesia drifts to the east, bringing warm water to Ecuador, where it spreads north and south along the South American coast.

Ten El Niño events occurred during the last half of the 20th century; most started in December or January—hence the name, El Niño, the Child, referring to Christmas time and Jesus's birth—and lasted from a few months to more than a year. During the more severe El Niños, as in 1992–93 and 1997–98, droughts and floods affected Australia, North America, South America, Asia, and the Pacific Rim. When atmospheric pressure increases in the western Pacific, onshore breezes fail and precipitation drops in Indonesia, Malaysia, and northern Australia; forest fires have been more common during El Niño because vegetation is drier. When the water warms and pressure drops off South America, convection and precipitation increase, occasionally causing flooding from Cellao, Peru, to Quito, Ecuador.

El Niño has long-distance effects on air pressure that link weather patterns in the United States, Canada, and elsewhere. As the ITCZ in the Pacific shifts south, the global circulation system follows, bringing horse latitude conditions and the associated dry weather to Hawaii. Warmer water on the west coast of North America tends to cause milder winters for coastal Alaska and British Columbia, and changing precipitation patterns have been linked to flooding in the southern United States.

La Niña occurs when equatorial waters in the Pacific become colder than normal. Stronger-than-normal trade winds off the west coast of South America cause more upwelling along the coast, which brings more cold water from the deep to the surface. La Niña sometimes, but not always, alternates with El Niño and causes opposite changes in weather around the world. In India, for example, monsoon rains decrease during an El Niño but increase during a La Niña.

Atmospheric Moisture

Water vapor in the atmosphere cools as it rises and condenses into liquid water or ice that forms dew, frost, fog, and clouds. When cloud droplets combine, they form rain and snow that fall to Earth or form dew and frost on the surface.

Hydrologic Cycle

Water vapor is the key element in the global energy and hydrologic systems. Vapor, the gaseous state of water, forms when liquid water or ice absorbs sufficient heat from the sun or Earth to change to a gas. The energy necessary for the change is stored in the water vapor as latent heat, which is released as sensible heat when the vapor changes form again, to either a solid or a liquid. As water vapor moves from one place to another, especially from tropical latitudes to the Polar regions, the stored energy is released as the vapor condenses, thus redistributing heat around Earth.

The movement of water in its different forms around the globe is called the hydrologic cycle, and this circulation connects oceans, continents, groundwater, and the atmosphere. (See Hydrologic Cycle diagram, opposite.)

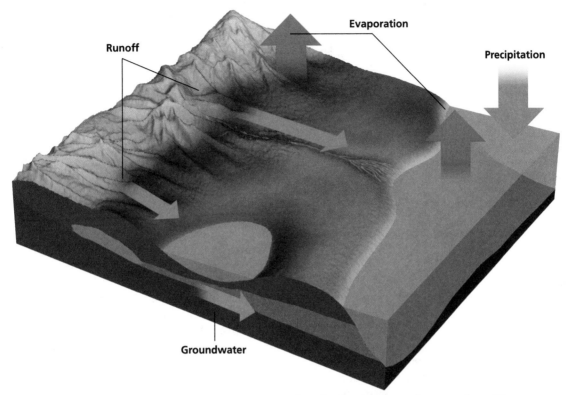

In the hydrologic cycle, evaporation transports water vapor from land and ocean to the atmosphere. Water returns to Earth in the form of precipitation. On land, water constantly seeks lower ground, often flowing into the ocean.

Although the water vapor in the atmosphere amounts to only .001 percent of all water on Earth, the rate of exchange of water between the atmosphere and the surface through condensation and precipitation is rapid, taking an average of ten days. Oceans contribute 85 percent of the water vapor in the atmosphere—almost 100 quadrillion gallons per year evaporate from ocean surfaces, or almost 3 gallons per square foot of ocean. The rest of the water vapor in the atmosphere comes from surface water evaporation on continents and transpiration from vegetation.

Atmospheric Humidity

The amount of water vapor contained in the atmosphere, or **humidity**, varies over space and time and is measured in terms of absolute and specific humidity. **Absolute humidity** is the ratio of the weight of water vapor to that of a given *volume* of air, and **specific humidity** is the ratio of the weight of water vapor of a given *weight* of air. A meteorologist can estimate how much potential precipitation exists when the specific humidity is known. The specific humidity can range from less than .02 ounces to nearly one ounce of water vapor per pound of atmosphere. Absolute humidity is not often mentioned in weather reports because the volume of a given mass of air will change as a function of temperature and therefore change the absolute humidity.

Condensation, precipitation, and evaporation result from changes in the **relative humidity** of the atmosphere—the ratio of the water vapor actually present to the maximum

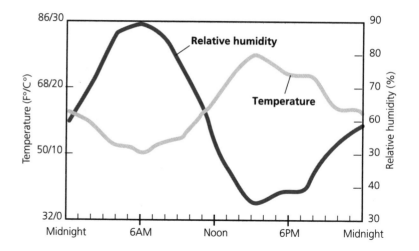

In calm air, relative humidity varies inversely with temperature. The percentage of water vapor in the air increases as temperatures fall and decreases as temperatures rise.

capacity at the same temperature. **Saturation pressure**, the maximum possible amount of water vapor in the air, depends on the temperature of the atmosphere: Warmer air contains more energy and therefore can contain more water vapor than cooler air. As air warms, the saturation pressure in the atmosphere increases and more water vapor can be held in the air. If the actual amount of water vapor remains the same, then the ratio between actual vapor pressure and saturation pressure changes and relative humidity drops. Conversely, as air cools, relative humidity increases because the saturation pressure decreases and approaches the actual amount of water vapor in the atmosphere.

Relative humidity can effect the physical and electrical properties of various objects, and relative humidity can be measured. Italian artist and scientist Leonardo da Vinci (1452–1519) measured relative humidity by comparing the weight of dry cotton to cotton that had absorbed water vapor from the air. **Hygrometers** (*hygro* is Greek for "wet") can measure relative humidity using a human hair because high relative humidity causes human hair to absorb water vapor and lengthen up to 2.5 percent. While some hygrometers still use human hair to control the location of a pointer on a gauge, others measure the electrical resistance of the air to determine the humidity. **Psy-**

chrometers measure relative humidity by using two thermometers: One registers the temperature of ambient air, and the second is wrapped in wet cloth. When the two thermometers are swung in the air, moisture evaporates from the wet cloth, causing the second thermometer inside to register a cooler temperature than the other thermometer because evaporation absorbs heat energy. The difference between the two temperatures can be compared to determine relative humidity; high relative humidity limits evaporation and therefore reduces the amount of evaporative cooling. (See Temperature Differences and Relative Humidity chart, above.)

Condensation and Adiabatic Processes

When the relative humidity of air reaches 100 percent, **saturation** occurs. At saturation, no more water vapor and therefore no more water-vapor pressure can be added to the air because the gases of the atmosphere do not have enough kinetic energy to evaporate more water. When relative humidity is high, people have difficulty cooling down because evaporation of perspiration, the process that cools the human body by absorbing heat energy, is prevented by the nearly saturated air.

As air cools below the saturation level of the atmosphere, the maximum capacity of the atmosphere drops below the actual amount of water vapor in the air and **condensation**, the phase change of water from a vapor to a liquid or solid, occurs. Condensation removes water vapor from the air and forms cloud droplets, dew, and frost. **Sublimation** refers to water vapor that changes directly to ice crystals at subfreezing temperatures. The process of condensation starts to occur at saturation and persists as long as the air continues to cool, during which time the relative humidity remains at 100 percent. Condensation creates clouds and the water droplets that form on a glass holding an icy drink after the cold glass has chilled the air next to it.

The **dew point** is the temperature at which condensation starts, and it depends on ambient air temperature and the specific humidity of the air. Warm air over a tropical ocean will have higher specific humidity than air the same temperature over a desert because of increased evaporation. The dew point for marine air may be 80°F while the dew point for desert air may be 35°F because its lower specific humidity provides so much less water vapor to start with. During summer in the United States, the lowest dew point temperatures are customarily registered in deserts and the Rocky Mountains, while the highest dew point temperatures are along the Gulf of Mexico.

Condensation of water vapor normally requires a surface on which water or ice— depending upon air temperature—can form. Without a surface, water vapor eventually forms water droplets, but the air must cool below the dew point level, thus becoming supersaturated. While dew and frost form on grass stems and windows, cloud droplets need microscopic particles on which to form. Almost all air contains **hygroscopic** particles—particles that attract water—and examples include sea salt in the atmosphere over oceans and dust, pollen, smoke, and bacteria in air over land. As a result, even rainwater is a solution

containing other substances; no water in nature is pure water. (See Weathering, page 159.)

As air temperature rises and falls throughout the day, relative humidity changes, too. As daily temperature drops after its mid-afternoon maximum, relative humidity begins to rise. When daily temperature reaches its minimum shortly after dawn, relative humidity peaks. Saturation of the air is most likely to be reached in surface air near dawn, and dew or frost tends to form then. Surfaces are also cooler than the atmosphere at dawn because they have cooled by radiation, while the air that absorbed the radiation has been warmed. As a result, dew or frost may form even if air temperatures reported by the Weather Service are not below the dew point.

In addition to changes caused by the daily insolation cycle, air temperature and relative humidity also change when air expands or compresses. In **adiabatic processes** the temperature changes without losing or gaining heat from surrounding air, and such processes include adiabatic cooling of air by the expansion of air and adiabatic warming when air is compressed. Adiabatic cooling is responsible for almost all clouds and precipitation on Earth and is caused by air rising to atmospheric levels with lower pressure. Adiabatic warming results from air descending to levels of higher atmospheric pressure. When air rises and expands, the energy to increase the air volume is taken from the kinetic energy of individual molecules, causing the air to cool. Air that descends is warmed by compression; the energy used in compression increases air density and is converted into heat absorbed by the gas molecules, thus warming the air. Thus, warmed air rises and cools, and cooled air sinks and warms.

Rising air cools at different rates depending upon whether the temperature of the rising air is above or below the dew point. At temperatures above the dew point, when the relative humidity is below 100 percent, air cools at a **dry adiabatic lapse rate** that averages 5.5°F per 1,000 feet of altitude or elevation. The term dry is used because water vapor is not yet condensing to form water droplets. The two-degree difference between the dry adiabatic lapse rate of 5.5°F and the environmental temperature lapse rate of 3.5°F per 1,000 feet affects how high warmed air can rise before it reaches the same temperature as ambient air. For example, if 70°F surface air is warmed 18°F to 86°F and rises, at 5,000 feet it has cooled 27.5°F—as a function of the dry adiabatic lapse rate—to 52.5°F. This is the same temperature as the ambient air at that altitude, after it has cooled 17.5° as a function of the environmental temperature lapse rate.

Atmospheric stability refers to how readily warmed air rises. In order to continue to rise, warmed air must remain warmer than the surrounding ambient air. Air is considered unstable when the dry adiabatic lapse rate is lower than the environmental lapse rate. Air is stable when the dry adiabatic lapse rate is higher than the environmental lapse rate; when this occurs, rising air cools faster than ambient air and therefore rapidly reaches the altitude where it will have the same temperature as ambient air.

When rising air is below the dew point temperature, the air cools at the **wet**—or saturated—**adiabatic lapse rate**, so named because saturation causes water vapor to condense and form either water droplets or ice crystals, depending on the air temperature. The wet adiabatic rate is lower than the dry adiabatic rate because the rate of cooling is offset by latent energy released when water vapor condenses. While on average the wet adiabatic rate is 3.3°F per 1,000 feet, the rate may be as low as 2.2°F per 1,000 feet for very warm air and as high as 9°F per 1,000 feet for cold air.

Wet adiabatic lapse rates vary according to ambient air temperatures because of the amount of water vapor that can be held at different temperatures. Warmer air usually has higher specific humidity than cooler air. When warmer air cools, a greater amount of vapor changes into water, releasing more latent heat

to offset the adiabatic cooling. As a result, the wet adiabatic lapse rate is lower for warmer air than for cooler air because more heat is released by condensation of warmer air than by condensation of cooler air.

When air descends and comes under greater atmospheric pressure, the air always warms at the dry adiabatic lapse rate. No condensation can occur because as the air warms its capacity for evaporation and water-vapor pressure increases. When absolute humidity is stable and air's capacity to hold water vapor increases, lower relative humidity results.

Areas of downdrafts and the leeward sides of mountains tend to have far fewer clouds and much less precipitation than areas of updrafts and the windward sides of mountains. Even in Hawaii, where rain forests dominate, western leeward sides of the islands have less precipitation. On Hawaii, the shrub and grasslands of the Kona coast on the west receive less than 20 inches of rain per year while Hilo, 60 miles to the east—and windward—receives 100 inches.

Clouds and Adiabatic Processes

Clouds are visible masses of water droplets or ice crystals that form when air rises and cools below saturation level, causing condensation. On average, about 52 percent of Earth is cloud-covered at any moment. Clouds provide rain and snow, the dominant types of precipitation. Dew and frost are also considered precipitation and are virtually the only water available for vegetation in deserts such as the Atacama in northern Chile. Different kinds of clouds result from different movements in Earth's atmosphere and are therefore associated with different types of weather and climates.

While clouds are almost always the result of the adiabatic cooling of air, the lifting of air is the result of convection, orographic uplift, frontal activity, or convergence. Each process occurs in different spatial and temporal patterns that may coexist and interact in different

Puffy cumulus clouds rise above Miller Peak, in the Huahuca Mountains of Arizona. Orographic uplift occurs when winds are forced to rise over hilly land.

locations. Different locations have predictable and seasonal types of atmospheric uplift, clouds, and precipitation.

Convection is the spontaneous rise of air after it has been warmed by surface radiation and has become less dense than the surrounding air. Equatorial regions receive more solar energy than elsewhere in the world and are more likely to experience convection consistently through the year. While regions in the midlatitudes also experience convection, it is usually greatest in summer, when land surfaces absorb the largest amounts of solar radiation.

Orographic uplift results when winds force air to rise over elevated land. Hilly islands, for example, cause orographic uplift, but the most important global patterns are associated with the windward coastlines of continents in the path of trade winds or the westerlies. British Columbia, Norway, and New Zealand have cloudy and wet coasts much of the year because of the dominant westerlies and mountain ranges parallel to their coastlines. The east slopes of the Hawaiian Islands, Madagascar, and the Bahamas also tend to be cloudy and wet because of the dominant trade winds, especially in the afternoons when heat causes convection to increase the rate of uplift.

Frontal activity occurs when two air masses of unequal temperatures meet; the colder air pushes under the warmer air, thereby lifting it. Where **fronts**, or boundaries, between the air masses exist, precipitation and winds occur. Frontal activity is most likely to take place in the midlatitudes, where warmer tropical and subtropical air masses meet colder subpolar air masses; the weather in North America and Eurasia is dominated by frontal activity. The polar-front jet stream, a high-altitude wind above the boundary of cold polar and warm tropical air, contributes to frontal activity by keeping the air masses moving.

The least common cause of adiabatic cooling occurs at the Equator, where the northeasterly and southeasterly trade winds converge, forcing the air to rise. Any **convergence** of air can contribute to rising, cooling, and condensation. Hurricanes and other cyclonic storms have a convergence of inflowing air that interacts with convection to cause condensation. (See Weather Systems, page 98.)

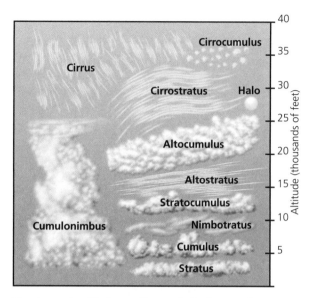

Clouds are classified according to their shape and the altitudes at which they are commonly found.

Classification of Clouds

Clouds created by adiabatic processes were classified in the early 1800s according to their appearance and altitude. Cloud shapes can be categorized as puffy (**cumulus**), layered (**stratus**), or wispy (**cirrus**), and these terms may also refer to their altitudes. Low clouds, or stratus, are below 6,500 feet (but not on the surface); middle clouds (marked by the prefix *alto*) are between 6,500 and 20,000 feet; and high clouds, cirrus, are above 20,000 feet. Cumulus clouds, which have extensive vertical development, are classified separately and may extend from near the surface to more than 50,000 feet. When precipitation falls from clouds, the cloud types have "nimbo" or "nimbus" added as a prefix or suffix to their names, such as **nimbostratus** and **cumulonimbus**. Clouds can be classified more narrowly: Small puffy clouds are called **cumulus humilis**, and irregularly layered clouds are called **stratus fractus**.

The appearances of clouds provide information on what atmospheric processes are most likely to be at work. Puffy cumulus clouds, including gigantic cumulonimbus storm clouds, are usually initiated by convection, although orographic and frontal activity can contribute

to lifting the air. Stratus clouds are most commonly associated with frontal activity, especially warm fronts, although convergence can also be involved. Uncommon atmospheric processes create uncommon clouds, such as the altocumulus lenticularis clouds that form when winds flow in waves over mountain ranges.

Fog is also classified as a cloud, but it is a surface cloud in which atmospheric cooling rarely occurs by adiabatic cooling. Fog is distinguished from mist, a less dense surface cloud, in that fog restricts visibility to 3,250 feet. **Radiation fogs** result when clear skies allow surface radiation to escape to space and the lowest part of the atmosphere cools rapidly. Valleys, such as coves in the Appalachians and much of California's San Joaquin Valley, often have radiation fogs, especially in winter when the ground is damp and surface humidity is high. **Advection fogs** occur when humid air advances from a warmer surface to a colder surface. San Francisco and the Grand Banks of Newfoundland experience advection fogs. Avalon, Newfoundland, is the foggiest location in Canada, and Cape Disappointment, Washington, is the foggiest location in the United States; each place has fog nearly 30 percent of the time. Fog occasionally forms along mountain slopes because of orographic uplift and is called upslope fog. If an upslope fog rises above the slope, it becomes a stratus cloud.

Precipitation

Precipitation returns water from the atmosphere to Earth's surface and continues the hydrologic cycle of water moving from oceans, to land, and to air. Rain and snow support life, carve landforms, and transport energy and material before returning to the atmosphere as water vapor through evaporation and transpiration. Other than dew and frost, which are precipitated directly on Earth, precipitation falls from clouds to the surface.

Rain and drizzle consist of droplets—an average raindrop has approximately one million droplets—that reach the surface. Individual cloud droplets are too small and too light to fall as rain, and each raindrop must be heavy enough to fall through slight updrafts and large enough not to evaporate during the fall through drier air. **Virga** is rain that evaporates before reaching the surface. In the midlatitudes, most raindrops start out as snowflakes that melt during their fall to Earth.

Two major processes create raindrops: collision-coalescence and Bergeron, named for Swedish meteorologist Tor Bergeron (1891–1977). Raindrops form by **collision-coalescence** when droplets collide and merge, or coalesce, as gravity pulls them to the ground. The droplets must be different sizes and weights so that they fall at different rates and collide. This process occurs most often over tropical oceans; warmer clouds prevent the formation of ice crystals, and the air contains more sea salt, which has particularly large hygroscopic particles that create larger, faster falling droplets.

In the mid- and upper latitudes, the **Bergeron process** is more common than collision-coalescence because the clouds are colder, and ice crystals and water droplets coexist in the same cloud. Some cloud droplets remain liquid at temperatures down to 4°F and others become ice. The vapor pressure of air around an ice crystal is lower than the vapor pressure around a water droplet because liquid droplets have very high surface tension. Water vapor molecules move to the lower pressure around ice crystals, freezing onto them, and the crystals grow into snowflakes. When atmospheric temperatures below the cloud are above freezing, falling snowflakes melt into rain before reaching the surface.

Snow occurs when the Bergeron process creates snowflakes that do not melt or evaporate during their fall to the surface. While snow falls at high elevations along the Equator—Chimborazo in Ecuador and Mount Kenya in Kenya are snowcapped year-round—snow is more common in higher latitudes and in colder seasons. When air is extremely cold—below minus 20°F—it has such low absolute humidity that little water vapor is available for ice-crystal growth, but even at these low temperatures snowflakes can form and fall.

Sleet and hail are different forms of frozen precipitation. Sleet is rain that freezes during

Rainmakers

Rainmaking has been a scientific undertaking only for the last half century, although rainmakers have existed for centuries.

Like fog dispersal and other types of weather modification, cloud-seeding (rainmaking) attempts to stimulate a natural process.

Cloud-seeding—the scattering of dry ice (frozen carbon dioxide) or silver iodide crystals (which have ice-like properties)—is most

commonly attempted with cold clouds to initiate the Bergeron process of ice-crystal growth.

its fall to Earth and requires a cold inversion layer thick enough to allow raindrops to freeze during their fall. Hail is another form of rain that freezes prior to reaching Earth's surface. Unlike sleet's raindrops that freeze as they fall, hail's raindrops freeze as strong updrafts in cumulonimbus clouds carry them up repeatedly into colder parts of the cloud. Sleet's appearance differs from that of hail: Sleet is a single frozen raindrop, but a hailstone is layers of ice that have frozen onto a central ice pellet during the several cycles of being lifted by updrafts to the freezing tops of clouds.

Global Precipitation Patterns

Global precipitation patterns are often seasonal and are related to global patterns of insolation, temperature, atmospheric pressure, wind, and ocean currents. Precipitation depends upon the adiabatic processes caused by surface warming (convection), low pressure (convergence), and uplift (orographic uplift and frontal activity). Ocean currents affect precipitation because the temperature of the water affects the rate of evaporation and the amount of water vapor available for condensation and precipitation. Regional winds and other factors affect precipitation patterns: In South and Southeast Asia, trade winds bring summer precipitation that is dramatically increased by the summer monsoon winds. (See Monsoons, page 79.)

Seasonal precipitation is higher near the solar equator and on the coasts of continents downwind from the trade winds and westerlies. During the Northern Hemisphere's winter, when the solar equator coincides with the Tropic of Capricorn, one band of high precipitation is centered at 5° to 10° south latitude, where convection and convergence from the trade winds occur. Regions at these latitudes, such as central Brazil and the Democratic Republic of the Congo, receive more than 40 inches of rain from January to March. East

coasts just north and south of the solar equator, such as northeastern Australia and Mozambique, receive orographic precipitation as the trade winds blow humid marine air over land. Finally, the west coasts struck by the westerlies also receive precipitation from orographic uplift; coastal California and northern Morocco usually receive just over 20 inches of rain in winter, almost all the precipitation for an entire year.

During the Northern Hemisphere's summer, when the solar equator shifts north to the Tropic of Cancer, precipitation patterns also shift north. Convection and convergence at the ITCZ result in a band of precipitation just north of the Equator. Nigeria and the coast of Guyana have their wettest months in June, July, and August. Trade winds also shift farther north in summer, bringing precipitation to Central America and Taiwan. The westerlies and the orographic precipitation caused by the trade winds are also displaced northward. Landforms affect precipitation from the trade winds and westerlies: Eastern Washington State and western Nicaragua are in the **rain shadows** on the leeward side of mountains and are far drier than windward western Washington and eastern Nicaragua.

Global patterns of precipitation are matched by global patterns of nonprecipitation, especially in areas of high atmospheric pressure. Air descending at the horse latitudes warms adiabatically and has decreasing relative humidity because its specific humidity remains constant. These latitudinal bands north and south of the Equator are therefore kept dry, affecting the Sahara, Mojave, and deserts of Australia. West coasts in the latitudes of the trade winds and regions east of the coastlines where the westerlies blow—for example, Montana and interior Siberia—are dry for the same reason: They are far from the source of humidity (oceans). Finally, the Arctic and Antarctic are extremely dry because of high pressure and low absolute humidity caused by low temperatures.

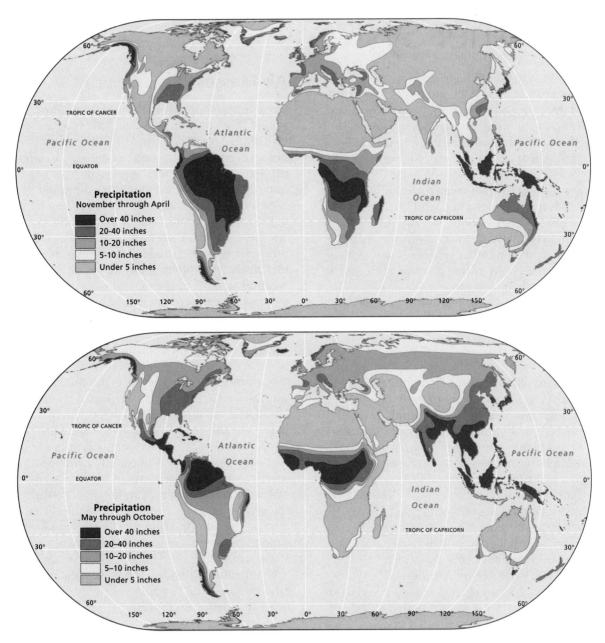

Global precipitation levels vary by season and are affected by insolation, temperature, atmospheric pressure, wind, and ocean currents.

Weather Systems

Weather systems are high- and low-pressure areas, such as air masses and fronts that form and dissolve over time as they move from one location to another. Frontal activity and variable weather are most common in the midlatitudes, where air masses from tropical and polar regions meet: The tropics and polar regions have more consistent weather conditions. Thunderstorms, tornadoes, and hurricanes—cyclonic weather systems that can be natural hazards—occur in distinct patterns on Earth. Understanding weather systems is key to understanding the spatial patterns of climate and atmospheric hazards.

Weather

Weather, in contrast to climate, is the short-term state of the atmosphere for an area, and **weather systems** are short-lived, regional combinations of temperature, wind, humidity, and precipitation that move as units. Weather systems such as hurricanes may cover thousands of square miles or, as in the case of a tornado, just a few acres; they may travel halfway around the world or dissipate after one mile. The dominant types of weather systems are high-pressure, anticyclonic systems characterized by clear skies and calm weather and low-pressure cyclonic systems characterized by cloudy skies and stormy weather.

Weather systems change as they travel over Earth because they contact different surfaces and encounter different weather systems. Their atmospheric components are related, and components change as systems form and dissipate over time. For example, a system that forms over a tropical ocean, such as a hurricane, changes rapidly by losing temperature and wind speed as it moves over relatively cold, upper-latitude landmasses.

Air Masses

Large units of air that may cover a million square miles or more are called **air masses**; cold air masses may extend only a few thousand feet up, and warm air masses may extend through the troposphere. Atmospheric conditions determine the stability of an air mass, how much precipitation it may have, how dense it is, and how it will interact with another air mass. Each air mass has relatively uniform atmospheric conditions and does not mix easily with different air masses. Most weather systems in the midlatitudes are either air masses or the frontal systems created by the interaction between different air masses. There are few frontal systems in polar and tropical latitudes because these regions have little variation in their atmospheric conditions.

Air masses form when air is stationary for several days over a **source region**, a relatively homogeneous surface such as an ocean or a landmass. During this time the air takes on the temperature and moisture characteristics of the surface with which it is in contact. Ordinarily there must be high pressure in the region to allow the air mass to remain in contact with the surface and to prevent other systems from moving in and displacing it. As a consequence, conditions conducive to the formation of stationary or longer term air masses are rare in the midlatitudes because the westerlies, upper-air westerlies, and the polar jet stream are continually moving air, preventing it from having sufficient time to reach equilibrium with the surface. Polar and tropical regions, on the other hand, lack persistent wind systems that bring in contrasting air; thus, most air masses form over these regions.

Air masses are categorized by their source regions and reflect the surface conditions in those regions. Most air masses form either in the tropics and are warm or in polar regions and are cold. For example, they may form at

Satellite images enable meteorologists to see large scale weather patterns, aiding not only immediate weather prediction but also long-term scientific research.

the Equator, in the Arctic, or in the Antarctic; these source regions generate the warmest and coldest air masses. The moisture content or humidity of air masses is related to whether the source region is maritime or continental.

Four types of air masses most often affect locations in North America: maritime-tropical air masses that form over the southern North Atlantic, the Gulf of Mexico, and the southern North Pacific; continental-tropical air masses from Mexico; maritime-polar air masses from the northern Pacific; and continental-polar air masses from Canada. Occasionally, maritime-polar air masses from the northern Atlantic, continental-polar masses from Siberia (the Siberian Express), and continental-arctic air masses from northern Canadian islands also affect the weather in North America. Different types of air masses are more common in different seasons: Continental-tropical air masses rarely develop in winter, and continental-arctic air masses rarely develop in summer.

The characteristics of air masses change as they move from their source region over surfaces that may have different temperatures and amounts of water, say from lakes or oceans to deserts. The changes are greater if air masses move slowly and have extended contact with new surface conditions. After several days or weeks an air mass either dissipates or becomes a different type of air mass based on the characteristics of its new source area. A continental-polar air mass from Canada, for example, will warm up, become more humid, and change into a maritime-tropical air mass if it stays over the Gulf of Mexico. Global winds such as the polar-front jet stream and upper-air winds are most important in moving air masses. Surface winds often reflect the pressure gradients of an individual weather system—the winds that flow inward to the low-pressure centers of a hurricane, for example—and therefore should not be interpreted as moving the weather system.

Fronts

A **front** is a boundary between two air masses with different densities. The front forms when air masses of different densities move and collide with each other. Although different air

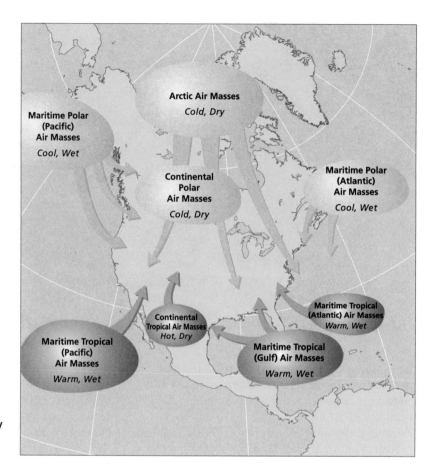

Air masses—named for where they are formed—vary seasonally and directly affect weather at midlatitudes.

masses may mix over a number of days, they do not do so easily: Differences in temperature and occasionally humidity cause differences in density that keep the air masses distinct. A front can range in size from hundreds of yards to several miles across, relatively short distances when compared to the size of air masses. A front is tilted up from the surface and moves with the air masses; how much a front tilts and how fast it moves depend upon the characteristics and motions of the air masses. Tilt and speed are responsible for the type of weather experienced on the surface.

Four types of fronts—cold, warm, occluded, and stationary—are associated with four different sets of atmospheric conditions. The most common type is a **cold front**, which results when a colder, denser air mass, such

as a continental-polar, moves into and under a warmer, less dense air mass, such as a maritime-tropical. A cold front may move at up to 30 miles per hour because of atmospheric pressure gradients and the pull of upper-air winds. As cold air forces warmer air up, the front that separates the two air masses may reach a slope with a ratio of as much as 1:50, a relatively steep slope for fronts, extending over the colder air mass. (See Diagram: Warm and Cold Fronts, opposite.) Squall lines, cumulonimbus clouds, thunderstorms, and drops in temperatures of 10°F or more are characteristics of cold fronts.

Warm fronts occur when relatively colder and warmer air masses meet. Unlike a cold front, the warmer, less dense air mass will move into and over the denser, colder air mass.

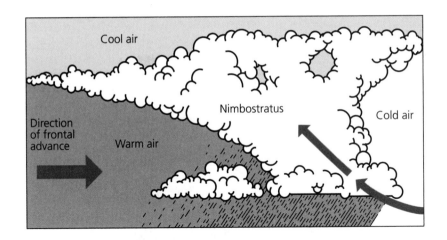

A warm front occurs when a relatively warm air mass moves into and over a cold, dense air mass. A cold front—the most common type of front—occurs when a cold, dense air mass moves into and under a warm air mass.

Warmer air can slowly push back colder air, but at the front the warmer air overrides the denser cold air mass. Warm fronts move at approximately half the speed of cold fronts because the less dense, warm air cannot push the cold air mass back easily. This slower speed produces a less steep angle than a cold front, at perhaps a 1:150 slope. Cirrus and stratus clouds precede a warm front, often by hundreds of miles, and rain or sleet can occur.

Occluded fronts result when a faster-moving cold front overtakes a slower warm front moving in the same direction: As the cold front reaches the warm front, the warm air mass is lifted entirely off Earth's surface. Warm fronts commonly become occluded in the mid-latitudes because weather systems often include cold fronts following warm fronts.

Lifting the warm air front can cause heavy rainfalls lasting a few days or less, depending on how much water vapor in the warm air mass condenses and precipitates.

Finally, **stationary fronts** occur when the boundary between two different air masses does not move, or is stationary, at the surface. Though neither air mass is moving as a unit, wind still blows from the pressure centers of each air mass into the frontal zone where the air is lifted by convergence. As a result of the uplift, rain occurs along stationary fronts, often in large amounts. During the 1993 flooding of the midwestern United States, much of the precipitation was associated with stationary fronts that persisted from June into August.

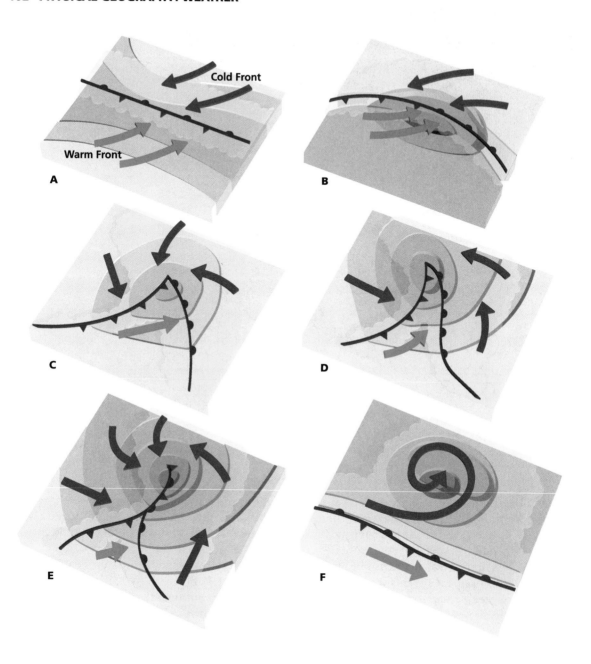

A **midlatitude cyclone** begins to form when a warm stationary front and a cold front collide (A) and curve poleward (B). The eastern side of the curve remains a warm front, while the western side becomes a cold front (C). As the faster moving cold front (D) overtakes the warm front, the storm reaches its peak (E). Finally, the occluded air mass breaks off, the storm dissipates, and the stationary front reforms (F).

Midlatitude Cyclonic Systems

Midlatitude cyclones are low-pressure systems, perhaps a thousand miles across, that form at the surface underneath meanders in the polar-front jet stream. A polar front, like cold and warm fronts, has relatively lower pressure than the polar and tropical air masses to the north and south, and winds flow outward (anticyclonic winds) from the high-pressure of the polar and tropical air masses. In the Northern Hemisphere, the Coriolis effect results in northeasterly winds from colder air masses and southwesterly winds from warmer air masses converging at the polar front from opposite directions. In addition, there is upper-air divergence above the polar front that perpetuates the low-pressure (cyclonic) zone and promotes the convergence of surface winds. When a bend or curve occurs in the polar front and upper winds change speed and direction, such as when a jet streak passes overhead, a pocket or trough of low pressure forms on the surface and can become the center of a cyclonic system.

Individual fronts in the midlatitudes often are components of larger weather systems traveling eastward along the polar front underneath the jet stream. On average, at any given time, ten of these low-pressure weather systems—called **midlatitude**, frontal, or extratropical cyclones—circle the Northern Hemisphere, and often circle the Southern Hemisphere. Some midlatitude cyclones promote convection that results in thunderstorms or can even generate **tornadoes**, potentially among the most powerful of cyclonic storms. High-pressure **anticyclones** are ordinarily paired with and follow each cyclonic system around the midlatitudes.

Each midlatitude cyclone follows a series of stages over a five- to six-day period, during which it forms different fronts with corresponding surface changes in temperatures, winds, and precipitation.(See Diagram: Midlatitude Cyclone Formation, opposite.) In the first stage of development, a stationary front underneath a polar front curves poleward, forming a wave;

the eastern side of the curve becomes a warm front, whereas the western side becomes a cold front. The warm front brings relatively warmer temperatures, southerly winds, and light but steady precipitation to areas over which it passes. Following the warm front is the cold front, which brings relatively colder temperatures, northerly or westerly winds, and brief but heavy precipitation. Eventually, the faster-moving cold front overtakes the warm front to form an occluded front, which brings heavy rains. Finally, as the occluded air mass is lifted off the ground, the cyclone dissipates and a stationary front reforms.

Anticyclones usually follow midlatitude cyclones along the polar front, bringing dry weather to the midlatitudes. Winds blow outward from the high-pressure centers of these anticyclones, preventing convection and keeping skies cloud-free. In winter, cold-core anticyclones form over polar surfaces and bring cold, clear weather to the midlatitudes; in summer, warm-core anticyclones from lower latitudes bring warm, clear weather.

Throughout their development, midlatitude cyclones follow a path determined primarily by upper-air winds, although surface features such as mountain ranges also have an effect. Upper-air westerlies dominate the midlatitudes and are strongest at the polar-front jet stream, so that most midlatitude cyclones move eastward. The meandering of the jet stream and surrounding upper-air westerlies causes midlatitude cyclones to move north and south as well as eastward. Seasonal shifts in the global-pressure and wind systems also shift the paths of cyclones poleward during the winter and equatorward in the summer.

The travel speed of midlatitude cyclones varies according to the season. In summer, they travel eastward at speeds averaging 20 to 30 miles per hour; surface friction caused by features such as trees and hills slows the eastward pull of the upper-air wind currents on the cyclones. In winter, midlatitude cyclones tend to travel faster, up to 40 miles per hour, because the cold air masses become even colder, creating greater temperature differences; the increased pressure gradients cause faster winds. Individual fronts associated with a midlatitude cyclone also have different rates of speed; cold fronts, in general, travel faster than warm fronts. (See Diagram: Warm and Cold Fronts, page 101.)

Thunderstorms

The most common weather systems on Earth are **thunderstorms**, low-pressure systems five to ten miles in diameter and sometimes extending to the tropopause. They are formed by convection, and accompanied by **lightning**, the electrical discharge that heats the atmosphere and causes thunder. Thunderstorms may also occur in conjunction with frontal or orographic lifting and are also associated with cold fronts, which are often components of midlatitude cyclones. At any given time approximately 2,000 thunderstorms are occurring on Earth. The storms are also accompanied by heavy precipitation, hail, strong winds, and occasionally tornadoes. Some exceptionally large thunderstorms can last for several hours, but most are short-lived and are over within an hour because precipitation causes downdrafts that interfere with the convectional uplift that creates and sustains the systems.

In order to form, thunderstorms require three conditions: High absolute humidity, instability, and rapid uplift; upper-air divergence and surface convergence of air can also be involved. Thunderstorm formation almost always involves equatorial or maritime-tropical air masses because they contain large amounts of water vapor. This large amount of water vapor releases more latent heat upon condensation and counteracts adiabatic, or expansion, cooling; this contributes to instability and allows the warm air to rise easily. Rapid uplift can be caused by frontal activity, such as a cold front, an occluded front, orographic uplift, convection, convergence, or a combination of these processes. When upper-air divergence

maintains the updraft of rising air, upper-air currents contribute to thunderstorm development by causing lower surface pressure.

Cumulus clouds towering six to nine miles high are the basis of thunderstorms. Surface warming and atmospheric instability initiate the rapid rate of uplift that creates the vertical cloud. The high absolute humidity found in the warm air maintains this uplift by releasing latent heat energy from condensing water and cloud droplets. Heating the air lowers the pressure so that the cumulus cloud extends higher into the atmosphere. At higher altitudes the cloud can meet upper-atmospheric winds that blow the top of the cloud downwind, giving it an anvil-shaped appearance.

The global distribution of thunderstorms shows the importance of warm, tropical air masses and the capacity of land to heat more quickly and cause more convection than water. (See Map: Global Distribution of Thunderstorms, opposite.) Central Africa, Brazil, and Southeast Asia have the highest number of thunderstorm days; in parts of Zaire, Cameroon, and Côte d'Ivoire thunderstorms occur on more than 180 days per year. Colder climates have far fewer thunderstorms in general, and very few occur poleward of 60° north and south latitudes or where inland temperatures are influenced by cold ocean currents. Oceans generally are cooler than land and in summer have fewer thunderstorms.

In the United States, thunderstorms are most common in Florida, but the Front Range on the eastern side of the Rocky Mountains in Colorado is a close second. Warm tropical air converges over Florida from the Atlantic to the east and the Gulf of Mexico to the west; as a result, atmospheric uplift above the central part of the state south of Orlando causes more than a hundred thunderstorm-days per year on average, most in the summer. On summer days in Colorado, south-facing slopes of the Front Range warm rapidly, and the resulting valley winds cause convection. When regional weather systems such as cold fronts intensify

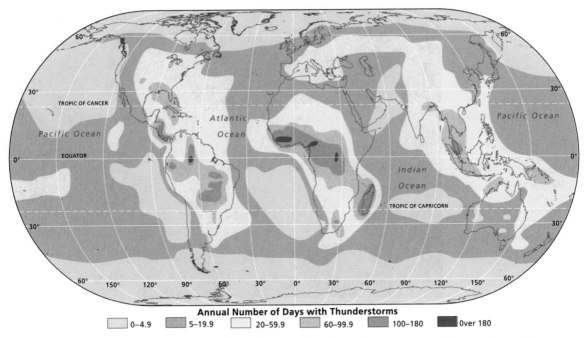

Annual Number of Days with Thunderstorms

0–4.9   5–19.9   20–59.9   60–99.9   100–180   Over 180

The global distribution of thunderstorms is shown in terms of number of days a year a region experiences them. Thunderstorms are the most common weather systems on Earth, with some 2,000 taking place at any given time somewhere on the planet.

this uplift, thunderstorms are most likely to occur.

Midlatitude thunderstorms across North America and Eurasia are often associated with cold fronts or with **squall lines**, lines of thunderstorms that precede cold fronts. When a cold front moves forward, the warm air mass rises rapidly through frontal uplift and is somewhat compressed by the incoming cold air mass. This convergence of air masses initiates uplift along a line ahead of the cold front and occasionally causes intense thunderstorms.

Thunderstorm Hazards

When heavy rains fall during a thunderstorm, rapid updrafts occur alongside downdrafts. Downdrafts are caused by the fall of rain and snow from the upper reaches of the cumulonimbus cloud. Not only does the falling precipitation cause air to descend, but some of the

precipitation evaporates in the lower reaches of the cloud when it reaches air of lower relative humidity. Evaporation absorbs heat energy from the air, causing it to cool, increase in density, and fall toward the surface. As these downdrafts reach Earth's surface, they spread outward and can gust ahead of the storm at speeds up to 60 miles per hour.

Hail develops when raindrops and ice pellets are carried by the up- and downdrafts within a mature thunderstorm cloud—one from which rain is falling. The temperature differences within the cloud, subfreezing near the top and above freezing closer to Earth's surface, allow layers of water to freeze onto and increase the size of ice pellets, called graupel, and form hailstones. When updrafts are especially strong, hailstones circulate repeatedly toward the top of the cloud before gravity and downdrafts carry them down again. Each round-trip through the cloud results in another layer of ice; hailstones with as many as 25 layers of ice

A single flash of lightning lasting one-quarter of a second may consist of dozens of main strokes. Thunder is produced as lightning instantly heats surrounding air to high temperatures, causing the air molecules to explode or expand rapidly. Sound travels more slowly than light, so thunder is always heard after lightning is seen.

have been discovered. The largest hailstones, including the record 1.67—pound stone found at Coffeyville, Kansas, in 1970, require the strongest updrafts to be able to lift the hailstones up to the tops of the clouds. Not all hail generated by thunderstorms falls as precipitation. Despite its number of thunderstorms, Florida is so warm that hail is extremely rare. Conversely, northeastern Colorado's frequent thunderstorms occur in much colder atmospheric temperatures—conditions that have earned it the nickname Hail Alley.

Lightning, a giant electrical spark or flow of electrons in the atmosphere, may be a side effect of lighter ice crystals and heavier ice pellets being separated within a cumulonimbus cloud by up- and downdrafts. For lightning to form, positive and negative charges must be separated until the difference in electrical charge is large enough to overcome air resistance. In thunderstorm clouds, ice pellets and ice crystals develop different charges: Heavy pellets fall faster through a cloud and strike lighter crystals; negatively charged electrons

Lightning and People

In an average year lightning in the United States kills nearly a hundred people, starts thousands of forest fires, and damages millions of dollars of electrical equipment. Death rates from lightning are greater in some tropical regions; in Kisii of western Kenya, some 30 people die each year from lightning strikes. Kisii's high rate of lightning fatalities occurs because of the frequency of thunderstorms and because many of the area's structures have metal roofs.

To avoid being struck by lightning, stay away from high areas, tall structures, and metallic objects such as golf clubs; these locations and objects are most likely to build up an electrical charge during a thunderstorm. Lightning can and does strike twice in the same place—the Empire State Building in New York City averages 20 strikes each year—and lightning can occur whether or not it is raining.

are transferred from the crystals to the pellets, which become negatively charged when temperatures are below 5°F. At higher temperatures, such as those in the lower parts of clouds, the negatively charged electrons transfer from the crystals to the pellets, which then become negatively charged.

As the lighter, positively charged ice crystals are carried to the upper cloud by updrafts, there is a spatial separation between this positively charged upper cloud and and the negatively charged lower cloud as well as between the lower cloud and the positively charged Earth's surface. The surface develops a positive charge to counter the negative field of the lower clouds. When the differences in charge between any two areas is large enough to overcome air's resistance to the flow of electricity, electrons flow as lightning between the charged areas to equalize the number of electrons. The path of the electrons is only an inch or so wide, which is why lightning occurs as a bolt; the presence of clouds and winds can change the appearance of lightning to look like sheets or ribbons. About 80 percent of all lightning discharges occur within clouds, but the 20 percent between clouds and Earth's surface can be a major natural hazard.

Tornadoes

The most violent cyclonic storm generated by a thunderstorm or by a hurricane is a **tornado**. Estimated rotational wind speeds may exceed 300 miles per hour, and the central pressure of a tornado's vortex may drop to 27.00 inches or lower, far below the standard 29.92-inch barometric pressure at sea level. Tornadoes extend from the ground up to about 20,000 feet and are ordinarily small with vortex diameters of about 300 feet, last less than five minutes, and travel less than one mile. A few tornadoes, however, can be nearly one mile in diameter, can last for hours, and can travel more than a hundred miles. Tornadoes may hopscotch from one location to another, but all travel along or near the ground.

The Fujita Tornado Intensity Scale

		ESTIMATED WIND SPEED	
F-SCALE	**CATEGORY**	**(km/hr)**	**(mi/hr)**
0	Weak	65–116	40–72
1		117–181	73–112
2	Strong	182–253	113–157
3		254–332	158–206
4	Violent	333–419	207–260
5		420–513	261–318

Tornadoes are categorized by the **F-scale**, their rotational wind speed, and the **P-scale**, the length of their path and width. University of Chicago meteorologist T. Theodore Fujita's scale ranges from F-0 (windspeeds from 40 to 72 miles per hour) to F-5 (wind speeds from 261 to 318 miles per hour). Almost 80 percent of all tornadoes are F-0 or F-1 and are considered weak; only one percent are F-4 or F-5 (violent). The P-scale, developed by Alan Pearson of the National Severe Storms Forecast Center, ranks tornadoes into six categories by the length and width of their path; categories range from a tornado 18 feet wide, with a path of 1,600 feet, to about 4,800 feet wide and a path of more than a hundred miles. Rare violent tornadoes, especially those with high P-rankings, cause the most deaths: A 1974 F-5 tornado in Xenia, Ohio, killed 34 people; another F-5 tornado killed 17 people in 1991 in Andover, Kansas.

Less than one percent of thunderstorms generate a strong tornado; extremely rapid updrafts and changes in wind direction with altitude are required. **Wind shear**, an abrupt change in wind direction or speed, creates a rotating tube of air at an altitude of about 20,000 feet. Thunderstorms, especially the largest—called supercells—can spawn tornadoes from wind shear because updrafts that can reach 150 miles per hour cause the rotating tube of wind to tilt. When the tilt straightens and becomes nearly vertical and reaches the surface, a tornado forms. Dust and

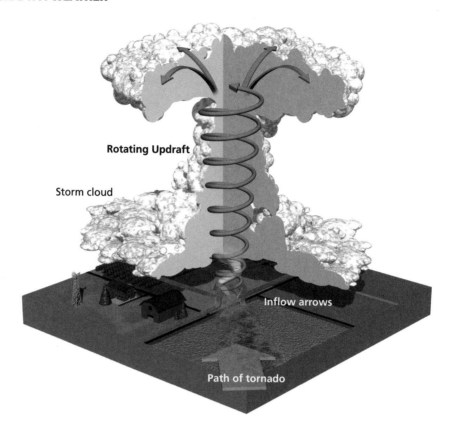

Rotating Updraft

Storm cloud

Inflow arrows

Path of tornado

Tornadoes are formed when a strong draft of wind in a thunderstorm catches a rotating tube of air formed by wind shear and lifts it to a vertical position, causing it to twist at the same time. When the tube touches the ground, a tornado forms.

water droplets caught in the winds of the vortex cause the tornado to become visible to an observer; tornadoes appear darker when the sun is behind them and lighter as they move away from the sun and reflect sunlight.

Tornadoes travel with the thunderstorm or hurricane that generated them, but accurate path prediction is not possible because they can take any direction, jump around on the surface, and move at speeds up to 75 miles per hour. Midlatitude tornadoes usually travel from southwest to northeast along with the cold front or squall line, at about 30 miles per hour.

Tornadoes occur in dozens of countries around the world, but the United States has by far the largest total number every year; Australia is a distant second. The location of the United States relative to the polar front, where thunderstorms are common and along which midlatitude cyclones travel, is the reason for the large number of tornadoes. Equatorial regions have fewer tornadoes because the

intertropical convergence zone (ITCZ) has diverging high-altitude air and therefore lacks the necessary wind shear; Eurasia has few because mountain ranges separate maritime-tropical and continental-polar air masses, resulting in less frontal activity and fewer midlatitude cyclones than in the United States.

Within the United States, tornadoes are most common in a region known as Tornado Alley, which extends from the Texas Panhandle to southeast Nebraska. All 50 states experience tornadoes, but Tornado Alley averages 20 per year. Despite its large number of thunderstorms, Florida has relatively few tornadoes because its thunderstorms are more often caused by converging air than by frontal activity. Tornado season in the United States varies by latitude; the season usually starts in early March when temperatures rise along the Gulf of Mexico, moves northward along with the polar front, and by midsummer has reached the United States–Canada boundary. Tornado

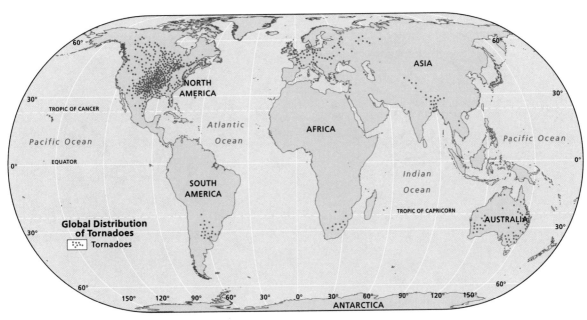

Many countries experience tornadoes, but the United States holds the record with between 700 and 1000 every year.

season ends at different latitudes as temperatures cool or as changes in the season cause the polar front and cyclonic storms to shift to different latitudes.

Tropical Systems and Hurricanes

Weather conditions in the tropics, between the horse latitudes centered on 30° north and south, are far more consistent and uniform than those in the midlatitudes, and traveling weather systems are far less common. The high pressure of the horse latitudes is a barrier that protects the tropics from the intrusion of colder polar air masses and the resultant frontal activity that dominates the weather of the midlatitudes. There is also less landmass over which continental air masses can form at these latitudes. Seasonal differences in insolation, temperature, and precipitation do occur, but in general warm tropical and warmer equatorial air masses dominate weather.

The weather systems that do occur in the tropics usually develop from **easterly waves**, westward moving, low-pressure disturbances in the trade-wind zone between 5° and 30° north and south latitudes from the Equator. During the late summer, as ocean temperatures increase slightly, a low-pressure system (which can appear as a linear trough hundreds of miles long) occasionally forms over tropical oceans, possibly over an island. As this system is blown westward by the trade winds, the normal easterly wind pattern curves into the low-pressure zone (convergence); as the system moves to the west, a wave-like disruption in the trade winds occurs.

A few of these easterly waves develop into larger cyclonic storms. If the low-pressure center intensifies and wind speed increases, then tropical depressions will form when winds reach 23 miles per hour. They become tropical storms when wind speeds reach 39 miles per hour and hurricanes when wind speeds reach 74 miles per hour. For the low pressure to intensify, the middle troposphere must contain sufficient water vapor to allow evaporation to occur, vertical wind shear must be limited, and subsiding air associated with the horse latitudes

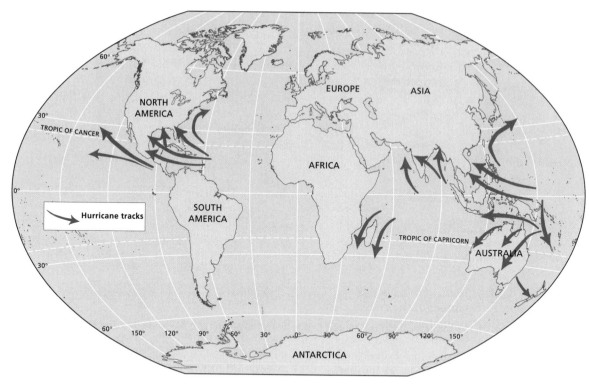

Tropical cyclonic storms develop over tropical waters in summer and autumn when ocean temperatures are warmest. Their movement is governed by the Coriolis effect and global and upper-atmosphere winds. Of the 100 or so storms that form near the west coast of Africa each year, only 10 percent reach Caribbean and American coasts as hurricanes.

on the eastern side of the oceans must be restricted to allow vertical development of the system. When these factors are present, convectional uplift increases, lowering surface atmospheric pressure and increasing surface-pressure gradients and cyclonic wind speeds.

Hurricanes, also called typhoons, cyclones, baguios, chubascos, and willy-willies, are tropical cyclonic wind systems that form over warm oceans. On average, the diameter of the area experiencing hurricane-force winds is 150 miles or less, although the overall wind system may be much larger. Winds flow into the low-pressure core of the hurricane (pressure down to 26.22 inches has been measured, far below the 29.92 average) and are curved counter-clockwise in the Northern Hemisphere and clockwise in the Southern Hemisphere. A calm eye is found at the center of the storm; the winds blow into this low-pressure system so

that rising air occurs around the eye, creating a wall of clouds but leaving the interior clear.

While hurricanes have traveled as far north as Canada and Hokkaido, Japan, they can form only over tropical—but not equatorial—waters. The energy supply for hurricanes is water with a temperature of 80°F or greater; evaporation from this warm water provides the latent heat released during condensation, and this heat perpetuates uplift and instability in the center of the hurricane. Although water along the Equator is also sufficiently warm, there is no Coriolis effect at the Equator so a cyclonic wind system cannot form. Most hurricanes therefore are generated between 5° and 20° north and south latitudes in the western North Atlantic, western Pacific, eastern North Pacific, and Indian Oceans; other tropical waters such as those off South America and the west coast of Africa are usually too cold due to the ocean currents that have traveled from polar regions. (See Map: Hurricane Tracks, opposite.)

The requirements for hurricane formation also affect their timing and duration. Hurricane season is usually in late summer and fall because ocean temperatures are at their maximum two months or so after the summer solstice. The U.S. National Hurricane Center, in Miami, Florida, describes the official season for Atlantic hurricanes as June 1 to November 30, while the Pacific season is May 15 to November 30. Most hurricanes lose wind speed and dissipate after one week, although a few may last up to three weeks. When hurricanes travel over colder water or inland, they weaken and die out because surface friction and lack of an energy supply slows wind speeds to below hurricane strength. Hurricanes usually dissipate before traveling to within 120 miles of the coast.

The storms follow a general path shaped by global and upper-atmospheric winds; their travel speed also reflects these influences. Early in their development, hurricanes tend to travel westward with the trade winds and upper atmospheric winds at speeds between 10 and 20 miles per hour. About two-thirds of all hurricanes eventually curve toward the Poles because of the Coriolis effect and slow down to 5 to 10 miles per hour when they no longer have the trade winds pushing them. The few that reach the zone of the westerlies curve back to the east and may travel more than 30 miles per hour.

Deaths and damages from hurricanes are most severe along coastlines. Hurricanes are destructive because of their wind speeds, accompanying tornadoes, large amounts of rain, and—perhaps most important—because of the storm surges they cause. As a hurricane approaches a coastline, the low-pressure center of the storm can cause ocean levels to rise three feet or more. The wind pattern of the hurricane also raises ocean levels by causing storm waves to be blown into the coast along the poleward side of the hurricane. Low pressure and wind can combine to cause storm surges that raise ocean levels an additional 25 feet. In 1900 Galveston, Texas, was flooded by the storm surge of a hurricane; 8,000 people died. The low-lying coast of Bangladesh is subject to hurricane storm surges, and the 1970 and 1991 hurricanes each caused hundreds of thousands of deaths.

Hurricanes are classified by the combined factors of wind speeds, atmospheric pressures, storm surges, and potential damage. The **Saffir-Simpson scale** (below), designed in the early 1970s by H. Saffir, an engineer, and R. Simpson, of the National Hurricane Center, rates hurricanes from one to five, where three to five are considered major. While level five hurricanes are uncommon, they are catastrophic. Hurricanes originating off the west coast of Africa, called Cape Verde hurricanes, are rare because water temperatures there are usually cool, but they tend to be especially destructive (frequently reaching level five); they increase their energy supply while traveling 3,000 miles across the tropical Atlantic Ocean to the Caribbean.

Saffir-Simpson Hurricane Intensity Scale

SCALE NUMBER (CATEGORY)	CENTRAL PRESSURE		WIND SPEED		STORM SURGE		DAMAGE
	MB	IN.	MI/HR	KM/HR	FT	M	
1	≥980	≥28.94	74–95	119–154	4–5	1–2	Minimal
2	965–979	28.50–28.91	96–110	155–178	6–8	2–3	Moderate
3	945–964	27.91–28.47	111–130	179–210	9–12	3–4	Extensive
4	920–944	27.17–27.88	131–155	211–250	13–18	4–6	Extreme
5	<920	<27.17	>155	>250	>18	>6	Catastrophic

Climate and Climatic Classifications

Climate

Climate is the average annual pattern of atmospheric conditions for a location, whereas weather is the short-term state of the atmosphere for the same location. Climate has a tremendous impact on vegetation, soil development, and agriculture, which in turn influence where and how humans live, including energy use and recreation. Classification systems based on meteorological criteria have been created to describe global patterns of climate and enable comparisons to be made between places.

Misinformation and myths about climate have influenced how people have settled and developed the planet. French and British farmers settled Nova Scotia and Newfoundland on Canada's east coast in the 1600s, mistakenly believing that latitudes similar to those of their homelands meant similar climates. Two centuries later and farther south, in the United States, settlement of lands west of the Mississippi slowed after parts of the region were shown as the Great American Desert on topographical engineer Stephen H. Long's map, which was based on travels in the West between 1817 and 1823. Farmers finally began to settle the region in the mid-1800s, believing the adage that "rain follows the plow"—that agriculture could change climate. Farmers on the Great

Plains did experience favorable growing conditions but eventually experienced droughts, especially during the Dust Bowl years of the 1930s.

Climates are usually classified according to basic elements of weather. Seasonal patterns of precipitation and temperature, for example, are key to most of the 30 or so classification systems because these data are important for the growth of vegetation, and knowing about these conditions enables people to grow crops and raise livestock. Other elements of weather, including wind, pressure, insolation, and humidity, have been used to set up classification systems.

Variations from year to year in precipitation and temperature make the averaging of data essential. For example, on July 4 in Kansas City, Missouri, maximum temperatures over a 30-year period have ranged from below 80°F to above 100°F, while precipitation on that date has ranged from zero to three inches. The **mean precipitation** and **mean temperature** are determined by adding all values on a date and then dividing by the number of years of data; this figure provides a basis for long-term planning. However, knowledge of the extremes in temperature and precipitation is useful for emergency planning. Means can be misleading: One major rainstorm in a desert can increase

Heavy snowfalls, brought by cold polar winds and high moisture levels, are a dependable feature of New England's climate.

the mean annual precipitation even though no rain may fall in nine out of ten years on a given date.

Thirty years of atmospheric data are ordinarily used to prevent shorter-term variations from skewing the averages. In the United States, beginning in 2001, the National Climate Data Center in Asheville, North Carolina, will use weather data from 1971 to 2000 for information about climates. Relying on shorter periods of time can give a misleading picture of climatic patterns: When water from the Colorado River was divided among California and other southwestern states in a 1922 interstate compact, data on average rainfall and average runoff were drawn from an 18-year period that proved to be especially wet. As a result, officials overestimated the amount of water available by about 50 percent, and withdrawals by states in the U.S. caused severe problems for residents of the Mexicali Valley downstream in Mexico.

Atmospheric data must be averaged for climatic classification, and monthly averages rather than annual averages are used. Seasonal and monthly variations are extremely important in defining types of climate because temperature and precipitation patterns affect the growing seasons of vegetation. (See Bioregions, page 227.) For example, Vancouver, British Columbia, and Springfield, Massachusetts, have annual average temperatures of 50°F and precipitation amounts of 45 inches. In Vancouver, however, the average January temperature (37°F) is 26° colder than the July average (63°F), far less than the 47° range in Springfield between January (26.5°F) and July (73.5°F). Seasonal precipitation patterns are also different: In Vancouver most rainfall occurs in winter, but precipitation is year-round in Springfield. Vegetation differs too: Douglas fir and hemlock dominate the natural vegetation near Vancouver, while maple and birch are the dominant trees in Springfield.

Although averaging data for climatic classification is very useful for understanding patterns of vegetation and for planning purposes, such data cannot be used to predict weather accurately. Research in the field of chaos theory has even shown that weather prediction for ten days in advance, much less a year, is unreliable because tiny variations in the levels or locations of atmospheric conditions—conditions too small to be accurately or systematically measured—lead to extremely different results. According to the American Meteorological Society, predictions beyond five days are increasingly limited in usefulness.

Climate Controls and Classification

Climatic classification systems enable meaningful comparisons to be made between locations; various systems use different criteria to emphasize different sets of weather elements. No single system meets the needs for all possible comparisons and analyses because different systems focus on different aspects and impacts of weather.

Geographic patterns of climates reflect the influences of the same controls that shape weather conditions, especially temperature and precipitation. Latitude, elevation, proximity to water bodies, ocean currents, topography, and prevailing winds are the most important climatic controls. Elevation, proximity to water bodies, ocean currents (despite conditions such as El Niño and La Niña), and topography are relatively unchanging over the centuries, and their impacts on climate are consistent year after year. Seasonal changes in insolation at each latitude and the shifting of prevailing winds at some locations provide the dynamic aspects of climate.

To be useful, climatic classification systems must be based on commonly available weather data, and they must capture differences and similarities between locations that are meaningful for a system's user. In order to create a global classification system, the amount and type of atmospheric data needed must be simplified in order to generalize the information. Simplification reduces the number of possible climatic types so that the geographic patterns of climates are not lost in excessive detail, and generalization is necessary for grouping climates to make comparisons between locations possible. Even though coastal cities in Uruguay, South Carolina, and southern China will have slightly different monthly temperatures and amounts of precipitation, the impacts of their climates on vegetation may be so similar that the areas can be grouped into one climatic category.

Different climates blend into each other because the influence of climatic controls, such as distance from an ocean, changes gradually. Establishing climatic regions includes defining boundaries between locations based on atmospheric data, and this results in dividing locations with similar atmospheric conditions into

Ancient Greek Climatic Classification

About 2,500 years ago the Greek philosopher Parmenides (born circa 515 B.C.) developed a climatic classification scheme based on weather conditions. He defined three zones of climate: torrid, for northern Africa; temperate, for southern Europe; and frigid, for northern Europe. Climatic mythology was incorporated into this system because the Greeks believed climates determined personal characteristics: People in the torrid zone were intelligent but lethargic; people in the frigid zone were energetic but unintelligent; and people in the temperate zone (which, coincidentally, included Greece) were intelligent and energetic. This philosophy of environmental determinism was fully discredited only in the mid-1900s.

Köppen's First System

Wladimir Köppen (1846–1940), a German botanist and climatologist, began to create a bioregional system of climates in 1900 that were characterized by a representative tree, plant, or animal found in each climate; he defined 24 climatic regions, ranging from baobab, fuchsia, and mesquite climates to oak, spruce, penguin, and yak. Köppen refined his classification system over the years, and a 1957 revision by University of Wisconsin climatologist Glenn Trewartha is the one widely used today.

different climatic regions. Hence, boundaries are understood to represent transition zones. For example, in many classification systems Lake Charles, Louisiana, and Washington, D.C., are included in the same category. Although Washington, D.C., is much closer to New York, New York City is in a different category because of definitions used to establish regions.

German botanist Wladimir Köppen's climatic classification system, developed in the early 1900s and revised many times since, is one system commonly used in the United States. In 1948 C. W. Thornthwaite proposed a

The vegetation of the Sonoran Desert near Tucson, Arizona, reflects the region's classification as a Mediterranean desert climate, one of the Type B climates.

system that focuses on the relationship of plants to climate; it links temperature and precipitation in a **moisture index** that compares actual and potential loss of moisture through evapotranspiration. Another system, proposed by Hermann Flohn in 1950, is based on global wind belts and precipitation. And in 1978 father and son Arthur and Alan Strahler began to classify climates by predominant patterns of air masses and fronts. Each of these climatic classification systems is designed to emphasize different atmospheric conditions and results in different spatial patterns of climatic regions.

Köppen's classification system focused on the climatic limits of vegetation and was based on temperature and precipitation patterns. Köppen and other climatologists revised the system numerous times to correspond more closely to vegetation patterns. The climates described below follow a 1957 revision by University of Wisconsin climatologist Glenn Trewartha.

The Köppen classification system employs temperature as the basis for four moist climatic regions: tropical rainy, humid mesothermal, humid microthermal, and polar. Lack of precipitation designates a fifth region (dry), and topography determines the sixth (highland). There are subclasses within each region, except for highland, that are usually distinguished on the basis of seasonal patterns of precipitation. In all, there are 15 major climates and the highland climate. (See Köppen classification system map, page 117).

Global Climate Patterns

Tropical Rainy Climates (A Climates)

TROPICAL RAIN FOREST (AF)

At the intertropical convergence zone (ITCZ) along the Equator, there are virtually no seasons; each month is hot (averaging 80°F) and wet (averaging eight inches of rain). The consistently high amount of insolation this equatorial region receives throughout the year causes high temperatures and daily precipitation. Precipitation usually peaks in the afternoons, when maximum daily temperatures increase convection. This climate promotes the growth of trees (rain forests, sometimes called selvas, from *silva*, Latin for wood) and insects because there is no cold season; insect-transmitted diseases, such as malaria and yellow fever, are endemic in many of these areas.

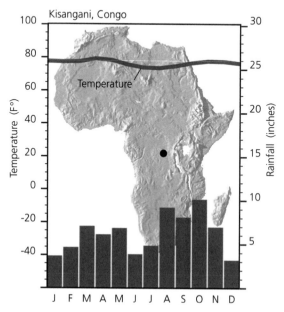

This climagraph for Kisangani, Congo, illustrates its seasonless tropical rain forest climate, which occurs at the ITCZ along the Equator.

TROPICAL SAVANNA (AW)

Immediately to the north and south of the Equator and the tropical rain forest climate, rainfall becomes seasonal. The ITCZ only dominates during summer, the wet season; the high-pressure horse latitudes shift slightly into these regions during the winter, the dry season. Temperature remains high year-round; monthly averages are between 70°F and 86°F, with slight cooling during the winter. Seasonal changes in precipitation result in fewer trees and more grasslands than in tropical rain forest.

TROPICAL MONSOON (AM)

In tropical monsoon climates (see Monsoons, page 79) precipitation patterns are intensified forms of those in tropical savanna climates, and wet summers average as much as 15 inches of rain each month. This seasonal precipitation is magnified by wind reversals caused by seasonal heating and cooling of a continental landmass. Monsoons are frequently associated with Asia, but this climate is also found in western Africa and eastern South America. Forest vegetation is most common in these regions; however, in areas where the dry season lasts longer, grasslands will form.

Dry Climates (B Climates)

TROPICAL STEPPE (BSH)

Tropical steppe climates are located poleward of tropical savannas (AW) and often surround the tropical desert (BWH) climate. A brief wet season may occur either in summer, as in southern Sudan, when the ITCZ is present, or in winter, as in coastal Libya, when westerlies bring precipitation. Grasses dominate this climatic region. A steppe, derived from the Russian word *step*, is a vast plain.

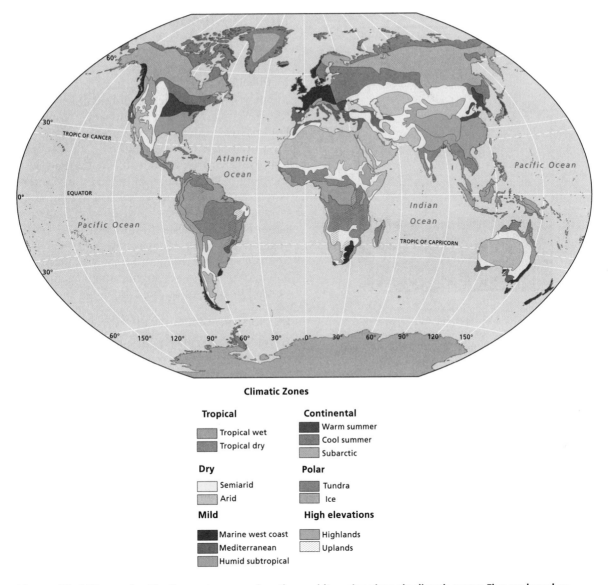

Climatic Zones

Tropical
- Tropical wet
- Tropical dry

Dry
- Semiarid
- Arid

Mild
- Marine west coast
- Mediterranean
- Humid subtropical

Continental
- Warm summer
- Cool summer
- Subarctic

Polar
- Tundra
- Ice

High elevations
- Highlands
- Uplands

The modified Köppen classification system organizes the world's regions into six climatic zones: Five are based on precipitation (four moist, one dry), and one is based on topography (highland).

MIDLATITUDE STEPPE (BSK)

Steppes also exist in the midlatitudes, where subfreezing temperatures are more common than in the tropics and where precipitation levels remain low, between 10 and 25 inches annually. Midlatitude steppes are often found in the rain shadow of a mountain range, as is the case east of the Cascade Range of Washington, Oregon, and northern California, or else so far downwind from an ocean, as in Kazakhstan, that frontal precipitation from maritime air masses is extremely limited.

TROPICAL DESERT (BWH)

Tropical deserts occur when annual precipitation is minimal (from near zero to ten inches

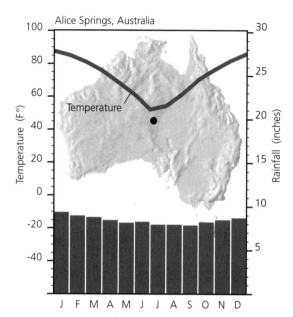

The climagraph for Alice Springs, Australia, shows a typical desert climate, which occurs because Australia's mountainous east coast prevents Pacific Ocean winds from penetrating the continent's interior.

per year) in regions centered on the Tropics of Cancer and Capricorn. High pressure from the horse latitudes prevents almost all forms of adiabatic cooling and precipitation. In most tropical deserts, such as the Atacama in Chile and the Gibson of Australia, some xerophytic, or drought-tolerant, vegetation, such as cactuses, is present, although individual plants are sparsely distributed.

MIDLATITUDE DESERT (BWK)

Midlatitude deserts are not as extensive as tropical deserts and are located farther from the Equator, where temperatures are lower in wintertime. Precipitation is rare because of rain shadows and distance from maritime air masses, as in the midlatitude steppes. With the exception of Patagonia, Argentina, all midlatitude deserts, such as the Gobi in northern China and southern Mongolia, are in the Northern Hemisphere, where there are continental landmasses at these latitudes.

Humid Mesothermal (C Climates)

MEDITERRANEAN (CS)

Mediterranean climates are found along the Mediterranean Sea and on the west coasts of landmasses bordered by cold ocean currents. They are poleward of tropical dry climates, and temperatures are mild but still cooler than in the tropics. Precipitation falls mainly in winter, when the westerlies move toward the Equator, while dry summers are caused by the high pressure of the horse latitudes. Native vegetation, such as chaparral in the U.S. Southwest, olive trees, and cork oaks, has adapted to summer droughts, and irrigation is needed to grow most crops.

HUMID SUBTROPICAL (CA)

Humid subtropical climates are found poleward of the tropics on east coasts bordered by warm ocean currents. In summer, trade winds bring

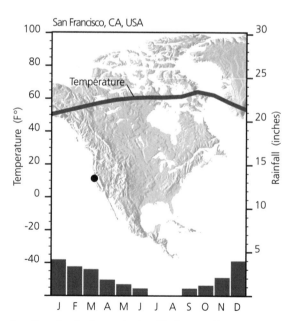

San Francisco's climate is classified as Mediterranean subtropical. The city's exposed coastal location accounts for its cool summers and mild winters—unusual for its latitude.

precipitation, while the high-pressure horse latitudes cause dry periods. In winter, frontal precipitation occurs when cold polar air masses move into these latitudes. Vegetation thrives in this temperate, humid climate, and crops such as rice can support large numbers of people, as in East Asia.

MARINE WEST COAST (CB, CC)

Marine west coast climates are found poleward of Mediterranean climates. Westerly winds dominate most of the year, and orographic precipitation, especially on the windward slopes, occurs year-round and supports coniferous forests. Maritime air masses keep temperatures mild, and the climate extends inland to mountains, such as the Cascade Range in the Pacific Northwest of the United States and the Coast Mountains of British Columbia, or to where air masses take on continental characteristics, as in Europe where the east-west trending Alps do not block westerly winds.

Humid Microthermal (D Climates)

HUMID CONTINENTAL–WARM SUMMER (DA)

Humid continental–warm summer climates are the first in a series of climates extending poleward of the humid subtropical climates on the east coasts of continents. Mean July temperatures are 71.6°F or warmer at latitudes about 40° north. Precipitation peaks in summer because the higher temperatures cause convection, although frontal precipitation occurs year-round. Deciduous forests such as those of Ohio and Pennsylvania are common in this climate, which is limited to the Northern Hemisphere because there are few landmasses at these latitudes in the Southern Hemisphere. In southern Argentina, where this climate might exist, the Andean rain shadow causes a desert climate.

HUMID CONTINENTAL–COOL SUMMER (DB)

Poleward of 40° north latitude, summer temperatures less than 71.6°F and humid continental–cool summer climates occur. This climate is absent in the Southern Hemisphere because there is no major landmass at those latitudes. Precipitation is lower than that of humid subtropical California climates because lower summer temperatures reduce convection, and colder air masses with lower specific humidity reduce frontal precipitation. Evergreens are found mixed with deciduous trees at these latitudes because of the cooler temperatures. Although this climate is not found on west coasts, it occurs in much of Sweden because the mountains of Norway exclude the moderating influence of maritime air masses, so continental air masses dominate.

SUBARCTIC (DC, DD)

The subarctic climate, also called the boreal forest or taiga climate for its type of vegetation, is an extremely cold climate, but it is one with

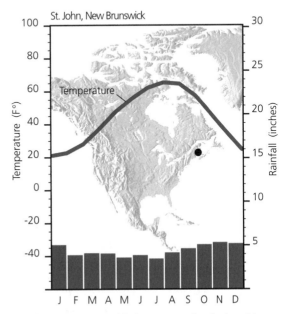

St. John, New Brunswick, is an example of a humid continental-cool summer climate. Its location on the North Atlantic storm track results in frequent heavy snowfalls in the winter months.

sufficient precipitation and a long enough growing season to support trees. Arctic and subarctic air masses dominate this area, with frontal activity in summer bringing limited precipitation of two to three inches per month. Evergreens are the most common trees, and forests can be an important natural resource; seasonal growth is limited by the short, cool summers.

Polar (E Climates)

TUNDRA (ET)

Tundra climates are found along the coastlines of the Arctic Ocean and on some coastlines of and islands off Antarctica. Frigid Arctic and Antarctic air masses dominate these regions but rarely produce precipitation because frontal activity is largely absent. Some climatic classification systems designate this region as a cold desert because it experiences a **meteorological drought**, receiving less than ten inches of precipitation a year. Temperatures are so consistently low that vegetation is limited to moss, lichen, and other hardy plants.

ICE CAP (EF)

Freezing temperatures keep the interiors of Greenland, Antarctica, and some northern Canadian islands ice covered year-round. Ice cap climates are extremely cold, dry, and

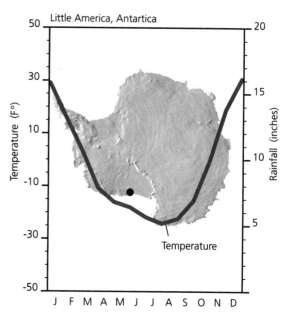

Antarctica is the coldest, driest, windiest continent. It is colder than the North Polar region and is almost completely covered by an ice sheet averaging one mile thick.

windy; no vegetation survives in this climate, but bacteria have been found in layers within the ice.

HIGHLAND (H CLIMATE)

Highland climates vary with changes in elevation and slope. Temperatures may be tropical at the base of mountains, such as the Andes in Ecuador, and cold enough for glaciers at the

Marine, Maritime, and Continental Climates

The moderating influence of oceans on climates is substantial, and proximity to oceans causes climate to be classified as marine or maritime. Continental climates are either far from or upwind from coastlines. Temperature extremes are moderated in maritime climates, in dramatic contrast to the much larger annual temperature range in continental climates. Even at higher latitudes, where seasonal variations in insolation are great, maritime climates are moderate. Tacoma, Washington, on Puget Sound and about 85 miles from the Pacific Ocean, has a moderate, 20°F annual temperature range, far less than the 56°F range of inland Montreal, Quebec—even though both cities are near the same latitude.

top. Precipitation may exceed 60 inches a year on a windward slope and be less than 10 inches on the leeward side. Individual locations may encompass one of the 15 other climates, but the area covered by each climate is too small to be included on a world map. Therefore, these regions' climates are designated as undifferentiated highlands.

Climatic Change

Climatic change, often associated specifically these days with global warming, includes increases and decreases in temperature, precipitation, and the frequency of extreme weather events such as drought. The exchanges of energy and water between the atmosphere, oceans, and land surfaces, especially ice sheets, make climatic change a complex phenomenon that is difficult to measure and predict accurately. Climatic changes need not affect all global locations, either: Warmer temperatures in some areas may melt glaciers even as colder temperatures elsewhere cause glaciers to grow.

Most, if not all, climatic changes can be traced to changes in Earth's radiation balance. (See Earth's Radiation Balance, page 58.) If the amount of insolation received at a latitude or in a region increases or if there is an increase in the amount of long-wave energy radiated out to space, surface temperatures will change. Changing temperatures will, in turn, cause changes in atmospheric pressure, wind patterns, humidity, and precipitation. Over millions of years, changes caused by geologic processes—such as plate movement to new latitudes and uplift to new elevations—will also bring about changes in climate.

Changes in Earth's radiation balance can be explained by changes in Earth's orbital patterns or changes in the composition of Earth's atmosphere. There have also been measurable changes in the amount of energy emitted from the sun during the 1980s, but this solar constant varies too little to cause climatic change on Earth. In 1893, however, British scientist E. Walter Maunder (1645–1715) established a relationship between the decreasing frequency of **sunspots**—large, cool blotches on the solar surface—and colder global temperatures. Two **minimums**, or periods of low sunspot activity—the Maunder minimum and the Sporer minimum —coincided with lower global temperatures; however, no causal relationship between sunspots and Earth's radiation balance has been confirmed.

In 1938 changes in Earth's orbital patterns were linked to global cooling and to the Pleistocene Ice Age. Milutin Milankovitch, a Serbian mathematician, discovered a statistical relationship among three factors: Earth's tilt, Earth's orbit around the sun, and glacial advances. He noted that three astronomic cycles are involved: Earth's tilt changes from 22.1 degrees to 24.5 degrees and back every 41,000 years; Earth's North and South Poles make one revolution, a **precession**, every 25,780 years; and Earth's orbit and distance from the sun change in a 100,000-year pattern, or **eccentricity**. John E. Kutzbach of the University of Wisconsin–Madison's Center for Climatic Resources theorized that these cycles could change the amount of insolation received at different latitudes by as much as 5 percent and apparently could allow the northern latitudes to cool sufficiently for glaciers to grow. Evidence in support of the **Milankovitch theory** has accumulated over the last 30 years: Fossils found in seafloor cores have provided evidence of changing ocean depths and the changing glacial coverage of

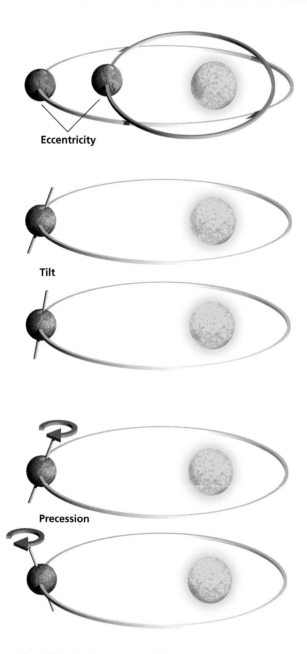

Eccentricity

Tilt

Precession

The **Milankovitch theory** links Earth's changing patterns of eccentricity, tilt, and precession to global cooling and the Pleistocene Ice Age.

continents during the past 500,000 years. When colder temperatures caused glaciers to expand on the continents, the decrease in runoff from streams and rivers caused ocean levels to drop.

American scientist, publisher, and diplomat Benjamin Franklin (1706-1790) linked changes in the composition of Earth's atmosphere and climatic changes following the 1783 eruption of Iceland's Laki volcano, arguing that volcanic ash in the atmosphere interfered with Earth's warming. Later volcanic eruptions, such as those of Tambora in 1815 and Pinatubo in 1991, were also followed by cooler temperatures, and they strengthened the link between eruptions and climatic change. Volcanic dust and ashes spewed into the atmosphere were once thought to reflect sunlight and therefore decrease insolation, but this is now considered an unlikely cause of global cooling because the particles settle out of the atmosphere too quickly to have lasting effects. The eruption of sulfur oxides, which are transformed into sulfurous aerosols, such as tiny drops of sulfuric acid in Earth's stratosphere, are of much greater concern. These aerosol droplets may stay in the stratosphere for months or years because there is no precipitation at this level, and they scatter and absorb solar radiation. The location of a volcanic eruption and the season in which it occurs are also factors in climatic change: Aerosols erupted from low-latitude volcanoes spread farther and with greater effect than those from high-latitude volcanoes, whereas summer wind patterns at lower latitudes disperse aerosols farther than during other seasons.

Human-caused changes to the atmosphere have contributed to global climatic changes. The United Nations Intergovernmental Panel on Climate Change reported in 1995 that global surface temperatures had risen one degree Fahrenheit since 1900 and that increased carbon dioxide from burning fossil fuels was partially responsible. Scientists continue to debate to what degree the burning of fossil fuels has damaged Earth's carbon cycle. (See Diagram: Carbon Cycle, page 231.)

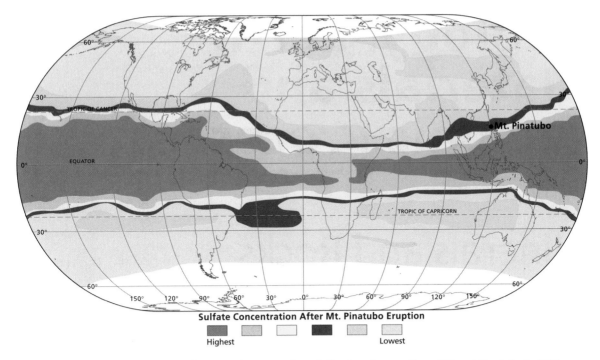

Sulfate Concentration After Mt. Pinatubo Eruption

Highest   Lowest

Clouds of sulfur dioxide were carried into Earth's atmosphere following the eruption of Mount Pinatubo in 1991. These clouds were transformed into droplets of sulfuric acid that spread around the globe, scattering sunlight back into space and absorbing heat from Earth, resulting in cooler surface temperatures.

Earth's climates have changed repeatedly in the past and will undoubtedly change in the future, but predicting the timing and amount of change is problematic. The cause-and-effect relationships between the different factors affecting climate—such as ocean temperatures, cloud cover, and atmospheric carbon dioxide— have not been quantified for modeling climatic change. (See Bioregions, page 227.) Scientists continue to work on our understanding of climatic change, but the scale and complexity of the system make efforts to predict and influence climate unreliable.

Urbanization and Climatic Change

At the local scale, climates in large cities are measurably different from climates in the surrounding countrysides. Warmer temperatures, especially at night and during winter, increasing clouds and rainfall (but not snowfall), slower wind speeds, and other changes in urban weather have been documented. The urban heat island phenomenon has been noted for more than a hundred years. (See Urban Heat Islands, page 65.) In cities, humans have changed atmospheric composition through pollution; they have changed ground surfaces with buildings, pavement, and the removal of vegetation; and they have increased the release of heat energy from buildings.

Geology: Earth Materials and Tectonic Processes

Minerals and Rocks

Minerals and the rocks they form combine to provide a history of the processes and patterns of Earth's environments. Minerals and rocks affect landform development and form natural resources such as gold, tin, iron, marble, and granite.

Minerals

So far more than 4,000 naturally occurring minerals have been identified on Earth. A **mineral** is an inorganic solid that has a characteristic chemical composition and specific crystal structure; these in turn affect its physical characteristics. Quartz, for example, is formed from silicon and oxygen, and halite, or salt, is a combination of sodium and chloride. A mineral's physical characteristics determine how resistant it is to weathering, how it influences landscape development, and how people decide to use it. The composition of quartz makes it very resistant to weathering, transparent, and a source for silicon used in computer chips. Although graphite and diamonds are composed of carbon atoms, the arrangement of atoms is different, which is why diamonds are the hardest minerals and graphite is one of the softest. Most mineral particles are small because they form within confined areas,

such as lava flows and between grains of sediments; large individual crystals found in geodes, pegmatites, and other rocks are relatively uncommon.

Only a few dozen of the 4,000 minerals recognized by the International Commission on New Minerals and Mineral Names are common on Earth. The most common minerals are combinations of the 112 elements—such as silicon, oxygen, and iron—that are also common on Earth. (See Planet Earth, page 45.) While many combinations of these elements are possible, only a limited number of combinations of minerals form under the environmental conditions found on Earth. Uranium, for example, is a rare element found most commonly in carnotite and uraninite.

Silicates, the most common class of minerals, are the major components of most rocks and include quartz, mica, olivine, and precious minerals such as emeralds, a subtype of beryl. Other major mineral classes are oxides, sulfides, sulfates, carbonates, halides, and native, or pure, elements such as gold.

Almost all minerals can form in more than one environment, but the existence of a particular mineral is ordinarily evidence of a limited range of conditions such as temperature, pressure, and the presence or absence of oxygen or water. As a result, minerals can be used to map a region's **paleogeography**, or prehistoric geologic processes. The spatial distribution of minerals, however, may not display easily identifiable patterns because the environmental conditions under which they formed were present over periods of hundreds of millions of years. Halite, for example, forms when salty bodies of water evaporate; salt deposits in Siberia and the midwestern United States are evidence of oceans and tropical locations. Diamonds form only under extremely high pressure hundreds of miles underground and are exposed on Earth's surface in very few locations, among them central South Africa, Yakutia in Russia, and northern Canada.

The Rock Cycle

Mixtures or clusters of minerals form **rocks** under specific sets of environmental conditions, and rocks are classified igneous, sedimentary, or metamorphic according to how they are formed. Minerals have very specific physical and chemical properties related to their composition; rocks have more diverse mineral components and therefore more variable properties. Sandstone, for example, is most often composed of quartz grains, although any other hard, rounded fragment in a limited size range from .002 to .08 inch in diameter, such as feldspar grains, can form sandstone. More specific names may be applied depending on the size and composition of grains comprising a rock: Quartzite refers to quartz sandstone with silicate cement between grains, and arkose refers to feldspar sandstone. The environmental conditions in which rocks form are often vastly different from the conditions in which their mineral components formed; the quartz grains of sandstone are usually formed miles below ground, whereas most sandstones are former beaches.

Rocks will not change unless their surroundings change. Their mineral components, stable in the original environment, do react to stresses from changes in temperature, pressure, and the presence of water and air. (See Diagram: Rock Cycle, page 126.) All rocks will change when environmental conditions cause sufficient stress, but the mineral composition of different rocks limits what their next forms may be. Silicates that form granite cannot change directly into the carbonates that form limestone. Once a rock changes, there is little evidence of the environmental conditions that existed when it was created.

IGNEOUS ROCKS AND RESOURCES

Igneous rocks form when **magma**, molten material below Earth's surface, or **lava,** magma on Earth's surface, cools. Not all minerals in magma or lava solidify at the same temperature when cooling occurs, so different igneous rocks can form from the same molten material. Olivine and augite solidify at warmer temperatures and form gabbro, whereas quartz and muscovite solidify at cooler temperatures and form granite.

Igneous rocks are classified by texture—evidence of their speed of cooling—and color—evidence of their chemical composition. In

Building Capitols

Some U.S. state capitol buildings have been constructed using stone from in-state quarries, as a matter of state pride and for economic reasons. Granite, an especially strong igneous rock, was used to build numerous capitols, and Barre granite from Barre, Vermont, started an industry. Limestone was also a popular choice in construction: Salem limestone, also called Indiana limestone, from Salem, Indiana, was used to construct not only the capitol of Indiana but also parts of the capitols of nine other states, including Alaska.

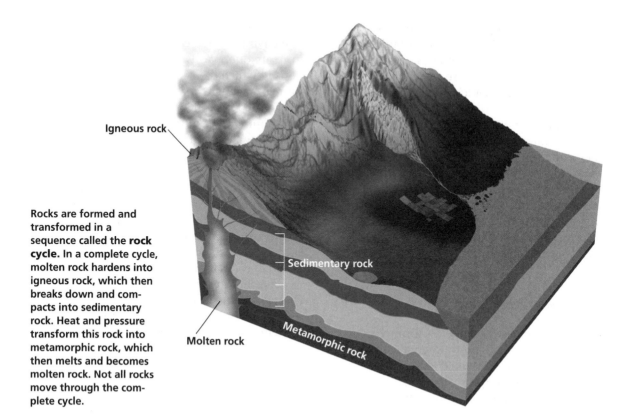

Igneous rock

Sedimentary rock

Molten rock

Metamorphic rock

Rocks are formed and transformed in a sequence called the **rock cycle**. In a complete cycle, molten rock hardens into igneous rock, which then breaks down and compacts into sedimentary rock. Heat and pressure transform this rock into metamorphic rock, which then melts and becomes molten rock. Not all rocks move through the complete cycle.

general, igneous rocks such as granite, with visible mineral crystals, form below the surface; igneous rocks with tiny crystals or a glassy appearance, such as obsidian, form at the surface. Cooling is usually very slow for magma because the **country rock**, the rock that surrounds the intrusive magma, is good insulation; in some cases, such as in the Sierra Nevada in California, it takes thousands of years for the magma to cool. Slow cooling allows mineral crystals in these rocks that formed below the surface—**intrusive**, or plutonic, rocks—such as granite, diorite, and gabbro—to grow large enough to be seen with the naked eye. Lava cools more quickly because it is exposed to air, and minerals in the resulting **extrusive**, or **volcanic**, rocks—such as rhyolite, andesite, and basalt—form much smaller crystals than intrusive rocks. Lighter-colored **felsic** rocks, such as granite, rhyolite, and andesite, have a greater percentage of quartz, micas, and silicate

than do darker **mafic** rocks such as gabbro and basalt; mafic rocks have a greater percentage of magnesium and iron. Lavas can be felsic or mafic, and their composition affects their rate of flow and how they may be erupted from a volcano. (See Igneous Structures and Volcanoes, page 150.) Despite different textures resulting from different rates of cooling, felsic igneous rocks have comparable mineral compositions. Gabbro is an intrusive rock whereas basalt is volcanic, but both are mafic and contain the minerals olivine, pyroxenes, and plagioclase feldspar.

The distribution of igneous rocks reflects Earth's tectonic history. (See Map: Global Distribution of Surface Rock Types, opposite.) Intrusive rocks dominate continental shields, the ancient cores of continents; the Canadian Shield, core of North America, is granite that is exposed over much of eastern Canada. Mountains, especially older chains such as the

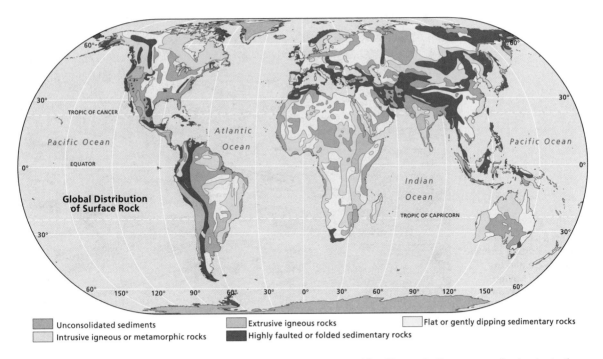

Unconsolidated sediments
Intrusive igneous or metamorphic rocks
Extrusive igneous rocks
Highly faulted or folded sedimentary rocks
Flat or gently dipping sedimentary rocks

Global distribution of surface rock types reflects geologic processes and landforms. Sedimentary rocks dominate the surface, covering most of the sea floor and much of the exposed land surface.

Appalachians and Urals, tend to have exposed intrusive rocks, laid bare by erosion. Extrusive rocks such as basalt are usually found where there has been volcanic activity; much of eastern Washington, Iceland, and western India have exposed basalt.

Igneous resources include many of Earth's deposits of diamonds and valuable metallic minerals such as titanium and chromium. As magma cools, heavier mineral crystals sink and concentrate at the bottom of the formation. Nickel deposits in Sudbury, Ontario, formed from pentlandite; platinum deposits in Bushveld, South Africa, formed from mineral crystal settling more than one billion years ago. Pegmatites, intrusive rocks with giant crystals, form during the final stage of magma cooling and include such rare metallic minerals as lithium and gems such as beryl and tourmaline. Some magmas generate superheated water—hydrothermal solutions—that carry rare metals such as gold, silver, and copper and deposit them as veins in rock fractures.

SEDIMENTARY ROCKS AND RESOURCES

Sedimentary rocks form from the accumulation of different types of sediments, including particles of minerals or rocks, ions in solution, and organic material. The majority of sedimentary rocks are created from sediments that settle or precipitate out of lakes, oceans, and seas; however, sand dunes, talus cones at the base of cliffs, and glacial deposits can also become sedimentary rocks. As sediments accumulate, they settle and eventually solidify to form layers, or **strata**. **Lithification**, the process of becoming rock, includes compaction of strata by burial and cementation by precipitating minerals such as calcite or hematite.

Sedimentary rocks are classified by their composition. **Clastic** sedimentary rocks, sometimes called detrital because they are made up

Cemented sand dunes carved by shifting prevailing winds created the cross-bedded Navajo sandstone formation in Zion National Park, Utah.

of fragments of other rocks, are accumulations of particles: Clay becomes shale, sand becomes sandstone, and gravel forms conglomerate. **Chemical** rocks form when ions in solution precipitate or become solid as evaporation or other changes reduce water's ability to hold ions in solution: Calcite forms from solution and combines with clay minerals to form limestone. **Organic** rocks form when dead plant and animal matter accumulates in bodies of water before it completely decomposes; organic processes are important in the formation of many limestones—especially chalk, which forms from the bodies of microscopic organisms such as foraminifera—and bituminous coal, which is made up of plant materials.

Changes in ocean levels relative to the continents have resulted in sedimentary rocks covering most of the continental surface, including **continental shelves**, the offshore extensions of continents. Ocean floors were originally basalt, an igneous rock, but over time sediments eroded and washed from the continents and eventually became sedimentary rocks that buried the basalt. Many of these sedimentary rocks formed hundreds of millions of years ago;

most of the rocks in the midwestern United States were formed in the Paleozoic Era, which ended 245 million years ago. In the past four billion years or so, tectonic activity has compressed and folded many former ocean floors into mountains, as evidenced by aquatic plant and animal fossils in sedimentary rocks found on mountain peaks in the Himalaya, Alps, and Rockies. (See Geologic Time Table, page 47.)

Many natural resources have their origins in sedimentary rocks; such as **fossil fuels** of coal, petroleum, and natural gas; construction materials such as limestone for cement; and metal deposits such as iron and gold. Coal is tropical swamp vegetation that accumulated in acidic water; the acidity killed bacteria that would otherwise have decomposed the vegetation. Most of the world's major coal deposits, including those in the central United States, Europe, and China, date to the late Paleozoic Era; their current locations, far from the tropics, are now known to be the result of tectonic plate movements and are evidence to support the theory that continents have shifted over time. (See Plate Tectonics, page 130.)

Petroleum, or crude oil, and natural gas

Banded Iron Formations

Perhaps the most important metal resource found in sedimentary rock is iron from banded iron formations (BIFs). About two billion years ago oxygen first began to accumulate in the ocean water. (See Atmosphere, page 54.) As the oxygen content in water rose, and as ocean currents caused deep ocean water to circulate to depths where oxygen was more plentiful, iron dissolved in the oceans precipitated as hematite onto continental shelves in layers interspersed with layers of chert, a silicate rock. These layered deposits are now the most important iron-ore deposits and are found in ancient rocks on all continents. Major iron-ore producers, including Australia, the Asian countries of India and China, and Brazil in South America obtain their iron from BIF.

formed in shallow oceans from microscopic organisms that settled and were covered by sediments that prevented decomposition. As the organisms were buried under deeper and deeper layers of sediments, pressure and heat converted the organisms to liquid and gaseous hydrocarbons. Petroleum starts to form at temperatures above 120°F; at temperatures above 212°F natural gas forms. There are major petroleum deposits in the Persian Gulf region and in Venezuela and western Russia where ocean floors have been uplifted and exposed.

METAMORPHIC ROCKS AND RESOURCES

When rocks are subjected to heat, pressure, and chemically active fluids (usually heated water infused with dissolved gases), they can become metamorphic rocks. Any rock can have its texture or its mineral composition changed: Limestone metamorphoses into marble when its texture changes because of increased heat, and basalt metamorphoses into greenstone when low heat and fluids alter its minerals. Different degrees of metamorphism can occur according to the amount of heat, pressure, and fluids present. Shale, a sedimentary rock composed of clay and silt, can progressively metamorphose into slate, phyllite, schist, and finally gneiss as an increasing percentage of the original clay changes to different minerals and more layering occurs.

Two major metamorphic processes, regional and contact metamorphism, are responsible for most metamorphism as well as for the two major types of metamorphic rocks—**foliated**, banded or layered rocks, and **nonfoliated rocks**. Less common metamorphic processes include **shock metamorphism** from meteorite impacts and **cataclastic metamorphism** from stress associated with faulting.

Regional metamorphism may affect areas of thousands of square miles and creates the layering found in foliated rocks through convergence and compression. (See Plate Tectonics, page 130.) When, for example, two continents come together, the rocks along the boundary where they converge are heated and compressed, causing sediments and minerals to align themselves at right angles to the pressure; Rocks such as slate, phyllite, and schist result.

Contact metamorphism is caused by heat from a magma body that forms nonfoliated rocks such as marble, greenstone, and hornfels. Pressure is not a factor, and less metamorphism of country rock occurs when the heat source is farther away. An **aureole**, or halo, forms around magma. Garnet and staurolite minerals form where the temperature is highest, and chlorite and biotite form farther away, where the temperature is cooler.

Metamorphic rocks are not common surface rocks because they form far below the surface and are exposed only after substantial erosion. Most often, metamorphic rocks are found alongside igneous rocks where tectonic convergence once occurred. Eroded mountain chains, such as the Appalachians and the Adirondacks in North America and the Urals in Europe, expose belts of metamorphic rocks. Shield areas of continents, such as the Canadian Shield, are the roots of ancient mountains, and they expose gneiss, greenstone, and other metamorphic rocks and granite, an igneous rock.

Most metal deposits created by metamorphism, including copper, lead, and zinc, are created by contact metamorphism involving superheated hydrothermal fluids commonly found where igneous rocks form. Other metamorphic minerals used as resources include graphite, used in pencil lead; talc, as talcum power; and asbestos, used in insulation. Slate, marble, and gneiss are metamorphic rocks used as construction materials, and precious stones formed by metamorphism include rubies, emeralds, and sapphires.

Plate Tectonics

The theory of plate tectonics links currents in the mantle to the location and formation of major geologic features on Earth's surface and to earthquakes and volcanic eruptions. Earth's continents, oceans, mountain ranges, and other major surface features change locations as tectonic processes continue.

Continental Drift

In 1620 English philosopher Sir Francis Bacon (1561–1626) noted in *Novanum Organum* that the shapes of eastern South America and western Africa matched one another. Over the years other authors noted the fit of these coastlines and hypothesized that the continents had once been joined and then drifted apart. German meteorologist and geophysicist Alfred Wegener (1880–1930) presented the first well-researched theory of continental drift in *The Origin of the Continents and Oceans* (1915). While his theory offered an explanation for many geographic and geologic patterns around the world, it generated a great debate among scientists because it challenged the accepted idea that continents had fixed locations.

Wegener theorized that all continents on Earth were united as a supercontinent, **Pangaea** (Greek *pan,* "all," and *ge,* "Earth"),

in a single super-ocean, Panthalassa, until the end of the Triassic geologic period, about 208 million years ago. When Pangaea began to drift apart, what is now Africa was at its center, with South America to the west; India, Antarctica, and Australia to the east; and North America and Eurasia to the north. Pangaea split first into two sections: Gondwanaland to the south and Laurasia to the north.

Wegener's evidence that the continents had once been attached included matching spatial

Alfred Wegener, shown here during a winter expedition to Greenland (1912–13), drew on much evidence to develop his theory of continental drift.

patterns of fossils and rock formations between continents. He pointed out that the fossils of two small Mesozoic reptiles, *Mesosaurus* and *Cynognathus*, are found only in limited areas of western Africa and eastern South America, and that coal deposits in Pennsylvania, France, and Siberia contain fossils of equatorial and tropical vegetation. Wegener inferred that rocks with grooves scratched by glaciers in southern India, central Australia, Africa's Kalahari Desert, and Uruguay may once have been attached to Antarctica. The Appalachian Mountains on the east coast of North America and mountains in Greenland, Ireland, and Norway have similar ages, rock layers, and fossils.

Despite the evidence Wegener gathered, most geologists rejected his theory of continental drift because he could not convincingly explain why or how the continents had sepa-

rated. Scientists derided his explanations that tidal forces caused continents to drift. Parts of his theory were inaccurate: The moon's gravity does cause tides, but it cannot cause continents to move; continents do not, as Wegener proposed, drift over or plow through ocean floors.

In the 1950s, 20 years after Wegener disappeared during an expedition to Greenland, new technology such as **magnetometers**, instruments that measure the magnetic field of the Earth, was used to examine seafloors. Researchers aboard ships measured and mapped the orientation of Earth's past magnetic fields as preserved in the basalt rocks from the ocean floors; their findings confirmed Wegener's basic claim that continents move. When basalt cools, the iron minerals in the molten rock align to the north and south magnetic poles in such a way that the basalt

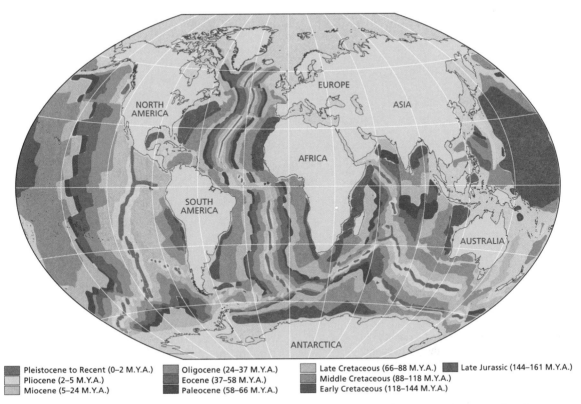

Pleistocene to Recent (0–2 M.Y.A.) Oligocene (24–37 M.Y.A.) Late Cretaceous (66–88 M.Y.A.) Late Jurassic (144–161 M.Y.A.)
Pliocene (2–5 M.Y.A.) Eocene (37–58 M.Y.A.) Middle Cretaceous (88–118 M.Y.A.)
Miocene (5–24 M.Y.A.) Paleocene (58–66 M.Y.A.) Early Cretaceous (118–144 M.Y.A.)

Scientists determine the ages of the Earth's ocean basins by noting magnetic anomalies in sea floor rocks. The youngest oceanic crust lies closest to the spreading ridges. The crust increases in age with distance from the ridges.

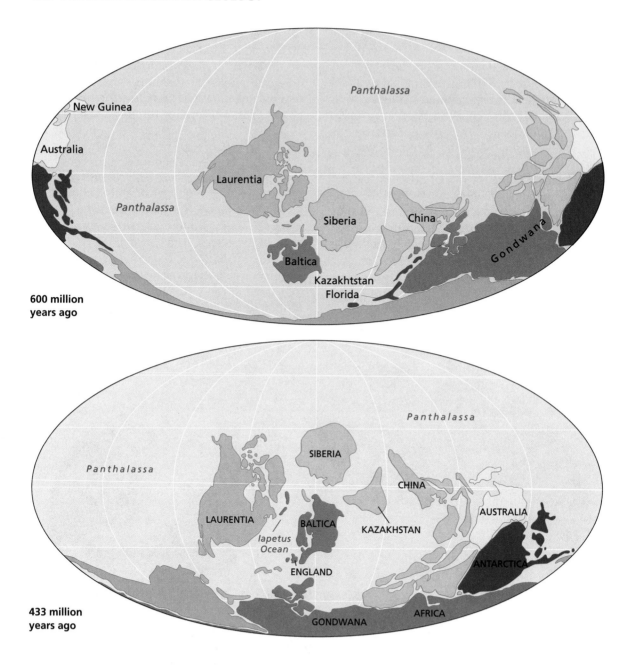

600 million years ago

433 million years ago

Evidence of plate tectonics can be seen in the shifting of land masses over the past 600 million years of Earth's history. The continents found their current positions only about 20 million years ago. Clues to the past positions of these land masses were derived from paleomagnetic information in rocks.

contains a record of the magnetic poles at the time of the rock's formation. Earth's magnetic poles reverse themselves every million years on average. Mapping the magnetic orientation of the minerals revealed that the sequence of reversing magnetic fields was

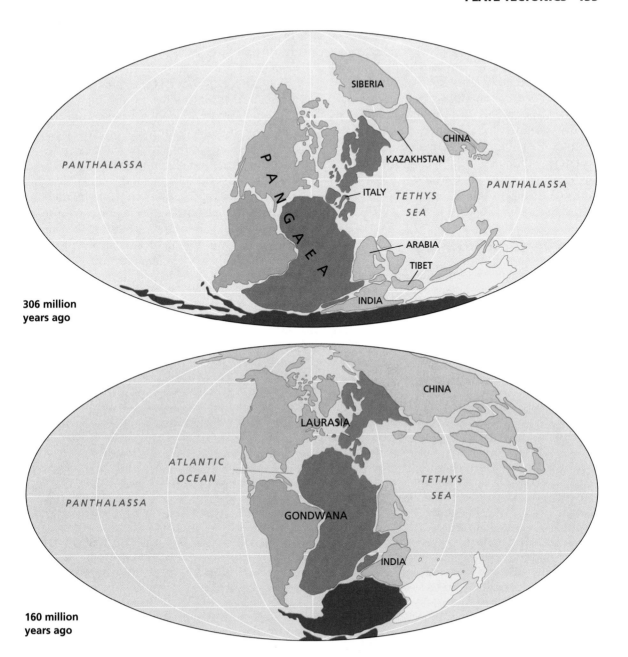

306 million years ago

160 million years ago

the same in rocks on both sides of the Mid-Atlantic Ridge.

These matching magnetic patterns are evidence that ocean floors are being created at the ridge and then are spreading slowly outward while new basalt forms at the ridge. In the 1960s, Princeton University geologist Harry Hess proposed the idea of seafloor spreading—that seafloors form at mid-ocean ridges and then move away, thus moving continents farther apart. New drilling technology enabled scientists to sample and date rocks on the ocean floors and to corroborate Hess's hypothesis with paleomagnetic evidence.

The youngest rocks were found along the mid-ocean ridges, and samples became progressively older with distance from the ridge. Sediments covering the basalt ocean floor are older, contain fossils from earlier geologic periods, and become thicker with increasing distance from the ridge because there has been more time for these sediments to accumulate. Continents would necessarily have been pushed farther apart as the seafloor between them spread.

Plate Tectonics Theory

The theory of plate tectonics that emerged after the 1950s and 1960s addresses many of the weaknesses of continental drift theory and explains additional spatial patterns of geologic features. **Plates** are sections of Earth's lithosphere—its rigid exterior—that form continents and ocean floors; **tectonics**, from the Greek *tecktonikos* (builder), is the study of Earth's structure. Tectonic processes of convergence and divergence, meeting and separating, create the largest surface features and link the formation of continents and oceans, their major surface features, the global distribution of rock types, and even past climatic changes. Understanding these processes also helps explain how and why earthquakes and volcanoes occur and helps predict geologic events. The theory of plate tectonics is still being refined as new information is collected and analyzed.

Geologists have identified several dozen

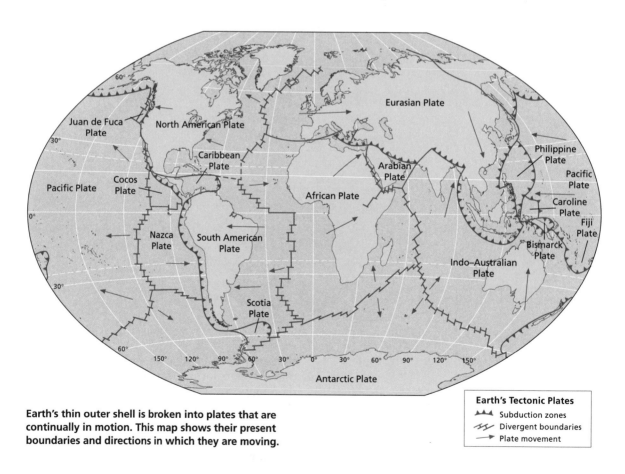

Earth's thin outer shell is broken into plates that are continually in motion. This map shows their present boundaries and directions in which they are moving.

Earth's Tectonic Plates
ᐃᐃᐃ Subduction zones
〰〰 Divergent boundaries
→ Plate movement

large and small tectonic plates that have stable interiors, move independently, and interact with each other at their boundaries. (See Map: Earth's Tectonic Plates, page 134.) Plates often are partly continental and partly oceanic; the North American plate extends from the Mid-Atlantic Ridge to the west coast of Canada and the United States (except for part of California's coast). The South American, North American, Eurasian, African, Pacific, Antarctic, Australian, Indian, and Nazca plates are the largest plates. Other plates, such as the Juan de Fuca (off the coast of Oregon and Washington), the Caribbean, the Philippine, and the Adriatic plates, are much smaller but are important tectonically because of their boundary interactions.

During Earth's history the number, size, and location of tectonic plates have changed dramatically. Smaller plates have merged into larger plates, and larger plates have divided into smaller plates. The supercontinent and superplate Rodinia existed from about 700 million to 600 million years ago, prior to the formation of Pangaea. Pangaea is the most recent example of a superplate that formed from smaller plates and is now divided into our current tectonic plates. The division of Pangaea into smaller plates started around 225 million years ago and continues today. (See Map sequence: Pangaea and Current Continents, pages 132-133.)

According to the theory of plate tectonics the Earth's **lithosphere**, its rigid outer layer, moves slowly—usually one to two inches a year—over the underlying, softer **asthenosphere**. The lithosphere includes the crust and the uppermost part of the mantle and can be classified as either oceanic or continental. (See Earth Structure, page 49.) The mostly granite continental lithosphere averages 45 miles in thickness and is more than 100 miles thick under mountain ranges. Basaltic oceanic sections of the lithosphere average 30 miles in thickness and may be only 12 miles thick in places. Oceanic basalt is about 10 percent denser than continental granite; when an oceanic section of a plate meets a continental section of a plate, the denser oceanic plate slides under the continental plate.

Radioactive decay of uranium and radium and the residual heat from Earth's formation cause temperatures in the asthenosphere to increase to more than 1,000°F. As a result the asthenosphere is softer than the lithosphere, and rock in the asthenosphere can flow, much as hot asphalt does. The lithosphere can glide over this underlying layer with reduced resistance from friction.

The ultimate source of energy for the movement of tectonic plates is heat from Earth's interior, but the exact mechanism for plate movement has not yet been discovered. One mechanism proposed in the 1960s is that heat in the mantle causes convection currents. Some geologists theorize that there may be two

The Balkans and Middle East

The region extending from the Adriatic Sea to northern Iran and the Sinai Peninsula is a collection of more than a half dozen small tectonic plates, some smaller than South Carolina's area of 31,113 square miles. Boundaries of individual plates—including the Caspian, Ionian, and Levantine—are being mapped based on earthquake locations. As these plates shift, they are being compressed by the African and Saudi plates, which are drifting north into Eurasia, and they have created numerous mountain chains, including the Caucasus, Zagros, and Taurus ranges. The plate movements cause earthquakes to be a continuing hazard.

other forces related to interactions between tectonic plates that provide mechanisms for plate movement. **Slab pull** may occur where plates meet: When one plate is pushed down at the boundary, it pulls the rest of the plate behind it. **Ridge push** may occur where plates are forming with a previously existing plate, and the plates are pushed away from each other.

The rate of movement of tectonic plates varies for different parts of the world and is apparently affected by the relative motions of plates. North America is moving away from Eurasia and South America is moving away from Africa at about 1 to 1.5 inches each year, whereas the Nazca plate, west of South America, pulls away from the Pacific plate at the rate of more than 7 inches per year. The faster speed of the Nazca plate seems to be because it lacks continental lithosphere, and the plate is being subducted under South America. In general, faster tectonic movements occur when one edge of the moving plate is being subducted under another plate and when slab pull is increased.

The differential movement of tectonic plates creates three types of tectonic boundaries: **divergent**, where plates move apart, or diverge; **transform**, where plates move sideways in relation to each other; and **convergent**, where plates move into one another, or converge. Earth's surface changes at tectonic boundaries. Over time, however, the convection currents within the mantle change, and boundaries can cease to function or change into different types of boundary. The boundary between Europe and Asia closed when the plates merged to form Eurasia, and the convergent boundary along the coast of California became a transform boundary when the Farallon plate was being subducted under the North American plate. If a boundary ceases to function, the relict boundary, locked within a new plate, can continue to have effects: The New Madrid Fault in southeastern Missouri, a former divergent boundary within

the North American plate, remains an earthquake hazard.

DIVERGENT BOUNDARIES AND LANDFORMS

When tectonic plates separate, they create a divergent boundary and new lithosphere. Initially, when a tectonic plate divides, its lithosphere thins from the tension; as a result there is less overlying pressure on the mantle beneath it. This reduced pressure allows part of the mantle to melt, rise through rifts caused by the tension, and fill the gaps between the two plates with basalt, creating basaltic lithosphere. Part of the newly created lithosphere attaches to the boundaries of both tectonic plates, so that each plate grows as it moves away from the line of divergence.

A predictable sequence of landforms results as divergence takes place. When divergence occurs within a continent, as is now happening in the Great Rift Valley of eastern Africa, a **rift valley** emerges. Rifts slowly widen as the plates pull apart and deepen because basaltic lithosphere at the boundary is thinner than the granitic, continental lithosphere. Gradually, the rift fills with water. At first lakes form, but over time, as the valley widens, the lakes become narrow seas; eventually oceans result if divergence continues. Lake Tanganyika and Lake Nyasa in East Africa have formed because the Great Rift Valley is lower than the surrounding highlands. The Red Sea is on the divergent boundary between the Arabian and African plates, which have been separating for about ten million years; if divergence continues the Red Sea will become an ocean.

Divergent boundaries also occur in the oceans, and, because magma that rises from the mantle is warmer and less dense than the existing oceanic crust, it creates a bulge, called a mid-oceanic ridge, while adding new tectonic plate material. Today's oceans were created by divergence, and all have mid-oceanic ridges. When Pangaea broke apart, the Atlantic Ocean formed; the Mid-Atlantic Ridge marks the divergent boundary between North America and South America on the west and Eurasia and Africa on the east. The Carlsberg, Mid-Indian, and Southeast Indian Ridges are found in the Indian Ocean and were formed between India, Africa, Australia, and Antarctica.

Not all divergent boundaries continue to spread apart; the driving forces can cease for reasons that are not yet known. The island of Madagascar, now part of the Africa plate, formed a smaller plate that separated from the east coast of Africa but stopped diverging about 90 million years ago; it is now 250 miles off the coast of Mozambique. Several rifts within continents ceased to develop, or failed, because divergence stopped, but thinned, weakened segments of lithosphere remain. In the United States, the lower Mississippi River Valley—including the New Madrid Fault—follows the edge of a **failed rift**; two other major rivers, the Amazon and the Niger, are also located in failed rifts.

TRANSFORM BOUNDARIES

Transform boundaries occur where two plates slide sideways past each other, along what are called strike-slip faults. (See Faulted Structures, page 142.) The San Andreas Fault in California is a boundary between the North American plate as it slides northwest relative to the Pacific plate as it slides southeast. Transform boundaries create no major landforms, but continual movement causes earthquakes along the entire boundary. (See Earthquakes, page 146.) Transform boundaries, like divergent boundaries, can cease to move. Loch Ness, a linear lake in northern Scotland, is on the Great Glen Fault, a relict transform boundary.

CONVERGENT BOUNDARIES AND LANDFORMS

Convergent boundaries occur when two tectonic plates move toward each other. Differing landforms result from convergent boundaries according to the speed of the plates and whether convergence is between continental plates, continental and oceanic plates, or oceanic plates. When one plate is **subducted**,

or forced below the other, it eventually melts into the mantle. The **Benioff zone**, named for American seismologist Hugo Benioff (1899–1968), marks the boundary between a subducted and an overriding plate. Globally, the loss of lithosphere through subduction balances the creation of lithosphere caused by divergence. The surface area of Earth neither grows nor shrinks: As new tectonic plate material is added, an equal area of tectonic plate material is destroyed.

When a continental tectonic plate converges with a denser oceanic tectonic plate, ocean floor is destroyed as the oceanic plate slides below the continental plate, and mountains rise along the boundary. As the oceanic plate bends down, the ocean floor angles down and forms a **trench**. Trenches are the deepest parts of oceans, and their location within a hundred miles of the coastlines of continents rather than in the middle of oceans supports the theory of plate tectonics: The Peru-Chile, Ryukyu, and Java Trenches all parallel coastlines.

As an oceanic plate is forced under a continental plate, the oceanic plate heats as it is subducted into the mantle. Much of the oceanic plate is eventually reabsorbed into the mantle, but the high pressure and temperatures in the upper mantle release water from the subducted rocks and melt felsic minerals, such as quartz, in the subducted plate and in the mantle above it. The resulting magma is less dense than the surrounding rock and rises toward the surface where it forms intrusive igneous rock bodies, such as the granite of the Sierra Nevada. (See Igneous Structures and Volcanoes, page 150.)

Mountains created by convergence between oceanic and continental plates are partly a result of volcanoes and intrusive igneous rock bodies and partly the result of other tectonic processes, such as compression. A **volcanic arc** results when a line of volcanoes forms parallel to a convergent boundary; the Cascade Range from Mount Lassen in California north to Mount Garibaldi in British Columbia, is one example. As an oceanic plate is subducted, part of its overlying sediments are scraped off and attached to the continent. In addition, islands that rise from the ocean floor are usually too light or too large to be subducted and therefore also attach or accrete to the continent. These island **terranes**, distinct geologic regions, make up much of the western edge of North America: There are about 40 or so terranes on the west coast, including Wrangellia, Stikine, and San Juan. The compression that results from two tectonic plates converging also causes the edge of the continent to fold into mountains. (See Geologic Structures and Earthquakes, page 139.)

Subduction of an oceanic plate beneath a continent can cause the continental plate to stretch like Silly Putty even as its edge compresses. This extension reduces the compressional effect that creates folded mountains at the boundary, making the mountains less prominent than they might have been.

The exact cause of the stretching is unknown, but it may be that melted plate material at the boundary creates small convection patterns and therefore some divergence below the edge of the continental plate. As a continent undergoes extension, part of its interior thins and may be flooded by an ocean that forms a **back-arc basin**, such as the Sea of Japan. The basin, on the west coast of Japan, exists because the Pacific plate is being subducted under Eurasia, stretching Eurasia's continental edge.

Convergence between two oceanic plates results in subduction of one of the plates and creates trenches and **volcanic island arcs**. Whichever oceanic plate is farther from the divergent boundary that created it has lost more of its original heat and so is colder and denser than the other oceanic plate. The colder plate subducts beneath the warmer plate and a trench forms. Nearly seven miles deep, the world's deepest trench—the Mariana Trench in the western Pacific—formed when the Pacific plate subducted the Philippine plate.

Volcanic island arcs form parallel to these trenches on the nonsubducted oceanic plate. Each island is a composite volcano formed from magma rising above the subducted plate, and is comparable to continental volcanoes forming in volcanic arcs.

Some island arcs, like the Aleutian Islands, are continuations of volcanic arcs found on land, in their case the Alaska Range. Other linear island arcs are the Marianas and Tonga in the Pacific and Lesser Antilles in the Caribbean. Not all volcanic islands are formed by convergence and subduction; like Hawaii, some formed over a hot spot of rising magma. (See Igneous Structures and Volcanoes, page 150.)

Convergent boundaries also occur between continental tectonic plates, but subduction cannot take place because neither plate is sufficiently dense to be forced down into the mantle. Continental plates converge only after intervening oceanic plates have been subducted; as a result, when the continents converge, intrusive igneous rock bodies and volcanic landforms will be found in the interior of the landmass.

When the continents meet, the highest mountains in the world form because lateral compression causes folding and therefore vertical uplift. The Himalaya contain the world's highest peaks and are the result of the Indian subcontinent converging with Eurasia about 50 million years ago.

Convergence between continental plates eventually slows and halts as mountains rise and their mass causes the lithosphere to thicken; this process is how tectonic plates merge and is how Pangaea and other superplates formed.

The mountain range created by convergence of continental plates becomes a **continental suture**, marking the former boundary between two plates. The Urals and Appalachians are examples.

The thickest parts of the lithosphere are found at these boundaries while they are active; after convergence stops, erosion eventually exposes the rock that was once buried miles beneath the mountains.

Geologic Structures and Earthquakes

Shifting tectonic plates stress rocks along their boundaries, causing folds, domes, and other geologic structures to form in rock layers that influence surface landforms such as mountains, cliffs, and valleys. Earthquakes, hazards to people, are also a result of tectonic shifting and stress. The relationship between tectonic boundaries and tectonic stress explains the spatial patterns of geologic structures, associated landforms, and earthquakes.

Stress, Strain, and Structures

Geologic structures are deformations, or changes, in the arrangement of rock layers. Geologic structures are most easily seen in sedimentary rocks, which are usually deposited in horizontal layers or strata. The assumption that the rocks were originally horizontal is called the principle of original horizontality;

thus, subsequent changes in the strata are readily apparent.

Three types of stress along tectonic boundaries cause geologic structures, and they usually occur singly: compression, tension, and shear or sideways stress. **Compression** causes rock layers to fold because it reduces surface area but not the amount of rock. **Tension** deforms rock by stretching it over a greater area, and **shear stress** causes deformation by applying force in opposing directions to rock layers.

Different types of tectonic boundaries cause different types of stress, and the resulting geologic structures are evidence of past stress and past tectonic boundaries. Compression occurs at convergent boundaries and is most evident when two continental plates collide and fold rock layers into mountains. Tension results at divergent boundaries and causes faulting along much of the ocean floor near mid-oceanic

A road cut reveals a fault, or break, in the rock layer below the surface. Faulting is more common in near-surface rocks because they are cooler and under less pressure than deeply buried rock.

ridges. Sufficient tension at convergent boundaries, with an oceanic plate being rapidly subducted under a continental plate, can create a back-arc basin. Shear stress, also called tangential stress, is caused by transform boundaries and is marked by offset surface features such as stream channels that bend dramatically. (See Diagram: Strike-Slip Fault, page 145.)

Deformation of rocks may be elastic, plastic, or fractured and is caused by compression, tension, and shear. The amount and duration of stress is a factor in the amount and permanency of deformation; the type of rock involved—and its strength—also affects the type of deformation.

Elastic deformation is temporary, and the rocks eventually return to their previous arrangement. Usually, elastic deformation is associated less with tectonic stress than with temporary kinds of stress, such as the weight of glaciers during an ice age. For example, Hudson Bay in Canada is in a temporary downfold that is slowly undergoing **isostatic rebound** to its above-water level; the glaciers that compressed the region of the bay melted 10,000 years ago. Isostatic rebound occurs because the lithosphere, which essentially floats on the asthenosphere, sinks when a region is weighted by glaciers, for instance, and rebounds upward when the weight is removed, as when glaciers melt.

Isostatic rebound also occurs when erosion wears away high peaks. The mountains rise and expose their roots because erosion causes peaks to weigh less and displace less of the mantle. The Appalachian Mountains probably averaged more than 14,000 feet high when they first formed, but most Appalachian peaks are now below 6,000 feet; erosion has removed between 15,000 and 24,000 feet of rock in this region but isostatic rebound caused the region to rise in compensation for the erosion.

Plastic deformation is permanent, and folded rock layers are records of the stress involved. As a rule, sedimentary rocks undergo plastic deformation when they are buried because heat and pressure from the burial and the millions of years involved allow the layers to reach equilibrium with the stress. Mountain roots, rock layers buried deep in a folded mountain but exposed by erosion, are excellent examples of plastic deformation. Continental shields, regions encompassing the oldest rock structures of all continents, were formed from the coalescence of many mountain roots when small tectonic plates converged. The Wopmay, Penokean, and Grenville regions of the Canadian Shield are ancient mountain roots.

A third type of deformation—**faulting**—occurs when rock layers are too brittle to fold. Faults are offset fractures or breaks in rocks where the sides of the break are displaced in any direction relative to each other. Near-surface rocks are generally more susceptible to fracture and faulting because they are colder and under less pressure than buried, hotter rock; however, earthquakes can occur at

Europe after the Pleistocene Ice Age

Europe, like North America, had huge glaciers covering much of the continent during the Pleistocene Ice Age, an event that lasted 2 million years, from 2 million years ago to about 10,000 years ago. Glaciers about 1.5 miles thick centered on Scandinavia and spread outward to the Bristol Channel on the south coast of Wales, the Harz Mountains in Germany, and the Carpathians in Poland. As the glaciers melted, Scandinavia began to rebound to its preglacial elevation; parts of the northern Baltic Sea continue to rise about four inches every decade, whereas the rebound rate is less than one inch per decade in the southern Baltic Sea.

depths greater than one hundred miles, evidence of faulting in the mantle.

Compression, tension, and shear cause geologic structures whose deformation can have a major influence on regional landforms. Deformation of rock layers can change their slope and expose layers that resist weathering and erosion differently. (See Weathering, page 159.) Parallel ridges in the Red Hills of Alabama and Mississippi lie between lowland valleys where folding tilted rock layers on Earth's surface; exposed layers of sandstone resisted erosion and formed ridges, but less resistant shale eroded to create valleys.

Although geologic structures affect landforms, other factors are involved and the landforms will not always mirror the underlying rock structure. Landforms are also the result of the surface erosion of exposed layers of rock and reflect the type and duration of erosion as well as the types of rock that are present. Similar types of folding may cause different landforms in different regions. For example, when the upper rock layer of a fold is resistant, a ridge forms, but when the upper layer is softer than underlying layers, then the top of the fold erodes away, and an anticlinal valley results.

FOLDED STRUCTURES

Rock layers that are lifted or pushed down relative to the surrounding area are called **folds**. Linear folds, domes and basins, and plunging folds are variations of folding and reflect different angles of pressure. Folds most often occur when Earth's surface is compressed by tectonic convergence, which causes the leading edges of continental plates to foreshorten and wrinkle like fabric as they contact another tectonic plate. In addition, convergence also causes subducted oceanic plates to melt, rise as magma bodies, and deform overlying rock layers.

Linear folds are the most common of folded structures and form at right angles to the compression of converging tectonic plates. With moderate compression, rock layers form a parallel series of **anticlines**, or upfolds, and **synclines**, or downfolds. As compression increases

over time, the folds can become more exaggerated and tilted sideways to the surface until they are complexly folded to form **recumbent** or **overturned folds**. The axis of a fold, which runs the length of the fold, can dip so that one end disappears beneath the surface. This is a **plunging fold**. (See diagram: Types of folds, page 142.)

Almost all major mountain ranges contain complex folded structures and often equally complex surface features. The Alps and Urals of Europe, the Zagros of Iran and Iraq, and Australia's Great Dividing Range are all intensely folded. In the United States, the Ridge and Valley region of the Appalachians developed from a series of folds extending from eastern Pennsylvania to northeastern Alabama. **Anticlinal valleys** and **synclinal ridges** are created in landscapes, as are **zigzag ridges** eroded from plunging folds.

Two variations of folds—domes and basins—occur when the stress is not linear but centers on a point. **Domes** are circular or elliptical anticlines and are the result of sedimentary rock layers being warped upward by rising fluids, such as magma or salt, rather than by tectonic compression. When less dense material rises underneath rock layers toward the surface, it can force the overlying rock layers to rise. In Louisiana and Texas, **salt domes** are common; they trap petroleum in porous rock such as sandstone when the petroleum floats upward toward the arch of the porous rock layer. The strategic petroleum reserve, established by the United States government as a hedge against disruption in the flow of imported oil from overseas, is stored in five salt domes and one salt mine on the Texas and Louisiana coasts.

Erosion tends to remove the center of a dome first; the higher elevation rocks at the center were fractured during uplift, and are therefore more susceptible to erosion. As a result, older rocks exposed in the central area of the dome are surrounded by tilted layers of younger rock. When the tilted layers, which may be resistant to erosion, are especially pro-

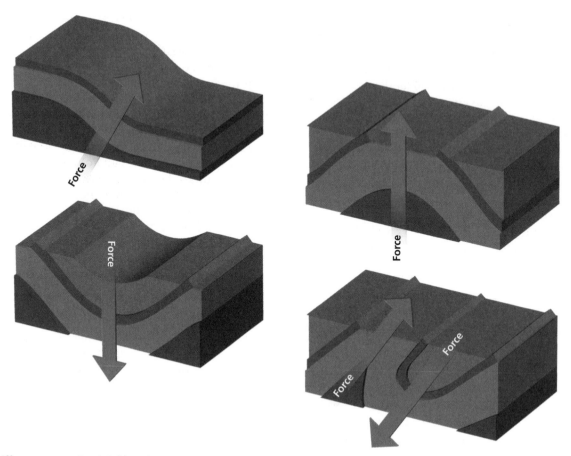

Different types of rock folds include, clockwise from top left, **monocline, anticline, overturned anticline** and **syncline,** and **syncline.** Folds result when tectonic plates meet, compressing the Earth's surface.

nounced, they are called **hogbacks**. The Black Hills of South Dakota and Wyoming, the Ozark Dome of southeastern Missouri, and the Aïr region of central Niger have domal structures.

Basins are circular or elliptical downwarps or **synclines** caused by a loss of supporting pressure, in some cases because the gradual accumulation of sediments on the surface becomes heavy enough to cause underlying rock layers to sink.

There are large structural basins in the mid-western United States, such as the Michigan Basin in Michigan, Williston Basin in North Dakota, and Permian Basin in Texas. In Europe, the Paris Basin extends southwest

from the Ardennes in southern Belgium to the Collines de Perch of Normandy in France. Many of these basins are hundreds of miles across and contain thick deposits of sedimentary rock.

FAULTED STRUCTURES
Almost all surface rock contains fractures or joints from expansion as erosion removes over-lying layers, but faulted structures represent past or present tectonic stress. Tremendous energy is required to overcome the strength of rocks and to cause the offset along a fracture that defines a fault. There is some gap between the two sides of a fault, but faults are mostly

two-dimensional features that are planes of contact between two displaced areas of rocks.

The movement that creates fault displacement can be extremely abrupt or very slow depending on the kind of tectonic stress involved, the rock's strength, the presence of groundwater along the **fault plane**, and the area of contact. Abrupt movement causes earthquakes, but in some cases, the rate of movement along a fault is so imperceptible that it is referred to as **fault creep**. (See Earthquakes, page 146.) In either case, cumulative movements can extend over hundreds of miles; along California's San Andreas Fault, matching rock layers have been found 350 miles apart.

A fault is classified according to the relative displacement of its two sides: Traditionally the side of a fault that tilts downward is called the **footwall**, and the ceiling is called the **hanging wall**. Distinct stresses related to different tectonic boundaries cause a footwall to move up, down, sideways, or in some combination of these movements relative to the hanging wall.

Normal faults, the most common type of fault, occur when the hanging wall slides down relative to the footwall. Tension associated with divergent boundaries and with the stretching of rock layers from warping up, or doming, causes normal faulting. Large areas can be affected by tension from these processes, and as a result normal faults usually occur in groups; rift valleys, such as the Great Rift Valley in East Africa, can have stepped sides from parallel normal faulting. If movements along the fault are slow, there may be no easily noticed resultant landforms; erosion and deposition will hide the displacement. More abrupt movements will create a **scarp**, or wall, where the upper part of the footwall is exposed. An 1819 earthquake near the mouth of the Indus River in India created a scarp almost 50 miles long and as much as 20 feet high; called the

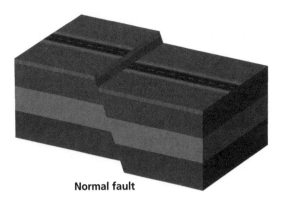

Normal fault

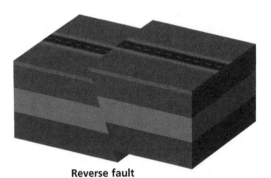

Reverse fault

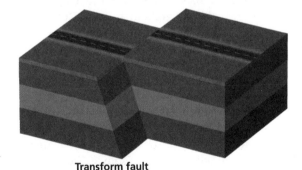

Transform fault

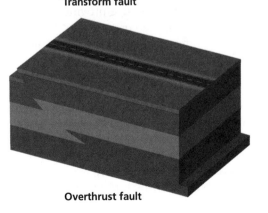

Overthrust fault

Hanging Walls and Footwalls

The names for the sides of faults were coined by miners who discovered that faults contained valuable minerals such as gold and silver. Hydrothermal solutions containing metals, including silver, lead, and zinc, form veins where they followed the easiest paths through rock, and faults allowed the fluids easy circulation. As miners dug down a fault, they named the side on which they walked, the footwall; and the side on which they hung their lanterns, the hanging wall. (See Diagram opposite)

Allah Bund, Dam of Allah, it caused the Indus to flood the region.

Multiple, parallel faults associated with divergent boundaries create horsts, grabens, and fault-block mountains. **Horsts** are linear ridges or land uplifted between parallel faults, and **grabens** are linear valleys that slipped down between parallel faults. The Black Forest in Germany and the Sinai Peninsula are horsts, and the Rhine Valley in Germany and Death Valley, California, are grabens. Grabens may become lakes because they drain adjacent areas; Lake Baikal in Siberia, the deepest lake in the world, is a graben, as is the Dead Sea.

Fault-block mountains form when blocks of land are tilted between parallel faults. This occurs when thousands of square miles come under tension by divergence or regional uplifting; the Aberdare Range in Kenya and the Tetons in the United States are classic examples. Ranges of fault-block mountains have formed in many of the world's large plateau areas, including those in Bolivia, Tibet, and Iran. The Basin and Range province in Nevada and Utah is composed of a series of fault-block mountain ranges between basins, or valleys. Uplift from rising magma may have caused the tension; another explanation for this tension lies in the change the west coast of the continent underwent 30 million years ago, moving from a convergent boundary to a transform boundary.

Reverse and thrust faults are caused when convergence forces a hanging wall to move up relative to its footwall. If the fault plane is close to vertical, most of the movement will also be vertical, and a **reverse fault**—compared to the movement on a normal fault—occurs. When the fault plane is within 45 degrees of horizontal, however, much of the movement is also horizontal, and a **thrust fault** results.

Thrust faults are often found in regions of extreme folding; when recumbent folds are compressed more, the fold material may break off and move sideways, forming a thrust fault.

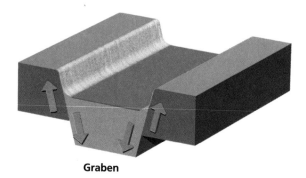

Graben

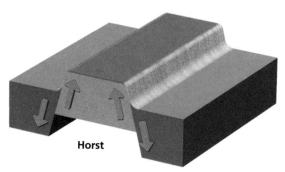

Horst

Grabens are linear valleys that slipped down between two parallel faults. **Horsts** are linear ridges between parallel faults.

The San Andreas fault slashes through California for more than 700 miles. The zone marks the boundary between the North American and Pacific tectonic plates.

Strike-slip faults below are formed by sideways displacement along vertical faults.

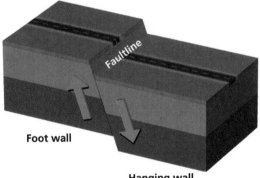

Foot wall

Hanging wall

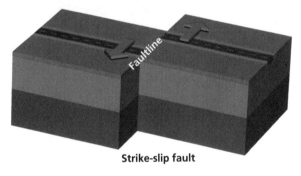

Strike-slip fault

Major mountain ranges have numerous thrust faults: The Alps are noted for having multiple layers of thrust faults caused by the convergence of the African and Eurasian plates. In Montana, the Lewis Overthrust moved a rock layer 30 miles eastward, where erosion has since isolated the end of the layer as Chief Mountain.

Strike-slip faults involve sideways displacement along nearly vertical faults. The shear stress that causes strike-slip faults is associated primarily with transform boundaries, although divergent boundaries on ocean floors also have numerous strike-slip faults. Different segments of a diverging plate can move at

slightly different rates, allowing some sideways displacement between faster- and slower-moving segments. Strike-slip faults can be either right-lateral or left-lateral, depending on whether the opposite side of the fault is displaced to the right or left. The Great Glen Fault in Scotland and the Dead Sea Fault are left-lateral faults. The San Andreas Fault is a right-lateral, because the coast of southern California moves right, or north, relative to the mainland. Lateral displacement offsets drainage patterns and rock formations, but does not create major landforms such as mountains.

Earthquakes

Earthquakes are vibrations caused by movement of rock along a fault. They are unavoidable effects of Earth's tectonic movements, and the pattern of earthquakes around the world nearly matches plate boundaries. More earthquakes occur along convergent and transform boundaries, where rocks are cold and more brittle, than along divergent boundaries, where rising magma warms rocks and makes them more pliant. Most earthquakes not occurring on current plate boundaries—such as the New Madrid earthquakes in Missouri in 1811–12, the Nova Scotia quake in 1929, and the 1886 quake in South Carolina—are responding to stress from a boundary hundreds of miles away or are associated with former tectonic boundaries. Other events cause surface vibrations—including bomb explosions, impacts of large meteorites, and even magma rising toward a volcano—but the release of tectonic stress along faults causes the majority of earthquakes.

Only a limited area of a fault—the **focus**—is under sufficient stress to move at any one time, causing an earthquake. Most foci are miles underground, so for mapping purposes geologists locate an **epicenter** on the surface directly above the focus. Occasionally the focus of an earthquake has included surface faulting: During the 1906 San Francisco earthquake, fences that had been built across the fault line were torn in half. When the focus shifts, the stress that had accumulated there is redistributed to adjacent areas of the fault. Rocks at the focus undergo **elastic rebound**, vibrations caused by shifting, as they adjust to a loss of stress, and nearby areas undergo small shifts known as **aftershocks** when they adjust to the redistribution of stress.

Most earthquakes occur in crustal rock within 40 miles of Earth's surface, although a few foci have been recorded as deep as 435 miles. In order for an earthquake to occur, rock must be brittle enough to break and shift along a fault; at greater depths increased heat and pressure cause rock to fold or flow instead of break and fault. Along convergent boundaries involving an oceanic plate, the foci of earthquakes follow the Benioff zone, the boundary between the subducting plate and the mantle, and correspond to the depth of the subducted plate. Of the more than one million earthquakes each year, the largest ones tend to occur closer to the surface.

Vibrations in and on Earth during an earthquake are caused by energy waves that radiate from the focus. Earthquake waves are either **surface waves**, which travel along Earth's surface, or **body waves**, which travel through the interior of Earth. Two types of surface waves—Love and Rayleigh waves—are especially important because they cause most of the damage directly associated with earthquakes. Hough Love (1863–1940) and physicist John William Strutt, third Baron Rayleigh (1842–1919), were English scientists who

A Three-Minute Earthquake: Alaska's Good Friday Earthquake, 1964

On March 28, 1964, Good Friday, southern Alaska suffered one of the largest earthquakes of the 20th century—8.5 on the Richter scale, or 9.2 magnitude on the moment-magnitude scale. Surface faulting caused some areas to rise more than 12 feet and other areas to subside more than 6 feet; landslides, tsunamis, and liquefaction destroyed homes and killed 131 people. Ordinarily, earthquakes last less than 60 seconds—the 1906 San Francisco earthquake, 8.3 on the Richter scale or 7.7 magnitude, lasted 40 seconds—but the Good Friday earthquake lasted more than three minutes, evidence of the large amount of energy that had accumulated.

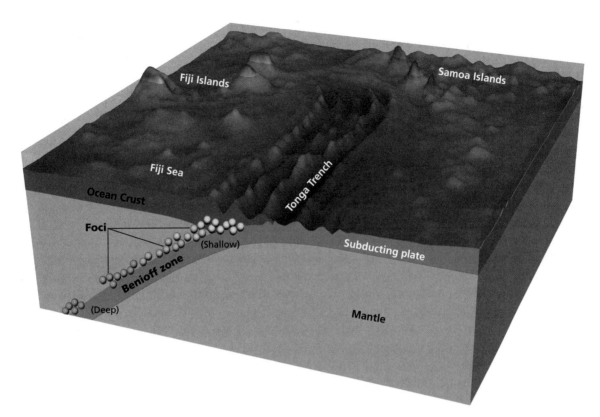

A cross section of the Tonga region of the South Pacific reveals the **Benioff zone,** the boundary between the subducting plate and the mantle. The **foci** of earthquakes follow the Benioff zone. Earthquakes with foci near the surface tend to be the strongest.

discovered the waves. **Love waves** have a shear or sideways motion on the surface, whereas **Rayleigh waves** move vertically, more like ocean waves.

The two types of body waves are especially important because seismologists can use them to triangulate earthquake epicenters: **Primary** or **P waves** are compressional body waves; they are faster than **secondary** or **S waves**, which are shear body waves. Seismographs register P and S waves and record the time that each arrived; the difference in arrival time can be translated into the distance from the seismograph station to the epicenter because the speeds of the two body waves are known. In the granite crust, P waves travel at an average rate of about 13,400 miles per hour, and S waves average about 8,000 miles per hour. Locating the epicenter of an earthquake requires triangulation—using the distances from a minimum of three stations to chart circles and find their intersection.

EARTHQUAKE SCALES

Scientists around the world use various scales to measure the size of earthquakes. The Japanese use the Wadati scale and Russians use the Medvedev scale. In the United States the moment-magnitude scale and the modified Mercalli scale are now used more frequently than the Richter scale. The moment-magnitude scale, developed by Hiro Kanamori and Thomas Hanks, is more accurate for large earthquakes than Charles Richter's scale,

Modified Mercalli Intensity Scale

I   Not felt except by a very few under especially favorable circumstances.

II   Felt only by a few persons at rest, especially on upper floors of buildings.

III   Felt quite noticeably indoors, especially on upper floors of buildings, but many people do not recognize it as an earthquake.

IV   During the day felt indoors by many, outdoors by few. Sensation like heavy truck striking building.

V   Felt by nearly everyone, many awakened. Disturbances of trees, poles, and other tall objects sometimes noticed.

VI   Felt by all; many frightened and run outdoors. Some heavy furniture moved; few instances of fallen plaster or damaged chimneys. Damage slight.

VII   Everybody runs outdoors. Damage negligible in buildings of good design and construction; slight to moderate in well-built ordinary structures; considerable in poorly built or badly designed structures.

VIII   Damage slight in specially designed structures; considerable in ordinary substantial buildings with partial collapse; great in poorly built structures. (Fall of chimneys, factory stacks, columns, monuments, walls.)

IX   Damage considerable in specially designed structures. Buildings shifted off foundations. Ground cracked conspicuously.

X   Some well-built wooden structures destroyed. Most masonry and frame structures destroyed. Ground badly cracked.

XI   Few, if any (masonry) structures remain standing. Bridges destroyed. Broad fissures in ground.

XII   Damage total. Waves seen on ground surfaces. Objects thrown upward into air.

---

designed in 1935 to determine the **magnitude**, or stress release, of an earthquake by measuring the amplitude of the S wave on a seismogram. The **moment-magnitude scale** is based on the seismic moment—the area of rock displaced, the rigidity of that rock, and the average distance of displacement.

In the **Richter scale** each increase in scale value, for example from one to two, denotes a tenfold increase in the amplitude of the S wave; however, the amount of energy released increases by 31.5 times for each unit increase in value. Although the Richter scale has no theoretical upper limit, the maximum value is limited by the strength of rocks undergoing tectonic stress and is probably near nine.

In 1902 Italian geologist Giuseppe Mercalli (1850–1914) developed a scale to measure the intensity of earthquakes that was modified by Americans H. O. Wood and Frank Neumann in 1931 and modified again in 1956. Mercalli used a scale of I to XII to measure the

intensity or damage caused by the earthquake: I, no damage; IV, pictures fall off walls and books fall from shelves, for example. The Modified Mercalli scale measures a range of values over a region because the degree of damage from an earthquake depends upon distance from the epicenter, type of bedrock, level of groundwater, and type of construction.

EARTHQUAKE HAZARDS

Destruction and deaths from earthquakes are caused by direct and indirect effects of surface vibrations. Love waves collapse rigid structures that are not designed to resist shear stress. Earthquakes in regions of Iran, Afghanistan, Armenia, and Turkey—where mud-brick construction is standard—are responsible for thousands of deaths due to the collapse of structures.

Indirect effects of earthquakes include liquefaction, landslides, avalanches, fires, and tsunamis. **Liquefaction** refers to the behavior

Comparison of Richter and Mercalli Scales, showing adjustments for famous earthquakes

EARTHQUAKE	RICHTER	MERCALLI
Chile, 1960	8.3	9.5
Alaska, 1964	8.4	9.2
New Madrid, 1812	8.7	8.1
Michoacán, 1985	8.1	8.1
San Francisco, 1906	8.3	7.7
Loma Prieta, 1989	7.1	7.0
Kobe, 1995	6.8	6.9
San Fernando, 1971	6.4	6.7
Northridge, 1994	6.4	6.7

of water-saturated soils when they are shaken by Love waves: Vibrations cause the soils to lose their weight-bearing capacity, allowing structures built on them to collapse. During the 1964 Good Friday earthquake in Alaska, sediment below Turnagain Heights, an Anchorage residential area, liquefied and 70 homes collapsed. Liquefaction contributed to damage at Vanadzor, Armenia, in 1988 and in San Francisco's Marina district in 1989; both places are built on landfills in marshes.

Landslides and **avalanches** result when earthquake vibrations upset the equilibrium of steep slopes in mountainous regions. In 1970 an earthquake in the Peruvian Andes caused a massive avalanche of ice, snow, and rock to break away high on Huascarán, the country's highest peak. The debris buried the town of Yungay in mud and rock, killing almost all its 20,000 inhabitants.

Earthquakes cause fires when water and natural-gas lines and electrical wires break. An earthquake in Japan in 1923 occurred during the noon lunch hour, when hibachis were lit. They were overturned and more than 140,000 people died in Tokyo and Yokohama, primarily in fires in residential areas where most homes were constructed of wood and paper. Fire also caused much of San Francisco's destruction after the 1906 earthquake, and for decades the disaster was referred to as the Great Fire, not the San Francisco earthquake.

Tsunamis, Japanese for harbor waves, are a series of sea waves caused by the vertical displacement of seafloor during an earthquake or volcanic eruption. The waves are sometimes

Alaska's 1964 Good Friday earthquake caused the ground to liquefy and homes to collapse in an Anchorage residential area.

misleadingly called tidal waves. In the Pacific Ocean, water averaging 3 miles deep allows tsunamis to travel more than 400 miles per hour but have wave heights of only a few feet. When tsunamis reach shallower water, friction from the seabed slows the waves, causing their wavelengths to decrease and heights to increase; when they strike a coastline, tsunamis average 30 feet high, and heights greater than 100 feet have been recorded. Tsunamis are most common in the Pacific Ocean because of convergent boundaries surrounding the Pacific plate. The most vulnerable coastlines are Honshu, Japan's northern coast, Hawaii, Alaska, Indonesia, Peru, and Ecuador. The Atlantic and Mediterranean have had memorable but rare tsunamis: The 1755 Lisbon tsunami killed thousands, and more that 8,000 Sicilians were killed by a tsunami in 1908.

Earthquakes are a certainty along tectonic boundaries around the world, and disasters like the July 17, 1998, earthquake and tsunami that killed more than 3,000 in Papua New Guinea are inevitable. In California, the San Andreas Fault in the San Francisco area has not had a substantial earthquake for decades and residents anticipate a big one; unfortunately, this **seismic gap**, the interval without significant earthquakes, means that the earthquake, when it arrives, is likely to be of greater magnitude because stress has been accumulating. The nearby Hayward Fault did generate a substantial earthquake in 1989, with an epicenter south of San Francisco. In southeastern Missouri, the New Madrid Fault, site of three powerful earthquakes in 1811 and 1812, is also accumulating stress that will eventually cause another large earthquake.

Earthquake prediction, by which the timing as well as the location and magnitude of an earthquake can be identified, is not yet a proven science. While some earthquakes have been successfully predicted, prediction is not consistently accurate. Chinese seismologists predicted the 1975 Haicheng earthquake by foreshocks but missed the 1976 Tangshan earthquake that killed 230,000 people. Research focuses on identifying changes that occur prior to an earthquake in **precursor phenomena**, including animal behavior, radon content in groundwater, and ground tilt. Recent studies on changes in the electrical resistance of rocks, caused perhaps by stress on quartz grains, are promising.

Igneous Structures and Volcanoes

Magma heated deep within Earth rises and forms igneous structures below the surface and volcanoes on the surface as a result of tectonic processes and hot spots. Igneous structures such as batholiths result from mantle plumes below the surface and also form near convergent boundaries; volcanoes form on the surface near convergent and divergent boundaries and at hot spots and are potentially serious hazards.

Plumes and Plate Tectonics

Magma rises from the upper mantle toward Earth's surface, where it creates and influences landforms. Mantle plumes, convergent boundaries, and divergent boundaries cause magma to form and rise. In order for mantle to melt, either temperatures must increase by about 400°F above the temperature of surrounding rock or pressure must decrease so that the

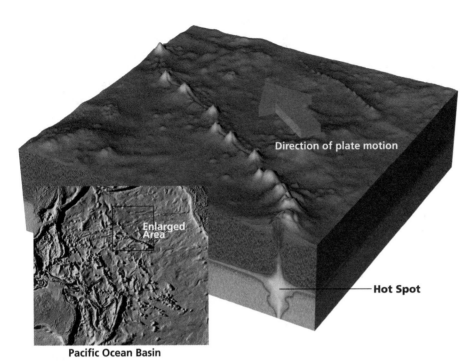

Direction of plate motion

Hot Spot

Pacific Ocean Basin

Enlarged Area

The islands and seamounts that stretch across the Pacific Ocean from the Hawaiian and Midway Islands to the Aleutian Islands increase in age toward the northwest, revealing the movement of the Pacific plate over a hot spot in the Earth's crust.

magma will become less dense and rise slowly through surrounding rock. Rock under high pressure remains solid, but once pressure decreases, it melts; on average, partial melting begins at a depth of 15 miles.

Geologists in the 1960s discovered that columns of heated material hundreds of miles in diameter rise from the boundary between the outer core and the mantle. When the molten outer core heats a section of the lower mantle it causes a column of heated rock, a **mantle plume**, to rise toward the surface at a rate of several inches to several feet each year. As the plume rises, pressure decreases, allowing some of the plume to melt as it continues to rise. (See Decompression Melting, page 152.)

The shape of a mantle plume changes as it rises toward—and eventually contacts—the lithosphere. In the mantle, a plume rises as a column with a slighter larger top. When the plume approaches the rigid lithosphere, the plume's top flattens out to a disklike form that can be 1,000 to 1,500 miles across and 100

miles thick. Below the top, the rising column or tail retains its columnar shape.

When magma from a plume reaches the lithosphere the spreading top of the plume causes the overlying lithosphere to bulge upward as much as 2,000 feet to form a huge plateau in the overlying plate. Faulting or rifting may begin, while magma extruded as lava pours from the rifts to cover the plateau with layers of basalt, adding height to the plateau. Unless the heat supply continues, the tail of the plume will reach the lithosphere in several million years, uplift will diminish, and lava will flow from a vent instead of a rift, creating a volcano. Eventually, after perhaps a hundred million years, the heat supply for the plume is exhausted, and magma will cease to rise to the surface.

Hot spots form at Earth's surface above mantle plumes. Mantle plumes and their surface hot spots are fixed in position above their source areas within continental and oceanic tectonic plates. As plates shift, however, landforms such as volcanoes, island arcs, and seamounts (underwater volcanoes) created above the hot spots move with the plates much like boxes on a conveyer belt.

The Galápagos in the Pacific and the Azores in the Atlantic are the result of hot-spot activity, and **flood basalts**, huge lava flows formed by past hot spots, exist in Siberia, Brazil, and India. Mantle plumes have created plateaus that cover much of the ocean floor. Active hot spots on continents are rare; the Yellowstone region of Montana, Wyoming, and Idaho is one of the few in North America.

Island chains formed by hot spots can be used to calculate the speed and direction of tectonic plate movement; scientists compare the ages and locations of past hot-spot landforms with the location of a hot spot today. In the Pacific, the chain of islands and **seamounts**, submerged volcanoes, gets progressively older from Hawaii to the northwest, past Midway to the Aleutian Islands. This indicates that the Pacific plate has been moving to the northwest at about four inches a year. Oahu is about 2.5 million years older than the big island of Hawaii. The movement of the Pacific plate was to the north until 43 million years ago, as indicated by the pattern and the ages of islands along the Emperor Seamount.

Magma created by subduction at convergent boundaries forms igneous bodies and surface volcanic landforms in the neighborhood of 60 or more miles away from and parallel to the convergent boundary. This happens because the subducted plate is not heated enough to form magma until it sinks about 100 miles below the surface, at which depth it has moved about 60 miles horizontally. The subducted plate tilts down into the mantle at angles ranging from 15 to 75 degrees, so the horizontal distance from the convergent boundary to the rising magma will vary.

Where plates diverge, a low-pressure zone is created that causes magma to form from **decompression melting** of hot mantle rock. At greater depths in the mantle, rock cannot fully melt because pressure is too great, even though the temperatures would melt rock at the surface; however, when the mantle rock nears the surface, pressure decreases and magma forms, welling up as it heats and expands.

When lava emerges through a fissure along a divergent boundary, the fissure may lie above a magma chamber that can average 0.5 mile to 3 miles wide, and it will have an inner core of magma. As plates continue to diverge, they widen the opening. Magma against the walls cools, adding a layer inside the fissure and chamber while lava continues to flow onto the surface from the opening marking the boundary. As a result, the fissure and chamber retain their dimensions. In addition to lava flowing from the opening, some lava may flow through vents along the boundary or flow from small volcanoes.

Plutons

Magma cools in chambers and openings below Earth's surface called **plutons**. Erosion and isostatic uplift may eventually expose the buried plutons. The igneous rocks that form plutons are often more resistant to erosion than surrounding sedimentary rocks, so plutons tend to form mountains, hills, or ridges in the landscape. Inclusions of country rock in plutons are called **xenoliths**.

Plutons are classified by their shape and relationship to the country rock. Massive plutons are **discordant**, or unshaped by the country rock, while flat, tabular plutons are **concordant**, or parallel to the country rock. **Batholiths**, the most massive plutons, have a minimum of 40 square miles of exposed surface. They are discordant and usually composed of felsic igneous rock, mostly granites and diorites. The Idaho Batholith covers more than 15,000 square miles and may have formed when a number of batholiths coalesced. Batholiths are created by converging boundaries and mantle plumes; the largest batholiths are formed when continental plates and oceanic plates converge. A **stock** is smaller than a pluton, with less than 40 square

The distinctive granite cliffs of the Yosemite Valley in California are part of the Sierra Nevada batholith.

miles of exposed igneous rock—usually granite and diorite. Stocks may be attached to or an extension of a batholith; Mount Ellsworth in Utah's Henry Mountains is a stock.

Most eroded mountains and continental shields include batholiths and stocks. Batholiths that formed 100 million years ago on the west coast of North America, from Baja California to the Alaska Panhandle, are now eroded mountain ranges. The Piedmont region of the Appalachians includes batholiths emplaced more than 300 million years ago.

The second type of pluton is **tabular**, or relatively flat, and may be concordant or discordant. Most tabular plutons form from the magma of a large chamber, which, when it cools completely, may form a batholith. Massive and tabular plutonic bodies are therefore often located near each other. Concordant tabular plutons form when magma follows bedding planes between sedimentary rocks; discordant plutons form when magma follows fractures in rocks that the magma chamber helped create by expanding and uplifting the country rock.

Laccoliths, lopoliths, and sills are concordant tabular plutons, but differences in their magma composition give each a different shape. A **laccolith** forms when viscous felsic magma is forced between rock layers and piles up in a mushroom shape, sometimes several miles across. On the surface the uplifted sedimentary rock and eventually the exposed laccolith can create a small mountain range, such as the Black Hills of South Dakota and Wyoming.

Lopoliths and sills form from more mafic and less viscous magma and therefore are flatter than laccoliths. **Lopoliths** are large, concave plutons injected up into country rock, and whose weight contributes to the sinking of the country rock. The Duluth lopolith beneath Lake Superior is 150 miles across, and the Bushveldt lopolith complex in South Africa is more than 100 miles across.

Sills are small and far more common than lopoliths. Unlike lopoliths, they form horizontally, varying in width from inches to hundreds of yards, and form only within 1 to 1.5 miles of the surface. Sills are common throughout mountain and shield regions. The Palisades along the Hudson River and the Giant's Causeway in Ireland are classic examples of

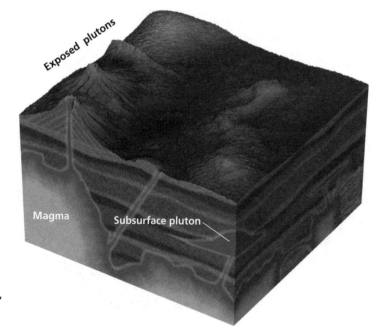

Magmatic plutons are formed when magma cools and hardens beneath the Earth's surface. As the surface is uplifted or eroded, these hard, igneous plutons are exposed, often taking the form of mountains, hills, and ridges.

sills; part of Hadrian's Wall in northeastern England is built upon the Great Whin Sill.

Dikes are the only major discordant tabular plutons and may be the most common plutonic bodies. Dikes are likely to form when a magma chamber fractures rocks, especially rocks at the surface. Different magmas can form dikes, but mafic magmas and basalt dikes are most common because felsic magmas are too viscous to flow easily. Generally, dikes and sills are similar in size, but dikes can be much larger. The Great Dike of Zimbabwe is 300 miles long and several miles thick.

Volcanic **pipes** or necks are cylindrical rem-

nants of conduits from magma chambers to the surface. In some cases, pipes are filled with erosion-resistant igneous rock that becomes isolated peaks in the landscape as weaker country rock is eroded away. Devils Tower, Wyoming, and Shiprock, New Mexico, are excellent examples. Other pipes that do not form prominent surface features may instead contain unusual minerals below the surface: Kimberlite pipes, such as those near Kimberly, South Africa, and pipes discovered in northern Canada during the 1990s, are sources for diamonds.

Gettysburg, Pennsylvania

Exposed plutonic bodies became strategically important during the Civil War battle at Gettysburg in 1863. Union troops camped on Cemetery Hill, an exposed sill, while Confederate troops were on Seminary Ridge, an exposed dike. These plutons provided each side with high ground, and Confederate troops led by Maj. Gen. George Pickett had to charge up Cemetery Ridge in their unsuccessful attempt to dislodge Union forces. The ironstone each side used to build walls was basalt from these two plutons.

Volcanic Landforms

When lava erupts onto Earth's surface from underlying magma chambers, it accumulates into different features or volcanic landforms according to whether the lava is felsic or mafic and whether the shape of the opening through which it emerges is a large, linear fissure or a small, circular vent. Volcanoes are landforms composed of lavas and other volcanic debris that flow or erupt onto Earth's surface; igneous structures such as plutons form beneath the surface and are exposed only by erosion.

Felsic lavas are more viscous and tend to contain more water vapor and other dissolved gases than mafic lavas. As a result, felsic lava does not flow easily; it explodes upon eruption. Mafic lavas are less viscous because they lack silicates and maintain a temperature averaging more than 1,700°F, enabling them to flow more readily and farther; they are less explosive on extrusion than felsic lavas. Linear fissures allow lava to cover larger areas than do vents. Mafic lava in eastern Washington has been found more than a hundred miles from its source.

Lava that flows from a fissure above a mantle plume forms **plateau basalts**, or **flood basalts**, and they may form on ocean floors or continents. Mafic lava from fissures at divergent boundaries between oceanic plates forms seafloor and mid-ocean ridges. A plateau basalt is composed of hundreds of layers of lava, each of which may be a hundred feet thick, from successive episodes of extrusion. The more than two-million-square-mile Ontong-Java Plateau east of the Solomon Islands is the largest basalt plateau on an ocean floor. Iceland lies over a hot spot as well as a divergent boundary and, as a result, is a volcanic island built on top of a huge flood basalt. Part of the same flood basalts cover eastern Greenland and northwestern Scotland and Ireland because the hot spot preceded the divergence that formed the northern Atlantic Ocean. (See Plate Tectonics, page 130.)

Tectonic shifting has moved many areas of flood basalts, sometimes called trap landscapes (from Swedish *trappa*, meaning "staircase"), away from the hot spots that created them. The Columbia River Plateau in North America formed 17 million years ago; since then the westward movement of the North American plate has caused the hot spot that created the plateau to shift eastward 500 miles to the Yellowstone region, where the tail of the mantle plume now creates geysers, hot springs, and an occasional huge explosion. The most recent explosion 620,000 years ago formed the Yellowstone Caldera and deposited ash over what is now the western U.S. Other flood basalts, including the Deccan of western India, between Bombay and Hyderabad, the Paraná in Brazil, and the Karoo in South Africa, also formed over hot spots that now lie elsewhere.

When lava, ash, and cinders erupt from a circular vent and accumulate around the opening, they form a **volcano**. Volcanoes are classified as shield volcanoes, cinder cones, or composite volcanoes, also called stratovolcanoes, depending upon whether the lava is mafic or felsic. The type of lava causes different shapes and sizes of volcanoes, and it also affects

Cascade Range Volcanoes

Mount St. Helens in Washington, like Mount Rainier, Mount Baker, and Glacier Peak, was one of several Cascade volcanoes scientists considered to be potentially dangerous prior to its dramatic eruption in 1980. St. Helens had last erupted in 1857, and it has been studied intensively since 1980 to understand its effects and potential for further eruption. California and western Oregon also face the threat of eruptions from volcanoes such as Mount Hood, 40 miles southeast of Portland, and Mount Lassen in northern California.

how explosive eruptions will be. Volcanoes are also classified as **active** (expected to erupt), **dormant** (capable of erupting), and **extinct** (incapable of erupting). Fewer than 1,500 of the 20,000 or so volcanoes on Earth are considered active; 550 of the active volcanoes are continental and the remainder are oceanic.

Shield volcanoes are the largest volcanoes on Earth and have slopes of only 10 degrees or so, with round bases shaped like shields. When the tail of a mantle plume under an oceanic plate reaches the ocean floor, a smaller column of rising magma may exit through a vent rather than through a fissure. This lava is extremely mafic and flows easily: Thousands of layers may accumulate over time and build up a volcano that rises miles above sea level. Mauna Loa, the largest volcano on the island of Hawaii, rises more than six miles from the ocean floor, and its base is more than a hundred miles wide.

Earth's shield volcanoes have formed primarily in the Pacific and Atlantic Oceans, because the two largest oceans contain the most hot spots, sources for magma. Many of these volcanoes are in linear patterns because, as a tectonic plate moves over a mantle plume,

the plate transports its volcanoes away from the plume as the next in the series of volcanoes form. Easter Island, Samoa, and the Galápagos Islands are Pacific Ocean shield volcanoes; Atlantic Ocean shield volcanoes include St. Helena, the Azores, and Bermuda.

Cinder cones are the smallest volcanoes, usually under a thousand feet high, and form over the tails of mantle plumes beneath continents. As magma melts through continental crust, it becomes more felsic: When silicate-enhanced magma reaches the surface, it has enhanced viscosity and tends to erupt explosively, ejecting cinders, ash, and other fragments. As fragments accumulate near the vent, they form a steep-sided hill with slopes between 30 and 40 degrees. Most cinder cones erode quickly and disappear from the landscape because they are piles of unconsolidated sediment. Paricutín, a cinder cone west of Mexico City, is famous because scientists were able to observe its formation between 1943 to 1952.

Most of the world's best-known volcanoes are **composite** volcanoes, formed from mafic and felsic lavas; they are large, steep-sided mountains found near coastlines and as islands in oceans. Subduction along convergent

The Mauna Loa volcano on the island of Hawaii rises more than six miles from the ocean floor. A shield volcano built layer by layer over time, Mauna Loa is still active and growing.

boundaries provides the magma that rises to form composite volcanoes. While the magma is mostly felsic, it may also combine melted mafic mantle and melted felsic sediments, and it may erupt as cinders and ash as well as flowing lava. Composite volcanoes tend to have the conical shape of a cinder cone but are larger because of lava flows. Mount Rainier, Washington, is more than 2 miles high and has a base 14 miles in diameter.

Composite volcanoes, like shield volcanoes, often occur in linear patterns because they parallel the convergent boundaries that formed them. There are chains of volcanoes along the west coasts of Central America, South America, and the Pacific Northwest, where the Cocos, Nazca, and Juan de Fuca plates are being subducted. The west side of the Pacific Ocean is also lined with composite volcanoes where the Pacific plate is subducted; the **Ring of Fire**, a nearly complete arc of volcanoes, circles much of the Pacific Ocean. Other lines of composite volcanoes are found in Indonesia and the Caribbean, with smaller concentrations in Italy and in the southern Sandwich Islands near the Falklands.

Volcanic Eruptions

Volcanic eruptions pose a serious and increasing hazard to humans, though not all active volcanoes and not all types of eruptions are dangerous. Many volcanoes, such as those in southern Alaska, are far from urban development and pose little threat to populations. In 1990, aircraft were threatened by high clouds of ash when they flew over erupting Redoubt Volcano southwest of Anchorage. Some eruptions, especially those of shield volcanoes, involve slow lava flows that miss development or can be diverted by barriers. During the 1973 eruption of Eldfell on Heimaey, Iceland, officials pumped seawater onto lava to cool and solidify it before it reached their homes in Vestmannaeyjar.

Eruptions can be classified based on the characteristics of past eruptions of specific volcanoes. Shield volcanoes may have Icelandic- or Hawaiian-type eruptions, which primarily involve lava flows. Hawaiian eruptions release more dissolved gases than Icelandic eruptions and can cause small ash falls. Eruptions of composite volcanoes can range from Strombolian—named for Stromboli, a volcano on an island of the same name off the west coast of Italy—which have moderate explosions and mostly steam eruptions, to ultra-Plinian, such as Vesuvius in A.D. 79, or Krakatoan for the Indonesian eruption in 1883, which are the largest types of explosive eruption.

Volcanic hazards include a number of secondary effects, such as tsunamis and landslides, but the primary effects involve the fall or flow of volcanic debris. Lava flows can cause substantial damage to property and land but cause few deaths. Few lava flows travel faster than five or ten miles per hour, although in 1977 the eruption of Nyiragonga in Zaire destroyed 400 houses and killed more than 70 people when lava spread at speeds reaching 25 miles per hour.

Lahars, volcanic mudflows, occur when water mixes with ash and cinders; the water can be from snow and glaciers melted by an eruption, from rain, or from the eruption of a water-filled crater. Lahars may be responsible for more than 10 percent of all volcano-related deaths; the 1985 lahar associated with the eruption of Nevado del Ruíz in Colombia killed more than 22,000 people. Both shield and composite volcanoes have generated lahars, and deaths have occurred in Iceland, Indonesia (the source of the term), Costa Rica, and the United States. The threat of future disasters is significant because lahars can be repetitive; the Seattle-Tacoma metropolitan area has expanded into a region that was covered by a lahar from Mount Rainier 500 years ago.

Pyroclastic falls, including ash, cinders, and larger fragments such as bombs and blocks, are associated with composite volcanoes whose magma is viscous and often sticks in its vent, causing explosive eruptions. The

The eruption of Mount St. Helens in Washington State in 1980 spread a hazardous cloud of super-heated gases and pyroclastic fragments known as nuée ardente.

eruption of Vesuvius in A.D. 79 is perhaps the best known example because the ash and cinders preserved Pompeii and the forms of some of the 16,000 victims. This century, pyroclastic falls have killed people in Guatemala, Indonesia, Italy (Vesuvius again), the Philippines, and the United States; many of the victims of the Mount St. Helens 1980 eruption died of asphyxiation from ash.

Eruptions have released toxic gases dissolved in magma and lava into the atmosphere and have been responsible for thousands of deaths this century. Carbon dioxide and sulfur oxides are among the more common gases, although hydrogen sulfide and other gases have also been emitted. Cameroon, in Africa, had nearly 2,000 deaths in 1986 when Lake Nyos, a crater filled with water, released carbon dioxide; Lake Manoun, a nearby crater, caused almost 40 deaths in 1984 by toxic gases.

One of the deadliest hazards from erupting volcanoes is a **nuée ardente**, a glowing cloud of superheated gases and pyroclastic fragments that can travel more than one hundred miles per hour. A nuée ardente usually explodes from the side of a composite volcano and may travel outward more than ten miles. The 1902 eruption of Mount Pelée on Martinique killed 29,000 people almost instantaneously and is the best known nuée ardente; others have occurred in Alaska, the Philippines, and New Guinea, where 3,000 people died in 1951 during the eruption of Mount Lamington.

Tsunamis caused by eruptions have resulted in thousands of deaths, including the coastal population of Crete when Santorini, an island volcano to the north, erupted in 1530 B.C. The explosive eruption that obliterated Krakatoa in 1883 killed more than 32,000 people. Famines may follow eruptions because ashfall may kill livestock and bury crops. Iceland suffered a famine in 1783, following the fissure eruption of Laki; 10,000 people and 130,000 head of livestock died.

Landforms and Landscapes

Weathering and Mass Wasting

Landforms are the visible record of geomorphic processes and part of the **landscape**, the natural and man-made surface features in a region. **Geomorphology** is the study of Earth's surface features; geomorphic processes include tectonic activity and volcanism, which may uplift land, and **gradation**, processes of weathering, mass wasting, and erosion that lower land. Streams, glaciers, waves, and wind erode, move, and deposit surface materials after weathering and mass wasting have already been at work and are treated separately.

Weathering

Weathering is a geomorphic process that disintegrates and decomposes surface rock and soil by physical and chemical processes. When rocks that were formed underground—at pressures and temperatures unlike those found at the surface and without the presence of atmospheric gases or surface water—reach the surface, they weather as they are exposed to rain, ice, snow, and wind. The minerals that comprise rocks and the rocks themselves are affected by changes in environment when they are exposed at the surface. Rocks disintegrate through mechanical processes, such as frost

action and root growth; they decompose chemically when mineral components change through oxidation, hydration, and solution.

The products of weathering include fragments of rocks, sediments, and dissolved ions. **Talus** and **scree**, boulders and rock fragments that break off from a cliff, accumulate at the cliff's base. Sand, silt, and clay-size sediments form from weathered rocks and become the basis of soils. (See Soils, page 218.) The mineral components of some rocks are soluble and can be dissolved by acidic water and transported in solution elsewhere. They can be precipitated as the basis for chemical sedimentary rocks or withdrawn by plants for nutrients. (See Sedimentary Rocks and Resources, page 127.)

There are two types of weathering: physical (or mechanical) and chemical. **Physical weathering** involves mechanical forces that break rocks into smaller pieces. **Chemical weathering** changes the mineral components of rocks into more stable minerals; for example, hematite, composed of iron and oxygen, becomes limonite, which is iron, oxygen, and water. Chemical weathering also dissolves soluble minerals, such as halite, into ions, which wash away. For example, when calcite dissolves, calcium and carbonate ions are formed. Both types of weathering affect man-made structures as well as rocks: Clay brick

The striking landforms seen in Bryce Canyon National Park, Utah, were formed by weathering, which gradually disintegrates and decomposes surface rocks.

eventually spalls when its outer layer flakes off because of physical weathering, and marble gravestones become unreadable over time because of chemical weathering.

Physical and chemical weathering interact, thus increasing each other's impact. Chemical weathering acts on the surface area of rocks, and physical weathering increases the surface area subject to weathering. When a block of rock is broken into eighths, the volume of rock remains the same but the surface area doubles. Physical weathering breaks rocks into fragments and sediments more readily when chemical weathering has weakened the rock by creating softer, less-resistant minerals.

PHYSICAL WEATHERING

The expansion of salt crystals, roots, and freezing water within a fracture or pore in a rock is a primary mechanism for breaking the rock into fragments. **Frost action**, also called ice wedging, is the most common example of expansion as a physical weathering process and occurs wherever there is water and the range of temperatures includes a freeze-thaw cycle. When water freezes, the molecules realign and expand about 9 percent in volume; in rock fractures, as in water pipes where water is confined, this expansion can create a force up to 1,400 pounds per square inch. Rock fractures are initially extremely small, so repeated freezing and thawing must occur before a crack expands enough to break off the outer part of the rock.

Salt-crystal growth is another example of physical weathering by expansion. Salt dissolved in water precipitates as the water evaporates and eventually accumulates as crystals of calcite, gypsum, and halite. Over time, as evaporation continues, the accumulation and growth of salt crystals within rock fractures can exert enough force to break off small fragments. Roots of trees growing in cracks in cliffs can expand as they grow and exert enough pressure to widen a fracture in a rock and break it, much the same way as tree roots buckle concrete sidewalks and streets.

Removing pressure from rocks can, like applying pressure through expansion, cause physical weathering. Rock formed under thousands of pounds of atmospheric pressure below the surface can undergo **unloading** when exposed to the much lower pressures at the surface. For example, as Stone Mountain, Georgia, was uncovered by millions of years of erosion, the granite batholith expanded because there was less pressure compressing the rock. The outer layer of the granite expands the most and can break off from the underlying rounded body of rock to form an **exfoliation dome;** this process, combined with glaciation, created Half Dome in Yosemite National Park, California.

Water that repeatedly freezes and thaws in rock cracks can ultimately break up the rocks, another example of physical weathering.

Patterned Ground

In polar regions and other regions of **permafrost,** where the subsurface is permanently frozen so that only the upper three to ten feet of soil thaws during summer, frost action creates a landform called patterned ground. Daily and seasonal freeze-thaw cycles cause lenses of ice to form below the surface. When the lenses expand as part of the freeze-thaw cycle, they cause low mounds to form on the surface; cobbles—rocks up to ten inches in diameter—and pebbles are also pushed to the surface. Once on the surface, rocks roll or slide away from a mound's center and form stone rings or polygons depending on the spacing of the mounds.

As the massive granite batholith forming Stone Mountain near Atlanta, Georgia, was uncovered by erosion, the granite expanded and and eventually formed an exfoliation dome. Stone Mountain rises about 700 feet above the relatively level surrounding landscape.

CHEMICAL WEATHERING

Chemical weathering occurs when water or atmospheric gases come in contact with the surface of a rock and change its mineral composition. Most chemical weathering takes place in the presence of water in which atmospheric gases are dissolved and within a dozen or so feet of Earth's surface. In climates with higher temperatures and higher precipitation, the rate of chemical weathering speeds up because the greater heat energy generally increases the rate of most chemical reactions. In humid tropical climates, chemical weathering can extend several hundred feet below Earth's surface; in deserts, chemical weathering may be limited to a depth of a few feet.

Chemical weathering causes minerals to change into different, usually softer, minerals or to divide into soluble ions. Hydrolysis, hydration, and oxidation often occur together, changing mineral composition and forming new types of minerals. **Hydrolysis** occurs when hydrogen ions contained in water (in Greek, *hydro*) replace ions in minerals; for example, some feldspars become clay minerals when hydrogen replaces potassium ions. **Hydration** results when a water molecule combines with one mineral and changes it into another mineral: With water, the sulfate mineral anhydrite becomes gypsum, a soft mineral used to make plaster. **Oxidation** occurs when oxygen combines with an ion; hematite, the red form of rust, is created when oxygen and iron combine. These three types of chemical weathering are closely linked: For example, hydrolysis will free iron ions from minerals; oxidation then changes the iron into hematite, after which hydration may change red rust (hematite) into yellow rust (limonite).

Chemical weathering by **solution** divides soluble minerals into ions, which can be removed by flowing water. Minerals such as gypsum, originally formed by the evaporation of oceans, usually dissolve easily. Solution always involves water and most often acids; water combines with dissolved gases and other ions to form carbonic acid, sulfuric acid, or **humic acid**, an acid formed by ions released from decomposing vegetation. Carbonic acid is particularly common in nature because it forms from a combination of water and carbon dioxide, both omnipresent in Earth's atmosphere. Carbonate minerals, such as calcite, which comprises most limestone and marble,

Gossan Zones

In 1993 two geologists working for a private company were in northern Labrador, Canada, searching for gold and diamonds, and discovered what turned out to be a ten-billion-dollar deposit of copper, nickel, and cobalt. While looking for kimberlite deposits, their serendipitous discovery happened when they recognized a rusty red **gossan zone** formed from hydrated iron-oxide minerals on a rock outcrop. Gossan zones (from *gossen*, Cornish for "blood") are associated with the chemical weathering of sulfide minerals such as pentlandite, composed of nickel, iron, and sulfur, and chalcopyrite, made of copper, iron, and sulfur.

are readily soluble in carbonic acid; they therefore weather quickly in warm, moist environments similar to those in caves. (See Groundwater, page 179.)

PATTERNS OF WEATHERING

Weathering varies geographically by type and rate depending upon climate, rock types, vegetation, and topography. Climate is the most significant factor affecting weathering because of the roles temperature and moisture play in chemical and physical weathering. Surface rocks and minerals vary in resistance to different types of weathering. Limestone, for example, weathers rapidly in moist climates and slowly in dry climates. Vegetation also affects weathering through root growth, which causes physical weathering, and humic acids, which come from the decomposition of vegetation and cause chemical weathering. Topography, especially the angle of slopes, affects runoff and drainage, and therefore the amount of water available for weathering.

Physical weathering occurs in all climates, but different types of weathering are associated with different climatic patterns. Frost action is most active in subpolar and mountainous regions where freeze-thaw cycles occur daily, at least during some seasons. Salt-crystal buildup is most pronounced in dry climates near water bodies: The Namibian coast on the Atlantic Ocean, the land around the Great Salt Lake in Utah, and the country near the Colorado River—at such places, precipitation is largely absent, but moisture is available for evaporation year-round. Root growth is most common where a warm, humid climate supports forests, as in the Ozarks of Arkansas, Missouri, and Oklahoma. (See Climate Controls and Climatic Classifications, page 114.)

Chemical weathering is most active in wet, warm climates; humid tropical climates have the highest rates of chemical weathering, mostly due to the climate but partly because of the large amount of vegetation supported by the climate. In contrast, chemical weathering in deserts is extremely limited because of the lack of water; **desert varnish,** a patina that forms on the surface of exposed rocks, occurs when iron and manganese in the rock oxidize. Rock type is also an important factor in chemical weathering rates. Sandstone, for example, is much more resistant to chemical change than is limestone because quartz sand grains are chemically stable, whereas calcite dissolves easily.

Mass Wasting

Mass wasting, also called mass movement or gravity transfer, is the downslope movement of rock, soil, and sediment in response to gravity; it is a component of the gradation process that lowers hills and mountains and works with erosional agents such as streams. All slopes experience mass wasting: Steep slopes may have dramatic landslides and rockfalls, but slopes with angles of only a few degrees also experience downslope movement of rocks and sediments. Creep, the slowest downslope movement, and slumps, the slow slippage of part of a slope, occur on virtually all slopes.

For mass wasting to occur, the pull of gravity must be greater than the resistance to gravity, or **shear strength,** of a slope's material. Shear strength is a composite of **cohesion** (molecular attraction) within a rock and friction between rock particles or between rock layers. As long as shear strength is sufficient to resist gravity's pull, a slope will remain stable. Strong rocks, granite for example, may form cliffs, while unstable sand dunes can have a maximum slope, or **angle of repose**, of about 35 degrees. The angle of repose varies with different sizes, shapes, and sortings of sediments: A talus cone at the base of a cliff, consisting of large, angular rock fragments, will have a much steeper slope than will piles of rounded pebbles along a coastline.

Most mass wasting is triggered by a catalyst—some change in the environment that either increases the gravitational force on or reduces the shear strength of a slope. Adding weight to a slope can cause it to fail. The weight may be heavy rainfall, snowfall, or houses or other structures on a slope. Water can also saturate the underlying rock and soil and trigger mass wasting; increased pore water pressure reduces the friction within the slope by separating sedimentary particles or rock layers. The slope's shear strength is reduced so that gravity causes materials composing the slope to be pulled downward. Earthquakes commonly set off landslides and rockfalls because vibrations unbalance slopes already at their angles of repose; they may also increase the pressure of groundwater and cause **liquefaction**, when the loss of shear strength causes soil to act like a liquid.

CLASSIFICATIONS OF MASS WASTING

Mass wasting is classified according to several criteria: motion, material, and speed. The

motions for rock and sediment include falls, slides, flow, and creep; materials include rocks, sediments, snow, and mud. Speeds can range from 0.1 inch per year to more than 100 miles per hour. The classification system used here is based on speed of movement to show a continuum of mass wasting and covers creep, solifluction, slumps, mudflows, and landslides.

The slowest and most common type of mass movement is soil creep. **Creep** occurs when soil expands *out*ward at right angles to a slope because of the addition or freezing of water; the soil then contracts *down*ward or vertically because of gravitational pull as water drains or frost melts. Depending upon the slope's angle, this will cause soil and rock layers within a few feet of the surface to move downslope between 0.1 inch and 0.5 inch per year.

Solifluction, the result of meltwater reducing friction and cohesion within the sediments of a slope, occurs in polar regions where the upper soil layer of permafrost thaws during the brief summers and then slowly slides downslope. Hillsides in regions near Fairbanks, Alaska, often appear to sag or bulge because of solifluction.

Slumps are faster than creep and solifluction but occur less often. Most slumps are rotational along a plane of weakness or **slip plane**.

These curved tree trunks are evidence of creep, a form of mass wasting in which a slope gradually slips downward in response to gravity.

Southern California is well-known for its destructive mudflows, which occur during periods of heavy rain following long dry periods or forest fires, both of which reduce protective vegetation cover.

As the lower section of a slope flows outward and downslope, the upper section slides downward; the entire slope section appears to rotate. Slumps may move a few feet a day and are often wet-season phenomena, occurring after water has infiltrated a slope and reduced friction between soil layers.

Mudflows, earthflows, and debris flows, like slumps, are faster than creep and solifluction and also involve sediments or rock fragments mixed with varying amounts of water. For flow to occur, there must be little or no vegetation on the slope because root systems increase slope strength and vegetation reduces the rate of water infiltrating the ground. **Lahars**, the flows of cinders and ash mixed with water from rain or snowmelt, are a volcanic version of mudflows. (See Volcanic Eruptions, page 157.)

Unlike slumps, the material in a mudflow does not move as a unit but has an internal fluid motion because water mixed with the sediments reduces friction throughout the mass of material. The increased weight from the water also increases gravitational pull on the material. Earthflows are viscous, with less water content than a mudflow, and debris flows are mostly rock fragments, have little water, and are slower than mudflows. The speed of mudflows, the fastest of the three types of flow, varies according to water content, slope, and surface roughness and may reach speeds up to 40 miles per hour.

Dry areas lacking vegetative cover experience mudflows during rare heavy rainfalls. In fall, southern California is subject to forest fires that reduce the amount of vegetation and droughts that precede winter rains; the region is vulnerable to mudflows, especially following forest fires on slopes in the Coast Ranges.

The fastest forms of mass wasting involve abrupt slides or falls of rocks, sediments, and snow. Landslides, rockslides, and avalanches are most common on steep mountainsides and often occur in tectonically active areas where earthquakes unbalance slopes. Slides along planes of weakness between rock layers in slopes and free-falling rockfalls are relatively common. Large **landslides** that move millions of cubic yards of debris and travel more than a

Rocky Mountain Slides

Several major avalanches and landslides have occurred in the Rocky Mountains of North America during the 1900s. In 1903 a rock avalanche on Turtle Mountain, Alberta, buried the town of Frank under a hundred feet of debris, killing 70 people. The Gros Ventre Slide in Wyoming, the largest slide in United States history, occurred in 1925 and moved more than 40 million cubic yards of debris.

hundred miles an hour are rare. Landslides and **avalanches**, a general term for extremely rapid slides and falls of snow, rocks, and trees, leave scars and may move debris miles downslope.

HUMAN ACTIVITIES AND MASS WASTING

Mudflows, landslides, avalanches, and rockfalls have always been hazardous to people. In 218 B.C. Hannibal, a Carthaginian general, may have lost as many as 18,000 soldiers to avalanches as he traveled across the Alps to attack Rome. People build homes, towns, cities, and roads on slopes that are subject to mass wasting. Such construction may reduce the shear strength of slopes by changing the angle of slopes, by lengthening slopes and forcing the lowest sections to support greater weight, and by increased soil moisture due to overwatering, leakage from swimming pools, and even, on occasion, septic tank overflow.

Mass wasting is often an unanticipated side effect of resource development that changes the water content of slopes. Clear-cutting in Oregon, Madagascar, and other forested regions has increased the frequency of landslides. The slides may cause few human deaths, but they change the local ecosystems: In Oregon increased mass wasting and erosion have made sediment deposits in streams greater, and the deposits have destroyed downstream salmon spawning grounds. Reservoirs behind dams also cause mass wasting when water infiltrates surrounding rock and reduces friction. In 1963 heavy rains caused a massive landslide into a reservoir on the Vaiont River in northern Italy. The landslide created a huge wave that broke over the dam and surged downstream, washing away towns along the river and killing nearly 2,000 people.

Almost all construction on mountainous terrain involves steepening one slope to create a level area for a building or road. Mountain roads often have retaining walls or wire mesh to prevent rockfalls; avalanche sheds protect travelers from falling and sliding rocks or avalanches. Mining, quarrying, and even ditchdigging can steepen and lengthen slopes, thus increasing stress at the slope's base.

The Cucaracha Formation and the Panama Canal

Construction of the Panama Canal at the turn of the 20th century was complicated by a tremendous number of landslides during excavation. The Cucaracha formation, a layer of clay, contributed to the problem. Clay in general (and wet clay in particular) has little cohesion and is likely to fail and slide. The canal's builders dredged clay to deepen the Chagres Valley and piled the clay along the canal, increasing the angle and the length of the slope. As a result, slopes along the canal failed repeatedly.

Streams, Fluvial Processes, and Landforms

Streams and rivers shape more of Earth's land surface than do glaciers or any other geomorphic agent. Even as streams wear away hills and mountains, they create new landforms from the eroded material, and each landform reflects the influences of climate and geology. Flooding, a normal aspect of stream activity, is important in landscape formation and is a hazard to humans. People attempt to control rivers and streams by building dams and levees, which affect wetlands and ecosystems downstream.

Stream Systems

Streams, flows of water in channels, range in size from backyard brooks and creeks to the longest rivers in the world: the 4,238-mile-long Nile and the 3,997-mile-long Amazon. Only the largest streams are called **rivers**. Landforms created by streams are common throughout the world, except for ice-covered regions and areas where bedrock such as chalk is so porous that water seeps directly into the ground. Streams even shape landforms in deserts where rainfall averages less than ten inches annually.

Streams are a major link between the atmosphere and the oceans as part of the hydrologic cycle. (See Atmospheric Moisture, page 88.) Almost one-third of all precipitation that falls on land eventually reaches the oceans, mostly via stream channels and the rest through groundwater. Evaporation and transpiration return the remaining two-thirds of precipitated water directly to the atmosphere.

Most streams flow when precipitation on land collects in channels rather than soaking into the ground or collecting in ponds and lakes. Groundwater flowing onto the surface from springs provides stream flow during drier

Extensive permafrost interrupts the drainage patterns of lakes and ponds in the tundra near Barrow, Alaska.

times. (See Groundwater, page 179.) The readiness with which water sinks into the ground depends upon the texture of soil and nonsoil sediment, the porosity of the surface rock, and the degree to which those surfaces are saturated. In dry, sandy areas, light rainfall infiltrates easily; almost all surfaces will be supersaturated after several days of heavy rain and block further infiltration. Water runs down a slope as overland flow and then, as it accumulates and flows faster, erodes a channel into the surface to form a stream.

Many separate channels form as water drains off a slope into streams, which then intersect and combine to become a **stream system**, consisting of a main channel and all the upstream tributaries that contribute water to it. Each system accumulates its runoff from a **drainage basin** or **watershed**. Drainage basins may range in size from a fraction of an acre draining into a creek to the 2,722,000-square-mile Amazon Basin, and they will change in size and shape over time. Sediments and surface contaminants in a drainage basin will eventually wash into a stream's main channel and flow downstream.

Elevated land, or **divides**, separate a watershed and stream system from adjoining watersheds and stream systems. Continental divides separate drainage systems flowing into different oceans and often follow the crests of mountain ranges. In North America the Continental Divide between the Pacific Ocean and Atlantic Ocean drainages follows the crest of the Rocky Mountains, and in South America the Andes form the continental divide. Hills and low ridges divide smaller watersheds and subdivide larger watersheds.

Streams and their tributaries form drainage patterns that reflect the geologic structure of a region. (See diagram: Drainage Patterns, page 170.) Different stream patterns develop depending on the tilting, folding, and fracturing of rock layers and on the presence of glaciers and volcanoes; these factors affect changes in surface slope or how resistant exposed rock layers are to erosion. **Dendritic patterns**

(from the Greek word *dendron*, meaning "tree") are most common, and they form on slightly tilted slopes of equally erosion-resistant rock layers with no significant structural variations, such as folds, that could affect drainage. **Trellis patterns** form when streams cut through folded rocks of various hardness and follow the path of least resistance. Streams in the Ouachita Mountains of Oklahoma and Arkansas and the Allegheny region of Appalachia follow this pattern. Streams that flow down the slopes of dome-shaped mountains and volcanoes, such as Mount Rainier in Washington or Haleakala in Hawaii, have **radial patterns**. Exposed laccoliths with surrounding hogbacks, such as the Black Hills of South Dakota and Wyoming, have **annular patterns** that combine the radial drainage characteristic of a central elevation with the trellis drainage characteristic of surrounding uptilted rock layers. **Rectangular drainage**, where tributaries meet at right angles, occurs on surfaces with intersecting rock fractures; **deranged drainage**, where stream patterns lack a definite pattern or organization, forms on irregular surfaces, such as on glacier-scoured parts of the Canadian Shield. (See Glaciers, page 189.)

The relationship of streams and stream patterns to the underlying geologic structures in an area can appear to be inconsistent because the structures may change over time. A river may exist for more than 50 million years, long enough for tectonic uplift or subsidence to change the slope of its channel and tributaries. Streams that exist before an area is uplifted or folded may retain their channels despite the new geologic structure because the streams erode their channels faster than the rocks are uplifted by folding. **Water gaps** form when streams erode through a ridge that is uplifting across their path and so cut through the ridge instead of flowing parallel to it. **Wind gaps** occur if the stream in a water gap loses its flow to **stream piracy** (one stream erodes into and intersects another, acquiring the upstream reach as a tributary), leaving the valley dry.

Tectonic processes create the geologic

Water flowing west of North America's Continental Divide, which follows the crest of the Rocky Mountains, flows into the Pacific Ocean, while water flowing east drains into the Atlantic Ocean.

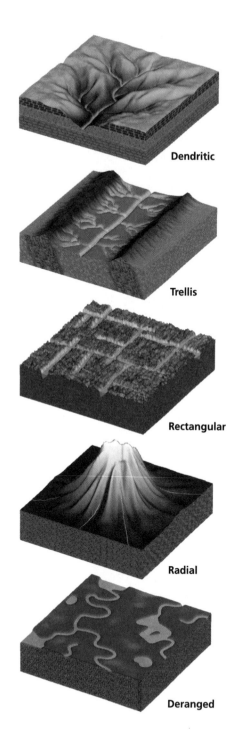

Dendritic

Trellis

Rectangular

Radial

Deranged

Drainage Patterns

structures that influence stream patterns and give rise to the mountains whose elevations determine the location of divides and drainage basins. The headwaters of nearly all major stream systems and the divides between them are in mountains: The major rivers of Asia— the Indus, Ganges, Brahmaputra, and Yangtze (Chang Jiang)—have their headwaters in the Himalaya. Converging tectonic plates are usually associated with one coastline—the west coasts of North America and South America, for example—and cause the world's largest rivers to flow to the opposite or **trailing coasts** of their continents. The 3,708-mile-long Mississippi-Missouri system, with headwaters in the Rocky Mountains, and the 2,634-mile-long Mackenzie-Peace system, with headwaters in the Stikine Mountains, flow to the eastern side of the continental divide. The world's second longest river, the 3,997-mile-long Amazon, flows east from headwaters in the Peruvian Andes.

Stream Flow

A stream's **velocity** is the key to understanding how land is lowered by erosion, how eroded material is transported to lower elevations, and how and where the eroded material will be deposited. The faster a stream flows, the greater its capacity to erode land and carry sediments and debris; decreased velocity causes the reverse and also increases the amount of deposition. Changes in a stream's velocity are a natural part of stream processes but are strongly affected by the building of dams and levees and the straightening of stream channels.

Slope angle, or **gradient**, is the most important factor affecting stream velocity, and gradient differences are why hilly, upstream areas have **fluvial**, or stream-formed, landscapes different from more level downstream areas. Streams in level plains areas may slope less than .01 degree, whereas mountain streams can have slopes averaging more than 5 degrees. Greater slope and the total amount of stream flow increase a stream's velocity, but the flow is restrained by friction against the stream's walls and channel bed, the **wetted perimeter**. Streams on steep slopes may average speeds of five to ten miles per hour; those on plains may flow at 0.5 mile per hour. No equation can calculate velocities for different slopes because of the differing effects of channel shapes and roughnesses on the wetted perimeter.

Most streams are **turbulent**—with swirls and eddies within the flow—rather than smooth, or **laminar;** turbulence increases the erosional and transport capabilities of a stream. Greater velocity increases turbulence, especially near the shoreline, because of friction between the water and the wetted perimeter of the channel. In fast-moving mountain streams and floodwaters, turbulence may be seen as white water, while in slower water turbulence exists as eddies.

A change in stream velocity also affects a stream's **competence**. Competence is the largest particle, based on its diameter, that a stream is capable of transporting, and it increases relative to the square or the cube of the velocity. If velocity doubles, for example, the competence increases between four times (two squared) and eight times (two cubed). The relationship between velocity and competence varies because particles on the streambed have different shapes and different amounts of surface area exposed to the force of the flow.

A stream's **capacity** is the total amount of sediment it can transport. Greater velocity increases capacity, as does increased stream **discharge,** the total amount of water passing through the channel in a given period of time. Slow-flowing rivers, such as the Platte in Nebraska or the Ob' in Siberia, will transport far more sediment and debris than their faster, smaller tributaries because, despite decreased velocity, the river has much greater discharge.

Changes in stream velocity occur seasonally and within a channel's length and cross section. For all streams, even those receiving water exclusively from springs, water supply is directly or indirectly atmospheric in origin. (See Diagram: Hydrologic Cycle, page 89.) The majority of climates have seasonal variations in precipitation, which are reflected in seasonal discharge rates and therefore velocities of stream flow. Streams in regions with humid climates are perennial, or year-round, but still display faster high-flow and slower low-flow seasons. In arid climates, streams may be **intermittent**, flowing only during the wet season, or **ephemeral**, flowing only after rainfalls. Flooding, a natural and recurring phenomenon, is a short-term large increase in flow discharge and velocity. (See Flood Processes, page 177.)

Velocity also varies within a stream's channel. As a rule, water flows faster in the headwaters of a stream and slows as the stream nears its **base level**, the lowest point to which it can erode. Sea level is the ultimate base level because channel flow is dissipated when stream water mingles with seawater. Within any curved section of a stream, velocities vary: Friction slows water on the inside of a curve, and centrifugal force accelerates it on the outside. The velocity of water in a straight portion of a stream is fastest near the surface in the middle of the channel, farthest away from the effects of friction along the streambed and sides.

Stream Processes

Streams create landforms by **erosion**, the removal of sediment, and by **deposition**, the dropping or laying down of sediment. These processes are functions of changes in the velocity and discharge of a stream's flow. When erosion or deposition starts and stops depends on the size of the sediments and at what velocity they can be moved or on their **critical erosion velocity:** Clay-size particles and small gravel require a flow velocity of five miles per hour to begin to erode. Clay particles are so flat that they adhere to each other, making them difficult to move, whereas fine sand—sand that is smaller than a pencil dot—is eroded at .75 mile per hour. Deposition begins at a **settling velocity** that also depends upon particle size; clay and fine sand are deposited when flow velocity slows below .25 mile per hour, while small gravel is deposited at velocities below 1.5 miles per hour.

A stream's erosion occurs only in its channel. There is some erosion before water reaches the channel: Large raindrops cause **splash erosion** when they hit loose sediment, and as water from raindrops accumulates into overland flow, **sheet erosion** occurs before the water collects in rills and gullies. Although bedrock channels are eroded by streams, much of the material transported within channels is sediment created by weathering of rocks often moved into the channel by slumping, creep, and other forms of mass wasting. (See Weathering and Mass Wasting, page 159.)

Three processes cause erosion in a stream: hydraulic action, corrosion, and abrasion. **Hydraulic action** removes sediments when moving water strikes and drags them, usually creating turbulence in the process; small sand grains are most easily eroded by hydraulic action because their cross sections are large enough to receive the force of the flow and their weights are too small to anchor them. **Corrosion** occurs when flowing water removes the ions of dissolved minerals; in some rivers, especially those flowing through limestone and other soluble rocks, corrosion may be responsible for more than half the total amount of sediments eroded. **Abrasion** results when particles carried by a stream strike the bedrock or other rocks on the streambed and sides, chipping off particles that are then washed away; potholes in bedrock streambeds are created by abrasion from rocks swirling in eddies. The degree to which each process affects erosion depends upon the type of rock in a region. Shale channels, for example, will

undergo little corrosion with relatively more hydraulic action and abrasion.

Erosion causes channels to widen, deepen, and lengthen, although not necessarily at the same time. **Lateral erosion** removes sediment and rocks on the sides of the channel and is most pronounced on the outer banks of curves. **Down cutting**, often by abrasion, erodes a streambed. When the base level of a stream changes after land has been raised tectonically or when ocean levels are lowered as during an ice age, the rate of down-cutting grows because the greater slope also increases stream velocity. The Grand Canyon is the result of one mile of down-cutting by the Colorado River following the tectonic lifting of the area.

Headward erosion, or erosion toward a stream's headwaters, extends the channel upslope and can expand the area drained by the stream. At the head of a stream and its tributaries, where overland flow enters the channels, the accumulating water flows quickly because of the steep gradient; the stream's higher competence and capacity therefore increase erosion.

Sediments are transported downstream until physical or chemical processes cause them to settle or precipitate out of the water. More than half of all transported sediments (mostly clays and silt) are suspended in the water; this **suspended load** causes turbidity and is why the Mississippi River is known as the Big Muddy; the Yellow, or Huang, River in China transports yellowish silt from upstream **loess** (wind-deposited silt) deposits to the Yellow Sea. A stream's **bed load** includes all particles moving via **saltation** (rolling, sliding, and skipping) along the streambed; larger, heavier particles may move seasonally or intermittently—for example, from an occasional flood—when faster high water is present. Ions transported as **dissolved load** in water may compose 30 percent of the total sediment load in streams traversing limestone regions.

Sediments transported as suspended loads or bed loads are deposited when stream velocity falls below their settling velocities; dissolved loads are deposited only when a chemical change occurs in the water. Settling of **alluvial deposits** (stream-carried deposits) occurs in slower and usually shallower sections of a channel, on floodplains, and in the lakes, ponds, or basins into which a stream flows. If the velocity decreases slowly, as in estuaries, transported sediments will be sorted by size. Larger particles, such as coarse sand, will settle when a stream's velocity is still fast enough to transport smaller particles. It may take smaller particles a long time to settle; clay may take a year to settle through a hundred feet of still water.

The dissolved load transported by a stream cannot settle out, even in still water; instead, it precipitates when ions combine and form mineral deposits. Salts such as sodium chloride, or table salt, and other dissolved minerals remain in solution, while alluvial deposits settle in slowed water. Only when water changes chemically, as when it evaporates, does precipitation occur; **alkali flats** (salt flats) in desert basins form from this process. Calcite, another mineral deposit and the basis of limestone, forms when water releases carbon dioxide to the atmosphere, allowing calcium and bicarbonate ions to combine.

Fluvial Landforms and Landscapes

Fluvial landforms are categorized by their location along a stream channel because slope usually decreases from the headwaters to the base level of a stream. In the upstream reaches, slopes are usually steep, and the water is fast and has not yet eroded much sediment; a stream is **underloaded** at this point, which means it has excess capacity for transporting sediment. Steep valleys and gorges dominate the upstream reaches as streams erode rapidly downward. The middle reaches of a stream have more moderate slopes than upstream,

and water velocities vary from fast to slow, depending on the season and location within the channel; erosion and deposition combine to create landforms such as **meanders**. Downstream, where a stream approaches base level, water slows and is **overloaded** with sediments that create depositional landforms, such as deltas.

UPPER-REACH LANDFORMS

In regions where tectonic uplift is relatively recent, streams tend to flow rapidly downslope in straight channels, generating erosional landfoms such as V-shaped valleys, gorges, waterfalls, and rapids. Streams in strong rocks such as granite, where the sides resist mass wasting and remain nearly vertical, downcut their

The Lower Falls of the Yellowstone River in Wyoming drops 308 feet into the V-shaped Yellowstone Valley below.

channels and create gorges. In areas with softer rock, such as shale, V-shaped valleys generally indicate the early stages of valley formation. Older valleys have softer, wider edges because mass wasting, including slumping and sliding, has occurred along the sides of the channel. Where rains are infrequent but cause flash floods, gullies and ravines may dominate the landscape, such as in the Badlands of South Dakota.

Waterfalls and rapids are commonly found in upstream locations, although both are also found at downstream **knickpoints**, sites where the slope increases because of a change from hard to soft rock or a blocking landslide or a man-made feature such as a dam. Waterfalls may be **cataracts**, with a single, long drop; the highest is the 3,212-foot cataract of Angel Falls, Venezuela, on a tributary of the Río Caroní. Waterfalls may also occur as a series of stair-step **cascades**, for which the Cascade Range in the Pacific Northwest is named. Niagara Falls, on the Niagara River between Canada and the United States, flows over a knickpoint formed by resistant Lockport dolostone, which overlies softer shale. More rapid erosion of the shale undercuts the dolostone, causing it to jut out and create the waterfall.

MID-REACH LANDFORMS

When slope and stream velocity decrease in the middle reaches of a stream, the channel begins to **meander**, or loop, and form a floodplain. Meanders begin when a slump or object such as a fallen tree temporarily blocks one side of the channel, pushing stream flow toward the opposite side of the channel. The force and turbulence of the water cause increased erosion on the opposite side, undercutting the bank and deepening that part of the channel. Stream flow enlarges this curve; water flowing on the outside travels farther and therefore must flow faster than the water flowing on the inside of the curve, much like a runner in the outside lane of a track. The difference in flow rates expands the curve, causing the meander to shift location because the faster, outside flow continues to erode while the slower, inside flow begins to deposit sediment.

Meanders grow outward during the high-flow season of a stream and are relatively stable during the low-flow season. Meanders slowly move downstream because stream velocity increases when water in a curve erodes more of the channel walls that interfere with its downslope movement. As meanders move sideways and downstream, they flatten the terrain on both banks.

The flattened terrain created by meandering is called the **floodplain;** such areas are

The Fall Line

On a line from New Jersey to Alabama, the sedimentary rocks of the coastal plain along the Atlantic Ocean meet the igneous and metamorphic rocks of the Piedmont region of Appalachia. This boundary drops toward the coast because the softer sedimentary rocks have eroded more than the igneous and metamorphic rocks—more resistant to erosion—of the Piedmont. Rapids and waterfalls along the boundary, known as the fall line, block upstream navigation by ships and barges; early European settlements located just downstream of the fall line enjoyed the benefits of ocean transport (limited to calmer and deeper downstream reaches) and used the rapids to drive waterwheels. Philadelphia, Baltimore, and Washington, D.C. are fall line cities; New England mill towns were often located at regional fall lines to obtain waterpower.

susceptible to flooding when heavy precipitation or snowmelt upstream causes a high-flow season. Floodplains may be backed by bluffs on either side of the channel. Floodplains may be less than a mile wide or, for rivers such as the Yangtze and Mississippi, may be more than 50 miles wide.

Along the banks of meandering streams, deposition from flooding creates ridges called **natural levees.** During floods, when water overflows the banks of a channel, it slows down quickly because of friction from the level terrain of the floodplain. This rapid decrease in velocity causes deposition immediately alongside the channel so that ridges, or levees, are built up; levees can be 20 feet higher than the floodplain and may contain smaller floods. Clays, silt, and other sediments accumulate as alluvium on a floodplain when floodwaters slow.

Deposition on a streambed occurs when the high-flow season ends, forming bars that may

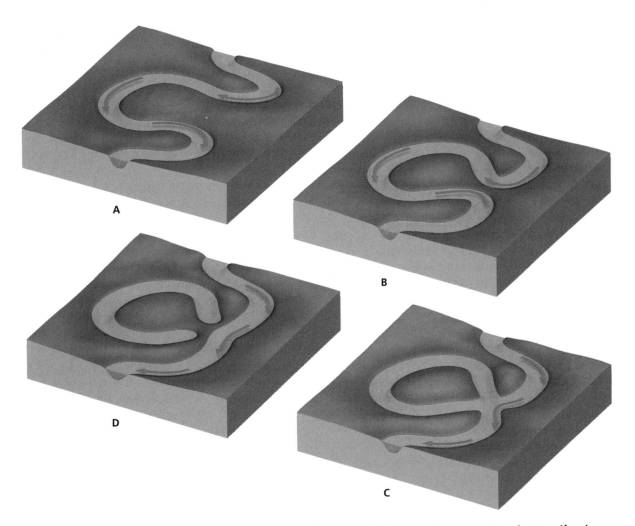

A stream meander develops in several stages. Clockwise from top left, the meander grows outward as centrifugal force deflects water flow toward the outside of the meander (A). Its neck becomes constricted (B). Eventually the meander is cut off from the main stream (C). Finally an **oxbow lake** forms (D).

The Mississippi River forms what is called a bird's-foot delta, named because its strings of sediment resemble a bird's foot when viewed from the air.

generate turbulence seen as riffles on the surface. Bars deposited on the inside curve of a meander are called **point bars;** bars deposited in a channel are classified by particle size and include mud bars, sandbars, and gravel bars. Bar deposits within a channel can be exposed during the low-flow season.

When streams are extremely shallow, in-channel sediment deposits separate the stream flow to form a **braided stream** with many channels. Such streams are most common downstream from glaciers because meltwater cannot transport larger particles, pebbles, rocks, or boulders very far from their source at the snout of the glacier.

DOWN-REACH LANDFORMS

As streams approach their base levels slopes continue to decrease, creating more depositional landforms. Meandering streams form oxbow lakes, yazoo streams, backswamps, and wetlands, and when a stream reaches its base level—either a temporary one, such as a lake, or its ultimate base level, the ocean—it may form a delta.

Oxbow lakes, sometimes called bayous in Louisiana and billabongs in Australia, are meander cutoffs. When a stream cuts through a **meander neck,** the narrow land between

two adjoining meander curves, the water in the cutoff meander forms a lake called an oxbow, named for the U-shaped collar that supports an ox yoke. (See Diagram: Characteristic Features of the Floodplain of a Meandering River, page 175.)

Yazoo streams and backswamps are caused by levees that parallel a stream channel and affect drainage patterns on floodplains. A **yazoo stream** forms when levees prevent a tributary from entering a river or stream. The tributary flows parallel to the main channel until it reaches a break or opening in the levee that allows it to join the main stream. Yazoo streams are named for the Yazoo River, which parallels the Mississippi River for more than one hundred miles before merging with it at Vicksburg, Mississippi. **Backswamps** are marshy areas that form in slight depressions on the floodplains behind levees.

When a stream flows into stationary waters, such as a pond, lake, reservoir, or calm ocean or sea, the decrease in velocity lowers the stream's competence and capacity, causing the bed load and suspended load to be deposited as a **delta**. Deltas form as a series of beds or layers of sediment; large particles settle first, and lighter sediments travel farther into the calmer water until stream velocity slows to the settling velocity for clays and silt.

Many of the major rivers of the world, including the Nile, Ganges, and Yangtze, form deltas as they reach, respectively, the Mediterranean, Bay of Bengal, and East China Sea; Russia's Volga River forms a wide delta as it flows into the Caspian Sea. In other cases, ocean currents prevent an accumulation of sediment, or a river lacks sufficient sediment; rivers such as the Amazon, St. Lawrence, and Zambezi do not form deltas. A river's main channel may separate into many branches, or **distributaries**, and deposit its sediment along smaller channels and breaks in levees to form the larger delta. The shape of a delta, named for the Greek letter Δ, reflects depositional processes, amounts and types of sediment load, and the influence of waves and tides. The

Mississippi River has a **bird's-foot delta** created by numerous distributaries and shifting channels, while the Nile River has an **arcuate delta**, a curved delta created by distributaries and modified by wave action.

Flood Processes

A **flood** occurs when a stream rises above its banks and covers part of the surrounding land. The water level in a stream usually varies seasonally because of the changes in the atmospheric sources of the water, such as rain or snowmelt. During the high-water season an especially large rainfall or snowmelt can cause water to rise above **flood stage**, which occurs when the water is level with the stream's banks. Flooding is a natural event in streams. When not modified by humans, streams naturally flood as often as every other year.

Different sections along the length of a stream may flood for different reasons. In the upper reaches of a stream, flooding is usually caused by a heavy rainfall or sudden snowmelt. In the lower reaches, flooding can result from the downstream movement of upstream floodwaters or from large weather systems that increase runoff over much of the drainage basin. For example, a blocking system may prevent a front from moving. (See Weather Systems, page 98.) **Flash floods,** rapid rises in stream levels, are limited to small watersheds, and are brief, usually lasting less than 24 hours.

People build cities, towns, highways, railroads, and farms on fertile deltas and floodplains, thus placing themselves in danger of floods, a major natural hazard worldwide and perhaps the most universally experienced natural disaster. In the United States more than 20 million people live on floodplains. In Bangladesh, which has 125 million people, 80 percent of the country's 55,598 square miles are classified as floodplain.

Natural and man-made levees prevent small rises in stream level from flowing onto floodplains, but high waters that overflow levees may become large floods. For this reason, levees have mixed consequences. The prevention of small floods may cause people to ignore the possibility of larger floods and therefore increase agricultural and residential development on floodplains. In like fashion, artificially increasing the height of natural levees and building artificial levees can prevent small floods but make the area more susceptible to the effects of larger ones.

Floods are described in terms of a number of years, such as a 10-year flood, 25-year flood, or 100-year flood. The terms are based on the frequency that high-water levels were reached in the past; these terms describe the likelihood of a stream reaching a given height during a given year. For example, if there were 100 years of data on stream levels, then the single greatest height reached would be called a 100-year flood, while a height reached on 10 out of 100 years would be called a 10-year flood. There is a 10 percent chance each year that the stream level will rise to the height of the 10-year flood—for example, three feet above

The Big Thompson and Nile Floods

Flood danger varies tremendously, depending on the frequency and predictability of the floods. On July 31, 1976, a cloudburst dropped more than ten inches of rain in four hours on the drainage basin of the Big Thompson River in Colorado, causing a flash flood that killed 140 people. The Nile River, prior to completion of the Aswan High Dam in 1971, flooded every fall when summer runoff from the Ethiopian highlands moved downstream. Few lives were lost because the flooding was expected.

flood stage—and a one percent chance each year that stream levels will rise to the 100-year flood level—for example, 20 feet above flood stage. These flood levels are not predictions but rather expressions of the possibility of particular flood levels being reached; the extremes of weather and other events that cause these flood levels cannot be accurately predicted.

Human Impact on Streams

Humans intentionally and unintentionally change stream flows when they develop water resources. Controlling stream flow enables humans to manage waterways for flood control, water supply, hydropower generation, recreation, irrigation, and other benefits. Changing stream flow, however, means that velocity and discharge also change; the new erosional and depositional characteristics of a stream can cause problems when they create new landforms. In Washington State, logging companies clear-cut large tracts of forest, exposing the ground to increased splash-and-sheet erosion and gullying. When runoff reached channels, the increased sediment load was deposited in shallower, slower portions of streams, often on gravel bars where fish such as salmon spawned; the unanticipated channel deposition seriously damaged fishing interests.

Varying surface characteristics within a watershed cause changes in stream flow by altering the amount and type of runoff. Urbanization is especially significant in moderating surfaces, although plowing also causes major surface changes. In cities, pavement may replace vegetation and cover well over 50 percent of the area, thus preventing precipitation from infiltrating the ground and relying on storm sewers and drains to carry runoff directly to nearby streams. As a result, both downstream flooding and in-stream erosion increase. A hydrograph shows the relationship between surface characteristics and the timing and amount of downstream flow. In a natural environment, runoff to a stream following precipitation is usually diminished by infiltration of the ground and slowed by vegetation hampering overland flow. After an area has been urbanized, however, the amount of runoff and therefore the stream level—during a flood, the **flood crest**—increases, and the lag time between precipitation and a rise in stream level decreases.

Water-control structures, especially dams, dramatically alter the flow characteristics of streams. Reservoirs behind dams act as new base levels and create knickpoints for streams, causing deposition within reservoirs. When water is released over spillways from dams, it has already deposited its sediment in its reservoir. Thus, because it is underloaded, the stream causes increased erosion below the dam. There are more than 58,000 dams in the United States. Damming California's streams and rivers has, in some cases, filled reservoirs to the tops of the dams with sediment and reduced beach size on the Pacific coast because

The Kissimmee River Restoration

Channelization of the Kissimmee River in Florida began in 1961; after the project's completion in 1971 it decreased flooding, drained wetlands and marshes, and provided more water for urban areas. Within 15 years, however, the side effects of channelization became apparent; water quality decreased because fewer wetlands were available to filter water, and wildlife disappeared alongside the river and downstream in the Everglades. The Kissimmee River is now being restored, and the project should be completed by 2009.

the sand that continually rebuilt the beaches has been trapped behind the dams.

Channelization, the straightening of stream channels for improved navigation and reduced flooding, has a major impact on a stream's channel as well as its surroundings. When streams are channelized by cutting off meanders, the shorter path results in a steeper slope along that stretch. The increased velocity erodes the channel and moves floodwaters downstream more rapidly. When the Blackwater River in Missouri was channelized, it reduced flooding along that stretch of the river but increased downstream flooding; several downstream bridges collapsed when increased lateral erosion from the faster flow widened the channel in some places from less than 90 feet to 200 feet.

Groundwater

Groundwater can flow below all types of land surfaces, including deserts and mountains, saturating fractures and pores in rocks and spaces between sediment particles. The water, which is mostly from rain and snowmelt, filters downward and collects above impermeable rock layers, forming an aquifer. Aquifers contain the largest supply of nonfrozen fresh water on Earth and supply much of the potable water used by people. Groundwater beneath a desert may be **fossil water** that accumulated when the region's climate was wetter. The Sahara's groundwater, one of the largest reservoirs, is likely the residual of precipitation from the wetter climate of the Pleistocene Ice Age.

Groundwater appears at the surface as springs, seeps, swamps, and thermal features such as geysers. It creates landforms such as caves and sinkholes by slowly dissolving minerals from rock and soil. The flow characteristics of groundwater are key to understanding how springs and caves are formed and how groundwater is an essential natural resource.

Groundwater Systems

Rain and snowmelt are the principal sources of groundwater, and some groundwater comes from surface streams when water seeps directly into rock through a streambed. Like streams on the surface, groundwater is part of the hydrologic cycle. (See diagram: Hydrologic Cycle, page 89.) Not all water that sinks into the ground becomes groundwater: Some water attaches to soil particles and rock fragments via surface tension, and plants absorb this **soil water** through their root systems before returning it to the atmosphere through evapotranspiration. The remainder of the water continues to sink until it saturates the soil or rock and becomes groundwater.

When raindrops fall through the atmosphere, some of the carbon dioxide in the air dissolves into the raindrops and forms diluted carbonic acid. This water becomes increasingly acidic as it percolates down through the soil layers, where decaying vegetation can increase the carbon dioxide content of the soil to more than a hundred times the normal concentration of the gas in the atmosphere. By the time water from the surface reaches the water table, it can be more than ten times as acidic as surface water, which increases its ability to dissolve soluble rocks such as limestone and marble. Groundwater flowing through rocks with high sulfur content can also dissolve the sulfur and form sulfuric acid.

Groundwater accumulates in rocks and sediments because they are porous; there are spaces between sediment particles and within rocks. For example, 60 percent of a pile of gravel, sand, or clay may be solid material, but the remaining 40 percent of the pile's volume consists of gaps between the irregularly shaped individual particles. Nearly all surface rocks have some **porosity**, or gaps in their mass; some rocks are porous because they formed under great pressure and cracked when the overlying rocks were eroded away. Sandstone is porous because of spaces between sand grains and **bedding planes** (breaks between layers of sediment); limestone is porous because of solution cavities. Granites may have porosity levels well below one percent, whereas some sandstones may have porosity levels as high as 30 percent.

Groundwater infiltrates until it reaches an impermeable layer of rock. There are two zones above the impermeable layer where infiltration slows or stops: The lower zone, the **zone of saturation**, is where groundwater collects, and the upper zone is the **zone of aeration**, where atmospheric gases occupy some of the space between sediments and in pores in rocks. The **water table** is the upper level of the zone of saturation. Water tables tend to mirror the topography of the surface; they are relatively higher under elevated areas and lower under valleys; they may be at the surface, in the case of swamps, or thousands of feet down in reservoirs under deserts. The level of a water table changes during the year, depending upon how much water is added or subtracted according to the climate or by irrigation. In dry seasons the water table may drop several feet in some areas before rising after the next wet season.

Groundwater Processes

Groundwater usually moves very slowly through rock at rates averaging between five feet per day and five feet per year. A combination of factors affects how groundwater moves: porosity, permeablity, and hydrostatic pressure. Porosity, the amount of space in rock fractures and pores and in gaps between sediments, changes with increasing depth as pressure from overlying rock increases; porosity decreases gradually as the pressure increases and compresses pore spaces, eventually closing them. **Permeability** is how easily water can travel vertically and horizontally through rock or sediment. To be permeable, pores need to be connected to each other and large enough for water drops to flow through without adhering to sediments or bedrock. Sand has porosity roughly equal to clay, but the permeability of sand is 20 times greater than that of clay because the gaps between sand particles are about .01 inch, larger than those between clay particles.

Hydrostatic pressure, the pressure on groundwater from overlying water, is the third factor that determines how groundwater flows. Horizontal differences in hydrostatic pressure control the direction of flow and—with permeability—the rate of flow. Groundwater flows from areas with higher water tables and greater hydrostatic pressure to areas with lower water tables. The greater the differences between water table levels, the faster the flow; greater permeability also increases the rate of flow. Flow rates range from 800 feet a day in porous limestone to a few inches a year in granites.

Rock layers that are highly permeable can be **aquifers,** or groundwater storage areas; most aquifers form in sandstone and limestone, although some aquifers form in highly fractured basalts. People drill wells to draw water from aquifers. For wells to continue to be productive, the aquifer needs to be sufficiently permeable to allow the wellhead to recharge rapidly. Shale, slate, and other less permeable rocks are considered **aquitards** when they slow or retard groundwater flow so that the rate of recharge is below useful levels or **aquicludes** if groundwater flow is negligible. Depending on rock type below the surface, some aquifers are perched on top of an aquiclude, and the upper level of the ground-

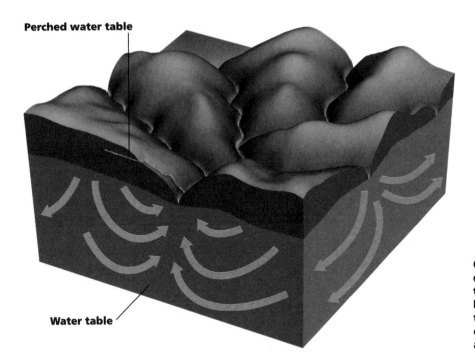

Perched water table

Water table

Groundwater first moves downward to the **water table** and then to areas of lower pressure. A water table's configuration often reflects the surface area of the land above it.

water in these aquifers is called a **perched water table**.

Surface water flow is turbulent and erodes by physical processes of abrasion and hydraulic force, whereas groundwater flow is **laminar**, or smooth, and erodes by dissolving limestone, marble, and other soluble rocks. The exception to erosion by solution is when groundwater-fed streams in caves have a turbulent flow; erosion by abrasion and hydraulic force can then take place.

Groundwater transports the ions of dissolved minerals until a change in the water (such as evaporation) causes the carbon dioxide to be removed from the water. The ions then recombine and precipitate onto solid surfaces as minerals. In caves, where the relative humidity can be 100 percent, precipitation of minerals often occurs as the groundwater drips from the rock ceiling. When the drop falls through the air, carbon dioxide moves from the water to the air because the cave air has less carbon dioxide, leaving minerals to precipi-

tate and accumulate as structures such as stalactites and stalagmites. (See Caves and Karst Topography, page 183.)

Groundwater and Landforms

Landforms created by groundwater may be found on or under 15 percent of the Earth's land surfaces. Springs, thermal springs, swamps, and geysers form when groundwater reaches Earth's surface. Caves and related surface features, such as sinkholes and rock bridges, form karst topography in humid regions where there are thick layers of limestone or other soluble rocks. The Kras—in German, Karst—is a region in Slovenia that parallels the Adriatic coast and is known for its caves, sinkholes, and underground streams.

SPRINGS AND ARTESIAN SPRINGS

Groundwater helps to recharge stream flow in most perennial streams, and it can also flow

Hard Water

Hard water develops in a given area because water percolating through limestone and other rocks dissolves calcium, magnesium, and other ions that prevent soap from lathering easily. When hard water drips into a sink or tub, the ions precipitate onto the surface. Water softeners contain insoluble substances, often resins, that attract the ions and remove them from solution and onto the substance by ion exchange.

onto the surface. **Springs** are surface flows of water caused by a water table—often a perched water table—intersecting a slope. (See Perched Water Table diagram, page 181.) Spring lines follow faults where permeable and impermeable rocks are next to each other. In many instances, springs hold only small amounts of water, called **seeps**, which flow slowly out of the ground and eventually into streams. In winter, ice formed on the walls of road cuts shows the locations of seeps. In the Thousand Springs region of Idaho and a few other locations, however, springs produce rivers pouring out of the ground; during the wet season, more than 35,000 gallons per minute pour out of the basalt layers of Thousand Springs into the Snake River Canyon.

Groundwater can also flow onto the surface when hydrostatic pressure forces water upward to create **artesian springs**, named after the Artois region of northern France, known as Artesium in Roman times. For an artesian spring to occur, groundwater must exist in a permeable rock layer overlain by an aquiclude, and both layers of rock must be tilted. Under these conditions, water infiltrates the aquifer at a higher elevation, flows slowly downward, and, because it cannot escape upward due to the overlying aquiclude, is under increasing hydrostatic pressure in the lower end of the aquifer.

When an opening—from faulting, for example—appears near the lower elevations of the tilted rock layers, groundwater rises to the surface because of hydrostatic pressure. Water from artesian springs rises to the **potentiometric surface**, or the height supported by the hydrostatic pressure of the water. Artesian wells are drilled to take advantage of this rise—in some cases several yards above the ground. Artesian springs are found in the Great Plains of the United States, especially near the Black Hills, as well as in Australia and northwestern Africa.

When a water table intersects a slope, a spring results. This is Pacific Springs near South Pass, Wyoming.

THERMAL SPRINGS AND GEYSERS

Springs can bring groundwater to the surface after it has been heated by contact with magma bodies near the surface or by contact with rock layers warmed at great depths. (See Earth Structure, page 48.) **Thermal springs** have higher water temperatures, usually more than 10°F warmer, than the average annual air temperature of a region; thermal springs may be called **hot springs** when their temperature is higher than the average human body temperature of 98.6°F. Such springs are found throughout the United States, but the majority are found in the West, where there is more tectonic and volcanic activity. Thermal springs are often used as spas because the heated water contains more dissolved minerals than colder water and is thought to have therapeutic value. Water that has been heated more than a half a mile below the surface in the Hollis quartzite formation issues from a thermal artesian spring in Warm Springs, Georgia; less than a mile away is Cold Spring, fed by groundwater from the same formation but rising from shallower depths.

Heated groundwater can produce **geysers**, a type of spring in which boiling water erupts into the air. Geysers, from the Icelandic term *geysir*, include Old Faithful in Yellowstone National Park and are relatively common in Iceland and Rotorua, New Zealand. For geysers to form, high water tables, groundwater heated to above-surface boiling temperatures, and an aquifer containing a large cavity or connected cavities are required. As groundwater fills a cavity, it begins to heat; water at the bottom of the cavity is under greater pressure than that at the top, and therefore its boiling point is higher than that of surface water, which is under less pressure. The same process is at work in a pressure cooker. When groundwater in the cavity approaches the boiling point (212°F), it expands and begins to flow out of the ground, decreasing pressure on the lower water, thus reducing the boiling point so that it flash-boils and erupts as steam at the surface. Geysers may erupt again and again; Old Faithful in Yellowstone is more predictable than most geysers, erupting every 50 to 100 minutes. Geyser fields may be tapped as an energy supply.

WETLANDS

When the water table intersects basins or lowlands, the depressions can be filled by groundwater, which saturates the ground to form **wetlands**. Floodplains and deltas commonly include wetlands; other low-lying areas are formed by tectonic activity, surface erosion by glaciers, and subsidence. Many of the lakes in Florida's lime sink region occupy sinkholes created by groundwater erosion. Swamps, such as the Okefenokee and the Great Dismal, are often found along coastal lowlands where fresh and saline groundwater intersects the surface.

CAVES AND KARST TOPOGRAPHY

Groundwater slowly dissolves limestone, marble, dolomite, and other soluble rocks, creating **caves** (underground cavities or chambers) usually with access to the surface. Cave formation is a time-consuming process because

Oases

In deserts adjacent to mountain ranges, precipitation in the mountains can feed artesian springs hundreds of miles away and form oases, local watered areas supporting vegetation. Rainfall in the Atlas Mountains of North Africa supports artesian springs forming oases in the Grand Erg region of the Sahara in Algeria. On Australia's east coast, precipitation on the Great Dividing Range eventually rises inland hundreds of miles away in the Great Artesian Basin, which covers nearly a fifth of the continent.

Old Faithful, in Yellowstone National Park, Wyoming, errrupts every 50 to 100 minutes. The eruptions, which last about 4 minutes, send up a spout of hot water and steam 115 to 175 feet high.

groundwater moves so slowly. It may take millions of years to form a large cave; Mammoth Cave, Kentucky, has more than 330 miles of passages, and the God Luck Cave in Sarawak, Indonesia, includes a room that is 2,300 feet long, 1,300 feet wide, and 900 feet high.

Caves begin when groundwater gradually dissolves soluble rock along a main channel that collects groundwater from numerous side channels or tributaries. Most solution takes place within a few feet below the water table because groundwater is still acidic from absorbing carbon dioxide from air in the soil. As long as the water table remains constant, cave passages and side channels continue to expand along joints or faults within the rock. Different spatial patterns of caves can result. The jointed rock near Hannibal, Missouri, caused the cave described in Mark Twain's *Tom Sawyer* to have a maze pattern, while other Missouri caves have rectilinear patterns.

When the water table moves downward (which occurs when precipitation decreases or surface stream erosion deepens a channel and siphons off groundwater), a cave drains, and

landforms called **speleothems**—cave deposits from precipitated minerals—are created. Minerals rarely precipitate in groundwater, so speleothems form only after a lowered water table allows a cave to have an atmosphere. Water dripping through a cave roof deposits calcite around itself, forming an icicle-like structure called a soda straw, which grows into a **stalactite**. When water drips from these formations onto the cave floor, mineral precipitation also occurs, and a **stalagmite** forms; over time the stalactite may meet the stalagmite to form a **column.** Other groundwater may flow along and drip from a fracture, precipitating a thin sheet of minerals that hangs down to form a **drapery.**

Caves may last only a few million years because walls and ceilings weaken and are unable to support overlying rock. When a cave collapses, it creates surface features called **karst topography**. Initially collapse occurs in limited areas referred to as **breakdown rooms.** Bowl-shaped depressions called **sinkholes**, or simply sinks, form on the surface above collapsed rooms. As more of a cave col-

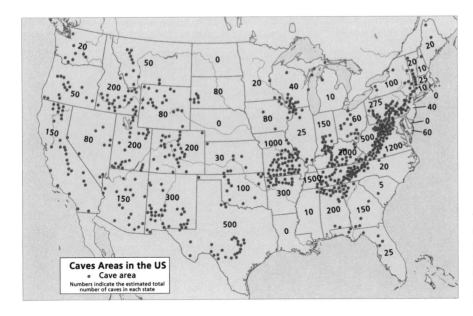

The dots indicate the distribution of karst caves in the continental United States; the numbers shown are the estimated number of caves in each state.

lapses, sinkholes expand along its channels to form **solution valleys** on the surface; occasionally a **rock bridge** will be created when a small part of a cave remains between two solution valleys. Runoff on the surface is erratic, and **disappearing streams**, also called sinking creeks, will flow into caves via surface openings known as **swallow holes**.

Karst topography is found throughout the world, but it is best developed in humid climates. (See Maps: Karst Caves in the U.S., page 185 and Karst Regions of the World, page 186.) In the United States caves and karst topography are found in many states, including Missouri, Kentucky, Indiana, and Florida, and globally karst topography is found in southern Europe, southern Australia, and southeastern Asia. In Puerto Rico and Cuba such topography is known as **cockpit karst** because the sinkholes have very steep sides and look like the pits or small amphitheaters used for cockfights. In more humid subtropical climates, such as the region near Guilin in southeastern China, this material is called **tower karst** because towers of more resistant rock dominate the landscape; the towers are what remain after

Carlsbad Caverns in New Mexico is an example of a karst cave.

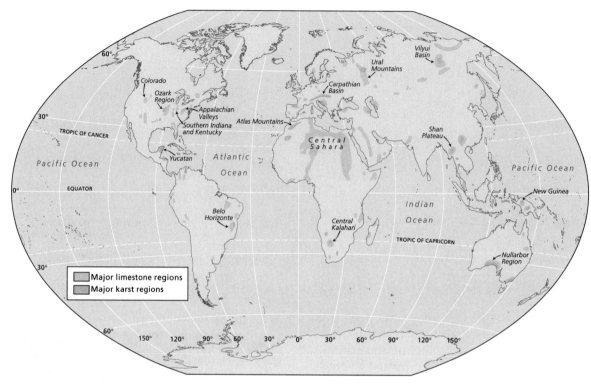

Limestone and karst regions occur worldwide but are especially prevalent in more humid climates.

groundwater removed all collapsed portions of the local cave system.

Groundwater Resources and Problems

Groundwater is a valuable source of **potable** (safe for drinking) water in the United States. In 1990 about 60 percent of all domestic and commercial users in the United States used groundwater rather than stream water, and more than one-third of the water used for irrigation was pumped from aquifers. The prairie states are most dependent on groundwater: Nebraska, Kansas, Oklahoma, and Texas obtain more of their domestic water supply from groundwater than from streams. California annually withdraws the largest amount of groundwater of all the states—and even more surface water for domestic use.

Groundwater resources throughout the country are vulnerable to depletion, saltwater intrusion, and contamination. The slow flow rate prevents rapid replenishment of aquifers where wells have been drilled and also prevents contaminants from being flushed rapidly out of aquifers. Water percolating into the ground can dissolve harmful ions from garbage in landfills and carry them into an aquifer.

Groundwater depletion is an increasingly serious problem because populations that are growing in areas such as the U.S. Southwest are dependent on groundwater. Technology

The scenic limestone formations along China's Li River are called tower karst.

has increased our ability to withdraw ground-water; wells can be drilled more than a thousand feet into the ground and can pump out millions of gallons per day, far faster than precipitation can recharge underground supplies. When a well is drilled, the groundwater around the wellhead is drawn off first, causing a **cone of depression** where the water table drops immediately; the water table drops less farther away from the wellhead. As more wells are drilled and water is pumped out, cones of depression intersect, and the water table lowers rapidly. This process is called **groundwater mining**.

Surface subsidence is a side effect of ground-water depletion in areas where aquifer materials include unconsolidated sediments. After groundwater has been pumped out of an aquifer, sediments may compact and cause the surface to lower. Cities on river deltas, including New Orleans, Venice in Italy, and Bangkok in Thailand, have experienced surface subsidence; Mexico City, built on a former lake bed, has subsided more than 25 feet in some places. Portions of the San Joaquin Valley in California have subsided more than 30 feet due to the withdrawal of groundwater for irrigation.

Groundwater withdrawal by coastal cities can also cause **saltwater intrusion** into the aquifer and therefore into the water supply.

Monster Sinkhole: Winter Park, Florida

In May 1981 a sinkhole formed so quickly in Winter Park, Florida, that three Porsches couldn't be moved before falling into a sinkhole. The hole was so large that it also swallowed a three-bedroom house. Sinkholes and circular lakes that are water-filled sinkholes are common in central Florida; as the population of the state increases and more groundwater is used, sinkholes are an increasing hazard in some urban areas.

Ogallala Aquifer

Farmers have used wells in West Texas since the 1930s to provide water for irrigation. But some of these wells have since run dry because of dropping water levels in the Ogallala aquifer, a subterranean ocean of freshwater that lies under eight states in the heart of America's breadbasket. In recent years some Texas farmers have abandoned irrigation on more than two million acres because the table has dropped as much as 200 feet. Others have switched to plants that require less irrigation. Scientists predict that overuse will cause the water level to fall as much as three feet a year in certain areas.

Saline ocean water is heavier than fresh groundwater because salt is dissolved in the seawater, and as a result saline water tends to flow slowly toward the bottom of a coastal aquifer. When a cone of depression occurs in these areas, the level of saltwater rises below the wellhead because of the reduction in water pressure there. Eventually, if the water table continues to fall, saltwater reaches the well and contaminates the freshwater supply. Long Island, New York, had severe problems with saltwater intrusion during the 1960s, and many cities on the Gulf of Mexico still face this problem.

Groundwater contamination is a serious problem in the United States as our use of this resource grows. Dumps and landfills used for storing waste, and mining and other industrial activities cause much of the contamination. When water infiltrates the ground and percolates down to the water table, it leaches chemical and biological contaminants from waste deposits, septic tanks, agricultural fields, and other surfaces. A **pollution plume** forms as the contaminated groundwater flows toward areas of lower hydrostatic pressure. Decontaminating a polluted aquifer is very difficult because the water is so inaccessible. The 1980 Comprehensive Environmental Response, Compensation, and Liability Act, called the Superfund Act, resulted in efforts to decontaminate groundwater at sites such as Cinnaminson, New Jersey, and Endicott, New York.

The San Joaquin Valley in California has experienced extreme subsidence over the years, a result of the withdrawal of groundwater in the area for irrigation.

Glacial Processes and Landforms

Glaciers

Glaciers, large accumulations of ice that move on land, cover about 10 percent of Earth's land surface; lakes and even oceans freeze (down to 15 feet or so), but neither is considered a glacier because the ice does not flow as a unit. Glaciers are customarily divided into two types based on their location and size. **Valley glaciers,** sometimes called **alpine glaciers,** are found at elevations above 15,000 feet in mountains near the Equator, and at progressively lower elevations at higher latitudes where average annual temperatures are cooler. Glaciers in the St. Elias Mountains of Alaska, including those in Glacier Bay National Park, flow down to the Gulf of Alaska. Alpine glaciers are much smaller than continental glaciers and are tongue-shaped because they follow and expand preexisting stream valleys out of the mountains. **Continental glaciers**, also called **ice sheets** or **ice caps**, are massive. Glaciers cover nearly 5 million square miles of Antarctica's 5.1 million square miles, with an average thickness of 7,000 feet. Greenland and Patagonia also have huge expanses of continental glaciers.

In order to form, glaciers require yearly snowfall plus temperatures cold enough throughout the year to allow annual snowfall to exceed annual melting and accumulate for hundreds of thousands of years. Each year's snowfall slowly compresses the previous season's snow, forcing air out to form a granular snow called **firn** (or névé), which is further compacted and over time recrystalizes into ice.

Glaciers move when an accumulation of ice is about 200 feet thick; the overlying weight causes bottom ice to flow. Such an accumulation of ice is only possible on land, where glaciers may be more than two miles thick, as in Greenland and Antarctica. Snow and ice accumulate on the upper two-thirds of a glacier, its **zone of accumulation**, and then are carried as if on a conveyor belt to the **zone of ablation**, where the glacier loses its mass by melting, **sublimation** (the process by which solid matter changes directly into a gas), or, in the case of glaciers that flow into the ocean, **calving** (breaking off chunks that float away as icebergs).

Ice in a glacier always moves downslope, away from higher elevations or higher pressure, but the distance the glacier travels and the location of its leading edge, or **snout**, vary over time. While glacial ice moves continually, the snout may advance, remain in one location, or retreat, depending on whether the climate cools (causing increased accumulation), remains stable, or warms (causing increased ablation). Theoretically, glaciers throughout the world would retreat if global warming occurs; most glaciers are in fact now retreating. Others, however, are advancing even in the same areas such as southern Chile, because cyclic surges are occurring.

Glaciers move slowly by sliding along Earth's surface over compressed water, while internally the ice glides along internal planes of weakness between the layers of ice formed by annual snowfalls and internal deformation. Average speeds of glaciers vary between one and ten feet per day—depending upon temperature, thickness of ice, and slope—although faster speeds are possible; glaciers in Greenland have been timed at up to 70 feet per day. Temporary rates up to 300 feet per day have occurred when increased temperature or overlying pressure caused bottom ice to melt and water to accumulate beneath a glacier.

Glaciers that experience these surges are called **galloping glaciers;** in coastal areas such surges increase the number of icebergs.

Most large glaciers are found in cold climates near the Arctic and in Antarctica, but Ecuador, Uganda, and Papua New Guinea—all within five degrees of the Equator—have small glaciers on their highest peaks. Not all cold regions have glaciers. Some lack sufficient snowfall, as is the case in parts of Ellesmere Island in the Arctic Ocean and in most of Siberia.

Glacial Processes

As glaciers move, they erode rock and sediment from the walls and beds of their routes. Physical weathering and mass wasting from valley walls above a glacier contribute to erosion by causing rock fragments to fall on the surface of the glacier. Glaciers erode by **plucking** rocks from the walls or bed (when meltwater freezes onto the rocks) or by **abrasion,**

when the plucked rocks embedded in ice scrape more rock and sediments from the walls and bed. **Glacial striations**, deep parallel grooves in bedrock, are caused by abrasion and can be found in British Columbia, where they date from the Pleistocene Ice Age; glacial striations can be found in South Africa that date from an ice age 300 million years ago, long before the Pleistocene.

Deposition by a glacier occurs at its edge and snout, where warmer air temperatures cause melting. All glacial deposits can be referred to as **glacial drift**, but deposits that are carried by meltwater and then layered, or sorted, as the streamflow slows are called **stratified drift**. Deposits that are dropped immediately or pushed aside and not sorted are called **till**. Sand and gravel deposits are often found in stratified drift; till contains all sediment sizes from clay to boulders.

Eroded rock and sediment can be moved hundreds of miles before deposition, and some sand and gravel deposits may be used as a valuable resource for construction

The movement of glaciers, such as the Ferrar Glacier in Arena Valley, Antarctica, causes erosion and abrasion, sometimes transporting rock and earth for several hundred miles.

purposes. Streams, lakes, and wetlands are often relocated when glaciers cover existing drainage patterns and meltwater creates new water features. After the Pleistocene, when some alpine glaciers melted away, water collected in the basins to form **tarns**, or lakes, such as the Enchantment Lakes in Washington State.

Glacial Landscapes—Alpine

Landforms created by alpine glaciers are restricted to higher elevations in mountainous areas where Pleistocene glaciers existed. Snowfall accumulates in **cirques.** Also called corries, coires, and cwms, these basins are in protected areas in the upper elevations and form the beginnings of glaciers that flow down preexisting valleys, widening and deepening them through erosion. The erosion creates distinct **U-shaped valleys**. Thousands of feet of rock can be eroded away in a valley; during the Pleistocene glaciers deepened California's

Yosemite Valley more than 3,200 feet, although almost 2,000 feet of glacial deposits now fill the valley. Smaller U-shaped valleys may become tributaries of larger U-shaped valleys. The surfaces of the glaciers may meet at the same elevation, but the larger glacier will erode a deeper valley. When the glaciers melt, the smaller and shallower valley becomes a **hanging valley** high above the more deeply cut larger valley. Waterfalls such as Bridalveil Fall in Yosemite are commonly found at the mouths of hanging valleys.

Deposition from alpine glaciers is usually limited to the lower valleys but may extend to adjacent flatlands. Conditions suitable for glaciers extend across the higher elevations of a mountain range, so the alpine landscape includes landforms caused by interactions between glaciers. When several glaciers form on different sides of the same peak, they erode cirques, arêtes, and horns into the landscape. **Arêtes** are steep-sided ridges separating cirques or U-shaped valleys; **horns** are pyramid-shaped peaks with three or more

The crest of the Sangre de Cristo Mountains in southern Colorado was carved into a continuous arête by Pleistocene glaciation.

Like most fjords, the Kenai Fjords of Alaska were formed by glacial carving. As glaciers melted and sea levels rose, carved coastal indentations filled with water. The walls of a fjord usually plunge deep below the surface of the water.

steep faces that are the back faces of cirques. The Matterhorn in the Swiss Alps is a classic example of a horn, as is Mount Assiniboine in the Canadian Rockies. In other circumstances two cirques may erode backward into each other, forming a **col** or low point; Tioga Pass in the Sierra Nevada and St. Bernard Pass in the Alps are cols.

Glaciers can erode below sea level on coasts but wave action eventually melts the glaciers. During the Pleistocene Ice Age oceans were lower because more of Earth's water supply was stored in the vast continental glaciers. When the glaciers melted, oceans rose and created **fjords** by flooding U-shaped valleys along the mountainous coasts of Alaska, British Columbia, southern Chile, Norway, and New Zealand.

Moraines, the ridgelike till deposits that mark the limits of glacial movement, are common in both alpine and continental glaciers. When alpine glaciers descend to the elevation at which ablation occurs, till is dropped as a **terminal moraine** at the snout of the glacier and as **lateral moraines** along the sides of the glacier. As a glacier retreats and the snout

recedes up the valley, till covers more of the ground below the snout and, if the retreat is spasmodic, may occur as a series of parallel **recessional moraines**.

Glacial Landscapes— Continental

Glaciers are now limited to high latitudes and high elevations, but their geographic extent during the Pleistocene and earlier ice ages was far greater and helped create our current landscapes. About two million years ago Earth's temperatures cooled enough for snowfall to accumulate and start forming the continental glaciers that covered North America south to Missouri and blanketed Europe south to London and Krakow; the Andes, the Himalaya, and all of Antarctica were also covered by glaciers. Most of these glaciers have melted, leaving only remnants, but the effects of the Pleistocene Ice Age on the land and water are ongoing and abundantly evident. More than 75 percent of the freshwater on Earth is currently stored as glacial ice, where it remains,

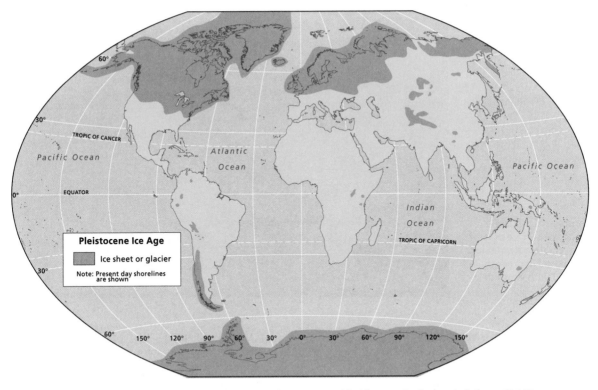

This map shows the maximum extent of Pleistocene glaciation worldwide, a cycle that ended about 10,000 years ago.

on average, for 10,000 years before melting. The large groundwater supplies under the Sahara and Utah's Great Salt Lake are but two legacies of the wetter climate of the Pleistocene Ice Age.

Continental glaciers are today limited to Antarctica, Greenland, Patagonia, and larger Arctic islands, but because of their spatial extent during the Pleistocene Ice Age, glacial landforms are found over much of Europe and North America. During the Pleistocene glaciers that arose from locations such as Hudson Bay and Labrador in North America and Scandinavia in Eurasia advanced and retreated several times. In North America the four major advances are labeled chronologically and by their extent as the Nebraskan, Kansan, Illinoisan, and Wisconsin periods. About 10,000 years ago the continental glaciers in the midlatitudes began to melt, ending the

Pleistocene Ice Age; previous cycles of retreats and advances, however, suggest this may be another temporary retreat that may be followed eventually by another advance.

The effects of Pleistocene glaciation are seen in the distribution of erosional and depositional landforms, changes in surface hydrology, and the global distributions of vegetation and animals. Erosional landforms created by continental glaciers are less dramatic in appearance than those of alpine glaciers and are distributed over much of Canada and northern Europe. Like alpine glaciers, continental glaciers pluck and abrade the surface as they flow outward from their centers, gouging depressions that later filled with water. Minnesota, known as The Land of 10,000 Lakes, was shaped by continental glaciers, as was Finland, with its more than 50,000 lakes.

Continental glaciers erode the surface as they flow, creating depressions in exposed bedrock that later fill with water to form lakes.

Glacial deposits cover much of the upper midwestern United States and northern Europe. Moraines were deposited by each glacial advance, and moraines from earlier advances were usually obliterated by later advances. Long Island, New York, and Denmark's Jutland Peninsula are primarily moraines; the Ronkonkoma moraine is part of Long Island and is also part of Martha's Vineyard and Nantucket. South of Lake Michigan and southwest of Lake Erie are a series of recessional moraines created when the glaciers melted after the Wisconsin advance; these moraines in central Illinois can be 20 feet high, 15 miles wide, and 200 miles long. **Till plains**,
level deposits of till, are also common in the Great Lakes area behind the terminal and recessional moraines.

When continental glaciers advanced over earlier till deposits, the glaciers shaped the till in some areas into low linear hills called **drumlins**, whose long axes paralleled the direction of the glaciers' movement. Although their formation process is still unclear, drumlins may also have formed around large boulders or other obstructions; they average 100 feet high and 0.5 mile long. The huge extent of till deposits during the Pleistocene resulted in numerous drumlin swarms in Ireland, New England, and Washington State.

The Great Lakes

Before the Pleistocene Ice Age, none of the Great Lakes existed; the entire area was a large drainage basin emptying into the St. Lawrence River. Glaciers moving from Canada into this area followed and deepened the major river channels. As temperatures warmed after each glacial advance, a series of lakes was formed: Lake Maumee was succeeded by Lake Whittlesey, which became Lake Erie. The current pattern of the Great Lakes appeared only in the last 14,000 years.

Low, linear hills called drumlins are formed when glaciers move over previously deposited till.

Eskers, sinuous ridges of deposited sediments, are formed by streams flowing through or under a melting glacier.

Bunker Hill in Boston, Massachusetts, is a drumlin, as is Breed's Hill, where Revolutionary War fighting occurred; several islands just off Boston's shore in Massachusetts Bay are drumlins as well.

Glacial **erratics**, rocks and boulders transported on or in the ice from distant sites, were deposited by Pleistocene glaciers. Large erratics in eastern Washington have been termed **haystack boulders;** they may be the size of a house and weigh several tons. Glacial erratics have been keys to locating valuable resources; a nickel deposit near Petsamo, Finland, was found by tracking nickel-rich erratics back to their source.

Landforms created from the stratified drift of melting Pleistocene glaciers include eskers, outwash plains, and kames. **Eskers** are long ridges formed by streams that flowed underneath the glaciers. Streams under glaciers form when water that melts in the zone of ablation sinks through crevasses in the ice and collects in tunnels running through and under the ice. As the water flows, heavier sediments such as sand and gravel settle in the streambed and may form deposits; some of these deposits are today mined for construction materials. Few eskers are more than a hundred feet high, but some in northern Canada measure more than 500 miles long.

Meltwater that flowed from the snouts of continental glaciers formed delta-like deposits called **outwash plains**, and deposits that collected between the lobes of a glacier (known as its **extensions**) formed low mounds called **kames**. Depositional landscapes from continental glaciers can be complex, with overlapping outwash plains and moraines and eskers that run through both. Small lakes called **kettles** are common in depositional landscapes; huge blocks of ice would break off the glaciers, become surrounded by accumulating sediments, and eventually melt, leaving a hole in the middle of the sediments. Walden Pond is one of the many kettles in New England.

The Pleistocene Ice Age dramatically changed the hydrology of both North America and Europe. It rerouted streams and changed precipitation patterns, resulting in new lakes.

Eskers and Arctic Life

Permafrost does not occur in eskers because they are composed of permeable sand and gravel and do not retain water and freeze. They are critical to the ecology of northern Canada. Several plants that grow on eskers, including bear root and cranberries, are important food for bears and migrating waterfowl; animals from grizzly bears to tundra wolves to ground squirrels can burrow into the eskers to survive the long winters.

Prior to the Pleistocene, streams north of what is now Nebraska drained northward, and the Missouri and the Mississippi Rivers did not exist as we know them. During the Pleistocene drainage to the north was halted by the wall of ice, and huge amounts of meltwater had to drain south. The Missouri River's tributary system eventually reached north to Saskatchewan, and the river developed a floodplain several miles across and more than 70 feet deep along much of its course. The Mississippi's sediment load was eventually deposited in the Gulf of Mexico and formed much of what is today's southern Louisiana.

Pluvial lakes, lakes created by rainfall, formed during the Pleistocene through much of what is now the arid American West. Precipitation patterns were different because global climatic patterns had shifted. Lake Bonneville occupied almost one-third of Utah during the Pleistocene, but it has since shrunk to become present-day Great Salt Lake. The Bonneville

Pleistocene glaciers dramatically modified the drainage systems of central North America. Before glaciation, much water drained northeastward. Afterward, the newly formed Mississippi drainage system channeled water to the south. In the north, meandering streams and numerous lakes characterize a deranged drainage pattern.

Salt Flats are evidence of Lake Bonneville's evaporation, which left behind extensive deposits of salt. Other western lakes have also evaporated, leaving small remnant lakes such as Pyramid Lake in Nevada and mineral deposits such as borax in Death Valley, California.

Throughout the northern United States and southern Canada evidence of Pleistocene glaciers is widespread. In addition to the landforms described above, a number of marshes and swampy areas are found from Saskatchewan to South Dakota; these are the hallmark of the Prairie Potholes region, a chain of ponds and marshes that provide habitat for migrating waterfowl. Eastern Washington contains huge dry channels called **coulees**, including the Grand Coulee, cut by gigantic floods when ice dams failed on the ancient glacial Lake Mis-

soula in Montana; the area is now named the Channeled Scablands because of these features.

The Pleistocene Ice Age also caused global changes in the distribution of animals and plants. Ocean levels may have dropped more than 400 feet along some coastlines because precipitation was trapped in the continental glaciers and could not flow in streams to the oceans. As a result, several landmasses now separated by water were connected by **land bridges** across which animals and people could travel; present-day Sri Lanka and India, New Guinea and Australia, and France and the British Isles were each connected. A land bridge between Siberia and Alaska enabled bison and humans to travel to North America; a land bridge connecting present-day Indonesia and the Malay Peninsula enabled elephants and other large mammals to reach the Indonesian archipelago.

Waves and Coastal Landforms

Shores and Coasts

The boundary or area of contact between continents and islands and seawater can be considered shore, a shoreline, and a coast. A **shore** is the actual contact *area* where waves wash over the land surface; the *line* of contact is the **shoreline**, which changes with the tides. A **coast** extends away from the shore as far as landforms created by waves or other marine processes reach inland. Coasts may be less than a half mile wide or dozens of miles wide, depending on past changes in sea level or land elevation. Wave-cut terraces, for example, may be found miles inland if sea levels have dropped since the terraces were formed.

Waves

Landforms along ocean shores and coasts are sculpted primarily by wave action, although in some areas tides can also cause erosion and

deposition. Friction and wind pressure create energy that moves through the water, creating **waves**—undulations in the water surface—that transport kinetic energy to shores. A minimum wind speed of about two miles per hour is needed to create waves; slower breezes cause ripples that die out rapidly.

In water deeper than 100 to 200 feet, energy from the wind is transferred downwind and down wave; the water, however, moves in vertical circles or loops, rising to a **crest** and falling into a **trough**. The dimensions of these **progressive waves**, also called waves of oscillation, can be characterized by their **wavelength** (distance between two crests), **wave height** (distance from trough to crest), and **wave period** (speed of waves). Waves also have a **base level**, a depth equal to half of the wave length under calm water level, below which water is not moved by wind. Submarines navigating below the base level are unaffected by surface storms.

Wave dimensions reflect wind speed and the

amount of energy transferred from the wind. Larger waves result when winds blow faster, for longer time periods, or over larger expanses of water (the **fetch** of the wind). The maximum height of a wave created by a given wind speed is limited because the amount of energy is limited by the speed, fetch, and duration of wind. As wind speed increases and waves transport more energy, waves steepen and eventually break, or fall over. When wind speeds reach ten miles per hour, some waves begin to break and form whitecaps. The energy transmitted from wind to water allows waves to travel well beyond the fetch of the wind itself; these **swells** have been known to travel for more than 6,000 miles, from just off Antarctica to the Alaskan shoreline.

As progressive waves approach shallower water along a shore, the base level of a wave meets the seafloor, and friction causes the onshore movement of the base to slow while the surface portion of the wave continues inland. As water gets increasingly shallow, the wavelength shortens because of the friction, but the wave height increases to compensate for the shortened wavelength (since little wave energy is lost). The entire wave begins to tilt

forward because its crest has moved ahead of its base. Eventually the top of the wave (now described as a **wave of translation**) plunges or spills forward, creating a **breaker**, and the water flows up the beach as **swash** before gravity pulls it back to sea level as **backwash**. When a series of waves, or a **wave train**, forms multiple breakers, **surf** is created.

Waves approach shorelines at various angles because shorelines are irregular. The angle at which most waves and shorelines actually meet, however, is usually about five degrees from parallel because of wave **refraction**. As each wave reaches shallow water, the friction of the seafloor slows down that part of the wave moving across it, causing it to angle into the shore. Each successive segment of the wave nearing the shoreline is also slowed so that the entire length of a wave meets the shore at almost the same angle.

Wave refraction is especially important in determining the direction in which sediments are transported by waves. As water from breakers swashes onto a beach, it does so at an angle of about five degrees, but when that water backwashes to the ocean, it flows at right angles to the slope of the beach because of the pull of

The cool coastal waters of California provide abundant commercially valuable fish. Here, smelt fishermen cast their nets.

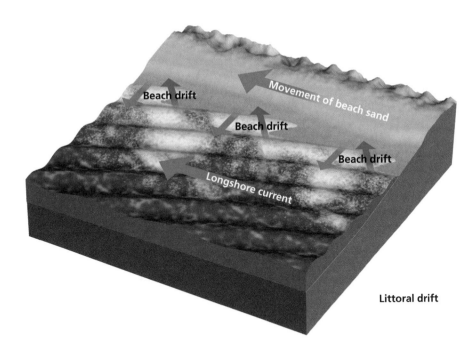

Beach drift

Movement of beach sand

Beach drift

Beach drift

Longshore current

Littoral drift

gravity. As a result, beach sediment is moved sideways by waves along a serrated path called **beach drift**, and the water nearest the shoreline also parallels this sideways movement, forming a **longshore current**. The combined movement of water and sediment is called a **littoral drift;** its direction reflects the dominant wave and wind pattern offshore.

Tides

In addition to waves, rising and falling ocean levels, or **tides**, also affect water along shorelines. Tides are the response of oceans to the gravitational pulls of the moon and sun. When tides rise (**flood tides**), water extends farther inshore; conversely, falling tides (**ebb tides**) uncover the shore. The timing of flood and ebb tides on shorelines is influenced by the relative location of the moon and sun and by the Coriolis effect. While few landforms are created directly by tides, erosion and deposition by waves do occur at sea level. The reach of the

high and low tides determines what portion of the shoreline is affected by the waves.

Despite the much larger size of the sun, the gravitational pull of the moon is slightly more than twice as strong because the moon is so much closer to Earth. As a result, the locations of high tides follow the path of the moon rather than that of the sun, and tides in general follow a monthly sequence based on the moon's revolution around Earth. It takes a **lunar month**, or 29.5 Earth days (an Earth day is 24 hours), for the moon to complete one orbit around Earth. During each Earth day the moon travels 12.2 degrees farther in its orbit around Earth. As a result, it takes 24 hours 50 minutes (one **lunar day**) for the moon to be directly over the same longitude.

As a rule, there are two high tides on Earth at the same time; ocean levels directly below the moon (a position relative to earth called the moon's **zenith**) are elevated, while on the opposite side of Earth (the moon's **nadir**) ocean levels are also elevated relative to other locations on Earth. The moon travels around Earth, but the moon and Earth also rotate as a

Undertow and Rip Currents

When a wave's backwash returns to the ocean, it contributes to a longshore current and also creates an **undertow** of offshore flow below incoming breakers. When low spots or undersea canyons are present on the seafloor, undertow can be channeled into fast-moving (more than five miles per hour) **rip currents** that transport sediments and unwary swimmers offshore.

pair around a common center located 2,919 miles above the middle of Earth and directly under the moon. Water levels below the moon's zenith rise because the gravitational pull of the moon is greater than the **centripetal force**—the force directed toward the center of the joint rotation—required to keep the moon and Earth in their joint orbit. Water levels at the moon's nadir rise because the moon's gravitational force is less than the required centripetal force; as a result the water rises because of centripetal force.

At the longitudes halfway between these two high tides, ocean levels are depressed because water has been pulled toward the areas below the nadir and zenith. Thus, two low tides exist as well at any given time. High and low tides are linked to the location of the moon relative to Earth. Therefore as Earth rotates on its axis, each longitude passes under two high and two low tides every lunar day.

In addition to the moon's gravitational pull, the sun's gravitational pull increases or decreases the levels that high and low tides reach. When the sun, moon, and Earth are in a line, that is in conjunction with one another, the gravitational pull on the oceans is compounded, and **spring tides** with the highest high tides and lowest low tides result. Spring tides occur during full moons and new moons. At the first and third quarters of the moon, the sun, moon, and Earth form a right angle so that the gravitational pulls on the oceans counteract each other, resulting in **neap tides** with small ranges.

Tidal ranges and timing are the result of many factors in addition to planetary alignment. For example, the latitude of the moon's zenith—the moon's orbit around Earth varies

Mean Sea Level

The level of the sea changes continuously because tides rise and fall twice daily and waves occur regularly. The average level of the water filling Earth's oceans relative to Earth's center basins and seas is the **mean sea level (MSL)**. It is determined by averaging the heights of high and low tides over a 19-year period. The 19-year time frame is called the Metonic cycle—for Meton, a fifth-century B.C. Greek astronomer—and it averages the effects of periodic changes in the moon's location relative to Earth. Mean sea level is the **datum**, or reference level, for elevations on topographic maps, but **hydrographic maps** (maps of water depths) use a reference level based on average low-tide levels—the **mean low water (MLW)**—to ensure that ships can clear obstacles on the seafloor.

from 28.5° north latitude to 28.5° south latitude—the topography of the seafloor, and the shape of the coastline affect tidal elevations and timing. In addition, high tides within a body of water such as the Mediterranean Sea move around a central point because the Coriolis effect deflects the movement of the water. Different shorelines along the same body of water can therefore have tremendous differences in the timing and range of tides. The Wash, a bay on the east coast of England, has a tidal range of more than 16 feet. The tidal range 450 miles and five hours later on the northwest coast of Denmark is within a range of only two feet.

On average, most shorelines have tidal

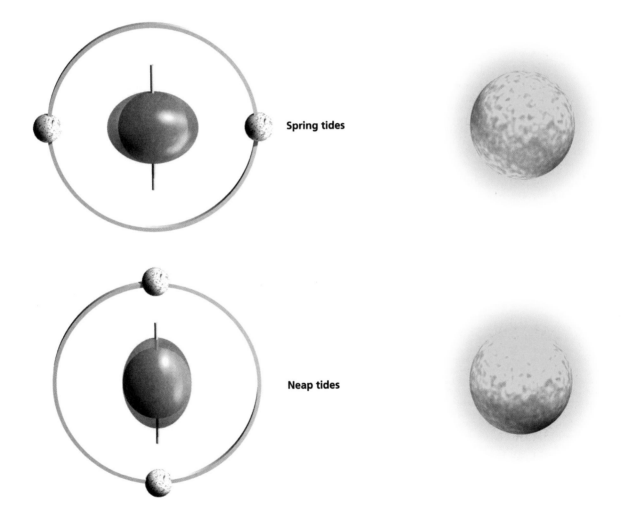

Spring tides

Neap tides

Tides result from the combined gravitational attraction of the moon and sun on Earth's oceans. Spring tides (the highest of the high tides) result when the sun and moon are aligned as shown in the top illustration. Neap tides (the lowest tides) result when the sun and moon are positioned at right angles to Earth.

Gulf of Saint-Malo

In the Gulf of Saint-Malo off the northwest coast of France, the tidal range reaches 44 feet. The inshore and offshore tidal flows drive the generators of a power plant on the Rance River which flows into the gulf. Mont-Saint-Michel lies one mile offshore and is connected to the mainland at low tide by exposed shore, but it is an island at high tide. Outgoing tides in the vicinity expose nearly nine miles of seafloor, and incoming tides move quickly enough to trap the unwary, a phenomenon author Aaron Elkins used as a central part of the plot in his award-winning mystery, *Old Bones*, published in 1987.

ranges between three and six feet and semidiurnal tides (two high and two low tides) every lunar day. Some locations, such as those on the Mediterranean, may have tidal ranges of one foot, and others, notably the Minas Basin in Nova Scotia's Bay of Fundy, have tidal ranges of more than 50 feet. The number of high and low tides per day is affected by the size and shape of the water body. The Gulf of Mexico has diurnal tides (one high tide and one low tide each day), but most of Earth's coasts, including the Pacific coast of North America, experience a mixed tide of semidiurnal tides most days and diurnal tides once or twice a lunar month.

Coastal Processes

Waves and, to a much lesser extent, tides create coastal landforms by eroding, transporting, and depositing sediments. A wave's energy is transferred to a shoreline when the wave breaks against it and causes erosion; when the water returns to the ocean, sediment is transported until the water slows and deposition occurs. Large storm waves contain great amounts of energy and therefore increase erosion; human-made changes in the characteristics of a coastline, such as artificial breakwaters offshore, slow wave movement and increase deposition.

EROSION

Waves erode rock along shorelines by abrasion, hydraulic action, and solution. Most wave erosion along steep shorelines is caused by **abrasion** from gravel and sand carried by waves. **Hydraulic action**, the physical force of moving water, causes erosion. Large storm waves can crash ashore with more than 2,000 pounds of pressure per square foot. The weight of the water in a wave also compresses air within rock fractures. Erosion by **solution** along shorelines is most significant where there are limestone and other carbonate rocks. All three types of erosion are concentrated on the shoreline elevation at which waves strike the shore. A change in sea level, such as the rise that occurred when ice age glaciers melted, moves the shoreline inland and so changes the elevation of wave erosion and the location of wave-induced landform development.

The rate of erosion is affected by wave size, rock strength, and the shape of the shoreline. Larger waves cause greater abrasion because more and larger particles can be hurled against the shoreline. Harder rocks have greater resistance to erosion than shales and other soft rocks. Erosion is greater on headlands that jut into an ocean than on the headlands of bays or coves because waves are refracted into the headlands.

Sediments that are eroded by waves or introduced into oceans by rivers are transported down the coast by longshore currents. Longshore currents along shorelines move sediments within the water as well as along the beach. The term "river of sand" is applicable to most beaches because the sand slowly and continuously moves downwave. Sediment is also transported offshore and onshore by seasonal storms. Off the coast of La Jolla, California, for example, winter storms transport sand offshore, where it remains as a sandbar until smaller summer waves transport it back onto the beach.

DEPOSITION

Waves deposit sediment when their speed decreases, which can occur when waves wash inland or when longshore currents reach slower water. Storm waves have greater energy and erosional power than regular waves and will deposit sediments if they wash so far inland that the water sinks into the ground before it flows back to the ocean. The barrier islands off the Atlantic coast of the United States are moving closer to the shore as storms erode their outer beach, overwash the islands, and deposit sediment on the inland side. Longshore currents slow when they reach calm water in bays or open water and deposit their loads at that point.

BIOLOGIC PROCESSES

Corals, tiny marine animals that live in undersea colonies, create landforms such as reefs. The colonies exist only in clean, shallow tropical seas with water temperatures averaging 64°F or higher. The animals have soft bodies surrounded by hard skeletons; along with deposits of certain algae, coral skeletons accumulate over centuries to form reefs.

Coastal Landforms and Landscapes

Coastal landscapes are composed of erosional landforms, depositional landforms, and biologic landforms such as coral reefs. The intensity of wave activity, type of rock material, type of tectonic boundary, water temperature, and changes in water level affect the landforms that occur along a shoreline.

Usually the coastal processes of erosion and deposition and therefore the landscapes are similar along long stretches of shoreline; for example, barrier islands and related landforms are common along the Gulf of Mexico shoreline. Onshore geologic processes also affect coastal landscapes. When ocean levels rose after Pleistocene glaciers melted, fjords were created when U-shaped glacial valleys along the coasts were flooded, such as those along the coast of British Columbia. **Ria** coastlines (ria is from the Spanish word *río*, for river) were created when river and stream valleys were flooded by rising oceans and seas. Ria coastlines can be seen along Tasmania's coast.

EROSIONAL LANDFORMS

Most shorelines dominated by erosional landforms have experienced geologically recent changes in sea level that caused wave action to strike at a different elevation than previously along the shoreline. Rising or falling ocean levels, tectonic uplift, and **isostatic rebound** (rising crust following glacier return) can have this effect. Other factors also affect the intensity of wave erosion, however, so that not all shorelines affected by changing ocean levels will be dominated by erosional landforms. For example, the Atlantic shoreline of the United States experiences a sealevel rise of about one foot each century, but the shoreline also has many depositional features because of sediments from streams and because of the gradual slope of the continental shelf.

Many of the erosional landforms found on shorelines develop from a wave-cut notch at the base of a cliff, where wave action is concentrated. If the rock forming the cliff is strong enough, the cliff will migrate inland as erosion undercuts it along the shoreline; weak rock, shale, or moraines will erode to form a slope. Fractures or other weak areas at the base of a cliff allow these notches to be expanded by erosion into **sea caves**, which can extend more than a hundred feet under the cliff.

Rising and Falling Sea Levels

Global warming has led to a rise in sea levels, which in turn have increased storm erosion along some of the world's most popular beaches. The Cape Hatteras Lighthouse on the Outer Banks of North Carolina was at risk of toppling into the ocean because more than 1,300 feet of shoreline had eroded since it was built in 1970, leaving just 120 feet between its foundation and the Atlantic. Using a hydraulic lift system, the National Park Service moved the lighthouse inland 2,900 feet in 1999. The lighthouse's beacon will continue to remind us that even the sturdiest man-made structures give way before the sea.

When a sea cave cuts across a narrow headland, the cave can be exposed at both ends until an **arch** is left. Eventually the roof of the arch will collapse, and the outlying part of the cliff becomes a **stack**. The west coasts of the United States and Canada and the southern coast of England have cliffs, stacks, and arches.

Other shorelines where wave erosion is (or was) occurring may have wave-cut terraces or an abundance of coves and islands. Waves striking a rocky shoreline leave a flattened offshore area over which waves break and below which waves are unable to erode. When ocean levels fall, these wave-cut platforms, or **terraces**, are exposed. If past ocean levels were at different heights for long enough periods, then a series of terraces may be eroded; more than ten terraces can be found on San Clemente Island, California.

Glacier- and stream-eroded areas that were flooded by rising ocean levels after the Pleistocene have distinctive erosional landforms created by processes other than wave action. Fjords are found along shorelines that were heavily glaciated during the Pleistocene, including the Panhandle of Alaska and the

Hikers climb a cliff near a large protrusion of volcanic rock on the shoreline of St. Helena Island in the South Atlantic Ocean.

west coasts of Norway and southern Chile. Erosional landforms dominate these coasts, but if a sufficient amount of glacial debris is available, **pocket beaches** may form in shallow bays where the waves' motion slows and sediments can collect. Ria coasts or shorelines form when river valleys are submerged or drowned by rising water levels. Some river valleys on the Atlantic coast of North America have drowned since Pleistocene glaciers melted. Drowning of the Potomac and James River Valleys formed the Chesapeake Bay, while the drowning of the Delaware River Valley formed the Delaware Bay.

DEPOSITIONAL LANDFORMS

When wave velocity slows—as when waves wash inland—sediments are deposited and depositional landforms result. Swash erosion, part of the swash-backwash transport system, is involved, but landforms such as beaches and spits are shaped by depositional processes. Deposition can be seasonal—some beaches are deposited in summer and eroded in winter—and changes in the amount of available

sediment (usually sand) will affect landform development.

Most depositional landforms created by wave action are extensions of beaches. **Beaches** are accumulations of sediments; the individual particles of a beach are usually sand size but range in size from clay to cobbles. These sediments are deposited by wave action on a shoreline between low- and high-tide marks. Quartz grains are the most common type of sand because of their resistance to abrasion and weathering; basalt grains create black-sand beaches, such as those on Hawaii, and crushed shells create white-sand beaches, such as those near Pensacola, Florida. Sediment deposits usually extend offshore, occasionally more than a mile. The sandy area above the high-tide mark is the **berm** or backshore, which often rises to a ridge or **dune** and is generated by storm waves and storm surges.

Beach drift transports sediment along beaches, parallel to the shoreline; this process creates new landforms when a coastline curves and the drift extends beaches offshore. **Spits** are beach extensions that form along shorelines with bays and other indentations; beach

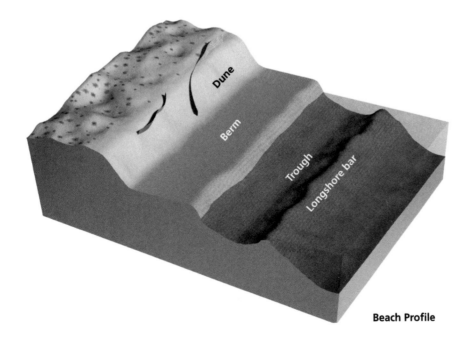

Beach Profile

sand is deposited in calm water offshore by wave swash in a low ridge that may be a few feet or yards above the average sea level. The growth rate of spits varies widely and depends on the rates of transport and deposition: On the shoreline of northern France growth rates have been measured at about 33 feet a year; on Long Island, New York, the rate of growth is more than 200 feet a year.

Variations of spits occur when they extend across bays, when offshore currents vary, and when nearshore islands exist. **Baymouth bars** are spits that extend all the way across the mouths of bays: If the bays are not fed by large streams, the bars cut the bays off from the ocean. When offshore currents cause a spit to curve inland, a **hook** is formed. Nearshore islands change depositional patterns by

causing incoming waves to refract and erode the island's seaward sides; at the same time wave speed on the shoreward side is slowed, thus allowing deposition. When a spit connects a beach and island, a **tombolo** is formed.

Barrier islands are long, linear wave deposits that form parallel to shorelines; Padre Island, Texas, is about a hundred miles long. A variety of geomorphic processes create barrier islands. Some are extended spits, some are berms that were isolated by rising ocean levels, and some are offshore deposits exposed by falling sea levels. The Frisian Islands along the northern coast of the Netherlands are barrier islands. Barrier islands from Cape Cod, Massachusetts, to Brownsville, Texas,

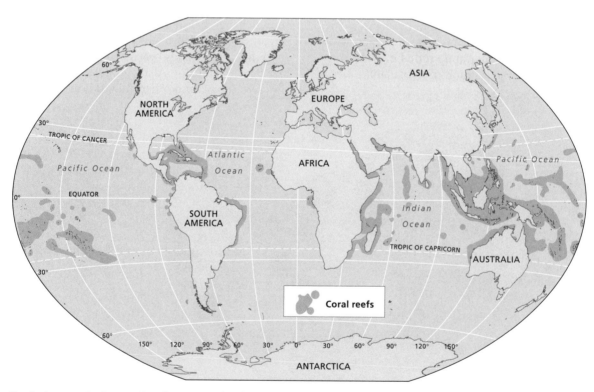

Tropical oceans harbor coral reefs, stony multicolored ridges constructed by tiny sea creatures called corals. Although reefs grow slowly, less than an inch a year, over millions of years they may grow to be hundreds of feet thick.

Bora-Bora, a volcanic island in French Polynesia, is ringed by a fringing reef that extends more than one thousand feet from shore.

protect the East and Gulf coasts from the brunt of storms.

Lagoons are narrow water bodies between barrier islands and the mainland; most are connected to the ocean by tidal inlets. The width of lagoons varies widely, from less than a hundred yards to more than a mile. A very narrow lagoon separates Palm Beach from the Florida mainland, while Pamlico Sound separates Cape Hatteras from the North Carolina mainland by more than a mile. Deposition in lagoons along the shoreline and barrier island sides creates marshes, swamps, and tidal flats, and diverse biologic communities thrive in these wetland environments.

BIOLOGIC LANDFORMS

Coral reefs are landforms created by corals, tiny, soft-bodied marine animals that have hard outer skeletons. Corals live in clean, shallow tropical oceans with water temperatures averaging 64°F or higher. Almost all coral reefs are found between 30° north latitude and 30° south latitude, along eastern shorelines that

have warm oceanic currents and where sediment deposits from streams are limited.

Corals cannot survive below depths of 500 feet, where the algae on which they depend lack sufficient sunlight to live. As a result, reefs are found along shorelines (these are called **fringing reefs**), are separated from shorelines by lagoons (**barrier reefs**), or exist as evidence of former shorelines that have since been submerged (**atolls**). Fringing reefs, such as those around the Society Islands in the western Pacific, range from 1,500 to 3,000 feet wide. Barrier reefs form around islands or off continents that are slowly subsiding; as the land sinks, the corals grow upward from one to three feet every hundred years.

Atoll formation, first explained by 19th-century British naturalist Charles Darwin, occurs when a volcanic island subsides below water level. A circular coral reef, paralleling the former shoreline of the island, grows upward at a rate equal to that of subsidence and forms the atoll. The Marshall Islands comprise many atolls in the western Pacific Ocean; one of them is Bikini Atoll, which has coral growing more than three-quarters of a mile above the rock of the former island. This landform implies more than 50 million years of subsidence and coral growth. There are more than 300 atolls worldwide, most of which are in the western Pacific and Indian Oceans.

Shorelines and Development

Shorelines are in a constant state of change as cliffs erode, beaches move, and spits are deposited, and they are being increasingly developed for housing, recreation and leisure activities, and shipping. In order to prevent damage to seaside structures and watercraft, people attempt to control or counteract normal shoreline processes, often with limited or temporary success, but sometimes with unanticipated—and often undesirable—results.

Seawalls have been built at the base of cliffs, especially cliffs composed of glacial deposits or soft sedimentary rocks, to prevent wave erosion from threatening buildings on top of the cliffs. Unfortunately erosion from wave turbulence increases when seawalls are built; the energy of waves is not distributed on a beach slope but remains undiminished until it strikes the seawall. During strong storms with high waves, erosion around the sides of seawalls may cause them to collapse; it may also undercut the cliffs.

The erosion, transport, and deposition of beach sediment by littoral drift is a perpetual concern for landowners, the recreation industry, and marinas and ports. **Groins**, piles of rock extending outward from a beach, have been used to prevent beach sand from migrating downwave. While a groin will accumulate beach sand on one side, littoral processes still operate down wave so that beaches begin to disappear when erosion is not matched by deposition; as a result, dozens or even hundreds of groins may be built along a shoreline as individual landowners attempt to prevent erosion of their beaches. Pairs of groins, called **jetties**, built around openings in a spit or barrier island to preserve access, also cause up wave deposition and down wave erosion.

Breakwaters, piles of rock built parallel to a shore to prevent wave damage to watercraft or construction, have mixed results. Waves are reflected off breakwaters, and marinas built on the landward side are protected

Many Chicago beaches have been re-formed with the help of beach groins. These groins prevent sand from migrating south, promoting beach growth on the north side of the groins.

from all but the highest storm waves. Slowing the waves, however, can cause deposition behind the breakwater of sediments being transported by littoral drift along the shoreline. In some coastal locations, such as southern California, where longshore currents transport more than 250,000,000 cubic yards of sediment annually, deposition can nearly fill a marina: The breakwater at Santa Monica has caused the beach behind the breakwater to expand tremendously.

In other coastal locations, cities have attempted to manage the gain or loss of beach sediments either by pumping out the sand or by trucking in sand to increase beach size. To prevent beach drift from closing its harbor, Santa Barbara, California, must regularly dredge the accumulation of sand, which averages 280,000 cubic yards a year. Miami Beach, Florida, and Ocean City, Maryland, have the opposite problem and bring in sand to replace eroded beaches, but this is also not a permanent solution.

Winds and Dryland Landforms

Dryland Landscapes

Regions with desert and steppe climates have limited precipitation and sparse vegetation; as a result, rates of gradational processes are different from those operating in regions where surface water supports more extensive plant cover. There are also variations within dryland regions because of differences in wind patterns, abundance and type of surface material, and amounts and timing of precipitation. Landforms created by wind erosion—called **eolian erosion**, after Aeolus, the Greek god of the winds—and deposition are almost exclusive to deserts; fluvial landforms in drylands are the result of occasional rainfall that creates ephemeral streams and temporary lakes that evaporate quickly.

Africa's Sahara, the largest desert in the world, is mostly covered by dunes. The volume of sand, geology of the landscape, and wind direction and strength determine dune size and shape.

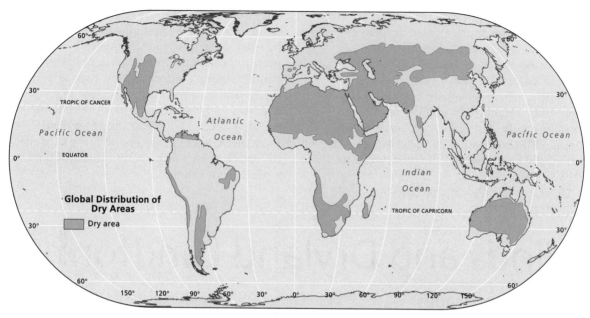

Arid regions cover about 20 percent of Earth's land surface, a percentage that may increase in the future due to human impact.

Deserts, regions that average less than 10 inches of precipitation annually, are found on every continent except Antarctica and cover about 20 percent of Earth's land surface. A **reg** is a stony desert while an **erg** is a sandy desert. **Steppes**, semiarid regions that receive between 10 and 20 inches of rain per year, cover about 15 percent of Earth's surface. (See Map: Climatic Zones, page 117.) Deserts grade into steppes, which in turn grade into more humid climates, and the landforms associated with these climates also grade into each other. About 75 percent of the world's desert regions are rocky or covered with thin soils and, along with steppe regions, are dominated by fluvial landforms; the remaining 25 percent of the world's deserts are sand covered and dominated by eolian landforms.

Today's desert and steppe climatic regions, like other climatic regions, are not permanent but may shift when climates change. During the Pleistocene Ice Age, wetter climates created lakes in what are now the Sahara, Mojave, and Australian deserts. Today humanity's impact on the environment is forcing a shift in the other direction—overgrazing, overfarming, and overlumbering are causing existing deserts to expand in a process called **desertification**. The effects of droughts in the Sahel region of northern Africa during the 1970s and 1980s were exacerbated by human activity and have resulted in desertification; Mauritania, Mali, Ethiopia, and Niger were especially hard hit.

Dryland Gradational Processes

WEATHERING AND MASS WASTING

Rates of weathering and mass wasting are far slower in drylands than in areas where water is more abundant. Landforms tend to be more angular than those in humid areas. Because there is less water, less chemical weathering by solution occurs. Limestone, for example, which is highly soluble and forms caves in humid

The Aral Sea

In an attempt to increase crop yields, particularly cotton, the Soviet Union diverted waters of the Syr Darya and Amu Darya—rivers that fed the Aral Sea—for irrigation in the 1960s. Since then, the sea has lost nearly 80 percent of its volume and more than 60 percent of its area. Desertification plagues the area around the lake, with salt buildup occurring on the former bed and dust storms feeding off eroding sediments. In 1997 the people of Kazakhstan, recognizing that their portion of the lake was fed by the cleaner Syr Darya River, built a 12-mile earthen dike that sealed off their healthier portion of water from the dangerously polluted lower sections of the lake. The World Bank hopes to fund a more permanent dike, which would save what the Kazakhstanis now call the Little Aral Sea, but might doom the larger southern portion.

environments, resists gradation in deserts; limestone strata can form caprock on cliffs over shales and softer sedimentary rocks. Atmospheric gases cause chemical weathering: Some oxidation occurs on rock surfaces and can accumulate to form a desert varnish of iron and manganese oxides. Physical weathering of surface rocks from salt-crystal growth does occur in dryland areas when saline groundwater rises and evaporates; the lack of surface water and vegetation means there is reduced opportunity for frost action and fracturing by root growth.

Mass wasting is particularly slow in deserts, where only thin soil layers can develop due to the lack of moisture and vegetation. Creep, slumps, and earth flows—the most common types of mass wasting—are rare in deserts. In steppes, however, they are more common. Occasional thunderstorms can cause mudslides, and small rockfalls loosened by physical weathering and minor downslope movements cause some accumulation of rocks and debris on talus slopes at the base of cliffs.

EOLIAN PROCESSES

Eolian processes include erosion by deflation and abrasion, transportation, and deposition of sediments. Wind erosion by **deflation** (from a Latin word meaning "to blow away") of sediments occurs after wind reaches the critical threshold speed for a sediment size. Small sand grains, for example, begin to be blown away when wind speed reaches about 11 miles per hour. Deflation usually needs wind turbulence to initiate movement by either lifting sediment particles into the wind or pulling them along the surface. Small, flat particles such as clay are not easily blown away because they lie flat on the surface, protected from wind by rocks and larger objects. Gravel and larger sediments are too heavy for deflation except when winds reach gale force, or at least 32 miles per hour. Deflation can lower land and create basins by blowing away sediments until the water table is reached; at this depth moistened sediments adhere to each other and resist deflation.

Abrasion involves windblown sediments (almost always sand grains) that strike rocks or other objects and chip away at them, thus creating **ventifacts**, stones or pebbles shaped, worn, or polished by abrasion. Abrasion is only operative within a few feet of the surface because most sand grains are too heavy to be lifted very high by the wind. As a result, rocks undercut by abrasion form **pedestal rocks**. In parts of Antarctica windblown snowflakes that are technically sediments have also caused abrasion of exposed rocks.

Sediments transported by winds may be suspended or bounced, depending upon wind speed and their weight. Lighter sediments such

Spires in Bryce Canyon national Park, Utah, were created by weathering processes that produced uneven erosion between the interbedding of soft siltstone and hard limestone.

as clay and silt are suspended by updrafts at altitudes that may reach 10,000 feet, and they may travel thousands of miles before they settle out or are rained out. **Black blizzards** occur when snow has been discolored by transported dust; dust storms are also evidence of sediments transported by wind. Heavier sediments such as sand and occasionally gravel are transported by **saltation** (skipping), rolling, and sliding along the surface. About 75 percent of all eolian surface transport is by saltation: When bouncing sand grains land, they may dislodge sand and other particles; the amount of sand in transport is thus increased.

When wind velocity slows, sediments are sorted and deposited on the surface. Sand and larger particles transported near the surface are deposited first and often collect in mounds or **dunes** near their source. Suspended dust particles require far lower wind speeds to stay aloft and travel farther, settling out days, weeks, or months later over large areas.

FLUVIAL PROCESSES

Most streamflow in drylands occurs rapidly and very sporadically. Thunderstorms and brief, heavy rains are characteristic of desert climates; though high temperatures cause convection, low absolute humidity reduces the number of convection events that can produce precipitation. Precipitation may cause flash

Dust Storms

Dust storms can carry more than 6,000 tons of sediment in one cubic mile of air. During the Dust Bowl years of the 1930s in the United States, winds blew clay and silt from midwestern states as far as the East Coast. Southeastern Australia is subject to brickfielders—dust storms named for winds that kicked up dust in brickfields near Sydney—from the interior deserts. Northern Africa has several winds, including khamsins, haboobs, siroccos, and simooms, that carry dust from the Sahara.

flooding because the thin soil and lack of vegetation reduce infiltration and increase runoff and erosion.

More than 90 percent of streams in deserts are ephemeral, and their channels contain water only a few days or hours each year. Fluvial processes in ephemeral streams are brief but intense. Streams can move large rocks and boulders down valleys during the high flow of flash floods; the average transport distance is shorter than in humid climates because the amount of water flowing in the channel is usually limited. Deposition occurs shortly after rainfalls, and most deposits are left within the stream channel, at the base of hills and mountains, and in depressions within the desert. Sediments are not sorted well because they are deposited abruptly. **Internal drainage**, where streams flow into landlocked basins within drylands, and deposition within dryland areas are common, occurring in the Mojave, Sahara, and Great Sandy and Gibson Deserts of Australia.

Dryland Landforms and Landscapes

EOLIAN LANDFORMS

Wind erosion by deflation creates landforms such as desert pavement and blowouts, and abrasion forms ventifacts. **Desert pavement**, found in the Sinai Peninsula and Death Valley, forms where all small surface sediments, including sand, have been blown away, leaving only pebbles and larger rocks on the surface. This surface layer of rock, also called lag gravel or desert armor, may take centuries to form; it is rarely more than the thickness of one pebble or cobble because underlying sediments are protected from the wind.

When wind turbulence removes exposed sediment, it may form shallow surface depressions called **blowouts** or **deflation hollows**. During the Dust Bowl years of the 1930s, blowouts were common in eastern Colorado and western Kansas, where drought had killed much of the vegetation and dried the soil before windstorms swept across the region.

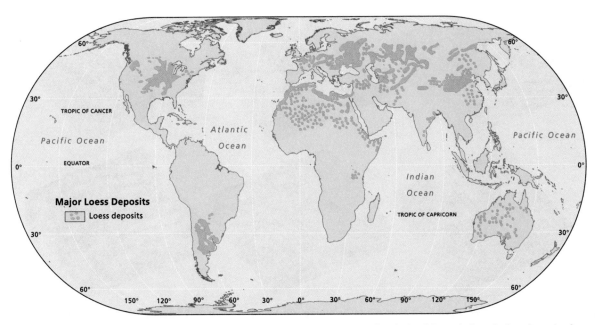

Loess, which is dust made up of silt and clay, has settled over large areas after being blown in by wind or deposited by glaciers in regions such as the midwestern United States.

Most of these Great Plains blowouts are like those in other deserts and on sandy coast-lines—less than three feet deep and ten feet across. Larger deflation hollows as much as several hundred feet deep have been found in the northern Sahara.

After pressure gradients change and a dust storm's winds slow, dust composed of mostly silt and clay may be deposited as **loess** over extensive areas. Many loess deposits are found in steppes, including the Palouse of eastern Washington and the Pampas of Argentina. Deserts, especially the Gobi, are common sources for the dust that forms loess, and the sediments are transported downwind hundreds or even thousands of miles from their sources. Areas alongside glaciers are also major sources for loess sediments; much of the loess deposited in the midwestern United States and Ukraine is composed of dust eroded from the outwash plains of Pleistocene glaciers. (See Glaciers, page 189.)

Loess deposits can cover hundreds of thousands of square miles; particles suspended in the wind take weeks or months to settle out and land at increasing distances from the source areas. The thickness of loess varies as a function of the amount of source material, its weight, and wind persistence. There are deposits a hundred feet thick in the Mississippi Valley and several hundred feet thick in northern China. The silt particles in loess are often composed of angular, interlocking particles of quartz and calcite; as a result, streams flowing over loess deposits eventually cut steep-sided channels. For years, people in the Shanxi Province of northern China and in Askole, Pakistan, a town in the foothills of the Karakoram Range, have occupied homes carved into loess bluffs.

Sand dunes are found in almost all deserts, although the sand-covered portion, or erg, of major deserts is rarely higher than 30 percent of the total area, as in the Arabian Desert, and may be less than 5 percent of the total area, as in the southwestern United States. Active

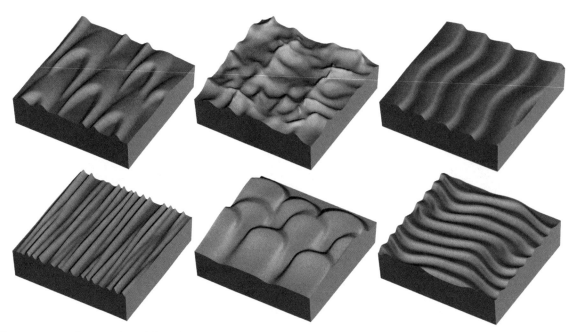

There are several types of sand dune formations, including (clockwise from upper left) **Barchan, Star, Longitudinal, Transverse, Parabolic,** and **Linear.**

dunes, in contrast to inactive dunes that have been stabilized by vegetation, migrate downwind as sand on the windward face is blown up and over the top of the dune, where it slides down the **slip face**. The slope on the windward face of a dune may average 10 degrees; on the slip face, the angle of repose may average 30 to 35 degrees. Migrating dunes usually travel less than 50 feet per year—although some walk 200 feet or more per year—and can be a major inconvenience; U.S. 95 north of Winnemucca, Nevada, runs through the Black Rock and Owyhee Deserts, and numerous dunes have crossed it in past decades.

Different types of sand dunes form depending on the direction of the wind, the amount of sand available, and the presence of vegetation. **Barchan dunes** form when wind blows constantly from one general direction, sand is limited, and vegetation is absent; if more sand is available, barchans merge to form **transverse dunes**. When wind blows from more than one quadrant—for example if it varies between a westerly and a northerly wind—then a **longitudinal dune** (large ones are called **seifs**) forms; central Australia is noted for its longitudinal dunes. A **star dune,** with multiple arms radiating from a central mound, forms when winds are highly variable in direction, as is the case in Egypt and on the Arabian Peninsula, especially in the Rub al Khali, the Empty Quarter, in southeastern Saudi Arabia. **Parabolic dunes** form when some vegetation is present to anchor the upwind horns of the dune; they are associated with blowouts on sandy coastlines.

The dimensions of sand dunes are highly variable because of differences in wind speed and the amounts of available sand. Barchans, the smallest dunes, are rarely higher than a hundred feet; seifs, which require far greater amounts of sand, may be more than 600 feet high and more than 50 miles long. Wind speed must be strong enough to blow sand upward to the tops of the dunes but not so strong and persistent that sand is unable to settle; wind

Mesas, such as this one on the Hopi Indian Reservation in Arizona, are defined as plateaus surrounded on all sides by scarps, or cliffs.

speed increases with altitude and eventually is fast enough that sand at the crest continues to saltate and does not accumulate.

FLUVIAL LANDFORMS

Stream erosion in deserts creates channels that are dry throughout much of the year. Dry channels are called **arroyos** or **washes** in the United States; in Arabic-speaking countries they are called wadi, and in South Africa, donga. Closely spaced, deeply eroded stream channels cut through areas of uniform weakness of shale or clay to create **badlands**. Badlands National Park in southwestern South Dakota is a well-known example in the United States, and badlands topography is also found in southern Israel.

Rommel and the Qattara Depression

The Qattara Depression lies 436 feet below sea level in northwestern Egypt and is more than a hundred miles across, with salt and sand deposits on its floor. In 1942 Nazi Field Marshal Erwin Rommel and the Afrika Korps had to travel around this huge basin to face British troops head-on at El-Alamein, located on a narrow stretch of land between the Mediterranean Sea and the Qattara. The resulting British victory was a turning point in World War II.

Stream erosion at the base of cliffs topped by resistant caprocks of limestone, for example, causes the cliffs (called **scarps**) to retreat and remain steep. **Plateaus**, extensive elevated areas, will over time have progressively smaller areas because fluvial erosion will undercut the surrounding cliffs; the cliffs will slowly retreat and eventually converge. **Mesas**, Spanish for "tables," are plateaus surrounded on all sides by scarps; mesas will eventually turn into

This alluvial fan in California's Death Valley is a classic example of how stream depositions near the base of mountains create the desert equivalent of river deltas.

buttes as they become smaller. Southern Argentina, western China, and the Four Corners area of the United States all contain these landforms. Over hundreds and thousands of years, fluvial erosion can also expose huge, resistant rock masses, such as Ayers Rock in central Australia; these prominent features are called **inselbergs** (German for "island mountain") or sometimes **bornhardts**, after F. Wilhelm C. E. Bornhardt (1864-1946), a German who described such features while exploring what is now Tanzania.

Stream deposition in and near channels emerging from the base of mountains, where channel gradients level out, creates **alluvial fans** (or alluvial cones if especially steep), the desert equivalent of deltas. Over time the sediments accumulating in nearby alluvial fans can merge and form a wide **bajada,** or apron. The bajada on the west side of California's Death Valley extends five miles from the Panamint Mountains and is 2,000 feet thick in some places.

Deposition also occurs in depressions or basins called **bolsons** (from a Spanish word meaning "large purse") in deserts where suspended sediments settle out in still water. The temporary, or ephemeral, lakes that form in bolsons after heavy rainfalls disappear rapidly as evaporation and infiltration remove the water, leaving **playas**. Salts dissolved in the lake water are precipitated onto the sediments during evaporation (very salty playas

The Badlands in South Dakota were created when eroded stream channels cut through areas of shale or clay.

are called **salinas**) and can form valuable mineral deposits; nitrates deposited in Chilean deserts were used to make gunpowder prior to World War I.

Several lakes now present in desert basins are remnants of much larger lakes that formed in wetter climates during the Pleistocene Ice Age. In Utah, for example, the Great Salt Lake is a remnant of the former Lake Bonneville while the Bonneville Salt Flats are a salina, from the same lake. Many other pluvial lakes, including former Lake Manley in what is now Death Valley, have since evaporated into playas and salinas.

Soils and Bioregions

Soils

Soils are surface layers of rock material and minerals that contain organic material and are capable of supporting the growth of rooted plants. Soils support vegetation that people and animals depend upon for survival, and historically the presence of fertile soils has strongly influenced settlement locations and the numbers of people. Plants, and therefore soils, also provide the chemical energy that supports Earth's animal populations, either directly in the case of herbivores or indirectly in the case of carnivores. Soil scientists, or **pedologists** (from the Greek word *pedon,* meaning "ground"), focus increasingly on understanding soil-forming or pedogenic processes rather than on soil qualities and characteristics. The pedogenic processes operating in a region produce all soil characteristics, and the spatial patterns of these processes are the basis for the distribution of soil types.

Soil Characteristics

The weathering processes and the available rock material in an area play a major role in the development of the physical, chemical, and biologic characteristics of soil. Physical characteristics of soil include composition, texture, and structure; chemical characteristics include

Soils form in distinctive layers, visible in a cross section. Shown here is a spodosol, in which a heavily leached lighter A horizon lies over a reddish-colored B horizon.

acidity/alkalinity and cation exchange capacity (CEC); and biologic characteristics include the number and types of organisms in the soil and the amount of humus. All the processes producing these characteristics are interrelated.

PHYSICAL CHARACTERISTICS

All soils are composed of weathered rock material or sediment, organic matter, water, and air. In a midlatitude forest with a cool, moist climate, 45 percent of the volume of the soil might be sediment, 25 percent water, 25 percent air, and 5 percent organic matter. Soil in a tropical rain forest near the Equator might be 60 percent sediment, 30 percent water, 9 percent air, and one percent organic matter. Water and air fill up the pore spaces in the gaps between the sediments and organic particles and replace each other as water percolates into the soil or as low humidity and drought evaporate the water.

The parent material of soil, the rock debris from which sediment derives, is either the decomposed and disintegrated bedrock in an area or transported **regolith** (rock debris or sediments moved into the area by water, wind, or glaciers); it can be a combination of the two. Different kinds of parent material contribute different minerals and different particle sizes to the soil; sandstone contributes quartz sand grains, whereas limestone contributes clays and calcite, a plant nutrient. Certain types of transported regolith, such as loess deposited by winds and alluvium deposited by floodwaters, can form soils very rapidly; in contrast is the slow soil formation on glacial debris.

The physical and chemical weathering of bedrock and regolith creates sediment particles of different sizes that determine soil texture. Texture affects the size of the pores between sediments and the ease with which water (and therefore dissolved ions and suspended particles) can move. There are three general ranges of sediment sizes: sand (.08 to .006 inches in diameter), silt (.006 to .0002 inches in diameter), and clay (.0002 to .00001 inches in diameter). Particles even smaller than clay, called

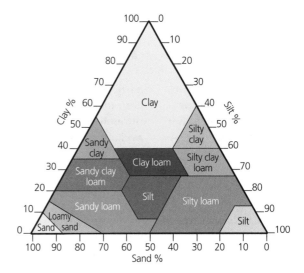

Geologists use this triangle to classify soil texture, taking into account a soil's proportions of sand, silt, and clay.

colloids, remain suspended in soil water and do not influence soil texture; colloids help transport nutrients within the soil. When sand dominates a soil, the large pores that result allow water to flow easily through to the water table, where it is not readily available for plant use. Clay has such small pores that water is retained easily, but the water will not sink easily into or flow through the soil. (See Groundwater, page 179.) The U.S. Department of Agriculture has developed a key to texture identification by depicting the relative proportions of soil sediments in the three size ranges; a relatively even mix creates a **loam** texture. (See diagram: U.S. Department of Agriculture Soil Textures, above.)

Soil structure is defined as the way soil particles clump together; it is a function of the amount of clay present, biotic activity, the mineral composition of the soil, and climate. A **ped,** or soil clump, can be flat (platy), linear (columnar, for example), blocky, or crumblike. If soils do not clump, such as loess, they are described as massive and lacking in structure. Soil water moves along the planes of weakness between soil clumps; for example, peds with

Field Capacity

As water sinks into soil, some drops attach to sediment particles by capillary tension. This water remains attached to the particles after gravity has pulled the rest through the soil and is available to plant roots. When only this water is present, the soil is at field capacity. In sand, field capacity equals about one cubic inch of water distributed through a column of twelve cubic inches of soil; field capacity for clay is about four cubic inches in a column of twelve cubic inches.

columnar structures allow rapid drainage between columns. Thus, soil structure affects a soil's fertility by determining how easily dissolved nutrients in soil water flow through it.

CHEMICAL CHARACTERISTICS

The chemical composition and solubility of the minerals within soil affect and are affected by chemical weathering and organic activity, including agriculture. Chemical weathering occurs within soil because air (including oxygen) and water (which is often slightly acidic after absorbing carbon dioxide from soil air) are present in pores within the soil. In addition to forming new minerals in soil—hematite, for example, forms when iron in soil oxidizes—chemical weathering creates ions, meaning atoms or molecules with a positive or negative charge. **Cations**, positively charged ions, include calcium, magnesium, and aluminum and are especially important to plant life; these cations are plant nutrients that can attach to negatively charged colloids and move with the flow of soil water.

Soil color, once used to classify soils, derives from the chemical as well as the biologic characteristics of soil. Iron oxides—hematite and limonite—commonly form in areas where warm, humid climates cause oxidation and hydration. In these areas soils are often red or yellow; Georgia, for example, is rich in red clay. In cooler areas with poor drainage, iron minerals change chemically to give a bluish color to the soil. White soil may be caused by the chemical precipitation of calcite or gypsum from water within the soil. **Humus**, decomposed vegetation, is black or dark brown, and therefore soils rich in humus are also dark. "Chernozem" (from *chernyi*, the Russian for "black," and *zemlya*, for "earth") was once commonly used to describe such soils.

Soil fertility depends on the number of **base cations** or nutrients available to plants in soil water. Calcium, magnesium, potassium, and sodium ions are base cations that plants can absorb through their root systems. Base cations can be dissolved from sediments or rock, such as calcium from limestone, or obtained from decomposing vegetation. They are attached to colloids in soil water; however, large amounts of water can leach nutrients from soil by washing out colloids.

The rate at which base cations are exchanged for other cations, such as hydrogen cations, is the **cation exchange capacity (CEC)** of a soil; it is a measure of soil fertility and of how well soils enable plants access to nutrients. Although water is required for cation exchange, the key to CEC is the mineral and organic content of the soil. For example, two types of clay—montmorillonite, found in west-central France and Georgia, among other places, and vermiculite, found in western Australia, Massachusetts, and other locations—have high CEC, making base cations more easily available to plants. Kaolinite, a clay found in China and Sardinia, for example, and quartz each have very low CEC and consequently make less fertile soils.

Hydrogen and aluminum cations also attach

to colloids, and the relative number of these cations present make soil either **acidic** or **alkaline**. Hydrogen and aluminum cations tend to replace base cations because hydrogen and aluminum have a greater attraction to colloids; the base cations then become dissolved in soil water and available to plants. The number of hydrogen ions present in a unit of soil water is measured on the **pH scale,** the power of hydrogen scale. The scale ranges from zero to 14, and a value of 7 is considered neutral. Values below 7 have greater numbers of hydrogen cations and are acidic; values above 7 have a decreased number of base cations and are alkaline. Highly acidic soils are usually infertile because of the lack of base cations; highly alkaline soils may be infertile because there are too few hydrogen ions to release enough base cations and make them available.

BIOLOGIC CHARACTERISTICS

Humus, the organic component of soil, can vary from nearly zero percent of soil volume in very dry areas where vegetation is scarce to more than 50 percent of soil volume in swampy areas where vegetation is plentiful. Vegetation that is alive or decaying usually composes the greatest volume of organic material in soil, but animals are also present: More than one million earthworms can inhabit an acre of topsoil. Bacteria, which are also present, decompose vegetation; 15 million bacteria can live in a cubic inch of soil.

Greater amounts of humus are present in midlatitude moist soils where vegetation is lush. In hot, rainy equatorial regions, bacteria rapidly decompose vegetation into base cations and organic compounds that are then washed from the soil, so that only minimal humus can accumulate. The soils in **peat bogs**, called muskegs in Canada, are mucks composed primarily of humus from moss, sedges, and other vegetation from surrounding pine and fir forests; cold temperatures and acidic water slow the decomposition process so that layers of humus accumulate.

Soil Formation

As soils form in a region, pedogenic processes cause soil characteristics to vary with depth and create soil layers or **horizons**, which can be seen in a soil cross section or profile. The vertical movement of material dissolved or suspended in soil water is most important in the formation of horizons; downward movement can remove or leach base cations from the area if the water reaches the groundwater. Surface material—volcanic ash, for example—may be added to soils in an area or removed by wind or stream erosion; at different depths within the soil, different types of chemical weathering can change minerals and organic debris.

Pedogenic processes are controlled by five interacting factors that may be remembered as **CLORPT**: climate, organic activity, relief, parent material, and time. Soils may be described as being in dynamic equilibrium with their environments because when the factors controlling pedogenic processes change, so do the soils. Parent material, whether bedrock or transported regolith, has decreasing influence on soil characteristics over time. Initially, parent material supplies the minerals (including cations) to the soil and therefore influences the rate of weathering and the amount of sand, silt, clay, and colloids that will be produced.

Time is critical in soil formation because pedogenic processes require time to change parent material to soil and to form horizons in the soil. The rates of these processes vary considerably around the world, and average rates for soil formation—for example, one inch per century—are misleading. In deserts almost no soil may form in a century, whereas soil may develop at the rate of 0.4 inch per year on volcanic ash in humid tropical locations. Recent studies of pedogenic activity on glacier deposits exposed at Glacier Bay, Alaska, found thin layers forming after 50 years, although only within 2.5 inches of the surface.

Over time, climate becomes the most important influence on the rate and type of soil formation because rates of weathering, levels of organic activity, and the transport of material within the soil are affected by the levels and timing of precipitation and temperature. Warm and wet climates experience more rapid weathering than do cold or dry climates and have more vegetation as well; bacteria are also increasingly active as temperatures rise. As a result, different kinds of parent material in similar climates tend to form similar soils over time, although factors such as flooding or a volcanic eruption can modify pedogenic processes in localized areas. Changes in climate affect soils too, although centuries or even millennia may pass before soils reach equilibrium with a new climate and soil horizons stabilize.

Organic activity and relief also affect processes of soil formation. Organic activity, especially the amount of humus available, is closely tied to climate. Relief, including a slope's angle and its aspect—the direction the slope faces, affects the rates of the soil formation process by affecting drainage, soil erosion, mass wasting, and **microclimates**, the near-surface atmospheric conditions for a local area. As a rule, steeper slopes have thinner soils because of erosion and mass wasting; slopes with angles greater than 45 degrees usually allow no soil to form. Aspect also affects microclimate and therefore the soil; south-facing slopes in the Northern Hemisphere are warmer and drier than north-facing slopes because of the greater intensity of sunlight.

HORIZONS

As soil water is drawn deeper into the soil by gravity or as it rises because surface evaporation causes water to ascend by capillary action, it transports ions and clay particles within the soil. As a result of these materials being lost from one soil level or gained by another, soil horizons develop: These are layers with different physical, chemical, and biologic characteristics. Climatic influences dominate the development of soil horizons, although not all soils have all horizons because of lack of time, moisture, or other factors.

Six horizons with subhorizons and intermediate horizons have been defined by the U.S. Department of Agriculture: O, A, E, B, C, and R.

SOIL HORIZONS

■ **O Horizon** The O horizon, which is nearest the surface, contains the highest percentage of organic debris of all the horizons, whether decomposed or unaltered. Little sediment is found in the O horizon, which may be extremely thin, such as the soil horizon in deserts, or several yards thick, as in peat bogs.

■ **A Horizon** The A horizon, commonly referred to as topsoil, consists mostly of sediment from weathered parent material but still may include considerable amounts of humus from the O horizon.

■ **E Horizon** Once considered part of the A horizon, the E horizon is distinguished by its loss of clay particles and ions to downward-

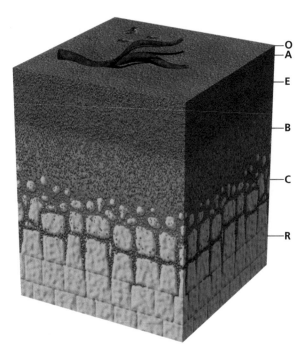

In an idealized diagram of a **soil profile,** the true soil is composed of the O, A, E, and B horizons. The C horizon is parent material and the R horizon is bedrock.

percolating soil water. This process of **eluviation** (from Latin *e*, "out," and *luere*, "wash") is called leaching if the material reaches the groundwater and is lost from the soil.

■ **B Horizon** Most B horizons are characterized by **illuviation**, the accumulation of material from overlying surface layers. Clays, base cations, or silica from the E horizon accumulate here. In some soil types, minerals such as calcite in the B horizon are lost to the A horizon when they rise because of capillary action.

■ **C Horizon** C horizons consist of weathered parent material or regolith, either transported or local, that has little if any organic content and is just beginning to be affected by pedogenic processes.

■ **R Horizon** This horizon consists of underlying, unweathered bedrock.

Soil Classification and Patterns

Soils, like climates, vary gradually between locations as the factors controlling rates and types of pedogenic processes change. Soil classification systems are therefore generalized so that the major characteristics of soils can be captured without being obscured by minor variations. One of the simplest systems is based on climates (humid temperate, dry temperate, and tropical), and soils are classified as **pedalfers** (dominated by ions of aluminum and iron), **pedocals** (dominated by base cations such as calcium), or **laterites** (highly weathered pedalfers).

The first soil classification system to recognize the influence of climate and vegetation on soils was developed around 1900 by Vasily Vasilyevich Dokuchayev (1846–1903), a Russian geologist. Dokuchayev's system was revised by another Russian, K. D. Glinka (1867–1927), and later by an American,

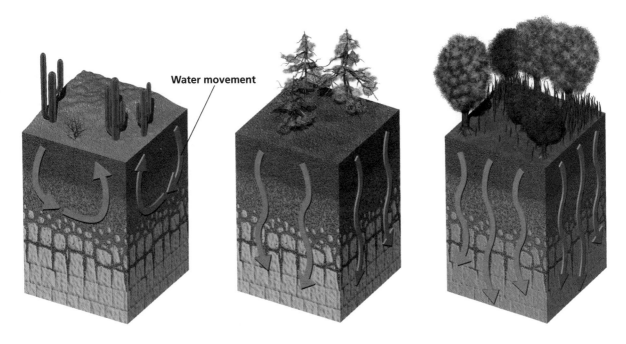

Water movement

Different soil types occur in different climates. From left to right, **podocal soils** form in dry climates; **pedalfer soils,** in moist climates; and **latertite soils,** in very wet climates, where considerable leaching takes place.

C. F. Marbut (1863–1935), whose expansion of Dokuchayev's work became the official system of the U.S. Department of Agriculture in 1938. Marbut's system was used until 1960 when, after ten years of work by the Soil Conservation Service, the U.S. Comprehensive Soil Classification System (referred to as the Soil Taxonomy system) was published. A revised form of the Soil Taxonomy is used today by the United States; other countries, including Canada, have developed their own classification systems.

Soil Taxonomy divides soils into 11 orders, the largest groupings of soils, then subdivides each order in a hierarchical system into suborders, great groups, subgroups, families, and series. With each level, soils are divided into classes on the basis of more specific information about the soil. For example, some soils on Puget Sound fall into the inceptisol order but belong to the haplumbrepts (*hapl,* "simple"; *umbr,* "dark"; "ept" is an abbreviation for

"inceptisol") great group. At the series level, more than 13,000 different kinds of soils have been identified; more will undoubtedly be identified as soils in different countries are analyzed.

The 11 orders, based on the physical and chemical characteristics of different soil horizons, are entisols, inceptisols, andisols, histosols, spodosols, aridisols, mollisols, alfisols, vertisols, ultisols, and oxisols. (The suffix, "-sol," is from Latin *solum,* "soil.")

Soils are not categorized specifically on the pedogenic process that formed them, but soil characteristics provide clues to their history of formation. Specifications for each order are quantified where possible, so that a soil falls into only one class.

SOIL TAXONOMY

■ Entisols—from Greek *ent,* meaning "recent" —have no distinctive soil horizons. They are usually very young. They may be only years or

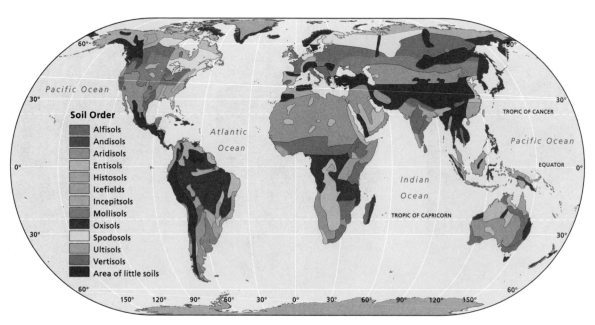

This world map shows the eleven orders of soil types that make up the U.S. Soil Taxonomy system, plus areas with icefields and minimal or missing soil cover.

decades old; however, in cold climates or other places where chemical weathering is slow, entisols may be much older. Different subtypes are found in Labrador's glacial deposits, northern China's flood deposits, and the Kalahari's dune deposits in Africa.

■ Inceptisols—from Latin *inceptum*, meaning "beginning"—form where sufficient soil water is available to start the development of horizons but the soils have not reached equilibrium with their environments. Inceptisols are found on steeper slopes, such as those in the Appalachians, where mass wasting is common and cold temperatures freeze soil water, thus slowing pedogenic processes, and on floodplains with frequent deposits of sediments.

■ Andisols (*ando* for "volcanic ash") form from the deposits of volcanic ash. They can be found in Hawaii as well as near Mount St. Helens in Washington's Cascade Range.

■ Histosols (*histos* for "tissue") form in poorly drained areas where organic material accumulates. During decomposition the organic material releases acids that kill the usually omnipresent bacteria that decompose gorganic material. Soils in the Florida Everglades and in Finnish peat bogs are examples of histosols.

■ Spodosols (*spodos* for "wood ash") have light gray E horizons dominated by silica left after eluviation. B horizons are dark because clays, iron oxides, and some base cations have illuviated. The eluviation of nutrients from the E

Aridisols, such as the one shown in this cross section from Utah, are dry and alkaline and exhibit poorly differentiated horizons.

This soil cross section is an example of mollisol, which features a thick, rich humus A horizon. It is from an area of central Iowa that developed on a glacial drift.

Expansive Soils

Soils containing large amounts of montmorillonite and related clays can expand as much as 50 percent in volume when water is absorbed. The water forms layers between the clay particles, and this clay-rich soil can expand and crack the foundation or walls of a house if not drained properly. In droughts, expansive soils shrink and can have cracks one inch wide and three feet deep.

horizon makes spodosols very infertile and unsuitable for agriculture; evergreens are common on these soils in moist northern forests, such as those in New England. Spodosols are very acidic because hydrogen ions have replaced the base cations washed into the B horizon.

■ Aridisols (*arid* for "dry") are alkaline soils that form in dry areas and have poorly differentiated horizons. Base cations, which accumulate in the A horizon because of surface evaporation and the capillary rise of soil water, can make the soil fertile if irrigated. **Salinization**, the accumulation of salts, can occur in aridisols when large amounts of bases accumulate on the surface. All major deserts, including the Mojave, Atacama, and Gobi, have aridisols.

■ Mollisols (*mollis* for "soft") are found in semiarid regions where water is available seasonally. A horizons in mollisols are dark from humus and are extremely fertile, while the base cations, including calcium, accumulate in the B horizon from the process of calcification. Many mollisols form on loess deposits in semiarid areas, such as the Great Plains of North America, northeastern China, and the Pampas in Argentina.

■ Alfisols ("alf," an abbreviation for aluminum and iron/ferrum) form mostly in midlatitude moist climates where precipitation has washed clays and most base cations to the B horizon, and the A and E horizons are reddish brown from the iron oxides. Sufficient cations remain available to make alfisols relatively fertile and good for agriculture. Northwestern France, southern Australia, and southern Michigan have alfisols.

■ Vertisols (*verto* for "turn") are distinguished by their high concentration of montmorillonite clay. Montmorillonite expands during moist weather, and it contracts and cracks in dry weather, causing surface soil to fall into the cracks. Essentially the soil turns over. Coastal Texas has vertisols, as does western India and southeastern Sudan.

■ Ultisols (*ultimus* for "ultimate") form in hot, wet climates where plant nutrients are rapidly washed out of the soil, iron oxides accumulate in the B horizon (giving it a red-brown color),

This example of an oxisol from Hawaii reveals that considerable leaching has taken place, a typical characteristic of soil in the Earth's hottest, wettest regions.

and clays accumulate in the B horizon. Southern Brazil, the southeastern United States, and Uganda have ultisols.

■ Oxisols (*oxi* for "oxide") are the most weathered soils, found where the hottest and wettest climates exist. Horizons are not well formed because the large amount of water leaches clays, base cations, and other ions out of the soil rather than allowing them to accumulate in the B horizon. Soils in equatorial rain forests, such as those in the Amazon and Congo Basins, are oxisols, and despite the massive amounts of vegetation, they are extremely infertile for agriculture.

Bioregions

Life on Earth

Biogeographers study the spatial distribution of individual organisms in **biotic communities**—composed of plants and animals—and of **ecosystems**—environmental systems that are associations of biotic communities interacting with their **environment**. An ecosystem may be defined and studied at scales ranging from a small pond to a global biome, such as prairies or tropical rain forests.

Organisms can have significantly different environmental requirements. A cactus, for example, can thrive in Arizona's Painted Desert in a climate that averages less than ten inches of rain per year. A mangrove tree, on the other hand, requires the hot, humid climate and huge amounts of water found in swamps such as Florida's Everglades. A cactus would not thrive in a swamp, nor would a mangrove thrive in a desert because their requirements for life are different. Different organisms such as pine trees, gray squirrels, and bacteria are able to share a single environment because they use different sources of energy, water, and nutrients.

Organisms can be classified as producers, consumers, or decomposers, according to how they acquire their energy. Green plants and some algae are producers; they use radiant energy from the sun to produce chemical energy by photosynthesis. Herbivores, animals such as rabbits and cattle that eat plants, and carnivores, animals such as lynx and hyenas that eat herbivores, are consumers that are directly or indirectly dependent upon plants to form energy. Bacteria and worms comprise another classification, decomposers, because they acquire energy by breaking down organic waste such as dead plants and animals, which also provide a supply of nutrients that may be used by other organisms.

Organisms can also be classified based on differences or similarities of anatomy, bodily functions and processes, and shared ancestry with other organisms; physiology and genetics are the basis for understanding how organisms have changed over time to adapt to different and changing environments. The biologic classification of organisms is based on the **Linnaean system** developed in the 1730s by Carolus Linnaeus (1707–1778), a Swedish naturalist. The Linnaean system has been revised over time and is hierarchical: At the broadest scale, organisms are grouped into one of five kingdoms: plant, animal, fungus, moneran (such as cyanobacteria), and protoctista (such as amoebas). Kingdoms are progressively sub-classified into phyla, classes, orders, and families, and more narrowly by genera and species. Organisms of the same species are able to reproduce and have fertile offspring. For example, horses and donkeys are classified in the same genus (*Equus*) and can mate, but their offspring (mules) are not fertile. Estimates of the total number of species on Earth

The Classification Scheme Now in Use Showing the Hierarchical Arrangement of the Categories
The gray bars include those animals to which the coyote, *Canis latrans*, is most closely related at
various levels in the classification scheme.

	COYOTE	WOLF	RED FOX	BOBCAT
Kingdom	Animalia	Animalia	Animalia	Animalia
Phylum	Chordata	Chordata	Chordata	Chordata
Subphylum	Vertebrata	Vertebrata	Vertebrata	Vertebrata
Class	Mammalia	Mammalia	Mammalia	Mammalia
Order	Carnivora	Carnivora	Carnivora	Carnivora
Family	Canidae	Canidae	Canidae	Felidae
Genus	*Canis*	*Canis*	*Vulpes*	*Lynx*
Species	*latrans*	*lupus*	*vulpes*	*rufus*

vary widely, from 4 million to more than
100 million.

Life first appeared on Earth about 3.5 billion
years ago and originated in the oceans because
water contained nutrients necessary for the
survival and growth of organisms and protected the earliest forms from ultraviolet radiation. (See Atmosphere, page 54.) The earliest
fossil evidence of life is from the Pilbara Shield
in northwestern Australia; microscopic structures in rocks there appear to be cells of cyanobacteria, a blue-green algae that lived in water.
Other rocks containing early fossils have been
discovered in eastern South Africa and
Ontario, and carbon found in 3.8-billion-year-
old rocks in Greenland may have been organi-
cally produced.

For nearly three billion years, life remained
simple, one-celled aquatic organisms; eventually multicellular organisms appeared, and over
time life moved onto land. The fossil record
from the Ediacara Hills in southeastern Australia shows that organisms resembling jelly-
fish, corals, and flatworms lived 630 million
years ago. About 570 million years ago, the
beginning of the Phanerozoic era, the rate of
change in organisms and the growth in species
diversity increased dramatically; within the
next 150 million years, life began to move
from the oceans onto land as plants developed

vascular systems. (See Table: Geologic Time
scale, page 47.) The fossil record is incomplete,
especially for the earliest time periods, but it
provides a broad outline of the kinds of organisms that existed at different times in different
environments.

Change in the biology of organisms over
time, where genetic changes are passed on to
offspring, is **evolution**. The theory of evolution was proposed in 1858 by Charles Darwin
(1809–1882)and fellow Englishman and naturalist Alfred Russell Wallace (1823–1913) and
has been revised as greater knowledge of
genetic processes has accumulated. Two key
concepts in explaining evolution are **natural
selection**, which holds that species better able
to survive and reproduce will replace competing species, and **mutation**, which holds that
the genetic makeup of an organism changes
randomly from that of its progenitors and with
varying effects on the ability of the organism to
survive and reproduce. Over time, mutations
that allow a species to compete better for
energy, water, and nutrients will accumulate as
offspring are selected for survival.

The evolution of plants and animals has led
to the adaptation of different species to diverse
environmental conditions; organisms now
inhabit nearly all Earth's surface environments,
except the vents of active volcanoes. Bacteria

HORSE	SNAPPING TURTLE	AMPHIOXUS	STARFISH	WHITE CLOVER
Animalia	Animalia	Animalia	Animalia	Plantae
Chordata	Chordata	Chordata	Eninodermata	Pterophyta
Vertebrata	Vertebrata	Cephalochordata	Eleutherozoa	
Mammalia	Reptilia	Leptocardii	Asteroidea	Angiospermae
Perissodactyla	Chelonia		Forcipulata	Rosales
Equidae	Chelydridae		Asteriidae	Leguminosae
Equus	*Chelydra*	*Branchiostoma*	*Asterias*	*Trifolium*
caballus	*serpentinia*	*virginiae*	*forbesi*	*repens*

are found in bedrock hundreds of feet below the surface, in Antarctic ice, and in ocean water miles deep. Animals, plants, and microscopic organisms have adapted to changing environmental conditions within an area: Peppered moths adapted to England's industrialization by gradually becoming darker, a camouflage that helps them avoid predators on soot-covered tree trunks. In other cases, organisms have adapted to new areas and environments; organisms either adapt to changes, migrate to a more hospitable environment, or eventually become extinct. When a flock of cattle egrets was blown from Africa to Brazil in the 19th century, the birds failed to survive. A similar event occurred in the 20th century, but this time the flock survived, perhaps because larger cattle herds carried the parasites used as food by the egrets.

Ecosystems

Organisms interact with other organisms and the physical environment in an area, forming an ecological system or ecosystem. Within an ecosystem each organism obtains the energy, water, nutrients, and space necessary for survival, growth, and reproduction. Nutrients required by organisms and the chemical energy stored within organisms flow through an ecosystem, cycling from producers to consumers to decomposers and back to producers. A **food chain** or **food web** exists within the ecosystem as the energy and nutrients move between organisms as they are eaten or decomposed.

The **carbon cycle** demonstrates how carbon, one of the basic nutrients required by living things, flows through an ecosystem. Carbon, in the form of carbon dioxide, is removed from the atmosphere by plants during photosynthesis and changed into carbohydrates in plant tissues. From plants the carbon travels through consumers and decomposers, cycling back to the air by respiration or oxidation; carbon from plants is also stored in fossil fuels such as coal, petroleum, and natural gas before returning to the environment after combustion. Carbon dioxide can also be removed from the air when it dissolves in water bodies, which act as carbon sinks or storage areas; this carbon, too, will eventually return to the active cycle. (See Carbon Cycle diagram, page 231.)

The environmental conditions within an ecosystem, including the presence of other organisms, form **habitats** for those species residing there. Each habitat has a specific physical location within an ecosystem, such as shallow water at the edge of a pond; the specific

Years ago (millions)	Geologic Time		Biologic Events
		Cenozoic	Age of mammals
65	Messzoic	Cretaceous	Massive extinctions First flowering plants Climax of dinosaurs and ammonites
		Jurassic	First birds Abundant dinosaurs and ammonites
		Triassic	First dinosaurs First mammals Abundant cycads
248	Late Paleozoic	Permian	Massive extinctions (including trilobites) Mammal-like reptiles
		Pennsylvanian	Great coal forests Conifers First reptiles
		Mississippian	Abundant amphibians and sharks Scale trees Seed ferns
		Devonian	Extinctions First insects First amphibians First forests First sharks
408	Early Paleozoic	Silurian	First jawed fishes First air-breathing arthropods
		Ordovician	Extinctions First land plants Expansion of marine shelled invertebrates
		Cambrian	First fishes Abundant shell bearing marine invertebrates Trilobites
570		Neoproterozoic	Rise of the metozoans

This geologic time scale relates the development of life-forms on Earth with the corresponding geologic periods.

environmental conditions of each habitat overlap with bordering habitats.

Field mice and great horned owls inhabit the same forest ecosystem and interact when owls hunt mice, but their habitats differ: Field mice occupy underground nests, whereas owls live in trees.

Different organisms also occupy different **niches** or functional roles within an ecosys-

tem; field mice, for example, are herbivores that consume seeds but are also an energy source for owls, carnivores that consume mice.

Each member species of the biotic community within an ecosystem fills a certain niche. The entire community relies on each niche function being performed so that there is interdependence among the species.

Animals and plants compete for and sometimes cooperate in obtaining resources within an ecosystem; some species behave in a **symbiotic** relationship that benefits both parties. The yucca and the yucca moth in the southwestern United States have a symbiotic relationship: The yucca moth benefits the yucca by pollinating the plant, and larvae of the moth benefit by feeding on yucca seeds.

Competition among species is a more common relationship; several species may compete in a single niche, as deer, rabbits, and pronghorns compete in high-plateau areas for grasses. Over time those species and individuals least able to compete successfully for energy (food) and water die out or migrate.

Climate and topography are the most significant environmental factors that determine an ecosystem. Climate has the greatest influence on an ecosystem because it controls the availability of energy, water, and nutrients. Daily and annual temperature ranges, sunlight for photosynthesis, precipitation, and soil characteristics are controlled principally by climatic factors, and plants in particular depend on climatic conditions for survival.

Topography influences environmental conditions because the angle and aspect of slopes, drainage patterns, and relief also affect temperatures, moisture, and sunlight. North- and south-facing slopes of mountains, for example, have slightly different temperatures and precipitation regimes and form microclimates; each, therefore, supports different ecosystems with different habitats.

Ecosystems vary in the quantity of organic matter or **biomass** they produce (**productivity**) and in the number of species present (**biodiversity**). Warm, wet environments tend to

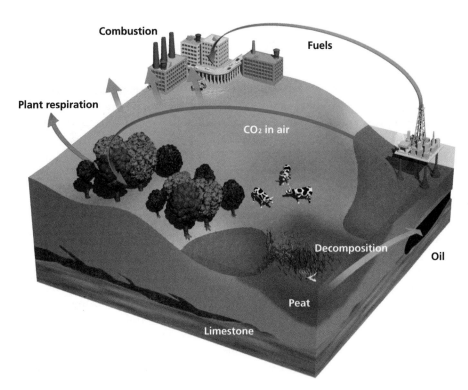

Carbon, in the form of carbon dioxide, is removed from the air by plants during photosynthesis and converted into carbohydrates. From plants, the carbon travels through consumers and decomposers, returning to the air via respiration or oxidation. Carbon is also stored in fossil fuels before returning to the environment after combustion. Some carbon dioxide is removed from the air when it dissolves in water bodies. This carbon, too, will eventually return to the active cycle.

have greater productivity and greater biodiversity than cooler, drier environments; plants that grow and reproduce more easily generate more chemical energy that can be used by other species in the ecosystem. Greater biodiversity, with more species interacting within an ecosystem, makes the food web more complex so that the loss of one species through drought, for example, or predation by animals or humans may not significantly interfere with the functioning of the entire ecosystem. Systems with limited biodiversity, such as deserts and tundra, are more vulnerable than tropical rain forests to disruption from the loss of a single species and its function in the ecosystem.

Ecosystems are geographically defined by the environmental conditions needed by members of the biological community; cave ecosystems, for example, provide the atmospheric conditions required by bats, blind cave fish, and other animals adapted to cave environments to survive. Each species has an optimum level of requirements, such as the amount of water, and also a **range of tolerance**, extremes of requirements within which the species can survive and reproduce and beyond which it cannot survive. As a species, the saguaro cactus can survive extremely low levels of moisture in southern Arizona, but it is particularly sensitive to cold temperatures: All new growth can be killed after 12 hours of −32°F temperatures. Ranges of tolerance are usually greater for mature members of a species than for the young.

Ecosystems are transformed into other ecosystems when environmental conditions, especially those associated with climate, change. **Ecotones** are the transition zones between ecosystems. Marshy areas, for instance, often surround ponds and are an example of a zone between an aquatic ecosystem and a terrestrial ecosystem; raccoons, snakes, and other animals will cross from the pond to the surrounding forest and back in search of food and water.

Ecosystems are not static; short-term

Locoweed and Selenium

Species have different nutrient requirements and tolerance levels for chemical elements, such as sodium or calcium, above and below which they cannot survive. Locoweed is one of the few plant species that tolerate soil with high concentrations of selenium, a rare element. Selenium is often associated with uranium so that geologists regard locoweed as an **indicator species** for uranium deposits.

disturbances, such as fires, droughts, and insect infestations, and long-term changes, such as climatic shifts, affect the flow of energy and nutrients through ecosystems. Temporary disturbances can change the availability of energy, water, or nutrients so that new species will expand their range into the area. If the newer species are more competitive than the resident species, the newcomers may displace them. Over time, however, if environmental conditions return to predisturbance levels, a sequence of plant and animal species more competitive in those conditions will return (**ecological succession**) until a stable ecosystem or **climax community** is reached. The term **mature community** is sometimes used to indicate a temporary stability. In midlatitude forests, for example, a field cleared within the forest may take 200 years to become a climax community of oak and hickory trees and associated animals. The sequence is that first the clearing fills with fast-growing weeds and grasses, then shrubs and fir trees move in,

shading out the smaller plants; shrubs and firs are then replaced by oaks and hickories, tree species that germinate better in shade.

Climatic changes can have longer-term effects on an ecosystem than a forest fire or volcanic eruption, changing it for hundreds of thousands of years or longer. During the Pleistocene Ice Age woodland and grassland ecosystems existed in the Sahara and the southwestern United States; tundra ecosystems thrived just south of the Great Lakes. If global warming continues at the current rate of about one degree Fahrenheit per ten years for several more centuries, the range of hemlock and sugar maples may reach several hundred miles farther north into Canada from their present limit at about 44° north latitude.

Humans affect ecosystems when they remove or add species to a region, as in the case of agriculture, or when they change the availability of water, nutrients, or sunlight. Commercial farming attempts to replace a diverse ecosystem with one crop

Adirondack Lakes

In upstate New York effects of changes in the environment were noticed by fishermen in lakes of the Adirondacks in the 1960s. Fewer fish were being caught, and all the fish that were being caught were older fish. A similar pattern had occurred in Scandinavia a decade earlier. The National Academy of Sciences in the United States eventually linked the change in fishing to increased acidity of lake water and, in turn, to acid precipitation. Acid levels in lakes in springtime were especially high because of the influx of snowmelt; many female fish were unable to produce eggs, and only mature fish could survive.

Wallace's Line

Boundaries between ecosystems can be abrupt if they are physically separated. In the Indonesian archipelago there is a boundary in the distribution of bird species between Borneo and Bali to the west and Celebes and Lombok to the east. Alfred Russell Wallace noted this boundary in the 1860s. It has since been called Wallace's Line and seems to mark Eurasia's continental shelf east of Bali and Borneo; the deeper water farther east was a barrier to the spread of species during the lowered ocean levels of the Pleistocene Ice Age.

(monoculture), and forestry may remove all mature tree species. Both of these activities drastically change the food web in a region and alter the amounts of moisture and sunlight available for surface plants. In Australia indigenous species such as the Javan tiger and Tasmanian wolf became extinct, and **exotic**, nonindigenous species such as rabbits were introduced; local ecosystems were changed by adding and removing consumers and producers from the food web.

Biomes: Global Distribution

Global patterns of mature ecosystems are studied at the **biome** scale—macroregional ecosystems based on life-forms (the form, structure, and function of the organisms) rather than on sets of particular species. Rain forests in Africa and South America, for example, contain vines, arboreal animals such as monkeys, and reptiles although the particular species present will be different on the two continents. Biomes enable comparisons between regions to improve the understanding of ecosystem processes and to establish management practices when species (crops, for example) are introduced from elsewhere.

Plant communities are more often used to identify biomes than are animals because vegetation is more visible, constitutes more of the biomass, and produces the chemical energy that flows through the food web. Although agriculture, forestry, and urban development have displaced native plant and animal species throughout much of the world, biomes are mapped based on the mature ecosystems that the environmental conditions would produce without human intervention. Biomes mirror climatic regions because vegetation reflects the amounts of precipitation,

The Biologic Invasion of Hawaii

Ecosystems in the Hawaiian Islands are especially vulnerable to introduced species because the islands have a limited area, which also limits the complexity of their food webs. Since 1778, when Capt. James Cook first visited the islands, nearly 4,000 species of plants and animals—including wild blackberry bushes, mongooses, Argentine ants, and cannibal snails—have been introduced, usually unintentionally, into the Hawaiian Islands. Native species have often been unable to compete with aggressive and prolific new species, and now 20 percent of native plant species and almost 50 percent of remaining bird species in Hawaii are endangered and at risk of extinction.

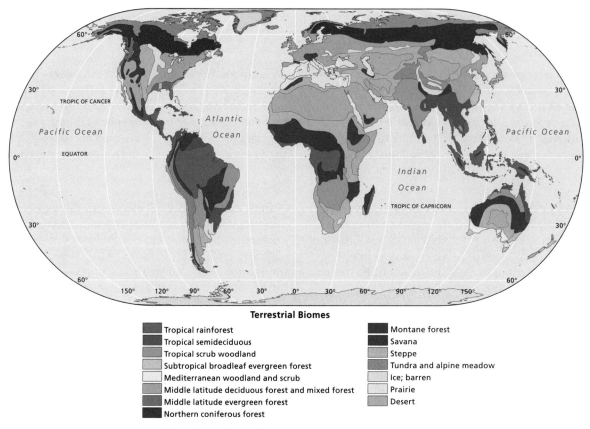

Terrestrial Biomes

Tropical rainforest
Tropical semideciduous
Tropical scrub woodland
Subtropical broadleaf evergreen forest
Mediterranean woodland and scrub
Middle latitude deciduous forest and mixed forest
Middle latitude evergreen forest
Northern coniferous forest

Montane forest
Savana
Steppe
Tundra and alpine meadow
Ice; barren
Prairie
Desert

The U.S. Forest Service system of classifying the Earth's biomes consists of four general categories—forest, grassland, desert, and tundra—which are further divided into 13 specific biomes. The list above numbers more than 13 biomes because montane forests include a range of these biomes at different elevations and ice areas lack biomes.

temperature, and sunlight that are available. Soil patterns, also strongly affected by climates, are similar to biome patterns. (See Climate Controls and Climatic Classifications, page 114, and Soils, page 218.)

Several classification systems for biomes have been developed, none of which are universally accepted. Early attempts to map biologic communities include a world vegetation map published in 1855, based on the work of Swiss botanist Augustin de Candolle (1778–1841), and an 1858 attempt at a global geography of animals produced by Philip Sclater. In 1976 the U.S. Forest Service mapped biomes, using the term "ecoregions," and began to use

the concepts of biomes to manage ecosystems within national forests in 1993. The Forest Service system, based on the work of geographer Robert G. Bailey of Fort Collins, Colorado, divides the world into domains. The polar domain, for example, is subdivided into the tundra division, and further subdivided into Bering tundra, northern province, to provide more specific information on the climate, soil, plants, and animals of smaller regions.

The U.S. Forest Service classification system, as revised by Ralph Scott, organizes biomes into four general categories: forest, grassland, desert, and tundra. The forest and grassland categories are divided into specific biomes,

The Seiplok Sanctuary on Borneo, East Malaysia, contains 10,000 acres of virgin rain forest. Here, animals recovered from poachers are returned to the wild.

such as tropical rain forests in the forest category and prairies in the grassland category, based on the life-forms of the vegetation; these biomes display significant differences in ecosystem productivity and biodiversity.

The 13 biomes—8 forest biomes, 3 grassland biomes, desert, and tundra—are discussed below.

FOREST BIOMES

TROPICAL RAIN FOREST

Tropical rain forests are found in the Amazon and Congo River Basins as well as in Southeast Asia, Central America, and Madagascar. Trees dominate this biome and are tall (often more than 200 feet), broad-leaved, and evergreen; the continuous warmth and rain in this biome means no seasonal stress or loss of leaves. Many animal species are arboreal, and insects thrive. These forests have the greatest biodiversity of any biome: At least several million species are found in them worldwide, and a single square mile may contain hundreds or even thousands of tree species.

TROPICAL SEMI-DECIDUOUS FOREST

In progressively drier regions of the tropics, vegetation changes to species that are more tolerant of dry periods. Tropical semi-deciduous forests, associated with humid subtropical climates, are found in Southeast

The Jungle

Jungles are extremely dense thickets that occur within tropical rain forests after some disruption, such as fire, creates a clearing. Pioneer species, the first to sprout in clearings, include low shrubs and thickets that grow so densely that they create a nearly impassable mass of vegetation. Ordinarily the lack of sunlight on the rain forest floor results in plenty of open ground under the canopy.

A salt marsh typical of the subtropical broadleaf evergreen biome can be seen through oak trees draped with Spanish moss at Fort King George State Historical Park in Darien, Georgia.

Asia, southeastern Brazil, northeastern Australia, and other regions. Semi-deciduous vegetation includes deciduous trees whose leaves drop during dry seasons and some evergreen trees that are also found in tropical rain forests. Animal species are comparable to those found in tropical rain forests, with more species living on the ground, including large cats such as panthers.

TROPICAL SCRUB WOODLAND

Longer dry seasons of four to seven months, associated with some monsoon climates and regions bordering deserts, create tropical scrub woodland biomes. Most trees are deciduous, and other vegetation, including grasses, becomes dormant during the annual droughts; **rain-green forests** lose leaves because of low rainfall rather than low temperatures. Tropical scrub woodlands are found in central India, Zambia, and northern Argentina; their animal populations often include larger herbivores such as antelopes and Africa's zebras and the carnivores that feed on them.

SUBTROPICAL BROADLEAF EVERGREEN

In a few locations along east coasts just poleward of the tropics, warm ocean currents provide sufficient moisture and temperatures are warm enough to support broadleaf, nondeciduous trees; these subtropical forests grow on the Sea Islands off Georgia, in eastern China, and in southern Japan, for example. Biodiversity is more limited in these forests (also called laurel forests) than in tropical rain forests, and trees are shorter and less dense than they are closer to the Equator. Magnolias, live oaks, and Spanish moss are found in this biome in the southeastern United States.

MEDITERRANEAN WOODLAND AND SCRUB

The Mediterranean climate, found on west coasts around 35° north and south latitude, creates a Mediterranean woodland and scrub biome. This biome is found in southern California, southern and southwest Australia, and central Chile and on Mediterranean coastlines. Vegetation, called chaparral in California and maquis in southern Europe, is limited to species that can tolerate the stress of high temperatures and summer drought. Other

New Hampshire's White Mountains, part of the Appalachians, are located in a biome region classified as midlatitude deciduous and mixed forest.

vegetation has small leaves and thick bark for protection from climatic stress; olive trees, cork oaks, and manzanitas are typical species.

MIDLATITUDE DECIDUOUS AND MIXED FOREST

In the cooler winters of the midlatitudes, an increasing number of cold-tolerant trees are found, including needle-leaf evergreens, such as pines, and deciduous broadleaf trees, such as oak, hickory, beech, and ash. Tree species in this biome have more deciduous varieties Equatorward and an increasing percentage of needle-leaf trees toward the Poles; the largest regions with this biome are found in the eastern United States, northern Europe to central Russia, and northeastern China.

MIDLATITUDE EVERGREEN FOREST

Midlatitude evergreen forests are found only in North America on the west coasts that have a marine west-coast climate and in parts of the southeastern United States. The west coast has far greater precipitation than the southeast and so tends to have larger trees; coastal redwoods include the tallest trees on Earth, some more

than 300 feet tall. In sandy areas between Texas and Virginia a southern pine forest includes loblolly and pitch pines as well as tupelo and cypress trees; armadillos and alligators inhabit this region.

NORTHERN CONIFEROUS FOREST

In northern latitudes with subarctic climates, northern coniferous forests, also called by the

This longleaf pine forest near Eglin Air Force Base, Florida, is an example of a midlatitude evergreen forest. It has been cleared and restored to its natural spacing by a program of regular burning.

Canyon Prairie, Iowa, is typical of a grassland biome called steppes. Steppe biomes also occur in the veldt of South Africa and the Caucasus of Eurasia.

Russian name "taiga," are found. Vegetation in these areas faces the stress of extremely cold winters. The trees—fir, spruce, and pine—mature to be shorter than normal because seasons are short and precipitation is limited. Much of northern North America and northern Eurasia are covered by this biome, which has very limited biodiversity because of climatic limitations on vegetation and therefore on the food web.

GRASSLAND BIOMES

SAVANNA

In tropical latitudes where low precipitation levels cannot support trees, shrubs and grasses dominate the ecosystems. Savanna biomes are usually located near and blend into tropical scrub woodland and tropical steppe biomes; much of central Africa, south-central Brazil, and inland Australia are covered by savanna. The lack of precipitation causes most vegetation to become dormant during the dry season, but the availability of grasses provides food for large herbivores, such as giraffes and zebras, plus associated predators, much as in tropical scrub woodlands.

STEPPE

Steppe biomes are short-grass grasslands found in either low latitudes or midlatitudes where rain shadows or the high pressure of the horse latitudes limit precipitation. Low annual precipitation creates steppes in South Africa (the veldt), the Sahel region south of the Sahara, the western Great Plains of North America, the Caucasus of Eurasia, and other locations. Trees

Like most deserts, Palm Desert, California, receives less than ten inches of rain each year, has a high average temperature, and experiences an evaporation rate that exceeds precipitation.

are found alongside streams; feather grass and buffalo grass are typical types of vegetation.

PRAIRIE

In the midlatitudes, tallgrass averaging three to four feet is found where precipitation is higher (up to 20 inches) than in the steppes but is still insufficient to support trees. Prairie biomes are limited to the midlatitudes between steppe and forest biomes. In addition to the eastern Great Plains, small prairie biomes are found in Uruguay, Manchuria, Hungary, and Ukraine. Bluestem and other grass species that dominate this biome once supported huge herds of grazing herbivores, such as bison on the Great Plains, but overhunting and agriculture have almost totally replaced such herds.

DESERT

In the dry climates of the Sahara, Atacama, Gibson, and other deserts, only **xerophytic** plants, those capable of tolerating annual precipitation levels below ten inches and occasionally prolonged droughts, can survive. In about 75 percent of regions with desert climates, some scattered vegetation exists, such as cactus, thornwood, and tamarisk. Vegetation is usually small and grows slowly, and many plants are ephemerals, grasses or herbs whose life cycles follow the rare rainfalls and include months or years of dormancy between weeks of blooming.

TUNDRA

Tundra climates are found along the shorelines of the Arctic Ocean and in the highest reaches of mountain ranges such as the Andes and Himalaya. Cold temperatures and two-month-long growing seasons severely limit biodiversity; however, the total number of organisms may be huge during summer, when reindeer, for example, and migratory birds converge and insects such as mosquitoes and blackflies are active. Vegetation grows slowly, and grasses, such as cotton grass, and lichens, including reindeer moss, are common types of vegetation. Permafrost, where soil temperatures remain below freezing most or all of the year, is common in tundra, affecting soil drainage and plant growth.

Summary

Geographers focus on spatial patterns from the global to the local scale, and the key to understanding places and environments lies in understanding the physical processes that shape the world. Physical geography studies past, present, and future environmental patterns on Earth, which are linked because physical processes act over space and time: Hurricanes do not form in a day, nor do canyons in a year or oceans in a century. Paleogeographers study the locations and patterns of continents, oceans, and landforms at different times in geologic history. Understanding how tectonic processes have moved continents and created oceans helps to explain present-day locations of mineral resources such as coal and copper as well as the locations of continents and oceans.

One of the most important applications of physical geography is to be able to predict future patterns and processes on Earth's surface. Physical processes of erosion and weathering are always at work, and Earth's surface is constantly changing. Many of the processes appear to be slow—the Atlantic Ocean widens one inch per year, and global temperatures rise one degree per century—but other processes are far faster. Understanding wave erosion helps to predict the retreat of coastal bluffs on the Atlantic coast, and understanding tectonic stress buildup may help to predict the sites of future earthquakes.

The natural environments in which we live do not control our behavior, but they influence and constrain many of our choices, such as where to live, what crops to grow, where to raise livestock, and where to build cities or seaports. Physical geography is basic to understanding how humans interact with their environments. Extremely cold climates, infertile soils, or subtropical deserts restrict the range of possible economic activities and lifestyles but rarely exclude all human activity. Despite their relative disadvantages, such environments as Siberia, the Mosquito Coast in Central America, and the Kalahari have been successfully occupied by different cultures for many centuries; in none of these areas, however, is urban development or commercial agriculture extensive. Perceived environmental advantages, on the other hand, attract people. Many older Americans are relocating from colder northern states to warmer Sunbelt states, while the beauty of coastal regions continues to attract more people than do nearby inland areas.

The geographer's concern with how humans interact with their environments relies on not only predicting changes in those environments but also anticipating the effects on human societies and their responses to those threats—from coastal erosion's effect on beach-front houses to the threat posed by earthquakes on densely populated metropolitan areas such as Kyoto, Japan, or Managua, Nicaragua. Physical geography provides the knowledge of where, how, and at what rate physical processes are likely to cause environmental changes that will necessitate societal adjustment. This basic knowledge is essential to all societies preparing for the future, even though their policies and responses may be very different.

The knowledge of physical processes and patterns is also essential to understanding and predicting the effects of resource development on Earth's systems. Clearing vegetation for construction sites affects soil characteristics, amounts of erosion, and distribution of plants and animals. Adding carbon dioxide and greenhouse gases to the atmosphere affects the carbon cycle and Earth's radiation balance. Building breakwaters to protect ships in a harbor causes wave erosion and deposition to be shifted to other parts of a beach. Humans have tremendous ability to affect physical processes and change the face of Earth, but they have not always accurately predicted the consequences of their actions.

Physical geography, like geography in general, is a wonderful challenge for the intellectually curious. Students can enjoy observing the world, appreciating its diversity and the beauty and complexity of its environments, preparing for changes, and abusing its environments less. Understanding Earth is the challenge and reward of physical geography.

SOURCES OF FURTHER INFORMATION

The Audubon Society Field Guide to North American Rocks and Minerals. New York: Alfred A. Knopf, 1995.
Comprehensive review with good photos.

The Audubon Society Field Guide to North American Weather. New York: Alfred A. Knopf, 1997.
Good photos and explanations of events.

Elsom, Derek. *Earth: The Making, Shaping and Workings of a Planet.* New York: Macmillan, 1992.
Good visuals with less detailed text.

Gates, David. *Climate Change and Its Biological Consequences.* Sunderland, MA: Sinauer Associates, 1993.
Specialized look at climate.

Junger, Sebastion. *The Perfect Storm.* New York: W. W. Norton, 1997.
Best-selling case study.

Lamb, Simon and David Sington. *Earth Story: The Shaping of Our World.* Princeton, NJ: Princeton University Press, 1998.
Good geologic history with illustrations.

Lambert, David and the Diagram Group. *The Field Guide to Geology.* New York: Facts on File, 1988.
Designed for younger readers.

Levy, Matthys and Mario Salvadori. *Why the Earth Quakes: The Story of Earthquakes and Volcanoes.* New York: W. W. Norton, 1995.
Good background and illustrations.

McPhee, John. *Assembling California.* New York: Farrar Straus & Giroux, 1993.

_____. *Basin and Range.* New York: Farrar Straus & Giroux, 1981.

_____. *In Suspect Terrain.* New York: Farrar Straus & Giroux, 1983.

Rees, Robin, ed. *The Way Nature Works.* New York: Macmillan, 1998.
Colorful and reader-friendly overview of Earth.

Restless Earth: Disasters of Nature. Washington, D.C.: National Geographic Society, 1997
Case studies; excellent photos.

Simon & Schuster's Guide to Rocks and Minerals. New York: Simon & Schuster, 1978.
Includes worldwide locations.

Roadside Geology Series. Missoula, MT: Mountain Press Publishing Company.
Descriptions and explanations of geology viewed from highways in an increasing number of states.

Watts, Alan. *The Weather Handbook.* Dobbs Ferry, NY: Sheridan House, 1994.
Good explanations, coverage, and diagrams.

Williams, Jack. *The Weather Book: An Easy-to-Understand Guide to the U.S.A.'s Weather.* New York: Vintage Books, 1992.
Good visuals.

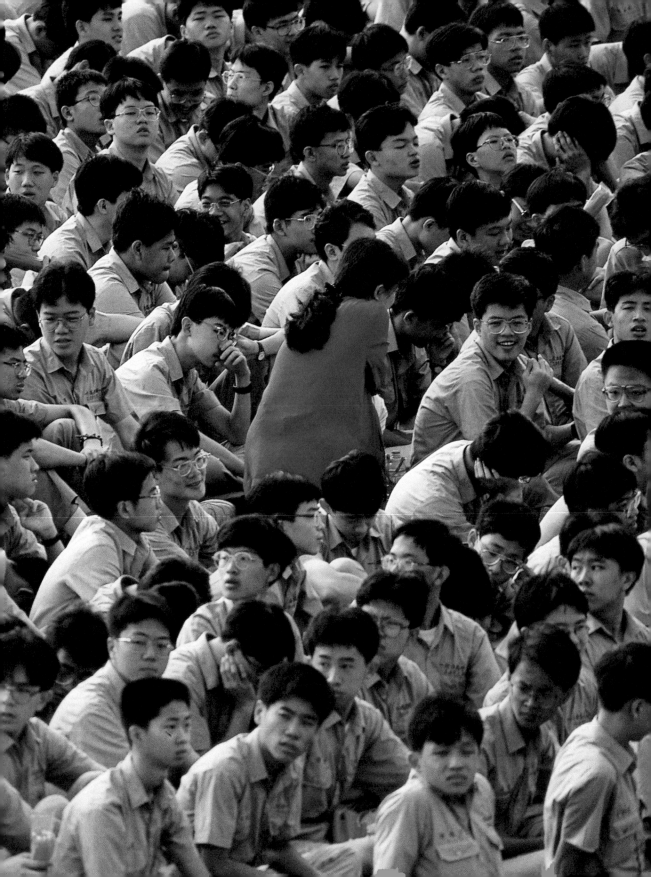

PART III

Human Geography

"Double Ten," or Taiwan's National Day, marks the October 10, 1911, anniversary of the Chinese Revolution. Taipei is the capital and largest city in Taiwan.

Introduction

Curiosity about the "the world and all that is in it" has guided the National Geographic Society since its founding in 1888. Human geographers share that goal of understanding the world, and by the world, human geographers mean the physical Earth as described in Part II, Physical Geography.

The surface of the physical Earth is composed of 29 percent land and 71 percent ocean. As people, we focus our attention on the land surface, although we do care about the ocean as a source of food, oil, other raw materials, transportation, and communication, and as habitat that supports an incredibly diverse range of life-forms. As human geographers, we concentrate, therefore, on a small portion of the habitable space of the world.

That land-based habitable space seems to be full of people. October 12, 1999, marked an important date in human history. It was the official "birthday" of the six billionth person born on Earth. Demographers, who study population, estimate that the number of people who have ever lived on Earth is about 105.7 billion people, so the six billionth person of today's population joins the 5.7 percent of all people ever born who are alive today.

Human geographers put people and space together. Today's population of six billion lives on a complex, highly fragmented land surface with an area of 57 billion square miles, thus each person has access to 9.5 square miles of Earth's land surface, but because of either inhospitable terrain or climate, only 80 percent of the surface is really usable, which reduces the habitable area to 7.6 square miles per person. However when you think about your neighborhood or look at maps and images from space, it is clear that people cluster together in dense concentrations, leaving vast areas of Earth's surface largely uninhabited.

And that is the key to what interests a human geographer: Where *do* people live? Why do they live in those places? How did they get there? What do they do for a living? For recreation? For retirement? Where do they move to and why do they move there? How—and why—do people in India, say, differ from people in Indiana in terms of language and culture and religion? Why are population growth rates so high in Africa and so low in parts of Europe?

As we look at our world, we realize that it is changing, sometimes quite dramatically. We now live in what already seems to be a crowded world: How many people can Earth's surface support? How much food can we produce? Our personal worlds are much smaller; we live in local places that we call home. What does it mean to put down roots in a place, to be attached to a place? Despite our parochial concerns, we also live in a world that is interconnected. Events in places far away have effects at home: What does it mean to "think globally, act locally?" Places are being created politically, such as the new Canadian territory of Nunavut, and places have come apart, such as Yugoslavia and the Soviet Union. How do we carve Earth's space into counties and states, nations and countries? Economies change as factories close and the work is transferred offshore to another country, as factories depend upon just-in-time shipments from faraway places, as people telecommute, working at home instead of in an office. How do high-tech and low-tech industrial regions develop, grow, and decline? We worry about deforestation in Amazonia, desertification in the Sahel, global warming: What have we done to the environment of Earth's surface, to our home?

All of these questions are the concern of human geography. We want to understand the Earth as the home of people. It is our world and we want to understand all that is in it, and this chapter will answer the questions that we have asked. The answers derive from the fundamental approach of a geographer: What is where, and how and why did it get there? And of course, we also want to know what it means, to us, to our children, to future generations.

Population

Introduction

An Indian from West Bengal and an American from Texas were arguing about family size and about the ability of the Earth to support six billion people. The American faulted India for its high birth rate and large families and population of nearly a billion. Earth, he added, cannot sustain the burden. The Indian responded: "One American consumes more, discards more, and pollutes the Earth more than five Indians."

In a debate on burdens of world population, both sides would score points. The world's **fertility rate**—the average number of live births per woman during her childbearing years—has fallen from about five in 1950 to about three at the end of the 20th century. The rate of world population growth has declined since the late 1960s, but the population is growing now at an astounding 84 million people a year. That means the Earth must accommodate an annual increase greater, by two million, than the population of Germany, Europe's second most populous country. The developing countries account for most of the world's population growth. Compared with developed countries, the developing countries have a larger proportion of their population in the reproductive years. In the 21st century the world's population growth will be concentrated in countries least able to support the increase.

The industrialized countries, although holding steady at below replacement fertility rates, also continue to grow in population and in their already high rate of consumption of the Earth's resources.

The burden on the Earth increases from both quarters: population growth and consumption. Geographers approach the study of human populations with a spatial perspective—an eye to the land. They try to understand why births, deaths, and migration vary from place to place. They study the changes in the physical environment prompted by changes in population size and composition. Because of their perspective, geographers express deep concern for Earth's ability to accommodate a population that passed the six billion mark at the end of the century.

This chapter reviews the debate over reasons for rapid population growth and addresses the varied national and regional population issues. For instance, while Japan devises plans for an aging population—projected to be the world's oldest by 2010 when 25 percent of the population is expected to be over 65—most African countries wrestle with prospects of expanding the job market to cope with overwhelming numbers of young people seeking employment.

Geographers examine interrelationships between people and their environment. In the early 20th century, geographers suggested that a favorable climate and adequate natural

Doubling Time

For most of human existence, the growth rate of the world's population has hovered near zero—births roughly equal to deaths. About 40,000 years ago, the world's population was perhaps as low as 1.5 million. The first major increase began around 8,000 B.C., when the number had jumped to between 5 million and 10 million, reflecting the capacity of agriculture to support denser populations. By the middle of the 18th century, at the dawn of the industrial revolution, world population stood at around 700 million, at which point it jumped again, because of productivity gains of industrialization and declining death rates. Historically, a rise in population entailed higher standards of living, larger markets, a finer division of labor, and economies of scale in the production process.

The issue of over-population is a relatively recent concern. At the close of the 20th century, the world population passed 6 billion, and the UN projected it could reach 8.9 billion by 2050, but that assumed a drop in the present world growth rate of 1.4 percent a year. More than half of the six billion people now on Earth are in Asia. At the beginning of the new millennium, more than a third of humanity lives in two countries—China at 1.25 billion and India at 1 billion.

The engines of population change are natural growth and net migration. Natural growth is defined as the difference between birth and death rates. (While crude rates, i.e., births or deaths per 1,000 people per year, are commonly used, demographers prefer age-specific rates, which are more accurate predictors.) Net migration is the difference between in-migration (immigration) and out-migration (emigration). The world's natural growth rate in 1999 was roughly 1.4 percent per year, which amounts to 137 million births and 53 million deaths for a net gain of 84 million people per year, or about 230,000 per day.

Growth rates can be used to estimate doubling times, the number of years a population requires to double in size. With a growth rate of 1 percent, a population would double in 70 years, or 35 years at 2 percent growth rate, and 23 years at 3 percent growth rate. Doubling time of a population, therefore, can be calculated by dividing 70 by the growth rate. If the world's annual natural growth rate continues at 1.4 percent, the population will double in 50 years to 12 billion, far more and slightly faster than present projections. (70/1.4 = 50) Doubling times tend to be long in the developed countries—an average of 583 years—where growth rates are low. Doubling times are short in the developing countries—an average of 40 years—where growth rates are generally high.

resources favored economic development in certain parts of the world. This position, applied to large regions, had considerable historical credibility. However, the belief that physical resources make or break a region is simplistic, and geographers were questioning its logic by the 1930s. The logic took a further beating with the phenomenal post-World War II economic success in Japan, South Korea, and Taiwan, all poor in natural resources and all coping with high population densities.

More recently, geographers have studied the effect that large, dense populations have on the quality of the environment and, by extension, the quality of life. The connections between the environment and the population vary considerably from region to region. Many countries of sub-Saharan Africa are faced with rapidly growing populations and dwindling resources. Persian Gulf countries, with small populations, have encouraged immigration of a large semipermanent work force to exploit bountiful sources of energy.

The World's Changing Population

The growth of the world's population over the last two centuries has been nothing short of phenomenal. Previously, few regions would have been able to support large populations. Early human populations were restricted to the number that could be supported by food gatherers. The work of geographer Friedrich Ratzel at the end of the 19th century suggested that prehistoric hunters and gatherers would require an average of one square mile per person for survival. Since recorded history, the Earth has supported a small population, estimated at up to 10 million around 8000 B.C., increasing—about the time that humans began farming and raising animals—to 200 million at the time of Jesus, 2,000 years ago, when the Roman Empire was well established. The slow growth of human population up to this time presupposes an infinitesimal growth rate. Tribal hostilities, famine, and changes in weather all kept human population in check, leading to a life expectancy at birth of 10 years. With such drastic "culling" of the population, the species could survive only with a very high birth rate—much higher than that found in African or other high fertility countries today.

A popular "shock fact" concerning population is that more people are alive today than were born in all human history. It's certainly shocking, but it's certainly no fact. In tracing the history of population growth, demographers have weighed dozens of variables, taken educated guesses, and estimated that the number of humans born since 50,000 B.C. is 105.7 billion. The human population at the beginning of the 21st century is slightly more than 6 billion, perhaps a huge burden on the Earth but only 5.7 percent of the total number of people who ever lived on Earth.

Early regional population growth often was associated with technological advances,

Three-child families   **Two-child families**

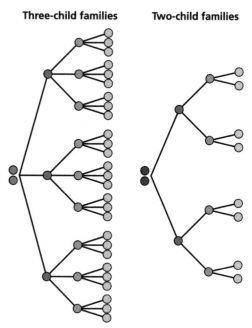

In just three generations, three-child families produce more than triple the number of kinsmen generated by two-child families.

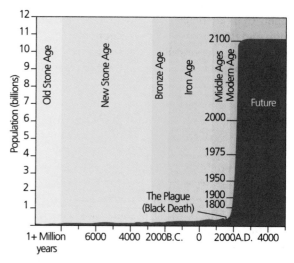

With the advance of industrialization the world has witnessed an ever accelerating population growth.

Two Approaches to Measuring Birth Rates

The two most common methods of measuring births are the crude birth rate and the total fertility rate. Both have distinct uses. The crude birth rate—given as the number of live births per 1,000 population—indicates the number of births relative to the entire population. Crude birth rates for the world range from about 8 in Latvia to about 54 in Niger. The rate helps in assessing the impact of births on population growth of an area.

The crude birth rate does not take the age or sex structure of the population into account. Age and sex , on the other hand, are crucial in computing the total fertility rate. This rate is the average number of children a woman would have in her lifetime given prevailing birth rates for each of her childbearing years. The total fertility rate ranges from 1.1 children in Italy, Latvia, Hong Kong, and Bulgaria to 7.1 children in Oman. The rate is the best birth indicator for comparing countries or places, because it considers births relative to the "population at risk," women of reproductive age, 15 to 44.

especially in agriculture. Population fluctuations in the Middle Ages, due largely to wars and pandemics, held world population to about 500 million in the mid-17th century. But from that time on, with the advance of industrialization, the world witnessed an ever accelerating population growth. The landmark number of one billion people was reached in the early 1800s. A population of two billion was attained in 1927. By 1960, the population had increased to three billion, then to four billion only 14 years later, in 1974. The five-billion landmark was reached in 1987, the six-billion mark in 1999. Note the smaller and smaller hiatus between each billion, even though the world's rate of natural increase (the difference between births and deaths) had been declining since the 1960s.

What underlies the population increase? First, small percentage increases in a population over a long period lead to large increases in actual numbers of people. This is a compounding effect. Greater and greater numbers of women reach childbearing age, then, their children grow up and produce a larger total number of children. Second, growth contains a built-in **population momentum**: Higher birth rates at a previous time and lower death rates at the present time keep populations growing even after families have achieved the average of 2.1 children known as **replacement fertility**. The level at which each person on average has a single successor in the next generation is defined as replacement fertility. Countries with high total fertility rates have births rates of up to seven children per woman over the woman's reproductive years. Countries with low total fertility rates have birth rates of fewer than two children per woman over the woman's reproductive years.

The **demographic equation** that measures population change comprises three components—births, deaths, and migration: Population change equals births minus deaths plus net migration. **Net migration** is the difference between in-migration (immigration) and out-migration (emigration). The equation calculates change in population growth rates, changes in the size of populations, and projections of future populations. A benefit of the demographic equation is its simplicity—only three components are needed to calculate population change.

Why and How Populations Change over Time

Limited space and resources define the finite Earth. How much longer can the Earth bear explosive growth in human population, even at the present small increase of 1.4 percent? Two divergent views have evolved with possible answers. One, the Malthusian theory of "overshoot and collapse," is pessimistic. The other, known as the cornucopians' view, a prediction of natural deceleration of population growth, is optimistic.

Thomas Malthus (1766-1834), an English economist, was alarmed by contemporary population data from France and England. He concluded that the world's population would inevitably increase to a point that would surpass the Earth's capacity to sustain it. He explained that population increased at an exponential rate, whereas food and shelter increased arithmetically, that is, by much smaller increments. Therefore, it would be only a matter of time until an "unholy trinity" of war, pestilence, and famine came onto the scene to control the population. In Malthus's theory, increased deaths would reduce the population to the Earth's carrying capacity. Then, the cycle would begin again. In the cornucopian view, forces in human society are expected to retard population growth before it exceeds Earth's carrying capacity. Human adaptability and aspirations for wealth, prestige, and a better life will prompt people to limit family size. In this scenario, technology will continue to squeeze more and more from the Earth's resources, in effect increasing its carrying capacity. In mathematical terms, population growth would follow a logistic curve.

This view is predicated on the demographic transition model of population change. Credited to Warren Thompson and Frank Notestein, the demographic transition postulates that declining death rates, the primary cause of population explosion, would be matched over time by falling birth rates. Several European countries, such as England and Sweden, had reached low birth rates by the mid-20th century. The demographic transition can both accompany and precede industrialization. (See Sidebar, page 253.) In France, for example, the onset of a decline in the birth rates in the 1820s preceded the industrial revolution. Thailand, a predominantly rural country, has witnessed in the last 30 years a rapid drop in birth rates to replacement levels without widespread industrialization.

Will the Malthusian view or the cornucopian view hold for the world's future? Recent developments help clarify the debate. World grain yields have jumped in the last three decades. High-yield rice and wheat, products of the "green revolution," have significantly increased food supplies in India, China, and Mexico, where populations long have pushed the limits of the land's capacity. Many developed countries, which typically have slow-growing populations, produce food in excess of their needs. The excess becomes a valuable export, helping to ease world hunger. In many developing countries, with the notable exception of the region of sub-Saharan Africa, food supply has begun to keep pace with or exceed population growth, tending to validate, over the short haul, the cornucopians' argument.

Perhaps the population explosion eventually will fizzle. The world's rate of natural increase peaked at 2.0 percent in the late 1960s and has since declined to 1.4 percent. But population momentum continues to increase the number of people in the world. The predominance of young people in most

Malthus: A Controversial Prophet

The causes of population change are linked to economic, social, and political circumstances. A pioneer in explaining the link was the English economist Thomas Malthus, known for his 1798 *Essay on the Principles of Population*. Malthus is credited with originating the theory of overpopulation. He argued that the population of nations tends to grow geometrically. The term used today is "exponential" growth, such as 4, 16, 64, 256, etc. In other words, Malthus postulated that given a constant rate of change, larger and larger absolute numbers of people will be added to the population each year. Such a reading implies that families had little choice in the number of children they bore; birth rates were taken as a biological given. Malthus said that the poor, because of their generally large families, were mainly responsible for spiraling growth in population. He further argued that food supplies increase arithmetically, that is, at a constant absolute rate over time, such as 4, 8, 12, 16, etc.

What happens when population increases by 4, 16, 64, 256...and food supplies increase by 4, 8, 12, 16...over the same period of time? Malthus said the future holds famine, unless population is held in check. He argued that catastrophe was avoidable only through negative checks, such as war and disease, which increase the death rate, and through positive checks, such as abstinence, which decreases the birth rate. (Malthus is largely responsible for the early label applied to political economy, "the dismal science," because of his pessimistic predictions.)

Malthus failed to foresee the enormous impact of the industrial revolution and great gains in agricultural productivity. Indeed, other than the Irish potato famine of the 1840s, large-scale famine in Europe ended with industrialization. Furthermore, the fertile lands of North America and Australia provided vast new food sources.

More important, he did not foresee the drop in birth rates and family size associated with industrialization and the growth of urban society. Birth rates reflect economic and social circumstances, not biological inevitabilities. Malthus also could have little idea of the effect that advanced methods of contraception would have on the birth rate. Consistent with the main method of lowering fertility in his time, Malthus advocated that people delay marriage. People in early 19th-century Europe married as late as in their 30s, and older women would often marry younger men.

Malthus's theories helped mold public policies after World War II, particularly birth control programs in developing countries. Low rates of population growth were assumed to be a prerequisite to economic growth. Birth control became integral to foreign aid, but with minimal success because its proponents generally failed to take into account the cultural and economic motivations that lead to high birth rates.

Malthus's notions have been revived several times since his death. Most recently, high rates of natural increase in the 1950s and 1960s lead to worldwide concern about overpopulation. Two influential books appeared at that time: Paul Ehrlich's 1968 *The Population Bomb,* and *The Limits to Growth* by the Club of Rome in 1972. These neo-Malthusians believed that time will validate Malthus's theory of overpopulation, arguing that population growth eventually will be constrained by finite resources because ecosystems cannot withstand the accumulated assaults of industrialization, deforestation, and pollution. Others, loosely labeled "technological optimists," hold that new production techniques, such as aquaculture and genetic engineering to boost plant yields, will keep pace with population growth.

Relief workers in Somalia serve food to famine victims in 1993. War, drought, and ruined crops can wreak havoc on poverty-stricken populations.

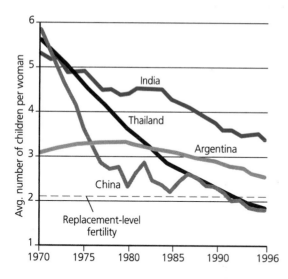

Patterns of fertility decline reflect falling birth rates in developing countries. Asian countries show more precipitous drops than Latin American countries.

South American, African, and Asian countries ensures that populations there will continue to increase even though families bear fewer children. Countries such as Taiwan, Thailand, South Korea, and China still will add appreciably to their populations in coming years, despite being at or below the replacement fertility level of 2.1 children per couple.

The United Nations 1998 *World Population Estimates and Projections* were revised downward from the 1996 projections by almost a half billion people, to 8.9 billion for the year 2050. The downward revisions occurred in developing countries, primarily Africa where it is now assumed that declines in the birth rate and the mortality tolls from AIDS will be more dramatic than previously expected.

Industrialization and Population Dynamics

An alternative to Malthusian interpretations of population growth is the demographic transition model, made famous by demographers after World War II. Based on the historical experience of the Western world as it industrialized, the demographic transition model ties birth, death, and natural growth rates to the changing socioeconomic circumstances faced by households in the midst of the shift from a predominantly rural, impoverished society to an urbanized, relatively wealthy society.

Societies typically pass through four stages en route to industrialization. (See Diagram, page 260) The first stage involves an agrarian economy. Birth rates tend to be high and family size large, often with ten or more births per family. Children provide labor for farm families. High birth rates also reflect the reliance on children as a form of social insurance in old age, for which organized programs are generally lacking in poorer countries. Finally, high infant mortality rates lead families to bear large numbers of children in the hopes that a substantial proportion will survive to adulthood. Thus, poverty is a major cause of high fertility rates; "overpopulation" may be the consequence, not simply the cause, of low standards of living. Death rates are high and life expectancies are low, largely due to inadequate nutrition, tainted water supplies, high infant mortality, and widespread prevalence of infectious bacterial diseases. Although birth and death rates are high, the difference between them—natural growth—is low. Pre-industrial societies grew slowly.

The second stage, often associated with early industrialization, includes a gradual decline in death rates and a gradual rise in life expectancy. Improved medical care is generally thought to be the primary cause. However, historical evidence suggests that the primary cause is improved diets as a result of mechanized agriculture. Antibiotics and public health measures, such as improved sanitation and potable water, also play a role, particularly in lowering infant mortality rates. Birth rates remain high; natural growth increases.

The third stage witnesses a decline in birth rates, usually after the death rate has declined. The reasons for declining birth rates in the face of industrialization, contrary to Malthus's theory, lay largely in the changing cost-benefit ratio of children. As mothers join the labor force, the utility of child labor declines and the cost of raising children rises. (Computing cost includes foregone incomes while mothers stay home to care for children.) Birth rates typically decline as per capita incomes rise. The natural growth rate falls.

The final stage, stage four, commonly occurs with advanced urbanization and industrialization, accompanied by low death rates and long life expectancies. Modern populations, apppreciably older than earlier ones, die most commonly from degenerative diseases such as heart disease, cancer, and stroke. Birth rates are also low; the nuclear family replaces the extended family. While both birth and death rates are low, the difference is negligible. Therefore, natural growth rates in the developed world are uniformly low. Contrary to developing countries, where population policies emphasize birth control, demographic incentives in industrialized countries typically seek to increase birth rates through subsidies for childbirth and rearing. Recently industrialized countries are going through this demographic transition far faster than Europe did, resulting in a larger gap between birth and death rates and therefore a higher population growth rate. The demographic transition postulates a fall in rates of natural growth and acknowledges the social, rather than purely biological, determinants of fertility.

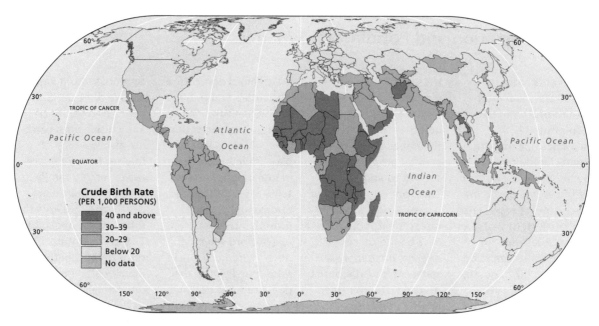

The crude birth rate is the ratio of total live births to total population in a geographic area over a determined period of time. It is expressed as the number of live births per one thousand people per year.

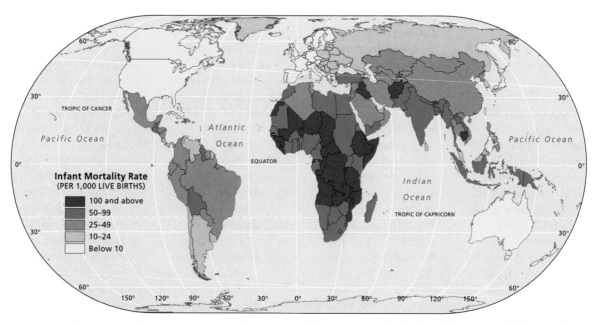

Health education, prenatal care, proper diet and hygiene, and the presence of trained medical personnel all contribute to lower levels of infant mortality.

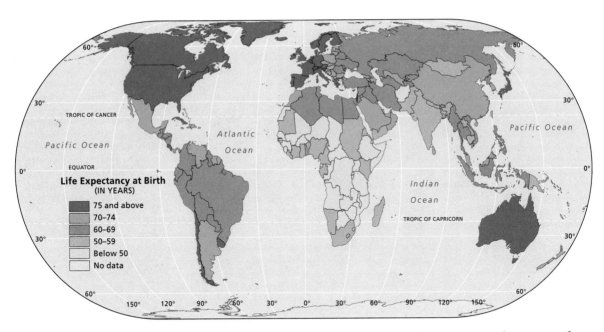

Much of the world benefits from improved medical care and in many industrialized countries extensive systems of social welfare have improved the quality of life for elderly citizens.

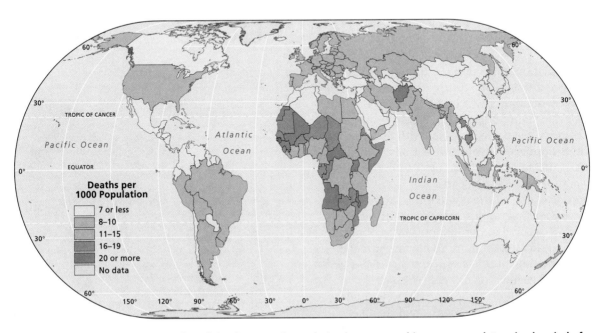

The crude death rate is the ratio of total deaths to total population in a geographic area over a determined period of time. It is expressed as the number of deaths per one thousand people per year.

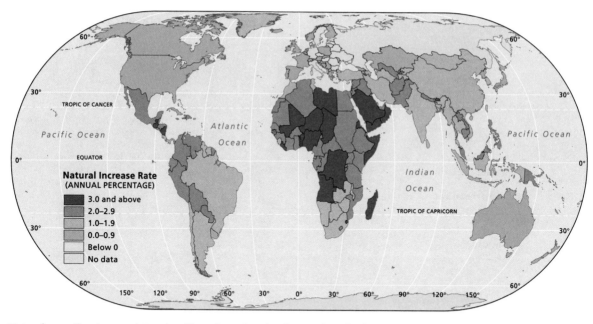

Natural growth rates are determined by subtracting death rates from birth rates. Growth rates are used to predict future population numbers and requirements for social services and food.

Population Projections

A population projection is a numerically derived estimate of a future population. Projections commonly cover up to 30 years. Beyond that the chance of error increases significantly. Accuracy generally increases with large populations projected over short periods, say ten years. Relatively accurate projections are possible if the calculation begins with recent and precise counts of the population, broken down by such demographic components as numbers in each age and sex group, plus rates of birth, death, and migration. More recent estimates from the time of the latest census can also be based on changes of address (often easily traced through drivers' licenses), new utility hookups, school enrollments, and the like.

Far more difficult to project are populations in small areas of rapidly growing regions. Short-period growth rates, because they are so

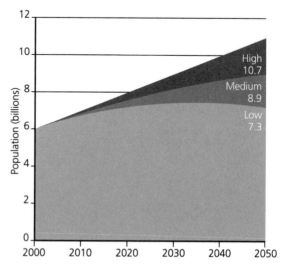

The UN projections for global population depend on anticipated total fertility rates (TFR) or the average number of children per woman in her lifetime.

recent and rapid, are often contingent on local economic booms, which are imprecise indicators of possible change. A new suburb offers a clear example of the techniques used to project future population. Calculations might start with the latest census, adjusted according to information gleaned from housing starts and demolitions, and average household size to help estimate a population at the moment. Then, population size can be projected with the latest rates of growth, along with adjustments for the maximum population an area can hold, given average residential lot size.

Dozens of other statistical methods can be used for projections, from a simple, straight-line extension of a growth curve to intricate procedures of matrix multiplication. Of the three demographic components (births, deaths, and migration) used in projections, migration is by far the trickiest to gauge. Vicissitudes of the local economy—such as the opening of a major industrial plant, or drought and the consequent monetary loss to farmers—can cause wild fluctuations in migration. Mortality schedules for most populations, on the other hand, are fairly well established; and births can be estimated with adequate information on age structure and other vital statistics of a population.

Population: Asset or Liability?

Population growth often brings with it economic growth, specialization, and material gain. However, it can also bring with it major problems. Social services—roads, schools, housing, law enforcement—often fail to keep pace with population growth, especially the increasingly dense populations in cities of developing countries during the last four decades. Governments at times appear powerless as urban areas spread, transforming highway runoff ditches into slow moving streams of human waste and debris. Indeed, the massive breakdown of basic urban services prompted the Nigerian government to move its capital in 1975 far from the seemingly uncontrollable sprawl of Lagos, now home to more than 12 million people. Rapid growth and high density exacerbate environmental problems. Governments, however, are not powerless. Japan has grown to be one of the world's top economic powers while successfully coping with high population densities and the related strain on the environment.

Is population growth the primary cause of environmental problems? Or is the culprit a complex combination of population size, affluence, and technology? Paul Ehrlich, author of the widely quoted *Population Bomb*, posits that the adverse impact of population on the Earth relates to the population's size, affluence, and technological sophistication. He expressed the relationship in the formula "Impact equals Population multiplied by Affluence multiplied by Technology ($I = P \times A \times T$)." Evironmentalist Barry Commoner strongly agrees that technology continues to ravage the environment with nitrogen fertilizers, throwaway plastic containers, and the like. However, he revised the import of Ehrlich's formula by arguing that technology also has the potential to dampen a population's negative impact on the Earth. He said that technological advances in the 1970s helped improve fuel efficiency, which in turn reduced car emissions and improved air quality. The "T" in Ehrlich's formula, Commoner argued, has an up side for the health of the Earth.

Some people maintain that population growth is beneficial to economic growth. Most notably, Julian Simon has popularized this view in his book, *Population: The Ultimate Resource*. Simon argues that the great advances of civilizations, such as ancient Rome and classical Greece, were propelled by technological innovation, which was in turn fueled by increased population size. Anthropologist Ester Boserup's evidence from 16th- and 17th-century Tokugawa, Japan, and 15th- and 16th-century Holland contains strong evidence in favor of the "beneficial" argument. She showed that a doubling of the population of Holland from 1550 to 1650 and a concomitant increase in demands on productivity were met with more efficient agricultural practices, including the expansion of the country's dikes to open more land to farming. Somewhat contradicting these findings, anthropologist Clifford Geertz found that on the densely populated island of Java, Indonesia, food per person decreased even though more and more people worked the land as the population grew in the 20th century.

World Population Distributions

Exact records are lacking for the spatial distribution of world population in ancient times. Studies indicate that preindustrial urban centers were small, incomparable to today's metropolitan areas. The Mesopotamian metropolis of Ur had up to 50,000 people in the 22nd century B.C., while Thebes, capital of Egypt at its zenith in the 14th century B.C., contained 225,000 inhabitants, by a liberal estimate. Rome, the largest city of antiquity, may have reached 350,000 around A.D. 200. Medieval Paris contained a mere 30,000 to 60,000 people, and commercially vibrant Venice probably counted no more than 70,000 in the 14th century.

Empires outside Europe could claim notable populations. China, which routinely conducted a census, beginning with the Han dynasty (206 B.C. to A.D. 220), grew to almost 60 million around the time of Christ, more than tripling to over 200 million by 1760. In the eighth century, the Tang Dynasty's capital, Ch'ang-an (Xi'an), held almost a million people within its walls. The 17th-century Thai capital of Ayutthaya contained hundreds of thousands of people before its destruction by Burmese armies in 1767. By the 18th century the thriving commercial city of Edo (precursor of modern Tokyo) was one of the largest cities of the world with more than a million people.

In the 19th century Europe's population burgeoned because of industrialization and because medical breakthroughs, better diets, and improved sanitation contributed to a reduction in the death rate. Paris, London, and Berlin emerged as the world's leading urban centers, their culture spread throughout the world by colonization. National populations of developing countries grew rapidly in the 20th century, initiated by a rapid drop in the death rate, first in South America, later in Asia and Africa. The onslaught of AIDS, however, has begun to push East Africa's death rate back up in the last two decades.

Pushed by generally precipitous drops in the death rate, the population growth of the developing countries in the 20th century has far surpassed growth in the developed countries, which experienced an earlier, more drawn out, demographic transition. World population reached more than 6 billion by 2000, increasing by 84 million annually, or roughly 1.4 percent per year. China, with 1.25 billion, and India, with about a billion, together account for about 37 percent of the world's people. The population division generally broke down to 4.8 billion in the developing countries and 1.2 billion in the developed countries at the end of the 20th century.

Asia accounts for 60 percent of the world's population. Distribution by other regions is 12 percent for Europe and former USSR countries, 5 percent for the United States and Canada together, 9 percent for Latin America, 13 percent for Africa (sub-Saharan Africa 10.5 percent), and 1 percent for Oceania.

During the last 100 years, Europe, the U.S.,

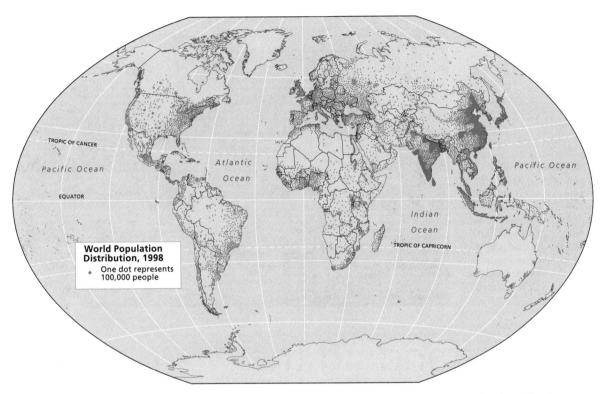

**World Population
Distribution, 1998**
• One dot represents
    100,000 people

The distribution of the world's population reveals not only the most populated countries, but also the inclination or necessity for populations to settle near coastlines and significant waterways such as the Nile River in Africa.

and Canada have sharply diminished in their relative share of the world's population, from 30 percent to 17 percent. Population increases have been most notable in the last several decades in Indonesia, Brazil, Pakistan, and Bangladesh. Several mid-size Asian countries— for example, Vietnam, the Philippines, and Thailand—with populations exceeding 60 million have overtaken all the major European countries in size, with the exception of Germany and Russia.

The future will most likely witness increasing relative importance of the African populations. Africa is the only region of developing countries not yet experiencing a major decline in birth rates. The United Nations has indicated that despite increases in deaths from AIDS, Africa still will go from 9 percent of the world's population in 1950 to almost 20 percent by the year 2050. With 98 percent of the current population growth today, developing countries will continue to become an increasingly larger proportion of the world's total population by the middle of the 21st century.

More than 125 million people live in Bangladesh, a country just slightly smaller than Wisconsin. Rural Bangladeshis have flocked to the capital city of Dhaka seeking jobs. Bangladesh remains one of the world's poorest and most densely populated nations.

Understanding the Demographic Transition

A decline in mortality, not an increase in fertility, has produced the rapid population growth of the last two centuries. In the demographic transition, the decline in birth rates has lagged behind the drop in death rates. The speed at which a country can lower its birth rate is critical to closing the gap between mortality and fertility. Otherwise, such countries are saddled with disproportionate numbers of children, rapid rural to urban migration, and continued strain on limited resources—all the socioeconomic problems associated with population growth at the turn of the century.

Places with high infant and child death rates tend to have persistently high birth rates. For example, in rural India, where infant death rates remain high, couples must bear several children to insure that at least two sons reach adulthood. This could be accomplished, when allowing for infant and child mortality, with the birth of up to seven children. Children provide families with farm labor, security in

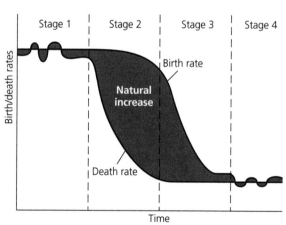

As a country develops, high birth and death rates give way to a drop in death rates followed by a drop in birth rates. In the developed country, both rates are low.

old age, and a chance to get ahead if the child succeeds in school and in work outside the home. Sons are especially crucial, because they carry on the family name and business. In

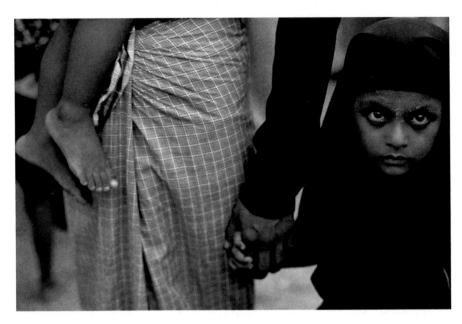

In Myanmar, a developing country, women give birth to an average of 3.8 children during their lifetimes. A full 33 percent of the population is under 15 years of age.

Hindu India, male heirs are especially important because they have the sacred duty of cremating the parents. Despite such supports for large families, the transition to smaller families is under way. The fertility rate in rural India has dropped from 4.7 to 4.0 between 1973 and 1992. Rates in urban India at that time were 2.7, closer to replacement fertility.

Fertility rates continue to decline in most of the regions of the world as we enter the 21st century. A number of countries have completed the demographic transition, or are close to it. Industrialization and the money economy helped foster the transition to lower fertility in Europe. Young 19th-century Europeans eager to get ahead began to move to the city, delay marriage, and then limit their family size. In more recent times, the trend toward smaller families has taken on a cost-benefit calculation: joy of children versus expense of children, happiness of family life versus lost career opportunities; relatively stable home atmosphere versus freedom to travel, to socialize, even to job hop in search of advancement.

Women's changing role in societies is the crux of the change in fertility rates. In societies that emphasize family and women's role in the home, the fertility rates have remained high. For example, Islamic countries, where women generally are restricted to domestic life, have some of the highest birth rates in the world. In the West, where women generally participate extensively in work outside the home, the fertility rates are low and continue to drop. A woman's educational level is closely associated with her family size. Increased education has changed women's values and heightened women's awareness of opportunities outside the home. In countries with greater educational opportunities, women delay marriage and childbearing. They typically find better jobs, which in turn lessens their incentive to adopt the domestic life of house and children. Indications are, therefore, that as women continue to gain equality with men, birth rates will decline. Where women have been allowed a place in the work force, yet given little support in their roles as homemakers, the drop in fertility can be dramatic. The extremely low birth rates in Russia today are in good part due to the change in society's attitude toward women. Russian women with demanding jobs and domestic responsibilities are finding that one child is quite enough.

Most developed countries experience low rates of birth and death. In Denmark, only 18 percent of the population is under 15 years old and approximately 15 percent is over 65. Life expectancy averages 75 years.

Regional Trends in Population Change

The 21st century sees the world in various stages of the demographic transition—from agrarian economies with high birth rates at one end to economies of advanced urbanization and industrialization with low death rates and long life expectancies at the other end.

Europe

Europe, with a population of 728 million, has some of the more densely populated lands in the world outside of South and East Asia. The Europeans were the first to complete the transition from high birth and death rates to low birth and death rates. Europe went through the demographic transition during the last two centuries while building up substantial numbers of people, despite losing many millions as emigrants, primarily to North America.

Europe's decline in the death rate began about 200 years ago. Total fertility rates continued to decline into the Depression era to replacement level, fluctuated in the 1940s and 1950s, and then began a persistent decline after the mid-1960s to below replacement levels. Rates in Northern and Western Europe declined to below replacement levels in the 1970s, while Eastern Europe experienced a precipitous drop in the 1990s with a regional fertility rate of 1.3.

Associated with Europe's decline in fertility has been a progressive aging of the population and the need for foreign workers. Although favorable levels of mortality have been achieved in Western Europe, life expectancy recently has dropped in Eastern Europe and Russia, particularly for males in their later working years, a trend partly blamed on alcohol consumption and industrial pollution.

South Asia

Second only to China in population, India had grown to about one billion people at the turn of the century. The populations of Pakistan and Bangladesh are more than 120 million each, making these two nations among the world's ten most populous countries. India's population has grown from 250 million at the beginning of the 20th century to 350 million at independence in 1947, and 996 million in 1999, almost a fourfold increase during the last 100 years. Both rapid population growth and high densities prompted the government of India in 1952 to establish a national family planning program, the first in the world. Fertility, however, remained high until the 1960s, then gradually decreased from 5.7 children per woman in the latter part of that decade to 3.4 in 1999. Bangladesh also has witnessed a transition to lower fertility. Birth rates remain high in Pakistan.

East Asia

China's population has been historically large, with almost 60 million during the Han dynasty 2,000 years ago, more than 200 million by the mid-18th century, and one billion in 1981. After the Communist takeover, China's population increased by more than 125 percent in 49 years, from 529 million in 1950 to 1.25 billion in 1999.

The government, concerned with the country's ability to support such rapid growth, adopted pervasive birth control in 1970. Family planning and abortion services were widely accessible and inexpensive. The new policies included neighborhood goals (such as production goals for factories, only in reverse), incentives and disincentives for couples, massive propaganda efforts, and open doors to education and health care. All this and the flood of affordable new consumer items for the average Chinese set the stage for a drop in the fertility rate from 6.06 children per woman between 1965 and 1970 to 3.32 children per woman between 1975 and 1980, a monumental social change in but a dozen years.

China's successful birth planning program, however, has not been without insidious side effects. China started to experience "missing females." The ratio of male babies to female babies, which typically has been about 105

Population Pyramids

The age structure of any population can quickly be understood by looking at its pyramid, two bar graphs of the proportions of men and women in each age group. The shape of the pyramid can show whether the population is predominately young, as in Uganda, middle-age as in the United States, or older, as in Germany. The pyramid also suggests the demo- graphic history of a country, typically over 80 years, the span of a few generations. The graph illustrates such information as age groups with low birth rates and the proportion of the sexes, most notably the pre- ponderance of older women in most societies and the significantly greater numbers of boys in certain East Asian countries, such as China and South Korea.

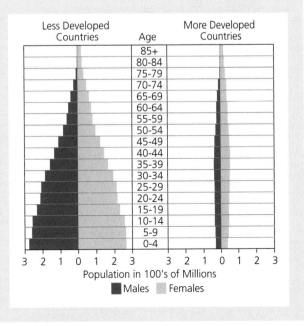

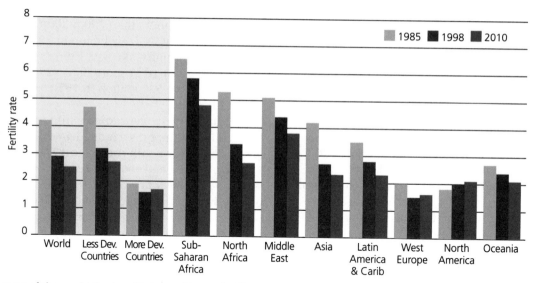

In most of the world the trend is toward lower fertility rates, with some of the most dramatic decreases in less developed countries. In North America and Europe, where fertility rates are below replacement levels, a rise is predicted in the next decade.

boys to 100 girls worldwide, had risen from 106 in 1979 to 114 by 1989. The ratio—boys to girls—for the fourth born was 132 to 100. Although stories of female infanticide proliferated, most likely the major reason for the unusual ratio was abortions of female fetuses and unreported female births. Women eligible for marriage soon will become a premium, which should help control China's population growth, if not also leading to another form of social disruption. China likely will have too few workers to support the aging "baby boom" generation in its later years. Now, however, a large proportion of the population is in the prime labor-force ages, auguring well for continued growth of China's economy.

Japan's 126 million people are highly concentrated; less than a fifth of the land is suitable for settlement. Japan's preindustrial population was reasonably stable. Between 1726 and 1852 it remained close to 25 million, with lower birth rates partly realized through infanticide and by Japanese women delaying marriage until their mid-20s. During Japan's initial period of rapid industrialization, from the 1870s to the end of World War I, the population grew by 60 percent, from 35 million to

56 million, an increase of 21 million. Birth rates in the period of maturation of the Japanese economy, the 1920s, actually increased, contrary to the model of demographic transition and the usual effects of industrialization. Government propaganda exhorted Japanese women to reproduce. They responded in the 1930s by pushing the birth rate to a high of about 31 children per 1,000 women.

Before the onset of World War II in 1939, Japan's population stood at 72 million. After the war, Japan quickly reduced its fertility from 4.5 children per woman in 1946 to 2.0 children in the late1950s, primarily through the use of condoms and abortion. In 1990 the Japanese media created a stir with the expression "1.57 shock," reminding the country that Japanese women, on average in their lifetimes, were bearing children at a rate far below replacement fertility. Young Japanese women, now delaying marriage several years and becoming less accepting of traditional domestic roles, have responded to such talk of "shock" by asserting that they are not "baby machines."

Given that Japan has among the highest life expectancy rates in the world and that the age groups born between 1930 and 1950 are analogous to the U.S. "baby boomers" of post World War II, Japan will not only have the world's oldest population in the next few decades, but it also will have a smaller labor base to support the disproportionately large number of elderly. The large aging population soon will increase the country's death rate and initiate a natural decrease in the population beginning about 2006.

The Middle East and North Africa

North Africa and the Middle East together contain 350 million people, about 5 percent of the world's population. Predominantly Islamic, these regions have experienced high fertility rates since World War II. Contributing factors are early marriage and strong family customs. Despite the wealth gained from oil revenues during recent decades and the improvement in health and literacy, the fertility rate has held steady. Many countries of the region, especially the oil-rich ones, such as Saudi Arabia and Kuwait, are relatively small, requiring migrants to supplement the labor force.

Sub-Saharan Africa

Sub-Saharan Africa shares with its neighboring region to the north the distinction of the world's most rapidly growing population. Its 48 countries cover less than 20 percent of the Earth's land surface, yet possess 10.5 percent of its population. Given the rapid rate of population growth in recent decades and the cultural preference for large families, regional growth rates probably will remain high. From the 16th to the 19th centuries, Africa lost up to 15 million people, primarily in their reproductive years, to the slave trade. As recently as 1950, the sub-Saharan population stood at only 177 million, more than tripling by the end of the century to about 630 million. Projections

indicate the population may rise to 804 million by the year 2010.

Use of contraceptives is up from 5 percent of married women of parental age to 18 percent, dropping the region's fertility rate from 6.7 in the early 1960s to about 5.7 in the mid-1990s. However, significant declines in the fertility rate do not appear imminent. Population growth will be slowed somewhat by a rise in the death rate because of the region's high incidence of AIDS. In the countries hardest hit by autoimmune deficiency syndrome, the average life expectancy at birth has decreased by seven years.

Latin America

At the end of the 20th century, Latin America had more than 500 million people, about 9 percent of the world's total. The fertility rate has decreased from 5.9 in the early 1960s to 3 percent near the end of the century. Four major groups account for the cultural origins in the region. The indigenous Indian population is most prevalent in the highlands, particularly in the Andes. Blacks are numerous in Brazil and parts of the Caribbean. European stock predominates in southern Brazil, Uruguay, Argentina, and Chile. People of mixed ethnic background are common throughout the region. Indian and black populations have distinctly higher fertility rates, while South American whites have fertility rates similar to those in European countries.

Mexico and Brazil together contain more than half of the region's population. Both experienced rapid declines in birth rates, from around 6 in the 1960s to 3.1 for Mexico and 2.5 for Brazil in 1998. In Argentina, Costa Rica, and Colombia total fertility rates have remained near replacement levels (2.5 to 3.0), for the last decade. The rapid decline in Latin America's crude birth rates since the 1950s has been somewhat unexpected, given the pronatalist governments that existed before the 1980s and the influence of the Catholic Church. In terms of population growth, the region's rate increased from 2.6 percent in the

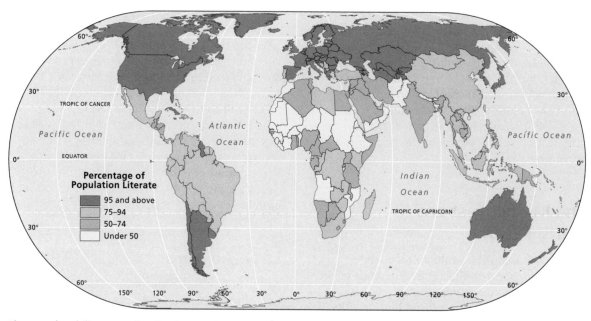

Percentage of Population Literate
- 95 and above
- 75–94
- 50–74
- Under 50

Literacy, the ability to read and write at a determined level of proficiency, is a learned skill usually obtained in a formal educational setting. Illiteracy is more prevalent in poor and less developed countries.

early 1950s to 2.75 percent a decade later. In the late 1970s, the rate had dropped to 2.3 percent. By the early 1990s, Latin America's growth rate was 1.72 percent.

Anglo America

Canada and the United States have completed the demographic transition and have low birth and death rates. Their combined population entering the new millennium is 303 million, 5 percent of the world's population. Life expectancy at birth is 78 years for Canada and 76 for the United States, compared with an average life expectancy of 66 years for the world. Fertility is at replacement level in the United States; slightly lower in Canada. Growth will depend on population momentum (caused by the larger proportions of the population presently in the reproductive ages) and immigration. At least two major demographic issues face North America. One, society must accom-

modate baby boomers as they retire and begin to collect Social Security. Baby boomers, born between 1946 and 1964, make up almost 30 percent of the population in the United States. Two, both countries must adjust to the shift in ethnicity as the European stock begins to yield population dominance, particularly to Asians, Hispanics, and African Americans. As interaction increases between Latin America and Anglo America, the Hispanic population will become increasingly important and is expected to supplant African Americans as the most numerous minority group in the United States.

Oceania

Throughout history, Oceania's relative share of the world's population has been only about 0.5 percent, and today, with approximately 30 million people, this large, spread-out region of islands contains only three counties of significant population size.

Sources of Population Data

The field of population geography is rich with data. The most comprehensive sources are national censuses, taken every ten years in most countries. A census contains information on housing, race, economic status, sex, age, education, and more. The ancient Romans and the Chinese dynasties of thousands of years ago conducted a regular census. Sweden has taken a census since 1749—the longest continual demographic count for a major modern country.

A trove of population data is available through government records of vital statistics—births, deaths, marriages, diseases, etc. The extent of vital statistics varies considerably among countries. Contributing to the study of human populations are sample surveys, covering a myriad of topics, such as personal decisions behind migrations, the size of families, the reasons for marriage, choice of job, income related to time of retirement. Governments, universities, and private organizations often finance institutes devoted to conducting surveys, most carried out repeatedly to monitor change. Princeton University researchers, for example, have traced the change in attitudes on birth control and reproduction behavior in the American family. The University of Chicago has a continuous study on the changes in health and medical care practices in the United States. The World Fertility Survey, conducted in the 1970s by the International Statistical Institute, London, measured attitudes and behavior on family planning, interviewing more than 400,000 women in 43 developing countries and 20 developed countries.

Technology is rapidly changing the form in which statistical reports appear. The U.S. census for the year 2000 has only one printed summary per state. However, the entire census will be accessible only on the Internet. Previously, thousands of printed volumes were available to the public. Some countries, Singapore, for example, are considering conducting and publishing their next census entirely over the Internet.

Australia, with 19 million people—about two-thirds of the region's population—and New Zealand , with close to 4 million people, have both completed the demographic transition. Historically, their changes in birth and death rates have generally been similar to those of Western Europe, consistent with the European, especially British, origins of most of their people. Australia augmented its population earlier in this century through immigration from the British Isles, and more recently from a diversity of places. In the early 1990s, Australia was the world's fifth most important country in net international migration. The Polynesian and Melanesian island countries in the region have higher birth, death, and population growth rates. Of these, only Papua New Guinea, with approximately 5 million people, has a statistically notable national population size.

Conclusion

At the end of the 20th century, which may go down in history as "the century of population growth," hope prevailed for the state of the Earth and its demanding human population. Although there is still great concern about the environmental damage inflicted by rapidly growing, densely settled populations, the consensus is that birth rates will continue to decline toward stabilization in the 21st century. The situation in Africa, however, is highly uncertain and may allow the world's population to continue to increase.

Migration

Introduction

Mold, which gives us bread and wine and penicillin, has a significant role in the history of human migration. Mold pushed as many as 1.5 million Irish out of Ireland, many of them across the Atlantic and onto the shores of the United States in the late 1840s. Their migration can be explained by the classic push and pull factors. The potato blight, brought on by a plant disease and combined with other economic factors, pushed the Irish out of their homeland by destroying their main source of food. The Irish were pulled to a new land by the possibility for economic opportunity in place of economic ruin.

Migration is the changing of one's place of habitation for a substantial time, normally across a political boundary. People react to the push of natural disasters such as war, overpopulation, religious persecution, politics, and slavery and respond to the pull of economic opportunity, religious freedom, social equality, democracy, safety, food sources, and open land.

Migration has redistributed people over the Earth for millions of years. Prehistoric humans migrated far in search of food, found favorable conditions, settled, multiplied, and depleted their sources of meat and fur. Their actions in turn changed the ecosystem, establishing a new mix of flora and fauna. Migrations of an industrialized people have led to the leveling of mountains in West Virginia for the purpose of

extracting coal. Brazilians in the last several decades have migrated to the rain forests, cleared the land for farms and ranches, and diverted rivers for crops and cattle, markedly changing the Earth's surface and sparking a worldwide debate on the destruction of species and the endangerment of one of the Earth's larger sources of oxygen.

Large tribes—such as the Vandals in Europe and northern Africa during the 5th century and the Mongols of the early 13th century in Asia—capitalized on military might and mobility to migrate long distances in search of conquest. During the great age of exploration, European navigators and adventurers of the 15th, 16th, and 17th centuries expanded the frontiers of Europe and diffused European culture and peoples to the Western and Eastern Hemispheres and to Australia.

The 20th century has experienced several forced mass migrations, including the transplanting of tens of millions of urban dwellers to the countryside during China's Great Leap Forward and Cultural Revolution, and the exodus of ethnic Albanians from Kosovo in 1999 in the ethnic cleansing of Yugoslavia. One of the most significant migration patterns of the 20th century has been the enormous rural to urban migration that has occurred in countries around the world.

In the first half of the 19th century, Tasmania was the recipient of about 68,000 British convicts. Agriculture was a primary means of subsistence for forced migrants.

Models For the Study of Migration

The most popular explanation of human migration is the **push-pull model:** Migrants are pushed out of one place and pulled to another. People's decisions are based on a calculation of the pluses and minuses of staying put and the pluses and minuses of moving. Travel costs also figures into the calculations. Terrain, cultural barriers, distance, modes of transportation, and time of travel all stand between migrants and their destination, and all usually weigh heavily on the decision to move or to stay. E. G. Ravenstein is credited as the first to suggest the push-pull framework. His celebrated paper on the "Laws of Migration" presented to the Royal Statistical Society on March 17, 1885, maintains that pull factors take precedence in the decision to migrate. "Bad or oppressive laws, heavy taxation, an

unattractive climate, uncongenial social surroundings, and even compulsion—all have produced and are still producing currents of migration, but none of those currents can compare in volume to that which arises from the desire inherent in most men to 'better' themselves in material respects."

Geographer Julian Wolpert takes a behavioral approach to the reasons behind migration. He suggests focusing on the individual rather than on the statistics, stressing migrants' search behavior, their "stress threshold," and their perception of a place's utility.

Migration is selective; that is, people who move tend to have characteristics in common. Better-educated, white-collar, and military personnel tend to move more often. Historically, women have moved less often than men and

When the winter winds howl in Montreal, hundreds of thousands of Canadian snowbirds fly to their favorite rookery on the Atlantic coast of Florida where they dance to familiar tunes at Le Club Canadien.

have moved shorter distances, on average, but now have approximately the same migration rates as men in most countries. People in formative stages of life—graduation, marriage, birth, separation, divorce—are associated with a greater likelihood of moving. Migration is selective for certain ages, most notably younger adults, 18 to 30 years old, and their young children, who must move with them.

The study of migration has been enriched by a movement in geography in the 1980s and 1990s toward social and humanistic concerns. Geographer Kevin McHugh, for example, has compiled recollections of retired Americans who seasonally migrate to Arizona. The study provides a personal view of the motivations of these "snowbirds." Migration, normally associated with displacement and travail, takes on an

Peterson's Typology of Migration

CATEGORY OF MIGRATION	TYPE OF INTERACTION	MIGRATORY FORCE
Primitive	Nature and man	Ecological push
Impelled	State (or equivalent) and man	Migration policy
Forced	State (or equivalent) and man	Migration policy
Free	Man and his norms	Higher aspirations
Mass	Collective behavior	Social momentum

entirely different meaning for snowbirds. Typically, they are an Anglo couple from the northern United States or Canada. With retirement, snowbirds flee their family home of several decades, flee the cold winters of the north, leave their grown children, jump in an RV (recreation vehicle), and drive the highways to Arizona, Texas, and other warm regions of the South and Southwest. Along their leisurely way, snowbirds stop at recreational areas and trailer parks to meet old friends. They continue on to their winter home for sunshine and more social activities. The migration is reversed in summer. Their extended trips back and forth are recreation all the way. Indeed, snowbirds celebrate a culture of migration. Movement is their life.

Recent studies of migration have countered behaviorism in favor of collective experiences of migrants. Geographer Bruce Moon argues that geographers should adopt a keener appreciation of cultural influences that bind people to a place or spur them to leave. For example, a recent survey of western women who married Sherpas of Nepal and then decided to leave the country found that the women left not for their personal happiness but for the welfare of their immediate family and their children's education.

The economist Michael Todaro, focusing on migration in developing countries, concluded that when workers migrate from low-wage regions to regions with higher wages, wage rates then rise in in the formerly low-wage areas in response to a shortage of workers so that wage equilibrium is eventually reached. Such a theoretical approach allows a clearer interpretation of longer-distance, interregional flows of economic migrants.An example is the mass migration of destitute workers in southern Africa to mining regions in South Africa.

Demographer William Petersen has classified migration into five categories on the basis of degree of choice. (See diagram, opposite.)

1) **Primitive migration** is the movement of preindustrial peoples in response to the physical environment, e.g., the effort to find sufficient land for hunting or farming.

Galway, Ireland, like many fast-growing cities in northern Europe, contends with the suburban sprawl that often occurs as a result of rural-to-urban migration.

2) **Impelled migration** involves relatively powerless people, such as indentured servants of the 18th century and workers under the pejorative title "coolie contracts" of the 19th century.

3) **Forced migration** includes people who are completely powerless, such as African slaves and the Jews of Nazi Germany.

4) **Free migration**, in which the unforced will of the migrant is the decisive factor, describes early pioneer movements in the settlement of the American West.

5) **Mass migration** often has involved persecuted minorities deported from their homes. Such was the case of the Poles, Germans, Crimean Tatars, and many others in Stalinist Soviet Union. Mass migration also finds impetus in politically and economically disenfranchised peoples. Millions of Germans migrated to the United States in the 18th and 19th centuries seeking religious and political freedom and the chance to own land.

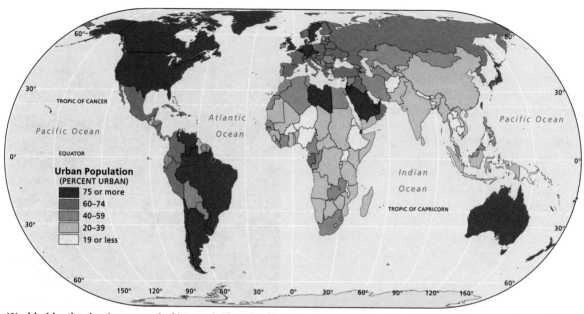

Urban Population
(PERCENT URBAN)
- 75 or more
- 60–74
- 40–59
- 20–39
- 19 or less

Worldwide, the dominant trend of internal migration has been from rural to urban locations. Experts estimate that 45 percent of the world's population live in urban areas.

Measuring Migration

Migration is measured in many ways, each with varying degrees of success. Measuring rates of migration according to a set time frame (one-year and five-year rates are routine) raises problems. For instance, what time span is appropriate for measuring migration rates? Studies of short periods might easily miss the infrequent mover. Studies using a longer span may miss multiple moves. How does one count multiple moves? Is distance definitely a criterion of migration? It even can be difficult to determine a person's permanent residence. How does a census measure the homeless in America, who have no permanent address and often wander from city to city?

A rich source of migration data is a recurrent national census, highlighting information on origins and destinations. Population registries also provide valuable statistics in the study of changes in residence by requiring migrants to transfer their records from one local registry office to another. In Japan the resident registration system contains monthly migration statistics dating to 1954. In China, the household registration system initiated in the early 1950s has provided important annual data for the world's most populous country. (The system, however, was used primarily to deny rural Chinese access to government subsidies for rice, cooking oil, housing, and urban transportation.) Place-of-birth statistics can serve as the best available movement data in some developing countries.

Surveys provide insight into cultural and behavioral influences on decisions to migrate. In measuring migrations, geographers work with numbers and rates, including in-migration and out-migration, gross migration (the total number of in-migrants and out-migrants) and **net migration** (the difference between the number of in-migrants and out-migrants). Indirect methods for estimating migrations involve birth and death statistics.

Movin' on up—or out?

Demographers study migrations between neighborhoods, counties, regions, and countries. The scale of migrations differs widely. Studies of migration in the United States between city neighborhoods have shown the importance of socioeconomic and educational considerations in decisions to move. In the 19th and 20th centuries, various ethnic groups migrated to areas of inexpensive housing near city centers. Over time, and with increasing affluence, the groups moved progressively outward, triggering an overlay of cultures throughout the cities. "Moving up" in the United States was often equated with "moving out," resulting in the socioeconomic homogeneity of suburban neighborhoods.

Migration within urban areas has been an integral building block of cities in North America. Geographer Richard Morrill showed that by approximating the factors that influence decisions to migrate, a geographer can build models of city areas most likely to become ethnic enclaves. Morrill's model simulated the spread of the African-American ghetto in Seattle in the 1950s, using such factors as land values, housing, and proximity to existing African-American neighborhoods. Analytical models such as Morrill's have the potential to predict urban dynamics, as in the clustering and spread of ethnic and income groups in urban areas. Recent studies have traced the spread of gentrification (rehabilitated housing in city centers) in relation to crime in Austin, Texas, in the1990s.

Study of county-to-county migration in the United States has been facilitated by extensive data of the Census Bureau. Summarized on maps, the information traces the redistribution of Americans since the 1960s toward the South and the West, pushed by retirement and drawn by coastal counties rich in amenities.

Geographers also have analyzed state-to-state and region-to-region movements. Studies at these larger scales have provided little insight into migrants' behavior, but considerable insight into the relationship of regional population flows and economic cycles. In the United States, the exodus of migrants from the Northeast and Midwest during the last few decades can be traced to a concentration of outmoded infrastructure, lack of new, high-tech industries, shift in job openings, and appreciation of the dollar in the early 1980s. Between 1970 and 1985, the Northeast lost more than a million jobs; the Midwest lost 700,000. Economic restructuring and downsizing in the Midwest in the late 1980s, however, led to a balance of migration.

The South, with lower taxes, wages, and land costs, continued to prosper, recording its largest population growth in the late 1980s. Trends in the 1990s show the continuing economic and demographic strength of the South. California started to lose migrants in the late 1980s and early 1990s partly because of inflated housing prices.

In the late 1970s about two million "boat people," many of whom were ethnic Chinese, fled from persecution in Vietnam to ports such as Hong Kong. Here, Hong Kong's Government Dockyard Transit Centre is filled with refugees.

Distance, Time, and Boundary Considerations

Distance is an major factor in migration flows. For instance, short-distance moves are more common than long-distance moves. A move across town has a minor impact on a person's life compared with a move abroad.

Decisions based on economic factors predominate in the regional relocation of people in the United States. The push of job dissatisfaction or unemployment and the pull of good or higher paying jobs often entice people to move long distances. Next, the migrants must decide on a new home. Factors include distance for commuting to the job, housing costs, social groups, and quality of schools. The perception that the new South Han River area of Seoul, Korea, contained high quality schools caused a massive relocation of urban middle- and upper-class Koreans in the 1990s.

Migration can be either temporary or per-

manent. How long does one have to live in a new place to be classified as an immigrant? Demographers generally define migration as a permanent change in residence. A majority of Tokyo residents spend more than two hours traveling to and from work. Whereas daily commuting is not counted as migration, demographers do count commuting as migration when workers change residence for several weeks in response to work conditions. Thai farmers become seasonal migrants to Bangkok as construction workers, taxi drivers, and the like. The income is an important supplement for farmers in the off-season. Seasonal migration, including the annual winter flight of snowbirds to warmer southern climates of the United States, usually involves two residences. Such seasonal migrations are perhaps better defined as circular, short-term,

The settlement of the American West was a voluntary migration. Unforseen circumstances forced many settlers to move again during the 1930s Dust Bowl era.

repetitive, or cyclic movements, without a declared intention of permanent change in residence. In a broad definition, **circular migrants** also include those who return to their homeland after years of absence. History is replete with stories about the vast numbers of European immigrants who passed through Ellis Island; but little is written about the fact that nearly a third of these immigrants returned to their homeland later in life.

Migration involves the crossing of a political, or some other, definite boundary. If, in the study of migration, the sampled geographic units are small, relatively few migrants will be missed in the counting. However, chances of missing migration streams increases when the sampled geographic units are large. For

example, within a county, a notable stream of migrants may move from the city proper to the suburbs. The movers may not be counted as migrants, however, if the tabulations include only people who have crossed county borders. In addition, people's proximity to a border increases the possibility that they will be included as a migration statistic. After all, one need not move far to be counted if one is close to a boundary. A further twist to this cross-boundary problem is that people have been statistically classified as migrants without moving. When boundaries themselves migrate—that is, change location—residents are counted as members of a new place or even a new country, as occurred with the breakup of Yugoslavia.

Foreigners and Foreign Workers in Selected European Countries, 1999

COUNTRY	POPULATION (1,000)			LABOR FORCE (1.000)		
	TOTAL	FOREIGN	PERCENT FOREIGN	TOTAL	FOREIGN	PERCENT FOREIGN
Total	366,745	18,678	5.2	136,294	8,161	6.0
Austria	8,087	690	8.6	3,177	30S	9.6
Belgium	10,225	921	9.1	4,096	340	8.3
Denmark	5,325	189	3.6	2,842	54	1.9
Finland	5,170	56	1.1	—	—	—
France	59,087	3,597	6.3	24,903	1,544	6.2
Germany	81,950	6,878	8.5	39,000	3,432	8.8
Ireland	3,734	94	2.7	1,333	40	3.0
Italy	57,717	987	1.7	—	—	—
Luxembourg	432	125	31.1	168	65	38.6
Netherlands	15,799	780	5.1	7,128	278	3.9
Norway	4,462	162	3.8	1,067	48	4.5
Spain	39,418	430	1.1	16,400	82	0.5
Sweden	8,856	508	5.8	4,333	221	5.1
Switzerland	7,119	1,260	18.1	3,346	726	21.7
United Kingdom	59,364	2,001	3.5	28,500	1,026	3.6

Refugees and Temporary Labor Migrants

A refugee is a category of migrant. War and persecutions have swelled the ranks of refugees. Host countries that have signed the 1951 Geneva Convention may not force refugees back to their homeland. Therefore, the host country must determine whether the migrants qualify as refugees, that is, whether they, in the words of the Geneva Convention, have "a well founded fear of being persecuted for reasons of race, religion, nationality, membership of a particular social group or political opinion." Determining who qualifies as a refugee is a daunting task. Many migrants claim to be refugees in order to stay in the host country, not for fear of harm back home but for a desire to find a better job, or better housing, or for another one of the various "pull" factors.

Nearly 70 percent of the 16 million refugees in the world were in the Middle East and Africa in the mid-1990s, according to the U.S. Committee for Refugees. Like migrants stimulated by economic factors, refugees often apply for membership in their host country; and often, if their application is denied, refugees remain illegally.

Temporary labor migrants, known as guest workers, have become common in a world that prospers on a flexible labor force. Migrants help turn the wheels of industry: In some oil-rich Middle Eastern countries, foreign workers form a majority of the labor force and in South Africa about 15 percent of the labor force; Germany, France, Israel, and the United States have relied heavily on labor migrants to bring in the harvest and to take over many unskilled jobs that the local population has abandoned.

At the beginning of World War II, U.S. farmers were asked to step up food production. Pressure on the farmers increased when the United States continued to expand the armed forces as the war continued, leading to a shortage of farm labor. In response, the United States recruited Mexican farmworkers under the so-called *bracero* program of 1942. Mexico and the United States agreed on rules governing transportation, pay, housing, working conditions, and medical care for the contract workers, who were called braceros. The program was resurrected in 1951 when the Korean War again took workers from U.S. farms, but was ended in 1964.

Labor Exporters and Importers in Asia, 1995

COUNTRY	WORKERS (THOUSANDS)	MIGRANTS AS % OF LABOR FORCE
Labor importers	Imported	
Singapore	310	18.3
Malaysia	954	12.2
Hong Kong	300	10.1
Taiwan	223	2.5
Thailand	650	2.0
Japan	529	0.8
Korea	103	0.5
Labor exporters	Exported	
Philippines	4,200	15.3
Bangladesh	1,600	3.1
Malaysia	250	3.0
Indonesia	1,200	1.5
Thailand	500	1.5
Vietnam	20	0.1
China	270	0

Major Migration Patterns of World Regions

International migration today involves greater numbers than ever before. About 120 million migrants, slightly more than the combined population of Italy and France, lived outside their country of citizenship or birth at the end of the 20th century. Migrants are not spread evenly in the world: One third live in seven of the world's wealthiest countries—Canada, United States, France, Italy, Germany, United Kingdom, and Japan.

Europe

Europe has absorbed millions of immigrants, France and Germany the most, with close to 45 percent of Europe's almost 25 million immigrants in the mid-1990s. Albania accepted hundreds of thousands of Kosovo refugees during the ethnic cleansing by the Serbs and NATO bombing of Yugoslavia in 1999. Agricultural economist Philip Martin and immigration specialist Jonas Widgren have outlined four stages of international migration for Europe in the period after World War II.

1) The first stage, during reconstruction from 1945 to 1960, involved displaced persons relocating or returning home. The largest of these movements was the 13 million ethnic Germans resettled to West Germany in 1945 to 1950, mainly from portions of Eastern Europe formerly tied to Germany.

2) The opening of borders and the rapid economic growth associated with the formation of the European Economic Community in 1957 stimulated the second stage, 1961 to 1974. Migrants from southern Europe and outside Europe formed a large cadre of foreign workers, commonly referred to as guest workers. The most notable migrations at this time were Turks to West Germany and Algerians to France. Many Slavs from Yugoslavia also migrated north to work in several European countries, most often on assembly lines, or in construction.

3) A less distinct stage of European migration involved the slowdown of the regional economy from 1975 to 1985 and the consequent public backlash against guest workers, which lead to government attempts at repatriation.

4) By the late 1980s, the last stage of international migration occurred with the breakdown of communist regimes in Eastern Europe. Martin and Widgren's description of this period as one of "mass asylum, illegal immigration and ethnic returns" relates the political and demographic turmoil as Eastern Europeans sought economic opportunity beyond their borders. The most affected country was Germany, which initially allowed free return to all ethnic Germans.

South and East Asia

In Asia five major displacements of peoples have resulted from regional conflict since World War II.

1) With the surrender of Japan in 1945, eight million Japanese were repatriated to their devastated homeland from the far stretches of the empire.

2) A massive refugee movement in Asia emanated from the partition of the British Indian Empire. In 1947 India and Pakistan were established as independent dominions of the British Commonwealth of Nations. With civil war brewing, some 15 million people fled to the land of their religion, Hindus and Sikhs to India and Muslims to Pakistan.

3) Millions of North Koreans fled to South Korea after the Korean War in 1953.

4) The Vietnam War, 1950s to 1970s, accelerated the movement of refugees, especially Catholics and ethnic Chinese, first southward within Vietnam and later abroad. Huge resettlement camps were set up on the Thai border to help relocate the refugees. About a million Southeast Asians were admitted to the United States between 1980 and 1994.

5) The Soviet occupation of Afghanistan in 1979 and the subsequent civil war created vast movements across national borders. Five million Afghanis fled to Iran and Pakistan, transforming Peshawar into an outpost of 1.5 million refugees. When the Soviets withdrew and an Islamic government again took power in 1992, about half of the refugees returned to Afghanistan.

Although an educated class of South and East Asians are prevalent throughout the world, the most notable migration of Asians has been of laborers often encouraged by governments and business opportunities. Asian workers swept into the Middle East in the 1970s to help build the infrastructure in response to huge oil revenues. South Korea, with the maturation of an economy based on exports, has evolved from a labor exporter in the 1970s and early 1980s to a labor importer in the 1990s. Several other Asian countries, Thailand and Malaysia included, import and export labor and appear to be approaching the "migration transition" experienced by South Korea. North America has accepted many "free-will" migrants from Asian countries.

Migration Statistics

- The number of Mexicans who died trying to cross illegally into the United States from 1993 to 1996 is 1,185, according to Worldwatch Institute. The approximate number of people who died trying to cross the Berlin Wall from 1961 to 1989 is 100, according to the Institute.
- Foreign workers form the majority of the labor force in several Middle Eastern countries, and about one-seventh of the labor force in South America.
- Africa and western Asia contain more than half of the world total of 15 million refugees and displaced persons.
- Newly arriving immigrants account for all the population growth in Germany and about a third of the annual growth in the United States.
- The United States had a migrant stock of almost 22 million in 1999, about 8 percent of the national population of 273 million.
- In the 1990s Europe, North America, Australia, and New Zealand had net population gain from migration. Africa, Asia, and Latin America experienced a net loss.
- Countries hosting the most refugees include:
  - Iran, 2.2 million, mostly Afghanis.
  - Democratic Republic of Congo, 1.5 million, mostly Rwandans.
  - Pakistan, 1.2 million, mostly Afghanis.
  - Jordan, 1.2 million Palestinians.
- Refugees from three countries or geographic areas accounted for nearly half the world's refugees in 1994: Palestinians 3.1 million, Afghanis 2.8 million, and Rwandans 1.7 million.
- Although their population is only about 5 percent of the world population, the United States and Canada contain about 20 percent of the world's migrant stock.
- More than 50 million Europeans immigrated, primarily to North America, South America, and Australia, between the mid-1800s and the outbreak of World War I. The trend was reversed in the 1960s, when millions of immigrants flowed into the countries of Northern and Western Europe as guest workers, asylum seekers from former communist countries, and unauthorized aliens or refugees from the violence in former Yugoslavia.
- In much of Europe, a foreigner is defined not by birthplace, but by ethnicity or ancestry.
- The high-income industrial democracies contain about 60 million immigrants, refugees and asylees, and authorized and unauthorized migrant workers.
- The percentage of countries whose policies in 1976 were aimed at reducing immigration was 6, increasing to 33 in 1995, according to Worldwatch Institute.
- Since 1960 the percentage of people living in urban areas has gone up about 30 percent.
- In developing countries, urban populations have more than doubled since 1950 to 39 percent.
- Currently, Oceania has the highest percentage of migrants in its population (17.8 percent). Yet those 4.7 million migrants are only one-tenth the number of migrants in Asia (43 million).
- The industrialized countries' native labor pool is expected to shrink as the developing world's workforce doubles.

Filipinos, Indians, Chinese, and Koreans recently have grown to significant minorities in the large cities and on the west coasts of the United States and Canada.

The Middle East

Political refugees and economic migrants have played a major role in the politics of the Middle East. The Palestinians, disenfranchised after the Middle Eastern wars of 1948 and 1967, arguably are the world's most famous refugee group. By varying accounts, they have numbered up to 3.75 million, some spending up to 50 years as refugees in Arab countries surrounding Israel. With the evolution of autonomy and with the semblance of a homeland in the West Bank and Gaza, the Palestinian refugee problem may be on the way to resolution. The Palestinians, arguably the best educated of the Arab peoples, have prospered as foreign workers in the oil-rich countries of the Persian Gulf. Indeed, the group in Kuwait most devastated by the 1991 Kuwait-Iraq War was not the ethnic Kuwaitis but the Palestinians, numbering about 300,000, who lost their homes and much of their life savings. They were not allowed back into Kuwait after the war because a small number of the Palestinians were suspected of sympathizing with the Iraqis.

The Middle East is a magnet for workers. Petrodollars from OPEC price increases of 1973 and 1979 spawned prodigious economic growth and a concomitant flow of foreign workers into countries of the Persian Gulf. Different nationals often filled different job classifications. It is not uncommon to find Yemeni day laborers, Egyptian teachers and college professors, and Palestinian bureaucrats. Pakistanis make up a large number of the construction laborers. Koreans and Thais have

tended to work in semiskilled jobs. Filipinos are popular as entertainers and musicians. Bengalis have worked as domestics and hotel employees. Large numbers of Egyptian farmers migrated to Iraq, partly because of a familiarity with irrigated river-basin agriculture. In the less populated countries of the Persian Gulf, such as Kuwait and the United Arab Emirates, foreign workers often make up the bulk of the labor force.

Africa

Wars, ethnic hatred, and economic disparities have instigated much of the African international migration since World War II. Independence movements of the 1950s to the 1970s prompted the small British, French, and Portuguese colonial populations to return to their native countries.

Independence also led to civil strife, which frequently turned a large portion of the population into refugees. In the last two decades, millions of refugees from Uganda, Rwanda, Democratic Republic of the Congo, Liberia, Sierra Leone, and Angola have fled to neighboring countries to escape civil wars. Guinea, with a population of only 7.5 million, harbored 700,000 refugees in 1999 from civil wars in four neighboring states; about 350,000 of the refugees are from Sierra Leone. Kenya provided haven for 420,000 refugees during the worst of the civil war and famine in Somalia in 1992. In 1994 more than two million Rwandans fled to Tanzania and Zaire (now the Democratic Republic of the Congo) to escape the genocidal war between the Hutus and Tutsis. By 1999 Africa, with but 12 percent of the world's population, harbored more than 20 percent of the world's refugees. Drought and degradation of farm and grazing lands also have driven large numbers of Africans from the Sahel, the southern fringe of the Sahara.

Foreign Labor Force in Persian Gulf Countries, 1975, 1990, and 1995

COUNTRY	FOREIGNERS AS PERCENT OF LABOR FORCE		
	1975	1990	1995
Total	47	68	—
Bahrain	46	51	60
Kuwait	70	86	82
Oman	54	70	60
Qatar	83	92	83
Saudi Arabia	32	60	60
United Arab Emirates	84	89	90

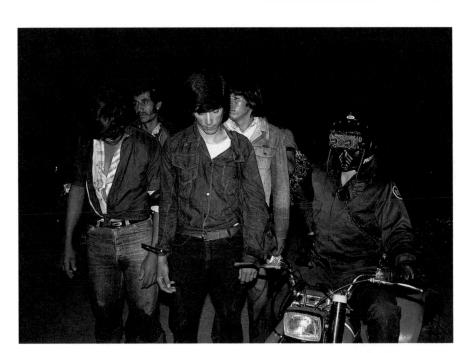

Wearing night-vision goggles, U.S. Border Patrol agents attempt to stem the flow of illegal immigrants from Tijuana, Mexico, to southern California.

Latin America

African and European migrants have populated North and South America during the last two centuries. Large numbers of African slaves were imported to the Caribbean and to Brazil for work on sugar plantations. Portuguese slavers brought between three million and four million Africans into Brazil, accounting for about a fifth of all African slave labor in the Western Hemisphere. The European colonial era brought disease, starvation, and war to the hemisphere, devastating indigenous populations. Mexico and Central America contained 25 million people when the Spanish arrived early in the 16th century, but was reduced to 2.5 million only one century later. Early migrants to South America were primarily Spanish and Portuguese. Later movements added other Europeans, primarily Germans and Italians, to the dominant classes, especially in Argentina and Brazil.

The most important stream of international migrants in the region in recent times has been from Mexico and Central America to the United States. Jobs, higher wages, and better living conditions have been the major draws. Civil wars in El Salvador and Nicaragua have turned thousands of residents into refugees. Almost 600,000 Central Americans sought political asylum in the United States between 1987 and 1996. Several hundred thousand Cubans and Haitians have fled to the United States to escape political and economic oppression. The refugees often have been contained in camps and then deported. More than 150,000 Hondurans and Nicaraguans were allowed to work in the United States for up to 18 months to earn money to help impoverished people in their homeland after the devastation of Hurricane Mitch in 1998.

Hispanics, already close to 30 percent of the population in Texas, will most likely be the largest minority in the United States in the second decade of the 21st century. In recent years the U.S. government has tried to stem migration from Latin America, primarily Mexico, with tough border controls. Areas of the Southwest have been unable to provide the infrastructure to keep up with the influx.

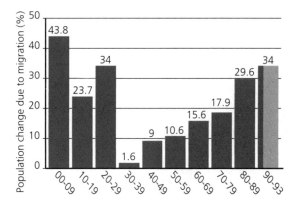

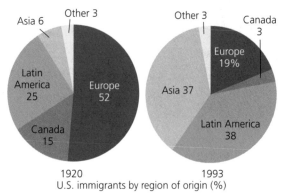

1920   1993
U.S. immigrants by region of origin (%)

Perceived economic opportunity, war, and immigration policy all contribute to fluctuating levels in the flow of migrants.

Migrations from Latin America to the United States will continue as long as stark wage disparities exist between the regions.

United States

Land, resources, political and religious tolerance, and economic opportunity all draw immigrants to the United States. Net flows into the country during the 1990s were at historical highs, with somewhat less than one million persons per year added to the U.S. population by migration. As birthrates continue to hover around replacement and as baby boomers move beyond the parenting years, the United

States, like Germany, will depend primarily on migration for population growth.

The historical migrations to the United States comprise four major waves, mainly based on the home region of the immigrants.

1) Northwest Europe and Africa—1600s to the 1850s. Northwestern Europeans and Africans built the American economy during its first 200 years of foreign settlement. Africans came as slaves, a trade abolished in 1807. The Native American population, decimated by wars and European diseases, was pushed west onto marginal lands in Oklahoma and the northern Great Plains. The population of Native Americans dwindled from about 7.5 million at the time of the first European settlements at the end of the 16th and the beginning of the 17th century to less than 250,000 by 1900. Settlers from the British Isles and Germany account for the largest number of European migrants to North America during the late 18th and early 19th centuries. Irish were pushed out of their homeland in the 1840s potato blight. Ireland's population in 1844 was 8.4 million. Today, it is close to 4 million. About 23 million people of direct Irish descent live in the United States today.

2) Southeast Europe—1880s to 1914. The second major wave of migrants to the United States comprised mainly southeastern Europeans. Unlike the earlier migrants who came to a land scarcely settled, the southeastern Europeans arrived in a country in the midst of intense industrial and agricultural growth. Slavs and southern Italians accounted for most of the immigrants to the United States from the 1880s to the start of World War I. They worked in the fields, in mines, and in factories of a growing America. This was the era of the Statue of Liberty, built between 1875 and 1885 and glorified almost mythically in the message of Emma Lazarus, "Give me your tired, your poor, your huddled masses yearning to breathe free...". The first decade of the 20th century witnessed the greatest impact of migrants on U.S. demographics. The number of immigrants was highest relative to the resident population.

On a farm near El Paso, Texas, workers from both sides of the border harvest peppers.

The 1920 census found that 58 percent of residents in big cities (100,000 plus) were of foreign birth or foreign parents. Immigrants played a role in population increase approaching that of natural increase of the resident population.

3) The 20th-century Trough. From 1914 to 1964, international migrations slowed appreciably, particularly to the United States. During the era, sometimes referred to as the "20th-century trough," migration was slowed by World War I, regaining momentum nearly 30 years later with the end of World War II. The depression years of the 1930s brought immigration almost to a standstill; in fact, during the 1930s, earlier immigrants to the United States, especially those from Southeast Europe, chose to return to their homeland. In 1929 the United States placed quotas on immigrants based on each ethnic group's share of the U.S. population in 1920. The quota system and other exclusionary laws effectively prevented the entrance into the country of anyone not of European, particularly northwestern European, origins. During the time when foreign immigration was low, the Great Migration of African Americans from the South to the North took place—a huge movement that contributed much to the redistribution of African Americans.

4) Asia and Latin America—1965 to the present. The liberalization of immigration laws in 1965 opened the door to more migrants from outside Europe. This most recent wave of immigrants from developing countries is changing the cultural fabric of the United States. Asians, such as Chinese, Filipinos, and Koreans, have become influential minorities, most notably in California. Texas and California are home to a recent and large influx of Hispanic immigrants. Indians have become the cultural group with the highest median income, according to the 1990 U.S. Census. Asians and Latin Americans, predominantly Mexicans, account for 40 percent each—that is, a full 80 percent together—of all immigrants to the United States. Indications are that this trend will hold for the immediate future.

Impact of Migration on Sending Countries

In the 1950s and 1960s, the "brain drain" was commonly cited as a major problem for developing countries that lost their educated citizens, primarily to Europe and the United States. High wages, modern lifestyles, and other amenities drew professionals and skilled workers to the western countries, where they often had received their education. It appears, however, that the negative impact of the brain drain has been attenuated. Many of the highly educated return to their home countries, albeit later in life. The Korean government, through generous incentives, has successfully enticed many of its scientists and engineers to return home. Near the end of the century, many immigrants had little desire to stay in the country in which they were trained. For example, the vast majority of Thai professionals chose to return home after receiving education in western countries because they preferred their homeland.

Countries can benefit when their citizens emigrate. In 1980 Cuba transported about 125,000 people, many of them poor and politically unwanted, to the southern shores of the United States during the Mariel Boatlift. The exodus from Europe of the political losers in the revolutions of 1848 benefited the power structure. Those who might have been competitors for power were far away in such countries as the United States.

In recent years emigrant countries have earned substantial income from remittances, money sent by guest workers and immigrants to their homeland. In 1990 annual worldwide remittances amounted to $71 billion. During this decade, Egyptians working abroad sent home what amounted to almost a third of their homeland's foreign earnings. Some 4.2 million Filipinos were working overseas, often with both the blessing and training of their

The Great Wall of China, built as a defense against raids by nomadic peoples, was constructed chiefly between the years of about 221 to 210 B.C. During the Ming Dynasty, from A.D. 1368-1644, the Great Wall was repaired and extended to its final length of about 4,500 miles.

Government Programs/Policies Affecting Population Redistribution

Many countries have found it in their best interests to either promote or discourage migration. For three centuries, Russian czars fostered frontier settlement in Siberia. The U.S. Homestead Act of 1862 promoted settlement of the Midwest by guaranteeing permanent settlers 160 acres. On the other hand, the Great Wall of China is a classic example of a government's use of a physical barrier to block migrations—in this case movement of the Mongols from the north to the south. The Great Wall also had the effect of stemming the flow of Chinese northward.

In this century China, Brazil, the Philippines, Indonesia, and Malaysia have implemented major rural settlement programs. Perhaps best known is Indonesia's effort to resettle residents of densely populated Java to the outer islands. Migrants have been provided with free transportation, land, and provisions for their first harvest. But the program has been plagued with administrative problems as well as political suspicions of a Javanese attempt to dominate the outer islands. While Indonesia has relocated more than a million people, a comparable government program in Malaysia, started in 1957, has been more successful, although it has been accused of ignoring the needs of the rural population.

In Brazil the Transamazonian highway was intended to help settle western Amazonia. However, the more than 200,000 annual migrants to this territory have settled mostly in the southwestern rim of the Amazon basin. Furthermore, the lure of riches, such as the discovery of gold in the northern Amazon in the 1980s, provided a stronger pull for migrants to the interior than the convenience of modern highways and other government incentives. The Mahaweli Dam project in Sri Lanka, started in the 1960s, involved building up a rural region in the center of the island, eventually to hold one million people. Large settlement projects on China's frontier have moved several million people to Xinjiang in the northeast and other sparsely populated regions during the last four decades.

Some nations want to staunch the flow of people from the countryside to urban areas. Often, these attempts are unpopular and ineffective. Before the economic reforms of the late 1970s, China tried to restrict migration to the cities by putting up railroad checkpoints where officials would turn back unauthorized migrants. The government also established a population register and rationed food. During the same period, the Philippine government tried to stop the rush to the cities by withholding residence certificates, which were necessary for free schooling. South Korea recently went after the pocketbook when it applied a graduated residence tax based on city size.

Governments have razed urban slums and kicked squatters and indigents out of cities. In Bangkok and Jakarta, officials have loaded hawkers and tricycle taxi drivers onto trucks and shipped them off to the countryside. But such efforts have been in vain because governments are treating the symptoms of overcrowding instead of the causes—rural poverty and urban opportunity.

Most countries and international agencies prefer to improve living standards in rural areas. Although these intentions are good, programs that try to do such a thing often fall short because of insufficient financing and organization.

government. Remittances by the Filipinos are estimated at eight billion dollars annually, almost three times the amount of foreign aid received by the Philippines. The Philippine government, however, has been criticized for its licensing of "entertainers," thousands of women who migrate to Japan for a few years to work in bars and clubs.

Immigration tends to be selective of age and gender. It is often the young and educated who strike out for opportunities elsewhere. This selective emigration has had devastating demographic effects on small towns and rural counties in the American Midwest. People with upward social mobility often have little choice but to migrate to cities. Bangkok and Rangoon in Thailand and Myanmar are urban demographic magnets. Urban growth strategies have been quite popular in national and regional planning schemes, but sometimes unsuccessful in practice. South Korea's investment in industry away from Seoul, primarily for national defense, has led to the growth of a vibrant network of cities of intermediate size throughout the country. Brazil's capital, Brasilia, was founded to divert population growth from coastal Rio de Janeiro and São Paulo. Abuja was dedicated as the Nigerian capital to lessen the seeming intractable urban problems of the overgrown metropolis of Lagos. Several other countries have relocated national capitals as a way of directing urban growth. India has developed two state capitals at Chandigarh and Bhubaneswar. Planned satellite cities are common around the world. Shenzhen, for example, has grown in China over the last 20 years from rice fields to a metropolis of several million people.

Conclusion

Sharp disparities in population and economic growth probably will continue to divide nations far into the new millennium. So long as they do, migration pressures will mount, fomenting disruption throughout the world. Political unrest, persecutions, ethnic friction, and regional economic downturns will most likely continue. So long as they persist, migration will offer an escape route.

Certainly, migrants can add a sort of "hybrid vigor" to receiving countries, which routinely have been the industrialized democracies. However, the increasing difficulty of assimilating migrants and the increasing sense of resentment from the established population has prompted the industrialized democracies to try to control the flow. Strengthened border patrols and more restrictive immigration laws are gaining in popularity. Will the clampdown be enough? Is the clampdown even fair or beneficial? Political leaders from the have and have-not countries are beginning to consider how to correct the root causes of large migrations because high barriers and strict laws will be ineffective if hundreds of millions of the world's population continue to wake each morning to civil unrest, unsanitary conditions, and poverty. Emigrant countries can help reduce migration pressures by reducing the factors that push their people out. They must consider adopting enlightened, vigorous economic policies, protecting human rights, and promoting peace at home. The industrial democracies began in the early 1990s to explore prospects of freer trade, expanded aid programs, and broad international investments as a means to lessen migration pressures. If these prospects become reality and are successful, the imbalance in living standards will be somewhat righted, taking much of the power out of the push and pull factors of migration.

Cultural Geography

Introduction

Cultural geography has changed over the last century from descriptive studies of traditional folk cultures in exotic locations to analytical studies of the spatial context of cultural identities. For last 20 years cultural geographers have focused increasingly on cultural meanings and values, as well as on the spread of modern cultures at the expense of traditional ones. They study landscapes, for example, not just for the artifacts created by residents, but for the symbolic meanings that provide a *sense of place* to residents and which perpetuate cultural values. For example log cabins may convey a rural, family-oriented lifestyle, whereas a football stadium conveys competitiveness. Despite these changes in cultural geography the objective remains the same: to better understand the formation, transformation, and significance of spatial patterns of cultures.

Culture is a group's way of life, including the shared system of social meanings, values, and relations that is transmitted between generations. Culture incorporates such traits or distinguishable attributes as language, religion, clothing, music, courtesy, legal systems, sports, tools, and other material and nonmaterial components. Culture includes all learned behavior. Visually, one can distinguish between Mennonites and Sikhs as well as the landscapes in which they typically live. However, the values and beliefs that underlie the formation of these landscapes are more important to understanding cultural identity and conflicts between cultures. Even as a culture unites members of *a* community, it can separate communities.

Cultural identity shared by members of a culture form in a region as members of the group interact with each other and with their shared environment; cultures change with exposure to other cultures. Spatial patterns of culture continually evolve as contact between cultures causes mixing as well as conflicts between them. Today, the process of globalization is creating more and different economic and political links between different regions and cultures, yet regional cultural identities remain extremely important: Serbians remain different from Bosnians, Hutus from Tutsis, and Canadians from Americans. The idea of a global village sharing a global culture may be a useful and appropriate metaphor for understanding the spread of Western culture around the world by mass media, but local, regional, and national cultural identities remain strong.

Three concepts—race, ethnicity, and society—are often linked to culture. **Race** is used to refer to biological differences between humans, *Homo sapiens sapiens*, which are not genetically significant, but are often visible, such as skin color, eye shape, and hair color. These differences form the basis of **racism**, the social practice of discrimination based on appearance. While *race* is biological and therefore not cultural, it is associated with culture and ethnicity because *racism* can be a value of one cultural group and can change the way of life of another group, creating a separate identity for it. Americans of African ancestry, Britons of Pakistani ancestry, and Indonesians of Chinese ancestry have faced discrimination and therefore may not share all the cultural values and traits of their larger cultures.

Ethnicity refers to a minority group with a collective self-identity within a larger host population. Within the United States, ethnic groups—often composed of recent immigrants—exist in most large cities, and some ethnic groups preserve their cultural traditions to form ethnic communities, such as Italians in Little Italy in New York and Cubans in Little Havana in Miami. While these examples of ethnic communities are culturally based, African Americans have been described as forming an ethnic group whose group identity is based on appearance. Ethnic communities often reside apart from the host population, by choice or by coercion, and may be found in ethnic islands. Jews, for example, were forced to live in segregated neighborhoods, or ghettos in 16th-century Italy, and today they can choose to live in Jewish neighborhoods in the United States.

A **society** is a system of interactions, including rules of conduct and class distinctions, among individuals as well as among groups. Every culture can be viewed as a society because status and conduct are based on cultural values. The status and role of women or of royalty, for example, are components of society. Societies, however, are not limited to members of one cultural group but can include members of numerous cultures and ethnic groups. American society incorporates members of Navajo, Jewish, and Amish ethnic groups as well as members of the majority Euro-American, Christian, capitalistic culture; for the Inuit, however, society and culture are identical. The distinctions between society and culture are increasingly fuzzy, and cultural geographers study both.

The societal role, status, and opportunities established for men and women create **gender** differences that are closely associated with culture and cultural values. Differences in level of education, infant mortality rates, income, and political power between men and women are described in terms of a **gender gap**, with women almost always at a disadvantage. Overall, African and Latin American countries place lowest in terms of gender equality and Scandanavian countries place highest. Religion can be extremely important in defining gender roles, but generalizations can be misleading. For example, women in Muslim Afghanistan have been compelled by the ruling Taliban to cease economic activities outside their homes and to wear shape-concealing clothing, while in Pakistan and Bangladesh, also Muslim countries, women have been able to serve as prime ministers.

Geographic aspects of gender roles are also evident within societies. Households remain the primary responsibility of women worldwide and usually serve as the geographic focus of their activities. During the 1960s, American suburbs were sometimes referred to as "pink ghettos," where many housewives were available as cheap labor because their household responsibilities limited their ability to travel farther to better jobs.

Culture has a strong spatial dimension because members of cultural groups often share a physical location and attribute similar meanings and values to it. Cultural regions based on these cultural groups range from covering a small neighborhood to much larger areas that cultures claim as homelands. (See Nations, page 400.) Ordinarily, cultural similarities between people and ties to place are stronger at local scales where interactions among members of the culture are more frequent and face-to-face; communities require this type of interaction. **Cyberspace,** the computer-linked global network, may create future placeless cultures whose members share cultural values and are linked electronically rather than by geographic proximity.

Neighborhoods are typically differentiated by cultural groups, by social (class) divisions, or by both. In inner cities of developed countries, neighborhoods are often inhabited by recent immigrants and by the poor, often poor minorities; ethnic segregation remains the rule in neighborhoods. (See Urban Geography, page 370.) Culturally based neighborhoods, such as those of Koreans and Vietnamese in Los Angeles, can provide residents with support groups, economic opportunities, and a defense against threats by other cultural groups.

To be useful in understanding the development of geographic patterns of cultural identity and conflicts, culture is generalized by geographers at different spatial scales. At a national scale, individuals will often share enough culture traits so that a national culture—such as Turkish, French, or Japanese—is a valid description. In countries where cultural diversity results in far less sharing of traits—as in Sudan—the idea of a national culture would be misleading: Sudan's population can be most accurately generalized into two major groupings—the Muslim north and the Christian and animist south.

Regional cultures exist within many countries and may be in conflict with the larger, dominating culture. Corsicans in France and Kurds in Turkey are seeking autonomy. **Subcultures,** variations of the dominant culture,

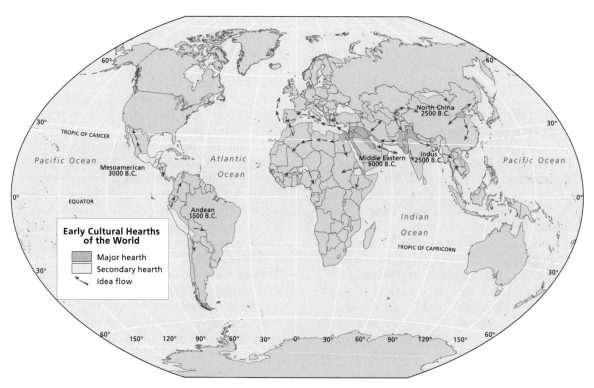

Cultural hearths reveal the origins of today's dominant cultural regions. Throughout history, as populations grew and expanded beyond their origins, contact with other cultures meant exchange of ideas and materials. Modern communications and transportation rapidly accelerate this process.

Environmental Determinism

The idea that the natural environment determines cultural development was used by Plato and Aristotle to explain why Greeks were so much more developed than cultures in colder or hotter climates. This concept of environmental determinism was redeveloped in geography by German geographer Friedrich Ratzel (1844–1904), following Charles Darwin's *Origin of Species* (1859). It became a major theme of geography when his students, including Americans Ellen Churchill Semple (1863–1932) and Ellsworth Huntington (1876–1947), expanded on Ratzel's work. (See Growth of Geography, page 15.) By the 1950s, however, environmental determinism was debunked as geographers recognized that environmental factors could not explain patterns of development.

also exist, such as the Bible Belt region of the southeastern United States. At more local scales ethnic groups and subcultures can also be distinguished. The **subcultural theory** argues that interpersonal conflicts found in large cities promote the formation of subcultures, such as of gays and lesbians and of artists and bohemians. Greenwich Village in New York City, for example, is well-known as a residential area for subcultures of artists and bohemians.

Culture Hearths and Diffusion

Cultures form as groups become separated spatially or socially, adapt to a new physical and human environment, and develop customs, values, and ways of life that are passed on to succeeding generations. Dominant cultures are those that expand outward from their **hearths**, regions where cultural traits such as religion and agriculture originate, transforming other cultures as well as themselves. The region around Mecca, for example, is the hearth of Islamic culture from which Muslims traveled to convert hundreds of millions of people to Islam around the world. Cultural changes are usually the result of contact and sharing ideas, practices, and artifacts with other cultures, although innovations also occur. At any time, global patterns of cultural regions can be detected in the landscape as the result of cultures adapting to and transforming their environments.

Innovations and Culture Hearths

The concept of **cultural divergence** explains the formation of new cultures as the result of groups dividing, migrating to seek resources, territory, or other advantages, and slowly changing in response to environmental stresses and new ideas. During prehistory, small tribes are believed to have emerged from Africa to wander across Eurasia and later to Australia and the Americas, and to have encountered a variety of environments. Over many generations changes accumulated, such as new vocabularies, beliefs, and technologies, that were handed down in each tribe until new cultures had evolved. The ancestors of modern Iranians, Greeks, Spaniards, and Swedes, for example, are believed to have emerged initially from what is now Anatolia, Turkey, around 7,000 years ago; similarities in their modern

At a McDonald's restaurant in Hong Kong, Extra Value Meals are advertised in both Chinese and English. Since Ray Kroc opened his first franchise in 1955, McDonald's has grown to more than 24,500 restaurants in 116 countries, often conforming to cultural differences through menu item changes.

languages provide evidence that they evolved from a single language and therefore a single cultural group. (See Language, page 297.)

Those cultural groups with the populations, attitudes, and resources most conducive to generating and fostering new ideas and other innovations, especially in agriculture, established Earth's major civilizations.

In the hearth areas for civilizations, such as the Nile and Indus Valleys, new weapons, tools, and social structures increased the ability of the civilizations to further develop their own environments and to dominate neighboring cultures. Iron tools and weapons, for example, were first used perhaps 3,500 years ago in what are now Turkey and Iran and proved superior to bronze weapons then in use.

Biologist and anthropologist Jared Diamond argues in *Guns, Germs, and Steel* published in 1997 that the development of early dominant civilizations was dependent on the presence of certain locational and environmental factors, including climates favorable to agriculture, the presence of domesticable animals (which were disease reservoirs and, as such, helped build up the population's immunity), and regions easy to traverse.

Ancient culture hearths, based on agricultural productivity, were able to conquer and dominate surrounding areas, thereby increasing their access to labor and resources; early hearths in the Middle East relied on wheat as their food staple, and those in Middle America relied on maize (corn). Increased food supplies allowed greater numbers of people to specialize in activities other than food production, such as arts and crafts. Armies as well as innovators were supported by having individuals freed from concern over sustenance, thus enabling them to focus their energy and attention on specialized activities.

Culture hearths have developed and declined over time as wars and disasters have caused civilizations to rise and fall. The United States and the Soviet Union were the two dominant cultures—referred to as superpowers—dominating the post-World War II-Cold War era, with each trying to spread their cultural values to other countries. After the rapid decline of the Soviet Union, the United States

Social institutions such as schools are important transmitters of culture. In most schools, curriculum is standardized or set by the state. Textbooks, therefore, carry much of the same information. Consequently, large numbers of students are taught the same information at the same time.

assumed a **hegemonic**, or ideologically dominant, role in the world, but other centers of innovation remain, such as the European Union and Japan.

Cultural Diffusion

Cultures and cultural traits spread and interact with other cultures through the process of diffusion, while barriers—both physical and cultural—prevent or channel diffusion. Historically, the spread of culture relied on direct contact between members of different cultures and on the migration of members of a culture. Modern technology has not replaced direct human contact as the means of diffusion, but mass communication and rapid transportation allow cultural diffusion to occur much faster and over far greater areas.

One result of these technological improvements has been to reduce spatial and temporal constraints on diffusion. Television, radio, and the Internet make new ideas more accessible to more members of more cultures. A culture can spread into new regions by expansion or by relocation diffusion.

Expansion diffusion occurs where contact causes cultural traits to be adopted, as when the Spanish converted indigenous Middle Americans to Roman Catholicism in the 16th and 17th centuries, and results in increased populations sharing those traits. **Relocation diffusion** is the result of migration, where the members of one culture change locations, but the total number of members does not increase. Settling English prisoners in Australia beginning in 1788 expanded the English cultural region but not the number of Englishmen; over generations the culture of the descendents of these expatriates changed and an Australian culture evolved.

Conquest and trade have undoubtedly been the causes of most expansion diffusion over history, and trade—as part of the global economy—is now increasingly important in spreading culture. The spread of McDonald's restaurants around the world is an example of how a concept and products developed within one culture can be accepted or imposed elsewhere. Blue jeans, Coca-Cola and Pepsi, jazz, and numerous other components of American culture have spread around the world, evidence of the role of the United States as a culture hearth.

While physical barriers such as mountains and deserts may hinder cultural diffusion, those barriers are more easily overcome with improved technology than are cultural barriers such as traditions and values. In some cases, members of a culture may intentionally bar innovations from outside in an attempt to remain unchanged. Mennonites, for example, reside in ethnic islands, in contact with but mostly unchanged by the larger American culture. Cultural barriers may be relatively permeable where members of a culture accept some new cultural traits, but not others. McDonald's restaurants are not welcomed by members of India's mostly vegetarian culture, although blue jeans are.

New ideas that directly challenge the traditions of a culture may meet strong resistance from its members: In the United States the diffusion of the concept of women's right to vote in 1919 and 1920 met great resistance among Congressional representatives from the South, all of whom were male.

As members of one culture interact with members of another, cultural traits may be adopted on both sides. When individuals enter into a new society and culture, as when migrants move to a new country, they—or at least their children—may undergo assimilation and adopt the identity—the values, meanings, and way of life—of the new culture. Other families may retain their old culture and form part of an ethnic community within the larger society. Some cultural traits brought by migrants may be adopted, at least in a revised version, by members of the dominant culture and result in syncretism, a fusion between the two cultures. As Mexicans migrate to the United States, Tex-Mex food and music become incorporated into American culture.

Culture is transmitted or passed on to individuals from a number of sources, but primarily it is transmitted from family, peers, and social institutions. Governments have a vested interest in their citizens sharing cultural values in order to reduce the potential for cultural conflicts. Social institutions, such as schools, are therefore especially important in transmitting culture. Large numbers of young, receptive individuals are introduced simultaneously to the same information and in the same language. (See Political Geography, page 391.) Much of the history taught in grade schools in the U.S. reflects this concern for shared values, and myths about Betsy Ross, George Washington, and other American heroes are part of the

Growing food and flowers in a garden such as this and sharing the bounty with neighbors and friends are still important cultural values for many urbanites today.

Rural cultural values often dictate how neighboring farmers cooperate—for example, in contouring the land to trap rainwater and check erosion as shown here.

Canadians and Americans

Americans and Canadians are often thought by Americans to share a single, American culture. However, Canadians—even Anglo-Canadians—have distinctive societal values, heroes, and traditions despite sharing language, religion, technology, and other cultural traits with the United States.

Canadians are in some ways the original anti-Americans, because they refused to support American independence in 1776. The American principles of "life, liberty, and the pursuit of happiness" are a strong contrast to the Canadian principles of "peace, order, and good government."

This difference in values is oversimplified in the symbol each country has of its settlement years: the lone gunslinger in the United States and the lone Mountie in Canada.

cultural heritage. The importance of public schooling in promoting cultural values is evident when there are disagreements within state and local schoolboards in the United States over the choice of textbooks, and how subjects such as the Vietnam War, evolution, and the legacy of past Presidents, are to be presented; all are part of the ongoing process of defining a national identity.

In some cases where members of one culture have been overwhelmed by a dominant culture, **cultural revivalism** may emerge decades or centuries afterward as those members seek to regain economic or political status. The rediscoveries of former cultural identities may include celebrations and festivals or have revolutionary overtones as members of the resurgent culture seek to establish a new relationship with the larger society. In New Zealand, for example, the integration of the indigenous Maoris into the dominant culture has progressed slowly, and a Maori revival has taken place during the 20th century.

Traditional Quebec culture was rural, Roman Catholic, French-speaking, and dominated by Anglo-Canadian culture. During the 1960s the "quiet revolution" revived the French identity of many Québécois and led to calls for independence. These separatist aspirations were further mobilized when French president Charles DeGaulle visited in 1967 and announced his support for a free Quebec. In the 1980s and 1990s there were several attempts to reconcile these political demands with the interests of the larger Canadian society, but the issue is still unresolved. (See Nationalism and Separatist Movements, page 402.)

Cultural Regions and Landscapes

Cultural regions is a general term for areas where some portion of the population shares some degree of cultural identity. How and by whom cultural regions are defined determines the nature of the region and its extent and boundaries. To be useful, the criteria must be selected carefully. In some cases a single criterion will suffice because it is linked to so many other traits. Cultural regions based on the Basque language or on blowgun usage—found in Brazil, New Guinea, and the Caroline Islands—are valid means of locating specific cultures, because the Basque language and the blowgun are both limited to small, traditional societies sharing a common history, ancestry, and culture. In other cases one criterion, such as the use of the English language, is useful only at the broadest scale because of the diversity of peoples—including Scots, Nigerians, Jamaicans, and Indians—for whom English is the primary language.

The members of most cultures tend to be concentrated within a core area and have a decreasing presence in the periphery, and the cultural region may be defined as incorporating all, part, or none of the periphery. Peripheral areas may be divided into a surrounding **cultural domain** where the cultural identity is still prominent and a **cultural sphere** farther away, where it is still influential. In a 1965 study of the spatial extent of the Mormon cultural region, geographer Donald Meinig examined population characteristics (for example, the percentage that are Mormon) and placed the regional core around Salt Lake City, the domain over most of Utah and southeastern Idaho, and the sphere south to Mexico and north to eastern Oregon.

The spatial scale of cultural regions can be expanded to the global perspective of realms, based on generalized perceptions of cultural similarities rather than on the spatial distribution of specific cultural traits. As a result, the usefulness of realms in understanding cultural variations is limited, but they can be used to show historical and societal linkages among populations. The Anglo-American realm of Canada and the United States has limited linguistic and religious diversity and many shared values, technologies, and other traits. In contrast, the sub-Saharan realm includes many dozens of different countries, hundreds of language groups, and tremendous cultural diversity but generalizations about the sub-Sahara's level of material culture and colonial legacy do have some validity and utility.

Members of cultures interact with and transform their environments through agriculture, land demarcation, construction, and transport systems to create cultural landscapes. Housing styles, street patterns, crop choices, and land ownership patterns are all components of the cultural landscape and reflections of cultural values. In the United States, for example, superhighways, front lawns, skyscrapers, and football stadiums are part of and reinforce the dominant cultural preferences. Regional differences in culture are also visible in the U.S.: Shotgun houses, that is houses that are one room wide, are traditionally found in Louisiana and Cape Cod cottages are found in the Northeast.

Landscapes not only reveal current cultural traits and values, such as choice of sport, religion, and transport, they also provide a partial history of previous cultural preferences in the area. Larger buildings, often with religious significance, may last centuries as evidence of an earlier culture. For example, Angkor Wat and other Hindu temples in Buddhist Cambodia and the Alhambra and other Muslim buildings in Catholic Spain attest to religious changes. Land use patterns also reflect past cultural values. In the United States, the 1800s division and sale of land in the West by 40-acre and 160-acre lots for farming remains evident in today's grid patterns of county roads. On the other hand, contrasting land use patterns can be found in the East where metes-and-bounds surveying, that is following streams and other natural features, was used. In Quebec the long-lots system, which established narrow fields, all with access to navigable rivers, was used.

Cultural Identities

Modern-day cultural identities are the result of centuries of cultural divergence and diffusion. Two components of culture—language and religion—are especially important in understanding cultural identities and appreciating the processes that have led to existing cultural patterns.

Esperanto

One solution to the problems of communicating between cultures is to create a new language.

Esperanto, one such created language, was developed in 1887 by L. L. Zamenhof (1859–1917), a Polish philologist, from a number of European languages.

Despite being endorsed for use by the League of Nations, Esperanto failed to gain wide acceptance and now has only about two million speakers.

Language

Language is the key means by which culture is transmitted and a cultural identity gained. Differences in language mean differences in culture and are a potential source of misunderstanding and conflict between peoples.

The geographic study of language focuses on current distributions of language and on the evolution of languages and language patterns over time and space. Studies focus especially on source areas and paths of diffusion.

Contact between cultures is increasingly common in our world economy, and this causes languages to be in constant change. Still, concerted efforts are made by some groups to preserve their linguistic identities.

SIGNIFICANCE OF LANGUAGE

Language is a system of spoken communication using sounds to transmit meanings. Now a language is almost always matched by a written system, and language is a critical component of cultural identity. Translation between languages can be extremely difficult. One reason is that meanings are often contained in phrases rather than single words.

The Ten Leading Languages in Numbers of Native Speakers

LANGUAGE	FAMILY	SPEAKERS (IN MILLIONS)	MAIN AREAS WHERE SPOKEN
Han Chinese (Mandarin)	Sino-Tibetan	874	China, Taiwan, Singapore
Hindi	Indo-European	366	Northern India
Spanish	Indo-European	358	Spain, Latin America, southwestern United States
English	Indo-European	341	British Isles, Anglo-America, Australia, New Zealand, South Africa, former British colonies in tropical Asia and Africa, Philippines
Bengali	Indo-European	207	Bangladesh, eastern India
Arabic	Afro-Asiatic	206	Middle East, North Africa
Portuguese	Indo-European	176	Portugal, Brazil, southern Africa
Russian	Indo-European	167	Russia, Kazakhstan, parts of Ukraine and other former Soviet republics
Japanese	Nipponese	125	Japan
German	Indo-European	100	Germany, Austria, Switzerland, Luxembourg, eastern France, northern Italy

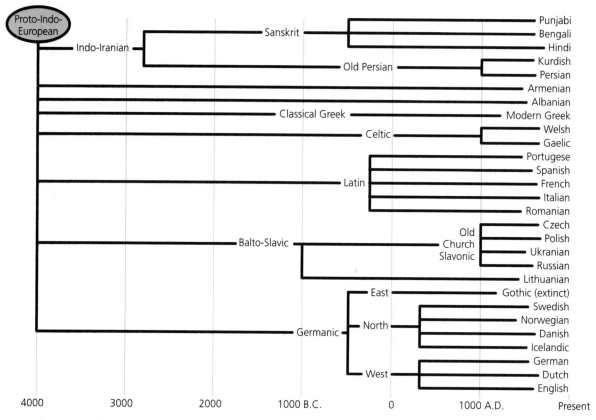

Over thousands of years numerous languages have developed through cultural divergence. This process continues today as some languages disappear—when the cultural group diminishes or is absorbed by another group—and others grow.

For example, translation of the words in the phrase "out in left field" to another language will miss the connotative meaning entirely. Values, experiences, and meanings of a cultural group are contained in its language. Finding similar words for similar meanings in different languages is one key to determining if they evolved from a single root language. (See Language Families, page 300.)

Estimates of the number of languages spoken today range from about 3,000 up to 6,500 because of differences in differentiating distinct languages from the dialects of one single language. **Dialects** are versions of one language with different vocabularies, pronunciations, accents, and sometimes syntaxes; most dialects are regionally based, such as the Southern accent in the United States, but dialects can

also be class- or gender-based. The majority of languages have relatively few speakers, numbering in the tens or hundreds of thousands. Mandarin Chinese has the most **native speakers**, those for whom it is their first language, but is not the most commonly spoken language. English is the primary or second language of choice for more people because of the legacy of the British Empire and American dominance in economics, military power, and computers.

During the last several centuries, hundreds of languages and the knowledge they contain have become extinct as the last speakers have died. Younger generations learned other languages so they could participate in the larger society and consequently adopted different cultural identities.

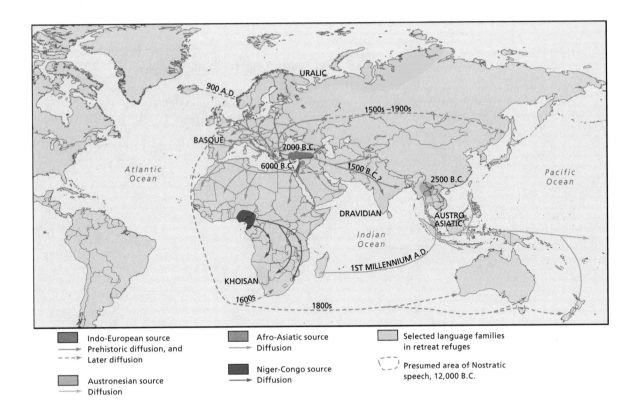

Studying the origin of early language families, as well as their diffusion and the timing of that diffusion, is another way the movement of people and cultures can be revealed to geographers.

In the United States, European settlers, with their weapons and diseases, caused the disappearance of probably 200 languages and their speakers; more recently, in 1995, the last speaker of North Pomo died in California, and her language died with her. The loss of these and other languages—including Gothic, Manx, and Cornish in Europe—means the loss of meanings and experiences that were contained in their vocabularies.

Researchers in the Amazon Basin who are engaged in chemical prospecting, that is searching for medicinal plants, question native Brazilians whose languages contain the knowledge of local plants and their uses.

Dialects evolve from a single language as populations separate and the frequency and intensity of interactions decline. Over time, if the vocabulary, pronunciations, and accents of the dialects become sufficiently different, then they have evolved into related but different languages, and the speakers into members of related but different cultures. British English and American English have different accents and use different vocabularies—British say "lift" instead of "elevator," for example.

But within both the United Kingdom and the United States regional dialects exist. East and West Midland are two dialects in the United Kingdom, and Southern and Bronx dialects are found in the United States.

Romans, who spoke Latin, settled in what are now Spain, France, and Portugal; dialects arose in each of these Roman provinces, influenced by local conditions and populations, and became Spanish, French, and Portuguese.

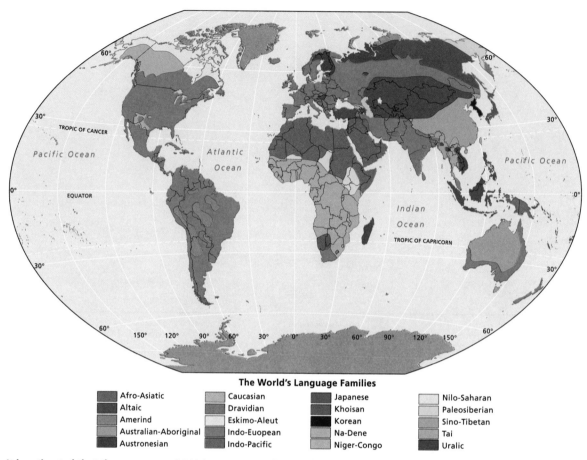

The World's Language Families

Afro-Asiatic	Caucasian	Japanese	Nilo-Saharan
Altaic	Dravidian	Khoisan	Paleosiberian
Amerind	Eskimo-Aleut	Korean	Sino-Tibetan
Australian-Aboriginal	Indo-Euopean	Na-Dene	Tai
Austronesian	Indo-Pacific	Niger-Congo	Uralic

It is estimated that there are up to 6,500 languages spoken in the world today. Mandarin Chinese, Hindi, Spanish, English, Bengali, Arabic, Portuguese, Russian, Japanese, German, French, and Malay-Indonesian are thought to be the 12 most widely spoken.

Contact between speakers of different languages—or in some cases between dialects—creates difficulties in communication and generates a need for a mutually intelligible language. A simplified version of one language, called a **pidgin** language, may be used during exchanges between different cultures, but not among members of the same culture. A pidgin English, for example, developed in the Caribbean for use between African slaves and English speakers. If a pidgin is used enough to become the primary language of a population, then it has become a **creole**. Swahili, which evolved from Arabic and Bantu languages, in eastern Africa, and Bazaar Malay

in Malaysia are creoles. **Lingua francas**—literally "Frankish languages"—are existing languages adopted by members of different cultures, and are an alternative to pidgins and creoles. Several lingua francas have been used in different regions and at different times. Latin, Arabic, and Hindi were or are lingua francas. Lingala is now used in the western Congo, and English is the most commonly used lingua franca today.

When a country is formed from a mixture of cultural groups with different languages, a **polyglot state** is created and an official language may be needed. In a number of former British colonies, such as Fiji, Ghana, and

India, English has become an official language to enable communication among the diverse groups and to avoid recognizing one tribal language above others. French, Dutch, and Portuguese are used as official languages in many of the former colonies of those countries.

Language is also evident in the cultural landscape as place-names, and the choice of language on signs is another visible symbol of culture on the landscape. **Toponymy**, the study of place-names, can reveal the history of a region and the values of the people. Throughout the United States places have been named by immigrants in honor of their native lands, such as New Rochelle, New York (France) and New Bern, North Carolina (Switzerland). Pakistan's capital of Islamabad, translated as "the place of Islam," is clear evidence of that country's Muslim religious values.

LANGUAGE FAMILIES

Different languages evolved over perhaps the last 200,000 years as members of cultural groups separated and language divergence occurred. The earliest languages have long been extinct, but by comparing vocabularies and sound shifts among modern languages some earlier languages, called **proto-languages**, have been reconstructed. One protolanguage, Nostratic, spoken perhaps 15,000 years ago, has been reconstructed from such modern languages as English, Turkish, Finnish, Arabic, and scores of other modern languages; the original location of Nostratic, in the Middle East, has not yet been determined.

Languages that diverged from a single ancestral language are related and can be grouped into **language families**. The **Indo-European family** of which English, Russian, Hindi, and Greek are members evolved from proto-Indo-European, a language that apparently evolved in turn from Nostratic perhaps 9,000 years ago. Different languages diverge at different times, so some languages are more closely related than others. For example,

English and German, both of which evolved from a proto-Germanic language, are more closely related to each other than to Spanish, Italian, and other Romance languages, which evolved from Latin.

The emergence of new languages was probably never a smooth transition but involved a number of competing influences. The English language can be traced to Germanic tribes—especially the Angles, Saxons, and Jutes—who invaded Britain some 1,500 years ago, and it has also been strongly influenced by Latin, which was brought along with Christianity about 1,400 years ago, and by French, brought by William the Conqueror in 1066. The Vikings also influenced the development of the language during their invasions of Britain from the 9th to the 11th centuries. Today's English, of which British Received Pronunciation (BRP) is the standard dialect in the United Kingdom, is the result of 1,500 years of linguistic development and cultural evolution.

While the routes and timing by which members of a language family diffused into new locations can be estimated from linguistic similarities, the causes of the diffusion are not as easily determined. For example, two major theories have been used to explain the spread of Indo-European languages from their core area: the conquest theory and the agriculture theory. According to the **conquest theory**, Indo-European evolved among pastoral nomads in the steppes of what is now Ukraine and spread west into Europe as the nomads conquered neighboring populations. More recently, L. Luca Cavalli-Sforza and Robert Ammerman proposed the **agriculture theory**, arguing that Indo-European started among farmers in the Caucasus Mountain region who migrated slowly outward to Iran and India as well as to Russia and Europe. The linguistic, genetic, and geographic data available are not yet conclusive as to which, if either, theory is more correct.

The current spatial distribution of language families reveals the global spread of

In Montreal, Quebec, two languages—French and English—are widely spoken and reflect the sharp division between the city's distinct cultural groups. Before a recent political referendum, people cast their votes in French and English on city walls.

Indo-European—the most widespread of all language families—and a set of large and small regions dominated by about 20 other language families. Even a few centuries ago, before European colonization overtook the Americas and the Niger-Congo speaking Bantu peoples expanded southward in Africa, this map would have been far different. Minor language families, from which few modern languages evolved, also exist but do not appear on global scale maps. Within Europe, for example, the Basque language is found in a small region from Biarritz, France, to Bilbao, Spain, and is unrelated to any other known language, suggesting long isolation of this cultural group.

The ability to trace languages back to earlier forms enables geographers and linguists also to trace populations back to earlier locations. Linking modern populations to an ancestral group provides evidence of earlier migrations and may be useful in suggesting genetic similarities. Natives of Madagascar, for example, speak an Austronesian language that

Disappearing Languages

Globalization in communication and economics is increasing the rate at which world languages are disappearing. In 1995 linguistic experts predicted that as many as half of the 3,000 to 6,500 languages would disappear by 2100 because children are learning other languages—such as English, Spanish, and Arabic—to communicate and interact with larger populations than their ethnic associations. Most of these losses will come in tropical regions in Africa and Indonesia where cultural groups have lost their isolation. California, however, will also lose languages as the remaining speakers of perhaps 50 Native-American languages die.

diffused westward from the Pacific and links them with Filipino and Vietnamese populations. In recent centuries, however, the diffusion of languages has become increasingly associated with global economic and political influences rather than with the relocation of cultural groups.

Language Conflicts

The importance of language as a cultural identifier involves language issues in numerous political conflicts, ranging from regional autonomy to the selection of languages in which school classes should be taught. As a symbol of their culture, members of an ethnic group may seek to protect their language from being overwhelmed by the language of the dominant society; in France, for example, efforts by speakers of Provençal to protect their language were finally granted government support for bilingual education in 1990. Dominant societies, on the other hand, may try to reduce the use and importance of minority languages in order to acculturate members of minority groups and strengthen the larger, national identity. Thus, before the breakup of the Soviet Union learning the Russian language was compulsory in all Soviet republics.

In the United States, which has as yet no official language, numerous language-based political issues have arisen in recent years. The choice of which language(s) to use in grade schools has become contentious as the number of Spanish-speaking residents has increased by about a half million per year for the last two decades, and as some schools have defined Black English Vernacular, referred to as Ebonics, as a separate language necessitating bilingual education. Several groups, such as English First and English Only oppose the use of other languages and seek to have national legislation passed to establish English as the sole official language of the United States.

In a number of countries, languages that had been suppressed are now being revived for future generations. In Wales ("Cymru" in Welsh) and Ireland ("Eire" in Gaelic) the number of speakers of Welsh and Irish Gaelic is growing because of compulsory language education. In the 1990s a number of cities in western India were renamed in the regional Gujarati language in response to a Hindi cultural revival; Bombay, for example, is now Mumbai. The struggle for greater adoption of French within Quebec resulted in the passage of Bill 101 in 1977, requiring education of most immigrant children in French, and the use of French in workplaces, on signs, and in public places.

English as the world's lingua franca is seen as a threat to some cultures for whom language is symbolically very important. Beginning in 1975, the French government has attempted to protect its language from the intrusion of English words, banning them from television and radio broadcasts if French terms were available. In the 1990s, not only has the French government made French its official language, but it has also instituted laws to prevent English vocabulary from invading the French language.

Wherever an ethnic group is seeking greater political or economic power within a dominant society, language divisions may arise; this is usually evidence of the larger cultural split rather than the cause. The split of the island of Cyprus between the Turkish north and the Greek south in 1974 is easily mapped linguistically, but the cultural differences across the Green Line dividing the island are far more complex. In Belgium, a bilingual and bicultural country, the Flemish north and Walloon south are divided by economics and history as well as by language and culture.

Language is critical in perpetuating a culture and its values, symbolism, and meanings. Many of the key values of cultural identity, however, derive from the religious beliefs held by most members of that culture. Cultural identities therefore nearly always include both language and religion.

Mecca is the birthplace of the Prophet Muhammad, founder of Islam, and therefore the most sacred of the Muslim holy cities. In the courtyard of the city's great mosque stands the Kaaba, a windowless cube-shaped structure. The faithful turn toward Mecca each day to pray.

Geography of Religion

Religion, like language, can be a defining component of a cultural identity and one that provides the basis for choice of clothing, food, tools, and occupation. Religion may also be more or less replaced by secularism in some modern societies.

As a social system based on a concept of the divine and involving beliefs, values, and behaviors, religion organizes many aspects of a culture. Shared beliefs and values establish strong group identification, and, because groups can also be linked to specific areas, geographic patterns of different religions result. Conflicts between religious groups also emerge, some because of differing religious beliefs—as between Hindus and Muslims over a sacred site in Ayodhya, India—and others based on economic or political relations—as between Armenian Christians and

Azerbaijani Muslims over possession of Nagorno-Karabakh.

Religious groups tend to be concentrated in regions, and the global distribution of these regions reflects past migrations of peoples and the diffusion of their religions. Religions originate in localized areas and expand outward with the local practitioners. Islam, for example, started in western Saudi Arabia around A.D. 610 and within three centuries was dominant in Spain, Turkmenistan, and northern Sudan as Arabs carried this new religion outward. More recently, following the collapse of communist governments in Eastern Europe and Russia, representatives from numerous Christian denominations have traveled as missionaries to this region to try to convert local populations and spread their religions.

Spatial patterns of religion are also

apparent in the location of **sacred spaces**, sites associated with holy or divine events. Sacred spaces may be either features in the natural environment or structures designed to honor a religion.

Rivers and mountains are commonly designated as sacred spaces by religions: The Jordan River is sacred to Christians, and the Ganges River sacred to Hindus, as Mount Fuji is holy to Shintoists, and Uluru (Ayers Rock) is to Australian animists. Structures such as the Western Wall, or Wailing Wall, in Jerusalem, the Dhamek pagoda in Sarnath, India, and the Kaaba in Mecca, Saudi Arabia, are sacred to Jews, Buddhists, and Muslims, respectively.

Pilgrimages are often made by members of a religion to visit its sacred spaces. All Muslims, for example, are expected to make one pilgrimage to Mecca during their life if possible, and so each year more than a million Muslim pilgrims make this journey. Many Hindus travel to Varanasi (Banaras), India, and Shintoists to Ise, Japan, as part of their religious observances.

Minor sacred spaces also inspire pilgrimages; hundreds of shrines are located in Western Europe—primarily in Roman Catholic regions—some of which are visited by hundreds of thousands of pilgrims each year.

Religion changes landscapes through the construction of religious buildings and patterns of land use. Choice of clothing, facial hair, and other visible personal characteristics also indicate differences in the cultural landscape. Mosques with their towering minarets are visibly different from churches and contribute to the difference between Muslim and Christian landscapes. Bo trees, symbolic of the tree under which the Buddha reached enlightenment, are found throughout Buddhist regions.

The absence of particular types of buildings can also be part of a religious landscape: Muslim communities lack both taverns and hog farms because alcohol and pork are taboo in Islam. Clothing, such as the concealing chador worn by Muslim women, and headwear, such as the turbans worn by Sikh men, are personal signs of those religions.

Types and Diffusion of Religion

Religions, and therefore religious patterns, can be differentiated in a number of ways, such as by the number of deities that are worshiped; some religions are linked in their shared worship of deities. **Monotheistic religions** worship one deity; Judaism, Christianity, and Islam are all monotheistic and are related in their worship of the same God. **Polytheistic religions**, such as many animist religions, worship multiple deities, but this may be a misleading description of some

Feng Shui

Some religions view the physical environment as containing divine energy or spirits that must be respected. Traditional Chinese and Korean religious beliefs, which merged with Buddhism, Taoism, and other religions, include the principle of *feng shui*, whereby settlements, buildings, and even graves must be located and oriented in harmony with the surrounding environment. As Chinese have migrated to North America, their belief in feng shui has affected their choice of real-estate development, including the location and placement of factories, restaurants, and residences.

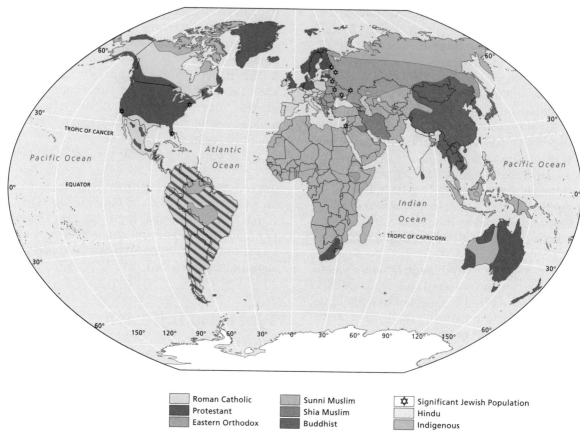

▦	Roman Catholic	▦	Sunni Muslim	✡	Significant Jewish Population
▦	Protestant	▦	Shia Muslim	▦	Hindu
▦	Eastern Orthodox	▦	Buddhist	▦	Indigenous

Christianity, Islam, and Buddhism are the world's most widely practiced religions with a combined following of more than three billion. Like languages and regional dialects, major religions and branches can be cultural indicators of the origin and history of an area's population.

religious beliefs. Hinduism is often described as polytheistic and Vishnu, Siva, and Brahma are all major deities, but Hindus also believe in one supreme consciousness of which these three are different aspects.

One important distinction among religions that affects their spatial distributions and the potential for conflicts between them is the role that proselytizing plays in the religion. **Universalizing** or **proselytizing religions** actively seek converts, and the social structure of the religion often includes missionary activity. Conflicts arise when other religious groups object to this activity.

Christianity, Islam, and Buddhism are the three major universalizing religions and have more than three billion followers. Christianity claims the largest number of followers worldwide at just nearly two billion, of whom some one billion are Roman Catholic.

The numbers of followers are affected by how each religion defines membership: Roman Catholicism counts all who are baptized in the church, and some Protestant churches count only those who are baptized as adults.

Membership in non-proselytizing religions is limited mostly to individuals raised within the specific cultural group practicing that religion, because conversion of outsiders is not actively sought. Larger religions of this kind, those with millions of followers, are labeled **cultural, regional,** or **ethnic religions** because they are associated with a single distinct cultural group, such as Hinduism, Sikhism, and Judaism. Religions associated with small and often isolated groups are termed **traditional** or **local religions**, such as Totemism and Druidism. Many traditional religions are **animist**, with followers believing in the presence of divine forces throughout nature; Central Africans, Native Americans, and residents of Oceania are often animists.

Not all religions are easily placed in one category, nor do all religions remain in one category through history. **Syncretic** religions meld beliefs from different religions; voodoo in Haiti and the Caribbean includes traditional beliefs from African and American local religions and beliefs from Roman Catholicism.

Hinduism, though now a cultural religion that is found almost exclusively among Indians, was proselytizing thousands of years ago as it spread eastward from the upper Indus Valley and converted local populations.

The diffusion or spread of religion is outward from the hearth area where the religion originated. All religions spread through relocation diffusion when followers relocate and bring their religion with them. British settlers in North America, South Africa, and Australia brought Christianity to those areas.

Universalizing religions also undergo expansion diffusion as additional populations are converted to the religion, adding to or expanding the total number of followers. The Spanish converted natives of Mexico, the Philippines, and other Spanish colonies to Roman Catholicism.

As religions moved outward from their hearths, they were occasionally replaced in those hearths. Christianity started in what is now Israel, but despite being the dominant religion of Europe, has relatively few followers in the Middle East.

Buddhism started in northeastern India near Nepal, but it is now nearly absent in India because Hindus regained their influence in this region. Islam and Judaism are still found in their hearth areas, but while Islam has remained dominant in the Arabian Peninsula, Judaism and Jews returned to Israel in the 20th century after being absent for nearly 2,000 years.

Trade and war have been important historically in the expansion of religions. Arab traders, who were Muslim, brought Islam to the eastern coast of Africa, to Indonesia, and to the southern Philippines by 1200, and Muslim armies captured and converted populations in northern Africa, the Iberian Peninsula, and parts of the Balkan Peninsula.

The Pentecostal Movement

A new Protestant sect based on the religious experience of "spirit baptism" or being "born again" started in the United States in the early 20th century.

In 1901 students at Bethel Bible College in Topeka, Kansas, began speaking in tongues. This action was attributed to Christ's original 12 disciples during Pentecost, the seventh day after Easter, according to the Christian calendar. Five years after the 1901 event, a mission was established on Azusa Street in Los Angeles.

As Pentecostalism began to receive greater exposure, it expanded rapidly. Now the church counts more than a hundred million members worldwide.

European colonialism involved both trade and conquest and has resulted in Christianity being the dominant religion over the largest area of Earth.

The diffusion of religions is rarely unimpeded as cultural and, historically, physical environmental barriers slow or stop religions from spreading into new regions. Christians in their mountainous region of Ethiopia have preserved their religion for centuries from surrounding Islamic influences.

When Islam was spreading into Southern Europe, a Muslim army was met by a Christian army and defeated at the Battle of Poitiers in 732, and thus barred from further expansion into Western Europe. More recently, the Russian government has threatened to pass laws to prevent missionaries of evangelic Protestant faiths from spreading their religions into Russia and competing with the Russian Orthodox church.

The spatial pattern of religions is made more complex by the divisions that exist within every major religion. The largest divisions are branches, such as the division of Christianity into Roman Catholic, Eastern Orthodox, and Protestant faiths, and are often based on major differences among followers over who should head the religion and interpret the faith.

As followers of the different branches migrate, different spatial patterns develop. For example, Roman Catholicism rather than Protestantism diffused to Latin America because Spain and Portugal, both Roman Catholic countries, colonized this area.

Branches can be further subdivided into denominations, such as the Baptist, Congregationalist, and Lutheran denominations of the Protestant branch, which may also have different spatial patterns. Lutherans are concentrated in the upper Great Plains region, where immigrants from Norway and Sweden, two Lutheran countries, settled.

Smaller divisions are often termed sects, and if dominated by a single personality may be referred to as cults.

Distributions of Religions

Although numerous religions can be found within any region, including Jews in Iraq and Buddhists in Peru, generalized global patterns of the major religions and their branches exist. Each pattern reflects centuries of diffusion and will probably continue to change in centuries to come. The current diffusion of Protestantism into traditionally Roman Catholic Latin America is one example of an ongoing change.

Two major source areas account for all major religions—the Middle East and South Asia. The three major monotheistic religions—Judaism, Christianity, and Islam—started in the Middle East and, despite their differences, share many key beliefs as well as some prophets. Hinduism evolved into a major religion in South Asia, after being brought there millennia ago from Central Asia, and Buddhism originated as an offshoot of Hinduism.

MIDDLE EASTERN RELIGIONS

Judaism, the oldest of the three major monotheistic religions originating in the Middle East, is concentrated in Israel, but large Jewish populations exist in many major European and American cities. The religious hearth of Judaism is centered in Jerusalem and includes the area Jews consider their Promised Land from God. When the Jews were driven from this area by the Romans in the Diaspora of the first century, other groups inhabited the area. For centuries, until the 1900s, the region was called Palestine and was populated by Muslims (Palestinians). In the 1880s, the **Zionist** movement started whereby Jews began returning in steadily increasing numbers to their ancestral home, eventually gaining control over the area when Israel was recognized in 1948. The Palestinian issue was created by this return of the Jews and the displacement of the Palestinians; there are currently about 530,000 Palestinians in the Gaza Strip, 430,000 in the

Within the city limits of Rome is Vatican City, the smallest independent state in the world. The most important edifice is St. Peter's Basilica, world center of Roman Catholic worship.

West Bank, 960,00 in Jordan, and 600,000 in Lebanon and Syria.

Christianity evolved from Judaism with the teachings of Jesus, a Jew born in Bethlehem, raised in Nazareth, and crucified in Jerusalem—three locations in Israel and the West Bank. The spread of Christianity to Europe was due to the proselytizing of the Apostle Paul and other missionaries and later to the influence of the Roman Empire after the Emperor Constantine converted to Christianity in 313. The global diffusion of this religion was due primarily to the establishment of empires by European countries.

Each of the three major branches of Christianity—Roman Catholicism, Eastern Orthodox, and Protestantism—tends to dominate certain regions within the global Christian realm. Roman Catholicism dominates Southern Europe, where Roman influence was strongest, and the countries in Latin America colonized by Spain and Portugal. The Eastern Orthodox Church separated from Roman Catholicism in the Great Schism of 1054 and now dominates Eastern Europe and the former Russian Empire of the tsars; this division separated churches following the Greek rite in the east from those following the Latin rite. In the 16th century Martin Luther of Germany and John Calvin of Switzerland started the Protestant movement which separated from Roman Catholicism during the Reformation; Protestantism now dominates Northern European countries and their former colonies.

In recent polls, about one-quarter billion North Americans define themselves as Christians; numerous other religions are also present, including more than four million Muslims and nearly six million Jews. Regional concentrations of different Christian branches and denominations have developed: In the U.S., Baptists dominate the Southeast. Roman Catholics dominate New England and areas bordering Mexico, which is nearly 90 percent Roman Catholic, Lutherans the upper Great Plains, and Latter Day Saints—Mormons—Utah and counties in bordering states. Migrations have changed these distributions over the years; the Latter Day Saints originated in New York, moved to Ohio, Missouri, and Illinois before relocating to Utah to escape persecution by other Christian denominations and find their promised land.

Islam, the third major religion originating in the Middle East, has western Saudi Arabia as its hearth. Islam started in Mecca with the revelations of Mohammed around 610, which became verses of the Koran (Quran). Mecca, Medina, where Mohammed found sanctuary after being driven from Mecca in 622, and Jerusalem are the three holiest cities of Islam. A proselytizing religion, Islam was spread by Muslim armies outward from Saudi Arabia as part of a **jihad**, holy war, to secure the peace of Islam. At one point, Islam dominated much of India as well as Spain, Portugal, and Yugoslavia. Islam is currently the fastest growing major religion due more to contact conversion by individuals rather than from organized missionary efforts.

Islam has two major branches, Sunni and Shiite, which separated during the seventh century over leadership of the religion. Sunnis compose about 84 percent of all Muslims and dominate the Arabian Peninsula, northern Africa, and most Muslim countries around the world. Shiites are the majority of the population in Iran, which is about 90 percent Shiite, and in Iraq, which is some 60 to 65 percent Shiite.

SOUTH ASIAN RELIGIONS

Hinduism is the oldest major religion, originating in Central Asia before being brought by Aryan tribes migrating to the Indus Valley perhaps 3,500 years ago. Although now a cultural religion, Hinduism diffused eastward toward the Ganges Valley, and missionaries spread the religion to much of Southeast Asia, including Malaysia and Indonesia. Bali in Indonesia is still predominantly Hindu and Angkor Wat is one of several ancient Hindu temples in what is now Cambodia. Regional variations in Hinduism are not as spatially discrete as in the Muslim and Christian religions but do exist; for example, the deities Siva and Shakti are venerated more in the north of India and

Vishnu more in the west. Hinduism has spread over the last few centuries primarily by Indians migrating to other countries, and sizable Hindu populations are found in Fiji, northern Sri Lanka, and South Africa. The majority of India's nearly one billion people are Hindu, which is why Hinduism is the third largest religion despite no longer being universalizing.

Indian society has been very much shaped by Hinduism, especially its caste system of social and religious status. Hindus believe in reincarnation in which an individual is born into a caste based on the **karma** or totality of actions by the individual during his or her prior life. There are four major castes—priests, warriors, tradesmen, and laborers—and interactions between the castes, such as marriage, are religiously defined. In recent years, problems have arisen in India because the national constitution does not recognize Hinduism as a state religion. Riots erupted in Gujarat in the 1980s and nationally in the 1990s in protest against laws enforcing the rights of the lowest caste, called pariahs or untouchables, to obtain higher education, government positions, and other opportunities.

Buddhism is an offshoot of Hinduism based on the teachings of Siddhartha Gautama, born a member of the Hindu priestly caste about 563 B.C. Buddhism started near the border of what are now India and Nepal where Siddhartha was born, reached enlightenment, and died. Lumbini, now in Nepal, and Bodh Gaya and Kusinagara in India are sacred places in this religious hearth based on these three events.

Missionaries carried Buddhism to eastern Asia following the conversion of Asoka, Emperor of India, around 261 B.C. Different branches developed, and Buddhism also merged with other religions. The number of Buddhists worldwide is consequently uncertain because individuals often practice Buddhism along with cultural Chinese and Japanese religions. Theravada Buddhism, the more conservative branch of the religion, diverged from Mahayana Buddhism over

A crowd gathers before the Western Wall in the Old City, Jerusalem, to celebrate the Jewish festival of Shauvot. Jerusalem's greatest concentration of religious and historical sites is in the Old City, which is surrounded by modern Jerusalem.

different interpretations of Buddha's teachings. Theravada now dominates Southeast Asia. Mahayana is most common in China, Korea, and Japan, and Lamaism, which also evolved from Mahayana, dominates Tibet despite Chinese oppression. Mahayana Buddhism merged with Taoist and Confucianist thought in China and with Shinto in Japan where a version of Buddhism referred to as Zen in Japan or Ch'an in China, also emerged.

Sikhism, a second offshoot of Hinduism, has relatively few followers—around 22 million worldwide—but it is important because of the conflicts between it and Hinduism. Founded in the 1500s and based on the teachings of Guru Nanak, the religious hearth of Sikhism is in the Punjab region on the border of India and Pakistan; Sikhism attempts to reconcile Hinduism and Islam. Currently, many Sikhs are seeking an independent homeland—Khalistan—separate from Hindu-dominated India and have been involved in a sometimes violent campaign to secede.

Three East Asian religions are closely associated with Buddhist practices. **Confucianism** and **Taoism**, two philosophical religions that arose in the sixth century, were dominant in China until the 20th century. Their influences have declined markedly since the country became communist in 1949. **Shinto** is an ethnic Japanese religion in which ancestors are venerated, but it lost influence following World War II and has become less popular in recent decades.

Religious Conflicts

Members of different religions coexist without problems in many areas of the world, but religious conflicts can arise where different religious communities come into contact. Many conflicts between members of different religions, such as that between Buddhist Sinhalese and Hindu Tamils in Sri Lanka, are struggles over economic opportunities and political justice between groups identified by their religions. Other conflicts are primarily over beliefs and values. In 1989 more than 400 people died in Ayodhya, India, when Muslims and Hindus fought over whether a mosque or a Hindu shrine should be located on a site sacred to both religions. In 1992 a Hindu mob destroyed the mosque, causing numerous riots in India. Disputes between religious and secular groups are also common; Islamic fundamentalists are currently battling the government of Egypt on the grounds that it is not adequately following the principles of Islam.

Religious conflicts usually occur when boundaries between religious regions do not match political boundaries, thus allowing one religious group to dominate another economically and politically. **Interfaith boundaries** are those between different religions and exist between branches or denominations of one religion. Within Chad, Ghana, and many other countries in the Sahel region of northern Africa, interfaith boundaries separate the Muslims in the northern areas from the animists and Christians in the southern areas. Muslims often are the national majority and dominate the governments. When the Sudanese government implemented **Sharia**, the Islamic rule of law, in the 1980s southern Sudanese, who are Christians and animists, protested, and the ensuing conflict has since claimed thousands of lives.

The ongoing dispute between Jews and Muslim Palestinians in Israel has clear economic and political components, but to a large degree is based on different beliefs about who should possess this territory. Muslims claim the land based on centuries of possession, and Jews claim that God promised it to them. Despite this ongoing conflict, Jerusalem remains a city sacred to both Jews and Muslims—as well as to Christians—and mosques, churches, and temples are located close to each other in the Old Town.

Territorial claims by religious groups are the basis for numerous conflicts around the world. Fighting between Sikhs and Hindus in the Indian state of Punjab is over political control of territory as is the fighting between Muslim Kosovars and Christian Serbians in Yugoslavia. **Ethnic cleansing**, the removal of one ethnic—often religious—group from an area, was used by the Serbians against Kosovars in 1999, much

as the Serbians and Croatians removed Muslim Bosnians from territory during the early 1990s.

Many current religious disputes have long histories and consequently cannot be resolved easily or quickly. Centuries of economic and political dominance by Protestants, mostly Scottish and English immigrants, created the conflict between Roman Catholics and Protestants in Northern Ireland. The island on which Ireland (Eire) and Northern Ireland (Ulster) coexist was divided in 1922 after counties voted individually on whether to become self-governing or to remain fully part of the United Kingdom. Irish Catholics were the majority in most counties and voted for dominion status, and the majority populations in the northern counties were Protestant and voted to stay in the United Kingdom. Establishing a lasting peace in Ulster is complicated by the continuing desire of most Roman Catholics to join Ireland, now a sovereign country, and the desire of most Protestants to remain part of the United Kingdom; armed groups still support each of these positions.

Political control by one religious group often leads to conflict when minority religious groups seek power. In **theocracies**, where the leader of the dominant religion is also the political leader, members of minority religions may be persecuted or reject the imposition of laws from another religion. When the Ayatollah Khomeini came to political and religious power in Iran in 1979, Iranians of the Baha'i religion faced tremendous discrimination. Baha'i originated in Iran (Persia) in 1844 and teaches that all religions are in ultimate agreement.

In some countries, including Norway, Ireland, and Peru, there may be an established church or an official state religion, but religious and government authorities remain separate. In these countries political discrimination against minority religions can still occur. Judaism is the state religion of Israel, and Muslims who live in Israel complain about limitations on voting and other civil rights.

In a number of countries **fundamentalist members** of religions, those who believe in literal interpretation of religious writings, have

come into political conflict with the less fundamentalist and more secular members of the
larger society. In Algeria, a civil war has been
waged for years between fundamentalist Muslims and the government; the conflict grew
deadly after the government canceled an election in 1992 that would have brought the fundamentalists to power. Not all disputes between
fundamentalist and moderate members of a religion involve civil war. In the United States,
protests are the dominant form of dispute
between fundamentalist Christians and other
groups of the population over issues such as
women's rights and abortion.

Religion and language remain vital components of cultural identities and societal relations,
but increasing contacts among members of the
global community have led to changes in all
aspects of culture. The spread of new cultural
traits and values is part of a larger process of
modernization, in which the political, economic, social, and cultural values of the world's
more developed societies diffuse to its less developed societies. Members of formerly isolated
folk cultures are increasingly adopting aspects
of more modern popular cultures.

A father and his daughter in her first kimono celebrate
Japan's traditional Seven-Five-Three Day. These ages
were milestones in times of high child mortality.

Folk and Popular Culture

Improvements in communications, transportation, and production have increasingly exposed
populations to new products, new ideas, and
new cultures during the 20th century. As a
result, many people have moved from rural
conservative, local folk communities into
urban, dynamic, popular societies. While no
global culture has yet emerged, cultures from
around the world share some material components as well as cultural values; blue jeans,
computers, and democratic ideals—all associated with American culture—are increasingly

common, part of what some cultures complain
is the process of **Americanization**.

Folk culture refers to isolated populations
whose cultures are traditionally based on kinship groups or clans, and which utilize artifacts
and **mentifacts**—beliefs, ideas, and their
expressions such as religion, music, and folk-
lore handed down over generations. The
spread of folk cultures has traditionally been
associated with migrations. For example, the
diffusion of the Mennonite culture in the
United States has been restricted almost

exclusively to relocation of members of this ethnic group. Individual components of folk culture, such as music, myths, and medical knowledge are passed down orally between generations.

Popular culture, on the other hand, refers to large urban populations, mass production of artifacts, and change. Ideas, activities, fashions, and other cultural traits diffuse rapidly through the mass media and can be adopted and discarded rapidly as well; fads and trends are considered components of popular culture.

Modern technology allows a far greater number of connections among individuals within their larger culture, but most of these connections are less developed than in a folk culture, thus making urban society more impersonal.

Much of popular culture derives from the United States, the world leader in technology and economics, although all developed industrial societies contribute their own innovations. The latest rap and rock music, colorful hair styles, newest computer games, and hippest cuisines are all components of popular culture that diffuse through the United States and often to the rest of the world. At the same time as cowboy boots and beepers appear in Russia, however, Japanese appliances and Parisian fashions appear in the United States, as innovations arise and diffuse from around the world.

Popular culture is often seen as a threat to folk values, and therefore cultures attempting to protect established beliefs may erect barriers to the diffusion of new ideas. Satellite television dishes have been seen as a direct threat by the Chinese, Saudi Arabians, and Iranians because of the type of American programming available. Iran outlawed satellite dishes in 1995, China banned private individuals from owning them, and Saudi Arabia dismantled 150,000 dishes.

The contrast between folk and popular cultures is easily visible in the material aspects of each one. Houses, barns, and other structures, as well as instruments, furniture, and household items are usually handcrafted in folk cultures rather than mass-produced or purchased. The resulting cultural landscapes of folk cultures are more strongly influenced by environmental considerations, such as resource availability, than are the landscapes of popular cultures, which are more reflective of franchised styles, standardized designs, and architectural fashions.

In isolated areas of the world, such as in Nunavut (Canada), Kalimantan (Borneo), and the Kalahari Desert (Africa), folk cultures continue to exist, though they do not thrive. There

The skyscraper was an American innovation, first seen in Chicago and New York City. Now, skyscrapers are found in nearly every major city in the world.

In today's well-connected world, people borrow easily from other cultures. In Washington State, a quaint Swiss chalet-style village is decorated for Christmas.

Enthusiasm for local sports teams, a distinct regional choice, links sports fans culturally and means big business.

are often development pressures on these areas, and folk societies such as the Yanomami in the Amazon are losing territory and the security of isolation to prospectors and other settlers. As members of these cultures change in the face of modernity, the cultures increasingly incorporate popular items and activities as folk items and activities are slowly retired. In Nunavut and other Inuit (Eskimo) societies, sled dogs are replaced by snowmobiles and skin tents by prefabricated houses.

Pure folk cultures may not exist anymore within the United States because our economic and social systems make isolation nearly impossible. Amish teenagers, for example, still do not drive cars, but some do use in-line skates. Isolated regions that at one time sheltered folk cultures have been invaded by telecommunications and highways so that former folk cultures, such as that of the hill people in the Ozarks, are in steady decline. Small communities and individual members of these cultures still exist, but younger generations are discovering new options.

Since the same fads and trends become available to populations throughout most countries, if not the world, a standardization of culture can occur. The convergence hypothesis argues that as different populations are exposed to the same products and ideas their cultures become increasingly similar, perhaps converging toward a single culture. As the cultural landscapes converge the result is termed placelessness, in which places become indistinguishable because malls, fast-food restaurants, and service stations are mass-produced and standardized.

Despite the standardization implicit in many aspects of popular culture, regional cultural identities still exist because not all folk values or traits are replaced by popular ones. At the international scale, Japanese, Americans, and Palestinians will react differently to new ideas and products as variations in cultural values affect the adoption of these innovations. Even in the United States, there remain clear regional differences in choice of magazines, fast food, and sports, among other things; traditional values and interests derived from folk cultures have not disappeared.

Conclusion

Culture provides the identity that links members of one society together and can also divide those members from other cultures. Cultural geography analyzes the spatial context of these cultural processes—where cultures originate, how they diffuse over Earth, what regional identities are created, and what conflicts arise between cultural groups.

Despite the increasing globalization of popular culture, there is no world culture yet, and regional differences remain extremely important for understanding how the world works. Increased economic and political ties between cultures will, however, help to increase mutual appreciation of different cultures and reduce the risk of future conflicts.

Economic Geography

Introduction

Economic geography concerns the ways societies create economic landscapes and generate spatial patterns of economic activity at scales ranging from the local to the global. This set of topics involves not only traditional issues such as resource use and population growth, but also the way in which businesses decide where to locate, how governments and private firms form regional and national development strategies, international trade, technological change, public policy, and the world economy.

There are several ways to interpret economic landscapes, including simple empirical description, classical location theory and quantitative modeling, and political economy. The approach here combines aspects of all of these, but stresses political economy because of its conceptual understanding of place.

Political economy views the economy and economic landscapes as historically created social institutions tightly linked to prevailing cultural and political relations, so that issues of spatial development are portrayed as the products of the organization of society as a totality rather than the aggregate decisions of individual actors.

This chapter provides an overview of economic geography, focusing primarily on global patterns of production, trade, and development, with particular reference to the United States. Throughout, it concentrates on capitalism, a type of political economy originating in the 15th century. Under capitalism the means of production are privately owned and production is organized around profit maximization. Production is for exchange rather than for subsistence. Capitalism has produced and changed economic landscapes at different spatial scales. Although there have been many types of economic systems throughout human history, capitalism has largely eclipsed other forms of economic organization, including such early forms as hunting and gathering, feudalism, or more recently, socialism.

Economic Sectors and Economic Geography

Economic activity is frequently classified into three sectors: the primary, secondary, and tertiary sectors. In general, **primary sector** activities are the cluster of economic activities that pertain to extracting raw materials from Earth's surface, including agriculture, forestry, fishing, and mining. In preindustrial economies this sector accounts for the bulk of employment; today, however, such activities tend to be highly capital-intensive and account for less than 5 percent of employment in economically developed nations.

Secondary sector activities include manufacturing and construction industries that transform raw materials into finished goods, and **tertiary sector** activities revolve around the production of intangibles such as services, including finance, producer and consumer services such as wholesale and retail trade, transportation and communications, education and health care, nonprofit organizations, and the public sector. Tertiary sector activities compose most of the economic activity of developed nations as well as of many developing ones.

While there is considerable overlap among these sectors and enormous diversity within them, economic theory has traditionally viewed development as a sequential movement from the primary to the secondary (industrialization) to the tertiary (postindustrial society). In the U.S., for example, the sectoral distribution of employment over time decreased the proportion of the workforce engaged in primary sector activities and increased the proportion of tertiary ones. However, this approach has questionable application in the developing world today, given that the employment structure of many developing countries moves directly from the primary to the tertiary sector,

a reflection of their historical trajectories and the timing of their entrance into the global economy, which often differ markedly from those in the economically developed world. Developing countries, or **Third World countries** are those with varying cultures and economies and consist of the majority of the world's population. Essentially, former European colonies in Latin America, Africa, and Asia, with the exception of Japan, comprise the Third World.

Primary Sector Activities

The **primary economic sector** involves extracting raw materials from the surface of Earth and includes agriculture, fishing, forestry, and mining. Historically, primary sector activities, particularly agriculture, involved the majority of the labor force of most societies, a reflection of the labor-intensive nature of the production process. In many underdeveloped parts of the world today, these activities still compose a large share, often the majority, of employment, much of it organized around local subsistence systems. With the global expansion of capitalism that began in the 16th century, primary sector activities became steadily integrated into a planetary network of commodity production, including the plantation system and colonial mining operations such as Spanish silver mines in Mexico and Bolivia.

AGRICULTURE

One of the most important facets of economic geography is the way societies procure food supplies for themselves. For the last several millennia, agriculture has been the primary

Hunting and Gathering

Hunting and gathering was the mode of production that sustained human beings for more than 95 percent of their existence on Earth. Characteristically organized around a division of labor in which men hunt game and fish, and women gather edible plants, this form of economy involved frequent migration, virtually no private property, kinship bonds as the essential social organization, and low population densities. (See Migration, page 268.) Almost extinct today, hunting and gathering began to be displaced by various agricultural systems following the Neolithic Revolution that began around 10,000 B.C.

means by and for which people transformed the natural environment. In many places, rising population levels necessitated the creation of new farmland by clearing forests and draining wetlands. Agriculture is a major agent in soil erosion and nonpoint source water pollution today. Irrigation systems in dry climates such as the American West often involve large-scale aqueducts or groundwater extraction.

THE ORIGINS OF AGRICULTURE

The origins of agriculture date back to the Stone Age, or Neolithic Revolution, beginning about 10,000 B.C., in which several societies independently discovered the process of **domestication,** the selective breeding of plants and animals such that they require human intervention in order to reproduce. Because agriculture allowed more calories to be harvested per unit area, thus sustaining denser population levels, it eventually displaced hunting and gathering as the mode of production that had endured for tens of thousands of years, if not more.

Different crops and animals were domesticated in different parts of the world (see Chart: Primary Areas of Crop and Livestock Domestication, page 320), some in more than one place simultaneously.

These societies were located in the Fertile Crescent of Southwest Asia and in Egypt, China, Southeast Asia, the Indus River Valley, the Mediterranean parts of western and southern Africa and, somewhat later, among cultures such as the Olmec and Maya in Central America, the moundbuilding Mississippian culture of the Mississippi River Valley (of which Cahokia is a major example), and the Incas of the Andean region of South America. From these culture hearths, farming diffused to surrounding regions, and different cultures based their agricultural systems around different complexes of crops. In Southwest Asia, for example, wheat and barley dominated; in East Asia, rice and millet; in Africa, diets centered on a millet–yam–sorghum combination; in Central America, maize, beans, and squash were most important; in South America, the potato was the primary staple.

The importance of agriculture in the historic emergence of human civilization cannot be overstated: Farming provided the **social surplus** that allowed the subsequent development of class society, cities, the state, a supply of products that exceeded demand, and innovations such as writing and metalworking. Population levels, densities, standards of living (including free time and experimentation), and life expectancies rose markedly during this first agricultural revolution. Anthropologist Ester Boserup theorized that rising population levels led to an intensification of agriculture, in which rising productivity via improved tools, irrigation, and labor specialization reflected Malthusian pressures for more food. (See Sidebar: Malthus, page 251.)

Primary Areas of Crop and Livestock Domestication

SOUTHWEST ASIA	MEDITERRA-NEAN	SOUTHEAST ASIA	CHINA	WEST AFRICA	CENTRAL AMERICA	SOUTH AMERICA
Barley	Celery	Bananas	Apricots	Cotton	Beans	Alpaca
Beans	Dates	Chicken	Barley	Coffee	Chilis	Guinea pig
Carrots	Garlic	Citrus fruits	Cabbage	Melons	Cotton	Llamas
Cattle	Grapes	Cucumbers	Peaches	Millet	Dogs	Papayas
Ducks	Lentils	Coconuts	Plums	Oil palm	Maize	Pineapples
Goats	Lettuce	Dogs	Soybeans	Okra	Manioc	Potatoes
Horses	Olives	Eggplant		Pigs	Squash	Pumpkins
Oats	Hemp			Sorghum	Sweet potatoes	Tobacco
Onions	Pigs			Yams	Turkeys	Tomatoes
Rye	Rice					
Sheep	Sugar cane					
Wheat	Tea					
	Water buffalo					

PREINDUSTRIAL AGRICULTURE

Despite the worldwide dominance of **commercial farming** today (farming that is industrialized and for profit) preindustrial agricultural systems continue to persist in several forms. Most common among these is slash-and-burn, which is found in the humid tropics of central and western Africa, Central America and Brazilian Amazonia, and parts of Southeast Asia. Roughly 40 million people live today on the basis of this technique. Because tropical soils are notoriously low in nutrients—most of the nutrients are contained in the living biomass—slash-and-burn agriculture is well developed for maximizing short-term yields in such environments. Typically, the sequence involved in this type of farming involves cutting down much of the vegetation in small clearings, burning it to release the nutrients into the soil and to clear farmland, then planting a mixed group of crops. Such a system may work for up to four or five years in a given site, until the crops exhaust the available nutrient supply. Then it becomes necessary to clear new land through the same means. When population levels are constant, this form of agriculture is quite effective.

Another preindustrial agricultural system is terraced rice farming, which is widely practiced in Asia from eastern India through southern China, Japan, Korea, Indochina, and Indonesia, and currently feeds almost two billion people. Terraced rice paddies are carved into hillsides as a means of creating arable land and involve intricate irrigation systems to control the flow of water, especially when rice plants are young. The system of dikes and levees used for this purpose, as well as the terraces themselves, have been constructed over millennia. This method is labor-intensive and involves working relatively small plots of land. There are few **economies of scale,** or productivity gains from producing in large quantities. Today rice is grown widely in East Asia, a prime example of intensive agriculture with high inputs per unit area, resulting in high outputs, as opposed to **extensive agriculture,** which involves few inputs scattered over large areas.

The preindustrial system of terraced rice farming, such as this one in Bhutan, has been practiced for thousands of years in much of Asia. Terraced fields demand intense labor, a relatively inexpensive commodity, but produce high yields, currently feeding nearly two billion people worldwide.

(See Map: World Wheat and Rice production, page 322.)

Finally, preindustrial agriculture includes various forms of pastoral nomadic herding generally practiced in arid or semiarid regions in Central Asia and Africa in which livestock rather than crops are the primary form of sustenance. The Masai of East Africa, for example raise cattle, and the Kirghiz of Central Asia migrate with herds of goats. Frequently such cultures, which are often in areas inhospitable to crops, may follow natural migratory cycles of their animals and trade with local settled communities.

Until the industrial revolution in the 18th and 19th centuries, agriculture was relatively unproductive in terms of output per unit area and, consequently, so labor-intensive that the majority of people were farmers. Even today, agriculture is the largest single form of employment throughout the world.

Historically, with the emergence of slave-based systems in the Middle East, China, and the Roman Empire, and later with the development of serf-based feudalism in Europe and elsewhere, agriculture was organized around small-plot subsistence systems relying on animate sources of energy, such as animals to pull plows and people to plant seeds, harvest crops, and fetch water. European agriculture was gradually transformed throughout the millennium of feudalism starting in the sixth century with a number of factors: rising population levels, technological changes such as the plow and stirrup, the replacement of oxen with horses, and the open-field system, in which several large fields surrounding a village were farmed.

COMMERCIALIZED AGRICULTURE

By the 17th century, **commercial agriculture** began to make its appearance in Europe: The motive for profit displaced subsistence production. Techniques included growing crops for profit, enclosing fields by fences and hedgerows, improvements in breeding stock and seeds, crop rotation rather than fallow fields. Commercial agriculture was also boosted by the introduction of new species such as the potato—via South America to Spain, then Britain and Ireland—and by the 19th century,

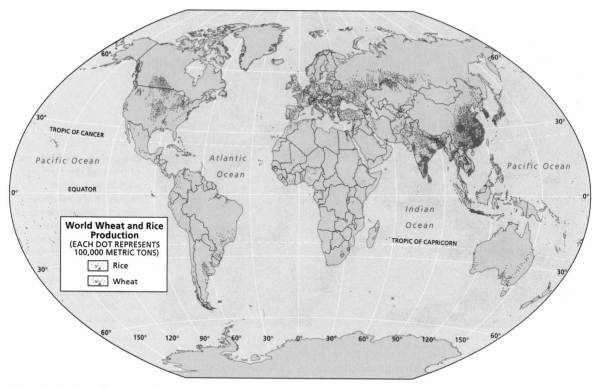

The principal growing areas of wheat, found at cooler latitudes, and rice, found at very warm latitudes, supply most of the world with grain. While wheat cultivation has become largely commercialized and highly mechanized, rice still involves labor-intensive, hands-on cultivation in most places. In the U.S. rice is grown with little human labor.

European cereals to the grasslands of North America and Australia.

The worldwide expansion of commercial agriculture was intricately linked to the plantation system, the primary institution through which foods and commodities grown or produced for profit were transplanted to European colonies elsewhere. Examples include the fruit and sugar plantations of the Caribbean and Latin America, cotton and tobacco in the southern U.S., groundnuts and cocoa in west Africa, cotton and tea in east Africa, cotton in Egypt, tea in India and Ceylon—today's Sri Lanka—and rubber, tobacco, sugar, and other crops in Southeast Asia.

Low-cost food imports from European colonies accelerated a transformation in agriculture in Europe, driving many laborers out of work and into cities, encouraging a wholesale reconstruction in agricultural organization and in productivity.

Capitalist agriculture—farming for a profit—is typified by intense pressure to mechanize production, making contemporary agriculture among the most capital-intensive industries in the world. Mechanization throughout the 19th century drastically reduced the number of workers needed per unit area of land, driving countless rural families off farms and freeing up a labor supply for the industrializing cities.

The 19th and 20th centuries experienced the widespread use of spectacular technological innovations such as the cotton gin and threshing machine and concomitant increases in productivity. High yields per unit of land or labor are also largely attributable to vast expenditures of energy through petroleum-dependent farming systems, including the production and operation of farming machinery—especially tractors but also airplanes, combines, harvesters, trucks, diesel pumps, and other equipment—as well as artificial petroleum-derived fertilizers.

Linkage to the petrochemical industry has made industrialized agriculture sensitive to world fluctuations in the price of petroleum, such as the oil crises of the 1970s.

In Japan agriculture today employs only 2 percent of the labor force, whereas in China 50 percent of the population is employed in the production of food.

The emergence of a wheat-based industrialized farming system was highly uneven geographically. In the late 19th century, Russia and Ukraine were important sources of wheat for the expanding markets of Western Europe.

But this supply was severed when the Bolshevik Revolution broke out in 1917 and, subsequently, when the Soviet Union withdrew from the world economy. Simultaneously, the vast grasslands of the Midwestern U.S. and Canada, blessed with rich soils and long growing seasons, became the core of the global cereal producing system.

Several subsystems characterize commercial agriculture in the U.S. including wheat, corn and hogs, fruits and vegetables, dairy farming, and cattle ranching, each of which exhibits a unique cluster of labor and management

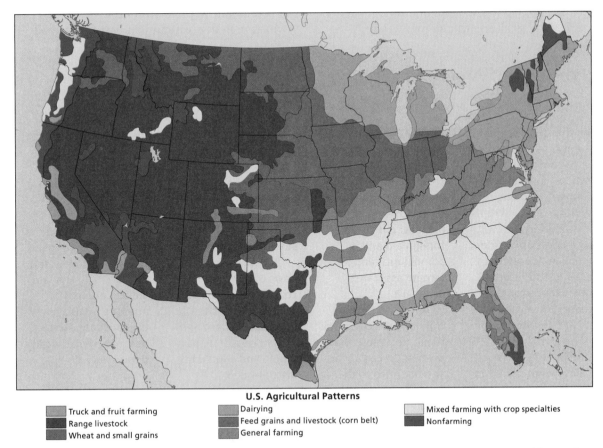

U.S. Agricultural Patterns

- Truck and fruit farming
- Range livestock
- Wheat and small grains
- Dairying
- Feed grains and livestock (corn belt)
- General farming
- Mixed farming with crop specialties
- Nonfarming

Approximately 44 percent of U.S. land area, more than a million square miles, is used to produce crops and livestock. Agricultural patterns depend largely on geography: Soil, the slope of the terrain, climate, distance to market, and storage and marketing facilities all play significant roles.

practices, land uses, geographic location, technologies, and market structure.

Recently, agriculture, particularly in the U.S., has been steadily reshaped by new technologies. The computer revolution introduced digital controls for irrigation, the application of pesticides, and harvesting. Innovations—including fertilizers, hybrid seeds, agrochemicals, and biotechnologies in pharmaceuticals, recombinant DNA techniques, and genetic alteration of crops—have increased productivity yet further. Conversely, industrial substitutes—such as artificial sweeteners for sugar—have dampened the demand for some agricultural goods.

Today, the U.S. is by far the world's largest producer of agricultural commodities, exporting half the world's volume of traded foodstuffs; in agriculture, there is only one superpower. U.S. output in agriculture exceeds most industries, including construction and automobiles. These exports, primarily wheat, rice, corn, and soybeans, are plant rather than animal products, and are concentrated at the bottom of the food chain. In contrast, the U.S. is a net importer of meats, which are located higher in the food chain and require far more calories to produce, even though the U.S. has an enormous domestic meat-processing industry. This is a reflection of the nation's high demand for meat; further, a large share of cereals output, for example half of corn output, is dedicated to feed for cattle, pigs, and chickens.

Despite its numerous assets, American farming has been periodically beset by crises, including the Dust Bowl of the 1930s and the severe financial problems of the 1980s, in which high interest rates and an overvalued

Subsidies of American Farming

In the 1930s economic and climatic catastrophes combined to devastate American farmers, resulting in widespread bankruptcies and foreclosures.

As part of President Franklin Roosevelt's attempts to resurrect this vital sector, the federal government passed the Agricultural Adjustment Act of 1933, the first of a series of measures designed to alleviate the crisis in agriculture.

Essentially, the law sets price supports for each type of farm commodity above the market price. If there are surpluses of subsidized commodities, the government is obligated to buy them. These surpluses can be used as foreign aid and in school lunch and low-income assistance programs.

American farmers still have the capacity to produce more than the market can absorb at a fair price to them. Trying to balance the supply and demand of U.S. commodities continues to be a challenge.

Supporters of government subsidies contend that financial help to the farm sector ensures consumers an abundant supply of reasonably priced food and stabilizes farm income.

But critics say that basic U.S. farm policies, conceived in the 1930s, no longer meet the needs of modern agriculture or society as a whole and should be discontinued.

Congress has frequently amended the early law in response to changing conditions in the farm sector and in an attempt to balance supply and demand. The latest farm law, passed in 1996, provided a more market-oriented system.

The level of income support is no longer related to current farm prices. But in the late 1990s Congress approved massive aid packages for farmers because of historically depressed prices, droughts, and political pressure.

In Siberia, Russia, the Nenets depend almost entirely on reindeer for their livelihood. The hardy, subarctic deer provide them with food, clothing, shelter, and transportation.

dollar drove thousands of farmers out of business. Due in part to its enormously high levels of efficiency, U.S. agricultural output frequently exceeds demand, creating a chronic surplus. This situation is also due in part to a series of federal government incentives implemented during the Depression of the 1930s, particularly price supports that encourage farmers to grow more than the market can absorb, thus creating a surplus the government is obligated to purchase. Some of this surplus is used as foreign aid or in domestic U.S. Department of Agriculture subsidized food programs.

The U.S. is not the only country to subsidize its farmers. Japan, for example, with very limited quantities of arable land, is self-sufficient in rice largely because of subsidies, and most of the budget for the European Union (EU) goes to agricultural subsidies. Persistent surpluses have led to long-term declines in prices, part of a worldwide glut of primary sector products.

The combination of low prices, the advantages enjoyed by large firms, and technological change has steadily eroded the number of family farms. In the 20th century, the number of farms in the U.S. has declined from 5.5 million

in 1950 to 1.5 million in 1995, and the average size has risen from 200 acres in 1950 to 500 in 1995. Long-term challenges to American farming include shortages of groundwater, soil erosion, and rural-to-urban land conversion.

Globally, concerns about agriculture are tied to impending limits to the world supply of arable land and fears that global food stocks will fail to keep pace with rising population levels. Large parts of Earth's surface are too dry, too steep, too wet, or too cold to sustain agriculture. The supply of arable land varies widely around the world and changes over time as prices and technologies allow crops to be grown in marginal environments. As farming encroaches upon such environments, however, diminishing returns make harvests there costly and inefficient to sustain in the long run.

The principle of **diminishing returns,** first articulated by 18th century English economist Thomas Malthus (1766-1834), is that increased investments in production capacity yield steadily smaller marginal increases in output, that is rising inefficiency. Often invoked in conjunction with limited supplies of arable farm land and fears of overpopulation, another

The Green Revolution

During and shortly after World War II, the Rockefeller Foundation based in New York City initiated attempts to stimulate agricultural productivity in developing countries, beginning in Mexico. Led by Norman Borlaug, the application of scientific knowledge to agriculture, including selective breeding of high-yield, high-protein "miracle crops," produced numerous new strains of rice and wheat that grew more rapidly than earlier varieties.

Miracle crops often yielded two or three harvests per year, compared to one for most traditional breeds, and each crop was two to three times larger; often they were more drought- and disease-resistant as well. Limited in their ability to absorb nitrogen, however, they required nitrogen-based fertilizers to grow properly. In the 1960s these efforts culminated in the green revolution, a sustained effort to introduce these crops in nations with rapidly growing populations such as Mexico, India, the Philippines, Indonesia, Bangladesh, Egypt, and elsewhere. Critics pointed out that such crops often required more water, fertilizer, pesticides, and capital inputs than did indigenous crops, thus increasing costs for small farmers and magnifying social inequalities and increasing their dependence upon the global petroleum industry.

In the long run, however, the results have been indisputable: Asian rice productivity almost doubled, and green revolution crops accounted for most of the world's agricultural productivity gains in the 1960s and 1970s, and 80 percent in the 1980s. The program has not been an unqualified success everywhere, however: In Africa such crops have been thwarted by wars, poor soils, and drought.

Recent research has concentrated upon other crops grown in tropical environments, such as cassava, soybeans, sorghum, and millet.

thesis advocated by Malthus, diminishing returns may be offset by continuous technological change and improved productivity. The effect of **overpopulation,** according to Malthus, was that the world, or some part thereof, could not sustain a current or future population as determined by the carrying capacity of a place, including Earth. (See Population, page 246.)

Because the world supply of arable land is essentially fixed, future gains in supply must occur through productivity increases. Persistent Malthusian fears that the world cannot feed its people have thus far been countered by technological changes that have overcome diminishing returns. In developing countries irrigation, tractors, hybrid crops improved during the **green revolution** of the 1960s, and better storage facilities as simple as concrete storage bins have led to continuous productivity gains. Many areas, notably Africa, have suffered declining food consumption per capita since World War II, largely due to wars that have disrupted farming systems there.

The globalization of agriculture links different production and consumption regions in an integrated industrial complex that spans the world. A network of corporate ties binds farmers, intermediaries, and consumers into an interdependent totality. U.S. wheat exports to the Soviet Union in the 1970s and 1980s, for example, illustrated the reliance of American farmers on foreign markets.

Global agribusiness is heavily shaped by multinational distribution companies such as Cargill and Archer-Daniels-Midland, which are rarely involved in direct production but can negotiate the complexities of multiple clients and markets, distribution systems, exchange-rate fluctuations, product prices, and different national farming systems. These firms dominate the distribution of cereals in the First World, including 80 percent of the world wheat trade. The **First World** includes the economically developed nations in Europe and North America, and Japan, Australia, and New Zealand, slightly more than one-sixth of the world's population, in contrast to the developing or underdeveloped Third World. The First World produces the majority of the world's industrial products and enjoys a relatively high standard of living.

A globalized agro-food system has been augmented by the standardization of consumption that has accompanied the growing popularity of mostly American fast-food outlets worldwide. Agriculture has also become increasingly linked to financial markets, including widespread speculation in commodities. The globalization of agriculture is also evident in worldwide attempts to reduce trade tariffs and quotas, by organizations such as the World Trade Organization, the European Union, and trade pacts such as the North American Free Trade Agreement (NAFTA).

Tariffs and quotas have powerfully affected prices and the competitiveness of local farmers in complex ways. **Tariffs** are a form of domestic protectionism in which nations levy a surcharge on imports designed to increase their market price and thus inhibit consumption of imports. **Quotas** are another form of protectionism in which governments limit the absolute volume of imports in an industry, effectively driving up the market price. Technically different from a tariff, quotas have much the same impact economically. Tariffs generate government revenues and have thus been more popular among countries.

MINING AND ENERGY

Minerals and petroleum constitute two of the world's most important nonrenewable natural resources. Metals are indispensable to the production systems of contemporary society. Many of the world's richest mineral deposits have been depleted, and others are

Worldwide Annual Production and Estimated Reserves of Selected Minerals, 1998 (millions of metric tons).

METAL	ANNUAL PRODUCTION	ESTIMATED RESERVE BASE
Iron ore	1,020	300,000
Aluminum	22.2	34,000*
Copper	11.9	650
Zinc	7.8	440
Lead	3.08	140
Nickel	1.17	140
Tin	0.216	12

*Bauxite

insufficiently concentrated to be economically recoverable except at high prices to consumers. This is particularly true of metallic minerals, of which iron is the most important, but also includes lead, aluminum, copper, nickel, tin, bauxite, manganese, and zinc.

The largest deposits of **strategic minerals,** those essential to industrial production, are concentrated in five nations: Canada, the U.S., Russia, South Africa, and Australia. In contrast, nonmetallic minerals such as potash, clay, and nitrogen are in abundant supply worldwide. To a degree, limited supplies of minerals have been offset by declining consumption per capita because industrialized economies utilize more efficient production methods, find viable substitutes such as plastics and ceramics, and accelerate their reuse and recycling efforts.

In nonindustrial societies, energy needs are satisfied primarily through renewable sources such as wood, charcoal, or dung. Industrialized nations, in contrast, rely on nonrenewable sources, primarily fossil fuels. The ability to mine Europe's abundant coal deposits, for example, was a defining moment of the industrial revolution, which increased the demand for energy exponentially. Indeed, the industrialization of Europe was made possible in part

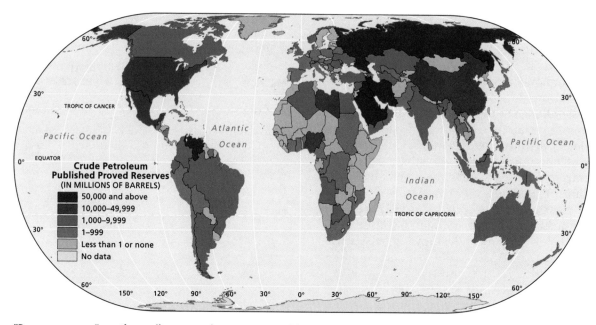

Crude Petroleum Published Proved Reserves (IN MILLIONS OF BARRELS)
- 50,000 and above
- 10,000–49,999
- 1,000–9,999
- 1–999
- Less than 1 or none
- No data

"Proven reserves" are those oil reserves that are recoverable with present technology and prices. "Explored reserves" may include proven, probable, and possible oil sources.

due to the large deposits of coal that underlay the North European lowlands.

The world's most abundant and commonly used fuel source remains coal, located in vast seams in northern Europe, Russia, China, and North America, especially in Appalachia and the Rocky Mountains. Similarly, natural gas deposits are concentrated primarily in Russia, North America, and the Middle East. U.S. energy production in the 20th century has shifted significantly away from a 19th-century reliance on coal and into petroleum and natural gas.

The modern petroleum industry dates from 1870, when American entrepreneur John D. Rockefeller (1839-1937) founded Standard Oil. European firms were motivated by the discovery of Middle Eastern deposits around 1914, the beginning of World War I. The widespread adoption of the automobile increased the demand for petroleum enormously. Today, multinational oil companies such as Exxon, Mobil, Gulf, Texaco, Arco, Phillips, Royal

Dutch Shell, and British Petroleum are among the largest firms in the world in terms of sales.

Because the industry is highly capital-intensive, with high initial investment costs, it tends to be very **oligopolistic,** from Greek, *oligo*, "few," as well: Production and sales are dominated by a few large firms with considerable influence over the market price. An oligopoly is a market structure in which a handful of firms dominate output in a particular industry, thus acting as price-setters rather than competitive price-takers. Oligopolies—rather than monopolies—tend to be the norm in many industries, particularly capital-intensive ones, such as the petroleum industry, in which economies of scale are critical to productivity.

The geographies of world oil production and consumption are highly uneven. Two-thirds of the world's proven reserves are located in the vicinity of the Persian Gulf, including Saudi Arabia, Iran, and Iraq, and North Africa. Secondary reserves are found around the Gulf of Mexico, Alaska, the North Sea, and the South China Sea. The largest petroleum consumers include the U.S.—where about 4 percent of the world's people consume 30 percent of its energy, largely for automobiles—Europe, and Japan.

The global petroleum industry has been dominated by the geopolitics of the Organization of Petroleum Exporting Countries (OPEC), which includes all the Middle Eastern and North African producers as well as Nigeria, Babon, Ecuador, Venezuela, and Indonesia. In 1973 and 1979, OPEC enforced oil embargoes on Western nations that raised the price of oil more than tenfold, creating dramatic oil crises with dire consequences for industrialized economies, including recession, inflation, and accelerated **deindustrialization,** which occurs when the loss of comparative advantage in manufacturing is brought about by technological displacement and the rise of foreign competitors.

Many oil importing nations were similarly affected, whereas the OPEC nations, particularly the lightly populated ones in the Middle East such as Saudi Arabia, Kuwait, and Qatar, enjoyed a substantial influx of funds. Large quantities of these petrodollars were deposited in Western banks, which promptly loaned them to clients in the developing world, paving the way for the debt crisis of the 1980s and 1990s among developing nations. However, by the mid-1980s the price of oil collapsed, due to

cheating on OPEC quotas; new non-OPEC oil sources such as those in the North Sea and South China Sea, on Alaska's North Slope, and in Mexico; growing non-oil alternatives such as coal, natural gas, and nuclear energy; and improved efficiency of production and consumption—conservation, for example. The low prices of fossil fuels in the 1970s have been highly detrimental to the economic health of both OPEC and non-OPEC oil producing nations, as well as to producers of substitutes such as coal.

Alternatives to fossil fuels include nuclear energy, hydropower, geothermal sources, and solar and wind energy. Nuclear energy in the form of fission—fusion is not yet technologically or economically feasible on a sustained basis—is used primarily in industrialized nations of Europe, although the proportion of total energy derived from this source varies widely. (See Table: Nuclear Energy as Percent of total Energy Supply, page 330.)

In the U.S., nuclear power provided about 20 percent of the energy supply in 1998. The use of nuclear energy is constrained by accidents such as those at Three Mile Island, Pennsylvania, in 1979 and Chernobyl, Ukraine, in 1986, the possibility of other accidents, and widespread concerns over the transport and storage of radioactive waste.

Hydropower is widely used in countries with adequate flows of water, but is constrained in the West by environmental

Deindustrialization

Deindustrialization involves plant closures and contractions in employment industries such as textiles, steel, automobiles, machine tools, shipbuilding, rubber, petrochemicals, and electronics. The process started in Great Britain shortly after the end of World War II because high costs and low productivity levels left Britain increasingly uncompetitive as other nations acquired manufacturing capacity. In the U.S. deindustrialization of the manufacturing belt, starting in the 1970s and later extending to most of the Sunbelt, accelerated the shift from blue-collar to white-collar jobs.

For communities dependent upon industry, deindustrialization is catastrophic because it results in high unemployment, poverty, depressed real estate markets, stressed families, and out-migration.

Nuclear Energy as Percent of Total Energy Supply, 1996.

France	72.7	Japan	23.8
Belgium	59.3	United States	21.7
Sweden	51.6	United Kingdom	20.6
Hungary	48.4	Argentina	19.1
South Korea	47.5	Russia	12.6
Switzerland	40.0	South Africa	5.9
Spain	35.9	Netherlands	4.9
Bulgaria	34.0	Mexico	3.6
Finland	33.3	India	1.8
Czech Republic	28.7	Brazil	0.6
Germany	27.6		

concerns associated with large dams; further, most large rivers have already been harnessed in this way. Geothermal energy is rarely used except in nations with large resources of hot groundwater, such as Iceland. Solar and wind energy are inexhaustible and ubiquitous, but economically difficult to obtain in sufficient quantities. (See Renewable and Inexhaustible Resources, page 422.)

Continued debates over the existence of a global-resource supply crisis involve fears of the limited supply of nonrenewable resources, growing population and per capita energy consumption levels, and the environmental consequences of high-volume consumption. The primary means to postponing resource crises historically has been the spatial expansion of extractive industries into increasingly marginal areas such as the expansion of farming in dry climates, timber harvests in secondary-growth regions, or use of low-grade iron ore deposits in inaccessible regions, with attendant concerns about ecological and social disruption as new regions are incorporated into the world economy.

In the late 20th century, fears of impending shortages have been alleviated by a global glut in raw materials, including petroleum and foodstuffs, which has severely depressed prices. In many nations, economic development has been constrained by concerns over environmental degradation, including pollution, wildlife habitat destruction, and the biophysical limits to growth such as soil erosion.

Secondary Sector Activities

Since the industrial revolution, manufacturing has become a vital part of the U.S. and world economies. Unlike primary sector industries, manufacturing involves transforming raw materials into finished goods, although on occasion the distinction between the primary and secondary sectors is difficult to draw. The evolution of large manufacturing systems was made possible by harnessing the inanimate energy of water power and increasing use of coal in the 18th and 19th centuries, and petroleum in the 20th century.

THE INDUSTRIAL REVOLUTION

Capitalism as a form of economic and social organization preceded the industrial revolution by several centuries. Beginning in the mid-18th century, the industrial revolution marked an enormously significant qualitative change in the social and spatial organization of society.

Industrialization began in Great Britain and was characterized by enormous technological change, including innovations such as the steam engine, cotton gin, railroad, electric generator, telegraph, refrigeration, gasoline engine, the telephone, and the automobile, all of which converted inputs into outputs more efficiently. As a result, productivity levels soared exponentially, raising the average standard of living as the costs of products declined relative to incomes. Food became cheaper with the industrialization of agriculture, and famine in Europe ended with the exception of the potato famine in Ireland of the late 1840s. (See Migration, page 268.)

The factory system brought large numbers of workers together for the first time, creating an

The Von Thünen Model

Location modeling in economic geography has a long history. One of the first examples was created by a German landowner, Johann Heinrich von Thünen (1783–1850), who analyzed land use patterns on his estates. Von Thünen's model of land use related the economic rent, or maximum potential amount of profit per unit area that a crop could generate, to the market price,

production costs, and transportation costs to the market.

Hypothetically, different crops competing for a limited supply of land form concentric rings of land use centered upon the market, ranging from high-profit, intensive land uses near the market to low-profit, extensive uses relatively far from the center. The model is easily illustrated using graphs of different bid–

rent lines (reflecting the economic rent each land use generates with distance from the center). This ideal pattern is disrupted by local variations in soil fertility and transportation costs. The model has long been popular among location analysts for its simplicity and elegance.

In the 20th century neoclassical economic analysis of land markets extended this concept

to include consumer demand in the study of intra-urban household and residential location behavior. Although the applicability of the Von Thünen model to the analysis of agricultural land has passed, given that cities today rely on national and global circuits of food production, it does serve as a useful pedagogic device to illustrate the rent-maximizing behavior of land markets.

urbanized workforce and accentuating rural-to-urban migration. In due course, automated assembly lines and use of interchangeable parts accelerated the development of the division of labor in industry, increasing productivity yet more through specialization.

Even the experience of time changed as workers exchanged the rhythms of the seasons for the standardized time of clocks, watches, bells, and factory whistles.

Great Britain, as the world's first industrialized nation, enjoyed a monopoly over industrialization for several decades late in the 18th century. English cities such as Manchester, Sheffield, Leeds, and Birmingham became the "workhorses of the world," particularly in the garment, textile, and metalworking sectors.

In the 19th century, industrialization spread to regions of Europe including the lower Seine River in France, the Ruhr Valley in Germany, and the Po River Valley in Italy. By the 1840s North America, starting with New England and later with the manufacturing belt stretching from southern Ontario along the southern

shores of the Great Lakes to Milwaukee, became another large concentration of manufacturing, including light industry and shipbuilding on the East Coast and steel, agricultural implements, machine tools, rubber, and automobiles in the Midwest.

After 1868 Japan also industrialized, the only non-Western nation to do so. Industrialization spread to include Russia after Joseph Stalin (1879-1953) became dictator. He launched a succession of five-year plans in the Soviet Union, beginning in 1928.

In the 1960s newly industrializing countries (NICs) included South Korea, China, Mexico, and Brazil.

LOCATIONAL UNDERPINNINGS OF MANUFACTURING

Unlike agriculture, climate and soil type are irrelevant to the geography of manufacturing whereas location of raw materials, labor costs, transport costs, and markets are more significant. Traditional **location theory,** developed by German economist Alfred Weber, emphasized the transportation costs of inputs and outputs, which have declined steadily today as shipping, air, and trucking technologies have lowered transport costs. Perhaps most important to the location decisions of manufacturing and service firms is the need to **agglomerate**—or cluster together—a geographic phenomenon that offers advantages such as a common labor pool, shared **infrastructure**—the public works on which companies rely such as sewers, water, and schools as well as the transportation and communications network that allows goods, people, and information to flow across space—access to specialized information, and minimal transport costs of inputs and outputs.

Essential to economic activity, the infrastructure is invariably publicly constructed and operated, allowing costs to be socialized but benefits to remain privatized. The degree of dependence upon agglomeration varies considerably, however, among industries.

Typically, large, capital-intensive sectors—the steel industry, for example—tend to be more **vertically integrated,** that is produc-

tion processes are located within the confines of an individual corporation, rather than relying upon proximity to suppliers and clients. Smaller, more labor-intensive firms, such as garment producers, tend to require close ties functionally and spatially.

Labor costs are also important in understanding the geography of manufacturing, although this factor varies with the degree of labor- and capital-intensity of the production process. For labor-intensive firms such as the garment industry, the cost of labor is critical; for others, such as petroleum, where labor makes up 3 percent of total costs, it is unimportant. Labor as a factor of location also involves the skill levels, education, training, experience, and productivity of workers, which vary considerably among industries and locations. Firms do not inevitably seek out the cheapest sources of labor; they seek the most profitable ones, which may be better-paid but more skilled, productive workers.

The geography of labor markets is also highly variable with respect to the local supply of labor, which in turn reflects birthrates,

Many of the garments sold in the U.S. are manufactured overseas, in clothing factories such as this one in Kowloon, Hong Kong, where labor costs—40 to 50 percent of total costs—are far below those in the U.S.

The U.S. Garment and Textile Industry

The textile and garment industry of the U.S. has long revealed a changing set of locations. In the 19th century, textiles were centered in southern New England in cities such as Manchester, New Hampshire, and Lowell, Massachusetts, where they employed thousands of young Irish women immigrants and women from Quebec.

Garment production was concentrated in New York, particularly the Lower East Side of Manhattan, where it generated jobs for Jewish immigrants from Eastern Europe. In 1900 more than half of U.S. garment output originated there.

Between the 1920s and World War II, however, the textile industry relocated to the South, particularly North and South Carolina and Georgia, where labor was cheaper and not as likely to be unionized. Today, most U.S. textiles employment remains concentrated in those states, although foreign competition and technological displacement have steadily reduced its size.

Garment production, however, remains largely concentrated in urban areas, particularly in New York and Los Angeles, where large numbers of unskilled immigrant women, primarily from China and Latin America, work in sweatshops, under deplorable, often illegal, conditions.

Long New York's largest form of manufacturing employment, the garment industry has contracted steadily, and today the metropolitan region employs about 100,000 people in this sector.

Many large U.S. clothing retailers are linked to global supply chains in which they purchase garments produced in East Asia or Central America.

schools and training systems, housing costs, and propensities to migrate among regions. Regions with a high quality of life may attract large numbers of in-migrants, while those with steep housing prices may be constrained, especially for low-income workers. Labor skills are critical to productivity and play an enormous role in defining different occupations with very limited substitutability: Labor markets are often specific to individual types of jobs with unique constellations of skills.

INDUSTRY-SPECIFIC ANALYSES OF MANUFACTURING

The geography of manufacturing varies considerably among industrial sectors. The textile and garment sector, for example, illustrates how a competitive, labor-intensive sector relies upon a high degree of spatial mobility and the resulting fluid geographies of production. Textiles were the leading edge of the industrial revolution in Europe, the U.S., and Japan, and have continued to be so in industrializing nations of East Asia today. Because the total investment capital in this sector is relatively low, start-up costs are not formidable, entry and exit are rapid, and the industry's market structure is therefore competitive.

The historical geography of textile production has thus been typified by a constant search for low labor costs, often creating exceptionally exploitative working environments. In Europe, for example, textile factories developed first in England during the late 18th century, then spread throughout the continent.

In the U.S., the textile industry dominated southern New England throughout the 19th and early 20th centuries, with garment production clustered in New York. By the 1920s and 1930s, however, the industry left New England in favor of the South, particularly North and South Carolina. The industry also has a long presence in East Asia, beginning with Japan in the late 19th century and

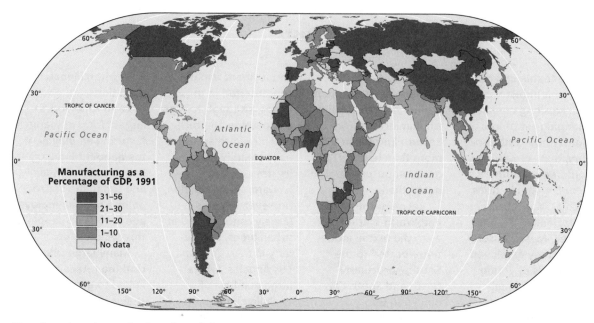

Manufacturing, the production of goods from raw materials, contributes significantly to the economy of the U.S. and other highly industrialized societies. Iron and steel, textiles, lumber, automobiles, electronics, and chemicals are some of the world's most significant manufacturing products.

continuing with garment production in Taiwan, Hong Kong, southern China, and more recently Indonesia. In Latin America, garments are produced in Mexico, Guatemala, and Honduras.

In contrast, the iron and steel industry is characterized by high degrees of capital intensity and low degrees of geographical mobility. Few industries are as critical to industrial society as this one, which has linkages to construction, agriculture, manufacturing, and transportation. With very high start-up costs, the industry has long been oligopolistic, as exemplified by the enormous U.S. Steel Corporation (now USX), which produced 60 percent of U.S. steel at the turn of the 20th century.

In the 1880s steel became the mainstay of the economies of the U.S. manufacturing belt, particularly Pittsburgh but also including southern Ontario, Buffalo, Cleveland, Youngstown, and Chicago, where producers obtained iron ore easily, transported cheaply by lake freighters from Minnesota and upper

Michigan across the Great Lakes, and coal by rail from Appalachia. In the South, only Birmingham was a significant steel producer, and it never rivaled the cities of the North.

During World War II, steel production emerged in California and Maryland in plants that were often publicly subsidized and located near coastal areas to facilitate receiving imported iron ore. By the 1970s in the wake of rising energy costs, old technology and equipment, higher labor costs, and rising imports from Japan and Europe, the U.S. steel industry began a dramatic contraction that devastated many manufacturing belt economies, part of the broader process of de-industrialization or loss of manufacturing jobs in the developed nations.

Japan is the largest producer of steel in the world, although other nations such as South Korea and Brazil have also become important producers. In the 1990s the U.S. steel industry experienced a moderate revival as technological changes such as **minimills**—small, highly automated plants—restored some degree of competitiveness by relying upon scrap metal inputs, the computerization of production, and specialized outputs.

The geography of the automobile industry is also significant. Invented in the 1890s by German and French engineers, the automobile in Europe was long produced primarily for the luxury market. Germany remains the largest European automobile producer, although other nations that make automobiles include Sweden, France, Britain, and Italy.

American automobile maker Henry Ford (1863-1947) perfected the production technique, which made automobiles more affordable for the mass market rather than luxury customers. He opened an auto factory in 1903 in Dearborn, Michigan, where he had access to a well-developed rail network and parts suppliers such as tire makers in Akron, Ohio. Ford's success was largely predicated upon a finely grained division of labor and standardized job tasks, or **Taylorism,** an idea developed by American efficiency manager Frederick W. Taylor (1856-1915). His method was so widely imitated that the particular form of production ultimately became known as **Fordism.**

Early automobile production was highly vertically integrated—Ford owned his own ships and rail lines—but it has become steadily more disintegrated over time. Today, automobile assemblers put together roughly 15,000 parts produced by separate firms in the textiles, metals, rubber, glass, chemicals, and electronics industries. And ancillary services such as engineering, finance, advertising, and legal became increasingly important to car manufacturing.

As the automobile gained popularity, particularly after World War I, it dramatically reshaped the social and spatial nature of American cities, including the waves of suburbanization that followed World War II, which was also encouraged by and facilitated by the federal interstate highway system. The industry also became steadily more oligopolized, until by the 1980s only three U.S. firms—General Motors, Ford, and Chrysler—remained, and Mercedes-Benz bought Chrysler in 1998.

American automobile firms, like steel corporations, were unprepared for the 1970s oil shocks, which provided an opportunity for foreign producers, notably those in Germany and Japan, to penetrate the U.S. market with smaller, more fuel-efficient cars.

Today, imports constitute roughly one-third of U.S. automobile purchases, although the globalization of the industry and location of foreign, particularly Japanese, assembly plants in the U.S. has made national origins notoriously difficult to ascertain.

The production and assembly of parts has spread to many nations, including assembly plants in Mexico, Spain, and Britain. Japan remains the largest automobile producer in the world (28 percent), and provided much of the capital and expertise for the growing

Henry Ford and Fordism

American automobile maker Henry Ford (1863–1947) developed a form of economic organization characterized by the vertically integrated production of homogeneous goods, automated assembly lines, mass markets, and large economies of scale. Adopted by many industries in the early and mid-20th century, Fordism was accompanied by political innovations such as the Keynsian welfare state and internationally by expanding trade and reduced protectionism. Today Fordist production systems have been largely displaced by systems that integrate computerized technology such as just-in-time delivery systems and niche marketing rather than homogeneous, mass-produced goods.

Car manufacturing technology has evolved from Ford's addition of the conveyor belt to assembly lines in 1913 to today's advanced electronic automation techniques that utilize sophisticated computers and robots.

productive capacity in South Korea and Southeast Asia.

The electronics sector is among the most important and rapidly growing industries in the world today. Unlike heavy industry such as steel or automobiles, transport costs are insignificant to electronics production, while labor skills, agglomerative economies, and military spending are critical. While some electronic technologies, such as the telegraph and telephone, date to the 19th century, the mass production of electronic goods can be traced to the development of the radio industry in the northeastern U.S. in the 1920s.

World War II delivered a major boost to electronics with the invention of radar, the computer, and the vacuum tube. In 1947 Americans William Shockley, John Bardeen, and Walter Brattain of Bell Laboratories invented the transistor, which ushered in a new round of innovations and led, in conjunction with the engineering school at Stanford University in Palo Alto, California, and substantial military expenditures, to the formation of the Silicon Valley complex south of San Francisco, the largest agglomeration of electronics production in the world. Other major U.S. centers include southern California, where the industry is heavily linked to the aerospace sector; what was Boston's Massachusetts Route 128 (now I-95); Austin, Texas, with Texas Instruments; Phoenix, Arizona, with Motorola; and North Carolina's Research Triangle of Raleigh, Durham, and Chapel Hill.

The semiconductor revolution of the 1970s and 1980s, which allowed for the digitization of information, revolutionized the electronics industry, dramatically lowering production costs, greatly enhancing computer speed and memory, and triggering numerous applications in other sectors. So great have been the uses of microelectronics in agriculture, manufacturing with the use of robotics and inventory control, airline and hotel reservations, medical care, finance, retail trade, and innumerable other sectors, that electronics has often been labeled *the* key industry of the late 20th century. As the industry steadily internationalized in its location and markets, low-wage, low-skilled assembly functions decentralized to selected developing nations, including Mexico but particularly South Korea and Malaysia, for example. Japan is the largest producer of electronics in the world, particularly in consumer goods, although China has acquired a growing capacity as well. The U.S. remains very competitive in this industry, however, as it dominates the high-end research part of the industry as well as software production, for example Microsoft near Seattle. (See Map: World Manufacturing, page 334.)

Tertiary Sector Activities

The tertiary economic sector is synonymous with services, which encompass a diversity of occupations and industries, ranging from professors to plumbers. Indeed, so great is the variation among firms and occupations within services that the term threatens to lose meaning in an economic context. **Post-industrial theory,** which attempted to chart the rise of a service-based economy, was widely influential in the 1970s and 1980s. It erroneously equated services with information-processing activities, including clerical activity, executive decision-making, telecommunications, and the media. Whereas many service jobs do involve the collection, processing, and transmission of information, clearly others do not: A trash collector, restaurant chef, security guard, and janitor all work in services, but the degree to which their activities center around information processing is minimal.

Services also include the transportation of goods and people. Despite the vast size of services (80 percent of the labor force in most industrialized nations), there has been a long-standing bias against the production of intangibles, which have been dismissed as "unproductive" since Scottish economist Adam Smith (1723-1790), who regarded them as "residual" activity compared to "real" economic activities such as agriculture and manufacturing. Even today, many economists and urban planners equate services with local consumption and minimize them as a viable source of regional development.

DEFINITIONS AND CONSIDERATIONS

Services involve the production of intangible outputs, and thus stand in contrast to manufacturing, the product of which can be "dropped on one's foot." What, for example, is the output of a lawyer? a teacher? a social worker? a doctor? It is impossible to measure these outputs accurately and quantitatively, yet they are real nonetheless. To complicate matters, many services generate tangible and intangible outputs. Consider a fast-food franchise: The output is assuredly tangible, yet it is considered a service; the same is true for a computer software firm, in which the output is stored on disks.

The fact that it is difficult to measure output in services has serious implications. For example, some critics of the service sector argue that the slowdown in U.S. productivity growth in the late 20th century reflected the growth of services. Yet if output in services cannot be adequately measured, how can one argue that output per employee in services is high or low, rising or falling? If wages reflect productivity levels, what is the relation between services output and incomes?

Services encompass so many different industries that it is misleading to speak of *the* service sector, as if the industries were all the same. However, a broad consensus exists as to the major components of services:

■ **Finance, insurance, and real estate,** including commercial, savings, and investment banking, insurance of all types, and commercial and residential real estate.

■ **Business services** subsume legal services, advertising, engineering and architecture, public relations, accounting, research and development, computer services, and consulting. Financial and business services are often labeled **producer services,** those that primarily sell their output to other firms rather than to households.

■ **Transportation and communications** include telecommunications, trucking, shipping, railroads, airlines, and local transportation such as taxis, and buses.

■ **Wholesale and retail** trade firms are the intermediaries between producers and consumers; closely affiliated are eating and drinking establishments, personal services such as beauticians, income tax consultants, veterinarians, and repair and maintenance services.

■ **Entertainment** related industries, including film, television and radio, publishing, and lodging, are also an important part of services, segments of this are part of tourism, the world's largest industry in employment terms.

■ **Government** at the national, state, and local levels includes state bureaucracies, the armed forces, and all those who provide public services.

■ **Nonprofit agencies** include charities, churches, museums, membership organizations, and private, nonprofit health care agencies.

Every definition of services is slippery, however. For example, does the term refer to a set of industries or occupations? Many workers in manufacturing are in fact service-sector workers, including administrative personnel in headquarters and clerical functions and research. Is the secretary who works for an automobile company part of manufacturing, while the secretary who works for a bank part of services?

The use of industrial versus occupational definitions is particularly critical given the growth of "nondirect" production workers within many manufacturing firms, that is, those not directly involved in the creation of goods such as clerical, administrative, research, advertising, and maintenance functions.

REASONS FOR THE GROWTH OF SERVICES

Services employment has increased steadily in developed countries throughout the 20th century despite low rates of population growth and significant manufacturing job losses. While services and manufacturing are intimately intertwined, services exhibit growth and locational dynamics somewhat different from those in manufacturing, although both constitute commodity production in varying forms. The reasons for the increase in services employment throughout the world may be:

First, rising per capita incomes, particularly in the industrialized world, have contributed markedly to rising services employment. The demand for many services is **income-elastic,** that is, increases in real (post-inflationary) personal income tend to generate proportionately larger increases in the demand for many kinds of services rather than a demand for manufactured goods.

Services with particularly high income-elasticities include entertainment, health care, and transportation. U.S. households, for example, spend slightly more on services (about 51 percent of disposable income) than they do on durable goods such as cars and refrigerators and nondurable goods such as food and clothing combined. An important reason contributing to this growth is the increasing value of time that accompanies rising incomes—especially with two income earners per family. As the value of time climbs relative to other commodities, consumers generally minimize the time needed to accomplish ordinary tasks. This phenomenon also explains the demand for washing machines, dishwashers, and automobiles, and it is especially important for the growth of personal and retail services, such as fast-food restaurants. Similarly, the growth of repair services reflects increasingly sophisticated technologies—automobiles or televisions, for example—and limited quantities of free time. Thus, the increasing value of time has led to more household functions being accomplished outside of the home: What was once taken care of at home is now a commodity to be purchased.

Second, rising levels of demand for health and educational services compose an important part of the broader growth of the service economy. The provision and consumption of health care has increased steadily, in large part because of the changing demographic composition of the populations of industrialized nations. The most rapidly growing age groups in the industrialized West today are the middle-aged and the elderly, precisely those demographic segments that require relatively high per capita levels of medical care. Consequently, medical services as a proportion of **gross national product (GNP),** the sum total of the value of goods and services produced by a nation-state in one year, have increased steadily throughout Europe, North America, and Japan, often leading to political conflicts about how to contain the associated costs. Medical services in the U.S. composed 13 percent of the GNP in 1998.

Similarly, a changing labor market and increasing demand for literacy, mathematical literacy, and computer skills at the workplace have driven the increasing demand for educational services at all levels, a process reflected in higher enrollments in universities, degrees from which have become prerequisites to obtain middle-class jobs. Thus, today almost 66 percent of secondary-school graduates in the U.S. start a college or university education, and the proportion of the labor force with a college degree has risen to almost 30 percent.

Third, the growth of services reflects the rising proportion of nondirect production workers, including firms in manufacturing. Most corporations devote considerable resources to dealing with highly segmented and rapidly changing markets and legal environments, including specialized clients, complex tax codes, environmental and labor restrictions, international competition, sophisticated financial systems, and real estate purchases. To do so, they require administrative bureaucracies to collect and process information and make strategic decisions: clerical workers process paperwork, sales people and researchers study market demand and create new products, and legions of advertisers, public relations experts,

accountants, lawyers, and financial experts assist in a complicated decision-making environment.

A fourth reason underpinning the growth of services is the increasing size and role of the public sector. Despite oft-repeated claims that capitalism is synonymous with the "free market," the state, in fact, is a major actor, subsidizing firms and framing the broader legal and institutional context of economic activity. Government contributes to the growth of services in two ways: In the United States, for example, public sector employment has increased steadily, especially since the New Deal of the 1930s, due to rising demands for the services that it provides, ranging from defense to local libraries. Today, the federal government is the largest single employer in the U.S., employing more than 2.5 million people, and federal employment is dwarfed by state, county, and municipal government employment, which totals more than 15 million. A second way in which government contributes to the growth of services is indirectly, through a labyrinth of laws, rules, restrictions, and regulations, contributing to the increase in specialists such as tax attorneys, accountants, consultants, and others who assist firms in negotiating with the legal environment.

A fifth reason for the growth of services is rising levels of service exports within and among nations. Many cities, regions, and nations derive a substantial portion of their aggregate revenues from the sale of services to clients located elsewhere in the same nation or overseas, as an example New York banks make loans to clients around the U.S. and abroad. Services are extensively traded on a global basis, composing roughly 20 percent of international trade. Internationally, the U.S. is a net exporter of services (but runs major trade deficits in manufactured goods), which is one reason services employment has expanded domestically; services compose roughly one-third of total U.S. export revenues. These sales overseas take many forms, including tourism, fees and royalties, sales of business services,

Central Place Theory

Central place theory is an interpretation of city-systems first articulated by German geographer Walter Christaller in 1933, which centers upon consumer demand, including the maximum distance consumers will travel for a given item and the minimum market size necessary to sustain distributors of different goods. A hierarchy of central places arises to distribute a hierarchy of goods from places with varying degrees of specialization. Influential in economic and urban geography, the central place theory that urban hinterlands should form nested hexagons has been supplanted by approaches more historically sensitive.

and repatriated profits from bank loans. Foreign service exports do not generate jobs and revenues in all places equally: Cities such as New York and London, for example, which are critical to global capital markets, have benefited the most.

LABOR MARKET AND GEOGRAPHIC STRUCTURE OF SERVICES

The emergence of services has changed labor markets in the Western world in several important respects. First, services tend to employ far larger numbers of women than did manufacturing, which was predominantly a male domain. The labor force participation rate of women has risen so that they compose 45 percent of the U.S. labor force.

Many women, however, work in low-paying occupations such as retail trade or daycare, leading to concerns of their concentration in pink-collar ghettos. Second, services tend to be less unionized than manufacturing; deindustrialization and rising services employment have lowered the share of the labor force in unions from 45 percent in 1948 to 14 percent in 1999. Some services, such as public employees, teachers, and medical workers, are partly unionized, but most are not. Third, services on the whole tend to pay less than manufacturing, leading to fears that the transition to a service-based economy may depress household incomes. On average, clerical jobs, for example, pay 60 percent of what manufacturing pays, and retail trade only 50 percent as much. Some

services, of course, consist of well-paying professional jobs, but the more rapid growth has been in part-time, low-skilled, and low-paying jobs.

The geography of services can be approached from several perspectives. Traditionally, the subject was analyzed through **central place theory,** created by German geographer Walter Christaller in the 1930s, which centered upon the spatial dynamics of retail consumption and the hierarchy of central places that distribute them to surrounding hinterlands.

Location of consumer services essentially is dictated by the location of their client base, typically segmented demographically by age, sex, ethnicity, and purchasing power. Thus, the suburbanization of consumer services—mainly through the shopping mall—has occurred in tandem with the movement of the middle class to the periphery of cities.

The geography of retail trade is a complex topic in its own right. It involves not only traditional marketing variables such as the size of the client base, purchasing power, and transportation networks, all of which change through time, but also the design, location, and symbolic meanings of shopping malls and strip-mall developments, which have come to dominate the American retail landscape. This geography is continually reworked by the development of franchises, the homogenization of consumer tastes, changing incomes and prices, demographic shifts, and advertising,

Two hundred miles of freeways reveal Houston's reliance upon the automobile for primary transportation. A major industrial, commercial, and financial hub, Houston is the center of the U.S. aerospace industry, the national petroleum industry, and one of the nation's busiest ports.

which plays a critical role in the social construction of demand.

The location of producer services is somewhat more complex than that of retailing. Overwhelmingly, the most important factor in this regard is the economies that firms enjoy when they agglomerate, largely to minimize transactions costs in the form of face-to-face meetings and access to specialized forms of information and ancillary services such as repair, consulting, and legal services.

The urban infrastructure may contribute to this tendency by providing ready access to fiber-optic lines or airports in large cities. For this reason, producer services tend to be concentrated in metropolitan areas, particularly the skyscrapers of a downtown, although the most rapid rates of growth have occurred on the urban periphery. The potential for telecommunications to affect this locational pattern is only partly understood. In general, high value-added service functions such as headquarters and administrative functions tend to cluster in metropolitan areas, whereas relatively low-wage, low value-added functions such as data

entry have largely dispersed to the urban periphery and beyond.

Financial services are a particularly important part of the national and global economic landscape. These include commercial, savings, and investment banks, and insurance companies of various types. They provide credit, allowing the costs of production and purchasing goods and services to be separated over space and time, and linking borrowers and savers with widely varying needs. The origins of the banking industry can be traced to Renaissance Italy, when goldsmiths and money changers stored precious metals for their clients and issued deposit certificates payable upon demand, then loaned some of those deposits to people who needed investment capital.

With the expanding world-system, merchant-bankers created innovations such as double-entry accounting, letters of credit, and deferred payment systems. In the 1970s American sociologist Immanuel Wallerstein first proposed the notion that a **world-system** was the only meaningful unit of social analysis in the global system of states and markets. Thus, individual places can only be meaningfully understood via their position within this worldwide system. The world-system of capitalism, which originated in the 15th and 16th centuries, differs from earlier world empires in that the world-system lacks a central coordinating authority such as a world state apparatus and is truly global in scope. (See also World-Systems Theory, page 366.)

Because banking is so critical to national economies, it is highly regulated throughout the world. Banks play important roles in determining national money supplies, which in turn heavily affect interest, inflation, and currency exchange rates. In the U.S., banking has been shaped by the Federal Reserve System, created in 1913, which forms the equivalent of a national bank.

During the 1970s and 1980s, several factors reshaped banking worldwide. These changes included the 1971 collapse of the Bretton Woods system, which had enabled the World Bank and International Monetary Fund to peg international currencies to the U.S. dollar—and the dollar, in turn, to gold, at $35 per ounce—since World War II, and the subsequent shift to floating exchange rates in 1973. Following the OPEC oil crisis of the 1970s, many oil-producing states, flush with excess funds, deposited them in western banks, which in turn loaned them to developing nations, laying the groundwork for the global debt crises.

American fiscal policy changed in the 1980s as enormous federal government budget deficits drove up interest rates, attracting foreign—largely Japanese—capital to the U.S. The deregulation of banking, initiated in the U.S. and imitated worldwide, removed restrictions on lending practices, facilitated the entrance of new sources of investment capital such as pension and mutual funds, encouraged competition between banking and other sectors such as retail trade—over credit cards, for example—and lured foreign firms to invest in stock markets.

Financial services were particularly affected by the new telecommunications technologies—especially fiber optics—that came into play in the 1980s. Because they are very information-intensive, financial services have been at the forefront of the construction of an extensive worldwide network of leased and private communication networks. Electronic funds transfer networks form the nervous system of the international economy, enabling banks to move capital around at a moment's notice, make money by playing on interest-rate differentials, take advantage of favorable exchange rates, and avoid political unrest.

With the breakdown of the Bretton Woods agreement and the shift to floating exchange rates, electronic trade in national currencies skyrocketed. Subject to digitization, information and capital became two sides of the same coin. This process was essential to the rapid internationalization of banking that has

Securities Markets

Securities markets, one of a series of financial markets and institutions involved in buying and selling equities (stocks and bonds), foreign currency exchange, and investment management (takeovers, buyouts, and mergers) in the U.S. are legally differentiated from banking by the Glass-Steagall Act of 1933, which prohibits commercial banks from trading stocks. Deregulation of finance, globalization of markets, and new telecommunication systems have restructured the industry—long dominated by London, New York, and Tokyo—including screen-based trading on the National Association of Securities Dealers Automated Quotation system (NASDAQ) stock market.

occurred since the 1970s. In the securities markets, telecommunications systems facilitated the linking of stock and bond dealers through computerized trading programs. The volume and volatility of these markets rose accordingly. Trade on the New York Stock Exchange, the world's largest, rose from 10 million shares per day in the 1960s to more than 1 billion per day in the 1990s, and brokers buy and sell to foreign clients with as much ease as they sell to clients next door.

The ascendancy of electronic money shifted the function of finance from investing to transacting, institutionalizing volatility in the process. Traveling at the speed of light, as nothing but assemblages of zeros and ones, global money performs an electronic dance around the world's neural networks in astonishing volumes. The world's currency markets, for example, trade roughly $800 billion every day, dwarfing the $25 billion that changes hands daily to cover global trade in goods and services. The boundaries of nation-states have little significance in this context: It is much easier, say, to move a billion dollars from London to New York than a truckload of oranges from Florida to Georgia.

These circumstances also favored the growth of **offshore banking,** financial activities in deregulated sites that seek to lure foreign accounts with liberal tax and regulatory legislation. Offshore banking has become important to many small countries including the Bahamas in the Caribbean, Luxembourg, San Marino, and Liechtenstein in Europe, Cyprus and Bahrain in the Middle East, and Vanuatu in the South Pacific. Thus, as the technological barriers to moving money around internationally have fallen, legal and regulatory ones have increased in importance, and financial firms have found the topography of regulation to be of the utmost significance in choosing locations.

Within the U.S., banking has exhibited a distinct and changing geography. With about 8,700 commercial banks, the American banking system is not spatially concentrated: Most

banks are small and serve local customers, although more than 50 percent of bank assets are owned by the largest 73 banks. Until the 1980s banking was strictly regulated by prohibitions against interstate banking, a measure designed to protect small banks from their large counterparts in the nation's banking capital, New York.

From World War II to the 1980s, the banking sector was stable, with few failures. The deregulation of banking included the gradual elimination of restrictions on interstate banking, resulting in a wave of mergers as successful banks enjoyed economies of scale. Charlotte, North Carolina, was a major beneficiary of this process, largely due to the business acumen of its financial community. With the commercial real estate boom of the 1980s, many banks heavily invested in urban hotels, offices, waterfront developments, and shopping centers. In the early 1990s, however, a glut of office space depressed commercial rents during an economic downturn; the rate of bank failures soared to the highest levels since the Great Depression. This trend was echoed in the savings and loan (S&L) sector, which was protected from mass bankruptcy by the federal government bailout. The majority of S&L failures—and bailout dollars—was concentrated in Texas and surrounding states, which had enjoyed rapid growth when the price of oil was high but suffered acutely from the collapse of oil prices in the 1980s.

TELECOMMUNICATIONS

As economic activities have expanded over ever larger distances, including the worldwide spaces of the global economy, the need and means to transmit information have grown accordingly. As a result, contemporary economic landscapes are closely tied to the deployment of telecommunications systems. Geography is the study of how societies are stretched over Earth's surface, and a vital part of that phenomenon is how people come to know and feel about space and time.

Although space and time appear as "natural"

and outside of society, they are in fact social constructions; every society develops different ways of dealing with and perceiving them. In this reading, time and space are socially created, plastic, mutable institutions that profoundly shape individual perceptions and social relations. For example, urbanites accustomed to the hustle and bustle of city life tend to view time and distance in markedly different terms from those who live in the relative quiet of rural areas.

Telecommunications have been critical to the ongoing reconfiguration of time and space for more than 150 years, accelerating the flow of information across distance and bringing places closer to one another in relative space through the process of time-space compression. **Time-space compression** is the notion that distance can be measured in terms of the time required to cross it via transportation and communications. Time-space compression signifies that space can be best understood using relative, not absolute, metrics that change over time and involve subjective, psychological interpretations. Steady improvements in the velocity of transportation and communications under capitalism have reduced the time required to interact among places, as well as the cost, leading to cost-space compression .

Telecommunications are not a new phenomenon. With the invention of the telegraph in 1837, the transmission of information over long distances was made possible, and communications became detached from transportation. For decades after the invention of the telephone in 1876, telecommunications was synonymous with simple telephone service. Just as the telegraph was instrumental to the

A Brief History of the Internet

The Internet can be traced to 1969, when the U.S. Department of Defense founded ARPANET (Advanced Research Projects Administration Net) at Menlo Park, California, a series of electronically connected computers with high-capacity transmission lines designed to withstand a nuclear onslaught.

The durability and high quality of much of today's network owes its existence to its military origins. In 1984, ARPANET was expanded and opened to the scientific community when it was taken over by the National Science Foundation.

The foundation incorporated ARPANET into its system, NSFNET, and other Internet backbones that linked supercomputers in New York, Washington, Chicago, Dallas, San Francisco, and Los Angeles.

Networking allowed previously independent personal computers, then rapidly declining in price, to be connected through modems and copper cable, and, later, fiber-optic lines of great capacity. Early uses of the Internet, such as e-mail, rapidly were complemented by graphical interfaces made possible by hyper text markup language (HTML), which allowed the creation of the World Wide Web in 1989.

When NSFNET was decommissioned in 1995 and the Internet was privatized, several telecommunications companies were providing backbone, including MCI and Sprint. The corporate presence has grown rapidly, with electronic advertising and shopping. In 1998 40 percent of U.S. households owned personal computers, although only 12 percent were connected to the Internet. The Internet grew rapidly on a global scale through the integration of existing telephone, fiber-optic and satellite systems, a task made possible by the technological innovation of packet switching, in which individual messages may be decomposed, the constituent parts transmitted by various technologies, and then reassembled, virtually instantaneously, at the destination.

Personal computers have proliferated, as have Internet hosts, which numbered 23.6 million in the U.S. in 1999. Here, at the Word Perfect Corporation in Provo, Utah, programmers work on a software application.

colonization of the American West, in the late 19th century the telephone was critical to the growth of the American city-system, enabling firms to centralize their headquarters functions while they spun-off branch plants to smaller towns. Even today, despite the proliferation of new technologies, the telephone remains by far the most commonly used form of telecommunications.

During the early and mid-20th century, the American Telegraph & Telephone Company (AT&T) enjoyed a monopoly over the U.S. telephone industry and had few incentives to change; the primary focus was upon guaranteeing universal access, resulting in a 95 percent penetration rate among U.S. households. In 1984 AT&T was broken up into one long-distance and several local-service providers, and new firms such as MCI and Sprint entered the field. Faced with mounting competition, telephone companies have steadily upgraded their copper cable systems to include fiber-optic lines, which allow large quantities of data to be transmitted rapidly, securely, and virtually error free.

With the digitization of information in the late 20th century, telecommunications steadily merged with computers to form integrated networks, most spectacularly through the Internet. Incontestably, the Internet is the largest electronic network on the planet, connecting an estimated 100 million people in more than 100 countries.

The Internet emerged upon a global scale via its integration with existing telephone, fiber optic and satellite systems. Popular access systems in the U.S. such as Compuserve and America On-Line allow any individual with a microcomputer and modem to plug into cyberspace, the world of electronic computerized spaces encompassed by the Internet and related technologies such as the World Wide Web. Cyberspace may exist in an office, a sailboat, or virtually anywhere.

As millions of new users log onto the Internet each year, cyberspace has expanded rapidly in size and in use and importance, including e-mail and electronic commerce. While popular mythology holds that cyberspace exists "everywhere," in fact access is uneven socially and geographically. Within the U.S., the heaviest users tend to be white, middle-class males. Inequalities in access to the Internet internationally reflect the long-standing bifurcation between developed and developing countries.

The notion that "telecommunications will render geography meaningless" is naive. This view holds that electronic communications are a viable substitute for virtually all activities, allowing everyone to work at home via telecommuting, dispersing economic functions, and spelling the obsolescence of cities.

This argument has fallen flat in the face of persistent growth of dense, urbanized places. In fact, telecommunications are generally a poor substitute for face-to-face meetings, the medium through which most corporate interaction occurs, particularly when the information involved is proprietary and unstandardized in nature. For this reason, a century of technological change, from the telephone to fiber optics, has left most high-wage, white collar, administrative command and control functions clustered in downtown areas, despite their high rents.

In contrast, telecommunications is ideally suited for the transmission of routinized, standardized forms of data, facilitating the dispersal of functions involved with their processing. Whereas the costs of communications have decreased, other factors have risen in importance, including local regulations, the cost and skills of the labor force, and infrastructural investments.

Economic space, in short, will not evaporate because of the telecommunications revolution.

Back offices, an example of dispersed function to low-wage regions, are the part of large service corporations that involve unskilled clerical functions, typically filled by women, such as data entry and processing of medical, insurance, or billing records.

Historically back offices were located next to headquarters activities in downtown areas to ensure close management supervision and rapid turnaround of information. Today back offices have become increasingly detached through the deployment of telecommunications systems and currently employ about 250,000 people in the U.S., frequently operating on a 24-hour basis.

In the 1980s and 1990s, many firms uncoupled their headquarters and back-office functions, moving the latter out of downtowns to cheaper locations on the urban periphery.

Recently, back offices have also begun to relocate on a much broader, continental scale, making them increasingly footloose. Many financial and insurance firms and airlines moved their back offices from New York, San Francisco, and Los Angeles to communities in the Midwest and South, which have lower wages and lower rents. Kansas City, and Omaha have been particularly significant beneficiaries of this trend.

Internationally, this trend has taken the form of the offshore office, which generates cost savings for U.S. firms by tapping labor pools in developing countries. Several New York-based life insurance companies, for example, relocated back office facilities to Ireland, shipping in documents by express mail services and exporting the digitized records back via satellite or one of the numerous fiber-optic lines that connect New York and London.

Likewise, the Caribbean, particularly English-speaking countries such as Jamaica and Barbados, has become an important locus for American back offices. Such trends indicate that telecommunications may accelerate exporting many low-wage, low value-added jobs from the U.S., with dire consequences for unskilled workers.

Specialization and Trade in the World Economy

Understanding economic geography necessitates an awareness of how regions and nations are sutured together into an integrated totality by flows of goods and services, corporations, and investments. Since the expansion of capitalism in the 16th and 17th centuries, the economic structure of local places has been increasingly tied to their role in the global economy; this trend is particularly true in the 20th century and will be even more relevant in the future.

Theoretical Concerns

A central theme in understanding where and why industries locate where they do is **comparative advantage,** which is the ability of a place to produce an output more cheaply, efficiently, or profitably than other places. The theory of comparative advantage, first articulated by English economist David Ricardo (1772–1823) explains the spatial division of labor and the specialization of places in the production of some types of goods and services and not others. When linked to trade, comparative advantage induces a specialization of production that rewards efficient producers and punishes inefficient ones. Early theories held it to be a natural aspect of places, whereas contemporary accounts stress its construction historically.

Comparative advantage is readily evident across the globe: Developing nations frequently produce and sell primary sector materials (foodstuffs and mineral ores) in return for manufactured goods; OPEC nations produce oil; South Africa exports gold and diamonds. Within the U.S., Appalachia has long been a coal producing region, the Southeast a producer of cotton and tobacco, the agricultural

Midwest is a world-renowned wheat, corn, and dairy producing region. Individual cities often specialize too. New York, for example, is the nation's leading producer of financial and producer services, and during the heyday of the manufacturing belt, Pittsburgh was the world's leading steel-making city; Akron, Ohio, the rubber-making capital of the world; and Memphis the leading cotton seed oil processing center.

The Ricardian theory of comparative advantage holds that specialization and trade allow resources—land and labor, for example—to be reallocated toward a region's or nation's most efficient or profitable uses. To realize comparative advantage, trade networks must thus be well developed. Specialization improves the efficiency of production, lowering costs to consumers and raising standards of living. Specialization may entail costs for inefficient regional producers who, facing decline at the hands of imports from other, more competitive regions, frequently call for protectionism.

Protectionism is government policy designed to protect domestic producers from foreign competition by limiting imports through tariffs, quotas, and nontariff barriers. Arguments for protectionism center around job protection in threatened industries, infant industries just initiating production, and national defense; critics, including most economists, argue that protectionism rewards inefficiency and removes incentives to become competitive internationally.

For this reason, economists typically favor unrestricted trade; tariffs and quotas are often seen as excuses to protect inefficiency. In turn, to realize a comparative advantage and become part of the global system, places must forfeit their economic independence and become reliant upon purchases of goods and services from other places. The original ideas of how comparative advantages might occur centered heavily upon the natural environment, although contemporary interpretations stress government policy, research and development efforts, human capital formation, and infrastructures. In short, comparative advantage is created, not simply found.

Comparative advantage leads naturally to the role of exports in regional and national growth. Exports in this context do not necessarily mean foreign sales of goods and services, although they might, but rather extra-local sales of locally produced outputs. Thus, states and cities in the U.S. "export" to one another all the time. Nor are exports synonymous with manufactured or agricultural goods. Cities frequently export services, including financial services, advertising, legal, and medical services, entertainment and tourism, or government services. Because they generate revenues, and thus sustain firms and generate jobs, exports are often taken to be the engine that drives local and national economic growth.

This conception is often approached through export base analysis, which links nonlocal exports to local economic structures. Regional economics can be divided into the basic sector, in which a region enjoys a comparative advantage, and the nonbasic sector (largely retailing), which caters to local demand and recycles revenues locally. Industries or firms that export most of their output from a region—called the **export base**—capitalize upon its comparative advantage and earn nonlocal revenues. The export base sector may include agriculture, manufacturing, and services and is linked to the rest of the regional economy through a series of interindustry backward linkages. Backward linkages involve purchases of inputs from other sectors, giving rise to **multiplier effects,** or total changes in revenues, output, and employment as the initial changes in the export-related sectors reverberate through interfirm linkages.

Linkages bind firms and industries together into integrated production complexes and play

a critical role in job generation. Firms purchasing large volumes and many types of goods and services locally have large multiplier effects.

Most employment in most regions is found in the nonbasic sectors, although from the viewpoint of export base theory, it is the export base that is most vital economically to the region. The role of the export base in generating regional growth depends largely on its relative size in the local economy, its organizational and technological structure, and the number and types of backward linkages to supplying firms, particularly the degree to which exporting firms purchase inputs locally rather than extralocally.

Small changes in the basic sector create larger changes in the surrounding economy by generating revenues and jobs in supplying firms that sell their output to companies within the export base. Conversely, firms that purchase goods or subcontract services from firms located extralocally will have correspondingly smaller multipliers. The size of multipliers reflects the relative importance of the export base, the technology of production—that is, capital- or labor-intensity—the spatial structure of backward linkages, and can be measured in terms of employment, revenues, and output and incomes.

Comparative advantages do not remain fixed in one place indefinitely. Regions may see their comparative advantages and export bases decline as other regions acquire them when capital flows across space. Some regions are abandoned and new ones created, typically through spatial differences in firm birth and death rates rather than corporate movements. For example, the decline of the textile industry in New England in the 1930s and 1940s was matched by its corresponding growth in parts of the South, particularly the Carolinas and Georgia. The rise of the East Asian newly industrializing entities such as Hong Kong and Singapore, as well as Mexico, coincided with the deindustrialization of much of the manufacturing belt in the U.S. In this way, the flow of capital across space reproduces uneven

Kondratieff Waves

Named for Russian economist Nikolai Kondratieff who first identified them in the 1920s, Kondratieff waves reflect the instability of capitalist economies over time. Rather than smooth, continuous changes in output, prices, and employment, capitalism is typified by business cycles, swings and oscillations of varying amplitudes and durations. Kondratieff identified long-term cycles in which commodity prices and output change in episodes lasting roughly 50 years.

He linked these to clusters of innovations and innovative industries. While there is disagreement as to the precise dates that demarcate these cycles, most social scientists agree that the history of capitalism has seen roughly four waves: The first cycle, approximately 1770 to 1820, was linked to the textile industry; the second—about 1820 to 1880—reflected the introduction of steam power to steamships and railroads; the third—about 1880 to 1930—in which electricity and the modern

steel industries were critical; and the fourth—about 1930 to the 1970s—in which the automobile, petrochemicals, and aerospace industries were significant. Many social scientists conclude that the 1970s marked the end of the Fordist Kondratieff wave and the beginning of a fifth, post-Fordist one in which electronics and producer services and telecommunications are highly important.

Geographically, Kondratieff waves help to explain changes in the comparative advantage

of individual places as their competitiveness rises or falls with the introduction of new products, industries, and production technologies. More recent interpretations of business cycles have added other, shorter term cycles to these long-term ones of roughly 15 to 20 years' duration, linked to aggregate patterns in the formation and depreciation of investment capital.

development, as some regions gain while others lose.

Temporal fluctuations in capitalist economies have been approached from many theoretical angles. Product-cycle interpretations, for example, hold that industries progress through stages from infancy to maturation, with different markets, production techniques, labor relations, and locations in each. The comparative advantage of regions in the early stages, when intensive research and skilled labor are critical, are quite different from those in the mature stages, in which unskilled, low-wage assembly jobs predominate.

The rise and fall of regional comparative advantages reflects cyclical oscillations in investment, output, prices, and employment found in various types of business cycles, most

famously the long Kondratieff waves of roughly 50 years' duration that have largely characterized the historical geography of capitalism.

Kondratieff waves, named for Soviet economist Nikolai Kondratieff, who first identified them in the 1920s, refer to long-term—about 50 years—periodicities in capitalist production, including changes in innovations, output, prices, and employment, linked to the emergence of critical new industries.

Several Kondratieff waves have been identified since the industrial revolution began in the mid-18th century and have been linked—in order—to the textile industry, steam power and railroads, electricity and steel, and computers.

One of the more intriguing theoretical issues in economic geography today is the interrelationship between changing cycles of capital investment and the construction of regional landscapes. A metaphor to illustrate this process is the palimpsest, the parchment upon which Romans repeatedly inscribed, erased, and inscribed messages anew.

In analogous fashion, regional landscapes may be thought of as consisting of numerous layers of investment, each corresponding to a different regional comparative advantage with its associated export base, labor markets, infrastructure, and landscape, that become "sedimented" over time much as geological strata are deposited successively one atop the other. For example, New England's textile industry was followed by the rise in the electronics industry, which nestled within the vestiges of textile production, sometimes literally in old factories such as those in Lowell, Massachusetts, creating a landscape that reflects the superimposition of one on top of the other.

In this way, each phase in a region's historical trajectory leaves a distinct imprint intertwined with the legacies of previous phases of accumulation and lays the groundwork for future rounds. In such a conception, the broad contours of capitalist development—the uneven spatial division of labor—are thoroughly intertwined with the local specificity of different places.

As specialization became more pronounced and as transport costs and protectionist barriers have declined throughout the 20th century, world trade has increased in magnitude and importance. Since World War II, world trade has grown more rapidly than total world output, reflecting the increased integration of national economies. Today, roughly 25 percent of the world's total output is traded among nation-states. Foreign trade is equivalent to roughly 24 percent of the U.S. economy, including exports (11 percent) and imports (13 percent), a difference manifested in the nation's persistent, large trade deficits in recent decades—often more than 100 billion dollars annually.

The largest bilateral trading partners for the U.S. are Canada, Japan, Mexico, China, Britain, and Germany.

The majority of international trade is among industrialized countries, particularly the three major centers of Europe, North America, and Japan, all of which have the requisite purchasing power and productive capacities. Fluctuations in the volume and type of trade reflect many variables, including the global supply, demand, and prices of goods, the locations of production, currency exchange rates, levels of protectionism, and transport costs, all of which change regularly.

The Multinational Corporation

Increasing global economic integration since World War II has largely been accomplished through a handful of large firms that conduct business in more than one nation, that is, multinational corporations (MNCs), also called transnational corporations. **Multinational corporations** are large firms with operations in more than one nation-state. Despite the stereotype of MNCs as inevitably global in scope, most operate within a handful of countries. Most originate in the industrialized nations—the U.S., Japan, Britain, France, and Germany—and concentrate their investments in other industrialized nations, generating foreign direct investment, with mixed costs and benefits to the host nation. **Foreign direct investments (FDI)** are tangible investments in productive capacity, such as buildings and equipment owned by firms from one nation but located in another. Most FDI originates from industrialized nations and is located in other industrialized countries.

MNCs dominate global trade, finance and investment, research and development, technology transfer, and the commodity chains that permeate the world economy. In this capacity, they are the most important force in the acceleration of globalization, although the extent of their reach varies widely around the world.

MNCs are, by definition, not bound to a

particular country, although all are headquartered in individual nations. In the 1990s, total MNC employment worldwide was estimated to be roughly 65 million, of which 43 million, or 66 percent, was located in developed nations. Many MNCs have a gross output larger than that of small nations.

MNCs vary widely in their organizational structure, managerial behavior, and strategic orientation. Mining and manufacturing dominated MNC activity in the decades after World War II. More recently investment in services and real estate has increased most rapidly, as banks, insurance, advertising, law, credit card, and hotel companies steadily globalize.

Such firms invest overseas for reasons that center around maximizing profit, including the quest for low-cost labor, resources, and markets. Frequently, they enter into joint ventures and strategic alliances with one another or with local firms. MNCs usually have operations in relatively few nations, generally no more than two or three; only a few of the largest MNCs are truly global in scope.

Foreign direct investment by MNCs may take the form of direct investments, affiliates and subsidiaries, or acquisitions of existing firms and facilities. Since World War II, FDI has increased significantly. As with trade, most MNC investment globally is made by developed nations and is located in other developed nations in Europe, Asia (Japan), and North America.

American firms lead the world in FDI, although their share of the world total has gradually declined. Roughly 50 percent of FDI by U.S. firms is located in Europe, 20 percent is in Canada, and only 3 percent is in Japan, although the most rapid rate of growth is in East Asia, which, since the shift to export-promotion in the 1960s, has eagerly courted foreign capital.

Conversely, many foreign firms invest in the U.S., including Japanese, British, Dutch, Canadian, and German companies, to gain access to the large American market and to escape possible protectionist measures and exchange rate fluctuations. In 1996 total FDI in the U.S.

amounted to roughly $500 billion, primarily in manufacturing.

In developing nations, MNCs are major sources of investment capital and the primary drivers behind the industrialization of selected countries, most notably the East Asian newly industrializing countries (NICs) and Mexico. One major difference between the industrialization of the developed and underdeveloped nations is the domination of foreign capital in the latter.

The relative benefits and costs of MNC presence have been widely debated. Proponents and opponents have seen them as a force to expand or exploit local and national economies. The benefits include enhanced pools of investment capital, often in short supply in developing countries; greater employment opportunities, including job training and human capital formation (skills and experience); technical and managerial expertise; access to more productive machinery and equipment, technology transfer (FDI being the primary means in the world today); superior distribution, marketing, maintenance, and sales networks; and improved balance of payments as exports increase in volume and value.

Disadvantages include potential disruptions of local producers and subsequent distortions of local, indigenous economic relations; the not inconsiderable incentives that most nations offer to attract foreign capital; and, given the long history of involvement by MNCs in foreign political affairs, possible decline in national sovereignty.

For small, relatively weak nations, large foreign corporations can be intimidating. Often, linkages with local producers, such as subcontracting, are minimal, resulting in small multiplier effects. In the eyes of dependency theorists , capital-intensive MNCs generate relatively few jobs and tend to fill skilled managerial positions with personnel from the home country. The jobs created may not exceed the jobs displaced by foreign competition. (See Dependency Theory, page 360.)

If MNCs remit the bulk of their profits to their home base, the host nation stands to gain little from the reverse flow of capital. Many developing countries therefore regulate MNC activity and require profits to be reinvested locally. Because the net benefits of MNC presence are often unclear, there is frequently tension between an MNC's drive to maximize profits and the host country's needs for national economic development and integration. The impacts are both a product of the nature of the particular MNC in question and that of the host country in which it invests, as well as the bargaining and negotiating skills of both parties.

Regional Trade Blocs

Because there is widespread recognition that protectionist barriers to trade are detrimental to national economies, most governments have reduced tariffs and quotas on imports. Many countries, for example, have simple, bilateral agreements with trading partners in which trade barriers are minimized or eradicated on a product-by-product basis.

Since World War II, the primary vehicle for serving this purpose on a global basis has been the **General Agreement on Trade and Tariffs (GATT),** which, through a series of negotiations, systematically lowered tariff rates worldwide, contributing to the post-World War II global economic boom. GATT members originally were almost exclusively developed nations, but expanded to include the developing world; today, most countries in the world are members.

In 1995 the GATT metamorphosed into the **World Trade Organization (WTO),** a permanent rather than ad hoc organization in Geneva that also regulates trade disputes. The WTO regulates trade in services, but has yet to include important nontariff barriers, such as export restraints, inspection requirements, health and safety standards, and import licensing, which inhibit imports.

In addition to these broad global agreements, many nations have joined **regional trading blocs,** associations of countries designed to reduce protectionism and enhance economic intercourse among member states. Nation-states hope that such blocs will enhance their competitiveness internationally, lower the costs of imports, and lead to gains in national income and purchasing power.

The most well developed regional trading bloc is the European Union (EU) headquartered in Brussels. Founded in 1957 by six members (Italy, France, West Germany, Belgium, the Netherlands, and Luxembourg), the European Economic Community (EEC), as it was originally known, expanded to include most of Western Europe.

The EEC became an important factor in the continent's attempts to recover from the 1970s petroshocks and slow economic growth, particularly in the face of intense Japanese and U.S. competition.

In 1992 the EEC launched an ambitious plan that extended far beyond simple annihilation of trade barriers among its members to include free movement of factor inputs, which include capital and labor, land, raw materials, and energy: Corporations from member states may invest anywhere within the EEC without restriction, and workers may seek employment without restraint.

In addition, the EEC, which became the European Union in 1995, harmonized many production and trade regulations and has moved steadily, if unevenly, toward a common currency, the euro, launched in early 1999, effectively binding diverse countries into a single economy.

With 400 million people, the EU is the largest single market in the world. The long run consequences are likely to be accelerated growth rates as specialization intensifies and firms achieve economies of scale. Within Europe, the Mediterranean states may benefit more than their northern counterparts as labor moves north and capital flows south. Whether this trade regime will succeed in ironing out the uneven development long persistent within Europe is unclear.

Maquiladoras

In the 1980s, given the global glut of petroleum, the industry upon which Mexico had staked its economic future in the 1970s, that nation undertook a systematic expansion in the diversity of its economy.

During this period, many countries opened varying forms of export-processing platforms—small, tax-free, often subsidized centers designed to attract foreign capital, stimulate jobs, and increase foreign revenues. These broadly corresponded to the shift from import-substitution to export-promotion globally. A *maquiladora* is a branch plant (mostly U.S. or Japanese) corporation in northern Mexico, which assembles goods or electronics components and relies on local women as the workforce. In northern Mexico maquiladoras were fueled in large part by American corporations seeking low-wage labor.

Many U.S. firms paired their operations in Mexico with cities along the U.S.–Mexican border in California and Texas.

With the low price of petroleum in the 1990s, the maquiladoras have become the largest source of foreign revenues for Mexico. Despite occasionally deplorable standards of living, the region, long one of the poorer parts of Mexico, has gained in income, and the northern states have become the wealthiest part of the country.

Mexico's entrance into NAFTA with the U.S. and Canada in 1994 will have uncertain effects, because flows of capital (but not labor or goods) were already relatively unrestricted.

Over the long run more rapid rates of growth on both sides of the border are possible.

Compared to the EU, the North American Free Trade Agreement (NAFTA) is considerably more modest. NAFTA's origins lay in the 1988 U.S.-Canada Free Trade Agreement, which gradually eliminated trade restrictions between the world's two largest trading partners.

In 1994 NAFTA was expanded to include Mexico, the first time a developing nation was included in the same trade bloc as developed ones. However, whereas the EU allows free movements of labor, NAFTA does not, largely due to U.S. fears of unrestricted flows of Mexican labor northward.

As critics of NAFTA have emphasized, freedom of capital movements, however, are guaranteed, accelerating the growth of the *maquiladora* assembly plants located in northern Mexico that utilize Mexico's cheap labor. Maquiladoras are branch plants of foreign (mostly U.S. or Japanese) corporations located in northern Mexico. They are typically automobile or electronics assembly plants employing young women laborers. The possibility exists that NAFTA may be extended into other parts of Latin America, perhaps creating a free trade zone extending from Alaska to Tierra del Fuego.

Several other trade blocs are found across the world. The Association of Southeast Asian Nations (ASEAN) is composed of most of the countries of one of the world's most rapidly growing areas. In Latin America, the Andean Common Market was envisioned as a means of enhancing investment and growth.

In West Africa, the French-speaking nations formed the *Union Douaniere et Economique de l'Afrique Centrale,* the UDEAC (Central African Customs and Economic Union) with a central bank, and in southern Africa, the Southern Africa Development Coordination Conference (SADCC) seeks to integrate several national economies.

Developing Nations' Economic Problems

A considerable part of economic geography is concerned with the origins and nature of poverty in developing countries and the possibilities of its alleviation through economic development. The division of Earth into a relatively small group of wealthy countries comprising one-quarter of the world's population and a large number of relatively poor countries is perhaps the defining characteristic of the world's economic geography today. This section explores this important issue by reviewing colonialism and neocolonialism, examining the differences between developed and undeveloped nations, summarizing the major economic problems confronting developing countries, and reviewing three major ways in which these issues have been analyzed conceptually.

Colonialism

The emergence of capitalism worldwide occurred through the growth of the large European colonial empires that reproduced uneven development on a planetary scale. **Colonialism** is the economic and political system by which some nations dominate others. Although colonialism is not an exclusively European phenomenon—for example, the Japanese colonialism in Korea and Taiwan—it was typified by Europe's conquest of the Americas, Africa, and Asia and the subsequent formation of a world economy that disproportionately benefited Europe.

In 1500, Europeans politically and economically dominated 9 percent of the world's land surface; by 1914 they dominated 85 percent, including the Americas, Africa, the Arab world, Asia, Australia, and the Pacific. Only Japan escaped completely and managed, not coinci-

dentally, to become the only non-European nation to rival the West on its own terms.

Colonialism was resisted everywhere by non-Europeans, including Inca revolts against the Spanish following Francisco Pizarro's conquest between 1532 and 1536, Zulu attacks on the Boers in South Africa in the late 19th century, the Indian Sepoy Mutiny against the British in 1857-59, China's Boxer Rebellion, and various nationalist movements in the 20th century.

The incentives for Europeans to colonize were the resources, including labor, the colonies offered, as well as the markets they provided, which were essential to expanding capitalist enterprises. These economic considerations were overlain with other motivations, such as religious conversions. The means by which Europe accomplished this feat are not well understood, but include technological superiority—better ships, guns, horses, and after the industrial revolution, inanimate energy sources—and the inadvertent introduction of diseases—particularly in the Americas, where 98 percent of the native population succumbed to smallpox and measles within a century of the Columbian encounter.

Two major waves of colonialism may be identified, which correspond to Europe's expansion before and during the industrial revolution. The size of these empires varied considerably among the colonizers as well as over time. (see Map: European Empires, page 356.)

The Spanish and Portuguese established the first great empires. Spain conquered much of what is now the southwestern U.S. and Florida, as well as Guam, the Philippines, Cuba, Puerto Rico, Mexico, and Central America, and the western parts of South America. Portugal took what are now Brazil, Guinea-Bissau, Angola, Mozambique, Goa, Timor, and

Macau. The Spanish empire provided vast quantities of silver and gold for its rulers; the empire largely disintegrated after the Napoleonic invasion in the early 19th century and ended altogether with the Spanish-American War of 1898.

France also conquered vast domains in Quebec, West and Central Africa, Madagascar, Indochina, some islands in the Caribbean, as well as portions of the Arab world, including what are now Syria, Lebanon, and Algeria, during the protracted collapse of the Ottoman Empire in the decades prior to World War I. France's empire effectively ended with their defeat in Vietnam in 1954 and the independence of Algeria in 1962.

In the 18th century the British claimed that "the sun never sets on the British Empire," which stretched over one-quarter of Earth, including, at various times, most of North America, parts of the Caribbean, Guyana, large parts of Africa (Ghana, Sierra Leone, Nigeria, Kenya, Sudan, Rhodesia, Southern Africa), portions of the Arab world (Egypt, Iraq, Palestine, the Persian Gulf, Yemen), southern Asia (Afghanistan to what is now Bangladesh), Burma (now Myanmar), Malaya, Hong Kong, Australia, New Zealand, and many islands of the Pacific.

The Dutch were successful in New Amsterdam (later New York), Suriname and Curaçao, South Africa, and above all, Indonesia. The Belgians were confined to the Congo. Germany's short-lived excursions overseas saw it take what are now Togo, Rwanda and Burundi, Namibia, and portions of Tanzania and New Guinea, only to lose it all after World War I. Finally, Italy made brief conquests in Libya, Somalia, and Ethiopia.

Although the broad contours were similar, colonialism took different forms in different regions. In the Americas, disease (particularly smallpox and measles) and genocide effectively depopulated two continents, resulting in the deaths of 50 to 80 million Native Americans. From Africa, the slave trade brutally shipped 15 million people to the labor-short New

World, particularly to South America and the Caribbean.

Africa's colonial boundaries, drawn during the Berlin Conference of 1884, collapsed roughly a thousand tribes into 50 states. In Africa, states (for they are not true nation-states) generally consist of disparate ethnic, linguistic, or religious groups lumped together with little obvious rationale, a factor that has greatly aggravated contemporary civil wars and secessionist movements (see Map: Stateless Nations, page 403).

India, a vast British colony that stretched from Afghanistan to Burma), provided resources and a market for textiles. The Arab world, long dominated by the Ottomans, saw the British and French enter relatively late, after World War I, and became a source of cotton (in Egypt) and petroleum.

China was never formally colonized, except for a string of treaty ports along the coasts following the Opium Wars of the mid-19th century, but was effectively controlled by the West through the weak Manchu dynasty, which collapsed in the revolution of 1911–12.

Australia was originally a British penal colony, with colonization beginning in 1788. Colonial policies toward native rights, land ownership, infrastructural development, and military rule varied among the powers and colonies as well as over time.

Colonialism had profound economic, political, and social effects. In large part, production systems in colonies became centered exclusively around exports of primary sector goods, particularly minerals and foodstuffs.

The plantation system—including cotton and tobacco in North America, sugar and coffee in Latin America, cotton in Egypt, peanuts, tea, and cocoa in Africa, tea in India and Ceylon (now Sri Lanka), and rubber and coffee in Southeast Asia—saw **cash crops,** crops grown for sale for profit, displace subsistence agriculture in many regions. Silver mines in Mexico and Bolivia, copper in Chile and southern Africa, gold and diamonds in South Africa, and tin in Borneo exemplified a different form

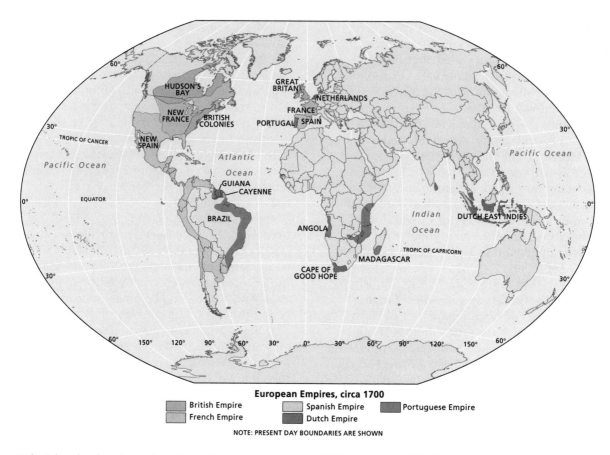

European Empires, circa 1700

- British Empire
- French Empire
- Spanish Empire
- Dutch Empire
- Portuguese Empire

NOTE: PRESENT DAY BOUNDARIES ARE SHOWN

Colonialism has long been the subject of intense controversy. While European civilization may have brought certain economic, technical, and educational benefits, entire societies were disrupted and cultures destroyed.

of resource extraction. Even Canada was colonized primarily around exports of lumber, fish, furs, and wheat. This restructuring has had long-term consequences for many developing countries that find their exports confined to relatively cheap commodities that generate few foreign revenues, resulting in poor terms of trade.

Politically, colonialism accentuated the power of small groups of local people who prospered by cooperating with the colonizers. The assistance of this elite in governance, taxation, military rule, and administration was essential. Frequently, colonizers employed a particular ethnic minority, such as the Alawites in Syria or Tutsi in Rwanda, to help in ruling their own people. For the bulk of the population living in rural areas, colonialism offered few benefits and generated unequal patterns of land ownership, taxation, job opportunities, and the disruption of indigenous agricultural systems.

Colonialism's social polarization was mirrored in its bifurcated geographies. Port cities, for example, became the primary centers of economic activity, including Buenos Aires, Lima, Lagos, Cape Town, Calcutta, Rangoon, Singapore, Jakarta, Saigon, and Hong Kong, often displacing indigenous landlocked capitals (such as Cuzco, Timbuktu, Mandalay, Delhi,

The Berlin Conference, 1884: Europe's Division of Africa

In 1884 the European powers, then busily colonizing Africa, met in Berlin to draw the boundaries of their possessions in an attempt to minimize rancor among them.

The Berlin Conference essentially established the boundaries of the current states of Africa, which were created with no consideration to the inhabitants of the places they demarcated.

Thus, Great Britain claimed West African colonies such as Ghana and Nigeria, East African ones such as Kenya, and in Southern Africa, Botswana and South Africa.

The French took a large swath of the states in West Africa stretching from Mauritania to Chad, as well as Central African regions such as Gabon and Brazzaville (Republic of Congo).

Belgium took over almost all of the Congo River Basin, which became the private reserve of King Leopold II (1835–1909), under whose rule more than half the people died.

Portugal retained its long-standing colonies in Guinea-Bissau, Angola, and Mozambique, leaving in 1975.

Italy, having invaded Ethiopia and Eritrea, briefly claimed Libya and part of Somalia.

Finally, Germany, a late colonial power, took control of Togo, Namibia,German West Africa, Rwanda, Tanzania, and a section of Mozambique, losing these as a result of its defeat during World War I.

The impacts of these borders long after the colonies became independent is difficult to exaggerate. Most African states are collections of varying cultures, with radically different languages, religions, and economic practices. Civil war, tribal conflict, and secessionism have wracked the continent.

For example, in the 1960s, the Igbo people of Nigeria, which has more than a hundred tribes, attempted to form the state of Biafra; a government-imposed ban on food imports left a million dead of starvation. The Sudan has been caught in a murderous civil war between the Arab north and Christian and animist south that has killed another million. Hutu and Tutsi in Rwanda and Burundi, lumped together in the same states, have repeatedly engaged in genocide. Congo consists of more than 200 tribal groups, and has degenerated into civil war and anarchy.

Such conflicts not only brought death and misery to tens of millions of people but also deterred foreign and domestic investment and economic progress.

The poverty of Africa is thus in part political in root, a reflection of the particular way in which its landscapes were divided administratively in the late 19th century.

and Jogjakarta). Railroads from these port centers offered access to the wealth of the interiors, allowing minerals and plantation products to be exported easily. As a result, rural-to-urban migration in colonized regions increased dramatically. These economic, political, and geographic predicaments were compounded by cultural forms of colonialism, including missionaries spreading Christianity, Western school systems, and lifestyles centered around commodity consumption.

Europe's colonial empires effectively came to an end in the aftermath of World War II, when many nationalist and independence movements succeeded in establishing nominally independent states.

Japanese conquests in Asia shattered the myth of European invincibility there. Often led by Western-educated intellectuals such as Ho Chi Minh (1890-1969) in Vietnam and Kwame Nkrumah (1909-72) in Ghana, these movements were frequently violent, although Mahatma Gandhi's program in India was a notable exception.

The rivalry between the U.S. and U.S.S.R. during the **Cold War,** the era following the end of World War II in 1945 to the 1991 collapse of the Soviet Union, created numerous openings as both superpowers sought to portray themselves as allies of nationalists in developing countries. From the 1940s through the 1980s the process of decolonization witnessed the emergence of dozens of independent states around the world, which today number nearly 200. (See Map: Dates of Independence, page 393.)

However, the formal end of colonial political rule did not automatically translate into de facto economic independence. Despite the rhetoric of independence, most colonies had little preparation, scarce investment capital (mostly owned by multinational corporations), no management experience, inadequate infrastructures, poor education systems, and could offer only cheap labor and raw materials. Competitively, then, most newly independent countries were disadvantaged in the world market from the outset. These economic problems were compounded by political instability, including unrest and civil wars, which complicates attempts to attract capital. Thus, formal colonialism is replaced by neocolonialism, that is independence in substance if not in form. Although the U.S. is not usually labeled a formal colonial power in the same sense as European powers were, the hegemony of American MNCs after World War II has made neocolonialism largely, but not exclusively, an American phenomenon.

North and South

The long-term consequences of colonialism are difficult to overemphasize in their significance for the contemporary world economy. In the bluntest terms, colonialism was the primary vehicle through which the so-called Third World was constructed historically. Thus, the bifurcation between the **First World** (Europe, Japan, North America, and Australia/New Zealand) and the **Third World** (Asia, Africa, and Latin America) corresponds closely to the developed former colonial powers and their underdeveloped former colonies.

The **Second World** originally referred to the Soviet Union and nations of the former Soviet bloc—the U.S.S.R., eastern Europe, Mongolia, and Cuba—a nomenclature that reflected Cold War geopolitics. With the disintegration of the U.S.S.R. in 1991, this term has fallen into disuse. Russia and some republics of the former U.S.S.R. (Belarus, Estonia, Latvia, and Lithuania) may be nominally classified as First World, although the collapse of the Russian economy, with a GNP roughly equal that of Belgium, makes this categorization suspect; other republics, such as Kazakhstan and Uzbekistan, are more appropriately considered part of the Third World. The First–Third World division, the most significant one of the world economy, must be seen as a product of the world-system, not a natural grouping of countries.

An alternative, widely used way to describe the schism between the world's have and have nots is that between the global North and South. **North,** in the context of the global North-South divide, is the economically developed nations (or First World) of Europe, Japan, and North America, including roughly one-quarter of the world's population. While countries of the North largely lie to the north of most of the developing world, they also include Australia and New Zealand, which lie in the Southern Hemisphere. **South,** in terms of the global North-South distinction, is essentially the Third World nations of Latin America, Africa, and Asia (except Japan), and includes roughly three-quarters of the world's population, most of which lie in the Northern Hemisphere but to the south of the more economically developed regions of Europe, North America, and Japan.

Such broad terms as First or Third World, or North and South, conceal as much as they reveal. The Third World, for example, consists of an enormously diverse collection of states

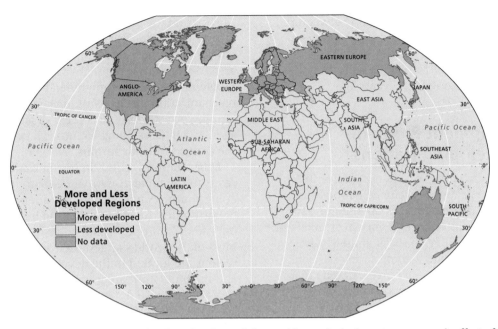

The geography of the more and less developed regions of the world reveals the long-term economic effect of European empires on subordinate colonies.

and societies in terms of their cultural heritage, languages and religions, ethnic and racial compositions, colonial experience, positions in the global economy, and standards of living. Some feel this heterogeneity is so great as to render the term virtually useless.

Economically, the Third World includes countries as desperately poor as Mali and as relatively prosperous as South Korea. Singapore has a higher standard of living than most of Europe, yet is often included in the Third World. Such discrepancies reflect the fact that, ultimately, all geographic labels are biased and somewhat arbitrary.

Whatever terminology one uses, and however one measures it, the division between the world's developed and developing nations is real. Using the flawed labels described above, about 20 percent of the world's 6 billion people live in the developed world and 80 percent live in the developing nations; in terms of global output of goods and services, however, 86 percent of the output is generated and consumed by developed nations and only 14 percent by the poorer nations of the South.

The poorest 20 percent of the planet consumes just 1.3 percent, while the richest 20 percent consumes 45 percent of all meat and fish, 58 percent of all energy, 84 percent of all paper, 74 percent of all telephones, and owns 87 percent of all automobiles. The most common measure of variations in income is per capita gross national product (GNP), which varies widely across the surface of Earth, ranging in 1996 from Norway's $34,910 (the U.S. stands at $28,495) to a low of $80 in Mozambique, a reflection not just of extreme poverty but also of largely unmeasured subsistence production.

Other indexes yield a similar geography, including key measures such as per capita energy consumption, life expectancy, infant mortality rates, and literacy levels, all of which mirror the enormous discrepancies between the global core of wealthy, industrialized countries and the world periphery of poor former colonies. Further, the gap between the world's richest and poorest people has been steadily widening for years; for example, in Africa, the average household consumes 20 percent less than it did 25 years ago.

Development Problems in Developing Nations

The majority of the world's people live in developing or underdeveloped nations, and most of them are poor. Although definitions and perceptions of poverty vary over time and are specific to different social and historical contexts, developing nations face a series of interlinked problems and predicaments that severely hamper their opportunities for economic progress and the improvement in the life chances for billions of people. This section details the major predicaments that confront developing societies, although the severity and prevalence of these problems vary widely across the world, and some of them may also be found within portions of the developed world, such as the inner cities of the U.S.

Unequal land distribution is a major political and economic issue in societies in which the bulk of the population lives in rural areas and in which land is the major source of wealth and income. Often, a small, wealthy oligarchy may own the bulk of arable land, as in Latin America, where the legacy of the colonial Spanish land grant system is still evident.

Much of this land is used to produce crops for export on the international market, leaving large numbers of the rural poor landless, able only to sell their labor at below-subsistence wages. Struggles and conflicts over land tenure are a major cause of social disruption. Conflicts over demands for land reform may cause social disruption and accelerate rural-to-urban migration.

Many nations that have achieved some degree of economic progress did so by first breaking up large land holdings, such as in

Mexico and the newly industrializing countries in East Asia. Rapid rates of population growth, which are more typical in rural than urban areas, add to the demand for farmland. This problem is further compounded by agricultural mechanization: In the West, mechanization of farming occurred in the context of labor shortages, and in developing countries it occurs in the context of labor surplus.

Urbanization without industrialization refers to the rapid growth of cities in the developing countries but without the attendant job opportunities that emerged in the industrializing cities of Europe, Japan, and North America. Most of the world's largest metropolitan regions are located in the developing world, and the bulk of urban growth in the 21st century will be located there as well.(See Table: World's Largest Metropolitan Areas, page 381.)The growth of these metropolitan areas is propelled largely by rural-to-urban migration, itself a reflection of problems in rural areas, rather than high natural growth. Within these cities, elevated rates of unemployment, underemployment, and poverty are common.

Frequently, urban economies of developing nations are divided into a relatively small, formal sector, which includes stable, relatively well-paying jobs with regular working hours—for example in multinational corporations or the government—and often consists of segments of the national economy directly linked to the world-system. The second segment is a larger, informal sector, with unstable, low-paying jobs—such as day laborers, black-market activities, prostitution and crime, street hawking, recycling of garbage. The size of the informal sector varies with the level of economic development; in the Asian NICs, for example, it is relatively small, whereas in much of Latin America, Africa, and South Asia it comprises the majority of employment.

Insufficient supply of housing plagues large numbers of people throughout the developing world. Because housing has become commodified—but, in developing nations, has few com-

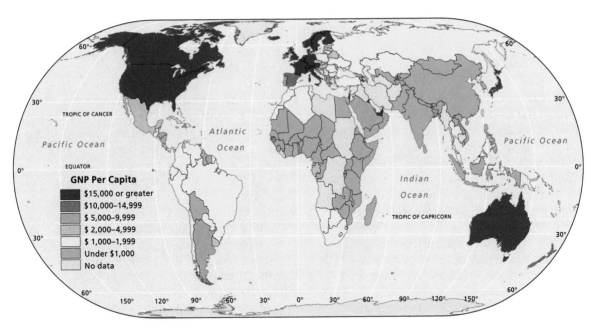

The term Gross National Product (GNP) is used to describe the economic value of the total annual flow of goods and services. GNP per capita is a measure of potential personal wealth.

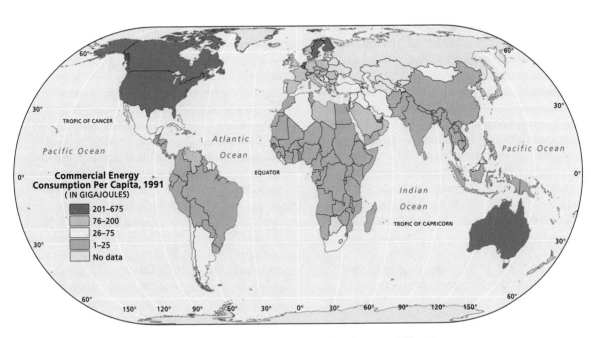

Energy consumption per capita is not only an economic indicator but also one of lifestyle.

mercial suppliers due to low levels of income—many urbanites construct their own housing out of locally available materials. The result is frequently poorly made, uncomfortable, or unsanitary dwellings that comprise vast slum districts or shantytowns, usually on the outskirts of the urban region, with inadequate electricity, transportation, clean water, or medical care. Densities in such neighborhoods greatly exceed those in Western cities. The morphology of such poor districts usually consists of a small cluster of the prosperous in the center and large rings of the poor on the outskirts. Whereas in most cities of the developed world the poor are a minority of the population, in many developing nations—depending upon overall levels of economic status—they comprise the majority.

Poor terms of trade refers to the relatively low value of most exported goods from, and higher-valued imports to, developing countries. Many developing nations export foodstuffs and minerals on the global market and import relatively expensive manufactured goods, resulting in a negative trade balance. This phenomenon is largely attributable to the colonial global division of labor and the critical role of the plantation and mining systems. Export revenues from raw materials are hampered by the numerous suppliers of such goods, low prices, and low-income elasticities of demand. **Elasticity of demand** is a measure of the degree to which the aggregate demand for a commodity rises or falls with changes in income or price. Income-elastic goods are those for which demand rises more than does income. Price-elasticities reflect how much demand falls if the price rises, or conversely, how much demand increases as the price falls.

The late 20th century global glut of commodities has severely lowered the prices of most such goods, hampering exporters' ability to generate foreign revenues and purchase badly needed imports, thus creating a cycle in which limited supplies of investment capital inhibit economic diversification and productivity growth.

Foreign debt is a significant shadow that hangs over the prospects of economic progress in many developing countries. The origins of this problem lie in the petroshocks of the 1970s, which halted a generation of development and created the conditions in which many Western banks loaned sizable quantities of funds to the governments of nations in Asia, Africa, and above all, Latin America. (See Map: Total Foreign Debt, page 364.)

Such loans often went to finance oil imports or large-scale, poorly managed development projects that yielded little in return due to corruption, mismanagement, or capital flight. For example, Brazil and India both borrowed billions of dollars in the 1980s for the construction of hydroelectric dams, which contributed little to national economic growth.

Nations that staked their economic future on petroleum exports, such as Mexico, were devastated by the collapse in oil prices in the 1980s and 1990s. Constrained by their low export earnings, many nations find the repayment of such loans to be difficult, and in the most dire cases have threatened default. The **International Monetary Fund (IMF),** with headquarters in Washington, D.C., has played a key role in managing the global debt crisis, frequently combining debt repayment rescheduling programs with austerity packages that include reduced government subsidies.

Inadequate public services and infrastructure are commonly encountered across the global South, although the level and quality of these vary dramatically with degree of economic development and government policy. Much of the infrastructure in developing nations was originally constructed by colonial powers, for example British rail lines in Africa and India and Japanese ports in Taiwan and Korea, although the primary focus was upon facilitating the colony's role in the colonial world-system. Insufficient maintenance of the infrastructure results in high transportation and communication costs. Inadequate health-care services, including, most critically, polluted-water supplies and sewer systems as well as severe shortages of physicians and pharmaceuticals, contribute to high death rates, particularly in the forms of infant mortality and prevalence of infectious diseases.

Educational systems in many developing countries are typically insufficiently funded, with poorly paid and trained teachers and large, underequipped classrooms, resulting in low literacy rates and unskilled labor supplies. This problem is particularly true for females, because many families in rural areas are more willing to invest scarce educational resources in their sons than in their daughters; as a result, female literacy rates are considerably lower than male ones around the world. (See Map: Literacy Rates Worldwide, page 265.)

Corrupt, inefficient governments with skewed budgetary priorities also plague many developing nations. This problem may be manifested in bloated, poorly managed public bureaucracies that often act as patronage systems for members of influential tribal groups or individuals. Lacking the social basis for democracy, many governments are repressive, curtailing civil rights, imprisoning dissidents, implementing press censorship, and savagely crushing ethnic, political, labor, religious, or regional opposition movements. One thesis holds that a large national middle class is the only secure anchor for democratic liberties. Many states have sadly misplaced spending priorities. For example, the average developing nation spends ten times as much on military expenditures as agricultural development; India has a nuclear-weapons program but not compulsory primary education.

Political instability is a frequent phenomenon in many developing nations, including military coups d'etat, tribal conflicts, civil wars, and secessionist movements. These problems are particularly acute in Africa—Angola, Sudan, and Sierra Leone, for example—where colonial boundaries exacerbated or created conflicts over land ownership and governance. The consequences of such turbulence include genocide, as in Rwanda, the disruption of agricultural

systems, and hampered efforts to attract foreign investment.

Ecological problems in developing nations are frequently much more severe than in developed countries. Their origins can be attributed to rapidly growing population levels and to inadequate attempts to preserve public open spaces and ecosystems; air pollution levels in many cities, which typically have few environmental safeguards, are often hazardous. Deforestation and soil erosion are severe problems in many countries when rural families seek sources of firewood or agricultural land or grazing for herds. These problems accentuate disasters such as mudslides or susceptibility to drought and contribute to the steady erosion of wildlife habitats around the globe. Many residents of developing nations regard ecological protection as a luxury that only wealthy countries can afford. Environmental destruction is, at root, a political phenomenon; to stop it, the structural origins of poverty must be changed.

Theories of Development Among Developing Nations

Any realistic understanding of poverty in developing nations and the possibilities for its alleviation must take into account the differing ways in which these conditions have been approached conceptually and as a matter of government policy. Explanations of development, and the lack of it, fall primarily into three major schools of thought, including modernization theory, with origins in neoclassical economics, and two left-inspired views, dependency theory and world-systems theory. Frequent, often heated, debates over these issues compose a significant part of economic geography today.

MODERNIZATION THEORY

The most frequently encountered approach to Third World development, **modernization theory,** has its origins in German Max Weber's (1864-1920) theory of capitalist development,

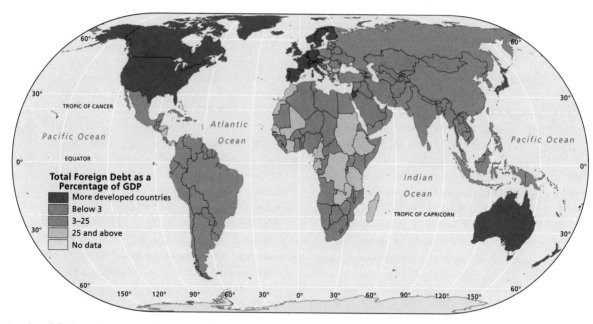

Total Foreign Debt as a Percentage of GDP
- More developed countries
- Below 3
- 3–25
- 25 and above
- No data

Foreign debt impedes economic progress in much of the developing world. The International Monetary Fund develops programs to help countries in Latin America, Asia, and Africa to manage debt crises.

which emphasized the process of "rationalization," the routinization of attitudes and behavior in politics (via the bureaucracy) and economics (via the market). Whereas Weber's concern was to explain the origins of capitalism in the West, by World War II sociologists such as American Talcott Parsons (1902–1979) of Harvard had applied it to the Third World. In this reading, Western rationality, including the values and ethics, scientific institutions, literacy levels, and economic and political systems of Europe and, particularly, the U.S., were seen as the only viable path to successful development.

Accordingly, development was portrayed as a "race" in which the West was the leader and the Third World "lagged behind" and must "catch up," that is, follow the historic trajectories of the developed world. In the context of Cold War superpower rivalry, this view celebrated capitalism as a system whose wealth created "a rising tide [that] lifts all boats" and that its absence was the primary explanation of poverty. Accordingly, the introduction of West-

ern rational ideas, technology, and economic and political institutions, through foreign aid, trade, and diffusion—from cities to the countryside, for example—was held to promote the gradual evolution of developing nations into prosperous, democratic states.

Modernization theory was influential in U.S.-led development initiatives after World War II, such as federal programs administered by the Agency for International Development and the Peace Corps. The most famous expression was American economist Walter Rostow's work, *The Stages of Economic Growth* (1960), which compared the development process to that of an airplane taking off. Rostow argued that traditional societies were not simply "primitive" or "backwards" in terms of available technologies and standards of living, but lacked a growth-oriented culture. During the "preconditions to take-off" many urban-centered groups and the government begin to create the conditions that favor growth, often by displacing conservative rural elites. The

Ecological problems confront developing countries. Most temperate forests are now protected by law, but many tropical forests are not. Here in Costa Rica, cleared rain forest abuts Coronado National Park.

"take-off" phase, akin to the U.S. in the late 19th century or the East Asian newly industrializing countries after World War II, sees growth become normalized and self-sustaining. In this phase, rapid technological change and capital investments, including foreign investment, create productivity growth rates that exceed population growth, resulting in rising standards of living.

Frequently, modernization theory was coupled with Malthusian-inspired population control programs. (See Thomas Malthus, page 251.) The emphasis was largely on the creation of a comparative advantage internationally and the promotion of exports. The fourth phase, the "drive to maturity," involves the creation of a literate, urbanized labor force and capacity to produce capital goods. Finally, the last phase, "mass consumption," sees widespread prosperity, a large middle class, and living conditions akin to those in the West.

Modernization theory has been roundly criticized by leftists for its obvious ethnocentrism, which denies the validity of non-Western value systems; developing nations are presumed to lack a meaningful history or capacity for development without the introduction of Western institutions, a notion belied by the facts historically. Its exclusive focus on the internal individualistic causes of poverty—culture—occurs at the expense of external structural features of global capitalism that have historically inhibited economic development, such as colonialism and neocolonialism. The primary responses to this school have argued that capitalism creates poverty as much as it creates wealth, and that these two phenomena consist of two sides of one coin.

DEPENDENCY THEORY

Drawing upon the intellectual tradition of Marxism developed by German philosopher Karl Marx (1818–1883), dependency theory arose—largely in Latin America—in part because of the obvious lack of economic development that had transpired in most of the Third World in the decades after World War II. This perspective emphasized the ways in which capitalism simultaneously creates both poverty and wealth through landscapes of uneven development. In this view, poverty is not "natural" and does not simply "happen," that is, it is hardly some inherent condition of the Third World; rather, it is actively created through colonialism and the mechanics of the contemporary neocolonial world economy.

In essence, by invoking the labor theory of value and interregional transfers of surplus value, dependency theory argued that the First World *made* the Third World poor, that the wealth of the former is the direct result of the poverty of the latter. The **labor theory of value** is the idea that all value is ultimately produced only through human labor. The classic theorization of how value is created was used by Adam Smith and David Ricardo and later popularized by Karl Marx. The Marxist version of this theory held that all class societies rely upon the extraction of surplus value from workers, which under capitalism occurs through the labor market. For example, colonialism often suppressed the development of manufacturing in colonized countries—such as the British and the Indian textile industry—restructuring them as centers of raw materials production. This notion was well captured in the phrase the "development of underdevelopment," which implies that underdevelopment is an active process, not a static state.

The Third World is held to be *under*developed, not simply undeveloped. Thus, the world economy is portrayed as a planetary mechanism for the transfer of surplus value from the developing nations to the developed ones. Notions such as comparative advantage and interdependence mask uneven power relations among states that foster exploitation of the weak and poor. The policy consequences of this perspective stressed self-sufficiency in the Third World, including a high degree of mistrust of foreign MNCs, and a focus on **import substitution**—once widely practiced in Asia and Latin America—in which prohibitively high tariffs designed to minimize imports were to protect domestic industries and foster growth fueled by the internal market.

Dependency theory has been criticized on several grounds, including its silence on the role of internal forces that may perpetuate poverty, such as local cultural and political systems. More importantly, this view erroneously holds that capitalism inevitably and inescapably generates poverty in developing nations and forecloses any possibility of increases in wealth associated with foreign investment and trade. However, colonial policies were not some monolithic entity that invariably impoverished nations, but varied greatly over time and space.

During the 1970s, the rapid growth of the East Asia NICs revealed the conceptual bankruptcy of the assumption that capitalism inevitably breeds poverty. More broadly, it is evident that economies that have opened up to the world-system—South Korea and Taiwan, for example—have prospered far more than those that remain isolated and attempt to practice self-sufficiency—North Korea, Bhutan, and Cuba, for example. By the 1980s, dependency theory had fallen into disuse, and export-promotion strategies designed to maximize foreign revenues and investment had displaced import-substitution ones throughout the developing world.

WORLD-SYSTEMS THEORY

The reincarnation of dependency theory occurred through the efforts of American sociologist Immanuel Wallerstein, who offered world-systems theory in its place in the 1970s. Where dependency theory examined only the developing nations, world-systems theory focuses upon the entire global economy, including the First World.

From this perspective, the global system of states and markets is an indispensable component in the explanation of events within individual areas: Local and national economies and societies can only be understood by reference to their position within the global division of labor. Unlike earlier "world-empires" such as Rome, in which the state acted as the primary vehicle for the extraction and transfer of surplus value, capitalism is a truly global system in which these flows are accomplished through the world market.

Wallerstein's original conception viewed the world-system as structured around a core of Western Europe, Japan, the U.S., a periphery of the poorer parts of the Third World, and an intermediate, quasi-developed semi-periphery of Eastern Europe, the former Soviet bloc, the East Asian NICs, and Mexico. The stability of the world-system is held to be secured through the efforts of a single hegemonic power at different historical moments, including Britain in the 19th century, for example, and the U.S. in the 20th.

Retaining the labor theory of value, this view also holds that capitalism creates wealth and poverty simultaneously through inter-regional and international flows of capital and surplus value. However, unlike dependency theorists, world-systems theory explicitly admits to the possibility of economic development in the developing nations, although global growth is still portrayed as a zero-sum game. Some places may "win," but only if others "lose."

Thus, some peripheral states may rise into the semi-periphery through industrialization, such as the Asian NICs, but such a transition could only occur through the deindustrialization of the global core, as developed nations passed the baton of certain industries to less developed ones. However, world-systems theory has been criticized for its neglect of culture, which can be critical to economic change, the functionalism that posits some necessary "role" for the semi-periphery as intermediary between core and periphery, and for conceptually privileging trade over production.

The growth of the East Asian NICs has clearly played an important role in debates over development theory. During the 1960s through the 1980s, Asia's "Four Tigers" of South Korea, Taiwan, Hong Kong, and Singapore enjoyed GNP growth rates of 8 to 10 percent per year, creating a large, urbanized middle class and a standard of living rivaling that of southern Europe. In the 1990s, despite the severe financial crisis that swept through East Asia, they have been joined by the new tigers of China, Thailand, Malaysia, and Indonesia.

The fastest growing part of the world economy since World War II, East Asia has become an inspiration for other aspiring Third World regions, especially Latin America. The reasons for the NICs' success have been hotly debated. The inability of dependency theory to account for this phenomenon largely led to its downfall. Some observers have suggested that the legacy of 50 years of Japanese colonialism, such as the infrastructures and centralized state bureaucracies, played a role, despite the harsh repression visited on Japan's colonies during World War II; indeed, Japan has long been a model for the NICs and continues to invest actively in East Asia.

Others point to the role of the U.S. during the Cold War, including development assistance. Yet others stress internal factors such as the Confucian cultural tradition, with its high rates of literacy, stress on education, and obedient labor forces, which allow for easily-exploited pools of cheap female labor and high national savings rates.

Finally, the NICs clearly were led by efficient, pro-growth governments that encouraged land reform, formed national banks, attracted foreign investment, and promoted exports. In contrast, Latin America has witnessed few attempts at land reform, has had many corrupt and inefficient governments, contradictory development policies, persistent import-substitution strategies—with the notable exception of Chile—numerous strikes, poorly developed credit markets, little foreign investment—except Mexico—and relatively little U.S. foreign assistance.

Conclusion

Economic landscapes are the complex result of influences from the natural environment, historical legacies, and contemporary political, economic, and cultural forces that intersect in highly uneven ways over space. With the spread of capitalism worldwide since the 16th century, these landscapes have become progressively restructured around the prerequisites of profit-maximization and the global economy, which tends to generate uneven economic development among and within regions and nations.

The expansion of colonial empires was a profound moment in the construction of the contemporary world-system, essentially generating the core-periphery schism between the developed and developing nations that continues to be the central feature of the world's economic geography today. The industrial revolution marked a qualitative change in this process, accelerating trade and deepening the formation of market relations in Europe,

Japan, and North America. Despite the traditional prominence of agricultural and manufacturing activities in economic geography, the bulk of output and employment worldwide today consists of the production of intangibles, that is of services of various sorts.

The specialization of regions and nations, linked by trade and investment and understood through the foundational principle of comparative advantage, has connected local areas together over time to an unprecedented degree, so that the consequences of action in one place inevitably reverberate to affect other places. Individual regions are linked to one another through dense networks of trade, investment, diffusion, migration, and communication, with numerous political and social consequences. Flows of capital across space are the primary means by which economic geographies are constructed and uneven spatial development is produced.

Dramatic reductions in the time and costs of

transportation and communications have created numerous rounds of time-space compression, which alters the relative positions of individual places within a broader grid of economic relations.

Despite the profound significance of technological change in this process, it is important to avoid the conceptual error of technological determinism, which assigns technological change an autonomous status independent of social and political relations. Other, equally important forces (institutional and cultural changes) are also at work, shaping and in turn being shaped by new technologies. Such processes play out at multiple spatial scales, from the neighborhood to the world-system, creating overlapping, nested patterns of differential access to wealth and power. Economic landscapes are thus in continual flux, changing both slowly, almost imperceptibly, as well as at the speed of light, as in global financial circles. These changes are not always beneficial, for capitalism is quite capable of generating poverty as well as wealth.

Urban Geography: Cities and Urbanization

Introduction

Almost half the world's population lives in cities. Between 1960 and 1998, the number of city dwellers rose from 800 million to 2.6 billion, a 307 percent increase, while the world's total population increased from just over 3 billion to 6 billion, a 195 percent increase. Analysts predict that there will be 5 billion urban dwellers by 2025, of whom 80 percent will live in developing countries.

Urbanization is not simply a process of demographic growth of villages, towns, and cities: It involves many other social and spatial changes, both quantitative and qualitative.

Cities are crucibles of social change, cultural transformation, and economic innovation. Urbanization typically involves, among other things, distinctive ways of life and subcultures and distinctive patterns of individual behavior and social interaction. Contemporary urbanization is a remarkable geographical phenomenon, and it involves some of the most important sets of processes shaping the world's landscapes. More and more of the world's economic, social, cultural, and political processes are played out within and between the world's villages, towns, and cities.

Cities in History

It has taken a long time for the world to become so heavily urbanized. Just after World War II, only 16 percent of the world's population lived in towns and cities; a century ago the figure was less than 10 percent. The earliest impulses toward urbanization developed independently in the various hearth areas of the first agricultural revolution. (See Cultural Geography, page 288; Economic Geography: Agriculture, page 318.) The first region of independent urban evolution was in the Middle East, in the valleys of the Tigris and Euphrates

Rivers (in Mesopotamia) and in the Nile Valley, beginning around 3500 B.C. Together, these intensively cultivated river valleys formed the Fertile Crescent. By 2500 B.C. towns and cities had appeared in the Indus Valley of Asia and by 1800 B.C. they were established in northern China. Other areas of independent urbanization include Central America and southwestern North America (from around 600 B.C.) and Andean America (from around A.D. 800). Meanwhile, the original Middle Eastern hearth continued to foster successive generations of city-based empires, including those of Athens, Rome, and Byzantium.

Experts differ in their explanations of the origins of these first city-based empires. The classical archaeological interpretation emphasizes the availability of an agricultural surplus large enough to enable the emergence of specialized, nonagricultural workers. Specifically, urbanization required the emergence of groups able to exact tributes, impose taxes, and control labor power throughout a region, usually through some form of religious persuasion, military coercion, or a combination of the two. Once established, these elite provided the stimulus for urban development by using their wealth to build palaces, arenas, and monuments as displays of their power and status.

The urbanized economies of these empires were a precarious phenomenon, however. In Europe the cities introduced by the Greeks and reestablished by the Romans almost collapsed during the early Medieval Age, from about A.D. 476 to 1000. Yet it was from this beginning that an elaborate system of towns and cities developed, the largest centers eventually growing into what have today become the centers of a global world economy. The **feudal system**, in which lords leased lands to subjects in exchange for military assistance, services, and loyalty, was displaced by a money economy predicated on trade, which provided the foundations for a new phase of urbanization.

Beginning with networks in northern Italy established by the merchants of Venice, Pisa, Genoa, and Florence and the trading partners of the **Hanseatic League**, a federation of **city-states** such as Hamburg, Lübeck, and Riga, around the North Sea and Baltic coasts, a trading system of immense complexity soon came to span Europe from Bergen to Athens and from Lisbon to Vienna. By 1400 Milan, Genoa, Venice, and Bruges had all grown to 100,000 or more, and Paris, a pre-Roman settlement, had grown to about 275,000.

The Spread of Urbanization

Between the 15th and 17th centuries, the cities of Europe and the world's economy were transformed. In Europe merchant capitalism, in contrast to industrial capitalism, increased in scale and sophistication. **Merchant capitalism** is a form of economic organization in which capital accumulation is based on trade in primary products such as agricultural, fish and forest products, minerals, and handicrafts. **Industrial capitalism** is a form of organization in which capital accumulation is based on manufacturing processes. Economic and social reorganization was accelerated by the Protestant reformation and the scientific revolution. Aggressive overseas colonization made Europeans the leaders, persuaders, and shapers of the rest of the world's economies and societies. (See Sidebar: Why Europe? page 372).

Between 1520 and 1580, the Spanish and Portuguese established colonial city systems in Latin America. The Spanish established colonial towns such as Bogotá (Colombia), Lima (Peru), and Quito (Ecuador) mainly as administrative and military centers from which they could occupy and exploit their claims in the New World. Spanish conquistadors founded towns on easily defensible sites such as hilltops and situated them strategically in relation to the populations they governed. Portuguese colonists, in contrast, founded their cities with commercial rather than administrative considerations in mind. They too were motivated by exploitation, but their strategy was to site towns to facilitate collection and export of products from mines and plantations. They thus sought coastal sites in Brazil with good harbors such as Recife, or inland sites along navigable rivers such as Belém on the Pará and Manaus on the Río Negro, a tributary of the Amazon. (See Age of Discovery, page 8 and Colonialism, page 354.)

Within Europe, Renaissance reorganization—from about the beginning of the 14th century to the 17th century—saw the centralization of political power and the formation of

Why Europe?

Why did Europe become the platform for the spread of urbanization and innovative political and economic changes in the 15th and 16th centuries? In particular, why not China? When European urbanization mushroomed, China had approximately the same total population as Europe. Well into the 15th century China was at least as far advanced in science and technology. Chinese ironmasters had developed blast furnaces that enabled them to cast iron as early as 200 B.C. Iron ploughs were introduced in the 6th century, the compass in the 10th century, and the water clock in the 11th century. The Chinese were also significantly more advanced than Europeans in medicine, papermaking and printing, and the production of explosives. In addition, because China had retained an imperial system, it held a potentially telling advantage in that its centralized decision-making, extensive state bureaucracy, well-developed internal communications, and unified financial system were potentially well suited to economic development and territorial expansion.

China's failure to take off in the way that Europe did must be attributed in part to its failure to pursue economic opportunities overseas. The Chinese had in fact matched early European exploratory successes by navigating the Indian Ocean from Java to Africa in a series of lucrative and informative voyages, but they simply lost interest in further exploration. One explanation offered by historians for this lack of a colonizing imperative is that Chinese authorities saw their own world as the only one that mattered. Another is that they were distracted by the growing menace of nomadic Mongol barbarians and Japanese pirates. A third explanation is that members of the centralized power structure of imperial China did not include those for whom overseas exploration was attractive: The administration and defense of such a huge population and landmass was a drain on the attention and energy of those with wealth and power. There is a link too between China's imperial framework and its failure to develop military technology in the way that enabled Europeans to turn exploration into domination: The imperial court suppressed the spread of knowledge of gunnery because it feared its use by bandits and in domestic uprisings within the country.

Another important difference between China and Europe was that European agriculture had become focused on raising cattle and wheat, whereas Chinese agriculture was dominated by rice production. Because rice production requires relatively little land, China's rulers did not see a great need for territorial expansion, but Europe's reliance on cattle and wheat, which required more land, provided a strong impetus for exploration and territorial expansion. Finally, some writers have emphasized the lack of autonomy of Chinese towns and cities compared to their European counterparts. The legal and political autonomy of European towns was a crucial "pull" factor in attracting rural migrants whose labor and initiative were central to the emergence of merchant capitalism. In contrast, the centralized decision-making of imperial China is seen by historians as having dampened the potential of China's estimated 1,700 city-states and principalities.

nation-states, the beginnings of industrialization, and the funneling of plunder and produce from distant colonies. In this new political and economic context, the port cities of the North Sea and Atlantic coasts enjoyed a decisive locational advantage. By 1700 London had grown to 500,000, while Lisbon and Amsterdam had each grown to about 175,000.

City Planning and Urban Design

Most ancient Greek and Roman settlements were laid out on **grid systems**, within which the siting of key buildings and the relationship of neighborhoods to one another were carefully thought out. In ancient China cities were laid out with strict regard to Taoist ideas about the natural order of the universe, with different quarters representing the four seasons of the year, and the placement of major streets and the interior layout of buildings designed to be in harmony with cosmic energy. This kind of mystical interpretation of the disposition and alignment of prominent landscape features and sacred sites, is **geomancy,** and its application in design is known as *feng shui.* (See Sidebar: Feng Shui, page 305.)

It was during the Renaissance and baroque periods in Europe (between the 15th and 17th centuries), that Western ideas of city planning and design were first applied by rich and powerful rulers who used urban design to create extravagant symbols of wealth, power, and destiny. At about the same time, dramatic advances in military ordnance, particularly cannon and artillery, brought a surge of planned urban redevelopment that featured impressive fortifications, geometrically shaped redoubts, or strongholds, and an extensive *glacis militaire*, or clear zones-of-fire.

Inside new walls, cities were recast according to a new aesthetic of grand design: Geometrical plans, streetscapes, gardens emphasizing views with dramatic perspectives, and palaces deliberately designed to show off the power and the glory of state and church. Cities of this era include Charleville (France), Copenhagen (Denmark), Karlsruhe (Germany), Nancy (France), and Philippeville (Belgium).

Colonialism and Gateway Cities

The most important aspect of urbanization during the 17th century, however, was the establishment of **gateway cities,** cities which because of their physical situation served as links between one country or region and others. These include, Boston, Charleston, Savannah, Georgetown, Recife, and Rio de Janeiro in the Americas; Luanda and Cape Town in Africa; Aden in Yemen; Masqat, Goa, Cochin, and Colombo around the Indian Ocean; and Malacca, Makassar (Ujungpandang), Manila, and Macau in the Far East. Protected by fortifications and European naval power, they began as trading posts and colonial administrative centers. Before long they developed their own manufacturing industries, along with more extensive commercial and financial services, in order to supply the pioneers' needs. (See Map: European Empires, page 356.)

As colonies were developed and trading networks expanded, some of these ports grew rapidly, acting as gateways for colonial expansion into continental interiors. Rio de Janeiro grew on the basis of gold mining in the Brazilian interior, São Paulo on the basis of coffee, Buenos Aires, Argentina, on mutton, wool, and cereals, Accra, now capital of Ghana, founded by the British and Dutch in the 17th century, grew on the basis of cocoa, and Calcutta, India, founded by the British in 1690, grew on the basis of jute, cotton, and textiles. As they became major population centers, they also became important markets for imported European manufactures, adding even more to their functions as gateways for international transport and trade.

First visited by Portuguese explorers in the early 16th century, Rio de Janiero began as a fort and trading outpost. It quickly grew to become capital of the colony of Brazil in 1763, of the Brazilian Empire in 1822, and of the independent republic in 1889. With a population of more than ten million, it is Brazil's second largest city, a major port and nucleus of business, and the country's leading cultural and tourist center.

Industrial Cities

Between the late 1700s and the end of the 1800s a distinctive phase of economic development took root in Europe and North America: **Industrialization** blossomed in towns and cities, driven by competition among small family businesses and with few constraints or controls imposed by governments or public authorities. Very quickly, it became evident that industrial economies could only be organized effectively with large pools of labor, transportation networks, physical infrastructure of factories, warehouses, stores, and offices, and the consumer markets provided by cities. As industrialization spread throughout Europe in the first half of the 19th century and then to other parts of the world, so urbanization increased at a faster pace. The higher wages and greater variety of opportunities in urban labor markets attracted migrants from rural areas. (See also Industrial Revolution, page 330.)

In Europe the demographic transition caused a rapid growth in population as death rates fell dramatically. The demographic transition is a period of change from high birth and death rates to low birth and death rates. The transition period is when birth rates decline more slowly than death rates, resulting, for a while, in a significant natural increase in population. (See Demographic Transition, page 260.) This growth in population provided a massive increase in the labor supply throughout the 19th century, further boosting the rate of urbanization, not only in Europe but also in Australia, Canada, New Zealand, South Africa, and the United States. Emigration carried industrialization and urbanization to the frontiers of the world economy. (See Migration, page 268.)

The paradigmatic city of 19th-century European industrialization was Manchester, England, which grew from a small town of 15,000 in 1750 to a town of 70,000 in 1801, a city of 500,000 in 1861, and a metropolis of 2.3 million by 1911. Cities like Manchester were engines of economic growth, and their prosperity attracted migrants and immigrants who made for rapid population growth. In this urbanization process, there was a close and positive relationship between rural and urban development. The appropriation of new land for agriculture, together with mechanization, resulted in increased agricultural productivity. This extra productivity prompted rural-urban migration, enabling surplus rural labor to work in the growing manufacturing sectors in towns and cities. At the same time, it provided the additional produce needed to feed growing urban populations. The whole process was further reinforced by the capacity of urban labor forces to produce agricultural tools, machinery, fertilizer, and other products that made for still greater increases in agricultural productivity. (See also Migration, page 268 and Agriculture, page 318.)

In this self-sustaining process of urbanization, the personal and corporate incomes generated by industrialization allowed for higher potential tax yields, which could be used to improve public utilities, roads, schools, health services, recreational amenities, and other components of the infrastructure. These investments improved the efficiency and attractiveness of cities for further rounds of private investment in industry. The whole process was one of **cumulative causation**, in which an upward spiral of advantages accumulated as a result of a city's development of external economies and localization economies. **External economies** are cost savings and other benefits that result from circumstances beyond a firm's own organization and methods of production—in particular, savings and benefits that accrue to producers from associating with similar producers in geographic settings that encompass the specialized business services that they need. For example, it is a financial advantage for a wire-making factory to locate near a steel mill, not just to save the cost of transporting steel for wire and to save on the cost of reheating the steel but also to have access to the specialized marketing, transportation, and engineering services associated with the steel industry. **Localization economies** are cost savings that accrue to particular

industries as a result of clustering at a specific location, for example being able to share a pool of labor with special skills or experience, or joining together to create a marketing organization or research institute. (See Economic Geography, page 317.).

Systems of Cities

By the late 18th century, the industrial revolution and European imperialism had created unprecedented concentrations of humanity that were intimately linked into networks and hierarchies of towns and cities that geographers describe as **urban systems**, which are an interdependent set of urban settlements within a specified region. (See Sidebar: Urban Systems, page 376.) Nation-states emerged to replace kingdoms, dukedoms, and principalities as entities to foster and regulate economic competition on a broad, geographic scale. (See Political Geography, page 391.) With nation states came national capitals. Within industrializing nation states such as the United States, Britain, France, and Germany, tight-knit networks of towns and cities evolved as production platforms. **Production platforms** are geographic settings in which specialized, interrelated manufacturing activities are bound together by the creation and exploitation of external economies. These settings became the bases of thriving national economies.

Elsewhere new gateway cities were founded, and, as European nation states sought to establish economic and political control over continental interiors, colonial cities such as Calcutta, Saigon (Ho Chi Minh City), Hong Kong, Jakarta, Lagos (Nigeria), Manila, and Singapore were established or reinforced as centers of administration, political control, and commerce.

Urban Systems

One of the most important ways in which geographers conceptualize urbanization processes is through the attributes and dynamics of urban systems. An urban system, or city system, is an interdependent set of urban settlements within a given region. Thus, for example, there is a German urban system, European urban system, and a global urban system. Every town and city is part of one of the interlocking urban systems that link local-, regional-, national- and international-scale human geographies in a complex web of economic interdependence. These urban systems organize space through hierarchies of cities of different sizes and functions. Many of these hierarchical urban systems have common attributes and features, particularly relative size and spacing of individual towns and cities.

Urban systems tend to exhibit clear functional differences within hierarchies of settlements of different sizes. The geographical division of labor resulting from processes of economic development means that many medium size and larger size cities perform quite specialized economic functions and so acquire quite distinctive characters, such as the steel-producing cities of Sheffield, England, and Pittsburgh, Pennsylvania. Some towns and cities, of course, do evolve as general-purpose urban centers, providing an evenly balanced range of functions for their own particular sphere of influence.

Within the American urban system, for example, the top tier of cities consists of centers of global importance (including Chicago, New York, and Los Angeles) which provide sophisticated functions to an international marketplace. A second tier consists of general-purpose cities with diverse functions but only regional importance, such as Atlanta, Miami, and Boston, while third and fourth tiers consist of more specialized centers of subregional and local importance, such as Charlotte, North Carolina, Memphis, Tennessee, and Richmond, Virginia.

Cities and Modernization

As societies and economies became more complex with the transition from merchant capitalism to industrial capitalism, national rulers and city leaders looked to city planning not just as a means of symbolizing new seats of power and authority but also as a means of imposing order, safety, and efficiency. One of the most important early precedents was set in Paris, by Napoléon III, who presided over a comprehensive program of urban redevelopment and monumental urban design. The work was carried out by a city administrator, Baron Georges Haussmann (1809–1891) who, between 1853 and 1870, demolished large sections of old Paris to make way for broad, new tree-lined avenues, with numer-ous public open spaces, including the Bois de Boulogne, the covered market, Les Halles, and monuments. His design set the precedent for the "Haussmannization" of other capital cities, including Berlin (Germany), Brussels (Belgium), and Vienna (Austria), wherein the objectives were not only to make them more efficient and a better place to live but also to make them more resistant to revolutionary politics: Wide boulevards were more difficult to barricade, and monuments and statues helped to instill national pride and identity.

In the United States the late 19th-century City Beautiful movement drew heavily on Haussmann's ideas and its associated Beaux Arts designs. The objective of the **City Beautiful movement** was to remake cities to reflect the higher values of society by using

Lights twinkle along the wide boulevards and foundation of the wrought iron Eiffel Tower in central Paris. More than 2,000 years old, Paris was redesigned during the mid-1800s under the direction of Baron Georges Haussmann for Emperor Napoléon III. A grand example of city planning, Paris stands as a symbol of power, authority, and national pride.

neoclassical architecture, grandiose street plans, parks, and inspirational monuments and statues. American architect Daniel Burnham (1846–1912) developed a plan for Chicago in 1909 that exploited urban design and planning as an uplifting and civilizing influence, emphasizing civic pride and power.

European imperial powers imposed similar designs on their colonial capitals and administrative centers, including the French in Casablanca (Morocco) and Saigon; the British in New Delhi (India) and Pretoria (South Africa) Rangoon, Burma (now called Yangon in Myanmar); and the Germans in Windhoek (Namibia).

In the early decades of the 20th century, a new labor process, known as Fordism, took hold in the world's industrialized countries. In 1913 and 1914, American Henry Ford pioneered the principle of mass production based on assembly-line techniques and "scientific" management, and linked it with mass consumption based on higher wages and sophisticated advertising techniques. He applied his ideas to manufacture the Model T at his plant

in Dearborn, Michigan. (See Sidebar: Henry Ford and Fordism, page 335.)

The role of government, meanwhile, had expanded significantly, partly to regulate the unwanted side effects of free-enterprise capitalism—exploitative wages and working conditions, cyclical unemployment, and threats to public health caused by unregulated urban growth and unregulated industrial processes— and partly to mediate the relationship between organized business and organized labor.

The cultural response to pressures of industrialization and urbanization was the **Modern movement**, which incorporated the idea that buildings and cities should be designed and run like machines. Equally important to Modernists was that urban design should not reflect prevailing social and political values but, rather, help to create a new moral and social order. This led to the idea of imposing order and creating safety and efficiency through building codes, planning regulations, and exclusionary land use zoning. **Zoning**, the basis for land-use planning and policy, identifies

Zoning

Exclusionary land use zoning has been a central tool of modern western city planning since the 1900s. Zoning is based on the idea that order and predictability of land uses within a city makes for efficiency, promotes investment by minimizing uncertainty, and lessens conflict between non-compatible land users. In 1924 the U.S. Department of Commerce drafted a model zoning law. Exclusionary zoning was tested by *Euclid* v. *Ambler.* The case went to the U.S. Supreme Court, which recognized, in 1926, single-purpose, land use zoning as a legitimate application of a local government's powers to police health, safety, and welfare issues. Specifically, it allowed local governments to protect the character of neighborhoods with single-family dwellings against the threat of lower property values and nuisances associated with apartment housing, commercial activities, and industrial land uses.

In practice, zoning in the United States, as in other developed countries, has also been motivated by the desire to exclude social, racial, or ethnic groups deemed undesirable. By the end of the 1970s, single-use exclusionary zoning came to be seen by critics as rigid and inflexible, and one of the reasons that caused city centers to lose their vitality. The cities had been planned to death. By then, zoning and other tools of western city planning had been exported to developing countries. Western-style land use planning was unable to cope with the pressure of urban growth in less developed countries, and it frequently forced land and property prices up, thus reducing most households' access to shelter. Nevertheless, zoning remains an important tool of urban planning.

preferred uses and/or proscribed uses for specific tracts of land.

Cities and Advanced Capitalism

After World War II, another important transformation in the nature of capitalism took place within developed countries: There was a shift away from industrial production toward services, particularly sophisticated business and financial services, as the basis for profitability. This was another step in the evolution of capitalism, from merchant capitalism, to industrial capitalism, and now to **advanced capitalism**. The decline in manufacturing jobs in developed countries, combined with the ability of huge multinational corporations to outmaneuver both governments and labor unions, contributed to a destabilization of urban and economic geographies throughout much of the world.

There are some 40,000 multinational corporations, which control about 180,000 foreign subsidiaries and account for more than six trillion dollars in worldwide sales. These multinational corporations have been central to a phase of global geographical restructuring that has been under way for the last 25 years or so. Firms of all sizes have had to adjust their operations by restructuring their activities and reorganizing and redeploying their resources among different countries, regions, and cities.

As a result, contemporary cities must be understood within the context of constantly changing networks of economic interdependence created by multinational corporate strategies. These networks are, effectively, international assembly lines spanning countries and continents and linking production and supply of raw materials, processing of raw materials, production of components, assembly of finished products, and distribution of finished products into vast webs of interdependence. Through these assembly lines, the world economy has been inscribed into local economies. At the top of the global urban hierarchy are **world cities** in which a dispropor-tionate part of the world's most important business is conducted. These cities—London, New York, and Tokyo—are, effectively, the control centers for the networked world economy.

World Cities in a World Economy

Ever since the advent of merchant capitalism in the world economy in the 15th century, certain cities have played key roles in organizing space beyond their own national boundaries. In earlier phases of urbanization, these roles involved organization of trade and execution of colonial, imperial, and geopolitical strategies. The world cities of the 17th century were London, Amsterdam, Antwerp, Genoa, Lisbon, and Venice. By the 18th century they included Paris, Rome, and Vienna; and Antwerp and Genoa had become less influential. Berlin, Chicago, Manchester, New York, and St. Petersburg became world cities in the 19th century, and Venice became less influential. Today, with the globalization of the economy, roles of world cities are less about deployment of imperial power and orchestration of trade and more about multinational corporate organization, international banking and finance, supranational government, and the work of international agencies.

London, New York, and Tokyo are at the peak of the current modern global urban system. The second tier is world cities with influence over large regions of the world economy, including Brussels, Chicago, Frankfurt, Los Angeles, Paris, Singapore, Washington, D.C., and Zürich; the third tier is important international cities with more limited or more specialized international functions, including Amsterdam, Houston, Madrid, Mexico City, Miami, San Francisco, Seoul, Sydney, Toronto, and Vancouver. The fourth tier is those cities with national importance and with some multinational functions, such as Barcelona, Boston, Dallas, Manchester, Montreal, Munich, and Philadelphia.

These cities have infrastructures essential for the delivery of services to clients whose activities are international in scope, such as specialized office space, financial exchanges, communications networks, and airports. They have also established a comparative advantage in two major areas: the availability of specialized firms and expert professionals and the availability of high-order cultural amenities for both high-paid workers and their out-of-town business visitors.

Above all, the cities have established themselves as centers of authority—with a critical mass of people-in-the-know about market conditions, trends, and innovations—people who can gain one another's trust through frequent face-to-face contact, not just in business settings but also in the informal settings of clubs and office bars.

They have become places that, in the globalized world economy, are able not only to generate powerful spirals of local economic development but also to act as pivotal points in the reorganization of global space. They are control centers for the flow of information, cultural products, and finance that, collectively, sustain the economic and cultural globalization of the world.

World cities also provide an interface between the global and the local. They contain the economic, cultural, and institutional apparatuses that channel national and regional resources into the global economy and that transmit the impulses of globalization back to national and regional centers.

As such, world cities are the settings for most of the leading global markets for commodities, commodity futures, investment capital, foreign exchange, equities, and bonds; for clusters of specialized, high-order business services such as advertising, design, and market research; for concentrations of corporate headquarters and national and international headquarters of trade and professional associations; for the most powerful and internationally influential media organizations, news and information services, and culture industries; and for most of the leading nongovernmental organizations (NGOs) and intergovernmental

organizations (IGOs) that are international in scope. Geneva, Switzerland, is base for such international NGOs as the World Council of Churches and the World Business Council for Sustainable Development, and Paris is headquarters for the Organization for Economic Cooperation and Development, an example of an international IGO.

There is synergy in these various functional components of world cities. New York, for example, attracts multinational corporations because it is a center of culture and communications, and it attracts specialized business services because it is a center of corporate headquarters and of global markets. Corporate headquarters and specialized legal, financial, and business services cluster in New York because of mutual cost savings. At the same time, different world cities fulfill specialized roles within the world system, making for differences in the nature of their world-city functions, as well as differences in their degree of importance as world cities.

Contemporary Patterns of Urbanization

There are thousands of cities functioning both as local centers of industry and commerce and as interdependent nodes in national, regional, and subregional urban systems. A 1996 United Nations document, *Global Report on Human Settlements: An Urbanizing World*, stated that the rate of urbanization of the world's population is accelerating significantly as a result of the global shift to technological, industrial, and service-based economies. It concluded that few countries are able to handle the consequent urban population crush, which is causing problems on an unprecedented scale: Ten million people die annually in densely populated urban areas from conditions produced by substandard housing and poor sanitation. About

500 million people, worldwide, are either homeless or living in unfit housing that is life threatening.

Rates of Urban Growth

In many parts of the world, urban growth is taking place at such a pace and under such chaotic conditions that it is impossible for geographers and demographers to do more than provide informed estimates of just how urbanized the world has become. National demographic statistics need to be analyzed cautiously because countries employ quite diverse definitions of what constitutes a town, a city, or a metropolitan region. The most comprehensive source of statistics is the United Nations, whose data suggest that almost half of the world's population is now urban. Taking 100,000 as a minimum size for an urban place, just over one third of the world's population is now urbanized. North America is the most urbanized continent, with almost 80 percent of its population living in cities of 100,000 or more. In contrast, Africa is 20 percent urban. To put these figures in perspective and using the same cutoff of 100,000 inhabitants to comprise an urban place, only 16 percent of the world's population was urbanized in 1950. In 1950 there were only 71 metropolitan areas of a million or more, and 6 cities of 5 million or more. Today there are approximately 350 metropolitan areas of a million or more and 40 metropolitan areas of 5 million or more. Looking ahead, population projections for 2010 suggest that more than 35 percent of the world's population will be living in cities of 100,000 or more, and there will be about 500 cities with a population of a million or more, including at least 60 cities of 5 million or more.

The most important aspect of world urbanization, from a geographical perspective, is the striking difference in trends and projections between the world's developed and developing regions. In 1950, 20 of the world's 30 largest metropolitan areas were located in developed countries—11 in Europe and 6 in North America. By 1980 the situation was reversed—with 19 of the largest 30 metropolitan area located in less developed regions. By 2010 all but 6 of the 30 largest metropolitan areas are expected to be located in developing regions.

Asia provides some of the most dramatic examples of this trend. From a region of villages, Asia is fast becoming a region of cities and towns. Its urban population rose nearly fivefold between 1950 and 1995, to 1.2 billion people. Already, Asia has more than 45 percent of the world's urban population and 16 of the 30 largest cities in the world.

By 2020 half of Asia's 4.6 billion projected population will be living in urban areas.

World's Largest Metropolitan Areas

METROPOLIS	POPULATION (MILLIONS)		
	1950	(estimate) 2000	(projected) 2015
Tokyo	6.2	27.7	28.7
Mumbai (Bombay)	2.8	16.9	27.4
Lagos	1.0	12.2	24.4
Shanghai	4.3	13.9	23.4
Jakarta	2.8	9.5	21.2
São Paulo	2.3	17.3	20.8
Karachi	1.1	11.0	20.6
Beijing	1.7	11.7	19.4
Dhaka	0.4	16.0	19.0
Mexico City	3.5	17.6	19.0
New York	12.0	16.5	17.6
Calcutta	4.45	12.5	17.3
Cairo	2.1	10.5	14.4
Los Angeles	4.0	12.9	14.2
Buenos Aires	5.25	12.2	13.9

Nowhere is the trend toward rapid urbanization more pronounced than in China, where for decades the communist government imposed strict controls on where people were allowed to live. The government feared the transformative and liberating effects that cities might have on rural migrants. By tying jobs, school admission, and even the right to buy food to the places where people were registered to live, the government made it almost impossible for rural residents to migrate to towns or cities. As a result, more than 70 percent of China's billion people still lived in the countryside in 1985. The Chinese government, having recognized that towns and cities can be engines of economic growth, has not only relaxed residency laws but also drawn up plans to establish more than 430 new cities. Between 1980 and 1996 the number of people living in cities in China more than doubled—

from 196 million, or about 20 percent of China's total population in 1980, to 388 million, or about 32 percent of China's total population in 1996.

Levels of Urbanization

In the world's industrialized regions, **levels of urbanization**, the percentage of the total population living in places designated as "urban" by a country's national census authorities, are high and have been high for some time. According to their government definitions, Belgium, the Netherlands, and the United Kingdom, reckon more than 90 percent of their populations are urbanized; the populations of Australia, Canada, Denmark, France, Germany, Japan, New Zealand, Spain, Sweden, and the United States are all more than 75 percent urbanized. Levels of urbanization are also very high in many of the world's newly-industrialized countries. Brazil, Hong Kong, Mexico, Taiwan, Singapore, and South Korea, for example, are all at least 75 percent urbanized. Almost all developing countries, meanwhile, are experiencing high rates of urbanization, with forecast growth of unprecedented speed and unmatched size. Karachi, Pakistan, a metropolis of 1.1 million in 1950, is estimated to reach 11 million in 2000, and 20.6 million in 2015. Likewise, it is estimated that Cairo, Egypt, will grow from 2.1 million to 10.5 million between 1950 and 2000 and may reach 14.4 million in 2015. Mumbai (Bombay), India's second largest city, Lagos, and São Paulo are all projected to have populations in excess of 20 million by 2015.

Many of the largest cities in developing regions are growing at annual rates of between 4 and 7 percent. Metropolitan areas such as Mexico City and São Paulo are adding half a million persons to their population each year, or nearly 10,000 every week, even after accounting for deaths and out-migrants. It took London 190 years to grow from half a million to ten million, and New York 140 years. By contrast, Mexico City, São Paulo, Buenos Aires, Calcutta, Rio de Janeiro, Seoul, and Mumbai all took less than 75 years to grow from half a million each to ten million inhabitants each. One consequence of such unprecedented growth is that these urban systems have become more volatile. They exhibit characteristics of greater **centrality**—the functional dominance of cities in terms of economic, political, and cultural activity within an urban system—than would be expected in comparison to the rank-size relationships that characterized the cities of the developed world.

The Demographic Transition and Rural-Urban Migration in Developing Regions

Urban growth processes in the world's developing regions have been entirely different from those in developed regions. In contrast to the self-sustaining urban growth of the world's industrial regions, the urbanization of developing regions has been a consequence of demographic growth that has *preceded* economic development. The unprecedented rates of urban growth in developing regions have been driven by rural push—overpopulation and the lack of employment opportunities in rural areas—rather than the pull of prospective jobs in towns and cities. (See Push-Pull Model, page 269.)

In much of the developing world, fast-growing rural populations, a result of the onset of the demographic transition, face an apparently hopeless future of drudgery and poverty. In the past, emigration provided a safety valve, but most of the more affluent countries have now put up barriers to immigration. The only option for the growing numbers of impoverished rural residents has been to move to relatively nearby towns and cities, where at least there is hope of employment and the prospect of access to schools, health clinics, a safe water supply, and the kinds of public facilities and services often unavailable in rural regions. The

Rank-Size Relationships, Primacy, and Centrality

Functional interdependency among places within urban systems tends to result in a distinctive relationship between the population size of cities and their ranking from largest to smallest within a particular urban system. This relationship is known as the **rank-size rule**, which describes a statistical regularity in the city-size distributions of countries and regions. The relationship is such that the nth largest city in a country or region is 1/n the size of the largest city in that country or region. In some urban systems, however, the top of the rank-size distribution is distorted as a result of the disproportionate size of the largest—and sometimes also the second-largest—city. In Argentina, for example, Buenos Aires is more than ten times the size of Rosario, the second-largest city. In the United Kingdom, London is more than three times the size of Birmingham. In France, Paris is nearly eight times the size of Marseilles. In Brazil, São Paulo is nearly five times the size of Belo Horizonte, the third-largest city. This condition is known as **primacy**, a situation in which the population of the largest city in an urban system is disproportionately large in relation to the second- and third-largest cities in that system. In a developing country, primacy is usually a consequence of the primate city's early role as a gateway city. Primacy in industrialized countries is usually a consequence of primate cities' roles as imperial capitals and centers of administration, politics, and trade for a much wider area than their own domestic system.

When cities' economic, political, and cultural functions are disproportionate to their population size, the condition is known as **centrality**, the functional dominance of cities within an urban system. Cities that account for a disproportionately high share of economic, political, and cultural activity have a high-degree of centrality within their urban systems. Bangkok, for instance, with 9 percent of the Thai population, accounts for approximately 38 percent of the country's overall **gross domestic product (GDP)**, more than 85 percent of the country's GDP in banking, insurance, and real estate, and 75 percent of its manufacturing. Very often, it is primate cities that exhibit centrality, but cities do not necessarily have to be primate in order to be functionally dominant within their urban systems.

lure of cities has, meanwhile, been intensified by images of modern amenities and consumer goods beamed into rural areas through satellite TV. Overall, the cities of developing regions have absorbed four out of five of the 1.2 billion city dwellers who have been added to the world's population since 1970.

Rural migrants have poured into cities out of desperation and hope, rather than being drawn by jobs and opportunities. Because these migration streams have been composed disproportionately of teenagers and young adults, an important additional component of urban growth has followed: exceptionally high rates of natural population increase. In most developing countries the rate of natural increase of urban populations exceeds the rate of net in-migration. On average, about 60 percent of current urban population growth in developing countries is attributable to natural increase.

One striking result of the combination of high rates of rural-urban migration and high rates of natural increase in urban populations has been the emergence of **megacities**, cities with populations of ten million or more. In 1960 New York and Tokyo were the only cities with ten million or more inhabitants. By the

Since 1980 Shenzhen, China, has gone from a farm town to a clamorous international finance center of three million people. An army of new-comers includes large numbers of workers from areas outside the city.

mid-1990s there were nearly a dozen more, including: Beijing, Cairo, Calcutta, Jakarta, Lagos, Manila, Mexico City, São Paulo, Shanghai, and Tehran. Most of these megacities provide important intermediate roles between the metropolises of the developed world and the provincial towns and villages of large regions of the less developed world. They not only link local and provincial economies with the global economy but also provide a point of contact between the traditional and the modern and between formal and informal economic sectors.

The **informal sector** is composed of economic activities that take place beyond official record and are not subject to formalized systems of regulation or remuneration. In addition to domestic labor, these activities include illegal activities such as drug peddling and prostitution, as well as legal activities such as casual labor in construction crews, domestic piecework, street trading, scavenging, and providing personal services such as shining shoes or writing letters. (See Economic Geography, page 317.)

Over-Urbanization

A consequence of urban population growth in developing countries has been that many cities have grown more rapidly than the jobs and housing they can sustain. This is called **over-urbanization**, and it produces instant **slums**, characterized by shacks set on unpaved streets, often with open sewers and no basic utilities. Shelters are constructed of any material that comes to hand, such as planks, cardboard, tar paper, thatch, mud, and corrugated iron. Such is the pressure of in-migration that many instant slums are squatter settlements, built illegally on land that is neither owned or rented by its occupants.

Squatter settlements are not necessarily slums, but many of them are. In Chile squatter settlements are called *callampas*, mushroom cities; in Turkey they are called *gecekondu*, meaning they were built after dusk and before dawn. In India they are called *bustees*; in Peru *barriadas*; in Brazil *favelas*, and in Argentina simply *villas miserias*, villages of misery. They typically accommodate well over one-third of

Mexico City is projected to be one of the world's largest metropolitan areas in the year 2000. It currently boasts more than 17 million inhabitants and exhibits strong growth. Like many developing countries, Mexico is highly urbanized, with almost 75 percent of its inhabitants living in cities.

the population and sometimes as much as three-quarters of the population of major cities in less developed countries. A 1996 United Nations conference report on human settlements estimated that 600 million people worldwide were living under health- and life-threatening situations in cities, with some 300 million people living in extreme poverty. The same report showed that, in some developing countries, including Bangladesh, El Salvador, Gambia, Guatemala, Haiti, and Honduras, more than 50 percent of the urban population live below their respective country's national poverty line.

Collectively, it is these slums and squatter settlements that have to absorb the unprecedented rates of urbanization in the megacities of the less developed regions. Many neighborhoods are able to develop self-help networks and organizations that form the basis of community amid dauntingly poor and crowded cities. Nevertheless, over-urbanization is causing acute problems throughout the less-developed world. A 1995 UNICEF report, *The Progress of Nations*, blamed "uncontrollable

Rio de Janiero has grown from a city of less than half a million to more than 10 million in less than 75 years. Squatter settlements, such as Rocinha's 50,000 hillside *favelados*, are clear examples of over-urbanization.

A child and a dog pick through the city dump in Ciudad Juárez, Mexico. In over-urbanized and poverty-stricken communities, the institutions that support children, such as jobs, housing, and schools, are often non-existent, and children are forced to become laborers, beggars, or worse. Work for many children means anything that contributes to survival—from dangerous factory work or street vending to selling drugs.

urbanization" in less developed countries for the widespread creation of "danger zones," where increasing numbers of children are forced to become beggars, prostitutes, and laborers before they reach their teens. Pointing out that urban populations are growing at twice the general population growth rate, the report concluded that too many people are being squeezed into cities that do not have the jobs, housing, or schools to accommodate them. As a consequence, the family and com-munity structures that support children are being destroyed, with the result that more and more young children have to work. For hundreds of thousands of street children in less developed countries, work means anything that contributes to survival, whether shining shoes, guiding cars into parking spaces, chasing other street kids away from patrons at an outdoor café, working as domestic help, making fireworks, or selling drugs.

Prosperous El Paso's high-rises contrast with the shacks of Ciudad Juárez. Shacks are often constructed from any available material—cardboard, tar paper, corrugated iron, wood boards, thatch, and mud. Each year, millions of people die worldwide from conditions caused by inadequate housing and poor sanitation.

Cities as Mirrors of Change: The Internal Structure of Cities

These broad processes of urbanization have not only produced systems of towns and cities of different sizes and with different economic functions but also have imprinted themselves into the physical fabric and cultural settings within individual cities. Cities acquire a distinctiveness that comes in large part from their physical characteristics: the layout of streets, the presence of monumental and symbolic structures, and the building types and architectural styles that fill out the built environment. The resulting urban landscapes reflect a city's history, its physical environment, and its people's social and cultural values.

Geographers are interested in urban landscapes because they can be read as multilayered texts that show how, when, and why cities have developed, how they are changing, and how people's values and intentions take expression in urban form. The built environ-

ment, whether it is planned or unplanned, is what gives expression, meaning, and identity to the various forces involved in urbanization—it becomes a biography of urban change. At the same time, the built environment provides people with cues and contexts for behavior, with landmarks for orientation, and with symbols that reinforce collective values such as civic pride and a sense of identity.

The distinctiveness of cities also stems in part from patterns of land use and the functional organization of economic and social subareas in cities. The resulting patterns of neighborhoods and districts are partly a product of the economic, political, and technological conditions at the time of the city's growth, and partly a product of regional cultural values. The most striking contrasts in such patterns are to be found between the cities of developing countries and those of developed countries.

The urban sprawl of Arizona's Sun City reflects the growth trends typical of the American Southwest since the 1960s.

The structure and urban landscapes of some cities in developing countries retain strong elements of traditional structure, such as Islamic towns and cities, which are organized around a central mosque, a citadel, and a main covered bazaar, or souk. Colonial towns may still have a fort, a cantonment, and **civil lines**, planned residential developments for officials and their families. In most cities in less developed regions, once-distinctive patterns of spatial organization and land use have all but disappeared as a result of congestion and over-crowding caused by over-urbanization, so that the dominant feature of their internal structure is their dualism. **Dualism** is the juxtaposition in geographic space of the formal and informal sectors of an economy, based on a core of modern commerce, retailing, service, and industry, and its associated residential areas, contrasted with an informal economy that is manifest in street markets and extensive areas of makeshift, shanty housing.

Urban Land Use Patterns

In the more developed regions of the world, urban structure has, from the onset of the industrial revolution, been strongly influenced by successive transportation technologies. In the mid-19th century, railways established a hub-and-spoke framework for urban development and prompted a realignment of manufacturing, warehousing, and central business district land uses around the main freight yards and railway stations. The **central business district (CBD)** is the nucleus of commercial land uses in a city.

At the end of the 19th century, streetcars triggered the first significant wave of suburbanization. Since the 1950s automobiles and trucks have allowed cities to sprawl ever outward, weaving ribbons and knots of retailing, services, and industry throughout the urban fabric. Meanwhile, household competitions for the best and most accessible sites, traded off against their desire for living space and modified by the tendency for different social and ethnic groups to cluster together, meant that the urban social patterns tended to develop into distinctive sectors and zones of neighborhoods, all organized around the city's commercial and industrial core.

The typical U.S. city, for example, has long been structured around the CBD, which is then surrounded by a **zone in transition**—a transitional area of mixed industrial, commercial, warehousing, and residential land uses, which, in turn is surrounded with tiers of successively more recent suburbs, then nodes of secondary business districts and strips of commercial development and industrial districts. Poorer households, unable to afford the recurrent costs of long journeys to work, tend to trade off amounts and qualities of living space for accessibility to jobs. As a result, poorer households end up living in poor, high-density conditions, at relatively expensive locations near their low-wage jobs.

Cities experiencing high rates of in-migration have tended to become structured into a series of concentric zones of neighborhoods of different ethnicity, demographic composition, and social status through processes of invasion and succession and congregation. **Invasion and succession** is a process of neighborhood change, whereby one social or ethnic group succeeds another in terms of numerical dominance. **Congregation** is the

Edge Cities

In the United States and some other developed countries, the decentralization of retailing and offices from central cities has reached the point where some suburban commercial centers have grown so large that they compete directly with the CBD for highly specialized functions such as mortgage banking, corporate legal offices, accounting services, publishing, luxury hotels, and exclusive clubs. The success of these suburban commercial centers has been paralleled by the development of private, master-planned residential subdivisions, new towns, and office parks and business campuses. With distinctive local labor markets and commuting patterns, they have collectively come to be known as edge cities. In northern Virginia, Tysons Corner, bounded by I-66, I-495 , (the Washington Beltway), and Virginia 267, (the toll road to Dulles International Airport), is the archetypal example. Administratively, it is still rural, an unincorporated area within Fairfax County, with almost 40,000 residents and almost 100,000 jobs. One of the ten largest concentrations of office and retailing space in the United States, it incorporates more than 25 million square feet of office space, several million square feet of retail space, ten major department stores, almost 4,000 hotel rooms, and parking for more than 90,000 cars. Yet, while this edge city incorporates the largest retail concentration on the East Coast with the exception of Manhattan, it has little of the apparatus of urban governance or civic affairs. It has a branch of Tiffany's but no public open space; an exclusive business club but no public forum; dozens of sportswear stores but no public recreation centers, swimming pools, or bicycle paths. It is a place of great affluence but at the same time a focus of intense concern over traffic congestion, inflated land values, service provision, and land use conflicts.

territorial and residential clustering of specific groups or subgroups of people in city neighborhoods. Distinctive neighborhoods emerge over time through these processes of **residential mobility** when similar kinds of households go through similar search patterns and make similar decisions about where to live. **Residential mobility** is a household's move from one residential location to another within a city. In cities where growth has been less dominated by successive waves of immigrant ethnic groups, neighborhood patterns have tended to be structured around the development of industrial corridors and high-class residential corridors.

Recently, however, the internal structure of cities in developed regions has been reorganized as a result of the economic transformation to postindustrial economies. Traditional manufacturing and related activities have closed or been moved out of central cities, leaving decaying neighborhoods and a growing, residual population of elderly and marginalized people. However, new, postindustrial activities such as business services have begun to cluster in redeveloped central business districts and in **edge cities**—nodes of commercial and residential development located on metropolitan fringes typically near major highway intersections.

In a few cases, metropolitan growth has become so complex and extensive that hundred-mile cities have begun to emerge, with half a dozen or more major commercial and industrial centers forming the nuclei of a series of interdependent urban realms. The archetype is **megalopolis**—the urbanized region extending from Washington, D.C., through Baltimore, Philadelphia, Newark, and New York to Boston. The avatar is Los Angeles, whose innovations and shocking extremes are staples in the way that cities of the 21st century are portrayed. The more likely progenitors of future urban forms and processes, however, are the likes of Mumbai, Hong Kong, Lagos, São Paulo, and Shanghai, which represent the dominant expression of urbanization in a world characterized by accelerating population growth and an increasingly global economy.

Conclusion

Urbanization is an important geographic phenomenon. Cities can be crucibles of economic development and cultural innovation. Cities and groups of cities also are fundamental organizers of space—not just their hinterland but, in some cases, national and even international space. The causes and consequences of urbanization, however, are very different in different parts of the world. The urban experience of the world's developing regions stands in sharp contrast to that of the developed countries, a contrast that is a reflection of the demographic, economic, and political dimensions of world geography.

Much of the developed world has become almost completely urbanized, with highly organized systems of cities. Today levels of urbanization are high throughout the world's more developed countries, while rates of urbanization are relatively low. At the top of the urban hierarchies of the world's developed regions are world cities such as London, New York, Tokyo, Frankfurt, and Milan, which have become the control centers for the flows of information, cultural products, and finance that, collectively, sustain the economic and cultural globalization of the world. In doing so, they help to consolidate the economic, cultural, and political dominance of the world's developed regions.

Few of the metropolises of the developing regions, on the other hand, occupy key roles in the organization of global economics and culture. Rather, they operate as links between provincial towns and villages and the world economy. They have innumerable economic, social, and cultural linkages to their own provinces on one side and to world cities on the other. Almost all developing countries, meanwhile, are experiencing high rates of urbanization, with forecast growth of unprecedented speed and unmatched size.

The most striking contrasts in the streetscapes and internal structure of cities are to be found between the developed and developing regions of the world. Similarly, the nature of urban problems is very different. In developed countries, urban change is dominated by the consequences of an economic transformation to a postindustrial economy. Many traditional manufacturing and related activities have been lost from central cities, leaving decaying neighborhoods and a residual population of disadvantaged households. The basic trend affecting the cities of the world's less developed regions, meanwhile, is demographic—the phenomenal rates of natural increase and in-migration that have given rise to over-urbanization. The corollary of this growth is an ever growing informal sector of the economy, in which people desperately seek economic survival and which is reflected in extensive areas of shanty housing. High levels of unemployment, underemployment, and poverty generate acute social problems that overwhelm under-staffed and under-funded city governments. If present trends continue, such problems are likely to characterize more and more of the world's largest settlements.

Political Geography

Introduction

Political geography examines the spatial and environmental contexts of political decisions made by entities such as governments, multinational corporations, and rebel organizations. Political decision-makers form policies and use power to implement those policies; these decisions inevitably have a geographic basis and geographic consequences. Annexation of a rural area outside of a city, redrawing boundaries for electoral districts, and occupation of territories by ethnic groups such as Kurds and Basques all involve political decisions that change the geography of an area. Geographic locations, such as of low-income residences or majestic landscapes, affect political decisions, such as where to locate landfills or whether to establish national parks. Political geographers analyze political activities at local, regional, national, and global or international scales.

Political decisions and their geographic contexts change constantly because of changes in the interests of populations and constituencies, in the groups making decisions, in the authority and power they wield, and in the boundaries of political units. In- and out-migration and aging change the demographic composition of regions and the priorities of their populations. Elections, uprisings, and coups may change the composition and priorities of those in power and even change political boundaries.

The United States is in the midst of major demographic changes: Hispanic Americans are becoming increasingly important in the Southwest, and political power will shift as a result. New Mexico, for example, is nearly 40 percent Hispanic. There are also movements for greater autonomy among native Hawaiians, white supremacists, as well as several Native-American tribes.

All political problems involve a scale dimension in which the consequences of political decisions impinge unequally on groups within or outside the political region. A government enforces political decisions within a physical territory, often one whose spatial limits were established by previous agreements or decisions. In some cases, enforcement of the decisions is opposed by internal regions and groups, who may also oppose the entire decision-making process. Calls for autonomy by Québécois in Canada, Basques in Spain, and Chechens in Russia are examples of ethnic groups who oppose the national decision-making process. In other cases, political decisions affect populations in areas outside the region who also object to the decision or to the decision-making process. For example, the national policies of the United States and Japan have created trade disputes between the two countries, political decisions by Germany on immigration have caused problems with Turkey, and political decisions on pollution policies by countries bordering the Mediterranean Sea affect people throughout the region regardless of boundaries.

Political geography, like politics itself, is shaped by the use of power by one group to affect the behavior of other groups and achieve specified goals. **Power** is the capacity to modify events and actions by others through the use of persuasion, purchase, barter, or coercion. Official power or **authority** is possessed by governments—recognized administrators of political units—and used to enforce compliance with laws and regulations. The federal government of the United States can impose laws regulating air pollution on all industries and can also influence manufacturing in Japan by imposing tariffs. Exxon, Intel, and Mitsubishi, examples of multinational corporations (MNCs), are unofficial bodies that have no power to establish official policy but can exert political power, and influence legislation in regions and countries where they do business. Rebel organizations, another example of unofficial bodies, such as the Irish Republican Army in Ulster and the Zapatistas in Mexico, have power to affect behavior within their homelands.

When political goals are not achieved by a government or other political entity or when the underlying policy is opposed by those affected, conflicts over decision-making may arise. Political conflict often involves regions where ethnic groups or other minorities are concentrated and whose opposition to political decisions may range from political protest to revolution. Neighborhoods within cities may protest zoning changes or creation of new grade-school districts and may vote politicians making the decisions out of office.

Political conflicts between a national government and regional interests can threaten national unity. The United States formed after a civil war with Great Britain over taxation and representation. Taxation by the U.S. federal government was one of the first internal conflicts of the fledgling country. The Whiskey Rebellion occurred when the federal government passed a tax on whiskey manufacturing in 1794. Revenue from the tax was to help pay off debt from the Revolutionary War. Western Pennsylvanians protested the tax because it rendered whiskey production unprofitable; they tarred and feathered tax collectors and marched on Pittsburgh. The federal government eventually sent troops to the region to confirm federal authority in the matter.

Political Organization of Territory

States

Political power exists at a variety of spatial levels, but it has been concentrated at the **state**—or national—level for centuries. State is used interchangeably with country in political science, but is also used in reference to a constituent unit within a state, such as Missouri in the United States or New South Wales in Australia. **Nation** refers to an ethnic group committed to a political area or homeland.

The English comprise a nation, and England—as well as Scotland, Wales, and Northern Ireland—combined to form a state, the United Kingdom.

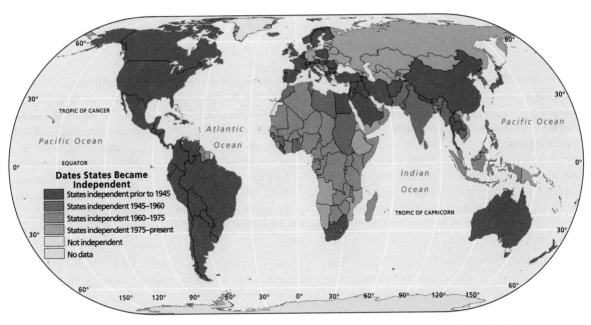

Political power is focused at the state or national level. Most of the world's major powers achieved independence prior to 1945. Independence has been more recent for many countries in historically colonized Africa and parts of Asia.

Even among predecessors to modern states—for example Greek city-states of Athens and Sparta and empires from China to the Andes—power was concentrated at the national level, albeit often in the person of an individual ruler rather than an institution of government. The defining moment in establishing the concept of modern states occurred at the Peace of Westphalia in 1648, which ended the Thirty Years' War. Combatants agreed on mutual recognition and on establishing boundaries for their principalities and duchies. This treaty recognized more than 300 princes as sovereigns, giving them the political authority to control both their internal and external affairs.

A state comes into existence when established states recognize it and when it possesses basic geographic characteristics. **Recognition** involves an established state acknowledging that the new state's government has specific authority to determine its internal affairs and external relations. Within China the

governments in Beijing and Taipei have claimed to represent all of mainland China and Taiwan since 1949, and each government seeks recognition by other states.

Geographically, each state must possess territory and a permanent population. An organized economy and transportation and communication systems are also important in the formation of a state. No minimum threshold of territory or of population is now required for a state, although a "threshold principle" was used by the victorious Allies in 1918 to justify combining Czechs and Slovaks into one country—Czechoslovakia—following the end of World War I. A state must be able to defend its territory from outside threats. Such a defense is called **territoriality,** although the term can be applied on a scale ranging from gangs protecting their turfs to armed forces defending their country from invasion.

During the latter half of the 20th century, a tremendous number of new states were

International Law

International law, the body of rules that has evolved to guide interstate relations, requires recognition before such international relations as trade or exchange of ambassadors may occur. Dutch scholar, Hugo Grotius (1583–1645), published *De jure belli ac Pacis*, the *Law of War and Peace*, in 1625, which became the basis for subsequent studies of international law. In 1778 France's decision to recognize and support the United States in its war against Great Britain was critical for the survival of the new state. More than a century and a half later, in 1948, the United States recognized Israel the day after the state of Israel was declared, and the U.S. could therefore, under international law, provide arms, materiel, and other resources to enable Israel to defend itself from attacks by its neighbors.

created, more than 40 in Africa alone, as independence movements by former colonies were successful. Fewer than 60 states existed prior to World War II, of which only 3 were in Africa: South Africa, Egypt, and Liberia. During the 1990s, as the Soviet Union and Yugoslavia dissolved, 19 new states were recognized by the world community and have since joined the United Nations, bringing the membership to a total of 185 countries. There remains, however, a number of would-be states. Despite the de facto division of Cyprus in 1974, the Turkish Republic of Northern Cyprus remains recognized only by Turkey. (See Map: Stateless Nations, page 403.)

Every state has institutions through which governmental power promotes and protects the interests of its citizens or, more specifically, the constituencies supporting the government. State institutions such as commerce departments, welfare agencies, and police forces can be viewed as "crisis-managers," which defuse potential societal conflicts and challenges to the state. Governments enact laws in reaction to events and situations that alarm the public or threaten public health, safety, or welfare. For example, following the 1996 mass murder of tourists at Port Arthur, Tasmania, the Australian government banned semiautomatic weapons to quiet public alarm and demonstrate its commitment to public safety. Political geographers are increasingly interested in how institutions are used to secure the support of society and to protect political and economic systems.

Capitals and Core Areas

National governments of states are physically located in capital cities. Political decisions are made by national institutions such as legislatures to ensure the stability of the political system by enacting and implementing policies and resolving conflicts. In the United States, the White House, residence of the chief executive, the elected head of government; the Capitol Building, where legislators, members of Congress work; and the Supreme Court Building, office for the justices of the judicial branch, are located in Washington, D.C. In Canada the Parliament buildings and the Supreme Court building are located in Ottawa. Well-known national government buildings, such as the Kremlin in Moscow and Whitehall in London, are commonly used when referring to the governments of Russia and the United Kingdom.

Capitals are symbols of the states as well as centers of power, and therefore the selection of a capital city is a major political decision. A number of capitals, especially in Europe, are located within traditional **core areas** of the states where population has historically been concentrated. The capital cities of Athens, Paris, and London are state capitals that have been dominant cities within the core areas of Greece, France, and the United Kingdom for centuries. Other capitals are located in capital territories, which are not part of a constituent state. This reduces competition between their cities. Canberra, Australia's capital city, for example, is located in the Australian Capital Territory midway between the country's two largest cities, Sydney and Melbourne, and it replaced Melbourne as the country's capital.

A number of national capitals have been relocated for symbolic reasons, and some relocations have been made for economic reasons. Moscow was the traditional capital of Russia, until Tsar Peter the Great moved it to the newly created city of St. Petersburg in 1712 to symbolize Russia's interest in Western Europe. The capital was returned to Moscow, again for symbolic reasons, in 1918 following the Bolshevik Revolution. Israel moved its capital from the seaport of Tel Aviv to the traditional Jewish capital of Jerusalem in 1980, despite resistance by Palestinians and surrounding Muslim populations for whom Jerusalem is also a sacred city. Other relocations of capitals have been made to shift the focus of economic development within the state: Brazil moved its capital from Rio de Janeiro to Brasília in 1960 for this reason, and Nigeria is building an interior capital in Abuja to shift the focus of development from Lagos.

Territorial Characteristics

Size, shape, and location of state territories relative to terrestrial features and to other states can affect the states' internal administration, the natural resources available to states, and external security. The United States, for example, has the fourth largest territory of any nation, a fragmented shape—since Hawaii and Alaska are separated from the main territory—two ocean coastlines, and it shares land borders with Canada and Mexico, two nonthreatening

states. The nearest hostile states have been the former Soviet Union, separated from the United States by the Bering Strait, and Cuba, across the Straits of Florida. In contrast, Belarus is one of the smaller states, with an area just a bit less than that of Kansas. It has a compact shape, no coastline, and is bordered by five states—Lithuania, Latvia, Poland, Ukraine, and Russia. Compared to the United States, the territorial characteristics of Belarus provide it with fewer resources, more external challenges, and relatively easier internal administration.

Size of territory has been traditionally associated with military and economic power, because greater area often meant more population and more abundant natural resources. Large countries such as China and the United States possess abundant natural resources and large populations, and both are world powers. But neither resources nor habitable environments are uniformly distributed over Earth, so that size alone can be a misleading indicator of power. Canada, despite possessing the second largest territory after Russia, the largest state, had a population of only 30 million in 1998 and is not a military power; yet based on total GNP, Canada's economy ranks as one of the highest in the world.

States with extremely small territories often have small populations and limited natural resources and economic diversity. As a result, **microstates** are often dependent on one or a very few industries. Tuvalu, an island nation in the South Pacific, relies on copra; Malta, in the Mediterranean Sea, relies on tourism and shipping; and Brunei, two enclaves on the island of Borneo, relies on petroleum. Vatican City, a state despite its name, is the smallest state, with a territory of 0.2 square miles and a population of fewer than a thousand, and it is economically dependent on the activities of the Roman Catholic Church.

Territorial shape can affect the number of bordering states—and therefore the number of potential conflicts—as well as internal administration, and ocean access. Political geographers traditionally categorize states by their shape: compact, elongated, fragmented, perforated, and prorupt. **Compact states,** such as Cambodia, Poland, and Uruguay, are roughly spherical, which facilitates internal control even if the capital is not centrally located, as in the case of Montevideo on Uruguay's coast. Topographic features such as mountains or an ethnically diverse population can interfere with administration, as in the case of Nigeria, which contains about 250 tribal groups and is divided in general between a Muslim north and a Christian and animist south.

Elongated states such as Chile, Italy, and Laos have narrow, linear shapes. Internal diversity is more likely to occur in elongated states, as seen in the economic division in Italy between the wealthy north and the poor south; and in the ethnic division in Laos between the northern Kha and southern mountain tribes. **Fragmented states** such as Angola, Malaysia, and Oman have territories separated by bodies of water or another state. Fragmentation can lead to regional identities and reduce linkages between territories, thus exacerbating administrative problems. Such problems were responsible for the breakup of the fragmented state of Pakistan, which was separated geographically into East and West Pakistan by India. East Pakistan became Bangladesh in 1971.

There are only a few states that are **perforated,** that is they totally surround another state. Italy surrounds San Marino, and South Africa surrounds Lesotho; the larger, surrounding states influence trade and transport systems of the smaller states. **Prorupt states** have extensions—proruptions—reaching outward from their main territories. Most proruptions provide access to resources, though some form buffers between neighboring states. The Caprivi Strip is Namibia's proruption and provides access to the Zambezi River, and the Shaba province of Republic of Congo (formerly Zaire) provides access to mineral resources such as cobalt and zinc. Afghanistan's proruption was designed by the British in the 1880s

to serve as a buffer between Russia's expanding territory and the United Kingdom's expanding influence in the Indian subcontinent.

A state's global location, especially with respect to ocean shorelines, is extremely important to the economic development of states. **Landlocked states,** of which there are 15 in Africa alone, lack direct access to oceans and therefore lack shipping, fishing, and other coastal opportunities. Many landlocked states, such as Niger, Bolivia, and Nepal, are among the poorest countries; Switzerland and Austria are exceptions. Russia, despite its huge size and long coastlines, has no ice-free ports in winter and therefore faces difficulties in shipping.

The proximity of more powerful or hostile bordering states is another important, though changing, aspect of global location. Canada's foreign relations with the United States are generally very friendly, but Canadian proximity to the U.S. was described by former Prime Minister Pierre Trudeau as "like sleeping with an elephant. No matter how friendly or even-tempered is the beast . . . one is affected by every twitch and grunt." Many of the states bordering Germany, Russia, and China have at one time been threatened by these three powerful states. States may also face economic or political threats when bordering states are far poorer or are attempting to export their political system through revolution. The United States has coped with illegal Mexican immigration for decades, and Laos was threatened by guerrilla activity from Vietnam during the 1970s. (See Domino Theory, page 414.)

Intrastate Political Organization

Political decision-making within every state includes the subdivision of the national territory into smaller political units administered by subnational governments. Not all problems and issues are national in scale and so policies and decisions addressing these issues may be more effectively formulated and implemented at the local or regional scale. Political disputes can arise when a problem involves a territory larger than that administered by a subnational government or when a political decision is enforced over a territory and population that disagrees with that decision. In Canada, for example, no province can eradicate gypsy moths and protect forest resources individually since the pests travel between jurisdictions, but the provincial governments have disputed national decisions on funding youth employment, maternal benefits, and other social services.

Various types of state organizations exist, differentiated primarily by the degree to which power is centralized in the national government. In **unitary states**, all political power derives from the national government; the majority of states have unitary systems. In **federal states**, political power is shared by both the national government and a number of subnational governments; fewer than 25 states can be classified as federal.

Unitary states, which include Paraguay, Libya, Japan, and Sweden, vary in how zealously the central governments protect their prerogatives. Central governments in unitary states may be elected, hereditary royalty, or controlled by military dictators. The most centralized unitary states are usually run by dictators who use their centralized power to counter internal diversity and challenges to their authority. In Iraq, for example, Saddam Hussein has used extreme measures to remain in power. In less centralized systems, assertions of centralized power are not needed to prevent regional challenges, and local governments are allowed more leeway in decision-making; Ireland and Denmark fall into this category.

Subnational administrative units exist in unitary states, but the powers of their governments are delegated from and controlled by the national government. France, for example, is divided into 22 administrative regions, which are subdivided into 96 *departements*. The departements are progressively subdivided into arrondissements, cantons, and communes.

There are about 3,600 communes. Local issues are dealt with at the commune level, and the larger administrative regions were established to address economic development and environmental issues.

Some unitary states have found it expedient to grant greater power, even autonomy, to regional territories and governments to increase national stability. In this process of **devolution** the national governments technically retain ultimate power, but in fact a hybrid form of government has been created. Devolution of authority has occurred in Brazil, Belgium, and Spain, for example; and Scotland and Wales within the United Kingdom were granted greater power in 1998. Although the national government in London could vote to reassert its powers, in doing so it would increase regional opposition to the national government.

In federal states, such as the United States and Australia, decision-making power is divided between a national government and subnational governments, and a **constitution** is the contract specifying what authority is held by each level of government. National governments in federal states ordinarily are responsible for decisions involving national defense, foreign relations, and foreign trade. Subnational governments usually make decisions concerning such regional concerns as health, welfare, and public safety that apply only within their individual territories, although these can also be dealt with at the national level. Subnational units have numerous designations, including provinces (Canada), cantons (Switzerland), and states (the United States and India.)

Within the United States, the national government and state governments have each established new political units and governing agencies with limited powers to address problems at intermediate spatial scales. For example, the national government created the Tennessee Valley Authority (TVA) in 1933 to coordinate development of the poverty-stricken part of Appalachia through which the

Tennessee River flowed; the TVA has limited authority over portions of seven states. The national government also has authority over outlying territories such as Guam, American Samoa, and the U.S. Virgin Islands, all of which are **unincorporated territories.**

All 50 states have established county subdivisions—called parishes in Louisiana and boroughs in Alaska—as well as municipalities and towns whose governments have varying degrees of authority. County governments have decreased in power as urban populations have outpaced those of rural areas, but most still have responsibilities in law enforcement, highway construction, and other concerns.

The number of municipalities is growing in the United States—nearly 20,000 have been incorporated as legal entities—and their governmental powers vary according to the state in which they exist. In Oregon municipalities of all sizes have equal powers; and in Missouri the degree of municipal authority—the power to pass certain bonds, for example—and responsibility—for sidewalks and parks, for example—varies with population. Cities often create **special purpose districts**, such as school and fire districts, within their municipal limits to manage regional services better, much as counties have used irrigation districts and soil conservation districts to improve the provision of those services.

Electoral Geography

Electoral geography is the analysis of the spatial patterns of voting and of representation in political systems. In nearly all representative governments, elected officials represent a political territory—called an electoral district in the United States and a riding in Canada—and are voted into office by residents of that territory. One notable exception is Israel, whose nationally elected officials represent the votes for particular parties rather than for individual representatives; this proportional representation ensures that a wide range of viewpoints is represented in the Knesset, the Israeli legislature, but makes it difficult to achieve majority approval on controversial issues.

Analyses of voting behavior in the United States have become increasingly important to political parties seeking to have their candidates elected and to special interest groups seeking to have an issue approved or refuted. At the national level, some candidates have extremely strong regional support. When George Wallace (1919-1998), former governor of Alabama, first ran for President in 1968, his support was almost exclusively from the Old South, states that had joined the Confederacy during the Civil War, such as Alabama and Mississippi. In 1984 presidential candidate Walter Mondale won only his home state of Minnesota. In recent years the voting patterns of growing ethnic groups have become of increasing interest. The rapid growth of the Hispanic population of the southern United States, of whom the majority vote Democratic, may increase their representation in Congress and cause both major political parties to revise their stands on immigration, welfare, and other issues of concern to Hispanic voters.

Studies of representation focus on voters' characteristics in electoral districts and changes in the areas, boundaries, and demographics of those districts. Shifts in population mean shifts in representation, political power, and federal monies. In the United States and Canada, there are constitutional requirements to redraw voting districts following every ten-year census to ensure their relatively equal populations. This process is called **reapportionment,** which can result in adding or subtracting the number of representatives from states and provinces as well as **redistricting,** or redrawing district boundaries within states and provinces. Voting tendencies of residents in electoral districts can be determined fairly accurately, and therefore incumbents who run for reelection may resist changes in district boundaries that will

Pork-Barrel Politics

The term **pork-barrel politics** dates back to the period before the Civil War and refers to Congressmen who draft bills that provide their state or electoral district with public-works projects. Congressional representatives with seniority and who chair committees have traditionally been able to bring public projects and associated federal jobs and funding to benefit their constituencies. This spatial bias in federal expenditures, also termed the **political representation effect,** can provide substantial support for local economies. Construction projects, including military weapons and transport, dams, and research centers, can bring millions of dollars into the districts of powerful senators and representatives.

threaten their chances in subsequent elections. In 1994 the Canadian House of Commons attempted to pass a bill that would delay adjusting ridings—or districts—until after the following national election. The delay would have benefitted incumbents running for reelection; the Canadian Senate prevented this bill from passing.

The U. S. Constitution requires Congress to reapportion the number of representatives to the House of Representatives (currently 435) among the states after each ten-year census, and then requires states to redistrict to ensure the equal populations of districts within the states. California, Florida, and Texas had the greatest increases in population between the 1980 and 1990 censuses and gained seven, four, and three representatives respectively; New York lost two representatives; many other northeastern states each lost representatives.

Redistricting the boundaries of the electoral districts can become an exercise in gerrymandering, which provides unfair advantage to one segment of voters over others. **Gerrymandering,** named after Governor Elbridge Gerry (1744–1814) of Massachusetts, who was known to support unfair redistricting, has

often been used by members of major political parties to ensure that their party remains in power. Electoral districts can be redrawn to divide the voting power of the competing party among several districts or to concentrate it into one district. In the early 1970s, Washington State had two competing redistricting plans, one from the Democratic House and one from the Republican Senate. Eventually a federal judge appointed geographer Richard Morrill to develop a nonpartisan plan.

Even attempts at righting past voting wrongs, such as trying to ensure minority representation from a state, can be determined to be gerrymandering. Following a 1982 amendment to the 1965 Voting Rights Act, several states created **majority-minority districts** to ensure that minority ethnic groups would have a majority vote in some congressional districts. North Carolina's 1st and 12th congressional districts were drawn to ensure African-American majorities, but the United States Supreme Court ruled in *Shaw* v. *Reno* (1993) and *Miller* v. *Johnson* (1996) that both of these districts used race unfairly as the basis of redistricting, which was considered to be unconstitutional gerrymandering.

Regionalism and Political Fragmentation

Nations and Nation-States

Distinct societies committed to their **homelands,** territories with which they identify a shared history and culture, form nations. A **nation** is usually an ethnic group, a people sharing the same language, religion, history, and icons—symbols of their distinctiveness. Flags, anthems, heroes, and heroines are icons. Old Glory, "The Star-Spangled Banner," George Washington, and Betsy Ross symbolize the United States. Maps, too, can be icons: Argentine maps have shown the Islas Malvinas (Falkland Islands) as Argentine territory, not British.

The identification of a nation with its homeland is often translated into proprietary behavior or defensive territorial behavior. Territoriality occurs at all spatial scales, including an individual defending his or her personal space, but it becomes political behavior and affects political geography when groups or nations act or seek to act as decision-makers for their homeland. Separatist actions taken by the Moros on Mindanao challenged the government of the Philippines much as actions taken by Corsicans challenge the French government. A peace was achieved in 1996 in the Philippines, but the Corsicans have not yet reached an accord with the French national government.

Ideally, the homelands of nations should coincide with the territories of states and form **nation-states,** thereby reducing potential conflicts, but few states approach this ideal. Island states such as Iceland and Japan, which can more easily control immigration, are close to the ideal of a nation-state. Japan is the classic example and has a population that is more than 99 percent ethnic Japanese; Ainu—an indigenous, aboriginal people—inhabit the northern island of Hokkaidō, and the number of Koreans in Japan is growing. In Western Europe, Denmark is nearly a nation-state, but Greenlanders (Inuit) and a growing population of Turkish laborers prevent a perfect match between nation and state.

Occasionally the territory of one state, occupied by members of its national group, is located within the boundaries of a second state, forming an **exclave** of the first state and an **enclave** within the second. West Berlin was a West German exclave contained in East Germany until the two countries recombined in 1990. Nagorno-Karabakh, an exclave of Armenia, is an enclave in Azerbaijan and was the scene of fierce fighting between the two states in the early 1990s. Typically, territory within one state includes part of the homeland of a nation dominating a neighboring state; the Albanian population of Kosovo in Yugoslavia and the Hungarian population of Transylvania in Romania are examples. Attempts by a state to incorporate outlying territories containing its nationals is called **irredentism** and has led to wars in the past and continues to threaten some areas. German incursions into Czechoslovakia and Poland in 1939 are examples of irredentism as are current efforts by Somalia to capture the Ogaden region of Ethiopia.

Most states are best described as multi-ethnic, which can create political problems, especially when ethnic groups occupy spatially discrete homelands within the state. In the United States, few ethnic groups are so geographically concentrated that they present a separatist challenge to the federal government. Native American tribes, however, do have limited decision-making authority over their reservations, although these territories are rarely their original homelands.

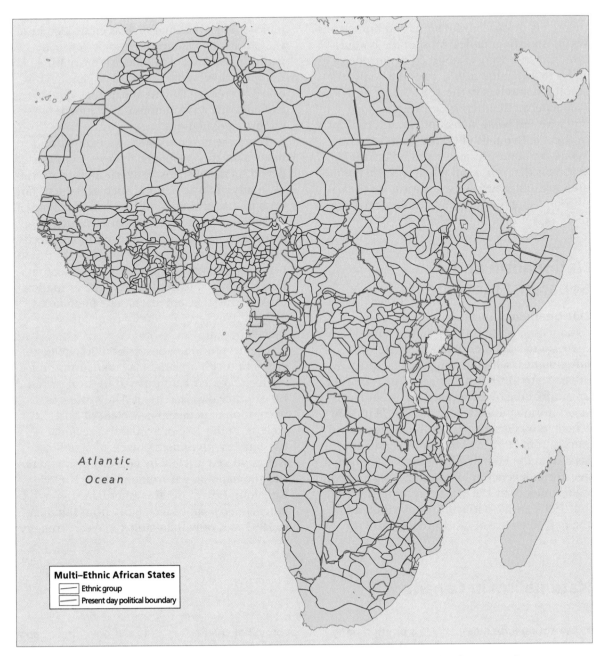

Multi–Ethnic African States
Ethnic group
Present day political boundary

African state boundaries, drawn principally by Europeans who sought to maximize profits from natural resources, ignored the boundaries of ethnic nations and homelands. The resulting political turmoil continues to this day.

In other states, especially those in Africa, there may be dozens of nations and homelands within state boundaries. Most of the boundaries in Africa were established by European states to divide the resources of the continent among themselves in the 1884 Treaty of Berlin. (See Sidebar: The Berlin Conference, page 357.) Recent political disruptions and civil wars in Nigeria, Republic of Congo (Zaire), Sierra Leone, and other African states reflect the problems that can result when political boundaries are designed to separate areas on the basis of conquest, resources, and economic development rather than on ethnicity.

Nationalism and Separatist Movements

Nationalism, sometimes specified as ethnic nationalism, is the concept that nations deserve the right to self-determination, as either autonomous, self-governing regions or as sovereign states. Ethnic nationalism instigated the breakup of the overseas empires of European states during the 20th century. The Mau Mau rebellion was waged against the British in Kenya from 1952 to1956, and Algerian guerrillas fought the French during the 1950s. Kenya became independent in 1963, and Algeria won independence in 1962. More recently, in 1990 and 1991, ethnic nationalism contributed to the independence of the 15 republics of the Union of Soviet Socialist Republics. This philosophy of nationalism was embedded in U.S. President Woodrow Wilson's Fourteen Points formula used to establish peace in Europe following World War I; several points called for recognizing nationalist movements and allowing autonomous development of minority populations.

There are dozens of stateless nations, and many actively seek political power from the governments of states in which their territories lie. Many of these nations, such as Baluchistan in southern Pakistan and Iran, are little known outside their region. Other nations, such as Kurdistan, have achieved much more publicity, partially as a continuing complication of the Persian Gulf War. Kurdistan, like many other homelands that existed prior to the formation of modern states, antedates state boundaries and overlaps several states—Iraq, Turkey, Syria, and Iran.

The devolution of power from a state government to a homeland may take forms ranging from limited authority—over local issues, for example—to statehood. The process of devolution may be either violent or nonviolent. In the case of Scotland, a regional legislature with limited powers of taxation was approved in 1997 by both Scottish voters and the national government of the United Kingdom. Eritrea, on the other hand, won independence and sovereignty from Ethiopia in 1993, but only following a 31-year struggle.

Nationalism in Canada

The struggle for independence by French-Canadians in Quebec has been nonviolent, except for a few terrorist acts by the Quebec Liberation Front (FLQ) in the late 1960s. In 1976 a political party, the Parti Québécois, was elected on the platform of Quebec independence and protection of the French language and culture; it continues to seek the approval of Quebec voters to separate from Canada. On another political front in Canada, the Inuit, a group of native Canadians in northern Canada, was granted the right to self-government and in 1999 the territory of Nunavat was created from the Northwest Territories.

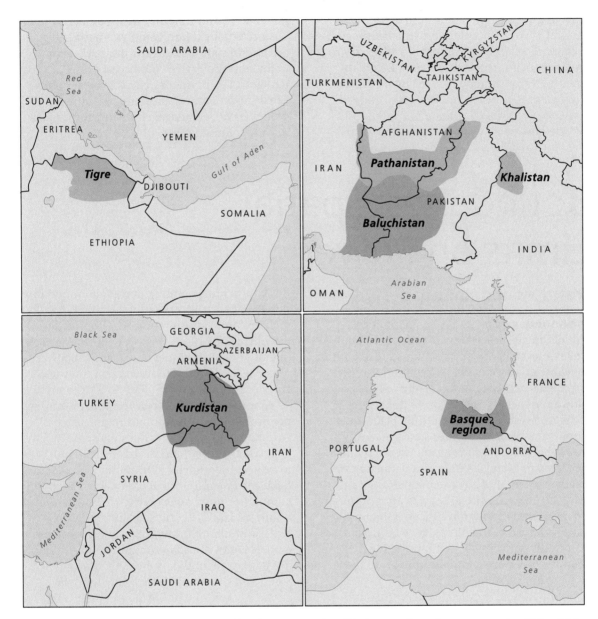

Dozens of stateless nations exist in the world today. Many seek political power from the governments within which their territories lie. This may be achieved through nonviolence or extended conflict.

In many cases, the political struggle of a nation for power becomes an armed struggle because the state governments involved try to preserve their territorial control. Guerrilla warfare and terrorism may be used by nationalist movements because states are better funded, manned, and armed; although in some cases outside powers may supply the nationalist movement with funding, weapons, and other resources. Libya, Iran, and Syria have been accused of sponsoring terrorist activities by nationalist groups. In recent years the Basque nation in Spain, the Chechens in Russia, the Corsicans in France, and numerous other groups have been engaged in armed struggles to gain political power.

Boundaries: Spatial Limits on Power

Frontiers and Boundaries

The **boundaries** of a state or any political unit define its jurisdiction and are the spatial limits of its ability to enforce compliance with political decisions. Laws, whether on taxation or criminal activities, can be enforced only within the spatial jurisdiction of the governing body. As a result, individuals may place their money in a bank in another state where tax laws are less costly, such as in Switzerland or the Cayman Islands, a British dependency, or a person accused of a crime in one state can flee to a different state to seek asylum. Agreements between states have made hiding money less secure and extraditing people accused of crimes less problematic, but international boundaries remain an important part of the international system.

Boundaries, also called borders, are both inclusive and exclusive. Governments use them as limits on the flow of goods, people, money, and communications both into and out of the state. Relationships with bordering states are managed along international boundaries, but political decisions on how an international boundary functions change with governments and situations. During the last century the United States has alternately excluded Mexicans and then allowed Mexican citizens into this country, depending upon economic conditions and on political sentiment. Mexicans were excluded during the Great Depression, but during the 1940s they were encouraged to migrate under the Emergency Farm Labor Program, also called the Bracero Program, which lasted until 1964.

Frontiers, undeveloped regions separating political units, are now almost nonexistent. Ancient civilizations were usually separated by frontiers because the civilizations were not able to project their power sufficiently to defend the territory. Expanding economies, growing populations, improving weaponry, and increasing claims on land have caused boundaries to replace frontiers throughout the world. A few neutral zones officially recognized by neighboring states remain today, including one between Spain and Gibraltar (United Kingdom) and another between Saudi Arabia and Kuwait.

Boundaries between states are understood to extend above the surface, beneath it, and, for those with coastlines, offshore. Airspace under the jurisdiction of a state currently extends to the limit of powered flight, so that overflights by satellites—at least for now—are not considered invasions of airspace. The downward extent of boundaries is theoretically to Earth's center and includes all resources, although fluid resources such as petroleum,

The Berlin Wall, maintained by East Germany from 1961 to 1989, divided soviet East Berlin from West Berlin, occupied by British, French, and United States forces. The 12-foot high concrete wall was an effective barrier for more than 25 years. In 1990 the wall came down as East Germany reunited with West Germany, forming the Federal Republic of Germany.

which can flow between states, may cause disputes. (See Boundary Disputes, page 407.)

The international consensus for offshore boundaries of states is the result of three United Nations Conferences on the Law of the Sea held in 1958, 1960, and from 1973 to 1982, known as UNCLOS I, II, and III. (See Alliances and Organizations, page 410.) Territorial seas, over which states have virtually the same authority as over land, extend 12 nautical miles offshore. States must, however, allow "innocent passage" of foreign ships through these waters. Each state's exclusive economic zone (EEZ), over which the state controls resource development, is the water and seabed within 200 nautical miles of shore. Problems with locating EEZ boundaries are common because many coastal states—such as Denmark, Germany, and Sweden—are not separated by 400 nautical miles of ocean, and therefore lines halfway between the nearest shorelines of the adjacent states must be determined. Beyond EEZs lie the high seas, open to all states for transport and resource development, although there is an international movement to have seabed resources under these

waters benefit all states, including landlocked ones. Open access to high-sea fisheries has been limited by specific treaties or organizations, such as the International Whaling Commission, but not by general international laws.

Formal establishment of a boundary occurs in stages, all of which may not take place. First, the boundary is defined by a treaty between bordering states that specifies the boundary's location. This written description is followed by **delimitation,** which means that the boundary is drawn on a map, and its location is recognized by the bordering states. Next, boundaries are **demarcated,** that is they are marked on the landscape by walls, posts, clearings, or other features. The United States, for example, has constructed walls along part of the border between California and Mexico's Baja California Norte to control the flow of people across that segment of their boundary. Finally, boundaries are administered by officials to fulfill such governmental functions as customs, health, and immigration checks.

Boundaries also separate subnational political units. Within the United States, boundaries separate states and limit the enforcement of state laws. Prostitution, for example, is legal only within Nevada, and states have different income taxes, except for Alaska, Florida, Nevada, South Dakota, Texas, Washington, and Wyoming, which have no state taxes. City limits are boundaries for city taxes, city services, and city laws—such as land-use planning ordinances—which are not enforced or provided beyond city limits. (See Sidebar: Zoning, page 378.) **Annexation** of adjacent rural areas expands city boundaries to include additional areas. While some cities, such as Chattanooga and Albuquerque, have been able to double their areas through annexation, some rural populations fight annexation to remain beyond city laws and taxes.

Types of Boundaries

Boundaries cause differences in the physical and human landscape because of differences in government policies on either side of the boundaries. As unrestricted as the United States-Canadian boundary is, differences in crops and livestock between the two countries reflect different agricultural-support policies of the two governments. Similarly, Canadian and American railroad lines often parallel each other along the border instead of joining to form an international rail network.

Boundaries can be classified, based on the surface features they follow, as physical, geometric, or ethnic. Each classification can affect boundary functions differentially and will have advantages and disadvantages in managing relations with bordering states. **Physical boundaries** follow natural features in the physical environment, such as rivers, mountains, and lakes. Rivers are easily recognized as boundaries, but questions of proportionate water use by the two states may come up, and rivers may also change location because of meandering. The United States and Mexico have negotiated the boundary along the Rio Grande, called Río Bravo in Mexico, numerous times in the 20th century to reflect changes in the location of the river's channel.

Geometric boundaries are usually straight lines, often lines of latitude or longitude, and only rarely follow other geometric shapes. The Gambia-Senegal boundary includes several arcs of circles centered on the Gambia River. The ease of establishing geometric boundaries is countered by the problems caused by dividing natural resources such as water and dividing ethnic populations and homelands. The 49th parallel dividing western Canada and the United States created problems with water development because it divided major watersheds, such as that of the Columbia River. The linear boundary between Ethiopia and Somalia resulted in the inclusion of a large Somali population in Ethiopia, which has created a major boundary dispute between the two states. (See Irredentism, page 400.)

Ethnic boundaries attempt to separate different ethnic groups to establish national identities and prevent irredentist claims. However, not only are ethnic settlements not grouped into discrete regions, but settlements often contain residents of different ethnicity. The difficulty in accurately defining ethnic boundaries became evident in the partitioning of the former Yugoslavia: Ethnic Bosnians in particular were dispersed throughout Bosnia and Herzegovina, and Croatian and Serbian settlements and families also were found in most parts of the new state.

Boundaries can also be classified according to the timing of their establishment and location relative to territorial development as antecedent, consequent, superimposed, and relict boundaries. **Antecedent boundaries** are those established prior to substantial development of the territory, and therefore state governments can influence the population and types of activities in the areas. For example the boundary on Borneo between Malaysia and Indonesia predates development of Borneo's resources.

Consequent boundaries are imposed

The Treaty of Tordesillas

Brazil is the only former Portuguese colony in South America because of a 1494 agreement brokered by the Pope between Portugal and Spain, two Roman Catholic states. This agreement, the Treaty of Tordesillas, named for a small Spanish town on the Douro River, established a north-south boundary 370 leagues west of the Cape Verde Islands and allocated lands east of the boundary to Portugal and those west to Spain.

subsequent to settlement within a territory and attempt to separate different ethnic groups. The boundaries between Ireland and Northern Ireland and between Pakistan and India were established to divide rival religious groups, and neither boundary was perfectly matched to the populations, despite the migration of millions of Muslims and Hindus between Pakistan and India, and problems remain today from these imperfect divisions.

Superimposed boundaries are also subsequent boundaries but are not concerned with patterns of ethnic settlements. The boundaries of most modern African states are the result of European colonial powers such as France, Portugal, the United Kingdom, and Spain dividing Africa to benefit themselves without concern for the homelands of the hundreds of African nations. A continuing legacy of these superimposed boundaries has been ethnic conflict. In Rwanda and Burundi, for example, the rivalry between Hutus and Tutsis resulted in hundreds of thousands of deaths in 1994; around one million died in the late 1960s as the Ibo nation attempted to separate from the rest of Nigeria.

Relict boundaries are inactive and represent earlier political units, nevertheless their impacts are often evident on landscapes. The reunification of Germany in 1990 erased the international boundary between West Germany and East Germany, but differences in industry and development between the two Germanies have not yet disappeared and will persist for decades because of the high costs of implementing policies to help the east reach parity with the west.

Boundary Disputes

Boundaries impose spatial limits on the power of states and other political units, yet the political, economic, and social interests of governments and their constituencies extend across boundaries. As a result, boundary disputes are extremely common between states as well as between subnational units. Claims to territory, to resources, and to populations across boundaries, and disagreements over boundary management, such as limiting imports or migrants, cause disputes and can cause wars. Ecuador's claims to territory now in northern Peru, Libya's claims to northern Chad, and the claims of Brunei, China, Malaysia, the Philippines, Taiwan, and Vietnam to the Spratly Islands are among the dozens of boundary disputes in the world.

Boundary disputes are categorized as positional, territorial, resource, and functional disputes, but the issues involved are rarely so straightforward. **Positional disputes** are based on different understandings of boundary definitions. An argument in the early 1900s between the United States and Canada over the position of the boundary between Alaska's Panhandle and British Columbia focused on the interpretation of 1824 treaties among Russia, the United States, and the United

Kingdom. A judgement by an international tribunal in 1903 gave the United States control over coastal areas and therefore over the ports of Dyea and Skagway serving miners arriving for the Yukon gold rush.

Territorial disputes arise when land is claimed by two or more states, each of which has historical claims to the territory. In Latin America alone there are nearly a dozen territorial disputes, many of which can be traced back to boundaries imprecisely defined in the 1800s. The 1982 Falkland Islands War between Argentina and the United Kingdom was the result of competing claims to these islands, dating back to 1833.

Resource disputes are a version of territorial disputes that involve natural resource development. The invasion of Kuwait by Iraq in 1990 was triggered by Kuwait pumping oil from the shared Rumaila oil field without a prior agreement with Iraq; several other factors were also involved, including Iraq's historic claims to Kuwaiti territory. Many recent resource disputes have arisen over the offshore extent of EEZs and authority over good fishing grounds. Canada and the United States disputed their offshore boundary and fishing rights in the Gulf of Maine until 1984, when they agreed to accept a judgment by the International Court of Justice.

Functional disputes revolve around policies one state enforces on trans-boundary movements, including immigration, imports, and smuggling, that result in inconveniences to another state. North Korea has barred South Koreans from visiting family members in the north since the two states divided in 1948. The United States has complained for years about the number of illegal immigrants and drug smugglers crossing the United States-Mexican border. Functional disputes are common, but usually remain at a low level of disturbance.

Imperialism, Multistate Organizations, and the World Order

State interests such as security and trade cannot be fully contained within state jurisdictions, so states have acted to exert their influence beyond their boundaries. Over the last five centuries, powerful states—especially European states—conquered lands and established colonies to improve their political, economic, and cultural influence.

During the 20th century most of these empires collapsed, and the colonies became independent thus changing the political and economic relationships between states and creating incentives for them to act jointly. During the last decades of the 20th century, the end of the Cold War and increases in biological weapons and terrorism created new threats to state security, and the growth of multinational corporations and expansion of the global economy generated new benefits from cooperative actions. The result has been the formation of a new political and economic order, a **new world order**.

Imperialism

Imperialism, the policy of dominating colonies or other states and maintaining those relationships to increase state power, was embraced by European states in the 15th

Lebensraum

Friedrich Ratzel (1844–1904) envisioned states as being similar to organisms requiring additional living space or **lebensraum** to remain healthy. Karl Haushofer (1869–1946), a German geographer and army officer, expanded Ratzel's work to justify German expansion in the first half of the 20th century. Haushofer specifically defended Germany's need to acquire parts of Poland and Czechoslovakia and coined the term *geopolitik* to justify Nazi aggression against its Slavic neighbors.

century. The reasons for imperialism are usually simplified to and rationalized by the phrase God, gold, and glory, because European states, driven by religious beliefs, cupidity, and nationalism, conquered much of the world. Earlier empires existed, such as the Inca, Roman, and Chinese empires, but imperialism during the last five centuries established unequal relationships between areas, which are now states, that remain in effect today. (See Map: European Empires Circa 1700, page 356.)

European imperialism at one time claimed almost the entire non-European world. The territories of North and South America, Australia, most of Africa, and much of Asia were claimed as colonies by European states. The phrase "The sun never sets on the British Empire" referred to the global extent of British colonies on all continents except Antarctica, as well as on Pacific and Atlantic islands. Russia's empire, unlike those of other Western European states, extended overland rather than overseas, which enabled Russian, and after 1917, Soviet forces, to maintain their presence and retain control in what are now central Asian states. Japan and the U.S. also had empires. Japan's empire in eastern and southeastern Asia was established between 1875 and World War II, and that of the United States, although rarely referred to as an empire, included Cuba, the Philippines, and other islands in both the Caribbean and the Pacific.

Colonies were controlled politically and economically by the imperial power. Often, colonies provided strategic locations for their rulers: Cape Town, Malta, and Singapore provided the British with critical locations for supplying and repairing ships. Economically, colonies provided raw materials for the industries of the imperial states; not only did this remove much of the wealth from the colony, but it established dominant-subordinate production and trading relationships that are still present today. Côte d'Ivoire, a former French colony, has France as its major trading partner, Ghana, a former British colony, has the United Kingdom as its major trading partner, and so on. (see Specialization and Trade, page 347.)

Empires began to break apart in the 19th century and continued to dissolve at the end of the 20th century, although some colonies had gained independence earlier. The United States, for example, declared independence from the British Empire in 1776. As recently as 1960 there were only four independent states in Africa: South Africa, Egypt, Ethiopia, and Liberia; all other territories were colonies. Now, however, the majority of colonies are recognized as states, as evidenced by their admissions to the United Nations, which had only 51 members at its beginning in 1945, and had 185 in 1999. (See Alliances and Organizations, page 410.)

One enduring legacy of imperialism is a global north-south division between less developed former colonies in Africa, Latin America, and southern Asia, and the more developed colonizing states of Europe, the U.S., and Japan.

Neo-colonialism, the economic dependence of former colonies on their former colonizers, is a modern form of imperialism which compromises the political sovereignty of the former colonies. Since the economies of former colonies remain dependent on supplying raw materials for the developed states, their financial policies are necessarily constrained. Attempts by former colonies to qualify for loans from the International Monetary Fund to build infrastructures and develop their economies involve complying with stringent requirements on national monetary and fiscal policy, which have been difficult to meet.

Alliances and Organizations

States have numerous incentives to cooperate with each other—to promote economic growth and military security, for example—but cooperation necessarily involves shared decision-making power and some loss of individual initiative. To preserve state powers, most alliances are established as international organizations that do not create a powerful central authority, but rely instead on collaborative decision-making. The British Commonwealth and the Organization of African States (OAU), for example, are international organizations. **Supranational organizations** have also been created, in which three or more member states delegate limited powers to a central authority. Although states lose some sovereignty, the organization has increased power to implement policies promoting joint interests. The United Nations and the European Union (EU), which establishes rules on the passage of labor, finances, and goods among member states, are supranational organizations.

As empires dissolved and international conflict and exchange increased in the 20th century, dozens of organizations formed as both new and old states sought to protect and promote their national interests. Most of these organizations postdate World War II, although a few formed earlier: the Economic Union of Belgium and Luxembourg (UEBL) (later the Benelux Economic Union) was established in 1921 to abolish customs checks between the two states, and their trade statistics are reported as a unit, rather than individually. In some instances the formation of one organization spurred the formation of another as the non-members grouped together to be economically or militarily competitive. Three years after Belgium, the Netherlands, Luxembourg, France, West Germany, and Italy formed the European Economic Community (EEC) in 1957, the European Free Trade Association (EFTA) was formed by the United Kingdom, Norway, Sweden, Denmark, Switzerland, Austria, and Portugal.

Organizations of states can be classified as primarily economic, military, or political in nature. Economic organizations are based on the premise that combining markets, resources, and production will create economies of scale, inspire greater productivity, and increase the organization's role in the international economy. The Central American Common Market (CACM), North American Free Trade Agreement (NAFTA), Economic Community of West African States (ECOWAS), Organization of Petroleum Exporting States (OPEC), and Asia-Pacific Economic Cooperative Group (APEC) are examples of economic groups.

The European Union (EU) has special status as an economic organization because of its commitment to social and political as well as economic integration. Building on such earlier organizations as UEBL and the European Coal and Steel Community, the EU is the latest name for the organization that started in 1957, when it was called the EEC or Common Market. By 1999 15 European states were members, with more requesting membership. Almost no restrictions or movements across members' boundaries remain, and the euro, a common currency, is now the official currency of 11 EU members, and plans for a common defense policy and coordinated social policies are under way.

Military organizations provide regional

Selected International Organizations (1999 Membership)

Asia-Pacific Economic Cooperation (APEC)

Australia, Brunei Darussalam, Canada, Chile, People's Republic of China, Hong Kong (China), Indonesia, Japan, Republic of Korea, Malaysia, Mexico, New Zealand, Papua New Guinea, Peru, Philippines, Russia, Singapore, Taiwan, Thailand, United States, Vietnam

Economic Community of West African States (ECOWAS)

Benin, Burkina Faso, Cape Verde, Côte d'Ivoire, Gambia, Ghana, Guinea, Guinea-Bissau, Liberia, Mali, Mauritania, Niger, Nigeria, Senegal, Sierra Leone, Togo

European Union (EU)

Austria, Belgium, Denmark, Finland, France, Germany, Greece, Ireland, Italy, Luxembourg, Netherlands, Portugal, Spain, Sweden, United Kingdom

North Atlantic Treaty Organization (NATO)

Belgium, Canada, Czech Republic, Denmark, France, Germany, Greece, Hungary, Iceland, Italy, Luxembourg, Netherlands, Norway, Poland, Portugal, Spain, Turkey, United Kingdom, United States

Organization of American States (OAS)

Antigua and Barbuda, Argentina, Bahamas, Barbados, Belize, Bolivia, Brazil, Canada, Chile, Colombia, Costa Rica, Cuba*, Dominica, Dominican Republic, Ecuador, El Salvador, Grenada, Guatemala, Guyana, Haiti, Honduras, Jamaica, Mexico, Nicaragua, Panama, Paraguay, Peru, Saint Lucia, Saint Vincent and the Grenadines, Suriname, St. Kitts and Nevis, Trinidad and Tobago, United States, Uruguay, Venezuela (*Cuba is excluded from participation)

Organization of Petroleum Exporting Countries (OPEC)

Algeria, Indonesia, Iran, Iraq, Kuwait, Libya, Nigeria, Qatar, Saudi Arabia, United Arab Emirates, Venezuela

security by committing members to a joint defense against an attack on any other member. Two such organizations, the North Atlantic Treaty Organization (NATO) and the Warsaw Pact, symbolized the Cold War because the United States dominated NATO and the Soviet Union dominated the Warsaw Pact. After the Soviet Union disintegrated in 1991, the Warsaw Pact also dissolved. NATO remains, in a changed role, and invited three former members of the Warsaw Pact—the Czech Republic, Hungary, and Poland—to join in 1997, while more states have requested membership.

Other organizations are designed to promote social, cultural, economic, and other links among members and are called political organizations. The Commonwealth (originally the British Commonwealth), Group of 77, Organization of the Islamic Conference (OIC), and Commonwealth of Independent States (CIS) are political groups with different agendas. The Commonwealth provides for discussions among its members, currently the United Kingdom and 53 other states, on political, economic, cultural, and scientific issues; the Group of 77 provides one voice for the interests of developing states, OIC promotes Islamic solidarity, and CIS was formed in 1991 to organize cooperation in foreign policy, transportation development, and other topics among 12 former republics of the Soviet Union.

Most organizations have a limited number

Completed in 1952, the United Nations headquarters in New York City is home to the international organization, whose members include most of the world's countries. The UN was founded in 1945 to promote world peace and human rights.

of members because the shared concerns are limited regionally or topically; a few organizations seek global participation. The United Nations (UN), founded in 1945 after the end of World War II and based in New York City, is the most important global organization and is the successor to the now defunct League of Nations formed after the end of World War I. Except for a very few states, most notably Switzerland, all states on Earth are members of the UN. Interpol, the International Criminal Police Organization established in 1923 to fight smugglers and drug traffickers, is one of the few other organizations to claim nearly global membership.

The purpose of the UN is to promote international peace, security, and cooperation among states, as well as to protect human rights. Two chambers are key to achieving these goals: the General Assembly and the Security Council. All members of the UN have a vote and the right to speak in the General Assembly, making it the most inclusive parliament in the world. While debates and speeches cannot resolve major issues, representatives from all states—and from some stateless nations awaiting recognition—are present and able to contact each other. The Security Council, with a membership of 15, has fewer members but more power than the General Assembly. Specifically, the council has the authority to investigate threats to international peace and to send UN troops on peacekeeping operations throughout the world. In 1949 and 1950 this meant involvement in conflicts in both Kashmir and Korea, and in 1999 UN troops were in 16 locations, including Sierra Leone, Haiti, Tajikistan, and Cyprus.

Other agencies with global concerns, including the Food and Agriculture Organization (FAO), the International Monetary Fund (IMF), and the International Bank for Reconstruction and Development (World Bank), work in tandem with the UN. The World Bank and IMF have become especially important because their decisions on loans for major projects and currency stabilization affect not just the states requesting assistance but, through financial linkages, the health of the global economic system.

Flanked by barbed wire, a United Nations peace-keeping guard from Austria keeps watch over the border between Israel and Syria in 1992.

Geopolitics and the New World Order

The global system of power relationships whereby more powerful states dominate and influence the actions of less powerful states, establishes a **world order. Geopolitics** is the study of international power relations from a spatial perspective. A similar term, geopolitik, refers to the philosophy developed by Karl Haushofer. (See Lebensraum, page 409.) At the beginning of the 20th century, the United Kingdom dominated much of the world, and at the end of the 20th century the United States took the dominant role. Other major powers have existed throughout this period, including Germany, Russia, Japan, and China, and Brazil and Nigeria are now considered examples of regional powers.

Geographers have long attempted to model global power relationships and Englishman Sir Halford Mackinder (1861–1947) developed one of the earliest geopolitical theories, the **heartland theory,** in 1904. Mackinder argued that the relative location and hostile environ-

ment of central Russia—the heartland—made it nearly impregnable to invasion by other states and was the key to world dominance. Eastern Europe, however, was the entryway to the heartland, and therefore the strategy of would-be global powers should be control over Eastern Europe. Some writers see the application of this philosophy in the Nazi invasions of Eastern Europe that began World War II.

Mackinder's theory oversimplified the influences of environment and distance and was rapidly outdated by the development of missiles and airpower, but it influenced numerous other writers. A competing view of world power relations was developed during World War II by Nicholas Spykman (1893–1943), a Dutch-American. Spykman's **rimland theory** argued that accessibility, productivity, and the history of relations among states meant that the coastal rimland of Eurasia, not its central part, was the key to world dominance. Preventing the rimland from uniting, Spykman argued, would also prevent any power from achieving world dominance; the policy of the United States during the Cold War to contain the spread of communism to rimland states reflects the viewpoint of this theory.

Following World War II, the world became increasingly perceived as bipolar, with states divided into the capitalist camp led by the United States and the communist camp led by the Soviet Union. A number of states, such as Indonesia, India, and other members of the Non-Aligned Movement, attempted to remain independent from both camps. A major concern of capitalists was that communist states would attack bordering capitalist states, overwhelm them, and then attack adjacent capitalist states. This perspective, the **domino theory,** originated in 1953 when the communist Viet Minh were attacking French forces in Vietnam, a French colony. The United States justified its involvement in Southeast Asia and later in undermining the Sandanista government of Nicaragua as fighting the spread of communism.

During the 1960s, American geographer Saul Cohen argued that there were four geostrategic regions on Earth, the **spheres of influence** of the United States, Maritime Europe, the Soviet Union, and China. During revisions of this theory over the next 30 years, other regions were noted, including independent regions such as South Asia, areas prone to political instability (**shatterbelts**) such as the Middle East and Southeast Asia, and regions linking the different spheres (**gateway regions**) such as Eastern Europe. In his later revisions, Cohen modified the divisions and

focused on cooperation among states within an increasingly interdependent world.

In 1991, even as the Union of Soviet Socialist Republics was beginning to disintegrate, the United States and the USSR agreed on the need to confront Iraq over its invasion of Kuwait and a New World Order began. The inflexible, bipolar aspects of the Cold War were over, and optimists believed increasing economic and political linkages between states and nations and the emergence of supranational organizations would create a balance of powers: Multinational actions would replace unilateral decisions and actions. The growing interconnectedness within the European Union and the United Nation's coalition against Iraq in 1991 were cited as evidence of these changes.

The decline of the USSR has dramatically changed power relations among the world's states, but there remains tremendous disparity between states in economic and military power, and powerful states still influence the actions of other states. The EU and Japan are major economic powers, and Russia, China, India, Pakistan, and several other states have nuclear arsenals; on the other hand most African states remain among the least powerful in the world. The United States still has the world's largest state economy and is considered the remaining superpower; but other states, organizations (the EU, for example), and even some multinational corporations (MNCs) are becoming increasingly capable of influencing events in the world.

Conclusion

Political geographers analyze the spatial aspects of political processes to understand past and present patterns of power and to predict future patterns. In recent decades two opposing trends seem most responsible for changing the world's political map and most likely to continue influencing political patterns: globalization and nationalism. Both trends have been accelerated by improvements in technology, especially in telecommunications and transport, and increasingly complex networks and linkages among states, regions, and groups.

Globalization is the increasing connection between states and places around the world and includes the development of worldwide financial markets, telecommunication networks, and the rise of multinational corporations. Economic integration has occurred faster than political integration because governments have accepted trade benefits but not greater loss of sovereignty, thus creating problems for governments: MNCs have become increasingly powerful actors in global politics, influencing regional and state decisions concerning financing, environmental protection, infrastructure, and other issues. All states, especially those with smaller economies, now find that decisions made in other states influence their national economic concerns and policies.

The power of individual state governments to effectively address national problems has declined somewhat in response to the rise of globalization and may continue to decline during the next decades as economies and security concerns become increasingly interconnected.

Threats to a state's economic security from environmental threats such as holes in the ozone layer, health threats such as the AIDS pandemic, and computer sabotage may come increasingly from indeterminate or multiple sources so that individual state responses may be ineffective. Multistate actions may be necessary to address these concerns but will result in further decline in individual state sovereignty.

State authority is likely to be increasingly challenged from internal sources as ethnic nationalism continues to thrive. Most states are multiethnic and vulnerable in some degree to this threat, and developed states are as vulnerable as less developed ones. The Zapatista challenge to Mexico and the Québécois challenge to Canada may be the rule in the future, not the exception.

Local governments, primarily municipalities, will face challenges in the future as they address problems whose causes are outside their jurisdictions. In metropolitan areas where annexation is no longer an option, cities will increasingly need to cooperate in councils of government or other forms of joint government to meet the needs of their residents.

Any number of future political geographies is possible. Global trends may change, new powers and threats arise, and unforeseen events occur. The tension between the desires of individuals and nations to have regional identities and autonomy and their desires to enjoy the benefits of global markets and productivity will continue to be a dynamic affecting local, regional, national, and global politics.

Environment and Society

Introduction

Geographers study interactions between human societies and natural environments, how societal—and individual—actions affect environmental processes, and how environmental processes affect societies. The flora and fauna in different regions and their physical milieus, including climate, soil, and hydrology comprise Earth's natural environments. Each component of the natural environment is linked to the others by flows of energy, water, and nutrients. For example, vegetation removes carbon dioxide from the atmosphere and nutrients from the soil while providing energy to grazing animals and oxygen and water vapor to the atmosphere. A system of interrelated processes is at work in each environment and creates resources such as forests, clean water, and fertile soils as well as hazards such as floods, tornadoes, and locust plagues.

Humans, more than any other species, can change natural environments. As a society inhabits a region and develops its resources, the society unavoidably interferes with environmental processes by displacing animal and plant species, interrupting cycles of nutrients,

and modifying water flows. The society may drain swamps to reduce disease, build dams to control flooding, construct power plants to provide energy, and apply pesticides to increase agricultural yields. All of these actions may benefit humans, but at the expense of other species. Drained swamps support far fewer species of plants and animals, dams prevent the migration of salmon and cannot prevent the largest floods, power plants pollute air and water, and pesticides kill far more creatures than the pests for which they were intended.

Societies cannot always predict the effects of their actions on the environment nor can they control many environmental processes. During the 1970s and 1980s, coal-burning power plants in the Ohio Valley contributed to acid rain in New England that killed fish, amphibians, and trees. Attempts to increase rainfall during droughts by intervening in atmospheric processes have met with limited and mixed success. Earthquakes, hurricanes, and other natural hazards threaten societies around the globe, and we are unable to control the environmental processes behind these events.

Resources and Resource Management

All societies rely on energy and materials extracted from the environment to maintain and improve their quality of life. Fuels, building materials, metals and industrial minerals, water, and food are all essential for modern society. Societies choose what components of their natural environment they will develop and how the resources will be extracted, processed, and used. Cotton growers in the short-grass prairie region of western Texas, for example, choose to pump groundwater to the surface to irrigate their crops, and farmers who live in a similar environment in central Turkey choose to graze livestock rather than raise crops. Natural gas from deposits in Siberia are transported to western Russia and Western Europe for use as fuel, and in parts of the Middle East natural gas has been treated as an inconvenient by-product of pumping oil and has been burned or flared off from oil wells.

Resource Management

Resources are substances, qualities, or organisms that have use and value to a society: Resources that are taken from the environment are **natural resources**. Societies perceive resources differently because of differences in cultural values, levels of technology, and economic concerns. Iron ores, fertile soils, coal deposits, and groundwater are considered resources by most societies. Clean air, diverse wildlife, wetlands, and beautiful views are also valued and may therefore be considered resources. A society makes choices when developing a resource that may prevent development of another. For example, iron ore is necessary for making steel, but mining the ore, processing it, and transporting it to factories scars the land and pollutes air and water unless specific preventive or restorative actions are taken.

Decisions on which natural resources should—and should not—be developed, to what degree, in what manner, and for whom are **resource-management** issues. Those who make resource-management decisions may be in the public or private sector, represent themselves or society in general, and be oriented toward economic gain, social welfare, or some other goals. Different weights will be assigned by corporations, federal governments, and other groups to concerns such as immediate financial gain, long-term productivity, and environmental protection. As a result, resource-management decisions vary tremendously in their impacts on society and the environment.

There are four major categories of resource-management strategies: exploitation, utilitarian, ecosystem, and preservation. **Exploitation** strategies focus on the immediate market value that will be realized by developing the resource. **Utilitarian,** or **conservation,** strategies emphasize ensuring long-term productivity by conserving resources for the future. **Ecosystem** strategies, another form of conservation, attempt to balance commercial and noncommercial values by developing resources without seriously affecting environmental processes. Finally, **preservation** strategies concentrate on managing resources to preserve noncommercial values of the environment such as species preservation and biodiversity.

Economic, political, and cultural considerations all play a role in resource-management strategies. Natural resources are nearly always limited in quality, quantity, and location, which means that development involves selecting among different, and often competing, management strategies. Economic concerns are compelling in many cases because resource development creates jobs, provides marketable products, and improves an economy—at least in the short run. Many, but not all, resources have had commercial values established that decision makers use to evaluate the costs and benefits of development. The market value of old-growth Douglas fir trees, for example, can be determined by the market demand for lumber. Resources such as clean air, biological diversity, and wilderness for which there is no market mechanism do not compete well with commercial resources that provide measurable financial benefits.

All resource decisions occur within and are influenced by political systems. In representative democracies, elected officials responsive to their constituents are ultimately responsible for establishing the laws regulating resource development. The USDA Forest Service manages some 191 million acres of national forests and grasslands; private loggers buy the rights to harvest timber, but Congress legislates the rules for multiple use—including recreation and wildlife protection and timber harvesting—and sustainable yield. In countries with centrally planned economies, resource strategies are determined by the government and imposed on the population. In the former Soviet Union, the government decided in the late 1950s to expand agricultural production into the drier region from northern Kazakhstan to western Siberia. This was called the Virgin and Idle Lands Project, which proved to be unsuccessful because precipitation levels and and growing seasons were too limited to support the crops.

Economic and political influences on resource-management strategies can be driven externally as well as internally. Countries are linked into a world system of trading patterns in which natural resources are often produced by less developed (peripheral) countries and traded to developed (core) countries. An unequal relationship exists between these two groups of nations: Developed countries have greater power than less developed countries because their economies are larger and more diversified. Less developed countries can be trapped into resource-based, boom or bust economies, which are vulnerable to changes in demand by the developed countries. Honduras, for example, exports mostly bananas and coffee, Uganda exports coffee, and Libya exports mostly petroleum. The value of these exports rises and falls depending on the demands by other countries.

The cultural values of a society affect resource management because management choices reflect the values of the decision-makers. During the 1960s in the United States, for example, the environmental movement gained strength when books such as *Silent Spring* by biologist Rachel Carson (1962) and *The Population Bomb* by Paul Ehrlich (1968) were published. Congress and various administrations reacted to this change in public values by passing laws such as the Clean Air Act (1965), the Endangered Species Act (1966, with amendments in 1973), and the National Environmental Policy Act (1969). Cultural values of different populations can also come into conflict and affect resource management. In 1986 the International Whaling Commission banned commercial whaling, but the Japanese—for whom eating whale meat is part of their cultural heritage—and a few other countries continued taking whales.

Natural resources and resource management strategies change over time as economics, politics, and culture change. When the price of steel drops, iron deposits that cannot be mined at a profit are no longer developed. Changes in a political administration can cause changes in resource decision. The definition of wetlands, lands saturated with water in which a majority of endangered species live, was changed in 1991 by the administration of President George Bush to include only half the areas that had previously been under federal protection. Cultural change, as seen in public opinion polls, was influential in slowing the development of nuclear power in Europe and United States following accidents at Pennsylvania's Three Mile Island reactor in 1979 and at the Ukraine's Chernobyl site in 1986, then managed by the agencies of the Soviet Union's central government in Moscow. The air pollution resulting from Chernobyl created an ecological disaster.

Resource-management strategies must also consider the type of resource being developed, especially the rate at which it regenerates. Metal ores, for example, form so slowly that deposits must be considered finite. In contrast, forests grow over decades and centuries so that supplies can be considered renewable. Strategies for future use of these and other resources are best addressed based on a division between nonrenewable and renewable—and inexhaustible—resources.

NONRENEWABLE RESOURCES

Mineral resources, such as coal and copper, that form from extremely slow geologic processes are considered **nonrenewable,** that is the amounts available will not appreciably increase for millions of years. Nonrenewable resources are also described as fund, stock, or inventory resources. When a mineral resource has been discovered, measured, and determined to be of commercial value, it is called a **proven reserve.** Subcommercial or as yet undiscovered—but inferred from past discoveries—deposits are potential reserves and are labeled resources.

Nonrenewable mineral resources can be divided into three groups based on their uses and physical properties: metals, fossil fuels, and industrial minerals. **Metal reserves** occur as ores, rocks composed primarily of a valuable mineral such as hematite (containing iron) or galena (containing lead) that can be mined and processed for commercial gain. The spatial distribution of metal resources on Earth reflects past geologic processes, processes often caused by plate-tectonic activity. (See Plate Tectonics, page 130.) As a result, some countries have larger reserves of more types of minerals

than other countries, a situation sometimes described as the geologic lottery. South Africa, Russia, and Canada all have substantial proven reserves of gold, nickel, chromite, and zinc. South Africa produces more than 25 percent of the world's gold, Russia 25 percent of the world's nickel, and Canada 17 percent of the world's zinc. The United States has substantial deposits of lead, copper, silver, and some other metals but imports all manganese, which is used in making steel, and 99 percent of bauxite, which is used to make aluminum.

The amount and distribution of metal reserves change over time because of discoveries of new deposits, exhaustion of old deposits, changes in societal demand, and improvements in mining and processing. A new deposit of nickel, copper, and cobalt valued at 10 billion dollars was discovered in Canada in 1993. New gold mines had opened in the 1970s after the price of gold was deregulated and prices rose dramatically; however, when the price of gold dropped from nearly $800 per ounce in 1980 to below $400 an ounce by 1985, mines closed because it was no longer profitable to mine them. Improved mining and processing techniques around 1950 enabled commercial development of taconite deposits, a low-grade iron mineral found near the Great Lakes, which greatly increased the iron ore reserves of the United States.

Future development of metal resources will be affected by a combination of factors, including the changing value of metals, size and location of proven reserves, ease of recycling metal products, availability of substitutable materials, and political concerns. Certain metals such as niobium and cobalt are labeled **strategic resources** because of their use in military, space, and energy programs. Such metals will retain their high value, and development of deposits of these metals will remain a national priority. Other metals, such as iron, should remain relatively inexpensive because they are widespread and abundant. Laws restricting environmental degradation, such as the 1977 Surface Mining Control and Reclamation Act,

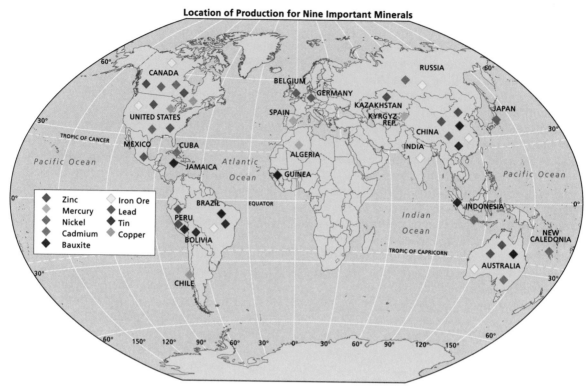

Location of Production for Nine Important Minerals

Minerals are considered to be nonrenewable resources. Formed from extremely slow geologic processes, they will not appreciably increase for millions of years.

increase the economic costs of resource development and therefore increase the search for substitute materials and recycling.

Nonrenewable mineral fuels, particularly fossil fuels, are the major source of energy used globally today, and fuels provide the energy to run machinery ranging from cars and combines to computers and canneries. The demand for energy is rising as populations increase and industrialization spreads. Between 1970 and the present, the total amount of energy used globally almost doubled to more than 150 quadrillion Btu (British thermal unit).

Three fossil fuels—petroleum, coal, and natural gas—account for more than 80 percent of global energy use, and uranium, the other major mineral fuel, accounts for another 5

percent. Renewable energy sources such as hydropower, wind, and solar energy provide the remaining 15 percent. Petroleum, also called oil or crude oil, is a mixture of liquid hydrocarbons derived from microscopic marine organisms trapped in seafloor sediments hundreds of millions of years ago. Natural gas, mostly methane, usually forms along with petroleum from the same organisms. Coal forms from swamp vegetation, and coal beds show the extent of ancient swamps. Uranium, usually the U235 isotope used in fission reactors, is created by igneous activity.

Unlike metal resources, mineral fuels are fully consumed when used and cannot be recycled. The amount of reserves is therefore extremely important for determining management strategies. Predictions on how

Since this photograph was taken, many factories have made significant progress in pollution control with new technology and careful monitoring and regulation of noxious gases.

long current reserves will last are based on assumptions about commercial values, resource discoveries, and patterns of usage, all of which are subject to change because of unexpected technical and social developments. However, at current rates of consumption and current technology, worldwide proven petroleum reserves should last until about 2040, coal reserves until 2200, natural gas reserves until 2060, and uranium until 3000 or later.

The spatial patterns of mineral-resource production and consumption rarely match; therefore, international trade in mineral resources—in fossil fuels, in particular—is a critical component of the world economy. More than half of Earth's petroleum reserves are located in the Middle East, and the major oil consumers are developed countries that must import petroleum. The United States now imports about 40 percent of its total consumption, nearly ten million barrels of petroleum per year, and Japan imports nearly 100 percent of its total consumption. Coal deposits are more widespread—the U.S. alone contains 23 percent of

the global reserves. The global exchange of coal is less extensive than of oil because of its widespread distribution and because of its greater weight per unit output of energy. Natural gas, the cleanest burning fossil fuel, is concentrated in Russia, which contains 40 percent of Earth's reserves and exports natural gas, mostly via pipelines, to European countries. Uranium deposits are found on all continents, but extensive data on reserves are not available because of security considerations. Australia, the United States, and South Africa may have the largest reserves.

In the future, as the reduction of petroleum reserves drives energy costs upward, the use of alternative sources of fossil fuels should increase, as should the use of renewable energy sources. In addition, increased conservation of fuel resources should result from increased technological efficiency; fuel economies of automobiles, for example, improved dramatically after the oil crises of the 1970s because auto manufacturers produced more energy efficient cars. Oil shales and tar sands are rock and sediment deposits

United States Strategic Petroleum Reserves

United States dependency on imported oil and its vulnerability to interrupted imports became evident during the 1973 oil embargo by members of the Organization of Petroleum Exporting Countries (OPEC), which decreased supplies and increased prices. In reaction, the United States government decided in 1975 to stockpile one billion barrels of oil by pumping it into salt domes in Louisiana. These strategic reserves started filling in 1977, but by the mid-1990s a leak formed in one of the salt domes and only 561 million barrels had been stored by December 1998.

containing fossil fuels and are alternatives to petroleum and natural gas. Today's high production costs make them noncompetitive with traditional fossil fuels, but they may become competitive in the future. Few oil shale resources have been identified worldwide, but Colorado's West Slope, Wyoming's Green River Basin, and the Uinta Basin in Utah contain most of the United States' deposits. Tar sands have been developed in pilot programs in Canada, where Alberta contains large reserves. World supplies are estimated to hold the equivalent of 75 percent of current petroleum reserves. (See Map: Proven Oil Reserves, page 328.)

Industrial minerals, minerals used in the construction and chemical industries, for example, are nonrenewable, but are for the most part plentiful. Sand, gravel, limestone, and other building materials are distributed across North America and Europe, and the weight of these materials increases transport costs so that mines and quarries are usually developed near areas of high, local demand. Salt, sulfur, phosphate, and other minerals are important to the chemical industry; salt and sulfur deposits are substantial and are widely distributed around the world, however only Morocco, South Africa, and the United States have major phosphate deposits.

RENEWABLE AND INEXHAUSTIBLE RESOURCES
Resources that are not limited by slow rates of geological formation are classified as either renewable, or inexhaustible. **Renewable resources,** such as fisheries, forests, and soils, are regenerated by either biologic reproduction or by environmental processes. However, mismanagement of these resources can cause depletion and destruction. **Inexhaustible resources** such as solar, wind, water, and tidal energy are generated continuously, and production is not reduced through mismanagement.

A variety of plant and animal species are valued as renewable resources for food and materials; and ecosystems, the interacting community of plants and animals in a region, are increasingly viewed as a resource in their own right. (Rain-forest ecosystems, for example, are valued for being wilderness, for producing oxygen through photosynthesis, and as the home of plants that are potential medicines.) Harvesting an individual species in an ecosystem, such as salmon and redwoods, raises the issue of how to establish the level of **sustained yield,** the amount that can be harvested annually without depletion. Over the past several decades, the USDA Forest Service has revised its definition of sustained yield and its management strategy of the national forests several times. The current definition of sustained yield includes no net loss of forested acres while maintaining productivity.

A major source of energy in many less-developed countries has been biomass, that is wood and biologic wastes (including animal dung) that can be burned as fuel or be processed into ethanol or gaseous fuels. In less

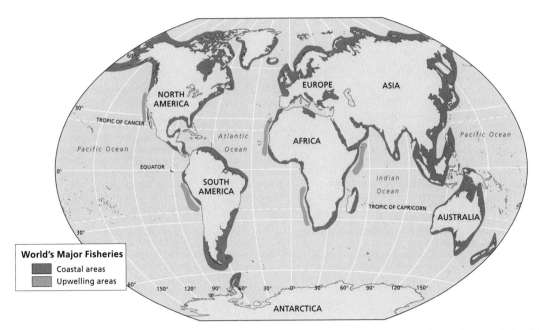

World's Major Fisheries
- Coastal areas
- Upwelling areas

Fisheries are considered to be renewable resources because they can be regenerated in fairly short periods of time. Proper management benefits many people with food and other products. Mismanagement, such as overfishing or pollution, can seriously deplete or even destroy these valuable resources.

developed countries such as Uganda and Haiti, biomass can supply more than 90 percent of local fuel demand, often in the form of wood. Globally, biomass provides about 15 percent of total energy consumption.

Attempts to establish sustained yields for fishing stocks are not easily achieved because of incomplete knowledge of all factors affecting fish populations and because of difficulties in limiting the amount of fish harvested. Managing ocean fisheries has been a major problem in the past because all coastal countries have access to the major fishing grounds around the world. The oceans were considered a commons, with free access to all, and with no authority to limit the amount of fish harvested. As a result, Pacific sardines, North Atlantic haddock, Atlantic bluefin tuna, and numerous other fish populations have been depleted. The 200-nautical mile exclusive economic zone (EEZ) each country claims off its shores has not resolved problems with overfishing because many fish species migrate to the open seas where fishing is not regulated.

Deforestation in Nepal

Overharvesting of wood in forests near towns and villages in Nepal has resulted in deforestation and depletion of local resources. In the 1980s more than 300 square miles were deforested each year, an annual loss rate of 3 percent. The side effects include increased soil erosion, loss of wildlife, and increased flooding downstream in India and Bangladesh.

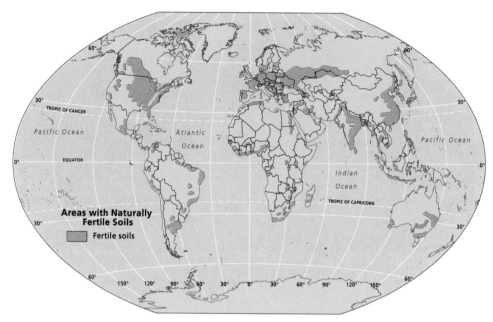

Soil fertility is governed by the amount of organic material—dead and decaying plant and animal debris—it contains. A renewable resource, soils retain their fertility if protected from erosion and overuse.

Fertile soils, clean air, and clean water are also renewable resources that can be perpetuated indefinitely if not abused. While soil, air, and water are always available, each can be degraded in the process of developing other resources, such as coal mining; this degradation is an unintentional side effect of the development process that is often omitted in considering costs and benefits of development. Soil formation and fertility are primarily the results of the climate in a region; soils retain their fertility if protected from erosion and overuse. Air, like water, has an **assimilative capacity,** the ability to remove particulates, chemicals, and other substances through settling and chemical changes, if the amounts are not excessive. Water, too, cleanses itself if protected from excessive additions of substances.

Inexhaustible resources are sources of energy that derive directly or indirectly from the sun, Earth's interior, or gravity. As a rule these are considered clean forms of energy

Wilderness

Wilderness areas are a relatively new type of resource, valued for their solitude, biological diversity, and scenery. The United States Wilderness Act of 1964 defined a wilderness as "an area where the earth and its community of life are untrammeled by humans, where humans themselves are visitors who do not remain." Unlike most other renewable resources, wilderness areas specifically need preservation, where no exploitation of individual resources occurs, rather than conservation, where resources such as rangelands are managed to benefit both humans and the environment.

Three Gorges Dam

In 2009 one of the largest hydroelectric and flood control dams ever constructed, the Three Gorges Dam on China's Yangtze River, is to be completed. Several major problems will be resolved by this dam. It should control floods that have plagued China for centuries and reduce the number of coal-powered generating plants that have created tremendous air pollution problems. At the same time, more than 1.2 million people will have to be resettled as the reservoir behind the dam fills, eventually to extend 400 miles, cover about 1.7 million acres of land, and modify the flow regime—the seasonal variations in flow levels of the river.

because they do not pollute the air or water while producing energy; hydropower, however, can cause other environmental problems. Each of these energy resources—solar, wind, hydropower, geothermal, fission, ocean thermal, and tidal—faces economic, technologic, or other difficulties, and so, despite high hopes by conservationists, they have not easily replaced fossil fuels as major sources of energy.

Solar energy uses radiation from the sun for heating or to generate electricity; wind power and hydropower both depend indirectly on the sun's radiation to create winds or the rainfall that accumulates behind dams. Solar heating is economically competitive with energy from fossil fuels in many regions, but producing electricity in large quantities using photovoltaic cells is not; photovoltaic energy was more than twice as expensive as traditional sources in the 1990s because of the cost of the cells. Wind power has been tapped for centuries—in the Netherlands to pump water out of polders behind dikes, and in the United States to grind grain—but improved storage facilities are needed to make wind-powered electricity competitive with fossil fuels because the timing of winds and of power demand do not always match. Hydroelectricity generated by water in reservoirs flowing through turbines is extremely important in a number of countries, such as Ghana, Laos, Canada, Austria, and other places where precipitation is high and rugged terrain provides good dam sites. Dams do, however, trap sediment and eventually lose their storage capacity and can disrupt local environments.

Inexhaustible energy is also derived from rising and falling tides, as at La Rance in France where 350 megawatts of electricity can be generated, and from tapping Earth's geothermal energy, as at Wairakei in New Zealand. Energy from nuclear fusion holds perhaps the greatest potential of all inexhaustible energy sources. Unlike nuclear fission, which relies mostly on splitting isotopes of uranium, fusion uses deuterium atoms that are available in all water bodies, a virtually unlimited supply. At this stage, however, technological problems remain, and environmental concerns abound over radioactive wastes, leaks, and disasters.

Development of natural resources is essential for modern societies. Over time populations have expanded numerically and spatially, technology has improved, and standards of living have risen. These factors have resulted in greater demand for resources and therefore have increased development activities in environments around the world. The effects of these increased activities include species extinctions, water and air pollution, and other forms of environmental degradation.

Human Degradation of the Environment

Whenever natural resources are developed for use by societies, the environment is changed, and when these changes interfere with existing biological and environmental processes **environmental degradation** results. Different levels and scales of degradation can occur. Clear-cutting a thousand acres of Panamanian rain forest causes far greater environmental damage than clearing ten acres of midlatitude deciduous forests. Soil and bedrock are removed and displaced by mining, species are harvested by fishing and forestry, and water is dammed for flood control; all these actions benefit human societies, but all affect local species and flows of water, energy, and nutrients.

Environmental degradation can be understood according to ecologist Barry Commoner's 1971 rules of ecology. First, everything is linked to everything else; for example, changes in air or water eventually affect groundwater, land, and ecosystems. Second, everything must go somewhere, thus incineration of garbage changes material from landfills into atmospheric pollutants because material cannot disappear. Third, nature knows best: The environment is a complex, interdependent, self-regulating system that will not be improved by human modification. Fourth, there is no such thing as a free lunch; all benefits obtained from the environment have associated costs, to humans or to other species.

Degradation is often an unintentional side effect of resource development, but development almost invariably results in a decrease in environmental quality. Some amount of degradation is unavoidable if a society wishes to survive and retain its standard of living, but resource-management strategies need to consider levels and locations of degradation. A common reaction by many individuals to the problems of environmental degradation is **not in my backyard (NIMBY),** and this approach seeks to have landfills, clear-cutting, and other losses in environmental quality occur elsewhere. However, every location is someone's backyard so even socially necessary activities such as sewage treatment plants, power plants, and sanitary landfills may be fought by local residents. In the U.S. decisions on placing undesirable activities can be delayed by legal challenges for years; Nevada has successfully fought the establishment of a nuclear waste depository at Yucca Mountain for more than a decade.

Human activities can degrade the atmosphere, water and groundwater, soils, and wildlife at local, regional, and even global scales. Although these different components of the environment will be treated separately below for convenience, changes in one component are necessarily transmitted by environmental cycles and food webs. (See Bioregions, page 227.) Over-farming without sufficient fallow periods in semiarid environments such as the Sahel region not only changes the local flora and fauna, but can lead to desertification, when changes in the soils and local water cycle make an area unable to support crops.

Atmosphere

Air pollution occurs when human activities add substances or energy—such as radiation—to the atmosphere in high enough concentrations or levels to harm organisms and cause other undesirable changes in the environment. Establishing pollution levels based on environmental quality is difficult; residents living near feedlots, for example, or corporate hog farms have lost their clean air, but odors are difficult to quantify. Specific levels of unsafe concentrations of pollutants, however, have been established by the United States Environmental Protection Agency (EPA)—sulfur dioxide, nitrogen oxides, particulates, carbon monoxide, and ozone—and these have been integrated into a Pollutant Standards Index (PSI). In the early 1990s the air in Los Angeles was rated as unhealthy because at least one of these five substances exceeded EPA standards more than 150 days each year; Honolulu had no unhealthy days.

Air pollution is a side effect of resource use, and much pollution results from the use of fossil fuels and industrial processes; the atmosphere is a commons for discarding wastes. Pollutants are classified by their chemical and physical composition and include hydrocarbons and toxics in addition to the five pollutants listed above; **toxics** include natural substances such as lead and asbestos and synthetic compounds such as ammonia, acetone, methanol, and toluene. **Photochemical smog,** a combination of dozens of different compounds plus ozone, is sometimes listed separately as a pollutant and is common in the Los Angeles Basin.

An unhealthy concentration of pollutants is usually caused by an increase in the production of pollutants combined with stable meteorological conditions such as temperature inversions. Air's assimilative capacity is a function of dispersing pollutants as well as rain washing out pollutants (scavenging) and gravity causing fallout. When an atmospheric inversion occurs, pollutants are unable to disperse and therefore accumulate; dangerous inversions are common in cities such as Mexico City, Santiago, and Los Angeles. (See Atmosphere, page 54)

The sources of pollutants vary between regions and countries depending on their levels of industrialization and technology; the amounts of pollutants introduced into the atmosphere reflect these factors as well as population size, level of affluence, and environmental values. In the United States about 55 percent of atmospheric pollutants are from vehicles, 21 percent from power plants and energy production, and 16 percent from industrial activities; incinerators and miscellaneous activities produce the rest. The concentration of population and industry in the northeastern states and other regions is mirrored in the concentration of pollution sources. Winds, however, can transport pollutants to other areas. Acid precipitation afflicting eastern Canada from the 1960s to the 1990s was caused by pollutants from power plants in the Ohio Valley; and haze near the Arctic Circle is the result of pollutants transported from industrial and urbanized regions in Europe and Russia.

Human health is affected by long-term, chronic exposure to air pollutants and by short-term, acute episodes of pollutants. Chronic exposure, especially in metropolitan

Tragedy of the Commons

In 1968 biologist Garrett Hardin compared Earth's global ecosystem to a commons, a public grazing land traditionally open to all residents of a village or town. Where there is no supervision or limitations on a commons, villagers may graze as many animals as possible to take as much advantage as possible of the land. What is individually rational, however, is collectively disastrous because overgrazing ultimately destroys the resource for all. Today's global commons, such as ocean fisheries, are also subject to collective disasters because individuals may act as though there is no limit to the use of the resource.

areas, can cause bronchitis and emphysema, and it is implicated in some lung cancers. Children are at greater risk than adults because their respiratory systems are smaller and immune systems less developed. Acute episodes of air pollution are associated with industrialized urban areas, valleys that trap air, and inversions. More than 2,500 people died in Bhopal, India, in 1984 when an insecticide manufacturing chemical plant accidentally released a cloud of methyl isocyanate gas at night, when residents were asleep.

Air pollution is a hazard to other species and to global atmospheric conditions, too. Trees in California's Sequoia National Park have been damaged, and yields of cotton, lemons, sweet corn, and other agricultural products in the state's Central Valley have been reduced due to ozone pollution. Ozone damages leaf cells and causes citrus fruits to fall prematurely. Increased levels of carbon dioxide and other greenhouse gases are slowly but measurably warming Earth's climate, and chlorofluorocarbons (CFCs) and halons released into the atmosphere from refrigerators and air conditioners are thinning the protective ozone layer 12 miles above Earth's surface. (See Atmosphere, page 54.)

Control of air pollution is primarily through restrictive legislation; perhaps the first law limiting air pollutants was a 1306 English law banning coal-burning in London. Local, state, national, and international laws have been established to fight air pollution problems at different spatial scales. Eighteen major U.S. cities had laws promoting carpools by the mid-1990s: California state law requires increasing sales of pollution-free cars each year until 2003, the federal Clean Air Act of 1970 was revised substantially in 1990, and 150 countries signed the Framework Convention on Climatic Change at the 1992 Earth Summit in Rio de Janeiro. The 1970 Clean Air Act was passed to limit pollutants from power plants, vehicles, and factories; the 1990 amendment introduced a new market approach to reduce pollution by establishing pollution allowances to major

electric utilities and then allowing bidding on air pollution permits. When utility companies purchase pollution permits they can increase the amount of air pollutants they can release without breaking federal regulations while the seller must reduce its pollution output. The total amount of air pollution remains the same, but regional differences result.

Air pollution control strategies can be either **end-of-pipe,** to capture pollutants after producing them, or **preventive,** to reduce the amount and type being produced. End-of-pipe strategies, such as catalytic converters on cars, protect the air by removing particulates and other pollutants for disposal elsewhere, such as to landfills. Preventive strategies, such as eliminating leaded gasoline to prevent lead from exhausts accumulating in the environment, seek to change the processes or materials in resource use.

Air pollution control raises several important issues, including the trade-off between environmental protection and jobs. The costs of lowering pollution can result in higher prices for goods or reduce profits, which can create concern among manufacturers. U.S. automobile makers Ford and General Motors strongly opposed federal standards to improve fuel efficiency in cars, arguing it would cause price increases. In the late 1990s, however, Harris public opinion polls show 80 percent of Americans were very or somewhat willing to pay higher taxes to protect the environment.

Water

Societal demands for greater amounts of unpolluted water are increasing around the world. Water is a renewable resource, which moves perpetually through the hydrologic cycle. (See Hydrologic Cycle, page 89.) It has the assimilative capacity to cleanse itself of pollutants, but the increasing demands and uses of water have made it a valuable and limited commodity in many parts of the world.

There are distinctions between demand for

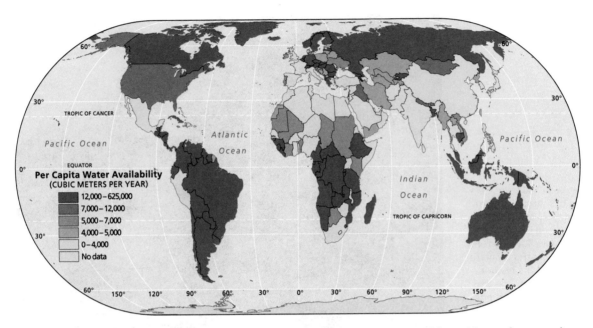

As world population grows, so does the demand for fresh, unpolluted water. Obtained from either surface or underground sources, water is a valuable but often limited renewable resource.

water and need for water and between withdrawal of water and consumption of water. **Demand** for water is the amount of water at a given quality that will be used at a given price; demand is higher when the price is lower, and water is usually underpriced in the United States because of government subsidies for storage and treatment. **Need** for water, on the other hand, is the amount of water necessary for survival, and the amount that would be used at any price. Demand has increased far faster than need because water contributes to development and more comfortable lifestyles.

Withdrawal of water refers to the amount of water removed from the environment, either from surface water or groundwater; **consumption** is that portion of withdrawn water not returned directly to its source but to another part of the hydrologic cycle, often by evaporation and transpiration. Water that is consumed by drinking or irrigation is unavailable to downstream users, and this can cause economic problems. The Colorado River in the

southwestern United States has an average annual flow of 13 million acre-feet, but only 1.5 million acre-feet reach Mexico downstream because the majority of the water is used for irrigation or used in municipalities such as Los Angeles and Phoenix.

Development of water resources almost inevitably results in changing the water regime, the seasonal variations in flow levels, and the water quality. Surface water supplies have high-flow and low-flow seasons; flooding may occur during high water, and water may be scarce during low-flow periods. Prior to the construction of large storage dams on the Ohio River, the average annual maximum flow was more than 300 times the discharge of its average annual minimum flow. Groundwater flow is far more consistent throughout the year because the low permeability of most rocks prevents groundwater from reacting quickly to seasonal changes in input.

River flow regimes are primarily controlled by dams that store water to meet societal

Between 1961 and 1971, the U.S. Army Corps of Engineers attempted to straighten Florida's Kissimmee River to form a flood-control canal. As a result of the historic decision to reverse that project, the river is now regaining its curves, marshes, and wildlife.

demands. Streams may be channelized and confined by levees to control their flows. The benefits of dams include flood control, hydropower, recreation, and a secure water supply; and the effects on the environment include changes in the amounts and locations of erosion and deposition by streams, interruption of anadromous fish migration—fish that move between fresh and saltwater environments—flooding of land covered by the reservoir, and drawdowns of reservoir water for power generation that affect shoreline ecosystems. Salmon populations of the entire Columbia and Snake River systems were destroyed by construction of the Grand Coulee, Bonneville, and other dams.

Groundwater supplies, unlike surface water, cannot be regulated by physical structures, and excessive withdrawal of groundwater affects future groundwater availability. In areas with dry climates, groundwater can be pumped out of aquifers far faster than environmental processes replace it. (See Groundwater, page 279.) As a result, the upper level of groundwater, the water table, drops, making further withdrawals more difficult and eventually uneconomic. In Texas overuse of the Ogallala aquifer has caused the water table in places to drop more than a hundred feet since the 1930s. Elsewhere, Beijing, New Delhi, and Mexico City are also depleting their groundwater supplies. Surface subsidence can be also be triggered by groundwater removal. Parts of New Orleans, for example, are now more than 15 feet below sea level because of subsidence.

Water quality is degraded by the introduction and concentration of substances and energy—especially heat—into water bodies. **Water pollution** occurs when concentrations of these substances are high enough to interfere with environmental processes or to make use of the water unsafe. Water pollution, like air pollution, is a relative term and therefore often defined relative to the type of use. The Environmental Protection Agency, for example, defines water as unhealthy for swimming when more than 200 coliform bacteria—associated with raw sewage—are found in each 100 milliliters of water. In less developed countries where rivers may also serve as

In 1989 the *Exxon Valdez* oil spill of 11 million gallons spelled ecological disaster in Prince William Sound, Alaska. Here, the *Exxon Baton Rouge* pumps remaining oil from undamaged cargo tanks.

sewers, water pollution can be extreme: Coliform bacteria levels as high as 7.3 million have been measured in the Bogotá River downstream from Bogotá, Colombia, and in India levels of 24 million have been measured in the Yamuna River downstream from New Delhi.

Water pollutants are generated by a wide range of activities. In the United States, agriculture, industry, mining, and municipalities generate the most pollutants. Agricultural activites contribute fertilizers, biocides, and excessive amounts of animal wastes such as waste from feedlots to water bodies and are linked to two specific pollution problems: nitrate pollution and eutrophication. A source of **nitrate pollution** is nitrates associated with fertilizers that can accumulate in groundwater supplies in agricultural areas. When such water is used in infant formulas, it can cause an anemic condition called methemoglobinemia, or blue baby syndrome. Agricultural areas in the United States, Israel, and eastern England have reported high levels of nitrates in their groundwater.

Eutrophication, a loss of dissolved oxygen (DO), occurs when large amounts of sewage, fertilizers, or animal wastes enter a stationary water body. Bacteria decompose the pollutants, aerobically at first, and then use up the DO in the water before anaerobic decomposition continues. In addition, nutrients from these pollutants cause the population of phytoplankton to bloom, which in turn causes the water to become cloudy and can kill sea grasses that produce DO. Although bacteria and other microorganisms survive without DO, fish die and eutrophication creates what are called dead lakes; even large water bodies can be affected by eutrophication, such as Lake Erie in the 1970s.

Industrial wastes include heavy metals such as mercury, synthetic chemicals such as PCBs (now banned in the United States), and other substances such as oil. Accumulation of these pollutants in water supplies creates health hazards for humans and for other species; polyaromatic hydrocarbons (PAHs) can cause cancer in humans, fish, and other wildlife. Sudden large releases of industrial pollutants can be devastating to the environment. For example,

1999 Endangered Rivers

An environmental group, American Rivers, releases an annual list of the top ten rivers threatened by development or pollution to enlist public and government support for more cleanup. The 1999 list, starting with the most endangered river, is: Lower Snake River, Missouri River, Alabama-Coosa-Tallapoosa River Basin, Upper San Pedro River, Yellowstone River, Cedar River, Fox River, Carmel River, Coal River, and Bear River.

accidental releases of mercury used in gold mining have sterilized sections of streams in the Amazon Basin. Oil tanker accidents, such as the 1989 grounding of the *Exxon Valdez* in Alaska's Prince William Sound, are responsible for the deaths of sea mammals, birds, and fish. While the *Exxon Valdez* was an ecological disaster and involved the release of 11 million gallons of oil that coated some 1,200 miles of shoreline, other oil spills have been far greater; some 69 million gallons were released from the wreck of the *Amoco Cadiz* off the French coast in 1978.

Residential and commercial activities in municipalities add detergents, salt, and chemicals to water, but sewage is a major water pollutant in the United States and throughout the world. Currently, only about half of the population of the United States lives in cities whose sewage is treated to meet federal water quality standards. Worldwide, more than 1.7 billion people return their sewage to the environment untreated, and waterborne diseases associated with sewage, such as cholera, typhoid, and dysentery, are linked to the deaths of perhaps 25 million people each year.

Water can cleanse itself of pollutants through its assimilative capacity if the amounts of pollution are not too great. Pollutants are removed from water, especially moving water, by gravity settling, by chemical changes or decomposition, and by dilution of the concentration to non-harmful levels. Stationary water sources, such as lakes and groundwater supplies in aquifers, are far slower in cleansing themselves than streams because their flow rates are

slower—just a few inches or feet per year for groundwater.

Some water pollution, like air pollution, can be treated by end-of-pipe processes; preventive strategies are necessary to control other types of water pollution. End-of-pipe controls work with **point source** pollution, where pollutants are emitted from a specific and limited area, such as a sewage pipe or factory. **Nonpoint sources,** which include runoff from streets, mining areas, and agricultural fields, are more difficult to control. Congress enacted legislation in 1987 requiring states to form management strategies to address nonpoint pollution.

Federal legislation to control water pollution in the United States was first passed in 1972 with the Federal Water Pollution Control Act, called the Clean Water Act (CWA) since it was amended in 1977. Under this legislation, Congress funded more sewage treatment facilities, required a minimum level of secondary sewage treatment, and established minimum quality standards for rivers and lakes. Water pollution levels have been drastically reduced since 1972 in a number of cases, including the Great Lakes, and the Hudson, Potomac, and Cuyahoga Rivers, but further protection of water resources is necessary to meet CWA standards.

Land and Soil

Earth's land and soil are degraded by both the development of mineral resources and by discarding material waste products of society. Mining alters surface topography through

In the People's Republic of China, a grid made from straw prevents sand from burying railroad lines in the Tengger Desert.

excavations and dumping of rock waste, with associated effects from acid mine drainage on soils, plants, wildlife, and hydrology; agriculture can increase erosion and change soil fertility. Discarding garbage into dumps and landfills degrades soil and groundwater through the introduction of toxic substances into an ecosystem, the addition of pollutants and odors into the atmosphere, and by lowering the aesthetic value of the environment.

The distribution of valuable metals within larger ore bodies necessitates the removal of large amounts of rock, which, after processing to remove the metals, is returned to the environment. Surface mining, which includes strip mining, hydraulic mining, and open-pit mining, scars Earth's surface, eliminates native vegetation and wildlife, and changes surface and subsurface drainage. Excavations may range from small quarries of less than an acre to the Bingham Canyon copper mine near Salt Lake City from which 160,000 tons of ore are mined daily; it is now more than half-a-mile deep and about two-and-a-half-miles across— the largest man-made excavation on Earth.

Subsurface mines are less obvious, but can cause major changes in subsurface drainage.

Overburden, uneconomic rock overlying coal or other valuable mineral resources, and **tailings,** uneconomic parts of a metal ore body, have often been merely dumped back onto the land, although laws in the U.S. increasingly regulate this activity. In an average year, about two billion tons of rock waste are returned to the environment in the United States.

Land reclamation, where mined land is recontoured, resoiled, and revegetated, alleviates much of the degradation caused by mining, but the costs involved can be substantial. In the United States, the 1977 Surface Mining Control and Reclamation Act was enacted that requires coal-mining companies to reclaim strip-mined land. Despite limited funding for inspections and enforcement, this law has been mostly successful; however, non-coal mines were not included in the legislation, and most of these excavations are not reclaimed.

Land degradation also occurs when fluid resources such as petroleum, natural gas, and

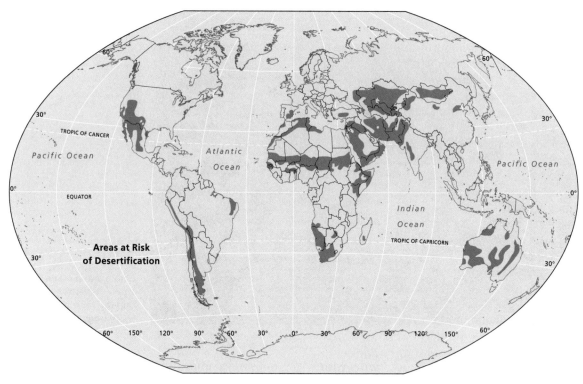

Desertification caused by overgrazing, the replacement of natural vegetation by food crops, and climate fluctuation turns semiarid grasslands into arid desert. Regions bordering tropical deserts are most vulnerable to this process.

groundwater are pumped from the ground. Compaction of sediments can cause surface subsidence, which endangers buildings as well as future subsurface fluid supplies. Coastal locations are particularly vulnerable because the sedimentary deposits found there are often saturated with water and compact readily after pumping removes fluids. Numerous cities have experienced subsidence, including Las Vegas, Pisa, and Niigata, Japan. Niigata, on the west coast of Honshu, has subsided nearly 44 inches because of the withdrawal of natural gas.

Soil loss and pollution due to agricultural practices occur throughout the world. In the United States about one third of all farmland is suffering from some soil erosion. The worst erosion, which involves loss of more than 75 percent of the topsoil and the presence of gullying, results from poor management of thick,

fertile soils, and is found mostly in Iowa and the Mississippi Valley south of Illinois. Worldwide, soil loss is most pronounced in a few countries such as El Salvador and Colombia, where steep slopes and high annual rainfall magnify the effects of poor soil management. Undoubtedly, growing population pressures will increase agriculture and agricultural erosion.

Mismanagement of soils can also cause salinization and desertification, both of which involve long-term loss of land use. **Salinization** of soils—when chloride and sulphate salts accumulate on or near the soil surface as soil water evaporates—is most common in dry areas with poorly drained soils, such as in Syria, Pakistan, and the Colorado River Basin. **Desertification**, the transition of a semiarid grassland region to arid desert conditions, was once thought to be solely climatic in nature, but overgrazing and changes in vegetation—crops—contribute to desertification by changing soil water availability. Regions adjacent to tropical deserts are most vulnerable to desertification as well as salinization, such as the Sahel region south of the Sahara and regions around the Thar Desert, in India.

Disposal of municipal and industrial waste degrades soil, water, and air through the volume of garbage involved and through the toxicity of some of the waste. In the U.S. Americans on average produce about 1,500 pounds of garbage a year, about twice as much as the average Japanese and four times as much as the average Pakistani or Indian. About one third of the volume of garbage in the United States consists of packaging—paper, plastic, and plastic foam—and another third consists of yard and food wastes and wood. While most of these substances are considered biodegradable, able to be decomposed by organisms in the environment, the dry conditions within landfills do not allow this to occur rapidly; phone books buried for 50 years in landfills can still be read.

In the United States the majority of garbage, currently around 67 percent, is deposited in landfills, about 10 percent is incinerated, and 23 percent is recycled. These relative proportions have changed over time: Until the Clean Air Act was enacted in 1970, incineration was far more common and occurred in open dumps. There are significant differences between states in the disposal of garbage because of political cultures, population pressures, and other factors. Landfills can account for as much as 95 percent of waste disposal in Arizona or as little as 20 percent in Maine. Disposal by incineration ranges from 63 percent in Connecticut to 0 percent in North Dakota, and recycling ranges from 44 percent in Minnesota to 5 percent in Arizona.

Sanitary landfills, where garbage is buried under a layer of soil, have replaced open dumps, but they still have a number of problems. Precipitation that percolates down through the garbage can dissolve or leach chemicals from the waste and become **leachate**; leachate then pollutes the groundwater unless downward drainage is controlled by an underlying and impermeable layer of clay, plastic, or other material. A problem for municipalities and industries seeking to dispose of garbage cheaply is the closing of landfills as they fill up. Between 1970 and 2000, the number of landfills in the United States has dropped from around 18,000 to about 3,500. The Fresh Kills landfill on Staten Island, where garbage from New York City is sent, is scheduled to close in 2002, and the city's garbage will need to be exported elsewhere or managed differently, perhaps recycled, for example. Solid waste disposal is a worldwide problem; more than half the countries represented at the 1992 Earth Summit in Rio de Janeiro listed waste disposal as a major environmental concern.

Few new landfills have opened in the U.S. in recent years, and most residents oppose opening them in their area. Passaic, New Jersey, trucks its garbage 250 miles to Johnstown, Pennsylvania, for disposal. In addition to the NIMBY attitude of residents, siting of new landfills is also opposed by politicians with a not in my term of office (NIMTOO) attitude. Landfills are often located in areas where residents are poor and have little political power or other economic opportunities; the location of many landfills in or near minority neighborhoods has led to charges of environmental racism. In recent years, some countries have paid others to allow dumping of solid waste. The United States and Japan have exported solid wastes to African and Latin American countries, and Canada was exporting almost 500,000 tons of garbage a year to the United States in the early 1990s.

Incineration of garbage can be used to reduce the volume by as much as 75 percent and generate electricity from the heat, but burning creates air pollution and ash that must still be disposed of. Ash from incinerators must now be tested for toxicity and, if levels are high enough, must be disposed of in licensed, hazardous waste landfills.

Recycling saves landfill space and energy used in processing and transporting raw materials. During the last decades, recycling has increased in the United States—especially for newspapers, glass, and metals—from about 7 percent of the total volume in 1970 to more than 20 percent in the mid-1990s. The types of substances recycled vary tremendously because of differences in convenience and market incentives. For example, almost 97 percent of lead is recycled and only about 2 percent of plastics are recycled. Greater public involvement is needed to expand recycling in the future to overcome the inconveniences

Hazardous waste can be extremely harmful to people and the environment. Here, a worker collects samples of toxic waste from open containers.

involved, and to generate markets for recycled material. State and city governments are working to encourage recycling: Washington State has created the Clean Washington Center for research and marketing on recycling, and Seattle currently recycles 48 percent of its municipal solid wastes.

Toxic, or hazardous, waste, which poses a substantial threat to human health or the environment, is a common component of industrial pollutants. The Environmental Protection Agency classifies more than 400 substances as hazardous wastes, including caustics, explosives, flammables, and poisons. Nuclear waste is a special category of hazardous waste. Leachate from hazardous waste landfills has polluted groundwater and has been responsible for health problems. In the 1970s, for example, miscarriages, birth defects, and nervous disorders among families living in Love Canal, New York, were traced to toxic pollutants buried in an abandoned canal in the 1930s and 1940s. The enactment of the Superfund Act—initially called the Comprehensive Environmental Response, Compensation, and Liability Act—in 1980 was in response to hazardous waste pollution, and it was used to clean up nearly 200 sites by the mid-1990s. Some experts believe that there are between 2,000 and 10,000 sites still in need of cleanup.

Nuclear waste disposal, particularly high-level radioactive waste, which will continue to be radioactive and a health hazard for more than 10,000 years, is problematic; low-level radioative wastes are relatively safe after a decade or so. No totally satisfactory disposal system has yet been found for high-level waste such as plutonium, most of which is from fuel assemblies of nuclear power plants or from development or dismantling of military weapons. An extensive search by the U.S. Department of Energy for an isolated and secure burial place proposed Yucca Mountain, Nevada, in 1987, but political resistance is delaying development of this site, and a site near Carlsbad, New Mexico, is now being used.

A clear-cut hillside in the Olympic Mountains of Washington reflects the controversy surrounding forest management. Valued resources of recreation, clean water, wilderness, and biodiversity, forests must be managed carefully to permit long-term, sustainable use.

Vegetation and Wildlife

Developing natural resources unavoidably affects native vegetation and wildlife and has led to regional losses and to global extinction of species. A change in any component of an ecosystem—soils, water, or atmosphere—changes the flow of energy or nutrients and therefore changes both the food web and the species most able to survive in the changed environment. Humans intentionally and unintentionally have also introduced new species into regions without fully appreciating the changes that might occur as a result. Greater awareness of the problems generated by these two processes has led to national and international attempts to protect and preserve not just species, but their habitats and ecosystems, too.

In the United States the Endangered Species Act (ESA), enacted in 1966 and amended in 1973, protects **endangered species,** those in immediate risk of extinction, from hunting and loss of habitat. The Department of the Interior's Fish and Wildlife Service is responsible for determining if species are **endangered** or **threatened,** at risk but not immediate risk;

decisions are based on political as well as biological factors. Placing a new species on the endangered list threatens resource development in regions where its habitat is found. During the 1990s a controversy raged in the Pacific Northwest when timber cutting was halted to protect spotted owl habitat. The controversy was resolved only when President Bill Clinton approved the Northwest Forestry Plan to protect the owl and to continue timber cutting. An earlier controversy, in the 1970s, occurred when construction of the Tellico Dam on the Little Tennessee River was nearly stopped in order to protect a tiny fish, the snail darter. This issue was resolved when Congress amended the ESA to allow the dam to be completed, and the snail darter population was successfully transplanted to nearby streams.

In 1997, nearly 900 species in the United States were considered endangered and 229 species threatened, with 3,700 more species awaiting full evaluation. Public awareness of endangered species is greatest for large mammals and birds, such as manatees and peregrine falcons, but insects, clams, and crustaceans are also endangered, and endangered plants outnumber endangered animals by a wide margin: Plants compose 90 percent of the 3,700 species on the list to be evaluated.

Worldwide, human activities contribute to about a thousand species becoming extinct each year, though estimates vary widely. Certain ecosystems, especially rain forests and wetlands, have especially high diversity, and their development threatens the loss of more species than development of rangeland ecosystems. The loss of any species affects an ecosystem, but when a **keystone species,** one whose activities affect large numbers of others, is lost, the effects are greater. The gopher tortoise is such a keystone species in the U.S. Southwest because its burrows provide shelter for at least 37 other species.

The major causes of extinction are loss of habitat, degradation of habitat, and overhunting. Deforestation, clearing for agriculture, and urbanization all cause the loss of habitat. As human populations grow around the world, increasing amounts of habitat are lost; Brazil's rain forest losses—now thought to be about 0.6 percent of the area each year—are well known, but clearing of rain forests in Indonesia, India, and China is also responsible for much loss of species. This problem is compounded by **fragmentation** of the ecosystems involved: **Ecological islands**, small acreages of habitat surrounded by developed land, are unable to support the diversity of life of larger areas. As a rule of thumb, the number of species in an ecosystem increases relative to the area protected, although **wildlife corridors** linking similar ecosystems reduce the negative pressure on species. Larger areas can support species such as grizzly bears that require more room and food, and maintain minimum **critical populations** that are necessary to support breeding and protect the genetic diversity within species.

Toxics, such as pesticides, and pollutants degrade habitats and cause unintentional deaths of wildlife. When the herbicide Diazinon was applied to a golf course in Hempstead, New York, in 1984, 700 Atlantic brant feeding on the greens died within two days. Many pesticides, such as DDT, pass through the food web and accumulate in predators at the top of the food chain by **biomagnification.** The decline of bald eagles and peregrine falcons in the United States prior to the banning of DDT in 1972 was partially the result of their consumption of prey that had eaten insects and worms containing DDT. In the larger birds, DDT caused eggshells to thin and break before hatching because they were calcium-deficient.

Overhunting has caused a number of birds and mammals to become extinct or endangered. The extinction of passenger pigeons in the 1900s is the classic example in the United States, and snowy egrets were almost wiped out in the 1800s for their plumage, which was used to decorate ladies' hats. Large mammals, such as blue whales, cheetahs, and black rhinoceroses, seem especially vulnerable to overhunting, and their extinctions would have unknown ripple effects in their ecosystems.

The value of species and ecosystems diversity to societies is not always commercial but can be philosophical or ethical in nature.

Tigers

Only about 5,000 to 7,200 tigers, the world's largest cat, still live in the wild, about 5 percent of the number in 1900. The demand for pelts, body parts for medicinal purposes, a continuing loss of habitat, and a shrinking gene pool are making extinction in the next ten years increasingly likely. Although tigers once roamed much of Asia, their spatial range is steadily shrinking, and the Bali, Caspian, and Javan tiger subspecies are already extinct.

Zebra Mussels

Although more than a hundred exotic species now live in the Great Lakes, the zebra mussel is often singled out as a classic example of problems introduced species may cause. Zebra mussels settle on hard surfaces where there is flowing water; therefore, they accumulate on and block intake pipes for water supplies and power stations. The damage caused by the mussels may reach into the billions of dollars within the next decade, especially if the species spreads farther into the Mississippi, Hudson, and St. Lawrence River systems.

American environmentalist and conservationist Aldo Leopold (1886–1948) wrote about a land ethic in *A Sand County Almanac,* published posthumously in 1949, arguing that humans are part of their larger environment and therefore need to value it and treat other species with respect. Loss of species also means the loss of gene pools and potential resources. Plants provide a large number of medicines: Jimsonweed, for example, provides scopolamine for motion sickness, and rosy periwinkle provides vinblastine for Hodgkin's disease. The loss of rain forest and wetland is particularly harmful to the search—chemical prospecting—for new medicines.

The introduction of an **alien species,** also called an **exotic species,** into a new environment changes the ecosystem and often results in the loss of native species. Every species is part of the food web within an ecosystem, and an exotic species is a competitor for food and, too often, a new predator. The introduction of rabbits into Australia in 1859 for hunting did not take into account the reproductive capabilities of rabbits, the amount of vegetation on which they would graze, or the lack of predators. One hundred years later there were nearly one billion rabbits in Australia so that farmers fenced off grazing land to protect it for livestock and finally introduced a disease virus to control the rabbit population.

Intentional introduction of alien species may provide initial benefits to humans in an area, but unanticipated problems often counteract these benefits. Kudzu, an Asian vine that helps prevent soil erosion by stabilizing slopes, was introduced into the southeastern United States early this century, but it has literally spread over the countryside, covering trees and buildings. Attempts are now being made to eradicate kudzu from many areas by using soybean looper caterpillars to eat it, since herbicides have been unsuccessful.

Unintentional introduction of alien species, especially insects, is almost unavoidable because of increasing exchange between regions. The Asian gypsy moth, Mediterranean fruit fly, and Asian cockroach have all been accidentally introduced into the United States. New species can exterminate native species: In Hawaii, cannibal snails are eliminating Oahu tree snails, and koa trees are being choked by banana poka vines and wild blackberries.

Survivors search for belongings in the wake of a violent earthquake in El Progreso, Guatemala. Natural hazards are often the most devastating to already economically stressed communities.

Natural Hazards

Natural environments are increasingly vulnerable to degradation by human actions, but this is not a one-way relationship. Humans are part of the environment and are therefore unavoidably affected by environmental processes. When local, global, or regional environmental processes such as earthquakes, tornadoes, or lightning threaten harm to humans or damage to developments, they are considered **natural hazards**: Blizzards in Antarctica, however, and volcanic eruptions in the Alaskan archipelago are natural events but not natural hazards.

All societies face risk from natural hazards, both to property and to persons because no location is immune to hazardous events. The choice of adjustment to these threats varies widely, from building more secure buildings to moving to different locations. Control over the environmental processes causing hazardous events is neither feasible nor possible, so future losses from hazards are inevitable but can be reduced by adopting more effective hazard-mitigation strategies.

Vulnerability to Hazards

Natural hazards are natural events that threaten the human system and range from avalanches to fog to plagues of locusts; hazards are often extreme events, such as large earthquakes rather than minor temblors or droughts rather than dry summers. In an average year, about 250,000 people die from natural hazards—more than 200,000 of these in less developed countries—and about 50 billion dollars is spent annually, mostly on recovery efforts, but also on prediction, prevention, and insurance premiums.

Defining a hazardous event is difficult and is often based on the event being statistically different in magnitude, frequency, or location from average—or mean—events. Snowstorms are normal winter events in the northeastern United States, but in January 1996 extended blizzard conditions in the Northeast killed one hundred people. Minor snowfalls, or even frosts, are extremely hazardous in normally warm regions such as Florida where neither people nor vegetation, orange groves for example, are prepared.

Natural hazards include meteorological, geological, and biological events; and although hazardous events, especially extreme events, are by definition uncommon, they are not abnormal. The environmental processes operating on Earth will generate high magnitude events, such as Category Five hurricanes and earthquakes with energy levels of 8.0 on the Moment Magnitude Scale, when conditions cause sufficient energy to accumulate. Fortunately, the frequency of extreme events is inversely related to their magnitude; small earthquakes, for example, far outnumber large earthquakes. (See Geologic Structures and Earthquakes, page 139.)

As humanity has spread over Earth, people of necessity settled in locations where extreme events will occur because natural resources are often found alongside natural hazards. The San Francisco Bay area of California has both earthquakes as well as a Mediterranean climate, that most people find very attractive. The midwestern United States has both tornadoes and fertile soils. Some locations experience greater numbers or more dangerous hazards than others. The coastline of Bangla-

desh, for example, is a low-lying delta that suffers from cyclones (hurricanes), floods, and an occasional tsunami. Residents evaluate how hazardous a place is against the benefits of living there and the opportunities to relocate. Societal concerns and policies may also be involved. Cities can zone floodplains to disallow residential development, and national governments can provide insurance or relief funding that indirectly supports continued residence in a hazardous area.

The interaction between the natural and human systems in natural hazards is not static but changes as societies develop and reevaluate their situations. Every hazard evokes a response, individually and collectively, that may be channeled into different activities, behavior patterns, or even locations. Societal values affect the choice of response, as do societal resources and social policies, so no universal strategy to address hazards is possible. Japanese, Armenian, and American responses to a major earthquake differ because the societies differ.

Worldwide, the risk of natural hazards is rising despite efforts by individual communities, countries, and international organizations to protect themselves. The United Nations declared 1990 to 2000 the International Decade for Natural Disaster Reduction, and the organization has been focusing on preventive measures and helping societies develop active disaster reduction plans. Two key factors underlie the rise in risk: growing populations in dangerous locations and increasing

Future Disasters

If the past is indeed prologue to the future, major natural disasters will befall cities in the United States and around the world. San Francisco will eventually have another big one, comparable to the 1906 earthquake, although the exact date cannot be predicted. It is also probable that New Orleans and Miami will eventually be struck by hurricanes; Columbus, Ohio, by a tornado; and Hilo, Hawaii, by a tsunami—all based on environmental processes active in these regions.

SUDDEN-IMPACT NATURAL DISASTERS IN LARGE CITIES, 1946–1988

COUNTRY	NUMBER OF DISASTERS	TYPES OF DISASTER	EXAMPLES OF CITIES AFFECTED
Brazil	15	floods, landslides	Rio de Janeiro, Recife
Philippines	8	hurricanes	Manila
Mexico	7	earthquakes, floods	Mexico City
Japan	6	hurricanes, earthquakes	Tokyo, Nagoya
India	6	hurricanes, floods	Madras
Indonesia	6	floods	Jakarta, Bandung
Rep. of Korea	5	floods	Seoul
Argentina	5	floods	Buenos Aires
Pakistan	3	floods, storms	Karachi
Peru	3	floods	Lima
Portugal	3	floods	Lisbon
Others	25	earthquakes	Bucharest, Tangshan, Tashkent
Total	**92**		

SUPERCITIES AFFECTED BY NATURAL HAZARD RISK

CITY AND COUNTRY	NATURAL HAZARD RISK
Mexico City, Mexico	Earthquake, subsidence
Chongqing, China	Earthquake, tsunami, flood, hurricane
Calcutta, India	Flood, hurricane
Beijing, China	Earthquake
Jakarta, Indonesia	Earthquake, flood, hurricane
Canton, China	Hurricane
Lima, Peru	Earthquake, flood
Delhi, India	Flood
Hong Kong, China	Hurricane, landslide

concentration of wealth in those locations. In the United States, the growth of population and income in Florida and along the rest of the Atlantic coastline increases the potential for disaster because of the hurricane hazard. In developing countries such as Chad, growing population pressure causes increased use of land that is subject to killing droughts.

If a natural hazard occurs and causes sufficient damage to humans then a natural disaster is said to have occurred. In the United States, the term disaster is commonly restricted to those events in which more than a hundred people die or more than a million dollars in damage occurs. On average the federal government declares 15 states of emergency each year

STRUCTURAL /ARCHITECTURAL RESPONSES TO NATURAL HAZARDS

1. Retrofitting of existing structures
2. Reinforcement of new structures: A. Design features
                                       B. Overdesign
3. Safety features: A. Structural safeguards
                                       B. Fail-safe design
4. Engineering phenomenology
5. Probabilistic prediction of impact strength

SOCIAL RESPONSES

SHORT-TERM

1. Emergency plans: A. Civil: a. coordinator(s)
                                        b. police and firefighters
                                        c. Red Cross and charities
                                        d. volunteer groups
                                        e. medical services
                           B. Military forces
2. Evacuation plans: A. Routes and reception centers for the general public
                           B. For vulnerable groups: the very young, elderly, sick or handicapped
3. Prediction of impact: A. Monitoring equipment
                           B. Forecasting methods and models
4. Warning processes: A. General message
                           B. Specialized warning (e.g. ethnic)

LONG-TERM

1. Building codes and construction norms
2. Hazard microzonation: A. Selected risks
                           B. All risks
3. Land use control: A. regulations, prohibitions, moratoria, compulsory purchase
4. Probabilistic risk analysis
5. Insurance
6. Taxation
7. Education and training

in response to requests by state governments. As a rule, financial losses are most common in developed countries and loss of life is greatest in less-developed countries because of the better warning systems and stronger structures in developed countries. Many of the deadliest disasters in human history have occurred in China where huge populations live on floodplains and in seismically active areas; hundreds of thousands of lives have been lost in individual earthquakes, as in 1556 and 1976, or floods, as in 1931 and 1939.

Hazard Adjustments

Adjusting to hazards requires individuals and societies to assess the risk of hazards at a location and then to choose among the available strategies that address those risks. In an ideal world, the statistical risk of each hazard would be known, the costs and benefits of each strategy measured and evaluated, and the final decision would be made rationally and objectively. None of these conditions exists in real life, and so management decisions can often be, or at least appear to be, inadequate.

The major factors affecting the choice of hazard adjustment are the perception of hazard risk and the limitations on choices economically, politically, and socially. Perception, the mental image held of both hazard risk and possible responses, is critical because people react to what they believe rather than to what is. The perceptions among individuals vary because of differences in knowledge base, which is associated with age, frequency of hazard experience, income and investments to be protected, and personal values and emotions. Individuals may be fatalistic about hazards or activists, risk-seekers or risk-avoiders, optimizers who seek satisfactory rather than optimum answers. In earthquake-prone regions, people may decide to buy insurance, build safer houses, relocate, or deny that the risk exists; each of these options will be considered sound by the individual selecting it.

Perception of risk is a major problem because data are often unreliable, anecdotal experiences and recent events are over-emphasized, and statistics misunderstood. Flood risk, for example, is based on records of flooding, and the records themselves may be incomplete and cover too short a time period. In addition, expected flood heights are probabilities rather than assertions of frequency: A hundred-year flood does not occur every hundredth year, but has a one percent chance of occurring each year. Residents were caught by surprise when the Patuxent River between Baltimore and Washington, D.C., flooded in 1971, an event expected less than once a century, and then had a comparable flood the following year.

Collective hazard adjustments are limited by the perceptions of the decision-makers on risks, possible adjustments, and on available resources and political support. Decision-makers are also influenced by the advice of technical experts and the public; studies show that officials' perceptions of hazards are often based on what officials believe is the public perception. Finances are also a limitation, especially for hazards that are not seen as imminent threats. When seismologists of the United States Geological Survey informed California officials in 1976 about the possibility of a major earthquake, it was several years before evacuation plans were completed and requirements established for building safety.

The range of possible hazard adjustments from which individuals and societies can choose focuses on accepting, reducing, or avoiding future losses. Both technological and social responses are used; technological responses involve construction and engineering—common in developed countries—and social responses involve regulating activities and the locations at which they occur. Incidental adjustments are made, not necessarily to reduce negative impacts of hazards but they do so anyway, such as improved construction, communication, and transportation. Purposeful adjustments, such as purchasing hazard insurance and building tornado warning systems, are made intentionally to cope with the hazard.

People make a conscious choice in selecting their purposeful adjustment to a hazard and, in addition to their perceptions, are affected by the magnitude, duration, and amount of forewarning of the hazard. Earthquakes, floods, and droughts may all cause comparable amounts of death and damage, but the duration of each hazard is so different that different types of adjustment should be expected. Acceptance of losses, personally or collectively through insurance or emergency aid, may be used in response to an earthquake. Reduction of loss, by modifying the event or preventing its negative effects by building dams for example, may be more appropriate for flood hazards. Choosing to change location of a land use or to move people may be required for survival in drought-prone areas, especially in developing countries.

Hazard adjustments are made not only by individuals and communities but also at national and international levels. After a severe earthquake in Managua in 1972, more than 70 countries contributed cash or services to Nicaragua. Humanitarian concerns are part of the reason for assistance from those outside the area of impact, but the increasing economic and political linkages between countries can cause losses from a disaster to be felt nationally and internationally, as well as regionally or locally. The 1995 earthquake in Kobe, Japan, resulted in the loss of 6,300 lives, destroyed the new port of Kobe thus interrupting exports and imports, and also caused the Nikkei Index to drop more than 5 percent. Loss of productivity, jobs, and investments add an economic dimension to the personal tragedies that disasters bring.

Conclusion

Humans are both dependent upon and interdependent with their environments. Natural resources remain the basis for economic growth and civilization even as development of those resources contributes to the loss of other environmental values. Natural hazards are everywhere and will cause future disasters.

Improved technology has helped humans to have far greater impacts on their environments, but the same technology has outstripped our knowledge of its affects on the environment; we cannot always predict the consequences of our actions.

Summary

The most striking modern image of our world shows Earth as a tiny blue dot in a sea of black, an image taken by the Voyager 1 spacecraft in 1977. Enlarge the image and you can see an underlying blue, from the oceans, and swirls of white, from clouds. We live in and on a world of water. Ours is the blue planet. We can appreciate that world as a whole, as essentially a closed system in terms of the amount of matter.

Since that image was taken, however, we have also come to appreciate just how much of an impact we have had—and more important—will have on Earth. Whether it is the Antarctic, and now the Arctic, ozone holes or the effects of global warming, we are beginning to recognize the human dimensions of global change in physical systems. At slightly smaller scales, we recognize the current and potential impacts of deforestation, as in the Amazon River Basin, or desertification, as in the southern Sahel. At yet smaller scales, we see the disastrous effects of agricultural policies and practices on the shrinking Aral Sea in Kazakhstan. At even smaller scales within the U.S., we can see wetlands being drained, beaches artificially created and maintained, and farmlands—which were once forests—being converted into suburban developments. At the smallest scale—the personal scale—we build an addition to a house, we travel and camp on a vacation trip, and we assume that the trash will be collected and caused to disappear on a regular basis.

The thread underpinning all of these

impacts is people. Our world is being reshaped by inexorable forces: increasing population, increasing affluence, increasing consumption, increasing technological capacity. Our activities have changed and will continue to change the surface of the Earth. We cannot escape the fact that we make an imprint on Earth's surface. We cannot be indifferent—whether those imprints are good or bad—to what we have done, to where we have done it, to why we did it, to why it looks that way, and to what it all means for us, now and in the future.

People do not just have an impact on the Earth: We also have an impact on each other. Consider language. Linguists believe that at least half of the world's 3,000 to 6,500 languages will die out in the next century. Alternatively, only about 5 percent of languages are safe in the sense that they are spoken by a significant number of people and receive support from nation-states. The loss of linguistic diversity is one result of globalization. As languages die, so too do cultures.

And in understanding the impacts of inexorable change, geography matters. We must answer the "why there" question? As a bumper sticker says, "Without geography, you're nowhere." Why, for example, is Federal Express based in Memphis, Tennessee? The answer is pure geography: Memphis is in the center of U.S. time-space, and it has a large airport. However, Memphis, unlike Chicago, is not a busy passenger hub.

Geography sets ideas into the twin contexts

of space and place. Space is the environmental stage upon which the drama of geography is played out, and places are particular points on the environmental stage where the action occurs. Human geography puts people at the center of space and place. It asks us to consider the effects of the varied roles that we play: as members of religious, ethnic, and linguistic groups, for example; as traders or workers or employers; as citizens of nations and states; as migrants or vacationers or refugees. It asks us to think about the costs and benefits of our actions in a local and a global context. It asks

us to understand the size of places. Siberia, for example, has been called the biggest place on Earth. It is equivalent in area to India, the U.S., and much of Western Europe added together, but it contains fewer people than the New York metropolitan area.

Parts II and III give you the essential information about our home as a physical space and as a human place. Part IV provides you with background information on the nation-states of the world. Taken together, the three parts give you the knowledge to satisfy your geographic curiosity about "the world and all that is in it."

SOURCES OF FURTHER INFORMATION

Angotti, Thomas. *Metropolis 2000*. New York: Rutledge, 1993.

Barber, Benjamin. *Jihad vs. McWorld*. New York: Ballantine Books, 1995.

Black, Jeremy. *Maps and Politics*. Chicago: University of Chicago, 1998.

Berry, Berry, Edgar Conkling, and D. Michael Ray. *The Global Economy in Transition*. Upper Saddle River, N.J.: Prentice Hall, 1997.

Boutros-Ghali, Boutros. *Unvanquished: A U.S.-U.N. Saga*. New York: Random House, 1999.

Brown, Lester, ed. *State of the World*. New York: W.W. Norton & Co, annual publication.

Brown, Lester R., Gary Gardner, and Brian Halweil. *Beyond Malthus: Nineteen Dimensions of the Population Challenge*. New York: W.W. Norton, 1999.

Brunn, S. and J. Williams, *Cities of the World*. New York: Harper & Row, 1992.

Cadwallader, M. T. *Urban Geography: An Analytical Perspective*. Englewood Cliffs, N.J.: Prentice Hall, 1996.

Carson, Rachel. *Silent Spring*. Boston: Houghton Mifflin Co., 1994.

Castells, Manuel. *The Rise of the Network Society*. Blackwell: Oxford, 1996.

Castles, Stephen and Mark J. Miller. *The Age of Migration*. New York: Guilford Press, 1993.

de Souza, Anthony and Frederick Stutz. *The World Economy*. New York: Macmillan, 1994.

Dicken, Peter. *Global Shift: The Internationalization of Economic Activity*. New York: Guilford Press, 1998.

Fadiman, Anne. *The Spirit Catches You and You Fall Down*. Farrar, Strauss, & Giroux, 1997.

Gebhard, Arlene, Carl Haub and Mary M. Kent. "World Population: Beyond Six Billion?" Population Bulletin 54 (1). Washington, D.C.: Population Reference Bureau.

Hall, P. *Cities in Civilization*. New York: Pantheon, 1998.

Hall, Ray and Paul White, editors. *Europe's Population: Toward the Next Century*. London: University College London Press, 1996.

Harr, Jonathan. *A Civil Action*. New York: Vintage Books, 1995.

Hiss, Tony. *The Experience of Place*. New York: Vintage Books, 1991.

Hugill, Peter. *World Trade since 1431: Geography, Technology, and Capitalism*. Baltimore: Johns Hopkins University Press, 1993.

Johnson, Ron, Peter Taylor and Michael Watts. *Geographies of Global Change*. Oxford: Blackwell, 1995.

Knox, Paul. *Urbanization: An Introduction to Urban Geography*. Englewood Cliffs, N.J.: Prentice Hall, 1994.

Knox, Paul and S. Marston. *Human Geography: Places and Regions in Global Context*. Englewood Cliffs, N. J.: Prentice Hall, 1998.

McCrum, Robert et al. *The Story of English*. New York: Penguin USA, 1993.

McPhee, John. *The Control of Nature*. New York: Farrar, Straus & Giroux, 1990.

Malecki, Edward. *Technology and Economic Development*. Essex, U.K.: Longman, 1991.

Martin, Philip and Elizabeth Midgley. "Immigration to the United States," Population Bulletin 54 (2). Washington, D.C.: Population Reference Bureau, 1999.

Martin, Philip and Jonas Widgen. "International Migration: A Global Challenge," Population Bulletin 51 (1). Washington, D.C.: Population Reference Bureau, 1996.

Monmonier, Mark. Cartographies of Danger: Mapping Hazards in America. Chicago: University of Chicago, 1997.

Moynihan, Daniel P. Pandemonium: Ethnicity in International Politics. New York: Oxford University Press, 1993.

Peterson, William. Population. New York: Macmillan Publishing Co., 1975

Plane, David A. and Peter A. Rogarson. The Geographical Analysis of Population: With Applications to Planning and Business. New York: John Wiley & Sons, 1994.

Robinson, Marilynne. Mother Country. New York: Farrar, Strauss, & Giroux, 1989.

Sassen, Saskia. Cities in a World Economy. Thousand Oaks, Cal.: Pine Forge Press, 1994.

Schlesinger, Arthur M., Jr. The Disuniting of America. New York: W.W. Norton & Co., 1998.

Shipler, David. Arab and Jew: Wounded Spirits in a Promised Land. New York: Penguin USA, 1987.

So, Alvin. Social Change and Development: Modernization, Dependency, and World-System Theories. Newbury Park, Thousand Oaks, Calif.: Sage Publications, 1990.

Stegner, Wallace. American West as Living Space. Ann Arbor: University of Michigan Press, 1987.

Suzuki, David and Amanda Mconnell. The Sacred Balance: Rediscovering Our Place in Nature. Amherst, N.Y.: Prometheus Books, 1998.

United Nations Centre for Human Settlements, An Urbanizing World

Report on Human Settlements 1996. New York: Oxford University Press, 1996.

Weeks, John R. Population: An Introduction to Concepts and Issues. Belmont, Calif.: Wadsworth Publishing Company, 1999.

Zelinsky, Wilbur. The Cultural Geography of the United States. Upper Saddle River, N.J: Prentice Hall, 1992.

PART IV

Places

Reading the World's Nations

The 191 independent countries of the world that follow are those counted in 1999 by the National Geographic Society, whose cartographic policy is to recognize de facto countries. The Lists of Independent Countries by Region on pages 454-457 are useful to determine the general location of countries; they also note dependencies and other sovereignties located by region. Maps of the world and its regions begin on page 676.

Countries vary widely in their ability and resources for collecting and tracking statistical information. Even when gathered efficiently and accurately, the data require revision as soon as they are published; human geography issues, by their nature, are in a constant state of flux. Every effort was made to ensure that the numbers provided in the *Desk Reference* are the most recent and reliable available. Further consideration was given to ensure comparability from country to country.

The **Country Name** listed is used by the National Geographic Society, which consults the U.S. Board on Geographic Names, country embassies, and country governments.

The **Official Name** is the conventional long form of the name in English translation.

Nationality is an identifying term for the country's citizens.

Capital gives the seat of government followed by the city's population. Where two figures are listed for capital cities the first is the population of the city proper, the second, in brackets, represents that of the metropolitan area. Definitions of city proper and metropolitan area vary from country to country.

When possible, *Major Cities* are listed in descending size order, largest cities first.

External Territories include all land outside of the entity's physical borders but under its political jurisdiction; this land is not included in the *Total Area*. External territories are listed within their respective regions on the List of Independent Countries by Region.

Location gives the country's placement relative to its nearest neighboring countries. More general placement within areas of the world is given on the List of Independent Countries by Region.

Physical Geography gives a general sense of topographic details and their approximate location within the country.

Total Area accounts for the sum of all land and inland water delimited by international boundaries, intranational boundaries, or coastlines.

Coastline gives the total length of the boundary between land and sea, including islands.

Land Use terms are defined as follows: Agricultural use includes all land that is cultivated, both arable land(crops are replanted after each harvest) and permanent crops. Meadows and pastures refers to land set aside for herbaceous forage crops. Forest and woodland is land under dense or open stands of trees.

Climate notes characteristic weather conditions, both regionally and seasonally.

Within **Population,** the figures are mid-1999 estimates from the Population Reference Bureau's *1999 World Population Data Sheet.*

Urban population is the percentage of a country's total population living in urban areas as defined by that country; typically, "urban" indicates a community with a population of 2,000 or more and in national or provincial capitals.

Rate of natural increase is the birth rate minus the death rate, expressed as a percentage of the base population. This statistic indicates the rate at which a population is increasing, or decreasing when expressed as a negative percentage, in a given year.

Age structure gives the percentage of the total population under age 15 and over age 65; it may be used to indicate how many people in that country are considered dependent—that is, not economically active. This number is the compound result of past trends in fertility, mortality, and migration.

Birth rate and *Death rate* are crude rates and as such do not consider a population's age structure; therefore, the death rate for a country with a large elderly population may seem higher than that for a country with fewer elders. Both rates are expressed per 1,000 population in a given year.

Infant mortality rate refers to the number of deaths of infants under one year of age per 1,000 live births.

Fertility rate represents the Population Reference Bureau's estimate of "Total Fertility Rate," or the average number of offspring born alive to a woman passing through her childbearing years conforming to the given year's age-specific fertility rates.

Life expectancy at birth refers to the average number of years an infant born in 1999 can be expected to live if current mortality trends remain constant in the future.

Under the heading **Religion,** the most widely practiced faith appears first. "Traditional" or "indigenous" connotes beliefs of important local sects, such as Maya in North America.

If a country has an official **Language**, it is listed first. Often, a country lists more than one official language; these instances are noted. Otherwise both **Religion** and **Language**, along with **Ethnic Divisions** listings, are in rank ordering.

Literacy Rate generally indicates the percentage of the population above the age of 15 who can read and write. There are no universal standards of literacy, so these U.S. Census Bureau estimates are based on the most common definition available for that nation, which makes comparisons among countries difficult.

Suffrage indicates who is allowed the right to vote in government elections, followed by the age at which this right commences.

Economy discusses the general economic conditions of the country: the size, development, and management of productive resources such as land, labor, and capital. It focuses on recent events, trends, and policy changes.

GDP per capita is derived by dividing the gross domestic product (GDP), which is the value of all final goods and services produced within a country in a given year, by midyear population estimates. GDP-per capita numbers for independent nations use the purchasing power parity (PPP) conversion factor designed to equalize the purchasing powers of different currencies. Because it is an average, it hides extremes of poverty and wealth and does not account for factors that also affect quality of life, such as environmental degradation, educational opportunites, and health care.

Inflation rate–CPI uses the consumer price index (CPI) method to note the percent change in consumer prices compared with the previous year's prices.

Agriculture, because of the structured nature of the text, serves as an umbrella term for not only crops but also livestock, products, and fish.

The dates given in **Public Holidays** are for legal or public holidays and widely observed religious holidays. The actual dates of many of these holidays vary from year to year because they are either tied to a particular day of the week or are based on religious traditions or calendars.

ABBREVIATIONS USED:

c.i.f.	cost, insurance, and freight
CPI	consumer price index
est.	estimate
EU	European Union
f.o.b.	free on board
ft.	feet
GDP	gross domestic product
km	kilometer (multiply by 0.621 to get miles)
m	meters
mi	mile (multiply by 1.609 to get kilometers)
N.A.	data not available
pop.	population
PPP	purchasing power parity
sq km	square kilometer (multiply by 0.39 to get square miles)
sq mi	square mile (multiply by 2.60 to get square kilometers)
U.K.	United Kingdom
UN	United Nations
U.S.	United States

Lists of Independent Countries by Region

North America

1 Antigua and Barbuda
2 Bahamas
3 Barbados
4 Belize
5 Canada
6 Costa Rica
7 Cuba
8 Dominica
9 Dominican Republic
10 El Salvador
11 Grenada
12 Guatemala
13 Haiti
14 Honduras
15 Jamaica
16 Mexico
17 Nicaragua
18 Panama
19 St. Kitts and Nevis
20 St. Lucia
21 St. Vincent and the Grenadines
22 Trinidad and Tobago
23 United States

DEPENDENCIES AND AREAS OF
SPECIAL SOVEREIGNTY:

Denmark:
Greenland: part of the Danish realm

France:
Guadeloupe: overseas department
Martinique: overseas department
St.-Pierre and Miquelon: territorial collectivity

Netherlands:
Aruba: part of the Netherlands realm
Netherlands Antilles: part of the Netherlands realm

United Kingdom:
Anguilla: dependent territory
Bermuda: dependent territory
British Virgin Islands: dependent territory
Cayman Islands: dependent territory
Montserrat: dependent territory
Turks and Caicos Islands: dependent territory

United States:
Puerto Rico: commonwealth associated with the U.S.
U.S. Virgin Islands: territory

South America

1 Argentina
2 Bolivia
3 Brazil
4 Chile
5 Colombia
6 Ecuador
7 Guyana
8 Paraguay
9 Peru
10 Suriname
11 Uruguay
12 Venezuela

DEPENDENCIES AND AREAS OF
SPECIAL SOVEREIGNTY:

France:
French Guiana: overseas department

United Kingdom:
Falkland Islands: dependent territory
South Georgia and the South Sandwich Islands: dependent territory

Europe

1 Albania	30 Poland
2 Andorra	31 Portugal
3 Austria	32 Romania
4 Belarus	33 Russia
5 Belgium	34 San Marino
6 Bosnia and Herzegovina	35 Slovakia
7 Bulgaria	36 Slovenia
8 Croatia	37 Spain
9 Czech Republic	38 Sweden
10 Denmark	39 Switzerland
11 Estonia	40 Ukraine
12 Finland	41 United Kingdom
13 France	42 Vatican City (The Holy See)
14 Germany	43 Yugoslavia
15 Greece	
16 Hungary	**DEPENDENCIES AND AREAS OF SPECIAL SOVEREIGNTY:**
17 Iceland	
18 Ireland	**Denmark:**
19 Italy	Faroe Islands: part of Danish realm
20 Latvia	
21 Liechtenstein	**Norway:**
22 Lithuania	Jan Mayen: Norwegian territory
23 Luxembourg	Svalbard: Norwegian territory
24 Macedonia	
25 Malta	**United Kingdom:**
26 Moldova	Channel Islands: crown dependency
27 Monaco	Gibraltar: dependent territory
28 Netherlands	Isle of Man: crown dependency
29 Norway	

Asia

1 Afghanistan	12 India
2 Armenia	13 Indonesia
3 Azerbaijan	14 Iran
4 Bahrain	15 Iraq
5 Bangladesh	16 Israel
6 Bhutan	17 Japan
7 Brunei	18 Jordan
8 Cambodia	19 Kazakhstan
9 China	20 Korea, North
10 Cyprus	21 Korea, South
11 Georgia	22 Kuwait

23 Kyrgyzstan
24 Laos
25 Lebanon
26 Malaysia
27 Maldives
28 Mongolia
29 Myanmar
30 Nepal
31 Oman
32 Pakistan
33 Philippines
34 Qatar
35 Saudi Arabia
36 Singapore
37 Sri Lanka
38 Syria
39 Tajikistan
40 Thailand
41 Turkey
42 Turkmenistan
43 United Arab Emirates
44 Uzebekistan
45 Vietnam
46 Yemen

DEPENDENCIES AND AREAS OF SPECIAL SOVEREIGNTY:

Northern Cyprus: By unilateral declaration of independence, the Turkish Cypriot minority created Northern Cyprus on November 15, 1983. Its capital is the divided city of Nicosia. Turkey is the only country to recognize this action.

Taiwan: The People's Republic of China claims Taiwan as its 23rd province. Taiwan maintains that there is only one China—but two political entities.

West Bank and Gaza Strip: Palestinians govern limited areas of the West Bank and Gaza Strip pending final status talks with Israel.

Portugal:

Macau: overseas territory; reverts to China, December 1999

Africa

 1 Algeria
 2 Angola
 3 Benin
 4 Botswana
 5 Burkina Faso
 6 Burundi
 7 Cameroon
 8 Cape Verde
 9 Central African Republic
10 Chad
11 Comoros
12 Congo
13 Congo, Democratic Republic of the
14 Côte d'Ivoire
15 Djibouti
16 Egypt
17 Equatorial Guinea
18 Eritrea
19 Ethiopia

20 Gabon
21 Gambia
22 Ghana
23 Guinea
24 Gunea-Bissau
25 Kenya
26 Lesotho
27 Liberia
28 Libya
29 Madagascar
30 Malawi
31 Mali
32 Mauritania
33 Mauritius
34 Morocco
35 Mozambique
36 Namibia
37 Niger
38 Nigeria

39 Rwanda
40 Sao Tome and Principe
41 Senegal
42 Seychelles
43 Sierra Leone
44 Somalia
45 South Africa
46 Sudan
47 Swaziland
48 Tanzania
49 Togo
50 Tunisia
51 Uganda
52 Zambia
53 Zimbabwe

DEPENDENCIES AND AREAS OF
SPECIAL SOVEREIGNTY:

France:
Mayotte: territorial collectivity
Réunion: overseas department

Morocco:
Western Sahara: administered by Morocco,
status of sovereignty unresolved

Spain:
Ceuta, Melilla: autonomous communities

Oceania

1 Australia
2 Fiji Islands
3 Kiribati
4 Marshall Islands
5 Micronesia
6 Nauru
7 New Zealand
8 Palau
9 Papua New Guinea
10 Samoa
11 Solomon Islands
12 Tonga
13 Tuvalu
14 Vanuatu

DEPENDENCIES AND AREAS OF
SPECIAL SOVEREIGNTY:

Australia:
Ashmore and Cartier Islands: territory
Christmas Island: territory
Cocos (Keeling) Islands: territory
Coral Sea Islands: territory
Heard and McDonald Islands: territory
Norfolk Island: territory

France:
French Polynesia: overseas territory
New Caledonia: overseas territory
Wallis and Futuna Islands: overseas territory

New Zealand:
Cook Islands: self-governing territory in free
association with New Zealand
Niue: self-governing territory in free association
with New Zealand
Tokelau Islands: territory

United Kingdom:
Pitcairn Islands: dependent territory

United States:
American Samoa: territory
Baker Island: territory
Guam: territory
Howland Island: territory
Jarvis Island: territory
Johnston Atoll: territory
Kingman Reef: territory
Midway Islands: territory
Northern Mariana Islands: commonwealth
in political union with U.S.
Palmyra Atoll: territory
Wake Island: territory

Afghanistan

Country Name: Afghanistan

Official Name: Islamic State of Afghanistan

Nationality: Afghan(s) (noun); Afghan (adjective)

Capital: Kabul, pop. 1,700,000

Major cities: Qandahār, Herāt, Māzar-e-Sharīf

External Territories: None

Location: Afghanistan, in southwestern Asia, is bordered on the north by Uzbekistan, Tajikistan, and Turkmenistan; on the northeast by China; on the east and south by Pakistan; and on the west by Iran.

Physical Geography: Northern plains rise to meet highlands, including the high mountains of the Hindu Kush; desert and semidesert lands lie in the southwest.

Total area: 251,773 sq mi (652,090 sq km)

Coastline: None

Land use: 46% of the land is meadows and pastures; 12% of the land is arable, and 3% is wooded.

Climate: Continental dry, with hot summers and cold winters; temperatures vary with elevation.

Population: 25,825,000

Urban population: 20%

Rate of natural increase: 2.49%

Age structure: 43% under 15; 3% over 65

Birth rate: 43/1000

Death rate: 18/1000

Infant mortality rate: 150/1000

Fertility rate: 6.1

Life expectancy at birth: 46 years (male); 45 years (female)

Religion: Sunni and Shiite Muslim

Language: Pashto, Dari, Turkik languages

Ethnic Divisions: Pathan, Tajik, Uzbek, Hazara, others

Literacy Rate: 32%

Government: Transitional government based on Islamic law, with a president and a unicameral legislature whose members are chosen by a national council (shura). There are 30 administrative provinces called velayat.

Armed services: N.A.

Suffrage: N.A.

Economy: Years of Soviet occupation and civil war have left a legacy of refugees (as many as six million Afghans may have fled to Pakistan and Iran between 1979 and 1989 and a million may still be in Pakistan and 1.2 million in Iran), inflation, a shattered infrastructure, and devastated manufacturing and agricultural sectors. Accurate information about the economic status of the country is difficult to obtain, and international aid has been essential to provide badly needed food and medical supplies in the past several years.

Unit of currency: Afghani; 100 puls = 1 afghani (AF)

GDP per capita: $800.

Inflation rate–CPI: 240% (1996 est.)

Workforce: 7.1 million (1980 est.)

Unemployment rate: 8% (1995 est.)

Exports: Goods worth more than $80 million (1996 est.) are sent to the F.S.U., Pakistan, Iran, Germany, India, the U.K., and other trading partners; exports include fruits, nuts, handwoven carpets, wool, cotton, hides and pelts, and gemstones.

Imports: Goods worth more than $150 million (1996 est.) are received from Pakistan, Iran, Japan, Singapore, India, South Korea, and Germany; imports include food, petroleum products, and consumer goods.

Agriculture: More than 67.8% (1980 est.) of the settled workforce participates in the agricultural sector. Livestock products, cotton, fruit, and nuts are raised for export. Food imports have been necessary in recent years.

Energy: Most energy is generated by imported fuels.

Natural Resources: Natural gas, petroleum, coal, copper, talc, sulfur, lead, zinc, gemstones

Environmental Issues: Deforestation, desertification

Transportation: 20 miles (30 km) of rail are in service. Less than 3,000 miles of the 13,000-mile (21,000 km) highway network are paved. The Amu Darya River adds another 750 miles (1,200 km) to available transport routes, with major ports at Kheyrabad and Shir Khan. Kabul and Qandahār have international airports.

Communications: A dozen daily papers are published in the country. There are 1.8 million radios (1996 est.) and 100,000 televisions (1993 est.) in use. Phone service,

---

AFGHANISTAN AN INVASION-PRONE LOCATION

The Soviet Union invaded Afghanistan in 1979, killing more than a million people during the eight years that followed. According to UN estimates, nearly 6 million Afghans left the country to escape the conflict; most fled to Pakistan and Iran. Long a trade crossroads between the Middle East and the rest of Asia—via the Khyber Pass—the country has been the target of invaders since the sixth century B.C.

with about 31,200 phones operating (1983), is limited.

Tourism: In 1993, about 6,000 visitors spent around $1 million (U.S.) in the country, drawn in part by the rugged beauty of the Hindu Kush.

Embassy in U.S.: (202) 234-3770

Public Holidays: First day of Ramadan (date varies, dependent on Islamic lunar calendar); End of Ramadan (date varies); New Year's Day (March 21); Feast of the Sacrifice (date varies, in April); Liberation Day (April 18); Revolution Day (April 27); Ashura (date varies, in May); Workers' Day (May 1); Birth of the Prophet (date varies, in July); Independence Day (August 18)

Albania

Country Name: Albania
Official Name: Republic of Albania
Nationality: Albanian(s) (noun); Albanian (adjective)
Capital: Tirana, pop. 244,200
Major cities: Durrës, Elbasan, Scutari
External Territories: None
Location: Albania, in southeastern Europe, is located on the Adriatic coast of the Balkan Peninsula and is bordered by Yugoslavia, Macedonia, and Greece.
Physical Geography: Most of Albania is mountainous, but the western coastal lowland provides better terrain for agriculture.
Total area: 11,100 sq mi (28,748 sq km)
Coastline: 225 mi (362 km)
Land use: About a quarter of the land in Albania is devoted to agriculture and permanent crops. An estimated 15% is meadows and pastures, and forests make up more than a third of the uncultivated land.
Climate: Mediterranean, with cool, wet winters and hot, dry summers; mountainous areas are subject to more extreme temperature ranges.
Population: 3,460,000
Urban population: 37%
Rate of natural increase: 1.2%
Age structure: 34% under 15; 6% over 65
Birth rate: 17/1000
Death rate: 5/1000
Infant mortality rate: 20.4/1000
Fertility rate: 2.0
Life expectancy at birth: 70 years (male); 76 years (female)
Religion: Muslim, Albanian Orthodox
Language: Albanian, Greek
Ethnic Divisions: Albanian
Literacy Rate: 72%
Government: Republic, with a unicameral legislature, the People's Assembly. The 155 members of the legislature are directly elected to office; they in turn elect the president of the republic. There are 26 administrative districts.
Armed services: 54,000 (1996); compulsory service for 12 months.
Suffrage: Universal and compulsory; 18 years old
Economy: Albania is changing its historical policy of economic self-sufficiency and is making a difficult transition to a market economy. Economic growth has resulted from strict fiscal measures as well as from remittances from Albanian citizens working in other countries.
Unit of currency: Lek; 100 qintars = 1 lek (L)
GDP per capita: $1,370
Inflation rate–CPI: 40% (1997 est.)
Workforce: 1.69million (1994 est.)
Unemployment rate: 14% (1997 est.)
Exports: Goods worth $228 million (f.o.b., 1996 est.) are sent to Italy, Greece, Germany, and the U.S.; exports include asphalt, metals and metallic ores, electricity, crude oil, and vegetables.
Imports: Goods worth $879 million (f.o.b., 1996 est.) are received from Italy, Greece, Bulgaria, Turkey, and the Former Yugoslav Republic of Macedonia; imports include machinery, consumer goods and grains.
Agriculture: Agricultural activities involve nearly 50% of the population; a wide range of temperate-zone crops and livestock are cultivated.
Energy: Hydroelectric power generates most of Albania's electricity.
Natural Resources: Chromium, petroleum, natural gas, coal, copper
Environmental Issues: Water pollution, deforestation, soil erosion
Transportation: More than 11,180 miles (17,990 km) of main and secondary roads cross Albania; many

ALBANIA UNIQUELY ETHNIC, THANKS TO GEOGRAPHY

Even though Albania has been ruled by outsiders for almost all of its past 2,000 years, 90 percent of the people remain ethnic Albanians, known as Shqiptarë. The Albanian language, with its two main dialects, Gheg and Tosk, forms its own branch of the Indo-European family of languages because it appears to be unrelated to any other language in that group. Geography helps explain this nation's isolation: The North Albanian Alps have long blocked the rest of the country from its neighbors to the east.

mountain roads are unsuitable for vehicles. Before 1991, private cars were banned. Railways connect many of the cities. Durrës, Vlorë, Sarande, and Shëngjin are major ports, and there is a small international airport near Tirana.

Communications: Three daily papers are published in Albania; telephone access is sparse. Albania has 577,000 radios (1991 est.) and 300,000 televisions (1993 est.).

Tourism: Growth of Albania's tourist industry is limited due to its primitive infrastructure and lack of foreign investment. Tourist attractions include the major cities, archaeological sites at Apollonia and Butrint, and the Roman amphitheater at Durrës.

Embassy in U.S.: (202) 223-4942

Public Holidays: End of Ramadan (date varies); International Women's Day (March 8); Catholic Easter (date varies, March or April); Orthodox Easter (date varies, in April); Feast of the Sacrifice (date varies, in late April); Independence and Liberation Day: from the Ottoman Empire, 1912 (November 28); Christmas (December 25)

Algeria

Country Name: Algeria
Official Name: Democratic and Popular Republic of Algeria
Nationality: Algerian(s) (noun); Algerian (adjective)
Capital: Algiers, pop. 2,168,000 [3,702,000]
Major cities: Oran, Constantine, Annaba

External Territories: None
Location: Algeria lies in northwestern Africa, bordered on the west by Morocco and Mauritania. Mali and Niger form its southern boundary, and Libya and Tunisia lie to the east. The Mediterranean Sea lies to the north.

Physical Geography: Along the Mediterranean coast, plains and rolling hills extend inland about 200 miles, terminating at the Tell Atlas Mountains. The High Plateaus extend south, where animals graze and shallow salt lakes form during rainy spells. To the south of the High Plateaus are the Atlas Mountains and the vast Sahara, which covers most of the country.

Total area: 919,595 sq mi (2,381,741 sq km)
Coastline: 620 mi (998 km)
Land use: Only 3% of the land in Algeria is used for agriculture; 13% is meadows and pastures.
Climate: Mediterranean climate along the coast, with mild, wet winters and hot, dry summers; farther south, conditions become hotter and drier as a desert climate predominates.

Population: 30,774,000
Urban population: 49%
Rate of natural increase: 2.4%
Age structure: 39% under 15; 4% over 65
Birth rate: 30/1000
Death rate: 6/1000
Infant mortality rate: 44/1000
Fertility rate: 4.1
Life expectancy at birth: 67 years (male); 69 years (female)

Religion: Sunni Muslim
Language: Arabic, French, Berber dialects
Ethnic Divisions: Arab, Berber
Literacy Rate: 62%
Government: Republic, with 48 provinces. In 1997, the legislative branch became bicameral with the National People's Assembly and the

Council of Nations. The president is elected by universal suffrage.
Armed services: 124,000 (1997 est.) in the army, navy, and air force; compulsory for 18 months
Suffrage: Universal; 18 years old

Economy: An oil- and natural-gas-based economy faltered in the 1980s, and government-sponsored recovery plans in the 1990s emphasized diversification, currency devaluation, and foreign investment. High unemployment levels and political unrest complicate recovery efforts.
Unit of currency: Algerian dinar; 100 centimes = 1 Algerian dinar (DA)
GDP per capita: $4,000
Inflation rate–CPI: 7% (1997 est.)
Workforce: 7.8 million (1996 est.)
Unemployment rate: 28% (1997 est.)

Exports: Oil and natural gas worth $13.1 billion (f.o.b., 1997 est.), which accounts for 97% of Algeria's export income, are sent to Italy, France, the U.S., Germany, and Spain.
Imports: Goods worth $10 billion (f.o.b., 1997 est.) are received from France, the U.S., Italy, Spain, Germany, and other countries; imports include agricultural products, machinery, iron, and steel.
Agriculture: Nearly a quarter of Algeria's workforce is employed in agriculture. Major products include wheat, barley, oats, olives, citrus fruit, grapes, and sheep.

Energy: Algeria has abundant supplies of petroleum and natural gas. A nuclear reactor was built in 1989.

Natural Resources: Petroleum, natural gas, iron, phosphates, uranium, lead, zinc. Algeria is fifth in the world for natural gas reserves and fourteenth in the world for oil reserves.

Environmental Issues: Soil erosion from poor agricultural practices, desertification, water pollution, inadequate potable water supplies

Transportation: More than 63,610 miles (102,420 km) of roads serve the country, but many are not surfaced. A limited rail network of just over 2,960 miles (4,770 km) provides transport for passengers and freight. Algiers is the major port; other ports are at Annaba, Arzew, Oran, and several other cities. The main international airport is located near Algiers; because of the oil industry, the country is well served with regional airports and airstrips.

Communications: Telephone service is standard in the north, but service becomes more sparse farther south. There are 17 daily papers and 6 million radios (1991 est.) and 2 million televisions (1993 est.) in service.

Tourism: The Mediterranean coast, Atlas Mountains, and Sahara all draw international visitors, who added $64 million (U.S.) to the economy in 1990.

Embassy in U.S.: (202) 265-2800

Public Holidays: Ramadan (date varies); End of Ramadan (date varies); Feast of the Sacrifice (date varies, in April); Ashura (date varies, in April or May); Islamic New Year (date varies, in May); Labour Day (May 1); Ben Bella's Overthrow, 1965 (June 19); Birth of Muhammad (date varies, in July); Independence: from France, 1962 (July 5); Anniversary of the Revolution (November 1); Ascension of Muhammad (date varies, in December)

Andorra

Country Name: Andorra
Official Name: Principality of Andorra
Nationality: Andorran(s) (noun); Andorran (adjective)
Capital: Andorra la Vella, pop. 22,000
Major cities: None
External Territories: None
Location: Andorra, in western Europe, is a tiny country in the Pyrenees mountains between France and Spain.
Physical Geography: Andorra is comprised of alpine mountains and valleys.
Total area: 175 sq mi (453 sq km)
Coastline: None
Land use: Only 2% of the land is cultivated; an estimated 56% of the country's area is meadows and pastures, and forests cover another 22%.
Climate: Continental, with heavy winter snows and warm, dry summers.
Population: 66,000
Urban population: 95%
Rate of natural increase: 0.82%
Age structure: 15% under 15 years; 12% over 65 years
Birth rate: 11/1000
Death rate: 3/1000
Infant mortality rate: 1.4/1000
Fertility rate: 1.7
Life expectancy at birth: 76 years (male); 82 years (female)
Religion: Roman Catholic

Language: Catalan, French, Spanish
Ethnic Divisions: Spanish, Andorran, French
Literacy Rate: N.A.
Government: Traditionally a co-principality of France and Spain, Andorra, a parliamentary democracy, has a legislative body of 28 elected councilors who compose the General Council of the Valleys and who serve for four years. The president of France and the Spanish Bishop of Urgel hold honorary positions as the heads of state. Andorra has seven parishes.
Armed services: None
Suffrage: Universal; 18 years of age
Economy: Andorra's stable economy profits mainly from tourism, banking, and the sale of duty-free goods.
Unit of currency: Spanish peseta; 100 centimos = 1 Spanish peseta (Pta); French franc; 100 centimes = 1 French franc (F)
GDP per capita: $18,000
Inflation rate–CPI: N.A.
Workforce: N.A.
Unemployment rate: 0%
Exports: Goods worth $47 million (f.o.b., 1995 est.) are sent primarily to France and Spain; exports include electricity, tobacco products and furniture.
Imports: Goods worth $1 billion (1995) are imported primarily from France and Spain; imports include consumer goods, food, and electrical equipment.
Agriculture: Andorra must import food to meet domestic demand; tobacco, rye, wheat, and livestock, particularly sheep, are traditional agricultural products.
Energy: Hydropower meets about one-quarter of the country's energy demands. Fuel and electricity are imported from France and Spain.
Natural Resources: Hydropower, mineral water, timber, iron ore

Environmental Issues: Deforestation, soil erosion from overgrazing

Transportation: A network of 170 miles (270 km) of roads connect Andorra's towns and capital; no railroads have been constructed in the country. The nearest airport is in Spain.

Communications: Both daily and weekly papers circulate in Andorra, and there are approximately 21,260 telephones in use, along with an estimated 10,000 radios and 7,000 televisions.

Tourism: An estimated 8 million tourists come every year to Andorra for the scenery, skiing, and duty-free shopping.

U.S. Tourist Office: (708) 674-3091
Embassy in U.S.: 202-750-8064

Public Holidays: Good Friday (date varies, in March or April); Easter Monday (date varies, in March or April); National Holiday: Mare de Deu de Meritxell (September 8); Christmas (December 25–26)

Angola

Country Name: Angola
Official Name: Republic of Angola
Nationality: Angolan(s) (noun); Angolan (adjective)
Capital: Luanda, pop. 2,081,000
Major cities: Huambo, Lobito, Benguela
External Territories: None
Location: Angola, in southwestern Africa, is bordered on the west by the South Atlantic Ocean, on the south by Namibia, on the east by Zambia, and on the north and east

ANGOLA DIAMONDS IN THE ROUGH

Once a center of the slave trade to Brazil, Angola (formerly Portuguese West Africa) won its independence from Portugal in 1975. Many were killed in the civil war that followed. Although the Marxist government that ruled was replaced by a social democracy in 1992, unrest continues. Almost twice the size of Texas, it has potentially rich mineral deposits of petroleum and diamonds.

by the Democratic Republic of the Congo. Cabinda Province is separated from the rest of the country by the Zaire (Congo) River and is bordered by the Democratic Republic of the Congo and Congo.

Physical Geography: A narrow coastal plain rises to meet a group of interior highlands, beyond which lie several plateaus that are part of Africa's large inland plateau.

Total area: 481,354 sq mi (1,246,700 sq km)
Coastline: 994 mi (1,600 km)
Land use: Only 2% of the land is used for agriculture and permanent cultivation. Almost 25% of the land is meadows and pastures, and more than 40% is forested.
Climate: Tropical along the coast, with seasonal rain that increases in amount from south to north; inland, the rainfall and temperatures decrease.

Population: 12,479,000
Urban population: 32%
Rate of natural increase: 2.9%
Age structure: 48% under 15; 3% over 65
Birth rate: 48.4/1000
Death rate: 18.8/1000
Infant mortality rate: 125/1000
Fertility rate: 6.8
Life expectancy at birth: 45 years (male); 48 years (female)
Religion: Indigenous beliefs, Roman Catholic, Protestant
Language: Portuguese (official), Bantu languages

Ethnic Divisions: Ovimbundu, Kimbundu, Bakongo, others
Literacy Rate: 42%
Government: Transitional multi-party republic, with a president directly elected for a five-year term. The National Assembly, the legislative branch, officially has 223 members elected to four-year terms. There are 18 provinces.
Armed services: 110,500 (1997 est.) in the army, navy, and air force
Suffrage: Universal; 18 years old
Economy: Despite oil deposits and other natural resources, Angola has been unable to develop stable economic growth because of civil war over the past several years and currency fluctuations. Much of the population relies on subsistence farming for survival.
Unit of currency: Kwanza; 100 lwei = 1 new kwanza (NKz)
GDP per capita: $800
Inflation rate–CPI: 92% (1997 est.)
Workforce: 2.8 million (1997 est.)
Unemployment rate: 50% (1997 est.)
Exports: Goods worth $4 billion (f.o.b., 1996 est.) are sent to the U.S., France, Germany, Netherlands, Brazil, and other countries; exports include crude oil, refined petroleum products, diamonds, gas, coffee.
Imports: Goods worth $1.7 billion (f.o.b., 1995 est.) are received from Portugal, Brazil, the U.S., France, Spain, and other countries; imports include machinery, electrical equip-

ment, food, medicines, vehicles, textiles, and military equipment.

Agriculture: About 85% (1997 est.) of the working population engages in subsistence and cash farming. Coffee, sugarcane, and fish are raised for cash, and cassava, bananas, maize, and sweet potatoes are grown for consumption.

Energy: Most of Angola's energy is derived from hydroelectric power.

Natural Resources: Petroleum, diamonds, iron ore, copper

Environmental Issues: Desertification, deforestation, soil erosion contributing to water pollution, land degradation from overuse, and inadequate potable water supplies

Transportation: There are more than 45,100 miles (72,630 km) of roads in Angola, but most are unpaved. Much of the 1,830 miles (2,950 km) of railway has been taken out of service because of the civil war. The main ports are at Lobito, Luanda, and Namibe; there are also plans for expanding Cabinda. Internal and international air travel is available from Luanda and other cities.

Communications: Two daily papers are published in Luanda, supplemented by weekly and monthly publications in Luanda and other cities. There are 320,000 radios and 70,000 televisions (1994 est.) in use. There are 53,000 telephones (1993) in use, mainly by government and business concerns.

Tourism: Although wildlife and a country rich with traditional culture holds tourist potential, the lack of infrastructure and the fallout from the civil war hinder the development of tourism.

Embassy in U.S.: (202) 785-1156

Public Holidays: Anniversary of colonial rebellion against Portugal (February 4); Victory Day (March 27); Youth Day (April 14); Workers' Day (May 1); National Hero's Day (September 17); Independence Day: from Portugal, 1975 (November 11);

Anniversary of the Foundation of the Movimento Popular de Libertção de Angola (MPLA), 1956 (December 10); Family Day (December 25)

Antigua and Barbuda

Country Name: Antigua and Barbuda

Official Name: Antigua and Barbuda

Nationality: Antiguan(s), Barbudan(s) (noun); Antiguan, Barbudan (adjective)

Capital: St. John's, pop. 22,300

Major cities: None

External Territories: None

Location: Antigua and Barbuda is a country made up of three islands in the Caribbean Sea along the eastern edge of the Leeward Islands.

Physical Geography: The three low-lying islands have some hilly terrain; Redonda, the smallest, has little vegetation and no inhabitants.

Total area: 170 sq mi (440 sq km)

Coastline: 95 mi (153 km)

Land use: Nearly 20% of the land is used for agricultural purposes, 11% is forest and woodland, and an estimated 9% is meadows and pastures.

Climate: Tropical

Population: 67,000

Urban population: 37%

Rate of natural increase: 1.52%

Age structure: 28% under 15; 8% over 65

Birth rate: 21.6/1000

Death rate: 6.4/1000

Infant mortality rate: 17.1/1000

Fertility rate: 1.7%

Life expectancy at birth: 72 years (male); 76 years (female)

Religion: Protestant, Roman Catholic

Language: English, local dialects

Ethnic Divisions: Black, British, Portuguese

Literacy Rate: 89%

Government: Constitutional monarchy with six parishes and two dependencies; the governor-general represents the British sovereign, and the prime minister is the head of state. The bicameral Parliament consists of 17 House of Representative members elected every five years and 17 Senate members who are appointed by the governor-general.

Armed services: 150

Suffrage: Universal; 18 years old

Economy: Tourism continues to be the backbone of Antigua and Barbuda's economy, but manufacturing is being developed. Since the 1970s, the economy has grown slowly but steadily.

Unit of currency: East Caribbean dollar; 100 cents = 1 East Caribbean dollar (EC$)

GDP per capita: $7,400

Inflation rate–CPI: 2.5% (1996)

Workforce: 30,000 (1996 est.)

Unemployment rate: 5% to 10% (1995 est.)

Exports: Goods worth $45 million (f.o.b., 1996 est.) are sent to other Caribbean countries, the OECS, the U.S., and other trading partners; exports include petroleum products, manufactures, food and animals, machinery and transportation equipment.

Imports: Goods worth $350.8 million (f.o.b., 1996 est.) are received from Canada, OECS, the U.K., the U.S., and other countries; imports include food, livestock, oil, machinery and transport equipment, chemicals, and manufactured goods.

Agriculture: Main crops include cucumbers, mangoes, coconuts, cotton, fruits, vegetables, bananas, sugarcane.

Energy: Mineral fuels are imported.

Natural Resources: Negligible

Environmental Issues: Newly cleared fields encourage the runoff of rainfall, thus reducing the amount of water available to recharge the limited fresh water supplies.

Transportation: An estimated 160 miles (240 km) of roads cross the islands, and a 50-mile-long (80 km) narrow-gauge railway is used primarily to transport sugarcane. The international port at St. John's handles passenger and cargo vessels. The country also has three major airports.

Communications: There are almost 7,000 telephones in the country, with international service available. There are 28,000 radios and 28,000 televisions (1993 est.) in use. One daily newspaper (1990) is published, supplemented by several weekly and monthly publications.

Tourism: An abundance of beaches, Carnival week, sailing regattas, and wildlife drew more than half a million tourists to Antigua and Barbuda in 1994.

U.S. Tourist Office: (212) 541-4117

Embassy in U.S.: (202) 362-5122

Public Holidays: Good Friday (date varies, in March or April); Easter Monday (date varies, in March or April); Labor Day (May 6); Whit Monday (May 27); Caribbean Community and Common Market (CARICOM) Day (July 1); Carnival (first week in August); Independence Day (November 1); Christmas (December 25–26)

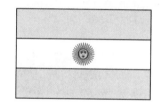

Argentina

Country Name: Argentina

Official Name: Argentine Republic

Nationality: Argentine(s) (noun); Argentine(s) (adjective)

Capital: Buenos Aires, pop. 2,965,400; [11,298,000]

Major cities: Córdoba, Rosario, Mendoza

External Territories: None

Location: Argentina, the second largest country in South America, occupies most of the southern part of the continent. It is bordered on the east by the Atlantic Ocean and on the west by Chile; Bolivia, Paraguay, Brazil, and Uruguay border Argentina on the north and northeast.

Physical Geography: Argentina extends about 2,300 miles from

lowland plains, a portion of the Gran Chaco region in the north, to the rugged island of Tierra del Fuego in the south. South of the plains are the fertile grasslands of the Pampas. The Patagonia plateau, south of the Pampas, supports extensive ranching. The Andes, which include the highest peak in the Americas, Cerro Aconcagua at 22,272 feet (6,690 m), are along the country's western boundary with Chile.

Total area: 1,068,302 sq mi (2,766,889 sq km)

Coastline: 3,100 mi (4,989 km)

Land use: Slightly more than half of Argentina's land is meadows and pastures; from 10% is cultivated or used for other agricultural practices, and 20% is forested.

Climate: Ranges from subtropical in the north to subarctic in the south; generally temperate, with rainfall decreasing from the north to the south

Population: 36,568,000

Urban population: 89%

Rate of natural increase: 1.2%

Age structure: 29% under 15; 9% over 65

ARGENTINA BUENOS AIRES: SOUTH AMERICAN MELTING POT

Buenos Aires, Argentina's capital, was founded by the Spaniards in 1580 but didn't begin to grow until more than 300 years later, when it became an important port city for shipping beef, hides, grains, and wool from the Pampas region. The metropolitan area now is home to more than one-third of the country's population and spreads out over 1,500 square miles (3,885 sq km). European in culture and architecture, Buenos Aires reflects the traditions of its many immigrants—the waves of Spaniards and Italians in the late 1800s and early 1900s were accompanied by Irish, Swiss, French, Arabs, and Armenians. It is also home to a large Jewish community of about 300,000 who came beginning around 1890 from Russia, Poland, Turkey, Syria, Lebanon, and Africa. More recently, immigrants have come from Korea and the surrounding countries in South America.

Birth rate: 20/1000

Death rate: 8/1000

Infant mortality rate: 21.8/1000

Fertility rate: 2.6

Life expectancy at birth: 70 years (male); 77 years (female)

Religion: Roman Catholic

Language: Spanish, English, Italian, German

Ethnic Divisions: White, mestizo

Literacy Rate: 96%

Government: Argentina is a republic, with an elected president and bicameral Congress. The president is elected to a four-year term; the 257 members of the Chamber of Deputies serve four-year terms as well, while members of the Senate—three each from the 23 provinces and Federal District of Buenos Aires—currently serve for nine years.

Armed services: 73,000 (1997 est.) in the army, navy, air force, others; voluntary

Suffrage: Universal; 18 years old

Economy: Extreme inflation between 1985 and 1994 and large international debt led Argentina into strict financial restructuring; a high unemployment rate still contributes to limited economic recovery and growth.

Unit of currency: Nuevo peso argentino; 100 centavos = 1 nuevo peso argentino

GDP Per capita: $9,700

Inflation rate–CPI: 0.3% (1997 est.)

Workforce: 14.3 million (1995 est.)

Unemployment rate: 13.7% (1997)

Exports: Goods worth $25.4 billion (f.o.b., 1997) are exported to Brazil, the U.S., Chile, the Netherlands, and other countries; exports include meat, wheat, corn, oilseed, manufactures, fuel.

Imports: Goods worth $30.3 billion (c.i.f., 1997) are received from the Brazil, the U.S., Italy, Germany, and France; imports include machinery and equipment, chemicals, metals, and agriculture products.

Agriculture: Agriculture, both for at-home consumption and export, employs more than 12% (1985) of the workforce. Argentina is one of the world's biggest producers of wheat and beef; maize, soybeans, sugar beets, and sorghum are also cultivated.

Energy: Hydroelectric power and coal provide Argentina with the majority of its energy. Two nuclear power stations, in operation since 1993, supply 11% of the country's energy.

Natural Resources: Fertile plains, lead, zinc, tin, copper, iron ore.

Environmental Issues: Desertification, soil degradation, soil erosion, air pollution in urban areas, water pollution from pesticides and fertilizers

Transportation: More than 40% of Argentina's 135,550 miles (218,000 km) of roads are paved, and the Pan-American Highway connects Buenos Aires with Chile, Bolivia, Paraguay, and Brazil. Railways also provide international transportation with 23,560 miles (37,900 km) of track. Inland water traffic is used extensively for commercial shipping, and Argentina's large merchant fleet is serviced by many ports. There are ten international airports and scores of smaller airports throughout the country.

Communications: There are 22.3 million radios and 7.1 million televisions (1991 est.) in use. There are more than 200 television broadcast stations and more than 100 FM radio stations. More than a dozen daily papers are published in Buenos Aires. There are approximately 4.6 million telephones (1990).

Tourism: Tourists visit Argentina for the wildlife in Patagonia, the festivals in the cities, the beaches, the mountains, and Iguazú Falls on the border with Brazil. An estimated 4.3 million visitors came to Argentina in 1996.

U.S. Tourist Office: (212) 603-0443

Embassy in U.S.: (202) 939-6400

Public Holidays: Good Friday (date varies, in March or April); Labor Day (May 1); Anniversary of the 1810 Revolution (May 25); Occupation of the Islas Malvinas (Falkland Islands) (June 10); Flag Day (June 24); Independence Day: from Spain, 1816 (July 9); Anniversary of the death of General José de San Martín (August 17); Columbus Day (October 12); Christmas (December 25)

Armenia

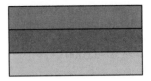

Country Name: Armenia

Official Name: Republic of Armenia

Nationality: Armenian(s) (noun); Armenian (adjective)

Capital: Yerevan, pop. 1,254,400

Major cities: Vanadzor, Gyumri

External Territories: None

Location: Armenia is located in southwestern Asia. It is bordered on the south and west by Turkey, on the east and south by Azerbaijan, and on the north by Georgia. A small part of its southern border is shared with Iran.

Physical Geography: The Lesser Caucasus Mountains cross Armenia from north to south, and the county has an average elevation of 5,900 feet with fertile valleys. Lake Sevan in the east covers 525 square miles (1,360 sq km).

Total area: 11,583 sq mi (30,000 sq km)

Coastline: None

Land use: About 20% of the land is used for agriculture and permanent crops; another 24% is meadows

ARMENIA DISASTER-PRONE ARMENIA

Armenia, the smallest of the 15 republics of the former Soviet Union, has long suffered from disasters political and physical. An estimated 1.5 million Armenians died between 1915 and 1918 during war with Ottoman Turks, and more than a million Armenians fled or were deported to other countries. In 1988, a devastating earthquake caused 55,000 deaths and much destruction. It has few natural resources, little industry, and relatively poor agricultural output. A much larger kingdom in ancient times, Armenia became a Christian region in the late second century A.D.

and pastures, and 15% is forest and woodlands.

Climate: Continental dry, with cold winters and hot summers; precipitation is greater at higher elevations.

Population: 3,802,000

Urban population: 67%

Rate of natural increase: 0.54%

Age structure: 27% under 15; 8% over 65

Birth rate: 12/1000

Death rate: 6/1000

Infant mortality rate: 15/1000

Fertility rate: 1.5%

Life expectancy at birth: 69 years (male); 76 years (female)

Religion: Armenian Orthodox

Language: Armenian, Russian

Ethnic Divisions: Armenian, Azeri, Kurd

Literacy Rate: 99%

Government: Republic, with a unicameral National Assembly, whose 131 members are elected by universal suffrage to four-year terms. The president is directly elected for a five-year term. The country is divided into eleven administrative regions called marz.

Armed services: 18 months of military service is compulsory. Some mobilization by conscription reported.

Suffrage: Universal; 18 years old

Economy: Despite severe economic decline between 1991 and 1994, economic reforms began to pay off

in 1994. Inflation decreased and exports increased. However, limited fuel and food imports continue to hinder a full economic recovery.

Unit of currency: Dram; 100 louma = 1 dram

GDP per capita: $2,750

Inflation rate–CPI: 13.2% (1997 est.)

Workforce: 1.6 million (1997)

Unemployment rate: 10.6% (1997)

Exports: Goods worth $290 million (f.o.b., 1996) are sent to Russia, Georgia, Turkmenistan, and Iran; exports include machinery, chemicals, jewelry, aluminum, and gold.

Imports: Goods worth $727 million (c.i.f., 1996) are received from Russia, Georgia, Turkmenistan, Iran, the U.S., and other European Union countries; imports include industrial products, food, grain, fuel and other energy

Agriculture: About one-third of Armenia's working population is currently involved in subsistence and cash farming, cultivating fruits, cereals, other vegetables, and livestock.

Energy: Russia is Armenia's main supplier of imported petroleum, and Turkmenistan is Armenia's primary source for natural gas. Nearly two-thirds (1994) of the country's electricity is derived from domestic hydropower. One nuclear plant is in operation.

Natural Resources: Gold, copper, zinc, aluminum, molybdenum

Environmental Issues: Water, air, and soil pollution; deforestation

Transportation: Estimates of the road network range between 4,760 miles (7,660 km) and 6,800 miles (11,000 km); the country has 510 miles (830 km) of rail track for internal and international travel.

Communications: Several daily newspapers circulate in Armenia, and the ratio of televisions, radios, and telephones is one for every five people (1993 est.).

Tourism: Because of complex internal problems, little attention is currently given to Armenia's tourist potential.

Embassy in U.S.: (202) 319-1976

Public Holidays: Christmas (January 6); Easter (date varies, in March or April); Armenian Genocide Commemoration Day (April 24); Anniversary of the Declaration of First Armenian Republic, 1918 (May 28); Independence Day: from the Soviet Union, 1990 (September 21); Day of Remembrance of the 1988 Earthquake (December 7)

Australia

Country Name: Australia

Official Name: Commonwealth of Australia

Nationality: Australian(s) (noun); Australian (adjective)

Capital: Canberra, pop. 298,200

Major cities: Sydney, Melbourne, Brisbane, Perth, Adelaide

External Territories: Several in the Indian Ocean, including Ashmore and Cartier Islands, Christmas Island, Cocos (Keeling) Islands, Heard and McDonald Islands, and, in the

South Pacific, Norfolk Island, and the Coral Sea Islands

Location: A country occupying the smallest of the continents, Australia is located between the Indian Ocean and the South Pacific Ocean; Papua New Guinea, to the north, is its nearest neighbor.

Physical Geography: The east coast, where the majority of the large cities are located, is bordered by mountains of the Great Dividing Range. The highest mountain on the continent, Mount Kosciusko at 7,310 feet (2,228 m), is in the Australian Alps at the southern end of the Great Dividing Range. Large ranches occupy Australia's vast Western Plateau and Great Artesian Basin.

Total area: 2,966,153 sq mi (7,682,300 sq km)

Coastline: 16,100 mi (25,760 km)

Land use: Nearly 60% of the land is meadows and pastures, 14% is forest and woodland, and 6% is used for agriculture.

Climate: The northern portion of Australia is tropical, with seasonal summer rains (November through February); rainfall gradually decreases southward into the desert; hot summers and mild winters with some precipitation along the southeastern coast; warm summers and cool winters along the east coast

Population: 18,981,000

Urban population: 85%

Rate of natural increase: 0.7%

Age structure: 21% under 15; 12% over 65

Birth rate: 13/1000

Death rate: 7/1000

Infant mortality rate: 5.3/1000

Fertility rate: 1.7

Life expectancy at birth: 76 years (male); 81 years (female)

Religion: Protestant, Roman Catholic

Language: English, Indigenous languages

AUSTRALIA LAND OF PADEMELONS, MONOTREMES, WOMBATS, AND QUOLLS

Tasmania, the island Australian state 150 miles south of the mainland, is home to many unusual animals: The Tasmanian devil, which looks like a cross between a small dog and a pig and is the world's largest carnivorous marsupial; wallabies and pademelons (small wallabies); wombats; quolls (squirrel-like animals with spots); and monotremes (egg-laying mammals), echidnas, and platypuses. Almost one-third of the island is protected within 14 national parks and reserves. The second-oldest living things on Earth (after the North American bristlecone pines) are found here as well: huon pines, which can live up to 4,000 years.

Ethnic Divisions: Caucasian, Asian, Aborigine

Literacy Rate: 100%

Government: Federal parliamentary state, with an appointed governor-general and a bicameral legislature, the Federal Parliament. The Senate has 76 members, whose term limits vary; the House of Representatives has 148 members, elected for three years. There are six states and two territories.

Armed services: 57,400 troops (1997) in the army, navy, and air force; voluntary

Suffrage: Universal and compulsory; 18 years old

Economy: Australia enjoys a generally healthy and diverse economy. In the early 1990s, the government attempted to decrease unemployment with government subsidies and to reduce the deficit with public spending reductions. Despite a mild recession, the economy regained strength from increased industrial output and business investments.

Unit of currency: Australian dollar; 100 cents = 1 Australian dollar ($A)

GDP per capita: $21,400

Inflation rate–CPI: 1% (1997 est.)

Workforce: 9.2 million (1997 est.)

Unemployment rate: 8.8% (1996 est.)

Exports: Goods worth $68 billion (f.o.b., 1997 est.) are sent to Japan, ASEAN., South Korea, the U.S., New Zealand, the U.K., and other trading partners; exports include coal, gold, meat, alumina, iron ore, wheat.

Imports: Goods worth $67 billion (f.o.b., 1997 est.) are received from the U.S., Japan, the U.K., New Zealand, China, and other countries; imports include machinery, computers and office machines, crude oil, and chemicals.

Agriculture: Australia is the world's leading producer of wool. It exports large amounts of wheat, barley, sugarcane, fruits, cattle sheep and poultry, all of which contributed 4% to the GDP in 1997.

Energy: Australia's energy needs are met by petroleum, natural gas, and coal.

Natural Resources: Minerals, including bauxite, coal, iron ore, gold, and silver; petroleum and natural gas

Environmental Issues: Degradation of the Great Barrier Reef, the world's largest coral reef, off the east coast

Transportation: The country is well served by a network of 567,000 miles (913,000 km) of roads and 24,200 miles (39,000 km) of railways. Because of the great distances involved, small airplanes are used to cross the interior. Most large cities have domestic and international airports. Major ports include Adelaide, Brisbane, Carins, Darwin, Melbourne, and Sydney.

Communications: Dozens of daily, weekly, and monthly newspapers and periodicals are published in Australia. There are 8.9 million telephones (1994) that provided standard service for the majority of the population; radios and televisions are widely available.

Tourism: Water sports along the Pacific beaches, wildlife, and mountain sports all draw domestic and foreign travelers to Australia.

U.S. Tourist Office: (212) 687-6300

Embassy in U.S.: (202) 895-6700

Public Holidays: Australia Day (January 26); Easter (date varies, in March or April); Anzac Day (April 25); Queen's Official Birthday (June 10); Christmas (December 25); Boxing Day (December 26)

Austria

Country Name: Austria

Official Name: Republic of Austria

Nationality: Austrian(s) (noun); Austrian (adjective)

Capital: Vienna, pop. 1,560,500

Major cities: Graz, Linz, Salzburg

External Territories: None

Location: A landlocked central European country, Austria is bordered by Switzerland, Liechtenstein, Germany, Hungary, Italy, Slovenia, the Czech Republic, and Slovakia.

Physical Geography: Almost three-fourths of Austria is covered by the Alps and their foothills, lakes,

---

AUSTRIA EUROPE'S CENTURIES-OLD CROSSROADS

Austria's location in central Europe has been key to its evolution as a nation. Vienna, in the Danube corridor, has long been an important European crossroads—the city's origins can be traced back to the Roman settlement of Vindobona about A.D. 50. The Austrian territory was first established in the tenth century by Charlemagne as a defensive border area against the Hungarians. The Hapsburgs later controlled the Alpine passes and the Vienna basin, building an empire that lasted from 1278 to 1918. In 1919, the Austro-Hungarian Empire was ended by the Treaty of St. Germain, which set Austria's present boundaries. It joined the European Union on January 1, 1995.

---

and valleys. Gentler slopes lie along the northern and eastern parts of the country. Most of the country is drained by the Danube River.

Total area: 32,377 sq mi (83,856 sq km)

Coastline: None

Land use: About 18% of land is devoted to agriculture and permanent crops. Nearly 25% is meadows and pastures, and almost 40% is forested.

Climate: Continental, but variable, due to mountains; cold winters with snow or rain, and cool summers

Population: 8,087,000

Urban population: 65%

Rate of natural increase: 0.03%

Age structure: 17% under 15; 15% over 65

Birth rate: 10/1000

Death rate: 10/1000

Infant mortality rate: 5/1000

Fertility rate: 1.3

Life expectancy at birth: 74 years (male); 81 years (female)

Religion: Roman Catholic, Protestant

Language: German

Ethnic Divisions: German

Literacy Rate: 99%

Government: Austria is a federal republic with nine states. Its bicam-

---

eral Federal Assembly consists of the Federal Council, whose 64 members' term lengths vary, and the National Council, whose 183 members serve for four years. Federal Council members are elected by the state assemblies, and National Council members are elected by universal suffrage. The Federal president is elected every six years by popular vote.

Armed services: 45,500 troops (1997 est.); compulsory with seven months of training and some reserve training

Suffrage: Universal; 18 years old; compulsory voting in presidential elections

Economy: After a period of slow economic growth in 1992, Austria's generally stable economy rebounded with the resurgence of exports and expanded privatization plans. Additional reductions in spending have been announced in order to bring down the budget deficit.

Unit of currency: Schilling; 100 groschen = 1 schilling (AS)

GDP per capita: $21,400

Inflation rate–CPI: 1.3 (1997)

Workforce: 3.65 million (1996)

Unemployment rate: 7.1% (January 1998)

Exports: Goods worth $57.8 billion (1996) are sent to Germany, Austria's primary export market, as well as to Italy, Eastern Europe, Japan, and the U.S.; exports include machinery and equipment, iron and steel, lumber, textiles, paper products, and chemicals.

Imports: Goods worth $67.3 billion (1996) are received from Germany, Italy, other eastern European countries, Japan, and the U.S.; imports include petroleum, foodstuffs, machinery and equipment, vehicles, chemicals, textiles and clothing, and pharmaceuticals.

Agriculture: Austria is nearly self-sufficient in food production. Grains, potatoes, sugar beets, wine, cattle, and brown wood are among its primary agricultural products.

Energy: Energy is derived from a combination of hydropower, coal, petroleum, and natural gas, with hydroelectric power the most important source of domestic energy.

Natural Resources: Iron ore, oil, coal, magnesite, lead, timber, lignite, copper, hydropower

Environmental Issues: Forest degradation from air and soil pollution, soil pollution from agricultural chemicals

Transportation: Austrian cities and towns are linked by a network of 80,140 miles (128,920km) of primary and secondary roads and 3,500 miles (5,640 km) of rail tracks. International flights arrive at Vienna, Innsbruck, Salzburg, Graz, Klagenfurt, and Linz.

Communications: Several national dailies are published, supplemented with a dozen national weeklies and other periodicals. The government's daily newspaper, *Wiener Zeitung,* founded in 1703, is the world's oldest daily newspaper. Radios, telephones, and television are widely available.

Tourism: Austria draws tourists with winter sports, arts festivals in Vienna and Salzburg, and mountain scenery, making tourism a leading source of revenue. Tourism, however-

er, declined in the early 1990s from 19.1 million visitors in 1992 to 17.1 million visitors in 1996.

U.S. Tourist Office: (800) 474-9696

Embassy in U.S.: (202) 483-4474

Public Holidays: Epiphany (January 6); Easter Monday (date varies, in March or April); Ascension Day (date varies, in May); Whit Monday (date varies, in May); Labor Day (May 1); Corpus Christi (date varies, in May or June); Assumption (August 15); National Holiday (October 26); All Saints' Day (November 1); Immaculate Conception (December 8); Christmas (December 25); St. Stephen's Day (December 26)

Azerbaijan

Country Name: Azerbaijan

Official Name: Azerbaijani Republic

Nationality: Azerbaijani(s) (noun); Azerbaijani (adjective)

Capital: Baku, pop. 1,149,000

Major cities: Gramfa, Sumgait

External Territories: None

Location: Azerbaijan, in southwestern Asia, is on the eastern shore of the Caspian Sea and between Russia, to the north, and Iran, to the south. Georgia and Armenia lie to its west.

Physical Geography: The Caucasus Mountains run along the northern border, and the Lesser Caucasus rise in the southwest. Steppe and semidesert lands are found in the lowlands along the Kura River. The Caspian coast is subtropical.

Total area: 33,591 sq mi (87,000 sq km)

Coastline: 500 mi (800 km) along the Caspian Sea

Land use: About 23% of the land is used for agriculture and permanent cultivation. Another 25% is meadows and pastures and 11% is forests and woodlands.

Climate: Dry subtropical in eastern and central regions, with mild winters and hot summers; the coast has more precipitation, mostly in the winter; in the mountains, temperatures vary with elevation.

Population: 7,734,000

Urban population: 52%

Rate of natural increase: 1.1%

Age structure: 33% under 15; 6% over 65

Birth rate: 17/1000

Death rate: 6/1000

Infant mortality rate: 20/1000

Fertility rate: 2.1

Life expectancy at birth: 67 years (male); 75 years (female)

Religion: Muslim, Russian Orthodox, Armenian Orthodox

Language: Azeri, Russian, Armenian

Ethnic Divisions: Azeri, Dagestani Peoples, Russian, Armenian, other

Literacy Rate: 97%

Government: Republic, with a directly elected president and a unicameral legislative body, the 125-member National Assembly. Members of the National Assembly are directly elected for five-year terms. Azerbaijan is divided into 70 administrative areas, including Naxçivan, which is located in Armenia, on its western boundary with Iran.

Armed services: Seventeen-month military service in the army, navy, and air force

Suffrage: Universal; 18 years old

Economy: The country is making the transition to a market economy. Government reforms are aimed at stabilizing currency, reducing inflation, and privatizing industry. Oil reserves offer future prosperity, but extraction infrastructures need to be overhauled before petroleum can revitalize the economy.

Unit of currency: Manat; 100 gopik = 1 manat

GDP per capita: $1,460

Inflation rate–CPI: 3.7% (1997 est.)

Workforce: 2.8 million (1995 est.)

Unemployment rate: 20% (1996 est.)

Exports: Goods worth $789 million (f.o.b., 1996 est) are sent to CIS, European countries and Turkey; exports include oil and gas, chemicals, and textiles.

Imports: Goods worth $1.3 billion (c.i.f., 1996 est.) are received from Russia, CIS, European countries, Turkey,and other countries; imports include petroleum products, machinery, food, and chemicals.

Agriculture: Nearly 32% of the working population is involved in agriculture, cultivating grains, grapes and other fruit, vegetables, and cotton.

Energy: Almost 60% of energy is derived from natural gas supplies, and almost 33% is derived from nuclear power. Petroleum and hydroelectric power also provide energy.

Natural Resources: Petroleum, natural gas, iron ore, nonferrous metals, alumina

Environmental Issues: Severe water pollution in the Caspian Sea, soil pollution from pesticide use, air pollution

Transportation: Estimates of roads in Azerbaijan range from 22,800 miles (36,680 km) to 37,100 miles (59,250 km); most are paved or graveled. More than 1,250 miles (2,000 km) of railway track carry passengers and freight, providing both internal and international connections. Baku is a major port on the Caspian Sea. Air service is available in Baku and 39 other airports around the country have paved runways.

Communications: Several daily newspapers are published, along with weeklies and periodicals, mainly in Baku. There are 710,000 telephones (1991 est.) and one out of every five persons has access to a television or radio.

Tourism: Caspian Sea resorts draw international visitors, but there are few other tourist facilities.

Embassy in U.S.: (202) 842-0001

Public Holidays: International Women's Day (March 8); Republic Day (May 28); Day of the Armed Services (October 9); Day of Statehood (October 18); Day of National Survival (November 17); Day of Azerbaijani Solidarity Worldwide (December 31)

Bahamas

Country Name: Bahamas

Official Name: Commonwealth of the Bahamas

Nationality: Bahamian(s) (noun); Bahamian (adjective)

Capital: Nassau, pop. 172,200

Major cities: Freeport

External Territories: None

Location: The Bahamas is made up of a chain of 2,700 islands and cays in the Atlantic Ocean off the southeast coast of Florida and north of Cuba.

Physical Geography: The Bahamas are generally low, coral islands with no rivers.

Total area: 5,382 sq mi (13,939 sq km)

Coastline: 2,200 mi (3,542 km)

Land use: Forests cover about a third of the country's area, and only 1% of the land is used for agriculture.

Climate: Mild, subtropical climate, with hurricane season from mid-July through mid-November

Population: 301,000

Urban population: 84%

Rate of natural increase: 1.53%

Age structure: 32% under 15; 5% over 65

Birth rate: 20.72/1000

Death rate: 5.4/1000

Infant mortality rate: 18.4/1000

Fertility rate: 2

Life expectancy at birth: 68 years (male); 77 years (female)

Religion: Protestant, Roman Catholic

Language: English, Creole

Ethnic Divisions: Black, white

Literacy Rate: 98%

Government: Constitutional monarchy, with the British monarch represented by an appointed governor-general and a bicameral Parliament. The 16 members of the Senate are appointed by the governor-general, and the 40 members of the House of Assembly are elected to five-year terms. There are 21 administrative districts.

Armed services: 860 (1997 est.) in the Royal Bahamian Defense Force

Suffrage: Universal; 18 years old

Economy: Tourism, offshore banking, and shipping are key activities fueling the stable economy, even though tourism has declined somewhat in recent years. Attempts have been made to diversify the economic base with commercial fishing and other ventures, including garment manufacturing, furniture, purified water, and plastic containers.

Unit of currency: Bahamian dollar; 100 cents = 1 Bahamian dollar (B$)

GDP per capita: $119,400

Inflation rate–CPI: 4% (1997)

Workforce: 146,600 (1996)

Unemployment rate: 10% (1995 est.)

Exports: Goods worth $201.7 million (f.o.b., 1996 est.) are sent to the U.S., United Kingdom, Norway, France, Spain, and Italy; exports include pharmaceuticals, cement, rum, crayfish, and refined petroleum.

Imports: Goods worth $1.26 billion (c.i.f., 1996 est.) are received from the U.S., Finland, Iran, and Denmark; imports include foodstuffs, manufactured goods, crude oil, vehicles, and electronics.

Agriculture: An estimated 5% (1995) of the workforce is employed by agriculture. The government is encouraging development to lessen dependence on food imports. Crops include citrus and vegetables. Crayfish are harvested commercially.

Energy: The Bahamas obtains most of its petroleum for its energy needs from Mexico and Venezuela.

Natural Resources: Salt, aragonite, timber

Environmental Issues: Decay of coral reefs; solid waste disposal

Transportation: Almost half of the paved roads, an estimated 600 miles (960 km) are on New Providence Island; another 850 miles (1,370 km) of roads are found on several of the other island population centers. There are no railroads. Two international airports at Nassau and Freeport are important tourist terminals, with 60 smaller airports located throughout the islands. Nassau, on New Providence Island, is the country's most important seaport; Freeport, on Grand Bahama Island, and Matthew Town, on Great Inagua Island, also draw significant traffic. Cruise ships also call at Potters Cay on New Providence, Governor's Harbour on Eleuthera, and George Town on Great Exuma.

Communications: Two daily papers are published in Nassau and one in Freeport. Telephone service is very good, and radios and televisions are generally available. Limited broadcasting services are supplemented by international broadcasts.

Tourism: Tourists have long been a mainstay of the economy of the Bahamas, bringing in $1.3 billion (U.S.) (1994 est.). Of the 4.5 million tourists who came to the Bahamas in 1994, more than 80% came from the U.S. Beaches, water sports, and casinos are key attractions.

U.S. Tourist Office: (800) 422-4262

Embassy in U.S.: (202) 319-2660

Public Holidays: Good Friday (date varies, in March or April); Easter Monday (date varies, in March or April); Whit Monday (date varies, in May); Labour Day (June); Independence Day (July 10); Emancipation Day (August 4); Discovery Day/Columbus Day (October 12); Christmas (December 25–26)

Bahrain

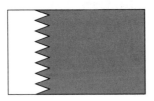

Country Name: Bahrain

Official Name: State of Bahrain

Nationality: Bahraini(s) (noun); Bahraini (adjective)

Capital: Manama, pop. 127,600

Major cities: Al Maharraq

External Territories: None

Location: Bahrain is made up of 35 islands in the Persian Gulf. Saudi Arabia is to the west and Qatar to the east.

Physical Geography: Bahrain's islands are desert with freshwater springs in the north.

Total area: 267 sq mi (691 sq km)

Coastline: 100 mi (161 km)

Land use: About 2% of the land is used for agriculture and another 6% for meadows and pastures.

Climate: Dry, with humid, hot summers and mild winters

Population: 661,000

Urban population: 88%

Rate of natural increase: 2%

Age structure: 31% under 15; 2% over 65

Birth rate: 22/1000

Death rate: 3/1000

Infant mortality rate: 8/1000

Fertility rate: 2.8

Life expectancy at birth: 68 years (male); 71 years (female)

Religion: Shiite and Sunni Muslim

Language: Arabic (official), English, Farsi, Urdu

Ethnic Divisions: Arab, Asian, Iranian

Literacy Rate: 85%

Government: Monarchy, with an appointed cabinet. There are 12 administrative districts.

Armed services: 11,000 (1997 est.) in the Bahrain Defense Force, which includes the army, navy, and air force; voluntary

Suffrage: None

Economy: Bahrain has a very stable economy traditionally based on the production and export of petroleum, but it has been developing alternate economic activities against the day its oil supply runs dry. Foreign investments, banking, communications industries, and port facilities have all been encouraged by the government.

Unit of currency: Bahraini dinar; 1,000 fils = 1 Bahraini dinar (BD)

GDP per capita $13,700

Inflation rate–CPI: -0.2% (1996 est.)

Workforce: 140,000 (1991); nearly 60% of the workforce is foreign-born

Unemployment rate: 15% (1996)

Exports: Goods worth $4.6 billion (f.o.b., 1996) are sent to India, Japan, Saudi Arabia, U.S., and other countries; exports include petroleum and petroleum products.

Imports: Goods worth $3.7 billion (f.o.b., 1996) are received from Saudi Arabia, the U.S., the U.K., Japan, and Switzerland; imports include nonoil products and crude oil.

Agriculture: Only 1% (1994) of the workforce engages in agriculture, producing a large part of the country's demand for vegetables and poultry. Dates, tomatoes, and melons are the principle crops.

Energy: Internal petroleum reserves are being depleted rapidly. If 1994 production levels continue, known reserves of crude oil will be exhausted by 2000 and natural gas reserves by 2050.

Natural Resources: oil, associated and nonassociated natural gas, fish

Environmental Issues: Limited freshwater, coastal pollution from oil refineries and shipping, farmland desertification

Transportation: There are 1,870 miles (3,010 km) of roads in Bahrain, of which 1,420 miles (2,280 km) are paved (1996). The King Fahd Causeway links Umm an Na'san and Al Muharraq Islands to Saudi Arabia at Al Khubar. International ports are at Mina Salman, Manama, and Sitrah, and an international airport is located on Al Muharraq Island.

Communications: Bahrain has four daily papers and an ample distribution of radios and televisions.

Tourism: Significant archaeological sites of the ancient Dilmun trading culture and other amenities brought an estimated 2.3 million tourists to Bahrain in 1994.

Embassy in U.S.: (202) 342-0741

Public Holidays: Beginning of Ramadan (date varies); End of Ramadan (date varies); Feast of the Sacrifice (date varies, in April); Islamic New Year (date varies, in May); Ashura (date varies, in May); Birth of the Prophet (date varies, in July); Ascension of the Prophet (date varies, in November or December); National Day (December 16)

Bangladesh

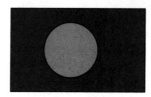

Country Name: Bangladesh

Official Name: People's Republic of Bangladesh

Nationality: Bangladeshi(s) (noun); Bangladesh (adjective)

Capital: Dhaka, pop. 8,545,000

Major cities: Chittagong, Khulna, Rajshahi, Rangpur

External Territories: None

Location: Bangladesh, on the Indian Ocean's Bay of Bengal, is located in southern Asia and is almost encompassed by India. It shares only a small portion of its southeastern land border with Myanmar.

Physical Geography: Bangladesh is mostly low-lying, alluvial plains, with some hills in the northeast and southeast. The country is crossed by many rivers that are subject to seasonal flooding. Two major rivers, the Ganges (Pama) and the Brahmaputra (Jamuna), form a broad delta at the Bay of Bengal.

Total area: 55,598 sq mi (143,998 sq km)

Coastline: 360 mi (580 km)

Land use: Nearly 73% of the land is used for agriculture, and 15% is wooded. Only 5% is meadows and pastures.

Climate: Warm and humid throughout the year, with monsoons from June through October

Population: 125,721,000

Urban population: 16%

Rate of natural increase: 20%

Age structure: 43% under 15; 3% over 65

Birth rate: 27/1000

Death rate: 8/1000

Infant mortality rate: 82/1000

Fertility rate: 3.3

Life expectancy at birth: 59 years (male); 58 years (female)

Religion: Muslim, Hindu

Language: Bengali, English

Ethnic Divisions: Bengali

Literacy Rate: 38%

Government: Republic, with an elected president and a 330-member unicameral Parliament (Jatiya Sangsad). Three hundred Parliament members are elected, and the remaining 30 seats are filled by women appointed by Parliament members; Parliament members and the president serve five-year terms. There are currently four administrative divisions.

Armed services: 117,500 (1996 est.) in the army, navy, and air force; voluntary

Suffrage: Universal; 18 years old

Economy: Most Bangladeshis are subsistence farmers who may also raise some cash crops. Frequent floods, overpopulation, worker unrest, and a lack of energy sources impede economic growth despite government intervention.

Unit of currency: Taka; 100 poiska = 1 taka (TK)

GDP per capita: $1,330

Inflation rate–CPI: 2.5% (1996)

Workforce: 56 million (1996 est.)

Unemployment rate: 35.2% (1996)

Exports: Goods worth some $3.9 billion (1996) are sent to Western, Europe, the U.S., Hong Kong, and Japan; exports include clothing, jute goods, and leather products, as well as frozen fish and seafood.

Imports: Goods worth some $6.9 billion (1996) are received mainly from Singapore, India, China, Western Europe, Hong Kong, Singapore imports include capital goods, petroleum products, food, and textiles.

Agriculture: About two-thirds (1994) of the economically active population engages in farming. Rice is the most important subsistence crop; cash crops include jute (Bangladesh is the world's largest producer) and tea.

Energy: Some natural gas reserves

Natural Resources: Natural gas, arable land, timber

Environmental Issues: Overpopulation, severe flooding during monsoon season and in the fall (when cyclones form), water pollution, deforestation

Transportation: About 1,780 miles (2,890 km) of railroads provide passenger and cargo transport. There are an estimated 138,730 miles (223,390 km) of roads and nearly 5,000 mi (8,000 km) of navigable inland waterways, of which about 1,800 mi (3,000 km) are used to transport an estimated 70% of domestic and foreign cargo. Dhaka, Narayanganj, Chandpur, and Barisal are major river ports. An airport at Dhaka offers international service, and most major cities have airports for domestic flights.

Communications: Nearly 200 daily papers are published throughout the country, but access to radios, television, and telephone service is severely limited.

Tourism: In 1995, tourist activities brought an estimated $24 million (U.S.) into the economy; tourists visit Dhaka, Chittagong, and the 74-mile-long (120 km) beach at Cox's Bazar, on the Bay of Bengal.

Embassy in U.S.: (202) 342-8372

Public Holidays: End of Ramadan (date varies); National Mourning Day (February 21); Independence Day (March 26); Good Friday (date varies, in March or April); Easter Monday (date varies, in March or April); Feast of the Sacrifice (date varies, in April); Buddha Purinama (date varies, in May); Islamic New Year (date varies, in May); May Day (May 1); Jamat Wida (date varies, in July); Birth of the Prophet (date varies, in July); Janmashtami (dates vary, in August or September); Shab-i-Bharat (date varies, in September); Durga Puja (dates vary, in September or October); National Revolution Day (November 7); National Day (December 16); Christmas (December 25); Boxing Day (December 26)

Barbados

Country Name: Barbados

Official Name: Barbados

Nationality: Barbadian(s) (noun); Barbadian (adjective)

Capital: Bridgetown, pop. 7,500

Major cities: None

External Territories: None

Location: A Caribbean island east of St. Vincent and the Grenadines and northeast of Trinidad and Tobago, Barbados is the easternmost of the West Indies.

Physical Geography: A coral island, with some high terrain in the northeast that gives way to a lowland plateau, Barbados has beaches on the west and southwest.

Total area: 166 sq mi (430 sq km)

Coastline: 60 miles (97 km)

Land use: More than one-third of the land is used for agriculture; over one-tenth is forest and woodland.

Climate: Tropical, with a summer rainy season from as early as June to as late as November; occasional hurricanes

Population: 269,000

Urban population: 38%

Rate of natural increase: 0.53%

Age structure: 24% under 15; 11% over 65

Birth rate: 14.1/1000

Death rate: 8.76/1000

Infant mortality rate: 14.2/1000

Fertility rate: 1.8

Life expectancy at birth: 72 years (male); 77 years (female)

Religion: Protestant, Roman Catholic

BANGLADESH CYCLONE CENTRAL

Bangladesh, formerly East Pakistan before gaining its independence from Pakistan in 1971, is about the size of Wisconsin and is one of the poorest and most densely populated countries in the world. It is situated on top of a huge river delta—where the Ganges, Jamuna (Brahmaputra), Padma, and Meghna Rivers and tributaries meet. The land, only a few feet above sea level, floods every year thanks to monsoon rains, and tropical cyclones destroy homes and farms. Bangladesh lies in the path of the world's most powerful storms—about five cyclones a year intensify in the Bay of Bengal. The cyclone that killed 139,000 people and left some 10 million homeless in 1991 was referred to as a super cyclone, equivalent to several thousand atom bombs of megaton strength. The floods bring life as well, renewing fish stocks, groundwater, and soil—some of the most fertile in the world; the rivers carry two billion tons of fertile silt each year and help balance erosion by forming new land through silt accretion.

Language: English

Ethnic Divisions: Black, white

Literacy Rate: 97%

Government: Constitutional monarchy, with the British monarch represented by a governor-general. The bicameral Parliament is made up of a 21-member Senate (appointed by the governor-general) and the 28 members of the House of Assembly (elected for five-year terms). Barbados is divided into 11 parishes.

Armed services: A small defense force patrols the island and its coastline; also a reserve forces

Suffrage: Universal; 18 years old

Economy: A relatively prosperous Caribbean nation, Barbados is expanding its economic base from tourism and sugar exports to offshore banking, and international business.

Unit of currency: Barbados dollar; 100 cents = 1 Barbados dollar (Bds$)

GDP per capita: $10,900

Inflation rate–CPI: 2.4% (1996)

Workforce: 68,900 (1996)

Unemployment rate: 16.2% (1996)

Exports: Goods worth $235 million (f.o.b., 1995 est.) are sent to the U.S., the U.K., and Trinidad and Tobago; exports include sugar and molasses, rum, other foods and beverages, as well as chemicals, electrical components, and clothing.

Imports: Goods worth $763 million (c.i.f., 1995 est.) are received from the U.S., the U.K., Trinidad and Tobago, and Japan, ; imports include machinery, foodstuffs, construction materials, chemicals, fuels, and electrical components and consumer goods.

Agriculture: About 10% of the economically active population is involved in agricultural production. Sugar continues to be the traditional main cash crop, but sea-island cotton is also important; vegetables are raised for local consumption

Energy: Internal reserves of petroleum and natural gas are supplemented by fuel imports.

Natural Resources: Petroleum, fish, natural gas

Environmental Issues: Coastal pollution, soil erosion, water-supply contamination

Transportation: There are more than 1,000 miles (1,600 km) of roads on Barbados, most of which are paved. There are no railroads. An international airport is at Seawell, 10 miles east of Bridgetown. Bridgetown also serves as port of call for tourists and cargo.

Communications: Two daily papers are published, supplemented by eight other publications. There are 69,400 televisions (1993 est.) in use; there are 87,340 telephones (1991 est.) in service.

Tourism: Tourists come to Barbados for the beaches, scenery, and variety of sports activities. In 1994, tourist receipts totaled an estimated $1.45 billion (U.S.).

U.S. Tourist Office: (800) 221-9831

Embassy in U.S.: (202) 939-9200

Public Holidays: Errol Barrow Day (date varies, in January); Good Friday (date varies, in March or April); Easter Monday (date varies, in March or April); Whit Monday (May); Labor Day (date varies, in May); Kadooment Day (date varies, in August); United Nations Day (date varies, in October); Independence Day: from the U.K. (November 30); Christmas (December 25–26)

Belarus

Country Name: Belarus

Official Name: Republic of Belarus

Nationality: Belarusian(s) (noun); Belarusian (adjective)

Capital: Minsk, pop. 1,671,600 [1,708,300]

Major cities: Homyel, Mahilyow, Vitsyebsk, Hrodná

External Territories: None

Location: Formerly part of the Soviet Union, Belarus is in eastern Europe, bordered on the northwest by Lithuania and Latvia, on the south by Ukraine, on the west by Poland, and on the east by Russia.

Physical Geography: Belarus is mostly low-lying plains, including the Polotsk Lowland in the north and Dnieper Lowland in the southeast, with numerous rivers, lakes, swamps, and marshes.

Total area: 80,154 sq mi (207,598 sq km)

Coastline: None

Land use: Arable land and crop land account for almost one-third of the land; about one-sixth is meadows and pastures.

Climate: Cool continental; cold winters and humid summers with ample precipitation

Population: 10,167,000

Urban population: 70%

Rate of natural increase: -0.4%

Age structure: 20% under 15; 13% over 65

Birth rate: 9/1000

Death rate: 13/1000

Infant mortality rate: 11/1000

Fertility rate: 1.3

Life expectancy at birth: 63 years (male); 74 years (female)

Religion: Eastern Orthodox

Language: Belorussian, Russian

Ethnic Divisions: Belarusian, Russian

Literacy Rate: 98%

Government: Republic, with six regions, called oblasts, and the capital city, Minsk. Legislation is the responsibility of the bicameral National Assembly which consists of 110

elected members of the House of Representatives and 64 members of the Council of the Republic. The president is elected by popular vote for a five-year term.

Armed services: 81,800 troops (1997) in the army, air force, and others; compulsory

Suffrage: Universal; 18 years old

Economy: Engineering and agriculture, mainstays of the Belarusian economy before independence from the Soviet Union in late 1991, did not continue to perform well due in part to difficulties in enacting economic reforms, such as privatizing state businesses and encouraging foreign investment. A program of strict economic measures was started in 1994 to reduce inflation and stabilize business, but the International Monetary Fund (IMF) has criticized the effectiveness of the measures and suspended a $300 million (U.S.) support program.

Unit of currency: Rubel; 100 kopeks = 1 new Belarusian rubel (BR)

GDP per capita: $4,800

Inflation rate–CPI: 65% (1997 est.)

Workforce: 4.3 million

Unemployment rate: 3.3% (1997)

Exports: Goods worth $5.4 billion (f.o.b., 1996) are sent to Russia, Ukraine, Poland, and Germany; exports include machinery and transport equipment, chemicals and foodstuffs.

Imports: Goods worth $6.7 billion (c.i.f., 1994) are received from Russia, Ukraine, Poland, Germany, and other trading partners; imports include fuel, natural gas, industrial raw materials, textiles, and sugar.

Agriculture: About 20% of the working population is involved in agricultural production, particularly raising cattle and pigs; potatoes, grains, and sugar beets are the primary field crops. Privatization of state farms continues to be an issue; about 80% (1995) of the agricultural land is run by state farms and collectives. Nearly four million acres of arable land have been taken out of production because of fallout from the 1986 nuclear reactor accident at Chornobyl, Ukraine.

Energy: Most (85%) of the energy needs of Belarus are met by Russian imports, including petroleum and natural gas, supplemented with coal.

Natural Resources: Forests, peat reserves, small deposits of oil and natural gas

Environmental Issues: Pesticide pollution in the soil, contamination of air and soil from the 1986 Chornobyl, Ukraine, nuclear reactor accident

Transportation: Most of the 32,380 miles (52,110 km) of roads are paved, and railroads run on an estimated 3,400 miles (5,500 km) of track. Two airports at Minsk provide international and domestic flights; there are about 120 airports in the country, of which 36 have paved runways. Rivers and canals are used extensively.

Communications: There are 12 (1996) daily papers in the country published in Russian or Belarusian or both. There are 3.2 million radios (1991 est.) and 3.5 million televisions (1992 est.). Telephone service is inadequate, with only around 1.8 million telephones serving the population.

Tourism: Tourists visit the museums in Minsk; the historic sites in Zhirovitsa; Nesvizh; Brest; and Hrodná; the Braslaw lake district, which offers hiking and water sports; and the Pripyat Nature Reserve, a UN-protected biosphere of forests, marshes, and rivers.

Embassy in U.S.: (202) 986-1606

Public Holidays: Orthodox Christmas (January 7); International Women's Day (March 8); Labor Day (May 1); Victory Day (May 9); Anniversary of Liberation from the Nazis, 1944 (July 3); Independence Day (July 27); Day of Commemoration (November 2); Christmas (December 25)

Belgium

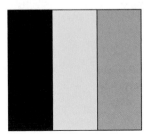

Country Name: Belgium

Official Name: Kingdom of Belgium

Nationality: Belgian(s) (noun); Belgian (adjective)

Capital: Brussels, pop. 136,500 [960,300]

Major cities: Antwerp, Gent, Charleroi, Liège, Brugge

External Territories: None

Location: Belgium, in western Europe, is bordered on the south and southwest by France, on the northwest by the North Sea, on the north and northeast by the Netherlands, on the east by Germany, and on the southeast by Luxembourg. Because of Belgium's central location, its capital, Brussels, is headquarters for the European Union and NATO.

Physical Geography: In the southeast, the hilly region of the Ardennes Forest gives way to a low plateau in central Belgium. Reclaimed land along the North Sea coast is used for farming and is protected from the sea's encroachment by sand dunes, seawalls, and dikes. Major rivers include the Schelde and Meuse.

Total area: 11,783 sq mi (30,518 sq km)

Coastline: 40 mi (64 km)

Land use: Arable land makes up almost one-quarter of Belgium territory, with forests and meadows each covering one-fifth.

Climate: Maritime, with mild summers and cool winters

Population: 10,225,000

Urban population: 97%

Rate of natural increase: 0.1%

Age structure: 18% under 15; 16% over 65

Birth rate: 11/1000

Death rate: 10/1000

Infant mortality rate: 6.1/1000

Fertility rate: 1.5/1000

Life expectancy at birth: 74 years (male); 81 years (female)

Religion: Roman Catholic, Protestant

Language: Flemish, French, German

Ethnic Divisions: Fleming, Walloon

Literacy Rate: 99%

Government: Constitutional monarchy, with a bicameral Parliament. The 150 members of the Chamber of Representatives are directly elected, and the 71-member Senate is partially elected and partially appointed; members of both houses serve four-year terms. There are ten administrative provinces divided among two ethnic regions and the city of Brussels.

Armed services: 44,450 troops (1997) in the army, navy, and air force

Suffrage: Universal and compulsory; 18 years old

Economy: Despite a traditionally strong and diverse economy, Belgium fell into a recession in the early 1990s and initiated economic measures to reduce the deficit and transfer state-owned business to private owners. By the mid-1990s, exports were again increasing and spending was reduced, but relatively high levels of unemployment continue.

Unit of currency: Belgian franc; 100 centimes = 1 Belgian franc (BF)

GDP per capita: $23,200

Inflation rate–CPI: 1% (1997 est.)

Workforce: 4.28 million (1997)

Unemployment rate: 12.75% (1997)

Exports: Goods worth $172 billion (f.o.b., 1997) are sent to the EU, predominantly Germany, and the U.S.; exports include iron and steel, transportation equipment, tractors, diamonds, and petroleum products.

Imports: Goods worth $158.5 billion (c.i.f., 1997) are received from the EU, primarily Germany, and the U.S.; imports include fuels, grains, chemicals, and foodstuffs.

Agriculture: Farming employs 2.6% (1992 est.) of the workforce and yields crops that include vegetables, fruits, grain, tobacco; beef, veal, and pork

Energy: Domestic nuclear power meets nearly 60% of Belgium's energy needs, supplemented by petroleum and natural gas imports.

Natural Resources: Coal and natural gas

Environmental Issues: Air and water pollution (including the Meuse River, a major source of drinking water) from industrial and agricultural activities

Transportation: An extensive railroad network for passengers and freight, with an estimated 2,100 miles (3,410 km) of track, is augmented by shipping on Belgium's 1,270 miles (2,040 km) of navigable rivers and inland waterways. An estimated 88,910 miles (143,190 km) of roads also cross the country. Antwerp, a rail center, is the second largest port for shipping in Europe. There are international airports at Brussels, Antwerp, Ostend, Liège, and Charleroi.

Communications: An advanced telephone system provides excellent service, and more than 3.3 million televisions and 100,000 radios receive broadcasts from dozens of television and radio stations. There are 28 daily papers (1994) published.

Tourism: Over 5 million tourists came to Belgium in 1995 to visit seaside resorts, the Ardennes Forest, and cultural centers such as Brussels, Antwerp, Liège, Gent, and Brugge.

U.S. Tourist Office: (212) 758-8130

Embassy in U.S.: (202) 333-6900

Public Holidays: Easter Monday (date varies, in April); Ascension Day (date varies, in May); Whit Monday

BELGIUM DIVIDED IT STANDS

Belgium's capital city, Brussels, is a symbol of European unity both economically and politically: It serves as headquarters for both the European Union (EU)—Belgium was one of its founders—and NATO, the North Atlantic Treaty Organization. It is also part of the Belgium Luxembourg Economic Union (BLEU). Internal unity has been more elusive, however. Belgium has long been divided by language. The Flemings, who are of Germanic heritage, speak Flemish, a language closely related to Dutch. The Walloons, whose ancestors were Celtic, speak French. Brussels divides the two areas, with the Flemings to the north and the Walloons to the south. About 10 percent of the population is bilingual, and Brussels is officially bilingual. In addition to the national government in Brussels, there are regional assemblies in Flanders and Wallonia. The country divided itself into three regions in 1993, although there are still ten official provinces.

(date varies, in May); Labor Day (May 1); National Day (July 21); Assumption (August 15); All Saints' Day (November 1); Armistice Day (November 11); Christmas (December 25)

Belize

Country Name: Belize

Official Name: Belize

Nationality: Belizean(s) (noun); Belizean (adjective)

Capital: Belmopan, pop. 6,800

Major cities: Belize City, Orange Walk, San Ignacio, Corozal

External Territories: None

Location: Belize, in Central America, is bordered on the east by the Caribbean Sea, on the south and west by Guatemala, and on the northwest by Mexico.

Physical Geography: In the north, swampy lowlands predominate, which give way to hilly country. The Maya Mountains extend from the south-central part of the country southwest to Guatemala. Many small islands and the second longest barrier reef in the world lie just off the Caribbean coast.

Total area: 8,867 sq mi (22,965 sq km)

Coastline: 240 mi (386 km)

Land use: Tropical hardwood forests cover 92% of the land. About 2% of the land is used for agriculture and 2% is meadows and pastures.

Climate: Hot and humid, with dry winters and a rainy season from May to February; hurricanes threaten from September to December.

Population: 248,000

BELIZE ENGLISH SPOKEN HERE

Belize, a former colony of Great Britain known from 1840 to 1973 as British Honduras, is growing in popularity as an ecotourism destination. Visitors come to see its 75-mile-long coral reef—the world's second longest—and tropical forests full of a variety of animals, including jaguars, monkeys, crocodiles, parrots, and toucans. Belize is also the location of the ruins of the Maya city of Caracol, and the ceremonial center at Cuello, known to have been in use from ca 2200 B.C. to A.D. 300–400. Belize is the only English-speaking country in Spanish-speaking Central America.

Urban population: 50%

Rate of natural increase: 2.58%

Age structure: 41% under 15; 5% over 65

Birth rate: 30.1/1000

Death rate: 4.3/1000

Infant mortality rate: 33.94/1000

Fertility rate: 3.9

Life expectancy at birth: 70 years (male); 74 years (female)

Religion: Roman Catholic, Protestant

Language: English, Creole, Spanish, Mayan, Carib

Ethnic Divisions: Mestizo, Creole, Maya, Garifuna

Literacy Rate: 70%

Government: Constitutional monarchy, with a governor-general appointed by the British sovereign and a bicameral National Assembly. The 8 Senate members are appointed, and the 29 members of the National Assembly are elected to five-year terms. There are six administrative districts.

Armed services: 1,050 troops (1997 est.) in the Belize Defense Force, including air and maritime wings; voluntary

Suffrage: Universal; 18 years old

Economy: Belize is attempting to reduce its reliance on agriculture by encouraging foreign investment, tourism, international shipping, and other service industries. Revenue from citizens working abroad are a significant source of national income. The withdrawal of British troops in 1994 meant a loss of some $60 million (BZ).

Unit of currency: Belizean dollar; 100 cents = 1 Belizean dollar (BZ$)

GDP per capita: $3000

Inflation rate–CPI: 1% (1997 est.)

Workforce: 71,000 (1996 est.)

Unemployment rate: 13% (1997 est.)

Exports: Goods worth $166 million (f.o.b., 1996 est.) are sent to the U.S., Canada, the U.K., and other European Community countries; exports include sugar, citrus fruits, bananas, clothing, fish products, molasses, and wood.

Imports: Goods worth $262 million (c.i.f., 1996 est.) are received from the U.S., the U.K., and Mexico; imports include machinery, transport equipment, food, manufactured goods, fuels, chemicals and pharmaceuticals.

Agriculture: Agricultural goods continue to dominate Belizean exports; 30% (1997) of the workforce is involved in agriculture and fishing. Cash crops include sugar, coca, citrus fruits, and bananas.

Energy: Wood has been the only domestic source of energy in Belize, but some attempts have been made to look for petroleum in the interior. Petroleum imports may soon be supplemented by domestic hydro-electric energy production.

Natural Resources: Arable land potential, timber, fish

Environmental Issues: Deforestation, water pollution

Transportation: There are 44 airports which serve Belize, three with paved runways. An estimated 1,400 miles (2,250 km) of roads cross the country, of which over 80% are unpaved. There is no rail service. About 520 miles (830 km) of rivers are navigable in season. A deepwater port at Belize City accommodates international shipping, Big Creek is used for banana exports, and Corozol and Punta Gorda have port facilities.

Communications: While there are no daily papers published, there are seven weeklies. There are 29,000 telephones (1996 est.) in service. Several television stations broadcast to an estimated 27,000 televisions.

Tourism: Belize is encouraging the development of ecotourism, including bird-watching, other wildlife observation, and diving along the barrier reef; Maya ruins and the tropical forests are other tourist draws. In 1996, nearly 350,000 visitors contributed $167.1 million (BZ) to the economy.

U.S. Tourist Office: (800) 624-0686

Embassy in U.S.: (202) 332-9636

Public Holidays: Baron Bliss Day (March 9); Easter (date varies, in March or April); Labor Day (May 1); Commonwealth Day (May 24); St. George's Caye Day (September 10); Independence Day: from Great Britain, 1981 (September 21); Columbus Day (October 12); Garifuna Settlement Day (November 19); Christmas (December 25–26)

Benin

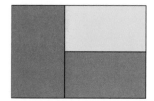

Country Name: Benin

Official Name: Republic of Benin

Nationality: Beninese (singular and plural noun); Beninese (adjective)

Capital: Porto-Novo (official), pop. 177,600; Cotonou (de facto), pop. 533,200

Major cities: Djougou, Parakou, Natitingou, Abomey, Kandi

External Territories: None

Location: Benin, on the west coast of Africa, is on the Gulf of Benin of the North Atlantic Ocean and lies between Togo to the west and Nigeria to the east. Burkina Faso is to the northwest and Niger is to the northeast.

Physical Geography: Coastal lagoons and tidal marshes give way to a flat and wooded expanse that terminates in a large inland marsh. The Chaine de l'Atakora, a low mountain range, crosses the northwest part of the country. In the north, the Niger River forms the boundary between Benin and Niger, flowing through arid savannas to the southeast.

Total area: 43,484 sq mi (112,622 sq km)

Coastline: 75 mi (121 km)

Land use: About 31% of the country is forested, and 21% is used for agricultural purposes.

Climate: Tropical; hot and humid along the coast, with the rainiest seasons from May to October; greater daily temperature variations farther north where the rainy season lasts from June to September

Population: 6,186,000

Urban population: 38%

Rate of natural increase: 2.98%

Age structure: 49% under 15; 3% over 65

Birth rate: 44.2/1000

Death rate: 14.4/1000

Infant mortality rate: 93.9/1000

Fertility rate: 6.3

Life expectancy at birth: 51 years (male); 56 years (female)

Religion: Traditional, Muslim, Christian

Language: French, Fon, Yoruba, tribal languages

Ethnic Divisions: Fon, Yoruba, Adja, Bariba, others

Literacy Rate: 37%

Government: Republic, with a president elected to a five-year term, and a unicameral legislature, the National Assembly, which has 64 members elected to four-year terms. There are six administrative departments.

Armed services: 4,800 troops (1997 est.) on active duty in the army, navy, and air force; men and women subject to selective conscription for an 18-month tour of duty

Suffrage: Universal; 18 years old

Economy: Since 1991 the country has been working with the World Bank to privatize industry and reduce foreign debt. Attempts to change an economy based on subsistence and regional trade have been hindered by rapid population growth, a costly civil service, unprofitable state enterprises, and high inflation rates.

Unit of currency: CFA franc; 100 centimes =1 franc de la Communauté financière africaine (CFA)

GDP per capita: $1900

Inflation rate–CPI: 3.5% (1997 est.)

Workforce: 2,085,446 (1992 est.)

Unemployment rate: 32,318 (1992 est.)

Exports: Goods worth $192 million (f.o.b., 1995 est.) are sent to France, Morocco, Portugal, Italy, the U.K., the U.S., and Libya; exports include cotton, crude oil, palm products, and cocoa.

Imports: Goods worth $693 million (c.i.f., 1995 est.) are received from France, Thailand, the Netherlands, the U.S., China, and Hong Kong; imports include foodstuffs, beverages, tobacco, and petroleum products.

Agriculture: Nearly 60% (1992) of the workforce engages in agriculture, and the country's demand for food crops is met by domestic production. Export crops include cotton, peanuts, rice, and cocoa; food crops include sorghum, cassava, yams, corn, and beans. An estimated 90% of agricultural products is produced on small farms.

Energy: Benin imports about 90% of its hydroelectricity from Ghana and supplements the rest with domestic production. Some offshore oil reserves are also exploited.

Natural Resources: Offshore oil, limestone, marble, timber

Environmental Issues: Drought, wildlife poaching, deforestation, desertification

Transportation: There are about 4,220 miles (6,790 km) of roads, of which about 20% are paved. About 360 miles (580 km) of railroad carry passengers and freight. Cotonou and Porto-Novo have port facilities. There are six airports in the country: Abomey, Natitingou, Kandi, and Parakou, and international flights arrive at Cotonou.

Communications: There are 24,000 telephones, 480,000 radios, and 29,000 televisions (1994 est.) with broadcasts from four radio and two television stations. About 50 newspapers (mid-1990) are published throughout the country.

Tourism: The tourist industry is developing. About 130,000 visitors arrived in 1992 and 140,000 in 1993. Museums in Porto-Novo, Abomey, and Parakou exhibit traditional carved wooden masks, tapestries, bronzes, and pottery. There are two national parks in the north.

Embassy in U.S.: (202) 232-6656

Public Holidays: End of Ramadam (date varies); Voudoun national holiday (January 10); Martyrs' Day (January 16); Good Friday (date varies, in March or April); Easter (date varies, in March or April); Feast of the Sacrifice (date varies, in April); Youth Day (April 1); Ascension Day (date varies, in May); Whit Monday (date varies, in May); Workers' Day (May 1); Independence Day: from France, 1960 (August 1); Assumption (August 15); Armed Forces Day (October 26); All Saints' Day (November 1); National Day (November 30); Christmas (December 25); Harvest Day (December 31)

Bhutan

Country Name: Bhutan

Official Name: Kingdom of Bhutan

Nationality: Bhutanese (singular and plural noun); Bhutanese (adjective)

Capital: Thimphu, pop. 22,000

Major cities: Phuntsholing

External Territories: None

Location: Bhutan, in southern Asia, is bordered on the north and northwest by China and on the south and southwest by India.

Physical Geography: In the south, plains and river valleys are suitable for cultivation of tropical fruits and rice. The Himalayas rise in the central and northern part of the country, and the highest peak is Khula Kangri I at 24,170 feet (7,553 m).

Total area: 18,147 sq mi (47,000 sq km)

Coastline: None

Land use: More than two-thirds of the country is forested, and one-tenth is used for livestock and crop production.

Climate: Humid subtropical in the south; temperate in the middle elevations; alpine, with permanent snow and glaciers, at higher elevations

Population: 800,000

Urban population: 15%

Rate of natural increase: 3.1%

Age structure: 43% under 15; 2% over 65

Birth rate: 40/1000

Death rate: 9/1000

Infant mortality rate: 71/1000

Fertility rate: 5.6

Life expectancy at birth: 52 years (average)

Religion: Lamaistic Buddhist, Indian- and Nepalese- influenced Hindu

Language: Dzongkha , Tibetan and Nepali dialects

Ethnic Divisions: Bhotia, Nepalese

Literacy Rate: 42%

Government: Absolute monarchy. The 151-members of the unicameral National Assembly serve three-year terms. Of the members, 106 are elected by adult suffrage, 10 are religious, and 33 are appointed by the king. There are 18 administrative districts.

Armed services: 5,000 troops (1996) in the Royal Bhutan Army

Suffrage: One vote per family in village-level elections

Economy: Bhutan's economy is primarily based on agricultural production for domestic consumption. Some cottage industries such as woodworking, metalworking, and weaving produce exports, mainly for India. Tourism is strictly controlled, but the government is loosening controls over public sector firms, trade agreements, and licensing agreements.

Unit of currency: Ngultrum; 100 chetrum = 1 ngultrum (Nu)

GDP per capita: $730

Inflation rate–CPI: 7% (1996 est.)

Workforce: N.A.

Unemployment rate: N.A.

Exports: Goods worth $77.4 million (f.o.b., 1996 est.) are sent to India and Bangladesh; exports include cardamon, gypsum, timber, handicrafts, cement, fruit, and electricity to India.

Imports: Goods worth $104.1 million (c.i.f., 1996 est.) are received from India, Japan, the U.K., Germany, and the U.S.; imports include fuel and lubricants, grains, machinery and parts, vehicles, fabrics, and rice.

Agriculture: About 93% of the workforce is involved in agriculture. Subsistence crops and livestock, particularly cattle, are the backbone of Bhutan's economy and culture. Some foods, such as citrus fruits and bananas, are grown for export.

Energy: Hydroelectricity is supplemented by coal mining and imported fuels.

Natural Resources: Timber, hydropower, gypsum, calcium carbonate

Environmental Issues: Soil erosion, limited potable water

Transportation: The rugged terrain seriously limits road construction; an estimated 2,040 miles (3,285 km) of roads exist, of which about 1,240 miles (2000 km) are paved. There are no railroads; one of the two airports in the country has scheduled international flights.

Communications: There are 4,600 telephones (1991 est.) in service, and there are few televisions and an estimated 23,000 radios (1989). There are no daily papers, but one weekly paper is published in English, Dzongkha, and Nepali.

Tourism: Forbidden to tourists until 1975, Bhutan restricts visitors to fewer than 5,000 every year. Visitors come to see wildlife and to trek or climb the mountains. In 1995, 4,795 visitors added $5.83 million (U.S.) to the Bhutanese economy.

Embassy in U.S.: None

Public Holidays: Dussehra (moveable Hindu feast day); Birthday of His Majesty Jigme Singye Wangchuck (November 11); National Day (December 17)

Bolivia

Country Name: Bolivia

Official Name: Republic of Bolivia

Nationality: Bolivian(s) (noun); Bolivian (adjective)

Capital: La Paz (administrative) pop. 739,500; Sucre (legal and judicial) pop. 149,100

Major cities: Santa Cruz, Cochabamba, El Alto

External Territories: None

Location: A landlocked country in South America, Bolivia shares an extensive border on the north and northeast with Brazil. It is bordered on the west by Peru and Chile, on the south by Argentina, and on the southeast by Paraguay.

Physical Geography: The western part of the country is mostly the Altiplano, a high plateau, which lies between western and eastern ranges of the Andes and extends south from Lake Titicaca on the Peruvian border, almost to Argentina. East of the Andes, the country slopes into the Amazon Basin where, in the northeast, subtropical forests grow on hills and in gorges. To the south, open grasslands, gentle hills, and wide valleys of the Gran Chaco support agriculture.

Total area: 424,164 sq mi (1,098,581 sq km)

Coastline: None

Land use: More than half of Bolivia is covered with forest, about 25% of the land is meadows and pastures, and only 2% is arable land.

Climate: Varies greatly with elevation: the highlands are cool and dry; the northeast is warm and humid; the southeast is somewhat drier; the rainy season is generally from December through February.

Population: 8,090,000

Urban population: 61%

Rate of natural increase: 2.0%

Age structure: 40% under 15; 4% over 65

Birth rate: 30.4/1000

Death rate: 10/1000

Infant mortality rate: 67/1000

Fertility rate: 4.2

Life expectancy at birth: 59 years (male); 62 years (female)

Religion: Roman Catholic

Language: Spanish, Quechua, Aymara (all official)

Ethnic Divisions: Quechua, Aymara, mestizo

Literacy Rate: 83%

Government: Republic, with an elected president and bicameral legislature, the Congresso Nacional, which is composed of the 130-member Chamber of Deputies and the 27-member Senate. The president and members of the legislature are elected to five-year terms. There are nine administrative departments.

Armed services: 33,500 troops (1997) in the army, navy, air force; citizens subject to selective conscription for a 12-month tour

Suffrage: Universal and compulsory; 18 years old if married and 21 years old if single

Economy: Controlling inflation and molding a free-market economy have been the primary objectives of Bolivian officials since 1983. Moves have been made to privatize industry, stabilize currency, and improve international trade. By 1995, 15 of 157

BOLIVIA   SAILING HIGH ON LAKE TITICACA

Bolivia's administrative capital, La Paz ("The Peace"), at more than 12,000 feet (3,660 m) is the highest capital city in the world. When the local people won their independence from Spain in 1824, they named their country after Simón Bolívar, the man who had led other South American countries to independence. Lake Titicaca lies on Bolivia's border with Peru, high in the Altiplano plateau. It is the largest lake in South America, covering some 3,200 square miles (8,300 sq km), as well as the world's highest navigable waterway.

state-owned companies had been transferred to private ownership.

Unit of currency: Boliviano; 100 centavos = 1 boliviano ($B)

GDP per capita: $3000

Inflation rate–CPI: 7%

Workforce: 2.5 million

Unemployment rate: 6% (1993 est.)

Exports: Goods worth $1.4 billion (f.o.b., 1997) are sent mainly to the U.S., the U.K., and Colombia; exports include metals, natural gas, soybeans, jewelry, and wood. The illegal export of coca and cocaine is valued at $600 million (U.S.) (1990 est.).

Imports: Goods worth $1.7 billion (c.i.f., 1997) are received principally from the U.S., Japan, Brazil, and Chile; imports include capital goods, chemicals, petroleum, and food.

Agriculture: Nearly 45% (1996) of Bolivia's workforce is involved in agriculture, producing enough to ensure Bolivia's self-sufficiency. Cash crops include soybeans, sugar, cotton, corn, and coffee; wood earns 7% (1994) of Bolivia's export earnings. Illegally grown coca continues to be a significant cash crop.

Energy: Primary power is generated by domestic petroleum and natural gas.

Natural Resources: Tin, natural gas, petroleum, timber; metals, including zinc, silver, iron, lead, gold

Environmental Issues: Deforestation, soil erosion, desertification, water pollution

Transportation: A network of an estimated 32,230 miles (52,000 km) of roads is augmented by 2,300 miles (3,700 km) of rail track. There are 6,210 miles (10,000 km) of navigable waters in the country, including Lake Titicaca. Airports at La Paz and Santa Cruz have international flights, and there are numerous airports and airstrips throughout the country with domestic service.

Communications: Urban phone service is adequate once it is installed. There are nearly 150 radio stations and 43 television stations (1993). More than a dozen daily papers and periodicals are published.

Tourism: One of the most popular tourist attractions in Bolivia is Lake Titicaca, At an elevation of 12,192 feet (3,810 m), it is the world's highest navigable lake. Other attractions include skiing and visiting pre-Inca ruins and colonial Spanish settlements. There are UNESCO World Heritage sites at Potosí and Sucre. Nearly 320,000 overnight visitors brought an estimated $135 million (U.S.) in 1994.

Embassy in U.S.: (202) 483-4410

Public Holidays: Good Friday (date varies, in March or April); Labor Day (May 1); Corpus Christi (date varies, in May or June); Independence Day: from Spain, 1825 (August 6); All Saints' Day (November 1); Christmas (December 25)

Bosnia and Herzegovina

Country Name: Bosnia and Herzegovina

Official Name: Bosnia and Herzegovina

Nationality: Bosnian(s), Herzegovinian(s) (noun); Bosnian, Herzegovinian (adjective)

Capital: Sarajevo, pop. 529,000

Major cities: Banja Luka

External Territories: None

Location: In southeastern Europe, Bosnia and Herzegovina is bordered on the north, west, and southwest by Croatia and on the east and southeast by Yugoslavia. A narrow corridor in the southwest gives access to the Adriatic Sea.

Physical Geography: The mountainous country, with ranges including the Dinaric Alps, Kozara Mountains, and the Vlasic Mountains, is mostly forested. Farming is possible on some flat terrain in the southwest.

Total area: 19,741 sq mi (51,129 sq km)

Coastline: 12 mi (20 km)

Land use: Nearly 40% of the land is forest and woodland, 20% is meadows and pastures, and nearly 20% is used for agriculture.

Climate: Continental, with precipitation throughout the year, cold winters, and hot summers; drier and more moderate temperatures near the Adriatic coast; colder temperatures at higher elevations

BOSNIA AND HERZEGOVINA SYMBOL OF UNITY LOST TO STRIFE

The Stari Most Bridge over the Neretva River in Mostar, Bosnia, survived more than 400 years of earthquakes, floods, and wars (it was built by Süleyman the Magnificent in 1566) but was finally destroyed by Croatian shelling in 1993. For centuries the graceful arched limestone and marble bridge was the scene of a local rite of passage—a diving competition—among Muslims, Croats, and Serbs. Until ethnic warfare began in the states of the former Yugoslavia, the bridge was a symbol that linked the country's various cultures.

Population: 3,839,000
Urban population: 40%
Rate of natural increase: 0.49%
Age structure: 22% under 15; 8% over 65
Birth rate: 13/1000
Death rate: 8/1000
Infant mortality rate: 12/1000
Fertility rate: 1.6
Life expectancy at birth: 71 years (male); 76 years (female)
Religion: Muslim, Orthodox, Catholic
Language: Serbo-Croat (Bosnian)
Ethnic Divisions: Serb, Muslim, Croat
Literacy Rate: N.A.
Government: Republic, with a bicameral National Assembly consisting of the National House of Representatives with 42 seats (14 Serb, 14 Croat, 14 Muslim) where members serve two-year terms and the House of Peoples with 15 members (5 Muslim, 5 Croat, 5 Serb) also serving two-year terms. A civil war erupted in 1991 just before independence from Yugoslavia in 1992; an uneasy peace has followed since the Dayton Accord was signed in December 1995. A three-member presidency is in place with one representative from each ethnic group in the country: Bosniack (Muslim), Croat, and Serb.

Armed services: 45,000 (1997) in the army
Suffrage: Universal; 16 years old if employed and 18 years old if unemployed
Economy: Before independence from Yugoslavia in 1992, minimal economic development had taken place in Bosnia and Herzegovina. After independence, the country's economic standing was devastated by inflation, blockades, and destruction resulting from civil war that continued until December 1995. Despite financial assistance from the international community, the inadequate infrastructure, external debt, and lack of foreign funds continue to hinder economic recovery.
Unit of currency: 1 convertible marka = 100 convertible pfenniga; former currencies still used.
GDP per capita: $1690
Inflation rate–CPI: N.A.
Workforce: 1,026,000
Unemployment rate: 40-50% (1996 est.)
Exports: N.A.
Imports: N.A.
Agriculture: Small-scale farming is a traditional occupation in Bosnia and Herzegovina. Due to civil war, food imports have been necessary to meet domestic demand. Wheat corn, fruits, vegetables, and livestock are important component of agricultural production.
Energy: N.A.
Natural Resources: Coal, iron, bauxite, copper, manganese, forests
Environmental Issues: Air pollution, widespread damage from civil war
Transportation: An estimated 35% of the transportation infrastructure was affected by the war. There are an estimated 13,570 miles (21,840 km) of roads and 640 miles (1,030 km) of railroads. International flights have resumed from Sarajevo.
Communications: There are 840,000 radios and 1.1 million televisions (1990 est.) in service; telephone service remains minimal compared to other European countries.
Tourism: Minimal development of visitor facilities and sites, and current post-war conditions are not suitable for touring.
Embassy in U.S.: (202) 833-3612
Public Holidays: Independence Day (March 1); Labor Day(s) (May 1–2); Birth of the Prophet (date varies, in July)

Botswana

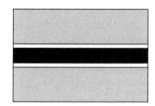

Country Name: Botswana
Official Name: Republic of Botswana
Nationality: Motswana (singular noun), Batswana (plural noun); Motswana (singular adjective), Batswana (plural adjective)
Capital: Gaborone, pop. 133,500 [286,800]
Major cities: Francistown, Selebi Phikwe

External Territories: None

Location: Botswana, in southern Africa, is bordered on the west and north by Namibia, on the east by Zimbabwe, and on the east and south by South Africa.

Physical Geography: Except for hills in the east, most of the country is a flat plateau with a mean elevation of 3,900 feet (1,186 m). Much of the Kalahari Desert is in Botswana; it spreads from the southwest across the central part of the country. In the north, the Okavango River drains into the Okavango Delta, one of the largest inland deltas in the world. Most of the population lives in the eastern part of the country.

Total area: 231,805 sq mi (600,372 sq km)

Coastline: None

Land use: Much of the land is either desert or semiarid; about 1% is used for agriculture.

Climate: Dry subtropical, with rains from December to April, hot summers, and frequent droughts

Population: 1,464,000

Urban population: 50%

Rate of natural increase: 1.18%

Age structure: 39% under 15; 5% over 65

Birth rate: 32.6/1000

Death rate: 20.8/1000

Infant mortality rate: 55.9/1000

Fertility rate: 4.1

Life expectancy at birth: 40 years (male); 41 years (female)

Religion: Indigenous beliefs, Christian

Language: English, Setswana

Ethnic Divisions: Batswana, Kalanga, Basarwa, Kgalagadi

Literacy Rate: 70%

Government: Parliamentary republic, with a president elected to a five-year term by the bicameral legislative body. The fifteen members of the House of Chiefs represent the eight principal tribes with four elected sub-chiefs and three members

BOTSWANA A MOST FAMOUS OASIS

Botswana, which was the British colony of Bechuanaland until 1966, contains two of the world's unique places: the Kalahari Desert and the Okavango Delta. The Kalahari—the world's longest continuous stretch of sand—covers most of Botswana and extends northward into Namibia and beyond. It has been home to the Bushmen, or San, people for 25,000 years, one of the last hunter-gatherer societies left on Earth, and a huge variety of birds and mammals. The Okavanga Delta, in north-central Botswana, is fed by the Okavango River, which in turn gets its water from the Cubango River. The delta—known as the world's largest oasis—is replenished with water every March, when the Cubango floods and spreads its waters over 8,500 square miles (22,000 sq km) of the Kalahari. About the size of France, Botswana has set aside 17 percent of its land area for wildlife parks and reserves.

elected by the other twelve. The forty members of the National Assembly are elected,and four are appointed, all for five-year terms. There are ten administrative districts and four town councils.

Armed services: 7,500 (1997 est.) in the army and air force; voluntary

Suffrage: Universal; 18 years old

Economy: Traditionally a livestock and agricultural economy, the development of diamond mining—Botswana is one of the world's leading diamond exporters—led to a high rate of growth in the 1980s. Partially in response to the 1990s recession, the government is now encouraging economic diversification with private investment incentives and discouraging government subsidies for unprofitable ventures.

Unit of currency: Pula, 100 thebe = 1 pula (P)

GDP per capita: $3,300

Inflation rate–CPI: 10% (1996 est.)

Workforce: 441,000 (1991 est.)

Unemployment rate: 21% (1997 est.)

Exports: Goods worth $2.31 billion (f.o.b., 1996) are sent to Switzerland, the U.K., and members of the Southern African Customs

Union; exports include diamonds, copper, nickel, and meat. Diamonds earn about 71% (1996 est.) of the value of all exports.

Imports: Goods worth $1.6 billion (c.i.f., 1996 est.) are received from Switzerland, members of the Southern African Customs Union, the U.K., and the Republic of Korea.; imports include food, vehicles and transport equipment, textiles, and petroleum.

Agriculture: Almost one-quarter (1991) of the working population engages in agricultural production and cattle raising. The country is not self-sufficient, but farmers support about half of the population. Subsistence crops include sorghum, maize,millet, pulses, peanuts, and beans.

Energy: Coal and wood fuels are the major sources of energy in Botswana, and petroleum is imported.

Natural Resources: Diamonds, copper, nickel, salt, soda ash, coal, silver

Environmental Issues: Overgrazing, desertification, limited fresh water resources

Transportation: There are 11,480 miles (18,480 km) (1996 est.) of roads, of which about 2,610 miles (4,340 km) are paved. There are 600 miles (970 km) (1995 est.) of rail track. There are regional airstrips throughout the country; Gaborone handles international flights and there is another major airport at Kasane.

Communications: One or two daily papers are supplemented by the publication of weekly and monthly periodicals. There are 22,000 televisions (1992 est.) in Botswana; however, there are no broadcast stations. There are 160,000 radios that receive broadcasts from about 20 stations.

Tourism: Botswana's wildlife, protected within national parks and reserves in the Okavango Delta and Kalahari, is a powerful tourist draw. In 1995, 1,021,000 visitors brought in $35 million (U.S.).

Embassy in U.S.: (202) 244-4990

Public Holidays: Easter (date varies, in March or April); Ascension Day (date varies, in May); President's Day (July 15–16); Botswana Day: independence from the U.K., 1966 (September 30–October 1); Christmas (December 25–26)

Brazil

Country Name: Brazil

Official Name: Federative Republic of Brazil

Nationality: Brazilian(s) (noun); Brazilian (adjective)

Capital: Brasília, pop. 1,737,800

Major cities: São Paulo, Rio de Janeiro, Salvador, Belo Horizonte

External Territories: None

BRAZIL   THE FAST-FLOWING, DELTA-LESS AMAZON

The 4,000-mile-long Amazon River discharges 4.5 trillion gallons a day into the Atlantic Ocean at its mouth in north-central Brazil—an amount that could supply every household in the United States with enough water for more than five months. The Amazon's flow is too strong to form a true delta. On average, it discharges 7.1 million cubic feet per second at its mouth, far surpassing the second-place Congo River in the Democratic Republic of the Congo, which discharges an average 1.6 million cubic feet per second. The Amazon drains one-sixth of the Earth's runoff into the ocean, carrying sediment 60 miles out to sea.

Location: Brazil, the largest country in South America, is in the east and has a long Atlantic Ocean coastline. Countries along its northern border are Venezuela, Guyana, Suriname, and French Guiana; to the south are Paraguay, Uruguay, and Argentina. Bolivia and Peru are on the west and Colombia is on the northwest.

Physical Geography: The world's fifth largest country in land area, Brazil varies from rain forest in the Amazon Basin to the drier plains and plateaus of the Brazilian Highlands and Mato Grosso. Ranges of mountains parallel the southeastern Atlantic coast.

Total area: 3,286,488 sq mi (8,511,965 sq km)

Coastline: 4,652 mi (7,491 km)

Land use: More than two-thirds of Brazil is forest and woodland, one-fifth is meadows and pastures, and less than one-tenth is used for agriculture.

Climate: Mostly tropical, with heavy rains in the Amazon Basin from December to May; warm coastal temperatures in the drier northeast; temperatures fluctuate more in the interior; slightly cooler average temperatures with some snow in the south

Population: 167,988,000

Urban population: 78%

Rate of natural increase: 1.54%

Age structure: 32% under 15; 5% over 65

Birth rate: 21.3/1000

Death rate: 5.9/1000

Infant mortality rate: 40.5/1000

Fertility rate: 2.3

Life expectancy at birth: 63 years (male); 70 years (female)

Religion: Roman Catholic

Language: Portuguese, Spanish, English

Ethnic Divisions: White, mulatto, black

Literacy Rate: 83%

Government: Federal republic, with a bicameral National Congress; the president is elected by popular vote for a four-year term. The 513 members of the Chamber of Deputies are elected to four-year terms, and the 81 members of the Federal Senate are elected for eight years. There are 26 states and one federal district.

Armed services: 314,700 (1997) in the army, navy, and air force; compulsory 12 month tour required of all men from 18 to 45 years of age

Suffrage: Voluntary between 16 and 18 years of age and over 70 years of age; compulsory between 18 and 70 years of age

Economy: Once one of the world's largest debtor nations, Brazil began to stabilize the economy in mid-

1994 by introducing a new currency, increasing privatization plans, encouraging foreign investment, and making other efforts at economic deregulation. A four-year spending plan may help shore up the infrastructure, social services, telecommunications, and other areas.

Unit of currency: Real (singular); reais (plural); 100 centavos = 1 real (R$)

GDP per capita: $6,300

Inflation rate–CPI: 4.8%

Workforce: 57 million (1989 est.)

Unemployment rate: 7% (1997 est.)

Exports: Goods worth $53 billion (f.o.b., 1997) are sent to the EU, other Latin American countries, the U.S., and Argentina; exports include iron ore, soybeans, bran, orange juice, footwear, and coffee.

Imports: Goods worth $61.4 billion (f.o.b., 1997) are received from members of the EU, the U.S., Argentina, and Japan; imports include crude oil, capital goods, chemicals, food, and coal.

Agriculture: Agriculture employs 25% (1996) of the workforce; soybeans, coffee, tobacco, sugarcane, and cocoa are cultivated for export.

Energy: More than 90% of Brazil's energy is generated by hydropower. Other sources include petroleum, wood, charcoal, and coal.

Natural Resources: Minerals, including bauxite, gold, iron, manganese, nickel; petroleum, hydropower, timber

Environmental Issues: Amazon Basin deforestation, air and water pollution in large urban areas

Transportation: There are 16,700 miles (26,900 km) of railroads and 1,229,580 miles (1,980,000 km) of roads in Brazil. Less than 10% of the roads are paved; however, more than 95% (1995) of the people travel by road and about 60% of the country's freight is transported by road. There are 31,050 (50,000

km) of navigable waterways in Brazil, including all of the Amazon River's main channel. There are more than 40 deep-water ports for domestic and international shipping. While there are more than 20 airports handling international flights, the principal international airports are at Rio de Janeiro and São Paulo. There are numerous airports and airstrips throughout the country.

Communications: Almost 400 daily papers are published in Brazil. The country has one of the world's largest television broadcasting systems: there are more than 110 stations broadcasting to an estimated 30 million televisions (1993). There are nearly 1,400 radio stations and 60 million radios (1993). Telephone distribution and service are good.

Tourism: Brazil is a popular tourist destination because of the Amazon rain forest, the beaches of Rio de Janeiro, and the pre-Lenten Carnival season. In 1997, 2.8 million visitors spent an estimated $972 million (U.S.).

U.S. Tourist Office: (800) 544-5503

Embassy in U.S.: (202) 238-2700

Public Holidays: Carnival (date varies, in February); Good Friday (date varies, in March or April): Tiradentes Day: Discovery of Brazil (April 21); Labor Day (May 1); Corpus Christi (date varies, in May or June); Independence Day: from Portugal, 1822 (September 7); Day of Our Lady Aparecida, patron saint of Brazil (October 12); All Souls' Day (November 2); Proclamation of the Republic, 1889 (November 15); Christmas (December 25)

Brunei

Country Name: Brunei

Official Name: Negara Brunei Darussalam

Nationality: Bruneian(s) (noun); Bruneian (adjective)

Capital: Bandar Seri Begawan, pop. 75,000

Major cities: Kuala Belait, Seria, Tutong

External Territories: None

Location: Brunei, in southeastern Asia, is on the South China Sea coast of the island of Borneo. The country is divided into two enclaves by Malaysia.

Physical Geography: Hilly forested interiors, intersected with rivers, give way to a narrow coastal plain. The country's two sections are divided by the Limbang River Valley.

Total area: 2,226 sq mi (5,765 sq km)

Coastline: 100 mi (161 km)

Land use: About 85% of the land is forested and 3% is used for agriculture and livestock production.

Climate: Tropical, with high humidity and frequent heavy rains

Population: 323,000

Urban population: 67%

Rate of natural increase: 2.2%

BRUNEI A CONCENTRATION OF RICHES

About the size of Delaware, Brunei gained its independence from Great Britain in 1984. The Sultan of Brunei—Hassanal Bolkiah—is one of the wealthiest men in the world. The country's oil and gas wealth provides its citizens with cradle-to-grave care.

Age structure: 34% under 15; 3% over 65

Birth rate: 25/1000

Death rate: 3/1000

Infant mortality rate: 24/1000

Fertility rate: 3.4

Life expectancy at birth: 70 years (male); 73 years (female)

Religion: Muslim, Buddhist, Christian, traditional indigenous

Language: Malay, English, Chinese

Ethnic Divisions: Malay, Chinese

Literacy Rate: 88%

Government: Constitutional sultanate; the sultan presides over four councils. There are four administrative districts.

Armed services: 5,000 troops (1997) in the army, navy, and air force; voluntary military service open only to Malays

Suffrage: None

Economy: The economy currently depends on oil and gas production. The government is developing finance and banking industries and encouraging foreign investments and industrial diversification.

Unit of currency: Brunei dollar; 100 sens = 1 Brunei dollar (B$)

GDP per capita: $18,000

Inflation rate–CPI: 2% (1997 est.)

Workforce: 144,000 (1995 est.)

Unemployment rate: 4.8% (1994 est.)

Exports: Goods worth $2.6 billion (f.o.b., 1996 est.) are sent to Japan, the U.K., Thailand, and Singapore; exports include mainly crude oil, natural gas, and petroleum products.

Imports: Goods worth $2.65 billion (c.i.f., 1996 est.) are received from Singapore, the U.K., the U.S., and Japan; imports include machinery, food, manufactured goods and chemicals.

Agriculture: Only 4% (1991) of the working population engages in agricultural production; the principal crops are rice, cassava, and bananas.

Energy: Brunei is self-sufficient in petroleum and natural gas.

Natural Resources: Oil, natural gas, timber

Environmental Issues: N.A.

Transportation: An estimated 710 miles (1,150 km) of roads are used by 168,000 vehicles (1995); about half the roadways are paved. There are no railroads. There is a deep-water port at Muara and other ports at Bandar Seri Begawan, Kuala Berlait, Seria, and Tutong. About 130 miles (209 km) of inland rivers are navigable by shallow draft craft. One airport near the capital accommodates international flights.

Communications: One daily paper (1995) is published. There are eight radio stations and one television station broadcasting to 284,000 radios and 173,000 televisions (1995 est). Phone service, with an estimated 90,000 telephones (1997), is adequate.

Tourism: Tourist attractions in Brunei include mosques and museums in and around Bandar Seri Begawan, beaches, and nature reserves along the coast and in the interior. Tourists numbered nearly 53,000 in 1994; in 1993, income from tourists was about $36 million (U.S.).

Embassy in U.S.: (202) 342-0159

Public Holidays: Beginning of Ramadan (dates vary); End of Ramadan (date varies); Chinese New Year (dates vary, in January or February); Anniversary of the Revelation of the Koran (dates vary, in February); National Day (February 23); Feast of the Sacrifice (date varies, in April); Islamic New Year (date varies, in May); Royal Brunei Armed Forces Day (June 1); Sultan's Birthday (July 15); Birth of the Prophet (date varies, in July); Ascension of the Prophet (date varies, in December); Christmas (December 25)

Bulgaria

Country Name: Bulgaria

Official Name: Republic of Bulgaria

Nationality: Bulgarian(s) (noun); Bulgarian (adjective)

Capital: Sofia, pop. 1,116,800 [1,193,700]

Major cities: Plovdiv, Varna, Burgas

External Territories: None

Location: Bulgaria, in southeastern Europe, is on the west coast of the Black Sea; Romania is to the north, Turkey and Greece are to the south, and Yugoslavia and Macedonia are to the west.

Physical Geography: The fertile lowland of the Danubian Plain extends from the Danube River on Bulgaria's border with Romania to the Balkan Mountains, which run east-west across the central part of the country. Another plain lies between the Balkan Mountains and the Rhodope Mountains on the Greek border.

Total area: 42,823 sq mi (110,912 sq km)

Coastline: 220 mi (354 km)

Land use: More than one-third of the land is forested, nearly 40% is used for agricultural production, and 16% is meadows and pastures.

Climate: Mixed temperate: continental weather in the north and northwest; warmer, drier weather in the southeast and in some river valleys; generally heavier precipitation in the mountains

Population: 8,188,000

Urban population: 68%

Rate of natural increase: -0.6%

Age structure: 17% under 15; 16% over 65

Birth rate: 8/1000

Death rate: 14/1000

Infant mortality rate: 14.4/1000

Fertility rate: 1.1

Life expectancy at birth: 67 years (male); 74 years (female)

Religion: Bulgarian Orthodox, Muslim

Language: Bulgarian

Ethnic Divisions: Bulgarian, Turk, Gypsy, Macedonian

Literacy Rate: 98%

Government: Republic, with an elected president and a unicameral legislative body, the National Assembly. The president serves for a five-year term; the 240 members of the National Assembly are elected to four-year terms. There are nine administrative provinces.

Armed services: 101,500 troops (1997 est.) in the army, air force, and navy; compulsory service for 18 months

Suffrage: Universal and compulsory; 18 years old

Economy: Trying to recover from severe economic decline in the late 1980s and early 1990s, as well as make the transition to a market economy, the Bulgarian government enacted several measures to revitalize the economy, including encouraging privatization, foreign investment, banking reform, developing tourism, and stabilizing price fluctuations. Industry privatization is not proceeding as quickly as planned, and a large foreign debt hinders recovery attempts.

Unit of currency: Lev (singular); leva (plural); 100 stotinki (stotinka, singular) = 1 lev (Lv)

GDP per capita: $4,100

Inflation rate–CPI: 579% (1997 est.)

Workforce: 3.57 million (1996 est.)

Unemployment rate: 14% (1997)

Exports: Goods worth $4.9 billion (f.o.b., 1997) are sent to Russia, Germany, Italy, and Greece; exports include agricultural and food products, metals and ores, chemicals, textiles and apparel, machinery and equipment, and minerals and fuels.

Imports: Goods worth $4.5 billion (f.o.b., 1997 est.) are received from Russia, Germany, and Italy; imports include fuels, minerals, raw materials, machinery and equipment, textiles and apparel, and agricultural products.

Agriculture: Privatized farms provide 75.4% (1996) of agricultural production and employ 181% of the workforce. Crops included grain, oilseed, vegetables, fruits, and tobacco. Viticulture is being encouraged; Bulgaria is the fourth largest (1989) exporter of wine in the world.

Energy: Coal and nuclear energy produce 44% (1992 est.) of the country's needs; other fuels are imported.

Natural Resources: Bauxite, copper, lead, zinc, coal, timber, arable land

Environmental Issues: Air and water pollution, deforestation, soil contamination

Transportation: There are an estimated 23,000 miles (37,000 km) of roads in Bulgaria, including two major international highways, and an estimated 2,500 miles (4,000 km) of railroads. Airports at Sofia, Varna, and Bourgas handle international flights, and there are seven other airports elsewhere in the country. Nearly 300 miles (470 km) of waterways carry cargo and passengers, including the Danube River. Black Sea ports include Varna and Burgas.

Communications: At least 26 daily papers are published, many of which came into existence following the liberalization of laws in 1990. There are 2.1 million televisions (1990 est.). Telephones number almost 3 million (1993), but the infrastructure needs updating.

Tourism: Black Sea resorts, mountain scenery, and tours of Sofia and other cultural areas draw visitors to Bulgaria. In 1996, there were 6.8 million visitors.

U.S. Tourist Office: (800) 852-0944

Embassy in U.S.: (202) 387-7969

Public Holidays: National Day (March 3): Easter Monday (date varies, in March or April): Labor Day (May 1); Education Day (May 24); Commemoration of the Leaders of the Bulgarian National Revival (November 1); Christmas (December 24–25)

Burkina Faso

Country Name: Burkina Faso

Official Name: Burkina Faso

Nationality: Burkinabe (singular and plural noun); Burkinabe (adjective)

Capital: Ouagadougou, pop. 634,500

Major cities: Bobo Dioulasso, Koudougou

External Territories: None

Location: Landlocked Burkina Faso, in western Africa, is bordered on the northwest by Mali, on the northeast by Niger, and on the south by Benin, Togo, Ghana, and Côte d'Ivoire.

Physical Geography: The Nazinan, Nakanbe, and Mouhoun Rivers flow south and cut through the plateau that covers most of Burkina Faso. There is some hilly country in the north and northeast; part of the Sahel lies in the north as well, where

BURKINA FASO THE LAND OF THE UPRIGHT MEN

Burkina Faso means "land of the upright men" and was once known as Mossi, an east African state dating back to 1100. The Mossi tribe is predominant today. The country gained its independence from France in 1960; before then, it was known as Upper Volta.

overgrazing and overcultivation has led to desertification.

Total area: 105,869 sq mi (274,200 sq km)

Coastline: None

Land use: Land use estimates vary; about 37% of the land is meadows and pastures, and an estimated 10% is cultivated. Estimates of woodlands range from 26% to 50%.

Climate: Hot and usually dry, with a rainy season from June to October; rainfall increasing from north to south

Population: 11,576,000

Urban population: 15%

Rate of natural increase: 2.89%

Age structure: 48% under 15; 3% over 65

Birth rate: 46.7/1000

Death rate: 17.8/1000

Infant mortality rate: 93.9/1000

Fertility rate: 6.7

Life expectancy at birth: 46 years (male); 47 years (female)

Religion: Indigenous beliefs, Muslim, Roman Catholic

Language: French, tribal languages

Ethnic Divisions: More than 50 groups including Mossi, Mande, Fulani, Lobi, Bobo

Literacy Rate: 19%

Government: Parliamentary, with a president and bicameral legislature; however, since independence, in 1960, the country has generally been under military rule. There are 30 administrative provinces.

Armed services: 10,000 troops (1997) in the army, air force, and

gendarmerie; voluntary, with a two-year, part-time enlistment

Suffrage: Universal; adult

Economy: In trying to improve the country's economy, Burkina Faso is battling the effects of a high population growth rate, poor infrastructure, and few natural resources. Subsistence farming is the main source of income for the majority of the population. There are attempts to exploit Burkina Faso's mineral resources, eliminate business monopolies, and encourage foreign investment.

Unit of currency: CFA franc; 100 centimes = 1 franc de la Communauté financière africaine (CFAF)

GDP per capita: $950

Inflation rate–CPI: 3% (1996 est.)

Workforce: 4,679,000 (1991 est.)

Unemployment rate: N.A.

Exports: Goods worth $298 million (f.o.b., 1995 est.) are sent to France, Côte d'Ivoire, and other trading partners; exports include cotton, gold, and animal products.

Imports: Goods worth $500 million (f.o.b., 1995 est.) are received from France, Côte d'Ivoire, Japan, and other trading partners; imports include machinery, transportation equipment, food, and petroleum products.

Agriculture: Agricultural products are raised both for consumption and for cash, and Burkina Faso can be self-sufficient depending on drought conditions. Cash crops include cotton, peanuts, and sesame; subsistence crops include millet, sorghum, and maize. More than 80% (1994)

of the working population is involved with farming.

Energy: Except for some internal generation of hydroelectricity, Burkina Faso depends upon petroleum imports.

Natural Resources: Manganese, limestone, marble, gold, antimony, copper

Environmental Issues: Desertification in the north, deforestation, soil degradation, overgrazing

Transportation: Less than 10% of the country's 7,770 miles (12,510 km) of roads are paved. There are nearly 390 miles (620 km) of railroad lines. Ouagadougou and Bobo Dioulasso have international airports, and there are smaller airports and airstrips for domestic flights.

Communications: Access to telephones, radios, and televisions is poor, although there are three radio stations and two television stations broadcasting in Burkina Faso. Four daily papers are published in Ouagadougou.

Tourism: In 1993, nearly 155,000 tourists, who came for big game hunting along the Mouhoun River, brought an estimated $15 million to the country. A pan-African biennial film festival is held in Ouagadougou.

Embassy in U.S.: (202) 332-5577

Public Holidays: Anniversary of the 1966 coup d'état (January 3); End of Ramadan (February); International Women's Day (March 8); Easter Monday (March or April); Feast of the Sacrifice (April); Ascension Day (May); Labor Day (May 1); Birth of the Prophet (July); National Day: independence from France, 1960 (August 5); Assumption (August 15); Anniversary of the 1987 coup d'état (October 15); All Saints' Day (November 1); Proclamation of the Republic (December 11); Christmas (December 25)

Burundi

Country Name: Burundi
Official Name: Republic of Burundi
Nationality: Burundian(s) (noun); Burundi (adjective)
Capital: Bujumbura, pop. 235,400
Major cities: Gitega
External Territories: None
Location: Landlocked Burundi, in central Africa, is bordered on the east by Tanzania, on the north by Rwanda, on the west by the Democratic Republic of the Congo, and the southwest by Lake Tanganyika.
Physical Geography: Burundi is mostly a high plateau along the eastern edge of the Great Rift Valley, with some escarpments and swamps in the east and central part of the country.
Total area: 10,747 sq mi (27,834 sq km)
Coastline: None
Land use: About 53% of the land is used for agriculture, 36% is meadows and pastures, and 3% is forested.
Climate: Tropical, with cooler temperatures at higher elevations
Population: 5,736,000
Urban population: 5%
Rate of natural increase: 2.46%
Age structure: 48% under 15; 3% over 65
Birth rate: 42.1/1000
Death rate: 17.5/1000
Infant mortality rate: 104.8/1000
Fertility rate: 6.5
Life expectancy at birth: 44 years (male); 47 years (female)

Religion: Roman Catholic, Protestant, indigenous beliefs
Language: Kirundi, French (both official)
Ethnic Divisions: Hutu, Tutsi, Twa
Literacy Rate: 35%
Government: Republic, with a president elected for a five-year term and unicameral legislature, the 81-member National Assembly, whose members are elected to five-year terms. There are 15 administrative provinces.
Armed services: 22,000 troops (1997) in the army, air force, and gendarmerie
Suffrage: Universal
Economy: Burundi's economy has traditionally depended on coffee for revenue, which makes up an estimated 80% of its export earnings. Political and ethnic civil war have severely hindered attempts at economic development from the 1960s into the 1990s. The country began to try to diversify its agricultural cash base, attract foreign investment, and update budget practices beginning in 1991.
Unit of currency: Burundian franc; 100 centimes = 1 Burundian franc (FBu)
GDP per capita: $660
Inflation rate–CPI: 26% (1996 est.)
Workforce: 2,765,000 (1990 est.)
Unemployment rate: N.A .
Exports: Goods worth $40 million (f.o.b., 1996 est.) are sent to the U.S., France, Germany, and other trading partners; exports include coffee, which earns about 81% of the value of exports, tea, cotton, and hides and skins.
Imports: Goods worth $127 million (c.i.f., 1996 est.) are received from Belgium, France, Luxembourg, and other trading partners; imports include petroleum, food, and consumer goods.
Agriculture: More than 93% (1990 est.) of the economically active population engages in agricultural pro-

duction. Coffee, tea, and animal hides are the main cash products, while subsistence crops include cassava, corn, and sweet potatoes. Prior to civil war, the country was self-sufficient.
Energy: Wood, hydropower, and peat supply energy; nearly 50% of hydropower is imported.
Natural Resources: Minerals, including nickel, uranium, peat, cobalt, copper, vanadium
Environmental Issues: Soil erosion, deforestation, wildlife habitat loss
Transportation: A dense network of about 9,000 miles (14,500 km) of roads crosses the country; there are no railroads. Bujumbura is the country's principal port on Lake Tanganyika through which pass passengers and international freight; there are other ports at Rumonge and Nyanza Lac. Bujumbura has an international airport.
Communications: Telephones and televisions are scarce. There are 9,000 television sets (1994 est.) in the country, and 400,000 radios ease communications difficulties somewhat. One daily paper and two weeklies are published in Bujumbura.
Tourism: Although 29,000 visitors brought an estimated $3 million to Burundi in 1994, the industry is underdeveloped, and political instability has prompted State Department warnings about traveling to the country.
Embassy in U.S.: (202) 342-2574
Public Holidays: Easter Monday (date varies, in March or April); Ascension Day (date varies, in May); Labor Day (May 1); Independence Day (July 1); Assumption (August 15); Victory of Union pour le progrès national (UPRONA) Day, vote for independence, 1958 (September 18); All Saints' Day (November 1); Christmas (December 25)

Cambodia

Country Name: Cambodia
Official Name: Kingdom of Cambodia
Nationality: Cambodian(s), Khmer (noun); Cambodian, Khmer (adjective)
Capital: Phnom Penh, pop. [920,000]
Major cities: Battambang, Kampong Cham, Pursat
External Territories: None
Location: Cambodia, in southeastern Asia, is on the Gulf of Thailand; it lies between Thailand and Vietnam, with Laos on the north.
Physical Geography: The Mekong River floodplains and lowlands around the 87-mile-long (140 km) Tonle Sap (Great Lake) rise to meet the Dangrek Range to the north. The Cardamon Mountains and Elephant Range are in the southwest.
Total area: 69,898 sq mi (181,035 sq km)
Coastline: 275 mi (443 km)
Land use: Almost 70% of Cambodia's land is covered with forest or woodlands, 13% of the land is arable or under cultivation, and 11% is meadows and pastures.
Climate: Tropical; monsoon from June through October, with heaviest rains in September
Population: 11,851,000
Urban population: 16%
Rate of natural increase: 2.39%
Age structure: 44% under 15; 4% over 65
Birth rate: 38/1000
Death rate: 14/1000

Infant mortality rate: 103/1000
Fertility rate: 5.2
Life expectancy at birth: 52 years (male); 55 years (female)
Religion: Theravada Buddhist
Language: Khmer, French
Ethnic Divisions: Khmer, Vietnamese, Chinese
Literacy Rate: 35%
Government: Constitutional monarchy, with a king selected from three royal lines, and a unicameral legislature, the National Assembly. The 120 members of the legislature are directly elected to five-year terms. There are 20 administrative provinces.
Armed services: 140,000 troops (1997) in the army, navy, and air force; five-year conscription for those between ages 18 and 35 years of age.
Suffrage: Universal; 18 years old
Economy: Economic reforms, reduced inflation, lifting trade and aid embargos, and encouraging the private sector and foreign investors beginning in 1993 have helped the country begin building a modern economy. However, 90% of the population is rural; the infrastructure remains underdeveloped in these areas.
Unit of currency: Riel; 100 sen = 1 new riel

GDP per capita: $715
Inflation rate–CPI: 9.5% (1997 est.)
Workforce: 2.3 million (19973 est.)
Unemployment rate: N.A.
Exports: Goods worth $615 million (1996 est.) are sent to Singapore, Japan, Thailand, Hong Kong, Indonesia, Malaysia and the U.S.; exports include timber, rubber, soybeans, and sesame.
Imports: Goods worth $1 billion (1996 est.) are received from Singapore, Vietnam, Japan, Australia, Hong Kong, and Indonesia; imports include cigarettes, construction materials, petroleum products, machinery, and motor vehicles.
Agriculture: Almost 80% (1995 est.) of the workforce is employed in the agricultural sector. Crops include rice, maize, sugar, cassava, and bananas.
Energy: Wood is the principal fuel, with some electricity generated with hydropower.
Natural Resources: Timber, gemstones, some iron ore, manganese, phosphates, potential for hydropower
Environmental Issues: Deforestation, soil erosion
Transportation: There are about 22,200 miles (35,800 km) of road, of which 8% (1996 est.) are paved; 375 miles (600 km) of railroads, and 2,300 miles (3,700 km) of in-

CAMBODIA ANGKOR WAT: ANCIENT STORIES IN STONE

In the mid-to-late 1970s, when the country was known as Democratic Kampuchea, Pol Pot's Khmer Rouge dictatorship was responsible for the deaths of some one to three million Cambodians. The Vietnamese overthrew Pol Pot in 1978.

The Hindu temple of Angkor Wat (pictured on the Cambodian flag), along with the Ankgor Thom, make up the world's largest group of religious buildings—some 600 were built in the 12th century, during the height of the Khmer empire. Currently undergoing restoration, Angkor Wat once housed priests and libraries, and its elaborate stone exterior features reliefs of Hindu epics and legends.

land waterways, including the Mekong River and Tonle Sap. The main seaport is at Kompong Som. Phnom Penh has an international airport, and a dozen other airports and airstrips are scattered around the country.

Communications: There are about 21 weekly and biweekly papers published in the country, most of which are published in Phnom Penh. An estimated 1.5 million radios and 800,000 televisions (1996) are in operation, and an estimated 7,000 telephones (1981) provide only minimal service.

Tourism: The ruins of Hindu shrines at Angkor Wat, pagodas, cultural exhibits, and holiday celebrations at Buddhist temples and elsewhere attracted about 220,000 visitors in 1995; 176,617 visitors brought $70 million (U.S.) into the country in 1994.

Embassy in U.S.: (202) 726-7742

Public Holidays: January 7 Day (January 7); National Day (January 9); New Year (date varies, in April); Victory Day (April 17); Labor Day (May 1); Constitution Day (September 24); Anniversary of Paris Peace Agreement on Cambodia (October 23); Independence Day: from France, 1953 (November 9)

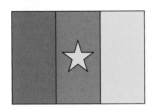

Cameroon

Country Name: Cameroon
Official Name: Republic of Cameroon
Nationality: Cameroonian(s) (noun); Cameroonian (adjective)
Capital: Yaoundé, pop. 1,000,000

Major cities: Douala, Nkongsamba, Maroua, Garoua
External Territories: None
Location: Cameroon, in west-central Africa, is between Nigeria to the west and Chad and the Central African Republic to the east. The Atlantic Ocean is on the southwest, and Congo, Gabon, and Equatorial Guinea are on the south.
Physical Geography: The Mandara Mountains in the northwest give way to savannas that slope down to Lake Chad; plateaus and a coastal plain characterize the central and southern regions; volcanic Cameroon Mountain, at 13,452 feet (4,100 m), near the coast and north of Douala, is the highest mountain in western sub-Saharan Africa.
Total area: 183,569 sq mi (475,442 sq km)
Coastline: 250 mi (402 km)
Land use: Woodlands cover more than 78% of the country, about 15% of the land is under agricultural cultivation, and 4% is meadows and pastures.
Climate: Tropical in the south; drier in the north, with greater fluctuations in temperature
Population: 15,456,000
Urban population: 44%
Rate of natural increase: 2.7%
Age structure: 44% under 15; 4% over 65
Birth rate: 39.4/1000
Death rate: 12.4/1000
Infant mortality rate: 77/1000
Fertility rate: 5.2
Life expectancy at birth: 53 years (male); 56 years (female)
Religion: Indigenous beliefs, Christian, Muslim
Language: French, English (both official), many African languages
Ethnic Divisions: Some 200 ethnic groups, including Cameroon Highlanders, Equatorial Bantu, Kirdi, and Fulani
Literacy Rate: 63%

Government: Unitary Republic, with an elected president and a unicameral legislature, the 180-member National Assembly. The president and National Assembly members are elected to seven-year and five-year terms, respectively.There are ten administrative provinces.
Armed services: 22,100 troops (1997 est.) in the army, navy, and air force
Suffrage: Universal; 21 years old
Economy: Cameroon's stable export-based economy was derailed when prices for coffee, cocoa, and petroleum dropped in the late 1980s. Reforms have been hindered by corruption within the government and political instability; in 1994, a devaluation of the CFA franc and other economic restructuring measures failed, but the recovery of the value of exports has since improved the economy.
Unit of currency: CFA franc; 100 centimes = 1 franc de la Communauté financière africaine (CFAF)
GDP per capita: $2,100
Inflation rate–CPI: 3% (1997 est.)
Workforce: 5,515,000 (1996 est.)
Unemployment rate: 5.8% (1985 est.)
Exports: Goods worth $1.9 billion (f.o.b., 1996 est.) are sent to the European Union (especially France), African countries, and the U.S.; exports include crude oil, petroleum products, lumber, cocoa beans, rubber, aluminum, coffee, and cotton.
Imports: Goods worth $1.5 billion (f.o.b., 1996 est.) are received from France, Germany, and the U.S.; imports include machinery, electrical equipment, food, consumer goods, transportation equipment, and petroleum products.
Agriculture: An estimated 68% (1996) of the labor force is involved in agricultural production for export and for domestic consumption. Leading export crops include coffee,

cocoa, and cotton; subsistence production includes roots, bananas, millet, sorghum, and livestock.

Energy: Cameroon's energy is derived largely from hydroelectric power.

Natural Resources: Minerals, including petroleum, limestone, natural gas, bauxite, iron, uranium, tin; timber and hydropower

Environmental Issues: Waterbourne disease, deforestation, desertification, overgrazing, poaching, overfishing

Transportation: About 690 miles (1,100 km) of railroads and 21,300 miles (34,300 km) of roads cross the country, of which about 12% are paved. Several river and ocean ports handle domestic and international cargo; the main port is Bonaberi. International airports are located at Douala, Garoua, and Yaoundé.

Communications: The government publishes the country's one daily newspaper; there are about 40 other weekly papers and periodicals. There are 309,000 televisions, 1.9 million radios, and 57,000 telephones (1994 est.).

Tourism: About 84,000 visitors in 1994, drawn by the beaches, national parks, wildlife, and cultural diversity of the Cameroon people, brought an estimated $49 million (U.S.) to Cameroon's economy.

Embassy in U.S.: (202) 265-8790

Public Holidays: Youth Day (February 11); End of Ramadan (date varies, in February); Good Friday (date varies, in March or April); Easter Monday (date varies, in March or April); Festival of Sheep (date varies, in April); Ascension Day (date varies, in May); Labor Day (May 1); National Day (May 20); Reunification Day (December 10); Christmas (December 25)

Canada

Country Name: Canada

Official Name: Canada

Nationality: Canadian(s) (noun); Canadian (adjective)

Capital: Ottawa, pop. 314,000 [1,039,000]

Major cities: Toronto, Montreal, Vancouver, Edmonton, Calgary

External Territories: None

Location: The second largest country in the world in area (after Russia), Canada, in North America, is bordered on the south by the coterminous United States, on the east by the Atlantic Ocean, on the west by the Pacific Ocean and by the U.S. state of Alaska, and on the north by the Arctic Ocean.

Physical Geography: The Coast Mountain and Rocky Mountains make up much of Canada's west, vast prairies cover the interior, and lowlands border the Great Lakes and St. Lawrence River. Baffin Island, above the Arctic Circle, and Ellesmere Island are two of the largest islands in the Arctic Ocean. The Atlantic provinces are generally hilly.

Total area: 3,849,670 sq mi (9,970,610 sq km)

Coastline: 151,394 mi (243,645 km)

Land use: Estimates of forest and woodland cover over half of Canada's land use. 5% of the land is used for agriculture, and 3% is meadows and pastures.

Climate: Varies from a moist maritime climate along the southwest coast to continental climates with extremes in temperatures in the interior; generally very cold winters; in the far north, temperatures often remain below freezing even in summer; high humidity in the southeast

Population: 30,589,000

Urban population: 77%

Rate of natural increase: 0.43%

Age structure: 20% under 15; 12% over 65

Birth rate: 11.49/1000

Death rate: 7.2/1000

Infant mortality rate: 5.6/1000

Fertility rate: 1.5

Life expectancy at birth: 76 years (male); 82 years (female)

Religion: Roman Catholic, Protestant

Language: English, French (both official)

Ethnic Divisions: British, French, other European origin, Native American, Asian

Literacy Rate: 97%

Government: Federal state, with a bicameral Parliament, the 104-member Senate and 301-member House of Commons. House members are elected to five-year terms, and Senate members are appointed by the governor-general, who in turn is appointed by the British monarch at the advice of the Canadian prime minister. There are ten provinces and three territories.

Armed services: 123,200 troops (1997 est.) in the army, navy, air force, other branches; voluntary

Suffrage: Universal; 18 years old

Economy: The growth of Canada's diverse, free-market economy based on abundant natural resources and modern technology has been affected by unemployment, inflation, debt, and questions about the political future of Quebec. Much of the economy is based on the export of raw materials that are subject to fluctuations in world prices. Canada is one of the richest countries in the world.

Unit of currency: Canadian dollar; 100 cents = 1 Canadian dollar (C$ or Can$)

CANADA BLAZING A CONTINENTAL (T)RAIL

The Canadian Pacific Railroad was the key to opening up the vastness of the country's interior to farming and other development. Begun in 1876, it was completed in Revelstoke, British Columbia, in 1885. The cities of Winnipeg and Regina grew because of the railway's presence. Today the system—which no longer carries passengers—traverses 19,000 miles through 80 tunnels and across 3,000 bridges. A 9.1-mile route through Mount Macdonald opened in 1989. Banff National Park, Canada's first, was created in 1885 after the railroad opened up the area.

GDP per capita: $21,700

Inflation rate–CPI: 1.8% (1997)

Workforce: 15,300,000 (1997)

Unemployment rate: 8.6% (1997)

Exports: Goods worth $208.6 billion (f.o.b., 1997 est.) are sent to the U.S., Japan, the U.K., Germany, South Korea, the Netherlands, and China; exports include crude petroleum, natural gas, aluminum, motor vehicles and parts, telecommunications equipment, machinery, and wood products such as newsprint, pulp, and timber.

Imports: Goods worth $194.4 billion (c.i.f., 1997 est.) are received from the U.S., Japan, the U.K., Germany, France, Mexico, Taiwan, and South Korea; imports include crude oil, chemicals, motor vehicles and parts, durable consumer goods, computers, and telecommunications equipment.

Agriculture: About 3% of the workforce engages in agriculture, forestry, and fishing. Wheat, barley, timber, dairy products, and fish are significant exports.

Energy: Nearly 70% (1985) of Canada's energy is generated by hydropower; coal-fired plants and nuclear power stations are also in use. Canada exports energy to the U.S.

Natural Resources: Minerals, including zinc, nickel, potash, petroleum, gold, and silver; fish and timber

Environmental Issues: Air pollution, water pollution, acid rain, soil degradation from industrial activities

Transportation: Canada is well served by a vast network of an estimated 634,040 miles (1,020,3900 km) of roads, more than 72,960 miles (117,420 km) of rail, and domestic and international airports throughout the country. The St. Lawrence Seaway and the Great Lakes provide access to ocean-going vessels from the Atlantic for domestic and international cargo to ports at Quebec, Montreal, Toronto, and Thunder Bay. Vancouver is an important international seaport on the west coast and east coast seaports include Halifax, St. John's, and Churchill.

Communications: Communications systems are generally excellent throughout the country, with an array of local and national television stations, radio stations, and newspapers. Phone service is also widely available.

Tourism: Visitors come to such eastern cities as Quebec, Ottawa, and Montreal, and the rugged Atlantic coast; in the west, the Canadian Rockies, the Pacific coast, Vancouver, and the wilds of the Yukon Territory are popular draws.

17.3 million tourists came to Canada in 1996.

U.S. Tourist Office: Canadian Tourism Commission (888) 456-5555: Alberta: (800) 661-8888; British Columbia: (800) 663-6000; Manitoba: (800) 665-0040; New Brunswick: (800) 561-0123; Newfoundland: (800) 563-6353; Northwest Territories: (800) 661-0494; Nova Scotia: (800) 565-0000; Nunavut (800) 491-7910; Ontario: (800) 668-2746; Prince Edward Island: (888) 734-7529; Quebec: (800) 363-7777; Saskatchewan: (877) 237-2273; Yukon Territory: (403) 667-5340

Embassy in U.S.: (202) 682-1740

Public Holidays: Good Friday (date varies, in March or April); Easter Monday (date varies, in March or April); Victoria Day (date varies, in May); Canada Day: independence from Britain, 1867 (July 1); Labor Day (date varies, in September); Thanksgiving (date varies, in October); Remembrance Day (November 11); Christmas (December 25); Boxing Day (December 26)

Cape Verde

Country Name: Cape Verde

Official Name: Republic of Cape Verde

Nationality: Cape Verdeans(s) (noun); Cape Verdean (adjective)

Capital: Praia, pop. 61,600

Major cities: Mindelo, São Filipe

External Territories: None

Location: Cape Verde is made up of a group of 15 islands in the North Atlantic Ocean about 310 miles off the coast of Senegal in west Africa.

Physical Geography: Cape Verde is comprised of mountainous, mostly barren volcanic islands.

Total area: 1,557 sq mi (4,033 sq km)

Coastline: 599 mi (965 km)

Land use: About 11% of the land is used for agriculture, 6% is meadows and pastures, and less than 1% is wooded.

Climate: Warm and arid, with periodic droughts

Population: 406,000

Urban population: 44%

Rate of natural increase: 2.8%

Age structure: 45% under 15; 6% over 65

Birth rate: 36.49/1000

Death rate: 7.58/1000

Infant mortality rate: 51.58/1000

Fertility rate: 5.3

Life expectancy at birth: 66 years (male); 73 years (female)

Religion: Roman Catholic fused with indigenous beliefs

Language: Portuguese, Crioulo

Ethnic Divisions: Creole, African

Literacy Rate: 72%

Government: Republic, with an elected president and a unicameral legislative body, the 72-member People's National Assembly. The president and deputies of the National Assembly are elected to five-year terms. There are 14 administrative districts.

Armed services: 1,100 troops (1997 est.) in the army and air force; selective conscription

Suffrage: Universal; 18 years old

Economy: Remittances from citizens working abroad and foreign aid have been vital in keeping the Cape Verde economy afloat. Extended droughts severely affect agricultural production; more than 85% of the country's food is imported. Plans to expand tourist facilities and offshore banking and financial services have been in place since 1990.

Unit of currency: Cape Verde escudo; 100 centavos = 1 Cape Verde escudo (CVEsc)

GDP per capita: $1,370

Inflation rate–CPI: 6.2% (1996 est.)

Workforce: 120,600 (1990 est.)

Unemployment rate: 26% (1990 est.)

Exports: Goods worth $12.8 million (f.o.b., 1996 est.) are sent to France, Portugal, Spain, and the U.S.; crustaceans and fish provide about half of Cape Verde's export value; 25% of value is from shoes and garments.

Imports: Goods worth $237 million (f.o.b., 1996 est.) are received from Portugal, the Netherlands and France; imports include food, beverages, vegetable products, and minerals, including petroleum and petroleum products.

Agriculture: About 40% (1994) of the labor force engages in agriculture and fishing. Export products include lobsters and tuna as well as bananas; subsistence crops include corn, beans, potatoes, cassava, and coconuts.

Energy: Most energy is obtained from hydropower and natural gas; some mineral fuels are imported.

Natural Resources: Salt, basalt rock, pozzuolana (volcanic ash), limestone, kaolin, fish

Environmental Issues: Soil erosion from overgrazing and cultivation on steep slopes, desertification, deforestation, habitat loss

Transportation: There were 2,860 passenger cars (1995 est.) using the 680 miles (1,100 km) of roads. There are no railroads. The main islands have domestic airports, and the airport at Espargos on Sal handles international flights and another is under construction at Santiago. Cruise and cargo ships call at Mindelo and Praia; other ports are under construction.

Communications: Broadcasts from one television station and several radio stations are received by

1,000 televisions and 67,000 radios (1994 est.). There are 21,500 telephones (1995 est.). Two daily papers are published.

Tourism: Mountain scenery and sandy beaches are prime attractions in Cape Verde, as are sailing, fishing, windsurfing, and hiking.

Embassy in U.S.: (202) 965-6820

Public Holidays: National Heroes' Day (January 20); Labor Day (May 1); Independence Day: from Portugal, 1975 (July 5); Assumption (date varies, in August); All Saints' Day (November 1); Christmas (December 25)

Central African Republic

Country Name: Central African Republic

Official Name: Central African Republic

Nationality: Central African(s) (noun); Central African (adjective)

Capital: Bangui, pop. 524,000

Major cities: Berbérati, Bouar, Bambari

External Territories: None

Location: The Central African Republic, landlocked in equatorial Africa, is bordered on the northeast by Sudan, on the south by the Democratic Republic of the Congo and Congo, on the southwest by Cameroon, and on the northwest by Chad.

Physical Geography: The Central African Republic's low plateau is covered by vast areas of forests and savanna.

Total area: 240,535 sq mi (622,984 sq km)

Coastline: None

Land use: About 75% of the country is forested, 5% is meadows and pastures, and 3% is used for agriculture.

Climate: Tropical, with heavy rains from March to October; heavier precipitation in the south and southwest

Population: 3,445,000

Urban population: 39%

Rate of natural increase: 2.14%

Age structure: 44% under 15; 4% over 65

Birth rate: 38.4/1000

Death rate: 17/1000

Infant mortality rate: 96.9/1000

Fertility rate: 5.1

Life expectancy at birth: 44 years (male); 48 years (female)

Religion: Indigenous beliefs, Protestant, Roman Catholic, Muslim

Language: French, Sango, Arabic, Hunsa, Swahili

Ethnic Divisions: Baya, Banda, Mandjia, Sara

Literacy Rate: 60%

Government: Republic, with an elected president and an 85-member National Assembly with other advisory councils. The president and National Assembly members are elected to terms of six years and five years, respectively. There are 16 administrative prefectures.

Armed services: 2,650 troops (1996) in the army and air force; selective two-year service; France also has troops in the country.

Suffrage: Universal; 21 years old

Economy: Although the Central African Republic has valuable natural resources such as timber and diamonds, the country's economy is sustained by subsistence agriculture and foreign assistance. The 1994 devaluation of the CFA franc led to a sharp rise in consumer prices; government programs to revamp investment regulations and reform civil

service programs have been announced, but the mostly unskilled workforce and inadequate infrastructure impede economic progress.

Unit of currency: CFA franc; 100 centimes = 1 franc de la Communauté financière africaine (CFAF)

GDP per capita: $1,000

Inflation rate–CPI: 4% (1996 est.)

Workforce: 1,611,000 (1996 est.)

Unemployment rate: 6% (1993)

Exports: Goods worth $171 million (f.o.b., 1995) are sent to France, Belgium, Luxembourg, Switzerland, Sudan, and Spain; exports include diamonds, timber, cotton, and coffee.

Imports: Goods worth $174 million (f.o.b., 1995.) are received from France, other European Union members, Japan, Cameroon, and Zaire; imports include food, textiles, petroleum, machinery, vehicles, and chemicals.

Agriculture: Almost 80% (1996) of the workforce engages in agriculture, raising coffee, cotton, livestock, and tobacco for cash, and cassava and yams for domestic consumption.

Energy: Most of the country's energy needs are met by domestic hydropower production; some fuel is imported.

Natural Resources: Minerals, including diamonds, gold, uranium, iron, copper, manganese; timber

Environmental Issues: Contaminated tap water, wildlife poaching, desertification

Transportation: The country has about 14,790 miles (23,810 km) of roads, most of which are unpaved; there are no railways. There are about 500 miles (800 km) of navigable rivers, including stretches of the Oubangui and Sangha. Bangui on the Oubangui and Salo on the Sangha are river ports, and other ports are being planned. About four dozen airports handle domestic flights , and the airport at Bangui handles international flights.

Communications: One daily paper, with a circulation of about 2,000, is published in Bangui. There are 235,000 radios in the country and 16,000 televisions (1994 est.); there are two radio stations and at least one television station. Telephone service is fair; there are 16,900 phones in service (1992 est.).

Tourism: In 1994, tourists brought an estimated $6 million (U.S.) to the country, attracted by the scenery, wildlife, hunting, and fishing.

Embassy in U.S.: (202) 483-7800

Public Holidays: Anniversary of the 1959 death of Barthélemy Boganda, first prime minister (March 29); Easter Monday (date varies, in March or April); Ascension Day (date varies, in May); Whit Monday (date varies, in May); May Day (May 1); National Day of Prayer (June 30); Independence Day (August 13); Assumption (August 15); All Saints' Day (November 1); National Day (December 1); Christmas (December 25)

Chad

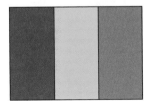

Country Name: Chad

Official Name: Republic of Chad

Nationality: Chadian(s) (noun); Chadian (adjective)

Capital: N'Djamena, pop. 531,000

Major cities: Sarh, Moundou, Abéché

External Territories: None

Location: Chad, in northwestern Africa, is bordered on the north by Libya, on the east by Sudan, on the south by the Central African Republic, and on the west by Cameroon, Nigeria, and Niger.

Physical Geography: The Sahara covers much of the northern half of the country; savanna separates the desert region from the tropical south. Lake Chad, on the country's southwest border, varies seasonally in area from about 3,800 square miles (9,842 sq km) to about 9,900 square miles (25,641 sq km); it is one of the largest inland deltas in the world.

Total area: 495,755 sq mi (1,284,000 sq km)

Coastline: None

Land use: Only 3% of the land is used for agriculture. Estimates of forest and woodland vary from 10% to 25% and about 36% is meadows and pastures.

Climate: Hot, arid conditions in the desert north; semiarid in the south-central region; tropical in the south

Population: 7,714,000

Urban population: 22%

Rate of natural increase: 3.29%

Age structure: 44% under 15; 3% over 65

Birth rate: 50/1000

Death rate: 17.1/1000

Infant mortality rate: 123/1000

Fertility rate: 6.6

Life expectancy at birth: 45 years (male); 50 years (female)

Religion: Muslim, Christian, indigenous beliefs

Language: French, Arabic (both official), Sara, Sango, many African languages

Ethnic Divisions: Sara, many others

Literacy Rate: 48%

Government: Republic, with transitional provisions in effect. There are 14 administrative prefectures.

Armed services: 30,350 (1996 est.); troops selected by conscription for a three-year tour of duty

Suffrage: Universal; 18 years old

Economy: Chad's economy has been hindered by civil war since independence from France in 1960, an inadequate infrastructure, external debt, international fluctuations in the prices of the cotton (the main cash crop), and drought. Attempts to control the economy with austerity measures have led to public strikes, and currency devaluation in 1994 pushed up inflation rates; foreign assistance is key to Chad's financial survival. The international community is working with Chad to improve economic growth and development.

Unit of currency: CFA franc; 100 centimes = 1 franc de la Communauté financière africaine (CFAF)

GDP per capita $600

Inflation rate–CPI: 15 % (1997 est.)

Workforce: 3,161,000 (1996 est.) .

Unemployment rate: N.A.

Exports: Goods worth $259 million (f.o.b., 1996 est.) are sent to France, Nigeria, Cameroon, and other African trading partners; exports include cotton, cattle, textiles, and fish.

Imports: Goods worth $301 million (f.o.b., 1996 est.) are received from the U.S., France, Nigeria, Cameroon, Italy, and Germany; imports include machinery and transportation equipment, industrial goods, petroleum products, food, pharmaceuticals, and chemicals.

Agriculture: More than three-quarters (1996) of the workforce engages in agriculture and fishing; cotton, the main cash crop, provides half the value of all exports. Livestock and fish from Lake Chad are also exported; millet, sorghum, and peanuts are produced for domestic consumption.

Energy: Forests have been significantly reduced by the use of wood for fuel. Chad imports petroleum to meet most of its energy requirements.

Natural Resources: Minerals, including petroleum, uranium, natron, kaolin; fish from Lake Chad

Environmental Issues: Inadequate potable water, water and soil pollution, desertification, deforestation

Transportation: There are no railroads in Chad. There are about 20,300 miles (32,700 km) of roads with an additional 12,420 miles (20,000 km) of tracks that are passable during the October to July dry season. International flights arrive at N'Djamena, and many smaller airfields throughout the country handle domestic traffic. There are about 1,240 miles (2,000 km) of navigable water on rivers such as the Chari and Logone.

Communications: One daily newspaper has a circulation of about 2,000. There are 5,000 telephones (1994 est.) and minimal service. There are 1.5 million radios and 9,000 televisions (1994 est.).

Tourism: In the north, tourists can visit prehistoric rock paintings and engravings; wildlife in the southern part of the country and traditional arts such as basket weaving and metalworking also draw visitors. In 1994, 19,000 visitors brought an estimated $36 million (U.S.) to the economy.

Embassy in U.S.: (202) 462-4009

Public Holidays: End of Ramadan (date varies, in February); Easter Monday (date varies, in March or April); Feast of the Sacrifice (date varies, in April); Whit Monday (date varies, in May); Labor Day (May 1); Liberation of Africa Day: recognizes foundation of Organization of African Unity, 1963 (May 25); Birth of the Prophet (date varies in July); Independence Day: from France, 1960 (August 11); Assumption (August 15); All Saints' Day (November 1); Proclamation of the Republic, 1958 (November 28); Christmas (December 25)

Chile

Country Name: Chile
Official Name: Republic of Chile
Nationality: Chilean(s) (noun); Chilean (adjective)
Capital: Santiago, pop. [4,640,000]
Major cities: Concepción, Viña del Mar, Puente Alto, Valparaíso
External Territories: None
Location: Chile, on the Pacific coast of South America, is bordered on the north by Peru and on the east by Bolivia and Argentina. Easter Island is 2,347 miles (3,780 km) to the west.
Physical Geography: Chile stretches narrowly about 2,650 miles (4,265 km) from the Atacama Desert in the north to Cape Horn and islands in the South Atlantic Ocean. The country is only 217 miles (350 km) at its widest: west from the Pacific coast to the rugged, high peaks of the Andes on its eastern boundary. The central part of the country is a fertile valley dotted with lakes.
Total area: 292,135 sq mi (756,626 sq km)
Coastline: 3,996 mi (6,435 km)
Land use: About 20% of the land is forested, 15% to 20% is meadows and pastures, and about 5% is cultivated.
Climate: Precipitation increases from north to south: the Atacama Desert receives almost no rainfall and the southern islands receive more than 160 inches of rain a year; mild, rainy winters and dry summers in the central valley
Population: 15,018,000
Urban population: 85%

Rate of natural increase: 1.4%
Age structure: 29% under 15; 7% over 65
Birth rate: 19.9/1000
Death rate: 5.6/1000
Infant mortality rate: 11.7/1000
Fertility rate: 2.4
Life expectancy at birth: 72 years (male); 78 years (female)
Religion: Roman Catholic, Protestant
Language: Spanish
Ethnic Divisions: Mestizo, white, Indian
Literacy Rate: 95%
Government: Republic, with a president and a bicameral legislature, the National Congress. The president is directly elected for a six-year term; the 48 Senate members are both appointed and elected to eight-year terms, and the 120 members of the Chamber of Deputies are elected to four-year terms. Twelve regions and one metropolitan area are designated as administrative areas.
Armed services: 94,300 (1997) in the army, navy, and air force; navy and air force enlistments are twenty-two months and army is one year; compulsory for men 19 years old
Suffrage: Universal and compulsory; 18 years old
Economy: Chile's free-market economy has privately-owned and state-owned businesses. The economy is relatively stable and has grown steadily in the past several years due to the government's conservative fiscal stance. There has also been a significant level of debt reduction. Economic diversification and foreign investment have been encouraged, but copper, whose price fluctuates on the world market, remains the key to the economy's health.
Unit of currency: Chilean peso; 100 centavos = 1 Chilean peso (Ch$)
GDP per capita: $11,600
Inflation rate–CPI: 6.0% (1997)
Workforce: 5.7 million (1997 est.)

Unemployment rate: 6.1% (1997 est.)
Exports: Goods worth $16.9 billion (f.o.b., 1997) are sent to Asia, the EU, other Latin American countries, and the U.S.; exports include copper (37% of the value of Chile's total exports) and other metals and minerals, fish, fruits, and wood products.
Imports: Goods worth $18.2 billion (f.o.b., 1997) are received from other Latin American countries, the U.S., the EU, and Asia; imports include capital goods, spare parts, raw materials, petroleum, and foodstuffs.
Agriculture: Chile is mostly self-sufficient; 33.8% of the workforce (1990 est.) engages in agriculture, forestry, and fishing. Agricultural exports include fruits and vegetables, seafood, and timber products, and Chile's export of wine continues to increase.
Energy: About 9% (1995) of Chile's energy is generated with imported petroleum. Domestic hydropower, coal, and natural gas are also used to generate energy.
Natural Resources: Minerals, including copper (Chile is the world's largest producer of copper), gold, silver, iron ore, nitrates, and others; timber and seafood
Environmental Issues: Air and water pollution, deforestation, soil erosion, desertification
Transportation: The railroad, primarily state-owned, has about 4,230 miles (6,800 km) of track and there are nearly 49,680 miles (80,000 km) of roads, including 2,150 miles (3,460 km) of the Pan-American Highway. An estimated 90% (1995) of the country's exports are shipped from such Pacific ports as Valparaíso, Talcahuano, Antofagasta, San Antonio, and Arica. There are international airports at Santiago and Arica and nearly 350 airfields throughout the country.
Communications: Many of the major cities have daily newspapers. There are 4.8 million radios and

2.9 million televisions in the country, with nearly 175 radio stations and 135 television stations (1994 est.). Telephone service is good, with an estimated 1.5 million lines in operation.

Tourism: Ski areas in the Andes west of Santiago are popular, as are Pacific beaches; Easter Island and islands in the south also attract tourists.

Embassy in U.S.: (202) 785-1746

Public Holidays: Good Friday (date varies, in March or April); Easter Saturday (date varies, in March or April); Labor Day (May 1); Battle of Iquique: with Peru, 1879 (May 21); Assumption (August 15); 1973 coup anniversary (September 11); Independence Day: from Spain, 1818 (September 18); Day of the Race: anniversary of the discovery of America (October 12); All Saints' Day (November 1); Immaculate Conception (December 8); Christmas (December 25)

China

Country Name: China

Official Name: People's Republic of China

Nationality: Chinese (singular and plural noun); Chinese (adjective)

Capital: Beijing, pop. 7,362,400

Major cities: More than 40 Chinese cities have populations estimated at 1 million or more (1990); the largest are Beijing, Shanghai, Tianjin, Shenyang, Wuhan, Guangzhou, Chongqing, Harbin, Chengdu, and Xi'an. Hong Kong became part of the country in July 1997.

CHINA LOVELY LI RIVER LANDSCAPES

The dreamlike landscape so often seen in books and films about China—green rivers and jagged limestone peaks—is near the city of Guilin, on the Li River in subtropical southeastern China. The peaks are karst formations that rose millions of years ago from the limestone seabed. The area is popular with tourists, who also visit the many interesting caves in the area.

External Territories: China claims Taiwan as its 23rd province. Taiwan maintains that there is only one China—but two political entities.

Location: China, in eastern Asia, is the third largest country in the world in land area, after Russia and Canada. It is bordered on the north by Mongolia and Russia; on the east by North Korea and the Pacific Ocean; on the south by Macau, Vietnam, Laos, Myanmar, India, Bhutan, and Nepal; and on the west by Pakistan, Afghanistan, Tajikistan, Kyrgyzstan, and Kazakhstan.

Physical Geography: Three general topographic regions are found in China. The Tibetan Plateau, in the southwest, is sometimes called "the roof of the world." The world's highest mountain, Mount Everest at 29,028 feet (8,848 meters), is on the border with Nepal. Arid uplands in the northwest contain deserts, such as the Taklimakan and part of the Gobi, and two large basins, the Tarim and Dzungarian. Plains and lowlands in the east are interspersed with several mountain chains and plateaus.

Total area: 3,705,829 sq mi (9,598,053 sq km) (including Hong Kong)

Coastline: 9,062 mi (14,500 km)

Land use: Between 30% and 40% is meadows and pastures, about 14% is forested, and an estimated 10% is used for agriculture.

Climate: Varies widely, with rainfall generally decreasing from east to west; tropical conditions in the southeastern coastal areas; temper-

atures stay cool even in the summer in the southwest; coldest winter temperatures are in the northeast

Population: 1,254,062,000 (including Hong Kong; 6.4 million)

Urban population: 30%

Rate of natural increase: 1.0%

Age structure: 26% under 15; 7% over 65

Birth rate: 16/1000

Death rate: 7/1000

Infant mortality rate: 31/1000

Fertility rate: 1.8

Life expectancy at birth: 69 years (male); 73 years (female)

Religion: Buddhist, Daoism, Muslim

Language: Mandarin-Chinese , many other dialects

Ethnic Divisions: Han Chinese, 55 minorities

Literacy Rate: 82%

Government: One-party republic; a unicameral legislature, the National People's Congress, has almost 3,000 deputies who are elected indirectly for five-year terms by provinces, autonomous regions, and municipalities. The State Council, appointed by the National People's Congress, holds executive power. For administrative purposes, there are twenty-three provinces, five autonomous regions, four municipalities, and one special administrative region.

Armed services: 2,935,000 regular troops and 1,275,000 conscripts (1996) in the army, navy, marines, and air force; selective conscription for four years in the air force and navy and three years in the army and marines

Suffrage: Universal; 18 years old

Economy: Reforms begun in the late 1970s have attracted foreign investments, introduced market-driven production, and established diverse international commercial links. As a result, economic growth has taken place in excess of the government's expectations. Government plans continue to emphasize growth, reduce inflation, and reform unprofitable state enterprises. Attempts are being made to distribute economic growth more evenly throughout the country by encouraging development in the interior. The addition of Hong Kong's wealth as a financial center and port in July 1997 should boost the economy.

Unit of currency: Yuan; 100 fen = 10 jiao = 1 renminbiao (People's Bank dollar, a yuan) (Y)

GDP per capita: $3,460

Inflation rate–CPI 2.8% (1997 est.)

Workforce: 623.9 million (1995 est.)

Unemployment rate: Urban workforce: 4% (1996 est.); rural workforce: between 60 and 100 million (1995 est.)

Exports: Goods worth $182.7 billion (f.o.b., 1997 est.) are sent to Hong Kong, Japan, the U.S., Germany, South Korea, and Singapore; exports include clothing and textiles, toys, and machinery.

Imports: Goods worth $142.4 billion (c.i.f., 1996 est.) are received from Japan, Taiwan, the U.S., Hong Kong, South Korea, and Germany; imports include cotton and yarn, mineral fuels, fabrics, mechanical appliances, electrical machinery.

Agriculture: Nearly 53% (1994) of the workforce engages in agriculture, forestry, and fishing; rice, accounting for one-third (1994) of the world's total harvest, is the main crop; peanuts, potatoes, wheat, sorghum, tea, millet, corn, soybeans, sugarcane cotton, and jute are also raised. China is self-sufficient in food production. The fish catch in 1993 totaled 18 million tons, the largest in the world.

Energy: China meets 75.5% (1995) of its energy requirements with domestic coal; the country also utilizes oil, hydropower, and natural gas.

Natural Resources: Coal, iron ore, oil, mercury, tin, tungsten, antimony, manganese, and other minerals; hydropower

Environmental Issues: Air, water, and soil pollution; water shortages; deforestation; desertification; trade in endangered animals

Transportation: Extensive transportation networks service much of the country, with 33,907 miles (54,600 km) of railroad track and 718,497 miles (1,157,000 km) of roads, most of them paved. There are 68,683 miles (110,600 km) of navigable inland waterways, including the Chang Jiang (Yangtze) and Zhu (Pearl) Rivers. Important seaports include Hong Kong, Dalian, Shanghai, Ningbo, and Guangzhou. There are about 200 airports and airfields throughout the country with major international service at Hong Kong, Beijing, Shanghai, Xi'an, and Guangzhou.

Communications: More than 70 daily papers are published in the country. There are 1,200 radio stations and 200 television stations (1995 est.), including 500 cable television stations, a few satellite services, and a state-run network television station. There are 216.9 million radios (1993) and 75 million televisions (1992 est.).

Tourism: The Great Wall of China, the historical treasures of Beijing, the terra-cotta warriors at Xi'an, and the gradual opening of Tibet are just a few of the enticements bringing visitors to China. Group tours are available, and many tourist hotels have been built in recent years. In 1996, nearly 51.1 million tourists brought an estimated $10.2 million (U.S.) to the economy.

U.S. Tourist Office: (212) 760-9700; (818) 545-7505

Embassy in U.S.: (202) 328-2500

Public Holidays: Lunar New Year (date varies, in February); International Women's Day (March 8); Labor Day (May 1); Army Day (August 1); Teachers' Day (September 9); National Days: proclamation of the People's Republic of China, 1949 (October 1–2)

Colombia

Country Name: Colombia

Official Name: Republic of Colombia

Nationality: Colombian(s) (noun); Colombian (adjective)

Capital: Bogotá, pop. 4,945,500 [5,399,000]

Major cities: Cali, Medellín, Barranquilla, Cartagena

External Territories: None

Location: Colombia, in northwestern South America, is bordered on the northwest by Panama, on the north by the Caribbean Sea, on the east by Venezuela, on the southeast by Brazil, on the south by Peru and Ecuador, and on the west by the Pacific Ocean.

Physical Geography: Three ranges of the Andes parallel the Pacific coast and separate the eastern coastal lowlands from the grasslands and the Amazon Basin to the west.

Total area: 439,737 sq mi (1,138,914 sq km)

Coastline: 1,992 mi (3,208 km)

Land use: Almost half of the land is forested, about 40% is meadows and pastures, and 5% is used for agriculture.

Climate: Mostly tropical in the lowlands; precipitation and temperature vary with elevation

Population: 38,581,000

Urban population: 71%

Rate of natural increase: 2.0%

Age structure: 33% under 15; 4% over 65

Birth rate: 26/1000

Death rate: 5.9/1000

Infant mortality rate: 28/1000

Fertility rate: 3.0

Life expectancy at birth: 65 years (male); 73 years (female)

Religion: Roman Catholic

Language: Spanish

Ethnic Divisions: Mestizo, white, mulatto, black

Literacy Rate: 91%

Government: Republic, with a president and bicameral legislature. The president is elected for a four-year term, as are the 102 Senate members and the more than 160 members of the House of Representatives. The country is divided into 32 administrative departments and one capital district.

Armed services: 146,300 troops (1997 est.) in the army, navy, and air force; selective conscription for one- or two-year tours of duty

Suffrage: Universal and compulsory; 18 years old

Economy: Colombia's economy is growing at a steady rate. Expanded oil and gas production in the early 1990s has helped to foster growth, and government plans to restrain inflation, restructure the industrial and financial sectors, and increase foreign investment promise to sustain growth.

Unit of currency: Colombian peso; 100 centavos = 1 Colombian peso (Col$)

GDP per capita: $6,200

Inflation rate–CPI: 17.7% (1997 est.)

COLOMBIA THE MINE AT MUZO: THE REAL EMERALD CITY

About half of the world's emeralds come from mines in Colombia. Considered more valuable than diamonds and second only to rubies, emeralds are the most treasured of the beryls, minerals composed of beryllium aluminum silicate. The emerald mine at Muzo has been producing the largest and finest emeralds in the world for perhaps a thousand years. Spanish conquistadors searched for the mine and finally found it in 1558, after almost 20 years of looting emeralds from the Indians in the area.

Workforce: 16.8 million (1997 est.)

Unemployment rate: 12.2% (1997 est.)

Exports: Goods worth $11.4 billion (f.o.b., 1997 est.) are sent to the U.S., the European Community, Venezuela, and Japan; exports include petroleum, coffee, coal, bananas, and cut flowers.

Imports: Goods worth $13.5 billion (c.i.f., 1997 est.) are received from the U.S., the European Community, Japan, Venezuela, and Brazil; imports include industrial equipment, vehicles, consumer goods, chemicals, and paper products.

Agriculture: 30% (1990) of the workforce engages in agriculture, forestry, and fishing. Coffee is the principal export crop, and cocoa, sugar, bananas, tobacco, cotton, and cut flowers are also important exports. Rice, cassava, plantains, potatoes, and livestock are primary subsistence products.

Energy: Most of Colombia's energy is generated by hydropower; the country is self-sufficient in petroleum and coal.

Natural Resources: Minerals, including petroleum, natural gas, coal, nickel, emeralds, gold

Environmental Issues: Deforestation, air pollution, soil pollution

Transportation: An estimated 66,500 miles (107,000 km) of roads cross the country; the majority are unpaved. There are about 2,110 miles (3,400 km) of rail track. There

are about 8,880 miles (14,300 km) of navigable waterways on river systems such as the Magdalena, Cauca, and Atrato. International seaports are located at Buenaventura on the Pacific coast and Santa Marta, Barranquilla, and Cartagena on the Caribbean. There are international airports in almost a dozen cities, including Bogotá, Medellín, Cali, and Cartagena.

Communications: Most major cities have daily newspapers, and a modern telephone system has 3.9 million lines (1986 est.). There are an estimated 6.1 million radios and 4.1 million televisions (1994 est.).

Tourism: Caribbean beaches and Amazon forests lure many tourists, while others visit pre-Columbian sites and colonial cities such as Cartagena. In 1996, 1.25 million tourists visited Columbia.

U.S. Tourist Office: (202) 868-7752

Embassy in U.S.: (202) 387-8338

Public Holidays: Epiphany (date varies, in January); St. Joseph's Day (date varies, in March); Maundy Thursday (date varies, in March or April); Good Friday (date varies, in March or April); Ascension Day (date varies, in May); Labor Day (May 1); Corpus Christi (date varies, in June); Saints Peter and Paul (date varies, in July); Independence Day: from Spain, 1810 (July 20); Battle of Boyacá, 1819 (August 7); Assumption (date varies, in August); Discovery of America (date varies, in

October); All Saints' Day (date varies, in November); Immaculate Conception (December 8); Christmas (December 25)

Comoros

Country Name: Comoros

Official Name: Federal Islamic Republic of the Comoros

Nationality: Comoran(s) (noun); Comoran (adjective)

Capital: Moroni, pop. 30,000

Major cities: Mutsamudu, Fomboni

External Territories: None

Location: Three main islands comprise Comoros, which is in the Mozambique Channel between Madagascar and Mozambique on the southeast African coast.

Physical Geography: The Comoros islands are volcanic with some forest.

Total area: 719 sq mi (1,862 sq km)

Coastline: 211 mi (340 km)

Land use: About 35% of the land is arable and 10% is under permanent cultivation; 18% is forested and 7% is meadows and pastures.

Climate: Tropical, with a dry season from May through October and a hot rainy season from November through April

Population: 563,000

Urban population: 29%

Rate of natural increase: 2.78%

Age structure: 42% under 15; 3% over 65

Birth rate: 37.6/1000

Death rate: 9.8/1000

Infant mortality rate: 77.3/1000

Fertility rate: 5.1

Life expectancy at birth: 57 years (male); 62 years (female)

Religion: Sunni Muslim, Roman Catholic

Language: Arabic, French (both official), Comoran

Ethnic Divisions: Anatalote, Cafre, Makoa, Oimatsha, Sakalawa

Literacy Rate: 57%

Government: Independent Republic, with a president and unicameral legislature. The president and members of the 42-seat Federal Assembly are directly elected for five-year terms. Three islands make up the administrative districts.

Armed services: 1,500 troops (1997)

Suffrage: Universal; 18 years old

Economy: Foreign assistance is essential to the economic survival of the Comoros, an agricultural country that is not self-sufficient in food production. Strict government measures to control public spending have resulted in serious unrest, and political instability in the early 1990s hindered the establishment of sound financial procedures and economic development plans.

Unit of currency: Comoroan franc; 100 centimes = 1 Comoran franc

GDP per capita: $685

Inflation rate–CPI: 3.5% (1996)

Workforce: 126,510 (1991)

Unemployment rate: 20% (1996 est.)

Exports: Goods worth $11.4 million (f.o.b., 1996 est.) are sent to France, the U.S., and Germany; exports include vanilla, ylang-ylang (an essence for perfumes), perfume oil, cloves, and copra.

Imports: Goods worth $70 million (f.o.b., 1996 est.) are received from France, South Africa, Kenya, and Singapore; imports included rice and other foods, petroleum, consumer goods, iron and steel, and cement.

Agriculture: An estimated 75% (1996) of the workforce engages in agriculture, fishing, and forestry. Export crops include vanilla, ylang-ylang, cloves, and copra; subsistence crops include cassava, bananas, coconuts, and sweet potatoes.

Energy: Energy is derived from wood and thermal installations.

Natural Resources: Few natural resources

Environmental Issues: Soil erosion and degradation, deforestation

Transportation: There are no railroads. There are 550 miles (880 km) of roads. Moroni has an international airport, and there are airfields on the other islands. Moroni, Fomboni, and Mutsamudu are ports.

Communications: There are no daily newspapers; however, the government publishes a weekly paper in Moroni and one independently owned weekly is published. There are 81,000 (1994 est.) radios receiving local and international broadcasts and an estimated 200 televisions. Phone service, with 4,000 lines (1994 est.), is sparse.

Tourism: Beaches, fishing, and mountains attract tourists; in 1994,

---

COMOROS THE LIVING FOSSIL FISH

The coelacanth, which was thought to have been extinct for more than 70 million years, was discovered by the crew of a South African fishing trawler in 1938. This is the only area in the world where it is has been found alive. National Geographic supported research that located and photographed coelacanths off the west coast of Njazidja, largest island of Comoros, in 1987.

27,000 tourists brought in about $9 million (U.S.).

Embassy in U.S.: (212) 972-8010

Public Holidays: Beginning of Ramadan (date varies); End of Ramadan (date varies, in February); Feast of the Sacrifice (date varies, in April); Islamic New Year (date varies, in May); Ashura (date varies, in May); Birth of the Prophet (date varies, in July); Independence Day: from France, 1975 (July 6); Anniversary of the assassination of Ahmed Abdallah, the country's first president, 1989 (November 27); Ascension of the Prophet (date varies, in December)

Congo

Country Name: Congo

Official Name: Republic of the Congo

Nationality: Congolese (singular and plural noun); Congolese, Congo (adjective)

Capital: Brazzaville, pop. 937,600

Major cities: Pointe-Noire

External Territories: None

Location: Congo, in equatorial Africa and on the Atlantic Ocean, is between Gabon and Cameroon on the west and the Democratic Republic of the Congo on the east; the Central African Republic is on the north and Angola on the south.

Physical Geography: The coastal plain gives way to escarpments of the Crystal Mountains; beyond the escarpments are forests and savanna. The Oubangui (Ubangi) and Congo (Zaire) Rivers form the coun-

try's eastern border with the Democratic Republic of the Congo.

Total area: 132,047 sq mi (342,000 sq km)

Coastline: 105 mi (169 km)

Land use: More than 60% of the land is forest and woodland, almost 30% is meadows and pastures, and less than 1% is arable.

Climate: Tropical, with rainfall most of the year; cooler coastal areas due to the cold ocean current

Population: 2,717,000

Urban population: 41%

Rate of natural increase: 2.269%

Age structure: 43% under 15; 3% over 65

Birth rate: 39.36/1000

Death rate: 16.67/1000

Infant mortality rate: 107/1000

Fertility rate: 5.1

Life expectancy at birth: 45 years (male); 49 years (female)

Religion: Christian, animist, Muslim

Language: French, Lingala, Monokutuba, many local dialects

Ethnic Divisions: BaKongo, Sangha, Teke, Mboshi

Literacy Rate: 75%

Government: Republic, with a president and bicameral legislature. The president and the 125-member National Assembly are elected to five-year terms, and the 60 Senate members are elected to six-year terms. There are nine administrative regions and one commune. As of January 1998, a transitional advisory parliament is in place.

Armed services: 8,000 troops (1997) in the army, navy, and air force; two years of voluntary national service open to men and women

Suffrage: Universal; 18 years old

Economy: Crude oil provides about 90% of the country's income from exports. The government is making efforts to diversify the economy and increase social services for citizens. Plans have been made for industry privatization and austerity

measures, but a high external debt continues to hamper development.

Unit of currency: CFA franc; 100 centimes = 1 franc de la Communauté financière africaine (CFAF)

GDP per capita: $2,000

Inflation rate–CPI: 3% (1996 est.)

Workforce: 1,107,000 (1996 est.)

Unemployment rate: N.A.

Exports: Goods worth $1.2 billion (f.o.b., 1995 est.) are sent to the U.S., Italy, France, Spain, and other trading partners; exports include crude oil, lumber, plywood, sugar, cocoa, coffee, and diamonds.

Imports: Goods worth $670 million (f.o.b., 1995 est.) are received from France, Italy, the U.S., Japan, and other trading partners; imports include manufactured goods, construction materials, foodstuffs, and petroleum products.

Agriculture: Almost half (1996) the workforce engages in agriculture, forestry, and fishing. Coffee, cocoa, sugarcane, and oil palm are grown for export, while cassava and bananas are grown for domestic consumption. Timber provides 8.4% (1995) of value of Congo's total exports. The Congo imports food to meet domestic needs.

Energy: Most energy demands are met by hydroelectricity.

Natural Resources: Minerals, including petroleum, natural gas, lead, zinc, gold, copper, phosphate, iron, potash, bauxite; timber

Environmental Issues: Air and water pollution, potable drinking water, deforestation

Transportation: Less than 10% of the country's 7,950 miles (12,800 km) of roads are paved; there are nearly 500 miles (800 km) of railroad track. The Congo and Oubangui Rivers and their tributaries are important inland waterways for commercial and local traffic. Brazzaville, on the Oubangui, is the principal river port and has one of the two international airports in the country. Pointe-Noire, the country's principal seaport, also has an international airport.

Communications: Four daily papers are published, three in Brazzaville and one in Point-Noire. There are 21,000 telephone lines in use, as well as 290,000 radios and 18,000 televisions (1994 est.).

Tourism: Tourism brought an estimated $8 million (U.S.) to the economy in 1994. Attractions include national parks and reserves, and there are plans to expand tourist accommodations.

Embassy in U.S.: (202) 726-5500

Public Holidays: Good Friday (date varies, in March or April); Easter Monday (date varies, in March or April); Labor Day (May 1); Independence Day: from France, 1960 (August 15); Christmas (December 25)

Costa Rica

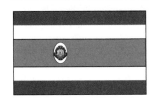

Country Name: Costa Rica
Official Name: Republic of Costa Rica
Nationality: Costa Rican(s) (noun); Costa Rican (adjective)
Capital: San José, pop. 324,000 [1,220,400]
Major cities: Puntarenas, Alajuela, Cartago
External Territories: None
Location: Costa Rica, in Central America, is between the South Pacific Ocean to the west and the Caribbean Sea to the northeast. Nicaragua is to the north and Panama to the east.
Physical Geography: Running from the northwest to the south-

east, the Cordillera Guanacaste and the Cordillera Talamanca form a continental divide. Highlands on the east slope give way to coastal plains and Caribbean beaches. The Pacific coastal strip, also with beaches, is much narrower than the Caribbean coast.
Total area: 19,730 sq mi (51,100 sq km)
Coastline: 801 mi (1,290 km)
Land use: 6% of the land is used for agriculture, 5% is in permanent crops, 46% is meadows and pastures, and 31% is forest and woodland.
Climate: Tropical along the Caribbean and Pacific coasts, with heavy rainfall especially from May to November; milder in the highlands, with less rain
Population: 3,594,000
Urban population: 45%
Rate of natural increase: 1.84%
Age structure: 33% under 15; 5% over 65
Birth rate: 22.52/1000
Death rate: 4.12/1000
Infant mortality rate: 14.2/1000
Fertility rate: 2.7
Life expectancy at birth: 75 years (male); 79 years (female)
Religion: Roman Catholic
Language: Spanish, English
Ethnic Divisions: White, (including mestizo), black, Native American, Chinese
Literacy Rate: 95%
Government: Republic, with a president and unicameral legislature, the 57 member Legislative Assembly, or Asamblea Legislativa. The members of the legislature are elected to four-year terms. There are seven administrative provinces.
Armed services: Constitution outlawed a national army in 1948; 7,000 (1997 est.) members of civil guard units and border police
Suffrage: Universal and compulsory; 18 years old

Economy: Costa Rica's economy derives the majority of its revenues from agricultural exports and tourism. In 1994, large debts forced the government into austerity measures, such as reducing the public workforce by 25,000 and reducing government spending. Other measures included pension system and tax administration reforms and the promotion of foreign investment.
Unit of currency: Costa Rican colón; colones (plural); 100 centimos = 1 Costa Rican colón (C)
GDP per capita: $5,500
Inflation rate–CPI: 11.2% (1997 est.)
Workforce: 868,300
Unemployment rate: 5.7% (1997 est.)
Exports: Goods worth $2.9 billion (f.o.b., 1996 est.) are sent to the U.S., Germany, Italy, Guatemala, El Salvador, Netherlands, UK, and France; exports include coffee, bananas, textiles, and sugar.
Imports: Goods worth $3.4 billion (c.i.f., 1996 est.) are received from the U.S., Japan, Mexico, Guatemala, Venezuela, and Germany; imports include petroleum, raw materials, and consumer goods.
Agriculture: An estimated 27% (1995) of the workforce engages in agriculture, fishing, and forestry. Crops for export include bananas, coffee, and sugar, as well as beef. Maize, rice, and beans are grown for domestic consumption.
Energy: Hydropower and imported petroleum are the two main energy sources.
Natural Resources: Hydropower potential
Environmental Issues: Deforestation, soil erosion
Transportation: An estimated 22,110 miles (35,580 km) of roads, not including 420 miles (660 km) of the Pan-American Highway, cross the country; there are 590 miles (950 km) of rail track. The main Pacific port is at Caldera and a secondary

port at Puntarenas; Puerto Limón is the main Caribbean port. There are also ports at Golfito, Moin, and Puerto Quepos. Some rivers are navigable for small craft during the rainy season. There are international airports, at San José and Liberia, and 156 regional airports throughout the country.

Communications: Five daily newspapers with a circulation of 333,000 (1994) are published. There are 364,000 telephone lines in service (1993 est.). Radios and televisions are widely distributed.

Tourism: Costa Rica promotes ecotourism to its many national parks and preserves; volcanoes and beaches are also big draws. In 1995, an estimated 792,000 tourists visited the country and added $664.4 million to the economy.

U.S. Tourist Office: (800) 327-7033

Embassy in U.S.: (202) 234-2945

Public Holidays: Feast of St. Joseph (March 19); Maundy Thursday (date varies, in March or April); Good Friday (date varies, in March or April); Anniversary of the Battle of Rivas, 1856 (April 11); Labor Day (May 1); Corpus Christi (date varies, in June); St. Peter and St. Paul (June 29); Anniversary of the annexation of Guanacaste Province (July 25); Our Lady of the Angels (August 2); Assumption (August 15); Independence Day: from Spain, 1821 (September 15); Columbus Day (October 12); Abolition of the Armed Forces Day, 1948 (December 1); Immaculate Conception (December 8); Christmas (December 25)

Côte d'Ivoire

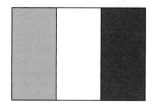

Country Name: Côte d'Ivoire

Official Name: Republic of Côte d'Ivoire

Nationality: Ivorian(s) (noun); Ivorian (adjective)

Capital: Yamoussoukro (official), pop. 106,800 [126,200]; Abidjan (administrative), pop. [2,793,000]

Major cities: Bouaké, Daloa, Korhogo

External Territories: None

Location: Côte d'Ivoire, in west Africa, is on the Atlantic Ocean between Liberia and Guinea on the west and Ghana on the east; Burkina Faso and Mali are on the north.

Physical Geography: Northern savanna gives way to tropical forests and lands cleared for agriculture. A coastal plain not more than 40 miles (64 km) wide with lagoons parallels the coast.

Total area: 124,504 sq mi (322,463 sq km)

Coastline: 320 mi (515 km)

Land use: About 22% of the land is forested, and 12% is used for agriculture. Estimates of grazing areas range from 9% to more than 40%.

Climate: Tropical; hot and humid along the coast; rainfall decreasing from south to north

Population: 15,818,000

Urban population: 46%

Rate of natural increase: 2.65%

Age structure: 43% under 15; 3% over 65

Birth rate: 42.6/1000

Death rate: 16.1/1000

Infant mortality rate: 97.7/1000

Fertility rate: 6.1

Life expectancy at birth: 45 years (male); 48 years (female)

Religion: Muslim, indigenous beliefs, Christian

Language: French, Dioula, many other African languages

Ethnic Divisions: Malinke, Baoule, Bete, Senoufou, many others

Literacy Rate: 40%

Government: Republic, with a president and unicameral legislature, the 175-member National Assembly, or Assemblée Nationale. The president and members of the National Assembly are directly elected to five-year terms. There are 16 regions subdivided into 50 administrative departments.

Armed services: 13,900 troops (1997) in the army, navy, air force, other government forces; selective conscription for six months

Suffrage: Universal; 21 years old

Economy: After several years of recession in the late 1980s, Côte d'Ivoire's economy began to pick up in 1994, in part because of rising prices for coffee and cocoa (its leading exports). The development of petroleum reserves, privatization initiatives, and growth in service industries such as banking have also given the economy a boost.

Unit of currency: CFA franc; 100 centimes = 1 franc de la Communauté financière africaine (CFAF)

GDP per capita: $1,700

Inflation rate–CPI: 3.4% (1997 est.)

Workforce: 5,098,000 (1996 est.)

Unemployment rate: N.A.

Exports: Goods worth $4.2 billion (f.o.b., 1996 are sent to France, the Netherlands, Germany, Italy, Burkina Faso, Mali, and the U.S.; exports include cocoa, coffee, tropical woods, petroleum, cotton, bananas, pineapples, palm oil, and fish.

Imports: Goods worth $3.2 billion (f.o.b., 1996) are received from France, Nigeria, Japan, the Nether-

CÔTE D'IVOIRE A COUNTRY NAMED FOR ELEPHANTS

Côte d'Ivoire (its official name until 1985 was the Ivory Coast) was named for the herds of elephants that roamed there at one time. A former French colony that achieved independence in 1960, it has been one of the more prosperous African countries. The largest Christian church in the world was completed in 1990 in Yamoussoukro. Higher than the dome of St. Peter's Basilica in Rome, the basilica of Notre Dame de la Paix was built in just three years. It can seat 7,000 people inside, with standing room for another 11,000. St. Peter's holds 50,000 people inside.

lands, the U.S., and Italy; imports include food, fuels, machinery, and chemicals.

Agriculture: Côte d'Ivoire is the world's largest producer of cocoa (1,254,000 metric tons in 1996) and among the top producers of coffee; other export crops include cotton, rubber, palm oil, timber, bananas, and pineapples. Crops for domestic consumption include yams, plantains, cassava, and rice. Just over half (1996 est.) of the workforce engages in agriculture, timber, and fishing. The government's objective is that the country becomes self-sufficient.

Energy: Hydropower, thermal power; petroleum and natural gas

Natural Resources: Minerals, including petroleum, natural gas, diamonds, gold, manganese, iron, bauxite, copper; timber

Environmental Issues: Deforestation, water pollution

Transportation: An estimated 31,300 miles (50,400 km) of roads and 410 miles (660 km) of rails cross the country; nearly 10% of the roads are paved. Abidjan and San Pedro are major seaports, and some inland waterways are also navigable. International airports are located at Abidjan, Bouaké, and Yamoussoukro, and several smaller airports serve domestic traffic.

Communications: Several daily newspapers are published. Tele-

phone access, with 108,000 lines (1994), is good. There are almost 2 million radios and about 822,000 televisions (1994); broadcasting capacities have recently expanded to include international providers.

Tourism: About 200,000 tourists brought in $66 million (U.S.) in 1994 while visiting game reserves, forests, and seeing cultural activities in Abidjan.

Embassy in U.S.: (202) 797-0300

Public Holidays: End of Ramadan (date varies, in February); Good Friday (date varies, in March or April); Easter Monday (date varies, in March or April); Feast of the Sacrifice (date varies, in April); Ascension Day (date varies, in May); Whit Monday (date varies, in May); Labor Day (May 1); National Day: fully independent from France, 1960 (August 7); Assumption (August 15); All Saints' Day (November 1); Féliz Houphouët-Boigny Remembrance Day: first president of the republic (1960–1993) (December 7); Christmas (December 25)

Croatia

Country Name: Croatia
Official Name: Republic of Croatia
Nationality: Croat(s) (noun); Croatian (adjective)
Capital: Zagreb, pop. 867,700
Major cities: Split, Rijeka, Osijek, Zadar
External Territories: None
Location: On the eastern shore of the Adriatic Sea in southeastern Europe, Croatia is bordered on the north by Slovenia and Hungary and on the east by Yugoslavia and Bosnia and Herzegovina.
Physical Geography: The Dinaric Alps parallel the Adriatic coast with its many islands, and more mountains rise in the central part of the country. The northeast has rolling hills, and eastern plains are suited for farming.
Total area: 21,829 sq mi (56,538 sq km)
Coastline: 3,596 mi (5,790 km); mainland 1,104 mi (1,778 km), islands 2,492 mi (4,012 km)
Land use: About 25% of the land is used for agriculture, 20% is meadows and pastures, and forests and woodlands make up 38% of the land cover.
Climate: Mediterranean climate, with mild, rainy winters and warm, dry summers, in coastal areas; continental climate in the interior, with hot summers and cold winters
Population: 4,600,000
Urban population: 54%
Rate of natural increase: 0.1%
Age structure: 20% under 15; 12% over 65
Birth rate: 12/1000

Death rate: 11/1000

Infant mortality rate: 8.7/1000

Fertility rate: 1.7

Life expectancy at birth: 69 years (male); 76 years (female)

Religion: Catholic, Orthodox

Language: Serbo-Croat

Ethnic Divisions: Croat, Serb

Literacy Rate: 97%

Government: Parliamentary democracy, with a president and bicameral legislature, the Assembly, or Sabor. The president is directly elected for a five-year term, and members of both chambers, the 80-member Chamber of Representatives and 68-member Chamber of Counties, are directly elected, with the exception of five members of the Chamber of Counties who are appointed by the president, to four-year terms. There are 21 administrative counties for electoral purposes and 420 municipalities.

Armed services: 58,000 men (1997 est.) in the army, navy, and air force; compulsory ten-month enlistment for all males

Suffrage: Universal; 18 years old for all citizens; 16 years old if employed

Economy: Civil war, which began following independence from Yugoslavia in 1991, has severely damaged much of Croatia's infrastructure, factories, farmland, and tourist centers, but the international community has made substantial loans to help the country regain its economic footing. Hyperinflation in the early 1990s was halted by the introduction of a new currency in May 1994. There are large numbers of refugees in the country from Bosnia and Herzegovina as well as Croatian refugees. New financial ties need to be established among international traders to replace markets lost through separation from the former Yugoslavia. There are plans to privatize state utilities and to begin to rebuild the infrastructure.

Unit of currency: Croatian kuna; 100 lipas =1 Croatian kuna (HRK)

GDP per capita: $4,500

Inflation rate–CPI: 3.7% (1997 est.)

Workforce: 1,444,000 (1995 est.)

Unemployment rate: 15.9% (1997 est.)

Exports: Goods worth $4.3 billion (f.o.b., 1997) are sent to Slovenia, Germany, and Italy; exports include machinery and transport equipment, miscellaneous manufactures, chemicals, food and live animals.

Imports: Goods worth $9.1 billion (c.i.f., 1997) are received from Germany, and Italy; imports include machinery and transport equipment, fuels and lubricants, food and live animals, chemicals.

Agriculture: About 14.3% (1996) of the workforce engages in agriculture, fishing, and forestry. The main crops include maize, wheat, and sugar beets; traditional farming also includes dairies, and raising livestock.

Energy: About 30% of Croatia's electricity generating capacity has been destroyed since 1991; although Croatia has petroleum reserves, imported fuel supplies nearly 11% (1996) of the country's energy.

Natural Resources: Minerals, including petroleum, coal, natural gas, bauxite, iron ore, calcium

Environmental Issues: Air and water pollution, destruction from civil war

Transportation: Much of the country's 1,180 miles (1,900 km) of railway are out of service because of the war. There are about 16,770 miles (27,000 km) of roads; 490 miles (790 km) of waterways are open year round. Sea ports include Dubrovnik, Rijeka, Split, and Zadar.

Communications: Zagreb has five daily newspapers, and many of the larger cities also have dailies. There are 1.2 million telephone lines (1993 est.), and 1.1 million radios and 1.52 million televisions (1992 est.) receive

broadcasts from state-run stations and independent broadcasters.

Tourism: Tourism decreased from 2,293,000 visitors in 1994 to 1,324,000 in 1995. The Adriatic coast and islands are popular destinations.

Embassy in U.S.: (202) 588-5899

Public Holidays: Epiphany (January 6); Good Friday (date varies, in March or April); Easter Monday (date varies, in March or April); Labor Day (May 1); Independence Day: from Yugoslavia, 1991 (May 30); National Holiday (August 5); Assumption (August 15); All Saints' Day (November 1); Christmas (December 25–26)

Cuba

Country Name: Cuba

Official Name: Republic of Cuba

Nationality: Cuban(s) (noun); Cuban (adjective)

Capital: Havana, pop. 2,185,000

Major cities: Santiago de Cuba, Camagüey, Holguín, Guantanamo

External Territories: None

Location: Cuba, the largest island in the West Indies, lies 90 miles south of Florida, between the Caribbean Sea and the North Atlantic Ocean.

Physical Geography: There are three mountain systems on the western, central, and eastern sections of the island; plains, hills, and valleys make up the rest of the country. About 3,700 smaller islands surround the main island.

Total area: 42,804 sq mi (110,861 sq km)

Coastline: 2,319 mi (3,735 km)

CUBA LAND OF BEE-SIZE BIRDS, SEE-THROUGH BUTTERFLIES, AND BLUE LIZARDS

The world's smallest bird, the bee hummingbird, lives in Cuba, along with clear-wing butterflies. Cuba has the most varied flora and fauna of any Caribbean country. A large blue lizard and a pupfish are two of the dozens of new species and subspecies found there in the 1990s.

Land use: About 24% of the land is used for agriculture, 27% is meadows and pastures, and 24% is forest and woodland.

Climate: Warm, semitropical, with dry winters and wet summers; greater temperature fluctuations in the interior

Population: 11,178,000

Urban population: 75%

Rate of natural increase: 0.67%

Age structure: 22% under 15; 9% over 65

Birth rate: 13.7/1000

Death rate: 7/1000

Infant mortality rate: 7.2/1000

Fertility rate: 1.6

Life expectancy at birth: 73 years (male); 78 years (female)

Religion: Roman Catholic, Protestant, Jewish, Santeriá

Language: Spanish

Ethnic Divisions: Mulatto, white, black, Chinese

Literacy Rate: 96%

Government: Communist, with a unicameral legislature, the National Assembly of People's Power, or Asamblea Nacional del Poder Popular. The 601 members of the legislature are directly elected to five-year terms. Fidel Castro has led the government since 1959, first as prime minister, then, from 1976, as president. There are 14 administrative provinces and one special municipality.

Armed services: 53,000 troops (1997) in the army, navy, and air force; selection by conscription for two years, including some nonmilitary duties

Suffrage: Universal; 16 years old

Economy: Cuba's economy has relied on sugar exports and was dependent on foreign aid from the Soviet Bloc until the collapse of the Soviet Union in 1990; the country is now deviating from its planned centralized economy in an attempt to find a new financial footing. Opening of foreign investment options, new taxes, the creation of free zones, and reorganization of the banking system have been considered or implemented.

Unit of currency: Cuban peso; 100 centavos = 1 Cuban peso (Cu$)

GDP per capita $1,540

Inflation rate–CPI: N.A.

Workforce: 4.5 million (1996 est.)

Unemployment rate: 8% (1996 est.)

Exports: Goods worth $1.9 billion (f.o.b., 1996 est.) are sent to Russia, Canada, and the Netherlands; exports include sugar, nickel, shellfish, tobacco, medical products, citrus, and coffee.

Imports: Goods worth $3.2 billion (c.i.f., 1997 est.) are received from Spain, Mexico, Russia; imports include petroleum, food, machinery, and chemicals. In 1989, about 68% of the value of Cuba's total imports came from the U.S.S.R.; in 1997, imports from Russia made up only 12% of the total.

Agriculture: Nearly 20% (1990 est.) of the workforce engages in agriculture, fishing, and forestry; sugar is the main agricultural export crop, with other exports such as tobacco, rice, and citrus.

Energy: Most energy is generated using imported petroleum and natural gas.

Natural Resources: Minerals, including cobalt, nickel, iron ore, copper, manganese, petroleum; timber

Environmental Issues: Deforestation, water pollution, overhunting of wildlife

Transportation: More than half of Cuba's 2,900 miles (4,670 km) of railways are used privately by plantations; an estimated 9,610 miles (15,480 km) of paved roads are supplemented by an estimated 7,410 miles (12,220 km) of unpaved roads, which are often impassable during the May to October rainy season. The port of Havana handles more than half of the country's shipping cargo; Santiago de Cuba, Cienfuegos, and Nuevitas are a few of Cuba's other significant sea ports. International airports are located at Havana, Santiago de Cuba, Camagüey, Varadero, and Holquín.

Communications: One national daily newspaper is published in Havana by the government. Phone service, with 229,000 telephones, is rudimentary. There are 2,140,000 radios and 2,500,000 televisions (1993 est.).

Tourism: Tourism development began after the U.S. repealed travel restictions in 1977. In 1996, an estimated 1,001,740 visitors brought $1.38 billion (U.S.) to the country while touring Caribbean beaches and Havana.

Information: Swiss Cubans Interest Section (202) 364-6781

Public Holidays: Liberation Day: establishment of communist government, 1959 (January 1); Labor Day (May 1); Anniversary of the 1953 Revolution (July 25–27); Wars of Independence Day (October 10)

Cyprus

Country Name: Cyprus

Official Name: Republic of Cyprus

Nationality: Cypriot(s) (noun); Cypriot (adjective)

Capital: Nicosia, pop. [193,000]

Major cities: Limassol, Larnaca

External Territories: None (*Note:* The northern part of the island claims independence as the Turkish Republic of Northern Cyprus.)

Location: Cyprus, in southwest Asia, is an island in the northeast Mediterranean Sea about 40 miles south of Turkey's mainland.

Physical Geography: A plain in the central part of the island separates the Troodos Mountains in the southwest and the Kyrenia Range, which parallels the northern coast.

Total area: 5,897 sq mi (9,250 sq km); Greek portion of the island 2,277 sq mi (5,897 sq km)

Coastline: 402 mi (648 km)

Land use: About 12% of the land is arable, 13% is wooded, and 5% is used for permanent crops.

Climate: Mediterranean climate, with hot, dry summers and mild winters; snowfall at higher elevations

Population: 875,000

Urban population: 64%

Rate of natural increase: 0.7%

Age structure: 23% under 15; 8% over 65

Birth rate: 14/1000

Death rate: 8/1000

Infant mortality rate: 9/1000

Fertility rate: 2.0

Life expectancy at birth: 74 years (male); 79 years (female)

Religion: Greek Orthodox, Sunni Muslim

Language: Greek, Turkish (both official), English

Ethnic Divisions: Greek, Turk

Literacy Rate: 94%

Government: The island is divided along ethnic lines into two political sectors: the Greek southern section and the Turkish northern section, which proclaims itself as the independent Turkish Republic of Northern Cyprus. (Turkey is the only country to recognize the claim.) In the south, a president is elected to a five-year term, as are the 56 members of the unicameral legislature, the House of Representatives. The president and 50 members of the unicameral legislative assembly are elected to five-year terms in the Turkish Republic of Northern Cyprus.

Armed services: Greek Cyprus: 10,000 (1996) men between 18 and 50 years of age serving 26-month tours of duty; Turkish Republic of Northern Cyprus: 4,000 (1996) men between 18 and 50 years of age serving 24-month tours of duty; 1,200 troop UN peacekeeping force

Suffrage: Universal; 18 years old

Economy: Tourism is a significant source of income for both sections of the island; the economy of the Greek Cypriots is more diverse than that of the northern Turks. In the

south, shipping and other service industries have contributed to a high rate of economic growth, even though imports exceed exports and there is a shortage of skilled labor. In the north, however, the economy relies on income from agriculture and support from Turkey, and the use of the Turkish lira as currency has led to a high rate of inflation.

Unit of currency: Cypriot pound: 100 cents = 1 Cypriot pound (Cyprus £); Turkish lira: 100 kurus = 1 Turkish lira (TL)

GDP per capita: $13,500

Inflation rate–CPI: Greek Cypriot: 3.5% (1997 est); Turkish Republic of Northern Cyprus: 87.5% (1997 est.)

Workforce: Greek Cypriot: 299,700 (1997); Turkish Republic of Northern Cyprus: 76,500 (1996)

Unemployment rate: Greek Cypriot: 3.3% (1997 est.); Turkish Republic of Northern Cyprus: 6.4% (1996)

Exports: Goods worth $1.3 billion (f.o.b., 19964 est.) are sent to the Russia, Bulgaria, the U.K, Greece, and other trading partners from Greek Cyprus; exports include citrus fruits, potatoes, clothing, and wine. Goods worth $70.5 million (f.o.b., 1996 est.) are sent to the U.K. and Turkey from the Turkish Republic of Northern Cyprus; exports include citrus fruits, potatoes, and textiles.

CYPRUS   A DIVIDED ISLAND NATION

Cyprus has a long history of outside rule, beginning with the Egyptians, the Assyrians, the Phoenicians, the Greeks, the Persians, the Romans, and the Syrians, who were drawn to the island by its supply of copper. It became independent from Great Britain in 1960. Nearly 80 percent of the population is Greek, with the rest forming the Turkish minority. In 1974, Turkish forces invaded and took over the northern third of the island, which proclaimed itself the Turkish Republic of Northern Cyprus in 1983. Only Turkey recognizes Northern Cyprus; a UN peacekeeping force has been stationed there since 1964.

Imports: Goods worth $3.6 billion (f.o.b., 1996 est.) are received by Greek Cypriot from the U.S., the U.K., and other trading partners; imports include consumer goods, petroleum, food, and machinery. Goods worth $318.4 million (f.o.b., 1996 est.) are received by the Turkish Cypriot from Turkey and the U.K.; imports include food, minerals, chemicals, and machinery.

Agriculture: In Greek Cyprus, 13% (1995) of the workforce engages in agricultural production, and 23% (1995) in the Turkish area. Principal crops include potatoes, grapes, and citrus.

Energy: Imported petroleum is used for most energy needs.

Natural Resources: Copper, pyrites, asbestos, gypsum timber, salt, marble, clay, earth pigment

Environmental Issues: Inadequate water supplies, water pollution, wildlife habitat loss

Transportation: There are 6,521 miles (10,500 km) of roads in the Greek Cypriot sector, of which 3,536 miles (5,694 km) are paved. There are 3,800 miles (6,120 km) of roads in the Turkish area, of which more than 85% are paved. There are no railroads. The main shipping ports in the Greek Cypriot area are Larnaca and Limassol. In the Turkish section, Famagusta is open only to domestic shipping. There are international airports at Nicosia (currently closed), Larnaca, and Paphos.

Communications: There are several daily newspapers published in Greek and Turkish. There are 300,000 televisions (1996 est.) in the Greek Cypriot area and 90,000 (1996 est.) in the Turkish area. There are 500,000 (1996 est.) radios in the Greek Cypriot area and130,000 (1996 est.) in the Turkish area.

Tourism: Tourists come to the island for beaches, archaeological sites, and historic churches. More than 2 million tourists came to the southern part of the island in 1996,

and 352,000 tourists visited the north in 1994.

U.S. Tourist Office: (212) 683-5280

Embassy in U.S.: (202) 462-5772

Public Holidays: Epiphany (January 6); End of Ramadan (date varies, in February); Green Monday (date varies, in February or March); Greek Independence Day (March 25); Easter (date varies, in March or April); Feast of the Sacrifice (dates vary, in April); Anniversary of Cyprus Liberation Struggle (April 1); National Sovereignty and Children's Day (April 23); May Day (May 1); Youth and Sports Day (May 19); Peace and Freedom Day: anniversary of Turkish invasion, 1974 (July 20); Birth of the Prophet (date varies, in July or August); Communal Resistance Day (August 1); Victory Day (August 30); Independence Day (October 1); Greek National Day (October 28); Turkish Republic Day (October 29); Turkish Republic of Northern Cyprus Day (November 15); Christmas (December 25–26)

Czech Republic

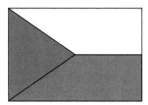

Country Name: Czech Republic

Official Name: Czech Republic

Nationality: Czech(s) (noun); Czech (adjective)

Capital: Prague, pop. 1,200,500

Major cities: Brno, Ostrava, Plzeň

External Territories: None

Location: The Czech Republic, in central Europe, is bordered on the east by Slovakia, on the south by Austria, on the west and northwest by Germany, and on the north by Poland.

Physical Geography: The Bohemian Woods on the western border with Germany and the Ore and Sudenten Mountains on the north rim the Bohemian Basin. The Bohemian highlands lie to the south of the basin, and lowlands extend to the east.

Total area: 30,450 sq mi (78,864 sq km)

Coastline: None

Land use: Nearly 45% of the land is arable, 11% is meadows and pastures and about 33% is forests and woodlands.

Climate: Continental, with warm summers and cold winters

Population: 10,284,000

Urban population: 77%

Rate of natural increase: -0.18%

Age structure: 17% under 15; 14% over 65

Birth rate: 9/1000

Death rate: 11/1000

Infant mortality rate: 5/1000

Fertility rate: 1.2

Life expectancy at birth: 71 years (male); 78 years (female)

Religion: Roman Catholic, Protestant

Language: Czech, Slovak

Ethnic Divisions: Czech, Slovak

Literacy Rate: 99%

Government: Parliamentary democracy, with a president elected to a five-year term by the bicameral legislature. The 200 members of the Chamber of Deputies are elected to four year-terms; the 81 members of the Senate are elected to two-, four-, and six-year terms. There are eight administrative regions.

Armed services: 61,700 troops (1997) in the army, air force, and other branches; compulsory for 12 months

Suffrage: Universal; 18 years old

Economy: The Czech Republic's new market economy is thriving due to rapid privatization, a growing service industry, tourist dollars, and low unemployment rates. Although some of this success brought about

CZECH REPUBLIC CZECHOSLOVAKIA'S VELVET DIVORCE

In an amicable split popularly referred to as a "velvet divorce," Czechoslovakia split in 1993 to become the Czech Republic and the Republic of Slovakia. Joined in 1918 after the collapse of the Austro-Hungarian empire, they were split again during World War II and rejoined under the Soviets in 1948. The two countries had been separate entities for most of their histories, with the Slovaks under Hungarian rule for nearly a thousand years.

Congo, Democratic Republic of the

a large number of bankruptcies, the continuing flow of international investments indicates confidence in the economy's stability and growth potential.

Unit of currency: Koruna (singular), (koruny, plural); 100 halér (haléy, singular) = 1 Czech koruna (Kc)

GDP per capita: $10,800

Inflation rate–CPI: 10% (1997)

Workforce: 5.12 million (1997)

Unemployment rate: 5% (1997 est.)

Exports: Goods worth $21.7 billion (f.o.b., 1996) are sent to Germany, Slovakia, Austria, and other trading partners; exports include manufactured goods, machinery and equipment, fuels, and raw materials.

Imports: Goods worth $27.7 billion (f.o.b., 1996) are received from Germany, Slovakia, Russia, Austria, and other trading partners; imports include machinery, manufactured goods, fuels, and raw materials.

Agriculture: 6% of the workforce (1996) engages in agriculture. Crops include grains, potatoes, sugar beets, hops, and fruit; livestock also provides income.

Energy: Nuclear power supplies 21% (1993) of the country's energy needs, and thermal power supplies about 76%. Mineral fuels are imported.

Natural Resources: Minerals, including coal, clay, graphite

Environmental Issues: Air and water pollution, acid rain

Transportation: The Czech Republic has about 35,000 miles (56,000 km) of roads and 5,800 miles (9,400 km) of railways. Navigable inland waterways include the Labe (Elbe), Vltava, and Odra (Oder); Prague, Kolín, Mělnik, Děčín, and Ústí nad Labem are the major river ports on the Labe. The main airports are at Prague, Brno, Karlovy Vary, and Ostrava.

Communications: More than ninety daily newspapers are published in the country; six are published in Prague. There are over 3 million telephones in use (1993 est.) Statistics for radio and televisions are not available.

Tourism: Visitors are drawn to the Czech Republic by winter sports in the mountains; historic towns such as Prague, Karlovy Vary, and Olomouc; as well as castles, cathedrals, and spas. About 4.6 million tourists came to the country in 1996.

U.S. Tourist Office: (212) 689-9720

Embassy in U.S.: (202) 363-6315

Public Holidays: Easter Monday (date varies, in March or April); Labor Day (May 1); Day of the Apostles St. Cyril and St. Methoduis (July 5); Anniversary of the martyrdom of religious leader Jan Hus, 1415 (July 6); Christmas (December 24–25); St. Stephen's Day (December 26)

Country Name: Democratic Republic of the Congo

Official Name: Democratic Republic of the Congo

Nationality: N.A.

Capital: Kinshasa, pop. 4,655,300

Major cities: Lubumbashi, Mbuji-Mayi, Kananga, Kisangani

External Territories: None

Location: The Democratic Republic of the Congo, in equatorial Africa, has a narrow coast on the Atlantic Ocean's Gulf of Guinea. It is bordered on the north by the Central African Republic and Sudan; on the east by Uganda, Rwanda, Burundi, and Tanzania; on the south by Zambia and Angola; and on the west by Congo.

Physical Geography: The Congo Basin spreads out over about three-fifths of the country; the headwaters of the 2,714 mile-long (4,370 km) Zaire (Congo) River, the eighth longest river in the world, are in the Mitumba Mountains in the east. One of the world's largest tropical rain forests occupies the northwestern part of the country.

Total area: 905,568 sq mi (2,345,409 sq km)

Coastline: 23 mi (37 km)

Land use: Nearly 80% of the country is forested, 7% is meadows and pastures, and about 3% of the land is arable.

Climate: Tropical, with wet and dry seasons alternating north and south of the Equator; humid along the Equator; cooler in the highlands

Population: 50,481,000

Urban population: 29%

Population growth rate: 3.21%

Age structure: 48% under 15; 3% over 65

Birth rate: 47.77/1000

Death rate: 15.64/1000

Infant mortality rate: 105.9/1000

Fertility rate: 6.6

Life expectancy at birth: 47 years (male); 51 years (female)

Religion: Roman Catholic, Protestant, Kimbanquist, Muslim, traditional

Language: French, Lingala, Kingwana

Ethnic Divisions: More than 200 groups, mostly Bantu

Literacy Rate: 77%

Government: After ruling from 1965 to 1997, Mobutu Sese Seko's government of the country of Zaire was overthrown. Laurent Kabila, new president of the country now called the Democratic Republic of the Congo, promised a referendum on a new constitution for the country by December 1998 and presidential and legislative elections by April 1999. Before the new government took over, there were ten administrative regions and one town, Kinshasa.

Armed services: 20,000 to 40,000 troops (1997 est.) in the army, navy, and air force; service in the military was compulsory prior to 1997

Suffrage: Universal and compulsory; 18 years old

Economy: Its status as one of the world's poorest countries led in part to Mobutu's ouster as president in 1997. Large deficits and high inflation rates weakened the country's financial base; bartering and subsistence farming have been key to the economy for years. If the new government formulates acceptable economic policies, the country, potentially one of the richest in Africa in terms of agriculture, mineral wealth, and timber, may see international financial aid and foreign investments resume.

DEMOCRATIC REPUBLIC OF THE CONGO
THE CONFUSING CONGOS

Known as Zaire since 1971, the Democratic Republic of the Congo was renamed by Laurent Kabila after he took over the country in 1997. Before its independence in 1960, the country was known as the Belgian Congo. To confuse matters, the former French colony across the Congo River is known as the Republic of Congo and is a much smaller country. The Portuguese, who arrived in the area in the 15th century, named it after the Kongo kingdom that ruled the region at the time.

Unit of currency: Zaire (to 1997); 100 new makuta (likuta, singular) = 1 new Zaire (NZ)

GDP per capita: $400

Inflation rate–CPI: 1,091% (1985–1995 average)

Workforce: 19,595,000 (1996 est.)

Unemployment rate: N.A.

Exports: Goods worth $1.9 billion (f.o.b., 1996 est.) are sent to the U.S., Belgium, France, Germany, Italy, the U.K., and the Netherlands; exports include copper, coffee, diamonds, cobalt, and oil.

Imports: Goods worth $1.1 billion (c.i.f., 1996 est.) are received from the U.S., Belgium, France, Japan, the U.K., and Brazil; imports include consumer goods, food, mining equipment, transportation equipment and fuel.

Agriculture: About two-thirds (1996) of the workforce engages in agriculture, forestry, and fishing; export crops include coffee, palm oil, sugar, tea, rubber, and cotton. Bananas, cassava, root crops, and maize are grown for domestic use. There are efforts to revitalize the timber industry.

Energy: Hydropower supplies 99.9% of the country's energy.

Natural Resources: Minerals, including diamonds, copper, oil, cobalt (65% of world's reserves), manganese, zinc, uranium, tin, gold; timber

Environmental Issues: Water pollution, deforestation, poaching

Transportation: About 90,050 miles (145,000 km) of roads, of which about 1550 miles (2,500 km) are paved, and an estimated 3,200 miles (5,100 km) of railways cross the country. The Zaire (Congo) River, its tributaries, the Ubangi (Oubanugi), and lakes including Lake Tanganyika, Albert, and Edward serve as major inland waterways, with 9,320 miles (15,000 km) of navigable waters. Main seaports, all on the Zaire River, are upriver at Matadi, Boma, and Banana. Zaire River ports include Kinshasa, Kisangani, and Mbandaka. There are international airports at Kinshasa, Lubumbashi, Bukavu, Goma, and Kisangani.

Communications: Nine daily newspapers are published (1994). There are 4.2 million radios and 63,000 televisions (1994 est.). Telephone service, with 36,000 phones (1994 est.) in service, is very poor.

Tourism: An estimated 18,000 visitors spent some $5 million (U.S.) in 1994. Tourist attractions include lakes, mountains, and wildlife parks, such as Garamba National Park, where rare rhinoceroses are protected from poachers and trained elephants are available for rides through the grasslands.

Embassy in U.S.: (202) 234-7690

Public Holidays: Commemoration of the Martyrs of Independence

(January 4); Labor Day (May 1); Anniversary of the Revolution (May 20); Promulgation of the 1967 Constitution and Day of the Fisherman (June 24); Independence Day: from Belgium, 1960 (June 30); Parents' Day (August 1); Youth Day (October 14); Army Day (November 17); Anniversary of the Second Republic (November 24); Christmas (December 25)

DENMARK DENMARK AND SWEDEN: A NEW GEOGRAPHICAL LINK

Denmark and Sweden will be linked geographically in 2000 by a 10-mile-long bridge and tunnel system known as the Öresund Link. The link will drastically cut travel time between the two countries; many positive economic benefits are expected. The link consists of three bridges and one tunnel that will connect Malmö, in southern Sweden, directly to the Copenhagen airport.

Denmark

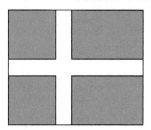

Country Name: Denmark

Official Name: Kingdom of Denmark

Nationality: Dane(s) (noun); Danish (adjective)

Capital: Copenhagen, pop. 632,200 [1,362,300]

Major cities: Århus, Odense, Ålborg

External Territories: Greenland, in North America, northeast of Canada between the Arctic Ocean and the North Atlantic Ocean (836,330 sq mi, 2,166,068 sq km; pop. 57,000); the Faroe Islands, in northern Europe between the Norwegian Sea and the North Atlantic Ocean (540 sq mi, 1,399 sq km; pop. 45,000)

Location: Denmark, in northern Europe, comprises Jutland, a peninsula between the North Sea and the Kattegat and Skagerrak (bodies of water) of the Baltic Sea and hundreds of islands. The only land border it shares is on the south with Germany.

Physical Geography: Denmark is mainly lowlands, with fertile soils in the north and east and sand and gravel deposits in the west; two

of the larger islands, Fyn and Sjælland, lie between the mainland and Sweden.

Total area: 16,638 sq mi (43,092 sq km)

Coastline: 4,542 mi (7,314 km)

Land use: About 60% of the land is used for agriculture, 10% is woodland, and 5% is meadows and pastures.

Climate: Temperate, with cool summers and mild, rainy winters

Population: 5,325,000

Urban population: 85%

Rate of natural increase: 0.1%

Age structure: 18% under 15; 15% over 65

Birth rate: 12/1000

Death rate: 11/1000

Infant mortality rate: 5.2/1000

Fertility rate: 1.7

Life expectancy at birth: 73 years (male); 78 years (female)

Religion: Evangelical Lutheran

Language: Danish, Faeroese, Greenlandic

Ethnic Divisions: Danish

Literacy Rate: 99%

Government: Constitutional monarchy, with a 179-member unicameral Parliament (Folketing) and Queen Margrethe II, a hereditary monarch, who holds only ceremonial powers. Parliament members are elected by proportional representation for four-year terms. There are 14 administrative counties; Greenland and the Faroe Islands, although

possessions of Denmark with parliamentary representation, are self-governing.

Armed services: 19,000 troops (1997) in the army, navy, and air force; some conscription for 9 to 12 months

Suffrage: Universal; 18 years old

Economy: Though unemployment rates are relatively high and future changes in the European economy have caused some concern, Denmark has a stable economy based on modern industrial and agricultural practices. Current goals are to reduce unemployment, income taxes, and inflation, privatize industry, and increase infrastructure investment.

Unit of currency: Danish krone (singular), kroner (plural), 100 øre = 1 Danish krone (DKr)

GDP per capita: $23,200

Inflation rate–CPI: 2.2% (1997 est.)

Workforce: 2.9 million

Unemployment rate: 7.9% (1997 est.)

Exports: Goods worth $48.8 billion (f.o.b, 1996 est.) are sent to Germany, the U.K., Sweden, Norway, and other trading partners; exports include meat and meat products, dairy products, machinery, ships, fish, and chemicals.

Imports: Goods worth $43.2 billion (c.i.f., 1996 est.) are received from Germany, the U.K., Sweden, Norway, and other trading partners; imports include petroleum, machinery,

chemicals, grains, foodstuffs, textiles, and paper.

Agriculture: Nearly 5% (1995) of
the workforce engages in agriculture, particularly pig and dairy farming; fishing provides 5% (1995) of
the total value of Denmark's exports. Grain, potatoes, rape, and
sugar beets, are the main crops.

Energy: Domestic petroleum and
natural gas and some imports provide most of Denmark's energy; the
government encourages renewable
energy sources such as wind power.

Natural Resources: Petroleum,
natural gas, fish, salt, limestone

Environmental Issues: Air and
water pollution, contamination of
drinking water

Transportation: An estimated
44,470 miles (71,570 km) of roads,
all paved, and 2,090 miles (3,360
km) of railways cross the country; a
system of train and car ferries runs
between Denmark and neighboring
countries. Ports include Fredericia,
Copenhagen, Århus, and Ålborg;
major airports are located at Copenhagen, Århus, Ålborg, Odense, and
other large cities.

Communications: About 220
newspapers are published in the
country, including 37 dailies with
an average weekday circulation of
1,610,000. Phone distribution and
service is excellent. There are 3
million televisions (1996 est.) in
operation.

Tourism: There were over 27 million visitors to Denmark in 1997; visitors come to see the attractions of
Copenhagen, historical cities such as
Odense, and coastal resorts.

U.S. Tourist Office: (212) 949-2333

Embassy in U.S.: (202) 234-4300

Public Holidays: Easter (date varies,
in March or April, three-day holiday);
Queen's Birthday (April 16); General
Prayer Day (date varies, in April or
May); Ascension Day (date varies, in
May); Whit Monday (date varies, in
May); Constitution Day (June 5);
Christmas (December 25–26)

Djibouti

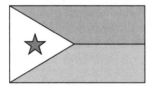

Country Name: Djibouti
Official Name: Republic of Djibouti
Nationality: Djiboutian(s) (noun);
Djiboutian (adjective)
Capital: Djibouti, pop. 383,000
Major cities: Dikhil, Ali-Sabieh, Tad-
joura
External Territories: None
Location: Djibouti, in northeast
Africa, is on the Gulf of Aden at the
entrance to the Red Sea; it is bordered on the northwest by Eritrea,
on the southeast by Somalia, and on
the west and southwest by Ethiopia.
Physical Geography: A coastal
plain gives way to mountains in the
north and volcanic plateaus in the
south and center of the country;
there is little vegetation.
Total area: 8,958 sq mi (23,200 sq
km)
Coastline: 195 mi (314 km)
Land use: There is no arable land or
forests; 9% of the land is meadows
and pastures.

Climate: Hot and dry; rainfall aver-
ages five inches per year
Population: 629,000
Urban population: 83%
Rate of natural increase: 2.28%
Age structure: 41% under 15; 3%
over 65
Birth rate: 39/1000
Death rate: 16.2/1000
Infant mortality rate: 115/1000
Fertility rate: 5.8
Life expectancy at birth: 47 years
(male); 50 years (female)
Religion: Muslim, Christian
Language: French, Arabic (both
official)
Ethnic Divisions: Somali, Afar,
French, Arab
Literacy Rate: 46%
Government: Republic, with a
president and unicameral legisla-
ture, the 65-member Chamber of
Deputies. The president is directly
elected to a six-year term, and
chamber members are elected for
five-year terms. There are five ad-
ministrative districts.
Armed services: 13,800 troops
(1997) in the army, navy, air force,
and other branches
Suffrage: Universal; adult
Economy: Djibouti's capital has developed as a major port because of

DJIBOUTI A TOURIST DESTINATION—FOR GEOGRAPHERS,
ANYWAY

Djibouti is one of the poorest, hottest, and most barren countries in
the world, but it has a few unique geographic features. The country
occupies one of the most geologically active places on Earth, known
as the Afar Triangle, where the Great Rift of Africa, the Red Sea,
and the Gulf of Aden meet. About 20 million years ago, the Arabian and African tectonic plates began to separate, eventually forming the Red Sea and the Gulf of Aden. At about 500 feet (152 m)
below sea level, Djibouti's Lake Assal is both the lowest place on the
African continent and the world's saltiest body of water—it's ten
times saltier than ocean water.

its strategic location on the Gulf of Aden; much of the country's economy is based on income derived from this service industry. Droughts, floods, civil war, and an influx of immigrants and refugees from Eritrea and Somalia have slowed Djibouti's economic growth. The government has reduced spending and increased taxes, but Djibouti remains dependent on foreign aid to meet its domestic and international obligations.

Unit of currency: Djiboutian franc; 100 centimes = 1 Djiboutian franc (DF)

GDP per capita: $1,200

Inflation rate–CPI: 3% (1997 est.)

Workforce: 282,000 (1991 est.)

Unemployment rate: 50% (1996 est.)

Exports: Goods worth $39.6 million (f.o.b., 1996 est.) are sent chiefly to Somalia, Ethiopia, France, Saudi Arabia and Yemen; exports include hides and skins and coffee.

Imports: Goods worth $200.5 million (f.o.b., 1996 est.) are received from Thailand, France, the U.K., Saudi Arabia, Japan, and Italy; imports include food, beverages, transport equipment, petroleum, and chemicals.

Agriculture: About 75% (1991) of Djibouti's workforce is involved in agriculture, mainly raising camels, sheep and goats; domestic production meets about 3% of the country's requirements for food, mostly fruits and vegetables. The country imports food to meet domestic demands.

Energy: Besides geothermal energy, 90% of Djibouti's energy needs are met by imported petroleum.

Natural Resources: Geothermal energy

Environmental Issues: Insufficient potable water, desertification

Transportation: There are about 1,800 miles (2,900 km) of roads, of which about 220 miles (360 km) are paved. About 60 miles (100 km) of the 550-mile (880 km) railroad link

between the city of Djibouti and Addis Ababa in Ethiopia are in Djibouti. An international airport is located outside Djibouti. Djibouti operates as a free port.

Communications: Two non-daily papers are published in Djibouti; there are no daily papers. Telephone service is adequate; there are nearly 8,200 main lines (1996). An estimated 46,000 radios and 25,000 televisions (1994) are in operation.

Tourism: Water sports attract tourists to the Djibouti coast; in 1993, visitors brought $13 million (U.S.) to the economy.

Embassy in U.S.: (202) 331-0270

Public Holidays: End of Ramadan (date varies, in February); Feast of the Sacrifice (date varies, in April); Workers' Day (May 1); Islamic New Year (date varies, in May); Independence Day: from France, 1977 (June 27); Birth of the Prophet (date varies, in July); Christmas (December 25)

Dominica

Country Name: Dominica

Official Name: Commonwealth of Dominica

Nationality: Dominican(s) (noun); Dominican (adjective)

Capital: Roseau, pop. 16,200

Major cities: none

External Territories: None

Location: Dominica, in the West Indies, lies between the Caribbean Sea and the North Atlantic Ocean. Guadeloupe is to the north and Martinique is to the south.

Physical Geography: Dominica is a volcanic island; a mountain range runs north and south.

Total area: 290 sq mi (751 sq km)

Coastline: 88 mi (148 km)

Land use: About 67% of the country is forested, 9% of the land is arable, and 3% is meadows and pastures.

Climate: Tropical, with heavy rainfall in the mountains; hurricane season July to September.

Population: 71,000

Urban population: N.A.

Rate of natural increase: 1.14%

Age structure: 38% under 15; 7% over 65

Birth rate: 19.1/1000

Death rate: 7.7/1000

Infant mortality rate: 16.2/1000

Fertility rate: 1.9

Life expectancy at birth: 75 years (male); 80 years (female)

Religion: Roman Catholic, Protestant

Language: English, French patois

Ethnic Divisions: Black, Carib Amerindian

Literacy Rate: 94%

Government: Parliamentary democracy, with a unicameral legislature, the House of Assembly. The president is elected to a five-year term by the 30-member House of Assembly. House members serve five-year terms; 9 senators are appointed and 21 representatives are elected. There are ten administrative parishes.

Armed services: Disbanded in 1981
Suffrage: Universal; 18 years old
Economy: Dominica's economy is based on agriculture, principally bananas and coconut-based products. Hurricanes destroy banana crops from time to time, most recently in 1995. The government has encouraged cultivation of other cash crops such as mangoes, avocados, and papayas since 1995 and is also promoting privatizing industry and expanding tourist facilities.

Unit of currency: East Caribbean dollar; 100 cents = 1 East Caribbean dollar (EC$)
GDP per capita: $2,500
Inflation rate–CPI: 1.7% (1996)
Workforce: 25,000
Unemployment rate: 15% (1996 est.)
Exports: Goods worth $51.8 million (f.o.b., 1996 est.) are sent to the U.K., members of Caribbean Community and Common Market (CARICOM), and the U.S.; exports include bananas, soap, bay oil, vegetables, grapefruits, and oranges.
Imports: Goods worth $98.1 million (f.o.b., 1996 est.) are received from members of CARICOM, the U.S., the U.K., Netherlands, and Canada; imports include machinery, food, and chemicals.
Agriculture: An estimated 4% (1984) of the workforce is employed in agriculture and fishing. Bananas, coconuts, mangoes, and citrus are the main cash crops; fish, vegetables, and livestock supply domestic needs. Timber and fishery resources are not exploited.

Energy: Dominica relies on hydropower, supplemented by some imported fuels. There is also geothermal potential.
Natural Resources: Timber
Environmental Issues: N.A.
Transportation: There are about 490 miles (790 km) of roads on the island and no railroads. Two airports provide regional service. The principal port is Roseau, and Portsmith handles cruise ships and bananas.
Communications: There are 45,000 radios, 5,200 televisions, and 14,613 telephones (1993 est.). Three non-daily newspapers are published on the island.
Tourism: Tourists, mostly cruise ship passengers, come for the scenery and bird-watching in rain forest habitat. In 1996, visitors added $30.8 million (U.S.) to the economy; in 1996, visitors numbered about 262,123.
Embassy in U.S.: (202) 364-6781
Public Holidays: Carnival (dates vary, in February); Good Friday (date varies, in March or April); Easter Monday (date varies, in March or April); Whit Monday (date varies, in May); Labor Day (May 6); Emancipation (date varies, in August); Independence Day: from the U.K., 1978 (November 3); Community Service Day (November 4); Christmas (December 25–26)

Country Name: Dominican Republic
Official Name: Dominican Republic

Nationality: Dominican(s) (noun); Dominican (adjective)
Capital: Santo Domingo, pop. (2,134,800)
Major cities: Santiago de los Caballeros, La Romana, San Pedro de Macorís
External Territories: None
Location: The Dominican Republic shares the West Indian island of Hispaniola with Haiti, which is on its western border. The island is between Cuba to the northwest and Puerto Rico to the east.
Physical Geography: The Cordillera Central (mountain range) separates drier western lands from fertile northern and eastern plains.
Total area: 18,816 sq mi (48,734 sq km)
Coastline: 800 miles (1,288 km)
Land use: About 12% of the land is forested, 21% is arable, and 43% is meadows and pastures.
Climate: Tropical, with precipitation decreasing from east to west
Population: 8,299,000
Urban population: 56%
Rate of natural increase: 2.4%
Age structure: 36% under 15; 4% over 65
Birth rate: 27/1000
Death rate: 5.6/1000
Infant mortality rate: 46.6/1000
Fertility rate: 3.2
Life expectancy at birth: 68 years (male); 72 years (female)
Religion: Roman Catholic
Language: Spanish
Ethnic Divisions: White, black, mixed
Literacy Rate: 82%
Government: Republic, with an elected president and a bicameral legislature, the National Congress. The president is elected by direct vote to a four-year term; 30 members of the Senate and 120 members of the Chamber of Deputies comprise the National Congress;

DOMINICAN REPUBLIC COLUMBUS'S AMERICAN HOME

The oldest surviving European construction in the Americas is the ruins of Christopher Columbus's house in La Isabela, on the Caribbean island of Hispaniola, in what is now the Dominican Republic. Columbus founded La Isabela in 1494, in the hopes of finding gold on the island but abandoned it four years later. Nearly a million Taino Indians lived on the island when Columbus arrived, but 30 years later almost all were gone, victims of European disease and warfare.

they are popularly elected to four-year terms. There are 29 administrative provinces and one district.

Armed services: 24,500 (1997) in the army, air force, and navy; voluntary for four years

Suffrage: Universal and compulsory; 18 years old or any age if married; members of the armed forces and police cannot vote.

Economy: In the 1990's the country's unstable electric supply and an ailing sugar industry greatly affected the economy. GDP, however, continued to increase in the late 1990s due to tourism and free trade zone expansion.

Unit of currency: Dominican peso; 100 centavos = 1 Dominican peso (RD$)

GDP per capita: $4,700

Inflation rate–CPI : 10.9% (1997)

Workforce: 2.3-2.6 million

Unemployment rate: 30% (1996 est.)

Exports: Goods worth $815 million (f.o.b., 1996 est.) are sent to the U.S., the European Union, Puerto Rico, Canada and Japan; exports include ferronickel, sugar, gold, coffee, and cocoa.

Imports: Goods worth $3.7 billion (f.o.b., 1996 est.) are received from the U.S., Venezuela, Mexico, Japan, EU, and Netherlands Antilles; imports include food, petroleum, textiles, chemicals, and pharmaceuticals.

Agriculture: An estimated 50% (1991) of the working population engages in agriculture, fishing, and timber. Sugar, coffee, and cocoa are the main cash crops; rice, beans, potatoes, and livestock are raised for domestic consumption.

Energy: Imported petroleum, about 13.2% (1996) of the total value of imports, is used to generate most energy.

Natural Resources: Minerals, including gold, silver, bauxite, nickel

Environmental Issues: Insufficient water supplies, deforestation, soil erosion causing reef degradation

Transportation: There are about 7,450 miles (12,000 km) of roads, of which about half are paved. There are 470 miles (760 km) of railroads; of which 150 miles (240 km) are privately held and used for transporting sugar. Santo Domingo is the most important seaport; international flights land at Santo Domingo, Puerto Plata, and Barahona.

Communications: There are 11 daily newspapers, eight of which are published in Santo Domingo (1994). There are 728,000 televisions (1993 est.) receiving broadcasts from government and commercial stations. Telephone service is good; there are 190,000 main lines (1987 est.) in service.

Tourism: Sportfishing, beaches, and Spanish colonial architecture draw visitors to the Dominican Republic;

in 1995, visitors added $1.490 million (U.S.) to the economy.

U.S. Tourist Office: (212) 575-4966

Embassy in U.S.: (202) 332-6280

Public Holidays: Epiphany (January 6); Our Lady of Altagracia (January 21); Duarte (January 26); Independence: from Haiti, 1844 (February 27); Good Friday (date varies, in March or April); Pan-American Day (April 14); Labor Day (May 1); Foundation of Sociedad la Trinitaria (July 16); Restoration Day (August 16); Our Lady of Mercedes (September 24); Columbus Day (October 12); United Nations Day (October 24); All Saints' Day (November 1); Christmas (December 25)

Ecuador

Country Name: Ecuador

Official Name: Republic of Ecuador

Nationality: Ecuadorian(s) (noun); Ecuadorian (adjective)

Capital: Quito, pop. 1,444,400

Major cities: Guayaquil, Cuenca, Machala

External Territories: None

Location: Ecuador, on South America's Pacific coast at the Equator, is between Colombia on the north and Peru on the south and east. The Galápagos Islands, about 600 miles (965 km) west of the mainland, are Ecuadorian possessions.

Physical Geography: Parallel ranges of the Andes run north and south and include the volcanic peaks of Chimborazo, 20,561 feet (6,267 m) and Cotopaxi, 19,347 feet (5,897 m). A high plateau lies between the ranges; the Amazon

ECUADOR A COUNTRY NAMED FOR AN IMAGINARY LINE

Ecuador is named after the Equator, which passes through the northern part of the country. The capital, Quito, lies 14 miles south of the Equator and is one of the Western Hemisphere's oldest continuously inhabited cities. About the size of Colorado, Ecuador is the world's biggest producer and exporter of bananas and balsa wood.

Basin lies to the east and the Pacific coast's lowlands lie to the west.

Total area: 109,484 sq mi (283,561 sq km)

Coastline: 1,380 miles (2,237 km)

Land use: Over 50% of the country is forested, 18% is meadows and pastures, and nearly 10% of the land is arable or permanent crops.

Climate: Wet, tropical climate in the Amazon Basin; slightly cooler along the Pacific coast; springlike conditions in the Andes highlands year-round

Population: 12,411,000

Urban population: 62%

Rate of natural increase: 2.1%

Age structure: 35% under 15; 4% over 65

Birth rate: 27/1000

Death rate: 6.1/1000

Infant mortality rate: 40/1000

Fertility rate: 3.3

Life expectancy at birth: 67 years (male); 72 years (female)

Religion: Roman Catholic

Language: Spanish, Quechua

Ethnic Divisions: Mestizo, Indian, white, black

Literacy Rate: 90% (1995 est.)

Government: Republic, with a president and unicameral legislature, the National Congress. The president is directly elected for one four-year term. Members of the 82-seat Congress are elected either by provinces for two-year terms or on a national basis for four-year terms. There are 21 administrative provinces.

Armed services: 57,100 (1997) in the army, navy, and air force; selective conscription for one-year tour of duty for 20-year-old males

Suffrage: Universal and compulsory for literate citizens 18 to 65 years of age; optional for other eligible voters

Economy: Petroleum, tourism, and exports, particularly of fish and fruit, are key to maintaining Ecuador's economy. Austerity measures begun in 1992 helped to reduce inflation from almost 50% to 22% in 1995. Foreign investment has declined, and political instability has complicated the government's efforts to restructure national finances.

Unit of currency: Sucre; 100 centavos = 1 sucre (S)

GDP per capita: $4,400

Inflation rate–CPI: 31% (1997 est.)

Workforce: 4.2 million (1990 est.)

Unemployment: 6.9% (1997 est.)

Exports: Goods worth $3.4 billion (f.o.b., 1997) are sent to the U.S., other Latin American countries, and the EU; exports include petroleum, bananas, seafood (principally shrimp), coffee, and cocoa.

Imports: Goods worth $2.9 billion (c.i.f., 1997) are received from other Latin American countries, the U.S., and the EU, and Asia; imports include transportation equipment, consumer goods, vehicles, machinery, and chemicals.

Agriculture: 29% (1990) of the working population engages in agriculture. Bananas, shrimp, cocoa, coffee, and timber, especially balsa wood, are important exports. Ecuador is the world's largest exporter of bananas and the second largest exporter of shrimp.

Energy: Energy is primarily derived from thermoelectric, and hydropower.

Natural Resources: Petroleum, seafood, timber

Environmental Issues: Deforestation, desertification, soil erosion, water pollution

Transportation: Ecuador has an estimated 26,700 miles (43,000 km) of roads, of which about 3,600 miles (5,800 km) are paved; 600 miles (970 km) of railroads are in service. Quito and Guayaquil have international airports. Key seaports include Guayaquil, Esmeraldas, Manta, and Puerto Bolívar, and there are 930 miles (1,500 km) of navigable waterways.

Communications: Four daily newspapers are published in Quito and four in Guayaquil. The country has 3.7 million radios and 990,000 televisions (1994 est.). Telephone service and distribution (586,300 in 1994) is inadequate.

Tourism: Quito's Spanish colonial architecture and Galápagos wildlife are two of Ecuador's primary attractions. In 1994, 482,000 tourists spent an estimated $252 million.

U.S. Tourist Office: (305) 461-2363

Embassy in U.S.: (202) 234-7200

Public Holidays: Epiphany (January 6); Carnival (dates vary, in February); Good Friday (date varies, in March or April); Easter (date varies, in March or April); Holy Thursday (date varies, in April); Labor Day (May 1); Battle of Pichincha: independence from Spain, 1822 (May 24); Birth of Simon Bolívar, leader against Spain (July 24); Independence of Quito, 1809 (August 10); Independence of Guayaquil (October 9); Discovery of America (October 12); All Saints' Day (November 1); All Souls' Day (November 2); Independence of Cuenca (November 3); Foundation of Quito (December 6); Christmas (December 25)

Egypt

Country Name: Egypt

Official Name: Arab Republic of Egypt

Nationality: Egyptian(s) (noun); Egyptian (adjective)

Capital: Cairo, pop. [6,800,000]

Major cities: Alexandria, Gîza, Shoubra el-Kheima

External Territories: None

Location: Egypt, in north Africa, is bordered on the west by Libya, on the south by Sudan, on the east by Israel and the Red Sea, and on the north by the Mediterranean Sea.

Physical Geography: Except for the northern 15,000 square mile (39,000 sq km) Nile Delta, most of Egypt is desert. Part of the Sahara, the Western Desert, which is south of the delta and west of the Nile and the Eastern Desert between the Nile and the Red Sea, has many dry riverbeds. The Sinai Peninsula is a mountainous desert. Most of the population lives in the Nile Valley and Delta.

Total area: 386,662 sq mi (1,001,449 sq km)

Coastline: 1,522 mi (2,450 km)

Land use: Over 90% of the country is desert; 2% is used for agriculture.

Climate: Arid, with hot summers and mild winters

Population: 66,924,000

Urban population: 44%

Rate of natural increase: 1.98%

Age structure: 39% under 15; 4% over 65

Birth rate: 26/1000

Death rate: 6.2/1000

Infant mortality rate: 52.3/1000

Fertility rate: 3.3

Life expectancy at birth: 64 years (male); 67 years (female)

Religion: Sunni Muslim, Coptic Christian

Language: Arabic, English, French

Ethnic Divisions: Egyptian, Bedouin, Berber, Nubian

Literacy Rate: 51%

Government: Republic, with a president elected by popular referendum for a six-year term and a unicameral legislature, the People's Assembly. Of the 454 members of the legislature, 444 are elected and 10 are nominated by the president, both for five-year terms. There are 26 administrative governorates.

Armed services: 450,000 troops (1997) in the army, air force, navy, and other branches; selective service for three years

Suffrage: Universal and compulsory; 18 years old

Economy: Since 1990, the Egyptian government has tried to reduce international debt with privatization plans and trade liberalization, but efforts are undermined by unemployment, population pressures, and political instability. Although about 40% of the workforce is in agriculture, most grow cotton and food must be imported to meet domestic demand.

Unit of currency: Egyptian pound; 100 piasters = 1 Egyptian pound (#E or £E)

GDP per capita: $4,400

Inflation rate–CPI: 4.9% (1997)

Workforce: 17 million (1995 est.)

Unemployment rate: 9.4% (1997 est.)

Exports: Goods worth $5.1 billion (f.o.b., 1996-1997 est.) are sent to the U.S., Italy, Israel, and the Netherlands; exports include petroleum, cotton textiles, chemicals, and food.

Imports: Goods worth $15.5 billion (c.i.f., 1996-1997 est.) are received from the U.S., Germany, France, and other trading partners; imports include machinery, food, fertilizers, iron and steel, wood products, and consumer items.

Agriculture: 40% of the workforce engages in agriculture and fishing. Crops include cotton, rice, wheat, beans, fruits, and maize.

Energy: Hydropower and coal are the main sources of Egypt's energy.

Natural Resources: Minerals, including petroleum, natural gas, phosphates, manganese, uranium, coal, iron ore

Environmental Issues: Desertification, soil pollution, urbanization, water pollution, limited water resources in most of the country

Transportation: Railroads and roads are most numerous in the Nile Delta, where most of the population lives. There are 39,740 miles (64,000 km) of roads, of which 31,040 miles (49,980 km) are paved; 2,950 miles (4,751 km) of railways are in service. The 120 mile-long (193.5 km) Suez

Canal connects the Mediterranean and Red Sea. Alexandria and Suez, on the Mediterranean, and Port Said, on the Gulf of Aden, are key ports. Cairo and Alexandria have international airports.

Communications: Several daily newspapers are published: Cairo has 10 daily newspapers and Alexandria has five. There are 19 million radios and 6.7 million televisions (1994 est.). There are 2,456,000 main telephone lines (1994 est.) in service.

Tourism: Egypt is famous for archaeological sites such as the pyramids at Gîza and the Valley of the Kings; coastal resorts along the Mediterranean also draw visitors. While tourism increased during the 1980s, recent attacks on tourists by Islamic fundamentalists have caused tourism to decrease. In 1993, tourism added $1.384 billion (U.S.) to Egypt's economy.

U.S. Tourist Office: (212) 332-2570

Embassy in U.S.: (202) 895-5400

Public Holidays: End of Ramadan (date varies, in February); Coptic Easter Monday (date varies, in April); Feast of the Sacrifice (date varies, in April); Islamic New Year (date varies, in May); Evacuation Day: proclamation of the republic, 1953 (June 18); Birth of Muhammad (date varies, in July); Revolution Day: overthrow of King Farouk, 1952 (July 23); Armed Forces Day (October 6); Popular Resistance Day (October 24); Ascen-

sion of Muhammad (date varies, in November or December); Victory Day (December 23)

El Salvador

Country Name: El Salvador

Official Name: Republic of El Salvador

Nationality: Salvadoran(s) (noun); Salvadoran (adjective)

Capital: San Salvador, pop. 415,300

Major cities: Soyapango, Santa Ana, San Miguel

External Territories: None

Location: El Salvador, on the Pacific coast of Central America, is bordered on the north and east by Honduras and on the west by Guatemala.

Physical Geography: El Salvador is a mountainous country; the Pacific coastal lowlands give way to a range of volcanos and elevated plateaus. To the north are the volcanic interior highlands.

Total area: 8,124 sq mi (21,041 sq km)

Coastline: 191 mi (307 km)

Land use: About 5% of the land is wooded, 27% is used for agriculture, and 29% is meadows and pastures.

Climate: Tropical along the coast, with most rain falling in the summer; generally more precipitation in mountains; temperate temperatures in the highlands

Population: 5,859,000

Urban population: 50%

Rate of natural increase: 2.33%

Age structure: 39% under 15; 5% over 65

Birth rate: 28.5/1000

Death rate: 5.2/1000

Infant mortality rate: 35/1000

Fertility rate: 3.6

Life expectancy at birth: 67 years (male); 73 years (female)

Religion: Roman Catholic, Protestant

Language: Spanish, Nahuatl

Ethnic Divisions: Mestizo, Indian, white, Amerindian

Literacy Rate: 72%

Government: Republic, with a president and unicameral legislature, the Legislative Assembly, or Asamblea Legislativa. The president is directly elected for a five-year term; the 84 members of the Assembly are directly elected for three-year terms. There are 14 administrative departments.

Armed services: 28,400 troops (1997) in the army, navy, and air force; men between 18 and 30 years of age; compulsory service abolished in 1992

Suffrage: Universal; 18 years old

Economy: Civil war raged in El Salvador from 1979 to 1992 and severely disrupted the country's economy; natural disasters, including an earthquake in 1986, a hurricane in 1988, and recurring draught, have compounded the problem. International aid has been approved to help support financial and economic programs; since 1989, progress has been made in

EL SALVADOR DISAPPEARING RAIN FORESTS

Slightly smaller than Massachusetts and with almost the same number of people, El Salvador is the smallest and most densely populated country on the New World mainland. Its rain forest area is rapidly dwindling—in 1995 rain forests made up only three percent of the total land area, mainly because residents had cut down trees to use as firewood or timber or to clear land for agriculture. As a result, erosion is becoming severe and the wildlife population is dwindling.

moving from agriculture to manufacturing, encouraging private investment, liberalizing trade, and attempting to stem poverty and reduce inflation.

Unit of currency: Salvadoran colon (singular), colones (plural); 100 centavos = 1 Salvadoran colon

GDP per capita: $3,000

Inflation rate–CPI: 2% (1997)

Workforce: 2,260,000 (1997)

Unemployment rate: 7.7% (1997)

Exports: Goods worth $1.96 billion (f.o.b., 1997 est.) are sent to the U.S., Guatemala, Costa Rica, Germany, and Honduras; exports include coffee, sugar, textiles, and shrimp.

Imports: Goods worth $3.5 billion (c.i.f., 1997 est.) are received from the U.S. Guatemala, Mexico, Venezuela, Japan, and Panama; imports include raw materials, fuel, consumer goods, and capital goods.

Agriculture: About 40% (1997 est.) of the workforce is employed in agriculture, fishing, hunting, and forestry. Cash crops raised include coffee, sugarcane, and cotton. Rice, corn, and beans are grown for domestic consumption.

Energy: Most energy is generated from imported fuel, and hydropower provides about 46.9% of total electricty production (1994 est.).

Natural Resources: Hydropower, geothermal power, petroleum

Environmental Issues: Deforestation, soil erosion and contamination, water pollution

Transportation: There are nearly 420 miles (670 km) of railroads in El Salvador and 6,200 miles (10,000 km) of roads, of which about 1,240 miles (1,990 km) are paved. The Rio Lempa is partially navigable and seaports include Acajutla, La Union, and La Libertad. An international airport is at San Salvador.

Communications: Six daily newspapers are published (1994). An estimated 1.5 million radios and 700,000 televisions (1997) are in operation and receiving broadcasts from government and commercial stations.

Tourism: Pacific beaches, Maya ruins, and volcanos are draws for tourists; in 1994, 181,000 tourists added an estimated $86 million (U.S.) to the economy.

Embassy in U.S.: (202) 265-9671

Public Holidays: Easter (date varies, in March or April, three-day holiday); Labor Day (May 1); Corpus Christi (date varies, in May or June); San Salvador Festival (dates vary, in August by city); Independence Day: from Spain, 1821 (September 15)); Discovery of America (October 12); All Souls' Day (November 2); First Call of Independence (November 5); Christmas (December 24–25)

Equatorial Guinea

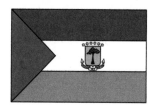

Country Name: Equatorial Guinea

Official Name: Republic of Equatorial Guinea

Nationality: Equatorial Guinean(s) or Equatoguineans(s) (noun); Equatorial Guinean or Equatoguinean (adjective)

Capital: Malabo, pop. 30,400

Major cities: Bata, Ebebiyin, Evinayong

External Territories: None

Location: Mainland Equatorial Guinea, in equatorial Africa, is bordered on the north by Cameroon, on the east and south by Gabon, and on the west by the Gulf of Guinea of the North Atlantic Ocean. The island of Bioko, to the north and east, and several smaller islands

off the southeast coast are also part of the country.

Physical Geography: On the mainland, called Río Muni, coastal plains lead to hills and inland plateaus; Bioko and the other islands are volcanic.

Total area: 10,831 sq mi (28,051 sq km)

Coastline: 184 mi (296 km)

Land use: Forests cover 46% of the country, 9% is arable or under cultivation, and 4% is meadows and pastures.

Climate: Tropical, hot and humid, little variation in temperature, alternating wet and dry seasons

Population: 442,000

Urban population: 37%

Rate of natural increase: 2.55%

Age structure: 43% under 15; 4% over 65

Birth rate: 43.5/1000

Death rate: 18/1000

Infant mortality rate: 117/1000

Fertility rate: 5.9

Life expectancy at birth: 46 years (male); 50 years (female)

Religion: Roman Catholic, pagan practices

Language: Spanish, French (both official), pidgin English, Fang, Bubi, Ibo

Ethnic Divisions: Fang, Bubi

Literacy Rate: 79%

Government: Republic, with a president and a unicameral legislature, the House of People's Representatives. The president is elected to a seven-year term; the 80 members of the House are directly elected to five-year terms. There are seven administrative provinces.

Armed services: 1,300 volunteers (1996) in the army, navy, and air force

Suffrage: Universal; 18 years old

Economy: Although petroleum exports, begun in 1992, hold promise for the economic future, an estimated 72.8% of the working population is involved in agriculture. Political instability in the past has discouraged foreign investment, and international aid is essential to the country's financial survival.

Unit of currency: CFA franc; 100 centimes = 1 franc de la Communauté financière africaine (CFAF)

GDP per capita: $1,500

Inflation rate–CPI: 6% (1996 est.)

Workforce: 102,500 (1983 est.)

Unemployment rate: 24% (1983)

Exports: Goods worth $197 million (f.o.b., 1996 est.) are sent to Spain, Nigeria, Cameroon, and other trading partners; exports include cocoa, timber, and petroleum.

Imports: Goods worth $248 million (c.i.f., 1996 est.) are received from Cameroon, Spain, Liberia, the U.S., and other trading partners; imports include petroleum, food, beverages, clothing, and machinery.

Agriculture: About 75% of the population engages in agriculture, hunting, and fishing. Fishing and timber are important to the econo-

my. Cash crops include cocoa and coffee; cassava and sweet potatoes are grown for domestic use.

Energy: Imported fuels supplement hydropower, the principal source of energy.

Natural Resources: Timber, petroleum, natural gas, gold, manganese, uranium

Environmental Issues: Inadequate potable water, desertification

Transportation: There are no railroads. Of 1,750 miles (2,820 km) of roads, none are paved. Ports, all on Bioko, include Malabo, Bata, and Luba. There are international airports at Malabo and Bata.

Communications: One daily newspaper (1994) is published in Malabo. There are 165,000 radios and 4,000 televisions (1994 est.) in operation. There are 3,000 telephones (1994) in service.

Tourism: Few tourists visit the country, and facilities for visitors are rudimentary. However, hardy travelers recommend the beaches and volcanic islands as out-of-the-way destinations.

Embassy in U.S.: (202) 393-0525

Public Holidays: Independence Day (March 5); Easter (date varies, in March or April); Labor Day (May 1); Organization of African Unity (OAU) Day (May 25); Human Rights Day (December 10); Christmas (December 25)

Eritrea

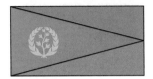

Country Name: Eritrea
Official Name: State of Eritrea
Nationality: Eritrean(s) (noun); Eritrean (adjective)
Capital: Asmara, pop. 358,100
Major cities: Massawa
External Territories: None
Location: Eritrea, in northeastern Africa, is on the Red Sea. Djibouti and Ethiopia are on the south and Sudan on the west. The Dahlak Archipelago, in the Red Sea, is Eritrean territory.
Physical Geography: There is a long, narrow coastal plain on the Red Sea; the interior has high plateaus.
Total area: 46,842 sq mi (121,320 sq km)
Coastline: 1,387 mi (2,234 km)
Land use: About 48% of the country is meadows and pastures, 20% is woodland and forest, and 13% is arable or under permanent cultivation.
Climate: Arid and hot along the coast, rainfall increasing and temperatures decrease with elevation
Population: 3,985,000
Urban population: 16%
Rate of natural increase: 2.98%
Age structure: 43% under 15; 3% over 65
Birth rate: 42.8/1000
Death rate: 13/1000
Infant mortality rate: 81.8/1000
Fertility rate: 6.1
Life expectancy at birth: 52 years (male); 57 years (female)
Religion: Muslim, Coptic Christian, Roman Catholic, Protestant

ERITREA AGAINST ALL ODDS, INDEPENDENCE AT LAST

The longest fight for independence in modern African history took place over three decades between Eritrea and Ethiopia. An Italian colony between 1890 and 1941, Eritrea was ruled by Great Britain during World War II. In 1952, the UN made Eritrea an autonomous federated state within Ethiopia, but when the Ethiopians tried to annex the northern part of the country in 1961 to gain access to the Red Sea, war broke out. With the odds against them, the under-equipped Eritreans eventually won the war and voted for independence in 1993.

Language: Afar, Amharic, Arabic,Tigrinya, Tigré

Ethnic Divisions: Tigrinya, Tigré, Kunama, Afar, Saho

Literacy Rate: N.A.

Government: Transitional since 1993. Plans for national government include a president and an elected unicameral legislative National Assembly.

Armed services: 46,000 troops (1997 est.); 18-month compulsory service plus a 6-month training period for all citizens 18–40 years of age

Suffrage: N.A.

Economy: Eritrea is one of the poorest countries in Africa. Its task since independence from Ethiopia in 1993 has been to build an economy that can provide its citizens with adequate resources. Most Eritreans depend on subsistence agriculture. Remittances from those working abroad significantly add to the country's economy. International assistance allows the country to bolster its infrastructure, and the provisional government is working to privatize existing industry and encourage international investments.

Unit of currency: Ethiopian birr; 100 cents = 1 birr (Br)

GDP per capita: $600

Inflation rate–CPI: 4% (1997 est.)

Workforce: N.A.

Unemployment rate: 50% (1996 est.)

Exports: Goods worth $71 million (f.o.b., 1996 est.) are sent to Ethiopia, Sudan, Saudi Arabia, the U.K., the U.S., Italy, and other trading partners; exports include livestock, sorghum, textiles, shoes, food, and manufactured goods.

Imports: Goods worth $499 million (1996 est.) are received from Ethiopia, Germany, Italy, Saudi Arabia and United Arab Emirates. Imports include petroleum, processed goods, machinery, and transportation equipment.

Agriculture: Subsistence agriculture supports an estimated 90% of the population. Because crop success depends upon rainfall, water conservation and management is a government priority. Food crops include maize, wheat, sorghum, millet, and teff (a native grain). Livestock is important, and fish in the Red Sea are a potential commodity.

Energy: Energy is derived from imported petroleum, firewood, and animal products.

Natural Resources: Minerals, including gold, copper, potash; seafood

Environmental Issues: Deforestation, desertification, soil erosion, overgrazing

Transportation: Of 190 miles (310 km) of railroads, about 3 miles (5 km) are in operation. There are 2,490 miles (4,010 km) of roads, of which 500 miles (870 km) are paved. Massawa and Assab are the principal seaports. An international airport is at Asmara.

Communications: There are 15,000 phone lines, 300,000 radios, and 1000 televisions (1994 est.) in service.

Tourism: About 315,000 tourists visited Eritrea in 1995. Potential tourist attractions include the Dahlak Islands and the striking landscape of the country's interior. The government is improving tourist amenities and privatizing hotels.

Embassy in U.S.: (202) 319-1991

Public Holidays: Epiphany (January 6); End of Ramadan (date varies, in February); Feast of the Sacrifice (date varies, in April); Independence Day: from Ethiopia, 1993 (May 24); Martyrs' Day (June 20); Anniversary of the beginning of armed struggle (September 1); Christmas (December 25)

Estonia

Country Name: Estonia

Official Name: Republic of Estonia

Nationality: Estonian(s) (noun); Estonian (adjective)

Capital: Tallinn, pop. 424,000

Major cities: Tartu, Narva, Kohtla-Järve

External Territories: None

Location: Estonia, in northern Europe, is bordered on the east by Russian, on the south by Latvia, on the west by the Baltic Sea, and on the north by the Gulf of Finland.

Physical Geography: Estonia is primarily a lowland, with marshes, many lakes, and small hills.

Total area: 17,413 sq mi (45,099 sq km)

Coastline: 865 mi (1,393 km)

Land use: Forest and woodland cover 31% of the land, 22% is arable or under cultivation, and 11% is meadows and pastures.

Climate: Moderate maritime, with cool summers and wet, mild winters

Population: 1,441,000

Urban population: 70%

Rate of natural increase: -0.4%

Age structure: 19% under 15; 14% over 65

Birth rate: 9/1000

Death rate: 13/1000

Infant mortality rate: 10/1000

Fertility rate: 1.2

Life expectancy at birth: 65 years (male); 76 years (female)

Religion: Evangelical Lutheran, Russian Orthodox, Estonian Orthodox

Language: Estonian, Russian, Ukrainian

Ethnic Divisions: Estonian, Russian, Ukrainian

Literacy Rate: 100%

Government: Republic, with a president and a State Assembly, or Riggikogu. The 101 members of the State Assembly are universally elected to four-year terms; they are responsible for electing the president, who serves a five-year term. There are 15 administrative counties.

Armed services: 3,510 troops (1997) in the army and navy; 12-month enlistment

Suffrage: Universal; 18 years old

Economy: Although Estonia suffered economic decline in the early 1990s after the breakup of the Soviet Union, the government's immediate and aggressive efforts, including monetary reform, privatization, increasing exports, and encouraging foreign investments, have succeeded in promoting the country's economic renewal. Western trading partners have replaced those of the former Soviet bloc, and industrial output is rapidly taking a backseat to the service sector.

Unit of currency: Estonian kroon ; 100 cents = 1 Estonian kroon (EEK)

GDP per capita: $6,450

Inflation rate–CPI: 11.2% (1997 est.)

Workforce: 785,100 (1996 est.)

Unemployment rate: 3.6% (1997 est.)

Exports: Goods worth $2 billion (f.o.b., 1996) are sent to Russia, Finland, Sweden, Germany, and other trading partners; exports include food, textiles, machinery and equipment, and metals.

Imports: Goods worth $3.2 billion (c.i.f., 1996) are received from Finland, Russia, Germany, Sweden, and other trading partners; imports include machinery and equipment, foodstuffs, minerals, textiles, and metals.

Agriculture: Nearly 10% (1996) of the working population engages in agriculture, fishing, and forestry. Raising livestock, especially pigs, cattle, and poultry, is the most important agricultural activity. Potatoes, fruits and vegetables are cash crops.

Energy: Domestic oil provides up to 65% of the energy requirements.

Natural Resources: Oil shale, peat, phosphorite, amber

Environmental Issues: Air, soil, and groundwater pollution

Transportation: There are 640 miles (1,030 km) of railroads and 9,500 miles (15,300 km) of roads, of which 53% are paved. Tallinn's port handles freight and has passenger ferry service to Finland and Sweden. There is an international airport at Tallinn.

Communications: There are 15 daily papers (1996) published in Tallinn and other major cities. There are 710,00 radios and 600,000 televisions (1996 est.). There are 400,000 main telephone lines (1994) and demand for phone service exceeds supply.

Tourism: Coastal resorts, nature reserves, and the historic cities of Tallinn and Tartu draw tourists. In 1997, there were an estimated 2.7 million visitors to Estonia.

Embassy in U.S.: (202) 588-0101

Public Holidays: Independence Day: from Germany, 1918 (February 24); Good Friday (date varies, in March or April); Labor Day (May 1); Victory Day: anniversary of Battle of Võnnu, 1919 (June 23); Midsummer Day (June 24); Christmas (December 25–26)

Ethiopia

Country Name: Ethiopia

Official Name: Federal Democratic Republic of Ethiopia

Nationality: Ethiopian(s) (noun); Ethiopian (adjective)

Capital: Addis Ababa, pop. 2,084,600

Major cities: Dire Dawa, Harar, Nazret, Gondar

External Territories: None

Location: Ethiopia, in northeastern Africa, is bordered on the north by Eritrea, on the northwest by Djibouti, on the east by Somalia, on the south by Kenya, and on the west by Sudan.

ETHIOPIA WORLD'S OLDEST HUMAN HOME?

Ethiopia has been home to humans for at least one million years; today it is the oldest independent state in Africa. The country has suffered for years from drought, soil erosion, deforestation, economic instability, and political violence. It has been mostly Christian since the fourth century. Haile Selassie, who was overthrown in 1974, was its last emperor. Under military rule until 1990, Ethiopians endured transitional rule until 1993, when a new socialist government was organized.

Africa's Great Rift cuts through the country's central plateau. The three-million-year-old fossil Lucy, which may be a member of the earliest known hominid species to walk upright, was found in the Hadar region in 1974.

Physical Geography: The Great Rift Valley extends the length of the country, dividing it into eastern and western highlands. Arid lowlands, including the Denakil Depression, are in the north and southeast.

Total area: 424,934 sq mi (1,100,580 sq km)

Coastline: None

Land use: Nearly 40% of the land is meadows and pastures, 25% is forested, and 13% is arable or under cultivation.

Climate: Varies with elevation; temperate to cool in highlands, hot in lowlands; rainy season from June to September; rainfall varies with elevation

Population: 59,680,000

Urban population: 14%

Rate of natural increase: 2.462%

Age structure: 46% under 15; 3% over 65

Birth rate: 45.5/1000

Death rate: 20.88/1000

Infant mortality rate: 128/1000

Fertility rate: 7

Life expectancy at birth: 41 years (male); 42 years (female)

Religion: Muslim, Ethiopian Orthodox, animist

Language: Amharic, Tigrinya, Orominga, Guaraginga, Somali, Arabic

Ethnic Divisions: Omoro, Amhara, Tigré, others

Literacy Rate: 36%

Government: Federation, with a bicameral legislative body, the Federal Parliamentary Assembly. The Assembly is responsible for electing the president, who holds a largely ceremonial position. The 548 members of the Council of People's Deputies are elected; the 117 members of the Council of the Federation are selected by state assemblies. Members of the legislature are elected to five-year terms. There are nine administrative states and one metropolitan area.

Armed services: 120,000 troops (1993 est.) in the army

Suffrage: Universal; 18 years old

Economy: Droughts and internal wars from 1961 to 1991 severely derailed the economy of Ethiopia, one of Africa's least developed countries. International aid, an increase in the service structure, and a move away from a centralized planned economy have helped stimulate some economic growth, but the need to raise interest rates and devalue the currency leaves citizens vulnerable to monetary hardship. The economy is based on agriculture, and the government has made self-sufficiency a goal. There are also plans to exploit natural gas and geothermal resources.

Unit of currency: Birr; 100 cents = 1 birr (Br)

GDP per capita: $530

Inflation rate–CPI: 0% (1996 est.)

Workforce: 24,396,000 (1995 est.)

Unemployment rate: N.A.

Exports: Goods worth $418 million (f.o.b., 1996) are sent to Germany, the U.S., Italy, Japan, Saudi Arabia, and other trading partners; exports include coffee, leather products and gold.

Imports: Goods worth $1.23 billion (f.o.b., 1996 est.) are received from Saudi Arabia, the U.S., Italy, Japan, Germany, and other trading partners; imports include food, petroleum, machinery, vehicles, and chemicals.

Agriculture: Nearly 90% (1996) of the working population engages in agriculture, fishing, and forestry. Coffee, grown for export, earns over 60% of the total value of exports. Barley, maize, sugarcane and sorghum are cultivated for domestic use. Livestock is raised for domestic use and for export.

Energy: Energy is generated with imported fuels and, when rainfall is adequate, hydropower. Firewood, charcoal, and animal dung are also used.

Natural Resources: Gold, copper, platinum, potash, salt, and petroleum.

Environmental Issues: Deforestation, desertification, soil erosion, overgrazing

Transportation: There are 420 miles (680 km) of railroads and 17,700 miles (28,500 km) of roads, the majority of which are unpaved. International airports are at Addis Ababa and Dire Dawa. Ethiopia uses its former ports of Massawa and Assab, which are now in Eritrea.

Communications: Several daily newspapers are published. There are 10.5 million radios and 230,000 televisions (1994 est.). With 138,000 main lines (1994 est.), telephone service is sparse.

Tourism: Historic early Christian churches and monuments and national parks are prompting greater tourist activity in Ethiopia. In 1994, 98,000 visitors spent $23 million (U.S.) in the country.

Embassy in U.S.: (202) 234-2281

Public Holidays: Coptic Christmas (January 7); End of Ramadan (date varies, in February); Epiphany (February 9); Battle of Adwa, 1896 (March 2); Palm Monday (date varies, in March or April); Good Friday (date varies, in March or April); Easter Monday (date varies, in March or April); Feast of the Sacrifice (date varies, in April); Victory Day (April 6); May Day (May 6); Birth of the Prophet (date varies, in July); New Year's Day (September 11); Feast of the True Cross (September 27)

Fiji Islands

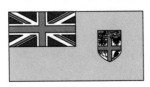

Country Name: Fiji Islands

Official Name: Republic of the Fiji Islands

Nationality: Fijian(s) (noun); Fijian (adjective)

Capital: Suva, pop. (167,400)

Major cities: Lautoka, Nadi, Ba, Labasa

External Territories: None

Location: Fiji, with an estimated 320 islands, is located in the South Pacific Ocean. About 100 of the islands are populated.

Physical Geography: Most of Fiji's islands are volcanic; some are mountainous. Some smaller islands are flat and sandy or fringed with coral reefs. The larger islands are Viti Levu, where about 70% of the population lives, Taveuni, and Kadavu.

Total area: 7,056 sq mi (18,274 sq km)

Coastline: 701 mi (1,129 km)

Land use: About 65% of the land is forested, 14% is arable or under cultivation, and less than 10% is meadows and pastures.

Climate: Tropical, hot and humid, with much rain and some hurricanes, precipitation decreasing from east to west

Population: 794,000

Urban population: 46%

Rate of natural increase: 1.8%

Age structure: 35% under 15; 3% over 65

Birth rate: 24/1000

Death rate: 6/1000

Infant mortality rate: 22/1000

Fertility rate: 3.3

Life expectancy at birth: 61 years (male); 65 years (female)

Religion: Christian, Hindu, Muslim

Language: English, Fijian, Hindi

Ethnic Divisions: Fijian, Indian

Literacy Rate: 92%

Government: Republic, with a president and bicameral Parliament. The 34 members of the Senate are appointed by the president (24 of those are nominated by the 80 member Great Council of Chiefs and one is nominated by the Rotuma Island Council). The 70 members of the House of Representatives are elected. Members of both Houses serve five-year terms. The president is also elected to a five-year term. There are four administrative divisions and one dependency.

Armed services: 3,600 troops (1996) in the army and navy

Suffrage: Universal; 21 years old

Economy: Fiji's economy is based on agriculture (including fishing for subsistence and export) and tourism; both were hurt by the world recession in the 1980s and the political instability at home during the same period. However, in the 1990s, foreign investment increased, sugar prices rose, and tourism regained its footing. Political instability and the resultant emigration continues to inhibit economic growth, but manufacturing is increasing, adding to Fiji's cash flow.

Unit of currency: Fijian dollar; 100 cents = 1 Fijian dollar ($F)

GDP per capita: $2,440

Inflation rate–CPI: 3% (1994)

Workforce: 98,112 (1995 est.)

Unemployment rate: 5.8% (1994 est.)

Exports: Goods worth $639 million (f.o.b., 1996 est.) are sent to the European Community, Australia, other Pacific islands, Japan, and other trading partners; exports include sugar, clothing, gold, processed fish, and timber.

Imports: Goods worth $947 million (c.i.f., 1996 est.) are received from Australia, New Zealand, Japan, and other trading partners; imports include machinery, fuels, food, chemicals, and consumer goods.

Agriculture: 67% (1987) of the working population engages in agriculture and fishing. Sugarcane, coconuts, cassava, rice; cattle and pigs.

Energy: Hydropower, supplemented by fuel imports, generates most of Fiji's energy needs.

Natural Resources: Timber, gold, copper, seafood, offshore oil potential

Environmental Issues: Deforestation, soil erosion

Transportation: A small 370-mile (595 km) railway serves the sugar industry. There are 2,140 miles (3,440 km) of roads. Ports include Suva and Lautoka, on Viti Levu, and Levuka, on Ovalau. An international airport is at Nadi on Viti Levu.

Communications: Fiji has one daily newspaper and seven non-dailies. There are 470,000 radios and 13,000 televisions (1994 est.). Telephone distribution, with 59,000 main lines (1994 est.), is adequate for business.

Tourism: Tropical amenities, including beaches, fishing, and diving, are prime tourist attractions. Firewalking ceremonies and other cultural traditions also draw visitors. Tourism is the country's greatest source of foreign exchange; in 1996, 339,560 tourists brought $442.3 million (U.S.) to the economy.

U.S. Tourist office: (800) 932-3454

Embassy in U.S.: (202) 337-8320

Public Holidays: National Youth Day (date varies, in March); Easter (date varies, in March or April); Ratu Sir Lala Sukuna Day (date varies, in May or June); Queen's official birthday (date varies, in June); Birth of the Prophet (date varies, in July); Constitution Day (July 21); Fiji Day: independence from United Kingdom, 1970 (October 10); Diwali

(November 11); Christmas (December 25–26)

Finland

Country Name: Finland

Official Name: Republic of Finland

Nationality: Finn(s) (noun); Finnish (adjective)

Capital: Helsinki, 532,100 [905,600]

Major cities: Espoo, Tampere, Vantaa, Turku

External Territories: None

Location: Finland, in northern Europe, is bordered on the east by Russia, on the south by the Baltic Sea, on the west by the Gulf of Bothnia and Sweden, and on the north by Norway and the Barents Sea.

Physical Geography: The country is mostly forested lowland, with many lakes, marshes, and low hills. A small highland lies in the northwest. There are thousands of coastal islands.

Total area: 130,558 sq mi (338,144 sq km)

Coastline: 699 mi (1,126 km), not including coastal indentations or islands

Land use: Three-quarters of the land is forested and 8% is arable. There are no meadows and pastures.

Climate: Warm summers and cold winters, temperatures decrease from south to north. In the north snow may remain on the ground for as long as six months.

Population: 5,170,000

Urban population: 59%

Rate of natural increase: 0.2%

FINLAND THE FINNISH-HUNGARIAN LINK

Finland is the northernmost country in Europe—so far north, in fact, that in its Arctic region the sun never sets in the month of June. Truly a land of lakes, Finland has at least 60,000, primarily in the southern part of the country, which is slightly smaller than Montana. Finland was ruled by Sweden from 1150 until 1809, when it became a grand duchy in the Russian Empire. It gained independence in 1919 but was invaded by the Soviet Union 20 years later. A treaty of mutual assistance with the Soviet Union was nullified in 1992. The Finnish language is similar to Magyar, Hungary's native tongue, and is unlike other Scandinavian languages. The first settlers to the area are thought to have come from the Urals about 2,000 years ago.

Age structure: 19% under 15; 15% over 65

Birth rate: 11/1000

Death rate: 10/1000

Infant mortality rate: 4.2/1000

Fertility rate: 1.7

Life expectancy at birth: 73 years (male); 81 years (female)

Religion: Evangelical Lutheran

Language: Finnish, Swedish

Ethnic Divisions: Finns, Swedes

Literacy Rate: 100%

Government: Republic, with a president and a unicameral legislature, the Parliament, or Eduskunta. The president is directly elected for a six-year term; the 200 members of the Parliament are elected for four-year terms. There are 12 administrative provinces.

Armed services: 36,00 troops, including 21,00 conscripts (1996) in the army, air force, and navy; 11-month conscription

Suffrage: Universal; 18 years old

Economy: Although Finland's economy has a strong base in manufacturing and service industries, high unemployment and budget deficits have prompted the government to devise programs to create jobs and reduce the deficit, as well as to increase exports and partially privatize state industries.

Unit of currency: Markka or Finmark; 100 penniä (penni, singular) = 1 markka or Finnmark (FMk)

GDP per capita: $20,000

Inflation rate–CPI: 1.2% (1997 est.)

Workforce: 2.53 million

Unemployment rate: 14.6% (1997 est.)

Exports: Goods worth $38.4 billion (f.o.b., 1996 est.) are sent to Germany, the U.K., Sweden, the U.S., and other trading partners; exports include paper and pulp, machinery, chemicals, metals, and timber.

Imports: Goods worth $29.3 billion (c.i.f., 1996 est.) are received from Germany, the U.K., Sweden, the U.S., Japan, and other trading partners; imports include food, petroleum, chemicals, and transportation equipment.

Agriculture: Nearly 9% of the working population engages in agriculture, fishing, and forestry. Forestry, which earns 31% (1996) of Finland's total exports, is the main agricultural activity. Cereals, sugar beets, and potatoes are raised, and livestock is also important.

Energy: Finland meets the majority of its energy needs with nuclear power, petroleum, wood fuels, coal, natural gas, and peat.

Natural Resources: Timber, copper, zinc, iron ore, silver

Environmental Issues: Air and water pollution, wildlife habitat loss

Transportation: The majority of the country's 48,300 miles (77,780 km) of roads are paved. There are 3,640 miles (5,860 km) of railroads, and an extensive 4,150 mile (6,680 km) inland waterway system of canals and channels. Kotka is the most important export port; imports generally pass through Helsinki. Other significant ports include Turku, Rauma, and Hamina. An international airport is at Helsinki.

Communications: Daily newspapers are published in 22 cities; 8 are published in Helsinki. There are 5 million radios and 1.9 million televisions (1995 est.) in use. Telephone service and distribution, with 2.5 million lines (1995 est.), is good.

Tourism: The inland waterway, scenery, and vast forests draw visitors to Finland. Tourism brought $1.2 billion (U.S.) to the country in 1993.

U.S. Tourist office: (212) 949-2333

Embassy in U.S.: (202) 298-5800

Public Holidays: Epiphany (January 6); Good Friday (date varies, in March or April); Easter Monday (date varies, in March or April); May Day (April 30–May1); Ascension Day (date varies, in May); Whit Sunday (date varies, in May); Midsummer Day (June 21–22); All Saints'

Day (date varies, in November); Independence Day: from Soviet Union, 1917 (December 6); Christmas (December 24–26)

France

Country Name: France

Official Name: French Republic

Nationality: Frenchman/Frenchwoman (noun); French (adjective)

Capital: Paris, pop. 2,152,300, [9,139,400]

Major cities: Marseille, Lyon, Toulouse, Nice

External Territories: Guadeloupe and Martinique, islands in the Caribbean Sea (1,112 sq mi, 2,880 sq km; pop. 800,000); French Guiana, on the northern coast of South America (32,253 sq mi, 83,534 sq km; pop. 185,000); Réunion, an island east of Madagascar in the Indian Ocean (968 sq mi, 2,507 sq km; pop. 705,000); Mayotte, part of the Comoros island group in the Indian Ocean (144 sq mi, 362 sq km; pop. 109,600); St.-Pierre and Miquelon, comprising eight islands in the North Atlantic

Ocean off the southern coast of Newfoundland (93 sq mi, 242 sq km; pop. 6,800); New Caledonia in the South Pacific Ocean (7,172 sq mi, 18,576 sq km; pop. 183,200); French Polynesia, in the Pacific Ocean (1,359 sq mi, 3,521 sq km; pop. 216,600); Wallis and Futuna Islands, in the South Pacific Ocean (106 sq mi, 274 sq km; pop. 14,400)

Location: France, in western Europe, is bordered on the north by the English Channel, Belgium, Luxembourg, and Germany; on the east by Germany, Switzerland, and Italy; on the south by the Mediterranean Sea, Spain, Monaco, and Andorra; and on the west by the Atlantic Ocean. The island of Corsica, in the Mediterranean, is about 100 miles (160 km) southeast of Cannes.

Physical Geography: The Pyrenees form the southern border of France; the Jura mountains and the Alps form part of its eastern border. Plains spread over the north and west. Farther south, Atlantic-facing lowlands give way to the central highlands, and lowlands also extend along the Mediterranean coast. Another plateau, edged by the Rhine Valley, rises in the northeast.

Total area: 210,026 sq mi (543,965 sq km)

Coastline: 2,142 mi (3,427 km)

Land use: About 35% of the land is arable or under permanent cultivation, 27% is forested, and 20% is meadows and pastures.

Climate: Temperate, with cool winters and mild summers in much of the country; hot, sunny summers and mild, wet winters along the Mediterranean coast; generally colder conditions in the east

Population: 59,067,000

Urban population: 74%

Rate of natural increase: 0.3%

Age structure: 19% under 15; 16% over 65

Birth rate: 12/1000

Death rate: 9/1000

FRANCE LYON'S HIDDEN ROMAN PAST

Lyon was founded as the capital of Roman Gaul, known as Lugdunum, but it wasn't until the 1930s that many of the ancient city's ruins, including a 10,700-seat Roman amphitheater, were accidentally discovered by a nun walking the grounds of a convent on the site, in the hills of the Fourvière district. Today the French government owns the site, which has been restored. A museum on the grounds displays a huge collection of Roman artifacts found there.

Infant mortality rate: 5/1000

Fertility rate: 1.7

Life expectancy at birth: 74 years (male); 82 years (female)

Religion: Roman Catholic

Language: French

Ethnic Divisions: French, Celtic and Latin with Teutomic, Slavic, North African, Indochine, Basques minorities

Literacy Rate: 99%

Government: Republic, with a bicameral legislature and a president. The president is directly elected to a seven-year term; the 321 members of the Senate are elected by an electoral college for nine-year terms, and the 577 members of the National Assembly are directly elected to five-year terms. There are 22 administrative regions.

Armed services: 380,820 troops (1997) in the army, navy, air force, and other military branches; compulsory ten-month tour

Suffrage: Universal; 18 years old

Economy: France has a diversified economy based on agriculture, manufacturing, and services, including tourism. The government has begun to deal with high levels of unemployment and budget deficits by implementing various spending plans, revenue-generating measures, and employment programs.

Unit of currency: French franc; 100 centimes = 1 French franc (F)

GDP per capita: $22,700

Inflation rate–CPI: 2% (1996)

Workforce: 25.5 million

Unemployment rate: 12.4% (1997 est.)

Exports: Goods worth $275 billion (f.o.b., 1997 est.) are sent to Germany, Italy, Spain, Belgium-Luxembourg, and other trading partners; exports include machinery and transportation equipment, chemicals, foodstuffs, agricultural products, and iron and steel products.

Imports: Goods worth $256 billion (f.o.b., 1997 est.) are received from Germany, Italy, the U.S., Belgium-Luxembourg, and other trading partners; imports include crude oil, machinery and equipment, agricultural products, and chemicals.

Agriculture: 5% (1995) of the labor force engages in agriculture; the country is almost self-sufficient in food production. Wheat, cereals, sugar beets, maize, barley, livestock, dairy products, and wine are all cash commodities.

Energy: Nuclear energy meets 75% (1994) of energy demands; hydropower and imported fuels are also used.

Natural Resources: Coal, iron ore, fish, timber, zinc, bauxite, potash

Environmental Issues: Air pollution, water pollution, forest damage from acid rain

Transportation: France is well served by all forms of transportation. An estimated 20,000 miles (32,000 km) of railways cross the country. There are about 750 miles (1,210 km) of high-speed train service, including service to the U.K. via a tunnel under the English Channel. About 554,240 miles (892,500 km) of paved roads and 9,270 miles (14,930 km) of inland waterways are also used. Main seaports include Marseille and Le Havre for cargo and Calais for passengers. The country has nearly 500 airports; international airports are located at Paris, Bordeaux, Lille, Lyon, Marseille, Nice, Strasbourg, and Toulouse.

Communications: Daily newspapers are published in nearly 40 cities, and Paris has more than a dozen. There are 49 million radios and 29.3 million televisions (1993 est.) in operation. The telephone system is highly developed. In 1987 there were 35 million telephones in use.

Tourism: A favored tourist country, visitors come to France to tour the museums and monuments of Paris, the Mediterranean coast, and the

wine country; winter sports in the mountains and resort spas are also big draws. In 1996, 62 million visitors brought in $28.2 billion (U.S.).

U.S. Tourist Office: (212) 838-7800

Embassy in U.S.: (202) 944-6000

Public Holidays: Easter Monday (date varies, in March or April); Whit Monday (date varies, in May); Labor Day (May 1); Liberation Day (May 8); National Day: taking of the Bastille in Paris, 1789 (July 14); Assumption (August 15); All Saints' Day (November 1); Armistice Day (November 11); Christmas (December 25)

Gabon

Country Name: Gabon

Official Name: Gabonese Republic

Nationality: Gabonese (singular and plural noun); Gabonese (adjective)

Capital: Libreville, pop. 362,400

Major cities: Port-Gentil, Franceville

External Territories: None

Location: Gabon, on the Equator in Africa, is bordered on the north by Equatorial Guinea and Cameroon, on the east and south by Congo, and on the west by the Atlantic Ocean.

Physical Geography: A narrow coastal plain of sandbars and lagoons gives way to rolling hills in the interior.

Total area: 103,347 sq mi (267,667 sq km)

Coastline: 550 mi (885 km)

Land use: Forest and woodland cover 77% of the country, 18% is meadows and pastures, and 2% is used for farming.

Climate: Tropical, with heavy seasonal rainfalls

Population: 1,197,000

Urban population: 73%

Rate of natural increase: 2.16%

Age structure: 39% under 15; 6% over 65

Birth rate: 37.5/1000

Death rate: 15.9/1000

Infant mortality rate: 87/1000

Fertility rate: 5.4

Life expectancy at birth: 51 years (male); 54 years (female)

Religion: Christian, Muslim

Language: French, Fang, Myene, Bateke, Bapounou/Eschira, Bandjabi

Ethnic Divisions: About 40 Bantu groups

Literacy Rate: 63%

Government: Republic, with an elected president and a bicameral legislature, made of the National Assembly and Senate. The president, the 120 members of the National Assembly, and the 91 members of Senate are directly elected to five-year terms. There are nine administrative provinces.

Armed services: 4,700 troops (1997) in the army, air force, and navy; voluntary

Suffrage: Universal; 21 years old

Economy: Natural resources, such as petroleum and timber, hold potential as a base for expanding Gabon's economic development, but international price fluctuations in these commodities have left the country vulnerable to budget deficits. The government is hoping to encourage foreign investment in other industries and is trying to control spending and keep inflation low to spur economic growth.

Unit of currency: CFA franc; 100 centimes = 1 franc de la Communauté financière africaine (CFAF)

GDP per capita: $5,000

Inflation rate–CPI: 6.2% (1996 est.)

Workforce: 512,000 (1996 est.)

Unemployment rate: 20% (1996 est.)

Exports: Goods worth $3.1 billion (f.o.b., 1996 est.) are sent to the U.S., France, Germany, Japan, and other trading partners; exports include crude, timber, manganese, and uranium.

Imports: Goods worth $969 million (f.o.b., 1996 est.) are received from France, the U.S., Japan, and other trading partners; imports include food, petroleum products, chemicals, construction materials, manufactured goods, machinery, and transportation equipment.

Agriculture: 45% (1996 est.) of the working population is involved with agriculture for subsistence and export. Timber, particularly okoumé, is the most important agricultural export, and cocoa, coffee, rubber, sugar, and palm oil are also grown for cash. Cassava and maize are raised for domestic consumption.

Energy: Most (75%) electricity is generated through hydropower and is supplemented by imported fuels.

Natural Resources: Petroleum, manganese, uranium, gold, timber, iron ore

Environmental Issues: Deforestation, poaching

Transportation: Nearly 400 miles (650 km) of railway are in operation, and 390 miles (630 km) of the 4,760 miles (7,670 km) of roads are paved. There are about 997 miles (1,600 km) of navigable inland waterways, including about 193 miles (310 km) on the Ogooué. Seaports include Port-Gentil, Owendo, and Libreville. International airports are at Libreville, Port-Gentil, and Franceville.

Communications: Libreville has two daily newspapers. There are 195,000 radios, 51,000 televisions, and 31,000 (1994 est.) telephone mainlines in service.

Tourism: The government is actively developing the tourist industry; attractions include the markets in Libreville, national parks and ani-

mal reserves, coastal villages, and the mountains. In 1994, 103,000 visitors brought an estimated $5 million (U.S.) to the country.

U.S. Tourist Office: (212) 447-6701

Embassy in U.S.: (202) 797-1000

Public Holidays: End of Ramadan (date varies, in February); anniversary of the Renovation: establishment of the Gabonese Democratic Party, 1968 (March 12); Easter Monday (date varies, in March or April); Feast of the Sacrifice (date varies, in April); Whit Monday (date varies, in May); Labor Day (May 1); Birth of the Prophet (date varies, in July); Anniversary of Independence: from France, 1960 (August 17); All Saints' Day (November 1); Christmas (December 25)

Gambia

Country Name: Gambia

Official Name: Republic of the Gambia

Nationality: Gambian(s) (noun); Gambian (adjective)

Capital: Banjul, pop. (42,300) [270,500]

Major cities: Serrekunda, Brikama, Bakau

External Territories: None

Location: Gambia, in western Africa, is surrounded by Senegal except for its western border on the Atlantic Ocean.

Physical Geography: The Gambia River flows into the country on its eastern border and divides the country north and its south. Broad, low hills and narrow valleys form the eastern part of the country; in the

GAMBIA   ONE SLAVE'S ROOTS UNEARTHED

Although lack of adequate records makes it virtually impossible for African Americans today to trace their ancestors to particular ethnic groups in Africa, author Alex Haley was apparently able to track down a Mandinka ancestor who was taken by slave traders from the Gambia, whose story he told in the book *Roots.*

west, mangrove swamps line the river and give way to sandy plateaus.

Total area: 4,361 sq mi (11,295 sq km)

Coastline: 50 mi (80 km)

Land use: Forests cover 28% of the land, 18% is arable, and 9% is meadows and pastures.

Climate: Tropical, with a wet season (June to November) and dry season (November to May)

Population: 1,268,000

Urban population: 37%

Rate of natural increase: 2.41%

Age structure: 41% under 15; 3% over 65

Birth rate: 43.3/1000

Death rate: 19.2/1000

Infant mortality rate: 130/1000

Fertility rate: 5.6

Life expectancy at birth: 43 years (male); 47 years (female)

Religion: Muslim, Christian

Language: English, Mandinka, Wolof, Fula

Ethnic Divisions: Mandinka, Jola, Wolof, Fula

Literacy Rate: 39%

Government: Republic, with a president and unicameral legislature, the National Assembly. The president is directly elected to a five-year term; of the 49 members of the House, 45 are elected and 4 are appointed to office. There are five administrative divisions and one city. A military coup suspended the government in 1994.

Armed services: 800 troops (1997); compulsory as of January

Suffrage: Universal; 18 years old

Economy: Agriculture and tourism are key components of the country's economy. The government is striving to develop the country's infrastructure and develop new industry, but political instability has threatened the tourist trade, and economic misfortunes have been compounded by unemployment, currency devaluation, and inflation.

Unit of currency: Dalasi; 100 butut = 1 dalasi (D)

GDP per capita: $1,000

Inflation rate–CPI: 2.2% (1997)

Workforce: 576,000 (1996 est.)

Unemployment rate: N.A.

Exports: Goods worth $160 million (f.o.b., 1995) are sent to Japan, Guinea, the U.K., Belgium, and France; exports include peanuts and their products, fish, cotton lint, and palm kernels.

Imports: Goods worth $140 million (c.i.f., 1995) are received from China, the U.K., Belgium, Senegal, and other trading partners; imports include food, fuels, machinery, and other manufactured goods.

Agriculture: Nearly 80% (1996) of the labor force engages in agriculture and fishing. Peanuts (groundnuts) are the main cash crop; cotton, citrus fruit, avocados, sesame seeds, and cattle are also raised for cash. Fish and fish products are important exports. Subsistence crops include rice, sorghum, millet, and maize.

Energy: Imported fuels power energy generation.

Natural Resources: Fish

Environmental Issues: Deforestation, desertification, water-borne diseases

Transportation: No railroads operate in the country; there are about 1,680 miles (2,700 km) of roads, of which one-third are paved. Much transport takes place on the 200 miles (320 km) of the Gambia River. Banjul is the major port and has an international airport nearby.

Communications: Newspaper publishing is in a state of flux because of the government overthrow in 1994. There are 176,000 (1994 est.) radios and 3000 televisions. There are about 18,000 (1994-5) telephones; telephone service is adequate, but distribution is sparse.

Tourism: Sandy beaches, tropical gardens, bird-watching, nature reserves, and craft markets draw visitors; tourism decreased sharply in 1994, but rebounded in 1995-96.

Embassy in U.S.: (202) 785-1399

Public Holidays: End of Ramadan (date varies, in February); Independence Day: from the U.K., 1965 (February 18); Easter (dates vary, in March or April); Feast of the Sacrifice (date varies, in April); Labor Day (May 1); Birth of the Prophet (date varies, in July); Assumption (August 15); Christmas (December 25)

Georgia

Country Name: Georgia

Official Name: Georgia

Nationality: Georgian(s) (noun); Georgian (adjective)

Capital: T'bilisi, pop. 1,268,000 (1990)

Major cities: K'ut'aisi, Rust'avi, Bat'umi

External Territories: None

Location: Georgia, in Transcaucasia (western Asia), is bordered on the north by Russia; on the east by Azerbaijan; on the south by Azerbaijan, Armenia, and Turkey; and on the west by the Black Sea.

Physical Geography: The country is mountainous, with the Great Caucasus Mountains in the north and Lesser Caucasus in the south. Lowlands lie along the Black Sea coast.

Total area: 27,027 sq mi (70,000 sq km)

Coastline: 193 mi (310 km)

Land use: Almost 34% of the land is forested, 25% is pasture, and 13% is arable or under cultivation.

Climate: Humid subtropical in the west, with humidity decreasing from west to east; cold winters and hot summers in the east

Population: 5,448,000

Urban population: 56%

Rate of natural increase: 0.3%

Age structure: 24% under 15; 11% over 65

Birth rate: 10.70/1000

Death rate: 7.5/1000

Infant mortality rate: 15.3/1000

Fertility rate: 1.3

Life expectancy at birth: 69 years (male); 76 years (female)

Religion: Christian Orthodox, Muslim, Armenian Apolistic

Language: Georgian, Russian, Armenian

Ethnic Divisions: Georgian, Armenian, Russian

Literacy Rate: 99%

Government: Republic, with a president and unicameral legislature, the Georgian Parliament. The president is directly elected to a five-year term; the 235 members of the parliament are directly elected to four-year terms. Two autonomous republics compose the administrative divisions.

Armed services: 33,200 troops (1997) in the army, navy, and air force; compulsory for two years

Suffrage: Universal; 18 years old

Economy: Internal conflicts have severely damaged Georgia's economy since independence from the Soviet Union in 1991. Fighting has disrupted manufacturing, farming, and tourism; energy supplies have diminished; and humanitarian aid is essential for adequate food supplies. The economy grew slightly in 1995, and inflation was somewhat curtailed.

Unit of currency: Lari; 100 tetri = 1 lari

GDP per capita: $1,570

Inflation rate–CPI: 7.1% (1997)

Workforce: 2.2 million (1996)

Unemployment rate: 16% (1996 est.) .

Exports: Goods worth $400 million (f.o.b., 1996 est.) are sent to Russia, Turkey, Armenia, Azerbaijan, and Bulgaria; exports include citrus fruits, tea, wine, other agricultural products, machinery, and metals.

Imports: Goods worth $773 million (c.i.f., 1996 est.) are received from Russia, Turkey, Azerbaijan, the U.S., and EU; imports include fuels, grain and other food, machinery, and transportation equipment.

Agriculture: 25% (1990) of the workforce is involved in agriculture; cash crops include citrus, grapes for wine, tea, vegetables, potatoes. Livestock, mostly sheep and goats, are raised in mountain areas.

Energy: Imported fuels produce supply significant amounts of energy; hydropower, coal, and natural gas are also used for energy generation.

Natural Resources: Forests, hydropower, manganese, iron, copper, coal

Environmental Issues: Air, water, and soil pollution

Transportation: Although an estimated 1,000 miles (1,600 km) of railways exist, many are in poor condition; 88% of the 12,850 miles (20,700 km) of roads are paved, but many roads are in need of repair. Major Black Sea ports include Bat'umi, P'oi'i, and Sokhumi, and an international airport is located in T'bilisi.

Communications: T'bilisi has several daily newspapers. There are 3,760,000 million radios and televisions (1990 est.) in operation. Phone distribution, 672,000 (1993, est.), is inadequate to meet demand and service is poor.

Tourism: Resorts along the Black Sea, medieval monasteries, castles, and the old city of T'bilisi are draws for tourists, but internal fighting has severely restricted tourism.

Embassy in U.S.: (202) 393-5959

Public Holidays: Orthodox Christmas (January 6); Easter (date varies, in March or April); Independence Day: from the Soviet Union, 1991 (May 26)

Germany

Country Name: Germany

Official Name: Federal Republic of Germany

Nationality: German(s) (noun); German (adjective)

Capital: Berlin, pop. 3,458,800

Major cities: Hamburg, München, Köln, Frankfurt

External Territories: None

Location: Germany, in northern Europe, is bordered on the north by Denmark and the Baltic Sea, on the east by Poland and the Czech Republic, on the south by Austria and Switzerland, and on the west by

France, Luxembourg, Belgium, the Netherlands, and the North Sea.

Physical Geography: Plains in the north give way to central highlands; in the south, further highlands meet the Bavarian Alps along the southern border with Austria.

Land use: Agricultural lands comprise 34% of the country, 31% is forested, and 15% is meadows and pastures.

Total area: 137,857 sq mi (357,046 sq km)

Coastline: 1,484 mi (2,389 km)

Climate: Moist temperate and marine, with cool summers and cold winters

Population: 81,950,000

Urban population: 86%

Rate of natural increase: -0.1%

Age structure: 16% under 15; 16% over 65

Birth rate: 10/1000

Death rate: 10/1000

Infant mortality rate: 5.1/1000

Fertility rate: 1.3

Life expectancy at birth: 73 years (male); 80 years (female)

Religion: Protestant, Roman Catholic

Language: German

Ethnic Divisions: German

Literacy Rate: 99%

Government: Federal republic, with a president and a bicameral legislature. The president is elected by the legislature and other local authorities. The 69 members of the Federal Council (Bundesrat) are ap-

pointed by state governments and their term lengths vary; the 672 members of the Federal Assembly (Bundestag) are elected to four-year terms by direct vote. There are 16 administrative states (Länder). The country's official capital is Berlin; however, prior to the 1990 reunification, West Germany's capital was Bonn, and the government is still in the process of moving to Berlin.

Armed services: 347,100 troops (1997) in the army, navy, and air force; compulsory for ten months

Suffrage: Universal; 18 years old

Economy: After unification in October 1990, the former German Democratic Republic began to receive massive amounts of financial aid from the Federal Republic of Germany, which has a stable economy based on manufacturing and service industries. Drastic business and market restructuring in the east has begun to generate much needed economic growth, while the country as a whole grapples with tax increases, unemployment, and financial austerity measures to reduce the deficit.

Unit of currency: Deutsche Mark; 100 Pfennige = 1 Deutsche Mark (DM)

GDP per capita: $20,800 (western: $23,600; eastern: $9,100)

Inflation rate–CPI: 1.8% (1997)

Workforce: 38.7 million

Unemployment rate: 12% (1997 est.)

Exports: Goods worth $521.1 billion (f.o.b., 1996 est.) are sent to

France, the Netherlands, Italy, the U.K., and other trading partners; exports include manufactures (including machines and machine tools, chemicals, motor vehicles, iron and steel products), agricultural products, and raw materials

Imports: Goods worth $455.7 billion (f.o.b., 1996 est.) are received from France, the Netherlands, Italy, the U.K., and other trading partners; imports include manufactures, agricultural products, fuels, and raw materials.

Agriculture: 3.2% (1995) of the workforce engages in agriculture, fishing, and forestry. Potatoes, sugar beets, barley, wheat, and wine are all key cash commodities.

Energy: Petroleum and natural gas account for over 60% of the total energy consumption. Coal, nuclear power, and lignite (primarily in eastern Germany) are also used

Natural Resources: Iron, coal, potash, timber, lignite, uranium, copper, natural gas, salt, nickel

Environmental Issues: Air and water pollution

Transportation: Roads, railways, and inland waterways provide Germany with an extensive transportation network. Nearly 27,320 miles (44,000 km) of railways and 393,090 miles (633,000 km) of roads cross the country; inland traffic also travels on about 4,700 miles (7,500 km) of waterways, including the Rhine and Elbe Rivers, the Kiel Canal that links the North and Baltic Seas, and the Main-Danube Canal, linking the North Sea to the Black Sea. Major North Sea ports include Bremen, Wilhelmshafen, Bremerhaven, and Hamburg; Baltic ports include Lübeck and Rostock. International airports are located at Berlin, Frankfurt, Köln, Dresden, Düsseldorf, Hamburg, Hannover, Leipzig, München, and Stuttgart.

Communications: More than 400 daily newspapers are published in the country. An estimated 77 million

GERMANY A NEW CAPITAL'S IMPROVEMENTS

Checkpoint Charlie, for 28 years the most famous crossing point in the Berlin Wall, is today the site of the American Business Center, a five-building, $680 million complex of offices, apartments, and shops. Berlin, a city of 3.5 million people, embarked on a huge building boom in the 1990s to prepare for its role as the new capital of a unified Germany by the end of the century.

radios and 46 million televisions (1995) are in operation. Phone service and distribution is excellent.

Tourism: Visitors to Germany flock to spas, mountain resorts for skiing and other winter sports, medieval towns, castles, and scenic regions such as the Black Forest, the Rhine Valley, and Bavaria. München, Berlin, Dresden, and Köln attract visitors. An estimated 14 million tourists visited Germany in 1996.

U.S. Tourist Office: (212) 661-7200

Embassy in U.S.: (202) 298-4000

Public Holidays: Good Friday (date varies, in March or April); Easter Monday (date varies, in March or April); Whit Monday (date varies, in May); Labor Day (May 1); Ascension Day (May 16); Unification Day: Federal Republic of Germany with German Democratic Republic, 1990 (October 3); Day of Unity (October 15); Christmas (December 25–26)

Ghana

Country Name: Ghana

Official Name: Republic of Ghana

Nationality: Ghanaian(s) (noun); Ghanaian (adjective)

Capital: Accra, pop. [1,673,000]

Major cities: Kumasi, Tamale, Tema

External Territories: None

Location: Ghana, in west Africa, is on the Atlantic Ocean between Côte d'Ivoire on the west and Togo on the east; Burkina Faso is on the north.

Physical Geography: Ghana has plains at low elevations, with a central plateau. Rivers include the Black and White Volta. Lake Volta, created by a dam on the White Volta, is about 300 miles long (485 km).

Total area: 92,100 sq mi (238,537 sq km)

Coastline: 335 mi (539 km)

Land use: Nearly 35% of the country is forested, 22% is meadows and pastures, and 19% is used for agriculture.

Climate: Tropical, except for the northern part of the country; two rainy seasons a year

Population: 19,678,000

Urban population: 37%

Rate of natural increase: 2.88%

Age structure: 46% under 15; 3% over 65

Birth rate: 38.8/1000

Death rate: 10/1000

Infant mortality rate: 66.4/1000

Fertility rate: 5.4

Life expectancy at birth: 57 years (male); 61 years (female)

Religion: Indigenous beliefs, Muslim, Christian

Language: English, Akan, Moshi-Dagomba, Ewe, and Ga

Ethnic Divisions: Akan, Moshi-Dagomba, Ewe, and Ga

Literacy Rate: 65%

Government: Democracy, with a president and a unicameral legislature, the Parliament. The president and the 200 members of the Parliament are directly elected to four-year terms. There are ten administrative regions.

Armed services: 7,000 troops (1997 est.) in the army, navy, and air force

Suffrage: Universal; 18 years old

Economy: Although Ghana's economy, based on agriculture and mining, is stronger than many of its neighbors, political instability, weather fluctuations, and commodity price swings hinder desired growth. International aid has been extended to support diversification of the export base and to encourage the transfer of industries from public to private owners. Although the government has been trying to bring down spending, some inflationary measures have had to be rescinded because of public protests over high prices.

Unit of currency: Cedi; 100 pesewas = 1 new cedi (C)

GDP per capita: $2,000

Inflation rate–CPI: 27.7% (1997 est.)

Workforce: 8.3 million (1996 est.)

Unemployment rate: 20% (1997 est.)

Exports: Goods worth $1.57 billion (f.o.b., 1996 est.) are sent to Germany, the Netherlands, the U.K., Switzerland, and other trading partners; exports include gold, cocoa, timber, tuna, and bauxite.

Imports: Goods worth $1.84 billion (c.i.f., 1995) are received from the U.K., the U.S., Germany, Nigeria, and other trading partners; imports include petroleum, food, chemicals, and machinery.

Agriculture: About 55% (1996 est.) of the working population engages in agriculture and fishing. Cash crops include cocoa, coffee, bananas, coconuts, limes, and timber. Food crops include rice, cassava, corn, and peanuts.

Energy: Hydroelectricity contributes about 90% of Ghana's energy.

Natural Resources: Minerals, including gold, diamonds, bauxite, manganese; timber; fish

Environmental Issues: Deforestation, soil erosion, water pollution, wildlife habitat loss, inadequate potable water

Transportation: There are about 590 miles (960 km) of railroads and 24,470 miles (39,400 km) of roads in Ghana, about 30% of which are paved. Seaports are at Tema and Sekondi-Takoradi. There are about 810 miles (1,300 km) of navigable waterways, most of which are on Lake Volta. There is an international airport at Accra.

Communications: Accra has two daily newspapers (1996). An estimated 4.0 million radios and 1.6 million televisions (1995) are in operation. An estimated 50,000 (1994) telephones in operation provide only fair service.

Tourism: In 1996, an estimated 300,000 tourists spent about $248 million (U.S.); important tourist draws include national parks for wildlife, cultural and historical sites in Accra and along the coast, and beaches.

Embassy in U.S.: (202) 686-4520

Public Holidays: Independence Day: from Great Britain, 1957 (March 6); Easter (date varies, in March or April); Labor Day (May 1); Republic Day (July 1); National Farmer's Day (December 1); Christmas (December 25–26)

Greece

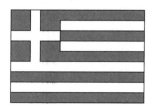

Country Name: Greece

Official Name: Hellenic Republic

Nationality: Greek(s) (noun); Greek (adjective)

Capital: Athens, pop. 772,100 [3,027,900]

Major cities: Thessaloníki, Piraeus, Pátrai

External Territories: None

Location: Greece, on the Mediterranean in southeastern Europe, is between the Aegean Sea on the east and Ionian Sea on the west; it is bordered on the north by Macedonia and Bulgaria and on the west by Albania.

Physical Geography: Mainland Greece is mostly mountainous, with rugged coastlines and some coastal plains and lowlands along river valleys. There are also more than 400 islands, including Crete, the largest, in the Aegean Sea, the Ionian Sea, and the Mediterranean Sea.

Total area: 50,962 sq mi (131,990 sq km)

Coastline: 8,493 mi (13,676 km)

Land use: An estimated 40% of land is meadows and pastures and 27% is used for agriculture; 20% is forested.

Climate: Mediterranean, with hot, dry summers and mild, rainy winters; temperature and precipitation vary with elevation, especially in the northern mountains where cold winters with deep snow prevail

Population: 10,539,000

Urban population: 59%

Rate of natural increase: 0.0%

Age structure: 16% under 15; 16% over 65

Birth rate: 10/1000

Death rate: 10/1000

Infant mortality rate: 6.3/1000

Fertility rate: 1.3

Life expectancy at birth: 75 years (male); 80 years (female)

Religion: Greek Orthodox

Language: Greek, English, French

Ethnic Divisions: Greek

Literacy Rate: 95%

Government: Democracy, with a president and a unicameral legislature, the Chamber of Deputies. The president is elected by the legislature for a five-year term, and the 300 members of the Chamber of Deputies are elected to four-year terms. There are ten administrative regions and Athens.

Armed services: 162,300 troops (1997) in the army, navy, and air force; compulsory service for men 18 to 40 years of age; women may volunteer; enlistments range from 19 to 23 months, depending on the branch of service

Suffrage: Universal and compulsory; 18 years old

Economy: Although Greece has significant revenue from tourism and agriculture, the budget deficit continues to be the overriding factor restricting economic growth. The government implemented plans beginning in the late 1980s to reduce the deficit, reduce inflation, and reform government management of the public sector. Nevertheless, international monetary assistance is still needed to sustain the economy.

Unit of currency: Drachma (singular), drachmae (plural); 100 lepta (lepton, singular) = 1 drachma (Dr)

GDP per capita: $13,000

Inflation rate–CPI: 6% (1997 est.)

Workforce: 4.1 million

Unemployment rate: 10% (1997 est.)

Exports: Goods worth $9.8 billion (f.o.b., 1997 est.) are sent to Germany, Italy, France, the U.K., and other trading partners; exports include manufactured goods, foodstuffs, and fuels.

Imports: Goods worth $27 billion (c.i.f., 1997 est.) are received from Germany, Italy, France, and other trading partners; imports include manufactured goods, foodstuffs and fuels.

Agriculture: An estimated 23% (1994) of the workforce is involved in agriculture and fishing. Cash crop include fruits and vegetables. Main crops are wheat, corn, barley, sugar beets, olives, tomatoes, wine, and tobacco.

Energy: Petroleum and domestic lignite provide fuel for most energy generation; hydropower is being developed.

Natural Resources: Minerals, including lignite, bauxite, magnesite, petroleum, marble

Environmental Issues: Air and water pollution

Transportation: Most of the 72,660 miles (117,000 km) of roads in Greece are paved, and there are 1,540 miles (2,480 km) of railways in operation. The 3.7-mile (6 km) Corinth Canal connects the Corinthian and Saronic Gulfs; seaports include Pátrai, Piraeus, Thessaloníki, and Iraklion on Crete. Athens, Thessaloníki, and Alexandroupolis, among others, have international airports.

Communications: 168 daily newspapers (1994) are published in Greece; Athens has more than two dozen. An estimated 4.3 million radios (1995) and 2.3 million televisions (1993) are in operation, receiving broadcasts from government and private stations. Phone service is good, with an estimated 5.6 million phones in use.

Tourism: Tourism is an important source of income; 11.2 million tourists brought $3.9 billion (U.S.) to Greece in 1994. Attractions include antiquities and museums in Athens and other cities, cultural events, and winter getaways in the Greek islands.

U.S. Tourist Office: (212) 421-5777
Embassy in U.S.: (202) 939-5800

Public Holidays: Epiphany (January 6); Clean Monday (date varies, in February or March); Independence Day: 1821 proclamation of war of independence, from Ottoman Empire (March 25); Greek Orthodox Easter (date varies, in April); Labor Day (May 1); Whit Monday (date varies, in June); Assumption (August 15); *Ochi* Day: anniversary of Greek defiance of 1940 Italian ultimatum (October 28); Christmas (December 25–26)

Grenada

Country Name: Grenada
Official Name: Grenada
Nationality: Grenadian(s) (noun); Grenadian (adjective)
Capital: St. George's, pop. 4,800
Major cities: N.A.
External Territories: None
Location: Grenada, an island country in the Caribbean Sea, is about 100 miles (160 km) north of Venezuela.
Physical Geography: Grenada is a mountainous volcanic island, with gorges and waterfalls; several smaller islands to the north are also part of the country.
Total area: 133 sq mi (344 sq km)
Coastline: 75 mi (121 km)
Land use: More than one-third of the land is arable and under permanent cultivation; 3% is meadows and pastures, and 9% is forest and woodland.
Climate: Tropical, with a rainy season from June through November; occasional hurricanes
Population: 97,000
Urban population: 34%.
Rate of natural increase: 2.34%
Age structure: 38% under 15; 6% over 65

Birth rate: 29.13/1000
Death rate: 5.74/1000
Infant mortality rate: 12/1000
Fertility rate: 3.8
Life expectancy at birth: 68 years (male); 73 years (female)
Religion: Roman Catholic, Protestant
Language: English, French patois
Ethnic Divisions: Black
Literacy Rate: 98%
Government: Parliamentary democracy, with a governor-general appointed by Queen Elizabeth II of the U.K., and bicameral legislature, the Parliament. The 13 members of the Senate are appointed, and the 15 members of the House of Representatives are popularly elected for five-year terms. There are six administrative parishes and one dependency.
Armed services: Regional Security trained by the British; parliamentary defense contingent trained by the U.S.
Suffrage: Universal; 18 years old
Economy: Tourism and agriculture are the backbone of Grenada's economy, which is hampered by large national and international debts and severe unemployment. The government plans to generate additional revenue by enhancing investment and is working with Indonesia to stabilize world prices for nutmeg, a key agricultural commodity.
Unit of currency: East Caribbean dollar; 100 cents = 1 East Caribbean dollar (EC$)
GDP per capita: $3,200
Inflation rate–CPI: 3.2% (1996 est.)
Workforce: 36,000
Unemployment rate: 20% (1996)
Exports: Goods worth $24 million (f.o.b., 1996 est.) are sent to Caribbean Community and Common Market (CARICOM) countries, the U.K., U.S., and the Netherlands; exports include bananas, cocoa, nutmeg, clothing, and mace.

GRENADA NUTMEG CAPITAL OF THE WORLD

Grenada is a Caribbean island about twice the size of the District of Columbia that has the distinction of being the smallest country in the Western Hemisphere. Often called the Spice Island, Grenada is the world's largest producer of nutmeg.

Imports: Goods worth $128 million (f.o.b., 1996 est.) are received from the U.S., the U.K., Japan, and CARICOM countries; imports include food, manufactured goods, machinery, chemicals, and fuels.

Agriculture: 24% (1985) of the workforce engages in agriculture. Nutmeg (a pod is on the national flag) and mace are key cash crops. Other export crops include bananas, cocoa, and other tropical fruits and vegetables.

Energy: Grenada uses imported fuels for energy generation.

Natural Resources: Timber, tropical fruit, and deepwater harbors

Environmental Issues: N.A.

Transportation: There are an estimated 650 miles (1,040 km) of roads, of which more than half are paved. There are no railroads. St. George's and Grenville the main seaports; an international airport is located at Point Salines.

Communications: There are no daily newspapers; several weekly and monthly newspapers are published in St. George's. About 80,000 radios and 30,000 televisions (1993) are in use. Phone service is good, with some 5,650 telephones (1988) in operation.

Tourism: In 1996, nearly 386,000 visitors, mostly cruise-ship passengers, came to Grenada, lured by tropical beaches and mountain forests. In 1996, visitors brought $161 million (E.C.) to the country.

U.S. Tourist Office: (800) 927-9554

Embassy in U.S.: (202) 265-2561

Public Holidays: Independence Day: from Great Britain, 1974 (February 7); Good Friday (date varies, in March or April); Easter Monday (date varies, in March or April); Labor Day (date varies, in May); Whit Monday (date varies, in May or June); Corpus Christi (date varies, in May or June); Emancipation Holidays (date varies, in early August); Thanksgiving Day (October 25); Christmas (December 25–26); New Year's Eve (December 31)

Guatemala

Country Name: Guatemala

Official Name: Republic of Guatemala

Nationality: Guatemalan(s) (noun); Guatemalan (adjective)

Capital: Guatemala City, pop. 1,675,600

Major cities: Quetzaltenango, Escuintla, Mazatenango, Retalhuleu

External Territories: None

Location: Guatemala, in Central America, is bordered on the north and west by Mexico, on the east by Belize, and on the southeast by Honduras and El Salvador; the Pacific Ocean is to the south, and the Caribbean is to the east.

Physical Geography: Plains in the north give way to the Sierra Madre, with some active volcanos, that cross the country from east to west. Lowlands line the Pacific coast.

Total area: 42,042 sq mi (108,889 sq km)

Coastline: 248 mi (400 km)

Land use: 54% of the land is forested, 24% is meadows and pastures, and 12% is arable.

Climate: Tropical, with a rainy season from May to October; temperatures and precipitation vary with elevation

Population: 12,336,000

Urban population: 38%

Rate of natural increase: 2.94%

Age structure: 44% under 15; 3% over 65

Birth rate: 36.7/1000

Death rate: 7.3/1000

Infant mortality rate: 51/1000

Fertility rate: 5.1

Life expectancy at birth: 63 years (male); 68 years (female)

Religion: Roman Catholic, Protestant, traditional Maya

Language: Spanish, Amerindian languages

Ethnic Divisions: Amerindian, mestizo

Literacy Rate: 56%

Government: Republic, with a president and a unicameral legislature, the Congress of the Republic. The president is directly elected to a four-year term, and the 80 members of the legislature are also elected to four-year terms. There are 22 administrative departments.

Armed services: 40,700 troops (1997) in the army, navy, and air force, and a paramilitary force of 9,800; 30-month selective conscription

Suffrage: Universal; 18 years old

Economy: Political stabilization in 1995 resulted in economic recovery. By 1997 the government had committed to raising tax revenue to 12% of the GDP. International aid for reconstruction has been accompanied by demands for strict tax reforms.

Unit of currency: Quetzal (singular), quetzales (plural); 100 centavos = 1 quetzal (Q)

GDP per capita: $4,000

GUATEMALA
UNIQUELY INDIAN

Once the center of the Maya Empire, Guatemala today is unique in North America in that its population remains predominantly Indian.

Inflation rate–CPI: 9% (1997 est.)

Workforce: 3.32 million (1997 est.)

Unemployment rate: 2% (1997 est.)

Exports: Goods worth $2.9 billion (f.o.b., 1997 est.) are sent to the U.S., El Salvador, Costa Rica, Germany, and Honduras; exports include coffee, sugar, bananas, cardamom, and petroleum.

Imports: Goods worth $3.3 billion (c.i.f., 1997 est.) are received from the U.S., Mexico, Venezuela, Japan, and Germany; imports include fuels, machinery, grain, fertilizers, and motor vehicles.

Agriculture: Nearly 60% (1995) of the labor force engages in agriculture and fishing. Cash crops include coffee, sugar, bananas, and cardamom.

Energy: Guatemala generates most of its energy using petroleum, largely imported, and other fuels; hydropower meets some energy needs.

Natural Resources: Petroleum, nickel, rare woods, fish, chicle

Environmental Issues: Deforestation, soil erosion, water pollution

Transportation: About 25% of Guatemala's 8,140 miles (13,100 km) of roads are paved, including over 300 miles (480 km) of the Pan American Highway. There are more than 500 miles (800 km) of railways. About 160 miles (260 km) of waterways are navigable year-round. Pacific seaports include San José and Champerico; the Caribbean port is Puerto Barrios. An international airport is at Guatemala City.

Communications: Half a dozen daily papers are published in Guatemala City. There are 400,000 radios and 475,000 televisions (1993) in operation. Telephone service is fairly good in urban areas, but phone distribution, an estimated 210,000 (1993), is limited.

Tourism: War during the 1980s discouraged tourists; now tourists come to the great Maya ruins at Tikal and to tour Guatemala City. In 1995,

585,000 visitors brought an estimated $276 million (U.S.) to the country.

U.S. Tourist Office: (800) 742-4529

Embassy in U.S.: (202) 745-4952

Public Holidays: Epiphany (January 6); Easter (date varies, in March or April); Labor Day (May 1); Anniversary of the Revolution (June 30); Independence Day: from Spain, 1821 (September 15); Columbus Day (October 12); Revolution Day (October 20); All Saints' Day (November 1); Christmas (December 24–25)

Guinea

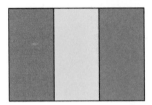

Country Name: Guinea

Official Name: Republic of Guinea

Nationality: Guinean(s) (noun); Guinean (adjective)

Capital: Conakry, pop. 1,090,600

Major cities: Kankan, Nzérékoré, Kindia

External Territories: None

Location: Guinea, in western Africa, is bordered on the north by Senegal and Mali, on the east by Côte d'Ivoire, on the south by Liberia and Sierra Leone, on the west by the North Atlantic Ocean, and on the northwest by Guinea-Bissau.

Physical Geography: The Fouta Djallon highlands rise in the northeast from coastal plains; plains also stretch to the north. A small forested region rises in the southeast highlands.

Total area: 94,926 sq mi (245,857 sq km)

Coastline: 199 mi (320 km)

Land use: Forest estimated area is 59%, 22% of the land is meadows and pastures, and 2% of the land is arable or used for agriculture.

Climate: Tropical, with heavy rains from May until November; decreasing precipitation and temperatures inland

Population: 7,539,000

Urban population: 26%

Rate of natural increase: 2.38%

Age structure: 46% under 15; 3% over 65

Birth rate: 42/1000

Death rate: 18.2/1000

Infant mortality rate: 134/1000

Fertility rate: 5.7

Life expectancy at birth: 43 years (male); 48 years (female)

Religion: Muslim, Christian, indigenous beliefs

Language: French, tribal languages

Ethnic Divisions: Peuhl, Malinke, Soussou, others

Literacy Rate: 36%

Government: Republic, with a president and a unicameral legislature, the National Assembly. The president and the 114 members of

---

GUINEA BUILDING ON BAUXITE

In 1958 Guinea became the first French colony in Africa to achieve independence. Today Muslims comprise 87 percent of the population. One of the world's largest bauxite (the mineral used to make aluminum) deposits is found here, which constitutes 25 percent of the world's reserves.

the National Assembly are directly elected. There are eight administrative provinces.

Armed services: 9,700 troops (1997 est.) in the army, navy, and air force; two-year compulsory service for citizens

Suffrage: Universal; 18 years old

Economy: Guinea's export revenue comes primarily from the sale of bauxite, and abundant mineral resources hold promise for Guinea's economy, prompting programs to attract foreign investment. Other plans are in the works to improve the country's infrastructure and provide greater educational and health services for citizens. However, strict budgetary measures and overall political stability will be essential for the development and diversification of the country's economic base.

Unit of currency: Guinean franc; 100 centimes = 1 Guinean franc (FG)

GDP per capita: $1,100

Inflation rate–CPI: 3.5% (1996 est.)

Workforce: 3,614,000 (1996 est.)

Unemployment rate: N.A.

Exports: Goods worth $748 million (1995 est.) are sent to the U.S., Belgium, Ireland, Spain, and other trading partners; exports include bauxite, alumina, diamonds, gold, and coffee.

Imports: Goods worth $809 million (1995 est.) are received from France, Côte d'Ivoire,Belguim, the U.S., and other trading partners; imports include petroleum, metals, machinery, transportation equipment, textiles, and food.

Agriculture: Just over 80% (1996 est.) of the workforce engages in agricultural production. Export crops include pineapples, palm kernels, and coffee; food crops include rice, cassava, and vegetables. Timber and fishing are potential as export earners.

Energy: Despite significant hydropower potential, electricity output fails to meet demand. Fuel imports are currently needed for most of Guinea's energy.

Natural Resources: Minerals, including bauxite, iron, diamonds, gold, uranium; hydropower; fish

Environmental Issues: Deforestation, desertification, soil pollution, erosion, inadequate drinking water supplies, overpopulation in forested regions

Transportation: About 670 miles (1090 km) of railroads and 18,940 miles (30,500 km) of roads cross the country; about 3,110 miles (5,000 km) of the roads are paved. About 808 miles (1,300 km) of waterways are navigable. The main sea ports are Conakry and Kamsar. An international airport is at Conakry.

Communications: Several weekly and monthly papers are published in Conakry. There are 280,000 radios, 50,000 televisions, and about 9,000 telephones (1994 est.) in operation.

Tourism: Tourists are able to see a rich variety of cultural arts, including musical performances, dance troupes, and handicrafts, in the larger cities. Visitors brought an estimated $6 million (U.S.) to the country in 1993.

Embassy in U.S.: (202) 483-9420

Public Holidays: End of Ramadan (date varies, in February); Easter Monday (date varies, in March or April); Labor Day (May 1); Birth of the Prophet (date varies, in July); Anniversary of Women's Revolt (August 27); Referendum Day (September 28); Republic Day: independence from France, 1958 (October 2); All Saints' Day (November 1); Day of Invasion: by Portuguese, 1970 (November 22); Christmas (December 25)

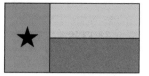

Guinea-Bissau

Country Name: Guinea-Bissau

Official Name: Republic of Guinea-Bissau

Nationality: Guinea-Bissauan(s) (noun); Guinea-Bissauan (adjective)

Capital: Bissau, pop. 223,000

Major cities: Bafatá, Gabú, Mansôa

External Territories: None

Location: Guinea-Bissau, in western Africa, is between Senegal to the north and Guinea to the south; the Atlantic Ocean is on the south and southwest.

Physical Geography: Highlands in the northeast give way to savannas in the interior, and coastal lowlands are covered by forests and mangrove swamps. The Arquipélago dos Bijagós, to the west, is also part of the country.

Total area: 13,948 sq mi (36,125 sq km)

Coastline: 217 mi (350 km)

Land use: About 38% is meadows and pastures, 38% is forested, and 12% is arable and under cultivation.

Climate: Tropical, with a rainy season from June to November

Population: 1,187,000

Urban population: 22%

Rate of natural increase: 2.2%

Age structure: 43% under 15; 4% over 65

Birth rate: 42.7/1000

Death rate: 20.7/1000

Infant mortality rate: 135.5/1000

Fertility rate: 5.9

Life expectancy at birth: 43 years (male); 46 years (female)

Religion: Indigenous beliefs, Muslim

GUINEA-BISSAU
YOUNG TEEN VOTERS

A Portuguese colony until 1974, Guinea-Bissau allows everyone 15 years of age and older the right to vote.

Language: Portuguese, Crioulo, African languages

Ethnic Divisions: Balanta, Fula, Manjaca, Mandinga, others

Literacy Rate: 54%

Government: Republic, with a president and a unicameral legislature, the National People's Assembly. The president is directly elected to a five-year term; the 100 members of the legislature are directly elected to four-year terms. There are nine administrative regions.

Armed services: 9,250 troops (1997 est.) in the army, navy, air force, and other military branches; selective conscription

Suffrage: Universal; 15 years old

Economy: An extremely poor country, the economy of Guinea-Bissau is based on farming and fishing. International aid has been essential for economic survival, and plans are being implemented to privatize state-run operations, improve the country's infrastructure, and create small businesses.

Unit of currency: CFA franc; 100 centimes = 1 franc de la Communauté financière africaine (CFAC)

GDP per capita: $975

Inflation rate–CPI: 65% (1996)

Workforce: 517,000 (1996 est.)

Unemployment rate: N.A.

Exports: Goods worth $25.8 million (f.o.b., 1996 est.) are sent to Spain, India, Thailand, Italy, and other trading partners; exports include cashews, peanuts, fish, and palm kernels.

Imports: Goods worth $63 million (f.o.b., 1996 est.) are received from Thailand, Portugal, Japan, and other trading partners; imports include food, transportation equipment, fuels, and machinery.

Agriculture: More than three-quarters (1996) of the working population engages in agriculture. Cashew nuts provide 85.8% (1995) of the total value of export earnings. Other cash crops include palm kernels, cotton, and peanuts. Rice, corn, beans, cassava, millet, sorghum, and other food crops are grown for domestic use. Fish and timber are becoming key exports.

Energy: Most energy is generated with hydropower and imported fuels.

Natural Resources: Phosphates, bauxite, and petroleum; fish; timber

Environmental Issues: Deforestation, soil erosion, overgrazing; overfishing

Transportation: There are no railroads. There are 2,730 miles (4400 km) of roads, of which 280 miles (450 km) are paved. Bissau is the main seaport, and rivers such as the Gêba and Cacheu are navigable. There is an international airport at Bissau.

Communications: One daily paper and one weekly paper are published in Bissau. There are 42,000 radios (1994 est.) and 9,000 phones (1993 est.) in service.

Tourism: Although tourists are welcome, there is little information about visitor attractions in Guinea-Bissau.

Embassy in U.S.: (202) 347-3950

Public Holidays: Death of Amílcar Cabral, founder of Partido Africano da Independência da Guinée Cabo Verde (January 20); End of Ramadan (date varies, in February); Feast of the Sacrifice (date varies, in April); Labor Day (May 1); Anniversary of the Killing of Pidjiguiti (August 3); National Day (September 24); Anniversary of the Movement of Readjustment (November 14); Christmas (December 25)

Guyana

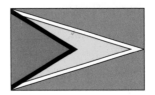

Country Name: Guyana

Official Name: Co-operative Republic of Guyana

Nationality: Guyanese (singular and plural noun); Guyanese (adjective)

Capital: Georgetown, pop. 72,000 [187,100]

Major cities: Linden, New Amsterdam, Rose Hall

External Territories: None

Location: Guyana, on the northeast coast of South America, is between Suriname on the east, Venezuela on the west, and Brazil on the south and west. The Atlantic Ocean is to the northeast.

Physical Geography: Protected coastal plains give way to an inland tropical forest that covers about 80% of the country. South of the forest are the Pakarima Mountains and savannas.

Total area: 83,000 sq mi (214,969 sq km)

Coastline: 285 mi (459 km)

Land use: About 80% of the land is covered with rain forest; 6% is meadows and pastures, and 2% is used for agriculture.

Climate: Tropical, with two rainy seasons from April to August and November to January

Population: 705,000

Urban population: 36%

Rate of natural increase: 1.7%

Age structure: 35% under 15; 4% over 65

Birth rate: 24.2/1000

Death rate: 6.9/1000

Infant mortality rate: 63/1000

Fertility rate: 2.7

Life expectancy at birth: 63 years (male); 69 years (female)

Religion: Christian, Hindu, Muslim

Language: English, Amerindian dialects

Ethnic Divisions: East Indian, black, mixed, Indian

Literacy Rate: 98%

Government: Republic, with a president and unicameral legislature, the National Assembly. The president is the leader of the majority party in the National Assembly; of the 65 members of the legislature, 53 are directly elected and 12 are appointed from their regional governments. There are ten administrative regions.

Armed services: 1,600 troops (1997 est.) in the Combined Guyanese Defense Force

Suffrage: Universal; 18 years old

Economy: Despite the challenges of managing a large external debt and moving toward industry privatization, Guyana is committed to bolstering its infrastructure and increasing its pool of skilled labor to sustain the favorable economic growth rate achieved in the early 1990s. A high emigration rate of about 15,000 per year has drained the country of skilled labor. International aid has been given to support the restructuring of the financial sector, and the government continues its attempts to bring down international debt and control inflation.

Unit of currency: Guyanese dollar; 100 cents = 1 Guyanese dollar ($G)

GDP per capita: $2,500

Inflation rate–CPI: 4.5% (1997)

Workforce: N.A.

Unemployment rate: 12% (1992 est.)

Exports: Goods worth $546 million (f.o.b., 1996) are sent to Canada, the U.K., the U.S, and other trading partners; exports include sugar, bauxite, rice, shrimp, and molasses.

Imports: Goods worth $589 million (c.i.f., 1996) are received from the U.S., Trinidad and Tobago, Netherlands Antilles, the U.K., and other trading partners; imports include manufactured goods, machinery, petroleum, and food.

Agriculture: About 39% (1995 est.) of the working population engages in agricultural production. Key exports include sugarcane, rice, timber, and seafood; beef, maize, fruits, and vegetables are raised for domestic consumption. Timber exports increased by 70% between 1993 and 1994.

Energy: Most energy is generated using imported fuel.

Natural Resources: Bauxite, gold, diamonds, timber, shrimp, fish

Environmental Issues: Deforestation, water pollution

Transportation: There are 55 miles (88 km) of railroad; however, there is no passenger service. There are 4,950 miles (7,970 km) of roads, most of which are on the coast. There are 3,725 miles (6,000 km) of navigable waterways, including the Essequibo, Mazaruni, and Berbice Rivers. Georgetown and New Amsterdam are the main shipping ports. An international airport is near Georgetown.

Communications: One daily newspaper is published in Georgetown. There are 400,000 radios, 32,000 televisions (1992, est.), and 33,000 phones (1987 est.) in service.

Tourism: Visitor facilities are limited in Guyana, but the rain forest holds potential as an ecotourist site. About 113,000 tourists brought $47 million (U.S.) to the country in 1994.

Embassy in U.S.: (202) 265-6900

Public Holidays: End of Ramadan (date varies, in February); Republic Day: independence from the U.K., 1966 (February 23); Good Friday (date varies, in March or April); Easter Monday (date varies, in March or April); Feast of the Sacrifice (date varies, in April); Labor Day (May 1); Caribbean Day (June 30); Birth of the Prophet (date varies, in July); Freedom Day (August 5); Christmas (December 25)

Haiti

Country Name: Haiti

Official Name: Republic of Haiti

Nationality: Haitian(s) (noun); Haitian (adjective)

Capital: Port-au-Prince, pop. 884,500

Major cities: N.A.

External Territories: None

Location: Haiti, in the West Indies, is on the western third of the island of Hispaniola. The Dominican Republic occupies the eastern two-thirds of the island. Cuba is less than 50 miles (80 km) to the west.

Physical Geography: Mostly mountainous lands are separated by an alluvial plain.

Total area: 10,714 sq mi (27,750 sq km)

Coastline: 1,100 mi (l,771 km)

Land use: Only 5% of the land is forested, 18% is meadows and pastures, and 33% is arable or under cultivation.

Climate: Tropical, with drier conditions on the lee sides of mountains; rainy season May to November

Population: 7,751,000

Urban population: 34%

Rate of natural increase: 2.09%

Age structure: 40% under 15; 4% over 65

Birth rate: 34/1000

Death rate: 13.1/1000

Infant mortality rate: 73.9/1000

Fertility rate: 4.8

Life expectancy at birth: 52 years (male); 56 years (female)

Religion: Roman Catholic, Protestant, Voodoo

Language: French, Creole

Ethnic Divisions: Black, mulatto

Literacy Rate: 45%

Government: Republic, with a president and a bicameral legislature, the National Assembly. The president is directly elected for a five-year term. The 27 members of the Senate are elected to six-year terms, and the 83 members of the Chamber of Deputies are elected to four-year terms. There are nine administrative departments.

Armed services: Effectively dissolved in 1995 and replaced with a 4,000-man police force

Suffrage: Universal; 18 years old

Economy: Struggling to regain its footing after years of political instability, the Haitian government faces a daunting task in providing food and adequate medical care for its citizens, aside from devising plans to increase economic growth. International aid is essential as the government attempts to stem inflation and restructure public businesses.

Unit of currency: Gourde; 100 centimes = 1 gourde (G)

GDP per capita: $1,070

Inflation rate–CPI: 17% (1997 est.)

Workforce: 3,600,000 (1995 est.)

Unemployment rate: 60% (1996 est.)

Exports: Goods worth $90 million (f.o.b., 1996 est.) are sent to the U.S.and EU; exports include manufactured items, coffee, and other agriculture.

Imports: Goods worth $665 million (f.o.b., 1996 est.) are received from the U.S.and EU; imports include machinery, manufactured goods, food, petroleum, fats and oils, and chemicals.

Agriculture: An estimated 66% of the workforce engages in agriculture and fishing. Domestic crops include sugar, maize, mangoes, sorghum, and rice.

Energy: Fuels are imported. Local timber and charcoal are extensively used.

Natural Resources: N.A.

Environmental Issues: Deforestation, soil erosion, insufficient potable water supply

Transportation: No public railroads operate in the country. Over 2,500 miles (4,000 km) of roads connect the country, of which nearly one quarter are paved. Port-au-Prince and Cap-Haïtien are the primary shipping ports, and there is an international airport near Port-au-Prince.

Communications: Two daily newspapers are published in Port-au-Prince. There are 330,000 radios, 33,000 televisions, and 45,000 phone lines (1993 est.) in service.

Tourism: Port-au-Prince is noted for its gingerbread-style houses and nearby beaches; Jacmel offers quiet beach resorts; and Cap-Haïtien has a historic citadel with a breathtaking view of the surrounding countryside. Visitors brought an estimated $46 million (U.S.) to the country in 1994.

Embassy in U.S.: (202) 332-4090

Public Holidays: Heroes of Independence: from France, 1804 (January 2); Shrove Monday (date varies, in February); Shrove Tuesday (date varies, in February); Good Friday (date varies, in March or April); Pan-American Day (April 14); Labor Day (May 1); Flag Day (May 18); National Sovereignty (May 22); Assumption (August 15); United Nations Day (October 24); All Souls' Day (November 2); Army Day and Comemoration of the Battle of Vertières (November 18); Discovery Day (December 5); Christmas (December 25)

Honduras

Country Name: Honduras

Official Name: Republic of Honduras

Nationality: Honduran(s) (noun); Honduran (adjective)

Capital: Tegucigalpa, pop. 813,900

Major cities: San Pedro Sula, La Ceiba, El Progreso

External Territories: None

Location: Honduras, in Central America, is bordered on the north by the Caribbean Sea, on the southeast by Nicaragua, on the southwest by El Salvador, on the south by the Pacific Ocean, and on the west by Guatemala.

Physical Geography: Honduras is mostly mountainous, with coastal plains on the Caribbean and the Pacific.

HONDURAS COPÁN: MAYA METROPOLIS

The ancient Maya city of Copán (A.D. 250 to 900) in Honduras was discovered in 1839 and has undergone extensive excavations and restoration over the past 100 years. Once a major center of Classic Maya civilization, it appears that its growing population—about 20,000 at its peak—may have led to its demise, as farmland and forests became exhausted and unable to support the inhabitants.

Total area: 43,277 sq mi (112,088 sq km)

Coastline: 509 mi (820 km)

Land use: About 54% the country is forested, 14% is meadows and pastures, and 18% is arable or under cultivation.

Climate: Tropical, with temperatures decreasing inland from the coast; two rainy seasons in the mountains, May through July and September through October

Population: 5,901,000

Urban population: 44%

Rate of natural increase: 2.76%

Age structure: 44% under 15; 3% over 65

Birth rate: 33.4/1000

Death rate: 5.8/1000

Infant mortality rate: 41.82/1000

Fertility rate: 4.4

Life expectancy at birth: 66 years (male); 71 years (female)

Religion: Roman Catholic, Protestant

Language: Spanish, American Indian dialects

Ethnic Divisions: Mestizo, Amerindian, black, white

Literacy Rate: 73%

Government: Republic, with a president and a unicameral legislature, the National Assembly. The president and the 128 members of the legislature are directly elected to four-year terms. There are 18 administrative departments.

Armed services: 18,800 (1997 est.) in the army, navy, air force; 5,500 paramilitary; voluntary service for eight months

Suffrage: Universal and compulsory; 18 years old

Economy: Large international debt, a large and inefficient public sector, and rapid population growth hinder the Honduran economy as the government tries massive restructuring to stimulate growth, encourage privatization, reduce inflation, and increase revenue through taxation.

Unit of currency: Lempira; 100 centavos = 1 lempira (L)

GDP per capita: $2,200

Inflation rate–CPI: 15% (1997)

Workforce: 1,300,000 (1997 est.)

Unemployment rate: 6.3% (1997); underemployed 30% (1997 est.)

Exports: Goods worth $1.3 billion (f.o.b., 1996 est.) are sent to the U.S., Germany, Belgium, Japan, Spain, and other trading partners; exports include bananas, coffee, shrimp and lobster, minerals, and lumber.

Imports: Goods worth $1.8 billion (c.i.f., 1996 est.) are received from the U.S., Mexico, Guatemala, and other trading partners; imports include machinery, transport equipment, chemicals, manufactured goods, fuels, and food.

Agriculture: 62% (1985) of the workforce engages in agriculture, fishing, and forestry. Export crops include coffee, bananas, seafood, and timber.

Energy: Fuel imports and domestic hydropower and fuel wood generate most of the country's electricity.

Natural Resources: Timber; fish; minerals, including gold, silver, copper, lead, zinc, iron, antimony; coal

Environmental Issues: Deforestation, water pollution, soil erosion

Transportation: Some 380 miles (610 km) of railways transport fruit rather than passengers. There are 9,560 miles (15,400 km) of roads, of which 1,940 miles (3,130 km) are paved. Caribbean ports include La Ceiba, Puerto Castilla, Puerto Cortés, Tela, and Puerto Lempira; San Lorenzo is on the Pacific. The country has four international airports.

Communications: Five daily newspapers are published. There are 2.12 million radios and 400,000 televisions (1992 est.) in operation. There are 105,000 phones in service (1992 est.).

Tourism: In 1994, 232,680 visitors spent $33 million (U.S.) in Honduras, drawn by beaches and diving along the Caribbean, fishing and boating facilities, and the Maya ruins at Copán.

Embassy in U.S.: (202) 966-7702

Public Holidays: Easter (date varies, in March or April); Pan-American Day (April 14); Labor Day (May 1); Independence Day: from Spain, 1821 (September 15); Morazán Day (October 3); Discovery Day (October 12); Army Day (October 21); Christmas (December 25)

Hungary

Country Name: Hungary

Official Name: Republic of Hungary

Nationality: Hungarian(s) (noun); Hungarian (adjective)

Capital: Budapest, pop. 1,896,500

Major cities: Debrecen, Miskolc, Szeged

External Territories: None

Location: Hungary, a landlocked country in eastern Europe, is bordered on the north by Slovakia, on the east by Ukraine and Romania, on the south by Yugoslavia and Croatia, and on the west by Slovenia and Austria.

Physical Geography: The Great Hungarian Plain, in the southeast, covers almost half the country. Central highlands separate this large plain from a smaller plain in the northwest. Another highland area in the northeast forms part of the Carpathian Mountains system. Major rivers include the Duna (Danube) and Tisza.

Total area: 35,919 sq mi (93,030 sq km)

Coastline: None

Land use: About 53% is arable or under cultivation, 19% is wooded, and 13% is meadows and pastures.

Climate: Continental, with cold winters and hot summers

Population: 10,076,000

Urban population: 64%

Rate of natural increase: -0.4%

Age structure: 17% under 15; 15% over 65

Birth rate: 10/1000

Death rate: 14/1000

Infant mortality rate: 9.7/1000

Fertility rate: 1.3

Life expectancy at birth: 66 years (male); 75 years (female)

Religion: Roman Catholic, Calvinist

Language: Hungarian

Ethnic Divisions: Hungarian

Literacy Rate: 99%

Government: Republic, with a president and a unicameral legislature, the National Assembly, or Országgyülés. The president is elected for a five-year term by the National Assembly; the 386 members of the legislature are directly elected to four-year terms. There are 19 administrative counties and Budapest, the capital.

Armed services: 49,100 troops (1997) in the army, air force, and other branches; 9-month conscription

Suffrage: Universal; 18 years old

Economy: A large budget deficit, high inflation rates, and limited economic growth continue despite the transition to a market economy that was begun in mid-1990. Economic reforms have resulted in some political unrest, hindering attempts to chart a monetary course for the future.

Unit of currency: Forint; 100 fillér = 1 forint (Ft)

GDP per capita: $7,400

Inflation rate–CPI: 18% (1997 est.)

Workforce: 4.5 million (1996 est.)

Unemployment rate: 9% (1997 est.)

Exports: Goods worth $16 billion (f.o.b., 1996 est.) are sent to Germany, Austria, Italy, and other trading partners; exports include machinery and equipment, other manufactures, agriculture and food products, and raw materials.

Imports: Goods worth $18.6 billion (f.o.b., 1996 est.) are received from Germany, Italy, Austria, and other trading partners; imports include machinery and equipment, other manufactures, fuels and electricity, and agricultural and food products.

Agriculture: An estimated 8.3% (1996) of the workforce engages in agriculture. Main crops include wheat, corn, sunflower seed, potatoes, and sugar beets.

Energy: Nuclear power generates much of Hungary's electricity (43% in 1993); imported and domestic fuels, including coal and natural gas, are also used.

Natural Resources: Minerals, including bauxite, coal, natural gas

Environmental Issues: Air, soil, and water pollution

Transportation: Hungary has 4,7203 miles (7,610 km) of railroads and 98,510 miles (158,630 km) of roads. Rivers and waterways provide an additional 1,010 miles (1,620 km) for transportation. There are international airports at Budapest and Siófok.

Communications: Many cities publish daily newspapers; Budapest has more than a dozen. There are 6 million radios and 4.4 million televisions (1993 est.) in operation. Phone service is good, with 2.16 million in service.

Tourism: The historical and cultural amenities of Budapest, the sporting facilities at Lake Balaton, and health spas attract visitors to Hungary. In 1995, visitors spent $1.724 billion (U.S.).

U.S. Tourist Office: (212) 355-0240

Embassy in U.S.: (202) 362-6730

Public Holidays: Anniversary of 1848 uprising against Austrian rule (March 15); Easter Monday (date varies, in March or April); Labor Day (May 1); Constitution Day and St. Stephen's Day: marking unification, 1001 (August 20); Day of the Proclamation of the Republic (October 23); Christmas (December 25–26)

Iceland

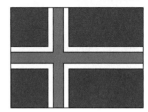

Country Name: Iceland
Official Name: Republic of Iceland
Nationality: Icelander(s) (noun); Icelandic (adjective)
Capital: Reykjavík, pop. 105,000 [160,100]
Major cities: N.A.

ICELAND LAND OF FIRE AND ICE

Iceland sits on top of the Mid-Atlantic Ridge, a seafloor mountain range where the North American plate and the Eurasian plate are moving away from each other. The country also lies above a hot spot, where magma flows up from deep inside the Earth, creating a zone of 36 volcanoes spread across one-third of the island.

External Territories: None

Location: An island in northern Europe between the North Atlantic Ocean and the Greenland Sea, Iceland is located just south of the Arctic Circle, southeast of Greenland.

Physical Geography: Coastal lowlands, with some fiords, give way to an inland plateau, which has glaciers and active volcanos.

Total area: 39,769 sq mi (103,001 sq km)

Coastline: 3,098 mi (4,988 km)

Land use: An estimated 23% of the land is meadows and pastures and forests make up another 1%.

Climate: Temperate maritime, moderated by the North Atlantic Drift Current, with heavier precipitation inland

Population: 277,000

Urban population: 92%

Rate of natural increase: 0.9%

Age structure: 24% under 15; 12% over 65

Birth rate: 15/1000

Death rate: 7/1000

Infant mortality rate: 2.6/1000

Fertility rate: 2.0

Life expectancy at birth: 76 years (male); 81 years (female)

Religion: Evangelical Lutheran

Language: Icelandic

Ethnic Divisions: Icelander

Literacy Rate: 100%

Government: Republic, with a president and unicameral legislature, the Althing. Both the president and the 63 members of the Althing are directly elected to four-year terms. There are seven administrative districts.

Armed services: 120 members in the coast guard

Suffrage: Universal; 18 years old

Economy: The fishing industry is a major part of Iceland's economy; in the late 1980s and early 1990s, allowable fish catches were reduced to permit fish stocks to replenish

themselves. Government plans continue to reduce the budget deficit, support the expansion of manufacturing and tourism, and continue the privatization of industry.

Unit of currency: Icelandic króná (singular), krónur (plural); 100 aurar (eyrir, singular) = 1 new Icelandic Króna (IKr)

GDP per capita: $21,000

Inflation rate–CPI: 2.3% (1996 est.)

Workforce: 131,000 (1996 est.)

Unemployment rate: 3.8% (1997 est.)

Exports: Goods worth $1.8 billion (f.o.b., 1996 est.) are sent to the U.K., Germany, Japan, the U.S., and other trading partners; exports include fish and fish products, animal products, aluminum, ferrosilicon and diatomite.

Imports: Goods worth $2 billion (f.o.b., 1996 est.) are received from the U.K., Germany, Denmark, Norway, and other trading partners; imports include machinery, transportation equipment, petroleum products, and foodstuffs.

Agriculture: 9.3% (1996) of the workforce engages in agriculture and fishing; the main farm products include potatoes, turnips, cattle and sheep. The fisheries account for 64.2% (1996) of the total value of exports.

Energy: 85% of domestic energy is provided through geothermal generation and hydropower.

Natural Resources: Fish, hydropower, geothermal power, diatomite

Environmental Issues: Water pollution

Transportation: No railroads operate in the country. There are 7,660 miles (12,340 km) of roads, mostly along the coast. Reykjavík is the main seaport, and an international airport is at Keflavík.

Communications: There are three daily newspapers published in Reykjavík. There are 91,500 radios and 96,100 televisions (1993 est.) in op-

eration. Telephone service, with 143,600 lines (1993 est.) in operation, is adequate for domestic needs.

Tourism: Tourists come to Iceland to see the spectacular geothermal scenery of geysers, volcanos, hot springs, as well as glaciers. Over 200,000 visitors came to Iceland in 1996.

U.S. Tourist Office: (212) 949-2333

Embassy in U.S.: (202) 265-6653

Public Holidays: Maundy Thursday (date varies, in March or April); Good Friday (date varies, in March or April); Easter Monday (date varies, in March or April); Ascension Day (date varies, in May); Whit Monday (date varies, in May); National Day: independence from Denmark, 1944 (June 17); Bank Holiday (date varies, in August); Christmas (December 24–26); New Year's Eve (December 31)

India

Country Name: India

Official Name: Republic of India

Nationality: Indian(s) (noun); Indian (adjective)

Capital: New Delhi, pop. 301,000 [8,419,100]

Major cities: Bombay, Delhi, Calcutta, Madras, Bangalore (cities with at least 3,000,000 population)

External Territories: None

Location: India, in southern Asia, is between the Bay of Bengal on the east and the Arabian and Laccadive Seas on the west. Land borders are Nepal, Bhutan, and China on the north, Myanmar on the east, and

INDIA MANY PEOPLE, MANY BELIEFS, MANY LANGUAGES

India is the world's largest democracy and the second most populous country after China, in an area only one-third the size of the United States. Its population is growing rapidly—the country adds the equivalent of about half the population of Canada every month. Many diverse ethnic groups, religious beliefs, and languages divide the country. It became independent from Great Britain in 1947, when its eastern and western parts were split to form West and East Pakistan. Today, Sikh separatists want to form their own independent state.

Pakistan on the northwest. Bangladesh is an enclave in the northeast.

Physical Geography: The southern peninsula includes the Deccan Plateau between mountain ranges on the east and west coasts. To the east and north of the Deccan Plateau is the Chota Nagpur Plateau. Farther north, the Great Indian Desert is to the west and the Ganges Plain is to the northeast. The Himalaya run along the border with China and Pakistan.

Total area: 1,269,346 sq mi (3,287,590 sq km)

Coastline: 4,347 mi (7,000 km)

Land use: About 57% of the land is arable or under cultivation, 23% is forested, and about 4% is meadows and pastures.

Climate: Tropical monsoon, with a monsoon season from June to September; cool, dry season from October until February; hot, dry season from March to May

Population: 986,611,000

Urban population: 26%

Rate of natural increase: 1.9%

Age structure: 34% under 15; 5% over 65

Birth rate: 26/1000

Death rate: 9/1000

Infant mortality rate: 63/1000

Fertility rate: 3.4

Life expectancy at birth: 60 years (male); 61 years (female)

Religion: Hindu, Muslim, Christian, Sikh, others

Language: Hindi, 14 other official

Ethnic Divisions: Indo-Aryan, Dravidian

Literacy Rate: 52%

Government: Republic, with a president and bicameral legislature, the Parliament or Sansad. The president is elected by an electoral college for a five-year term. Of the members of the Council of States (250 at a maximum are permitted), up to 12 are appointed by the president and the rest are indirectly elected by regional governments for six-year terms. Of the 545 members of the House of the People, 543 are directly elected to five-year terms and 2 are appointed. There are 25 self-governing states and 7 territories.

Armed services: 1,145,000 troops (1996) in the army, navy, and air force; voluntary service

Suffrage: Universal; 18 years old

Economy: Reforms introduced in the 1990s were successful at increasing foreign exchange reserves and exports and prompting growth in both the agricultural and manufacturing sectors of the economy. Bank reforms were supported with international loans, and plans are in the works to reform the system of tariffs. However, it is difficult for the benefits of national economic growth to affect much of the Indian population, many of whom lack basic food supplies and medical care.

Unit of currency: Indian rupee; 100 paise (paisa, singular) = 1 Indian rupee (Re)

GDP per capita: $1,600

Inflation rate–CPI: 7% (1997 est.)

Workforce: 390 million (1997 est.)

Unemployment rate: N.A.

Exports: Goods worth $33.9 billion (f.o.b., 1997) are sent to the U.S., Hong Kong, UK, and Germany; exports include gems and jewelry, clothing, engineering products, chemicals, leather manufactures, cotton yarn, and fabric.

Imports: Goods worth $39.7 billion (c.i.f., 1997) are received from the U.S., Belguim, Germany, Kuwait, Saudi Arabia, UK and Japan; imports include crude oil and petroleum products, machinery, gems, fertilizer, and chemicals.

Agriculture: An estimated 67% (1995) of the working population engages in agriculture. Cash commodities include rice, wheat, oilseed, cotton, jute, tea, sugarcane, potatoes; livestock; fish

Energy: Petroleum and coal, both imported and domestic supplies, are used for energy generation. There are also nuclear and hydroelectric plants in operation.

Natural Resources: Minerals, including coal, iron, manganese, mica, bauxite, titanium, chromite, diamonds, petroleum, limestone

Environmental Issues: Deforestation, soil erosion, desertification, air and water pollution, overpopulation, nonpotable tap water

Transportation: India's railway system, one of the largest in the world, has 40,117 miles (64,600 km) of track. There are also about 1.3 million miles (2.1 million km) of roads, of which 609,719 miles (981,834 km) are paved. There are nearly 9,936 miles (16,000 km) of navigable waterways, including the Ganges and Brahmaputra Rivers and some of their tributaries. Major seaports include Vishakhapatnam and Madras on the east coast, and Bombay on the west coast. International airports are located at New Delhi, Bombay, Calcutta, Madras, and Trivandum.

Communications: Daily newspapers are published in many cities, including 22 in Delhi and New Delhi. There are 70 million radios and 33 million televisions (1992 est.) in operation. Phone distribution, 12 million (1996 est.), is inadequate and service is poor.

Tourism: Tourists come to India for its temples, wildlife, palaces, and spectacular displays during festivals and holidays. In 1993, 2.3 million visitors added an estimated $1.5 billion (U.S.) to the economy.

U.S. Tourist Office: (800) 953-9399

Embassy in U.S.: (202) 939-7000

Public Holidays: Vary locally; Delhi holidays are as follows: Republic Day: anniversary of proclamation, 1950 (January 26); End of Ramadan (date varies, in February); Holi (date varies, in March); Ram Navami and Mahabir Jayanti (dates vary, in March or April); Good Friday (date varies, in March or April); Easter Monday (date varies, in March or April); Feast of the Sacrifice (date varies, in April); Islamic New Year (date varies, in April or May); Buddha Purnima (date varies, in May); Birth of the Prophet (date varies, in July); Janmashtami (date varies, in August); Independence Day: from Great Britain, 1947 (August 15); Dussehra, Diwali, and Guru Nanak Jayanti (dates vary, in October and November); Mahatma Gandhi's birthday: born 1869, he led the struggle for nationhood (October 2); Christmas (December 25–26)

Indonesia

Country Name: Indonesia

Official Name: Republic of Indonesia

Nationality: Indonesian(s) (noun); Indonesian (adjective)

Capital: Jakarta, pop. 9,113,000

Major cities: Surabaya, Bandung, Medan, Palembang

External Territories: None

Location: Indonesia, in southeast Asia between the Indian and Pacific Oceans, is made up of more than 13,660 islands. The main islands are Java, the Moluccas, Sumatra, Sulawesi, and Timor. Kalimantan, on the island of Borneo, is bordered on the north by two Malaysian states. Irian Jaya is on New Guinea, and Papua New Guinea is on its eastern border.

Physical Geography: The major islands are volcanic; there are hundreds of smaller coral islands and atolls. Indonesia's rain forests are the second largest in the world, after Brazil.

Total area: 741,101 sq mi (1,919,443 sq km)

Coastline: 33,979 mi (54,716 km)

Land use: Almost 62% of the land is forested, 17% is arable or under cultivation, and 7% is meadows and pastures.

Climate: Tropical monsoon, with a rainy season from October to April

Population: 212,941, 810

Urban population: 38%

Rate of natural increase: 1.6%

Age structure: 31% under 15; 4% over 65

Birth rate: 23/1000

Death rate: 8/1000

Infant mortality rate: 59/1000

Fertility rate: 2.6

Life expectancy at birth: 60 years (male); 65 years (female)

Religion: Muslim, Protestant, Roman Catholic, Hindu, Buddhist

Language: Bahasa Indonesia, English, Dutch, Javanese

Ethnic Divisions: Javanese, Sundanese, Madurese, coastal Malays

Literacy Rate: 84%

Government: Republic, with a president and a unicameral legislature, the House of Representatives. The president is elected for a five-year term by the legislature and by the 1,000-member People's Consultative Assembly, the Majelis Permusyawaratan Rakyat, which is indirectly elected to the assembly. Of the 500 members of the legislature, 425 are elected and 75 are appointed from the military. There are 24 administrative provinces.

Armed services: 284,000 troops (1996) in the army, navy, and air force

INDONESIA   A NATION OF ISLANDS

Indonesia is home to the world's largest Muslim population, but even though about 90% of its people are Muslim, Indonesia is not officially Muslim. It was once known as the Dutch East Indies, and the islands were united for the first time as a republic after World War II. Java, one of the larger islands, has 61 volcanoes, of which more than a dozen are active; Java is also one of the world's most densely populated places.

Suffrage: Universal; 17 years of age; married people of any age may vote

Economy: The Asian financial crisis in 1997/8 revealed a weak economy with an unhealthy bank sector, untenable levels of foreign debt, and untenable practices that favored the former President Soeharto's family and friends. Although Indonesia brokered a $42 million IMF bailout package, the program was jeopardized by restricting IMF reforms.

Unit of currency: Rupiah; 100 sen = 1 rupiah (Rp)

GDP per capita: $4,600

Inflation rate–CPI: 50% (1998 est.)

Workforce: 67 million

Unemployment rate: 15% ; 50% underemployed (1998 est.)

Exports: Goods worth $53.4 billion (f.o.b., 1997) are sent to Japan, the U.S., Singapore, South Korea, Taiwan, China, Hong Kong; exports include textiles/garments, wood products, electronics, footwear.

Imports: Goods worth $41.6 billion (f.o.b., 1997) are received from Japan, the U.S., Germany, South Korea, Singapore, Australia, Taiwan; imports include manufactures, raw materials, food, and fuels.

Agriculture: About 44% (1994) of the workforce engages in agriculture, fishing, and forestry. Cash commodities include rubber (Indonesia was second only to Thailand in rubber production in 1995), palm oil (second in production to Malaysia in 1995), peanuts, cocoa, coffee. Crops grown for domestic use include rice and cassava.

Energy: Energy is generated through hydroelectricity, geothermal energy, coal, and petroleum.

Natural Resources: Minerals, including petroleum, tin, natural gas, nickel, bauxite, copper, coal, gold, silver; fertile soils; timber

Environmental Issues: Deforestation, water and air pollution

Transportation: Java, Madura, and Sumatra have 4,037 miles (6,500 km) of railways. There are 254,000 miles (393,000 km) of roads, of which 107,850 miles (178,800 km) are paved. Most of the roads are on the islands of Java, Sumatra, Sualwesi, Bali, Madura, and in Kalimantan. Many other islands use inland water traffic. Major seaports include Jakarta and Surabaya on Java; Cilacap, Cirebon, Kupang, and Palembang on Sumatra; Ujungpandang on Sulawesi; and Semarang. There are international airports on the larger islands.

Communications: There are many daily newspapers published on the main islands. There are 28.1 million radios and 11.5 million televisions (1992 est.). Phone service, with 1,276,600 lines in operation (1993 est.), is fair.

Tourism: Beaches, temples, cultural exhibits, and mountain vistas attract tourists. In 1996, 5.03 million tourists brought $6.1 billion (U.S.) to the country.

U.S. Tourist Office: (213) 387-2078

Embassy in U.S.: (202) 775-5200

Public Holidays: End of Ramadan (date varies, in February); Good Friday (date varies, in March or April); Feast of the Sacrifice (date varies, in April); Islamic New Year (date varies, in April or May); Ascension (date varies, in May); Birth of the Prophet (date varies, in July); Indonesian National Day: proclamation of independence from the Netherlands, 1945 (August 17); Ascension of the Prophet (date varies, in November or December); Christmas (December 25)

Iran

Country Name: Iran

Official Name: Islamic Republic of Iran

Nationality: Iranian(s) (noun); Iranian (adjective)

Capital: Tehran, pop. 6,750,000

Major cities: Mashhad, Eşfahān, Tabrīz, Shīrāz

External Territories: None

Location: Iran, in the Middle East, is bordered on the north by Turkmenistan, the Caspian Sea, Azerbaijan, and Armenia; on the east by Afghanistan and Pakistan; on the south by the Gulf of Oman; and on the west by the Persian Gulf, Iraq, and Turkey.

Physical Geography: An interior plateau, the Iranian Plateau and salt deserts, make up more than half of the country; the Zagros Mountains border the west to the Persian Gulf and the Elbruz Mountains the north to the Caspian Sea. A coastal strip along the Caspian Sea is suitable for farming.

Total area: 636,296 sq mi (1,648,000 sq km)

Coastline: 1,525 mi (2,440 km)

IRAN IN A PRECARIOUS POSITION ATOP PLATES

Arid and prone to earthquakes due to its location over the colliding Arabian and Eurasian tectonic plates, Iran was known as Persia until 1935 and was once the center of a huge empire that extended east to India and north to what is now Austria. Its highest point, at 18,386 feet (5,671m), is Mount Damavand; its lowest, at 92 feet (28.4m) below sea level, is the Caspian Sea.

Land use: Meadows and pastures cover 27% of the country, 10% is arable or under cultivation, and 10% is forested.

Climate: Mostly arid or semiarid; subtropical along Caspian coast; temperatures range widely with seasons and elevation differences

Population: 66,208,000

Urban population: 58%

Rate of natural increase: 2.04%

Age structure: 43% under 15; 4% over 65

Birth rate: 31/1000

Death rate: 6/1000

Infant mortality rate: 49/1000

Fertility rate: 4.31

Life expectancy at birth: 67 years (male); 70 (female)

Religion: Shiite and Sunni Muslim

Language: Persian (Farsi; official), Turkic languages, Kurdish, Luri

Ethnic Divisions: Persian, Azerbaijani, Gilaki and Mazandarani, Kurd, others

Literacy Rate: 72%

Government: Republic, with a president and a unicameral legislature, the Islamic Consultative Assembly, the Majlis. The president and the 270 members of the legislature are directly elected to four-year terms. There are 25 administrative provinces.

Armed services: 518,260 troops (1997) in the army, navy, air force, and other branches; two-year compulsory service

Suffrage: Universal; 15 years old

Economy: Government plans to reduce economic dependence on petroleum production, continue industry privatization, and reduce foreign debt partially hinge on improved relations with its neighbors. Until Iran succeeds in diversifying its economy, it will remain subject to the vagaries of the rise and fall of international oil prices.

Unit of currency: Iranian rial; 100 dinars = 1 Iranian rial (IR)

GDP per capita: $5,500

Inflation rate–CPI: 23% (1996)

Workforce: 15.4 million (1998 est.)

Unemployment rate: more than 30% (1998 est.)

Exports: Goods worth $19 billion (f.o.b., 1997 est.) are sent to Japan, the U.S., the U K., Germany, South Korea, and the U.A.E.; exports include petroleum (80% of the total value of 1994 exports), carpets, fruits, nuts, and hides.

Imports: Goods worth $15.6 billion (f.o.b., 1997 est.) are received from Germany, Italy, Japan, the U.A.E., the U.K., and Belguim; imports include machinery, military supplies, metal works, food, pharmaceuticals, and refined oil products.

Agriculture: About 33% (1998 est.) of the labor force engages in agriculture. Cash commodities include fresh and dried fruit. Subsistence crops include wheat, rice, and sugar beet; dairy products, wool; caviar.

Energy: Energy is generated with domestic natural gas, and coal.

Natural Resources: Minerals, including petroleum, natural gas (reserves second only to former Soviet Union republics), coal, chromium, copper, iron ore, lead, manganese, zinc, sulfur

Environmental Issues: Air and water pollution, deforestation, overgrazing, desertification, inadequate drinking-water supplies

Transportation: There are about 4,520 miles (7,290 km) of railways in Iran, and 100,600 miles (162,000 km) of roads, of which 50,300 miles (81,000 km) are paved. Rivers such as the Kārūn and Karkheh are navigable. The principal shipping port is on Khārk, an island in the north Persian Gulf, and a Caspian port is Bandar Anzalī. International airports are located at Tehran, Eşfahān, and Abādān.

Communications: Nine daily newspapers are published in Tehran⁻n, and one each in Eʃfahān and Shīrāz. There are 14.3 million

radios and 3.9 million televisions (1992 est.) in operation. Telephone service, with 3.02 million phones (1992 est.), is limited.

Tourism: Historic cities, such as Rasht, and Tabrīz, draw visitors, 362,000 of whom added $153 million (U.S.) to the country's economy in 1994.

Embassy in U.S.: Contact Iranian Interest Section, Embassy of Pakistan (202) 965-4990

Public Holidays: National Day: fall of the Shah Reza Pahlavi, 1979 (February 11); End of Ramadan (date varies, in February); Oil Nationalization Day, 1951 (March 20); Iranian New Year (March 21–24); Feast of the Sacrifice (date varies, in April); Islamic Republic Day: proclaimed, 1979 (April 1); Revolution Day (April 2); Ashoura (date varies, in April or May); Birth of the Prophet (date varies, in July); Martyrdom of Imam Ali (July 14); Ascension of the Prophet (date varies, in December)

Iraq

Country Name: Iraq

Official Name: Republic of Iraq

Nationality: Iraqi(s) (noun); Iraqi (adjective)

Capital: Baghdād, pop. [4,336,000]

Major cities: Al Başrah, Al Mawşil, Kirkūk

External Territories: None

Location: Iraq, in western Asia, is bordered on the east by Iran; on the south by Kuwait, a narrow section of the Persian Gulf, and Saudi Arabia; on the west by Jordan and Syria; and on the north by Turkey.

IRAQ   BIRTHPLACE OF CIVILIZATION

The world's first farming villages and later its first city-states began here, along the Fertile Crescent formed by the Tigris and Euphrates Rivers, some 10,000 years ago. Ancient residents included the Akkadians, the Sumerians, the Bablyonians, the Parthians, and the Assyrians. Part of the Ottoman Empire, Iraq was taken over by the British after World War I; a revolution ended British rule in 1958.

Physical Geography: Alluvial plains along the Tigris and Euphrates Rivers in central and south-central Iraq are bordered to the south and west by the Syrian Desert, which covers about 40% of the land. Highlands in the northeast border Iran; between the highlands and the river plains is an arid plateau, the Al Jazirah.

Total area: 169,235 sq mi (438,317 sq km)

Coastline: 36 mi (58 km)

Land use: About 12% of the land is arable and cultivated, 9% is meadows and pastures. None of the country is forested.

Climate: Desert in the south and west, tropical in the east and southeast, temperate in the north

Population: 22,450,000

Urban population: 70%

Rate of natural increase: 3.2%

Age structure: 44% under 15; 3% over 65

Birth rate: 39/1000

Death rate: 7/1000

Infant mortality rate: 62/1000

Fertility rate: 5.2

Life expectancy at birth: 66 years (male); 68 years (female)

Religion: Shiite and Sunni Muslim

Language: Arabic, Kurdish (official in Kurdish regions), Assyrian, Armenian

Ethnic Divisions: Arab, Kurdish,other

Literacy Rate: 58%

Government: Republic, with a president and a unicameral legislature, the National Assembly. The president is elected to office by the 8-member Revolutionary Command Council; 250 members of the legislature are directly elected to four-year terms and 30 are appointed by the president. There are 18 administrative governorates.

Armed services: 382,500 troops (1996) in the army, air force, and navy; compulsory service for 18 months to two years

Suffrage: Universal; 18 years old

Economy: Iraq's infrastructure was heavily damaged during the Persian Gulf War in 1991, and its production of petroleum, on which its economy is based, is a fraction of its prewar volume. The economic problem of a huge foreign debt is compounded by the fact that many Iraqi citizens are unable to obtain adequate supplies of food. However, Iraq has resisted most international demands that would allow it to return to the world marketplace, leaving its population vulnerable to continued poverty and its economy unable to develop.

Unit of currency: Iraqi dinar; 1,000 fils = 20 dirhams = 1 Iraqui dinar (ID)

GDP per capita: $2,000

Inflation rate–CPI: N.A.

Workforce: 4.4 million (1989 est.)

Unemployment rate: N.A.

Exports: Goods are sent to Jordan and, Turkey,; exports include oil (98% of the value of exports).

Imports: Goods are received from France, Turkey, Jordan, Vietnam, and Australia; imports include manufactured goods and food .

Agriculture: 30% (1989) of the labor force engages in agriculture. Dates are a key cash commodity; wheat, barley, rice, vegetables, dates and cotton are also cultivated.

Energy: Hydropower is the primary source of energy generation; oil-fired power stations also contribute.

Natural Resources: Petroleum, natural gas, phosphates, sulfur

Environmental Issues: Water and air pollution, inadequate water supplies, desertification, soil erosion, habitat loss (especially in marsh areas)

Transportation: There are 1,262 miles (2,032 km) of railways in the country; and 28,910 miles (47,400 km) of roads, of which 25,380 miles (40,870 km) are paved. The Tigris and Euphrates Rivers, which join to form the Shatt al Arab, are navigable. Al Başrah, on the Shatt al Arab, is considered a Persian Gulf port and has partially reopened since 1991. Umm Qaşr is another important Persian Gulf port. There is an international airport at Baghdād.

Communications: Nine daily newspapers are published in Baghdād. There are 4 million radios (1989 est.) and 1 million televisions (1992 est.) in use. An estimated 632,000 telephones (1987) provide adequate service, but distribution is poor.

Embassy in U.S.: 202-483-7500

Tourism: Archaeological ruins of ancient cities are major attractions; Iraq earned $12 million (U.S.) from 330,000 visitors in 1994.

Public Holidays: Army Day (January 6); 14 Ramadan Revolution, 1963 (February 8); End of Ramadan (date varies, in February); Feast of the Sacrifice (date varies, in April);

Islamic New Year (date varies, in April or May); Ashoura (date varies, in April or May); Birth of the Prophet (date varies, in July); Republic Day, 1968 (July 14); Ascension of the Prophet (date varies, in December)

Ireland

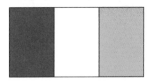

Country Name: Ireland
Official Name: Republic of Ireland
Nationality: Irish (singular and plural noun); Irish (adjective)
Capital: Dublin, pop. 481,900 [952,700]
Major cities: Cork, Limerick, Galway, Waterford
External Territories: None
Location: The republic is on the island of Ireland and is considered one of the British Isles. The Irish Sea separates the island from England, Scotland, and Wales to the east. Northern Ireland, on the north end of the island, is administered as part of the U.K. The Atlantic Ocean is to the west.
Physical Geography: Inland lowlands, with hills, lakes, and bogs, are edged by coastal highlands; there are small islands off the west coast, which has sea cliffs and many inlets and bays.
Total area: 27,137 sq mi (70,284 sq km)
Coastline: 899 mi (1,448 km)
Land use: Meadows and pastures cover 68% of the country, 13% is arable, and forests cover 5%.
Climate: Temperate maritime, with mild winters and cool summers
Population: 3,734,000
Urban population: 58%
Rate of natural increase: 0.6%

Age structure: 23% under 15; 11% over 65
Birth rate: 14/1000
Death rate: 9/1000
Infant mortality rate: 6.2/1000
*Fertility rate:*1.9
Life expectancy at birth: 72 years (male); 78 years (female)
Religion: Roman Catholic
Language: English, Irish (Gaelic)
Ethnic Divisions: Celtic, English
Literacy Rate: 98%
Government: Republic, with a president and a bicameral legislature, the National Parliament, or Oireachtas. The president is directly elected for a seven-year term. The 60 members of the Senate are either nominated or indirectly elected for five-year terms; the 166 members of the House of Representatives are directly elected for five-years terms. There are 26 administrative counties.
Armed services: 12,700 troops (1997) in the army, navy, and air force; voluntary service
Suffrage: Universal; 18 years old
Economy: Although unemployment is a major concern, Ireland's economy is growing steadily, assisted by government programs that attract foreign investment and encourage small business. Exports fuel continued economic expansion, and inflation has dropped substantially.
Unit of currency: Irish pound or punt; 100 pence (penny, singular) = 1 Irish pound or punt (£Ir)
GDP per capita: $18,600

Inflation rate–CPI: 1.6% (1997 est.)
Workforce: 1.52 million (1996 est.)
Unemployment rate: 11.8% (1997 est.)
Exports: Goods worth $54.8 billion (f.o.b., 1996 est.) are sent to the U.K., Germany, France, the U.S., and other trading partners; exports include chemicals, data processing equipment, industrial machinery, live animals, and animal products.
Imports: Goods worth $44.9 billion (c.i.f., 1997 est.) are received from the U.K., the U.S., Germany, France, and other trading partners; imports include food, animal feed, data processing equipment, petroleum and petroleum products, machinery, textiles, and clothing.
Agriculture: An estimated 10% (1996) of the workforce engages in agriculture and fishing. Cash commodities include turnips, barley, potatoes, sugar beets, wheat, and meat and dairy products.
Energy: Domestic natural gas provides about 54% of fuel for energy generation; petroleum, peat, and hydropower are also used.
Natural Resources: Minerals, including natural gas, zinc, lead barite, copper, gypsum, limestone, dolomite, silver; peat
Environmental Issues: Water pollution
Transportation: There are 1,210 miles (1,950 km) of rails and 57,440 miles (92,500 km) of roads, of which 54,050 miles (87,040 km) are paved. Inland waterways provide an additional 440 miles (7100 km) of

IRELAND   IRELAND'S SHRINKING ARAN ISLANDS

The three Aran Islands—Inishmore, Inishmaan, and Inishmeer—off Ireland's western coast have slowly lost most of their population to emigration over the past 100 years and today depend largely on tourism to help support those who remain. Some 200,000 people a year visit these islands. Life is simple, with farming and fishing the primary occupations. Many residents still speak Irish.

transportation routes. Dublin, Cork, Waterford, Limerick, Foynes, and Galway are among the main shipping ports. International airports are at Shannon, Dublin, and Cork.

Communications: Four daily newspapers are published in Dublin and two in Cork. There are 1 million televisions and 2.2 million radios (1990 est.) in service. Phone service, with 1,426,500 lines (1997), is adequate.

Tourism: Tourism is a key source of income. Drawn by the lush countryside, historic cities, and cultural exhibits, over 5 million visitors came to Ireland in 1997.

U.S. Tourist Office: (800) 223-6470
Embassy in U.S.: (202) 462-3939

Public Holidays: St. Patrick's Day (March 17); Good Friday (date varies, in March or April); Easter Monday (date varies, in March or April); June Bank Holiday (date varies, in June); August Bank Holiday (date varies, in August); October Bank Holiday (date varies, in October); Christmas (December 25–26)

Israel

Country Name: Israel
Official Name: State of Israel
Nationality: Israeli(s) (noun); Israeli (adjective)
Capital: Jerusalem, pop. [702,000]
Major cities: Tel Aviv-Yafo, Haifa, Holon
External Territories: None
Location: Israel, in southwestern Asia, is bordered on the west by the Mediterranean Sea, on the north by Lebanon, on the northeast by Syria,

ISRAEL GROWING FROM THE OUTSIDE IN

The United Nations established Israel as a Jewish state in 1948 in a partitioned part of Palestine to provide the Jewish people with a homeland. Surrounded by Arab states, Israel has been the site of unceasing conflict since its founding. Its population continues to grow because it actively encourages Jews from all parts of the world to settle there; all Jewish refugees are granted immediate citizenship. About the size of Massachusetts, Israel lies in the biblical region of Palestine, once known as Canaan.

on the east by Jordan, and on the southwest by Egypt. To the south is a narrow coast on the Red Sea's Gulf of Aqaba.

Physical Geography: The desert region of the Negev makes up almost all of the southern part of Israel; a narrow coastal plain borders the Mediterranean Sea. Highlands extend eastward to the northern portion of the Great Rift Valley, which runs along Israel's eastern border and is the basin for the Dead Sea and the Sea of Galilee.

Total area: 8,019 sq mi (20,770 sq km); Gaza Strip and West Bank 3,850 mi (6,200 sq km)
Coastline: 170 mi (273 km)
Land use: About 40% of land is meadows and pastures, 21% is arable or under cultivation, and 6% is forested.
Climate: Mediterranean, with mild, wet winters and hot, dry summers
Population: 6,135,000; includes West Bank 155,000, Golan Heights 17,000, Gaza Strip 6,000, and East Jerusalem 164,000
Urban population: 90%
Rate of natural increase: 1.9%
Age structure: 28% under 15; 10% over 65
Birth rate: 20/1000
Death rate: 6/1000
Infant mortality rate: 8/1000
Fertility rate: 2.7

Life expectancy at birth: 77 years (male); 80 years (female)
Religion: Judaism, Islam, Christian, Druze and others
Language: Hebrew, Arabic (used officially for Arab minority), English
Ethnic Divisions: Jewish, Arab
Literacy Rate: 95%
Government: Republic, with a president and unicameral legislature, the Assembly, or Knesset. The president is elected to a five-year term by the 120 members of the Knesset. Knesset members are directly elected to four-year terms. There are six administrative districts.
Armed services: 175,000 regular troops and 430,000 reserves (1996) in the army, navy, and air force; voluntary service for Christians, Circassians, Muslims; compulsory service for Jews, Druzes; men serve for 36 months and women for 21 months
Suffrage: Universal; 18 years old
Economy: Israel, though aiming for increased industry privatization and lower inflation rates, attracts foreign investments because of its impressive growth in the early 1990s. The U.S. continues to contribute substantial economic aid. Israel is focusing on increasing international trade with the production of high-tech equipment.
Unit of currency: New Israeli shekel; 100 new agorot (agora, singular) = 1 new Israeli shekel (NIS)
GDP per capita: $17,500

Inflation rate–CPI: 9% (1997)

Workforce: 2.3 million (1997)

Unemployment rate: 7.7% (1997)

Exports: Goods worth $20.7 billion (f.o.b., 1997) are sent to the EU, the U.S., and Japan; exports include machinery, cut diamonds, chemicals, textiles, agricultural products, and metals.

Imports: Goods worth $28.6 billion (c.i.f., 1997) are received from the the EU, the U.S., and Japan; imports include military equipment, investment goods, rough diamonds, oil, and consumer goods.

Agriculture: 2.6% (1996) of the workforce engages in agriculture, fishing, and forestry. Israel is largely self-sufficient. Cash crops include citrus fruit, vegetables, cotton; beef, poultry, dairy products.

Energy: Most energy is generated using imported oil, which is 6.1% (1994) of the total value of Israel's imports.

Natural Resources: Minerals, including copper, phosphates, bromide, potash, clay, sand, sulfur, asphalt, manganese

Environmental Issues: Desertification, air and groundwater pollution

Transportation: There are 380 miles (610 km) of rails and 9,355 miles (15,065 km) of roads, all of which are paved. Important seaports include the Mediterranean ports of Haifa and Ashdod and Elat on the Gulf of Aqaba. An international airport is at Tel Aviv-Yafo.

Communications: Many daily newspapers are published in Hebrew and Arabic; Tel Aviv-Yafo has more than a dozen dailies. There are 2.25 million radios and 1.5 million televisions (1993 est.) in operation. With 2.6 million telephones (1996) in service, telephone service is good.

Tourism: Jerusalem is an important pilgrimage for Christian, Muslim, and Jewish tourists. Haifa and Tel Aviv-Yafo are cultural draws, and beaches along the Mediterranean

coast and spas on the Dead Sea are additional attractions. In 1996, 1,919,604 tourists visited Israel

U.S. Tourist Office: (800) 596-1199

Embassy in U.S.: (202) 364-5500

Public Holidays: Passover (dates vary, in April); Independence Day, 1948 (date varies, in April or May); Shavuot (date varies, in May or June); Jewish New Year, Rosh Hashanah (date varies, in September or October); Yom Kippur (date varies, in September or October); Succot (date varies, in September or October); Simhat Torah (date varies, in October)

Italy

Country Name: Italy

Official Name: Italian Republic

Nationality: Italian(s) (noun); Italian (adjective)

Capital: Rome, pop. [2,648,800]

Major cities: Naples, Milan, Turin

External Territories: None

Location: Italy, in southern Europe, is a peninsula in the Mediterranean Sea. It is bordered on the northwest by France, on the north by Switzerland and Austria, and on the northeast by Slovenia.

Physical Geography: Italy's northern border is formed by ranges of the Alps. The Apennines run the length of the country from north to south. The Po River Valley stretches from the northwest to the Adriatic coast on the northeast. The Ligurian and Tyrrhenian Seas are on the southwest coast. The island of Sardinia lies off the west coast, and

Sicily is beyond the southern tip of the peninsula.

Total area: 116,324 sq mi (301,277 sq km)

Coastline: 4,720 mi (7,600 km)

Land use: Just over 40% of the land is arable or under cultivation, 23% is forested, and 15% is meadows and pastures.

Climate: Southern regions generally hot and dry; hot summers and cold winters, with more precipitation in northern region

Population: 57,717,000

Urban population: 90%

Rate of natural increase: 0%

Age structure: 15% under 15; 17% over 65

Birth rate: 9/1000

Death rate: 10/1000

Infant mortality rate: 5.5/1000

Fertility rate: 1.2

Life expectancy at birth: 75 years (male); 81 years (female)

Religion: Roman Catholic

Language: Italian, German, French

Ethnic Divisions: Italian

Literacy Rate: 97%

Government: Republic, with a president and a bicameral legislature, the Parliament, Parlamento. The president is elected to a seven-year term by the legislature and 58 regional representatives. The 630 members of the Chamber of Deputies are directly elected for five-year terms. Of the 326 members of the Senate, 315 are directly elected and 11 are appointed for life. There are 20 administrative regions.

Armed services: 325,150 troops (1997) in the army, navy, and air force; 10-month tour of duty

Suffrage: Universal; 18 years old; 25 year old minimum for senatorial elections

Economy: Scaling back on generous pension and health-care benefits and encouraging industry privatization are two tactics being used by the government to reduce the budget deficit and promote economic growth. Italy's industrial center is in the north; the southern part of the country remains agricultural.

Unit of currency: Italian lira (singular), lire (plural); 100 centèsimi (centèsimo, singular) = 1 Italian lira (Lit)

GDP per capita: $21,500

Inflation rate–CPI: 1.9% (1997 est.)

Workforce: 22,851,000 (1994 est.)

Unemployment rate: 12.2% (1997 est.)

Exports: Goods worth $250.8 billion (f.o.b., 1996 est.) are sent to the U.S., Germany, France, the U.K., and other trading partners; exports include metals, textiles nad clothing, production machinery, motor vehicles and other transportation equipment, and chemicals.

Imports: Goods worth $190 billion (c.i.f., 1996 est.) are received from Germany, France, the U.K., and other trading partners; imports include industrial machinery, chemicals, transportation equipment, petroleum, metals, food, and agricultural products.

Agriculture: 7% (1996) of the labor force engages in agriculture, fishing, and forestry; crops include fruits, vegetables, grapes, potatoes, sugar beets, soybeans, grain, and olives.

Energy: Italy imports more than 80% of its energy needs; coal, natural gas, and nuclear power are primary sources.

Natural Resources: Petroleum, mercury, potash, marble, sulfur, coal, fish

Environmental Issues: Air and water pollution, acid rain

Transportation: There are 12,070 miles (19,440 km) of rails and 196,860 miles (317,000 km) of roads. The principal seaports are Genoa, Naples, Palermo, and Trieste.

Communications: There are 74 daily newspapers; Rome has 13 dailies and Milan 7. There are 45.7 million radios and 17 million televisions (1996 est.) in use. Telephone service, with 25.6 million phone lines (1996 est. in service, is good.

Tourism: Italy is a celebrated tourist destination because of its history, art, scenery, and its famous cities. The country earned $20.5 billion (U.S.) from tourism in 1993; 56.3 million tourists visited the country in 1996.

U.S. Tourist Office: (212) 245-4822

Embassy in U.S.: (202) 328-5500

Public Holidays: Epiphany (January 6); Easter Monday (date varies, in March or April); Liberation Day (April 25); Labor Day (May 1); Anniversary of the republic, 1946 (June 2); Assumption (August 15); All Saints' Day (November 1); National Unity Day (November 5); Immaculate Conception (December 8); Christmas (December 25); St. Stephen's Day (December 26)

Jamaica

Country Name: Jamaica

Official Name: Jamaica

Nationality: Jamaican(s) (noun); Jamaican (adjective)

Capital: Kingston, pop. 104,000 [538,100]

Major cities: Spanish Town, Montego Bay, May Pen

External Territories: None

Location: Jamaica, in the Caribbean Sea, is in the West Indies; Cuba is 90 miles (145 km) north and Haiti is 124 miles (200 km) west.

Physical Geography: Coastal lowlands rise to a limestone plateau with sinkholes, caves, and underground streams. The Blue Mountains rise north of Kingston on the eastern end of the island.

Total area: 4,244 sq mi (10,991 sq km)

Coastline: 635 mi (1,022 km)

Land use: About 20% of the land is arable or under cultivation, 17% is meadows and pastures, and forests cover 30% of the island.

Climate: Tropical in the lowlands, temperate in the mountains

Population: 2,621,000

Urban population: 50%

Rate of natural increase: 1.72%

Age structure: 32% under 15; 7% over 65

Birth rate: 23.4/1000

Death rate: 6.2/1000

Infant mortality rate: 24.4/1000

Fertility rate: 2.8

Life expectancy at birth: 70 years (male); 73 years (female)

Religion: Protestant, Roman Catholic

ITALY MANY MILES MEAN MANY CULTURES

The Italy of today was not a unified state until 1871. Before that time it was made up of several kingdoms and alliances; for example, the region known as Venetia belonged to Austria until 1866. As such, the country's language, food, and cultures vary greatly even today. Great distances between regions have also played a role: More than 700 miles separate Italy's northern border with Switzerland from its southernmost coast. In fact, Milan is closer to London than it is to Reggio, a city in the toe of Italy's "boot."

Language: English, Creole
Ethnic Divisions: Black, mixed
Literacy Rate: 85%
Government: Parliamentary democracy, with a governor-general appointed by the British monarch, and a bicameral Parliament. Of the 21 members of the Senate, 13 are held by the ruling party and 8 by the opposition. The 60 members of the House of Representatives are popularly elected to five-year terms. There are 14 administrative parishes.
Armed services: 3,320 troops (1997) in the army, coast guard, and air wing
Suffrage: Universal; 18 years old
Economy: Tourism and exports of bauxite, alumina, sugar, and tropical produce are the main sources of Jamaica's income. Economic growth is hampered by high inflation rates, budget deficits, and unemployment; however, the Jamaican government is encouraging foreign investment. Debt rescheduling and debt forgiveness have helped to ease the government's financial pressures.
Unit of currency: Jamaican dollar; 100 cents = 1 Jamaican dollar (J$)
GDP per capita: $3,660
Inflation rate–CPI: 17% (1996 est.)
Workforce: 1.14 million (1996 est.)
Unemployment rate: 16% (1996 est.)
Exports: Goods worth $1.4 billion (f.o.b., 1996 est.) are sent to the U.S., the U.K., Canada, Norway, and the Netherlands; exports include bauxite, alumina, sugar, rum, and bananas.
Imports: Goods worth $2.9 billion (f.o.b., 1996 est.) are received from the U.S., Japan, the U.K., and Trinidad and Tobago; imports include machinery, construction materials, fuels, food, and chemicals.
Agriculture: Nearly one-quarter (1989) of the labor force engages in agriculture. Sugarcane, bananas, citrus fruit, coffee, and vegetables are cultivated.

Energy: Most energy is generated using imported fuels.
Natural Resources: Minerals, including bauxite, gypsum, limestone
Environmental Issues: Deforestation, coastal water and air pollution, damage to coral reefs
Transportation: There are 230 miles (370 km) of railroads used to transport bauxite rather than passengers. There are 11,610 miles (18,700 km) of roads, of which miles (13,100 km) are paved. The main seaports are Kingston on the south coast and Montego Bay and Port Antonio on the north coast. International airports are at Kingston and Montego Bay.
Communications: Three daily newspapers are published in Kingston. There are 1.97 million radios (1997) and 330,000 televisions (1992 est.) in operation. Phone service is good, with 350,000 main lines (1997 est.) in service.
Tourism: Jamaica draws considerable income from tourists, who come because of the country's scenic beaches and mountains and cultural heritage. In 1996/7, 1.75 million visitors generated $1.13 million (U.S.) in revenue.
U.S. Tourist Office: (212) 856-9727
Embassy in U.S.: (202) 452-0660
Public Holidays: Ash Wednesday (date varies, in February); Good Friday (date varies, in March or April); Easter Monday (date varies, in March or April); National Labor Day (May 23); Independence Day: from the U.K., 1962 (August); National Heroes' Day (October 6); Christmas (December 25–26)

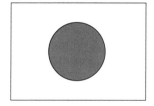

Japan

Country Name: Japan
Official Name: Japan
Nationality: Japanese (singular and plural noun); Japanese (adjective)
Capital: Tōkyō, pop. 11,573,000 [32,332,000]
Major cities: Yokohama, Ōsaka, Nagoya, Sapporo, Kyōto, Kōbe
External Territories: None
Location: Japan, in eastern Asia, is an island chain made up of four major islands and as many as 4,000 smaller islands between the Sea of Japan and the North Pacific Ocean off the Korean and Russian coasts.
Physical Geography: Typically the islands have mountainous interiors and narrow coastal lowlands, with a few plains. From north to south, the main islands are Hokkaidō, Honshū (where the majority of the population lives), Shikoku, and Kyūshū.
Total area: 145,875 sq mi (377,815 sq km)
Coastline: 18,476 mi (29,751 km)
Land use: Forests cover 67%, 12% of the land is arable or under cultivation, and 1% is meadows and pastures.
Climate: Temperate, with warm summers; winters cold in the north

JAPAN   LONG-LIVED WOMEN

Japan's 126.7 million people—nearly half the size of the U.S. population—live in an area smaller than California. In 1999, Japanese women had the world's longest life expectancy at birth—84 years.

and mild in the south; precipitation heaviest in summer

Population: 126,745,000

Urban population: 79%

Rate of natural increase: 0.2%

Age structure: 15% under 15; 16% over 65

Birth rate: 10/1000

Death rate: 8/1000

Infant mortality rate: 4/1000

Fertility rate: 1.46

Life expectancy at birth: 77 years (male); 83 years (female)

Religion: Shinto, Buddhist, Christian

Language: Japanese

Ethnic Divisions: Japanese

Literacy Rate: 99%

Government: Constitutional monarchy, with a hereditary emperor, Emperor Akihito, and a bicameral legislature, the Diet. The 500 members of the House of Representatives are elected to four-year terms, and the 252 members of the House of Councillors are elected to six-year terms. There are 47 administrative prefectures.

Armed services: 235,600 troops (1997) in the army, navy, and air force; voluntary service

Suffrage: Universal; 20 years old

Economy: One of the strongest economies in the world, Japan's production of high-quality electronic goods and other exports has yielded a trade surplus large enough to create friction with some of its trading partners, including the U.S. Inflation and unemployment is low, and the service industry remains a key component of the economy.

Unit of currency: Yen; 100 sen = 1 yen (Y)

GDP per capita: $24,500

Inflation rate–CPI: 1.7% (1997)

Workforce: 67.23 million (1997.)

Unemployment rate: 3.4% (1997)

Exports: Goods worth $421 billion (f.o.b., 1997 est.) are sent to the U.S., Southeast Asia, the EU and China; exports include machinery, motor vehicles, and electronic goods.

Imports: Goods worth $339 billion (c.i.f., 1997 est.) are received from the U.S., Southeast Asia, the EU, and China; imports include manufactured goods, food, and raw materials, fossil fuels.

Agriculture: 6% (1994) of the workforce engages in agriculture, fishing, and forestry. Farmers and fishermen meet 62% (1994) of domestic food requirements; however, about 50% of rice is imported. Crops include rice, sugar beets, vegetables, fruit; pork, poultry, dairy products, eggs.

Energy: Most energy is generated using imported oil; nuclear energy supplies 31.7% (1996) of Japan's power.

Natural Resources: Fish

Environmental Issues: Air and water pollution, acid rain

Transportation: There are 16,560 miles (26,670 km) of railroads, including track for high-speed trains, and 720,360 miles (1,160,000 km) of roads. The world's longest suspension bridge, 5.84 miles (9.4 km), connects Honshū and Shikoku. Major ports include Tokyō, Yokohama, Nagoya, and ōsaka; the port city of Kōbe was severely damaged by an earthquake in 1995. Tokyō, Ōsaka, and Narita have international airports, and more are planned.

Communications: There are 121 (1996) daily newspapers published, of which 5 are national. Most major cities have dailies; Tokyō has 22. There are 97 million radios and 100 million televisions (1993 est.) in operation. Phone service, with 64 million phones, is excellent.

Tourism: The historic buildings and gardens of Kyōto are major tourist draws, as are cultural events, traditional architecture, and mountain scenery throughout the country. In 1996, 3.83 million visitors added $4 billion (U.S.) to the economy.

U.S. Tourist Office: (212) 757-5640

Embassy in U.S.: (202) 238-6700

Public Holidays: Coming of Age Day (January 15); National Foundation Day (February 11); Vernal Equinox Day (March 21); Greenery Day (April 29); Constitution Memorial Day (May 3); Children's Day (May 5); Marine Day (July 20); Respect for the Aged Day (September 15); Autumnal Equinox Day (September 22); Sports Day (October 10); Culture Day (November 3); Labor Thanksgiving Day (November 23); Emperor's Birthday (December 23)

Jordan

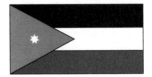

Country Name: Jordan

Official Name: Hashemite Kingdom of Jordan

Nationality: Jordanian(s) (noun); Jordanian (adjective)

Capital: Ammān, pop. 965,000

Major cities: Az Zarqā', Irbid

External Territories: None

Location: Jordan, in the Middle East, is bordered on the north by Syria, on the northeast by Iraq, on the east and south by Saudi Arabia and the Gulf of Aqaba, and on the west by Israel and the West Bank.

Physical Geography: The Jordan River Valley, part of the Great Rift system, drains south into the Dead Sea; uplands extend from the Jordan eastward and meet the Syrian Desert, which makes up most of the eastern and southern sections of the country.

Total area: 35,467 sq mi (91,860 sq km)

Coastline: 16 mi (26 km)

Land use: Jordan has 5% arable land and permanent crops, 1% is forested, and 9% is meadows and pastures.

JORDAN   A PEACE-LOVING NATION BORN OF WAR

Jordan was formed after World War I, when the League of Nations divided up the Arab territories of the Ottoman Empire and gave the area east of the Jordan River, which was part of Palestine and became known as Transjordan, to Great Britain. Jordan became independent in 1946. King Hussein ruled from 1952 until his death in 1999. Before King Hussein died, he named his eldest son Abdullah to succeed him.

Climate: Mostly Mediterranean, with mild rainy winters and hot dry summers; hotter summers and warmer winters in the Jordan River valley; rainfall generally more abundant in the north than in the south

Population: 4,,731,000

Urban population: 78%

Rate of natural increase: 2.5%

Age structure: 43% under 15; 3% over 65

Birth rate: 35/1000

Death rate: 4/1000

Infant mortality rate: 33/1000

Fertility rate: 4.8

Life expectancy at birth: 71 years (male); 75 years (female)

Religion: Sunni Muslim, Christian

Language: Arabic, English understood

Ethnic Divisions: Arab

Literacy Rate: 867%

Government: Constitutional monarchy, with a hereditary king—King Abdullah, since 1999—and a bicameral legislature, the National Assembly, or Majlis al 'Umma. The 40 members of the Senate are appointed to eight-year terms by the king; the 80 members of the House of Deputies are directly elected to four-year terms. There are eight administrative governorates.

Armed services: 98,560 troops (1996) in the army, air force, and navy; selective conscription

Suffrage: Universal; 20 years old

Economy: Unemployment, foreign debt, and an inadequate infrastructure hinders Jordan's efforts to increase economic growth and provide its growing population with sufficient services. Tourism, international grants and loans, and remittances sent back by Jordanians working abroad help mitigate the worst of the country's financial struggles.

Unit of currency: Jordanian dinar; 1,000 fils = 1 Jordanian dinar (JD)

GDP per capita: $4,800

Inflation rate–CPI: 3% (1997 est.)

Workforce: 1.15 million plus 300,000 foreign workers (1997 est.)

Unemployment rate: 15% is official, 20%-25% actual (1997 est.)

Exports: Goods worth $1.53 billion (f.o.b., 1997.) are sent to Iraq, India, Saudi Arabia, the EU, and Indonesia, and U.A.E.; exports include phosphates, fertilizers, potash, and agricultural products and manufactures.

Imports: Goods worth $3.7 billion (c.i.f., 1997) are received from the EU, Iraq, the U.S., Japan, and Turkey; imports include oil, machinery, transportation equipment, food, live animals, and manufactured goods.

Agriculture: 8.7% (1992) of the workforce engages in agriculture. Cash crops, include wheat, barley, citrus, tomatoes, melons, olives; sheep, goats, poultry.

Energy: Most energy is generated using imported oil; wind and solar power are also in use.

Natural Resources: Phosphates, potash, shale oil

Environmental Issues: Limited freshwater, deforestation, overgrazing, soil erosion

Transportation: The country has 420 miles (680 km) of rail and 4,120 miles (6,640 km) of roads, all of which are paved. Al 'Aqabah is the country's seaport, and Ammān and Al 'Aqabah have international airports.

Communications: Four daily newspapers are published in Ammān. There are 1.1 million radios and 350,000 televisions (1992 est.) in use. Phone service, with 81,500 in operation (1987 est.), is adequate.

Tourism: The ancient cities of Petra and Jarash draw tourists, and Dead Sea spas are also strong attractions. In 1993, 3,098,938 visitors brought $563 million (U.S.) to Jordan.

U.S. Tourist Office: (202) 265-1606

Embassy in U.S.: (202) 966-2664

Public Holidays: Arbor Day (January 15); End of Ramadan (date varies, in February); Arab League Day (March 22); Feast of the Sacrifice (date varies, in April); Islamic New Year (date varies, in April or May); Independence Day: as a League of Nations mandate with a new constitution, 1946 (May 25); Birth of the Prophet (date varies, in July); King Hussein's Accession, 1953 (August 11); King Hussein's birthday (November 14); Ascension of the Prophet (date varies, in November or December)

Kazakhstan

Country Name: Kazakhstan

Official Name: Republic of Kazakhstan

Nationality: Kazakhstani(s) (noun); Kazakhstani (adjective)

Capital: Astana, pop. 270,400

Major cities: Qaraghandy, Shymkent, Pavlodar

External Territories: None

Location: Kazakhstan, in Central Asia, is bordered on the north and northwest by Russia; on the east by China; on the south by Kyrgyzstan, Uzbekistsan, the Aral Sea, and Turkmenistan; and on the west by the Caspian Sea.

Physical Geography: Desert and steppes cover most of Kazkhstan; the Tian Shan mountains border the southeast.

Total area: 1,049,039 sq mi (2,716,998 sq km)

Coastline: None

Land use: Meadows and pastures cover 57% of the country, 12% is arable or under cultivation, and 4% is forested.

Climate: Continental, with cold winters and hot summers

Population: 15,417,000

Urban population: 56%

Rate of natural increase: 0.5%

Age structure: 30% under 15; 7% over 65

Birth rate: 14/1000

Death rate: 10/1000

Infant mortality rate: 25/1000

Fertility rate: 2.0

Life expectancy at birth: 59 years (male); 70 years (female)

Religion: Muslim, Russian Orthodox

Language: Kazakh, Russian, others

Ethnic Divisions: Kazakh, Russian

Literacy Rate: 98%

Government: Republic, with a president and bicameral legislature, the Parliament. The president is directly elected to a five-year term. Of the 47 members of the Senate, 40 are elected and 7 are appointed to office by the president. The 67 members of the Assembly are elected to four-year terms. There are 15 administrative regions.

Armed services: 35,100 troops (1997) in the army and air force

Suffrage: Universal; 18 years old

Economy: Because of its large reserves of coal, oil, and natural gas, Kazakhstan has attracted considerable foreign investment since becoming independent. Following the collapse of the Soviet Union in 1991, economic growth was restricted by the transition from a planned economy to a market economy and by high inflation rates, but government programs to control inflation and shift industry from public to private ownership have resulted in renewed growth.

Unit of currency: Tenge; 100 tiyn = 1 tenge

GDP per capita: $3,000

Inflation rate–CPI: 12% (1997 est.)

Workforce: 6.9 million (1996 est.)

Unemployment rate: 2.6% (1996 est.)

Exports: Goods worth $5.6 billion (1996) are sent to Russia, Ukraine, Uzbekistan, and other trading partners; exports include oil, ferrous, and nonferrous metals.

Imports: Goods worth $6 billion (1996) are received from Russia, Ukraine, Uzbekistan, Turkey, Germany, and other trading partners; imports include machinery, industrial parts, fuels, and food.

Agriculture: 23% (1996) of the working population is employed in agriculture. Cash commodities include fruits, sugar beets, vegetables, potatoes, cereals, cotton, and wool.

Energy: Coal supplies 54.4% (1991) of the country's energy; petroleum, natural gas, and hydropower supply much of the rest; nuclear power supplies about 1%.

Natural Resources: Minerals, including petroleum, coal, iron, manganese, chrome, nickel, cobalt, copper, lead, zinc, bauxite, gold, uranium

Environmental Issues: Soil, air, and water pollution from chemicals and radioactive materials; soil salinization

Transportation: There are 8,600 miles (13,840 km) of railroads and 87,610 miles (141,080 km) of roads in the country. Waterways, including the Syr Darya and Ertis Rivers, add 2,484 miles (4,000 km) to the

KAZAKHSTAN SHEDDING RUSSIAN RULE

When Kazakhstan gained its independence after the dissolution of the Soviet Union in 1991, many Kazakhs whose forebears had fled to Mongolia after the 1917 Russian Revolution returned to their homeland. Russia's control over the Kazakhs, a Turkic people, began in the 1700s. By the late 1800s, many Russians and Ukrainians had moved there to farm, and until recently Russians outnumbered Kazakhs. Today, Kazakhs are in the majority and are working to restore their ethnic identity. For example, they have made Kazakh the country's official language.

transportation network. There are more than 350 airports; international airports are at Almaty, Aktau, and Atyrau.

Communications: There are three daily newspapers published in the capital. There are 4.75 million televisions and 4.1 million radios in operation. Phone service, with 2.2 million lines (1993), is poor.

Tourism: Trekking and skiing in the mountains, an Olympic training center for winter events, and archaeological sites in the southern part of the country attract hardy tourists.

Embassy in U.S.: (202) 333-4504

Public Holidays: International Women's Day (March 8); Spring Holiday (March 22); Day of Unity (May 1); Victory Day (May 9); Constitution Day (August 30); Republic Day (October 25); Independence Day: from the Soviet Union, 1991 (December 16)

Kenya

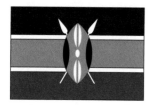

Country Name: Kenya
Official Name: Republic of Kenya
Nationality: Kenyan(s) (noun); Kenyan (adjective)
Capital: Nairobi, pop. 1,504,900
Major cities: Mombasa, Kisumu, Nakuru
External Territories: None
Location: Kenya, on the Equator in east Africa, is bordered on the north by Ethiopia and Sudan, on the east by Somalia and the Indian Ocean, on the south by Tanzania, and on the west by Uganda.
Physical Geography: A coastal strip along the Indian Ocean is

---

KENYA MANY CULTURES, ONE LANGUAGE

The site of many important archaeological finds of early humans, some dating back nearly two million years, Kenya was a British colony until its independence in 1963. Although some 40 ethnic groups make up the population, each with its own language and culture, they all speak Swahili. Nearly 40 percent of the population is Protestant.

---

bounded on the west by low hills; beyond these hills, the land rises gradually to meet central highlands that form the eastern border of the Great Rift Valley. The western escarpment of the Great Rift Valley ranges to the borders of Uganda and Tanzania, and the basin associated with Lake Victoria reaches from the southwestern corner of Kenya to the central highlands.

Total area: 228,861 sq mi (592,747 sq km)

Coastline: 333 mi (536 km)

Land use: Of Kenya's land, 37% is meadows and pastures, 8% is arable or under cultivation, and 30% is forested.

Climate: Generally hot, but with varying temperature and precipitation; rainy seasons from March until May and from October until December in the south; little rainfall in the north; cooler in highlands than coastal areas

Population: 28,809,000
Urban population: 20%
Rate of natural increase: 2.1%
Age structure: 46% under 15; 3% over 65
Birth rate: 34.8/1000
Death rate: 13.8/1000
Infant mortality rate: 73.7/1000
Fertility rate: 4.7
Life expectancy at birth: 48 years (male); 49 years (female)
Religion: Protestant, Roman Catholic, indigenous beliefs, Muslim
Language: English, Swahili (both official), indigenous languages

Ethnic Divisions: Kikuyu, Luhya, Luo, Kalenjin, Kamba, Kisii, Meru, others

Literacy Rate: 78%

Government: Republic, with a president and unicameral legislature, the National Assembly, or Bunge. The president is directly elected to a five-year term; of the 222 members of the legislature 210 are directly elected and 12 are nominated by the president, both for five years. There are seven administrative provinces and the capital city.

Armed services: 24,200 troops (1997) in the army, air force, and navy; voluntary service

Suffrage: Universal; 18 years old

Economy: Internal unrest, unemployment, a large and growing population, and corruption in financial circles have all blocked needed economic growth in Kenya, which gets most of its cash from agriculture and tourism. The foreign debt also continues to grow, but the international community has at times insisted on seeing some measure of economic and political reform before providing additional funds.

Unit of currency: Kenyan shilling; 100 cents = 1 Kenyan shilling; 20 Kenyan shillings = 1 Kenyan pound (K£)

GDP per capita: $1,600
Inflation rate–CPI: 8.8% (1996)
Workforce: 13,417,000 (1996 est.)
Unemployment rate: 35% urban (1994 est.)

Exports: Goods worth $2.1 billion (f.o.b., 1996) are sent to the U.K., Uganda, Tanzania, Germany, Pakistan, and other trading partners; exports include tea, coffee, petroleum products, fruits, and vegetables.

Imports: Goods worth $2.9 billion (f.o.b., 1996) are received from the U.S., the U.K., Japan, Germany, and other trading partners; imports include machinery, transportation equipment, oil, iron and steel, raw materials, food, and consumer goods.

Agriculture: 78% (1996 est.) of the workforce engages in agriculture and fishing. Export crops include tea, coffee, pyrethrum, sisal, sugarcane, and cotton. Maize and livestock are raised for domestic use.

Energy: Hydropower supplies over 80% of Kenya's energy needs. Geothermal energy supplies 15%, and wood and charcoal are important household fuels.

Natural Resources: Minerals, including gold, limestone, soda ash, salt barytes, rubies, fluospar, garnets

Environmental Issues: Water pollution, deforestation, soil erosion, desertification, wildlife poaching

Transportation: Of 39,620 miles (63,800 km) of roads, 5,510 miles (8,870 km) are paved; there are 1,650 miles (2,650 km) of railroads operating. There is ferry travel on Lake Victoria. Mombasa is the main seaport, and Nairobi operates an inland container depot. International airports are located outside Nairobi and at Mombasa.

Communications: Nairobi has five daily newspapers. There are 2.6 million radios and 500,000 televisions (1995) in use. Phones, with 229,000 in service (1994), are sparsely distributed, but service is comparatively good for the region.

Tourism: Wildlife parks, game reserves, and beaches along the Indian Ocean are key tourist attractions in Kenya, which earned $505 million (U.S.) from 863,000 visitors in 1993.

U.S. Tourist Office: (212) 486-1300

Embassy in U.S.: (202) 387-6101

Public Holidays: End of Ramadan (date varies, in February); Easter (date varies, in March or April); Feast of the Sacrifice (date varies, in April); Labor Day (May 1); Anniversary of self-government (June 1); Kenyatta Day: for Jomo Kenyatta, the first president, 1964 (October 20); Independence Day: from United Kingdom, 1963 (December 12); Christmas (December 25–26)

Kiribati

Country Name: Kiribati

Official Name: Republic of Kiribati

Nationality: I-Kiribati (singular and plural noun); I-Kiribati (adjective)

Capital: Tarawa, pop. 25,200

Major cities: N.A.

External Territories: None

Location: Kiribati, an island country in the central Pacific Ocean, has 33 islands that are located in three main groups: the Gilbert Islands, Phoenix Islands, and Line Islands.

Physical Geography: Most of the islands are low-lying coral atolls encircled by reefs.

Total area: 277 sq mi (717 sq km)

Coastline: 710 mi (1,143 km)

Land use: There is no arable land and no meadows or pastures, but 51% is in permanent crops and 3% is forested.

Climate: Tropical; variable rainfall with precipitation heaviest from October to March

Population: 82,000

Urban population: 35%

Rate of natural increase: 2.3%

Age structure: N.A.

Birth rate: 32/1000

Death rate: 9/1000

Infant mortality rate: 65/1000

Fertility rate: 3.8

Life expectancy at birth: 53 years (male); 56 years (female)

Religion: Roman Catholic, Protestant

Language: English, Gilbertese

Ethnic Divisions: Micronesian

Literacy Rate: N.A.

Government: Republic, with a president and unicameral legislature, the Maneaba ni Maungatabu, or House of Assembly. The president is directly elected; of the 41 members of the legislature, 39 are elected, 1 is nominated by the president and one is an ex-officio member, all serve four-year terms. There are three administrative units.

Armed services: No active military forces

Suffrage: Universal; 18 years old

Economy: Fishing, copra, and tourism are key components in Kiribati's economy; foreign aid is vital for Kiribati's survival.

Unit of currency: Australian dollar; 100 cents = 1 Australian dollar ($A)

GDP per capita: $800

Inflation rate–CPI: -0.6%

Workforce: 7,870 (not including subsistence farmers)

Unemployment rate: 2% (1990 est.); 70% underemployed (1990 est.)

Exports: Goods worth $6.7 million (f.o.b., 1996 est.) are sent to the U.S., Australia , New Zealand, and other trading partners; exports include copra, seaweed, and seafood.

Imports: Goods worth $37.4 million (c.i.f., 1996 est.) are received from Australia, Fiji, Japan, New Zealand, and other trading partners; imports include food, machinery, manufactured goods, and fuels.

Agriculture: Most of the workforce engages in agriculture and fishing. Coconuts (for copra) earn 68.1%

(1996) of the total value of exports; taro, breadfruit, sweet potatoes, and vegetables are raised for domestic use. Some income is derived from selling fishing licenses and from seaweed cultivation.

Energy: Mineral fuels are imported.

Natural Resources: Phosphate production ceased in 1979.

Environmental Issues: Water pollution

Transportation: There are 420 miles (670 km) of roads. Main seaports are located on Banaba and Betio, at English Harbor on Tabuaeran, and Kanton in the Phoenix Islands. There is an international airport at Tawara and five on other islands.

Communications: There are some weekly and monthly publications, but no daily newspapers are published. There are 15,000 radios (1992) in use, and 1,400 phones (1994) provide limited service.

Tourism: Bird-watching, fishing, and World War II battle sites are key draws for tourists coming to Kiribati; in 1994, 3,900 visitors added $2 million (U.S.) to the country's economy.

Public Holidays: Easter (date varies, in March or April); Independence Day: from the U.K., 1979 (July 12); Youth Day (August 4); Christmas (December 25–26)

Korea, North

Country Name: Korea, North
Official Name: Democratic People's Republic of Korea
Nationality: Korean(s) (noun); Korean (adjective)
Capital: Pyongyang, pop. 2,741,300

Major cities: Hamhung, Chongjin, Sinuiju, Kaesong

External Territories: None

Location: North Korea, on the Korean peninsula in eastern Asia, is bordered on the north by China and Russia and on the south by South Korea. The Sea of Japan is on the east and the Yellow Sea is on the west.

Physical Geography: An upland plateau is in the northeast; mountain ranges extend along the southeast coast and through the middle of the country from north to south. Plains in the southwest and coastal plains occupy only about one-fifth of the country.

Total area: 46,540 sq mi (120,538 sq km)

Coastline: 1,549 miles (2,495 km)

Land use: Forests cover 61% of the land and 16% is arable or under cultivation. There are no meadows and pastures.

Climate: Temperate, with cold winters and wet summers

Population: 21,386,000

Urban population: 59%

Rate of natural increase: 1.5%

Age structure: 28% under 15; 6% over 65

Birth rate: 21/1000

Death rate: 7/1000

Infant mortality rate: 26/1000

Fertility rate: 2.3

Life expectancy at birth: 67 years (male); 73 years (female)

Religion: Buddhist, Confucianist

Language: Korean

Ethnic Divisions: Korean

Literacy Rate: 99%

Government: Communist state, with a president and a unicameral legislature, the Supreme People's Assembly. The 687 members of the Assembly are directly elected to five-year terms, and Assembly members elect the president to a four-year term. There are nine administrative provinces and three cities.

Armed services: 1,054,000 troops (1996) in the army, air force, and navy; citizens subject to conscription for service lasting from three to ten years; 3.5 million in the Red Guards, a peasant militia

Suffrage: Universal; 17 years old

Economy: A centrally planned economy has not been able to forestall financial difficulties stemming from the 1991 collapse of the Soviet Union, a key trading partner, as well as chronic food shortages and continued investments in military support. Industrial development since World War II has been based on mineral production and the utilization of hydropower; living standards lag behind those of South Korea.

Unit of currency: North Korean won; 100 chon = 1 North Korean won (Wn)

GDP per capita: $900

Inflation rate–CPI: N.A.

Workforce: N.A.

Unemployment rate: N.A.

Exports: Goods worth $912 million (f.o.b., 1996 est.) are sent to China, Japan, Russia, South Korea, and other trading partners; exports include minerals, metal products, agricultural and fish products.

Imports: Goods worth $1.95 billion (c.i.f., 1996 est.) are received from China, Japan, Russia, Hong Kong, Germany, and other trading partners; imports include oil, grains, coking coal, machinery, and consumer goods.

Agriculture: An estimated 36% of the working force engages in agriculture, fishing, and forestry. Main crops include rice, corn, potatoes, and soybeans; cattle and pigs are also raised. North Korea must import food to meet domestic demand.

Energy: Coal generates about 70% of the country's energy needs; hydropower supplies 21% and petroleum 10%. Nuclear power is also being developed.

Natural Resources: Minerals, including coal, lead, tungsten, zinc, graphite, magnesite, iron, copper, gold, pyrite, salt, fluospar; hydropower

Environmental Issues: Air and water pollution, limited potable water

Transportation: The country has 3,170 miles (5,110 km) of railroad track and 19,380 miles (31,200 km) of roads, of which 1,160 miles (1,860 km) are paved. Major seaports include Nampo, Wonsan, Chongjin, Hungnam, Songnim, and Haeju. There are 1,400 miles (2,260 km) of rivers, such as the Yalung and Taedon, that are navigable by small craft. There are nearly 50 airports and airfields in the country, and an international airport is at Sunan, 15 miles (24 km) from Pyongyang.

Communications: There are nearly a dozen (1992) daily newspapers published in the capital and elsewhere. There are 3.5 million radios and 400,000 televisions (1992) in operation. There are 30,000 phones (1990 est.) in service, probably available only to government officials.

Tourism: The government plans to enhance tourist facilities; there are museums in Pyongyang and recreation at Mount Kumgang. In 1991, 100,000 visitors came to North Korea.

Public Holidays: Kim Jong Il's birthday (February 16–17); International Women's Day (March 8); Kim Il Sung's birthday, first premier, 1947 (April 15); May Day (May 1); Anniversary of Liberation: from Japan, 1945 (August 15); Independence Day: proclamation of the People's Republic, 1948 (September 9); Anniversary of the Foundation of the Korean Worker's Party (October 10); Anniversary of the Constitution (December 27)

Korea, South

Country Name: Korea, South

Official Name: Republic of Korea

Nationality: Korean(s) (noun); Korean (adjective)

Capital: Seoul, pop. 10,231,000

Major cities: Pusan, Taegu, Inchon, Taejon

External Territories: None

Location: South Korea, on the Korean peninsula in eastern Asia, is bordered on the north by North Korea. The Sea of Japan is on the east and the Yellow Sea is on the west.

Physical Geography: Mountains extend from the north-central and northeast border to a southern plain that occupies the entire southern coast. Plains and rolling hills run along the western coast, and many islands lie off the southern and western coasts.

Total area: 38,230 sq mi (99,016 sq km)

Coastline: 1,499 (2,413 km)

Land use: Forests cover 65% of the land, 19% is arable or under cultivation, and 2% is meadows and pastures.

Climate: Temperate, with cold winters and wet summers

Population: 46,873,000

Urban population: 79%

Rate of natural increase: 0.9%

Age structure: 22% under 15; 7% over 65

Birth rate: 15/1000

Death rate: 6/1000

Infant mortality rate: 11/1000

Fertility rate: 1.6

Life expectancy at birth: 70 years (male); 77 years (female)

Religion: Christian, Buddhist, Confucian, traditional

Language: Korean, English widely taught

Ethnic Divisions: Korean

Literacy Rate: 98%

Government: Republic, with a president and a unicameral legislature, the National Assembly, or Kuk Hoe. The president is directly elected to a five-year term, and the 299 members of the legislature are directly elected to four-year terms. There are nine administrative provinces and six cities.

Armed services: 672,000 troops (1997) in the army, navy, and air force; conscription lasts from 26 months for the army to 30 months for the navy

Suffrage: Universal; 20 years old

Economy: South Korea's booming economy, based on export manufacturing, slowed slightly in the 1990s from the effects of inflation and external debt. Although economic growth has recovered its pace, government plans are in the works to encourage foreign investment, promote small and medium-size businesses, and improve industrial efficiency.

Unit of currency: South Korean won; 100 chun = 1 Sourh Korean won (W)

GDP per capita: $13,700

Inflation rate–CPI: 5% (1996)

Workforce: 20 million (1991 est.)

Unemployment rate: 2% (1996 est.)

Exports: Goods worth $129.8 billion (f.o.b., 1996 est.) are sent to the U.S., the EU, Japan, and other trading partners; exports include electronic and electrical equipment, machinery, steel, cars, ships, textiles, clothing, and fish.

Imports: Goods worth $150.2 billion (c.i.f., 1996 est.) are received from the U.S., Japan, the EU, and other trading partners; imports include machinery, electronics, oil, steel, transport equipment, and textiles.

Agriculture: 21% (1996) of the workforce engages in agriculture, fishing, and forestry. Rice, maize, barley, potatoes, sweet potatoes, fruit, and livestock are raised for domestic consumption. South Korea's fishing fleet brings in the seventh largest catch in the world.

Energy: Domestic and imported fuels and nuclear power, which supplies 40% of power requirements, are used for most energy generation.

Natural Resources: Minerals, including coal, tungsten, graphite, molybdenum, lead, hydropower

Environmental Issues: Air and water pollution, drift net fishing

Transportation: There are 51,790 miles (83,400 km) of roads, of which 39,410 miles (63,470 km) are paved, and 1,910 miles (3,080 km) of railroads in the country. There are 994 miles (1,600 km) of waterways navigable for small craft on rivers such as the Han. Key seaports include Pusan, Inchon, Donghae,

Masan, Yeosu, Gunsen, Mokpo, Pohang, Ulsan, and Cheju. There are more than 100 airports and airfields in the country; international airports are at Seoul, Pusan, and Cheju.

Communications: There are over 60 national dailies published in the country. There are 42 million radios and 9.3 million televisions (1992 est.) in operation. There are 16.6 million telephone lines in service, providing good domestic and international communications.

Tourism: Tourists visit mountain resorts, Buddhist temples, and historic sites in Seoul and elsewhere; Cheju, an island off the South Korean coast, is a popular honeymoon spot. In 1996, 3.7 million visitors spent an estimated $3.8 billion (U.S.) in South Korea.

U.S. Tourist Office: (213) 382-3435

Embassy in U.S.: (202) 939-5600

Public Holidays: Lunar New Year (date varies, in February); Independence Movement Day (March 1); Arbor Day (April 5); Children's Day (May 5); Buddha's birthday (date varies, in May); Memorial Day (June 6); Constitution Day (July 17); Liberation Day (August 15); Korean Thanksgiving Day (date varies, in September); National Foundation Day (October 3); Christmas (December 25)

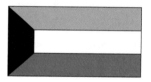

Kuwait

Country Name: Kuwait
Official Name: State of Kuwait
Nationality: Kuwaiti(s) (noun); Kuwaiti (adjective)
Capital: Kuwait, pop. [1,090,000]
Major cities: Al Jahrah, Salmiya, Hawalli

External Territories: None.

Location: Kuwait, in the Middle East, is bordered on the north and west by Iraq, on the south by Saudi Arabia, and on the east by the Persian Gulf.

Physical Geography: Kuwait consists of mostly desert plains.

Total area: 6,880 sq mi (17,818 sq km)

Coastline: 310 mi (499 km)

Land use: Desert and urban areas make up about 92% of the country and 8% is meadows and pastures. There are no arable lands or forests.

Climate: Hot, humid summers and cool, dry winters

Population: 2,076,000

Urban population: 100%

Rate of natural increase: 2.2%

Age structure: 29% under 15; 1% over 65

Birth rate: 24/1000

Death rate: 2/1000

Infant mortality rate: 13/1000

Fertility rate: 3.2

Life expectancy at birth: 72 years (male); 73 years (female)

Religion: Muslim, Christian, Hindu, Parsi

Language: Arabic, English

Ethnic Divisions: Kuwaiti, Arab, South Asian, Iranian

Literacy Rate: 79%

Government: Constitutional monarchy, with a king and a unicameral legislature, the National Assembly, or Majlis al-Umma. The 50 members of the legislature are elected to four-year terms. There are five administrative governorates.

Armed services: 15,300 troops (1997) in the army, air force, and navy; two-year compulsory service; one year for university students

Suffrage: Males; 21 years old

Economy: Kuwait has managed to regain its footing after the damages it suffered during the Persian Gulf War, 1990–1991; the government is

KUWAIT   A NATION OF OUTSIDERS

Kuwait's defense and foreign relations were managed by the British from 1899 until the country's independence in 1961. Oil was discovered there in 1938. The al-Sabah dynasty of rulers was established in 1756 and they continue to rule today. Most of the people living and working in Kuwait are guest workers from other parts of the Middle East and Europe.

promoting industry privatization and increasing its military strength. Petroleum production continues to dominate the economy, providing Kuwaiti citizens with a relatively high standard of living.

Unit of currency: Kuwaiti dinar; 1,000 fils = 1 Kuwaiti dinar (KD)

GDP per capita: $22,300

Inflation rate–CPI: 3.2% (1996)

Workforce: 1.1 million (1996 est.; nearly 70% of workers are non-Kuwaiti)

Unemployment rate: 1.8% (1996)

Exports: Goods worth $14.7 billion (f.o.b., 1996) are sent to Japan, the U.S., Germany, the U.K., the Netherlands, and other trading partners; oil and refined products, fertilizer.

Imports: Goods worth $7.7 billion (f.o.b., 1996) are received from the U.S., the U.K., Japan, Germany, Italy, and other trading partners; imports include food, construction materials, vehicles, and clothing.

Agriculture: Practically no crops; extensive fishing. Most food is imported.

Energy: Energy is generated using domestic petroleum and natural gas.

Natural Resources: Petroleum, natural gas, shrimp, fish

Environmental Issues: Limited freshwater, air and water pollution, desertification

Transportation: Of the 2,760 miles (4,450 km) of roads in Kuwait, 2230 miles (3,590 km) are paved. There are no railways. Shuwaikh, Doha, Kuwait , and Al Ahmadī are key seaports, and an international airport is near the capital.

Communications: Nine daily newspapers are published in the capital. There are 720,000 radios (1992) and 800,000 televisions (1993) in operation. Phone service, with 548,000 lines in service (1991 est.), is still undergoing repair for damages suffered during the Persian Gulf War.

Tourism: Museums in Kuwait have Muslim and Bedouin cultural exhibits. In 1993, visitors spent an estimated $83 million (U.S.) in Kuwait.

Embassy in U.S.: (202) 966-0702

Public Holidays: Beginning of Ramadan (date varies); End of Ramadan (date varies, in February); Kuwaiti National Day (February 25); Feast of the Sacrifice (date varies, in April); Islamic New Year (date varies, in April or May); Birth of the Prophet (date varies, in July); Ascension of the Prophet (date varies, in November)

Kyrgyzstan

Country Name: Kyrgyzstan

Official Name: Kyrgyz Republic

Nationality: Kyrgyzstani(s) (noun); Kyrgyzstani (adjective)

Capital: Bishkek, pop. 589,000

Major cities: Osh, Jalal-Abad, Tokmak

External Territories: None

Location: Kyrgyzstan, in Central Asia, is bordered on the north by Kazakhstan, on the southeast by China, on the south and west by Tajikistan, and on the west by Uzbekistan.

Physical Geography: Parallel ranges of the Tian Shan trend east and west, covering most of the country. Jengish Chokusu (Pik Pobody), at 24,567 feet (7,439 m), is the highest point. Ysk Köl, the country's largest lake, remains ice-free year round.

Total area: 76,834 sq mi (198,999 sq km)

Coastline: None

Land use: Meadows and pastures cover 44% of the country and 7% of the land is arable or under cultivation. There is less than 5% woodlands.

Climate: Conditions vary with elevation and aspect; temperatures generally decrease with elevation, dropping to polar extremes at the highest elevations; high peaks and some valleys are dry; other valleys and slopes receive enough moisture to permit some farming

Population: 4,728,000

Urban population: 34%

Rate of natural increase: 1.5%

Age structure: 37% under 15; 6% over 65

Birth rate: 22/1000

Death rate: 7/1000

Infant mortality rate: 26/1000

Fertility rate: 3.0

Life expectancy at birth: 63 years (male); 71 years (female)

Religion: Muslim, Russian Orthodox

Language: Kirghiz, Russian (both official)

Ethnic Divisions: Kyrgyz, Russian, Uzbek, Ukrainian

Literacy Rate: 97%

Government: Republic, with a president and a bicameral legislature, the Supreme Council, or Zhougorku Kenesh. The president is directly elected to a five-year term. The 35 members of the Legislative Assembly and the 70 members of the People's Assembly are also directly elected to five-year terms. There are six administrative oblasts and one city, the capital.

Armed services: 12,200 troops (1997) in the army; compulsory service from 12 to 18 months

Suffrage: Universal; 18 years old

Economy: Creating new trade links and encouraging foreign investment has helped the economy of Kyrgyzstan rebound from the decline following separation from the Soviet Union in 1991. Prior to that, shortages of food and other commodities hindered economic development. The economy is mostly agricultural, based on cotton, wool, and meat. The government is working to implement privatization, restructuring to reduce inflation rates, and encouraging foreign investment in industries.

Unit of currency: Kyrgyzstani Som; 100 tyiyn = 1 Kyrgyzstani som

GDP per capita: $2,100

Inflation rate–CPI: 15% (1997 est.)

Workforce: 1.7 million (1995 est.)

Unemployment rate: 8% (1996 est.)

Exports: Goods worth $506 million (1996) are sent to China, the U.K., and other trading partners; exports include cotton, wool, meat, tobacco, gold, mercury, uranium, hydroelectricity, machinery, and shoes.

Imports: Goods worth $890 million (1996) are received from Turkey, Cuba, the US, Germany, and other trading partners; imports include grain, lumber, fuels, metals, and industrial products.

Agriculture: 40% (1995 est.) of the labor force engages in agriculture. The most important livestock raised is sheep; fruit, cotton, tobacco, grains, potatoes, and vegetables are cultivated.

Energy: Most energy is derived from hydropower; imported mineral fuels are also used.

Natural Resources: Minerals, including gold, coal, oil, natural gas, mercury, bismuth, lead, zinc; hydropower, which is 10% (1995) of the total value of the country's exports

Environmental Issues: Water and soil pollution

Transportation: There are 230 miles (370 km) of rails in operation; over 90% of the 11,500 miles (18,500 km) of roads are paved. International airports are at Bishkek and Osh.

Communications: Seven weekly papers are published in the country; two are published five times a week. There are 825,000 radios and 875,000 televisions in use; telephone service, with 342,000 lines operating (1991 est.), does not meet demand.

Tourism: Ysyk-Köl, in northeast Kyrgyzstan, is one of the deepest mountain lakes in the world and is a key tourist attraction; the high peaks of the Tian Shan attract mountaineers and tourists who prefer to explore more remote regions.

Embassy in U.S.: (202) 338-5141

Public Holidays: Christmas (January 7); Orozo Ait, end of Ramadan (date varies, in February); International Women's Day (March 8); Mooruz, Kyrgyz New Year (March 21); Kurban Ait, Feast of the Sacrifice (date varies, in April); International Labor Day (May 1); Victory Day (May 9); Independence Day: from Soviet Union, 1991 (August 31)

Transportation: There are 1,713 miles (2,759 km) of railroads and 57,008 (91,800 km) of roads, of which 9,161 (14,752 km) are paved. Lake Kariba is navigable and has ports at Binga and Kariba. International airports are at Harare, Bulawayo, and Victoria Falls.

Communications: There are two daily newspapers. There are 945,000 radios and 297,000 televisions (1994) in operation; phone service, with 135,000 telephones, is poorly maintained.

Tourism: Some 10% of Zimbabwe is devoted to parks, gardens, and sanctuaries; the spectacular Victoria Falls and mountain retreats draw visitors to the country, which earned $153 million (U.S.) from 1.1 million tourists in 1994.

U.S. Tourist Office: (800) 621-2381

Embassy in U.S.: (202) 332-7100

Public Holidays: Easter (date varies, in March or April); Independence Day (April 18); Worker's Day (May 1); Africa Day (May 25); Heroes' Day (August 11–12); Christmas (December 25–26)

Laos

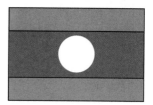

Country Name: Laos

Official Name: Lao People's Democratic Republic

Nationality: Lao(s) or Laotian(s) (noun); Lao or Laotian (adjective)

Capital: Vientiane, pop. [534,000]

Major cities: Savannakhet, Louangphrabang, Pakxe

External Territories: None

Location: Laos, a landlocked country in southeastern Asia, is bordered on the east and northeast by Vietnam, on the south by Cambodia, on the west by Thailand and Myanmar, and on the northwest by China.

Physical Geography: Mountains, generally higher in the north, cover most of the country. Floodplains along the banks of the Mekong River in the west provide land for farming, extending to higher plateaus that rise to the Annam Cordillera on the border with Vietnam.

Total area: 91,429 sq mi (236,800 sq km)

Coastline: None

Land use: Forests covered 54% of the country in 1993. An estimated 3% of the land is arable or under cultivation, and 3% is meadows and pastures.

Climate: Tropical monsoon, with rain from May to October; dry from December to April

Population: 5,000,000

Urban population: 17%

Rate of natural increase: 2.7%

Age structure: 44% under 15; 4% over 65

Birth rate: 43/1000

Death rate: 15/1000

Infant mortality rate: 104/1000

Fertility rate: 5.6

Life expectancy at birth: 50 years (male); 52 years (female)

Religion: Buddhist, animist

Language: Lao, French, English, ethnic

Ethnic Divisions: Lao Loum, Lao Theung, Lao Soung

Literacy Rate: 57%

Government: Communist state, with a president and a unicameral legislature, the National Assembly. The president is elected by the members of the legislature for a five-year term; the 99 members of the National Assembly are directly elected to five-year terms. There are 16 administrative provinces and one municipality.

Armed services: 29,000 troops (1997) in the army, navy, and air force; 18-month compulsory service

Suffrage: Universal; 18 years old

Economy: Agriculture and forestry are the primary economic activities in Laos; however, even with the majority of workers engaged in this sector, rice imports are necessary in some

LAOS A LONG ROAD TO INDEPENDENCE

Laos has a long history of outside rule: the Khmer of ancient Cambodia, the Burmese, the Chinese, the Vietnamese, and the French, who took it as a protectorate in 1893. The country became independent in 1954. Laos is relatively unspoiled by the development and overcrowding found elsewhere in Southeast Asia and is growing in popularity as a tourist destination.

years to meet demand. In 1986, the government began a transition from a centrally planned economy to a market economy. Market reforms have been made and foreign investment encouraged, but international aid is essential while Laos works to modernize its infrastructure and revamp its financial institutions.

Unit of currency: New kip; 100 at = 1 new kip (NK)

GDP per capita: $1,150

Inflation rate- CPI: 16% (1997 est.)

Workforce: 1 million to 1.5 million (1997 est.)

Unemployment rate: 1.7% (1995 est.)

Exports: Goods worth $313.1 million (f.o.b., 1996) are sent to Vietnam, Thailand, Germany, France, and other trading partners; exports include electricity, wood products, garments, electricity, coffee.

Imports: Goods worth $678 million (c.i.f., 1996) are received from Thailand, Japan, Vietnam, China, Singapore, and other trading partners; imports include machinery and equipment, vehicles, fuel.

Agriculture: 80% (1997 est.) of the workforce engages in agriculture, forestry, and fishing. Rice is the primary crop; corn, cassava, potatoes, and sweet potatoes are also grown, and livestock is raised. Exports include coffee and wood products; logs and wood products earn 32% (1994) of the total value of the country's exports.

Energy: Most energy is generated using hydropower; imported mineral fuels are also used.

Natural Resources: Minerals, including gypsum, tin, gold, gemstones; timber; hydropower

Environmental Issues: Deforestation, soil erosion, inadequate access to potable water

Transportation: No railroads are currently operating, but there are 13,860 miles (22,320 km) of roads, of which 2,170 miles (3,500 km) are paved. The Mekong River and its tributaries add an additional 2,850 miles (4,590 km) to the country's transportation network. An international airport is located at Vientiane.

Communications: Several biweekly and monthly newspapers are published in Vientiane and elsewhere. There are 560,000 radios and 32,000 televisions (1993 est.) in use. Telephone distribution and service, with 19,333 lines in service (1996 est.), is poor.

Tourism: Wildlife, trekking in mountain forests, Buddhist shrines, classical architecture from the 14th to 19th centuries, the Hindu temple of Wat Phu Champasak, and other archaeological sites are all tourist draws. Tourists were excluded from the country until 1989; in 1996, over 400,000 visitors came to Laos.

Embassy in U.S.: (202) 332-6416

Public Holidays: Army Day (January 24); Lao New Year (April 13–15); Labor Day (May 1); National Day: proclamation of People's Republic, 1975 (December 2)

Latvia

Country Name: Latvia

Official Name: Republic of Latvia

Nationality: Latvian(s) (noun); Latvian (adjective)

Capital: Rīga, pop. 821,200

Major cities: Daugavpils, Liepāja, Jelgava

External Territories: None

Location: Latvia, in northwestern Europe, is bordered on the north by Estonia, on the east by Russia and Belarus, on the south by Lithuania, and on the west by the Baltic Sea.

Physical Geography: Latvia encompasses generally flat lowlands and hills with lakes and swamps.

Total area: 24,942 sq mi (64,599 sq km)

Coastline: 330 mi (531 km)

Land use: Nearly 46% of the land is wooded, 27% is arable or under cultivation, and 13% is meadows and pastures.

Climate: Maritime, with cold winters and cool summers

Population: 2,430,000

Urban population: 69%

Rate of natural increase: -0.6%

Age structure: 19% under 15; 14% over 65

Birth rate: 8/1000

Death rate: 14/1000

Infant mortality rate: 14.8/1000

Fertility rate: 1.1

Life expectancy at birth: 64 years (male); 76 years (female)

Religion: Lutheran, Roman Catholic, Russian Orthodox

Language: Latvian, Lithuanian, Russian

Ethnic Divisions: Latvian, Russian, Byelorussian

Literacy Rate: 100%

Government: Republic, with a president and a unicameral legislature, the Parliament, or Saeima. The president is elected by the 100 members of Parliament for a three-year term; Parliament members are directly elected to three-year terms. There are 26 administrative districts and seven towns.

Armed services: 4,500 troops (1997) in the army, navy, air force, and other military branches; 12-month compulsory service from 19 years of age; voluntary at 18 years of age

Suffrage: Universal; 18 years old

Economy: A diverse industrial base has helped Latvia make the transition from a planned to a market economy, and government programs to reduce inflation and increase foreign trade helped the economy recover from an economic slowdown in the early 1990s. A series of bank failures in 1995 caused a larger than expected budget deficit; however, monetary policies have eased the situation. The government supports industrial privatization to compliment the already completed agricultural privatization.

Unit of currency: Lats (singular), lati (plural); 100 santimi = 1 lats

GDP per capita: $4,260

Inflation rate–CPI: 7.4% (1997 est.)

Workforce: 1.4 million (1997)

Unemployment rate: 7% (1996 est.)

Exports: Goods worth $1.4 billion (f.o.b., 1996 est.) are sent to Russia, Germany, Sweden, the U.K., and other trading partners; exports include wood and wood products, textiles and foodstuffs.

Imports: Goods worth $2.3 billion (c.i.f., 1996 est.) are received from Russia, Germany, Sweden, and other trading partners; imports include fuels, cars, machinery and equipment, and chemicals.

Agriculture: Nearly 16% (1990) of the labor force engages in agriculture, fishing, and forestry. Dairy farming and pig farming are the main agricultural activities; grain, sugar beets, potatoes, and vegetables are also raised.

Energy: Electricity is imported from Estonia and Lithuania and supplemented by petroleum imports.

Natural Resources: Amber, peat, limestone, dolomite

Environmental Issues: Air, water, and soil pollution

Transportation: There are 1,500 miles (2,410 km) of rail track and 37,290 miles (60,050 km) of roads, of which 14,280 miles (23,000 km) are paved. Main seaports are located at Ventspils, Rīga, and Liepāja. There are international airports at Rīga and Jelgava.

Communications: The country has 14 daily newspapers and 6 are published in Rīga. There are 1.4 million radios and 1.1 million televisions (1993 est.) in operation. Phone service, with 600,000 phones in use (1993 est.), is adequate.

Tourism: Baltic beaches, castles, the medieval and art nouveau architecture in Rīga, and winter sports in Sigulda are among the country's tourist attractions. In 1997, 1.4 million visitors came to Latvia.

Embassy in U.S.: (202) 726-8213

Public Holidays: Good Friday (date varies, in March or April); Labor Day (May 1); Midsummer Festival (June 23–24); National Day: proclamation of the republic, 1918 (November 18); Christmas (December 25–26)

Lebanon

Country Name: Lebanon

Official Name: Lebanese Republic

Nationality: Lebanese (singular and plural noun); Lebanese (adjective)

Capital: Beirut, pop. (1,826,000)

Major cities: Tripoli, Zahleh, Sidon (1975 est.)

External Territories: None

Location: Lebanon, in the Middle East, is bordered on the north and east by Syria, on the south and southeast by Israel, and on the west by the Mediterranean Sea.

Physical Geography: The Bekka Valley separates the Anti-Lebanon Mountains on the eastern border from the Lebanon Mountains, to the east of the coastal plain along the Mediterranean Sea.

Total area: 4,015 sq mi (10,400 sq km)

Coastline: 140 mi (225 km)

Land use: Of the country's land, 30% is arable or under cultivation, 8% is wooded, and 1% is meadows and pastures.

Climate: Mediterranean, with hot, dry summers and mild, wet winters; winter snow in mountain areas

Population: 4,070,000

Urban population: 88%

Rate of natural increase: 1.6%

Age structure: 30% under 15; 6% over 65

Birth rate: 23/1000

Death rate: 7/1000

Infant mortality rate: 35/1000

Fertility rate: 2.4

Life expectancy at birth: 68 years (male); 73 years (female)

Religion: Muslim, Christian

Language: Arabic, French, English

Ethnic Divisions: Arab, Armenian

Literacy Rate: 86%

Government: Republic, with a president and a unicameral legislature, the Majilis Alnuwab, or National Assembly. The president is elected by the 128 members of the National Assembly to a six-year term; Assembly members are directly elected to four-year terms. There are five administrative governorates.

Armed services: 55,100 troops (1996) in the army, air force, and navy; 12-month conscription

Suffrage: Compulsory for males at 21 years of age; voluntary for women with an elementary education at 21 years of age

Economy: International assistance and revenues from banking, remittances from abroad, and other sources are rebuilding Lebanon's infrastructure after the civil war that lasted from 1975 to 1991. The government has been concentrating on stabilizing the value of the Lebanese pound and encouraging foreign investment, but continued political stability will be essential for Lebanon's economic growth to continue.

Unit of currency: Lebanese pound; 100 piastres = 1 Lebanese pound (£L)

GDP per capita: $4,400

Inflation rate–CPI: 9% (1997 est.)

Workforce: 938,000 (1994 est.)

Unemployment rate: 18% (1997 est.)

Exports: Goods worth $1 billion (f.o.b., 1996 est.) are sent to Saudi Arabia, Jordan, Kuwait, and other trading partners; exports include paper, paper products, foodstuffs, jewelry, textiles, and metals.

Imports: Goods worth $7.559 billion (c.i.f., 1996 est.) are received from Italy, France, the U.S., Germany, Syria, the U.K., and Japan; imports include consumer goods, machinery and transport equipment, and oil.

Agriculture: 7% (1994) of the labor force engages in agriculture. Citrus fruit, potatoes, olives, tobacco, and hemp are cultivated for export.

Energy: Imported oil is used for most energy generation.

Natural Resources: Limestone, iron, salt

Environmental Issues: Water and air pollution, deforestation, soil erosion

Transportation: Of the 260 miles (420 km) of railways in Lebanon, only 140 miles (220 km) are in service. Of the 3,950 miles (6,360 km) of roads, 3,890 miles (6,260 km) are paved. Beirut, Tripoli, and Jounieh are key seaports, and an international airport is located at Beirut.

Communications: Nearly 40 daily newspapers are published in the country, mostly in Beirut. There are 2.32 million radios and 4.1 million televisions (1992 est.) in operation. Phone service, with an estimated 150,000 phones in operation, is still undergoing repair for damages suffered during the civil war.

Tourism: Since the end of the civil war, archaeological sites, ancient churches and mosques, beaches, and winter sports are drawing tourists back to Lebanon. Prior to the civil war, tourism earned about 20% of the country's income.

Embassy in U.S.: (202) 939-6300

Public Holidays: Feast of St. Maron (February 9); End of Ramadan (date varies, in February); Arab League Anniversary (March 22); Easter (date varies, in March or April); Feast of the Sacrifice (date varies, in April); Islamic New Year (date varies, in April or May); Ashura (date varies, in April or May); Ascension (date varies, in May); Birth of the Prophet (date varies, in July); Assumption (August 15); All Saints' Day (November 1); Independence Day, 1943 (November 22); Ascension of the Prophet (date varies, in December); Christmas (December 25)

Lesotho

Country Name: Lesotho

Official Name: Kingdom of Lesotho

Nationality: Mosotho (singular noun), Basotho (plural noun); Basotho (adjective)

Capital: Maseru, pop. 109,400

Major cities: Teyateyaneng, Mafeteng, Qacha's Nek

External Territories: None

Location: Lesotho, in southern Africa, is surrounded by the country of South Africa.

Physical Geography: Lesotho is a mountainous country. The Drakensberg in the north and east reach elevations of more than 11,000 feet and include the summit of Lesotho's highest point, Thabana Ntlenyana at 11,425 feet (3,482 m). The Orange and the Caledon Rivers form Lesotho's western boundary.

Total area: 11,720 sq mi (30,355 sq km)

Coastline: None

Land use: Meadows and pastures cover 66% of the land and 11% is arable or under cultivation. There are no forests or woodlands.

Climate: Temperate subtropical, with dry, cold winters and warm, wet summers; decreasing precipitation from west to east

Population: 2,129,000

Urban population: 16%

Rate of natural increase: 2.115%

Age structure: 41% under 15; 5% over 65

Birth rate: 32.99/1000

Death rate: 11.84/1000

Infant mortality rate: 72.79/1000

Fertility rate: 4.3

Life expectancy at birth: 54 years (male); 58 years (female)

Religion: Christian, indigenous beliefs

Language: Sesotho, Zulu, Xhosa, English

Ethnic Divisions: Basotho

Literacy Rate: 71%

Government: Parliamentary constitutional monarchy, with a hereditary monarch, King Letsie III, who has ruled since 1996, and a bicameral legislature, with the National Assembly and the Senate. The 65 members of the Assembly are elected to five-year terms by direct vote; the Senate has 22 chiefs and 11 members nominated by the ruling party. There are ten administrative districts.

Armed services: 2,000 troops (1997); voluntary service

Suffrage: Universal; 18 years old

Economy: Political unrest, a large and growing population, limited land resources, and economic dependence on South Africa have all hindered independent economic development in Lesotho. International assistance has supported economic reforms, resulting in lower inflation rates and a budget surplus. The government continues to strengthen the economy with civil service reforms, industrial privatization, and the development of export crops. 35% of adult males (1996 est.) work in South Africa and send money home; such remittances are significant for the economy.

Unit of currency: Loti (singular), maloti (plural); 100 lisente (sente, singular) = 1 loti (L)

GDP per capita: $2,500

Inflation rate–CPI: 8.7% (1996 est.)

Workforce: 849,000 (1996 est.)

Unemployment rate: >50% (1996 est.)

Exports: Goods worth $218 million (f.o.b., 1996 est.) are sent mainly to South African countries; exports include clothing, mohair, road vehicles, and footwear.

Imports: Goods worth $1.1 billion (c.i.f., 1996 est.) are received from South African countries and other trading partners; imports include maize, construction materials, clothing, road vehicles, machinery, and oil.

Agriculture: 39% (1996 est.) of the workforce engages in agriculture, fishing, and forestry. Cattle and other animals are raised for export. Wool and mohair are also exported. Corn, sorghum, pulses, barley, and wheat are grown for domestic use. The country is subject to drought and must import foodstuffs.

Energy: South Africa provides Lesotho with 90% of its mineral fuels.

Natural Resources: Minerals, including diamonds, lead, uranium, iron ore; water

Environmental Issues: Population pressures resulting in soil erosion and degradation, deforestation; desertification

Transportation: A 1.6-mile link (2.6 km) connects Maseru to the Blomfontein and Natal line in South Africa. Of the 3,080 miles (4,960 km) of roads, 18% are paved. An international airport is located at Thota-Moli, 12 miles (20 km) from Maseru.

Communications: A daily newspaper is published in the capital, as are three weeklies and one biweekly. There are 75,000 radios and 56,000 televisions (1995) in operation. Telephone service is minimal, with 12,000 main lines (1993).

Tourism: Lesotho's mountains are a key draw for visitors from South Africa and elsewhere; in 1994, 253,000 visitors came to the country and spent $17 million (U.S.).

Embassy in U.S.: (202) 797-5533

Public Holidays: Moshoeshoe Day (March 11); Easter (date varies, in March or April); Heroes' Day (April

4); Ascension (date varies, in May); Worker's Day (May 1); King's birthday (July 17); National Independence Day: from the U.K., 1966 (October 4); Christmas (December 25); Boxing Day (December 26)

Liberia

Country Name: Liberia
Official Name: Republic of Liberia
Nationality: Liberian(s) (noun); Liberian (adjective)
Capital: Monrovia, pop. 850,000
Major cities: Gbarnga, Buchanan
External Territories: None
Location: Liberia, on the western coast of Africa, is bordered on the north by Sierra Leone and Guinea, on the east by Côte d'Ivoire, and on the south and west by the North Atlantic Ocean.
Physical Geography: Mountainous plateaus in the north and northwest descend to rolling hills that parallel the coast; the coastal plain has many lagoons and swamps.
Total area: 43,000 sq mi (111,369 sq km)
Coastline: 360 mi (579 km)
Land use: Nearly 18% of the country is wooded, 4% of the land is arable or under cultivation, and 59% is meadows and pastures.
Climate: Equatorial, with high temperatures and wet summers; dry season from November to April
Population: 2,924,000
Urban population: 45%
Rate of natural increase: 3.08%
Age structure: 45% under 15; 4% over 65
Birth rate: 42.3/1000

Death rate: 11.5/1000
Infant mortality rate: 105.6/1000
Fertility rate: 6.2
Life expectancy at birth: 56 years (male); 61 years (female)
Religion: Traditional, Muslim, Christian
Language: English, African languages
Ethnic Divisions: Kpelle, Bassa, Grebo, others
Literacy Rate: 38%
Government: A transitional government established in 1995 has since been disrupted by continued political violence. The 1986 constitution calls for a president elected to a six-year term, and a bicameral legislature, the National Assembly, with a 26-member Senate and 64-member House of Representatives. There are 13 administrative counties.
Armed services: 24,000 troops (1995, during civil war); 13,000 troops (1997 est.) in the Cease-Fire Monitoring Group
Suffrage: Universal; 18 years old
Economy: Civil war began in 1989 and came to an uneasy truce in 1996. Food shortages, the destruction of the country's infrastructure, high inflation rates, and large numbers of unemployed workers continue to undermine Liberia's economy. Continued fighting prevents efforts to regain economic stability, and international aid is essential for survival.
Unit of currency: Liberian dollar; 100 cents = 1 Liberian dollar (L$)
GDP per capita: $1,000

Inflation rate–CPI: 4.6% (1980–1989 average); 1,000% (during civil war)
Workforce: 886,000 (1996 est.)
Unemployment rate: 90% (1995 est.)
Exports: Goods worth $667 million (f.o.b., 1995 est.) are sent to the U.S., the European Union, Singapore, and other trading partners; exports include diamonds, iron ore, rubber, timber, and coffee.
Imports: Goods worth $5.8 billion (f.o.b., 1995 est.) are received from the U.S., Germany, the Belgium-Luxembourg, the Netherlands, and other trading partners; imports include mineral fuels, chemicals, machinery, transportation equipment, manufactured goods, and food.
Agriculture: 70% (1996 est.) of the labor force engages in agriculture, fishing, and forestry. Rubber, coffee, cocoa, and timber are key export crops, and rice, cassava, and sheep are raised for domestic consumption.
Energy: Most energy is generated using hydropower, and imported mineral fuels, nearly 20% (1994) of the value of all imports, are also used.
Natural Resources: Iron, timber, diamonds, gold
Environmental Issues: Deforestation, soil erosion, loss of biodiversity, water pollution
Transportation: Many transportation routes have been disrupted by the civil war. Operations on the 304 miles (490 km) of railway stopped in 1990. Of 6,580 miles (10,600 km)

LIBERIA AN AFRICAN NATION'S U.S. ORIGINS

Liberia successfully resisted both French and British colonialism; its founders were freed American slaves backed by private U.S. interests. Almost as large as Tennessee, it became Africa's first independent republic in 1847. The capital city, Monrovia, was named after U.S. President James Monroe.

of roads, 410 miles (660 km) are paved. Buchanan, Greenville, Harper, and Monrovia are key seaports, but most port activity has been halted. Liberia has the largest merchant fleet in the world, with 1,680 vessels (1996), because of its open registry policy. An international airport is at Monrovia.

Communications: Several newspapers are published in Monrovia. About 675,000 radios and 56,000 televisions (1995). An estimated 5,000 main phone lines (1993) provide minimal service.

Tourism: Political instability has disrupted tourist visits in the 1990s, and visitors are discouraged from traveling to Liberia until internal fighting has ceased.

Embassy in U.S.: (202) 723-0437

Public Holidays: Armed Forces Day (February 11); Decoration Day (March 12); J .J. Robert's birthday (March 15); Good Friday (date varies, in March or April); Fast and Prayer Day (April 11); National Unification Day (May 14); Independence Day, 1847 (July 26); Flag Day (August 24); Thanksgiving Day (November 6); National Memorial Day (November 12); President William V. Tubman's Birthday, president, 1944–1971 (November 29); Christmas (December 25)

Libya

Country Name: Libya

Official Name: Socialist People's Libyan Arab Jamahiriya

Nationality: Libyan(s) (noun); Libyan (adjective)

Capital: Tripoli, pop. [1,682,000]

Major cities: Banghazi, Misrātah

External Territories: None

Location: Libya, in northern Africa, is between Egypt and Sudan on the east, Chad and Niger on the south, Algeria and Tunisia on the west, and the Mediterranean Sea on the north.

Physical Geography: The Sahara covers much of the country. Sand dunes in the southwest and mountains in the far south merge with the barren rocks and sand of the central Libyan desert region. To the north, grasslands eventually meet coastal oases.

Total area: 679,362 sq mi (1,759,540 sq km)

Coastline: 1,106 mi (1,770 km)

Land use: The country's land is 8% meadows and pastures and 1% is arable or under cultivation. There are no woodlands.

Climate: Hot and arid in most of the country; more moderate temperatures and greater precipitation along the coast

Population: 4,992,000

Urban population: 86%

Rate of natural increase: 2.48%

Age structure: 39% under 15; 4% over 65

Birth rate: 28.2/1000

Death rate: 3.4/1000

Infant mortality rate: 33.3/1000

Fertility rate: 4.1

Life expectancy at birth: 73 years (male); 77 years (female)

Religion: Sunni Muslim

Language: Arabic, Italian, English,

Ethnic Divisions: Arab

Literacy Rate: 76%

Government: Socialist republic, theoretically governed by local councils. A unicameral General People's Congress has 3,000 members who elect the Revolutionary Leader as head of state. Since 1969, Muammar Qaddafi has exercised considerable control over the government, either as its head or as an advisor. There are ten administrative governorates.

Armed services: 65,000 troops (1997); two-year selective conscription

Suffrage: Universal and compulsory; 18 years old

Economy: Oil production is the centerpiece of Libya's centrally planned economy and is supplemented by the manufacture of iron and steel, and by agricultural processing. International embargoes against Libyan oil, initiated in 1992, have begun to affect the country's ability to update infrastructure and industry, and foreign investment has dwindled.

Unit of currency: Libyan dinar; 1,000 dirhams = 1 Libyan dinar (LD)

GDP per capita: $6,700

Inflation rate–CPI: 30% (1997 est.)

Workforce: 1.2 million (1996 est.), including 132,000 (estimated) resident foreigners

Unemployment rate: 25% (1997 est.)

Exports: Goods worth $9.0 billion (f.o.b., 1995) are sent to Italy, Germany, Spain, France, Greece, and other trading partners; exports include crude oil, refined petroleum products, and natural gas.

Imports: Goods worth $6.2 billion (f.o.b., 1995) are received from Italy, Germany, the U.K., France, Turkey, and other trading partners; imports include machinery, vehicles, food, and manufactured goods.

Agriculture: An estimated 18% (1996) of the labor force engages in agriculture, fishing, and forestry. Raising livestock is the primary activity, but some barley, wheat, olives, dates, citrus, vegetables, and peanuts are grown for domestic use. The country imports 75% of its food.

Energy: Most energy is generated using domestic oil.

Natural Resources: Oil, natural gas, gypsum

Environmental Issues: Desertification, limited freshwater

Transportation: There are no railroads. Of the 51,670 miles (83,200 km) of roads, 29,550 miles (47,590 km) are paved. Main seaports include Tripoli, Banghazi, and Misrātah. There are international airports at Tripoli and Banghazi.

Communications: Two daily newspapers are published in Tripoli. There are 1.25 million radios and 550,000 televisions (1995) in operation, and an estimated 240,000 telephones (1993) provide modern phone service.

Tourism: Tripoli, with its marketplace, mosques, and architecture, is a key starting point for tourists, who also visit Mediterranean beaches, Roman ruins at Leptis Magna, and Cyrene, now called Shāḥḥāt. In 1993, visitors spent an estimated $5 million (U.S.) in Libya.

Public Holidays: End of Ramadan (date varies, in February); Evacuation Day (March 28); Feast of the Sacrifice (date varies, in April); Islamic New Year (date varies, in April or May); Ashoura (date varies, in April or May); Evacuation Day (June 11); Birth of the Prophet (date varies, in July); Revolution Day, 1969 (September 1); Evacuation Day (October 7); Ascension of the Prophet (date varies, in November or December)

Liechtenstein

Country Name: Liechtenstein
Official Name: Principality of Liechtenstein
Nationality: Liechtensteiner(s) (noun); Liechtenstein (adjective)
Capital: Vaduz, pop. 5,000

Major cities: Schaan, Balzers, Triesen
External Territories: None
Location: Liechtenstein, a landlocked country in central Europe, is bordered by Switzerland on the south and west and by Austria on the north and east.
Physical Geography: Alps in the eastern two-thirds of the country meet the Rhine River floodplain in the west.
Total area: 62 sq mi (160 sq km)
Coastline: None
Land use: About 16% of the land is meadows and pastures, 24% is arable or under cultivation, and 35% is wooded.
Climate: Alpine, with mild winters
Population: 32,000
Urban population: N.A.
Rate of natural increase: 0.7%
Age structure: 19% under 15; 10% over 65
Birth rate: 14/1000
Death rate: 7/1000
Infant mortality rate: 18.4/1000
Fertility rate: 1.6
Life expectancy at birth: 67 years (male); 78 years (female)
Religion: Roman Catholic
Language: German, Alemannic dialect
Ethnic Divisions: Alemannic, Italian
Literacy Rate: 100%
Government: Hereditary Constitutional monarchy—Prince Hans Adam II, since 1989—with a unicameral parliament, the Landtag. The 25 members of the parliament are directly elected to four-year terms. There are 11 administrative communes.
Armed services: No standing army since 1868; all citizens under 60 years of age liable for duty in an emergency
Suffrage: Universal; 20 years old

Economy: Light industry, financial and business services, and tourist revenues have provided Liechtenstein with a modern, stable economy, making it one of the wealthiest nations in the world.
Unit of currency: Swiss franc; 100 Rappen (centimes) = 1 Franken (Swiss franc) (SwF)
GDP per capita: $23,000
Inflation rate–CPI: 0.5% (1997 est.)
Workforce: 22,891 (13,847 are foreigners); 8,321 commute from Austria and Switzerland each day
Unemployment rate: 1.6% (1997 est.)
Exports: Goods worth $2.47 billion (1996 est.) are sent to Switzerland and other trading partners; exports include small specialty machinery, dental products, stamps, hardware, and pottery.
Imports: Goods worth $917.3 million (1996 est.) are received from Switzerland and other trading partners; imports include machinery, metal goods, textiles, foodstuffs, and motor vehicles.
Agriculture: 2% (1996) of the workforce engages in agriculture; wheat, barley, maize, and potatoes, are cultivated; livestock and dairy farming are important.
Energy: 92.5% (1995) of energy is imported.
Natural Resources: Potential for hydropower
Environmental Issues: N.A.
Transportation: There are 11.5 miles (18.5 km) of Austrian owned and operated railroads in the country; all 160 miles (250 km) of roads are paved. There are no international airports.
Communications: Three daily newspapers are published in the country. There are 12,130 radios, 11,790 televisions, and 22,880 telephones (1996) in use.
Tourism: Tourism is a key component of Liechtenstein's economy; tourists are drawn by mountains

and the Postal Museum in Vaduz. In 1996, 58,781 visitors came to the country.

Embassy: Contact the Swiss Embassy (202) 745-7900

Public Holidays: Epiphany (January 6); Candlemas (February 2); St. Joseph's Day (March 19); Good Friday (date varies, in March or April); Easter Monday (date varies, in March or April); Ascension (date varies, in May); Whit Monday (date varies, in May); Labor Day (May 1); Corpus Christi (date varies, in May or June); Assumption and National Holiday (August 15); Nativity of the Virgin Mary (September 8); All Saints' Day (November 1); Immaculate Conception (December 8); Christmas (December 25); St. Stephen's Day (December 26)

Lithuania

Country Name: Lithuania
Official Name: Republic of Lithuania
Nationality: Lithuanian(s) (noun); Lithuanian (adjective)
Capital: Vilnius, pop. 580,100
Major cities: Kaunas, Klaipėda, Šiaunliai
External Territories: None
Location: Lithuania, in northeast Europe, is bordered on the west by the Baltic Sea, on the north by Latvia, on the south and east by Belarus, and on the southwest by Poland and Russia's Kaliningrad Oblast.
Physical Geography: The gently rolling hills of the Baltic Highlands and lakes are in the east and southeast; low-lying plains cover the rest

of the country, and there are dunes along the Baltic coast.
Total area: 25,213 sq mi (65,301 sq km)
Coastline: 61 mi (99 km)
Land use: Almost half the land is arable or under cultivation, 7% is meadows and pastures, and forests cover 31% of the land.
Climate: Maritime, with wet, mild winters and summers
Population: 3,700,000
Urban population: 68%
Rate of natural increase: -0.1%
Age structure: 21% under 15; 13% over 65
Birth rate: 10/1000
Death rate: 11/1000
Infant mortality rate: 9.2/1000
Fertility rate: 1.4
Life expectancy at birth: 66 years (male); 77 years (female)
Religion: Roman Catholic, Lutheran, Russian Orthodox, Protestant
Language: Lithuanian, Polish, Russian
Ethnic Divisions: Lithuanian, Polish, Russian
Literacy Rate: 98%
Government: Republic, with a president and a unicameral legislature, the Seimas, or Parliament. The president is directly elected to a five-year term; the 141 members of Parliament are directly elected to four-year terms. There are 10 districts divided into 56 municipalities.
Armed services: 5,250 troops (1997) in the army, air force, and navy; 12-month compulsory service
Suffrage: Universal; 18 years old
Economy: Since independence, in 1990, the government has focused on rebuilding the economy through privatization, controlling inflation, cultivating new trading partners, and encouraging foreign investment. The country has few natural resources; however, manufacturing is a key component of its economy, and a skilled workforce further

strengthens Lithuania's potential for economic growth.
Unit of currency: Litas (singular), litai (plural); 100 centas = 1 litas
GDP per capita: $4,230
Inflation rate–CPI: 8.6% (1997 est.)
Workforce: 1.8 million
Unemployment rate: 6.7% (1998)
Exports: Goods worth $3.3 billion (1996) are sent to Russia, Ukraine, Germany, and other trading partners; exports include agricultural products, mineral products, textiles, machinery, and live animals.
Imports: Goods worth $4.4 billion (1996) are received from Russia, Germany, Poland, and other trading partners; imports include mineral production, machinery, transport equipment, chemicals, textiles, and foodstuffs.
Agriculture: 20% (1997) of the labor force engages in agriculture, forestry, and fishing. Livestock is raised, and grain, sugar beets, and vegetables are cultivated.
Energy: Nuclear power meets 83% (1996) of the country's needs and is supplemented by imported mineral fuels and hydropower.
Natural Resources: Peat
Environmental Issues: Soil and groundwater pollution
Transportation: The country has 1,240 miles (2,000 km) of railroads and 40,450 miles (65,140 km) of roads, the majority of which are paved. Main seaports are Kaunas and Klaipėda; international airports are located at Vilnius Kaunas, and Siauiai.
Communications: The country has 16 daily newspapers. There are 1.42 million radios and 1.77 million televisions (1993) in operation. Phone service, with 1.01 million main lines (1995) in use, is above average for former Soviet republics.
Tourism: Historic buildings in Vilnius, Kaunas, and other cities and resorts and spas along the Baltic coast are tourist draws. There were

222,000 visitors in 1994 who spent $70 million (U.S.).

Embassy in U.S.: (202) 234-5860

Public Holidays: Day of Restoration: of the Lithuanian State, 1918 (February 16); Day of the Reestablishment of Independence, 1990 (March 11); Easter Monday (date varies, in March or April); Labor Day (May 1); Coronation Anniversary: of Grand Duke Mindaugas of Lithuania, 1253 (July 6); All Saints' Day (November 1); Christmas (December 25–26)

Luxembourg

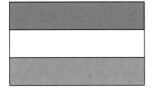

Country Name: Luxembourg

Official Name: Grand Duchy of Luxembourg

Nationality: Luxembourger(s); Luxembourg (adjective)

Capital: Luxembourg, pop. 77,400

Major cities: Esch, Differdange, Dudelange

External Territories: None

Location: Luxembourg, a landlocked country in western Europe, is bordered on the east by Germany, on the south by France, and on the west by Belgium.

Physical Geography: Forested mountains are in the north; rolling plateaus slope to the Moselle floodplain in the south and southeast.

Total area: 998 sq mi (2,586 sq km)

Coastline: None

Land use: About 25% of the land is arable or under cultivation, forests cover 21% of the land, and 20% is meadows and pastures.

Climate: Humid, with mild summers and winters

Population: 432,000

Urban population: 88%

Rate of natural increase: 0.4%

Age structure: 19% under 15; 14% over 65

Birth rate: 13/1000

Death rate: 9/1000

Infant mortality rate: 4.2/1000

Fertility rate: 1.7

Life expectancy at birth: 74 years (male); 80 years (female)

Religion: Roman Catholic

Language: Luxembourgian, German, French

Ethnic Divisions: Celtic base (with French and German blend), Portuguese, Italian

Literacy Rate: 100%

Government: Constitutional monarchy, with a unicameral legislature, the Chamber of Deputies. The monarchy is hereditary. The 60 members of the legislature are directly elected to five-year terms. There are three administrative cantons.

Armed services: 800 volunteer troops (1997)

Suffrage: Universal and compulsory; 18 years old

Economy: Financial services and manufacturing support Luxembourg's thriving economy, which is marked by low inflation and unemployment rates. Luxembourg, Belgium, and the Netherlands share close economic ties. The Belgium-Luxembourg Economic Union was formed in 1921, and trade statistics are for both countries.

Unit of currency: Luxembourg franc; 100 centimes = 1 Luxembourg franc (LuxF)

GDP per capita: $33,700

Inflation rate–CPI: 2.3% (1995)

Workforce: 213,100 (one-third of labor force is made up of foreign workers); (1997)

Unemployment rate: 3.5% (1997)

Exports: Goods worth $7.1 billion (f.o.b., 1996 est.) are sent to Germany, France, Belgium, the U.K., and other trading partners; exports include finished steel products, chemicals, rubber products, glass, and aluminum.

Imports: Goods worth $9.4 billion (c.i.f., 1996 est.) are received from Belgium, Germany, France, the Netherlands, and other trading partners; imports include minerals, metals, foodstuffs, and quality consumer goods.

Agriculture: 1% (1995 est.) of the labor force is employed in agriculture, fishing and forestry; barley, oats, potatoes, wheat, fruits and wine grapes are cultivated.

Energy: Nearly 60% (1990) of the country's energy needs are met by hydropower; imported oil is also used.

Natural Resources: Iron ore (no longer exploited)

Environmental Issues: Urban water and air pollution

Transportation: There are 170 miles (270 km) of railroads and 3,200 miles (5,160 km) of paved roads. The Moselle River is used for inland shipping; the main port is Mertert. An international airport is located near the capital.

Communications: Five daily newspapers are published in Luxembourg. There are 230,000 radios (1993) and 105,000 televisions (1993 est.). With 221,900 phones in use (1994 est.), telephone service is modern and efficient.

Tourism: In 1996, 484,000 visitors came to Luxembourg; key visitor attractions include medieval castles, health spas, walking trails in the mountains, and cultural activities in the capital.

U.S. Tourist Office: (212) 935-8888

Embassy in U.S.: (202) 265-4171

Public Holidays: Easter Monday (date varies, in March or April); Ascension (date varies, in May); Labor

Day (May 1); Whit Monday (date varies, in May or June); National Day (June 23); Assumption (August 15); All Saints' Day (November 1); Christmas (December 25); St. Stephen's Day (December 26)

Macedonia

Country Name: Macedonia
Official Name: The Former Yugoslav Republic of Macedonia
Nationality: Macedonian(s) (noun); Macedonian (adjective)
Capital: Skopje, pop. 430,000
Major cities: Bitola, Kumanovo, Prilep, Tetovo
External Territories: None
Location: Macedonia, a landlocked country in southeastern Europe, is bordered on the north by Yugoslavia, on the east by Bulgaria, on the south by Greece, and on the west by Albania.
Physical Geography: Macedonia is mainly mountainous with deep basins, including the Vardar River Basin that bisects the country. Two large lakes, Ohrid and Presya, are on the southern border.
Total area: 9,928 sq mi (25,713 sq km)
Coastline: None
Land use: About 40% of the land is wooded, 25% is meadows and pastures, and 26% is arable or cultivated.
Climate: Hot, dry summers; cold winters accompanied by heavy precipitation
Population: 2,019,000
Urban population: 59%
Rate of natural increase: 0.7%

Age structure: 24% under 15; 9% over 65
Birth rate: 15/1000
Death rate: 8/1000
Infant mortality rate: 15.7/1000
Fertility rate: 1. 8
Life expectancy at birth: 70 years (male); 75 years (female)
Religion: Eastern Orthodox, Muslim
Language: Macedonian, Albanian
Ethnic Divisions: Macedonian, Albanian
Literacy Rate: N.A.
Government: Republic, with a president and a unicameral legislature, Sobranje, or Assembly. The president is directly elected to office for a five-year term, and the 120 members of the Assembly are elected to four-year terms. There are 34 administrative counties.
Armed services: 15,400 troops (1997) in the army and other military branches; nine-month conscription
Suffrage: Universal; 18 years old
Economy: High unemployment rates, the lack of foreign investment, and political instability in the region work against Macedonia's attempts to generate economic growth since independence from Yugoslavia in 1991. The government has succeeded in encouraging some industrial privatization, lowering inflation rates, stabilizing the national currency, and reducing the deficit, and international funds continue to support economic restructuring.

Unit of currency: Denar; 100 deni = 1 new Macedonian denar
GDP per capita: $960
Inflation rate–CPI: 3.5% (1997 est.)
Workforce: 591,773 (1995 est.)
Unemployment rate: 30% (1997 est.)
Exports: Goods worth $1.2 billion (f.o.b., 1996 est.) are sent to Bulgaria, other Yugoslav republics, Germany, and Italy; exports include food, beverage, tobacco, machinery and transport equipment, and other manufactured goods.
Imports: Goods worth $1.6 billion (c.i.f., 1996 est.) are received from former Yugoslav republics, Germany, and other trading partners; imports include machinery equipment, food, chemicals, and fuel.
Agriculture: 16.5% (1996) of the labor force engages in agriculture, fishing, and forestry. Crops for export and domestic use include rice, tobacco, wheat, corn, millet, and beef, pork, poultry, and mutton.
Energy: Domestic coal and hydropower is used for most energy generation.
Natural Resources: Minerals, including chromium, lead, zinc, manganese, tungsten, nickel, iron, asbestos, sulfur; timber
Environmental Issues: Air pollution
Transportation: There are 570 miles (920 km) of railroads and 6,580 miles (10,590 km) of roads, of which 3,420 miles (5,500 km) are

MACEDONIA THE NAME GAME, YUGOSLAV STYLE

When Yugoslavia dissolved in 1991, one of its former republics kept the name of Macedonia. Greece, which has a province by the same name, was not pleased and placed a blockade on the country. A 1995 agreement to refer to the country as "the Former Yugolsav Republic of Macedonia" appears to have settled the dispute. The current Macedonia was once part of a larger region known as Macedonia that was ruled by the Turks from 1389 to 1912.

paved. International airports are located at Petrovets and Ohrid.

Communications: Five daily newspapers are published in the capital. There are 369,000 radios, 327,01 televisions, and 337,000 telephones (1992 est.) in service.

Tourism: Before independence in 1991, mountain scenery was a key tourist draw, but tourism has fallen because of regional conflicts. In 1997, 121,000 visitors came to the country.

Embassy in U.S.: (202) 337-3063

Public Holidays: Orthodox Christmas (date varies, in January); Orthodox Easter (date varies, in April or May); Labor Day (May 1–2); National Day (August 2); Independence Day: from Yugoslavia, 1995 (September 8–9); Rebellion Day (October 11)

Madagascar

Country Name: Madagascar

Official Name: Republic of Madagascar

Nationality: Malagasy (singular and plural noun); Malagasy (adjective)

Capital: Antananarivo, pop. 1,052,800

Major cities: Antsirabe, Toamasina, Fianarantsoa, Mahajanga

External Territories: None

Location: Madagascar, in the Indian Ocean, is an island country off the coast of southern Africa, east of Mozambique. It is the fourth largest island in the world, after Greenland, New Guinea, and Borneo.

Physical Geography: The Angavo Escarpment rises sharply from the

---

MADAGASCAR A CONCENTRATION OF CHAMELEONS

Probably once part of Africa geologically, Madagascar is rich in natural wonders; it is thought that some 150,000 of the 200,000 living things on the Texas-size island are found nowhere else in the world. In fact, half the world's species of chameleons are found there. A former French colony, it gained independence in 1960. It was the site of Arab colonies in the Middle Ages. Most of its citizens are of mixed Malay-Indonesian and African descent.

---

east coast to plateaus that slope to plains on the west.

Total area: 226,658 sq mi (587,041 sq km)

Coastline: 2,998 mi (4,828 km)

Land use: Meadows and pastures 41% of the country, 40% is wooded, and 5% of the land is arable or under cultivation.

Climate: Generally hot, but conditions vary; temperate central plateau; hot and humid eastern coast; distinct wet and dry seasons on the western coast; arid in the southern section of the island

Population: 14,417,000

Urban population: 22%

Rate of natural increase: 2.9%

Age structure: 44% under 15; 3% over 65

Birth rate: 43.5/1000

Death rate: 14.1/1000

Infant mortality rate: 96.4/1000

Fertility rate: 6.0

Life expectancy at birth: 51 years (male); 53 years (female)

Religion: Indigenous beliefs, Christian, Muslim

Language: Malagasy, French (both official)

Ethnic Divisions: Merina, Betsimisaraka, others

Literacy Rate: 80%

Government: Republic, with a president and a bicameral legislature. The president is elected for a five-year term. The 138 members of the National Assembly are directly

---

elected to four-year terms. Two-thirds of the Senate members are selected by an electoral college and one third are appointed to office by the president, both for four-year terms. There are six administrative provinces.

Armed services: 21,000 troops (1997) in the army, navy, and air force; conscription

Suffrage: Universal; 18 years old

Economy: Population pressures, foreign debt, political instability, and an economy driven by agriculture have all hindered Madagascar's quest for economic growth. International aid has been given with the stipulation that the government promote industrial privatization, continue to control inflation, and reorganize banking.

Unit of currency: Malagasy franc; 100 centimes = 1 Malagasy franc (FMG)

GDP per capita: $730

Inflation rate–CPI: 19.8% (1996)

Workforce: 7,306,000 (1996 est.)

Unemployment rate: 6% (1995 est.)

Exports: Goods worth $493 million (f.o.b., 1996 est.) are sent to France, Germany, the U.S., Japan, Reunion, and other trading partners; exports include coffee, vanilla, cloves, shellfish, and sugar.

Imports: Goods worth $612 million (f.o.b., 1996 est.) are received from France, Iran, Japan, the United States, China, and other trading partners; imports include manufactured and capital goods, oil, consumer goods, and food.

Agriculture: Over three-quarters (1996) of the workforce is employed in agriculture, fishing, and forestry. Coffee earns 19.1% (1996) of the total value of exports, and vanilla earns 4%. Other export crops include cloves, sugar, coconuts, fruits, cotton, and sisal. Rice and cattle are important domestic commodities, but rice imports are needed to meet demand. Fishing for tuna and prawns is expanding.

Energy: Most energy is generated using imported oil.

Natural Resources: Minerals, including graphite, chromite, coal, bauxite, salt, quartz, tar sands, gemstones, mica; fish

Environmental Issues: Deforestation, soil erosion, desertification, water pollution, habitat loss

Transportation: There are 550 miles (880 km) of railroads and 30,950 miles (49,840 km) of roads, of which 3,590 miles (5,780 km) are paved. The Panglanes Canal parallels the east coast between Toamasina and Farafangana. The main seaport is Toamasina. International airports are located at Antananarivo and at Mahajanga and Nosey Be on the west coast.

Communications: Several daily newspapers are published in the capital. There are 2,850 million radios and 295,000 televisions (1995); phone service, with 34,000 phones (1994 est.) in operation, is above average.

Tourism: Tourist attractions include Madagascar's festivals, wildlife, and landscapes; in 1996, 82,681 visitors spent $64.7 million (U.S.).

Embassy in U.S.: (202) 265-5525

Public Holidays: Commemoration of 1947 Rebellion (March 29); Good Friday (date varies, in March or April); Easter Monday (date varies, in March or April); Ascension (date varies, in May); Whit Sunday (date varies, in May); Labor Day

(May 1); Independence Day: from France, 1960 (June 26); All Saints' Day (November 1); Christmas (December 25); National Anniversary (December 30)

Malawi

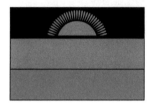

Country Name: Malawi
Official Name: Republic of Malawi
Nationality: Malawian(s) (noun); Malawian (adjective)
Capital: Lilongwe, pop. 395,500
Major cities: Blantyre, Mzuzu, Zomba
External Territories: None
Location: Malawi, in southeastern Africa, is on the western shore of Lake Malawi; on the north is Tanzania, on the east and south is Mozambique, and Zambia is on the west.
Physical Geography: The Great Rift Valley, on the east and south central part of the country, underlies Lake Malawi and the Shire River valley; the lake shore and river valley are characterized by lowlands and plateaus that rise to the west of the lake. The Nyika Plateau is in the north.
Total area: 45,747 sq mi (118,484 sq km)
Coastline: None
Land use: Forests cover 39% of the land, 18% is arable or cultivated, and 20% is meadows and pastures.
Climate: Tropical, with a dry season from May to October; cooler temperatures at higher elevations
Population: 10,000,000
Urban population: 20%
Rate of natural increase: 1.7%

Age structure: 48% under 15; 3% over 65
Birth rate: 41.56/1000
Death rate: 24.48/1000
Infant mortality rate: 137/1000
Fertility rate: 5.9
Life expectancy at birth: 36 years (male); 36 years (female)
Religion: Protestant, Roman Catholic, Muslim, traditional indigenous beliefs
Language: Chewa, English
Ethnic Divisions: Chewa, Nyanja, Tumbuko, Yao
Literacy Rate: 56%
Government: Multiparty democracy, with a president and a unicameral legislature, the National Assembly. The president and the 177 members of the Assembly are directly elected to five-year terms. There are three administrative regions.
Armed services: 6,000 troops (1997) in the army, air force, and other branches
Suffrage: Universal; 18 years old
Economy: A growing population, an economy based on agriculture, and an inefficient civil service hinder Malawi's quest for economic growth. Government plans include industrial privatization, the promotion of foreign investment, and fiscal reforms; however, austerity measures may interfere with providing citizens with basic health care and education, and the country remains dependent on foreign aid.
Unit of currency: Malawian kwacha; 100 tambala = 1 Malawian kwacha (K)
GDP per capita: $900
Inflation rate–CPI: 83.4% (1995)
Workforce: 4,788,000 (1995 est.)
Unemployment rate: 1.3% (1987)
Exports: Goods worth $405 million (f.o.b., 1995) are sent to the U.S., South Africa, Germany, Japan, and other trading partners; exports include tobacco, tea, sugar, and coffee.

Imports: Goods worth $475million (f.o.b., 1995) are received from South Africa, Germany, Zimbabwe, the U.K., and other trading partners; imports include food, oil, consumer goods, manufactured items, and transportation equipment.

Agriculture: 86.3% (1996) of the workforce is employed in agriculture, fishing, and forestry. Tobacco, which earned 64.4% (1996) of the total value of exports, tea, and sugarcane are the most important export crops; domestic crops include maize, cassava, and peanuts. The country is nearly self-sufficient; however, drought necessitates food imports.

Energy: Most electricity is generated using hydropower and imported fuels. Firewood is still used extensively by households.

Natural Resources: Minerals, including limestone, uranium, coal, bauxite

Environmental Issues: Deforestation, land degradation, water pollution

Transportation: About 490 miles (790 km) of rail track are in service; there are 17,640 miles (28,400 km) of roads. Lake Malawi and the Shire River are navigable; lake ports include Chipoka, Monkey Bay, Nkhotakota Bay, and Nkotakota. Lilongwe has an international airport.

Communications: One daily newspaper is published. There are 2.48 million radios (1995) in operation (no figures are available for televisions). Phone service, with 33,000 lines (1994) in use, is fair.

Tourism: National parks and game reserves are among the key attractions to Malawi's visitors; 154,000 visitors spent $5 million (U.S.) in the country in 1994.

Embassy in U.S.: (202) 797-1007

Public Holidays: John Chilembwe Day (January 15); Martyrs' Day (March 3); Easter (date varies, in March or April); Labor Day (date varies, in May); Freedom Day (June 14); Republic Day: independence

from the U.K., 1964 (July 6); Mother's Day (date varies, in October); Christmas (December 25–26)

Malaysia

Country Name: Malaysia
Official Name: Malaysia
Nationality: Malaysian(s) (noun); Malaysian (adjective)
Capital: Kuala Lumpur, pop. 1,145,100
Major cities: Ipoh, Johor Baharu
External Territories: None
Location: Malaysia, in southeastern Asia, is divided into West, or Peninsular, Malaysia on the Malay Peninsula, which is bordered on the north by Thailand and Singapore to the south, and East Malaysia, which is across the South China Sea on the island of Borneo. The Malaysian states of Sabah and Sarawak occupy northern Borneo and surround Brunei; Indonesian territory is on the south.
Physical Geography: West Malayisia is mountainous with coastal lowlands; East Malaysia, on Borneo, has wide coastal plains that rise to a series of hills and mountains.
Total area: 127,317 sq mi (329,749 sq km)

Coastline: West Malaysia: 2,903 mi (4,675 km); East Malaysia: 1,619 mi (2,607 km)
Land use: Nearly 70% of the land is wooded and 15% is arable or under cultivation. There are no meadows and pastures.
Climate: Tropical monsoon, with heavy rains from October to February along the eastern mainland coast; rain along the western coasts from May to September
Population: 22,710,000
Urban population: 57%
Rate of natural increase: 2.13%
Age structure: 34% under 15; 4% over 65
Birth rate: 26/1000
Death rate: 5/1000
Infant mortality rate: 8/1000
Fertility rate: 3.2
Life expectancy at birth: 70 years (male); 75 years (female)
Religion: Muslim, Buddhist, Hindu, Christian, Confucianist
Language: Malay, English, Chinese
Ethnic Divisions: Malay, Chinese, Indian
Literacy Rate: 84%
Government: Constitutional monarchy, with an elected monarch and a bicameral legislature, the Parliament. The monarch is elected to a five-year term by the 13 federation state rulers. Of the 69 members of the Senate, 26 are elected and 40 are appointed to office for six-year terms; the 192 members of the House of Representatives are

MALAYSIA KUALA LUMPUR: SKYSCRAPER RECORD BREAKER

The world's tallest buildings—the Petronas Twin Towers—were completed in 1997 in Malaysia's capital, Kuala Lumpur. At 1,483 feet (452 m), they surpass the Sears Tower in Chicago by 29 feet (8.85 m). Malaysia is one of the fastest developing nations in Southeast Asia and is one of the world's centers for semiconductor assembly. It gained its independence from Great Britain in 1957.

directly elected to five-year terms. There are 13 administrative states and 2 territories.

Armed services: 111,500 troops (1997) in the army, navy, and air force; voluntarily service

Suffrage: Universal; 21 years old

Economy: After a long period of economic growth, Malaysia was hit hard by the Asian financial crisis in 1997-1998. The government has invested nearly five billion dollars in the proposed Multimedia Super Corridor, Asia's version of the U.S.'s Silicon Valley. The recession may call for a scaling back. Subsistence farming is still key for the survival of many citizens.

Unit of currency: Ringgit or Malaysian dollar; 100 sen = 1 ringgit or Malaysian dollar (RM)

GDP per capita: $11,100

Inflation rate- CPI: 36% (1996 est.)

Workforce: 8,398,200 (1996 est.)

Unemployment rate: 2.6% (1996 est.)

Exports: Goods worth $78.2 billion (1996) are sent to Singapore, the U.S., Japan, the U.K., Thailand, and other trading partners; exports include electronic equipment, petroleum and petroleum products, palm oil, wood, rubber, and textiles.

Imports: Goods worth $78.4 billion (1996) are received from Japan, the U.S., Singapore, Taiwan, Germany, and other trading partners; imports include machinery, chemicals, food, and petroleum products.

Agriculture: 21% (1996) of the workforce engages in agriculture, fishing, and forestry, producing rice for domestic use and rubber, palm oil, cocoa, pepper, coconuts, tea, pineapples, and wood for export. Malaysia is the world's largest producer of palm oil (1995) and the world's third largest producer of rubber, after Thailand and Indonesia.

Energy: Most energy (38% in 1993) is derived from domestic petroleum; natural gas, hydropower, and coal are also used.

Natural Resources: Minerals, including tin, petroleum, copper, iron ore, bauxite, natural gas; timber

Environmental Issues: Air and water pollution, deforestation

Transportation: The country has 1,020miles (1,650 km) of railroads and 58,680 miles (94,500 km) of roads, of which 75% on the mainland are paved. Mainland seaports include Port Kelang on the west coast and Kuantan on the South China Sea; ports on Borneo include Labuan, Kota Kinabalu, Sandakan, Kuching, and Bintulu. An international airport is at Kuala Lumpur.

Communications: There are nearly 40 daily newspapers published in Malay, English, Chinese, and Tamil on the mainland and Borneo. There are 8.08 million radios and 2 million televisions (1993 est.) in operation. Phone distribution and service, with 2.55 million lines (1992 est.), is fair to good.

Tourism: Tourism is growing in Malaysia, in part because of the attraction of the diverse ethnic groups. Museums in Kuala Lumpur and elsewhere offer a range of cultural exhibits. In 1996, 7.1 million visitors brought $3.6 billion (U.S.) to the country.

U.S. Tourist Office: (213) 689-9702; (800) 336-6842

Embassy in U.S.: (202) 328-2700

Public Holidays: Chinese New Year (date varies, in January or February); End of Ramadan (date varies, in February); Vesak Day (date varies, in April or May); Labor Day (May 1); Feast of the Sacrifice (date varies, in May); Official Birthday of His Majesty, Yang di-Pertuan Agong (June 3); Birth of the Prophet (date varies, in July); National Day: independence from the U.K., 1957 (August 31); Deepavali (date varies, in October or November); Christmas (December 25)

Maldives

Country Name: Maldives

Official Name: Republic of Maldives

Nationality: Maldivian(s) (noun); Maldivian (adjective)

Capital: Male, pop. 63,000

Major cities: N.A.

External Territories: None

Location: Located in the Indian Ocean, this south Asian country is made up of 1,200 coral islands, of which 202 are inhabited. India and Sri Lanka are to the northeast.

Physical Geography: The low-lying coral islands are protected by barrier reefs.

Total area: 115 sq mi (298 sq km)

Coastline: 400 mi (644 km)

Land use: About 10% of the land is arable or under cultivation, 3% is wooded, and 3% is meadows and pastures.

Climate: Tropical monsoon, with heavy rains from May to August

Population: 278,000

Urban population: 26%

Rate of natural increase: 2.2%

Age structure: 45% under 15; 4% over 65

Birth rate: 26/1000

Death rate: 5/1000

Infant mortality rate: 27/1000

Fertility rate: 5.8

Life expectancy at birth: 69 years (male); 70 years (female)

Religion: Sunni Muslim

Language: Maldivian Divehi, English

Ethnic Divisions: Sinhalese, Dravidian, Arab, African

Literacy Rate: 93%

Government: Republic, with a president and a unicameral legislature, the Citizens' Council. The president is directly elected for a five-year term; of the 50 members of the legislature, 42 are elected and 8 are appointed by the president, all for five-year terms. There are 19 administrative districts and the capital.

Armed services: N.A.

Suffrage: Universal; 21 years old

Economy: Fishing and tourism have generated enough revenue for the government to undertake infrastructure improvements and to allow increased foreign investment. In the mid-1990s, thousands of foreign workers were employed in Maldives, and vocational courses were offered to residents in an effort to increase the labor pool.

Unit of currency: Rufiyaa; 100 laari (larees, singular) = 1 rufiyaa (Maldivian rupee)

GDP per capita: $1,800

Inflation rate–CPI: 6.3% (1996)

Workforce: 56,435 (1990 est.)

Unemployment rate: Negligible

Exports: Goods worth $59 million (f.o.b., 1996) are sent to Sri Lanka, the U.S., the U.K., Singapore, and other trading partners; exports include seafood and clothing.

Imports: Goods worth $302 million (f.o.b., 1996) are received from Singapore, Sri Lanka, India, Hong Kong, Japan, Thailand, and other trading partners; imports include consumer goods and petroleum products.

Agriculture: 5% of the workforce engages in agriculture and 15% in fishing. Fishing, especially for tuna, is important; fishing is the second largest source of foreign exchange. Coconuts are grown for export and some fruits, vegetables, and cereals for domestic use. The country began an afforestation program in 1996.

Energy: Petroleum imports are used to generate most electricity.

Natural Resources: Fish

Environmental Issues: Depletion of freshwater aquifers threatens water supplies

Transportation: There are no railroads in the country, and few roads. Main seaport at Male, and there is an international airport at Hulule Island, near Male.

Communications: Several newspapers are published in Male. There are 28,280 (1992 est.) radios and 1,310 televisions (1994) in operation. There are 8,520 main phone lines (1992 est.) in service.

Tourism: Tourism is growing in Maldives; 338,700 visitors came to the country in 1996 to enjoy its beaches and marine life.

Public Holidays: National Day (January 7); End of Ramadan (date varies, in February); Feast of the Sacrifice (date varies, in April); Islamic New Year (date varies, in April or May); Birth of the Prophet (date varies, in July); Independence Day: from the U.K., 1965 (July 26); Victory Day (November 3); Republic Day, 1968 (November 11); Fishermen's Day (December 10); Martyrs' Day (December 23)

Mali

Country Name: Mali

Official Name: Republic of Mali

Nationality: Malian(s) (noun); Malian (adjective)

Capital: Bamako, pop. [809,600]

Major cities: Ségou, Mopti, Sikasso, Kayes

External Territories: None

Location: Mali, a landlocked country in western Africa, is bordered on the north by Algeria; on the east and southeast by Niger; on the south by Burkina Faso, Côte d'Ivoire, and Guinea; and on the west by Senegal and Mauritania.

Physical Geography: Mali is mostly flat, with dissected plateaus in the south and southwest and hills in the east and southeast; the northern half of the country is part of the Sahara.

Total area: 478,841 sq mi (1,240,192 sq km)

Coastline: None

Land use: Meadows and pastures cover 25% of the land, 6% is wooded, and 2% is arable or under cultivation.

Climate: Varies from north to south; subtropical in the south, with 20 to 55 inches of rain annually; hotter and drier in the Sahara; almost no rain, with extreme ranges in daily

MALI THE DOGAN PEOPLE: A WORLD APART

The Bandiagara escarpment, which runs for 120 miles across central Mali, has been home to Africans since at least 300 B.C. Today about 300,000 Dogon live in the region, largely in seclusion from civilization. There are 35 Dogon dialects, some of which can't be understood 30 miles away. The Dogon have long resisted outside influence—their religion is animistic, and their calendar features a 5-day week.

temperatures, from more than 110° F in the day to below 40° F at night, in the north

Population: 10,960,000

Urban population: 26%

Rate of natural increase: 3.1%

Age structure: 47% under 15; 4% over 65

Birth rate: 47/1000

Death rate: 16/1000

Infant mortality rate: 122.5/1000

Fertility rate: 6.7

Life expectancy at birth: 45 years (male); 47 years (female)

Religion: Muslim, indigenous beliefs

Language: French, Bambara, numerous African languages

Ethnic Divisions: Bambara, Malinke, Sarakole, others

Literacy Rate: 31%

Government: Republic, with a president and a unicameral legislature, the National Assembly. The president and the 147 members of the legislature are directly elected to five-year terms. There are eight administrative and one governmental districts.

Armed services: 7,350 troops (1997) in the army and air force; two-year selective conscription

Suffrage: Universal; 21 years old

Economy: Mali's economy is dominated by subsistence agriculture and processing cotton, sugarcane, and other farm products. The country is hampered in its quest for economic growth by large foreign debts, but the government is pushing for industrial diversification with plans for industrial privatization and greater foreign investment.

Unit of currency: CFA franc; 100 centimes = 1 franc de la Communauté financière africaine (CFAF)

GDP per capita: $600

Inflation rate–CPI: 3% (1997 est.)

Workforce: 5,345,000 (1995 est.)

Unemployment rate: N.A.

Exports: Goods worth $473 million (f.o.b., 1996 est.) are sent to Belgium-Luxembourg, France, Spain, Côte d'Ivoire, and other trading partners; exports include cotton, livestock, and gold.

Imports: Goods worth $797 million (f.o.b., 1996 est.) are received from Côte d'Ivoire, France, the U.K., and other trading partners; imports include machinery, food, construction materials, oil, and textiles.

Agriculture: 83.7% (1996) of the workforce engages in agriculture; export crops include cotton, peanuts, vegetables, and mangoes, while millet, sorghum, rice, corn, and other cereals are raised for domestic use. Livestock and fish are also important domestic and export commodities. Cotton earns 59% (1996) of the total value of Mali's exports.

Energy: Hydropower generates 80% (1995) of the country's energy.

Natural Resources: Minerals, including gold, phosphates, uranium, bauxite, iron, manganese, tin, copper

Environmental Issues: Deforestation, desertification, soil erosion, potable water, poaching

Transportation: There are 400 miles (640 km) of railroads and 9,380 miles (15,100 km) of roads, of which 1,140 miles (1,830 km) are paved. The Niger and Senegal Rivers are navigable, with river ports at Gao, Tombouctou, Mopti, and Bamako. An international airport is at Bamako.

Communications: A daily newspaper and more than a dozen periodicals are published in the capital. There are 500,000 radios and 20,000 televisions (1995) in operation. Phone service, with 14,000 phones (1993) in use, is minimal.

Tourism: Cultural draws, including the architecture in the Niger River Valley and performances by the Malinke and other ethnic groups, earned Mali $18 million (U.S.) from 28,000 visitors in 1994.

Embassy in U.S.: (202) 332-2249

Public Holidays: Armed Forces Day (January 20); End of Ramadan (date varies, in February): Easter Monday (date varies, in March or April); Feast of the Sacrifice (date varies, in April); Labor Day (May 1); Africa Day (May 25); Birth of the Prophet (date varies, in July); Baptism of the Prophet (date varies, in August); Independence Day: independence from France and proclamation of republic, 1960 (September 22); 1968 coup anniversary (November 19); Christmas (December 25)

Malta

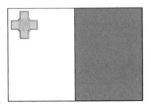

Country Name: Malta
Official Name: Republic of Malta
Nationality: Maltese (singular and plural noun); Maltese (adjective)
Capital: Valletta, pop. 9,100
Major cities: Birkirkara, Qormi, Mosta
External Territories: None
Location: Malta, a southern European island country in the Mediterranean Sea, consists of three main islands—Gozo, Comino, and Malta—and two minor islets; the largest island, Malta, is 60 miles (90 km) south of Sicily, Italy.
Physical Geography: Malta consists mainly of flat to dissected plains, with coastlines characterized by cliffs, harbors, bays, beaches, and coves.
Total area: 122 sq mi (316 sq km)
Coastline: 87 miles (140 km)
Land use: About 40% of the land is arable or under cultivation. There are no meadows and pastures or woodlands.
Climate: Mediterranean, with hot, dry summers and cool, rainy winters
Population: 380,000
Urban population: 89%
Rate of natural increase: 0.5%
Age structure: 21% under 15; 12% over 65
Birth rate: 13/1000
Death rate: 8/1000
Infant mortality rate: 6.4/1000
Fertility rate: 2.0
Life expectancy at birth: 75 years (male); 80 years (female)
Religion: Roman Catholic

Language: Maltese, English
Ethnic Divisions: Maltese
Literacy Rate: 88%
Government: Republic, with a president and a unicameral legislature, the House of Representatives. The president is elected by the 65 House members for a five-year term; the House members are directly elected to five-year terms. There are no local governments; all administration is from Valletta, on Malta.
Armed services: 1,950 troops (1997); voluntary service
Suffrage: Universal; 18 years old
Economy: Tourism, shipbuilding and repair, and light industry are all key sectors in Malta's economy, which virtually reinvented itself in 1979 after the withdrawal of British military operations. The government has encouraged foreign investment and sponsored the construction of a free port, stock exchange, and offshore business center.
Unit of currency: Maltese lira (singular), liri (plural); 1,000 mils = 100 cents = 1 Maltese lira (LM)
GDP per capita: $12,900
Inflation rate–CPI: 2.3% (1996)
Workforce: 148,100 (1994 est.)
Unemployment rate: 3.7% (1996)
Exports: Goods worth $1.7 billion (f.o.b., 1996 est.) are sent to Italy, Germany, the U.K., and other trading partners; exports include machinery and transport equipment, clothing, and printed matter.
Imports: Goods worth $2.8 billion (c.i.f., 1996 est.) are received from Italy, Germany, the U.K., and other trading partners; imports include food, petroleum, machinery and semi-manufactured goods.
Agriculture: Only about 2% (1996) of the labor force engages in agriculture. Potatoes, cauliflower, grapes, wheat, barley, tomatoes, and citrus are cultivated.
Energy: Most energy is generated with imported oil and coal.
Natural Resources: Limestone, salt

Environmental Issues: Limited freshwater
Transportation: No railroads operate in the country; there are 980 miles (1,580 km) of roads. Valletta and Marsaxlokk on Malta are key seaports. There is an international airport at Valletta.
Communications: Three daily newspapers (1996) are published. There are 189,000 radios and 300,000 televisions (1996) in operation. Phone service, with 191,876 lines in service (1992 est.), is excellent.
Tourism: An estimated 1,111,161 tourists visited Malta in 1997; attractions include scenic and historical sites and beaches.
U.S. Tourist Office: (212) 695-9520
Embassy in U.S.: (202) 462-3611
Public Holidays: St. Paul's Shipwreck (February 10); St. Joseph (March 19); Freedom Day (March 31); Easter Monday (date varies, in March or April); St. Joseph the Worker (May 1); Memorial of 1919 Riot (June 7); St. Peter and St. Paul (June 29); Assumption (August 15); Our Lady of Victories (September 8); Independence Day: from the U.K., 1964 (September 21); Immaculate Conception (December 8); Republic Day, 1974 (December 13); Christmas (December 25)

Marshall Islands

Country Name: Marshall Islands
Official Name: Republic of the Marshall Islands
Nationality: Marshallese (singular and plural noun); Marshallese (adjective)
Capital: Majuro, pop. 28,000

Major cities: None

External Territories: None

Location: The Marshall Islands is a group of some 1,200 islands, islets, and atolls in two parallel chains of islands—Ratak and Ralik—that span nearly 800 miles (1,285 km) in the western North Pacific Ocean.

Physical Geography: The country consists of low-lying islands of coral, limestone, and sand.

Total area: 70 sq mi (181 sq km)

Coastline: 230 miles (370 km)

Land use: Approximately 60% of the land is used for permanent crops. There are no meadows and pastures, woodlands, or arable land.

Climate: Tropical, with heavy rains from May to November; precipitation decreasing from south to north

Population: 62,000

Urban population: 65%

Rate of natural increase: 3.6%

Age structure: 49% under 15; 3% over 65

Birth rate: 43/1000

Death rate: 7/1000

Infant mortality rate: 26/1000

Fertility rate: 6.7

Life expectancy at birth: 60 years (male); 63 years (female)

Religion: Christian

Language: English, local dialects, Japanese

Ethnic Divisions: Micronesian

Literacy Rate: 93%

Government: Republic, with a president and a legislature, the Nitijela. The 33 members of the legislature are directly elected to four-year terms, and the president is elected to a four-year term by the legislature. There are no administrative divisions.

Armed services: The U.S. is responsible for the military defense of the Marshall Islands.

Suffrage: Universal; 18 years old

Economy: The economy of the Marshall Islands is based on tourism, agriculture, and foreign assistance

from the U.S.; tourist development is continuing, and plans are in the works for some industrial development.

Unit of currency: U.S. dollar; 100 cents = 1 U.S. dollar ($ U.S.)

GDP per capita: $1,680

Inflation rate–CPI: 4% (1995-1996)

Workforce: 4,800

Unemployment rate: 16% (1991 est.)

Exports: Goods worth $17.5 million (f.o.b., 1996 est.) are sent to the U.S., Japan, Australia, and other trading partners; exports include fish, coconut oil, and trochus shells.

Imports: Goods worth $71.8 million (c.i.f., 1996 est.) are received from the U.S., Japan, Australia, and other trading partners; imports include food, machinery, beverages and tobacco.

Agriculture: Fish and coconuts are important exports. Subsistence crops of cacao, taro, breadfruit, fruits, pigs, and chicken dominate the agriculture.

Energy: Energy is generated using imported fuels.

Natural Resources: Phosphates, seafood, seabed mineral deposits

Environmental Issues: Inadequate potable water

Transportation: There are no railroads; roads are paved on the major islands and stone and coral-surfaced tracks are also used. An international airport is located at Majuro, which is also the main seaport.

Communications: Several newspapers are published in the country. There are 2,000 phones in service (1997), three radio stations, and one television station.

Tourism: Tourist attractions in the country include beaches, lagoons, fishing, and World War II sites; in 1994, 4,910 visitors came to the Marshall Islands bringing $2 million (U.S.) to the country.

Embassy in U.S.: (202) 234-5414

Public Holidays: Proclamation of the Republic, 1979 (May 1)

Mauritania

Country Name: Mauritania

Official Name: Islamic Republic of Mauritania

Nationality: Mauritanian(s) (noun); Mauritanian (adjective)

Capital: Nouakchott, pop. 735,000

Major cities: Nouadhibou, Kaédi, Zouérate

External Territories: None

Location: Mauritania, in northwestern Africa, is bordered on the northeast by Algeria, on the northwest by Western Sahara, on the east by Mali, on the south by Mali and Senegal, and on the west by the Atlantic Ocean.

Physical Geography: Mauritania is mostly desert, part of which is the Sahara. About half the country is covered by sand dunes. Much of the population lives along the Sénégal River, which forms the border with Senegal.

Total area: 397,955 sq mi (1,030,700 sq km)

Coastline: 468 miles (754 km)

Land use: Meadows and pastures cover 38% of the country, 4% is wooded, and 1% is arable or under cultivation.

Climate: Hot and arid, with some coastal rains from July to September; widely ranging inland diurnal temperatures

Population: 2,598,000

Urban population: 54%

Rate of natural increase: 2.72%

Age structure: 45% under 15; 3% over 65

Birth rate: 40.5/1000

Death rate: 13.3/1000

Infant mortality rate: 92/1000

Fertility rate: 5.5

Life expectancy at birth: 52 years (male); 55 years (female)

Religion: Muslim

Language: Hasaniya Arabic, Wolof, Pular, Soninke

Ethnic Divisions: Maur, Fulani, Wolof, others

Literacy Rate: 38%

Government: Republic, with a president and a bicameral legislature. The president is directly elected to a six-year term. The 56 members of the Senate are elected by municipal leaders for six-year terms; the 79 members of the National Assembly are directly elected for five-year terms. There are 13 administrative provinces.

Armed services: 15,650 troops (1996) in the army, navy, and air force; two-year conscription

Suffrage: Universal; 18 years old

Economy: Foreign debt, rapid population growth, and recurring drought are obstacles in Mauritania's efforts to develop and diversify its economic base, which relies on agriculture and livestock. The government has launched programs to stabilize inflation rates, restructure the banking sector, and better manage fish resources, which is a major export item. However, because of the larger conditions working against economic growth, changes are slow in coming.

Unit of currency: Ouguiya; 5 khoums = 1 ouguiya (UM)

GDP per capita: $1,750

Inflation rate–CPI: 4.7% (1996)

Workforce: 1,071,000 (1996)

Unemployment rate: 23% (1995 est.)

Exports: Goods worth $494 million (f.o.b., 1996) are sent to Japan, Italy,

Belgium, France, Germany, and other trading partners; exports include iron ore, gold, fish, and fish products.

Imports: Goods worth $457 million (c.i.f., 1996) are received from Algeria, the U.S., France, and other trading partners; imports include food, consumer goods, and petroleum products.

Agriculture: About 48% (1996) of the workforce engages in agriculture and fishing. Dates, millet, sorghum, root crops, and livestock are raised for domestic use; fish, which earns 57% (1996) of the total value of exports, is very important. The country imports food; a government objective is to be self-sufficient by 2000.

Energy: There are plans to develop hydropower sources; imported fuels are currently used for energy generation.

Natural Resources: Minerals, including iron, gypsum, copper, gold, phosphate; fish

Environmental Issues: Deforestation, soil erosion, overgrazing, limited freshwater

Transportation: There are 416 miles (700 km) of railroads and 4,760 miles (7,660 km) of roads, of which 540 miles (870 km) are paved. Main seaports and international airports are at Nouakchott and Nouadhibou. Ferries ply the Sénégal River.

Communications: A daily newspaper is published in the capital, as are three weeklies. There are 340,000 radios and 57,000 televisions (1995) in operation. Phone service, with 8,000 phone lines (1994), is poor.

Tourism: National parks and game reserves draw tourists to Mauritania; visitors spent $15 million (U.S) in the country in 1993.

Embassy in U.S.: (202) 232-5700

Public Holidays: End of Ramadan (date varies, in February); Feast of the Sacrifice (date varies, in April); Islamic New Year (date varies, in April

or May); Labor Day (May 1); African Liberation Day (May 25); Birth of the Prophet (date varies, in July); National Day: independence from France, 1960 (November 28); Ascension of the Prophet (date varies, in November and December)

Mauritius

Country Name: Mauritius

Official Name: Republic of Mauritius

Nationality: Mauritian(s) (noun); Mauritian (adjective)

Capital: Port Louis, pop. 145,800

Major cities: Beau Bassin, Vacoas-Phoenix, Curepipe

External Territories: None

Location: Mauritius, in the Indian Ocean east of Madagascar, is composed of the islands of Mauritius, Caragados Carajos, Agalega, and Rodrigues.

Physical Geography: Coral reefs circle Mauritius; beaches edge the coastal plain, and an inland plateau is surrounded by mountains.

Total area: 788 sq mi (2,040 sq km)

Coastline: 110 mi (177 km)

Land use: The country's land is 52% arable or under cultivation and 3% is meadows and pastures. Woodlands comprise 22% of the land.

Climate: Humid subtropical, with most rainfall from November to May

Population: 1,172,000

Urban population: 43%

Rate of natural increase: 1.03%

Age structure: 26% under 15; 6% over 65

Birth rate: 17.1/1000

MAURITIUS   THE DODO BIRD'S ANCESTRAL HOME

A mountainous island about two-thirds the size of Rhode Island, Mauritius was a British, and earlier a French, colony of sugarcane plantations until 1968. Although English is the official language, most people speak a French patois. This island was once the home of the now-extinct dodo bird, which was hunted to extinction within 50 years of the arrival of the first Dutch settlers in 1658.

Death rate: 6.8/1000

Infant mortality rate: 19.7/1000

Fertility rate: 2.0

Life expectancy at birth: 66 years (male); 74 years (female)

Religion: Hindu, Roman Catholic, Muslim, Protestant

Language: English, Creole, French, Hindi, Urdu, Hakka, Bojpoori

Ethnic Divisions: Indo-Mauritian, Creole

Literacy Rate: 83%

Government: Republic, with a president and a unicameral legislature, the National Assembly. The president is elected by a majority vote of the legislature to a five-year term. The National Assembly has 62 members who are directly elected and 4 who are appointed to office. There are nine administrative districts and three dependencies.

Armed services: None; 1,300-member police force

Suffrage: Universal; 18 years old

Economy: Over the past few decades, Mauritius has maintained a steady rate of economic growth with a mixture of agriculture, manufacturing, and tourism. The government continues to encourage industrial and agricultural diversification, promote foreign investment, and control inflation rates.

Unit of currency: Mauritian rupee; 100 cents = 1 Mauritian rupee (MauR)

GDP per capita: $10,300

Inflation rate–CPI: 6.5% (1996)

Workforce: 514,600 (1995 est.)

Unemployment rate: 1.8% (1995)

Exports: Goods worth $1.6 billion (f.o.b., 1996 est.) are sent to the U.K., France, the U.S., Germany, Italy, and other trading partners; exports include textiles, sugar, and clothing.

Imports: Goods worth $2.2 billion (c.i.f., 1996 est.) are received from the European Union, the U.S., South Africa, India, and other trading partners; imports include manufactured goods, capital equipment, food, oil, and chemicals.

Agriculture: 13% (1995) of the workforce engages in agriculture and fishing. Sugarcane and tea are cultivated for export; potatoes, corn, bananas, pulses, and cattle are produced for domestic use. Sugar and molasses earn 24.1% (1995) of the total value of the country's exports.

Energy: Hydropower and imported oil are used for electrical generation; a sugarcane by-product, bagasse, is also used for energy.

Natural Resources: Arable land, fish

Environmental Issues: Water pollution

Transportation: There are 1,160 miles (1,860 km) of roads, of which 1,080 miles (1,730 km) are paved; there are no railroads. Port Louis, the main port, operates as a free port. An international airport is at Plaisance, near Mahébourg.

Communications: Eight daily newspapers are published in the capital. There are 410,000 radios and 248,000 televisions (1995) in

service. Phone service, with 129,000 phone lines in operation (1994), is relatively good.

Tourism: Tourism is an important sector of the economy; visitors come to Mauritius for its beaches, cultural blends, and scenic interiors. In 1993, tourists spent an estimated $301 million (U.S.); 487,000 visitors came to the country in 1996.

U.S. Tourist Office: (516) 944-3763

Embassy in U.S.: (202) 244-1491

Public Holidays: Chinese New Year (date varies, in January or February); End of Ramadan (date varies, in February); National Day: independent, 1968, from the U.K. (March 12); Good Friday (date varies, in March or April); Labor Day (May 1); All Saints' Day (November 1); Christmas (December 25)

Mexico

Country Name: Mexico

Official Name: United Mexican States

Nationality: Mexican(s) (noun); Mexican (adjective)

Capital: Mexico City, pop. 8,575,000 [18,202,300]

Major cities: Guadalajara, Netzahualcóyotl, Puebla, Monterrey

External Territories: None

Location: Mexico, in Middle America, is bordered on the north by the United States and on the south by Belize and Guatemala. The Gulf of Mexico is to the east and the Pacific Ocean to the west.

Physical Geography: In the north and central parts of the country, a large plateau is bordered on the east by the Sierra Madre Oriental and on the west by the Sierra Madre Occidental, mountain chains that parallel the coasts. An upland region extends south of the plateau to the Yucatán Peninsula, which is a lowland plateau in the far south; a coastal plain, along the Gulf of Mexico shore, reaches from Mexico's northern border with Texas to the Yucatán Peninsula.

Total area: 754,120 sq mi (1,953,162 sq km)

Coastline: 5,794 mi (9,330 km)

Land use: Meadows and pastures cover 39% of the land, 26% is forested, and 13% is arable or under cultivation.

Climate: Generally tropical or subtropical, with some arid regions; rainfall and temperature vary from north to south and with elevation; rains generally fall from May to November

Population: 99,734,000

Urban population: 74%

Rate of natural increase: 2.8%

Age structure: 35% under 15; 5% over 65

Birth rate: 28.6/1000

Death rate: 5/1000

Infant mortality rate: 31.5/1000

Fertility rate: 3.0

Life expectancy at birth: 69 years (male); 75 years (female)

Religion: Roman Catholic, Protestant

Language: Spanish, indigenous languages

Ethnic Divisions: Mestizo, American Indian, white

Literacy Rate: 90%

Government: Federal republic, with a president and a bicameral legislature, the Congreso de la Unión, or National Congress. The president is popularly elected to a six-year term. The 128 members of the Senate serve six year terms and the 500 members of the Chamber of Deputies serve three year terms. There are 31 administrative states and one federal district.

Armed services: 175,000 troops (1997) in the army, navy, and air force; compulsory service by one-year conscripts selected by lottery, serving four hours each week

Suffrage: Universal and compulsory; 18 years old

Economy: High levels of international debt, high inflation rates, political instability, and a large and growing population have slowed Mexico's economic growth, which is dependent on petroleum. The peso was devalued in 1994 to reduce Mexico's foreign debt. This led to unemployment, high domestic interest rates, and strict government spending; however, balance is beginning to return to the economy.

Unit of currency: New Mexican nuevo peso; 100 centavos = 1 New Mexican peso (Mex$)

GDP per capita: $7,700

Inflation rate–CPI: 15.7% (1997 est.)

Workforce: 36,600,000 (1996)

Unemployment rate: 3.7% (1997 est.) urban, plus considerable underemployment

Exports: Goods worth $110.4 billion (f.o.b., 1997 est.) are sent to the U.S., Japan, Canada, and other trading partners; exports include crude oil and oil products, coffee, silver, machinery, and cotton.

Imports: Goods worth $109.8 billion (f.o.b., 1997 est.) are received from the U.S., Japan, and other trading partners; imports include machinery, steel mill products, agricultural machinery, electrical equipment, and car parts for assembly.

Agriculture: 21.8% (1996) of the labor force engages in agriculture and fishing. Domestic crops include corn, wheat, soybeans, rice, and beans; coffee, cotton, sugarcane, fruit, and tomatoes are raised for export.

Energy: Domestic resources of mineral fuels, and hydropower are used for most energy generation; some nuclear power is also generated.

Natural Resources: Minerals, including silver, copper, gold, lead, zinc; petroleum, natural gas; timber

Environmental Issues: Limited freshwater, water and air pollution, deforestation, desertification, widespread erosion

Transportation: There are 12,770 miles (20,570 km) of railroads and 155,250 miles (250,000 km) roads, of which nearly 40% are paved. Major seaports include Gulf of Mexico ports Tampico and Veracruz; Pacific ports include Acapulco, Manzanillo, Salina Cruz, and Guyamas. International airports are located at many cities, including Mexico City and Toluca.

Communications: 309 daily newspapers (1994) are published in the capital and elsewhere. There are 22.5 million radios and 13.1 million televisions in operation and 11.9 million telephones (1992). Phone service is adequate for business and

MEXICO TEOTIHUACAN: ANCIENT CITY, MODERN PLAN

Mexico City, one of the world's largest and fastest growing urban areas, sits near the site of the New World's first metropolis, Teotihuacan. The oldest city in Mesoamerica, it dates to 200 B.C.; by A.D. 400, 125,000 people lived there in 2,000 apartment compounds ranging in size from 7,000 to 35,000 square feet. The city was laid out on a grid design and featured distinct neighborhoods for various crafts specialists and foreign residents.

government, but distribution falls short of demand.

Tourism: Tourists come to Mexico for the beaches, Aztec and Maya archaeological sites, and mountain scenery. In 1996, 8.98 million visitors spent $4.65 billion (U.S.).

U.S. Tourist Office: (800) 446-3942

Embassy in U.S.: (202) 728-1600

Public Holidays: New Year's Day (January 1); Constitution Day, 1917 (February 5); Benito Juárez's birthday (March 21); Easter (date varies, in March or April); Labor Day (May 1); Anniversary of the Battle of Puebla*, 1862 (May 5); Independence Day: from Spain, 1810 (September 16); Discovery of America Day (October 12); All Saints' Day (November 1); All Souls' Day* (November 2); Anniversary of the Revolution (November 20); Day of Our Lady of Guadalupe* (December 12); Christmas (December 25)
*Widely Celebrated; unofficial

Micronesia

Country Name: Micronesia
Official Name: Federated States of Micronesia
Nationality: Micronesian(s) (noun); Micronesian, Kosrae(s), Pohnpeian(s), Trukese, Yapese (adjective)
Capital: Palikir, pop. N.A.
Major cities: N.A.
External Territories: None
Location: The Federated States of Micronesia, in the Pacific Ocean, is a group of some 600 islands and atolls spanning more than 1,800 miles (2,900 km).

Physical Geography: Micronesia consists of islands, some with elevations as high as 2,000 feet (600 m), and low-lying coral atolls. The larger islands are Yap, Kosrae, Pohnpei, and Chuuk.
Total area: 271 sq mi (702 sq km)
Coastline: 3,796 mi (6,112 km)
Land use: N.A.
Climate: Tropical, with occasional typhoons; rainfall generally decreasing from east to west

Population: 117,000
Urban population: 27%
Rate of natural increase: 2.6%
Age structure: 44% under 15; 4% over 65
Birth rate: 33/1000
Death rate: 8/1000
Infant mortality rate: 46/1000
Fertility rate: 4.7
Life expectancy at birth: 61 years (male); 65 years (female)

Religion: Roman Catholic, Protestant

Language: English, Trukese, Pohnpeian, Yapese, Kosrean

Ethnic Divisions: Micronesian, Polynesian

Literacy Rate: 89%

Government: Constitutional government in free association with the U.S., with a president and unicameral legislature, the Congress. The president is elected from among the Congress members; the 14 senators in Congress are elected to either two- or four-year terms. There are four administrative states.
Armed services: Military defense is provided by the United States.
Suffrage: Universal; 18 years old

Economy: Although the country is isolated and relies heavily on U.S. assistance, the government is working to develop and diversify the economy to produce a wider variety of agricultural commodities, expand its potential as a tourist destination, develop its infrastructure, and attract foreign investment.

Unit of currency: U.S. dollar; 100 cents = 1 U.S. dollar ($U.S.)

GDP per capita: $1760

Inflation rate–CPI: 4% (1996 est.)

Workforce: 30,640 (1990)

Unemployment rate: 27% (1989 est.)

Exports: Goods worth $73 million (f.o.b., 1996 est.) are sent to Japan, the U.S., and other trading partners; exports include seafood, garments, bananas, and black pepper.

Imports: Goods worth $168 million (c.i.f., 1996 est.) are received from the U.S., Japan, Australia, and other trading partners; imports include food, manufactured goods, machinery, and beverages.

Agriculture: Crops for export include black pepper, bananas, copra, and seafood; coconuts, cassava, and sweet potatoes are raised for domestic use. Subsistence agriculture is a major sector of the economy. Micronesia is a major point for transshipment of fish to Japan.

Energy: Most energy is generated using imported fuels.

Natural Resources: Forests, marine products, seabed minerals

Environmental Issues: N.A.

Transportation: The larger islands have some paved roads. Main ports include Colonia on Yap, the former capital; Kolonia on Pohnpei; and Lele off Kosrae. International airports are located on Pohnpei, Chuuk, Yap, and Kosrae.

Communications: There are no daily newspapers published in the country. There are 17,000 radios and 1,300 televisions (1993) in operation and 960 phone lines in service. The islands also use shortwave radios for communication.

Tourism: World War II battlefields and scuba diving opportunities draw visitors to the country, which is developing a solid tourist infrastructure; in 1990, 20,475 visitors came to the islands.

Embassy in U.S.: (202) 223-4383

Public Holidays: Constitution Day, 1980, and proclamation of Federated States of Micronesia, 1979 (May 10); United Nations Day (October 24); Independence Day: from UN Trusteeship, 1986 (November 3); Christmas (December 25)

Moldova

Country Name: Moldova
Official Name: Republic of Moldova
Nationality: Moldovan(s) (noun); Moldovan (adjective)
Capital: Chişinău, pop. 655,900
Major cities: Tiráspol, Bălţi, Bender
External Territories: None
Location: Moldova, in southeastern Europe, is bordered on the north, south, and east by Ukraine and on the west by Romania.
Total area: 13,217 sq mi (33,999 sq km)
Coastline: None
Physical Geography: The country is mainly rolling hills. Rivers include the Nistru, Bac, and Prut, which forms the country's western border with Romania.
Land use: At least 67% of the land is arable or under cultivation and 13% is meadows and pasture, 13% forests or woodlands.
Climate: Continental, with mild winters
Population: 4,284,000
Urban population: 46%
Rate of natural increase: 0.1%
Age structure: 26% under 15; 9% over 65
Birth rate: 13/1000
Death rate: 12/1000

Infant mortality rate: 19.8/1000
Fertility rate: 1.7
Life expectancy at birth: 63 years (male); 70 (female)
Religion: Eastern Orthodox
Language: Moldovan, Russian
Ethnic Divisions: Moldovan, Romanian, Ukrainian, Russian
Literacy Rate: 96%
Government: Republic, with a president and a unicameral legislature, the Parliament. The president and the 104 members of the legislature are directly elected to four-year terms. There are 38 administrative districts, four municipalities, and one autonomous unit.
Armed services: 11,030 troops (1997) in the army and air force; 18-month compulsory service
Suffrage: Universal; 18 years old
Economy: Internal unrest, drought, and widespread poverty have prevented needed economic growth in Moldova since the breakup of the Soviet Union in 1991. The initial shift to a market economy and the loss of established trading partners in the Soviet bloc have hindered expansion, but the government is steadily working to continue industrial privatization, control inflation, and promote foreign investment.
Unit of currency: Moldovan leu (singular), lei (plural); 100 bani (ban, singular) = 1 Moldovan leu
GDP per capita: $2,400
Inflation rate–CPI: 11.2% (1997 est.)
Workforce: 2.42 million (1995)
Unemployment rate: 1.4% (1997)
Exports: Goods worth $816 million (1997) are sent to Russia, Kazakhstan, Ukraine, Romania, Germany, and other trading partners; exports include foodstuffs, wine, tobacco, textiles and footwear, and machinery.
Imports: Goods worth $1.16 billion (1997) are received from Russia, Ukraine, Uzbekistan, Romania, Germany, and other trading partners; imports include oil, gas, coal, steel,

machinery, foodstuffs, cars, and consumer durables.
Agriculture: 46.1% (1996) of the workforce engages in agriculture and fishing. Vegetables, fruits, wine, grain, and sugar beets are raised for domestic use and for export.
Energy: Imported fuels supply an estimated 40% (1995) of the country's energy.
Natural Resources: Lignite, phosphorites, gypsum
Environmental Issues: Soil erosion, soil and groundwater contamination
Transportation: There are 830 miles (1,340 km) of railways and 7,640 miles (12,300 km) of roads, the majority of which are paved. Rivers are also important transport routes, and Bender, is an important river port. An international airport is located at Chişinău.
Communications: Four daily newspapers (1995) are published in the country. There are 3 million radios and 1.2 million televisions (1995); 600,000 telephones (1996 est.) provide basic service.
Tourism: In 1994, 21,000 visitors to Moldova spent $2 million (U.S.).
Embassy in U.S.: (202) 667-1130
Public Holidays: Christmas (January 7–8); International Women's Day (March 8); Good Friday (date varies, in March or April); Easter Monday (date varies, in March or April); Victory and Commemoration Day (May 9); Independence Day: from the Soviet Union, 1991 (August 27); National Language Day (August 31)

Monaco

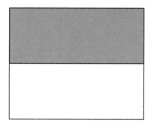

Country Name: Monaco
Official Name: Principality of Monaco
Nationality: Monacan(s) or Monégasque(s) (noun); Monacan or Monégasque (adjective)
Capital: Monaco
Major cities: Monaco is the only municipality in the country.
External Territories: None
Location: Monaco, in western Europe, is located on the coast of the Mediterranean Sea; it shares all land boundaries with France.
Physical Geography: The country is hilly and rocky.
Total area: 0.6 sq mi (1.9 sq km)
Coastline: 2.5 mi (4 km)
Land use: 100% urban
Climate: Mediterranean, with hot, dry summers and mild, wet winters
Population: 33,000
Urban population: 100%
Rate of natural increase: 0.3%
Age structure: 12% under 14; 22% over 65
Birth rate: 20/1000
Death rate: 17/1000
Infant mortality rate: N.A.
Fertility rate: N.A.
Life expectancy at birth: 78 years (average)
Religion: Roman Catholic
Language: French, English, Italian
Ethnic Divisions: French, Monégasque, Italian
Literacy Rate: N.A.

Government: Constitutional monarchy, Prince Rainier III, and a unicameral legislature, the National Council. The throne is hereditary; the 18 members of the legislature are elected to five-year terms. There are four administrative quarters.
Armed services: None
Suffrage: Universal; 21 years old
Economy: Monaco has a strong economy based on tourist revenue and light manufacturing. Low taxes encourage businesses to establish their offices in the country, and banking services have also expanded. Migrant workers make up the gap left by a labor shortage among Monaco's citizens.
Unit of currency: French franc; 100 centimes = 1 French franc
GDP per capita: $25,000
Inflation rate–CPI: N.A.
Unemployment rate: 3.1% (1994)
Workforce: 30,540 (1994)
Exports: N.A. Statistics are officially included with export figures for France.
Imports: N.A. Statistics are officially included with import figures for France; most imports are from France.
Agriculture: There is no agricultural production in this urban country.
Energy: N.A.
Natural Resources: N.A.
Environmental Issues: N.A.
Transportation: A short railway connects Monaco with France, and there are 30 miles (50 km) of roads. Monaco serves as a port; the nearest international airport is at Nice, France.
Communications: One daily paper is published in the country, and newspapers from France are distributed widely. There are 33,000 radios and 24,000 televisions (1994) in operation; phone service, with 53,180 telephones (1994 est.), is good.
Tourism: A famous vacation destination, Monaco is noted for its casi-

no, beaches, and sportscar races; in 1992, about 4 million people came to the country (including those on day trips) and spent $1.3 billion (U.S.).
U.S. Tourist Office: (212) 759-5227
Public Holidays: Feast of St. Dévote (January 27); Easter Monday (date varies, in March or April); Ascension Day (date varies, in May); Whit Monday (date varies, in May); Labor Day (May 1); Assumption (August 15); All Saints' Day (November 1); National Day (November 19); Immaculate Conception (December 8); Christmas (December 25–26)

Mongolia

Country Name: Mongolia
Official Name: Mongolia
Nationality: Mongolian(s) (noun); Mongolian (adjective)
Capital: Ulaanbaatar, pop. 627,000
Major cities: Darhan, Choybalsan, Erdenet
External Territories: None
Location: Mongolia, a landlocked country in north-central Asia, is bordered on the north by Russia and on the east, south, and west by China.
Physical Geography: Almost all the country is covered by highlands. Mountain ranges separated by basins are found in the north and west; there are deserts and plateaus in the east and the south. Part of the desert region of the Gobi is in the central and southeast.
Total area: 604,250 sq mi (1,565,000 sq km)
Coastline: None
Land use: Almost 80% of the country is meadows and pastures, 9% is

wooded, and 1% is arable or under cultivation.

Climate: Dry continental, with cold winters and cool summers

Population: 2,438,000

Urban population: 52%

Rate of natural increase: 1.3%

Age structure: 35% under 15; 4% over 65

Birth rate: 20/1000

Death rate: 6/1000

Infant mortality rate: 34/1000

Fertility rate: 2.7

Life expectancy at birth: 60 years (male); 66 years (female)

Religion: Tibetan Buddhist, Muslim

Language: Khalkha Mongo, Turkic, Russian, Chinese

Ethnic Divisions: Mongol, Kazakh, Chinese, Russian

Literacy Rate: 83%

Government: Republic, with a president and a unicameral legislature, The Great Hural. The president and the 76 members of the legislature are elected by universal vote to four-year terms. There are 21 administrative provinces and one municipality.

Armed services: 28,110 troops (1998 est.); one-year service

Suffrage: Universal; 18 years old

Economy: Foreign aid and mineral resources currently supply much needed money while Mongolia makes the transition from a planned to a market economy. The breakup of the Soviet Union in 1990 and 1991 caused temporary food rationing in the cities and meant the loss of a key trading partner. Financial conditions are improving. Some economic growth was noted in 1993, and inflation rates have declined. The government is working to privatize industry, improve environmental conditions, and soften the impact of the transition to a market economy.

Unit of currency: Tughrik; 100 möngö = 1 tögrög (tughrik) (Tug)

GDP per capita: $2,200

Inflation rate–CPI: 66% (1994); 53.2% (1996)

Workforce: 868,200 (1995 est.)

Unemployment rate: 6% (1995 est.)

Exports: Goods worth $418 million (f.o.b., 1997 est.) are sent to Russia, China, Japan, Kazakhstan, and other trading partners; exports include copper, livestock, animal products, cashmere, and wool.

Imports: Goods worth $443.4 million (f.o.b., 1997 est.) are received from Russia, Austria, China, and other trading partners; imports include machinery, fuels, food, consumer goods, building materials, sugar, and tea.

Agriculture: Nearly 45% (1995) of the labor force engages in agriculture and forestry. Livestock, including sheep, goats, horses, cattle, and camels, is the most important commodity and are raised by private individuals for domestic needs and for export. Livestock products include cashmere, wool, and hides. Cereals, potatoes, and vegetables are raised on state farms.

Energy: Coal is used for most electrical generation, and firewood and animal dung is gathered for home use in rural areas.

Natural Resources: Minerals, including oil, coal, copper, molybdenum, tungsten, phosphates, tin, nickel, zinc, gold

Environmental Issues: Limited freshwater, air pollution, deforestation, soil erosion, desertification

Transportation: About 2,000 miles (3,220 km) of railroads and 28,860 miles (46,470 km) of roads connect the country; about 2% of the roads are paved. The Selenge River in the north is navigable for nearly 250 miles (397 km), and Hövsgöl Nuur near the Russian border is also navigable. An international airport is located at Ulaanbaatar.

Communications: At least one daily newspaper and nearly 60 weekly and biweekly papers are published. There are 222,000 radios, 120,000 televisions, and 89,000 telephones (1995) in use.

Tourism: Tourists are drawn to Mongolia by its scenery; the traditional festival of Naadam, with horse riding, wrestling, and archery; and the museums and sites in Ulaanbaatar. In 1997, there were 15,000 visitors in Mongolia.

Embassy in U.S.: (202) 333-7117

Public Holidays: Lunar New Year (date varies, in February); National Day (July 11–13); Republic Day (November 26)

Morocco

Country Name: Morocco

Official Name: Kingdom of Morocco

Nationality: Moroccan(s) (noun); Moroccan (adjective)

Capital: Rabat, pop. [1,220,000]

Major cities: Casablanca, Fez, Marrakech, Oujda

External Territories: Claims to Western Sahara are in dispute.

Location: Morocco, in northern Africa, is bordered on the east and southeast by Algeria; the Mediterranean Sea is to the north and the Atlantic Ocean to the west. The disputed territory of Western Sahara is in the southwest and is bordered by Mauritania.

Physical Geography: Coastal plains along the Mediterranean Sea and the Atlantic Ocean rise to meet ranges of the Atlas Mountains that trend northeast and southwest. Beyond the Atlas lies the Sahara.

MOROCCO A BERBER HERITAGE, PRESERVED THROUGH LANGUAGE

Influenced over the centuries by the many cultures and nationalities that have passed through its lands—it's on the northwestern tip of Africa only eight miles from Europe—Arab-ruled Morocco has managed to retain its ancient Berber culture. Today, more than one-third of the population speaks at least one of the three Berber languages, reflecting a heritage that dates back to the country's glory days as a Berber empire between the mid-11th and mid-14th centuries.

Total area: 275,117 sq mi (712,550 sq km)

Coastline: 1,140 mi (1,835 km)

Land use: About 47% of the land is meadows and pastures, 22% is arable or under cultivation, and 20% is forested.

Climate: Mediterranean in the north and central regions, with hot, dry summers and mild, wet winters; arid inland conditions, with greater extremes in temperature

Population: 28,248,000

Urban population: 54%

Rate of natural increase: 1.69%

Age structure: 34% under 15; 5% over 65

Birth rate: 23.2/1000

Death rate: 6.3/1000

Infant mortality rate: 37/1000

Fertility rate: 3.1

Life expectancy at birth: 67 years (male); 71 years (female)

Religion: Muslim

Language: Arabic, Berber dialects, French

Ethnic Divisions: Arab, Berber, Moor

Literacy Rate: 44%

Government: Constitutional monarchy, with a king—Hassan II, whose reign began in 1961—and a bicameral legislature, the Chamber of Representatives and the Chamber of Counselors. The throne is hereditary, and the 325 members of the Representatives are elected for five-year terms. The 270 counselors are indirectly elected for nine year terms. There are 37 administrative provinces.

Armed services: 196,300 troops (1997) in the army, navy, and air force; 18-month compulsory service

Suffrage: Universal; 21 years old

Economy: Tourism, phosphate reserves, agriculture, and a growing manufacturing sector are spurring economic growth in Morocco, although the demands of a growing population at times outstrip economic output. Programs to encourage foreign investment, control inflation, reduce taxes, and privatize industry have all helped reduce international debt. Remittances from workers abroad also help the economy.

Unit of currency: Moroccan dirham; 100 centimes or santimat = 1 Moroccan dirham

GDP per capita: $3.500

Inflation rate–CPI: 3% (1997 est.)

Workforce: 10,564,000 (1996 est.)

Unemployment rate: 16% (1997 est.)

Exports: Goods worth $6.9 billion (f.o.b., 1996) are sent to the E.U., Japan, and India, and other trading partners; exports include food and beverages, semiprocessed goods, and consumer goods.

Imports: Goods worth $9.78 billion (c.i.f., 1996) are received from the E.U., the U.S., Saudi Arabia, and other trading partners; imports include capital goods, semiprocessed goods, raw materials, oil, food and beverages, and consumer goods.

Agriculture: 40% (1996) of the working population engages in agriculture, fishing, and forestry. Livestock is raised and barley, wheat, sugar beets, citrus fruit, tomatoes, and potatoes are cultivated for domestic use; seafood and selling fishing licenses are significant to the country's wealth.

Energy: Imported oil, gas, and coal generate about 94% of the country's energy. Hydropower is supplemental.

Natural Resources: Minerals, including phosphates, iron, manganese, lead, zinc; fish

Environmental Issues: Desertification, land degradation, water pollution

Transportation: There are 1,180 miles (1,910 km) of railroads and 37,650 miles (60,630 km) of roads, of which half are paved. Atlantic coast seaports include Casablanca, Mohammedia, Safi, and Tangier. International airports are at Casablanca, Rabat, Marrakech, Tangier, Oujda, Agadir, Al Hoceima, and Ouarzazate.

Communications: Seven daily newspapers are published in Rabat and five in Casablanca. There are 6.0 million radios and 2.5 million televisions (1995) in operation. With 1.1 million phone lines (1995), telephone service is good.

Tourism: In 1994, nearly 2.3 million tourists added $1.2 billion (U.S.) to Morocco's economy; visitors come to see the markets, ancient cities, and to stay at beach resorts.

U.S. Tourist Office: (212) 557-2520

Embassy in U.S.: (202) 462-7979

Public Holidays: Beginning of Ramadan (date varies); End of Ramadan (date varies, in February); Festival of the Throne: anniversary of King Hassan II's accession, 1961 (March 3); Feast of the Sacrifice (date varies, in April); Islamic New Year (date varies, in April or May); Ashura (date varies, in April or May); Labor Day (May 1); Birth of the Prophet (date varies, in July); Annexation Anniversary, 1979 (August 14); Anniversary of the Green March (November 6); Independence Day (November 18)

Mozambique

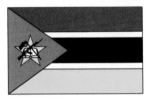

Country Name: Mozambique
Official Name: Republic of Mozambique
Nationality: Mozambican(s) (noun); Mozambican (adjective)
Capital: Maputo, pop. 931,600
Major cities: Beira, Nampula, Nacala
External Territories: None
Location: Mozambique, on the Indian Ocean's Mozambique Channel in southern Africa, is bordered on the north by Tanzania and on the west by South Africa, Swaziland, Zimbabwe, Zambia, and Malawi.
Physical Geography: There are lowlands in the south; the Mozambique Plateau in the north extends from the coastal lowlands to the mountains in the northwest. Rivers include the Shire and Zambezi.
Total area: 308,642 sq mi (799,380 sq km)
Coastline: 1,534 mi (2,470 km)
Land use: Almost 56% of the land is meadows and pastures, 18% is wooded, and 4% is arable or under cultivation.

Climate: Tropical, with rains from October to May; decreasing rainfall from north to south
Population: 19,124,000
Urban population: 28%
Rate of natural increase: 2.19%
Age structure: 46% under 15; 2% over 65
Birth rate: 40.7/1000
Death rate: 18.8/1000
Infant mortality rate: 133.9/1000
Fertility rate: 5.6
Life expectancy at birth: 43 years (male); 46 years (female)
Religion: Indigenous beliefs, Christian, Muslim
Language: Portuguese, indigenous dialects
Ethnic Divisions: Makua, Shangaan, Chokune, Sena
Literacy Rate: 40%
Government: Republic, with a president and a unicameral legislature, the Assembly of the Republic. The president and the 250 members of the legislature are directly elected to five-year terms. There are 11 administrative provinces.
Armed services: Troop numbers in flux since the end of civil war in 1992
Suffrage: Universal; 18 years old
Economy: Civil war from 1990 to 1992, the advent of new government in 1994, foreign debt, and a lack of skilled labor have left the citizens of Mozambique among the poorest in the world. The government has taken steps to curb inflation, encourage investment, and reduce debt, but foreign aid is essential, and austerity measures continue as the government strives to strengthen the economy.
Unit of currency: Metical (singular), meticais (plural); 100 centavos = 1 metical (Mt)
GDP per capita: $800
Inflation rate–CPI: 5.8% (1997)
Workforce: 9.328 million (1996 est.)

Unemployment rate: 118,000 (1996 est.)
Exports: Goods worth $226 million (f.o.b., 1996 est.) are sent to Spain, South Africa, the U.S., Portugal, and other trading partners; exports include shrimp, cashews, cotton, sugar, copra, and citrus.
Imports: Goods worth $802 million (c.i.f., 1996 est.) are received from South Africa, the U.K., France, Japan, and other trading partners; imports include food, clothing, farm equipment, and oil.
Agriculture: An estimated 81.0% (1996) of the labor pool engages in agriculture and fishing. Shrimp and prawns are the most important exports, earning 43.3% (1995) of the total value of Mozambique's exports; cotton, cashews, sugarcane, and copra are also significant exports. Cassava, tea, beef and other crops are raised for domestic use.
Energy: Hydropower, some of which is imported, is the main source of energy; petroleum is also imported.
Natural Resources: Coal, titanium, natural gas
Environmental Issues: Desertification, water pollution
Transportation: The country has 1,940 miles (3,130 km) of railroads and 18,880 miles (30,400 km) of roads, of which 3.530 miles (5,690 km) are paved. There are 2,330 miles (3,750 km) of navigable waterways, including the Zambezi, Shire, and Limpopo Rivers and Lake Malawi. Main seaports include Maputo, Beira Nacala, and Quelimane, and international airports are located at Maputo and Beira.
Communications: There are three daily newspapers. There are 660,000 radios and 60,000 televisions (1996) in operation; phone service, with an estimated 62,000 phones, is fair.
Tourism: Although tourist opportunities were limited during the civil war, attractions include beaches,

markets, game reserves, and national parks.

Embassy in U.S.: (202) 293-7146

Public Holidays: Heroes' Day: anniversary of assassination of Eduardo Mondlane, 1969 (February 3); End of Ramadan (date varies, in February); Feast of the Sacrifice (date varies, in April); Day of the Mozambican Woman (April 7); Worker's Day (May 1); Independence Day: from Portugal, 1975 (June 25); Victory Day (September 7); Armed Forces Day (September 25); National Family Day (December 25)

Myanmar

Country Name: Myanmar

Official Name: Union of Myanmar (Burma)

Nationality: Myanme (noun); Myanmar (adjective)

Capital: Yangon (Rangoon), pop. [3,873,000]

Major cities: Mandalay, Mawlamyine, Bago, Pathein

External Territories: None

Location: Myanmar, in southeastern Asia, is bordered on the east by China, Laos, and Thailand and on the northwest by Bangladesh and India. The Bay of Bengal and the Andaman Sea are on its west coast.

Physical Geography: Mountains in the north and west meet lowlands in the central part of the country; the broad valleys of the Ayeyarwady and Thanlwin Rivers run from north to south. A dissected plateau in the east rises from the central lowlands.

Total area: 261,218 sq mi (676,552 sq km)

MYANMAR A TREASURE IN TEAK

Myanmar's repressive military government—with one of the world's worst records on human rights—took over the country in 1989 and changed the nation's name from Burma. Nearly the size of Texas, Myanmar was a British colony until 1948, when it became independent. About three-quarters of the world's teak comes from its forests—one log can bring $20,000—and each year 30,000 acres of teak trees are replanted.

Coastline: 1,999 mi (1,930 km)

Land use: Almost 50% of the country is forested, 16% is arable or under cultivation, and 1% is meadows and pastures.

Climate: Tropical monsoon, with rains from June to September and December to April

Population: 48,081,000

Urban population: 26%

Rate of natural increase: 2.0%

Age structure: 33% under 15; 5% over 65

Birth rate: 29/1000

Death rate: 10/1000

Infant mortality rate: 82/1000

Fertility rate: 4.0

Life expectancy at birth: 60 years (male); 62 years (female)

Religion: Buddhist, Christian, Muslim

Language: Burmese

Ethnic Divisions: Burman, Shan, Karen

Literacy Rate: 83%

Government: Martial law was declared following a military coup in 1988; a new constitution is currently being drafted.

Armed services: 429,000 troops (1997) in the army, navy, and air force

Suffrage: Universal; 18 years old

Economy: Myanmar's centrally planned economy profits primarily from rice exports, timber production, and other commodities such as sugar, maize, peanuts, and cot-

ton. The government has begun to encourage private business and has courted foreign investment with some success. However, a large foreign debt must be paid, many financial transactions occur on the black market, and international criticism has arisen over the use of forced labor.

Unit of currency: Kyat; 100 pyas = 1 kyat (K)

GDP per capita: $1,190

Inflation rate–CPI: 22.8% (1985–1995 average)

Workforce: 17,582,000 (1995–1996 est.)

Unemployment rate: 3.1% (1993–1994 est.)

Exports: Goods worth $693 million (1996) are sent to Singapore, China, Thailand, India, and other trading partners; exports include pulses, beans, teak, and rice, and rubber.

Imports: Goods worth $1.4 billion (1997) are received from Japan, China, Thailand, Singapore, Malaysia, and other trading partners; imports include machinery, transportation equipment, construction materials, food products, and consumer goods.

Agriculture: Nearly 70% (1995–1996) of the labor force engages in agriculture, fishing, and forestry. Rice, the main export crop, is so important to the country that two rice ears are on the flag. Other important cash crops include sugarcane, maize, peanuts, pulses, rubber, and tobacco. Timber, especially teak, generates significant export revenue, and fishing is also important.

Energy: Natural gas and hydropower supplies most energy needs.

Natural Resources: Minerals, including oil, tin, antimony, zinc, copper, tungsten, lead, coal, precious stones; timber

Environmental Issues: Air and water pollution, deforestation

Transportation: There are 3,569 miles (5,750 km) of railroads and 17,510 miles (28,200 km) of roads in the country, of which about 16% are paved. Yangon is the main seaport, and the Ayeyarwady, Thanlwin, and Chindwin Rivers are navigable. An international airport is at Yangon, and more are planned.

Communications: Daily newspapers are currently published by the government. The statistics for radios is not available. 88,000 televisions (1992 est.) in operation. Phone service, with 122,000 lines (1993 est) in operation, is fair.

Tourism: Myanmar has shrines, palaces, wildlife parks, Buddhist temples, and scenic lakes and has recently begun promoting itself as a tourist destination. In 1993, 62,547 visitors spent an estimated $19 million (U.S.). Visitation increased in 1995 and 1996 to nearly 106,000.

Embassy in U.S.: (202) 332-9044

Public Holidays: Independence Day: from the U.K., 1948 (January 4); Union Day (February 12); Full Moon of Tabaung (date varies, in March); Peasants' Day (March 2); Dry Season Festival (March 10); Armed Forces Day (March 27); Water Festival (date varies, in April); Feast of the Sacrifice (date varies, in April); New Year (April 17); Full Moon of Kason (date varies, in May); Workers' Day (May 1); Martyrs' Day (July 19); Full Moon of Waso (date varies, in July or August); Full Moon of Thadingyut (date varies, in October); Devali (date varies, in October); Tazaungdaing Festival (date varies, in November); National Day (November 11); Christmas (December 25)

Namibia

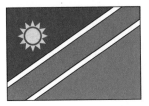

Country Name: Namibia

Official Name: Republic of Namibia

Nationality: Namibian(s) (noun); Namibian (adjective)

Capital: Windhoek, pop. 147,100

Major cities: Swakopmund, Rehoboth, Rundu, Keetmanshoop

External Territories: None

Location: Namibia, on the southwestern coast of Africa, is bordered on the north by Angola and Zambia, on the east by Botswana, on the south by South Africa, and on the west by the South Atlantic Ocean.

Physical Geography: The Namib Desert along the coast rises to an inland plateau; the Kalahari lies to the east of the plateau.

Total area: 318,261 sq mi (824,292 sq km)

Coastline: 976 mi (1,572 km)

Land use: At least 46% of the land is meadows and pastures, 22% is forested, and 1% is arable or under cultivation.

Climate: Continental; hot and dry, with large ranges in daily temperature

Population: 1,648,000

Urban population: 27%

Rate of natural increase: 1.667%

Age structure: 44% under 15; 4% over 65

Birth rate: 36.32/1000

Death rate: 19.65/1000

Infant mortality rate: 68.38/1000

Fertility rate: 5.1

Life expectancy at birth: 42 years (male); 42 years (female)

Religion: Christian, native religions

Language: English, Afrikaans, German, indigenous languages

Ethnic Divisions: Ovambo, Kavango, white, mixed

Literacy Rate: 38%

Government: Republic, with a president and a bicameral legislature. The president is directly elected to a five-year term. Of the National Assembly, 72 are directly elected to a maximum five-year term; up to 6 additional members may be appointed to office by the president. The National Council has 26 elected members serving six-year terms. There are 13 administrative regions.

Armed services: 5,800 troops (1997) in the army and coast guard

Suffrage: Universal; 18 years old

Economy: Mining, fishing, and farming are the main economic activities in Namibia; diamonds are the country's key export, and lead, zinc,

---

NAMIBIA A VERY OLD, VERY LONG, VERY DRY DESERT

The Namib Desert, which runs for 1,300 miles along Namibia's southwest coast, is one of the world's oldest (perhaps 55 million years) and driest (it receives an average of one-half inch of rain a year) deserts. It contains a group of usually dry riverbeds, which become linear oases when the rain comes. Water is trapped under the sand, which wildlife, including elephants, dig through to drink.

tin, silver, and tungsten also generate income. Since independence in 1990, the government has worked to diversify the economic base by expanding manufacturing activities and promoting tourism. However, there is a large gap between the rich and the poor, urban unemployment has increased, and Namibia must still import some food to meet domestic needs.

Unit of currency: Namibian dollar; 100 cents = 1 Namibian dollar (N$)

GDP per capita: $2,000

Inflation rate–CPI: 8% (1996 est.)

Workforce: 493,600 (1991 est.)

Unemployment rate: 30% to 40% (1997 est.)

Exports: Goods worth $1.45 billion (f.o.b., 1996 est.) are sent to Switzerland, South Africa, Germany, the U.K., and other trading partners; exports include diamonds, copper, gold, zinc, lead, uranium, cattle, and processed fish.

Imports: Goods worth $1.55 billion (f.o.b., 1996 est.) are received from South Africa, Germany, the U.S., Japan, and other trading partners; imports include food, petroleum products, machinery, and transportation equipment.

Agriculture: 44.3% (1996) of the workforce engages in agriculture and fishing. Seafood, beef, and karakul skins are all key commodities; millet, sorghum, and peanuts are grown for domestic use.

Energy: Imported oil and coal fuels most of the country's energy generation.

Natural Resources: Minerals, including diamonds, copper, uranium, gold, lead, tin, lithium, cadmium, zinc, salt, vanadium; fish

Environmental Issues: Limited freshwater, desertification

Transportation: There are about 1,480 miles (2,380 km) of railroads and 40,240 miles (64,800 km) of roads, of which 12% are paved. Main seaports are at Walvis Bay and

Lüderitz, and an international airport is at Windhoek.

Communications: Four daily newspapers are published. There are 215,000 radios and 50,000 televisions (1997) in operation. Phone service, with 85,000 phones in use (1996–1997), is fair to good in urban areas.

Tourism: Etosha National Park, known for its wildlife, is one of Namibia's prime attractions; visitors have a wide range of other parks and camps from which to choose. The Namibian government emphasizes its commitment to ecotourism by developing visitor amenities; in 1993, 255,000 tourists brought $95 million (U.S.) to the country.

Embassy in U.S.: (202) 986-0540

Public Holidays: Independence Day, 1990 (March 21); Easter (date varies, in March or April); Ascension Day (date varies, in May); Worker's Day (May 1); Casinga Day (May 4); Africa Day (May 25); Heroes' Day (August 26); Day of Goodwill (October 7); Human Rights Day (December 10); Christmas (December 25)

Nauru

Country Name: Nauru

Official Name: Republic of Nauru

Nationality: Nauruan(s) (noun); Nauruan (adjective)

Capital: Yaren, pop. 600

Major cities: None

External Territories: None

Location: Nauru, an island country in the South Pacific Ocean, lies south of the Equator, northeast of New Guinea and west of the Gilbert Islands in Kiribati.

Physical Geography: Nauru is a coral island with a central plateau and sandy beaches.

Total area: 8 sq mi (21 sq km)

Coastline: 19 mi (30 km)

Land use: N.A.

Climate: Tropical, with rains from November to February

Population: 11,000

Urban population: N.A.

Rate of natural increase: 1.4%

Age structure: N.A.

Birth rate: 19/1000

Death rate: 5/1000

Infant mortality rate: 25/1000

Fertility rate: 2.0

Life expectancy at birth: 64 years (male); 69 years (female)

Religion: Protestant, Roman Catholic

Language: Nauruan, English

Ethnic Divisions: Nauruan, other Pacific Islanders

Literacy Rate: N.A.

Government: Republic, with a president and a unicameral legislature, the Parliament. The 18 members of the legislature are directly elected for terms lasting up to three years; they in turn elect the president. There are 14 administrative districts.

Armed services: Military defense is provided by Australian armed forces.

Suffrage: Universal and compulsory; 20 years old

Economy: Phosphate mining has been the backbone of Nauru's economy since independence in 1968. However, the resource will soon be exhausted and the government is working to find other sources of income; phosphate trust fund investments will help the transition from mining. There are long-term plans to restore the mined areas.

Unit of currency: Australian dollar: 100 cents = 1 Australian dollar ($A)

GDP per capita: $10,000

Inflation rate–CPI: -3.6%

Workforce: N.A.

Unemployment rate: 0%

Exports: Goods worth $25.3 million (f.o.b., 1991) are sent to Australia, New Zealand, and other trading partners; phosphates are the main export of the country.

Imports: Goods worth $21.1 million (c.i.f., 1991) are received from Australia, New Zealand, the U.K., Japan, and other trading partners; imports include food, fuels, manufactured goods, building materials, and machinery.

Agriculture: Livestock is raised, and coconuts, bananas, and pineapples are cultivated for domestic use, but most food, including water, is imported.

Energy: Imported oil is the main source of energy.

Natural Resources: Phosphates

Environmental Issues: Limited freshwater, mining damage

Transportation: A short stretch of railroad is used for transporting phosphates. There are 20 miles (30 km) of paved roads. The island has an airport and a shipping facility with offshore moorings.

Communications: A weekly newspaper is published on the island. There is one radio station and one television station (1991). There are 2,000 phone lines (1989) in operation.

Tourism: Most of the island has been devoted to phosphate mining, but there are opportunities for sportfishing.

Embassy: None in U.S.

Public Holidays: Independence Day: from UN Trusteeship, 1968 (January 31); Easter (date varies, in March or April, four-day holiday); Constitution Day (May 17); Angam Day (October 26); Christmas (December 25–26)

Nepal

Country Name: Nepal

Official Name: Kingdom of Nepal

Nationality: Nepalese (singular and plural noun); Nepalese (adjective)

Capital: Kathmandu, pop. 421,100

Major cities: None

External Territories: None

Location: Nepal, a landlocked country in southern Asia, is bordered on the north by China and on the east, south, and west by India.

Physical Geography: The Terai, southern plains along the Indian border, extends north to foothills and low mountains in the central part of the country; the Himalayas—the world's highest peak, Mount Everest, at 29,028 feet (8,848 m)–run along the border with China.

Total area: 54,362 sq mi (140,797 sq km)

Coastline: None

Land use: Less than 42% of the land is forested, 17% is arable or under cultivation, and 15% is meadows and pastures.

Climate: Varies with elevation; tropical monsoon in the lowlands, with a rainy season from July to November; cool summers and severe winters at higher elevations

Population: 24,303,000

Urban population: 9%

Rate of natural increase: 2.4%

Age structure: 41% under 15; 3% over 65

Birth rate: 36/1000

Death rate: 10/1000

Infant mortality rate: 79/1000

Fertility rate: 4.6

Life expectancy at birth: 58 years (male); 57 years (female)

Religion: Hindu, Buddhist, Muslim

Language: Nepali, 20 others

Ethnic Divisions: Newars, Indians, Tibetans, Gurungs, Magars, Tamangs, Bhotias, Rais, Limbus, Sherpas

Literacy Rate: 28%

Government: Constitutional monarchy—King Birendra Bir Bikram Shah Dev came to the throne in 1972—with a bicameral legislature, the Parliament. The 205 members of the House of Representatives are elected to five-year terms. Of the 60 members of the National Council, 50 are appointed by the House of Representatives and 10 are appointed by the monarch, all for six-year terms. There are 14 administrative zones.

Armed services: 46,000 troops (1997) in the army and air force; voluntary service

---

NEPAL THE WORLD'S ONLY HINDU KING

Nepal, about the size of Arkansas, is one of the world's most remote and beautiful places and has one of the least developed economies. It is ruled by the world's only Hindu monarch, whom many Nepalese believe is the reincarnation of the Hindu god Vishnu. Many think that Buddha was born here.

Suffrage: Universal; 18 years old

Economy: Although Nepal's international debt is growing and foreign aid is essential for survival, Nepalese officials are intent on bolstering the country's economy with greater agricultural output, currency reforms, and foreign investment. Much of the workforce engages in subsistence farming, and Nepal's remote location and rugged terrain hinders greater economic growth.

Unit of currency: Nepalese rupee; 100 paisa (pice, singular) = 1 Nepalese rupee (NR)

GDP per capita: $1,370

Inflation rate–CPI: 7.5% (1997 est.)

Workforce: 10 million (1996 est.)

Unemployment rate: N.A.

Exports: Goods worth $419 million (f.o.b., 1997 est.) are sent to India, the U.S., Germany, and other trading partners; exports include carpets, clothing, leather goods, jute, and grain.

Imports: Goods worth $1.6 billion (c.i.f., 1997 est.) are received from India, Singapore, Japan, Germany, and other trading partners; imports include petroleum products, fertilizer, and machinery.

Agriculture: 81% of the labor force engages in agriculture and forestry. Rice, maize, barley, millet, wheat, sugarcane, tobacco, and potatoes are some of the main crops; livestock include cattle, buffalo, sheep, and goats.

Energy: Imported oil and hydropower are used for some energy generation, but wood is still an important source of household fuel.

Natural Resources: Timber, hydroelectric potential

Environmental Issues: Deforestation, soil erosion, water pollution

Transportation: There are 63 miles (101 km) of railroads in the southern part of the country and 4,780 miles (7,700 km) of roads, of which 1,990 miles (3,200 km) are paved. An international airport is at Kathmandu.

Communications: Several daily newspapers are published in the capital. There are 690,000 radios and 45,000 televisions (1992) in operation and 115,990 telephones (1996) in service.

Tourism: Tourism is a mainstay of the Nepalese economy; trekkers in the Himalaya, pilgrims visiting Hindu and Buddhist temples and shrines, and 393,600 visitors to Kathmandu and the many national parks set aside for wildlife brought $157 million (U.S.) to the country in 1993.

Embassy in U.S.: (202) 667-4550

Public Holidays: Martyrs' Day (date varies, in January); National Unity Day (January 11); Shivaratri (date varies, in February); National Democracy Day (date varies, in February); Holi (date varies, in March); Nepalese Women's Day (date varies, in March); Birthday of Lord Ram (date varies, in March or April); New Year's Day (date varies, in April); Birthday of Lord Buddha (date varies, in May); Festival of Rain God (date varies, in September); Durga Puja Festival (dates vary, in September and October); Queen Aishworya's birthday (date varies, in November); Constitution Day (November 9); King Birendra's birthday (December 29)

Netherlands

Country Name: The Netherlands

Official Name: Kingdom of the Netherlands

Nationality: Dutch (collective noun); Dutch (adjective)

Capital: Amsterdam, pop. 716,000 [1,102,300]

Major cities: Rotterdam, The Hague, Utrecht, Eindhoven

External Territories: Aruba, an island off the northern coast of Venezuela in the Caribbean Sea (75 sq mi, 193 sq km; pop. 69,000); Netherlands Antilles, five West Indies islands in the Caribbean Sea: Curaçao, Bonaire, Saba, St. Eustatius, and St. Maarten (shared with France as St-Martin) (309 sq mi, 800 sq km; pop. 199,000)

Location: The Netherlands, in western Europe, is bordered on the east by Germany, on the south by Belgium, and on the west by the North Sea.

Physical Geography: Plains and hills cover the southern and eastern parts of the country. In the north, an extensive river delta and coastal system lies below sea level, protected from flooding by seawalls, sand dunes, and mechanical pumps. Rivers include the Rhine, Meuse, and Schelde.

Total area: 16,023 sq mi (41,499 sq km)

Coastline: 280 mi (451 km)

Land use: Meadows and pastures cover 31% of the land, 28% is arable or under cultivation, and 10% is forested.

Climate: Temperate maritime, with cool summers, mild winters, and moderate rainfall

Population: 15,799,000

Urban population: 61%

Rate of natural increase: 0.4%

Age structure: 18% under 15; 13% over 65

Birth rate: 12/1000

Death rate: 9/1000

Infant mortality rate: 5.1/1000

Fertility rate: 1.5

Life expectancy at birth: 75 years (male); 80 years (female)

Religion: Roman Catholic, Protestant

Language: Dutch

Ethnic Divisions: Dutch

NETHERLANDS AMSTERDAM: A CITY BORN FOR BUSINESS

The city of Amsterdam, founded in the 13th century, began simply as a dam across the Amstel River, hence its name. Its importance as a port city can be traced back to 1602, when the Dutch East India Company was founded to bring spices, silk, porcelain, and other riches from the Far East. Amsterdam's famous canals were built to allow barges of these exotic goods to make direct deliveries to merchants and warehouses.

Literacy Rate: 99%

Government: Constitutional monarchy, with a hereditary monarch—Queen Beatrix Wilhelmina Armgard, since 1980—and a bicameral legislature, the States-General, or Staten General. The 75 members of the First Chamber are indirectly elected by provincial councils to four-year terms, and the 150 members of the Second Chamber are directly elected to four-year terms. There are 12 administrative provinces.

Armed services: 57,180 troops (1997) in the army, navy, and air force; no conscription since August 1996

Suffrage: Universal; 18 years old

Economy: Despite a large deficit and significant unemployment, the Netherlands possesses a healthy economy based on services, trade, and diversified agricultural and manufacturing sectors. The government continues to look for ways to reduce the deficit and reduce unemployment.

Unit of currency: Netherlands guilder/gulden/florin; 100 cents = 1 Netherlands gulden/guilder/florin

GDP per capita: $22,000

Inflation rate–CPI: 2% (1997)

Workforce: 6.6 million (1997)

Unemployment rate: 6.9% (1997)

Exports: Goods worth $203.1 billion (f.o.b., 1997 est.) are sent to Germany, Belgium, Luxembourg, the U.K., and other trading partners; exports include manufactures and machinery, chemicals, processed food, and tobacco and agricultural products.

Imports: Goods worth $1.79 trillion (c.i.f., 1997 est.) are received from Germany, Belgium, Luxembourg, the U.K., and other trading partners; imports include raw materials, semi-finished products, consumer goods, transportation equipment, oil, and food products.

Agriculture: 2% (1996) of the labor force engages in agriculture, fishing, and forestry. Agricultural exports earn 16.2% (1996) of the total value of earnings. Crops include grains, potatoes, sugar beets, fruits and vegetables.

Energy: The country relies on thermal and nuclear powerand imported fuels for energy..

Natural Resources: Oil, natural gas, fertile soil

Environmental Issues: Air and water pollution, acid rain

Transportation: There are 1,700 miles (2,740 km) of railroads and 78,870 miles (127,000 km) of roads, mostly paved, in the country. Canals and navigable rivers such as the Rhine and Scheldt expand the transportation network by 3,940 miles (6,340 km). Main seaports include Rotterdam (one of the world's busiest ports) and Amsterdam. International airports are at Amsterdam, Rotterdam, Maastricht, and Groningen.

Communications: There are 46 newspapers published in the country. There are 13.8 million radios and 7.4 million televisions (1992 est.) in use. Phone service, with 8.27 million phones in operation (1993 est.), is highly developed.

Tourism: In 1997, 4.7 million visitors came to the Netherlands. Tourist attractions include the many art museums in Amsterdam, The Hague, and Rotterdam; traditional architecture in the cities; and large fields of cultivated flowers.

U.S. Tourist Office: (212) 370-7360

Embassy in U.S.: (202) 244-5300

Public Holidays: Good Friday (date varies, in March or April); Easter Monday (date varies, in March or April); Queen's Day (April 30); Ascension Day (date varies, in May); Whit Monday (date varies, in May); National Liberation Day (May 5); Christmas (December 25–26)

New Zealand

Country Name: New Zealand

Official Name: New Zealand

Nationality: New Zealander(s) (noun); New Zealand (adjective)

Capital: Wellington, pop. 153,800

Major cities: Auckland, Christchurch, Hamilton, Dunedin, Tauranga

External Territories: In the South Pacific Ocean: Cook Islands (93 sq mi, 240 sq km; pop. 18,000); Niue (100 sq mi, 258 sq km; pop. 2,000); Tokelau Islands (4 sq m, 10 sq km; pop. 1,580)

Location: New Zealand is located in Oceania, in the South Pacific

Ocean, about 1,000 miles (1,600 km) southeast of Australia.

Physical Geography: The country consists of two main islands and several smaller islands. North Island has a central plateau, with mountains in the south and hilly northern sections. Much of South Island is also mountainous; the Southern Alps are in the south, with smaller hills in the north.

Total area: 103,883 sq mi (269,057 sq km)

Coastline: 9,398 mi (15,134 km)

Land use: Meadows and pastures cover 50% of the land, 28% is forested, and 14% is arable or under cultivation.

Climate: Temperate, with mostly mild winters; varying precipitation from east to west due to the mountains' rainshadow effect

Population: 3,817,000

Urban population: 85%

Rate of natural increase: 0.8%

Age structure: 23% under 15; 12% over 65

Birth rate: 15/1000

Death rate: 7/1000

Infant mortality rate: 5.3/1000

Fertility rate: 1.9

Life expectancy at birth: 74 years (male); 80 (female)

Religion: Protestant, Roman Catholic

Language: English, Maori

Ethnic Divisions: European, Maori, Pacific Islander

Literacy Rate: 99%

Government: Parliamentary democracy, with a governor-general appointed by the British monarch and a unicameral legislature, the House of Representatives. The 120 members of the legislature are directly elected to three-year terms.

Armed services: 9,550 troops (1997) in the army, navy, and air force

Suffrage: Universal; 18 years old

Economy: Inflation, unemployment, and budget deficits have all been

NEW ZEALAND RIDING TWO TECTONIC PLATES

Taken together, New Zealand's two main islands stretch 1,000 miles north to south and are 280 miles across at their widest point. Each rides a separate tectonic plate about halfway between the South Pole and the Equator. Discovered by the Dutchman Abel Tasman in 1642, New Zealand became a British colony in 1840 and gained independence in 1947. Maoris, whose Polynesian ancestors settled the islands in the sixth century, make up about 10 percent of the population.

targeted by the government as the economy of New Zealand attempts to diversify its traditionally agrarian economy and increase its international trade. Tourism contributes significantly to the national economy, and trade barriers have been eliminated between New Zealand and Australia. The beginning of annual budget surpluses should ease the pressures of foreign debt.

Unit of currency: New Zealand dollar; 100 cents = 1 New Zealand dollar (NZ$)

GDP per capita: $17,700

Inflation rate–CPI: 2% (1997 est.)

Workforce: 1,634,500 (1995)

Unemployment rate: 5.9% (1996)

Exports: Goods worth $18.5 billion (1997 est.) are sent to Australia, Japan, the U.S., the U.K., and other trading partners; exports include wool, lamb, mutton, beef, fish, cheese, chemicals, wood products, fruits, vegetables, and manufactured goods.

Imports: Goods worth $19.2 billion (1997 est.) are received from Australia, the U.S., Japan, the U.K., and other trading partners; imports include machinery and equipment, vehicles, aircraft, petroleum, and consumer goods.

Agriculture: 8.7% (1997) of the labor force engages in agriculture, fishing, and forestry. Crops include wheat, barley, potatoes, fruit, and vegetables. Wool, meat, and dairy products are key agricultural com-

modities; wood products and seafood are also increasing in importance.

Energy: Domestic hydropower, natural gas, coal, and petroleum are used for energy generation. Hydropower supplies 15% of the country's energy needs.

Natural Resources: Natural gas, iron ore, sand, coal, gold, limestone, silica, timber, hydropower

Environmental Issues: Deforestation, soil erosion

Transportation: There are 2,465 miles (3,970 km) of railroads and 57,255 miles (92,200 km) of roads, the majority of which are paved, in the country. Main North Island seaports include Auckland, Tauranga, and Wellington; main South Island ports include Lyttleton at Christchurch and Port Chalmers at Dunedin; Wellington, Christchurch, and Auckland have international airports.

Communications: The country has nearly 100 daily newspapers. There are 3.2 million radios and 1.5 million televisions (1992) in operation. Phone service, with 1.7 million phones (1986) in service, is excellent.

Tourism: Glaciers, geysers, mountain lakes, the city life in Wellington and other urban areas, historic areas of Christchurch, fishing, and beaches all draw tourists to New Zealand. More than 1.5 million visitors in 1996/97 spent $3.5 billion (U.S.).

U.S. Tourist Office: (800) 338-5494

Embassy in U.S.: (202) 328-4800

Public Holidays: Waitangi Day: anniversary of 1840 treaty establishing British sovereignty (February 6); Easter (date varies, in March or April, four-day holiday); Australia New Zealand (ANZAC) Day and Gallipoli landing anniversary, 1915 (April 25); Queen's Official Birthday (date varies, in June); Labor Day (date varies, in late October); Christmas (December 25); Boxing Day (December 26)

Nicaragua

Country Name: Nicaragua

Official Name: Republic of Nicaragua

Nationality: Nicaraguan(s) (noun); Nicaraguan (adjective)

Capital: Managua, pop. 864,200

Major cities: N.A.

External Territories: None

Location: Nicaragua, in Central America, is between Honduras on the north and Costa Rica on the south. The Pacific Ocean is to the west and the Caribbean Sea to the east.

Physical Geography: Lowlands along the Pacific coast give way to valleys and basins that are interspersed with the mountains in the western and central parts of the country; some volcanoes are still active. A wide band of marshy plains, the Costa de Mosquitos, runs along the Caribbean coast.

Total area: 46,430 sq mi (120,254 sq km)

Coastline: 565 mi (910 km)

Land use: Nearly 45% of the land is meadows and pastures, 27% is forested, and 10% is arable or under cultivation.

Climate: Tropical, with a rainy season from May to January

Population: 4,952,000

Urban population: 63%

Rate of natural increase: 3.18%

Age structure: 44% under 15; 3% over 65

Birth rate: 38/1000

Death rate: 6.18/1000

Infant mortality rate: 40/1000

Fertility rate: 3.9

Life expectancy at birth: 63 years (male); 68 years (female)

Religion: Roman Catholic, Protestant

Language: Spanish, English, Amerindian

Ethnic Divisions: Mestizo, white, black, Amerindian

Literacy Rate: 66%

Government: Republic, with a president and a unicameral legislature, the National Assembly. The president is directly elected to a five-year term, as are the 93 members of the legislature. There are 5 administrative departments and 2 autonomous regions.

Armed services: 17,000 troops (1996) in the army, navy, and air force; no compulsory service since 1990

Suffrage: Universal; 16 years old

Economy: The government has managed to reduce high rates of inflation and lower international debt, but Nicaragua's economy has still not begun to grow substantially since the beginning of the new government in 1990, following civil war that raged from 1980 to 1988. Ownership of much private property, confiscated by the previous government, has not been resolved, and many citizens live in poverty. However, the international community continues to work with the government by providing debt forgiveness and other financial assistance for needed health care and education.

Unit of currency: Córdoba; 100 centavos = 1 córdoba or gold córdoba (C$)

GDP per capita: $2,100

Inflation rate–CPI: 11.6% (1996)

Workforce: 1.5 million (1995 est.)

Unemployment rate: 16%; underemployment: 36% (1996 est.)

Exports: Goods worth $635 million (f.o.b., 1996 est.) are sent to the U.S., Canada, Germany, and other trading partners; exports include meat, coffee, sugar, cotton, seafood, gold, and bananas.

Imports: Goods worth $1.1 billion (c.i.f., 1996 est.) are received from the U.S., Japan, Venezuela, and other Central American trading partners; imports include consumer goods, machinery and equipment, and petroleum products.

Agriculture: 31% (1995) of the working population is employed in agriculture, fishing, and forestry. Coffee, sugarcane, bananas, and cotton are the primary cash crops, and meat and seafood are becoming important exports; beans, rice, and corn are grown for domestic use.

Energy: Imported petroleum is used to generate most of the country's energy, although hydroelectric plants produce about one third of the country's needs.

Natural Resources: Minerals, including gold, silver, copper, tungsten, lead, zinc; timber; seafood

Environmental Issues: Soil erosion, deforestation, water pollution

Transportation: There are no railroads in operation. Of the 11,180 miles (18,000 km) of roads, 1,130 miles (1,820 km) are unpaved. Pacific ports include Corinto, Puerto Sandino, and San Juan del Sur; ports on the Caribbean include Puerto Cabezas and El Bluff. An international airport is at Managua.

Communications: There are four daily newspapers in circulation.

There are 1.04 million radios (1995 est.) and 260,000 televisions 1992 est.) in operation and 66,800 telephones (1993).

Tourism: The country is working to develop its tourist attractions, including mountain and coastal amenities. In 1994, 238,000 visitors brought $40 million (U.S.) to the economy.

Embassy in U.S.: (202) 939-6570

Public Holidays: Maundy Thursday (date varies, in March or April); Good Friday (date varies, in March or April); Labor Day (date varies, in May); Liberation Day (July 19); Battle of San Jacinto (September 14); Independence Day: from Spain, 1821 (September 15); All Souls' Day (November 2); Christmas (December 25)

Niger

Country Name: Niger
Official Name: Republic of Niger
Nationality: Nigerien(s) (noun); Nigerien (adjective)
Capital: Niamey, pop. 391,900
Major cities: Zinder, Maradi, Tahoua
External Territories: None
Location: Niger, a landlocked country in western Africa, is bordered by Algeria on the northwest, by Libya on the northeast, by Chad on the east, by Benin and Nigeria on the south, and by Burkina Faso and Mali on the west.
Physical Geography: The Sahara and Djado Plateau in the north give way to the Sahel and lower southern plateaus. The Niger River crosses the southern part of the country

NIGER GOLD-TOTING TERMITES

Engineers for an international mining company tried a technique used by ancient African civilizations to locate gold deposits: check the contents of termite mounds—some of them six feet high—for traces of gold. The termites are known to dig as deep as 250 feet in their search for water, and whatever they encounter along the way eventually is brought back up to the surface.

and Lake Chad is in the country's southeastern corner, on the borders with Nigeria and Chad.

Total area: 489,191 sq mi (1,267,000 sq km)
Coastline: None
Land use: Meadows and pastures cover 7% of the land, 3% of the land is arable or under cultivation, and 2% is wooded.
Climate: Tropical and arid in much of the country; rainy season between June and October in southern areas; large fluctuations in daily temperatures in desert regions
Population: 9,962,000
Urban population: 17%
Rate of natural increase: 2.97%
Age structure: 48% under 15; 2% over 65
Birth rate: 53.7/1000
Death rate: 24/1000
Infant mortality rate: 123.1/1000
Fertility rate: 7.5
Life expectancy at birth: 41 years (male); 40 years (female)
Religion: Muslim, indigenous beliefs, Christian
Language: French, Hausa, Djerma
Ethnic Divisions: Hausa, Djerma, Tuareg, Fula
Literacy Rate: 14%
Government: Republic in transition, with a president and unicameral legislature, the National Assembly. The president and the 83 members of the National Assembly are to be directly elected to five-year terms.

There are seven administrative departments and a capital district.
Armed services: 5,300 troops (1997) in the army and air force; two-year selective conscription
Suffrage: Universal; 18 years old
Economy: Rapid population growth, external debt, political instability, and labor unrest hinder Niger's attempts at encouraging economic growth and diversity; subsistence agriculture, trade re-exports, and a dwindling trade in uranium are the country's key economic activities. International aid has helped, but the government continues to try to improve basic health and education services for its citizens, attract foreign investment, boost domestic tax revenues, and restore political stability.
Unit of currency: CFA franc; 100 centimes =1 franc de la Communauté financière africaine (CFAF)
GDP per capita: $670
Inflation rate–CPI: 5.3% (1996)
Workforce: 4,504,000 (1996 est.)
Unemployment rate: 20,926 (1991 est.)
Exports: Goods worth $188 million (f.o.b., 1995 est.) are sent to France, Nigeria, Burkina Faso, Côte d'Ivoire, Canada, and other trading partners; exports include uranium ore, livestock products, cowpeas, and onions.
Imports: Goods worth $374 million (c.i.f., 1996 est.) are received from France, Côte d'Ivoire, Japan, Germany, Italy, and other trading partners; imports include consumer

goods, machinery, vehicles, oil, and food.

Agriculture: Nearly 90% (1996) of the working population engages in agricultural production raising livestock and producing cowpeas, cotton, and peanuts for cash and millet, sorghum, cassava, and cattle for domestic use. In nondrought years, the country is nearly self-sufficient.

Energy: Almost half of Niger's energy requirements are met by electricity imports from Nigeria; coal and oil are used for additional energy generation.

Natural Resources: Many minerals, including uranium, coal, iron, tin, phosphates, gold, petroleum

Environmental Issues: Deforestation, desertification, soil erosion, poaching, over grazing

Transportation: There are no railroads. There are 6,270 miles (10,100 km) of roads, of which 500 miles (800 km) are paved. The Niger River is navigable for 190 miles (300 km) and provides access to ocean ports through Nigeria from September to March. Niamey and Agadez both offer international air service.

Communications: At least one daily newspaper is published. There are 620,000 radios, 105,000 televisions (1995), and 11,000 telephones (1993) in service.

Tourism: A museum in Niamey exhibits the country's cultural diversity, and a wildlife reserve protects animals native to the region. In 1994, 11,000 visitors added $16 million to the national economy.

Embassy in U.S.: (202) 483-4224

Public Holidays: End of Ramadan (date varies, in February); Easter Monday (date varies, in March or April); Feast of the Sacrifice (date varies, in April); Anniversary of the 1974 coup (April 15); National Concord Day (April 24); Islamic New Year (date varies, in April or May); Labor Day (May 1); Birth of the Prophet (date varies, in July); Independence Day: from France, 1960

(August 3); Republic Day (December 18); Christmas (December 25)

Nigeria

Country Name: Nigeria
Official Name: Federal Republic of Nigeria
Nationality: Nigerian(s) (noun); Nigerian (adjective)
Capital: Abuja, pop. 350,100
Major cities: Lagos, Ibadan, Ogbomosho
External Territories: None
Location: Nigeria, in western Africa, is bordered by Niger and Chad on the north, by Cameroon on the east, and by Benin on the west. The Gulf of Guinea and the North Atlantic Ocean are on the south.
Physical Geography: Coastal plains give way inland to higher plateaus and river lowlands. Lake Chad lies in the northeastern corner of the country.
Total area: 356,669 sq mi (923,768 sq km)
Coastline: 530 mi (853 km)
Land use: About 33% of the land is arable or under cultivation, nearly 44% is meadows and pastures, and 12% is forest and woodland.

Climate: Tropical, with rainfall heavy along the coast and decreasing inland; inland rainy season from April to October; shorter rainy season in the north
Population: 113,829,000
Urban population: 16%
Rate of natural increase: 2.97%
Age structure: 45% under 15; 3% over 65
Birth rate: 42.6/1000
Death rate: 12.9/1000
Infant mortality rate: 73/1000
Fertility rate: 6.2
Life expectancy at birth: 53 years (male); 55 years (female)
Religion: Muslim, Christian, indigenous beliefs
Language: English, Hausa, Yoruba, Igbo
Ethnic Divisions: Hausa, Fulani, Yoruba, Igbo; more than 300 groups
Literacy Rate: 57%
Government: Republic in transition, with an elected president and bicameral legislature, the National Assembly. When the existing Chief of State died in office, the Provisional Ruling Council appointed a new chief in June 1998 who promised to continue actions toward civilian rule. There are 30 administrative states.
Armed services: 77,100 troops (1997) in the army, navy, and air force; voluntary service
Suffrage: Universal; 21 years old
Economy: An economy dependent on oil exports has left Nigeria financially vulnerable in the case of de-

NIGERIA POPULATION BOOM IN PROGRESS
Nigeria is Africa's most populous country, with more than 107 million people living in an area about twice the size of California. It continues to grow at a rapid pace, with Nigerian women having an average of 6.2 children each. If demographic trends continue, Nigeria will be the world's seventh most populous country by 2025, with a UN projection of 231 million people.

clining prices, and an expanding population continues to outstrip economic growth. Government plans to encourage foreign investment, freeze interest rates, and better manage revenues have resulted in some budget surpluses; however, foreign debt continues to grow, and the country must import food to meet domestic demand.

Unit of currency: Naira; 100 kobo = 1 naira (N)

GDP per capita: $1,300

Inflation rate–CPI: 12% (1997 est.)

Workforce: 30.77 million (1986 est.)

Unemployment rate: 1.8% (1995 est.)

Exports: Goods worth $15 billion (f.o.b., 1996) are sent to the U.S., Spain, Germany, the Netherlands, Italy, and other trading partners; exports include petroleum, petroleum products, cocoa, and rubber.

Imports: Goods worth $8 billion (c.i.f., 1996) are received from Germany, the U.K., the U.S., Japan, and other trading partners; imports include machinery and transportation equipment, manufactured goods, chemicals, food, and animals.

Agriculture: 36.7% (1996) of the labor force engages in agriculture, forestry, and fishing. Cocoa, cattle, palm oil, and peanuts are raised for cash, and rice, maize, taro, yams, and cassava are grown for domestic use. Other livestock, fish farming, and timber also contribute significantly to this sector.

Energy: Most energy is generated using supplies of domestic oil, coal, and natural gas. Wood is also used in households.

Natural Resources: Minerals, including oil, coal, tin, columbite, iron, natural gas, uranium

Environmental Issues: Deforestation, desertification, soil degradation

Transportation: There are 2,210 miles (3,560 km) of railroads and 20,180 miles (32,500 km) of roads, of which 16,150 miles (26,010 km)

are paved. Navigable rivers such as the Niger expand the transportation network by 5,330 miles (8,580km). Port Harcourt, Calabar, Warri, Koko, Burutu, Sapele, Apapa, and Tin Can Island are significant seaports. Lagos, Kano, Port Harcount, Calabar, and Abuja have international airports.

Communications: More than a dozen daily newspapers are published in the capital and elsewhere. There are 22.0 million radios and 6.1 million televisions in operation (1995). Phone service, with 369,000 phone lines (1994), provides adequate service; the system is currently under expansion.

Tourism: Rain forests and their wildlife, the cultural diversity of Nigeria's many ethnic groups, and coastal getaways attract visitors to Nigeria; 193,000 tourists spent $34 million (U.S.) in the country in 1994.

Embassy in U.S.: (202) 986-8400

Public Holidays: End of Ramadan (date varies, in February); Easter (date varies, in March or April); Feast of the Sacrifice (date varies, in April); Birth of the Prophet (date varies, in July); National Day: independence from the U.K., 1960 (October 1); Christmas (December 25–26)

Norway

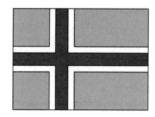

Country Name: Norway
Official Name: Kingdom of Norway
Nationality: Norwegian(s) (noun); Norwegian (adjective)
Capital: Oslo, pop. 421,700 [758,900]

Major cities: Bergen, Trondheim, Stavanger

External Territories: Arctic Ocean islands: Svalbard (pop. 2,900); Jan Mayen; South Atlantic islands: Bouvet Island (uninhabited); Peter Island (uninhabited); Queen Maud Land, Antarctica (disputed)

Location: Norway, in northern Europe, is bordered on the east by Russia, Finland, and Sweden; the Norwegian Sea is to the west.

Physical Geography: Norway is mountainous, with deep fjords along the northern and western coasts.

Total area: 125,182 sq mi (324,220 sq km)

Coastline: 13,615 mi (21,925 km)

Land use: More than 25% of the land is wooded, and 3% is arable or under cultivation; there are no meadows and pastures.

Climate: Variable; mild winters with heavy precipitation and cool summers on west coast; colder inland temperatures

Population: 4,462,000

Urban population: 74%

Rate of natural increase: 0.3%

Age structure: 20% under 15; 16% over 65

Birth rate: 13/1000

Death rate: 10/1000

Infant mortality rate: 4.1/1000

Fertility rate: 1.8

Life expectancy at birth: 75 years (male); 81 years (female)

Religion: Evangelical Lutheran

Language: Norwegian

Ethnic Divisions: Norwegian, Sami (Lapp)

Literacy Rate: 99%

Government: Constitutional monarchy—King Harald V, since 1991—with a unicameral legislature, the Parliament, or Storting. The 165 members of the legislature are directly elected to four-year terms. There are 19 administrative counties.

NORWAY LIVES LINKED TO THE SEA

Norway has the longest coastline in Europe, which helps explain why the sea has always been an important part of its history and culture, from the days of Viking exploration more than a thousand years ago to the country's involvement in shipbuilding, fishing, and shipping today. Its North Sea seabed has also provided the country with oil and natural gas for its own needs and for export; one of the world's largest oil platforms is there. The country's electricity comes from water power, however, some of which is harnessed from the many waterfalls in its steep-sloped fjords.

Armed services: 33,600 troops (1997) in the army, navy, and air force; compulsory service for 12 months; males from 19 to 44 years of age subject to periodic additional service

Suffrage: Universal; 18 years old

Economy: Oil and natural gas production is a key component of Norway's economy. The government has begun to explore different avenues of industrial diversification to help reduce unemployment and protect the country from oil price swings. Public expenditures for health care, education, and other components of social welfare are supported by a hefty tax burden, but the country as a whole has one of the highest standards of living in the world.

Unit of currency: Norwegian krone (singular), kroner (plural); 100 øre = 1 Norwegian krone (NKn)

GDP per capita: $27,400

Inflation rate–CPI: 2% (1997 est.)

Workforce: 2.13 million

Unemployment rate: 2.6% (1997)

Exports: Goods worth $49.3 billion (f.o.b., 1996 est.) are sent to the U.K., Germany, Sweden, and other trading partners; exports include petroleum and petroleum products, metals and products, foodstuffs (mostly fish), and chemicals,and raw materials.

Imports: Goods worth $35.1 billion (c.i.f., 1996 est.) are received from Sweden, Germany, the U.K., Denmark, and other trading partners; imports include machinery and equipment, manufactured consumer goods, and chemicals.

Agriculture: About 6% (1993) of the labor force engages in agriculture, fishing, and forestry. Livestock and fish, including those raised on fish farms, are the most important agricultural commodities. Oats and other grains are also cultivated.

Energy: Hydropower generates enough energy to meet almost all domestic demand; surplus energy is exported.

Natural Resources: Minerals, including petroleum, copper, natural gas, pyrites, nickel, iron ore, zinc, lead; fish; timber; hydropower

Environmental Issues: Water and air pollution, acid rain

Transportation: About 2,500 miles (4,020 km) of railroads and 56,710 miles (91,320 km) of roads, the majority of which are paved, connect the country. Seaports include Oslo, Bergen, Drammen, Hammerfest, Kristiansand, Larvik, Narvik, Stavanger, Tromsø, and Trondheim. There is an international airport in Oslo.

Communications: More than 60 daily newspapers are published throughout the country. There are 1.5 million televisions (1993 est.) and 3.3 million radios (1993 est.). Telephone service, with 2.39 million telephones (1994 est.) in service, is excellent.

Tourism: In 1996, 3.3 million tourists visited Norway, drawn by the dramatic scenery and winter-sports in the mountains.

U.S. Tourist Office: (212) 949-2333

Embassy in U.S.: (202) 333-6000

Public Holidays: Maundy Thursday (date varies, in March or April); Good Friday (date varies, in March or April); Easter Monday (date varies, in March or April); Ascension Day (date varies, in May); Whit Monday (date varies, in May); May Day (May 1); National Day (May 17); Christmas (December 25–26)

Oman

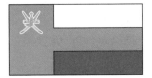

Country Name: Oman

Official Name: Sultanate of Oman

Nationality: Omani(s) (noun); Omani (adjective)

Capital: Muscat, pop. [635,000]

Major cities: Salālah

External Territories: None

Location: On the Arabian Peninsula, Oman, in the Middle East, is bordered on the southwest by Yemen and on the west by Saudi Arabia and the United Arab Emirates. The Arabian Sea is on the east. Omani territory, separated from the rest of the country by the United Arab Emirates, is at the northern end of the Musandam Peninsula, on the Strait of Hormuz between the Persian Gulf and Gulf of Oman.

Physical Geography: Much of the western part of the country is desert, part of the Ar Rub' al Khālī. Mountains parallel the northern and southwestern coasts. A northeastern coastal plain provides some land for cultivation.

Total area: 82,030 sq mi (212,457 sq km)

Coastline: 1,299 mi (2,092 km)

Land use: Meadows and pastures take up about 5% of the land. There is no arable land. The remaining land is either desert or developed areas.

Climate: Mostly desert, but with high humidity along the coasts; rainfall from May to September in the south

Population: 2,460,000

Urban population: 72%

Rate of natural increase: 3.8%

Age structure: 46% under 15; 3% over 65

Birth rate: 43/1000

Death rate: 5/1000

Infant mortality rate: 30/1000

Fertility rate: 7.1

Life expectancy at birth: 69 years (male); 73 years (female)

Religion: Ibadhi, Sunni, and Shi'a Muslim, Hindu

Language: Arabic, English, Baluchi, Urdu

Ethnic Divisions: Arab, Baluchi, Indian

Literacy Rate: 80%

Government: Hereditary monarchy, with an 80-member Consultative Council, the Majlis ash-Shoura, appointed by the sultan, Sultan Qaboos bin Said, since 1970. There are six administrative regions and two governorates.

Armed services: 43,500 volunteers (1996) in the army, navy, air force, and other military branches

Suffrage: None

Economy: Although Oman's economy is driven by oil exports, the government is promoting industrial diversification for the day when reserves run low. Foreign investment is encouraged, and job training for Omanis will reduce the need for foreign workers and increase employment among Omani citizens.

Unit of currency: Omani rial; 1,000 baiza = 1 Omani rial (RO)

GDP per capita: $8,000

Inflation rate–CPI: 1.5% (1996 est.)

Workforce: 636,400 (1993 est.), including 64.2% non-Omanis

Unemployment rate: 11.9% (1993 est.)

Exports: Goods worth $7.6 billion (f.o.b., 1997 est.) are sent to Japan, South Korea, the U.S., China, Thailand, and other trading partners; exports include petroleum, and reexports fish, copper, and textiles.

Imports: Goods worth $4.8 billion (f.o.b., 1997 est.) are received from the United Arab Emirates, Japan, the U.K., the U.S., and other trading partners; imports include machinery, transportation equipment, manufactured goods, food, and livestock.

Agriculture: Nearly 37% of the labor force engages in agriculture, hunting, and fishing, raising dates, limes, alfalfa, tobacco, and other fruits and vegetables; seafood and livestock are also produced. Most of the population relies on imported food.

Energy: Domestic petroleum fuels most energy generation.

Natural Resources: Minerals, including petroleum, copper, asbestos, marble, limestone, chromium, gypsum, natural gas

Environmental Issues: Soil and coastline pollution, limited freshwater

Transportation: There are no railroads. There are 16,115 miles (25,950 km) of roads, of which 3,062 miles (4,930 km) are paved. Port towns include Maṭraḥ and Mīnā' al Faḥl. International airports are at Seeb International and Salālah.

Communications: There are three Arabic daily newspapers and two English dailies. There are 1.043 million radios (1992 est.) and 1.195 million televisions in operation (1992 est.), and phone service, with 150,000 lines (1994), is good.

Tourism: Visitors come to see traditional souks and historic forts and to

enjoy beaches and museums in Muscat and other cities. In 1994, 358,000 visitors brought $88 million to the country.

Embassy in U.S.: (202) 387-1980

Public Holidays: Beginning of Ramadan (date varies); End of Ramadan (date varies, in February); Feast of the Sacrifice (date varies, in April); Islamic New Year (date varies, in April or May); Ashura (date varies, in April or May); Birth of the Prophet (date varies, in July); National Day (November 18); Birthday of Sultan Qaboos bin Said (November 19); Ascension of the Prophet (date varies, in November or December)

Pakistan

Country Name: Pakistan

Official Name: Islamic Republic of Pakistan

Nationality: Pakistani(s) (noun); Pakistani (adjective)

Capital: Islamabad, pop. [799,000]

Major cities: Karachi, Lahore, Faisalabad, Rawalpindi, Hyderabad

External Territories: None

Location: On the Arabian Sea in southern Asia, Pakistan is bordered on the north by China, on the east by India, and on the west by Iran and Afghanistan.

Physical Geography: High peaks of the Karakoram Range, on the border with China, include K2, the world's second-highest peak (after Mount Everest). The Hindu Kush are on the northwest, and dry highlands are found in the southwest and some parts of the west. The Indus River plain provides land for cultiva-

PAKISTAN THREE NATIONS FROM ONE

At the time of Indian Independence from Great Britain in 1947, the regions of India with large Muslim populations became East and West Pakistan. East Pakistan became the independent country of Bangladesh in 1971. Pakistan became the Islamic Republic of Pakistan in 1956. Punjabis are the largest single ethnic group.

tion, and the Great Indian Desert occupies much of the region east of the Indus.

Total area: 307,374 sq mi (796,095 sq km)

Coastline: 650 mi (1,046 km)

Land use: 25% of the land is arable or under cultivation, 6% is meadows and pastures, and 5% is forested.

Climate: Continental, with hot summers and mild winters (except for colder winters in the mountains); precipitation generally increasing inland

Population: 146,488,000

Urban population: 32%

Rate of natural increase: 2.8%

Age structure: 41% under 15; 4% over 65

Birth rate: 39/1000

Death rate: 11/1000

Infant mortality rate: 91/1000

Fertility rate: 5.6

Life expectancy at birth: 58 (male); 59 (female)

Religion: Muslim, Christian

Language: Urdu, English, Punjabi, Sindhi

Ethnic Divisions: Punjabi, Sindhi, Pashtun, Baluchi

Literacy Rate: 38%

Government: Republic, with a president and bicameral parliament. The president is elected to a five-year term by both houses of the parliament. Of the 217 members of the National Assembly are directly elected for five year terms, 207 are Muslims and 10 non-Muslim. The 87 members of the Senate are elect-

ed to six-year terms by provincial assemblies. Administrative areas are divided into four provinces, the federal district, and an area set aside to be administered as a tribal area.

Armed services: 587,000 volunteer troops (1997) in the army, navy, and air force

Suffrage: Universal; 21 years old

Economy: Although internal unrest, an expanding population, and a substandard infrastructure impede needed economic growth in Pakistan, the government began reforms in 1988 to encourage foreign investment, reduce the budget deficit, and privatize industry. In 1997, foreign aid was suspended until additional reforms could be made such as reducing taxes, relaxing import tariffs, and subsidizing wheat, rice, and oil seed farmers.

Unit of currency: Pakistani rupee; 100 paisa = 1 Pakistani rupee (PRs)

GDP per capita: $2,600

Inflation rate–CPI: 11.8% (1996-1997)

Workforce: 37.8 million (1998)

Unemployment rate: N.A.

Exports: Goods worth $8.2 billion (1996) are sent to the U.S., Japan, Hong Kong, and other European trading partners; exports include cotton, textiles, clothing, rice, leathers, and carpets.

Imports: Goods worth $11.4 billion (1996) are received from Japan, the U.S., Germany, the U.K., Saudi Arabia, Malaysia, South Korea, and other trading partners; imports include petroleum, machinery, trans-

portation equipment, vegetable oils, animal fats, and chemicals.

Agriculture: Nearly half of the workforce engages in agriculture, fishing, and forestry (1998). Rice, wheat, maize, sugarcane, and cotton are cash crops; leathers and fish are also significant export commodities. Cotton and cotton products earned 54.2% of the value of total exports in 1994–1995.

Energy: Domestic oil and natural gas supply 41% of the country's energy needs (1991).

Natural Resources: Natural gas, petroleum, coal, iron ore, copper, salt, limestone

Environmental Issues: Water pollution, soil erosion, deforestation and desertification, limited freshwater

Transportation: There are 5,100 miles (8,200 km) of railroads and 139,730 miles (225,000 km) of roads, of which more than half are paved. Major seaports include Karachi, Gwadar, and Pasni; international airports are at Karachi, Lahore, Peshawar, and Quetta.

Communications: 225 daily newspapers are published in cities throughout the country. There are 11.3 million radios and 2.08 million televisions (1993) in operation; there are nearly 2.55 million phones (1997) in service, and service is considered to be poor.

Tourism: The Hindu Kush and Karakoram mountains offer scenery, hiking, and challenging mountaineering opportunities; archaeological sites and structures from settlements dating from 3500 B.C. also draw visitors. In 1994, 239,889 visitors brought $117 million to Pakistan.

Embassy in U.S.: (202) 939-6200

Public Holidays: Beginning of Ramadan (date varies); End of Ramadan (date varies, in February); Pakistan Day, proclamation of republic, 1956 (March 23); Good Friday (date varies, in March or April); Easter Monday (date varies, in March or

April); Feast of the Sacrifice (date varies, in April); Islamic New Year (date varies, in April or May); Ashura (date varies, in April or May); Labor Day (May 1); Birth of the Prophet (date varies, in July); Independence Day: from the U.K., 1947 (August 14); Defense of Pakistan Day (September 6); Anniversary of the death of Quaid-i-Azam (Great Leader), the first governor-general, Muhammad Ali Jinnah, 1948 (September 11); Allama Iqbal Day (November 9); Birthday of Quaid-i-Azam (December 25), Christmas (December 25); Boxing Day (December 26)

Palau

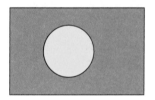

Country Name: Palau
Official Name: Republic of Palau
Nationality: Palauan(s); Palauan (adjective)
Capital: Koror, pop. 12,000
Major cities: N.A.
External Territories: None
Location: Palau, southeast of the Philippines, consists of more than 200 islands stretching more than 400 miles (650 km) between the Philippine Sea and the North Pacific Ocean.
Physical Geography: Palau's geography varies from mountainous islands to low coral islands with barrier reefs. Babelthaup is the largest island.
Total area: 188 sq mi (487 sq km)
Coastline: 943 mi (1,519 km)
Land use: N.A.
Climate: Tropical, with a rainy season from May to November
Population: 19,000

Urban population: 69%
Rate of natural increase: 1.0%
Age structure: 28% under 15; 6% over 65
Birth rate: 18.2/1000
Death rate: 8/1000
Infant mortality rate: 19.2/1000
Fertility rate: 2.5
Life expectancy at birth: 64 years (male); 71 years (female)
Religion: Roman Catholic, Protestant, Modekngei (indigenous)
Language: English, Palauan, three local official
Ethnic Divisions: Palauan
Literacy Rate: 92%
Government: Republic, with a president and a bicameral legislature, the Palau National Congress, the Olbiil era Kelulau. The president is directly elected to a four-year term. The 16 members of the House of Delegates and the 14 members of the Senate are also elected to office. There are 16 states.
Armed services: Defense is the responsibility of the U.S.
Suffrage: Universal; 18 years old
Economy: Palau, a former UN Trust Territory administered by the U.S., continues to receive considerable financial assistance from the U.S. since its independence in 1994. Most paid jobs are with the government, and subsistence farming is important. Tourism is also on the rise.
Unit of currency: U.S. dollar; 100 cents = 1 U.S. dollar ($)
GDP per capita: $8,800
Inflation rate–CPI: N.A.
Workforce: N.A.
Unemployment rate: 7%
Exports: Goods worth $14 million (f.o.b., 1996) are sent to the U.S., Japan, and other trading partners; exports include trochus, tuna, copra, and handicrafts.
Imports: Goods worth $72.4 million (f.o.b., 1996) are received from the U.S. and other trading partners; im-

ports include food and manufactured goods.
Agriculture: Subsistence farmers raise coconuts, copra, cassava, and sweet potatoes; copra is exported. Fishing licenses are sold to foreigners.
Energy: N.A.
Natural Resources: Forests, gold and other minerals, seafood
Environmental Issues: Inadequate solid waste treatment, water pollution
Transportation: The more important islands have concrete roads; 22 miles (36 km) of the 38-mile (61 km) road system are paved. Malakal Harbor is a main seaport, and there is an international airport near Koror, on Babelthaup.
Communications: There are no daily newspapers. There are 9,000 radios and 1,600 televisions (1993) in use. An estimated 1,500 telephones (1988) are in service.
Tourism: Diving, snorkeling, beaches, and island scenery (including the Rock Islands) draw visitors to Palau; in 1995, 44,850 tourists came to the country.
Embassy in U.S.: (202) 452-6814
Public Holidays: Senior Citizens' Day (March 5); Youth Day (March 15); President's Day (June 1); Constitution Day (July 9); United Nations Day (October 24); Thanksgiving (date varies, in November); Christmas (December 25)

Panama

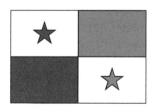

Country Name: Panama
Official Name: Republic of Panama

Nationality: Panamanian(s) (noun); Panamanian (adjective)

Capital: Panama City, pop. 464,900

Major cities: Colón, David, Penonomé, Santiago

External Territories: None

Location: Panama, the southern-most country of Central America, is bordered on the west by Costa Rica and on the east by Colombia; the Caribbean Sea is to the north and the Pacific Ocean to the south.

Physical Geography: Mountains occupy both the eastern and western regions of the country, as well as some of the interior. Plains extend from the Pacific and Caribbean coasts and along inland river valleys. The Panama Canal bisects the country and connects the Pacific and Atlantic Oceans.

Total area: 29,157 sq mi (77,517 sq km)

Coastline: 1,546 mi (2,490 km)

Land use: Forests cover 44% of the land, 20% is meadows and pastures, and 9% of the land is arable or under cultivation.

Climate: Tropical, with a rainy season from May to January

Population: 2,809,000

Urban population: 56%

Rate of natural increase: 1.77%

Age structure: 32% under 15; 5% over 65

Birth rate: 22.8/1000

Death rate: 5.1/1000

Infant mortality rate: 21.95/1000

Fertility rate: 2.7

Life expectancy at birth: 72 years (male); 76 years (female)

Religion: Roman Catholic, Protestant

Language: Spanish, English

Ethnic Divisions: Mestizo, Amerindian and mixed, white

Literacy Rate: 91%

Government: Constitutional Republic, with a president and a uni-cameral legislature, the Legislative Assembly, or Asamblea Legislativa. The president, two vice-presidents, and the 72 members of the legislature are directly elected to five-year terms. There are nine administrative provinces and two territories.

Armed services: 11,800 (1997) in the Public Force; national police, air service, and maritime service

Suffrage: Universal and compulsory; 18 years old

Economy: Panama's economy is largely fueled by the service revenue associated with the Panama Canal and the Colón Free Zone, which offers storage, assembly, and shipment services in one of the world's largest trading centers; international banking is also important. The government continues to work to reduce unemployment, attract additional foreign investment, and modernize other aspects of the economy.

Unit of currency: Balboa; 100 centésimos = 1 balboa (B)

GDP per capita: $6,700

Inflation rate–CPI: 1.2% (1997)

Workforce: 1,044,000 (1997 est.)

Unemployment rate: 13.1% (1997 est.)

Exports: Goods worth $592 million (f.o.b., 1997 est.) are sent to the U.S., the E.U., Central America and other Carribbean trading partners; exports include bananas, shrimp, sugar, clothing, and coffee.

Imports: Goods worth $2.95 billion (c.i.f., 1997 est.) are received from the U.S., Japan,and other E.U., Central American, and Caribbean trading partners; imports include capital goods, crude oil, food, and consumer goods.

Agriculture: 26.8% (1997) of the labor force engages in agriculture, hunting, fishing, and forestry. Cash commodities include bananas, sugar, and coffee; timber, shrimp, and livestock are also important. Bananas earned 43% (1997) of the total value of all exports. Rice, corn, and beans are the main crops grown for domestic use.

Energy: Hydropower is used for most energy generation.

Natural Resources: Copper, mahogany forests, shrimp

Environmental Issues: Water pollution, deforestation, land degradation

Transportation: There are 220 miles (360 km) of railroads and 6,890 miles (11,100 km) of roads, of which a third are paved. The 51-mile-long (82 km) Panama Canal, completed in 1914, carries 4% (1984 est.) of the world's total seaborne trade and connects Cristóbal on the Caribbean with Balboa on the Pacific. Other ports are Panama City on the Pacific and Colón on the Caribbean. An international airport is near Panama City.

Communications: Seven daily newspapers are published in Panama City. There are 298,000 radios, 10,000 televisions (1992 est.), and 63,200 phone lines (1986) in service. Telephone service is good.

Tourism: Panama City, beach resorts, and offshore tropical islands attract visitors to Panama, which earned $236 million (U.S.) from 412,000 visitors in 1996.

Embassy in U.S.: (202) 483-1407

Public Holidays: National Martyrs' Day (January 9); Carnival (dates vary, in February); Good Friday (date varies, in March or April); Labor Day (May 1); Revolution Day (October 11); National Anthem Day (November 1); All Souls' Day (November 2); Independence Day: from Colombia, 1903 (November 3); Flag Day (November 4); First Call of Independence (November 10); Independence Day: from Spain, 1821 (November 28); Immaculate Conception and Mothers' Day (December 8); Christmas (December 25)

Papua New Guinea

Country Name: Papua New Guinea

Official Name: Independent State of Papua New Guinea

Nationality: Papua New Guinean(s) (noun); Papua New Guinean (adjective)

Capital: Port Moresby, pop. 193,200

Major cities: N.A.

External Territories: None

Location: Papua New Guinea, in Oceania, lies north of Australia. The South Pacific Ocean is to the north and the Coral Sea to the south. It occupies the eastern half of the island of New Guinea; the Indonesian province of West Irian Jaya occupies the western half.

Physical Geography: Almost all of Papua New Guinea is on the island of New Guinea. New Guinea has high central mountains that descend to swampy lowlands on the north and south coasts and two major rivers: the Sepik on the north and the Fly on the south. Of the estimated 600 smaller islands, including the Bismarck Archipelago and Bougainville, some are volcanic and surrounded by coral formations.

Total area: 178,260 sq mi (461,691 sq km)

Coastline: 3,199 mi (5,152 km)

Land use: Forest and woodland cover 92.9% of the country; only 0.1% is considered arable.

Climate: Tropical, with rains from December to March and again from May to October; precipitation is heaviest along the coasts

Population: 4,669,000

Urban population: 15%

Rate of natural increase: 2.4%

Age structure: 40% under 15; 2% over 65

Birth rate: 34/1000

Death rate: 10/1000

Infant mortality rate: 77/1000

Fertility rate: 4.8

Life expectancy at birth: 56 years (male); 57 years (female)

Religion: Protestant, indigenous beliefs, Roman Catholic

Language: More than 700 indigenous languages

Ethnic Divisions: Melanesian, Papuan, negrito

Literacy Rate: 72%

Government: Parliamentary democracy, with a governor-general appointed by the British monarch and a unicameral legislature, the National Parliament. The 109 members of the legislature are directly elected to five-year terms. There are 20 administrative provinces.

Armed services: 4,300 volunteers (1997) in the army, navy, and air force

Suffrage: Universal; 18 years old

Economy: Minerals have provided much of the cash for Papua New Guinea's economy, but most of the the working population still labors in subsistence farming, and the economy has little income from manufacturing or service industries. International assistance is necessary, but the government is implementing programs to increase industrial privatization and decrease the deficit.

Unit of currency: Kina; 100 toea = 1 kina (K)

GDP per capita: $2,650

Inflation rate–CPI: 11.6% (1996)

Workforce: 1,941,000 (1995 est.)

Unemployment rate: N.A.

Exports: Goods worth $2.5 billion (f.o.b., 1996) are sent to Australia, the U.S., Japan, Singapore, the U.K., and other trading partners; exports include gold, copper ore, oil, logs, coffee, palm oil, cocoa, and lobster.

Imports: Goods worth $1.7 billion (c.i.f., 1996) are received from Australia, the United States, Singapore, Japan, the U.K., and other trading partners; imports include machinery, transportation equipment, manufactured goods, food, fuels, and chemicals.

Agriculture: 64% (1993) of the labor force engages in agriculture, forestry, and fishing. Cash commodities include coffee, cocoa, coconuts, palm oil, rubber, and tea. Vegetables, bananas, melons, and roots and tubers are grown for do-

PAPUA NEW GUINEA FOUR MILLION PEOPLE, 700 LANGUAGES

Papua New Guinea was once joined geologically and politically to Australia, which is less than 100 miles to its south. After nearly a century of colonial rule by Germany until 1947, when the region became a UN trust territory administered by Austria, the country became independent in 1975. Some 700 languages are spoken in Papua New Guinea, and although English is the official language, only a small percentage of the population speak it. The most widely spoken language is Enga, with more than 150,000 speakers; many Papuan languages have only a few hundred speakers.

mestic use. Timber earns 15.7% (1996) of the total value of exports.

Energy: Hydropower generates 30% of the country's energy, and ethanol is produced with sugar.

Natural Resources: Minerals, including gold, copper, silver, natural gas, oil; timber; mineral deposits account for 72% of total export earnings.

Environmental Issues: Deforestation, mining pollution

Transportation: There are no railroads. There are 12,180 miles (19,600 km) of roads, of which 430 miles (690 km) are paved. Main ports include Kieta on Bougainville, Lae, Madang, and Port Moresby on New Guinea and Rabaul on New Britian; an international airport is at Port Moresby.

Communications: There are numerous newspapers. There are 298,000 radios and 10,000 televisions (1992) in operation. Phone service, with 63,000 lines in service, is good.

Tourism: The country is developing a tourism plan to attract more visitors to enjoy forests, wildlife, and cultural exhibits (including a national museum and art gallery). In 1995, 42,328 tourist arrivals were noted.

Embassy in U.S.: (202) 745-3680

Public Holidays: Easter (date varies, in March or April); Queen's Official Birthday (date varies, in June); Remembrance Day (July 23); Independence Day and Constitution Day, 1975 (September 16); Christmas (December 25); Boxing Day (December 26)

Paraguay

Country Name: Paraguay

Official Name: Republic of Paraguay

Nationality: Paraguayan(s) (noun); Paraguayan (adjective)

Capital: Asunción, pop. 502,400

Major cities: San Lorenzo, Lambare, Fernando de la Mora, Caaguazú

External Territories: None

Location: Paraguay, a landlocked country in South America, is bordered on the northeast and east by Brazil, on the south and southwest by Argentina, and on the northwest by Bolivia.

Total area: 157,048 sq mi (406,752 sq km)

Coastline: None

Physical Geography: Hot and semiarid plains, part of the Gran Chaco that extends into Bolivia and Argentina, spread out from the western borders to the Paraguay River. Plateaus and hills cover the east, and mountains run along part of the border with Brazil. The Paraná River, in the east, forms Paraguaya's eastern border with Brazil and Argentina.

Land use: More than 50% of the land is meadows and pastures, 32% is wooded, and 6% is arable or used for crops.

Climate: Subtropical in the east; hotter in the west; rainfall generally decreasing from east to west

Population: 5,219,000

Urban population: 52%

Rate of natural increase: 2.7%

Age structure: 41% under 15; 4% over 65

Birth rate: 32.3/1000

Death rate: 5.6/1000

Infant mortality rate: 27/1000

Fertility rate: 4.5

Life expectancy at birth: 68 years (male); 72 years (female)

Religion: Roman Catholic

Language: Spanish, Guaraní

Ethnic Divisions: Mestizo, Indian

Literacy Rate: 92%

Government: Republic, with a president and a bicameral legislature, the National Congress. The president, 45 members of the Senate, and 80 members of the Chamber of Deputies are all directly elected to office for five-year terms. There are 17 administrative departments.

Armed services: 20,200 troops (1997) in the army, navy, and air force; compulsory service: one year in army, two years in navy

Suffrage: Universal; 18 years old; compulsory for people between 18 and 60 years of age

Economy: Agricultural exports and light industries are the keys to Paraguay's current economy. The government is working to modernize agricultural practices, encouraging domestic and foreign investment in other economic ventures, and promoting industrial privatization. However, some stringent financial measures have resulted in strikes and protests by workers, and the government is collaborating with the international community to find ways to resolve its external debt.

Unit of currency: Guaraní; 100 centimos = 1 guarani (G)

GDP per capita: $3,900

Inflation rate–CPI: 6.2 (1997)

Workforce: 1.8 million (1995 est.)

Unemployment rate: 8.2% (urban) (1996 est.)

Exports: Goods worth $1.1 billion (f.o.b., 1997) are sent to Brazil, the Netherlands, Argentina, Chile, the U.S., and other trading partners;

exports include cotton, soybeans, timber, vegetable oils, meat, coffee, and tung oil.

Imports: Goods worth $2.5 billion (c.i.f., 1996) are received from Brazil, Argentina, the U.S., Hong Kong, and other trading partners; imports include capital goods, foodstuffs, consumer goods, raw materials, and fuels.

Agriculture: 45% of the workforce engages in agriculture, fishing, and forestry. Cash crops include soybeans and other oil-seed crops, cotton, sugarcane, wheat, maize, rice, tobacco, timber, and beef.

Energy: Most energy is generated using hydropower; imported oil is also used. The Itaipú Dam on the Paraná, built cooperatively with Brazil, furnishes much of the country's energy.

Natural Resources: Minerals, including iron, manganese, limestone; timber; hydropower

Environmental Issues: Deforestation, water pollution

Transportation: There are 603 miles (971 km) of railroads and 18,320 miles (29,500 km) of roads, of which 1,740 miles (2,800 km) are paved. There are 1,930 miles (3,100 km) of navigable waters in the country, including the Paraguay and Paraná Rivers, and some ocean-going vessels can navigate the Paraná from its mouth north of Buenos Aires, Argentina, on the Atlantic Ocean. River ports include Asunción and Villeta on the Paraguay and Encarnación on the Paraná. International airports are at Asunción and Ciudad del Este.

Communications: Five daily newspapers are published in the capital (1994). There are 775,000 radios and 370,000 televisions (1992) in operation. There are 88,730 telephone lines (1985 est.), which provide rudimentary service.

Tourism: More than 405,000 visitors spent $197 million (U.S.) in Paraguay in 1994. Attractions include the spectacular Itaipú Dam, wildlife and fishing opportunities in the west, and the baroque church in Yaguarón.

Embassy in U.S.: (202) 483-6960

Public Holidays: Day of San Blás, Patron Saint of Paraguay (February 3); Heroes' Day (March 1); Maundy Thursday (date varies, in March or April); Good Friday (date varies, in March or April); Ascension Day (date varies, in May); Labor Day (May 1); Independence Day celebrations: from Spain, 1811 (May 14–15); Corpus Christi (date varies, in June); Peace of Chaco (June 12); Founding of Asunción, 1537 (August 15); Constitution Day (August 25); Battle of Boquerón (September 29); Day of the race: discovery of America Day (October 12); All Saints' Day (November 1); Immaculate Conception (December 8); Christmas (December 25)

Peru

Country Name: Peru

Official Name: Republic of Peru

Nationality: Peruvian(s) (noun); Peruvian (adjective)

Capital: Lima, pop. 5,681,900 [6,321,000]

Major cities: Arequipa, Trujillo, Callao

External Territories: None

Location: Peru, on the Pacific coast of South America, is bordered on the north by Ecuador and Colombia, on the east by Brazil and Bolivia, and on the south by Chile.

Physical Geography: A narrow and dry coastal strip meets ranges of the Andes, which run north to south through the central part of the country. In the east, the Andes descend to the Amazon River Basin. Lake Titicaca, in the south, is on the border with Bolivia. The Marañon and Ucayali Rivers, in the east, are tributaries of the Amazon.

Total area: 496,225 sq mi (1,285,217 sq km)

Coastline: 1,499 mi (2,414 km)

Land use: Forest and woodland cover 66% of the country, 21% is meadows and pastures, and 3% of the land is arable or used for agriculture.

Climate: Varies from east to west; tropical in the Amazon lowlands, with heavy rainfall; mostly temperate in the mountains, with large ranges in daily temperatures; permanent snow at higher elevations; dry and temperate on the coast; extremely dry in the south

Population: 26,624,000

Urban population: 72%

Rate of natural increase: 2.2%

Age structure: 35% under 15; 5% over 65

Birth rate: 27.8/1000

Death rate: 6/1000

Infant mortality rate: 43/1000

Fertility rate: 3.5

Life expectancy at birth: 66 years (male); 71 years (female)

Religion: Roman Catholic

Language: Spanish, Quechua (both official), Aymara

Ethnic Divisions: Indian, mestizo, white

Literacy Rate: 89%

Government: Republic, with a president and a unicameral legislature, the Congress. The president, two vice-presidents, and the 120 members of the legislature are elected to five-year terms. There are 24 administrative departments and one constitutional province.

Armed services: 125,000 troops (1997) in the army, navy, and air force; selective conscription

PERU MACHU PICCHU: A CELESTIALLY SIGNIFICANT SITE

Peru's best-known Inca site, the holy sanctuary of Machu Picchu high in the Andes Mountains, is a mystery of archaeology—no one knows for sure why it was built around 1500 or what it meant to the Inca. But it sits in a unique geographic location, surrounded on three sides by sacred Inca mountains that reveal the site's celestial significance. The summit of Salcantay points directly to the Southern Cross constellation—the Inca symbol of water and fertility—during the rainy season. On the day of the December solstice, at the beginning of the rainy season, the sun sets directly behind Pumasillo mountain. On the days of the fall and spring equinoxes, the sun rises behind Nevada Verónica, and on the day of the June solstice, the sun rises behind San Gabriel mountain.

Suffrage: Universal; 18 years old

Economy: Financial reforms, begun in 1990 and including tax reforms, debt restructuring, industrial privatization, and inflation restrictions, have convinced international lenders that Peru is committed to generating economic growth and repaying foreign debts. However, because many Peruvians still live in poverty and large numbers of the working population are unemployed, the government hopes to increase funding for social programs. Meanwhile, fishing, mining, and tourism are viewed as prime industries for additional growth.

Unit of currency: Nuevo sol; 100 céntimos = 1 nuevo sol (S/)

GDP per capita: $4,420

Inflation rate–CPI: 6.7%

Workforce: 7.6 million (1996 est.)

Unemployment rate: 8.2% (1996 est.); extensive underemployment (1996 est.)

Exports: Goods worth $5.9 billion (f.o.b, 1996) are sent to the U.S., Japan, the U.K., China, and other trading partners; exports include copper, zinc, fishmeal, oil, lead, silver, coffee, and cotton.

Imports: Goods worth $9.2 billion (f.o.b, 1996.) are received from the U.S., Colombia, Chile, Venezuela, and other trading partners; imports include machinery, transportation equipment, food, oil, iron and steel, chemicals, and pharmaceuticals.

Agriculture: 33% of the labor force engages in agriculture, fishing, and forestry. Rice, potatoes, and maize are principally raised for domestic use, and coffee is grown for export; seafood and seafood products are also important commodities. Coca, from which cocaine is derived, generates significant amounts of cash for its cultivators.

Energy: Domestic petroleum and hydropower are used for the majority of energy generation.

Natural Resources: Minerals, including copper, silver, gold, oil, iron ore, coal, phosphates, and potash; timber; seafood

Environmental Issues: Deforestation, desertification, air and water pollution

Transportation: There are 1,268 miles (2,041 km) of railroads and 45,210 miles (72,800 km) of roads, of which 8,345 miles (13,438 km) are paved. Callao, Salaverry, San Juan, and Paita are among 17 deepwater seaports. There are 5,341 miles (8,600 km) of navigable waters, including Lake Titicaca and Amazon River tributaries. Iquitos is an important Amazon port; other river ports include Pucallpa on the Uycayali and Yurimaguas on the Huallaga. International airports are at Lima, Cuzco, and Arequipa.

Communications: Twelve cities have daily newspapers; Lima has seven. There are 5.7 million radios and 2 million televisions (1993) in operation; 779,300 phone lines provide adequate service.

Tourism: The famed Inca ruins at Machu Picchu, the Inca city of Cuzco, and Lake Titicaca are three of Peru's prime tourist attractions. Museums, churches, and colonial buildings in Lima and Arequipa are also attractions. Iquitos is a popular Amazon stop. In 1994, 386,000 visitors spent $402 million (U.S) in Peru.

Embassy in U.S.: (202) 833-9860

Public Holidays: Maundy Thursday (date varies, in March or April); Good Friday (date varies, in March or April); Labor Day (May 1); Day of the Peasant (June 24); St. Peter and St. Paul (June 29); Independence: from Spain, 1821 (July 28–29); St. Rose of Lima (August 30); All Saints' Day (November 1); Immaculate Conception (December 8); Christmas (December 25)

Philippines

Country Name: Philippines

Official Name: Republic of the Philippines

Nationality: Filipino(s) (noun); Philippine (adjective)

Capital: Manila, pop. 1,654,800 [8,594,200]

Major cities: Quezon City, Davao, Cebu, Zamboanga

External Territories: None

Location: The Philippines, off mainland southeastern Asia, is an island country made up of some 7,100 islands in the Pacific Ocean, between the South China Sea and the Philippine Sea. The two largest islands are Luzon and Mindanao.

Physical Geography: The islands are mountainous, with narrow coastal plains; some volcanoes, such as Mount Pinatubo on Luzon, are active.

Total area: 115,831 sq mi (300,000 sq km)

Coastline: 22,536 mi (36,289 km)

Land use: About 45% of the land is forested, 31% is arable or under cultivation, and 4% is meadows and pastures.

Climate: Tropical; some parts of the country receive rain year round; dry season from November to April in other regions; temperatures vary with elevation

Population: 74,655,000

Urban population: 47%

Rate of natural increase: 2.3%

Age structure: 38% under 15; 4% over 65

Birth rate: 29/1000

Death rate: 7/1000

Infant mortality rate: 35/1000

Fertility rate: 3.7

Life expectancy at birth: 66 years (male); 69 years (female)

Religion: Roman Catholic, Protestant, Muslim, Buddhist

Language: Tagalog, English (both official)

Ethnic Divisions: Malay

Literacy Rate: 95%

Government: Republic, with a president and a bicameral legislature, the Congress, or the Kongreso. The president is directly elected for a single six-year term. The 24 members of the Senate are directly elected for six-year terms; of the 254 members of the House of Representatives, 204 are directly elected and 50 from minority groups are ap-

PHILIPPINES PREDICTING PINATUBO ERUPTION SAVED LIVES

One of the 20th century's biggest volcanic eruptions occurred in the Philippines on June 15, 1991, when Mount Pinatubo blew two cubic miles of ash into the atmosphere—enough to bury Washington, D.C., under a layer 150 feet thick. The sulfur dioxide cloud took 21 days to circle the globe, deflecting about 2 percent of the sun's light and leading to slightly lower temperatures, on average, around the world. Nearly 900 people died and more than 110,000 homes were destroyed. The death toll would have been greater, but scientists had predicted the eruption, allowing some 200,000 people to be evacuated.

pointed to office by the president. There are 16 administrative regions.

Armed services: 110,500 troops (1997) in the army, navy, and air force

Suffrage: Universal; 18 years old

Economy: Although economic reforms introduced in 1992 helped generate economic growth, the gap between rich and poor has generally widened, and inflation has risen as a result of food shortages and rising fuel prices. The effects of a generally unfavorable trade balance have been offset somewhat by remittances from citizens working abroad. Plans continue for deregulating industry, improving infrastructure, and overhauling the tax structure.

Unit of currency: Philippine peso; 100 centavos = 1 Philippine peso (P)

GDP per capita: $3,200

Inflation rate–CPI: 5.1% (1997)

Workforce: 29.13 million (1996 est.)

Unemployment rate: 8.7% (1997)

Exports: Goods worth $25 billion (f.o.b., 1997 est.) are sent to the U.S., Japan, Germany, Hong Kong, the U.K., and other trading partners; exports include telecommunications machinery and transport equipment.

Imports: Goods worth $34 billion (f.o.b., 1997 est.) are received from Japan, the U.S., Singapore, Taiwan, South Korea, and other trading

partners; imports include raw materials, capital goods, and oil products.

Agriculture: Nearly 45% (1996 est.) of the workforce engages in agriculture, fishing, and forestry. Rice, maize, and cassava are raised for domestic use; coconuts, sugarcane, bananas, and pineapples are key export commodities. Illegal logging, banned since 1989, also generates revenue.

Energy: Imported oil generates about 50% of the country's energy needs; the balance is supplemented by hydropower and some geothermal energy.

Natural Resources: Minerals, including oil, nickel, cobalt, silver, gold, salt, copper; timber

Environmental Issues: Deforestation, soil erosion, air and water pollution

Transportation: There are 5600 miles (900 km) of railroads, mostly on Luzon and Panay, and 96,500 miles (157,000 km). Waters navigable by shallow-draft boats total 2,000 miles (3,220 km). Main seaports include Manila, on Luzon; Cebu on Cebu; Iloilo, on Panay; and Cagayan de Oro, Davao, General Santos, and Zamboanga on Mindinao. International airports on Luzon are at Manila and Subic Bay; on Cebu at Cebu; on Mindinao at Davao and Zamboanga; and on Palawan at Puerto Princesa.

Communications: The country has nearly 45 daily newspapers, of which 25 are published in Manila. There are 9 million radios (1992 est.) and 9.2 million televisions (1998 est.); phone service, with some 1.9 million phones in use (1997), is adequate.

Tourism: Island resorts, with beaches, fishing, sailing, snorkeling, and windsurfing, are strong draws for visitors to the Philippines. Museums and parks in Manila and jungle getaways are popular options for tourists, who numbered 1.6 million in 1995 and spent $2.45 billion.

U.S. Tourist Office: (212) 575-7915

Embassy in U.S.: (202) 467-9300

Public Holidays: Freedom Day, anniversary of People's Revolution (February 25); Maundy Thursday (date varies, in March or April); Good Friday (date varies, in March or April); Labor Day (May 1); Araw ng Kagitingan (May 6); Independence Day (June 12); National Heroes' Day (August 27); Barangay Day (September 11); National Thanksgiving Day (September 21); All Saints' Day (November 1); Bonifacio Day (November 30); Christmas (December 25); Rizal Day (December 30); Last Day of the Year (December 31)

Poland

Country Name: Poland
Official Name: Republic of Poland
Nationality: Pole(s) (noun); Polish (adjective)
Capital: Warsaw, pop. 1,632,500
Major cities: Łódź, Kraków, Wrocław
External Territories: None

POLAND TREASURES OF SALT

Kraków is one of the few European cities to escape the bombings of World War II. One of its most intriguing tourist attractions is the Wieliczka salt mine near the city. Beginning in the 17th century, miners sculpted reliefs and statues of saints, kings, and heroes out of the rock salt, creating galleries of salt art. In recent years, pollution and humidity were causing the salt to dissolve, so air coolers and a dehumidifier have been installed to preserve these unusual art forms.

Location: Poland, in eastern Europe, is bordered on the north by the Baltic Sea, the Russian enclave of Kaliningrad Oblast, and Lithuania; on the east by Belarus and Ukraine; on the south by Slovakia and the Czech Republic, and on the west by Germany.

Physical Geography: The Carpathian Mountains in the south and southwest give way to smaller, low-lying hills. Central lowlands are bordered to the north by plains dotted with small lakes and peat bogs, and there are sand dunes and swamps along the Baltic coast. Major rivers include the Vistula, Oder, and Bug.

Total area: 120,725 sq mi (312,677 sq km)

Coastline: 305 mi (491 km)

Land use: Nearly 50% of the land is arable or under cultivation, 29% is wooded, and 13% is meadows and pastures.

Climate: Temperate, with cold, wet winters and warm summers

Population: 38,674,000

Urban population: 62%

Rate of natural increase: 0.1%

Age structure: 21% under 15; 12% over 65

Birth rate: 10/1000

Death rate: 10/1000

Infant mortality rate: 9.6/1000

Fertility rate: 1.5

Life expectancy at birth: 69 years (male); 77 years (female)

Religion: Roman Catholic
Language: Polish
Ethnic Divisions: Polish
Literacy Rate: 99%

Government: Republic, with a president and a bicameral legislature, the National Assembly. The president is directly elected to a five-year term. The 100 members of the Senat and the 460 members of the Sejm are elected to four-year terms. There are 49 administrative provinces, or voivodships.

Armed services: 241,750 troops (1997) in the army, navy, and air force; 18-month service

Suffrage: Universal; 18 years old

Economy: The transition from a planned to a market economy, begun with independence from the Soviet Union in 1989, has brought about high unemployment and other problems in the country; the government continues to focus on privatizing industry, reducing budget deficits and inflation, reforming social security, and restructuring and modernizing heavy industry. Foreign investment is encouraged, and exports to neighboring countries have increased.

Unit of currency: Złoty; 100 groszy (grosz, singular) = 1 new złoty (Zl)

GDP per capita: $2,250

Inflation rate–CPI: 15% (1997)

Workforce: 17.7 million (1997 est.)

Unemployment rate: 12% (1997)

Exports: Goods worth $26.4 billion (f.o.b., 1997 est.) are sent to Germany, the Netherlands, Russia, Italy, and other trading partners; exports include intermediate goods, machinery, transportation equipment, consumer goods, foodstuffs, and fuels.

Imports: Goods worth $44.5 billion (f.o.b., 1997 est.) are received from Germany, Italy, Russia, the U.K., and other trading partners; imports include machinery and transportation equipment, intermediate goods, chemicals, and consumer goods.

Agriculture: 26% (1996) of the workforce engages in agriculture, fishing, and forestry. Main crops include potatoes, fruits, vegetables. Livestock is also an important commodity.

Energy: Domestic coal generates 80% of the country's energy.

Natural Resources: Minerals, including coal, sulfur, copper, silver, lead, salt; natural gas

Environmental Issues: Air and water pollution

Transportation: There are 15,100 miles (24,310 km) of railroads and 232,870 miles (374,990) of roads, of which 152,300 miles (245,240 km) are paved. Many rivers, lakes, and canals in Poland are part of a substantial inland waterway network of 2,370 miles (3,810 km). Baltic seaports are Gdynia, Gdańsk, and Szczecin. Several international airports in the country provide service from Warsaw, Gdańsk, and Kraków.

Communications: Nearly 20 Polish cities publish daily newspapers; nine dailies are published in Warsaw. There are 9.9 million radios, 9.4 million televisions, and 8.2 million phone lines (1996). Phone service needs updating.

Tourism: Poland's attractions brought 87.4 million visitors in 1996. Health spas are a key attraction for other Europeans, while forests, and Kraków and other historic cities are also popular draws.

U.S. Tourist Office: (212) 338-9412
Embassy in U.S.: (202) 234-3800

Public Holidays: Easter Monday (date varies, in March or April); Labor Day (May 1); Polish National Day: proclamation of constitution, 1791 (May 3); Victory Day (May 9); Corpus Christi (date varies, in May or June); Assumption (August 15); All Saints' Day (November 1); Independence Day: proclamation of independent republic, 1918 (November 11); Christmas (December 25–26)

Portugal

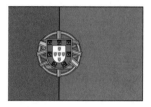

Country Name: Portugal
Official Name: Portuguese Republic
Nationality: Portuguese (singular and plural noun); Portuguese (adjective)
Capital: Lisbon, pop. 663,400 [2,561,200]
Major cities: Porto, Vila Nova de Gaia, Amadora, Cascais
External Territories: Macau, on the coast of the South China Sea, surrounded by China (6.5 sq mi, 17 sq km; pop. 429,152). Macau is scheduled to be returned to China in December 1999.

Location: Portugal, in southwestern Europe on the Iberian Peninsula, is bordered on the north and east by Spain and by the Atlantic Ocean on the west and south. The Azores and Madeira Islands are also Portuguese territory.

Physical Geography: Highlands and mountains are found in the northern part of the country; coastal lowlands and hills cover the south-ern section. Major rivers, from north to south, include the Douro, Tagus, and Guadiana.

Total area: 35,672 sq mi (92,389 sq km)
Coastline: 1,114 mi (1,793 km)
Land use: Woodland and forest cover 36% of the country, 35% is arable or under cultivation, and 9% is meadows and pastures.
Climate: Generally temperate, with cool winters and warm summers; temperatures increase and precipitation decreases from north to south

Population: 9,992,000
Urban population: 48%
Rate of natural increase: 0.1%
Age structure: 17% under 15; 15% over 65
Birth rate: 11/1000
Death rate: 11/1000
Infant mortality rate: 6.4/1000
Fertility rate: 1.5
Life expectancy at birth: 71 years (male); 79 years (female)
Religion: Roman Catholic
Language: Portuguese
Ethnic Divisions: Portuguese
Literacy Rate: 85%

Government: Republic, with a unicameral legislature, the Assembly of the Republic. The president is directly elected to a five-year term, and the 230 members of the Assembly are directly elected to four-year terms. There are nine administrative regions and two autonomous regions, the Azores and Madeira.
Armed services: 59,300 troops (1997) in the army, navy, and air force; compulsory service: 4–8 months in army, 4–18 months in navy and air force
Suffrage: Universal; 18 years old

Economy: In trying to spur economic growth and development in the country, which lags behind much of western Europe, Portugal's government has focused on efforts to decrease the budget deficit, increase social welfare spending, decrease unemployment, modernize industry and infrastructure, and privatize state-owned companies, especially telecommunication, electricity, and cement companies.

Unit of currency: Portuguese escudo; 100 centavos = 1 Portuguese escudo (Esc)

GDP per capita: $15,200

Inflation rate–CPI: 2.3% (1997 est.)

Workforce: 4.53 million (1996 est.)

Unemployment rate: 7% (1998 est.)

Exports: Goods worth $23.8 billion (f.o.b., 1996 est.) are sent to France, Germany, Spain, and other trading partners; exports include clothing, footwear, machinery, cork, paper products, and hides.

Imports: Goods worth $33.9 billion (c.i.f., 1996 est.) are received from France, Spain, Germany, and other trading partners; imports include machinery, transportation equipment, agricultural products, chemicals, oil, and textiles.

Agriculture: 11% (1995) of the labor force engages in agriculture, forestry, and fishing. Grain, potatoes, olives, grapes, and sheep are key commodities.

Energy: Imported oil and hydropower are used to generate energy.

Natural Resources: Fish, cork, iron ore, tungsten, uranium, marble

Environmental Issues: Soil erosion, air and water pollution

Transportation: There are 1,910 miles (3,070 km) of railroads and 42,680 miles (68,730 km) of roads, of which 36,710 (59,110 km) are paved. (Lisbon, Porto, Setúbal, and Funchal on Madeira are important seaports; passenger cruise ships call at Portimão and in the Azores. International airports are at Lisbon, Porto, Faro, Funchal on Madeira, and two in the Azores.

Communications: Daily newspapers are published in eight cities; Lisbon has seven dailies. There are 2.2 million radios and 2.97 million televisions in operation (1993 est.). Phone service, with 3.72 million telephones in operation (1996), is adequate.

Tourism: Portugal is a popular tourist destination and earned $4.34 billion (U.S.) from 23.1 million visitors in 1995, who came to tour Lisbon, winter along the warm and quiet southern coast, and visit resorts on the Madeira and Azores Islands.

U.S. Tourist Office: (800) 767-8842

Embassy in U.S.: (202) 328-8610

Public Holidays: Carnival Day (date varies, in February); Good Friday (date varies, in March or April); Liberty Day (April 25); Labor Day (May 1); Corpus Christi (date varies, in June); Portugal Day (June 10); Assumption (August 15); Proclamation of the Republic, 1910 (October 5); All Saints' Day (November 1); Restoration of In-

dependence (December 1); Immaculate Conception (December 8); Christmas (December 25)

Qatar

Country Name: Qatar

Official Name: State of Qatar

Nationality: Qatari(s) (noun); Qatari (adjective)

Capital: Doha, pop. [339,471]

Major cities: N.A.

External Territories: None

Location: Qatar, in the Middle East, is located on a peninsula in the Persian Gulf, on the northeastern coast of the Arabian Peninsula. It is bordered on the south by Saudi Arabia.

Physical Geography: Qatar is flat, with sand dunes in the southeast and desert in most of the rest of the country. Many islands and coral reefs in the Persian Gulf are also Qatari territory.

Total area: 4,247 sq mi (11,000 sq km)

Coastline: 350 mi (563 km)

Land use: Only 5% of the land can be used for meadows and pastures. Negligible arable land or forests and woodlands; most is desert.

Climate: Tropical, with dry winters and humid summers

Population: 541,000

Urban population: 91%

Rate of natural increase: 1.7%

Age structure: 27% under 15; 1% over 65

Birth rate: 19/1000

Death rate: 2/1000

Infant mortality rate: 20/1000

Fertility rate: 4.0

Life expectancy at birth: 70 years (male); 75 years (female)

PORTUGAL MACAU'S CASINOS HELP PAY THE WAY

Macau, a Portuguese colony since 1557 and the last European outpost in Asia, will be turned over to the Chinese in 1999. A Chinese official is said to have leased land to the Portuguese that is now part of Macau, and for nearly 100 years it was a trading hub for goods from China, Japan, the Spice Islands, India, and Europe. In the 1970's Portugal offered to return the island to China. Even though China frowns on gambling, Macau's main industry for 150 years has been its gambling casinos, and it appears that China is likely to let them remain—no doubt because the tax income they generate pays for more than one-third of the government's costs.

Religion: Muslim

Language: Arabic, English

Ethnic Divisions: Arab, Pakistani, Indian, Iranian

Literacy Rate: 79%

Government: Traditional monarchy —Amir Sheikh Hamad bin Khalifa Thani, since 1995—with an Advisory Council. Elections were proposed in 1970 for the 30 council seats but have not yet been held. There are nine administrative municipalities.

Armed services: 11,800 troops (1996) in the army, navy, and air force

Suffrage: None

Economy: Like many of its neighbors, Qatar's economy is dependent upon oil production, and the country also exports natural gas. The government is encouraging the development and diversification of other industrial enterprises, as well as building up the country's infrastructure.

Unit of currency: Qatari riyal; 100 dirhams = 1 Qatari riyal (QR)

GDP per capita: $16,700

Inflation rate–CPI: 2.5% (1996)

Workforce: 233,000 (1993 est.); non-Qataris make up much of the labor force

Unemployment rate: N.A.

Exports: Goods worth $5.8 billion (F.O.B., 1997 est.) are sent to Japan, Singapore, South Korea, and other trading partners; exports include petroleum products, steel, and fertilizers.

Imports: Goods worth $5 billion (f.o.b., 1997 est.) are received from Italy, the U.K., France, Japan, Germany, the U.S., and other trading partners; imports include machinery, consumer goods, food, and chemicals.

Agriculture: 3.1% of the workforce engages in agriculture and fishing. Cereal, vegetables, and fruits are cultivated for domestic consumption and some export. Livestock and fish are also significant; the country is nearly self-sufficient in vegetables.

Energy: Domestic petroleum and natural gas are used to generate energy; solar energy is also being developed.

Natural Resources: Oil, natural gas, seafood

Environmental Issues: Limited freshwater

Transportation: There are no railroads. There are 760 miles (1,230 km) of roads, of which the majority are paved. Doha, Umm Sa'īd, and Ḩālūl are key seaports, and there is an international airport at Doha.

Communications: Doha has six daily newspapers. There are 201,000 radios and 205,000 televisions (1992 est.); 160,700 main telephone lines provide modern service.

Tourism: Historic forts, beaches, and Doha museums and markets attract tourists to Qatar. There were 309,000 visitors to the country in 1995.

Embassy in U.S.: (202) 274-1600

Public Holidays: Beginning of Ramadan (date varies); End of Ramadan (date varies, in February); Feast of the Sacrifice (date varies, in April); Islamic New Year (date varies, in April or May); Anniversary of the Amir Sheikh Hamad bin Khalifa Al Thani's Accession, 1995 (June 27); National Day: independence from the U.K., 1971 (September 3); Ascension of the Prophet (date varies, in November or December)

Romania

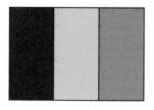

Country Name: Romania
Official Name: Romania

Nationality: Romanian(s) (noun); Romanian (adjective)

Capital: Bucharest, pop. 2,037,300

Major cities: Constanţa; Iaşi; Cluj-Napoca, Timişoara, Galaţi

External Territories: None

Location: Romania, in southeastern Europe, is bordered on the north by Ukraine, on the east by Moldova and the Black Sea, on the south by Bulgaria, on the southwest by Yugoslavia, and on the west by Hungary.

Total area: 92,699 sq mi (237,499 sq km)

Coastline: 140 mi (225 km)

Physical Geography: Ranges of the Carpathian Mountains run from the north through the central section of the country; the Transylvanian Alps, which trend east and west, surround the Transylvanian Basin in the country's midsection. Plains lie in the south and east. The Danube River forms the border with Bulgaria and flows into the Black Sea.

Land use: Nearly 45% of the land is arable or under cultivation, 29% is forested, and 21% is meadows and pastures.

Climate: Continental, with cold, wet winters and hot summers

Population: 22,460,000

Urban population: 55%

Rate of natural increase: -0.1%

Age structure: 19% under 15; 13% over 65

Birth rate: 11/1000

Death rate: 12/1000

Infant mortality rate: 20.5/1000

Fertility rate: 1.3

Life expectancy at birth: 65 years (male); 73 years (female)

Religion: Romanian Orthodox, Roman Catholic, Protestant

Language: Romanian, Hungarian, German

Ethnic Divisions: Romanian, Hungarian

Literacy Rate: 97%

Government: Republic, with a president and a bicameral legislature, the Parliament. The president, the 343 members of the Chamber of Deputies, and the 143 members of the Senate are all directly elected to four-year terms. There are 40 administrative counties and one municipality.

Armed services: 226,950 troops (1997) in the army, navy, and air force; compulsory service: lasts 12 months in army and air force; 18 months in the navy

Suffrage: Universal; 18 years old

Economy: Romania's switch from a planned to a market economy, begun in 1989, is slowly resulting in needed economic growth. Industry privatization, foreign investments, austerity measures, and an increase in exports have helped to bring about economic recovery, and the government is planning to develop and diversify agricultural and tourist industries.

Unit of currency: Leu (singular), lei (plural); 100 bani (ban, singular) = 1 leu (L)

GDP per capita: $15,300

Inflation rate–CPI: 151% (1997 est.)

Workforce: 10.1 million (1996 est.)

Unemployment rate: 8.8% (1997 est.)

Exports: Goods worth $8.4 billion (f.o.b., 1997 est.) are sent to Germany, Italy, France, China, Turkey, and other trading partners; exports include textiles and footwear, metals and metal products, and chemicals.

Imports: Goods worth $10.4 billion (f.o.b., 1997 est.) are received from Germany, Russia, Italy, Iran, France, and other trading partners; imports include fuels and minerals, machinery and transport equipment, food and agricultural products, and chemicals.

Agriculture: 34.4% (1995) of the labor force engages in agriculture, hunting, and forestry; wheat, corn, sugar beets, sunflower seed, and potatoes are significant cash crops. Wine, reeds, and fish farms are also important. About 80% of the farms have been privatized by 1995.

Energy: Domestic and imported oil, natural gas, and coal are used for energy generation. The country also uses hydroelectric power and has one nuclear power station.

Natural Resources: Petroleum (reserves declining), timber, natural gas, coal, iron ore, salt

Environmental Issues: Soil, water, and air pollution

Transportation: There are 7,060 miles (11,360 km) of railroads and 95,120 miles (153,170 km) of roads, of which about half are paved. The Danube River is an important inland waterway, with ports at Giurgiu, Brăila, Galaţi, and Tulcea; Constanţa is the principal Black Sea port. International airports are at Bucharest, Constanţa, Timişoara, and Arad.

Communications: Nearly 73 daily newspapers are published in the country; Bucharest has 14 dailies. There are 4.6 million radios and 4.6 million televisions in operation (1992); phone service, with 2.8 million phones in use, needs upgrading to meet demand.

Tourism: In 1994, 5.9 million visitors spent $414 million (U.S.). Visitors are drawn by Black Sea resorts, health spas, mountains, castles and sites associated with Dracula, including the town of Tirgovişte, the location of Dracula's palace.

U.S. Tourist Office:(212) 697-6971

Embassy in U.S.: (202) 332-4848

Public Holidays: Good Friday (date varies, in March or April); Easter Monday (date varies, in March or April); International Labor Day (May 1–2); National Day, 1990 (December 1); Christmas (December 25)

Russia

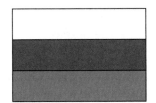

Country Name: Russia

Official Name: Russian Federation

Nationality: Russian(s) (noun); Russian (adjective)

Capital: Moscow, pop. 8,368,400 [8,598,900]

Major cities: St. Petersburg, Novosibirsk, Nizhniy Novgorod, Yekaterinburg, Samara, Omsk, Ufa

External Territories: None

Location: Russia stretches from the North Pacific Ocean in Asia to the Baltic Sea in Europe. The Arctic Ocean is on the north. Russia's Asian borders, from east to west, are North Korea, China, Mongolia, and Kazakhstan, the Caspian Sea, Azerbaijan, Georgia, and the Black Sea. European borders, north to south, are Norway, Finland, the Baltic Sea, Estonia, Latvia, Belarus, and Ukraine. An enclave on the Baltic is between Lithuania and Poland.

Physical Geography: The north-south trending Ural Mountains, traditionally regarded as the boundary between Europe and Asia, mark the extent of the Russian Plain in northeastern Europe. European Russia is further separated into the glaciated lowlands of the north, with many small lakes and swamps, and the southern plains, where rivers such as the Volga and Dnieper have formed more extensive valleys and ravines in the higher relief. The Caucasus Mountains, including El'brus, the highest point in Europe at 18,054 feet (5,642 m), border European Russia to the south. Siberia is east of the Urals, in Asia, and the West Siberian Plains gradually rise to meet

RUSSIA KAMCHATKA: RUSSIA'S FAR-FLUNG PACIFIC OUTPOST

The Russian peninsula of Kamchatka—a land twice the size of England, Scotland, and Wales combined—lies northeast of Japan, nine times zones away from Moscow, near the Aleutian Islands between the Bering Sea and the Okhotsk Sea. Now becoming important to Russian business interests in the Pacific Rim, the region is part of the Pacific's Ring of Fire. It features a 500-mile stretch of volcanoes, as well as forests and tundra, home to foxes, sables, deer, and brown bears.

the Central Siberian Plateau, which then slopes to the Arctic Ocean. Mountain ranges border the Pacific coast on the Sea of Japan, the Sea of Okhotsk, and the Bering Sea. Lake Baikal, the world's deepest lake at 5,238 feet (1,637 m), is in Siberia. The Yenisey-Angara, Lena, and Ob-Irtysh Rivers flow north into the Arctic Ocean.

Total area: 6,592,692 sq mi (17,074,993 sq km)

Coastline: 23,383 mi (37,653 km)

Land use: Woodland and forest cover 46% of the land, 8% is arable, and 4% is meadows and pastures.

Climate: Mostly continental, with severe winters (especially at the higher latitudes) and hot summers; across Siberia, precipitation generally increases from east to west; climatic conditions vary greatly with latitude and elevation

Population: 146,519,000

Urban population: 73%

Rate of natural increase: -0.5%

Age structure: 20% under 15; 13% over 65

Birth rate: 9/1000

Death rate: 14/1000

Infant mortality rate: 16.6/1000

Fertility rate: 1.2

Life expectancy at birth: 61 years (male); 73 years (female)

Religion: Russian Orthodox

Language: Russian

Ethnic Divisions: Russian, Tatar, many others

Literacy Rate: 98%

Government: Republic, with a president and a bicameral legislature, the Federal Assembly. The president is elected by direct vote to a four-year term. The 178 members of the Federation Council are appointed to office, and the 450 members of the State Duma are directly elected to four-year terms. There are 21 republics, 49 oblasts, 6 provinces, 10 autonomous districts, and one autonomous oblast.

Armed services: 1,240,000 troops (1997) in the army, air force, navy; compulsory service for 18 to 24 months

Suffrage: Universal; 18 years old

Economy: The transition from a planned to a market economy, begun in December 1991, is progressing slowly. Initial plans for privatizing industry have not been met, although some transitions have occurred. Foreign debt, unemployment, capital flight, and deteriorating manufacturing facilities hinder national economic growth. However, the country has abundant natural resources, a strong service sector, and ample workers, all of which are key in the quest for economic stability.

Unit of currency: Ruble; 100 kopeks = 1 ruble (R)

GDP per capita: $4,700

Inflation rate–CPI: 11% (1997 est.)

Workforce: 66 million (1997)

Unemployment rate: 9% (1997)

Exports: Goods worth $86.7 billion (1997) are sent to Europe, North America, Japan, Third World Countries; exports include petroleum, petroleum products, natural gas, wood and wood products, metals, and chemicals.

Imports: Goods worth $66.9 billion (1997) are received from Europe, North America, Japan, and Third World Countries, and other trading partners; imports include machinery, consumer goods, medicines, meat, grain, sugar, and semifinished metal products.

Agriculture: 15% (1995) of the workforce engages in agriculture and forestry. Grain, sugar beets, sunflower seeds, and meat are the main agricultural products. About 60% of state farms are now privately owned.

Energy: Most energy is generated using domestic oil, coal, natural gas, hydroelectricity, and nuclear power.

Natural Resources: Many minerals, including oil, coal, natural gas, and timber

Environmental Issues: Air, water, and soil pollution; soil erosion; deforestation; radioactive contamination

Transportation: There are 54,030 miles (86,950 km) of railroads used to transport people and 41,610 miles (67,000 km) for use by industries. There are 588,710 miles (948,000 km) of roads. Most of the roads are in European Russia. Pacific coast seaports include Vladivostok, Nakhodka, and Vostochnyy on the Sea of Japan; Magadan on the Sea of Okhotsk; and Petropavlovsk on the Bering Sea. St. Petersburg and Kalingrad serve Baltic Sea traffic; Murmansk, above the Arctic Circle on the Barents Sea, and Archangel'sk are key northern ports. Black Sea ports include Novorossiysk and Sochi. Navigable waters, including the Volga, Don, Lena, Amur, Ob, and Irtysh Rivers, as well as other tributaries and waterways, add 62,720 miles (108,980 km) to the transport network. Major international airports are at Moscow and St. Petersburg.

Communications: There are 292 daily newspapers published in the country and a total of more than 13,000 registered newspapers, most of which are weeklies or bi-weeklies. There are 50 million radios (1993 est.) and 54.85 million televisions (1992 est.). Telephone service, with 25.4 million lines in service (1993 est.), is being updated to meet demand. There are also 34,100 pay phones available for long distance calls.

Tourism: Historic churches, spas, Volga River cruises, museums in St. Petersburg, and the Cathedral of St. Basil in Moscow are only a few of the tourist sights in Russia. In 1994, 4.6 million visitors brought $1.161 billion (U.S.) into the country.

U.S. Tourist Office: (212) 757-3884

Embassy in U.S.: (202) 298-5700

Public Holidays: Christmas (January 7); International Women's Day (March 8); Orthodox Easter (date varies, in April); Day of Unity of the Peoples (April 2); Spring and Labor Day (May 1–2); Victory Day (May 9); Russian Independence Day (June 12); National Flag Day (August 22); Day of National Reconciliation (November 7)

Rwanda

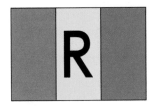

Country Name: Rwanda
Official Name: Rwandese Republic
Nationality: Rwandan(s) (noun); Rwandan (adjective)

Capital: Kigali, pop. 120,000
Major cities: Butare, Ruhengeri, Gisenyi
External Territories: None
Location: Rwanda, a landlocked country in central-eastern Africa, is bordered on the north by Uganda, on the east by Tanzania, on the south by Burundi, and on the west by the Democratic Republic of the Congo.

Physical Geography: Lake Kivu and the Ruzizi River, part of the Great Rift Valley system, form the western border with the Democratic Republic of the Congo. Marshy plains in the east rise gradually to a series of plateaus and the Virunga Mountains in the northwest. A depression in the southeastern corner has many lakes.

Total area: 10,169 sq mi (26,338 sq km)

Coastline: None

Land use: About 48% of the country is arable or under cultivation, 18% is meadows and pasture, and 22% is wooded.

Climate: Temperate, with rains from February to April and November to January; generally cooler temperatures at higher elevations

Population: 8,155,000
Urban population: 5%
Rate of natural increase: 2.08%
Age structure: 45% under 15; 3% over 65
Birth rate: 39.1/1000
Death rate: 18.3/1000
Infant mortality rate: 114/1000
Fertility rate: 6.0
Life expectancy at birth: 43 years (male); 44 years (female)
Religion: Roman Catholic, Protestant, indigenous beliefs
Language: Kinyarwanda, French, English, Kiswahili
Ethnic Divisions: Hutu, Tutsi, Twa
Literacy Rate: 61%
Government: Republic, with a president and a transitional 70-

member legislature, the National Assembly. Political turmoil has interfered with elections since the mid-1990s. In 1994 an estimated two million people fled to neighboring countries and one million people were victims of genocide. There are twelve administrative prefectures.

Armed services: 5,500 in the Army with an additional 7,000 paramilitary (1997).

Suffrage: Universal at adulthood (age unknown)

Economy: Ethnic civil war since 1990 has seriously damaged agricultural production, the base of Rwanda's economy, but international loans have helped restore a basic level of production. The displacement of the high-density population, continued political unrest, and damaged infrastructures severely impede economic growth in Rwanda, and international assistance is vital for survival.

Unit of currency: Rwandan franc; 100 centimes = 1 Rwandan franc (RF)

GDP per capita: $440
Inflation rate–CPI: 7.4% (1996)
Workforce: 2,874,000 (1996 est.)
Unemployment rate: N.A.

Exports: Goods worth $62.3 million (f.o.b., 1996 est.) are sent to Germany, Belgium, the Netherlands, Switzerland, the U.K., the U.S., and other trading partners; exports include coffee, tea, cassiterite, and wolframite.

Imports: Goods worth $202.4 million (f.o.b., 1996 est.) are received from the U.S., Belgium, Germany, Kenya, Japan, and other trading partners; imports include textiles, food, machines, capital goods, steel, oil products, cement, and construction materials.

Agriculture: 91% (1996 est.) of the workforce engages in agriculture. Plantains, sweet potatoes, cassava, and beans are grown for domestic use, and coffee, tea, pyrethrum, and livestock are grown for export. Coffee earned 75% (1995) of the total value of exports.

Energy: Imported hydropower supplies 54% (1990) of the country's energy. Additional energy supplied by imported fuel.

Natural Resources: Minerals, including gold, cassiterite, and wolframite (tungsten ore); natural gas; hydropower

Environmental Issues: Deforestation, soil erosion

Transportation: There are no railroads. Fighting has severely damaged the 7,450-mile (12,000 km) road network. Lake Kivu is navigable, and international flights leave from Kigali.

Communications: Although there are no daily newspapers, several periodicals are published in Kigali and elsewhere. There are 525,000 radios (1995) in operation; the number of televisions is not available. An estimated 15,000 phones (1994) are in service, but use is generally limited to business and government.

Tourism: Traveling in Rwanda is risky because of current political conflicts; the country is famed as one of the last strongholds of the mountain gorilla, which are found in Volcanoes National Park and elsewhere. Lake Kivu is a tourist attraction. In 1994, 1,000 visitors spent $2 million (U.S.).

Embassy in U.S.: (202) 232-2882

Public Holidays: Democracy Day (January 28); Easter Monday (date varies, in March or April); Ascension Day (date varies, in May); Whit Monday (date varies, in May); Labor Day (May 1); National Holiday: independence from a Belgian-administered UN Trustee Territory, 1962 (July 1); Assumption (August 15); Kamarampaka Day: anniversary of 1961 referendum to abolish the monarchy and establish a democracy (September 25); Armed Forces Day (date varies, in October); All Saints' Day (November 1); Christmas (December 25)

St. Kitts and Nevis

Country Name: St. Kitts and Nevis

Official Name: Federation of Saint Kitts and Nevis

Nationality: Kittitian(s), Nevisian(s) (noun); Kittitian, Nevisian (adjective)

Capital: Basseterre, pop. 12,600

Major cities: None

External Territories: None

Location: The country consists of two West Indian islands in the Lesser Antilles island chain in the Caribbean Sea. Antigua and Barbuda is to the east and the Virgin Islands are to the northwest.

Physical Geography: Both islands are volcanic and are separated by a two-mile-wide channel. Nevis has sandy beaches and is circled by coral reefs.

Total area: 101 sq mi (262 sq km)

Coastline: 84 mi (135 km)

Land use: Nearly 40% of the land is arable or under cultivation, 17% is wooded, and 3% is meadows and pastures.

Climate: Tropical, with rains from May to November

Population: 39,000

Urban population: 43%

Rate of natural increase: .85

Age structure: 31% under 15; 9% over 65

Birth rate: 19.7/1000

Death rate: 11.2/1000

Infant mortality rate: 24/1000

Fertility rate: 2.6

Life expectancy at birth: 64 years (male); 70 years (female)

Religion: Protestant, Roman Catholic

Language: English (official)

Ethnic Divisions: Black

Literacy Rate: 97%

Government: Constitutional monarchy, with a governor-general appointed by the British monarch, and a unicameral legislature, the National Assembly. Eleven representatives are directly elected to office for five years terms. Nevis has retained the option to secede from the federation. There are 14 administrative parishes.

Armed services: N.A.

Suffrage: Universal; 18 years old

Economy: Agriculture, mainly sugarcane, and tourism are the main supports of the economy; light manufacturing is being encouraged.

Unit of currency: East Caribbean dollar; 100 cents = 1 East Caribbean dollar (EC$)

GDP per capita: $5,700

Inflation rate–CPI: 3.1% (1996 est.)

Workforce: 18,172 (1995 est.)

Unemployment rate: 4.3% (1995 est.)

Exports: Goods worth $39.1 million (f.o.b., 1996 est.) are sent to the U.S., the U.K., Caribbean Community and Common Market (CARICOM) countries; exports include machinery, food, electronics, beverages, and tobacco.

Imports: Goods worth $131.5 million (f.o.b., 1996 est.) are received from the U.S., the U.K., Canada, Japan, and CARICOM countries; imports include machinery, basic manufactures, food, and fuel.

Agriculture: Sugarcane is the principal crop, and vegetables, and bananas are grown for domestic use. Sea-island cotton is also grown on Nevis. Fishing is increasingly important but not fully exploited.

Energy: Fuels are imported for energy generation.

Natural Resources: Negligible

Environmental Issues: N.A.

Transportation: There is no common carrier; a 40-mile (60 km) railroad serves the sugar industry on St. Kitts. There are 200 miles (320 km) of roads, of which about 40% are paved. Basseterre on St. Kitts is a deepwater port, and ships also call at Charlestown on Nevis. An international airport is near Basseterre.

Communications: There are no daily newspapers; two non-dailies are published in Basseterre. There are 25,000 radios and 9,500 televisions (1993 est.) in operation. Phone service, with 3,800 phones in use (1986), is adequate.

Tourism: Tourism, especially cruise ships, contributes significant revenue to the country; mountains, beaches, casinos, and quiet resorts attract visitors; 172,000 tourists added $180.4 million (EC) to the economy in 1996.

U.S. Tourist Office: (800) 582-6208

Embassy in U.S.: (202) 686-2630

Public Holidays: Carnival (January 2); Good Friday (date varies, in March or April); Easter Monday (date varies, in March or April); Whit Monday (date varies, in May); Labor Day (date varies, in May); Queen's Official Birthday (date varies, in June); August Monday (date varies, in August); Independence Day, from the U.K., 1983 (date varies, in September); Prince of Wales' Birthday (date varies, in November); Christmas (December 25–26)

St. Lucia

Country Name: St. Lucia

Official Name: Saint Lucia

Nationality: St. Lucian(s) (noun); St. Lucian (adjective)

Capital: Castries, pop. 2,000 [52,000]

Major cities: Vieux Fort, Soufrière

External Territories: None

Location: St. Lucia, an island in the Lesser Antilles in the Caribbean Sea, is between Martinique to the north and St. Vincent to the south.

Physical Geography: St. Lucia is a volcanic, mountainous island with wide valleys; there are sulfur springs in the southwest.

Total area: 238 sq mi (616 sq km)

Coastline: 98 mi (158 km)

Land use: Nearly 30% of the land is arable or under cultivation, 13% is forested, and 5% is meadows and pastures.

Climate: Tropical maritime, with most rain falling in November and December; temperature and precipitation vary with elevation

Population: 154,000

Urban population: 48%

Rate of natural increase: 1.58%

Age structure: 34% under 15; 5% over 65

Birth rate: 22.4/1000

Death rate: 6.6/1000

Infant mortality rate: 17.9/1000

Fertility rate: 2.5

Life expectancy at birth: 71 years (male); 73 years (female)

Religion: Roman Catholic, Protestant

Language: English, French patois

Ethnic Divisions: Black, mixed, East Indian, white

Literacy Rate: 67%

Government: Parliamentary democracy, with a governor-general appointed by the British monarch and a bicameral parliament, the Parliament. The 17 members of the House of Assembly are directly elected for terms of five years; the 11 Senate members are appointed, 6 on advice by the prime minister, 3

by the leader of the opposition and 2 after consultation with religious, economic and social groups. There are 11 administrative quarters.

Armed services: 300 (est.) in the Royal Saint Lucia Police Force, Coast Guard

Suffrage: Universal; 18 years old

Economy: Agriculture and tourism are the mainstays of St. Lucia's economy. Bananas, which are subject to drought and storm damage, are the main export crop. The government is encouraging diversification in agriculture and other sectors; investments in infrastructure have been especially beneficial for manufacturing and tourism.

Unit of currency: East Caribbean dollar; 100 cents = 1 East Caribbean dollar (EC$)

GDP per capita: $3,800

Inflation rate–CPI: -2.9% (1996 est.)

Workforce: 43,800 (1983 est.)

Unemployment rate: 15% (1996 est.)

Exports: Goods worth $79.5 million (f.o.b., 1996 est.) are sent to the U.K., the U.S., and other Caribbean Community and Common Market (CARICOM) countries; exports include bananas, clothing, cocoa, vegetables, fruits and coconut oil..

Imports: Goods worth $270.6 million (f.o.b., 1996 est.) are received from the U.S., the U.K., other CARICOM countries, Japan and Canada; imports include food, basic manufactures, fuels, and chemicals.

Agriculture: Nearly half (1983) of the labor force engages in agriculture, fishing, and forestry. Bananas, coconuts, vegetables, citrus fruits, cocoa, and root crops are raised.

Energy: Energy is generated using imported hydrocarbon fuels, and there is also petroleum transshipment terminal on the island.

Natural Resources: Forests, pumice, geothermal potential

Environmental Issues: Deforestation, soil erosion

Transportation: There are no rail-roads. There are 750 miles (1,210 km) of roads, of which about 5% are paved. The principal seaports are at Castries and Vieux Fort, and an international airports is near Castries.

Communications: There are no daily newspapers; five non-daily papers are published in Castries. There are 104,000 radios and 26,000 televisions (1992) in operation, and 26,000 telephone lines provide fair service.

Tourism: Sulfur springs, beaches, and mountains draw visitors to St. Lucia; visitors, who numbered 422,000 in 1996, spent $638.8 million (EC).

U.S. Tourist Office: (800) 456-3984

Embassy in U.S.: (202) 364-6792

Public Holidays: Carnival (date varies, in February); Independence Day: from the U.K., 1979 (February 22); Good Friday (date varies, in March or April); Easter Monday (date varies, in March or April); Whit Monday (date varies, in May); Labor Day (date varies, in May); Corpus Christi (date varies, in May or June); Queen's Official Birthday (date varies, in June); August Bank Holiday (date varies, in August); Thanksgiving Day (date varies, in October); St. Lucia Day (date varies, in December); Christmas (December 25–26)

St. Vincent and the Grenadines

Country Name: St. Vincent and the Grenadines

Official Name: Saint Vincent and the Grenadines

Nationality: St. Vincentian(s) or Vincentian(s) (noun); St. Vincentian or Vincentian (adjective)

Capital: Kingstown, pop. 15,500

Major cities: N.A.

External Territories: None

Location: St. Vincent and the Grenadines, in the Caribbean Sea's Lesser Antilles, consists of 32 islands and cays. The chain is between St. Lucia, to the north, Grenada to the south, and Barbados to the east.

Physical Geography: St. Vincent is mountainous, with active volcanoes, including Soufrière; the Grenadines have beaches and coral reefs. The principal islands are Bequia, Canouan, Mustique, Mayreau, and Union Island.

Total area: 151 sq mi (390 sq km)

Coastline: 52 mi (84 km)

Land use: Almost one-third of the country's land is arable or under cultivation, 36% is forested, and 5% is meadows and pastures.

Climate: Tropical, with a rainy season from May to November

Population: 114,000

Urban population: 25%

Rate of natural increase: 1.41%

Age structure: 37% under 15; 7% over 65

Birth rate: 20.7/1000

Death rate: 6.6/1000

Infant mortality rate: 17.7/1000

Fertility rate: 2.4

Life expectancy at birth: 71 years (male); 74 years (female)

Religion: Protestant, Roman Catholic

Language: English, French patois

Ethnic Divisions: Black, white East Indian, Carib, Amerindian

Literacy Rate: 96%

Government: Constitutional monarchy, with a governor-general appointed by the British monarch and a unicameral legislature, the House of Assembly. Of the 21 Assembly members, 6 Senators are appointed, and 15 Representatives are directly elected for terms lasting five years. There are six administrative parishes.

Armed services: Part of an East Caribbean regional defense group

Suffrage: Universal; 18 years old

Economy: Although the government is trying to encourage the growth of new industries, the banana export crop and a developing tourist sector are the main economic activities in the country. Farming for domestic markets is also important.

Unit of currency: East Caribbean dollar; 100 cents = 1 East Caribbean dollar (EC$)

GDP per capita: $2,200

Inflation rate–CPI: 3.6% (1996 est.)

Workforce: 67,000 (1984 est.)

Unemployment rate: 35%–40% (1994 est.)

Exports: Goods worth $46 million (f.o.b., 1996 est.) are sent to the U.K., other Caribbean Community and Common Market (CARICOM) countries, the U.S., and other trading partners; exports include bananas, taro, arrowroot starch and tennis racquets.

Imports: Goods worth $127 million (f.o.b., 1996 est.) are received from the U.S., other CARICOM countries, the U.K., and other trading partners; imports include food, machinery, chemicals and fertilizers, minerals, and fuels.

Agriculture: A quarter (1991) of the workforce engages in agriculture, fishing, and forestry. Bananas, sweet potatoes, coconuts, and spices are all commodities; a small fish catch is consumed domestically. Forestry is carefully controlled.

Energy: Nearly 90% (1992) of the country's energy is generated by using imported oil; some hydroelectricity is also used.

Natural Resources: Negligible

Environmental Issues: Water pollution

Transportation: There are no railroads. There are 650 miles (1,040 km) of roads, of which 200 miles (320 km) are paved. Kingstown on St. Vincent is the principal port, and there is an airport near Kingstown.

Communications: Five weekly papers are published. There are 76,000 radios and 20,600 televisions (1999 est.) in operation. Phone service, with 6,000 main lines (1983 est.) in use, is adequate.

Tourism: Yachting facilities, resorts, and beaches draw visitors to the country. In 1996, over 216,000 tourists brought $144.4 million (EC) to the country.

U.S. Tourist Office: (800) 729-1726

Embassy in U.S.: (202) 364-6730

Public Holidays: St. Vincent and the Grenadines Day (January 22); Good Friday (date varies, in March or April); Easter Monday (date varies, in March or April); Whit Monday (date varies, in May or June); Labor Day (date varies, in May); Caribbean Community and Common Market (CARICOM) Day (date varies, in July); Carnival (date varies, in July); Emancipation Day (date varies, in August); National Day: independence from the U.K., 1979 (October 27); Christmas (December 25)

Samoa

Country Name: Samoa

Official Name: Independent State of Samoa

Nationality: Samoan(s) (noun); Samoan (adjective)

Capital: Apia, pop. 34,100

Major cities: None

External Territories: None

Location: Samoa, a country of nine islands, is in the South Pacific Ocean. The largest islands are Sava'i and Upolu.

Physical Geography: The Western Samoan islands are volcanic with narrow coastal plains.

Total area: 1,093 sq mi (2,831 sq km)

Coastline: 250 mi (403 km)

Land use: Nearly 50% of the country is forested and 43% is arable or cultivated. There are no meadows and pastures.

Climate: Tropical, with rains from October to March

Population: 195,000

Urban population: 21%

Rate of natural increase: 2.4%

Age structure: 41% under 15; 4% over 65

Birth rate: 29/1000

Death rate: 5/1000

Infant mortality rate: 21/1000

Fertility rate: 4.2

Life expectancy at birth: 69 years (average)

Religion: Protestant, Roman Catholic

Language: Samoan (Polynesian), English

Ethnic Divisions: Samoan

Literacy Rate: 97%

Government: Constitutional monarchy—Chief Susuga Malietoa Tanumafilli II, since 1963—with a unicameral legislature, the Legislative Assembly, or Fono. The 49 members of the legislature, of whom 47 are chiefs (Matai) and 2 are non-Samoans, are directly elected to five-year terms. There are 11 districts.

Armed services: Protected by New Zealand forces

Suffrage: Universal; 21 years old

Economy: The export of coconut oil and copra, tourist revenues, and foreign aid fuels the economy of Western Samoa, which is ranked as one of the world's least developed countries by the United Nations. The government has attempted to attract foreign investment for industrial development beyond the country's existing light manufacturing activities, and new taxes have been levied to generate additional revenue.

Unit of currency: Tala; 100 sene = 1 tala (WS$)

GDP per capita: $2100

Inflation rate–CPI: 7.5% (1996)

Workforce: 82,500

Unemployment rate: N.A.

Exports: Goods worth $10 million (f.o.b., 1996) are sent to New Zealand, American Samoa, Australia, Germany, and other trading partners; exports include coconut oil and cream, copra, fish, beer.

Imports: Goods worth $100 million (c.i.f., 1996) are received from New Zealand, Australia, Fiji, the U.S., and other trading partners; imports include intermediate goods, food, and capital goods.

Agriculture: About 65% of the workforce engages in agriculture, forestry, and fishing (1995). Cash crops include coconuts and coconut products, taro, bananas, taamu, and cocoa which generally earn about 70% of the country's total export revenue. Breadfruit, yams, maize, mangos, passion fruit, and livestock are raised for domestic use. Timber is also exported.

Energy: Hydropower, thermal power and imported oil is used to generate most of the country's energy.

Natural Resources: Timber, seafood

Environmental Issues: Soil erosion

Transportation: There are no railroads. Of the 490 miles (790 km) of roads, 206 miles (332 km) are paved. Main seaports are at Apia, on Upolu, and Assau, on Savai'i. An international airport is at Faleolo, 39 miles (35 km) from Apia.

Communications: A daily newspaper is published in the capital. There are 76,000 radios and 6,000 televisions in operation and 7,500 telephones (1988) in service.

Tourism: Spectacular mountain waterfalls, beaches, traditional villages, and Robert Louis Stevenson's home in Vailima are some of Western Samoa's tourist attractions. In 1995, the country earned nearly $34 million (U.S.) from 68,392 visitors.

Embassy in U.S.: (212) 599-6196

Public Holidays: Easter (date varies, in March or April); ANZAC Day (April 25); Whit Monday (date varies, in May); Independence celebrations: as a UN Trust Territory administered by New Zealand, 1962 (June 1–3); Arbor Day (date varies, in November); National Women's Day (date varies, in November); Christmas (December 25); Boxing Day (December 26)

San Marino

Country Name: San Marino
Official Name: Republic of San Marino
Nationality: Sammarinese (singular and plural noun); Sammarinese (adjective)
Capital: San Marino, pop. 2,800 [4,400]
Major cities: None
External Territories: None
Location: San Marino, a landlocked country, is an enclave in central Italy.
Physical Geography: The country, in the Appenines, is mountainous,

with much of it on the slopes of Monte Titano.
Total area: 24 sq mi (61 sq km)
Coastline: None
Land use: Nearly 20% of the land is arable or under cultivation; there are no woodlands, meadows, or pastures.
Climate: Mediterranean, with mild winters and warm summers
Population: 26,000
Urban population: 89%
Rate of natural increase: 0.4%
Age structure: 15% under 15; 15% over 65
Birth rate: 11/1000
Death rate: 7/1000
Infant mortality rate: 6.8/1000
Fertility rate: 1.2
Life expectancy at birth: 73 years (male); 79 years (female)
Religion: Roman Catholic
Language: Italian
Ethnic Divisions: Sammarinese, Italian
Literacy Rate: 96%
Government: Republic, with a unicameral legislature, the Great and General Council. The 60 members of the legislature are elected for five-year terms. There are nine administrative parishes.
Armed services: Voluntary service
Suffrage: Universal; 18 years old
Economy: Tourism, banking, electronics, and ceramics are key components of San Marino's economy. The government is encouraging the development of light manufacturing and supports economic diversification in other sectors.
Unit of currency: Italian lira (singular), lire (plural); 100 centèsimi (plural; centèsimo, singular) = 1 lira
GDP per capita: $20,000.
Inflation rate–CPI: 5.3% (1995)
Workforce: 15,600 (1995)
Unemployment rate: 3.6% (1996)

Exports: San Marino exports building stone, lime and wood; trade data for the country is included with Italian trade data.
Imports: San Marino imports a wide variety of consumer manufactures and food.
Agriculture: 2% (1995) of the labor force engages in agriculture. Key crops include wheat, grapes, , maize, and olives.
Energy: Natural gas imported from Italy provides 75% of the country's energy.
Natural Resources: Building stones
Environmental Issues: N.A.
Transportation: There are no railroads. There are 140 miles (230 km) of roads; the nearest airport is in Rimini, Italy.
Communications: Four daily newspapers are published. There are 15,000 radios and 9,000 televisions (1994) in operation. Phone service, with 15,000 telephones (1995 est.), is good.
Tourism: Tourists come to San Marino, the world's oldest republic, since 301, to see medieval forts and mountains as well as to buy postage stamps and coins. In 1996, of the 3.3 million visitors who came to the country, 440,000 spent at least one night.
Public Holidays: Epiphany (January 6); Liberation Day and St. Agatha's Day (February 5); St. Joseph's Day (March 19); Anniversary of the Arengo (March 25); Easter Monday (date varies, in March or April); Investiture of the New Captains-Regent (April 1); Labor Day (May 1); Corpus Christi (date varies, in May or June); Fall of Fascism (July 28); Assumption (August 15); San Marino Day and Republic Day (September 3); Investiture of the New Captains-Regent (October 1); All Saints' Day (November 1); Commemoration of the Dead (November 2); Immaculate Conception (December 8); Christmas (December 25); St. Stephen's Day (December 26)

São Tomé and Príncipe

Country Name: São Tomé and Príncipe

Official Name: Democratic Republic of São Tomé and Príncipe

Nationality: São Toméan(s) (noun); São Toméan (adjective)

Capital: São Tomé, pop. 43,400

Major cities: None

External Territories: None

Location: The country of São Tomé and Príncipe consists of two islands at the Equator, off the coasts of Río Muni and Gabon of western Africa.

Physical Geography: Volcanic highlands, with lowlands in the northeast

Total area: 372 sq mi (964 sq km)

Coastline: 130 mi (209 km)

Land use: Forest and woodland coverage is unknown, 38% is arable or under cultivation, and 1% is meadows and pastures.

Climate: Tropical, with a rainy season from October to May

Population: 155,000

Urban population: 44%

Rate of natural increase: 3.4%

Age structure: 47% under 15; 4% over 65

Birth rate: 43/1000

Death rate: 9/1000

Infant mortality rate: 50.8/1000

Fertility rate: 6.2

Life expectancy at birth: 62 years (male); 65 years (female)

Religion: Roman Catholic

Language: Portuguese

Ethnic Divisions: Mixed African, Portuguese-African

Literacy Rate: 73%

Government: Republic, with a president and unicameral legislature, the National Assembly, or Assembléia Nacional. The president is directly elected to a five-year term; the 55 members of the legislature are directly elected to four-year terms. There are two administrative districts.

Armed services: 900 (1992) in a police force divided into a public order unit and a criminal investigation unit

Suffrage: Universal; 18 years old

Economy: The country's economy has traditionally depended on cocoa exports; however, cocoa exports have declined in recent years. The government is promoting agricultural diversification, increasing the number of private landholdings, and developing tourism. Austerity measures and increased prices of fuel have resulted in inflation and public protest, and international assistance and food imports are needed for the country's survival.

Unit of currency: Dobra; 100 cêntimos = 1 dobra (Db)

GDP per capita: $1,000

Inflation rate–CPI: 60% (1996 est.)

Workforce: 36,789 (1994)

Unemployment rate: 28% (1996 est.)

Exports: Goods worth $4.9 million (f.o.b., 1996 est.) are sent to the Netherlands, Germany, Portugal, and other trading partners; exports include cocoa, copra, coffee, and palm oil.

Imports: Goods worth $19.6 million (c.i.f., 1996 est.) are received from France, Belgium, Japan, Angola, Italy, Portugal, and other trading partners; imports include machinery, electrical equipment, food, and oil.

Agriculture: Nearly 32% (1994) of the labor force engages in the agricultural sector. Cocoa, coconuts, coffee, cinnamon, pepper, and palm kernals are raised for export; fishing is also important. Taro, corn, cassava, poultry, and breadfruit are raised for domestic use. Cocoa earned 96% (1996) of the total value of all exports.

Energy: Imported fuels and hydropower generate electricity; nearly 25% of the country's energy needs are supplied by hydropower.

Natural Resources: Fish, cinchona bark

Environmental Issues: Deforestation, soil erosion and exhaustion

Transportation: There are no railroads on the islands. There are 200 miles (320 km) of roads, of which 140 miles (220 km) are paved. The principal ports are the city of São Tomé on São Tomé and Santo António on Principé. The main airport is near São Tomé.

Communications: There are no daily newspapers. There are 36,000 radios and 21,000 televisions (1995) in use, and 2,457 phones provide minimal service.

Tourism: Mountains, beaches, and tropical flora and fauna hold potential for the tourist industry, which earned $2 million (U.S.) from 5 million visitors in 1994.

Embassy in U.S.: (212) 697-4211

Public Holidays: Shrove Tuesday (date varies, in February or March); Easter (date varies, in March or April); Labor Day (May 1); Corpus Christi (date varies, in June); Independence Day: from Portugal, 1975 (July 12); Assumption (August 15); Agricultural Nationalization Day (September 30); Christmas (December 25–26)

Saudi Arabia

Country Name: Saudi Arabia
Official Name: Kingdom of Saudi Arabia
Nationality: Saudi(s) (noun); Saudi or Saudi Arabian (adjective)
Capital: Riyadh, pop. [1,800,000]
Major cities: Jeddah, Makkah (Mecca), At Taif, Medina
External Territories: None
Location: Saudi Arabia, in the Middle East, is on the Arabian Peninsula, with the Red Sea on the west and the Persian Gulf on the east. Jordan, Iraq, and Kuwait are to the north; Qatar, the United Arab Emirates, and Oman are on the east; and Yemen is to the south.
Physical Geography: Lowland swamps and salt flats of the Hasa Plain along the Persian Gulf gradually rise to meet a central plateau. Deserts, including the An Nafūd lie to the north and Rub 'al Khālī to the south, and highlands separate the narrow Red Sea coast from the rest of the country.
Total area: 830,000 sq mi (2,149,690 sq km)
Coastline: 1,639 mi (2,640 km)
Land use: About 2% is arable or cultivated, 1% is wooded, and nearly 60% of the land is meadows and pastures.
Climate: Mostly desert, with cooler temperatures in winter
Population: 20,899,000
Urban population: 83%
Rate of natural increase: 3%
Age structure: 42% under 15; 3% over 65

Birth rate: 35/1000
Death rate: 5/1000
Infant mortality rate: 29/1000
Fertility rate: 6.4
Life expectancy at birth: 70 years (male); 73 years (female)
Religion: Muslim
Language: Arabic
Ethnic Divisions: Arab
Literacy Rate: 63%
Government: Monarchy—King Fahd bin al-Aziz Al Saud, since 1982—with a 60-member Council of Ministers appointed by the monarch for four-year terms. There are 13 administrative provinces.
Armed services: 105,500 voluntary troops (1997) in the army, air force, and navy
Suffrage: None
Economy: Industry is sustained primarily by oil production in Saudi Arabia, which is the largest oil producer in the world, but some industrial diversification and privatization is taking place. The government is increasing private industry, increasing oil production and refining capacities, and building up the national infrastructure.
Unit of currency: Saudi riyal; 100 halalah = 20 qurush = 1 riyal (SR)

GDP per capita: $10,300
Inflation rate–CPI: 0% (1997 est.)
Workforce: 7 million (1998 est.)
Unemployment rate: N.A.
Exports: Goods worth $56.4 billion (f.o.b., 1996) are sent to Japan, the U.S., South Korea, Singapore, France, and other trading partners; exports include petroleum and petroleum products.
Imports: Goods worth $25.4 billion (f.o.b., 1996 est.) are received from the U.S., the U.K., Japan, Germany, Italy, and other trading partners; imports include machinery, chemicals, food, vehicles, and textiles.
Agriculture: An estimated 5% (1998) of the labor force engages in the agricultural sector. Wheat is the principal crop, along with barley, sorghum, and millet; tomatoes, dates, and watermelons are also important crops.
Energy: Domestic oil is used to generate energy.
Natural Resources: Oil, natural gas, iron ore, gold, copper
Environmental Issues: Desertification, limited freshwater, water pollution
Transportation: There are 860 miles (1,390 km) of railroads in the

SAUDI ARABIA NEW NATION, ANCIENT CITIES

Saudi Arabia was founded in 1932 as a conservative Islamic kingdom, and its cities of Mecca and Medina are sacred to the world's Muslims. Muhammad, Islam's founder, was born in Mecca about 570; even then, the city had long been a religious center for various Arabian clans and tribes. They came there to worship a black stone, probably a meteorite, that had been placed in the Kabah, a pilgrimage shrine. After spending several years in Medina gaining and organizing converts to his religion, Muhammad defeated the leading tribe that had opposed him and returned to Mecca, taking with him the Kabah, as an Islamic shrine. Today, all the world's Muslims face Mecca during their daily regimen of prayers, and they are encouraged to make a pilgrimage to Mecca at least once in their lifetime. Non-Muslims are rarely allowed in Mecca.

country, as well as 100,600 miles (151,500 km) of roads, of which over 40% are paved. Ad Dammām and Al Jubayl on the Persian Gulf and Jeddah, Jīzān, and Yanbu 'al Ba[h]r on the Red Sea are major seaports. International airports are at Makkah and Riyadh.

Communications: Twelve daily newspapers are published. There are 5 million radios and 4.5 million televisions (1993 est.) in operation. Phone service, with 1.46 million lines (1993) in use, is good.

Tourism: Makkah (Mecca) and Medina are both holy cities for Muslims, who try to visit both places at least once in their lives. More than 2 million pilgrims visited the country in 1993 and 1994.

Embassy in U.S.: (202) 342-3800

Public Holidays: End of Ramadan (date varies, in February); Feast of the Sacrifice (dates vary, in April); Islamic New Year (date varies, in April or May); Ashura (date varies, in April or May); Birth of the Prophet (date varies, in July); Unification Day, 1932 (September 23); Ascension of the Prophet (date varies, in November or December)

Senegal

Country Name: Senegal
Official Name: Republic of Senegal
Nationality: Senegalese (singular and plural noun); Senegalese (adjective)
Capital: Dakar, pop. 1,641,400
Major cities: Thiès, Kaolack, Saint-Louis, Ziguinchor
External Territories: None

Location: Senegal, on the west coast of Africa, is bordered on the north by Mauritania, on the east by Mali, on the south by Guinea-Bissau and Guinea, and the west by the Atlantic Ocean. Senegal encloses Gambia on three sides.

Physical Geography: Beaches and marshes along the Atlantic coast give way to rolling sandy plains in the interior; foothills rise in the southeast. The Senegal River forms the border with Mauritania.

Total area: 75,955 sq mi (196,722 sq km)

Coastline: 330 mi (531 km)

Land use: Forest and woodland cover 54% of the land, 16% is meadows and pastures, and 12% of the land is arable or under cultivation.

Climate: Tropical, with rain from June to October

Population: 9,240,000

Urban population: 41%

Rate of natural increase: 2.79%

Age structure: 45% under 15; 3% over 65

Birth rate: 40.9/1000

Death rate: 13/1000

Infant mortality rate: 67.7/1000

Fertility rate: 5.7

Life expectancy at birth: 51 years (male); 54 years (female)

Religion: Muslim, indigenous beliefs

Language: French, Wolof, Pulaar, Diola

Ethnic Divisions: Wolof, Fulani, Serer, others

Literacy Rate: 33%

Government: Republic, with a president and a unicameral legislature, the National Assembly. The president is directly elected to a seven-year term, and the 140 members of the legislature are directly elected to five-year terms. There are ten administrative regions.

Armed services: 13,400 troops (1997) in the army, navy, and air force; two-year selective conscription

Suffrage: Universal; 18 years old

Economy: Tourism, agriculture, fishing, and mining provide much of Senegal's revenue. However, droughts often severely disrupt agricultural production, and the government plans to diversify the economy so that it is less vulnerable to climatic fluctuations. International aid has been given to help the country privatize industries and eliminate monopolies.

Unit of currency: CFA franc; 100 centimes = 1 franc de la Communauté financière africaine (CFAF)

GDP per capita: $1,850

Inflation rate–CPI: 2.5% (1997 est.)

Workforce: 3,815,000 (1996 est.)

Unemployment rate: 20% (late 1980's est.)

Exports: Goods worth $986 million (f.o.b., 1996) are sent to the E.U. (especially France), Côte d'Ivoire, and other trading partners; exports include fish, groundnuts, petroleum products, and phosphates.

Imports: Goods worth $1.4 billion (f.o.b., 1996 est.) are received from the E.U. (especially France), Nigeria, Côte d'Ivoire, Thailand, and other trading partners; imports include food, consumer goods, capital goods, and oil.

Agriculture: Nearly 75% (1996) of the workforce engages in agriculture, fishing, and forestry. Cash commodities include peanuts, cotton, cattle, and seafood. Crops for domestic use include peanuts, millet, sorghum, corn, rice, and vegetables; fish are also important. The government plans to be self-sufficient by 2000.

Energy: Imported oil is used for most energy generation; some domestic hydropower is also used.

Natural Resources: Fish; minerals, including phosphates, iron ore

Environmental Issues: Poaching, deforestation, soil erosion, overgrazing, desertification, overfishing

Transportation: There are 560 miles (900 km) of rails and 9,050 miles (14,580 km) of roads, of which 2,650 miles (4,270 km) are paved. The Senegal, Saloum, and Casamance Rivers are navigable. Dakar is the country's most important seaport, and the second-largest port in western Africa, after Abidjan, Côte d'Ivoire. An international airport is near Dakar.

Communications: Three daily newspapers are published in Dakar. There are 1,000,000 radios and 320,000 televisions in use, and 72,000 telephones (1995) provide adequate service.

Tourism: Beaches, museums, and restaurants in Dakar, the historic slave trading center on Gorée Island, and wildlife in the national parks are some of Senegal's tourist draws; in 1996, an estimated 305,000 visitors spent about $123 million (U.S.) in the country.

U.S. Tourist Office: (800) 443-2527
Embassy in U.S.: (202) 234-0540

Public Holidays: End of Ramadan (date varies, in February); Good Friday (date varies, in March or April); Easter Monday (date varies, in March or April); Feast of the Sacrifice (date varies, in April); National Day (April 4); Ascension Day (date varies, in May); Whit Monday (date varies, in May); Labor Day (May 1); Birth of the Prophet (date varies, in July); Day of Association (July 14); Assumption (August 15); All Saints' Day (November 1); Christmas (December 25)

Seychelles

Country Name: Seychelles
Official Name: Republic of Seychelles
Nationality: Seychellois (singular and plural noun); Seychelles (adjective)
Capital: Victoria, pop. 25,000
Major cities: None
External Territories: None
Location: Seychelles, off the east coast of Africa, is a country of more than 90 islands north of Madagascar in the western Indian Ocean.
Physical Geography: There are two main island groups: the larger granitic mountainous islands in the Mahé group and a group of flat, coral islands.
Total area: 175 sq mi (453 sq km)
Coastline: 305 mi (491 km)
Land use: About 15% of the land is arable or under cultivation and 11% is wooded. There are no meadows and pastures.
Climate: Tropical, with rainfall varying from island to island
Population: 80,000
Urban population: 59%
Rate of natural increase: 1.13%

Age structure: 28% under 15; 7% over 65
Birth rate: 19.1/1000
Death rate: 7.8/1000
Infant mortality rate: 8.1/1000
Fertility rate: 2.2
Life expectancy at birth: 67 years (male); 73 years (female)
Religion: Roman Catholic, Protestant
Language: English, French, Creole
Ethnic Divisions: Seychellois
Literacy Rate: 58%
Government: Republic, with a president and a unicameral legislature, the National Assembly. The president is directly elected for a five-year term. Of the 35 members of the legislature, 25 are directly elected for five-year terms and 10 are appointed to office. There are 23 administrative districts.
Armed services: 400 troops (1997) in the army and coast guard
Suffrage: Universal; 17 years old
Economy: While tourism generates the most income for Seychelles, the government is encouraging economic diversification by promoting farming, fishing, and small-scale manufactures. International debt hampers a greater degree of economic growth.
Unit of currency: Seychelles rupee; 100 cents = 1 Seychelles rupee (SRe)
GDP per capita: $7,000
Inflation rate–CPI: -0.3% (1995 est.)
Workforce: 26,276 (1996 est.)

SEYCHELLES UNUSUAL ISLANDS OF GRANITE

Seychelles is sometimes called the world's smallest continent, since it has a continental shelf; it may have been part of an ancient landmass. It became independent from Great Britain in 1976, and its population is a blend of Asian, African, and European, most of whom are Roman Catholic. Some of its islands are coral atolls and others are granite, making them very unusual oceanic islands. Granites are usually found on continental mainlands.

Unemployment rate: 8% (1993 est.)

Exports: Goods worth $56.1 million (f.o.b., 1995) are sent to Yemen, the U.K., Germany, and other trading partners; exports include fish, cinnamon bark, and copra.

Imports: Goods worth $238 million (c.i.f., 1995) are received from Singapore, Yemen, South African countries, the U.K., and other trading partners; imports include manufactured goods, food, oil products, tobacco, beverages, machinery, and transportation equipment.

Agriculture: Nearly 7% (1996) of the labor force engages in agriculture, fishing, and forestry. Fish, especially tuna, copra, cinnamon, vanilla, and coconuts are key exports. Sweet potatoes, cassava, yams, bananas, and chicken are raised for domestic use.

Energy: Imported oil is used for most energy generation.

Natural Resources: Fish, copra, cinnamon trees

Environmental Issues: No natural freshwater sources

Transportation: There are no railroads. There are 170 miles (280 km) of roads, of which most are paved. Ferry service is available between some of the islands. Victoria on Mahé is the main seaport. An international airport is near Victoria.

Communications: There is one daily newspaper. There are 40,000 radios and 10,000 televisions in operation and 12,000 telephones.

Tourism: Beaches, tropical scenery, and diverse and rare flora and fauna draw visitors to Seychelles; 131,000 visitors came to the country in 1996.

U.S. Tourist Office: (212) 687-9766

Embassy in U.S.: (212) 972-1785

Public Holidays: Easter (date varies, in March or April); Labor Day (May 1); Corpus Christi (date varies, in May or June); Liberation Day (June 5); National Day: adoption of constitution, 1993 (June 18); Independence Day: from the U.K., 1976

(June 29); Assumption (August 15); All Saints' Day (November 1); Immaculate Conception (December 8); Christmas (December 25)

Sierra Leone

Country Name: Sierra Leone

Official Name: Republic of Sierra Leone

Nationality: Sierra Leonean(s) (noun); Sierra Leonean (adjective)

Capital: Freetown, pop. 469,800

Major cities: Koindu, Bo, Kenema, Makeni

External Territories: None

Location: Sierra Leone, on the west coast of Africa, is bordered on the north and east by Guinea, the southeast by Liberia, and on the west by the Atlantic Ocean.

Physical Geography: Forested mountains slope to coastal mangrove swamps; beyond the mountains are interior plains, which extend to the Loma Mountains in the eastern section of the country.

Total area: 27,699 sq mi (71,740 sq km)

Coastline: 250 miles (402 km)

Land use: Meadows and pastures cover 31% of the country, 28% is

wooded, and 8% is arable or used for crops.

Climate: Tropical, with rains from April to November

Population: 5,297,000

Urban population: 37%

Rate of natural increase: 2.89%

Age structure: 45% under 15; 3% over 65

Birth rate: 46.7/1000

Death rate: 17.8/1000

Infant mortality rate: 135.6/1000

Fertility rate: 6.3

Life expectancy at birth: 45 years (male); 51 years (female)

Religion: Indigenous beliefs, Muslim, Christian

Language: English, Mende, Temne, Krio

Ethnic Divisions: Mende, Temne, Creole, others

Literacy Rate: 31%

Government: Constitutional democracy reinstated in 1998, after military coup. The 1991 constitution calls for a president and a unicameral legislature, the National Assembly. The president is elected to a five-year term. Of the 80 members of the legislature, 68 are directly elected for five-year terms and 12 chiefs serve five-year terms. There are four administrative regions.

Armed services: 14,200 troops (1997) in the army and navy

Suffrage: Universal; 18 years old

Economy: Agriculture and mining generate most of Sierra Leone's revenue. Civil war since May 1997 has disrupted agriculture and mining

---

SIERRA LEONE FREETOWN: FOUNDED FOR FREED SLAVES

Independent from Great Britain since 1961, Sierra Leone was a center of slave trade in the 17th and 18th centuries. Its capital, Freetown, was established as a refuge for freed slaves in 1787. Today it is a major exporter of industrial and commercial diamonds.

activities and interfered with the government's long-range economic goals. International aid had been given to help the country achieve needed reforms; however, until a stable government is in place, economic growth will remain a secondary concern. An influx of Liberian refugees has also strained the country's resources.

Unit of currency: Leone; 100 cents = 1 leone (Le)

GDP per capita: $540

Inflation rate–CPI: 40% (1997 est.)

Workforce: 6,680,000 (1995 est.)

Unemployment rate: 50% (1990 est.)

Exports: Goods worth $47 million (f.o.b., 1996) are sent to the U.S., the U.K., Belgium, Germany, and other trading partners; exports include rutile, diamonds, coffee, cocoa, and fish.

Imports: Goods worth $211 million (c.i.f., 1996) are received from the U.S., the E.U., Japan, China, Indonesia, and other trading partners; imports include food, machinery and equipment, and fuels.

Agriculture: Nearly 67% (1996) of the labor force engages in the agricultural sector. Coffee, cocoa, and fish are raised for export; cassava, rice, bananas, and poultry are raised for domestic use.

Energy: Imported oil is used for most energy generation; domestic sources include some solar energy and hydroelectricity.

Natural Resources: Minerals, including diamonds, titanium, bauxite, iron, gold, chromite

Environmental Issues: Deforestation, overfishing

Transportation: The country has no common carrier railroad service. There are 7,270 miles (11,700 km) of roads, of which 800 miles (1,290 km) are paved. Freetown is the largest seaport, and the Great and Little Scarcies Rivers are navigable.

An international airport is at Lungi, near Freetown.

Communications: One daily newspaper is published in Freetown. There are 1,050,000 radios and 49,000 televisions (1995) in operation; 16,000 telephones (1994) provide only marginal service.

Tourism: Tourists come to Sierra Leone to visit national parks and wildlife sanctuaries and Freetown's beaches, museums, markets, and architecture. In 1994, 72,000 visitors spent $10 million (U.S.).

Embassy in U.S.: (202) 939-9261

Public Holidays: End of Ramadan (date varies, in February); Easter (date varies, in March or April); Feast of the Sacrifice (date varies, in April); Independence Day: from the U.K., 1961 (April 27); Birth of the Prophet (date varies, in July); Christmas (December 25); Boxing Day (December 26)

Singapore

Country Name: Singapore

Official Name: Republic of Singapore

Nationality: Singaporean(s) (noun); Singapore (adjective)

Capital: Singapore, pop. 3,737,000

Major cities: N.A.

External Territories: None

Location: Singapore, a city-state, occupying Singapore Island and 57 islets off the southernmost tip of Malay Peninsula, is in southeastern Asia. Malaysia is on the north and to the south is Indonesian territory, across the Singapore Strait.

Physical Geography: Singapore Island, the largest island, has low-lying uplands in its center.

Total area: 239 sq mi (618 sq km)

Coastline: 120 mi (193 km)

Land use: Just over 10% of the land is arable or under cultivation and 5% is forested. There are no meadows and pastures.

Climate: Equatorial tropical, with little variation in temperature and rainfall

Population: 3,999,000

Urban population: 100%

Rate of natural increase: 1.1%

Age structure: 22% under 15; 7% over 65

Birth rate: 15/1000

Death rate: 5/1000

Infant mortality rate: 3/1000

Fertility rate: 1.6

Life expectancy at birth: 75 years (male); 79 years (female)

Religion: Buddhist, Muslim, Christian, Hindu, Sikh, Taoist, Confucianist

Language: Chinese, Malay, Tamil, English

Ethnic Divisions: Chinese, Malay, Indian

Literacy Rate: 91%

Government: Republic, with a president and a unicameral legislature, the Parliament. The president is directly elected to a six-year term, and the 83 members of the legislature are directly elected to five-year terms.

Armed services: 70,900 troops (1997) in the army, navy, and air force; compulsory service for 24–30 months

Suffrage: Universal and compulsory; 20 years old

Economy: Banking, trade, manufacturing, and other services help to make Singapore one of the wealthiest countries in the world per capita. The country has begun to locate some of its plants in other countries to take advantage of lower labor costs, and taxes have been scaled

SINGAPORE A PROSPEROUS ISLAND CITY-STATE

A British colony until 1959, Singapore is a world commercial and financial center, and its per capita Gross Domestic Product is one of the highest in the world. This island city-state is smaller in both area and population than New York City. Most of its citizens are Chinese, and the country has four official languages: Tamil, Malay, Chinese, and English.

Slovakia

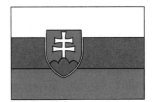

back in the 1990s to balance out rising production costs.

Unit of currency: Singapore dollar; 100 cents = 1 Singapore dollar (S$)

GDP per capita: $24,600

Inflation rate–CPI: 1.8% (1997 est.)

Workforce: 1,856,000 (1997 est.)

Unemployment rate: 3% (1997 est.)

Exports: Goods worth $126.5 billion (1997 est.) are sent to Malaysia, the U.S., Hong Kong, Japan, Thailand, and other trading partners; exports include computer and other office equipment, and rubber.

Imports: Goods worth $133.9 billion (1997 est.) are received from Japan, the U.S., Malaysia, Hong Kong, Japan, and other trading partners; imports include aircraft, oil, chemicals, and food.

Agriculture: Less than 1% (1994) of the workforce engages in the agricultural sector, raising vegetables and poultry for domestic consumption.

Energy: Most energy is generated using imported oil.

Natural Resources: Seafood

Environmental Issues: Air and water pollution, limited freshwater

Transportation: Singapore has 25 miles (40 km) of railways. There are 1,860 miles (3,000 km) of roads, of which almost all are paved. Singapore is one of the world's busiest seaports, and there is an international airport at Changi, on Singapore Island.

Communications: The government watches the press carefully;

there are at least eight daily newspapers published and a variety of other publications. About 1.05 million televisions (1992 est.) are in use. Phone service, with 1.4 million phone lines (1997 est.) in operation, is good.

Tourism: A nature reserve is located in the center of Singapore Island; shopping is another favored visitor pastime. There were 7.2 million visitors in 1997; in 1997, visitors spent about $5.79 billion (U.S.) in the country.

U.S. Tourist Office: (212) 302-4861

Embassy in U.S.: (202) 537-3100

Public Holidays: Chinese New Year (date varies, in January or February); End of Ramadan (date varies, in February); Good Friday (date varies, in March or April); Feast of the Sacrifice (date varies, in April); Vesak Day (date varies, in May); Labor Day (May 1); National Day: independence from Malaysia, 1965 (August 9); Deepavali (dates vary, in October or November); Christmas (December 25)

Country Name: Slovakia

Official Name: Slovak Republic

Nationality: Slovak(s) (noun); Slovak (adjective)

Capital: Bratislava, pop. 452,300

Major cities: Košice, Prešov, Nitra, Žilina

External Territories: None

Location: Slovakia, a landlocked country in central Europe, is bordered on the north by Poland, on the east by Ukraine, on the south by Hungary, on the southwest by Austria, and on the west by the Czech Republic.

Physical Geography: Slovakia is mostly mountainous, including the Tatra and Carpathians in the north, with some lower elevations in the southwest and southeast. The Danube River forms the southern boundary with Hungary.

Total area: 18,921 sq mi (49,006 sq km)

Coastline: None

Land use: About 40% of the country is forested, nearly 34% is arable or under cultivation, and 17 % is meadows and pastures.

Climate: Continental, with hot humid summers and cold dry winters

Population: 5,401,000

Urban population: 57%

Rate of natural increase: 0.1%

Age structure: 21% under 15; 11% over 65

Birth rate: 11/1000

Death rate: 10/1000

Infant mortality rate: 8.79/1000

Fertility rate: 1.4

Life expectancy at birth: 69 years (male); 77 years (female)

Religion: Roman Catholic, Protestant

Language: Slovak, Hungarian

Ethnic Divisions: Slovak, Hungarian

Literacy Rate: N.A.

Government: Republic, with a unicameral legislature, the National Council, or Narodma Rada. The president is elected by the legislature for a five-year term; the 150 members of the legislature are directly elected to four-year terms. There are eight regions and 79 administrative districts.

Armed services: 41,200 troops (1997) in the army and air force; compulsory service for one year

Suffrage: Universal; 18 years old

Economy: Mining and manufacturing provide the base for Slovakia's economy, which began the transition from a planned economy to a market economy upon independence from Czechoslovakia in 1993. The government has acted to reduce inflation, unemployment, and the budget deficit, but industry privatization and foreign investment are not taking place as quickly as originally forecast. However, the economy is gradually showing signs of growth, transport, communication networks, contribute to the countries growth.

Unit of currency: Slovak koruna (singular); koruny (plural); 100 halierov (halier, singular) = 1 Slovenská koruna (Sk)

GDP per capita: $8,600

Inflation rate–CPI: 6% (1997)

Workforce: 2.35 million

Unemployment rate: 12.8% (1997 est.)

Exports: Goods worth $8.8 billion (f.o.b., 1996 est.) are sent to the Czech Republic, Germany, Austria, and other trading partners; exports include machinery and transport equipment, chemicals, miscella-

neous manufactured goods and raw materials.

Imports: Goods worth $11.1 billion (f.o.b., 1996 est.) are received from the Czech Republic, Germany, Italy, and other trading partners; imports include machinery and transportation equipment, fuels, intermediate manufactured goods, and miscellaneous manufactured goods.

Agriculture: Nearly 9% (1994) of the workforce engages in the agricultural sector. Grains, potatoes, sugar beets, and livestock are all raised for domestic consumption. By 1995, more than 80% of the former state farms had been privatized.

Energy: Imported oil, nuclear power, brown coal lignite, and hydropower are used for energy generation.

Natural Resources: Minerals, including coal, iron ore, copper, manganese, salt

Environmental Issues: Air pollution, including acid rain

Transportation: There are 2,280 miles (3,670 km) of railroads in the country and 22,730 miles (36,610 km) of roads. The Danube River is navigable for 110 miles (180 km) with ports at Bratislava and Komárno. International airports are at Bratislava, Košice, Piešt'any, Poprad, and Sliač.

Communications: Twenty (1995) daily newspapers are published. There are 915,000 radios and 1.2 million televisions (1995 est.) in use and 1.36 million telephones (1992 est.).

Tourism: Ski resorts, health spas, castles, and historic towns, such as Bratislava, Košice, and Nitra, attract visitors to Slovakia; in 1994, 901,812 tourists spent $672 million (U.S.).

U.S. Tourist Office: (212) 689-9720

Embassy in U.S.: (202) 965-5160

Public Holidays: Easter Monday (date varies, in March or April); May Day (May 1); Anniversary of Liberation (May 8); Day of the Slav Apos-

tles (July 5); Anniversary of the Slovak National Uprising, 1944 (August 29); Reconciliation Day (November 1); Christmas (December 24–26)

Slovenia

Country Name: Slovenia

Official Name: Republic of Slovenia

Nationality: Slovene(s) (noun); Slovenian (adjective)

Capital: Ljubljana, pop. 273,000

Major cities: Maribor, Celje, Kranj

External Territories: None

Location: Slovenia, on the Adriatic Sea in south-central Europe, is bordered on the north by Austria, on the northeast by Hungary, on the east and south by Croatia, and on the west by Italy.

Physical Geography: Slovenia is mostly mountainous. The Julian Alps are in the north, with ranges cut by rivers such as the Sava and Drava. The profile of the country's highest point, Triglav at 9,162 feet (2,863 m), is on the nation's flag.

Total area: 7,819 sq mi (20,251 sq km)

Coastline: 29 mi (47 km)

Land use: 50% of the country is wooded, 28% is meadows and pastures, and 15% is arable or under cultivation.

Climate: Mediterranean along the coast, continental in the interior

Population: 1,978,000

Urban population: 50%

Rate of natural increase: -0.1 %

Age structure: 17% under 15; 13% over 65

Birth rate: 9/1000

Death rate: 9/1000

Infant mortality rate: 4.8/1000

Fertility rate: 1.2

Life expectancy at birth: 71 years (male); 79 years (female)

Religion: Roman Catholic

Language: Slovenian, Serbo-Croat

Ethnic Divisions: Slovene, Croat, Serb

Literacy Rate: 99%

Government: Republic, with a president and a bicameral legislature, the National Assembly. The president is directly elected to a five-year term, as are the 88 members of the State Assembly. Of the 40 members of the State Council, 22 are directly elected to five-year terms and 18 are selected by an electoral college. There are 48 administrative districts.

Armed services: 9,550 troops (1997) in the army, coastal defense, and air force; seven months' conscription

Suffrage: Universal; 18 years old; 16 years old if employed

Economy: Building on its preindependence prosperity, Slovenia, independent from Yugolavia since 1991, is experiencing solid economic growth. Industrial privatization is still in progress, and trading ties with other European countries have been maintained after independence. Inflation and unemployment are expected to decline in the next few years.

Unit of currency: Tolar; 100 stotins = 1 tolar (SIT)

GDP per capita: $10,000

Inflation rate–CPI: 9.7% (1996)

Workforce: 857,400

Unemployment rate: 7.1% (1997 est.)

Exports: Goods worth $8.3 billion (f.o.b., 1996 est.) are sent to Germany, Italy, Yugoslavia, France, Austria, and other trading partners; exports include manufactured goods, machinery and transport equipment, chemicals, and food.

Imports: Goods worth $9.5 billion (f.o.b., 1996 est.) are received from Germany, Italy, Austria, France, and other trading partners; imports include machinery and transport equipment, manufactured goods, chemicals, fuels and lubricants and food.

Agriculture: 2% (1995) of the workforce engages in agriculture. Crops include potatoes, hops, wheat, sugar beets, corn, and grapes.

Energy: Imported and domestic fuels, nuclear energy, and hydropower are used for electrical generation.

Natural Resources: Lignite coal, lead, zinc, mercury, uranium, silver

Environmental Issues: Water and air pollution, including acid rain

Transportation: There are 750 miles (1,210 km) of railroads. There are 9,260 miles (14,910 km) of roads, of which 7,590 miles (12,230 km) are paved. Adriatic ports are Izola, Koper, and Piran, and international airports are at Ljubljana and Portoroz.

Communications: Several daily newspapers are published. There are 596,100 radios and 454,400 televisions (1993) in operation. Phone service, with 691,240 telephones (1997 est.) in service, is adequate.

Tourism: Historic buildings in Ljubljana, Roman ruins in Ptuj, castles, and ski resorts are all tourist draws; the country earned $1.2 billion (U.S.) from 831,895 visitors in 1996.

Embassy in U.S.: (202) 667-5363

Public Holidays: Prešeren Day and National Culture Day (February 8); Easter Monday (date varies, in March or April); Resistance Day (April 27); Whit Sunday (date varies, in May); Labor Days (May 1–2); Statehood Day: independence from Yugoslavia, 1991 (June 25); Assumption (August 15); Reformation Day (October 31); Christmas (December 25); Independence Day (December 26)

Solomon Islands

Country Name: Solomon Islands

Official Name: Solomon Islands

Nationality: Solomon Islander(s) (noun); Solomon Islander (adjective)

Capital: Honiara, pop. 43,600

Major cities: None

External Territories: None

Location: Solomon Islands is an island country between the South Pacific Ocean and the Coral Sea. The six largest islands, northwest to southeast, are Choiseul, New Georgia, Santa Isabel, Malaita, Guadacanal, and San Cristobal. Papua New Guinea is to the west and Vanuatu to the southeast.

Physical Geography: The country is composed of volcanic islands (some still active) and atolls.

Total area: 10,985 sq mi (28,450 sq km)

Coastline: 3,299 mi (5,313 km)

Land use: Forests and woodlands cover 88% of the land, 2% is arable and under cultivation, and 1% is meadows and pastures.

Climate: Tropical, with rainfall throughout the year

Population: 430,000

Urban population: 13%

Rate of natural increase: 3.2%

Age structure: 47% under 15; 3% over 65

Birth rate: 37/1000

Death rate: 4/1000

Infant mortality rate: 28/1000

Fertility rate: 5.4

Life expectancy at birth: 68 years (male); 73 years (female)

Religion: Protestant, Roman Catholic, traditional

Language: Melanesian pidgin, 120 indigenous languages, English

Ethnic Divisions: Melanesian, Polynesian

Literacy Rate: N.A.

Government: Parliamentary democracy with a governor-general appointed by the British monarch and a unicameral legislature, the National Parliament. The 47 members of the legislature are directly elected to four-year terms. There are four administrative districts.

Armed services: No standing military force; the Police Field Force, a unit within the Police Force, patrols the country's territory

Suffrage: Universal; 21 years old

Economy: Subsistence farming, forestry, and fishing are key to the country's economy. Cyclones have severely damaged the country's infrastructure, and external debt and commodity price fluctuations have eroded the country's financial health. The government is promoting World War II battle sites as tourist attractions and is working to increase economic growth with industry privatization and other investments. The government has not adopted a policy of sustainable logging of its rain forests, which has caused international concern and the loss of some financial aid.

Unit of currency: Solomon Islands dollar; 100 cents = 1 Solomon Islands dollar (SI$)

GDP per capita: $3,000

Inflation rate–CPI: 11.8% (1996)

Workforce: 26,842 (1992 est.)

Unemployment rate: N.A.

Exports: Goods worth $168 million (f.o.b., 1995) are sent to Japan, the U.K., Thailand, Australia, and other trading partners; exports include timber, seafood, palm oil, cocoa, and copra.

Imports: Goods worth $152 million (c.i.f., 1995 est.) are received from Australia, Japan, Singapore, New Zealand, and other trading partners;

imports include machinery, manufactured goods, food, live animals, and fuels.

Agriculture: 41.5% (1995) of the working population engages in agriculture, fishing, and forestry. Livestock and subsistence crops of sweet potatoes, taro, yams, vegetables, and fruit are raised for domestic use. Coconuts, cocoa, rice, oil palm, and some spices and honey are produced for export; fish, timber, and seashells are also significant commodities.

Energy: Most energy is derived using hydropower.

Natural Resources: Seafood, timber, minerals, including gold, bauxite, phosphates, lead, zinc, nickel

Environmental Issues: Soil erosion; deforestation; dying coral reefs

Transportation: There are no railroads. There are 850 miles (1,360 km) of roads, of which 20 miles (35 km) are paved; most are on the main islands, particularly Guadacanal, Malaita, and Makira. Honiara, on Guadacanal, Yandina, and Gizo are the main seaports, and an international airport is at Honiara.

Communications: There are three weekly newspapers but no dailies. There are 38,000 radios and 2,000 televisions (1992) in operation. Phone service, with 5,000 lines (1991), is adequate.

Tourism: Wildlife, cultural exhibits, and World War II battlefields attract visitors, who spent an estimated $6 million in the country in 1994.

Embassy: (202) 599-6192

Public Holidays: Easter (date varies, in March or April); Whit Monday (date varies, in May); Queen's Official Birthday (date varies, in June); Independence Day: from the U.K., 1978 (July 7); Christmas (December 25); Boxing Day (December 26)

Somalia

Country Name: Somalia

Official Name: Somalia

Nationality: Somali(s) (noun); Somali (adjective)

Capital: Mogadishu, pop. 900,000

Major cities: Hargeysa, Kismaayo (Chisimayu), Berbera, Marka (Merca)

External Territories: None

Location: Somalia, on the Horn of Africa, with the Gulf of Aden to the north and the Indian Ocean to the east, is bordered on the northwest by Djibouti, on the west by Ethiopia, and on the southwest by Kenya.

Physical Geography: Coastal plains rise to mountains in the north; central plateaus slope to plains in the south.

Total area: 246,201 sq mi (637,657 sq km)

Coastline: 1,879 mi (3,025 km)

Land use: Nearly 70% of the land is meadows and pastures, 26% is forested, and 2% is arable or under cultivation.

Climate: Tropical to subtropical, generally more rainfall in the south, high temperatures along the northern coasts

Population: 7,141,000

Urban population: 24%

Rate of natural increase: 2.8%

Age structure: 44% under 15; 3% over 65

Birth rate: 47/1000

Death rate: 19/1000

Infant mortality rate: 125.8/1000

Fertility rate: 6.8

Life expectancy at birth: 49 years (male), 48 years (female)

Religion: Sunni Muslim

Language: Somali, Arabic, Italian, English

Ethnic Divisions: Somali

Literacy Rate: 24%

Government: No functioning government since 1991. A 41 member National Salvation Council is in place. There are 18 administrative regions.

Armed services: No national armed forces

Suffrage: Universal; 18 years old

Economy: Civil war, clan warfare, and external debt have had severe repercussions on the Somali economy since 1989. Most of the working population practices subsistence farming and livestock husbandry; international relief operations have been essential in providing Somali citizens with food and medical care. The country must achieve political stability before much needed economic growth and development can begin.

Unit of currency: Somali shilling; 100 cents = 1 Somali shilling (So sh)

GDP per capita: $600

Inflation rate–CPI: 45.7% (1980–1988 average); 100% (1991 est.)

Workforce: 4,290,000 (1996 est.) .

Unemployment rate: N.A.

Exports: Goods worth $130 million (1994 est.) are sent to Saudi Arabia, Germany, Italy, and other trading partners; exports include bananas, live animals, fish, and hides.

Imports: Goods worth $269 million (1994 est.) are received from the U.S., Italy, France, Kenya, the U.K., Saudi Arabia, and other trading partners; imports include manufactured products, petroleum products, food, and construction materials.

Agriculture: Nearly 73% (1996) of the labor force engages in agriculture. Cattle, fish, and bananas are the principal cash commodities raised.

Energy: Imported fuel is used for most energy generation.

Natural Resources: Minerals, including uranium, iron ore, tin, gypsum, bauxite, copper, salt

Environmental Issues: Deforestation, soil erosion, desertification, nonpotable water

Transportation: There are no railroads; of the 13,720 miles (22,100 km) of roads, 1,620 miles (2,610 km) are paved. Main seaports are Marka, Berbera, Mogadishu, and Kismaayo, and an international airport is at Mogadishu.

Communications: One daily paper is published in Mogadishu (1995). There are 400,000 radios and 124,000 televisions (1995) in operation. Telephone service, with 15,000 lines 1994, has been disrupted by the civil war.

Tourism: Game reserves and national parks, with some rare African animals, beaches, and fishing have been popular attractions; however, travel is not advised during the period of civil unrest.

Public Holidays: End of Ramadan (date varies, in February); Feast of the Sacrifice (date varies, in April); Ashura (date varies, in April or May); Labor Day (May 1); Independence Day: from the U.K., 1960 (June 26); Birth of the Prophet (date varies, in July); Foundation of the Republic, 1960 (July 1)

South Africa

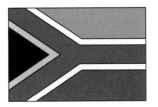

Country Name: South Africa

Official Name: Republic of South Africa

Nationality: South African(s) (noun); South African (adjective)

Capital: Pretoria (administrative), pop. 525,000 [822,900]; Cape Town (legislative), pop. [2,350,000]; Bloemfontein (judicial), pop. [126,900]

Major cities: Durban, Johannesburg, Port Elizabeth

External Territories: None

Location: South Africa, at the southern tip of Africa, with the Indian Ocean to the east and the South Atlantic Ocean to the west, is bordered on the north by Namibia, Botswana, and Zimbabwe, on the northeast by Mozambique, and on the east by Swaziland. Lesotho is surrounded by South Africa.

Physical Geography: Narrow coastal plains rise to the Drakensberg, a semicircular escarpment that borders the broad plateau occupying the interior of the country; the plateau slopes gradually to the northeast and northwest. The Great Karroo, coastal mountains, run along the southern coast. Part of the Namib Desert lies along the west coast and a strip of the Kalahari Desert borders Botswana in the north. The Orange River is tapped for irrigation.

Total area: 471,445 sq mi (1,221,037 sq km)

Coastline: 1,738 miles (2,798 km)

Land use: About 67% of the country is meadows and pastures, 11% is arable or under cultivation, and 7% is forested.

Climate: Mostly temperate subtropical; Mediterranean along the southwest coast, with hot summers and rainy winters; semiarid in the west

Population: 42,579,000

Urban population: 45%

Rate of natural increase: 1.61%

Age structure: 34% under 15; 5% over 65

Birth rate: 27.35/1000

Death rate: 11.25/1000

Infant mortality rate: 52.13/1000

Fertility rate: 3.3

Life expectancy at birth: 55 years (male); 60 years (female)

Religion: Christian, indigenous beliefs, Hindu, Muslim

Language: Afrikaans, English, Ndebele, Pedi, Sotho, Swazi, Tsonga, Tswana, Venda, Xhosa, Zulu (all official)

Ethnic Divisions: Black, white, mixed, Asian

Literacy Rate: 82%

Government: Republic, with a president and a bicameral legislature, the Parliament. The president is elected to office by the 400 members of the National Assembly who are elected by direct vote; the 90 members of the National Council of Provinces are elected by provincial governments. There are nine administrative provinces.

Armed services: 79,440 troops (1997) in the army, air force, and navy

Suffrage: Universal; 18 years old

Economy: South Africa's economy is based on mining , especially of diamonds and gold. International economic sanctions (due to apartheid) in the 1980s, including foreign disinvestment, seriously hindered the economy, and droughts affected crop production. Sanctions were repealed in 1993, and the country has rescheduled international debt payments, but high unemployment rates and continued civil unrest continue to impede economic growth.

Unit of currency: Rand; 100 cents = 1 rand (R)

GDP per capita: $6,200

Inflation rate–CPI: 9.7% (1997 est.)

Workforce: 14,356,000 (1995 est.)

Unemployment rate: 30% (1997 est.)

Exports: Goods worth $31.3 billion (f.o.b., 1997) are sent to Italy, Japan, the U.S., Germany, the U.K., Switzerland, and other trading partners; exports include gold and other

minerals, food, and chemicals. Gold earned 20% of the total value of exports in 1997.

Imports: Goods worth $28 billion - (f.o.b., 1997) are received from Germany, the U.S., Japan, the U.K., Italy, and other trading partners; imports include animistic machinery, transportation equipment, chemicals, oil, textiles, and scientific instruments.

Agriculture: Nearly 13% (1995) of the labor force engages in agriculture, fishing, and forestry. Export commodities include corn, fruit, wheat, sugarcane, vegetables and beef; corn is also a key subsistence crop.

Energy: Domestic coal generates most energy and is supplemented by hydropower and power from one nuclear plant.

Natural Resources: Gold, chromium, antimony, coal, iron, manganese, nickel, phosphates, tin, uranium, diamonds, platinum, copper, vanadium, salt, natural gas

Environmental Issues: Limited freshwater; air and water pollution, including acid rain; desertification, soil erosion

Transportation: There are 13,310 miles (21,430 km) of railroads and 205,720 miles (331,270km) of roads, of which 85,370 miles (137,480 km) are paved. Main Atlantic seaports are Cape Town and Saldanha Bay; Indian Ocean ports include Port Elizabeth, East London, Durban, and Richards Bay. Cape Town, Johannesburg, and Durban have international airports.

Communications: The country has 20 daily newspapers. There are 13.1 million radios and 2.3 million televisions (1995) in use. Telephone service, with 3,988,000 main lines (1995), provide the best service in Africa.

Tourism: Tourism is highly profitable for South Africa. Attractions include Johannesburg, Pretoria, and Cape Town, with their many parks, gardens, and museums. There are na-

ture reserves and wildlife excursions, and Kruger National Park is one of the country's best known sites. Nearly 5 million tourists and visitors in 1996 spent $2.1 billion (U.S.).

U.S. Tourist Office: (800) 822-5368

Embassy in U.S.: (202) 232-4400

Public Holidays: Human Rights Day (March 21); Good Friday (date varies, in March or April); Family Day (date varies, in March or April); Freedom Day (April 27); Workers' Day (May 1); Youth Day (June 16); National Women's Day (August 9); Heritage Day (September 24); Day of Reconciliation (December 16); Christmas (December 25); Day of Goodwill (December 26)

Spain

Country Name: Spain

Official Name: Kingdom of Spain

Nationality: Spaniard(s) (noun); Spanish (adjective)

Capital: Madrid, pop. [2,866,900]

Major cities: Barcelona, Valencia, Sevilla, Zaragoza, Málaga

External Territories: On the Mediterranean coast and bordered by Morocco in North Africa: Ceuta (8 sq mi, 20 sq km; pop. 67,600); Melilla (5 sq mi, 13 sq km; pop. 56,600)

Location: Spain occupies most of the Iberian Peninsula in southwestern Europe, with the Atlantic Ocean on the north and the Mediterranean on the south. It is bordered on the north by France and on the west by Portugal; the country of Andorra lies between France and Spain. The Canary Islands, in the Atlantic Ocean

SPAIN A BASQUE BALL GAMES GOES BIG TIME

The Basque people living in the Pyrenees Mountains that border Spain and France appear to be descended from some of the first people to live in Europe. Blood-typing and genetic studies have indicated that they are unrelated to any other people in Europe today and were probably living in the Pyrenees and Cantabrian Mountains before the first Indo-Europeans reached the area thousands of years ago. Most Basques today speak either French or Spanish, but about one-fourth speak one of the Basque language's eight dialects, which were banned by the Spanish government for almost 40 years. At times resorting to terrorism, the Basques have fought for years to preserve their culture and language. The ball sport jai alai, popular in many parts of the world, is a Basque invention.

off the coast of Morocco, and the Balearic Islands, in the Mediterranean Sea, are also Spanish territory.

Physical Geography: A large central plateau, the Meseta, is almost enclosed by mountains: the Cordillera Cantábrica and the Pyrenees are in the north, and the Sierra Moreno are to the south. Major rivers include the Tagus, Douro, Ebro, and the Guadalquivr.

Total area: 194,897 sq mi (504,782 sq km)

Coastline: 3,083 mi (4,964 km)

Land use: About 40% of the land is arable or under cultivation, 32% is forested, and 21% is meadows and pastures.

Climate: Temperate, with hot summers and cold winters; northern coast generally cooler in the summer, with rainfall throughout the year; dry summers and mild winters along southern coast

Population: 39,418,000

Urban population: 64%

Rate of natural increase: 0.0%

Age structure: 15% under 15; 16% over 65

Birth rate: 9/1000

Death rate: 9/1000

Infant mortality rate: 5.5/1000

Fertility rate: 1.2

Life expectancy at birth: 74 years (male); 82 years (female)

Religion: Roman Catholic

Language: Spanish, Catalan, Galician, Basque

Ethnic Divisions: Spanish, Catalan, Galician, Basque

Literacy Rate: 96%

Government: Parliamentary monarchy with a hereditary monarch, King Juan Carlos since 1975, and a bicameral legislature, the General Courts, or Las Cortes Generales. The 350 members of the Congress of Deputies are directly elected to four-year terms, and the 256 members of the Senate are elected to four-year terms. There are 17 administrative communities.

Armed services: 197,500 troops (1997) in the army, navy, and air force; compulsory service for nine months

Suffrage: Universal; 18 years old

Economy: Manufacturing, services, and agriculture are important components of the Spanish economy. Although affected by recession in the early 1990s, the country has experienced some recovery; however, unemployment is still a serious concern. The government is trying

to reduce its bureaucracy, increase revenues from tax collection, and turn over state industries to the private sector.

Unit of currency: Peseta; 100 céntimos = 1 Spanish peseta (Pta)

GDP per capita: $14,400 (

Inflation rate–CPI: 2.1% (1997 est.)

Workforce: 16.2 million

Unemployment rate: 21% (1997 est.)

Exports: Goods worth $94.5 billion (f.o.b., 1995 est.) are sent to The European Union, the U.S., and other trading partners; exports include cars, trucks, semifinished manufactured goods, foodstuffs, and machinery.

Imports: Goods worth $118.3 billion (c.i.f., 1995 est.) are received from the European Union, the U.S., the Middle East, and other trading partners; imports include machinery, transport equipment, fuels, semifinished goods, foodstuffs, consumer goods, and chemicals.

Agriculture: 8% (1997 est.) of the workforce engages in agriculture, fishing, and forestry. Principal crops are grain, vegetables, olives, wine grapes, sugar beets, and citrus. Wine, olive oil, and fishing are also important.

Energy: Imported oil fuels most energy generation; nuclear energy supplies 29.3% (1997) of the country's needs.

Natural Resources: Lignite coal, iron ore, uranium, mercury, pyrites, fluorspar, gypsum, zinc, lead, tungsten, copper, kaolin, potash, hydropower

Environmental Issues: Water and air pollution, deforestation, desertification

Transportation: There are 9,420 miles (15,170 km) of railroads and 214,150 miles (344,840 km) of roads, of which the majority are paved. Main seaports include Barcelona and Valencia on the Mediterranean, Bilbao on the

Atlantic, and Las Palmas and Santa Cruz de Tenerife in the Canary Islands. Madrid, Barcelona, Málaga, Alicante, Bilbao, Sevilla, Valencia, Santiago de Compostela, Palma de Mallorca, Menorca, Las Palmas, and Tenerife have international airports.

Communications: 85 daily newspapers are published. There are 12 million radios and 15.9 million televisions (1992 est.) in use. Phone service, with 12.6 million lines (1990 est.) in service, is generally good.

Tourism: Numerous attractions draw visitors to Spain, including historic cities, the running of the bulls in Pamplona, and Mediterranean beaches. In 1996, over 61.9 million tourists visited Spain.

U.S. Tourist Office: (212) 759-8822

Embassy in U.S.: (202) 452-0100

Public Holidays: Epiphany (January 6); St. Joseph the Workman (March 19); Good Friday (date varies, in March or April); Easter (date varies, in March or April); Labor Day (May 1); Corpus Christi (date varies, in May or June); King's Saint's Day (June 24); St. James of Compostela (July 25); Assumption (August 15); National Day (October 12); All Saints' Day (November 1); Constitution Day (date varies, in December); Immaculate Conception (December 8); Christmas (December 25)

Sri Lanka

Country Name: Sri Lanka

Official Name: Democratic Socialist Republic of Sri Lanka

Nationality: Sri Lankan(s) (noun); Sri Lankan (adjective)

Capital: Colombo, pop. 615,000

Major cities: Dehiwala-Mount Lavinia, Moratuwa, Jaffna

SRI LANKA STRUGGLES OVER SEPARATISM

The Buddhist majority, the Sinhalese, has been warring with the Hindu Tamil separatist minority since the 1980's; the Tamils want to establish a separate state in the country's northeast corner. Known as Ceylon before 1972, this island is about the size of West Virginia and was a Dutch colony from 1658–1796 and a British colony until independence in 1948.

External Territories: None

Location: Sri Lanka, in the Indian Ocean, is an island country off the southeastern tip of India.

Physical Geography: Central highlands extend to mountains in the southwest; rolling plains occupy the east, and lowlands are in the north.

Total area: 25,332 sq mi (65,610 sq km)

Coastline: 832 mi (1,340 km)

Land use: Nearly 35% of the country is forested, 29% is arable or under cultivation, and 7% is meadows and pastures.

Climate: Tropical monsoon

Population: 19,003,000

Urban population: 22%

Rate of natural increase: 1.2%

Age structure: 35% under 15; 4% over 65

Birth rate: 19/1000

Death rate: 7/1000

Infant mortality rate: 17/1000

Fertility rate: 2.3

Life expectancy at birth: 70 years (male); 74 years (female)

Religion: Theravada Buddhist, Hindu, Christian, Muslim

Language: Sinhalese, Tamil, English

Ethnic Divisions: Sinhalese, Tamil, Moor

Literacy Rate: 90%

Government: Republic, with a president and a unicameral legislature, the Parliament. The president is directly elected for a six-year term; the number of legislative representa-

tives varies, about 225, but all are directly elected to six-year terms. There are eight administrative provinces.

Armed services: 112,000–117,000 troops (1997 est.) in the army, navy, and air force

Suffrage: Universal; 18 years old

Economy: External debt, inflation, unemployment, and civil unrest have interfered with Sri Lanka's economic growth in the last decade. The country's economy is based on textile manufacturing and agriculture. Foreign investment is increasing, and the government is working to promote privatization. However, fighting between the Sinhala majority government and Tamil guerrillas, begun in the mid-1980s, continues to drain the country's resources.

Unit of currency: Sri Lankan rupee; 100 cents = 1 Sri Lankan rupee (SLRe)

GDP per capita: $3,800

Inflation rate–CPI: 9.6% average (1997 est.)

Workforce: 6.2 million (1997 est.)

Unemployment rate: 11% (1997 est.)

Exports: Goods worth $4.1 billion (f.o.b., 1996) are sent to the U.S., the U.K., Japan, Germany, Netherlands, and other trading partners; exports include garments, textiles, tea, and diamonds.

Imports: Goods worth $5.4 billion (c.i.f., 1996) are received from India, Japan, South Korea, Hong Kong, Taiwan, and other trading partners; imports include textiles, machinery, transportation equipment, food, oil, and construction materials.

Agriculture: Over one-third (1997 est.) the labor force engages in agriculture, fishing, and forestry. Tea, rubber, and coconuts are key export crops; rice and livestock are also raised. In 1995, tea earned 11.7% of the country's total value of exports.

Energy: Most energy is generated using hydropower.

Natural Resources: Limestone, graphite, mineral sand, gems, phosphates, clay

Environmental Issues: Water pollution, deforestation, soil erosion, poaching

Transportation: There are 930 miles (1,500 km) of railroads and 61,600 miles (99,200 km) of roads, of which 24,640 miles (39,680 km) are paved. There are also 270 miles (430 km) of canals and rivers navigable by shallow draft boats. Colombo, Trincomalee, Galle, and Jaffna are important seaports. There is an international airport at Colombo.

Communications: Nine daily newspapers are published (1995). There are 3.6 million radios and 1.6 million televisions (1996 est.) in operation; 352,000 telephones (1997 est.) provide poor domestic service.

Tourism: Sri Lanka's many beaches are a prime tourist draw. Buddhist and Hindu temples and shrines are also important tourist attractions, as are traditional hill country cultural activities.

Embassy in U.S.: (202) 483-4025

Public Holidays: Ramazan Festival Day (date varies, in February); Independence Commemoration Day: from the U.K., 1948 (February 4); Good Friday (date varies, in March or April); Easter Monday (date varies, in March or April); Hadji Festival Day (date varies, in April); May Day (May 1); National Heroes' Day (May 22); Special Bank Holiday (June 30); birth of the Prophet (date varies, in July); Christmas (December 25); Boxing Day (December 26); Special Bank Holiday (December 31)

Sudan

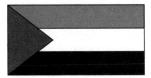

Country Name: Sudan
Official Name: Republic of the Sudan
Nationality: Sudanese (singular and plural noun); Sudanese (adjective)
Capital: Khartoum, pop. 947,500
Major cities: Nyala, Port Sudan, Kassala
External Territories: None
Location: Sudan, the largest country in Africa, is bordered on the north by Egypt; on the east by the Red Sea, Eritrea and Ethiopia; on the south by Kenya, Uganda, and the Democratic Republic of the Congo; and on the west by the Central African Republic, Chad, and Libya.
Physical Geography: There are Saharan plains in the north and sand dunes in the west; swamps and mountains occupy the central and southern sections of the country. The White Nile and the Blue Nile, flowing from the south, merge at Khartoum.
Total area: 963,600 sq mi (2,495,712 sq km)
Coastline: 530 mi (853 km)
Land use: Meadows and pastures cover 46% of the country, 19% is wooded, and 5% is arable or under cultivation.
Climate: Tropical, northern deserts, rainfall from April to October increasing southward
Population: 28,883,000
Urban population: 27%
Rate of natural increase: 2.16%
Age structure: 43% under 15; 3% over 65

Birth rate: 33.1/1000
Death rate: 11.5/1000
Infant mortality rate: 69.5/1000
Fertility rate: 4.6
Life expectancy at birth: 50 years (male); 52 years (female)
Religion: Sunni Muslim, indigenous beliefs, Christian
Language: Arabic, Nubian, Ta Bedawie
Ethnic Divisions: Arab, Nilotic groups, Beja, others
Literacy Rate: 46%
Government: Transitional republic, from a military junta to a president and unicameral legislature, the National Assembly. Of the 400 members of the transitional legislature, 275 were directly elected in 1996 and 125 appointed to office in 1992; a new constitution was presented in 1998. There are 26 administrative states.
Armed services: 79,700 troops (1997) in the army, navy, and air force; compulsory service up to 36 months for males 18–30 years of age
Suffrage: Universal, but non-compulsory
Economy: A large foreign debt substantially blocks Sudan's economic growth, and civil unrest, bad weather, high inflation, and poor economic policy management contribute to the country's financial plight. Most of the labor force works in agriculture, and the small industrial sector is in need of modernization. The country continues to set goals with the international financial community to pay its debts but has had trouble in meeting its obligations. Foreign investors are reluctant to do business.
Unit of currency: Sudanese pound; 1,000 millièmes = 100 piastres = 1 Sudanese pound (£S)
GDP per capita: $875
Inflation rate–CPI: 27% (1997 est.)
Workforce: 10.119 million (1996 est.)

Unemployment rate: 30% (1992–1993 est.)

Exports: Goods worth $620 million (f.o.b., 1996) are sent to the U.K., Saudi Arabia, China, the U.S., and other trading partners; exports include cotton, sesame, livestock, meat, and gum arabic.

Imports: Goods worth $1.5 billion (1996) are received from the South Korea, Germany, Egypt, Saudi Arabia, the U.S., and other trading partners; imports include food, oil products, manufactured goods, machinery, medicines, chemicals, and textiles.

Agriculture: 67% (1996) of the labor force engages in the agricultural sector. Cotton, the most important export crop, earned 23% of the total value of exports in 1996. Other cash crops include gum arabic, and sesame. Sorghum, groundnuts, millet, wheat, and sheed are raised for subsistence use.

Energy: Hydropower and imported oil are both used for energy generation.

Natural Resources: Oil, iron, copper, chromium, zinc, tungsten, mica, silver, gold

Environmental Issues: Desertification, soil erosion, limited potable water, overhunting

Transportation: There are 3,430 miles (5,520 km) of railroads and 7,390 miles (11,900 km) of roads, of which about 35% are paved. Weather conditions make roads impassable at times. The Blue Nile, White Nile, and Nile River are navigable in part: 2,530 miles (4,070 km) in times of high water and 1,070 miles (1,720 km) year-round. River ports include Khartoum on the Nile and Kusti on the White Nile. Port Sudan on the Red Sea is the main seaport. An international airport is at Khartoum.

Communications: Several daily newspapers, controlled by the government since 1989, are published. There are 7,200,000 radios and 2.2 million televisions (1995) in operation. Phone service, with about 64,000 phones in use (1993), is minimal.

Tourism: Tourist attractions in Sudan include Omdurman's camel market, the souk and the National Museum in Khartoum, and archaeological sites along the Nile River. Red Sea diving opportunities and marine gardens are another key draw, and national parks are full of wildlife. In 1994, visitors spent an estimated $3 million (U.S.) in the country.

Embassy in U.S.: (202) 338-8565

Public Holidays: Independence Day: from the U.K. and Egypt, 1956 (January 1); End of Ramadan (date varies, in February); Unity Day (March 3); Feast of the Sacrifice (date varies, in April); Coptic Easter Monday (date varies, in April); Uprising Day (April 6); Islamic New Year (date varies, in April or May); Decentralization Day (July 1); Birth of the Prophet (date varies, in July); Christmas (December 25)

Suriname

Country Name: Suriname

Official Name: Republic of Suriname

Nationality: Surinamer(s) (noun); Surinamese (adjective)

Capital: Paramaribo, pop. 216,600 [265,000]

Major cities: Nieuw Nickerie

External Territories: None

Location: Suriname, on South America's north coast, is bordered on the north by the Atlantic Ocean, on the east by French Guiana, on the south by Brazil, and on the west by Guyana.

Physical Geography: A narrow coastal plain rises to forested hills; mountains lie to the south of the hills. A small section of plains occupies the southwest. The Litani (Itany) River forms the border with French Guiana and the Koeroeni (Courantyne) River with Guyana.

Total area: 63,037 sq mi (163,265 sq km)

Coastline: 240 mi (386 km)

Land use: Forest and woodland cover 97% of the country; negligible areas are devoted to agriculture, meadows, and pastures.

Climate: Tropical

Population: 431,000

Urban population: 70%

Rate of natural increase: 1.8%

Age structure: 34% under 15; 5% over 65

Birth rate: 23.9/1000

Death rate: 5.9/1000

Infant mortality rate: 29.3/1000

Fertility rate: 2.6

Life expectancy at birth: 68 years (male); 73 years (female)

Religion: Hindu, Protestant, Roman Catholic, Muslim

Language: Dutch, English, Sranang Tongo (Taki-Taki), Hindustani, Javanese

Ethnic Divisions: Creole, East Indian, Javanese, black, Indian

Literacy Rate: 93%

Government: Republic, with a president and a unicameral legislature, the National Assembly. The 51 members of the legislature are directly elected to five-year terms; they in turn elect the president. There are ten administrative districts.

Armed services: 1,800 troops (1997) in the army, navy, and air force

Suffrage: Universal; 18 years old

Economy: Aluminum and aluminum industries have traditionally been the key support of Suriname's economy, but political coups and guerrilla activity since 1986 have led to massive industry destabilization, and the country has needed outside assistance to sustain economic growth and development. Inflation is somewhat under control, and the country has rescheduled international debt payments.

Unit of currency: Surinamese guilder or florin; 100 cents = 1 guilder or florin (Sf)

GDP per capita: $3,400

Inflation rate–CPI: 8% (1997 est.)

Workforce: N.A.

Unemployment rate: 20% (1997)

Exports: Goods worth $434.3 million (f.o.b., 1996 est.) are sent to Norway, the Netherlands, the U.S., Japan, Brazil, and other trading partners; exports include alumina and aluminum, shrimp, fish, rice, and bananas.

Imports: Goods worth $490 million (f.o.b., 1997 est.) are received from the U.S., the Netherlands, Trinidad and Tobago, Japan, and other trading partners; imports include capital equipment, oil, food, cotton, and consumer goods.

Agriculture: 20% (1996) of the labor force engages in agriculture, fishing, and forestry. Rice is the principal domestic and export crop, and seafood, principally shrimp, is also exported. Bananas, sugarcane, citrus, and plantains are also grown for cash; vegetables, coconuts, and livestock are raised for domestic use. The timber industry is being developed.

Energy: Most energy is generated using imported oil.

Natural Resources: Timber; seafood; hydropower; minerals, including bauxite, iron, nickel, copper, platinum, gold

Environmental Issues: Deforestation

Transportation: The nearly 105 miles (166 km) of railroads are for the timber and sugarcane industry

only. Of the 2,815 miles (4,530 km) of roads, about a quarter are paved. The 745 miles (1,200 km) of navigable rivers and canals are important links within the country. Paramaribo is the country's main seaport and the location of an international airport.

Communications: At least two daily newspapers are published in the capital. There are 290,000 radios and nearly 60,000 televisions (1993) in use. Phone service, with 43,500 phones operating, is good.

Tourism: Dutch colonial architecture in Paramaribo, along with its parks and museums, is an interesting tourist stop; nature reserves offer wildlife viewing opportunities. Suriname earned $11 million (U.S.) from visitors in 1994.

Embassy in U.S.: (202) 244-7488

Public Holidays: End of Ramadan (date varies, in February); Phagwa (date varies,in March); Easter (date varies, in March or April); Labor Day (May 1); National Union Day (July 1); Independence Day: from the Netherlands, 1975 (November 25); Christmas (December 25–26)

Swaziland

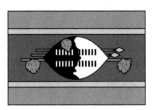

Country Name: Swaziland

Official Name: Kingdom of Swaziland

Nationality: Swazi(s) (noun); Swazi (adjective)

Capital: Mbabane, pop. 38,300

Major cities: Manzani

External Territories: None

Location: Swaziland, a landlocked country in southern Africa, is bor-

dered on three sides by South Africa, and Mozambique is to the east.

Physical Geography: Western highlands gradually descend to eastern plateaus; the Lebombo Mountains are on the border with Mozambique.

Total Area: 6,704 sq mi (17,364 sq km)

Coastline: None

Land use: Nearly two-thirds of the country is meadows and pastures, 11% is arable or under cultivation, and 7% is wooded.

Climate: Temperate to subtropical, with rain from November to March; precipitation generally increasing from east to west

Population: 985,000

Urban population: 22%

Rate of natural increase: 3.2%

Age structure: 44% under 15; 3% over 65

Birth rate: 41.9/1000

Death rate: 9.9/1000

Infant mortality rate: 72/1000

Fertility rate: 5.2

Life expectancy at birth: 38 years (male); 41 years (female)

Religion: Christian, indigenous beliefs

Language: English, Swazi (both official)

Ethnic Divisions: Swazi, Zulu

Literacy Rate: 77%

Government: Monarchy, with a king, Mswati III since 1986, and an advisory bicameral legislature, the Libandla. Of the 65 members of the National Assembly, 55 are elected and 10 are appointed by the monarch; of the 30 members of the Senate, 20 are appointed by the monarch and 10 are elected by the National Assembly. There are four administrative divisions.

Armed services: 2,657 troops (1983); compulsory service for two years

Suffrage: None

Economy: Swaziland's economy is dominated by South Africa, which provides about 90% of its imports. Agriculture, which is vulnerable to drought, occupies much of the workforce. Remittances from Swazis who work in South Africa are important to the economy. Tourism and mining hold potential for improving the country's finances. Strikes in 1996 and 1997 discouraged foreign investors and the budget deficit continues to hinder growth, but the government hopes to increase revenue through tax reform and other measures.

Unit of currency: Lilangeni (singular), emalangeni (plural); 100 cents = 1 lilangeni (E)

GDP per capita: $3,800

Inflation rate–CPI: 9.5%

Workforce: 315,000 (1996 est.)

Unemployment rate: 22% (1995 est.)

Exports: Goods worth $893 million (f.o.b., 1996) are sent to South Africa, the U.K., and other trading partners; exports include sugar, wood pulp, cotton yarn, and soft drink concentrates.

Imports: Goods worth $1.1 billion (f.o.b., 1996) are received from South Africa, Switzerland, the U.K., and other trading partners; imports include vehicles, machinery, oil products, food, and chemicals.

Agriculture: 32% (1996) of the workforce engages in agriculture and forestry. Sugarcane, cotton, citrus, pineapples, maize, tobacco, and rice are cash crops, and pulp wood is also important. The majority of farming is for subsistence and includes cattle.

Energy: South Africa provides most of the country's energy needs, and domestic hydropower is being developed.

Natural Resources: Hydropower; timber; minerals, including asbestos, coal, clay, cassiterite, gold, diamonds, talc

Environmental Issues: Soil erosion and degradation, overhunting, and potable water

Transportation: There are nearly 190 miles (300 km) of railroads and 1,790 miles (2,890 km) of roads, of which nearly 30% are paved. There is an international airport at Manzani.

Communications: Two daily newspapers are published. There are 140,000 radios and 18,000 televisions (1994) in operation. There are 30,400 (1993 est.) telephones in service, providing minimal service.

Tourism: Mineral springs, casinos, breathtaking scenery, waterfalls, and game sanctuaries are some of Swaziland's tourist attractions. In 1994, the country earned an estimated $29 million (U.S.) from visitors.

Embassy in U.S.: (202) 362-6683

Public Holidays: Commonwealth Day (date varies, in March); Easter (date varies, in March or April); King Mswati III's birthday (April 19); National Flag Day (April 25); Ascension Day (date varies, in May); Birthday of King Sobhuza, first hereditary monarch, who died in 1982 (July 22); Independence Day: from the U.K., 1968 (September 6); United Nations Day (October 24); Christmas (December 25); Boxing Day (December 26)

Sweden

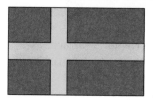

Country Name: Sweden

Official Name: Kingdom of Sweden

Nationality: Swede(s) (noun); Swedish (adjective)

Capital: Stockhom, pop. 718,500

Major cities: Göteborg, Malmö, Uppsala

External Territories: None

Location: Sweden, which takes up two-thirds of the Scandinavian Peninsula, is in northern Europe. Finland is on the northeast border and Norway is on the west. The Gulf of Bothnia and the Baltic Sea are on the east and the Skagerrak and Kattegat separate Sweden from Denmark on the south.

Physical Geography: Rugged mountains drained by many streams and rivers on the Norwegian border slope to inland hills. Plains with many lakes occupy the central and southern sections of the country. In the far south, a plateau rises from the lowlands.

Total area: 173,732 sq mi (449,964 sq km)

Coastline: 1,998 miles (3,218 km)

Land use: Nearly 70% of the country is forested, 7% is arable or under cultivation, and 1% is meadows and pastures.

Climate: Temperate, with mild summers and cold winters; subarctic zone, with severe winters, in the north

Population: 8,856,000

Urban population: 84%

Rate of natural increase: -0.1%

Age structure: 19% under 15; 17% over 65

Birth rate: 10/1000

Death rate: 11/1000

Infant mortality rate: 3.6/1000

Fertility rate: 1.5

Life expectancy at birth: 77 years (male); 82 years (female)

Religion: Evangelical Lutheran

Language: Swedish

Ethnic Divisions: white, Lapp (Sami), foreign born or first generation immigrants

Literacy Rate: 99%

Government: Constitutional monarchy, King Carl XVI Gustaf since 1973, and a unicameral legis-

SWEDEN   SCANDINAVIA DEFINED

Sweden is the largest country in Scandinavia, which is defined geographically as the peninsula shared by Sweden and Norway and politically as the five countries of the Nordic Council: Sweden, Norway, Denmark, Finland, and Iceland. Except for Finland, the languages of all these countries are related in some way.

lature, the Riksdag. The 349 members of the legislature are directly elected to four-year terms. There are 24 administrative counties.

Armed services: 53,350 troops (1997) in the army, navy, and air force; compulsory service for men, 19–47 years of age: 7–15 months for army and navy, 8–12 months for air force; voluntary service for women

Suffrage: Universal; 18 years old

Economy: Natural resources, including timber, iron ore, and hydropower, underlie the strength of the Swedish economy. In recent years unemployment, inflation, and a weakening export trade have somewhat eroded Sweden's economic strength. Austerity budgets have been proposed to help reduce the budget deficit, and the government is working to maintain Sweden's economic standing with other European countries.

Unit of currency: Swedish krona (singular), kronor (plural); 100 öre = 1 Swedish krona (SKr)

GDP per capita: $19,700

Inflation rate–CPI: 2% (1997)

Workforce: 4.55 million (1992)

Unemployment rate: 6.6% (1997 est.)

Exports: Goods worth $84.5 billion (f.o.b., 1996 est.) are sent to Germany, the U.K., Norway, Denmark, France, Finland, and other trading partners; exports include machinery, motor vehicles, paper products, pulp and wood, iron and steel products, chemicals, and petroleum and petroleum products.

Imports: Goods worth $66.6 billion (c.i.f., 1996 est.) are received from Germany, the U.K., the U.S., Denmark, Norway, Finland, and other trading partners; imports include machinery, petroleum and petroleum products, chemicals, vehicles, foodstuffs, iron and steel, and clothing.

Agriculture: 3.2% (1991) of the workforce engages in agriculture, fishing, and forestry. Grains, sugar beets, potatoes, meat, and milkare the main agricultural products.

Energy: Twelve nuclear reactors supply 47% (1996) of the country's energy needs; the reactors are to be phased out by 2010, and alternative energy sources are being investigated. Hydropower supplies 34% (1996) of energy needs, and imported oil is also used.

Natural Resources: Timber; hydropower; metals, including zinc, iron ore, lead, copper, silver, uranium

Environmental Issues: Water pollution, acid rain damage

Transportation: There are 7,350 miles (11,840 km) of railroads and 85,700 miles (138,000 km) of roads, mostly paved. Major ports include Stockholm, Malmö, Göteborg, and Helsingborg. Stockholm, Malmö and Göteborg have international airports.

Communications: Daily newspapers are published in many cities. There are 3.5 million televisions (1995) and 7.3 million radios (1993) in operation. Phone service, with 13 million telephones (1996 est.) in use, is good.

Tourism: Tourist attractions include the historic cities of Stockholm and Göteborg, as well as resorts along the coasts and in the mountains. Other attractions include the remote wilderness of northern Lappland and historical and archaeological sites throughout the country. Sweden earned an estimated $2.8 billion (U.S.) from visitors in 1995.

U.S. Tourist Office: (212) 949-2333

Embassy in U.S.: (202) 467-2600

Public Holidays: Epiphany (January 6); Good Friday (date varies, in March or April); Easter Monday (date varies, in March or April); Ascension Day (date varies, in May); Whit Monday (date varies, in May); May Day (May 1); Midsummer Holiday (date varies, in late June); All Saints' Day (date varies, in November); Christmas (December 25); St. Stephen's Day (December 26)

Switzerland

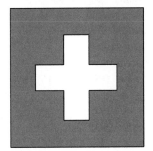

Country Name: Switzerland

Official Name: Swiss Confederation

Nationality: Swiss (singular and plural noun); Swiss (adjective)

Capital: Bern, pop. 128,900 [331,900]

Major cities: Zürich, Basel, Geneva, Lausanne

External Territories: None

Location: Switzerland, a landlocked country in central Europe, is bordered on the north by Germany, on the east by Austria and Liechten-

---

SWITZERLAND A MUSEUM OF MANY HOMES

The many traditional architectural styles of Switzerland are preserved full-size at the Swiss Open-Air Museum east of Interlaken near Brienz. The site contains more than 80 types of rural buildings, some of which date from the 15th century, from all parts of the country, reflecting its French, German, and Italian heritage.

---

stein, on the south by Italy, and on the west by France.

Physical Geography: A central plateau, with rolling hills, separates ranges of the Alps in the southern part of the country and the Jura Mountains in the north and west.

Total area: 15,941 sq mi (41,288 sq km)

Coastline: None

Land use: About 30% of the land is meadows and pastures, 32% is forested, and 12% is arable or under cultivation.

Climate: Temperate, temperature and precipitation varying with elevation

Population: 7,119,000

Urban population: 68%

Rate of natural increase: 0.3 %

Age structure: 18% under 15; 15% over 65

Birth rate: 11/1000

Death rate: 9/1000

Infant mortality rate: 4.8/1000

Fertility rate: 1.5

Life expectancy at birth: 76 years (male); 82 years (female)

Religion: Roman Catholic, Protestant

Language: German, French, Italian, Romansch

Ethnic Divisions: German, French, Italian

Literacy Rate: 99%

Government: Federal republic, with a president and bicameral legislature, the Federal Assembly. The president is appointed from within the Assembly for a one-year term by

Assembly members. The 46 members of the Council of States are elected for terms of three to four years, and the 200 members of the National Council are directly elected to four-year terms. There are 26 administrative cantons.

Armed services: No standing army; 357,460 army and air force troops (1997) ready for mobilization; compulsory service

Suffrage: Universal; 18 years old

Economy: Services, industry, and banking are key components of Switzerland's economy, which is one of the wealthiest per capita in the world. Although a recession developed in the early 1990s in response to inflation threats, the economy was in recovery by the mid-1990s. The government is devising measures to further prompt economic growth by removing anti-competitive practices, liberalizing commerce laws, and relaxing immigration policies in order to attract foreign workers.

Unit of currency: Swiss franc; 100 centimes = 1 Swiss franc (SFR)

GDP per capita: $23,800

Inflation rate–CPI: -0.1% (19975)

Workforce: 3.8 million

Unemployment rate: 5% (1997 est.)

Exports: Goods worth $99.2 billion (f.o.b., 1997 est.) are sent to the European Union, the U.S., Japan, and other trading partners; exports include machinery, chemicals, metals, and agricultural products.

Imports: Goods worth $86.6 billion (c.i.f., 1997 est.) are received from

the European Union, the U.S., and other trading partners; imports include machinery, chemicals, metals and agricultural products.

Agriculture: 4% of the workforce engages in agriculture. Grains, fruits, vegetables, meat, and eggs are important commodities.

Energy: Domestic hydropower, nuclear power, and imported oil are used for energy generation.

Natural Resources: Hydropower, timber, salt

Environmental Issues: Air and water pollution, including acid rain

Transportation: There are 1,860 miles (2,990 km) of state-owned railroads and 1,260 miles (2,030 km) of privately owned railroads; the 44,160 miles (71,120 km) of roads are all paved. The Rhine River is navigable for its 40 miles (65 km) within the country. Bern, Zürich, Geneva, and Basel have international airports.

Communications: 84 daily newspapers are published, and 10 have circulations of more than 50,000. There are 2.8 million radios and 2.6 million televisions (1996). Phone service is excellent, with 5.2 million lines in operation.

Tourism: Tourist attractions include ski resorts, alpine towns, and lake resorts. In 1994, visitors added $7.5 billion (U.S.) to the country's economy.

U.S. Tourist Office: (800) 467-9477

Embassy in U.S.: (202) 745-7900

Public Holidays: Good Friday (date varies, in March or April); Easter Monday (date varies, in March or April); Ascension Day (date varies, in May); Whit Monday (date varies, in May); Labor Day (May 1); National Day: foundation of Swiss Confederation, 1291 (August 1); Christmas (December 25–26)

Syria

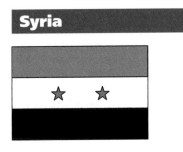

Country Name: Syria

Official Name: Syrian Arab Republic

Nationality: Syrian(s) (noun); Syrian (adjective)

Capital: Damascus, pop. 1,549,900

Major cities: Aleppo, Homs, Latakia, Hama

External Territories: None

Location: Syria, in western Asia, is bordered on the north by Turkey, on the east by Iraq, on the south by Jordan, and on the west by Israel, Lebanon, and the Mediterranean Sea.

Physical Geography: A narrow coastal strip rises to mountains that parallel the coast and extend northeast; the Syrian Desert lies to the east of the mountains. The Euphrates River flows from northwest to southeast.

Total area: 71,044 sq mi (184,004 sq km)

Coastline: 120 mi (193 km)

Land use: Nearly 45% of the land is meadows and pastures, 32% is arable or under cultivation, and 3% is wooded.

Climate: Varies from east to west, Mediterranean along the coast, precipitation generally decreasing and temperature ranges increasing in the east

Population: 16,033,000

Urban population: 50%

Rate of natural increase: 2.8%

Age structure: 45% under 15; 3% over 65

Birth rate: 34/1000

Death rate: 6/1000

Infant mortality rate: 39/1000

Fertility rate: 4.7

Life expectancy at birth: 67 years (male); 68 years (female)

Religion: Sunni, Alawite, and Druze Muslim, Christian

Language: Arabic, Kurdish, Armenian

Ethnic Divisions: Arab, Kurd, Armenian

Literacy Rate: 71%

Government: Republic, with a unicameral legislature, People's Assembly, or Majlis al-Chaab. The president is directly elected to a seven-year term; the 250 members of the legislature are directly elected to four-year terms. There are 14 administrative provinces.

Armed services: 320,000 troops (1997) in the army, air force, navy, and other branches; compulsory service for 30 months

Suffrage: Universal; 18 years old

Economy: Although Syria's private sector is generally more profitable than the public sector, the country is hindered in its quest for needed economic growth by a trade deficit, rising unemployment, and inflation. The region's political instability, although providing Syria with short-term profits during the Persian Gulf War in the early 1990s, also interferes with economic stability.

Unit of currency: Syrian pound; 100 piastres = 1 Syrian pound (£S)

GDP per capita: $6,600

Inflation rate–CPI: 15%–20% (1997 est.)

Workforce: 4.7 million (1995 est.)

Unemployment rate: 12% (1997 est.)

Exports: Goods worth $4.2 billion (f.o.b., 1997 est.) are sent to European Union countries, Lebanon, Saudi Arabia, and other trading partners; exports include oil and live animals.

Imports: Goods worth $5.7 billion (c.i.f., 1997 est.) are received from Japan, the U.S., and other trading partners; imports include machinery, metal products, transportation equipment, food, and textiles.

Agriculture: 40% of the labor force engages in the agricultural sector. Cotton, fruits, and vegetables are the main cash crops cultivated.

Energy: Most energy is generated by hydropower and, to a lesser degree, oil.

Natural Resources: Oil, phosphates, chrome, manganese, asphalt, iron ore, rock salt, marble, gypsum

Environmental Issues: Deforestation, overgrazing, soil erosion, desertification, water pollution, potable water

Transportation: There are 1,250 miles (2,000 km) of railroads and 25,140 miles (40,480 km) of roads, of which 5,780 miles (9,310 km) are paved. Principal seaports include Banias, Tartous, and Latakia. International flights are available out of Damascus and Aleppo. Much oil is moved through a network of pipelines crossing Syrian territory.

Communications: Daily newspapers are published in Damascus, Aleppo, and Hama. There are 3.4 million radios (1992) and 700,000 televisions (1993 est.) in operation. Phone service, with 541,500 phones in operation (1992), is fair.

Tourism: Damascus antiquities, the ancient Citadel at Aleppo, and beach and mountain resorts draw visitors to Syria. In 1996, 2.4 million tourists visited.

Embassy in U.S.: (202) 232-6313

Public Holidays: End of Ramadan (date varies, in February); Revolution Day (March 8); Feast of the Sacrifice (date varies, in April); Greek Orthodox Easter (date varies, in April); Islamic New Year (date varies, in April or May); Birth of the Prophet (date varies, in July); Egypt's Revolution Day (July 23); Union of Syria, Egypt, and Libya (September 1); Beginning of October War (October 6); National Day: independence: from League of Nations mandate, 1946 (November 16); Ascension of the Prophet (date varies, in November); Christmas (December 25)

Tajikistan

Country Name: Tajikistan

Official Name: Republic of Tajikistan

Nationality: Tajik(s) (noun); Tajik (adjective)

Capital: Dushanbe, pop. 582,600

Major cities: Khudzand, Kurgan-Tybe, Kulyab

External Territories: None

Location: Tajikistan, in Central Asia, is bordered on the north and west by Uzbekistan, on the north by Kyrgyzstan, on the east by China, and on the south by Afghanistan.

Physical Geography: Mostly mountainous, including the Pamirs on the south and east, which have three peaks with elevations greater than 22,400 feet (7,000 m) and Altai on the north. Most of the population live in the Feragana and Isfara Valleys.

Total area: 55,213 sq mi (143,000 sq km)

Coastline: None

Land use: Nearly 25% of the land is meadows and pastures and 7% is arable or under cultivation. There are no forests or woodlands.

Climate: Continental, with hot summers and mild winters; conditions vary with elevation, winters in the mountains often extremely cold

Population: 6,213,000

Urban population: 27%

Rate of natural increase: 1.9%

Age structure: 44% under 15; 4% over 65

Birth rate: 25/1000

Death rate: 6/1000

Infant mortality rate: 25/1000

Fertility rate: 3.2

Life expectancy at birth: 66 years (male); 71 years (female)

Religion: Sunni and Shiite Muslim

Language: Tajik, Russian

Ethnic Divisions: Tajik, Uzbek, Russian

Literacy Rate: 98%

Government: Republic, with a unicameral legislative body, the Supreme Assembly. The president and 181 members of the legislature are elected to five-year terms. There are three administrative provinces and one autonomous region.

Armed services: 5,000–7,000 troops (1996) in the army

Suffrage: Universal; 18 years old

Economy: Although the country has promising reserves of gold and other minerals, the breakup of the Soviet Union in 1990 and subsequent civil war for the newly independent republic have severely damaged Tajikistan's economy. Foreign investment has been minimal because of political unrest, and humanitarian assistance is essential to meet basic needs. However, the government is working to redesign the economy by revamping the tax system, encouraging land reform, and courting foreign investment.

Unit of currency: Tajik ruble; 100 kopeks = 1 Tajik ruble

GDP per capita: $700

Inflation rate–CPI: 40% (1995)

Workforce: 1,854,000 (1993 est.)

Unemployment rate: 3.3% (1996 est.)

Exports: Goods worth $768 million (1996 est.) are sent to Russia, Kazakhstan, Ukraine, Uzbekistan, Turkmenistan, and other trading partners; exports include cotton, aluminum, fruits, vegetable oil, and textiles.

Imports: Goods worth $657 million (1996 est.) are received from Russia, Uzbekistan, Kazakhstan, and other trading partners; imports include fuels, chemicals, machinery, transport equipment, textiles, and foodstuffs.

Agriculture: Nearly 50% (1993) of the workforce engages in agriculture. Cotton, grains, fruits, grapes, vegetables, are the main crops raised.

Energy: Hydropower supplies about 75% of energy needs. Imported oil and gas are also used.

Natural Resources: Hydropower, uranium, mercury, brown coal, lead, zinc, antimony, tungsten

Environmental Issues: Soil pollution, industrial pollution

Transportation: There are fewer than 310 miles (500 km) of common carrier railroads. Of the 40,480 miles (25,140 km) of roads, 9,310 miles (5,780 km) are paved. Dushanbe has an international airport.

Communications: Two daily newspapers are published (1994). There are 3.392 million radios (1992 est.)and 700,000 televisions (1993 est.) in use. Phone service, with 268,000 lines in operation (1994), is poor.

Tourism: The high, rugged summits of the Pamirs, including Lenin and Communism, are an appealing attraction for mountaineers. Historic sites in and about Dushanbe, mountain lakes, and Buddhist temple ruins are also attractions for visitors. Tajikistan is enhancing amenities for tourists.

Public Holidays: End of Ramadan (date varies, in February); Navrus (March 21); Independence Day: from the Soviet Union, 1991 (September 9)

Tanzania

Country Name: Tanzania

Official Name: United Republic of Tanzania

Nationality: Tanzanian(s) (noun); Tanzanian (adjective)

Capital: Dar es Salaam, pop. 1,360,900

Major cities: Mwanza, Tabora, Mbeya, Tanga, Zanzibar

External Territories: None

Location: Tanzania, in eastern Africa, is bordered on the north by Uganda and Kenya; on the east by the Indian Ocean; on the south by Mozambique, Malawi, and Zambia; and on the west by the Democratic Republic of the Congo, Burundi and Rwanda. The islands of Zanzibar and Pemba are off the northeast coast.

Physical Geography: Narrow coastal lowlands rise to inland steppes. The Great Rift Valley divides and holds the Lake Victoria Basin and Lake Tanganyika and Lake Malawi. The highest mountain in Africa, the volcanic Kilimanjaro at 18,864 feet (5,895 m), is in the north, and other ranges are found in the south and central parts of the country.

Total area: 364,900 sq mi (945,087 sq km)

Coastline: 884 miles (1,424 km)

Land use: Nearly 40% the land is forested, 40% is meadows and pastures, and 4% is arable or under cultivation.

Climate: Tropical along the coast, drier inland, more temperate in the mountains

Population: 31,271,000

Urban population: 21%

Rate of natural increase: 2.49%

Age structure: 45% under 15; 3% over 65

Birth rate: 41.52/1000

Death rate: 16.64/1000

Infant mortality rate: 100/1000

Fertility rate: 5.7

Life expectancy at birth: 45 years (male); 49 years (female)

Religion: Christian, Muslim, indigenous beliefs

Language: Swahili, English (both official), Arabic, many local languages

Ethnic Divisions: More than 120 groups: mostly Bantu, including Sukuma, Makonde, Chaga, Nyamwezi

Literacy Rate: 68%

Government: Republic, with a president and a unicameral legislature, the Bunge. Of the 274 members of the legislature, 232 are elected and 42 are appointed to five-year terms; the president is directly elected to a five-year term. There are 25 administrative regions.

Armed services: 34,600 troops (1997) in the army, navy, and air force; two-year service

Suffrage: Universal; 18 years old

Economy: An economy based on subsistence agriculture and light manufacturing has left Tanzania one of the poorest countries in the world. International loans are being used to raise the country's infrastructure to modern standards, and other economic reforms, including privatizing state businesses, have led to greater revenues. However, external debt remains high, and inflation runs in the double digits.

Unit of currency: Tanzanian shilling; 100 cents = 1 Tanzanian shilling (TSh)

GDP per capita: $700

Inflation rate–CPI: 15% (1997 est.)

Workforce: 15,299,000 (1995 est.)

Unemployment rate: N.A.

Exports: Goods worth $760 million (f.o.b., 1996) are sent to Germany, the U.K., Japan, the Netherlands, Kenya, and other trading partners; exports include coffee, cotton, cashew nuts, and manufactured goods.

Imports: Goods worth $1.4 billion (c.i.f., 1996) are received from Germany, the U.K., the U.S., Japan, Italy, Denmark, and other trading partners; imports include manufactured goods, machinery, vehicles, textiles, oil, and food.

Agriculture: Nearly 82% (1996) of the workforce engages in agricultural production. Coffee, sisal, cotton, cashew nuts, cloves, tobacco, tea, sisal, pyrethrum, coconuts, sugarcane, and cardamon are all impor-

---

TANZANIA A NATION OF NATURAL WONDERS

Tanzania is home to three of Africa's great places: Lake Tanganyika, which is some 20 million years old and larger than Belgium, is Africa's deepest lake; Mount Kilimanjaro is Africa's highest mountain; and Lake Victoria (the southern half of which lies in Tanzania) is the second-largest body of freshwater in the world. Another natural wonder is the Ngorongoro Crater, which is the caldera of an ancient volcano. At 11 miles (18 km) across, it is the sixth largest caldera in the world. Its high walls form a natural preserve for a variety of wildlife, including 50 species of mammals and 200 species of birds, in a 100-square-mile (260 sq km) area.

tant cash crops; cassava, maize, and cattle are grown for domestic use. Agricultural products account for 85% of the country's exports.

Energy: 70% of the country's electricity is generated using hydropower.

Natural Resources: Hydropower; natural gas; minerals, including tin, phosphates, iron, coal, diamonds and other gemstones, gold, nickel

Environmental Issues: Deforestation, desertification, soil degradation, destruction of coral reefs

Transportation: There are 2,220 miles (3,570 km) of railroads and 54,770 miles (88,200 km) of roads, of which 4% are paved. Steamers navigate on Lakes Tanganyika, Victoria, and Malawi. Coastal ports include Dar es Salaam, Mtwara, Tanga, and Bagamoyo; Zanzibar and Pemba also have ports. International flights can be taken from Dar es Salaam, Kilimanjaro, and Zanzibar.

Communications: There are three daily newspapers published in Dar es Salaam. There are 8.3 million radios and 70,000 televisions (1995) in use. Phone service, with about 88,000 phones in service (1994), is fair.

Tourism: Beaches, snorkeling and diving, big-game fishing, the spice island of Zanzibar, and 11 national parks, including the famed Serengeti National Park, draw tourists to Tanzania. The country earned $328 million (U.S.) from 280,000 visitors in 1995.

Embassy in U.S.: (202) 939-6125

Public Holidays: Zanzibar Revolution Day (January 12); End of Ramadan (date varies, in February); Chama Cha Mapinduzi Day (February 5); Easter (date varies, in March or April); Feast of the Sacrifice (date varies, in April); Union Day: merger of Tanganyika and Zanzibar, 1964 (April 26); International Labor Day (May 1); Birth of the Prophet (date varies, in July); Saba Saba Peasants' Day (July 7); Independence Day:

Tanganyika as a UN Trust Territory administered by the U.K., 1961 (December 9); Christmas (December 25)

Thailand

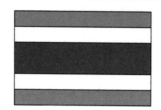

Country Name: Thailand
Official Name: Kingdom of Thailand
Nationality: Thai (singular and plural noun); Thai (adjective)
Capital: Bangkok, [6,547,000]
Major cities: Nakhon Ratchasima, Songkhla, Nonthaburi, Chiang Mai, Khon Kaen
External Territories: None
Location: Thailand, on the Gulf of Thailand and the Andaman Sea in Southeast Asia, is bordered to the northeast by Laos, to the east and southeast by Cambodia, and to the west and south by Myanmar.
Physical Geography: Mountains are in the north and northwest. The Khorat Plateau is in the northeast with the Mekong River as a boundary. The Ping and Yo Rivers flow south through plains to form the Chao-Phrara, which flows through lowlands to the Gulf of Thailand.

The southern part of the country, on the Malay Peninsula, is covered with a mix of mountains and hills.
Total area: 198,457 sq mi (514,000 sq km)
Coastline: 1,999 miles (3,219 km)
Land use: Nearly 26% of the land is arable or under cultivation, 30% is forested, and 2% is meadows and pastures.
Climate: Tropical monsoon, with rains from July to October
Population: 61,818,000
Urban population: 31%
Rate of natural increase: 1.1 %
Age structure: 27% under 15; 5% over 65
Birth rate: 18/1000
Death rate: 7/1000
Infant mortality rate: 25/1000
Fertility rate: 2.0
Life expectancy at birth: 70 years (male); 75 (female)
Religion: Buddhist Muslim, Christian
Language: Thai, English, regional dialects
Ethnic Divisions: Thai, Chinese
Literacy Rate: 94%
Government: Constitutional monarchy—the hereditary monarch is Bhumibol Adulyadej King Rama IX, since 1946—with a bicameral legislature, the National Assembly. The 270 members of the Senate are appointed to office by the king for a six-year term, and the 393 members of the House of Representatives are

THAILAND POPULATION CONTROL SUCCESS STORY

Thailand is the only southeast Asian country never colonized by a European power; it was known as Siam until 1939. One of the world's most significant reductions in the annual population growth rate has taken place in Thailand, the result of a highly successful family planning program: the rate dropped from 3.2 percent in 1972 to 1.1 percent in 1999. Women there are having an average of 2.0 children, just below replacement level.

directly elected to office for four-year terms. There are 76 administrative provinces.

Armed services: 266,000 troops (1996) in the army, navy, and air force; two-year compulsory military service for men 21–30 years of age

Suffrage: Universal; 18 years old

Economy: Although Thailand's economy has experienced considerable growth in the past several years, the country's infrastructure has not kept up with the demands this expansion has generated. The labor force also needs more education and technical training to sustain growth at this quick pace. The government controls the value of the national currency against other world currencies to manage potentially inflationary situations, and it is encouraging investments to further economic growth.

Unit of currency: Baht; 100 satangs = 1 baht (B)

GDP per capita: $8,800

Inflation rate–CPI: 5.6% (1997 est.)

Workforce: 32.6 million (1997 est.)

Unemployment rate: 3.5%

Exports: Goods worth $51.6 billion (f.o.b., 1996 est.) are sent to the U.S., Japan, Singapore, Hong Kong, and other trading partners; exports include manufactures, agricultural products, and fisheries.

Imports: Goods worth $73.5 billion (c.i.f., 1997 est.) are received from the U.S., Japan, Singapore, and other trading partners; imports include manufactured goods and fuels.

Agriculture: Over 50% (1996) of the workforce engages in agricultural production, fishing, hunting, and forestry. Rice, cassava, rubber, sugarcane, and maize are all important crops; seafood is also a cash commodity. Thailand was the world's largest exporter of rice and in 1996.

Energy: Most energy is generated using imported oil.

Natural Resources: Minerals, including tin, tungsten, lead, gypsum, lignite, fluorite; rubber; natural gas; timber; seafood

Environmental Issues: Air and water pollution, deforestation, soil erosion

Transportation: There are 2,871 miles (4,623 km) of railroads and 40,117 miles (64,600 km) of roads, of which 39,110 miles (62,980 km) are paved. Canals and navigable rivers add another 2,480 miles (4,000 km) to the transport network. Udon is the principal river port on the Mekong, and Bangkok is the main seaport for the country and a key port for Southeast Asia. International airports are at Bangkok, Chiang Mai, Chiang Rai, Hat Yai, Phuket, and Surat Thanai.

Communications: There are 35 daily newspapers published in Thai, English, and Chinese. There are 10.75 million radios and nearly 3.3 million televisions (1993 est.) in use. Phone service, with 1.55 million phones (1994), is still inadequate to meet demand.

Tourism: Bangkok's canals, temples, and night life are a key tourist draw; elsewhere in the country, festivals, wildlife parks, beach resorts, and jungles are prime attractions. In 1994, Thailand earned $8.65 billion (U.S.) from 7.2 million visitors.

U.S. Tourist Office: (800) 842-4526

Embassy in U.S.: (202) 944-3600

Public Holidays: Makhabuja (date varies, in February); Songkran Festival (dates vary, in April); Chakri Day (April 6); Coronation Day (May 5); Visakhabuja (date varies, in May or June); Asalhabuja (date varies, in July); Beginning of Buddhist Lent (date varies, in July); Queen's Birthday (August 12); Chulalongkorn Day (October 23); King's Birthday (December 5); Constitution Day (December 10); New Year's Eve (December 31)

Togo

Country Name: Togo

Official Name: Togolese Republic

Nationality: Togolese (singular and plural noun); Togolese (adjective)

Capital: Lomé, pop. 366,500

Major cities: Sokóde, Kpalimé, Atakpamé

External Territories: None

Location: Togo, in western Africa, is bordered on the north by Burkina Faso, on the east by Benin, on the south by the Gulf of Guinea, and on the west by Ghana.

Physical Geography: Mountains, the Chaine de l'Atakora, cross from the northeast to the southwest, and other highlands occupy the northwest. Central hills and southern plateaus slope to a narrow coastal plain with marshes and lagoons.

Total area: 21,925 sq mi (56,785 sq km)

Coastline: 35 mi (56 km)

Land use: About 17% of the land is wooded, 45% is arable or under cultivation, and 4% is meadows and pastures.

Climate: Tropical, with precipitation generally increasing from north to south

Population: 4,512,000

Urban population: 31%

Rate of natural increase: 2.62 %

Age structure: 46% under 15; 3% over 65

Birth rate: 41.6/1000

Death rate: 15.4/1000

Infant mortality rate: 79.7/1000

Fertility rate: 5.4

Life expectancy at birth: 48 years (male); 50 years (female)

Religion: Indigenous beliefs, Christian, Muslim

Language: French, Ewe, Mina, Kabye, Dagomba

Ethnic Divisions: Many groups, including Ewe and Mina

Literacy Rate: 52%

Government: Republic under transition, with a president and a unicameral legislature, the National Assembly. The president and the 81 members of the legislature are directly elected to five-year terms. There are 21 administrative circumscriptions.

Armed services: 6,950 troops (1997) in the army, air force, and navy; selective conscription for two-year service

Suffrage: Universal; adult (age N.A.)

Economy: After years of struggling, the Togolese economy, based on subsistence agriculture, experienced some growth in the mid-1990s, led by strong performances in the mining and manufacturing sectors. Political instability, international debts, and austerity measures have interfered with the country's ability to develop. Foreign aid diminished after general strikes in 1992 and 1993; however, some countries have agreed to cancel part of Togo's debt and provide financial support for new economic developments, including tax reform and industry privatization.

Unit of currency: CFA franc; 100 centimes = 1 franc de la Communauté financière africaine (CFAF)

GDP per capita: $1,300

Inflation rate–CPI: 15.7% (1995)

Workforce: 1.751 million (1996 est.)

Unemployment rate: 4.076 (1985)

Exports: Goods worth $196 million (f.o.b., 1996) are sent to Canada, Bolivia, Indonesia, the Philippines, France, and other trading partners; exports include phosphates, cotton, cocoa, and coffee.

Imports: Goods worth $404 million (c.i.f., 1996) are received from France, Germany, Côte d'Ivoire, the U.S., and other trading partners; imports include machinery, consumer goods, food, and chemicals.

Agriculture: Nearly 62% (1996 est.) of the labor force engages in the agricultural sector. Cash commodities include cotton, cocoa, and coffee; yams, maize, cassava, millet, and sorghum are the primary subsistence crops. Livestock and fish are also important. The country is generally self-sufficient in food crops.

Energy: Domestic hydropower and imported fuels are used for most energy generation.

Natural Resources: Phosphates, limestone, marble

Environmental Issues: Deforestation

Transportation: There are 330 miles (530 km) of railroads and 4,670 miles (7,520 km) of roads, of which some 1,480 miles (2,380 km) are paved. Lomé, the main seaport, also has an international airport.

Communications: Two daily newspapers are published in Lomé. There are 880,000 radios and 50,000 televisions (1995), and 21,000 telephones (1994) provide fair service.

Tourism: Colonial sites, markets, and national parks showcasing Togolese wildlife draw visitors to the country, which earned $18 million (U.S.) from tourism in 1994.

U.S. Tourist Office: (212) 490-3455

Embassy in U.S.: (202) 234-4212

Public Holidays: Liberation Day (January 13); Day of Victory (January 24); End of Ramadan (date varies, in February); Easter Monday (date varies, in March or April); Feast of the Sacrifice (date varies, in April); Day of Victory (April 24); Independence Day: as a French administered UN Trust Territory, 1960 (April 27); Ascension Day (date varies, in May); Whit Monday (date varies, in May); Labor Day (May 1); Assumption (August 15); Anniversary of the failed

attack on Lomé (September 24); All Saints' Day (November 1); Christmas (December 25)

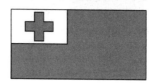

Tonga

Country Name: Tonga

Official Name: Kingdom of Tonga

Nationality: Tongan(s) (noun); Tongan (adjective)

Capital: Nuku'alofa, pop. [34,000]

Major cities: None

External Territories: None

Location: Tonga, in the South Pacific Ocean, is made up of some 170 islands, of which 36 are inhabited. The three principal islands, from north to south, are Vava'u, Ha'apai, and Tongatapu. Fiji is to the east and Samoa is to the north.

Physical Geography: Coral limestone formations underlie the eastern islands. Islands in the west are volcanic; some are still active.

Total area: 270 sq mi (699 sq km)

Coastline: 261 miles (419 km)

Land use: About 70% of the land is arable or under cultivation, 11% is wooded, and 6% is meadows and pastures.

Climate: Tropical, with rains from December to March

Population: 109,000 (1996 est.)

Urban population: N.A.

Rate of natural increase: 2.2%

Age structure: 38% under 15; 5% over 65

Birth rate: 26/1000

Death rate: 4/1000

Infant mortality rate: N.A.

Fertility rate: 3.7

Life expectancy at birth: 66 years (male); 71 years (female)

Religion: Christian

Language: Tongan, English

Ethnic Divisions: Tongan

Literacy Rate: 99%

Government: Constitutional monarchy, Taufa'ahau Tupou IV since 1965, with a unicameral legislature, the Legislative Assembly, or Fale Alea. Of the 30 members of the legislature, 12 are reserved for cabinet members, 9 are selected within the country's 33 nobles and 9 are elected by popular vote for three years. There are five administrative groups.

Armed services: Tonga has its own defense force

Suffrage: Universal; 21 years old

Economy: Agriculture for subsistence and cash provides the base for Tonga's economy. Tourism helps to bring in foreign exchange. Some Tongans emigrate to New Zealand, sending wages back home to their families. The government is promoting the development of an industrial base, but foreign aid is still needed.

Unit of currency: Pa'anga or Tongan dollar; 100 senti = 1 pa'anga or Tongan dollar ($T)

GDP per capita: $2,250

Inflation rate–CPI: 2.0% (1997)

Workforce: 36,665 (1994 est.)

Unemployment rate: 11.8% (1993-1994 est.)

Exports: Goods worth $15.3 million (f.o.b., 1996) are sent to Japan, the U.S., Canada, New Zealand, and other trading partners; exports include squash, seafood, vanilla, root crops, and coconut oil.

Imports: Goods worth $82.9 million (f.o.b., 1996) are received from New Zealand, Australia, the U.S., the U.K., and other trading partners; imports include food, animals, machinery, transportation equipment, basic manufactures, fuels, and chemicals.

Agriculture: Nearly 40% (1990) of the workforce engages in the agricultural sector. Coconuts, vanilla, and squash are the main cash crops. Taro, sweet potatoes, yams, water-melons, tomatoes, cassava, lemons, limes, oranges, peanuts, and breadfruit are grown for domestic use; livestock and seafood are also important local food sources.

Energy: Most energy is generated using imported fuels; solar power is being investigated.

Natural Resources: Seafood

Environmental Issues: Deforestation, coral reef damage

Transportation: There are no railroads. Most roads are paved: 123 miles (198 km) on Tongatapu; 46 miles (74 km) on Vava'u; 12 miles (20 km) on Ha'apai; and 12 miles (20 km) on 'Ewe. Nuku'alofa, on Tongatapu, and Neiafu Vava'u are the main seaports. An international airport is near Nuku'alofa.

Communications: One daily newspaper is published and several other publications are circulated. There are 66,000 radios, 2,000 televisions (1994, and 6,000 telephones (1993) in operation.

Tourism: Natural coastal formations called blowholes, beaches, underground caves, and bird-watching are some of Tonga's tourist attractions. The country earned an estimated $14 million (Tongan) in 1993-94 from 29,520 visitors.

Public Holidays: Easter (date varies, in March or April); Australia-New Zealand Day (April 25); Birthday of the Crown Prince (May 4); Independence Day: from the U.K., 1970 (June 4); Birthday of the King (July 4); Constitution Day (November 4); Tupou I Day (December 4); Christmas (December 25); Boxing Day (December 26)

Trinidad and Tobago

Country Name: Trinidad and Tobago

Official Name: Republic of Trinidad and Tobago

Nationality: Trinidadian(s), Tobagonian(s) (noun); Trinidadian, Tobagonian (adjective)

Capital: Port of Spain, pop. 43,400

Major cities: San Fernando, Arima

External Territories: None

Location: The country of Trinidad and Tobago, in the Caribbean Sea, is made up of two West Indian islands that lie just off the northern coast of Venezuela.

Physical Geography: Three low mountain ranges cross Trinidad, the larger of the country's two islands, and plains and hills occupy much of the rest of the island and Tobago.

Total area: 1,981 sq mi (5,131 sq km)

Coastline: 225 mi (362 km)

Land use: Nearly 46% of the land is wooded, 24% is arable or under cultivation, and 2% is meadows and pastures.

Climate: Tropical, with a wet season from July to December

Population: 1,285,000

Urban population: 72%

Rate of natural increase: 0.67%

Age structure: 28% under 15; 6% over 65

Birth rate: 14/1000

Death rate: 7.3/1000

Infant mortality rate: 16.2/1000

Fertility rate: 1.7

TRINIDAD AND TOBAGO SIR WALTER RALEIGH'S UNUSUAL ISLAND DISCOVERY

Trinidad and Tobago are among the more ethnically mixed Caribbean islands—Africans and East Indians each make up about 40 percent of the population; French, Spanish, Portuguese, Chinese, and Syrians also emigrated to this island. Sir Walter Raleigh discovered evidence of underground oil reservoirs there, and oil and natural gas have made Trinidad one of the Caribbean's strongest economies.

Life expectancy at birth: 68 years (male); 73 years (female)

Religion: Roman Catholic, Hindu, Protestant, Muslim

Language: English, Hindi, French, Spanish

Ethnic Divisions: African, East Indian, French, Spanish, Portuguese, Chinese, Syrian

Literacy Rate: 98%

Government: Parliamentary democracy, with a president and a bicameral legislature, the Parliament. The president is elected by the members of the legislature. The 31 members of the Senate are appointed by the President and the 36 members of the House of Representatives are directly elected to five-year terms. There are eight administrative counties, 3 municipalities, and 1 ward.

Armed services: 2,100 troops (1997) in the army, air force, and coast guard

Suffrage: Universal; 18 years old

Economy: Oil and natural gas support the country's economy, and the government has been working to diversify export manufacturing and to promote tourist traffic. Foreign investment has funded additional mineral exploration, and citizens enjoy a relatively high standard of living in comparison to neighboring countries.

Unit of currency: Trinidad and Tobagon dollar; 100 cents = 1 Trinidad and Tobagon dollar (TT$)

GDP per capita: $10,400

Inflation rate–CPI: 3.4% (1996)

Workforce: 404,500 (1993 est.)

Unemployment rate: 16.1% (1996)

Exports: Goods worth $2.5 billion (f.o.b., 1996 est.) are sent to other Caribbean Community and Common Market (CARICOM) countries, the U.S., European Union countries, and Latin America; exports include oil and oil products, chemicals, steel products, fertilizer, sugarcane, cocoa, coffee, citrus fruits, and flowers.

Imports: Goods worth $2.1 billion (c.i.f., 1996 est.) are received from the U.S., Venezuela, the U.K., and Germany, and Canada; imports include machinery, transportation equipment, manufactured goods, food, and live animals.

Agriculture: Nearly 11% (1995) of the labor force engages in agriculture. Sugarcane, coffee, cocoa, and citrus are cultivated for export. Poultry is raised for domestic use.

Energy: Most electricity is generated with domestic natural gas and petroleum.

Natural Resources: Petroleum, natural gas, asphalt

Environmental Issues: Water pollution, soil erosion, deforestation; oil pollution of beaches.

Transportation: No railroads have been in service since 1968. There are 5,170 miles (8,320 km) of roads, of which 2,640 miles (4,250 km) are paved. Main seaports include Port of Spain, Pointe-à-Pierre, and Point Lisas on Trinidad and Scarborough on Tobago. An international airport is near Port of Spain.

Communications: There are three daily newspapers, all published in Port of Spain. There are 700,000 radios (1993) and 400,000 televisions (1992) in operation. Phone service, with 170,000 phones in use (1992 est.), is good.

Tourism: Carnival celebrations, the cultural attractions of Caribbean cities, beaches, snorkeling, and diverse wildlife draw visitors to Trinidad and Tobago, which earned $1.05 billion (U.S.) from tourism in 1996.

U.S. Tourist Office: (800) 748-4224

Embassy in U.S.: (202) 467-6490

Public Holidays: New Year's Day (January 1), End of Ramadan (date varies, in January or February); Carnival (dates vary, in February); Easter (date varies, in March or April); Spiritual Baptist Shouters' Liberation Day (March 30); Corpus Christi (date varies, in May or June); Indian Arrival Day (May 30); Labor Day (June 19); Emancipation Day (August 1); Independence Day: from the U.K., 1962 (August 31); Divali (date varies, in October); Christmas (December 25–26)

Tunisia

Country Name: Tunisia

Official Name: Republic of Tunisia

Nationality: Tunisian(s) (noun); Tunisian (adjective)

Capital: Tunis, pop.674,100

Major cities: Sfax, Ariana, El Hamma, Sousse

External Territories: None

Location: Tunisia, on the Mediterranean coast of North Africa, is bordered on the southeast by Libya and on the west by Algeria.

Physical Geography: Northern mountains extend to a central plateau. Shallow salt lakes, the Shott el Jerid, lie south of the plateau, and the Sahara covers the southern portion of the country.

Total area: 63,170 sq mi (163,610 sq km)

Coastline: 713 mi (1,148 km)

Land use: About 32% of the land is arable or under cultivation, 20% is meadows and pastures, and 4% is forested.

Climate: Temperate in the north, with hot, dry summers and mild, rainy winters; precipitation decreasing and temperatures increasing to the south

Population: 9,498,000

Urban population: 61%

Rate of natural increase: 1.58%

Age structure: 35% under 15; 5% over 65

Birth rate: 22.35/1000

Death rate: 6.55/1000

Infant mortality rate: 35/1000

Fertility rate: 2.8

Life expectancy at birth: 67 years (male); 70 years (female)

Religion: Muslim

Language: Arabic, French

Ethnic Divisions: Arab

Literacy Rate: 67%

Government: Republic, with a president and a unicameral legislature, the National Assembly, or Majlis al-Nuwaab. The president is directly elected to a five-year term. Of the 163 members of the legislature, 144 are directly elected and 19 are proportionally elected to office from opposition parties. There are 23 administrative governorates.

Armed services: 35,000 troops (1997) in the army, navy, and air force; one-year selective conscription

Suffrage: Universal; 20 years old

Economy: Government encouragement of economic diversification has yielded strong sectors in manufacturing, tourism, and mining, although agricultural commodities (principally olive oil) are vulnerable to climatic fluctuations, international trade restrictions, and prices. Industry privatization continues at a measured pace, and foreign investment has been encouraged in manufacturing and mining.

Unit of currency: Tunisian dinar; 1,000 millimes = 1 Tunisian dinar (TD)

GDP per capita: $6,100

Inflation rate–CPI: 4.6% (1997 est.)

Workforce: 3,461,000 (1996 est.)

Unemployment rate: 15% (1997 est.)

Exports: Goods worth $5.6 billion (f.o.b., 1997 est.) are sent to France, Italy, Germany, Belgium, Spain, and other trading partners; exports include hydrocarbons, agricultural products, phosphates, chemicals, and textiles.

Imports: Goods worth $7.4 billion (c.i.f., 1997 est.) are received from France, Italy, Germany, the U.S., Belgium, and other trading partners; imports include industrial goods and equipment, oil, food, and consumer goods.

Agriculture: Nearly 22% (1996) of the labor force engages in the agricultural sector. Olives, oranges, almonds and dates are important export crops, and wheat and barley are also grown. Olive oil is the principal agricultural export.

Energy: Mineral fuels generate most of the country's electricity, and some hydropower plants are also operating.

Natural Resources: Oil, natural gas, phosphates, iron, lead, zinc, sea salt

Environmental Issues: Water pollution, limited freshwater resources, deforestation, desertification, soil erosion, overgrazing

Transportation: There are 1,400 (2,260 km) of railroads and 14,350 miles (23,100 km) of roads, of which 11,320 (18,230 km) are paved. Main seaports include Tunis, La Goulette, Bizerta, Sousse, Sfax, Gabès, and Zarzis. There are seven international airports, including ones at Tunis, Sfax, and Djerbo.

Communications: Several daily newspapers are published, including two in French and two in Arabic in Tunis. An estimated 1.8 million radios and 800,000 televisions (1995) are in operation. There are 474,000 phones (1994), providing above average service.

Tourism: Mediterranean resorts, the ancient city of Carthage, and oases in the central part of the country are some of Tunisia's tourist attractions. In 1996, 3.9 million visitors spent $1.2 billion (U.S.) in the country.

Embassy in U.S.: (202) 862-1850

Public Holidays: End of Ramadan (date varies, in February); Independence Day: from France, 1956 (March 20); Youth Day (March 21); Feast of the Sacrifice (date varies, in April); Martyrs' Day (April 9); Labor Day (May 1); Republic Day (July 25); Women's Day (August 13); Evacuation of Bizerta (October 15); President Ben Ali's accession, 1987 (November 7)

Turkey

Country Name: Turkey
Official Name: Republic of Turkey
Nationality: Turk(s) (noun); Turkish (adjective)

Capital: Ankara, pop. 2,938,000 [3,258,000]

Major cities: İstanbul, İzmir, Adana, Bursa

External Territories: None

Location: Turkey bridges the continents of Europe and Asia. It is bordered on the north by the Black Sea; on the east by Georgia, Armenia, Azerbaijan, and Iran; on the south by Iraq, Syria, and the Mediterranean Sea; and on the west by the Aegean Sea, Greece, and Bulgaria.

Physical Geography: The European portion of Turkey is mainly rolling grasslands. In Asia, the Anatolian Plateau is ringed by mountains, and higher peaks rise in the eastern section of the country. The Bosphorus Strait at İstanbul links the Black Sea and the Sea of Marmara.

Total area: 300,948 sq mi (779,452 sq km)

Coastline: 4,471 mi (7,200 km)

Land use: Nearly 35% of the land is arable or under cultivation, 26% is forested, and 12% is meadows and pastures.

Climate: Mediterranean along the southern and western coasts, with mild, rainy winters and hot, dry summers; the higher elevations have hot summers and cold winters

Population: 65,869,000

Urban population: 64%

Rate of natural increase: 1.5%

Age structure: 31% under 15; 5% over 65

Birth rate: 22/1000

Death rate: 7/1000

Infant mortality rate: 42/1000

Fertility rate: 2.6

Life expectancy at birth: 66 years (male); 71 years (female)

Religion: Muslim (mostly Sunni)

Language: Turkish, Kurdish, Arabic

Ethnic Divisions: Turkish, Kurdish

Literacy Rate: 82%

Government: Republic, with a president and a unicameral legislature, the Turkish Grand National Assembly. The president is elected by the legislature for a seven-year term; the 550 deputies of the Assembly are directly elected to five-year terms. There are 80 administrative provinces.

Armed services: 639,000 troops (1996) in the army, navy, and air force; 18-month conscription

Suffrage: Universal; 18 years old

Economy: A large budget deficit and high inflation rates have necessitated austerity programs by the government, which is trying to restore the rates of economic growth sustained in earlier years. The benefits of international loans and favorable trade concessions have been partially offset by internal political instability, but the government continues to work to improve its economic standing and provide better services for its citizens. An estimated 1.5 million workers who live abroad send remittances home which, in 1994, totaled an estimated $2.7 billion (U.S.).

Unit of currency: Turkish lira; 100 kuruş = 1 Turkish lira (TL)

GDP per capita: $6,100

Inflation rate–CPI: 99% (1997)

Workforce: 21.6 million

Unemployment rate: 5.9% (1997 est.)

Exports: Goods worth $26 billion (f.o.b., 1997 est.) are sent to Germany, the U.S., Russia, the U.K. and other trading partners; exports include textiles and apparel, steel products, and fruits and vegetables.

Imports: Goods worth $46.7 billion (f.o.b., 1997 est.) are received from Germany, Italy, the U.S., and other trading partners; imports include machinery, fuels, raw materials, and food.

Agriculture: Nearly 45% (1996) of the labor force engages in agriculture. Cotton, tobacco, wheat, fruit, and nuts are exported; barley, sunflower and other oilseeds, maize, sugar beets, potatoes, tea, and olives are also grown. Raising sheep, goats, cattle, and poultry is also important. The country is self-sufficient.

Energy: Domestic and imported oil, coal, and hydropower are used for energy production.

Natural Resources: Antimony, coal, chromium, mercury, borate, copper, oil, sulfur, iron ore

Environmental Issues: Air and water pollution, deforestation

Transportation: There are 6,450 miles (10,390 km) of railroads and

TURKEY ANCIENT LIFE-GIVING RIVERS OFFER HOPE ONCE MORE

A system of dams is being built along the Tigris and Euphrates rivers in southeastern Turkey to bring both electricity and water for irrigation to the region. More than five thousand years ago, these same rivers were the key to the growth of the world's first civilizations in Mesopotamia. Project planners hope the dams and plants will increase agricultural production by about 60 percent and stop people from migrating to the cities of Ankara and Istanbul, where shantytowns may soon house one of every two or three urban migrants. One of the largest public works projects in the world, the project consists of 19 hydroelectric plants and 22 dams. The Atatürk Dam on the Euphrates is the keystone of the project, with completion expected in 2005.

236,990 miles (381,360 km) of roads, of which 59,250 miles (95,410 km) are paved. There are about 750 miles (1,200 km) of navigable rivers, including stretches of the Tigris and Euphrates. Main ports include the Black Sea port of Samsum, İstanbul and Bandirma on the Sea of Marmara, the Aegean port of İzmir, and the Mediterranean ports of İskenderun and Mersin. İstanbul, İzmir, and Ankara have international airports.

Communications: Daily newspapers are published throughout the country. There are 9.4 million radios and 10.53 million televisions (1993); 14.3 million telephones provide adequate service.

Tourism: Tourist attractions include the gardens, museums, and buildings of İstanbul. Coastal resorts, ski resorts, and archaeological sites are also draws. In 1997, 9.67 million visitors spent $7.2 billion in the country.
U.S. Tourist Office: (202) 429-9844
Embassy in U.S.: (202) 659-8200

Public Holidays: End of Ramadan (date varies, in February); Feast of the Sacrifice (date varies, in April); National Sovereignty Day (April 23); Children's Day (April 23); Commemoration of Mustafa Kemal Atatürk, who died in 1938 (May 19); Youth and Sports Day (May 19); Victory Day (August 30); Republic Day: proclamation of the republic, 1923 (October 29)

Turkmenistan

Country Name: Turkmenistan
Official Name: Turkmenistan
Nationality: Turkmen(s) (noun); Turkmen (adjective)

TURKMENISTAN BIG FOOT, DINOSAUR STYLE

The longest set of dinosaur tracks discovered to date—1,020 feet—have been found in an area near the Turkmenistan-Uzbekistan border. The footprints—one of which measures 26 inches long—were left 155 million years ago by a group of huge, meat-eating megalosaurs of the Jurassic era that appeared to have roamed the entire Northern Hemisphere.

Capital: Ashgabat, pop. [462,000]
Major cities: Chärjew

External Territories: None

Location: Turkmenistan, in Central Asia, is bordered on the north by Kazakhstan and Uzbekistan, on the east and south by Afghanistan, on the south by Iran, and on the west by the Caspian Sea.

Physical Geography: The country is mostly desert, the Gargakum (Kara Kum). There are mountains and foothills in the south. The Amu Darya River flows parallel to the Uzbek border.

Land use: Nearly 70% of the land is meadows and pastures and 2% is arable or under cultivation. There is no woodland or forest.

Total area: 188,418 sq mi (488,000 sq km)

Coastline: None; Caspian Sea coast: 1,098 miles (1,768 km)

Climate: Continental, with hot summers and winters; little precipitation

Population: 4,779,000
Urban population: 44%
Rate of natural increase: 1.5%
Age structure: 40% under 15; 4% over 65
Birth rate: 22/1000
Death rate: 7/1000
Infant mortality rate: 38/1000
Fertility rate: 2.6
Life expectancy at birth: 62 years (male); 69 years (female)

Religion: Sunni Muslim

Language: Turkmenian, Russian Uzbek

Ethnic Divisions: Turkmen, Russian, Uzbek

Literacy Rate: 98%

Government: Republic, with a president and a unicameral legislature, the Assembly, or Majlis. The president is directly elected to a five-year term as are the 50 members of the legislature. There are five administrative regions.

Armed services: 16,000–18,000 troops (1997) in the army and air force; 18-month compulsory service

Suffrage: Universal; 18 years old

Economy: With an economy based on cotton exports and natural gas, Turkmenistan has faced difficulties since independence from the Soviet Union in 1991; its previous customers, principally other former members of the Soviet Union, have not been able to pay for goods that Turkmenistan has delivered. Economic reform has come slowly, and though extensive irrigation enables cotton cultivation and intensive farming on desert lands, food must be imported to meet domestic demand.

Unit of currency: Manat; 100 tenge = 1 Turkmen manat

GDP per capita: $3,000

Inflation rate–CPI: 992% (1996 est.)

Workforce: 2.34 million (1996 est.)

Unemployment rate: N.A.

Exports: Goods worth $1.7 billion (1996) are sent to Ukraine, Russia, Kazakhstan, Uzbekistan, Georgia, Azerbaijan, Armenia, and other trading partners; exports include natural gas, and cotton.

Imports: Goods worth $1.56 billion (1996) are received from Russia, Azerbaijan, Uzbekistan, Ukraine, Kazakhstan, Turkey, and other trading partners; imports include machinery, transportation equipment, food, plastics and rubber, consumer goods, and textiles.

Agriculture: Nearly 45% (1996) of the working population engages in agriculture. Irrigation permits the cultivation of cotton, grains, vegetables, and fruit; wool, livestock, and silkworms are also important commodities.

Energy: Domestic natural gas is used for most energy generation.

Natural Resources: Natural gas (the fifth largest reserve in the world), oil, coal, sulfur, salt

Environmental Issues: Soil and groundwater pollution, salinization, desertification, water pollution

Transportation: There are 1,360 miles (2,190 km) of common carrier railroads and 14,900 miles (24,000 km) of roads, of which 12,110 miles (19,500 km) are paved. The Amu Darya River carries a significant amount of inland water traffic. An international airport is at Ashgabat. Türkmenbashi is the key Caspian Sea port.

Communications: Many daily newspapers are published. Radio, television, and telephone statistics not available.

Tourism: Bazaars, horse races, archaeological sites, and coastal beaches are some of Turkmenistan's tourist attractions.

Embassy in U.S.: (202) 588-1500

Public Holidays: Remembrance Day (January 12); Birthday of the president (February 19); Navrus Bayram (date varies, in March); International Women's Day (March 8); Victory Day (May 9); Day of Revival and Unity (May 18); Gurban Bayram (May 28); Independence Day: from the Soviet Union, 1991 (October 27–28)

Tuvalu

Country Name: Tuvalu
Official Name: Tuvalu
Nationality: Tuvaluan(s) (noun); Tuvaluan (adjective)
Capital: Funafuti, pop. 4,000
Major cities: None
External Territories: None
Location: Tuvalu, in the South Pacific Ocean, is made up of nine islands about 2,500 miles (4,000 km) northeast of Australia. Fiji is to the south.
Physical Geography: Tuvalu's islands are low-lying coral atolls.
Total area: 10 sq mi (26 sq km)
Coastline: 15 miles (24 km)
Land use: There is enough soil to grow coconuts and to support subsistence agriculture, otherwise there is no measurable arable land, no forest and woodland, and no meadows and pastures. About three-fourths of the land is under cultivation.
Climate: Tropical, with rain from November to March
Population: 12,000
Urban population: N.A.

Rate of natural increase: 1.9 %
Age structure: 35% under 15; 6% over 65
Birth rate: 28/1000
Death rate: 9/1000
Infant mortality rate: 47/1000
Fertility rate: 3.1
Life expectancy at birth: 62 years (male); 65 years (female)
Religion: Protestant
Language: Tuvaluan, English
Ethnic Divisions: Polynesian
Literacy Rate: N.A.
Government: Constitutional monarchy, with a governor-general appointed by the British monarch and a unicameral legislature, the Parliament, or Fale I Fono. The 12 members of the legislature are directly elected to four-year terms. Local governments operate on eight islands.
Armed services: None
Suffrage: Universal; 18 years old
Economy: Subsistence farming and fishing are supplemented with international funds and remittances sent from citizens working abroad. The government is trying to diversify agricultural production and is searching for international investors who will support needed industrial development. Sales of stamps and coins are a major source of revenue.
Unit of currency: Tuvaluan dollar; 100 cents = 1 Tuvaluan dollar ($T) (Australian dollars are also used.)
GDP per capita: $800
Inflation rate–CPI: 3.9% (1985–1993 average)

TUVALU NO THRONGS OF TOURISTS ON THIS ISLAND—YET

This island nation is one of the world's most isolated and least visited places. Stretching some 360 miles, the island chain covers some 500,000 square miles of Pacific Ocean. It's land area covers only ten square miles. Tuvalu was formerly part of the British colony called the Gilbert and Ellice Islands; independence was gained in 1978.

Workforce: N.A.

Unemployment rate: N.A.

Exports: Goods worth $165,000 (f.o.b., 1989) are sent to Fiji, Australia, New Zealand, and other trading partners; copra is the only significant export.

Imports: Goods worth $4.4 million (c.i.f., 1989) are received from Fiji, Australia, New Zealand, and other trading partners; imports include food, livestock, fuels, machinery, and manufactured goods.

Agriculture: About 60% of the labor force engages in agriculture. Food crops include taro, papayas, and bananas; honey, livestock, and seafood are also used for domestic consumption. Copra, from coconuts, is the only significant cash commodity. Fishing licenses are sold for foreign exchange.

Energy: Imported fuels are used for most energy generation.

Natural Resources: Seafood

Environmental Issues: Coral reef damage, beach erosion, no potable groundwater

Transportation: There are no railroads; there are 5 miles (8 km) of roads. International flights leave from Funafuti, which is also the primary port of call.

Communications: There are two newspapers, with a circulation of 1,250. There are 4,000 radios (1993) in operation and 130 telephones (1983) in service. Figures for televisions are not available.

Tourism: Tropical lagoons, food, and lifestyle draw visitors to Tuvalu.

Embassy in U.S.: N.A.

Public Holidays: Commonwealth Day (date varies, in March); Easter (date varies, in March or April); Queen's Official Birthday (date varies, in June); National Children's Day (date varies, in August); Tuvalu Day: independence from the U.K., 1978 (October 1–2); Birthday of the Prince of Wales (November 14);

Christmas (December 25); Boxing Day (December 26)

Uganda

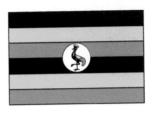

Country Name: Uganda

Official Name: Republic of Uganda

Nationality: Ugandan(s) (noun); Ugandan (adjective)

Capital: Kampala, pop. 773,000

Major cities: Jinja, Njera, Mbale

External Territories: None

Location: Uganda, a landlocked country in eastern Africa, is bordered on the north by Sudan; on the east by Kenya; on the south by Lake Victoria, Tanzania, and Rwanda; and on the west by Congo.

Physical Geography: Most of Uganda is a large plateau bordered by mountains; Lake Victoria, the third largest lake in the world and source of the White Nile, lies in the southeast.

Total area: 91,134 sq mi (236,036 sq km)

Coastline: None

Land use: Nearly 35% of the country is arable or under cultivation, 28% is forested, and 9% is meadows and pastures.

Climate: Tropical, with rains from March through May and from September through November

Population: 22,805,000

Urban population: 15%

Rate of natural increase: 2.86%

Age structure: 47% under 15; 3% over 65

Birth rate: 48.1/1000

Death rate: 19.5/1000

Infant mortality rate: 81.3/1000

Fertility rate: 6.9

Life expectancy at birth: 41 years (male); 42 years (female)

Religion: Roman Catholic, Protestant, MUslim, indigenous beliefs

Language: English,Ganda or Swahili, Luganda

Ethnic Divisions: 40 groups, including Bagando, Karamojong, others

Literacy Rate: 62%

Government: Republic in transition, with a president and a unicameral parliament, the National Resistance Council. The 278 members of the unicameral legislature elect the president. There are 39 administrative districts.

Armed services: 50,000 troops (1997 est.) in the army

Suffrage: Universal; 18 years old

Economy: With considerable help from the international financial community, Uganda is working to diversify its primarily agrarian economy, privatize industry, and reduce government bureaucracy. Since 1986, political unrest has lessened, and citizens are returning from exile and bringing additional cash into the economy. The government continues to work to improve the country's infrastructure, diversify export production, and keep inflation rates low.

Unit of currency: Ugandan shilling; 100 cents = 1 Ugandan shilling (USh)

GDP per capita: $1,700

Inflation rate–CPI: 6% (1997)

Workforce: 10.08 million (1996 est.)

Unemployment rate: N.A.

Exports: Goods worth $604 million (f.o.b., 1996) are sent to the U.S., the U.K., France, Spain, and other trading partners; exports include coffee, gold, cotton, tea, corn, and fish.

Imports: Goods worth $1.2 billion (c.i.f., 1996) are received from Kenya, the U.K., Italy, and other trading partners; imports include oil, machinery, cotton piece goods, metals, vehicles, and food.

Agriculture: 83% (1996) of the workforce engages in the agricultural sector. Coffee, cotton, tea, tobacco, and maize are key cash crops; coffee earned nearly 63% of the total value of export earnings in 1996. Cassava, sweet potatoes, millet, sorghum, maize, beans, peanuts, rice, and livestock are raised for domestic use.

Energy: Domestic hydropower is used for most energy production.

Natural Resources: Copper, gold, cobalt, limestone, salt

Environmental Issues: Deforestation, soil erosion, overgrazing, poaching; draining of wetlands for agricultural use

Transportation: There are 770 miles (1,240 km) of railroads and 16,770 miles (27,000 km) of roads, the majority of which are unpaved. Inland waterways include Lakes Victoria, Albert, Edward, and Kyoga. Entebbe, Jinja, and Port Bell, on Lake Victoria, are important ports. An international airport is at Entebbe.

Communications: There are more than a dozen daily and weekly newspapers published, mostly in Kampala. There are 2.3 million radios and 250,000 televisions (1995); 35,000 telephones (1994) provide fair service.

Tourism: Tourism earned $61 million for the country in 1994; attractions include game reserves, mountain hot springs, the wildlife and scenery in national parks, and the palaces, mosques, and museums in Kampala.

Embassy in U.S.: (202) 726-7100

Public Holidays: Liberation Day (January 26); End of Ramadan (date varies, in February); Easter (date varies, in March or April); International Women's Day (March 8); Feast of the Sacrifice (date varies, in April); Labor Day (May 1); Martyrs' Day (June 3); National Heroes' Day

(June 9); Independence Day: from the U.K., 1962 (October 9); Christmas (December 25); Boxing Day (December 26)

Ukraine

Country Name: Ukraine
Official Name: Ukraine
Nationality: Ukrainian(s) (noun); Ukrainian (adjective)
Capital: Kiev, pop. 2,630,000 (1995 est.)
Major cities: Kharkiv, Dnipropetrovs'k, Donets'k, Odesa
External Territories: None
Location: Ukraine, in eastern Europe, is bordered on the north by Belarus; on the east by Russia; the south by the Sea of Azov and the Black Sea; on the southwest by Moldova, Hungary, and Romania; and on the west by Poland and Slovakia.
Physical Geography: The country is mostly steppe. The Carpathian Mountains are in the west and the Crimean Mountains are on the

Crimean Peninsula in the south. The Dnipro River flows through the center of the country into the Black Sea.

Total area: 233,206 sq mi (604,001 sq km)
Coastline: 1,728 mi (2,782 km)
Land use: 60% of the land is arable or under cultivation and 13% is meadows and pastures. and 18% is forested.
Climate: Continental in most of the country, with warm summers and cold winters; Mediterranean along the Black Sea coast, with hot summers and mild winters
Population: 49,910,000
Urban population: 68%
Rate of natural increase: -0.6%
Age structure: 19% under 15; 14% over 65
Birth rate: 9/1000
Death rate: 15/1000
Infant mortality rate: 14/1000
Fertility rate: 1.3
Life expectancy at birth: 62 years (male); 73 years (female)
Religion: Ukrainian Orthodox, Ukrainian Catholic (Uniate), Protestant
Language: Ukrainian, Russian, Romanian
Ethnic Divisions: Ukrainian, Russian
Literacy Rate: 98%
Government: Republic, with a president and a unicameral legisla-

UKRAINE THE CRIMEA: LONG-TIME RUSSIAN GETAWAY

The Crimea, a peninsula of Ukraine about the size of Vermont, has been a resort for privileged Russians for centuries, thanks to its subtropical climate. The mild temperatures are made by the 90-mile long strip of the limestone Crimean Mountains, which protects a small strip of land along the water of the Black Sea. Near Yalta is the dacha used by Nikita Krushchev, Leonid Brezhnev, and Gorbachev; the palace at nearby Livadia was the summer home of Nicholas II and was the site of the 1945 Yalta Conference in which Stalin, Churchill, and Roosevelt remapped postwar Europe.

ture, the Supreme Council. The president is directly elected for a five-year term, and the 450 members of the legislature are also directly elected. There are 24 administrative provinces, the autonomous republic of Crimea, and Kiev, the capital.

Armed services: 387,400 troops (1997) in the army, navy, and air force; compulsory service for males over 18 years of age; 18 months in the army and air force, two in the navy

Suffrage: Universal; 18 years old

Economy: Like many of the other former Soviet republics, Ukraine's transition from a planned to a market economy, beginning in 1991, has been difficult. The country has ample farmland, raw materials, and heavy industry, but for several years following independence, internal dissent hindered economic growth. Recent efforts have successfully lowered inflation rates and unemployment and lessened government control of prices and foreign trade.

Unit of currency: Hryvnya; 100 kopiykas = 1 hryvnya

GDP per capita: $2,500

Inflation rate–CPI: 10% (1997 est.)

Workforce: 2.8 million (1997)

Unemployment rate: 2.6% officially registered, large number of underemployed workers (1997)

Exports: Goods worth $15.2 billion (1997 est.) are sent to Russia, China, Belarus, and other trading partners; exports include metals, chemicals, machinery , transport equipment, and food products.

Imports: Goods worth $20.2 billion (1997 est.) are received from Russia, Turkmenistan, Germany, and other trading partners; imports include energy, machinery and parts, transportation equipment, chemicals, plastics and rubber.

Agriculture: 24% (1996) of the labor force engages in the agricultural sector. Grain, sugar beets, sunflower seeds, and vegetables are the primary cultivated crops, and livestock is also raised. The country is self-sufficient. The abundance of grains is represented on the national flag, as golden grain fields under a blue sky.

Energy: Domestic nuclear power supplies 45% of Ukraine's energy. Imported oil, natural gas, and hydropower are also used.

Natural Resources: Iron ore, coal, manganese, natural gas, oil, sulfur

Environmental Issues: Air and water pollution, deforestation, radioactive contamination due to the nuclear disaster at Chornobyl in 1986, limited drinking water supplies

Transportation: There are 14,500 miles (23,350 km) of railroads and 107,160 miles (172,570 km) of roads, of which most are paved. Inland waterways, including the Dnipro River, are navigable for 2,730 miles (4,390 km). Main seaports are Odesa, Yalta, and Yevpatoriya. The main international airport is at Kiev.

Communications: 40 daily newspapers are published throughout the country. There are 15 million radios and 17.3 million televisions (1992) in use. Phone service is generally inadequate.

Tourism: Resorts along the Black Sea; churches, museums, and other historic sites in Odesa and Kiev; and L'viv, with its baroque and Renaissance architecture, are some of Ukraine's tourist draws. In 1994, 772,000 visitors brought $230 million (U.S.) into the country.

Embassy in U.S.: (202) 333-0606

Public Holidays: Christmas (January 7); International Women's Day (March 8); Easter (dates vary, in April or May); Spring and Labor Day (May 1–2); Victory Day (May 9); Constitution Day (June 28); Navy Day (August 1); Ukrainian Independence Day (August 24)

United Arab Emirates

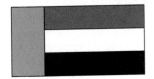

Country Name: United Arab Emirates

Official Name: United Arab Emirates

Nationality: Emiri(s) (noun); Emiri (adjective)

Capital: Abu Dhabi, pop. [799,000]

Major cities: Dubayy, Ash Shāriqah, Al 'Ayn, Ra's al Khaymah

External Territories: None

Location: The United Arab Emirates, in southwestern Asia, is bordered on the north by the Persian Gulf, on the east by the Gulf of Oman and Oman, and on the south and west by Saudi Arabia.

Physical Geography: The country is mainly part of the Ar Rub' al Khālī, a low-lying desert plain. There are some mountains in the east.

Total area: 32,278 sq mi (83,600 sq km)

Coastline: 819 mi (1,318 km)

Land use: About 2% of the land is meadows and pastures; there are no woodlands or arable lands.

Climate: Dry tropical

Population: 2,779,000

Urban population: 84%

Rate of natural increase: 2.1%

Age structure: 33% under 15; 2% over 65

Birth rate: 24/1000

Death rate: 2/1000

Infant mortality rate: 16/1000

Fertility rate: 4.9

Life expectancy at birth: 73 years (male); 76 years (female)

Religion: Muslim, Christian, Hindu

Language: Arabic, Persian, English, Hindu, Urdu

Ethnic Divisions: Emiri, Iranian

Literacy Rate: 79%

Government: South Asian Federation of seven emirates. The seven hereditary rulers of the emirates make up the Supreme Council of Rulers, who elect a president from their members. The 40 members of the Federal National Council are appointed to office by the president for two-year terms and review proposed legislation.

Armed services: 64,500 voluntary troops (1997) in the army, air force, and navy

Suffrage: None

Economy: Oil revenues and profits from Dubay, a regional port of trade, are the main supports of the wealthy U.A.E. economy. The emirates are attempting to promote industrial diversification and privatization in the less-developed regions. The government is also encouraging foreign investment in non–oil related industry; and the opening of a formal stock exchange has been considered.

Unit of currency: Emirian dirham; 100 fils = 1 Emirian dirham (Dh)

GDP per capita $24,000

Inflation rate–CPI: 3.6% (1997 est.)

Workforce: 1.05 million (1996)

Unemployment rate: N.A.

Exports: Goods worth $33.2 billion (f.o.b., 1996 est.) are sent to Japan, South Korea, Singapore, India, Oman, and other trading partners; exports include oil, natural gas, re-exports, dried fish.

Imports: Goods worth $23.5 billion (f.o.b., 1996 est.) are received from the U.S., Japan, the U.K., Italy, and other trading partners; imports include manufactured goods, machinery and transportation equipment, and food.

Agriculture: An estimated 5% of the workforce engages in the agricultural sector. The cultivation of dates, tomatoes, cucumbers, and eggplants, along with livestock and fishing, are the most important agricultural activities. The country is self-sufficient in vegetables, eggs, and poultry; however, 70% of the total food needs are imported.

Energy: Domestic oil and natural gas are used for energy generation.

Natural Resources: Oil and natural gas

Environmental Issues: Desertification, water pollution, little natural freshwater

Transportation: There are no railroads. The 3,000 miles (4,840 km) of roads are all paved. Main ports include Mīnā' Jabal 'Alī on the Persian Gulf and Al Fujayrah on the Gulf of Oman. International airports are at Abu Dhabi, Al Fujayrah, Dubayy, Ra's al Khaymah, and Ash Shāriqah.

Communications: Nearly a dozen daily newspapers are published. There are 545,000 radios (1992) and 170,000 televisions (1993); 677,800 telephones (1993) provide adequate service.

Tourism: In 1994, 1.9 million people visited the U.A.E.; tourist attractions include mosques, oasis towns, markets, snorkeling, and camel races in the desert.

Embassy in U.S.: (202) 995-7999

Public Holidays: Beginning of Ramadan (date varies, in January); End of Ramadan (date varies, in February); Feast of the Sacrifice (date varies, in April); Islamic New Year (date varies, in May); Birth of the Prophet (date varies, in July); Accession of the Ruler of Abu Dhabi (August 6); National Day: end of association with the U.K., 1971 (December 2); Ascension of the Prophet (date varies, in November or December); Christmas (December 25)

United Kingdom

Country Name: United Kingdom

Official Name: United Kingdom of Great Britain and Northern Ireland

Nationality: Briton(s), noun, British (collective plural noun); British (adjective)

Capital: London, pop. [7,074,300]

Major cities: Birmingham, Leeds, Glasgow, Sheffield, Bradford, Liverpool, Edinburgh, Manchester, Bristol

External Territories: Anguilla, in the Caribbean Sea's Leeward Islands (60 sq mi, 155 sq km; pop. 10,700); Bermuda, a group of about 138 islands in the North Atlantic Ocean off the coast of North Carolina (21 sq mi, 53 sq km; pop. 60,144); British Virgin Islands, 70 islands in the Greater Antilles chain in the Caribbean Sea (59 sq mi, 130 sq km; pop. 17,000); Cayman Islands, in the Caribbean Sea (100 sq mi, 260 sq km; pop. 31,900); Channel Islands, in the English Channel (75 sq mi, 194 sq km; pop. 135,300); Falkland Islands, in the South Atlantic Ocean off the coast of Argentina (5,700 sq mi, 22,002 sq km; pop.2,600); Gibraltar, an island in the Strait of Gibraltar between the Mediterranean Sea and the Atlantic Ocean (2.5 sq mi, 6.5 sq km; pop. 28,100); Isle of Man, in the Irish Sea (221 sq mi, 572 sq km; pop.72,700); Montserrat, in the Caribbean Sea (40 sq mi, 102 sq km; pop. 8,000, 1996 est.); Pitcairn Island, in the Pacific Ocean (2 sq mi, 5 sq km; pop. 50); St. Helena, in the South Atlantic Ocean (47 sq mi, 122 sq km; pop. 1,500); South Georgia and South Sandwich Islands in the South Atlantic Ocean (1,580 sq mi, 4,066 sq km; no permanent population);

Turks and Caicos Islands, 40 islands in the North Atlantic Ocean (192 sq mi, 497 sq km; pop. 12,350)

Location: The country of the United Kingdom, in western Europe, is located on the British Isles, which are west of the European continent, separated by the North Sea and English Channel. England, Scotland, and Wales are separated from Ireland, to the west, by the Irish Sea. Northern Ireland is bordered on the south by the Republic of Ireland.

Physical Geography: Lowlands cross the south and southeast of England. The Pennine Mountains run north and south in England, the Cheviot Hills are on the border between England and Scotland, and the Cambrian Mountains cover Wales and western England. Plains cover eastern and central England. Highlands cross northern Scotland, and the Southern Uplands are just north of the Cheviot Hills. Northern Ireland is a mix of lowlands and low mountains.

Total area: 94,248 sq mi (244,101 sq km)

Coastline: 7,718 mi (12,429 km)

Land use: Nearly 50% of the country is meadows and pastures, 25% is arable or under cultivation, and 10% is wooded.

Climate: Temperate, with mild winters and cool summers

Population: 59,364,000

Urban population: 89%

Rate of natural increase: 0.2%

Age structure: 19% under 15; 16% over 65

Birth rate: 12/1000

Death rate: 10/1000

Infant mortality rate: 5.9/1000

Fertility rate: 1.7

Life expectancy at birth: 74 years (male); 80 years (female)

Religion: Anglican, Roman Catholic

Language: English, Welsh, Gaelic

Ethnic Divisions: English, Scottish, Irish, Welsh

Literacy Rate: 99%

Government: Constitutional monarchy, Queen Elizabeth II since 1952, with a bicameral legislature, the Parliament. The 659 members of the House of Commons are directly elected to five-year terms. Of the 1,200 members of the House of Lords, 80% are hereditary peers and the rest are appointed by the monarch for life terms. There are 92 administrative divisions.

Armed services: 213,800 men and women (1997) in the army, navy, and air force; voluntary service

Suffrage: Universal; 18 years old

Economy: Agriculture, services, and industry are the basis of the United Kingdom's economy, but recessions in the past several years have slowed economic growth and raised unemployment rates. The government has increased taxes and interest rates and cut public spending to reduce the budget deficit. Inflation rates have dropped, and workers are gradually finding greater opportunities for employment.

Unit of currency: Pound sterling; 100 pence = 1 pound sterling (£)

GDP per capita: $21,200

Inflation rate–CPI: 3.1% (1997)

Workforce: 28.2 million (1997)

Unemployment rate: 8.2% (1996 est.)

Exports: Goods worth $268 billion (f.o.b., 1997) are sent to Germany, the U.S., France, the Netherlands, and other trading partners; exports include manufactured goods, machinery, fuels, chemicals, semifinished goods, and transport equipment.

Imports: Goods worth $283.5 billion (f.o.b., 1997) are received from Germany, France, the Netherlands, the U.S., and other trading partners; imports include manufactured goods, machinery, semifinished goods, food, and consumer goods.

Agriculture: 1.1% (1996) of the labor force engages in agricultural production. Cereals, oilseed, potatoes, vegetables, cattle, poultry, and fishing are the main commodities produced.

Energy: Domestic and imported oil, natural gas, and coal, as well

UNITED KINGDOM CHALK MARL: THE ONE EASY THING ABOUT BUILDING THE CHUNNEL

With the opening of the Channel Tunnel in 1994, Great Britain gained a physical link with the European continent for the first time since the last ice age some 10,000 years ago. The British and French had talked about building a tunnel for more than 200 years, but it took modern engineering and construction techniques, using navigation satellites and computer-guided lasers, to build the 31-mile-long tunnel between Folkestone, England, and Coquelles, France. The Chunnel, as it is popularly known, is actually three interconnected tunnels—two one-way rail tunnels for passenger trains and shuttle trains carrying cars, buses, and trucks, with a third tunnel for service. The engineers were blessed with a geologic advantage: The tunnel was cut through a thick layer of chalk marl, which was easy to drill through and impervious to water. It took seven years to build.

as some nuclear power, is used for energy generation.

Natural Resources: Coal, petroleum, natural gas, tin, limestone, iron ore, salt, clay, chalk, gypsum, lead, silica

Environmental Issues: Air and water pollution

Transportation: There are an estimated 10,480 miles (16,880 km) of railways, 231,010 miles (372,000 km) of mainly paved roads, and 1,987 miles (3,200 km) of inland waterways. Main seaports include London, Belfast, Liverpool, Aberdeen, Bristol, Cardiff, Grangemouth, Leith, and Manchester. London has two international airports, and international flights are available out of Manchester, Glasgow, Liverpool, Edinburgh, Leeds, and other large cities.

Communications: More than 100 daily newspapers are published throughout the country. There are 70 million radios and 20 million televisions in operation, and 29.5 million telephones provide good service.

Tourism: A renowned tourist destination, the U.K. offers an array of visitor options; among them are the highlands of Scotland, Welsh countryside and castles, coastal resorts throughout the country, England's Lake District, country villages and gardens in England, and London's theaters, shops, and museums. In 1997, 25.96 million visitors came to the country.

U.S. Tourist Office: (800) 462-2748
Embassy in U.S.: (202) 588-6500

Public Holidays: Good Friday (date varies, in March or April); Easter Monday (date varies, in March or April); Early May holiday (date varies, in May); Spring Holiday (date varies, in May); Queen's official birthday (date varies, in June); Summer Bank Holiday (date varies, in August); Christmas (December 25); Boxing Day (December 26)

United States

Country Name: United States
Official Name: United States of America
Nationality: American(s) (noun); American (adjective)
Capital: Washington, D.C., pop. 523,200 [4,563,100]
Major cities: New York, Los Angeles, Chicago, Houston, Philadelphia, San Diego, Phoenix, San Antonio, Dallas
External Territories: Self-governing commonwealths: Puerto Rico, in the Caribbean Sea Northern Mariana Islands, consisting of 14 islands in the Pacific Ocean, including Saipan, Tinian, and Rota, Territories: U.S. Virgin Islands, some 70 islands in the Caribbean Sea, including St. Thomas, St. Croix, and St. John; American Samoa, in the Pacific Ocean (77 sq mi, 199 sq km; pop. 57,000); several other islands in the Pacific Ocean, including Guam, Midway Islands, Johnston Atoll, Kingman Reef, Wake Island, and Baker, Howland, and Jarvis Islands. The Pacific islets of the Palmyra Atoll are privately owned.

Location: The United States, in North America, is bordered on the north by Canada, on the east by the Atlantic Ocean, on the south by the Gulf of Mexico and Mexico, and on the west by the Pacific Ocean. The state of Alaska, on the northwest part of the continent, is separated from the rest of the country by Canada and from Asia by the Bering Strait, with the Arctic Ocean to the north. The state of Hawaii is an archipelago in the central Pacific Ocean, 2,385 miles (3,840 km) off the mainland's west coast.

Physical Geography: The Appalachian Highlands stretch from Maine, in the northeast, to Georgia and Alabama in the southeast. Coastal plains along the Atlantic Ocean lie to the east of the Appalachian Highlands, in the southeast along the Gulf coasts of Alabama, Mississippi, Louisiana, and Texas. Gently rolling plains, drained by the Ohio, Mississippi, and Missouri Rivers, extend west of the Appalachians to the Rocky Mountains. The Ozark Plateaus are in Missouri and Arkansas. The Columbia Plateau, Basin and Range and the Colorado Plateau—drained by the Columbia, Snake, Green, Colorado, and Rio Grande—are between the western slopes of the Rocky Mountains and the eastern slopes of the Cascade Range and Sierra Nevada that parallel the Pacific coast. The five Great Lakes in the northeastern region of the plains are on the U.S.-Canadian border between Minnesota and New York and include Lake Superior, the second largest lake in the world. Hawaii consists of several volcanic islands in the Pacific Ocean. Alaska has interior plains, with mountains to the south (the Alaska Range, with Mount McKinley at 20,320 feet, the highest mountain in North America) and the Brooks Range on the north. The North Slope, north of the Brooks Range, lies along the Arctic Ocean coast.

Total area: 3,717,796 sq mi (9,629,091 sq km)
Coastline: 12,373 mi (19,924 km)
Land use: Woodland and forest cover 30% of the land, 25% is meadows and pastures, and 19% of the land is arable or under cultivation.
Climate: Varies considerably: subtropical in the southeast, with hot summers and mild winters; humid continental in the Great Lakes regions, with hot summers and cold winters; temperate maritime in the mid-Atlantic states, with hot summers and winters ranging from mild

to cold; cool temperate in the northeast, with cool summers and cold winters; continental in the plains states, with winter temperatures decreasing from south to north and hot summers; arid conditions generally dominate west of the 100th meridian, with average temperatures increasing from north to south; marine west coast climates in the northwest, with considerable rainfall and moderate temperatures from northern California to beyond the Canadian border; desert conditions in the southwest, with hot temperatures and little moisture; climate ranges in Alaska, from subarctic to polar in the far north, with cold winters and cool summers; tropical in Hawaii

Population: 270,933,000

Urban population: 75%

Rate of natural increase: 0.6%

Age structure: 21% under 15; 13% over 65

Birth rate: 14.62/1000

Death rate: 8.63/1000

Infant mortality rate: 7/1000

Fertility rate: 2.0

Life expectancy at birth: 74 years (male); 79 years (female)

Religion: Protestant, Roman Catholic, Jewish

Language: English, Spanish

Ethnic Divisions: White, African-American, Asian, Amerindian

Literacy Rate: 97%

Government: Federal republic, with a president and a bicameral legislature, the Congress. The president is elected to a four-year term by an electoral college. The 100 members of the Senate are popularly elected to six-year terms and the 435 members of the House of Representatives are elected to two-year terms. There are 50 administrative states and one federal district.

Armed services: 1,447,600 men and women (1997) in the army, navy, air force, and marines; voluntary service

Suffrage: Universal; 18 years old

Economy: A strong economy makes the U.S. one of the major players in the global market. Services, manufacturing, mining, tourism, and agriculture contribute to a robust gross national product, one of the highest in the world. Recessions led to unemployment in the 1980s and early 1990s, but the economy has shown steady growth in the past several years. Debates continue over eliminating the deficit and producing balanced budgets, and outlays for social spending are being reevaluated as the aging population creates a larger demand for services and benefits.

Unit of currency: United States dollar; 100 cents = 1 U.S. dollar (U.S.)

GDP per capita: $30,200 (1997)

Inflation rate–CPI: 3.7% (1980–1990 average); 2.8% (1995)

Workforce: 136.3 million (1997)

Unemployment rate: 4.9% (1997)

Exports: Goods worth $625.7 billion (f.o.b., 1996 est.) are sent to Canada, Japan, Mexico, Western Europe; exports include capital goods, vehicles, raw materials, consumer goods, and agricultural products.

Imports: Goods worth $882 billion (c.i.f., 1996 est.) are received from Canada, Japan, Mexico, Western Europe; imports include oil and oil products, machinery, vehicles, consumer goods, raw materials, and food and beverages.

Agriculture: Nearly 3% (1997) of the workforce engages in agriculture, fishing, and forestry. Wheat, potatoes, sugar beets, citrus, grains, cotton, and tobacco are all crops. Cattle, pigs, and poultry are the chief groups of livestock. Fishing also generates significant revenue.

Energy: Domestic and imported hydrocarbons are used for most energy generation; in 1995 22.5% of energy requirements are met by nuclear power.

Natural Resources: Minerals, including coal, copper, lead, molybdenum, phosphates, uranium, bauxite, gold, iron, mercury, nickel, potash, silver, tungsten, zinc, oil, natural gas; timber.

Environmental Issues: Air and water pollution, including acid rain; desertification

Transportation: There are 149,040 miles (240,000 km) of railroads and 4.08 million miles (6.42 million km) of roads, of which most are paved. Major rivers add 25,460 miles (40,970 km) of navigable waters; the St. Lawrence Seaway connecting the Great Lakes to the Atlantic Ocean is also an important waterway. Duluth on Lake Superior is the largest Great Lakes port. The seaports of New Orleans and Houston, on the Gulf of Mexico, and New York, on the Atlantic coast, handle the most traffic. Other important Atlantic coast ports are Baltimore, Philadelphia, Boston, Jacksonville, and Savannah; Pacific ports include San Francisco, Anchorage, Honolulu, Los Angeles, Portland, and Seattle. International airports are located in many of the larger cities.

Communications: About 1,500 cities and towns have daily newspapers. There are 540.5 million radios (1992) and 215 million televisions (1993) in use. Phone service, with an estimated 182,558 million telephones (1987 est.), is good in most areas.

Tourism: The U.S. is one of the world's top tourist destinations. In 1997, 49.1 million tourists brought $75.7 billion into the country.

Public Holidays: Martin Luther King, Jr., Day (date varies, in January); Presidents' Day (date varies, in February); Memorial Day (date varies, in May); Declaration of Independence Day: from England, 1776 (July 4); Labor Day (date varies, in September); Columbus Day (date varies, in October); Veterans' Day (November 11); Thanksgiving (date varies, in November); Christmas (December 25)

Uruguay

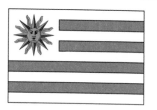

Country Name: Uruguay

Official Name: Oriental Republic of Uruguay

Nationality: Uruguayan(s) (noun); Uruguayan (adjective)

Capital: Montevideo, pop. 1,303,200

Major cities: Salto, Paysandú, Las Piedras, Rivera

External Territories: None

Location: Uruguay, on the southeastern coast of South America, is bordered on the northeast by Brazil, on the east by the Atlantic Ocean, on the south by the Río de la Plata estuary, and on the west by Argentina.

Physical Geography: Plains along the Atlantic coast extend to interior lowlands and rolling hills, including the Cuchilla de Santa Ana on the border with Brazil. The Uruguay River forms the boundary with Argentina, and the Negra River flows south, through the center of the country.

Total area: 68,037 sq mi (176,215 sq km)

Coastline: 410 mi (660 km)

Land use: Nearly 80% of the land is meadows and pastures, 7% is arable, and 6% is forested.

Climate: Temperate, with warm summers and mild winters; freezing temperatures are rare

Population: 3,351,000

Urban population: 91%

Rate of natural increase: 0.8%

Age structure: 25% under 15; 13% over 65

Birth rate: 17.8/1000

Death rate: 9.6/1000

Infant mortality rate: 16.6/1000

Fertility rate: 2.4

Life expectancy at birth: 70 years (male); 78 years (female)

Religion: Roman Catholic

Language: Spanish, Portunol, Brazilero

Ethnic Divisions: White, mestizo, black

Literacy Rate: 97%

Government: Republic, with a president and a bicameral legislature, the General Assembly, or Asemblea General, with a Senate and Chamber of Deputies. The president and vice-president (who also serves in the Senate) are elected to five-year terms by direct vote, as are 30 senators and 99 deputies. There are 19 administrative departments.

Armed services: 17,600 volunteers (1997) in the army, navy, and air force; one- to two-year service; 18 to 45 years of age

Suffrage: Universal and compulsory; 18 years old

Economy: Agriculture, light industry, and services (especially tourism) support Uruguay's economy, but high inflation, recessions, austerity programs, and internal protests have interfered with the country's economic growth in the early 1990s. The government, in 1990, began to reduce inflation rates and encourage industrial development in the private sector. The international financial community has provided funds to allow the country to further its economic recovery.

Unit of currency: Uruguayan peso; 100 centesimos = 1 peso ($Ur)

GDP per capita: $8,900

Inflation rate–CPI: 15.2% (1997)

Workforce: 1.38 million (1997 est.)

Unemployment rate: 10.3% (1997 est.)

Exports: Goods worth $2.7 billion (f.o.b., 1997 est.) are sent to Brazil, Argentina, the U.S., Germany, Italy, and other trading partners; exports include wool, textiles, beef, other animal products, fish, and rice.

Imports: Goods worth $3.7 billion (c.i.f., 1997 est.) are received from Brazil, Argentina, the U.S., Italy, and other trading partners; imports include machinery, vehicles, chemicals, mineral products, and plastics.

Agriculture: 11% of the labor force engages in agriculture, fishing, and forestry. Rice, sugarcane, sugar beets, wheat, barley, potatoes, sorghum, and maize are the main cultivated crops. Sheep and cattle are also important, earning nearly 40% (1996) of the total value of exports.

Energy: Most energy is generated using hydropower and imported fuels.

Natural Resources: Hydropower

Environmental Issues: Air and water pollution, including acid rain

Transportation: There are 1,292 miles (2,080 km) of railroads and 5,230 miles (8,420 km) of roads, of which 4,705 miles (7,578 km) are paved. Inland waterways, including the Uruguay and Negra Rivers, add 995 miles (1,600 km) to the transport network. Major river ports are Salto and Paysandu on the Uruguay. Montevideo is the country's primary seaport. There is an international airport near Montevideo.

Communications: Nearly two dozen daily newspapers are published in the capital and elsewhere. There are 1.89 million radios and 1.13 million televisions (1996) in use. Phone service, with 767,000 phones, is adequate.

Tourism: Beach resorts are the main draw for visitors coming to Uruguay. The country earned an estimated $632 million (U.S.) from nearly 2.2 million tourists in 1994.

U.S. Tourist Office: (212) 753-8581

Embassy in U.S.: (202) 331-1313

Public Holidays: Epiphany (January 6); Landing of the 33 Patriots (April 19); Labor Day (May 1); Battle of Las Piedras, 1811 (May 18); Birth of General José Gervasio Artigas, 1764 (June 19); Constitution Day (July 18); National Independence Day (August 25); Discovery of America (October 12); All Souls' Day (November 2); Blessing of the Waters (December 8); Christmas (December 25)

Uzbekistan

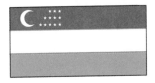

Country Name: Uzbekistan

Official Name: Republic of Uzbekistan

Nationality: Uzbek(s) (noun); Uzbek (adjective)

Capital: Tashkent, pop. 2,107,000 [2,282,000]

Major cities: Samarqand, Namangan, Andijon, Bukhoro (Bukhara)

External Territories: None

Location: Uzbekistan, in Central Asia, is bordered on the north and west by Kazakhstan, on the east by Kyrgyzstan and Tajikistan, on the south by Afghanistan, and on the southwest by Turkmenistan.

Physical Geography: Uzbekistan is mostly desert, the Qizilkum, and steppe. Mountain ranges, the Tian Shan and Pamirs, lie in the east. There are also some oases. The Syr Darya River flows through the Fergana Valley in the northeast; the Amu Darya flows into the Aral Sea in the northwest.

Total area: 172,588 sq mi (447,000 sq km)

Coastline: None; borders the inland Aral Sea for 261 miles (420 km)

Land use: Nearly 50% of the country is meadows and pastures and 10% is arable or cultivated. Less than 5% is forest or woodland.

Climate: Continental dry, with hot summers and cool to cold winters

Population: 24,416,000

Urban population: 38%

Rate of natural increase: 1.9%

Age structure: 40% under 15; 4% over 65

Birth rate: 26/1000

Death rate: 6/1000

Infant mortality rate: 23/1000

Fertility rate: 3.2

Life expectancy at birth: 66 years (male); 72 years (female)

Religion: Muslim, Eastern Orthodox

Language: Uzbek, Russian, Tajik

Ethnic Divisions: Uzbek, Russian

Literacy Rate: 97%

Government: Republic, with a unicameral legislature, the Supreme Assembly. The president is directly elected to a five-year term, and the 250 members of the legislature are also elected for five-year terms. There are 12 administrative regions, one city, and one autonomous republic, Qoraqalpoghiston.

Armed services: 65,000–70,000 troops (1997) in the army and air force; 18-month compulsory enlistment

Suffrage: Universal; 18 years old

Economy: Traditionally dependent on its exports of cotton, gold, and natural gas, Uzbekistan is attempting to diversify its economy with the development of electronics and textile manufacturing. After independence upon the dissolution of the Soviet Union in 1991, the government promoted industry privatization and developed plans for other needed economic reforms, which have been supported by loans from the international financial community.

Unit of currency: Som; 100 teen = 1 som

GDP per capita: $2,500

Inflation rate–CPI: 55% (1996)

Workforce: 8.6 million (1996 est.)

Unemployment rate: 5% (1996 est.)

Exports: Goods worth $3.8 billion (1996) are sent to Ukraine, Eastern Europe, and Western Europe; exports include cotton, gold, natural gas, fertilizers, metals, textiles, and food.

Imports: Goods worth $4.7 billion (1996) are received from the former Soviet Union, Czech Republic, and Western Europe, and other trading partners; imports include grains, machinery, consumer goods, and food.

Agriculture: More than 40% (1995) of the labor force engages in agriculture. Cotton, the primary cash crop, is grown by intensive irrigation

UZBEKISTAN TOURISTS REPLACE TRADERS ON THE SILK ROUTE

The famous Silk Route, the 5,000 miles (8,050 km) of roads that carried early trade between the Mediterranean area and China for more than a thousand years (Marco Polo was one of its famous travelers), passes through Uzbekistan. Some of the most famous Silk Route cities are there today: Khiva, Tashkent, Bukhara, and Samarkand. Although the route crosses wide expanses of desert, these cities and other Silk Route stops are becoming popular tourist destinations.

that is causing the Aral Sea to dry up. Grains, rice, vegetables, fruit, silkworms, and astrakhan wool are also important agricultural commodities. The country is nearly self-sufficient; farms are being privatized, and some acreage formerly devoted to cotton is being used to grow wheat.

Energy: Energy is generated with domestic supplies of oil, coal, natural gas, and hydropower.

Natural Resources: Oil, coal, gold, uranium, silver, copper, lead, zinc, tungsten, molybdenum, natural gas

Environmental Issues: Water pollution, desertification, salinization, soil contamination

Transportation: There are 2,100 miles (3,380 km) of railroads and 44,240 miles (71,240 km) of roads, the majority of which are paved. Some of the Amu Darya River is navigable. An international airport is at Tashkent.

Communications: There are several daily newspapers. Statistics on radios and televisions are not available; telephones number 1.46 million (1995 est.).

Tourism: Cities along the famed Silk Road, including Tashkent and Samarqand, have museums, mosques, and other cultural sites; Bukhoro and other cities are also of historic interest.

Embassy in U.S.: (202) 887-5300

Public Holidays: March 8 (International Women's Day); Navrus (March 21); Independence Day: from Soviet Union, 1991 (September 1); Constitution Day (December 8)

Vanuatu

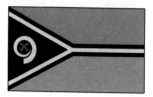

Country Name: Vanuatu

Official Name: Republic of Vanuatu

Nationality: Ni-Vanuatu (singular and plural noun); Ni-Vanuatu (adjective)

Capital: Port-Vila, pop. 31,800

Major cities: Luganville

External Territories: None

Location: The country of Vanuatu, in the South Pacific Ocean, includes some 80 islands. The largest islands, from north to south, are Espírito Santo, Éfaté, Malakula, and Erromango. The Solomon Islands are to the north and New Caledonia is to the south.

Physical Geography: Vanuatu's islands are mostly mountainous, including some active volcanoes, with some coastal plains.

Total area: 5,700 sq mi (14,760 sq km)

Coastline: 1,570 mi (2,528 km)

Land use: About 12% of the land is arable or under cultivation, 2% is meadows and pastures, and 75% is wooded.

Climate: Tropical, with occasional cyclones

Population: 186,000

Urban population: 18%

Rate of natural increase: 2.8%

Age structure: 41% under 15; 4% over 65

Birth rate: 29/1000

Death rate: 5/1000

Infant mortality rate: 21/1000

Fertility rate: 4.2

Life expectancy at birth: 63 years (average)

Religion: Protestant, Catholic, indigenous

Language: English, French, pidgin (Bislama)

Ethnic Divisions: Melanesian, French

Literacy Rate: 53%

Government: Republic, with a president and a unicameral legislature, the Parliament. An electoral college elects the president to a five-year term; the 52 members of the legislature are directly elected to four-year terms. There are six administrative provinces.

Armed services: No regular military forces

Suffrage: Universal; 18 years old

Economy: Subsistence farming, fishing, and tourism are the main sectors in Vanuatu's economy. The government has attempted to diversify the economic base of the country with foreign assistance, but there are few natural resources to support industrial development. International aid has been necessary to help pay for imports; tax increases have also been levied to generate revenue. The government is encouraging tourism, offshore banking, and serves as a flag of convenience for shipping.

Unit of currency: Vatu; 100 centimes = 1 vatu (VT)

GDP per capita: $1,300

Inflation rate–CPI: 2.2% (1997 est.)

Workforce: N.A.

Unemployment rate: N.A.

Exports: Goods worth $30 million (f.o.b., 1996) are sent to Japan, Spain, Germany, the U.K., Cote d'Ivoire and other trading partners; exports include copra, beef, cocoa, timber, and coffee.

Imports: Goods worth $97 million (f.o.b., 1996) are received from Japan, Australia, Singapore, New Zealand, France, and other trading partners; imports include machinery, vehicles, food, basic manufactures, raw materials, fuels, and chemicals.

Agriculture: 65% (1995 est.) of the workforce engages in the agricultural sector. Copra, beef, coffee, cocoa, squash, timber, and trochus shells have traditionally generated export revenue; yams, taro, cassava, breadfruit, and vegetables are grown for domestic use. Foreign exchange is gained by selling fishing rights.

Energy: Most energy is generated using imported fuels.

Natural Resources: Manganese, timber, seafood

Environmental Issues: Limited access to potable water

Transportation: There are no railroads. The islands have 665 miles (1,070 km) of roads, of which 160 miles (256 km) are paved. Port-Vila, on Éfaté, and Luganville, on Espírito Santo, are the main seaports. An international airport is at Port-Vila.

Communications: There are no dailies published, but there are a variety of weekly and monthly newspapers. There are 49,000 radios, 2,000 televisions, and 4,000 telephone main lines (1994 est.) in operation.

Tourism: Tourism is an important source of revenue. The country earned $55 million from visitors in 1994, and 46,000 visitors came to the islands in 1995. Attractions include World War II sites, cultural exhibits and artifact collections, volcanoes, beaches, bird-watching, and the village on Tanna Island.

Public Holidays: Easter (date varies, in March or April); Labor Day (date varies, in May); Ascension (date varies, in May); Independence Day: from France and the U.K., 1980 (July 30); Assumption (August 15); Constitution Day (October 5); Unity Day (November 29); Christmas (December 25)

Vatican City (Holy See)

Country Name: Vatican City (Holy See)

Official Name: The Holy See (State of the Vatican City)

Nationality: N.A.

External Territories: None

Location: Vatican City is enclosed within the limits of Rome, Italy's capital city.

Physical Geography: Urban

Total area: 0.2 sq mi (0.4 sq km)

Coastline: None

Land use: N.A.

Climate: Warm temperate, with hot summers and mild winters

Population: 1,000

Urban population: 100%

Rate of natural increase: N.A.

Age structure: N.A.

Birth rate: N.A.

Death rate: N.A.

Infant mortality rate: N.A.

Fertility rate: N.A.

Life expectancy at birth: N.A.

Religion: Roman Catholic

Language: Italian, Latin

Ethnic Divisions: Italian, Swiss, others

Literacy Rate: N.A.

Government: The Pope, who is elected for a life term by the College of Cardinals, has absolute legislative, executive, and judicial powers.

Armed services: Army of more than 100 Swiss Papal Guards

Suffrage: limited to Cardinals under 80 years old

Economy: Investments, donations, tourism, and the management of the Roman Catholic Church finances are the mainstays of the economy in Vatican City.

Unit of currency: Vatican lira, Italian currency; 100 centisimi =1 Vatican lira (Vlit)

GDP per capita: N.A.

Inflation rate–CPI: N.A.

Workforce: N.A.

Unemployment rate: N.A.

Exports: N.A.

Imports: Virtually all necessities are imported.

Agriculture: N.A.

Energy: Imported fuels and electricity are used.

Natural Resources: N.A.

Environmental Issues: N.A.

Transportation: A short railway, 2,760 feet (840 m), connects Italy with Vatican City; it is mainly used for freight. A heliport is used for transportation.

Communications: The country publishes extensively, including Roman Catholic Church bulletins, a daily newspaper, and scholarly books. A radio station was begun in 1931, and a television center produces and distributes religious programming.

Tourism: Tourists and religious pilgrims come to Vatican City to hear the Pope's addresses in St. Peter's Square, to tour St. Peter's Basilica (the largest Christian church in the world), to see the many antiquities and artworks housed in the Museum and Treasure House, and to view the Sistine Chapel and its famed paintings by Michelangelo.

Embassy in U.S.: (202) 333-7121

Public Holidays: Easter (date varies, in March or April); Assumption (August 15); All Saints' Day

(November 1); Immaculate Conception (December 8); Christmas (December 25)

Venezuela

Country Name: Venezuela

Official Name: Republic of Venezuela

Nationality: Venezuelan(s) (noun); Venezuelan (adjective)

Capital: Caracas, pop. [3,672,800]

Major cities: Maracaibo, Valencia, Maracay, Barquisimeto

External Territories: None

Location: Venezuela, on the north coast of South America, is bordered on the north by the Caribbean Sea and the Atlantic Ocean, on the east by Guyana, on the south by Brazil, and on the west by Colombia.

Physical Geography: Lake Maracaibo occupies the center of a lowland basin in the northwest; three separate highland systems, including the Cordillera de Mérida (which are, in part, extensions of the Andes), are southwest of the basin. Central plains, Llanos, separate these western highlands from the Guiana Highlands in the southeastern section of the country. The Orinoco River flows northeast to the Atlantic Ocean.

Total area: 352,144 sq mi (912,050 sq km)

Coastline: 1,739 mi (2,800 km)

Land use: Nearly 35% of the country is forested, 20% is meadows and pastures, and 5% is arable or cultivated.

Climate: Tropical to temperate, with cooler temperatures at higher elevations

Population: 23,707,000

Urban population: 86%

Rate of natural increase: 2.0%

Age structure: 39% under 15; 4% over 65

Birth rate: 24.9/1000

Death rate: 4.7/1000

Infant mortality rate: 21/1000

Fertility rate: 2.9

Life expectancy at birth: 70 years (male); 76 years (female)

Religion: Roman Catholic

Language: Spanish

Ethnic Divisions: Mestizo, white, black, Indian

Literacy Rate: 91%

Government: Federal republic, with a president and a bicameral legislature, the National Congress. The president, 53 senators, and 203 members of the Chamber of Deputies are directly elected to five-year terms; former presidents also serve as senators. There are 21 states, one territory, and one federal district.

Armed services: 79,000 troops (1997) in the army, navy, air force, and other branches; 2 1/2-year selective service for men 18–45 years of age

Suffrage: Universal; 18 years old

Economy: Oil, subject to international price fluctuations, is the source of 27% of the country's GDP and 78% of export earnings. In recent years price controls and fixed currency rates have been imposed to mitigate the effects of bank failures and the subsequent loss of foreign reserves. The government has also begun austerity measures in order to gain international assistance and reduce the budget deficit, and it hopes to encourage foreign partners in the oil industry.

Unit of currency: Bolívar; 100 céntimos = 1 bolívar (Bs)

GDP per capita: $8300

Inflation rate–CPI: 38% (1997)

Workforce: 9.2 million (1997 est.)

Unemployment rate: 11.5% (1997 est.)

Exports: Goods worth $20.8 billion (f.o.b., 1996) are sent to the U.S., Puerto Rico, the Netherlands, Japan, Italy, and other trading partners; exports include petroleum, bauxite, aluminum, steel, chemicals, agricultural products, and basic manufactures.

Imports: Goods worth $10.5 billion (f.o.b., 1996) are received from the U.S., Germany, Japan, the Netherlands, Canada, and other trading partners; imports include raw materials, machinery, transportation equipment, and construction materials.

Agriculture: 13% (1997) of the labor force engages in the agricultural sector. Corn, sorghum, sugarcane, rice, bananas, vegetables, and coffee. Cattle are raised on the central plains.

Energy: Domestic oil, coal, and hydropower generates most energy.

Natural Resources: Petroleum, natural gas, coal, iron, gold, bauxite, zinc, diamonds, hydropower

Environmental Issues: Water pollution, deforestation, soil degradation

Transportation: There are 363 miles (584 km) of railroads and 52,350 miles (84,300 km) of roads, more than a third of which are paved. Navigable waters, including the Orinoco River and Lake Maracaibo, total 4,410 miles (7,100 km). La Guaira, Maracaibo, Puerto Cabello, and Puerto Ordaz are major ports. There are eight international airports, including one at Caracas.

Communications: Daily newspapers are published in cities throughout the country; Caracas has eight daily papers. There are 9.04 million radios and 3.3 million televisions (1992 est.) in operation; 1.44 million telephones (1987 est.) provide modern service.

Tourism: Local festivals for patron saints, beaches, fishing, water sports, and the spectacular Angel Falls in the Guiana Highlands, the highest waterfall in the world, are some of Venezuela's key attractions. In 1995, some 600,000 visitors added $820 million (U.S.) to the country's economy.

U.S. Tourist Office: (212) 826-1678

Embassy in U.S.: (202) 342-2214

Public Holidays: Carnival (dates vary, in February); Easter (date varies, in March or April); Declaration of Independence (April 19); Labor Day (May 1); Battle of Carabobo (June 24); Independence Day (July 5); Battle of Lake Maracaibo and birth of Simón Bolívar, 1783 (July 24); Civil Servants' Day (September 4); Discovery of America (October 12); Christmas (December 25–26); New Year's Eve (December 31)

Vietnam

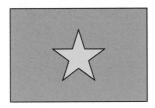

Country Name: Vietnam

Official Name: Socialist Republic of Vietnam

Nationality: Vietnamese (singular and plural noun); Vietnamese (adjective)

Capital: Hanoi, pop. 1,089,800 [3,056,000]

Major cities: Ho Chi Minh City, Haiphong, Da Nang

External Territories: None

Location: Vietnam, in Southeast Asia, is bordered on the north by China, on the east by the Gulf of Tonkin, on the south by the South China Sea, and on the west by Cambodia and Laos.

Physical Geography: Wide river deltas—the Hong (Red) River that flows into the Gulf of Tonkin in the north and the Mekong River that flows into the South China Sea in the south—are separated by the Annam Cordillera, a mountain chain that extends from the northwest to cover two-thirds of the country. Coastal lowlands run along the eastern perimeter of the mountains.

Total area: 127,242 sq mi (329,556 sq km)

Coastline: 2,139 mi (3,444 km)

Land use: Forests cover about 30% of the land, 21% is arable or cultivated, and 1% is meadows and pastures.

Climate: Tropical, with monsoons from May through September, cooler winters in the north

Population: 79,490,000

Urban population: 20%

Rate of natural increase: 1.5%

Age structure: 35% under 15; 5% over 65

Birth rate: 22/1000

Death rate: 7/1000

Infant mortality rate: 35/1000

Fertility rate: 2.7

Life expectancy at birth: 63 years (male); 69 years (female)

Religion: Buddhist, Taoist, Roman Catholic, traditional, Islam, Protestant

Language: Vietnamese, Chinese, English, French, Khmer, tribal languages

Ethnic Divisions: Vietnamese

Literacy Rate: 94%

Government: Socialist republic, with a president and unicameral legislature, the National Assembly, or Quoc-Hoi. The members of the 450 seat legislature are directly elected to five-year terms; the president is elected to a five-year term from the legislature by its members. There are 50 administrative provinces and 3 municipalities.

Armed services: 4922,000 troops (1997) in the army, navy, and air force; two-year compulsory service

Suffrage: Universal; 18 years old

VIETNAM HANOI: ONE MILLENNIUM OLD IN 2011

Vietnam, somewhat larger than Italy, has verdant hills and mountains running almost the 1,000-mile length of the country, with beaches and lagoons dotting the long coastlines. Hanoi, which was founded in 1011, is the oldest capital in southeast Asia and served as the capital of French Indonesia from 1887 to 1954. Vietnam is 2,000 years old and was ruled by China for 1,000 years, between 111 B.C. and A.D. 938.

Economy: Oil and rice are two of Vietnam's key exports; the production of both have benefitted from the government's shift from a central economy to a market economy, begun in 1986, in order to privatize industry and allow market rates to prevail for commodity prices. The international community has also contributed to the development of Vietnam's economic growth with investments, loan restructuring, and debt relief. The country is faced with the challenge of lowering unemployment and meeting the many demands of a growing population.

Unit of currency: Dông; 100 xu = 1 new dông (D)

GDP per capita: $1,700

Inflation rate–CPI: 5% (1997 est.)

Workforce: 32.7 million (1990 est.)

Unemployment rate: 25% (1995)

Exports: Goods worth $7.1 billion (f.o.b., 1996 est.) are sent to Japan, Germany, Singapore, Taiwan, Hong Kong, and other trading partners; exports include oil, rice, seafood, and coffee.

Imports: Goods worth $11.1 billion (f.o.b., 1996 est.) are received from Singapore, South Korea, Japan, France, Hong Kong, and other trading partners; imports include oil products, machinery, steel products, fertilizers, raw cotton, and grains.

Agriculture: The agricultural sector employs 65% (1990) of the workforce. Rice, coffee, rubber, tea, cotton, and peanuts are all cash crops; livestock and seafood are important exports. Timber exports have been banned since 1997.

Energy: Domestic hydropower and imported oil generates most of the country's energy.

Natural Resources: Minerals, including phosphates, oil, coal, tin, zinc, iron, antimony, chromium, phosphates, bauxite; timber

Environmental Issues: Deforestation, water and groundwater pollution, overfishing, soil degradation

Transportation: There are 1,760 miles (2,840 km) of railroads and 57,940 miles (93,300 km) of roads, of which about a quarter are paved. The Mekong and Hong Rivers and other inland waterways add 10,992 miles (17,700 km) to the transport network. Main seaports include Ho Chi Minh City, Da Nang, Haiphong, Hong Gai, Nha Trang, and Qui Nhon. International airports are at Hanoi and Ho Chi Minh City.

Communications: Daily newspapers are published in Hanoi and Ho Chi Minh City. There are 7.2 million radios and 2.9 million televisions (1992 est.) in use; phone service, with 800,000 lines, is inadequate to serve the growing demand.

Tourism: In 1994, 1.01 million tourists brought $363 million (U.S) to Vietnam. Temples, markets, and museums in Hanoi draw visitors, as do Hue's historic architecture and Citadel and the mixture of colonial and oriental cultures in Ho Chi Minh City.

Embassy in U.S.: (202) 861-0737

Public Holidays: Tet, lunar new year (date varies, in February); Liberation of Saigon (April 30); May Day (May 1); National Day: independence, from France, 1945 (September 1–2)

Yemen

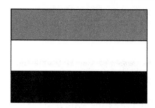

Country Name: Yemen

Official Name: Republic of Yemen

Nationality: Yemeni(s) (noun); Yemeni (adjective)

Capital: Sanaa (San'a), pop. [972,200]

Major cities: Adan (Aden), Ta'izz, Al Ḥudayadah, Al Mukallā

External Territories: None

Location: Yemen, in the Middle East, is on the south coast of the Arabian Peninsula, with the Gulf of Aden to the east and the Red Sea to the west. It is bordered on the north by Saudi Arabia and on the east by Oman.

Physical Geography: Narrow coastal plains merge with flat-topped hills, and the eastern plateau slopes to deserts. The Bab el Mandeb Strait links the Red Sea and the Gulf of Aden.

Total area: 203,850 sq mi (527,968 sq km)

Coastline: 1,191 mi (1,906 km)

Land use: About 30% of the land is meadows and pastures, 4% is forested, and 3% is arable or under cultivation.

Climate: Tropical dry, with more rainfall in the mountains

Population: 16,372,000

Urban population: 25%

Rate of natural increase: 2.9%

Age structure: 47% under 15; 3% over 65

Birth rate: 40/1000

Death rate: 11/1000

Infant mortality rate: 75/1000

Fertility rate: 6.7

Life expectancy at birth: 58 years (male); 61 years (female)

Religion: Shiite and Sunni Muslim

Language: Arabic

Ethnic Divisions: Arab

Literacy Rate: 38%

Government: Republic, with a president and a unicameral legislature, the House of Representatives. The president is directly elected for a five-year term; the 301 members of the legislature are elected to four-year terms. There are 17 governorates.

Armed services: 66,300 troops (1997) in the army, navy, and air force; two-year compulsory service

Suffrage: Universal; 18 years old

Economy: Since the establishment of the Yemen republic in 1990, the country has not been able to sustain economic growth because of political turmoil, including civil war in 1994, austerity measures, and low currency values. Yemen has oil reserves and the port of Aden has potential for generating substantial revenue. The government has devised several plans to prompt industry privatization, stabilize currency values, reduce subsidies, and keep inflation rates low; international funds have been allocated to help carry out these reforms.

Unit of currency: Yemeni rial; 100 fils = 1 Yemeni rial

GDP per capita: $2,300

Inflation rate–CPI: 5% (1997)

Workforce: N.A.

Unemployment rate: 30% (1995 est.)

Exports: Goods worth $2.3 billion (f.o.b., 1997 est.) are sent to the South Korea, Thailand, Brazil, China, and other trading partners; exports include oil, cotton, coffee, and dried and salted fish.

Imports: Goods worth $2.3 billion (f.o.b., 1997 est.) are received from the U.S., the U.A.E., Saudi Arabia, Japan, and other trading partners; imports include textiles, manufactured goods, consumer goods, oil, food, cement, machinery, and chemicals.

Agriculture: Almost half (1995) of the workforce engages in the agricultural sector. Sorghum, potatoes, coffee, cotton, and fruits are cash crops; wheat, barley, grapes, and watermelons are subsistence crops. Livestock and seafood are also exported. Kat, a shrubby plant with leaves that are chewed for their mild narcotic effect, is grown for domestic use and is replacing export crops of cotton, fruit, and vegetables. The

country, once self-sufficient, must now import food.

Energy: Domestic and imported oil is used for most energy generation.

Natural Resources: Oil, seafood, rock salt, marble

Environmental Issues: Limited freshwater, desertification, soil erosion

Transportation: There are no railroads in the country. There are 40,200 miles (64,730 km) of roads, the majority of which are unpaved. Seaports include Adan (Aden), Al Ḥudayadah, and Al Mukallā. International airports are at Sanaa, Adan, Ta'izz, Al Ḥudayadah, and Al Mukallā.

Communications: Three newspapers are published. There are 325,000 radios and 100,000 televisions (1993) in operation, and 131,660 main lines (1992 est.) provide basic phone service.

Tourism: Visitors, numbering 40,000 in 1994, spent $41 million (U.S.) in Yemen; attractions include the markets and historic buildings in Sanaa and other cities and mountain scenery.

Embassy in U.S.: (202) 965-4760

Public Holidays: Beginning of Ramadan (date varies, in December or January); End of Ramadan (date varies, in February); International Women's Day (March 8); Feast of the Sacrifice (date varies, in April); Islamic New Year (date varies, in April or May); Ashura (date varies, in April or May); Labor Day (May 1); Corrective Movement Anniversary (June 13); Birth of the Prophet (date varies, in July); National Day (October 14); Ascension of the Prophet (date varies, in November or December)

Yugoslavia

Country Name: Yugoslavia

Official Name: Federal Republic of Yugoslavia

Nationality: Serb(s) and Montenegrin(s) (noun); Serbian and Montenegrin (adjective)

Capital: Belgrade, pop. 1,168,500 [1,338,900]

Major cities: Novi Sad, Niš, Kragujevac, Priština

External Territories: None

Location: Yugoslavia, in southeastern Europe, is bordered on the north by Hungary, on the east by Romania and Bulgaria, on the south by Macedonia and Albania, and on the west by the Adriatic Sea, Bosnia and Herzegovina, and Croatia.

Physical Geography: There are plains in the north, part of the Pannonain Basin. There are river valleys, including drainages of the Sava, Tara, and Danube, and highlands throughout much of the rest of the country. The Dinaric Alps are along the coast.

Total area: 39,450 sq mi (102,173 sq km)

Coastline: 124 mi (199 km)

Land use: N.A.

Climate: Continental in the north and central part of the country, Mediterranean along the coast

Population: 10,646,000

Urban population: 51%

Rate of natural increase: 0.2%

Age structure: 21% under 15; 13% over 65

Birth rate: 12/1000

Death rate: 11/1000

Infant mortality rate: 12.7/1000

Fertility rate: 1.7

Life expectancy at birth: 70 years (male); 75 years (female)

Religion: Orthodox, Muslim

Language: Serbo-Croatian, Albanian

Ethnic Divisions: Serb, Albanian, Montenegrin, Hungarian

Literacy Rate: N.A.

Government: Federal republic, with a president and a bicameral legislature, the Federal Assembly. The president is elected by members of the legislature for a four-year term. The 138 members of the Chamber of Citizens are directly elected to office, and the 40 members of the Chamber of Republics are elected by two regional assemblies. There are two republics and two autonomous provinces.

Armed services: 114,200 troops (1997) in the army, navy, and air force; 12–15 month compulsory service for men; women may volunteer

Suffrage: Universal; 18 years old; 16 years old if employed

Economy: In 1991 and 1992 Croatia, Bosnia and Herzegovina, and Macedonia became independent from Yugoslavia, leaving Serbia and Montenegro as the principal republics within the country. This left the new state without its traditional trading partners and economic partnership. Political strife within the country exacerbated the economic crisis, as did UN sanctions between 1992 and 1994 against trade with Yugoslavia. However, austerity measures, the promise of industry privatization, the removal of international sanctions, and the introduction of a new currency have seeded some new economic stability.

Unit of currency: Yugoslav New Dinar; 100 paras = 1 Yugoslav New Dinar (YD)

GDP per capita: $2,280

Inflation rate–CPI: 7% (1997)

Workforce: 2.178 million

Unemployment rate: More than 35% (1995 est.)

Exports: Goods worth 2.8 billion (1996 est.) are sent to Italy, Russia, Germany; exports include manufactured goods, food and live animals, and raw materials.

Imports: Goods worth 6.2 billion (1996 est.) are received from Germany, Italy, and Russia; imports include machinery and transport equipment, fuels and lubricants, manufactured goods, chemicals, food an live animals and, raw materials.

Agriculture: An estimated 5% (1994) of the workforce engages in agriculture, Cereals, fruits, vegetables, tobacco, olives, sheep, and goats are the key agricultural commodities.

Energy: Thermal power stations (providing about 68% of the total electricity generated in 1994) and hydroelectric power (32%) are two primary sources of energy.

Natural Resources: Oil, natural gas, coal, antimony, copper, lead, zinc, nickel, gold, pyrite, chrome

Environmental Issues: Water and air pollution

Transportation: There are 2,480 miles (4,000 km) of railroads and 30,760 miles (49,530 km) of roads, of which 17,930 miles (28,870 km) are paved. Canals and rivers such as the Danube are navigable. River ports include Novi Sad and Belgrade on the Danube; the principal seaport is Bar on the Adriatic. International airports are at Belgrade and Podgorica.

Communications: Seventeen daily newspapers (1995) are published in the country. There are 2 million radios and 1 million televisions in operation, and 700,000 phones are in use.

Tourism: The country earned $31 million (U.S.) from 2.8 million tourists in 1994.

Attractions include museums in Belgrade, mosques and monastaries in other cities, and picturesque villages in the mountains and along the coast.

Embassy in U.S.: (202) 462-6566

Public Holidays: Labor Days (May 1–2); Republic Days (November 29–30)

Zambia

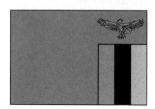

Country Name: Zambia

Official Name: Republic of Zambia

Nationality: Zambian(s) (noun); Zambian (adjective)

Capital: Lusaka, pop. 982,400

Major cities: Ndola, Kitwe, Kabwe, Chingola

External Territories: None

Location: Zambia, a landlocked country in south central Africa, is bordered on the north by the Democratic Republic of the Congo and Tanzania; on the east by Malawi; on the south by Mozambique, Zimbabwe, Botswana, and Namibia; and on the west by Angola.

Physical Geography: Zambia is mostly plateaus, characterized by hills and smaller ranges. The Muchinga Mountains are in the north. Lake Kariba, on the border with Zimbabwe in the south, was created by a dam on the Zambezi River. The terrain in the west is more level along the Zambezi River floodplain.

Total area: 290,586 sq mi (752,614 sq km)

Coastline: None

Land use: Nearly 40% of the land is meadows and pastures, 39% is wooded, and 7% is arable or cultivated.

Climate: Highland tropical, modified by elevation, with rains from October to April

Population: 9,664,000

Urban population: 38%

Rate of natural increase: 1.96%

Age structure: 45% under 15; 3% over 65

Birth rate: 42.2/1000

Death rate: 22.6/1000

Infant mortality rate: 109/1000

Fertility rate: 6.1

Life expectancy at birth: 37 years (male); 38 years (female)

Religion: Christian, Muslim, Hindu

Language: English, indigenous languages

Ethnic Divisions: More than 70 groups, mainly Bantu

Literacy Rate: 78%

Government: Republic, with a president and a unicameral legislature, the National Assembly. The president and 150 members of the legislature are directly elected to five-year terms. There are nine provinces.

Armed services: 21,600 volunteers (1997) in the army and air force

Suffrage: Universal; 18 years old

Economy: Zambia's economy in the past several years has suffered because of drought, a large external debt, and declining prices for copper, one of its chief export commodities. The government has worked diligently to administer an austerity program to reduce inflation and decentralize social services, and international aid has helped to pare down external debt.

Unit of currency: Zambian kwacha; 100 ngwee = 1 kwacha (ZK)

GDP per capita: $950

Inflation rate–CPI: 43.9% (1996)

Workforce: 3.5 million (1996 est.)

Unemployment rate: 22% (1991 est.)

Exports: Goods worth $975 million (f.o.b., 1996 est.) are sent to Japan, South Africa, Saudi Arabia, Thailand, India, and other trading partners; exports include copper, zinc, cobalt, lead, and tobacco.

Imports: Goods worth $990 million (f.o.b., 1996 est.) are received from South Africa, the U.K., Zimbabwe, Japan, the U.S., and other trading partners; imports include machinery, vehicles, food, fuels, and manufactured items.

Agriculture: An estimated 73% (1996) of the labor force engages in the agricultural sector. Corn, cassava, millet, sorghum, beans, rice, peanuts, sunflower seeds, cotton, sugarcane, beans, and livestock, especially cattle, are raised for domestic use. The country has had to import food in recent years because drought has affected crops.

Energy: Most energy is generated using domestic hydropower.

Natural Resources: Minerals, including copper, cobalt, zinc, lead, coal, emeralds, gold, silver, uranium; hydropower

Environmental Issues: Air pollution, acid rain, wildlife poaching, deforestation, desertification

Transportation: There are 1,340 miles (2,160km) of railroads and 24,650 miles (39,700 km) of roads, of which nearly 20% are paved. Navigable waterways, including stretches of the Zambezi and Luapula Rivers and Lake Tanganyika, add 1,400 miles (2,250 km) to the transportation network. Lusaka has an international airport.

Communications: Two daily newspapers are published in Lusaka. There are 800,000 radios and 260,000 televisions (1995) in use. Phone service, with 80,000 phones (1994/95) in operation, is above average for the region.

Tourism: National parks, with their array of flora and fauna, and the thundering Victoria Falls, on the border with Zimbabwe, earned Zambia $43 million (U.S.) from 134,000 tourists in 1994.

U.S. Tourist Office: (212) 758-1110

Embassy in U.S.: (202) 265-9717

Public Holidays: Youth Day (March 11); Easter (date varies, in March or April); Labor Day (May 1); African Freedom Day (May 24); Heroes' Day (July 5); Unity Day (July 8); Farmers' Day (August 5); Independence Day: from the U.K., 1964 (October 24); Christmas (December 25)

Zimbabwe

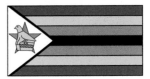

Country Name: Zimbabwe

Official Name: Republic of Zimbabwe

Nationality: Zimbabwean(s) (noun); Zimbabwean (adjective)

Capital: Harare, pop. 1,189,100

Major cities: Bulawayo, Chitungwiza, Gweru, Mutare

External Territories: None

Location: Zimbabwe, a landlocked country in southern Africa, is bordered on the north by Zambia, on the east by Mozambique, on the south by South Africa, and on the west by Botswana.

Physical Geography: Zimbabwe is mostly hilly plateaus, with mountains in the east. The Zambezi River forms the boundary with Zambia and the Kariba Dam forms Lake Kariba.

Total area: 150,804 sq mi (390,580 sq km)

Coastline: None

Land use: Nearly 23% of the country is forested, 13% is meadows and pastures, and 7% is arable or cultivated.

Climate: Tropical to subtropical, with temperatures moderated by elevation, rainy season from November to March

Population: 11,163,000

Urban population: 31%

ZIMBABWE CASTING OFF A COLONIAL PAST

Zimbabwe was originally named for Cecil Rhodes, whose fortune was created from South African diamonds. Known as South Rhodesia when it was a British Colony, the country was renamed when Zimbabwe's majority blacks took over in 1980.

Rate of natural increase: 1.22%

Age structure: 44% under 15; 3% over 65

Birth rate: 32/1000

Death rate: 19.8/1000

Infant mortality rate: 52.8/1000

Fertility rate: 4

Life expectancy at birth: 40 years (male); 40 years (female)

Religion: Syneretic (part Christian, part indigenous beliefs), Christian, indigenous beliefs

Language: English, Shona, Sindebele

Ethnic Divisions: Shona, Ndebele

Literacy Rate: 85%

Government: Parliamentary democracy, with a president and a unicameral legislature, the House of Assembly. The president is elected by the legislature for a six-year term. Of the 150-member legislature, 120 members are directly elected to office, 20 are nominated by the president, and 10 are chiefs. There are eight administrative provinces and two cities.

Armed services: 39,000 troops (1997 est.) in the army and air force

Suffrage: Universal; 18 years old

Economy: Although agriculture is central to the country's economy, manufacturing generates significant revenue, and an array of minerals supplement agricultural exports. The country has a well-developed infrastructure. The government has had difficulty maintaining austerity measures that would qualify the country for some forms of international aid. However, the country is encouraging additional economic growth via foreign investment and export development.

Unit of currency: Zimbabwean dollar; 100 cents = 1 Zimbabwean dollar (Z$)

GDP per capita: $2,200

Inflation rate–CPI: 21.4% (1996)

Workforce: 5.2 million (1995 est.)

Unemployment rate: 33% (1997 est.)

Exports: Goods worth $2.5 billion (f.o.b., 1996) are sent to the U.K., Germany, South African countries, Japan, and other trading partners; exports include tobacco and other agricultural products , manufactures, gold, and ferrochrome.

Imports: Goods worth $2.2 billion (f.o.b., 1996) are received from South African countries, the U.K., Germany, the U.S., Japan, and other trading partners; imports include machinery, transportation equipment, manufactured goods, chemicals, and fuels.

Agriculture: An estimated 67% (1996) of the labor force is engaged in the agricultural sector. Tobacco, cotton, corn, coffee, and sugarcane are the main cash crops; wheat, soybeans, peanuts, livestock, and other commodities are raised for domestic use. Tobacco earns 28% (1996 est.) of the total value of exports.

Energy: Hydropower and coal are used for most energy generation.

Natural Resources: Minerals, including coal, chromium, asbestos, gold, nickel, copper, iron, vanadium, tin, cobalt

Environmental Issues: Air and water pollution, deforestation, soil erosion, poaching

Transportation: There are 1,710 miles (2,760 km) of railroads and 11,390 (18,340 km) of roads, of which 5,400 (8,690 km) are paved. Lake Kariba is navigable and has ports at Binga and Kariba. International airports are at Harare, Bulawayo, and Victoria Falls.

Communications: There are two daily newspapers. There are 945,000 radios and 297,000 televisions (1994) in operation; phone service, with 135,000 telephones, is poorly maintained.

Tourism: Some 10% of Zimbabwe is devoted to parks, gardens, and sanctuaries; the spectacular Victoria Falls and mountain retreats draw visitors to the country, which earned $153 million (U.S.) from 1.1 million tourists in 1994.

U.S. Tourist Office: (800) 621-2381

Embassy in U.S.: (202) 332-7100

Public Holidays: Easter (date varies, in March or April); Independence Day (April 18); Worker's Day (May 1); Africa Day (May 25); Heroes' Day (August 11–12); Christmas (December 25–26)

Physical Map

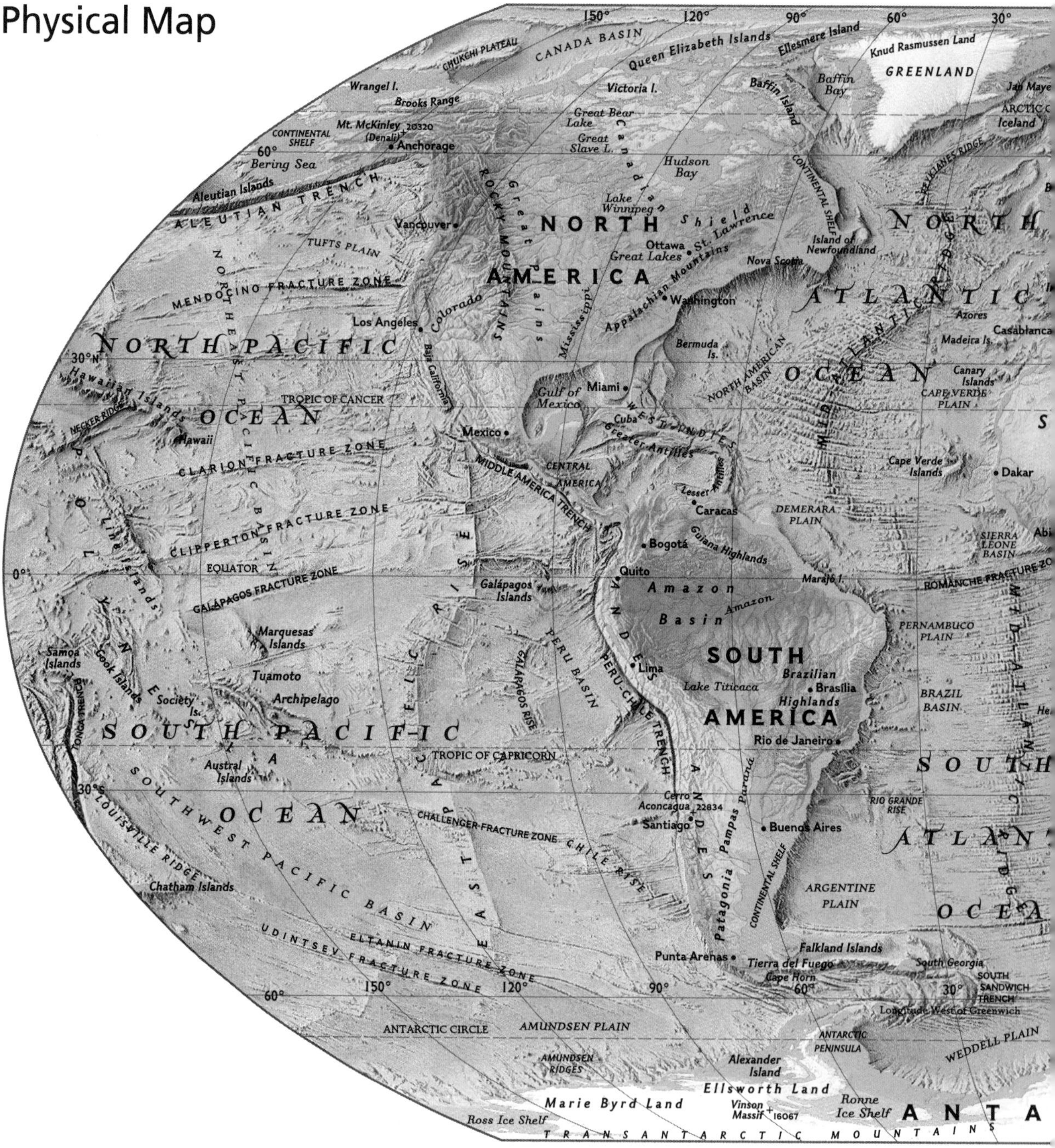

CANADA BASIN
CHUKCHI PLATEAU
Queen Elizabeth Islands
Ellesmere Island
Knud Rasmussen Land
GREENLAND
Wrangel I.
Brooks Range
Victoria I.
Baffin Island
Baffin Bay
Great Bear Lake
Great Slave L.
Mt. McKinley (Denali) 20320
Anchorage
CONTINENTAL SHELF
Bering Sea
Aleutian Islands
ALEUTIAN TRENCH
Hudson Bay
Canadian Shield
Lake Winnipeg
NORTH AMERICA
Vancouver
ROCKY MOUNTAINS
Great Plains
Ottawa
St. Lawrence
Great Lakes
Island of Newfoundland
Nova Scotia
Appalachian Mountains
Washington
Mississippi
Colorado
Los Angeles
Baja California
TUFTS PLAIN
MENDOCINO FRACTURE ZONE
NORTH PACIFIC OCEAN
NORTHEAST PACIFIC BASIN
Hawaiian Islands
NECKER RIDGE
Hawaii
TROPIC OF CANCER
Gulf of Mexico
Miami
Bermuda Is.
NORTH AMERICAN BASIN
Cuba
WEST INDIES
Greater Antilles
Lesser Antilles
Mexico
CENTRAL AMERICA
MIDDLE AMERICA TRENCH
CLARION FRACTURE ZONE
CLIPPERTON FRACTURE ZONE
EQUATOR
GALÁPAGOS FRACTURE ZONE
Galápagos Islands
Line Islands
Caracas
Bogotá
Quito
Guiana Highlands
DEMERARA PLAIN
Amazon Basin
Marajó I.
Lima
ANDES
SOUTH AMERICA
Brazilian Highlands
Brasília
Lake Titicaca
Rio de Janeiro
PERU BASIN
PERU-CHILE TRENCH
GALÁPAGOS RISE
EAST PACIFIC RISE
Marquesas Islands
Samoa Islands
Cook Islands
Tuamoto Archipelago
Society Is.
TONGA TRENCH
SOUTH PACIFIC OCEAN
Austral Islands
TROPIC OF CAPRICORN
Cerro Aconcagua 22834
Santiago
Pampas
Paraná
Buenos Aires
CHALLENGER FRACTURE ZONE
CHILE RISE
SOUTHWEST PACIFIC BASIN
LOUISVILLE RIDGE
Chatham Islands
Patagonia
CONTINENTAL SHELF
ARGENTINE PLAIN
RIO GRANDE RISE
Punta Arenas
Tierra del Fuego
Cape Horn
Falkland Islands
South Georgia
SOUTH SANDWICH TRENCH
ELTANIN FRACTURE ZONE
UDINTSEV FRACTURE ZONE
Longitude West of Greenwich
ANTARCTIC CIRCLE
AMUNDSEN PLAIN
AMUNDSEN RIDGES
ANTARCTIC PENINSULA
WEDDELL PLAIN
Alexander Island
Ellsworth Land
Marie Byrd Land
Vinson Massif 16067
Ronne Ice Shelf
Ross Ice Shelf
TRANSANTARCTIC MOUNTAINS
ANTA
NORTH ATLANTIC OCEAN
MID-ATLANTIC RIDGE
REYKJANES RIDGE
Iceland
Jan Mayen
Azores
Madeira Is.
Casablanca
Canary Islands
CAPE VERDE PLAIN
Cape Verde Islands
Dakar
SIERRA LEONE BASIN
ROMANCHE FRACTURE ZONE
PERNAMBUCO PLAIN
BRAZIL BASIN
SOUTH ATLANTIC OCEAN
150°
120°
90°
60°
30°
0°
30°N
30°S
60°

ARCTIC OCEAN

30° 60° 90° 120° 150°

Svalbard
CONTINENTAL SHELF
Barents Sea
Novya Zemlya
Kara Sea
North Land
Taymyr Peninsula
Laptev Sea
New Siberian Is.
East Siberian Sea

Scandinavia

Norilsk

SIBERIA

L. Onega
L. Ladoga
Moscow
Ural Mountains
Ob
West Siberian Plain
Yenisey
Central Siberian Plateau
Lena
Verkhoyansk Ra.

Kamchatka Peninsula
Sea of Okhotsk
Sakhalin
Central Ra.
Bering Sea
ALEUTIAN TRENCH

EUROPE

Baltic Sea
Northern European Plain
Volga
Danube
Aral Sea
L. Balkhash
Altay Mountains
Lake Baikal
Amur
Mongolian Plateau
GOBI
Beijing

NORTHWEST PACIFIC BASIN

Hokkaido
Sea of Japan
Honshu
Tokyo
NORTH

KURIL TRENCH

EMPEROR SEAMOUNTS

Rome
Black Sea
Istanbul
El'brus 18510
Caucasus Mts.
Tian Shan
Taklimakan Desert
Kunlun Mountains
Kyushu
East China Sea
Seoul

PACIFIC

OCEAN

ASIA

Mediterranean Sea
Sicily
Cyprus
Tigris
Zagros Mountains
Euphrates
Tehran
Plateau of Tibet
Mt. Everest 29028
Yellow
Yangtze
Taiwan
RYUKYU TRENCH

30°N

SAHARA
Cairo
Nile
Red Sea
ARABIAN PENINSULA
THE HIMALAYA
New Delhi
Ganges
Indus
Mekong

TROPIC OF CANCER

MID-PACIFIC MOUNTAINS

Haggar Mts.

SAHEL

AFRICA
Lake Chad
Ethiopian Highlands
OWEN FRACTURE ZONE
Arabian Sea
ARABIAN BASIN
Socotra
Western Ghats
INDIA
Bay of Bengal
Indochina Peninsula
Bangkok
South China Sea
Hainan
Philippine Sea
Luzon
Manila
Philippine Islands
Challenger Deep 35620
Guam
MARIANA TRENCH
PHILIPPINE TRENCH
KYUSHU-PALAU RIDGE

MICRONESIA

Marshall Is.

MELANESIA

Sri Lanka
CHAGOS-LACCADIVE PLATEAU
Maldive Is.
CEYLON PLAIN

Caroline Islands

EQUATOR

Kinshasa
Congo
Congo Basin
Lake Victoria
Lake Tanganyika
Nairobi
19340 Kilimanjaro
Seychelles
MID-INDIAN BASIN
Borneo
INDONESIA
Celebes
Greater Sunda Islands
Jakarta Java
New Guinea
Solomon Is.

Gilbert Is.
Tuvalu

0°

ANGOLA
Lake Malawi
Zambezi
Comoro Is.
Madagascar
MASCARENE PLATEAU
Sumatra
MOLUCCAS
JAVA TRENCH
Lesser Sunda Is.
Cape York
Coral Sea
Fiji Is.

Victoria Falls
Namib Desert
Kalahari Desert
Johannesburg
Orange
Reunion
Mauritius Is.
MID-INDIAN RIDGE
MADAGASCAR PLATEAU
NINETYEAST RIDGE
INVESTIGATOR RIDGE
WHARTON BASIN
Western AUSTRALIA Plateau
Lake Eyre
New Caledonia
GREAT DIVIDING RANGE
GREAT BARRIER REEF

TROPIC OF CAPRICORN

Cape of Good Hope
AGULHAS PLATEAU
AGULHAS RIDGE
NATAL PLAIN
INDIAN

OCEAN

PERTH BASIN
Perth
Sydney
Tasman Sea
North Island
NEW ZEALAND
Mt. Cook 12316
South Island

30°S

DAVIS RIDGE
Meridian of Greenwich (London)
ATLANTIC-INDIAN RIDGE
AGULHAS BASIN
SOUTHWEST INDIAN RIDGE
CROZET PLATEAU
Kerguélen Islands
KERGUELEN
Heard Island
PLATEAU
SOUTHEAST INDIAN RIDGE
Tasmania
MACQUARIE RIDGE

30° ENDERBY PLAIN 60°
90°
SOUTH INDIAN BASIN 120°
150°
60°

Longitude East of Greenwich

Elevations and depths in feet
Robinson Projection, Standard Parallels 38°N and 38°S
SCALE 1:98,675,000
1 INCH=1,557 MILES OR 1 CENTIMETER=986.7 KILOMETERS

0 mi   2000

0 km   2000

ANTARCTIC CIRCLE

Queen Maud Land
Victoria Land

ANTARCTICA

North America

Azimuthal Equidistant Projection

0 mi 600
0 km 600

MAP SYMBOLS

⊛ ★ ◉ Capitals
∴ Ruin
Below sea level
Dry salt lake
Glacier
Sand
Swamp

ARCTIC OCEAN

PACIFIC OCEAN

ATLANTIC OCEAN

BERING SEA

BEAUFORT SEA

LINCOLN SEA

GREENLAND SEA

BAFFIN Bay

LABRADOR SEA

HUDSON BAY

GULF OF ALASKA

Bristol Bay

GULF OF MEXICO

CARIBBEAN SEA

Gulf of California

Gulf of Tehuantepec

Gulf of Panama

ALEUTIAN ISLANDS

ALASKA

CANADA

UNITED STATES

MEXICO

GREENLAND (KALAALLIT NUNAAT) Denmark

YUKON TERRITORY

NORTHWEST TERRITORIES

NUNAVUT

BRITISH COLUMBIA

ALBERTA

SASK.

MANITOBA

ONTARIO

QUEBEC

NEWFOUNDLAND

LABRADOR

NOVA SCOTIA

Nord
Wandel Sea
Oodaaq I.
Peary Land
Daneborg
Ittoqqortoormiit
Alert
Eureka
Knud Rasmussen Land
Axel Heiberg I.
Ellesmere Island
SVERDRUP ISLANDS
Kangersuatsiaq
Qaanaaq
Qeqertarsuaq
Nuuk (Godthåb)
Qaqortoq
Nunap Isua (Kap Farvel)
Pangnirtung
Iqaluit
Kimmirut
Nain
Cartwright
St. Anthony
Island of Newfoundland
St. John's
Avalon Peninsula
Cape Breton Island
P.E.I.
Sydney
Halifax
Fredericton
Bangor
Concord, N.H.
Boston, MA.
Providence, R.I.
Hartford, CT.

Attu I.
Point Hope
Point Barrow
Point Barrow
Bering Strait
St. Lawrence I.
Seward Peninsula
Hooper Bay
Bethel
Togiak
Nunivak Island
Kaktovik
Sachs Harbour
Banks Island
Inuvik
Holman
Victoria Island
Boothia Peninsula
Melville Peninsula
Chesterfield Inlet
Baker Lake
Southampton Island
Arviat
Churchill
Gillam
Inukjuak
Belcher Islands
Chisasibi
Kuujjuarapik
Schefferville
Sept-Îles
Waskaganish
Baie-Comeau
Chicoutimi
Rouyn-Noranda
Fort Albany
Québec
Montréal
Ottawa ⊛
Toronto

North Magnetic Pole 2000
Mackenzie King I.
Prince Patrick I.
Borden Island
PARRY ISLANDS
Melville Island
Prince of Wales I.
Somerset I.
Brodeur Pen.
Borden Pen.
Arctic Bay
Clyde River
Devon I.

QUEEN ELIZABETH ISLANDS

Mt. McKinley (Denali) 6194 m 20320 ft
Fairbanks
Anchorage
Valdez
Sitka
Juneau
Skagway
Whitehorse
Mayo
Hay River
Yellowknife
Fort McMurray
Uranium City
Lupin

Umnak I.
Unalaska
Unimak I.
Alaska Peninsula
Kodiak I.
Glacier Bay
Alexander Archipelago
Queen Charlotte Islands
Kitimat
Prince George
Vancouver Island
Vancouver
Seattle
Portland
Eugene
Cape Mendocino

Great Bear L.
Mackenzie
Great Slave L.
Peace
Lake Winnipeg
Lake Superior
Lake Huron

Sacramento
San Francisco
San Jose
Fresno
Las Vegas
Los Angeles
San Diego
Tijuana
Tucson
Ciudad Juárez
Phoenix
El Paso
San Antonio
Austin
Houston
Dallas
Fort Worth
Oklahoma City
Tulsa
Wichita
Santa Fe
Denver
Salt Lake City
Reno
Boise
Idaho Falls
Butte
Spokane
Billings
Bismarck
Fargo
Minneapolis
St. Paul
Sioux Falls
Des Moines
Omaha
St. Louis
Louisville
Indianapolis
Chicago
Detroit
Columbus
Nashville
Memphis
Atlanta
Birmingham
Charlotte
Charleston, S.C.
Jacksonville
Tallahassee
Tampa
Miami
Key West
New Orleans
Jackson
New York
Philadelphia, PA.
Washington, D.C.
Richmond
Cheyenne

Edmonton
Red Deer
Calgary
Saskatoon
Regina
Medicine Hat
Winnipeg
Thunder Bay

Bermuda Islands U.K.

Sierra Nevada
Grand Canyon
Colorado
Great Salt L.
Rocky Mountains
Arkansas

WA. OR. CA. NV. ID. UT. AZ. N.M. CO. WY. MT. N.D. S.D. NE. KS. OK. TX. LA. AR. MO. IA. MN. WI. MI. IN. IL. KY. TN. MS. AL. GA. FL. S.C. N.C. VA. W.V. OH. PA. MD. DE. N.J. N.Y. VT. N.H. ME. MA. R.I. CT.

TROPIC OF CANCER

La Paz
Cabo San Lucas
Mazatlán
Guadalajara
Mexico ⊛
Acapulco
Monterrey
San Luis Potosí
Chihuahua
Veracruz
Mérida
Yucatan Pen.
Belize City
Belmopan
BELIZE
San Pedro Sula
Tegucigalpa
San Salvador
GUATEMALA
Guatemala ⊛
EL SALVADOR
HONDURAS
NICARAGUA
Managua
COSTA RICA
San José
PANAMA
Panama
PANAMA CANAL

I. Guadalupe Mexico
Punta Eugenia
Baja California
Sierra Madre Occidental
Sierra Madre Oriental
Islas Revillagigedo Mexico

Havana
CUBA
Santiago de Cuba
BAHAMAS
Nassau
HAITI
Port-au-Prince
DOMINICAN REPUBLIC
Santo Domingo
JAMAICA
Kingston
PUERTO RICO
San Juan
U.S.
U.K. Cayman Is.
Straits of Florida

Isla del Coco Costa Rica
I. de Coiba

EQUATOR

BARBADOS
DOMINICA
ANTIGUA AND BARBUDA
ST. KITTS & NEVIS
ST. LUCIA
ST. VINCENT AND THE GRENADINES
GRENADA
TRINIDAD AND TOBAGO
Port of Spain

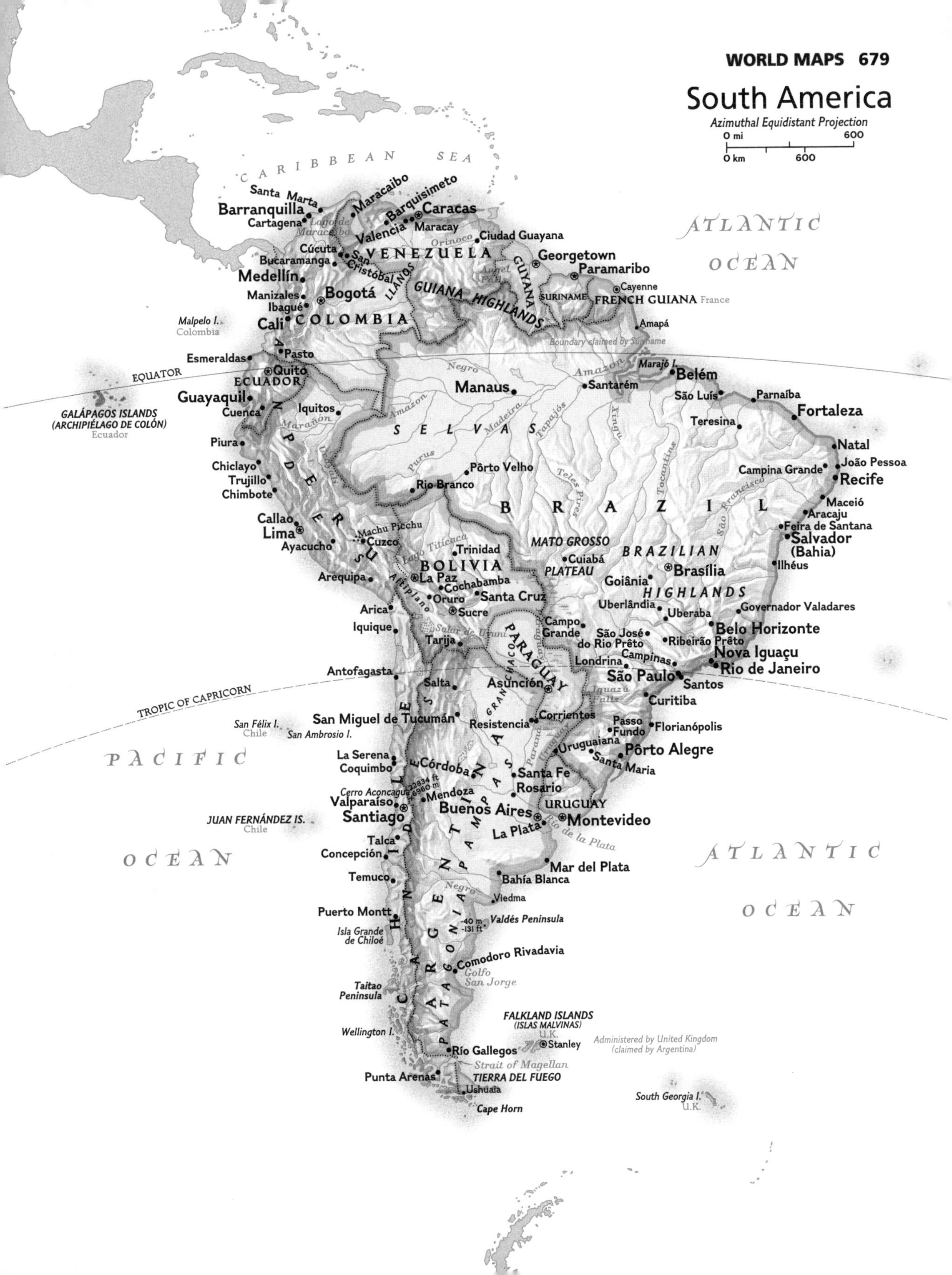

South America

Azimuthal Equidistant Projection

0 mi — 600
0 km — 600

CARIBBEAN SEA

ATLANTIC OCEAN

Santa Marta
Barranquilla
Cartagena
Maracaibo
Lago de Maracaibo
Valencia
Barquisimeto
Caracas
Maracay
Ciudad Guayana
Orinoco
Georgetown
Paramaribo
Cúcuta
Bucaramanga
San Cristóbal
VENEZUELA
LLANOS
GUIANA
SURINAME
Cayenne
FRENCH GUIANA France
Angel Falls
Medellín
Manizales
Ibagué
Bogotá
GUIANA HIGHLANDS
Cali
COLOMBIA
Malpelo I. Colombia
Pasto
Amapá
Boundary claimed by Suriname
Esmeraldas
Quito
ECUADOR
Negro
Amazon
Marajó I.
Belém
EQUATOR
Santarém
São Luís
Parnaíba
GALÁPAGOS ISLANDS
(ARCHIPIÉLAGO DE COLÓN)
Ecuador
Guayaquil
Cuenca
Iquitos
Marañón
Fortaleza
Piura
SELVAS
Teresina
Madeira
Tapajós
Xingu
Chiclayo
Trujillo
Chimbote
Pôrto Velho
Purus
Rio Branco
BRAZIL
Natal
João Pessoa
Campina Grande
Recife
Teles Pires
Tocantins
Callao
Lima
Ayacucho
Cuzco
Machu Picchu
MATO GROSSO
Cuiabá
PLATEAU
BRAZILIAN
São Francisco
Maceió
Aracaju
Feira de Santana
Salvador
(Bahia)
Ilhéus
Lago Titicaca
Trinidad
BOLIVIA
La Paz
Cochabamba
Oruro
Santa Cruz
Sucre
Goiânia
Brasília
HIGHLANDS
Uberlândia
Uberaba
Governador Valadares
Arequipa
Arica
Iquique
Altiplano
Salar de Uyuni
Tarija
Campo Grande
São José do Rio Prêto
Belo Horizonte
Ribeirão Prêto
Nova Iguaçu
Rio de Janeiro
Campinas
Londrina
São Paulo
Santos
Antofagasta
Salta
Asunción
PARAGUAY
Corrientes
Iguaçu Falls
Curitiba
TROPIC OF CAPRICORN
San Félix I. Chile
San Ambrosio I. Chile
San Miguel de Tucumán
Resistencia
Passo Fundo
Florianópolis
La Serena
Coquimbo
Córdoba
Uruguaiana
Santa Maria
Pôrto Alegre
Cerro Aconcagua 22,834 ft 6960 m
Mendoza
Santa Fe
Rosario
URUGUAY
PACIFIC
Valparaíso
Santiago
Buenos Aires
La Plata
Montevideo
Rio de la Plata
JUAN FERNÁNDEZ IS. Chile
Talca
Concepción
Mar del Plata
OCEAN
Temuco
Bahía Blanca
Viedma
ATLANTIC
Puerto Montt
ARGENTINA
PAMPAS
Negro
-40 m -131 ft
Valdés Peninsula
OCEAN
Isla Grande de Chiloé
PATAGONIA
Comodoro Rivadavia
Golfo San Jorge
Taitao Peninsula
ANDES
FALKLAND ISLANDS
(ISLAS MALVINAS)
U.K.
Stanley
Administered by United Kingdom
(claimed by Argentina)
Wellington I.
Río Gallegos
Strait of Magellan
Punta Arenas
TIERRA DEL FUEGO
Ushuaia
South Georgia I.
U.K.
Cape Horn

Europe

Azimuthal Equidistant Projection

0 mi   600
0 km   600

ARCTIC OCEAN

Zemlya Alexandra
Zemlya George
FRANZ JOSEF LAND
Russia

Ny Ålesund
Spitsbergen
Longyearbyen   Edgeøya
SVALBARD
Norway

Bear Island

Noril'sk

Yenisey

Gyda
Peninsula

Novyy Port

KARA
SEA

Yamal
Peninsula

NOVAYA ZEMLYA

Ob'

Jan Mayen
Norway

BARENTS
SEA

Amderma

Vorkuta

Tobseda

Surgut

Denmark Strait

Ísafjörður
Akureyri
Reykjavík ICELAND Vopnafjörður
Höfn

ARCTIC CIRCLE

North Cape
Hammerfest
Tromsø
Narvik

Vadsø Kirkenes
Pechenga
Ivalo Kirovsk
Murmansk
Kola
Peninsula

Pechora

Khanty
Mansiysk

EUROPE-ASIA
BOUNDARY

FAROE ISLANDS
Denmark Tórshavn

Namsos
Trondheim

Kiruna
FINLAND
Kemi
Luleå
Umeå
Åre

Umba

Kem'

White Sea

Lake Onega

Arkhangel'sk
Severodvinsk

Syktyvkar

RUSSIA

Serov
Nizhniy
Tagil
Perm'
Yekaterinburg
Chelyabinsk

URAL MOUNTAINS

SHETLAND
ISLANDS
Lerwick

Rockall
U.K.

Ålesund
Bergen
Stavanger

NORWAY

Sundsvall
SWEDEN
Vaasa
Pori
Turku
Tampere

Kuopio

Lake
Ladoga

Helsinki
Uppsala
Oslo
Stockholm

St. Petersburg

Velikiy
Novgorod

Yaroslavl'

Kirov

Kazan'

Ufa

ORKNEY ISLANDS
Isle of Lewis
Inverness
Aberdeen
UNITED
Glasgow SCOTLAND
Edinburgh
NORTHERN
IRELAND Belfast
IRELAND
Dublin
Cork
Liverpool Manchester
Birmingham
WALES
Cardiff ENGLAND
London
Southampton

Gulf of Bothnia

Tallinn
ESTONIA
LATVIA
Riga

Gotland

DENMARK Århus
Göteborg
Malmö
Copenhagen
Kiel

Daugavpils
Vitsyebsk
LITHUANIA
Vilnius
Kaunas

Moscow

Tver'

Nizhniy Novgorod

Samara

Orenburg

Saratov

Ryazan'
Smolensk
Penza

Oral

KAZAKHSTAN

Volga

Atyraü

Celtic
Sea

Irish
Sea

Land's End

North
Sea

Skagerrak

Baltic
Sea

RUSSIA

Minsk

BELARUS

Homyel'

Bryansk

Kursk

Volgograd

Astrakhan'

Le Havre
Brest
Nantes
La Rochelle

Rennes

Brussels
BELGIUM
Paris
Strasbourg

NETH.
Amsterdam
The
Hague
Bonn
Frankfurt
GERMANY

Hamburg
Berlin

Gdańsk
Bydgoszcz

POLAND
Łódź
Wrocław

Warsaw
Kraków

Chernihiv
Kiev
L'viv

Sumy

Kharkiv

Poltava

Donets'k

Rostov

ENGLISH CHANNEL

English Channel

Bordeaux

FRANCE

Limoges
Lyon
Geneva

Zürich
Bern
SWITZ.
LIECH.

Munich
Linz
AUSTRIA
Graz
Vienna
Prague
CZECH REP.
SLOVAKIA
Bratislava

Budapest

HUNGARY

Vinnytsya
UKRAINE

Dnipropetrovs'k

Dniester

Sea of Azov

Stavropol'

Groznyy

CASPIAN
SEA

Bay of
Biscay

A Coruña
Vigo
Oporto
Santander
Bilbao
San
Sebastián
Donostia-
San Sebastián

Santiago
Valladolid

Toulouse
Turin

Nice
Genoa
MONACO
ITALY

SLOVENIA
Ljubljana
Zagreb
CROATIA

BOSN.
HERZG.
Sarajevo

Belgrade
YUG.

ROMANIA
Bucharest

Chişinău
MOLDOVA

Odesa
Crimea
Kerch
Simferopol'
Sevastopol'
Yalta

El'brus
5642 m
18510 ft

Caucasus Mountains

GEORGIA

T'bilisi

AZERBAIJAN
Gäncä

Baku

Coimbra
Madrid

PORTUGAL

Lisbon
Cape
St. Vincent

SPAIN

Córdoba
Sevilla
Cádiz
Málaga

Zaragoza
Barcelona

Valencia
Murcia
Cartagena

ANDORRA

Marseille
Pyrenees

Milan
Venice
SAN
MARINO

Corsica
France

Sardinia
Italy

Cagliari

VATICAN
CITY
Rome

Naples

ADRIATIC SEA

Danube

Balkan Mts.

Sofia
BULGARIA

Tirana
ALBANIA
MACED.
Skopje

Constanța

Varna

BLACK SEA

Bat'umi

Trabzon

Erzurum

Samsun
Zonguldak

Istanbul
Bursa

Ankara

Sivas

Bitlis

Mardin

Balearic
Islands Sp.

Palma

Strait of Gibraltar

U.K. GIBRALTAR

MEDITERRANEAN SEA

Tyrrhenian
Sea

Palermo
Sicily
Catania

Messina

Ionian
Sea

MALTA

Pátrai
GREECE
Kalámai
Peloponnesus
Athens

Tirana

Thessaloníki

Aegean
Sea

İzmir

Antalya
Taurus Mts.

Konya
TURKEY
Eskişehir

Kayseri
Adana
Antioch

Crete
Dardanelles
Sea of
Crete

Irákleion

Rhodes

TROPIC OF CANCER

A commonly accepted division between Asia and
Europe--here marked by an orange line--is formed
by the Ural Mountains, Ural River, Caspian Sea,
Caucasus Mountains, and the Black Sea with its
outlets, the Bosporus and Dardanelles.

ATLANTIC
OCEAN

NORWEGIAN SEA

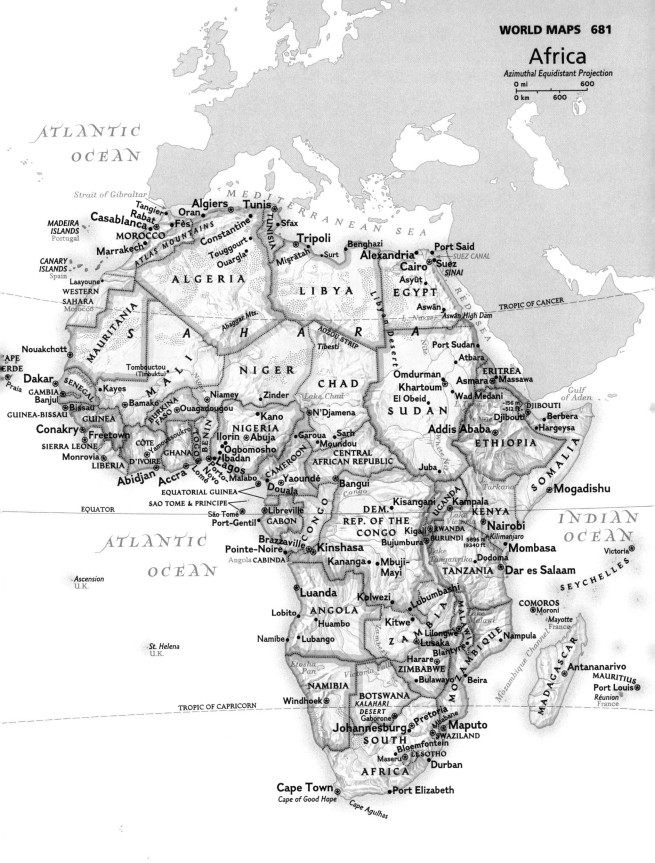

Africa

Azimuthal Equidistant Projection

0 mi   600
0 km   600

ATLANTIC
OCEAN

MADEIRA
ISLANDS
Portugal

CANARY
ISLANDS
Spain

CAPE
VERDE
⊛ Praia

MEDITERRANEAN SEA

Strait of Gibraltar

Tangier
Rabat
Casablanca ⊛
Fès ⊛
Oran ⊛
Algiers ⊛
Tunis ⊛
TUNISIA
Sfax ⊛

MOROCCO
Marrakech
Constantine
Touggourt
Ouargla

Tripoli
Benghazi
Miṣrātah
Surt

Port Said
Alexandria
Cairo ⊛
Asyût
Suez
SINAI
SUEZ CANAL

Laayoune
WESTERN
SAHARA
Morocco

ALGERIA

LIBYA

EGYPT

Aswân
Aswân High Dam
L. Nasser

TROPIC OF CANCER

ATLAS MOUNTAINS

Ahaggar Mts.

AOZOU STRIP

Tibesti

Libyan Desert

RED SEA

Nouakchott ⊛

MAURITANIA

S A H A R A

Tombouctou
(Timbuktu)

NIGER

CHAD

Lake Chad

Port Sudan
Atbara

Dakar ⊛
Kayes
GAMBIA
Banjul
GUINEA-BISSAU
Bissau ⊛
Conakry ⊛
Freetown ⊛
SIERRA LEONE
Monrovia ⊛
LIBERIA
Abidjan

SENEGAL
Bamako ⊛
GUINEA
CÔTE
D'IVOIRE
GHANA
Yamoussoukro
Accra

M A L I

BURKINA
FASO
Ouagadougou
Niamey
Zinder
Kano
N'Djamena

NIGERIA
Ilorin
Abuja
Ogbomosho
Ibadan
Lagos
Porto-
Novo
Lomé

BENIN

Garoua
Sarh
Moundou
CENTRAL
AFRICAN REPUBLIC

Omdurman
Khartoum ⊛
El Obeid

SUDAN

ERITREA
Asmara ⊛ Massawa
Wad Medani
-156 m/
-512 ft.
DJIBOUTI
Djibouti ⊛ Berbera
Hargeysa

Addis Ababa ⊛

ETHIOPIA

White Nile

Blue Nile

Gulf
of Aden

Malabo
EQUATORIAL GUINEA
SAO TOME & PRINCIPE
São Tomé
Port-Gentil

Yaoundé
Douala
CAMEROON

Bangui

Juba

SOMALIA
⊛ Mogadishu

EQUATOR

Libreville
GABON

CONGO

DEM.
REP. OF THE
CONGO

Kisangani
UGANDA
Kampala ⊛
Kigali
RWANDA
BURUNDI
Bujumbura

Lake
Victoria

KENYA
Nairobi ⊛

Turkana

INDIAN
OCEAN

ATLANTIC

OCEAN

Ascension
U.K.

Brazzaville
Pointe-Noire
Angola CABINDA

Kinshasa ⊛
Kananga
Mbuji-
Mayi

Kolwezi

Kigali
5895 m/
19340 ft
Kilimanjaro
Dodoma ⊛
TANZANIA

Mombasa
Dar es Salaam

SEYCHELLES
Victoria ⊛

St. Helena
U.K.

Luanda ⊛
Lobito
Namibe

ANGOLA
Huambo
Lubango

Lubumbashi
Kitwe

ZAMBIA
Lusaka ⊛

Lake
Tanganyika

Lake
Malawi

COMOROS
⊛ Moroni
Mayotte
France

Namibe

Zambezi

Victoria Falls

Etosha
Pan

Windhoek ⊛

NAMIBIA

KALAHARI
DESERT

BOTSWANA

Gaborone ⊛

Lilongwe ⊛
MALAWI
Blantyre
Harare ⊛
ZIMBABWE
Bulawayo

Nampula

MOZAMBIQUE

Beira

Mozambique Channel

MADAGASCAR

Antananarivo ⊛
MAURITIUS
Port Louis ⊛
Réunion
France

TROPIC OF CAPRICORN

Johannesburg ⊛ Pretoria ⊛
Mbabane
Maputo
SWAZILAND
SOUTH
Bloemfontein
Maseru LESOTHO Durban

AFRICA

Cape Town ⊛
Cape of Good Hope
Cape Agulhas

Port Elizabeth

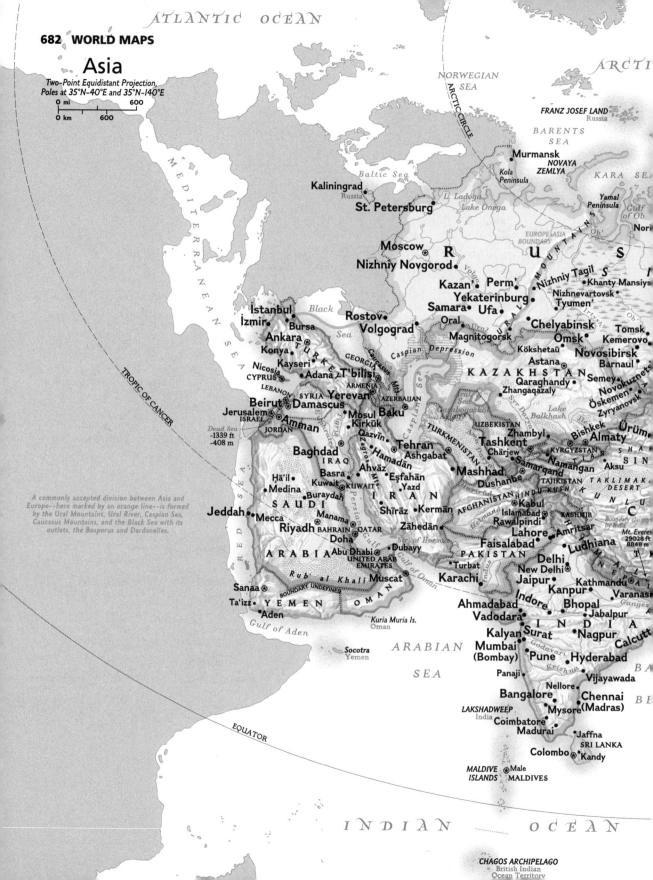

Asia

Two-Point Equidistant Projection,
Poles at 35°N-40°E and 35°N-140°E

Australia

Azimuthal Equidistant Projection

0 mi ——————— 600
0 km ——————— 600

PACIFIC OCEAN

MELANESIA

EQUATOR

Admiralty Islands

Manus

Mussau Is.

New Hanover

Kavieng

NEW GUINEA

Vanimo

Wewak

BISMARCK ARCHIPELAGO

New Ireland

Green Is.

Bismarck Sea

Madang

4509 m
14793 ft + Mt. Wilhelm

Rabaul

Hoskins

New Britain

Sohano

Kieta

PAPUA NEW GUINEA

Lae

Huon Gulf

Bougainville

Solomon

Daru

Popondetta

Port Moresby ⊚

Abau

Trobriand Islands

D'Entrecasteaux Islands

SOLOMON ISLANDS

Sea

Samarai

ARAFURA SEA

Torres Str.

Cape York

Weipa

Louisiade Archipelago

TIMOR SEA

Melville I.

Cobourg Pen.

Wessel Is.

C. Arnhem

Gulf of

Darwin ⊚

ARNHEM LAND

Groote Eylandt

Coen

CORAL

Joseph Bonaparte Gulf

Cape Talbot

Pine Creek

Carpentaria

Cooktown

Admiralty Gulf

Wyndham

Daly Waters

Borroloola

Karumba

Cairns

CORAL SEA ISLANDS TERRITORY
Australia

Collier Bay

King Sound

Newcastle Waters

Burketown

Normanton

Innisfail

Cape Leveque

Dampier Land

Derby

Fitzroy Crossing

Halls Creek

Croydon

Forsayth

Townsville

SEA

Broome

Tennant Creek

Camooweal

Cloncurry

Ayr

Charters Towers

Lagrange

NORTHERN

Mount Isa

Hughenden

Proserpine • Mackay

Great Sandy Desert

TERRITORY

Barrow Creek

Boulia

QUEENSLAND

Monte Bello Islands

Port Hedland

Barrow Island

Dampier

Marble Bar

Macdonnell Ranges

Winton

Aramac

Emerald

Rockhampton

North West Cape

Onslow

Alice Springs

Barcaldine

Mount Morgan

Gladstone

Exmouth

Blackall
Windorah

Bundaberg

Fraser Island

TROPIC OF CAPRICORN

WESTERN

Gibson Desert

Charleville

Maryborough

Kingaroy

Toowoomba

Shark Bay

Carnarvon

AUSTRALIA

Eromanga

Roma

Brisbane

Cape Inscription

Meekatharra

Wiluna

SOUTH

Cunnamulla

Goondiwindi

Gold Coast

Mount Magnet

Great Victoria Desert

AUSTRALIA

Lake Eyre
-16 m
-52 ft

Lismore

Geraldton

Mullewa

Laverton

Oodnadatta

Moree

Grafton

Dongara

Menzies

Marree

Armidale

Kalgoorlie

Nullarbor Plain

Haig

Ooldea

Woomera

Bourke

Coonamble

Tamworth

Southern Cross

Norseman

Eucla Motel

Penong

Ceduna

Port Augusta

Broken Hill

Dubbo

Muswellbrook

Perth ⊚

Northam

Geographe Bay

Narrogin

Ravensthorpe

Cape Pasley

Whyalla

Port Pirie

Wallaroo

Mildura

NEW SOUTH

Orange

Lord Howe I.

Newcastle

New South Wales

Bunbury

Esperance

Port Lincoln

WALES

Sydney

Ball's Pyramid

Cape Naturaliste

Augusta

Hopetoun

Murray

Wagga Wagga

Goulburn

Wollongong

Cape Leeuwin

Albany

Adelaide ⊚

Kangaroo I.

Bendigo

2228 m
7310 ft

Canberra, AUSTRALIAN CAPITAL TERRITORY

Cooma

West Cape Howe

Great Australian Bight

Ballarat VICTORIA Mt. Kosciuszko

Mount Gambier

Geelong

Melbourne ⊚

Warrnambool

Moe

TASMAN SEA

Port Phillip Bay

Bass Strait

Furneaux Group

King Island

Burnie Devonport

Launceston

St. Marys

Queenstown

Geeveston

TASMANIA

Hobart

South East Cape

NEW ZEALAND

INDIAN OCEAN

NEW ZEALAND

Three Kings Islands

North Cape

Kaitaia

Whangarei

Dargaville

Great Barrier Island

Hauraki Gulf

Auckland

Tauranga

NORTH ISLAND

Hamilton

Bay of Plenty

New Plymouth

East Cape

Gisborne

Wanganui

Napier

TASMAN SEA

Palmerston North

Hastings

Cape Farewell

PACIFIC OCEAN

Nelson

Wellington

Greymouth

Cook Strait

Hokitika

Kaikoura

Mt. Cook
3754 m
12316 ft

Christchurch

Ashburton

Chatham Is.

Chatham Island
N.Z.

SOUTH ISLAND

Timaru

Queenstown

Oamaru

Pitt Island

Gore

Dunedin

Puysegur Point

Invercargill

Stewart Island

Bounty Islands
N.Z.

The Snares

AUCKLAND ISLANDS
N.Z.

Macquarie I.
Tasmania

Campbell I.
N.Z.

Antarctica

Azimuthal Equidistant Projection

0 mi — 600
0 km — 600

ATLANTIC OCEAN

South Sandwich Is. U.K.

SCOTIA SEA

South Orkney Is.

South Shetland Islands

Joinville I.

ANTARCTIC CIRCLE

FIMBUL ICE SHELF

Cape Norvegia

RIISER-LARSEN ICE SHELF

Riiser-Larsen Peninsula

Lützow-Holm Bay

INDIAN OCEAN

QUEEN MAUD LAND

ENDERBY LAND

WEDDELL SEA

COATS LAND

LARSEN ICE SHELF

ANTARCTIC PENINSULA

4190m Mt. Jackson

Alexander I.

RONNE ICE SHELF

Berkner Island

PENSACOLA MTS.

Cape Darnley

AMERY ICE SHELF

Prydz Bay

AMERICAN HIGHLAND

BELLINGSHAUSEN SEA

ELLSWORTH LAND

TRANSANTARCTIC MOUNTAINS

POLAR PLATEAU

+ South Pole

EAST ANTARCTICA

WEST ICE SHELF

4897m Vinson Massif 16067ft

ELLSWORTH MTS.

WEST ANTARCTICA

SHACKLETON ICE SHELF

Thurston I.

MARIE BYRD LAND

AMUNDSEN SEA

+4528m

ROSS ICE SHELF

Roosevelt I.

WILKES LAND

Cape Poinsett

GETZ ICE SHELF

Ross I. Mt. Erebus 3794m

McMurdo Sound

ROSS SEA

VICTORIA LAND

Porpoise Bay

INDIAN OCEAN

4165m Mt. Minto

Cape Adare

* 2000 South Magnetic Pole

PACIFIC OCEAN

Balleny Islands

ANTARCTIC CIRCLE

GLOSSARY

A

adiabatic process the changing of sensible air temperature without the gain or loss of heat to or from surrounding air

albedo percentage of electromagnetic radiation reflected from a surface

alluvial fan feature found in deserts, the result of stream deposits accumulating where stream channels emerge from the base of mountains and channel gradients level out

angle of repose natural surface inclination of a slope consisting of loose, well-sorted rock or mineral fragments

anticline upfold of layered rocks in an archlike structure

anticyclone center of high atmospheric pressure; it spins in the opposite direction from a cyclone

antipode point that lies diametrically opposite a given point on the surface of the Earth

aphelion point on the Earth's elliptical orbit at which the sun is farthest from the Earth

aquifer rock mass or layer with high porosity and high permeability; stores and transmits ground water

Artesian spring groundwater that flows to the surface as a result of hydrostatic pressure that forces water upward

asthenosphere soft layer of the upper mantle of the Earth, beneath the lithosphere

atmosphere thin layer of gasses surrounding the Earth that is the medium for weather and climate

atoll circular coral reef enclosing a shallow lagoon

avalanche general term for extremely rapid slides and falls of snow, ice, rocks, and trees

B

bajada graded slope that is an alluvial fan, extending from mountain base to playa

barrier island landform created by long linear wave deposits that form parallel to shorelines

barrier reef coral reef separated from shoreline by a lagoon

biodiversity number of species present in an ecosystem

biogeography study of the distribution patterns of plants and animals and the processes that produce those patterns

biomass dry weight of living organic matter in a particular ecosystem; units are grams of organic matter per square meter

biotic communities local communities of interdependent plants and animals that are often found together

birth rate number of live births per 1,000 population in a given year

braided stream small waterway with shallow channels that carry multiple flows

breakwaters piles of rock built parallel to the shore to prevent damage to watercraft or construction

C

caldera steep-sided circular depression that results from the explosion and subsidence of a large composite volcano

calving breaking off of blocks of glacial ice into the ocean, forming icebergs

capitalism form of economic organization characterized by resource allocation primarily through markets. The means of production are privately owned, and production is organized around profit maximization.

carbon cycle material cycle in which carbon flows through an ecosystem

cartogram simplified map designed to present a single idea in a diagrammatic way, usually not to scale

cash crops crops grown for sale on the market, that is, for profit

catacract waterfall that forms a single long drop

cation positively charged ion

central business district (CBD) central nucleus of commercial land uses in a city.

central place theory interpretation of city systems set forth by German geographer Walter Christaller in 1933 that centers on consumer demand, including the maximum distance consumers will travel for a given good and the minimum market size necessary to sustain them

centrality functional domininace of cities, in terms of econmoic, political, and cultural activity, witin an urban system.

chinook very dry wind that occurs when air that is blown up the windward side of the Rocky Mountains descends

cirque bowl shaped basin that holds the collecting ground and firn of an Alpine glacier

City Beautiful movement early 20th century attempt to renovate cities to reflect the higher values of society, using neoclassical architecture, grandiose street plans, parks, and inspirational monuments and statues

colloids extremely small mineral particles that can remain in suspension in water indefinitely

colonialism economic and political system by which some nations dominate others

comparative advantage principle that some regions can produce some goods and services more efficiently or profitable than others

condensation change of water from vapor to a liquid or a solid.

congregation territorial and residential clustering of specific groups or subgroups of people in city neighborhoods

continental drift theory that today's continents were formed by the breakup of prehistoric supercontinents and slowly drifted to their present positions

continental shelf offshore extensions of continents.

continental suture mountain range formed by the convergence of continental plates—for example, the Appalachians, the Alps, and the Himalayas.

core area nation's or culture's historic homeland

Coriolis effect result of the Earth's rotation that causes any freely moving object or fluid to turn toward the right in the northern hemisphere and to the left in the southern hemisphere

creole any pidgin language used widely enough to become a population's primary tongue

cultural divergence theory that explains the formation of early cultures as the result of groups dividing, migrating, and slowly changing in response to new ideas and environmental stress

cultural realm region where a group's culture prevails

cultural revivalism rediscovery of a former cultural identity in which members of a culture that has been overwhelmed by a dominant culture seek to regain their former culture

culture way of life of a group that is transmitted between generations and includes a shared system of meanings, beliefs, values, and social relations; it includes such things as language, religion, clothing, music, laws, and entertainment.

culture hearth specific place where a distinctive culture originated

cumulative causation spiral buildup of mutually reinforcing advantages that occurs in specific geographic settings as a result of the development of external economies and localization economies

cyberspace world of electronic computerized spaces encompassed by the Internet and related technologies such as the World Wide Web

D

deindustrialization loss of comparative advantage in manufacturing, brought about by technological displacement and the rise of foreign competitors

delta flat, low-lying area formed by sediment deposited by a stream entering a body of standing water

demographic equation calculation of population change expressed as change equals births minus deaths plus net migration

demographic transition historical shift of birth and death rates from high to low levels in a population; the decline of mortality usually precedes the decline in fertility, thus resulting in rapid population growth during the transition period.

deposition laying down of sediment

desert region that has little or no vegetation and averages less that 10 inches of precipitation a year

desertification invasion of desert into nondesert regions.

devolution violent or nonviolent process in which power from a state government is returned to a political region or homeland, in forms ranging from limited authority (e.g., over local issues) to statehood

dialects regional variations of one language with differences in vocabulary, accent, pronunciation, and syntax

diminishing returns principle first set forth by Thomas Malthus: increased investments in production capacity yield steadily smaller marginal increases in output.

drumlin low, linear hill shaped by glaciers whose long axes parallel the direction of the glacier's movement

dualism juxtaposition in geographic space of the formal and informal sectors of the economy

E

earthquake intensity scale series of numbers indicating the intensity of earth shaking felt at a location during an earthquake; see Modified Mercalli scale

earthquake magnitude stress releases by a single earthquake at its focus; see Richter scale

ecosystem group of organisms and the environment with which they interact

ecotome transition zone between ecosystems

edge cities nodal concentrations of retail and office space that are situated on the outer fringes of metropolitan areas, typically near major highway intersections

El Niño periodic reversal of current flow and water temperatures in the mid-Pacific Ocean

elasticities of demand measure of the degree to which the aggregate demand for a commodity rises or falls with changes in income and price

endangered species species in immediate risk of extinction

energy ability to move solids, liquids, and gases

environment sum of the conditions that surround and influence an organism

environmental degradation damage to the environment resulting from human development and use of natural resources; human involvement that changes the environment or interferes with biological and environmental processes

environmental determinism often misapplied belief that the environment causes human events and activities

epicenter ground surface point directly above the earthquake focus, the point in the earth where the energy of the earthquake is first released

equinox an astronomical event occuring twice a year, when the subsolar point falls on the Earth's Equator and the circle of the sun's illumination passes through both poles. The vernal equinox occurs on March 20 or 21; the autumnal equinox occurs on September 22 or 23.

erosion general term for the removal of sediment by the force of water, air, or ice, or by the impact of solid particles carried by a fluid

erratic boulder large rock carried by glacial ice to a distant site

escarpment cliff or steep rock face that separates two comparatively level land surfaces

esker long ridge formed by the stress of water that flowed underneath a glacier

estuary broadened seaward end or extension of a river

ethnicity minority group with a collective self-identity within a larger host population

eutrophication process that occurs when large amounts of nutrients from fertilizers or animal wastes enter a water body and bacteria break down the nutrients. The bacterial action depletes the water of dissolved oxygen.

exponential growth constant rate of growth continuously applied to a growing base over a period of time

export base industry or group of firms that export most of their output from a region, capitalizing on its comparative advantage and earning nonlocal revenues

external economies cost savings and other benefits that result from circumstances beyond a firm's own organization and methods of production—in particular, savings and benefits that accrue to producers in geographic settings that encompass the specialized business services that they need

F

fault offset fractures or breaks in rock where the sides of the break are displaced in any direction relative to each other

federal state governmental organization in which political power is shared and derived from both the national government and a number of subnational governments

fertility actual reproductive performance of an individual, a couple, or a population.

fertility rate number of live births per 1,000 women ages 15–44 in a given year

fjord narrow, deep ocean valley that reaches far inland and partially fills a glacial trough

firn old snow that has become granular and forms a surface layer in a glacier

First World theoretical grouping that includes the economically developed nations of Europe, Japan, North America, and Australia and New Zealand, in contrast to the developing or underdeveloped Third World; also called the global North

flood basalts huge lava flows that produce thick accumulations of basalt layers over a large area

folds rock layers lifted up or pushed down relative to the surrounding area

food chain organization of an ecosystem through which energy flows as organisms at each level consume energy stored in the bodies of organisms of the next lower level

Fordism form of economic organization put in place by Henry Ford, characterized by the vertically integrated production of homogeneous goods, mass markets, and large economies of scale

foreign direct investment (FDI) tangible investments in productive capacity made by firms from one nation in another.

fossil fuels remains of ancient plants and animals trapped in sediment that are used for fuel in the form of coal, petroleum, and natural gas

front low-pressure boundary between two unlike high-pressure air masses

G

gateway city urban area that serves as a link between one country or region and others because of its physical situation.

geodesist mathematician who studies Earth measurements

geographic information system (GIS) computer system used to store, revise, analyze, manipulate, model, and display geographic data.

geomancy mystical interpretation of the disposition and alignment of prominent landscape features and sacred sites

geomorphology study of the Earth's surface features

gerrymandering redistricting of the boundaries of an electoral district to provide an unfair advantage to one political faction over others; named for a salamander-shaped district formed to favor Elbridge Gerry, a 19th-century Massachusetts politician

glacier large natural accumulation of ice on land that moves

global positioning system (GPS) space-based system of 24 satellites that provide three-dimensional positional, velocity, and time information to suitably equipped users anywhere at or near the Earth's surface

global village view of the world as a community in which distance and differences have been reduced by electronic media

great circle largest circle that can be drawn around a sphere such as a globe; a great circle route is the shortest route between two points

green revolution sustained effort to introduce high-yield, high-protein crops in Mexico, India, the Philippines, Indonesia, Bangladesh, and elsewhere in the 1960s

greenhouse effect property of the atmosphere that allows the short-wave radiation of sunlight to pass easily to the Earth's surface but makes it difficult for heat in the form of long-range radiation to escape back toward space

greenhouse gases group of gases including water vapor, carbon dioxide, ozone, nitrous oxide, and methane

groin a pile of rocks extending out from a beach.

gross national product (GNP) sum total of the value of goods and services produced by a nation-state in one year

growth rate rate at which a population is increasing or decreasing in a given year due to natural increase and net migration, expressed as a percentage of the base population

Gutenberg discontinuity the boundary of contact between the Earth's mantle and outer core where there are changes in the speed of seismic waves

gyre continuous, nearly circular flows of surface water centered on an oceanic subtropical high-pressure cell

H

habitat natural environment of a plant or animal having a certain combination of controlling physical factors

heartland theory assertion by Halford Mackinder (1861–1947) that the relative location and environmental challenges of Russia made it a nearly unconquerable area

hinterlands broadly, the area of influence surrounding a city.

hot spot intensely hot region deep within the Earth

hot springs thermal springs that discharge heated ground water at temperatures of more than 98.6 degrees Fahrenheit (average human body temperature)

humidity general term for the amount of water vapor present in the atmosphere

humus dark organic matter on or in the soil that is made up of decomposed vegetation

hunting and gathering mode of production that sustained human beings for more than 95 percent of their existence on Earth, characteristically organized around a division of labor (men hunt, women gather)

hurricane rotating tropical storm with winds of at least 74 mph (119km/h); called a typhoon when it forms in the Western Pacific Ocean, and called a cyclone when it forms over the Bay of Bengal and the northern Indian Ocean.

hydrosphere all of the Earth's water, including the oceans, surface water, ground water, and water held in the atmosphere

I

imperialism policy of dominating colonies or other states and maintaining those relationships to increase state power

inexhaustible resources natural resources such as solar and tidal energy that are generated continuously and production is not reduced through mismanagement

informal sector economic activities that take place beyond official record, not subject to formalized systems of regulation or remuneration

infrastructure transportation and communications networks that allow goods, people, and information to flow across space.

insolation sun's radiation emitted toward Earth

Intertropical convergence zone (ITCZ) low-pressure zone created by intense solar radiation and heating

invasion and succession process of neighborhood change, through residential mobility, whereby one social or ethnic group succeeds another in terms of numerical dominance

isobar line on a map connecting all points of equal atmospheric pressure

isotherm line on a map connecting all points of equal air temperature

J–K

jet stream high-speed winds flowing in narrow zones within the upper air westerlies

karst area of land underlain by limestone formations such as sinkholes, underground streams, and caves

Kondratieff waves long-term economic periodicities (50 to 75 years) in capitalist production, including changes in innovations, output, prices, and employment, linked to the emergence of critical new industries

L

La Niña meteoroligical event that occurs when the equatorial waters in the Pacific Ocean become colder than normal

labor theory of value classic theorization of how value is created; it holds that all value is ultimately produced only through human labor

lagoon shallow, narrow body of water lying between a barrier island and the mainland

lahar volcanic mudflow

land reclamation process in which mined land is recontoured, resoiled, and revegetated, thus alleviating much of the degradation caused by mining

language divergence evolution of different languages over the last 100,000 years as members of cultural groups separated

language families groups of languages that diverged from a single ancestral language, for example, the Indo-European family

lingua franca established language used by a population as a common language

lithification process of formation of sedimentary rock

lithosphere general term for the entire solid Earth; in plate tectonics, the rigid outer layer of Earth shell, above the asthenosphere

loam soil texture class in which the three size grades—sand, silt, and clay—are relatively equally mixed

localization economies cost savings that accrue to particular industries as a result of clustering together at a specific location

loess dust composed mostly of silt and clay

longshore current current in the breaker zone running parallel with the shoreline that transports and deposits sand to beaches and spits

M

mafic rocks igneous rocks rich in magnesium and iron.

magma molten, mobile rock that lies beneath the Earth's surface

map projection system of transferring information about a round object such as a globe to a flat piece of paper or other surface

maquilladores branch plants of foreign (mostly U.S. or Japanese) corporations located in northern Mexico, typically automobile or electronics assembly functions employing young women

mass wasting downward movement of rock, soil, and sediment in response to gravity

meanders winding bends of a river that form when it flows around a curve

merchant capitalism form of economic organization in which capital accumulation is based on trade in primary products (agricultural, fish, and forest products, minerals) and handicrafts

mesa broad, flat-topped landform surrounded by cliffs; they become buttes as they grow smaller

meteorology science of the atmosphere

microclimate climate of a shallow layer of air near the ground

migration movement of people across a specified boundary for the purpose of establishing a new residence

mineral inorganic solid that has a characteristic chemical composition and specific crystal structure that affect its physical characteristics

modern movement intellectual movement with origins in the early 20th century that incorporated the idea that buildings and cities should be designed and run like machines

Modified Mercalli scale earthquake intensity scale that uses 12 intensity levels relating to the phenomena observed during an earthquake

Moho (Mohorovii discontinuity) division between the Earth's crust and its mantle

monsoon seasonal change in the direction of the prevailing wind

moraine till deposits left behind by a glacier

mortality deaths as a component of population change

multinational corporations (MNCs) large firms with operations in more than one nation-state; also called transnational corporations

multiplier effects total impacts on revenues, output, and employment from initial changes in economic activity, particularly those of the export-related sectors

N

nation distinct society dedicated to its own region or homeland, whether or not it is a state; usually an ethnic group that shares the same language, religion, history, and icons, or symbols of their distinctiveness

nationalism concept that nations deserve the right to self-determination, as autonomous regions or as sovereign states

nation-state state in which the homeland of a nation coincides with the territory of a state

natural disaster a natural event that adversely affects humans; in the United States, the term is usually reserved for events in which more than 100 people die or more than $1,000,000 in damage occurs

natural increase surplus of births over deaths in a population in a given period

natural selection process by which organisms better able to survive and reproduce replace competing organisms

neo-colonialism economic dependence of former colonies on their former colonizers

New World Order an optimisitc view of the arrangement of power in the world. The New World Order ostensibly took effect in 1991, after the Union of Soviet Socialist Republics dissolved and Soviet communism was discredited. It holds that the bipolar aspects of the Cold War were over and could be replaced by increasing connections between states and nations, that supra-nationalist organizations would emerge to balance the superpowers, and that multinational actions would replace unilateral decisions and actions.

nonpoint source pollution pollutants that are emitted through runoff from streets and agricultural fields, for example

Nostratic a reconstructed proto-language that is assumed to have been spoken perhaps 15,000 years ago; from it, English, Korean, Arabic, and hundreds of other modern languages evolved

nuée ardente glowing cloud of superheated gas and pyroclastic fragments that explode from the steep side of a volcano

O

offshore banking financial activities in deregulated sites, often but not always located in small island states and nations

oligopoly market structure in which a handful of firms dominate output in a particular sector, thus acting as price setters

outgassing process in which volatiles are exuded as gases from the Earth's crust, largely through volcanic activity

overurbanization condition in which cities grow more rapidly than the jobs and housing they can sustain

oxbow lake crescent-shaped lake or swamp (such as a bayou) that occupies an abandoned channel left by a meandering stream

oxidation chemical weathering process in which oxygen combines with minerals to produce mineral oxides

ozone layer stratospheric area containing ozone, which protects life on Earth by absorbing the sun's ultraviolet rays

P

Pangaea hypothetical supercontinent that is thought to be the parent of today's continents

pedology science of soil

perihelion point on the Earth's orbit at which the Earth is closest to the sun

permafrost condition of permanently frozen ground in subarctic and arctic regions

pH measure of the concentration of hydrogen ions in a solution on a scale in which 7 represents neutrality. Lower numbers indicate increasing acidity and higher numbers indicate increasing alkalinity.

photogrammetry science of making measurements from photographs

photosynthesis process by which plants convert carbon dioxide to oxygen

pidgin language simplified version of language used among people who do not share a common language

plate tectonics theory that the Earth's lithospheric plates slide or shift slowly over the asthenosphere and that their interactions cause geologic events such as volcanic explosions, movement of landmasses, and earthquakes

plateau extensive elevated area bounded by a steep cliff

playa temporary lake or lake bed in a desert

pluton a mass of rock formed by the cooling of magma and the crystallization of igneous rock beneath the Earth's surface

point source pollution the emission of pollutants from a specific and limited area, such as a sewage pipe or factory

pollutant substance, usually a result of human waste or human activity, that contaminates the surrounding environment. A substance can become a pollutant when its concentration increases to levels that threaten the health of living things or change atmospheric conditions.

polyglot state country with a mixture of cultural groups with different languages

population momentum tendency for population growth to continue beyond the time that replacement level fertility has been achieved because of a relatively high concentration of people in the childbearing years

primacy condition in which the population of the largest city in an urban system is disproportionately large in relation to the second- and third-largest cities in that system

primary sector cluster of economic activities that pertain to the extraction of raw materials from Earth's surface, including agriculture, forestry, fishing, and mining

prime meridian line of 0 degrees longitude, which runs through Greenwich, England

producer services service industries that cater primarily to corporate clients rather than households

production platform geographic setting involving a tightly knit cluster of towns and cities with specialized, interrelated manufacturing activities bound together by the creation and exploitation of external economies

protectionism government policy or web of policies designed to protect domestic producers from foreign competition by limiting imports through tariffs, quotas, and nontariff barriers

push-pull hypothesis theory of migration stating that circumstances at the place of origin repel, or push, people out of that place to other places that exert a positive attraction, or pull

Q–R

quotas form of protectionism in which governments limit the absolute volume of imports in an industry, effectively driving up the market price

race visible differences or phenotypes among people such as skin color, eye shape, and hair color

racism social practice of discrimination based on appearance

radiation balance condition of balance between energy coming from the sun and energy radiated and reflected from the Earth

rain forest moist, densely wooded area usually found in a warm, tropical climate; annual rainfall is about 80 inches (200 cm) a year or more

rain shadow dry region on the downwind (leeward) side of a mountain range

rank-size rule statistical regularity in the population-size distribution of cities and regions

regional trading blocs associations of countries designed to reduce protectionism and enhance economic intercourse among member states

regolith layer of rock debris or sediment moved into an area by water, wind, or glaciers

relative humidity measure of the moisture content of the air, expressed as the amount of water vapor present relative to the maximum that can exist at the current temperature

remote sensing measurement of some property of an object by means other than direct contact, usually from aircraft or satellites

renewable resources natural resources that can be regenerated by either biologic reproduction or by environmental processes; mismanagement of these resources can cause their depletion

replacement level fertility average number of children needed to replace both parents in the population; in the United States today, total fertility rate of about 2.1 is considered to be the replacement level

residential mobility movement of households from one residential location to another within a city

resource management decisions made on what natural resources should (and should not) be developed, to what degree, in what manner, and for whom

resources substances, qualities, or organisms that have use and value to a society

ria coast river valley that has been partially submerged beneath the sea; it is highly indented

Richter scale logarithmic scale of numbers that represent the relative amount of energy released by an earthquake

rift valley long valley formed by the depression of a block between two parallel faults

Ring of Fire nearly complete arc of volcanoes that circles much of the Pacific Ocean

S

salinization accumulation of soluble salts in the soil

Santa Ana easterly winds, often hot and dry, that blow over the Sierra Nevada into southern California and the Pacific Ocean

savanna tropical grassland with widely spaced trees that experiences distinct wet and dry seasons

seamount submerged volcano

Second World now defunct theoretical grouping of the nations of the former Soviet bloc (USSR, eastern Europe, Mongolia, and Cuba) characterized by socialist economies

secondary sector industries that transform raw materials into finished goods; i.e., manufacturing and construction

securities markets one of a series of financial markets and institutions involved in buying and selling equities, foreign currency exchange, and investment management

seep small amount of water that flows slowly out of the ground and eventually into a stream

seismic waves waves emitted from the focus during an earthquake by faulting or other crustal disturbances

seismology scientific study of earthquakes

sensible heat heat felt or sensed as warmth, measurable by a thermometer

silt type of sediment transported and deposited by water, ice, or wind

sinkhole surface depression resulting from the ground collapsing into a cave

soil horizon horizontal layer of the soil that is set apart from other layers by differences in chemical and physical composition, organic content, structure, or a combination of those properties

solstice celestial event that occurs twice a year, when the sun appears directly overhead to observers at the Tropic of Cancer or the Tropic of Capricorn; summer solstice occurs on June 21 or 22, and winter solstice occurs on December 21 or 22.

spheres of influence theory popular in the 1960s that the United States, maritime Europe, the Soviet Union, and China were the Earth's four geostrategic regions

spit beach extension that forms along a shoreline with bays and other indentations

state independent political unit that claims jurisdiction over a defined territory and the people in it; used interchangeably with country

steppe semiarid treeless regions that receive between 10 and 20 inches of precipitation yearly

strait narrow passage of water that connects two larger bodies of water

subduction process by which the downbent edge of a crustal plate is forced underneath another plate

sublimation process by which water vapor (gas) changes to ice (solid) or vice versa

sustained yield amount of food and material species that can be harvested annually without depletion

T

tariffs a surcharge on imports levied by a state, a form of protectionism designed to increase imports' market price and thus inhibit their consumption

tarn small lake that occupies a basin in a cirque or glacial trough

temperature inversion atmospheric condition, caused by rapid reradiation, in which air at lower altitudes is cooler than air higher up

terrane large piece of crustal rock having a distinctive geology

territoriality societal action of defending a state's territory from outside threats

tertiary sector industries and activities that produce and transmit intangibles, i.e., services including finance, producer, and consumer services, transportation and communications, education, health care, nonprofit organizations, and the public sector

thermal inertia resistance of land and water to temperature change

Third World theoretical grouping roughly synonymous with the global South, essentially comprising former European colonies in Latin America, Africa, and Asia

threatened species species at some but not immediate risk of extinction

tide regular rise and fall of the ocean level, caused by gravitational pull between the Earth and moon in combination with Earth rotation

till unsorted mixture of rock fragments deposited beneath moving glacier ice

time-space compression idea that distance can be measured in terms of the time required to cross it via transportation and communications

toponymy study of place names

tornado violently rotating column of air that descends to the ground during intense thunderstorm activity

total fertility rate average number of children that would be born alive to a woman during her lifetime if she were to pass through all her childbearing years conforming to the age-specific fertility rates of a given year

tsunami series of ocean waves caused by the vertical displacement of the seafloor during an earthquake or volcanic explosion

tundra cold region characterized by low vegetation

U-V

unitary state political organization in which all power derives from the national government

urban heat island dome of heat over a city resulting from urban activities and conditions

urban system group of cities in which a disproportionate part of the world's most important business is conducted

vertical integration the consolidation of different stages in the production or distribution process within the confines of an individual corporation

volcanic arc long, narrow chain of composite volcanoes that forms parallel to a convergent boundary

W

water table upper level of the saturated zone of soil and rock, where it meets unsaturated soil and rock

wave refraction angle at which waves meet shorelines, usually about 5 degrees from parallel

weathering geomorphic process that causes physical disintegration and chemical decomposition of rock and soil

wetland area of land covered by water or saturated by water sufficiently enough to support vegetation adapted to wet conditions

world system theory that the only meaningful unit of social analysis is the global system of states and markets, and that individual places can only be understood via their position within this worldwide system

X-Z

xerophytes plants that can survive in a dry environment

zone in transition area of mixed commercial and residential land uses surrounding the central business district of a city

zoning process of subdividing urban areas as a basis for land-use planning and policy

INDEX

Water 424; albedo of 61; fossil 179; hard 182; pollution 428–32; potable 186; as precipitation 95–96; temperature changes of 67; see also Atmospheric moisture

Water gaps 168

Water table 179, 180, 181

Water vapor 64, 89

Waterfalls 174

Watershed (drainage basin) 168

Wavelength 59, 197

Waves 86, 198; defined 197; deposition by 203, 205–8; of earthquakes 146–47; erosion by 202–5; oceanic 197–99

Weather: defined 98; differential heating and 63; predicting 84, 113

Weather systems 98–111; air masses and 98–99; fronts and 99–100; hurricanes and 110–11; midlatitude cyclonic systems and 103; thunderstorms and 104–7; tornadoes and 107–8; tropical 109–10

Weathering 159–63; chemical 159–60, 162–63, 210–11; climate and 163; defined 159; mass wasting and 210–11; patterns of 163; physical 159–61, 163; by solution 162–63, 202

Weber, Alfred 331

Weber, Max 363

Westerlies 80, 81, 82; Rossby waves and 83–84

Wetted perimeter 171

Wheat-based farming systems 323

Widgren, Jonas 277

Wilderness areas 424

Wildlife 437–439

Wilson, Woodrow 402

Wind 74–80; atmospheric convergence, divergence and 72–73; atmospheric pressure and 71; circulation of latent energy by 58–59, 62; coriolis effect and 50, 75–77; defined 74; direction as characteristic of 75–76; energy from 329, 425; erosion by 209, 211–12; fetch of 198; friction and 75, 76, 77; global (see Global winds); landforms created by 213–15; local 77–79; monsoon 79; orographic uplift and 93; pressure gradient and 74, 75–76, 77; regional 77–79; speed of 75; surface 99; as thermals 75

Wind gaps 168

Wind shear 107

Windchill index 68–69

Wolpert, Julian 269

Women 260, 261, 313

World Aeronautical Chart 24

World cities 379–80

World order 413–14

World systems theory 341

World Trade Organization (WTO) 352

World-systems theory 366–67

X

Xenoliths 152

Xerophytic plants 239

Y

Yanomamo 314

Yazoo streams 176

Yugoslavia 312

Z

Zamenhof, L. L. 297

Zebra mussels 439

Zen Buddhism 310

Zigzag ridges 141

Zionist movement 308

Zonda wind 79

Zone: of ablation 189; of accumulation 189; of aeration 180; of saturation 180

Zoning 378

CREDITS

PART ONE: 5, George F. Mobley; 9 (top), J.W. Lothers; 9 (bottom), James L. Stanfield; 16, Royal Geographical Society, London; 19 (top), Pat Lanza; 19 (center), James P. Blair; 19 (bottom), Galen A. Rowell; 21, Semitic Museum, Harvard University; 22 (top), Joseph H. Bailey; 22 (bottom), W. M. Edwards; 23, Piri Reis; 25, Mark Thiessen; 27, Emory Kristof; 29 (left), Joseph H. Bailey; 29 (right), S. C. DeBrock/Lockheed Martin; 30, Stuart Armstrong/WORLDSAT International, Inc.; 31 (top), Joseph D. Lavenburg/Mark Thiessen; 31 (bottom), Miguel Luis Fairbanks; 32, Steve Raymer; 34, Jodi Cobb; 37, George F. Mobley.

PART TWO: 42, George Grall/Photo Researchers, Inc.; 47, James L. Amos; 54, NASA; 61, The Map Factory/Photo Researchers, Inc.; 65, Richard Nowitz; 66, George F. Mobley; 93, Rich Clarkson; 99, NOAA; 106, Bruce Dale; 113, Jodi Cobb; 115, Priit Vesilind/NGS Image Collection; 128, Robert F. Sisson; 130, Bilderchiv Preussicher Kulturbesitz; 139, Bruce Dale; 145, James L. Stanfield; 149, Win Parks; 153, Joseph H. Bailey; 156, James L. Amos ; 158, Steve Raymer; 160, W. M. Edward; 161, Craig Blacklock/Blacklock Nature Photography; 162, Photo Researchers, Inc.; 164, Catherine Ursillo/Photo Researchers Inc.; 165, Jodi Cobb; 167, W. R. Moore; 173, David S. Boyer; 176, NASA; 182, James L. Amos; 184, James L. Amos; 185, Jacob Gayer; 187, James Blair; 188, U.S. Geological Survey; 190, George F. Mobley; 191, Dick Durrance II; 192, Steve Raymer; 194, Richard C. Johnson/Visuals Unlimited; 195 (left), Dr. E. R. Degginger; 195 (right), Cary Wolinsky; 198, B. A. Stewart; 204, W. M. Edwards; 207, Jodi Cobb; 208, Gregory Heisler; 209, George F. Mobley; 212, George F. Mobley; 215, Rich Clarkson; 216, Visuals Unlimited; 217, Dan Westergren; 218, U.S. Department of Agriculture/Natural Resources Conservation Service; 225 (left), U.S. Department of Agriculture/Natural Resources Conservation Service; 225 (right), U.S. Department of Agriculture/Soil Conversation Service; 226, U.S. Department of Agriculture/Natural Resources Conservation Service; 235, James P. Blair; 236, Raymond Gehman; 237 (top), Richard Nowitz/Image Collection; 237 (bottom), Raymond Gehman; 238 (top), James R. Brandenburg; 238 (bottom), Bruce Dale.

PART THREE: 242, Jodi Cobb; 252, Robert Caputo; 260, Karen Kasmauski; 261, Steve McCurry; 262, Marie-Louise Brimberg; 268, Sam Abell; 270, Sarah Leen; 271, W. M. Edwards; 274, William Albert Allard; 275, Library of Congress; 281, Danny Lehman; 283, Gordon Gahan; 284, James L. Stanfield; 292, Sid Hastings; 293, Joseph H. Bailey; 294 (left), Sam Abell; 294 (right), James C. Richardson; 302, Maggie Steber; 304, Thomas J. Abercrombie; 309, James L. Stanfield; 311, James L. Stanfield; 313, David Alan Harvey; 314 (left), James P. Blair; 314 (right) David Boyer; 315, James P. Blair; 321, James L. Stanfield; 325, Maria Stenzel; 332, Jodi Cobb; 336, Bruce Dale; 341, Gordon Gahan; 345, James P. Blair; 365, Michael Melford; 374, Bruce Dale; 377, James L. Stanfield; 384, Michael Yamashita; 385 (top), Stuart Franklin; 385 (bottom),Stephanie Maze; 386, Bruce Dale; 387, Bruce Dale; 388, W. M. Edwards; 405, Anthony Suau/Black Star; 412, Jon Riley/Folio Inc.; 413, James L. Stanfield; 421, Robert Madden; 430, Kevin Fleming; 431, Michelle Barnes; 433, Bruce Dale; 436, Fred Ward; 437, James P. Blair; 440, Robert Madden.

The world's largest nonprofit scientific and educational organization, the National Geographic Society was founded in 1888 "for the increase and diffusion of geographic knowledge." Since then it has supported scientific exploration and spread information to its more than nine million members worldwide.

The National Geographic Society educates and inspires millions every day through magazines, books, television programs, videos, maps and atlases, research grants, the National Geography Bee, teacher workshops, and innovative classroom materials.

The Society is supported through membership dues and income from the sale of its educational products. Members receive NATIONAL GEOGRAPHIC magazine—the Society's official journal—discounts on Society products, and other benefits.

For more information about the National Geographic Society and its educational programs and publications, please call 1-800-NGS-LINE (647-5463), or write to the following address:
National Geographic Society, 1145 17th Street N.W., Washington, D.C. 20036-4688 U.S.A.
Visit the Society's Web site at www.nationalgeographic.com.

PUBLISHED BY
THE NATIONAL GEOGRAPHIC SOCIETY
John M. Fahey, Jr., *President and Chief Executive Officer*
Gilbert M. Grosvenor, *Chairman of the Board*
Nina D. Hoffman, *Senior Vice President*

Prepared by the Book Division
William R. Gray, *Vice President and Director of Book Division*
Charles Kogod, *Assistant Director*
Barbara A. Payne, *Editorial Director and Managing Editor*
David Griffin, *Design Director*

Staff for this book
Rebecca Lescaze, *Project Editor*
Sallie Greenwood, *Text Editor and Researcher*
Arnold Ajello, Elizabeth Booz, Martha C. Christian, *Contributing Editors*
Jean Redmond, *Legend Writer and Illustrations Researcher*
Alexander Cohn, Mary Collins, Kimberly DeLashmit, Dale-Marie Herring, Mary E. Jennings, Victoria Garrett Jones, Tracy Mangano, Jordan Monroe, Keith Moore, Ann Perry, Robin T. Reid, Johnna Rizzo, Karla Tucker, Diana Vanek, *Researchers*
Carl Mehler, *Director of Maps*

Kathleen Cole, *Design Assistant*
Thomas B. Powell, III, *Illustrations Editor*
Janet A. Dustin, *Illustrations Assistant*
Roger M. Downs, *Chief Consultant*
Sari Bennett, Alice Recklin Perkins, *Consultants*
National Geographic Maps, Magellan Geographix, *Cartography*

Manufacturing and Quality Control
George V. White, *Director*
John T. Dunn, *Associate Director*
Vincent P. Ryan, *Manager*
James J. Sorensen, *Budget Analyst*

STONESONG PRESS, INC.
Paul Fargis, *Director*
Ellen Scordato, *Managing Editor*
Martin Lubin, Martin Lubin Graphic Design, *Designer*
Andrea Sutcliffe, *Contributing Editor*
Brad Walrod, High Text Graphics, Inc., *Composition*
Martin Levick, *Photo Editing*
SlimFilms, *Illustrators*
William F. Sangrey, Ph.D., *Consultant*